KU-414-538

THE OFFICIAL ★ BIGGEST PUB QUIZ BOOK

Ever!

SECOND EDITION

CARLTON
BOOKS

Contents

Introduction

Over the past decade snugs and lounges in pubs the length and breadth of the country have become, if not seats of learning at least seats of intellect. Which makes a change from seats of worn leatherette (although these still prevail in some areas). The pub quiz has transformed the bar into an arena of knowledge where beery brethren battle to the final bell. The format is simple: some friends, acquaintances, even complete strangers, will do, a questioner, some paper, a collection of ragged Biros and a surfeit of beer and questions are all that is needed to create the perfect evening's entertainment. Wits are challenged, heads are huddled and patience is tested as teams attempt to outdo each other in their show of trivia retention. At these events you will learn that no fact is too small, no sport star too obscure and no war too insignificant to test the pub crowd's grey matter. In fact, the more obscure and wide-ranging the questions the greater the chance of involving the entire barroom – nothing will gain the pub idiot greater respect than showing that they have the entire cast, storyline and signature tune of "Emergency Ward 10" lodged in their head, except perhaps their switching from slip-ons to lace-ups. So take heart, and a copy of *The Official Biggest Pub Quiz Book Ever!* to the boozer and have a few warm up sessions and see if you can't organize your own pub quiz. You know it makes sense; it's the only way you'll know all the answers.

The main aim of *The Official Biggest Pub Quiz Book Ever!* is to entertain, so it is important that you retain a sense of humour and good sportsmanship as you play along, whether you are testing friends at home or setting a quiz for your local hostelry. That aside, you also have to ensure that you are fully in control of your questions and players: remain calm, speak in a steady voice and be constantly unflapped when challenged by any of the more heavily imbibed, as indeed you will be.

If the locals do get testy your best bet is to head for the door while throwing beer nuts in the air to confuse them, though this should happen in only the roughest pubs or on outings with the extended family – in which case you should attempt to rescue your spouse, if you can do so without spilling your drink and it isn't them causing the trouble.

The Official Biggest Pub Quiz Book Ever! is divided into three sections of Easy, Medium and Hard questions, which are all subdivided by specialist and pot-luck rounds. The former can be chosen either to help or hinder your players; giving Easy sports questions to the literature fanatics is bound to reveal some interesting answers but it is possibly more challenging to tailor your questions so that the experts receive the brain-wracking Hard questions and the novice the stupefyingly simple Easy questions. Nothing hurts a fanatic more than being beaten on their specialist subject and the division of questions gives you the chance to employ a handicap system. Other handicap systems will also become apparent as you continue as quiz master. The team that wins the Sunday-afternoon quiz will doubtless fail when it comes to Sunday night, although if you want to set a quiz on Friday night you should check pupil dilation first, as on that evening of great relaxation you may find your teams asleep or brawling before calling the whole thing quits and joining them in a drink ... or three.

In the interest of further clarification there follows a brief run-down of each section:

Easy

In this primary round the main objective is to keep breathing, these questions are so easy that even the most docile pub idiot could gurgle his way through them in the time it takes to down a pint and still have time left to knock over the stack of pennies on the bar.

Medium

On your toes people, things are getting tricky. By now even the ringers on the out-of-towners' team will be sweating. These questions make for a challenge, but you are bound to get the odd smug bar steward who will fancy his chances, for which you should continue on to section three.

Hard

Ask a full thirty of these questions and only the shrill wail of the pub cat fighting in the yard will be heard, brows will be furrowed, glances exchanged and beer stared into. To set an entire quiz using just these questions is a form of evil so dark-hearted Fu Manchu would blanch.

The Easy Questions

If you think that Louis Armstrong was the first man on the moon or that Uri Geller was the first man in space then you will no doubt struggle through the next few questions terribly. For the rest of us though these are the EASY questions, so called because if the quizzee falters on these they are either three sheets to the wind or far too young to be in the pub – either state rendering them toddling buffoons whose social graces will equal their breadth of knowledge. So beware their flailing arms as you attempt to collect the answers.

These questions are perfect when used in the first round of an open entry quiz as they lull everyone into a false sense of security, although you must ensure that contestants don't shout answers out, which creates a problematic precedent for the later, harder questions. Another way of placing these questions is to dot them about throughout the quiz, thus making sure that on every team everyone should know the answer to at least one question despite their age.

If you are running a league quiz then some of your team members may heap derision on such obvious questions, but don't worry: even the cleverest quiz team member can come a cropper, as was noted in a championship final when a contestant was asked to name the continents. He deliberated before eventually beaming out the answer, "A, E, I, O, U!"

Quiz 1

Pot-Luck 1

Answers – page 13

LEVEL 1

1 What is the highest number used in a Sudoku puzzle?
2 What is the term for a positive electrode?
3 In "Last of the Summer Wine" what was Nora's husband called?
4 Which swimming stroke is named after an insect?
5 Which English queen has the same name as a type of plum?
6 Which Rovers does veteran cartoon character Roy play for?
7 How many dots are used in each letter in the Braille system?
8 Who won the Oscar for best actor in both 1993 and 1994?
9 What is a female deer called?
10 What does the letter B stand for in an ASBO?
11 What can be an island, a sweater or a potato?
12 What unit is used to measure horses?
13 Who is Reg Dwight better known as?
14 Who provided Aslan's voice in the 2005 movie of "The Lion, the Witch and the Wardrobe"?
15 Which Eamonn left the GMTV sofa in the summer of 2005?
16 How many tenpin bowling skittles need knocking down for a strike?
17 How is 77 represented in Roman numerals?
18 Who is the patron saint of music?
19 What are birds of a feather said to do?
20 "Kiss Me Kate" is a musical version of which play by Shakespeare?
21 The single "Papa Don't Preach" came from which Madonna album?
22 Betz cells are found in which part of the body?
23 What is the only bird that can hover in the air and also fly backwards?
24 Who earned the nickname "Slow-hand"?
25 In the Bible who goes after Mark and before John?
26 Which country does opera singer Pavarotti come from?
27 Which is the third largest of the Channel Islands?
28 Who was Liverpool's skipper in the 2005 European Champions League triumph?
29 In which Puccini opera does Mimi appear?
30 How many sides has an octagon?

Answers	**Pot-Luck 2** *(see Quiz 3)*

1 Gregorian. 2 Guitar. 3 Portsmouth. 4 Katrina. 5 Seven. 6 Rome. 7 Goat. 8 25.
9 John Sullivan. 10 Four. 11 Australia. 12 Cher. 13 Waterloo. 14 The Diddymen. 15 Thursday. 16 Kevin Pietersen. 17 Lilliput. 18 Dish. 19 Aardvark. 20 Seven. 21 Dirty. 22 George Best. 23 Siesta. 24 Edgar Allan Poe. 25 One minute. 26 Harrow. 27 M. 28 Badger. 29 Madonna. 30 Fernando Alonso.

1 Which shirt number was linked with David Beckham at Man Utd?
2 In which area of London was David born?
3 Who was Man Utd boss when Beckham broke into Man Utd's team?
4 Beckham was first sent off for England in 1998, against which country?
5 What was wife Victoria's nickname in the Spice Girls?
6 Is Beckham's middle name Alex, Edward or Joseph?
7 The Beckham's first son was named after an area of which American city?
8 David's autobiography was called "My..." what?
9 Which Beckham baby shares a name with a Shakespeare character?
10 What was the second country in which Beckham played domestic football?
11 How many players before Beckham had been sent off twice playing for England?
12 What was Mrs Beckham's original surname?
13 Which TV soccer pundit Alan got it hopelessly wrong about Man Utd "kids" not winning anything?
14 What was the usual colour of the shorts during Beckham's Man Utd days?
15 Who are Ted and Sandra in relation to David?
16 Which country beginning with a "C" did Becks score against in France '98?
17 Victoria and David married at a castle in which country?
18 Which England soccer boss gave Beckham the captaincy?
19 Young Beckham was part of a side known as Fergie's what?
20 What was the nickname of the Beckhams' palatial home in Hertfordshire?
21 Beckham was sent off a second time for England against which country?
22 What was David's squad number at Real Madrid – 13, 23 or 43?
23 Against which Premiership side did David score from the half-way line in the 1996/7 season?
24 In which major 2002 sporting opening ceremony was David involved?
25 Beckham's transfer fee moving to Real Madrid – £10m, £15m or £25m?
26 Which team ended Beckham's and England's World Cup hopes in 2002?
27 Why was the game against Getafe on 3 December 2005 significant for Beckham?
28 Which English international Michael was with Becks at Real Madrid?
29 Which Englishman was England boss when Becks was first capped?
30 Who is the older – David or Victoria Beckham?

Answers	I'm a Celebrity ... *(see Quiz 4)*

1 Carol Thatcher. 2 Will Young. 3 Girls Aloud. 4 Strictly Come Dancing. 5 Aled Jones. 6 Hear'Say. 7 David Dickinson. 8 Chicago. 9 Nell McAndrew. 10 Sugar. 11 Australia. 12 Prince William's. 13 Louis Walsh. 14 Dragon's Den. 15 Will Young. 16 Pasquale. 17 Llewelyn Bowen. 18 Properties. 19 Hancock. 20 The Sun. 21 Jill Halfpenny. 22 Big Brother. 23 Sharon Osbourne. 24 Overhaul your wardrobe. 25 Kidman. 26 Ali G. 27 The Pussycat Dolls. 28 Hurley. 29 Colin Jackson. 30 Ant & Dec.

1 Which type of calendar is used today in the western world?
2 What instrument can be bass, electric or Spanish?
3 Think about this – which club did Harry Redknapp manage first – Portsmouth or Southampton?
4 Which female-named hurricane devastated New Orleans in September 2005?
5 What do the numbers add up to on the opposite sides of a dice?
6 Which city is said to have been founded by Romulus and Remus?
7 In the zodiac, which animal is linked with Capricorn?
8 How many years are involved in a silver anniversary?
9 Who scripted "Only Fools and Horses"?
10 In music, how many quavers equal a minim?
11 Which country originated the term "plonk" for wine?
12 How did Cherilyn Sarkasian LaPierre become better known?
13 What was the final battle that Napoleon fought in?
14 Which men used to perform with Ken Dodd?
15 On which day are British elections held?
16 Which member of the 2005 Ashes-winning side sported a diamond earring and a two-colour hairstyle?
17 What was the name of the land where Gulliver met the Little People?
18 In the nursery rhyme, who ran away with the spoon?
19 Which animal's name comes first in the dictionary?
20 How many sides has a 20-pence piece?
21 What is Den's nickname in "EastEnders"?
22 In the 1960s which footballer was called "The Fifth Beatle"?
23 In Spain what is the word for an afternoon nap?
24 Who wrote "The Pit and the Pendulum"?
25 How long is there between rounds in boxing?
26 Which public school did Sir Winston Churchill go to?
27 What is the thirteenth letter of the English alphabet?
28 Which is the largest land carnivore in Britain?
29 Who made the album "Confessions on a Dance Floor"?
30 Which Fernando became the youngest F1 World Champion in 2005?

Answers	**Pot-Luck 1** *(see Quiz 1)*

1 9. 2 Anode. 3 Wally. 4 Butterfly. 5 Victoria. 6 Melchester. 7 Six. 8 Tom Hanks. 9 Doe. 10 Behaviour. 11 Jersey. 12 Hands. 13 Elton John. 14 Liam Neeson. 15 Eamonn Holmes. 16 Ten. 17 LXXVII. 18 St Cecilia. 19 Flock together. 20 The Taming of the Shrew. 21 True Blue. 22 The brain. 23 Hummingbird. 24 Eric Clapton. 25 Luke. 26 Italy. 27 Alderney. 28 Steven Gerrard. 29 La Bohème. 30 Eight.

1 Which PM's daughter won the 2005 "I'm a Celebrity ... Get Me Out of Here"?
2 Who beat Gareth Gates to win "Pop Idol"?
3 Who were "Popstars: The Rivals" winners, Girls Aloud or Atomic Kitten?
4 It "Takes Two" is the follow-up programme about which show?
5 Which Welsh singer, famous for "Walking in the Air" appeared on "Strictly Come Dancing"?
6 Myleene Klass was part of which band?
7 Which antiques celebrity coined the phrase "cheap as chips" on TV?
8 Which musical about gangsters did Pop Idol's Darius Danesh join in 2005?
9 How is model Tracey Jane McAndrew better known?
10 Which entrepreneur Alan appeared in "The Apprentice"?
11 In which country was the third series of "I'm a Celebrity" held?
12 Kate Middleton was whose girlfriend when they graduated from St Andrews University in 2005?
13 Which juror walked out of "The X Factor" in autumn 2005?
14 Which was the reality TV show, "Dragon's Den" or "Lion's Den"?
15 Which "Pop Idol" winner appeared with Judi Dench in "Mrs Henderson Presents"?
16 Which comedian Joe has been voted King of the Jungle?
17 Which Lawrence was a star of "Changing Rooms"?
18 Does Sarah Beeny present programmes on properties or food?
19 Which Sheila, widow of John Thaw, appeared in "Grumpy Old Women"?
20 Rebekah Wade, Mrs Ross Kemp, edited which paper when they made front-page news concerning assault allegations?
21 Which Jill won "Strictly Come Dancing" in December 2004?
22 Which reality TV series had a family member's name in its title?
23 Which "X Factor" celebrity is married to Ozzy Osbourne?
24 Do Trinny and Susannah overhaul your wardrobe or clean your house?
25 Which actress Nicole advertised Omega watches?
26 Which Ali was created by Sacha Baron Cohen?
27 Which girl band is fronted by Carmen Electra?
28 Which Elizabeth did Gwyneth Paltrow replace as the face of Estee Lauder?
29 Which sprint hurdler was a 2005 "Strictly Come Dancing" contestant?
30 Which duo were booked to interview Princes Charles, William and Harry to mark the 30th anniversary of the Prince's Trust?

Answers	**David Beckham** *(see Quiz 2)*

1 No 7. **2** Leytonstone. **3** Alex Ferguson. **4** Argentina. **5** Posh Spice. **6** Joseph. **7** New York (Brooklyn). **8** My Side. **9** Romeo. **10** Spain. **11** None. **12** Adams. **13** Hansen. **14** White. **15** Parents. **16** Colombia. **17** Ireland. **18** Sven Goran Eriksson. **19** Fledglings. **20** Beckingham Palace. **21** Austria. **22** No 23. **23** Wimbledon. **24** Commonwealth Games. **25** £25m. **26** Brazil. **27** He was sent off. **28** Michael Owen. **29** Glenn Hoddle. **30** Victoria.

Quiz 5 Pot-Luck 3

Answers – page 17

1 In "EastEnders" what is the name of Den Watts' widow?
2 How many children were there in Enid Blyton's Famous Five?
3 Kerry Katona found fame in which all-girl band?
4 What kind of animal was Phillip Schofield's puppet pal Gordon?
5 What is the stage name of Harry Webb?
6 Which Sadie was married to Jude Law?
7 Which film gave Jack Nicholson his first Oscar?
8 Which season do Americans call the Fall?
9 The fabled bird the griffin had the head of which real bird?
10 On which Common would you find the Wombles?
11 Whose catchphrase is, "Nice to see, to see you nice"?
12 Who was the first Labour MP?
13 Whom did Boris Yeltsin make his Prime Minister in 1999?
14 Which country does Bryan Adams come from?
15 Who was known as the lady with the lamp?
16 What is the plural of the word sheep?
17 In golf, who won the British Open in 2005?
18 What is the symbol for the Gemini sign of the zodiac?
19 Where in a horse is the coffin joint?
20 What word can go before cheese, plant and roll?
21 Which Simon and Garfunkel song features the words "Jesus loves you more than you can say"?
22 Which "famous first" is attributed to asparagus in Britain?
23 Which substance is most used for pencil lead?
24 To ten years either way, in which year did Charles Dickens die?
25 Which long-running radio programme was devised by Roy Plomley?
26 Which Lloyd Webber musical does the song "Memory" come from?
27 What drink does pear juice make?
28 What name can be a lettuce or a mass of floating frozen water?
29 Which vegetable did Sir Walter Raleigh bring to England?
30 In the strip cartoon, what is the name of Snoopy's brother?

Answers	**Pot-Luck 4** *(see Quiz 7)*

1 Kipps. 2 Michael Vaughan. 3 Union. 4 Condoleezza Rice. 5 Gilbert and Sullivan. 6 Lucy Locket. 7 Edward Fox. 8 Blue. 9 Right. 10 Bruno Tonioli. 11 The General Lee. 12 Desdemona. 13 15. 14 Motor racing. 15 Japan. 16 Turkey. 17 The Doors. 18 12. 19 France. 20 Maria Callas. 21 Quarto. 22 Even numbers. 23 Two. 24 Hangman. 25 Kidneys. 26 Knot garden. 27 Billy J. Kramer. 28 17th. 29 Greta Garbo. 30 None.

1 What was the name of Bill Haley's backing group?
2 Which shoes did Elvis warn you not to step on in 1956?
3 What kind of doll was Cliff Richard's first No 1?
4 Which blonde film star sang about her Secret Love?
5 Where was the Doggie when Lita Roza asked how much it was?
6 What relation to each other were Don and Phil Everly?
7 Where were the tulips from, which Max Bygraves sang about?
8 According to Connie Francis where did she find lipstick?
9 Whom did the Beverley Sisters see kissing Santa Claus?
10 How were the Balls of Fire described by Jerry Lee Lewis?
11 According to Frank Sinatra how do Love and Marriage go together?
12 Which Buddy was killed in a plane crash?
13 What did Perry Como ask you to catch and put in your pocket?
14 Which Biblical Garden did Frankie Vaughan sing about?
15 Who sang "Oh Carol" about fellow singer/songwriter Carole King?
16 Who's Boy Child did Harry Belafonte sing about in 1958?
17 Which line follows "Be Bop A Lula" at the start of the Gene Vincent hit?
18 Which 1950s pop star is Kim Wilde's father?
19 Who had hits with "When I Fall In Love" and "Stardust"?
20 Where did the Lace which the Big Bopper sang about come from?
21 Who asked "What do you want, if you don't want money"?
22 Where did Pat Boone write his Love Letters?
23 Which late soul singer had a hit with "Reet Petite" in 1957?
24 How many steps are there to heaven?
25 What Blues ain't there no cure for, according to Eddie Cochran?
26 In the song title, what did Shirley Bassey ask her Honey Honey to do?
27 Which record machine appeared in coffee bars in the 1950s?
28 According to Lonnie Donegan what might lose its flavour on the bedpost overnight?
29 How many tons did Tennessee Ernie Ford sing about?
30 According to the Platters what gets in your eyes?

Answers | The Royal Family *(see Quiz 8)*

1 One. 2 Prince Charles. 3 Duchess. 4 France. 5 Army. 6 Balmoral. 7 Philip. 8 Andrew. 9 Princess Anne. 10 Two. 11 Eton. 12 Corgi. 13 Mrs Wallis Simpson. 14 Victoria. 15 Buckingham Palace. 16 Six. 17 Saturday. 18 Mark Phillips. 19 Prince Andrew, Duke of York. 20 Prince Edward. 21 Golden Jubilee. 22 Her sister (Princess Margaret). 23 Windsor. 24 Henry. 25 Princess Anne. 26 Prince Edward. 27 Cornwall. 28 Duke of Windsor. 29 Sandringham. 30 Horsewoman.

1 "Half a Sixpence" is based on which story by H. G. Wells?

2 Who captained England to their Ashes win in 2005?

3 Soyuz was the name of a Russian spacecraft, but what does the name mean?

4 Which lady became George W. Bush's Secretary of State in his second term of office?

5 Who wrote the Savoy operas?

6 Who lost her pocket?

7 In the film "The Day of the Jackal", who played the Jackal?

8 What colour is a sapphire?

9 Does Elizabeth II face to the left or right on a British coin?

10 Which Bruno is on the "Strictly Come Dancing" panel of judges?

11 What did Bo and Luke Duke call their car?

12 In Shakespeare's "Othello", who is the female lead?

13 In the pirate song, how many men were on the dead man's chest?

14 Mike Hawthorne was the first Briton to win the World Championship in which sport?

15 Venetian blinds originated in which country?

16 A poult is the young of which creature?

17 Which group recorded the original of "Light My Fire"?

18 In an English trial, how many people sit on the jury?

19 Marcel Desailly was a World Cup winner playing for which country?

20 Which great soprano earned the name of "La Divina"?

21 What measure of paper is 8 by 10 inches?

22 On a standard roulette wheel which numbers appear on the black?

23 What number is dos in Spanish?

24 In which game do you draw part of a gallows for every wrong answer?

25 Bright's disease affects which organs of the body?

26 What name is given to a garden with geometrically arranged beds and small hedges?

27 Who sang with the Dakotas?

28 In which century was 1658?

29 Which actress said, "I want to be alone"?

30 How many kings of England have been called Philip?

Answers	**Pot-Luck 3** *(see Quiz 5)*

1 Chrissie. 2 Four – one was a dog. 3 Atomic Kitten. 4 Gopher. 5 Cliff Richard. 6 Frost. 7 One Flew Over the Cuckoo's Nest. 8 Autumn. 9 Eagle. 10 Wimbledon. 11 Bruce Forsyth. 12 Keir Hardie. 13 Vladimir Putin. 14 Canada. 15 Florence Nightingale. 16 Sheep. 17 Tiger Woods. 18 Twins. 19 Foot. 20 Swiss. 21 Mrs Robinson. 22 First frozen food. 23 Graphite. 24 1870. 25 Desert Island Discs. 26 Cats. 27 Perry. 28 Iceberg. 29 Potato. 30 Spike.

1 How many daughters does Queen Elizabeth II have?
2 Who is the father of Princes William and Harry?
3 Did Camilla Parker Bowles use the title Duchess or Princess after she married Prince Charles?
4 In which country did Princess Diana tragically meet her death?
5 Did Prince Harry join the Navy or the Army after his gap year?
6 What is the Queen's residence in Scotland called?
7 Which Prince is Duke of Edinburgh?
8 Which Prince was a helicopter pilot in the Falklands War?
9 Who is the Princess Royal?
10 How many children does the Duchess of Cornwall have?
11 Which school did Prince William start at in 1995?
12 What is the Queen's favourite breed of dog?
13 What was the name of the woman for whom Edward VIII abdicated?
14 Which Queen was married to Prince Albert?
15 What is the name of the Queen's London residence?
16 How many English kings have been called George?
17 On what day of the week did Charles and Camilla marry?
18 What was Princess Anne's first husband called?
19 Who is the father of Princesses Beatrice and Eugenie?
20 Who is Queen Elizabeth II's youngest son?
21 Which Jubilee did the Queen celebrate in 2002?
22 In 2002, the Queen lost her mother and which other close relative?
23 Which castle was badly damaged by fire in 1992?
24 What is Prince Harry's proper first name?
25 Which Royal survived a kidnap attempt in 1974?
26 Which son of the Queen has a daughter called Louise?
27 Prince Charles is Duke of which county of southwest England?
28 Which title did Edward VIII take after he abdicated?
29 What is the name of the Queen's residence in Norfolk?
30 Is the Queen's granddaughter Zara Phillips an accomplished horsewoman or a top tennis player?

Answers	Pop: Sounds Of The 50s *(see Quiz 6)*

1 The Comets. 2 Blue Suede. 2 Livin'. 4 Doris Day. 5 In the Window. 6 Brothers. 7 Amsterdam. 8 On Your Collar. 9 Mommy. 10 Great. 11 Like a Horse and Carriage. 12 Holly. 12 A Falling Star. 14 Eden. 15 Neil Sedaka. 16 Mary's. 17 She's My Baby. 18 Marty Wilde. 19 Nat King Cole. 20 Chantilly. 21 Adam Faith. 22 In the Sand. 23 Jackie Wilson. 24 Three. 25 Summertime. 26 Kiss Me. 27 Jukebox. 28 Chewing Gum. 29 16. 30 Smoke.

1 Which cabinet minister resigned following visa allegations in 2004?
2 How many stomachs has a cow?
3 With which swimming stroke do races begin in the water?
4 What have you been doing if you finish by casting off?
5 How is the Roman city of Verulamium known today?
6 Roy Jenkins was a founder of which political party?
7 What does Susan Hampshire suffer from?
8 In which sport did Michael Phelps win gold at the Athens Olympics in 2004?
9 Which city in the world has the largest population?
10 Whose ship was the first to sail round the world?
11 In music hall, who was the "Prime Minister of Mirth"?
12 Who composed "The Flight of the Bumble Bee"?
13 "Freedom" was the first UK top ten hit for which Robbie?
14 What is the full name of BBC Radio 5?
15 What was invented by Lewis Waterman in the 1880s?
16 Which illustrator was famous for detailed drawings of weird and wonderful mechanical inventions?
17 Which US President was nicknamed "The Comeback Kid"?
18 Following the 1963 Peerage Act, who was the first peer to disclaim his title?
19 What was "Prisoner: Cell Block H" originally called?
20 Which instrument usually has 47 strings?
21 What is the name of Dennis the Menace's dog?
22 For over 30 years, which tobacco company gave its name to a football yearbook?
23 Who wrote "Help Me Make It Through the Night"?
24 Moving anti-clockwise on a dartboard what is the number next to 4?
25 Who created the detective Paul Temple?
26 Who pricked her finger on a spinning wheel and slept for 100 years?
27 Who became Earl of Stockton on his 90th birthday?
28 Which traffic light follows green?
29 In "My Friend Flicka" who or what was Flicka?
30 Which is the first month of the year to have exactly 30 days?

Answers	Pot-Luck 6 *(see Quiz 11)*

1 Angela Merkel. 2 Two. 24 Greek, 26 English. 3 Pancakes. 4 Leaves. 5 Perseus.
6 Noah. 7 John Peel. 8 John Curry. 9 1986. 10 Eight. 11 First test tube baby. 12 Excalibur (also referred to as Caliburn). 13 Russell Harty. 14 Desert island. 15 Tongue. 16 Richard Nixon. 17 Quentin Crisp. 18 Bob Hope. 19 Harry Palmer. 20 Private Eye. 21 Celine Dion. 22 Roker Park. 23 West Germany. 24 88. 25 Eight. 26 Pavement. 27 Crocodile. 28 Harold Pinter. 29 Fifty years. 30 Three.

1 The Severn, the Trent and the Ouse are all what?
2 In which county are all ten of England's highest peaks?
3 Which is the second largest city in England?
4 Which London station was named after a long-reigning Queen?
5 In which county are the seaside resorts of Clacton and Southend?
6 Leeds Castle is in Kent. Where is Leeds?
7 Which seaside resort is famous for its Tower and its Golden Mile?
8 What might you see at Regent's Park, Chester and Whipsnade?
9 What is the name of the famous cathedral in York?
10 Which is the largest island in England?
11 What did Sunderland become in 1992 which Manchester, Liverpool and Birmingham became in the 19th century?
12 Which river runs through London?
13 Which is further north, Southport or Northampton?
14 Which stretch of water divides England and France?
15 What do the letters NEC stand for?
16 What is the area around Stoke-on-Trent known as?
17 Which northern city is served by Ringway airport?
18 Which motorway starts south of Birmingham and goes northwest towards Scotland?
19 Which part of the country would a Geordie come from?
20 Near which large city would you find the Wirral?
21 Which two cities are the home of England's two oldest universities?
22 Which range of northern hills is called the backbone of England?
23 Which moorland area of southwest Devon is the site of a high-security prison?
24 What were Dagenham, Luton and Cowley famous for producing?
25 Where would a Manx person come from?
26 Which famous stones can be seen on Salisbury Plain?
27 Whose birthplace might you be visiting in Stratford-on-Avon?
28 In which county is the English terminal of the Channel Tunnel?
29 How many square miles is the City of London?
30 Which was England's smallest county before the 1974 changes?

Answers	**40s and 50s Films** *(see Quiz 12)*

1 Bambi. 2 80 days. 3 Over the River Kwai. 4 White Christmas. 5 Tramp. 6 Ben Hur. 7 Fantasia. 8 Gone with the Wind. 9 Bob Hope. 10 Casablanca. 11 Laurence Olivier. 12 Brief Encounter. 13 Hitchcock. 14 Welles. 15 Alec Guinness. 16 Ealing Comedies. 17 In the Rain. 18 Hot. 19 Genevieve. 20 James Dean. 21 Grace Kelly. 22 Brigitte Bardot. 23 Ten. 24 At the Top. 25 Elizabeth Taylor. 26 Rogers. 27 Brando. 28 Arsenic. 29 Love. 30 Eternity.

1 Which lady replaced Gerhard Schroeder as German Chancellor?
2 How many more letters are there in the English than the Greek alphabet?
3 Which food item is used in an annual race at Olney?
4 Which part of the mint plant is used to make mint sauce?
5 In legend, who slew the gorgon Medusa?
6 Who had sons called Ham, Shem and Japheth?
7 Which former Radio 1 DJ had a commemorative day on 12th October 2005?
8 Which British Olympic gold ice skating medallist died in 1995?
9 When did Halley's Comet last appear?
10 How many legs has a lobster?
11 Louise Brown will always hold which famous first?
12 What was the name of King Arthur's sword?
13 Who on TV often used the phrase "you are, are you not..."?
14 On the radio where are you sent with eight records of your choice?
15 Which part of its body does a snake use to detect noise?
16 Who was the first American president to resign from office?
17 In "The Naked Civil Servant" whom did John Hurt portray?
18 "Thanks for the Memory" was the theme song of which comedian?
19 Whom did Michael Caine play in "The Ipcress File"?
20 Which magazine has been edited by Richard Ingrams and Ian Hislop?
21 Who topped the US and UK charts with "My Heart Will Go On?"
22 Which soccer ground did Sunderland move from in 1997?
23 In which country was Checkpoint Charlie located?
24 What number in bingo is two fat ladies?
25 How many notes are there in an octave?
26 What is it that Americans call the sidewalk?
27 Which creature links Jimmy Nail's Shoes and Elton John's Rock?
28 Which Harold won the Nobel Prize for Literature in 2005?
29 How many years are involved in a golden celebration?
30 How many faults are incurred for a refusal in showjumping?

Answers | **Pot-Luck 5** *(see Quiz 9)*

1 David Blunkett. 2 Four. 3 Backstroke. 4 Knitting. 5 St Albans. 6 Social Democrat Party. 7 Dyslexia. 8 Swimming. 9 Tokyo. 10 Ferdinand Magellan. 11 George Robey. 12 Rimsky-Korsakov. 13 Robbie Williams. 14 Radio Five Live. 15 Fountain pen. 16 Heath Robinson. 17 Bill Clinton. 18 Tony Benn. 19 Prisoner. 20 Harp. 21 Gnasher. 22 Rothmans. 23 Kris Kristofferson. 24 18. 25 Francis Durbridge. 26 Sleeping Beauty. 27 Harold Macmillan. 28 Amber. 29 Horse. 30 April.

1 Which Disney film released in 1942 was about a little fawn?
2 How many days did it take David Niven to go Around the World?
3 In the 1957 film about Japanese prisoners of war, where was the Bridge?
4 Which yuletide classic was first sung by Bing Crosby in "Holiday Inn"?
5 If Lady is a pedigree spaniel what is the name of the mongrel?
6 Which Ben won 11 Oscars in 1959?
7 In which 1940 film did Mickey Mouse conduct the orchestra?
8 In which film did Vivien Leigh play Scarlett O'Hara?
9 Who starred in the Road films with Dorothy Lamour and Bing Crosby?
10 Which film set in Rick's Café starred Humphrey Bogart and Ingrid Bergman?
11 Which distinguished actor, later a Lord, played the lead in "Henry V"?
12 Which film starred Celia Johnson, Trevor Howard and a train station?
13 Which Alfred directed the thrillers "Rebecca" and "Notorious"?
14 Which actor Orson starred in "Citizen Kane" and "The Third Man"?
15 Who played eight different characters in "Kind Hearts and Coronets"?
16 What was the series of comedies made in West London studios called?
17 Where was Gene Kelly Singin' in 1952?
18 How did Some Like It in the film with Jack Lemmon, Tony Curtis and Marilyn Monroe?
19 What was the name of the car that involved Kenneth More and Dinah Sheridan in the London to Brighton road run?
20 Which young star of "East of Eden" died in a car crash aged 24?
21 Which actress married Prince Rainier of Monaco?
22 Which French "sex kitten" starred with Dirk Bogarde in "Doctor at Sea"?
23 In the Charlton Heston film how many commandments were there?
24 Where was there Room in the film starring Laurence Harvey?
25 Who was the young star of "National Velvet" in 1945?
26 Which dancer/actress Ginger won an Oscar in 1940?
27 Which actor Marlon starred in "On the Waterfront"?
28 What goes with Old Lace in the title of the Cary Grant film?
29 What is A Many Splendored Thing in the film about the Korean War?
30 From Here to where is the Oscar-winning movie with Deborah Kerr, Burt Lancaster and Frank Sinatra?

Answers	**Around England** *(see Quiz 10)*

1 Rivers. 2 Cumbria. 3 Birmingham. 4 Victoria. 5 Essex. 6 Yorkshire. 7 Blackpool. 8 Zoo. 9 The Minster. 10 Isle of Wight. 11 A city. 12 Thames. 13 Southport. 14 English Channel. 15 National Exhibition Centre. 16 The Potteries. 17 Manchester. 18 M6. 19 Northeast. 20 Liverpool. 21 Oxford. Cambridge. 22 Pennines. 23 Dartmoor. 24 Cars. 25 Isle of Man. 26 Stonehenge. 27 Shakespeare's. 28 Kent. 29 One. 30 Rutland.

1 What does an arctophile collect?
2 Which of Verdi's operas is set in Ancient Egypt?
3 What gives red blood cells their colour?
4 What was the name of Nintendo's 2005 canine computer game?
5 On TV, what kind of creature was Flipper?
6 Which animals took Hannibal over the Alps?
7 How is the auracaria tree more commonly known?
8 In which team game do you try to move backwards all the time?
9 Which country did the British and Irish Lions tour in 2005?
10 Who was the first British monarch to visit New Zealand?
11 Who recorded the albums "John Wesley Harding" and "Nashville Skyline"?
12 Who does the Beast fall in love with?
13 What is the main ingredient in a brick?
14 What hangs down from the roof of cave – a stalagmite or a stalactite?
15 What is the body of a penguin covered with?
16 How does Saturday's child work for a living?
17 Who presented the first series of "Big Brother"?
18 Which musical direction means at ease, at a slow comfortable pace?
19 Which bell said, "You owe me five farthings"?
20 Which king is said to have burnt the cakes?
21 Which British national daily newspaper ceased publication in 1995?
22 Which girl shares her name with a Christmas song?
23 How many edges in a cube?
24 Which dance comes from "Orpheus in the Underworld"?
25 At what age does a filly become classified as mare?
26 What type of creature is a Pacific sea wasp?
27 Who had a No 1 in 1995 with "You are Not Alone"?
28 How many are there in a baker's dozen?
29 Who is the eldest of the Corrs?
30 Is the South Pole at the Arctic or the Antarctic?

| **Answers** | Pot-Luck 8 *(see Quiz 15)* |

1 Rugby. 2 Mongoose in a Rudyard Kipling story. 3 Three. 4 Bedrock. 5 Australia. 6 Mrs Emery. 7 Richard Adams. 8 The giant tortoise. 9 Joseph. 10 Epidermis. 11 Sausages. 12 Robbie. 12 A backbone. 14 Little John. 15 Germaine Greer. 16 Nine. 17 Asia. 18 Perry Mason. 19 Istanbul. 20 Tottenham Hotspur. 21 Irving Berlin. 22 Taurus. 23 Windsor. 24 7-0. 25 Sandie Shaw. 26 Stamps. 27 Spandau. 28 Benjamin Britten. 29 Pay As You Earn. 30 Richard Beckinsale.

Quiz 14 — Sport: Football

1 Who plays home games at Ewood Park?
2 Which team are known as the Gunners?
3 What colour are Manchester United's home shirts?
4 Which European country was drawn in the group with England in the 2006 World Cup in Germany?
5 Wayne Rooney joined Man Utd from which club?
6 Which city has teams called Wednesday and United?
7 Jose Mourinho joined Chelsea from which club in Portugal?
8 Who plays against Rangers in an Auld Firm derby match?
9 How many minutes in the second half of a Premier League match?
10 What name is shared by Birmingham, Coventry and Leicester?
11 Which colour card is used to send a player off?
12 Which German city hosted the final of the 2006 World Cup?
13 Which country does Ryan Giggs play for?
14 Which Graeme has managed Blackburn, Liverpool, Newcastle and Rangers?
15 Which East Anglian team is nicknamed the Canaries?
16 How many players should be on the pitch at the start of a game?
17 Who won the World Cup in 1958, 1962, 1970 and 1990?
18 Which team plays home games at Villa Park?
19 Raphael Benitez managed which British club to win the 2005 Champions League?
20 Hearts and Hibs come from which Scottish city?
21 What number is traditionally worn on the goalie's shirt?
22 Which England keeper Paul moved from Leeds to Spurs?
23 Which country does Freddie Ljunberg play for?
24 If you were at Goodison Park who would be playing at home?
25 Martin O'Neill managed which club to the Scottish title?
26 Which Nottingham club was managed by Brian Clough?
27 What is the colour of the home strip of both Everton and Chelsea?
28 Who managed England during the 2002 World Cup campaign?
29 Can a goalkeeper score a goal for his own team?
30 At which Lane do Spurs play when at home?

Answers | Soups (see Quiz 16)

1 Queen Victoria. 2 Dingle. 3 The patio. 4 Ramsay. 5 Brown. 6 Emmerdale. 7 Frankie. 8 Falcon. 9 Ric Griffin. 10 Home and Away. 11 H. 12 Peyton. 13 Crossroads. 14 Fowler. 15 The Colbys. 16 Knot's. 17 Brookside. 18 Jason Donovan. 19 Jack and Vera Duckworth. 20 Angie Watts. 21 J.R. 22 Sadie. 23 Girl. 24 Emmerdale. 25 Melbourne. 26 The Bill. 27 Rita Sullivan. 28 Ena. 29 America. 20 Barbara Windsor.

1 Thomas Arnold was headmaster of which public school?
2 What kind of creature was Rikki-Tikki-Tavi?
3 In the story, how many men were in Jerome K. Jerome's boat?
4 In which town do the Flintstones live?
5 In 1930, which country did Amy Johnson fly to from England?
6 What is the name of the incontinent character in "Little Britain"?
7 Who wrote "Watership Down"?
8 Which animal is regarded as the one with the longest life span?
9 Who in the Bible had a coat of many colours?
10 What is the outer layer of skin called?
11 What meat appears in a Punch and Judy show?
12 Who left "Take That" in July 1995?
13 What does an invertebrate not have?
14 Who was the tallest of Robin Hood's Men?
15 Who wrote "The Female Eunuch"?
16 In "Countdown" how many letters are selected for the letters game?
17 Which continent suffered a devastating earthquake in October 2005?
18 Della Street was secretary to which famous legal character?
19 What did Constantinople become known as in March 1930?
20 Sol Campbell joined Arsenal from which club?
21 Who wrote the song "White Christmas"?
22 Which star sign has the bull as its symbol?
23 In which English town did Charles and Camilla marry?
24 In a tennis tie-break, what is the largest winning margin?
25 Who won the Eurovision Song Contest in bare feet?
26 What do philatelists collect?
27 Rudolf Hess was the last prisoner in which jail?
28 Who composed "Peter Grimes"?
29 What does PAYE stand for?
30 Who played student Alan Moore in "Rising Damp"?

Answers	Pot-Luck 7 *(see Quiz 13)*

1 Teddy bears. 2 Aida. 3 Haemoglobin. 4 Nintendogs. 5 Dolphin. 6 Elephants. 7 Monkey puzzle. 8 Tug of War. 9 New Zealand. 10 Elizabeth II. 11 Bob Dylan. 12 Beauty. 13 Clay. 14 Stalactite. 15 Feathers. 16 Hard. 17 Davina McCall. 18 Adagio. 19 St Martins. 20 Alfred. 21 Today. 22 Carol. 23 12. 24 The can-can. 25 Five. 26 Jellyfish. 27 Michael Jackson. 28 13. 29 Jim. 30 Antarctic.

1 What is the name of the pub in Albert Square?
2 Which "Emmerdale" family's members include Sam and Delilah?
3 What was Trevor Jordache buried under in "Brookside"?
4 In which street is "Neighbours" set?
5 What was Cilla's surname before she married "Coronation Street"s Les Battersby?
6 In which soap is there a pub called the Woolpack?
7 Who was Danny Baldwin's wife when they first moved into Coronation Street?
8 Which bird added to a Crest completes a soap series?
9 Who was Jess Griffin's dad in "Holby City"?
10 Which Australian soap is set in Summer Bay?
11 On which Cell Block might there be a Prisoner in an Australian soap?
12 Which Place was the the name of the first major US soap?
13 Which British soap was set in a motel?
14 In "EastEnders" what was Sonia's surname when she married Martin?
15 Which soap was a spin-off of "Dynasty"?
16 In which Landing did some members of Dallas's Ewing family settle?
17 Which soap has featured the Corkhills, the Grants and the Dixons?
18 Who left his role as Scott Robinson and became a West End Joseph?
19 Which couple took over the Rovers' Return after Bet Gilroy left?
20 Who was Sharon's mum in "EastEnders"?
21 By what initials was actor Larry Hagman known as in "Dallas"?
22 Which character in "Emmerdale" was played by Patsy Kensit?
23 In "Home and Away" was Bobby Simpson a boy or a girl?
24 Where was there a horrific air crash in December 1993?
25 In which Australian city is "Neighbours" set?
26 Which police series is based at Sun Hill police station?
27 In "Coronation Street" who owns the Kabin?
28 What was the first name of legendary Street character Mrs Sharples?
29 Which country did Michelle go to when she left Albert Square?
30 Which Carry On star became Phil and Grant's mum in "EastEnders"?

Answers	**Sport: Football** *(see Quiz 14)*

1 Blackburn Rovers. 2 Arsenal. 3 Red. 4 Sweden. 5 Everton. 6 Sheffield. 7 FC Porto. 8 Celtic. 9 45. 10 City. 11 Red. 12 Berlin. 13 Wales. 14 Souness. 15 Norwich City. 16 22. 17 Brazil. 18 Aston Villa. 19 Liverpool. 20 Edinburgh. 21 1. 22 Robinson. 23 Sweden. 24 Everton. 25 Celtic. 26 Forest. 27 Blue. 28 Sven Goran Eriksson. 29 Yes. 30 White Hart.

1 Which Girls took "Sound of the Underground" to No 1?
2 What is the zodiac sign of Pisces?
3 What is the fruity name of Gwyneth Paltrow's daughter?
4 Who had a No 1 hit with the song "Wuthering Heights"?
5 With which branch of medicine is Mesmer associated?
6 In recent years, which politician John punched an assailant in North Wales who threw an egg an him?
7 In the nursery rhyme, what did Tom, Tom the piper's son steal?
8 Who wrote "Where Have All the Flowers Gone"?
9 In "HMS Pinafore" whom did Sir Joseph Porter bring on boat along with his sisters?
10 According to the proverb, what begins at home?
11 Which birds are traditionally used by Japanese fishermen to help them catch fish?
12 Who played TV's Inspector Morse?
13 Called chequers in America, what's the name of this game in Britain?
14 Who was the last queen of England by succession before Elizabeth II?
15 What is the term for fear of enclosed spaces?
16 Name the consortium that runs the National Lottery?
17 What was the name of the Big River sung about by Jimmy Nail?
18 What is the name of the person who delivers the mail in Greendale?
19 Which city is the setting for "Saturday Night Fever"?
20 What was the No 1 recording made by Matthews Southern Comfort?
21 Which food item is most consumed by humans throughout the world?
22 Which boxer said, "Know what I mean, 'Arry"?
23 Which day of the week is named after the god Thor?
24 Who first recorded "A Whiter Shade of Pale"?
25 What is Sweden's national flower?
26 What do entomologists study?
27 What tree does a date grow on?
28 In the song, what did my true love send to me on the seventh day of Christmas?
29 Who was the famous son of Uther Pendragon?
30 How many goals did France score in the 1998 World Cup final?

Answers	Pot-Luck 10 *(see Quiz 19)*

1 Westlife. 2 The Rolling Stones. 3 Dennis Rickman. 4 Dire Straits. 5 Tennis. 6 Ethelred. 7 Phil. 8 Australia. 9 Abraham Lincoln. 10 Davy Crockett. 11 India. 12 New York. 13 Home on the Range. 14 Mars. 15 Wins. 16 Four. 17 Rin Tin Tin. 18 Toytown. 19 India. 20 Female. 21 Argentina. 22 Male. 23 Gordon Richards. 24 Saffron. 25 Chest. 26 American. 27 Blessed. 28 The Saint. 29 Honey bees. 30 Women's Royal Air Force.

Quiz 18 | Theatre and Musicals

1 Michael Crawford starred in the musical about "The Woman" in which colour?
2 Who wrote the long-running play "The Mousetrap"?
3 Complete the title of the comedy: "No Sex Please _____"
4 In "Starlight Express" what do the performers wear on their feet?
5 What was Jesus Christ according to Tim Rice and Andrew Lloyd Webber?
6 According to the comedy, There's a what in My Soup?
7 Where is the Fiddler in the musical which starred Topol?
8 Which London theatre's motto was, "We never closed"?
9 Which New York street is famous for its theatres?
10 Which musical about Professor Higgins and Eliza Doolittle is based on "Pygmalion"?
11 Who wrote the music in the comic operas for which Gilbert wrote the words?
12 What do the initials RSC stand for?
13 Which musical is based on T. S. Eliot's poems?
14 Who first played the title role in "Evita" in the West End?
15 Which musical is the name of a US state?
16 Which show includes "Climb Ev'ry Mountain"?
17 Which musical is the name of a fairground ride?
18 Which musical is about a circus impresario?
19 In which musical does Fagin appear?
20 Which Boulevard is the title of a musical?
21 Which part of the Pacific is the setting for a popular musical?
22 Which class of Society is a musical based on "The Philadelphia Story"?
23 Which Arthur wrote "Death of a Salesman", a play revived in the West End in 2005?
24 The Importance of Being what is the name of an Oscar Wilde play?
25 Who are with the Guys in the show about gangsters?
26 Which girl is the lecturer Educating in the play by Willy Russell?
27 Which Miss is a musical set in Vietnam?
28 What is the full name of the show often just referred to as Les Mis?
29 What do you say to Dolly in the title of the show?
30 Aspects of what are the theme of which Lloyd Webber musical?

Answers	40s and 50s Newsround *(see Quiz 20)*

1 Churchill. 2 Hitler. 3 The Blitz. 4 Prisoner of war. 5 Vera Lynn. 6 Dad's Army. 7 USSR. 8 Africa. 9 France. 10 Europe. 11 1945. 12 Princess Elizabeth. 13 Israel. 14 Miss World. 15 Jeans. 16 John F. Kennedy. 17 USSR. 18 Everest. 19 Hovercraft. 20 Premium Bonds. 21 Hula hoop. 22 Mini. 23 M1. 24 Teenagers. 25 Coffee. 26 Holiday camps. 27 Meters. 28 USSR. 29 Skiffle. 30 The Bomb.

1 Which boy band had a 2003 No 1 with "Mandy"?
2 What was the most famous group managed by Andrew Loog Oldham?
3 Who was Dirty Den's son as played by Nigel Harman?
4 Who recorded the album "Brothers in Arms"?
5 In which sport is the Davis Cup played for?
6 Which English king was said to be Unready?
7 Which of the Neville brothers was first to leave Man Utd?
8 Which team did England beat in the 2003 rugby World Cup final?
9 Which US president was assassinated in a Washington theatre?
10 Who had a rifle called "Old Betsy"?
11 David Lean's film was about a passage to which country?
12 Which city was "so good they named it twice"?
13 In song, where do the deer and the antelope play?
14 Which planet is fourth from the sun?
15 According to a Nick Berry song title every loser does what?
16 How many sides has a parallelogram?
17 Which film star dog had three names each containing three letters?
18 Where did Larry the Lamb live?
19 In which country did the Thuggee – from which we derive the word thug – operate?
20 Is Mickie a male or female character in Holby City?
21 Which country did Juan Perón rule?
22 Is it the male or female cuckoo that makes the "cuck-oo" call?
23 Which jockey was knighted in 1953?
24 On TV, what's the name of Edina's daughter?
25 What can be a box or part of the body?
26 What nationality was the notorious murderer Dr Crippen?
27 Which Brian appeared in "Z Cars" and "Cats" and is an authority on Mount Everest?
28 Which holy-sounding character was created by Leslie Charteris?
29 Which insects live in apiaries?
30 What does WRAF stand for?

Answers	**Pot-Luck 9** (see Quiz 17)

1 Girls Aloud. 2 Fish. 3 Apple. 4 Kate Bush. 5 Hypnotism. 6 John Prescott. 7 A pig. 8 Pete Seeger. 9 His cousins and his aunts. 10 Charity. 11 Cormorants. 12 John Thaw. 13 Draughts. 14 Queen Victoria. 15 Claustrophobia. 16 Camelot. 17 Tyne. 18 Postman Pat. 19 New York. 20 Woodstock. 21 Rice. 22 Frank Bruno. 23 Thursday. 24 Procol Harum. 25 Lily of the valley. 26 Insects. 27 Palm. 28 Seven swans a-swimming. 29 King Arthur. 30 Three.

1 Which Winston took over as prime minister in 1940?
2 Who was the German leader throughout World War II?
3 What name was given to the persistent air attack on London?
4 What does POW stand for?
5 Who was known as the Forces' Sweetheart?
6 What was the popular name for the Home Guard?
7 Which country was Stalin leader of?
8 Which continent was El Alamein in?
9 In which country did the D Day landings take place?
10 V-E Day commemorated victory on which continent?
11 World War II ended in which year?
12 Whose engagement to Philip Mountbatten was announced in 1947?
13 Which Jewish state was founded in 1948?
14 Which competition did Miss Sweden win the first of in 1951?
15 Which type of denim trousers took Britain by storm in 1955?
16 Which future US president did Jacqueline Bouvier marry in 1953?
17 Which country launched the first satellite – Sputnik 1 – in space?
18 What was climbed by Edmund Hillary and Tensing in 1953?
19 Which craft which floats on an air cushion was invented in 1958?
20 What type of prize-winning Bonds were introduced?
21 Which large plastic hoop became a sports craze in the 1950s?
22 Which small car did Austin and Morris launch in 1959?
23 What was the name of the London to Birmingham motorway?
24 Which word for 13- to 19-year-olds was first coined in the 1950s?
25 A frothy version of which non-alcoholic drink became popular in this era?
26 What did Billy Butlin found in the 1950s?
27 What type of parking payment machine was introduced in London?
28 Where did spies Burgess, Maclean and Philby defect to?
29 Which type of 1950s music used a washboard?
30 What did CND marchers on the way to Aldermaston want to ban?

Answers | Theatre and Musicals *(see Quiz 18)*

1 White. 2 Agatha Christie. 3 We're British. 4 Skates. 5 Superstar. 6 Girl. 7 On the Roof. 8 The Windmill. 9 Broadway. 10 My Fair Lady. 11 Sullivan. 12 Royal Shakespeare Company. 13 Cats. 14 Elaine Paige. 15 Oklahoma! 16 The Sound of Music. 17 Carousel. 18 Barnum. 19 Oliver! 20 Sunset. 21 South. 22 High. 23 Miller. 24 Earnest. 25 Dolls. 26 Rita. 27 Saigon. 28 Les Misérables. 29 Hello. 30 Love.

1 What type of singing voice does Russell Watson have?
2 In which TV programme do Patsy and Edina appear?
3 Which band had a chart hit with "Speed of Sound"?
4 In which month does the grouse shooting season start in Britain?
5 What type of racing has only two cars competing on the track at the same time?
6 How many years are celebrated by a platinum anniversary?
7 What is an oblong bar of gold called?
8 Harry Kewell is a football international for which country?
9 Which European soccer trophy did Spurs become the first British team to win?
10 In the Paul McCartney/Stevie Wonder hit what went with ebony?
11 In which month is Twelfth Night?
12 In which city is the Whitney art gallery?
13 In which soap do the Sugdens appear?
14 What are the initials of thriller writer James?
15 Who recorded the album "The Immaculate Collection"?
16 In the book title, whom did writer Laurie Lee have cider with?
17 Which musical does "I Know Him So Well" come from?
18 Which fictional Scottish doctor kept a casebook?
19 Who made up Abba with Benny, Bjorn and Annifrid?
20 Which traveller had the unusual first name of Lemuel?
21 Who wrote the words to "The Boxer"?
22 In which country is Hampden Park Stadium?
23 What can be upside down, ginger or Dundee?
24 What was the name of the musical show about Frank Sinatra, Sammy Davis and Dean Martin?
25 Who was the lead singer with Culture Club?
26 What do the French words au revoir mean ?
27 Who said, "Am I dying beyond my means?"?
28 Who played the character of Mrs Fawlty?
29 Which Marie is supposed to have said, "Let them eat cake"?
30 What do the initials TB stand for?

Answers | Pot-Luck 12 *(see Quiz 23)*

1 Andrew. 2 300. 3 Spain. 4 Edward VIII. 5 Dido. 6 Valhalla. 7 Iron. 8 Rommel.
9 Mrs Dale's Diary. 10 January. 11 Queen Vic. 12 Piano. 13 Mick McCarthy. 14 Haddock. 15 Avocado. 16 Austria. 17 Plimsoll Line. 18 Soup. 19 Lorna Doone. 20 Vivaldi. 21 Dublin. 22 Richmal Crompton. 23 XIV. 24 Chair. 25 Alexander the Great. 26 Karen. 27 Intelligence. 28 Spencer. 29 Jerusalem. 30 Bonsai.

1 Is Australia in the northern or the southern hemisphere?
2 What does each star on the flag of the United States stand for?
3 Which country does the holiday island of Ibiza belong to?
4 Which island would you visit to kiss the Blarney Stone?
5 In which country would you be if you were visiting the Taj Mahal?
6 The south of which continent is closest to the Falkland Islands?
7 In which mountain range would you find Mount Everest?
8 Which country is Luxembourg the capital of?
9 What colour is the spot in the middle of the Japanese flag?
10 The island of Sicily is at the toe of which country?
11 Which country is also known as the Netherlands?
12 In which country are Maoris the indigenous population?
13 In which Scandinavian country would you find fjords?
14 Which country's languages include English, Zulu and Afrikaans?
15 Which country's name could be part of a Christmas dinner?
16 In which city is the Vatican City?
17 What is K2?
18 In which country is the Yellow River, also known as Huang He?
19 Which country has four letters, the last one q?
20 Which country, capital Bangkok, used to be called Siam?
21 Which ocean lies between Europe and America?
22 Which European country has an area called Flanders?
23 Which stretch of water separates Anglesey and Wales?
24 Which Rock is on the south coast of Spain?
25 Which isle lies between England and Northern Ireland?
26 Which island to the south of India used to be called Ceylon?
27 Which sea separates Europe and Africa?
28 In which ocean is Fiji?
29 Which island, in the Arctic Ocean, is the largest in the world?
30 In which continent is the world's longest river, the Nile?

Answers	Sounds of the 60s (see Quiz 24)

1 Happiness. 2 Blue Jeans. 3 Dustman. 4 Downtown. 5 Congratulations. 6 Sonny. 7 Diana Ross. 8 Pins. 9 Whiter. 10 The Pacemakers. 11 24. 12 Freddie. 13 Herman. 14 Roy Orbison. 15 Go. 16 Lollipop. 17 Fashion. 18 Billy J. Kramer. 19 The Rising Sun. 20 Lulu. 21 Four. 22 Cilla Black. 23 The Monkees. 24 Nights. 25 Dusty Springfield. 26 The Who. 27 Yellow. 28 The Shadows. 29 The Beach Boys. 30 Papas.

1 At the end of 2005, which was the only son of the Queen who was unmarried?

2 How many minutes in five hours?

3 A car with the international registration letter E comes from where?

4 Who came first, King Edward VIII or George VI?

5 Who recorded the million-selling album "Life for Rent"?

6 Where were Norse gods said to live?

7 Fe is the symbol of which chemical element?

8 Which army commander was known as "The Desert Fox"?

9 In which early radio soap was Mary worried about Jim?

10 What is the first month of the year to have exactly 31 days?

11 Under the floor of which building did Chrissie bury Dirty Den's body?

12 Which musical instrument has dampers, hammers and strings?

13 Who was the Republic of Ireland's World Cup manager in 2002?

14 Which fish is smoked and cured and called "finnan"?

15 Which pear-shaped tropical fruit has given its name to a bathroom suite colouring?

16 The Spanish Riding School is in which country?

17 What was the original name of the line on a ship showing the level to which it could be loaded?

18 Bouillabaisse is what kind of fish dish?

19 John Ridd is the male lead in which book with a girl's name as its title?

20 Who wrote the music "The Four Seasons"?

21 In which city in 1916 was the Easter Rising?

22 Who wrote the stories about a schoolboy named William Brown?

23 Which King Louis built the palace at Versailles?

24 Sedan, arm and high are all types of what?

25 Who had a horse called Bucephalus?

26 What was the first name of the female singer in the Carpenters?

27 In the USA what does the I stand for in CIA?

28 What was the surname of Frank in "Some Mothers Do 'Ave 'Em"?

29 "Walk upon England's mountains green" is the second line of which rousing song?

30 What name is given to the Japanese skill of growing miniature trees?

Answers | **Pot-Luck 11** *(see Quiz 21)*

1 Tenor. 2 Absolutely Fabulous. 3 Coldplay. 4 August. 5 Drag Racing. 6 70. 7 Ingot. 8 Australia. 9 European Cup Winners' Cup. 10 Ivory. 11 January. 12 New York. 13 Emmerdale. 14 P. D. 15 Madonna. 16 Rosie. 17 Chess. 18 Doctor Finlay. 19 Agnetha. 20 Gulliver. 21 Paul Simon. 22 Scotland. 23 Cake. 24 The Rat Pack. 25 Boy George. 26 Until we meet again. 27 Oscar Wilde. 28 Prunella Scales. 29 Antoinette. 30 Tuberculosis.

1 What was Helen Shapiro Walking Back to in 1961?
2 What was Venus wearing in 1962 according to Mark Wynter?
3 What was the occupation of Lonnie Donegan's old man?
4 In which part of town was Petula Clark in the 1960s?
5 What was the title of Cliff Richard's 1968 Eurovision song?
6 Who was Cher's first singing partner with a hit song?
7 Who was lead singer with the Supremes?
8 What did the Searchers sing about along with Needles?
9 What shade of Pale did Procol Harum sing about?
10 Who was Gerry's backing group?
11 How many Hours was Gene Pitney from Tulsa?
12 Who sang with the Dreamers?
13 Who had Hermits?
14 Who was known as "The Big O"?
15 What followed Ready, Steady in the title of the pop show?
16 My Boy, according to Millie, is called what?
17 What were the Kinks Dedicated Followers of in 1966?
18 Who sang with the Dakotas?
19 According to the Animals, what was the name of The House in New Orleans?
20 Who was heard to "Shout" in 1964?
21 How many were there in the Tops, Pennies and Seasons?
22 Which Liverpool lady took "Anyone Who Had a Heart" to No 1?
23 Which US band "aped" the Beatles and sang "Daydream Believer"?
24 What was in White Satin according to the Moody Blues?
25 Who left her two group members and sang "I Only Want to be with You"?
26 Which group wrote the rock opera "Tommy"?
27 What colour was the Beatles' Submarine?
28 Who was Cliff Richard's backing group?
29 Who felt "Good Vibrations" in 1966?
30 Who sang with the Mamas?

Answers	Geography *(see Quiz 22)*

1 Southern. 2 A state. 3 Spain. 4 Ireland. 5 India. 6 South America. 7 Himalayas.
8 Luxembourg. 9 Red. 10 Italy. 11 Holland. 12 New Zealand. 13 Norway. 14
South Africa. 15 Turkey. 16 Rome. 17 Mountain. 18 China. 19 Iraq. 20 Thailand.
21 Atlantic. 22 Belgium. 23 Menai Strait. 24 Gibraltar. 25 Isle of Man. 26 Sri Lanka.
27 Mediterranean. 28 Pacific. 29 Greenland. 30 Africa.

1 Who was the only woman on the "Strictly Come Dancing" panel of judges for 2005?
2 Which country was the first to win the World Cup five times?
3 Which former British Prime Minister who died in 2005 was a keen yachtsman?
4 Who had a No 1 hit with the song "I Just Called to Say I Love You"?
5 Who wrote "The Owl and the Pussycat"?
6 What are beds of snooker tables traditionally made of?
7 By what name was travelling show tap dancer Luther Robinson known?
8 What was the name of the "Neighbours" character played by Kylie Minogue?
9 What word describes the permanent disappearance of a species?
10 The Star of Africa is what type of gem?
11 In education, what does BA stand for?
12 In the human body, what has four chambers?
13 Which creature can turn its stomach inside out?
14 There are 78 cards in which type of pack?
15 What is arachnophobia the fear of?
16 Which two writers created "Auf Wiedersehen, Pet"?
17 How many cards of the same suit are needed for a flush in poker?
18 What name is given to an athletics event such as running or hurdling?
19 Which war in Europe took place between 1936–9?
20 Under what name did Samuel Clemens write?
21 Who recorded the album "Tubular Bells"?
22 In which city is the Obelisk of Luxor?
23 Which day of the week is named after the moon?
24 In the USA what is a greenback?
25 October 2005 witnessed events to mark the bicentenary of which admiral's death?
26 Which Charles wrote "The Origin of Species"?
27 Donnerstag is German for which day?
28 Jennyanydots was what kind of cat?
29 What is the federal republic of Switzerland divided into?
30 Who wrote "Rebecca"?

Answers | **Pot-Luck 14** *(see Quiz 27)*

1 Confessions on a Dance Floor. 2 Schilling. 3 Measles. 4 Oasis. 5 Bob Geldof. 6 Cabriolet. 7 Clock. 8 Cilla Black. 9 Scott Joplin. 10 Bell. 11 Enya. 12 1931. 13 Bread. 14 Cabbage. 15 Derby County. 16 Three. 17 Radioactivity. 18 Larry Grayson. 19 Tyne. 20 Anthony Quinn. 21 Sex change. 22 Blue. 23 Lawson. 24 Cruet. 25 Nap. 26 The Blue Angel. 27 Prince Charles. 28 Captain W. E. Johns. 29 Fifty. 30 World Boxing Association.

1 In which Italian city were the 1960 Olympic Games held?
2 What nationality were 1961 Wimbledon finalists Christine Trueman and Angela Mortimer?
3 What was the first name of heavyweight boxing champion Liston?
4 Who won the FA Cup for the first time, under Bill Shankly?
5 What was the surname of cricketer Fiery Fred who retired in 1968?
6 What nationality was 1962 Wimbledon champion Rod Laver?
7 In what kind of racing was Jim Clark world champion?
8 Which Stanley retired from playing football aged 50?
9 Who won the World Cup in 1966?
10 Which Glasgow soccer team were the first British side to win the European Cup?
11 In 1969 Tony Jacklin was US Open Champion in which sport?
12 What was the surname of boxer Cassius?
13 What was the first name of British Wimbledon champion Mrs Jones?
14 What was the first name of US golfer Palmer?
15 Which Henry was British heavyweight champion in 1963?
16 Which father of Damon won the World Drivers championship in 1962?
17 What was the surname of Wimbledon singles champion Billie-Jean?
18 Which country does 1969 motor racing champion Jackie Stewart come from?
19 What was the surname of former Manchester United legend George?
20 How did Anita Lonsborough win an Olympic gold medal in 1960?
21 Which country was banned from the Olympics because of apartheid?
22 Which jump won Mary Rand a gold medal at the 1964 Olympics?
23 What was the surname of international footballers Jackie and Bobby?
24 Which international football trophy was stolen in 1966?
25 At which sport were Margaret Court and Maria Bueno champions?
26 Who were the runners-up in the 1966 World Cup?
27 What sport was Jack Brabham famous for?
28 Which England manager Alf received a knighthood?
29 Which UK tennis championship was the first to be seen on TV in colour in 1967?
30 Sir Matt Busby retired as manager of which football club?

Answers | The 60s *(see Quiz 28)*

1 Coronation Street. 2 Z Cars. 3 Forsyte Saga. 4 University Challenge. 5 Your Lucky Stars. 6 Dr Who. 7 Dr Finlay. 8 Flintstones. 9 Liver Birds. 10 Magic Roundabout. 11 Man from UNCLE. 12 Match of the Day. 13 Horse. 14 Adam. 15 The Avengers. 16 Home. 17 That was the Week That was. 18 Mason. 19 Peyton Place. 20 The Saint. 21 Songs of Praise 22 Star Trek. 23 Till Death Us Do Part. 24 Tomorrow's. 25 Top of the Pops. 26 Williams. 27 England, West Germany. 28 Dudley Moore. 29 Winters. 30 The Beatles.

1 "Hung Up" was a track featured on which Madonna album?
2 What is the currency of Austria?
3 Which childhood disease is also known as rubella?
4 Who recorded the album "Definitely, Maybe"?
5 Who was presented a 2005 MTV award, for organizing the Live8 concert?
6 Cab is a shortening of which word?
7 In rhyming slang what is meant by dickory dock?
8 How is Priscilla White better known?
9 Who wrote "Maple Leaf Rag"?
10 The Tsar Kolokol is the biggest what in the world?
11 In November 2005, which Irish singer released her album "Amarantine"?
12 To five years either way, when was the Empire State Building finished?
13 Which comedy series featured the Boswell family?
14 Brassica oleracea is better known as what?
15 Which club once played soccer home games at the Baseball Ground?
16 How many sides has an isosceles triangle?
17 What does a Geiger counter detect?
18 Whose catchphrase was, "Shut that door!"?
19 Which major river flows through Newcastle?
20 Who was the star of "Zorba the Greek"?
21 Which much-publicized operation did Doctor Richard Raskind undergo?
22 In the song, what colour are Crystal Gale's brown eyes made?
23 Which Nigel is a former Chancellor of the Exchequer?
24 What is the word for a condiment container?
25 What can be a sleep or how fabric lies?
26 In which film did Dietrich sing "Falling in Love Again"?
27 Which Prince visited Ground Zero with his wife in the autumn of 2005?
28 Who created Biggles?
29 According to Paul Simon, how many ways are there to leave your lover?
30 In boxing, what does WBA stand for?

| **Answers** | **Pot-Luck 13** *(see Quiz 25)* |

1 Arlene Phillips. 2 Brazil. 3 Edward Heath. 4 Stevie Wonder. 5 Edward Lear. 6 Slate. 7 Bojangles. 8 Charlene. 9 Extinction. 10 Diamond. 11 Bachelor of Arts. 12 The heart. 13 Starfish. 14 Tarot. 15 Spiders. 16 Clement and La Frenais. 17 Five. 18 Track. 19 Spanish Civil War. 20 Mark Twain. 21 Mike Oldfield. 22 Paris. 23 Monday. 24 A dollar bill. 25 Nelson. 26 Darwin. 27 Thursday. 28 Gumbie Cat. 29 Cantons. 30 Daphne du Maurier.

1 Which soap, which started in 1960, tells of life in Weatherfield?
2 Which Cars were at the heart of a long-running police drama series?
3 Which family Saga spanned the Victorian and Edwardian eras?
4 Which university quiz was hosted by Bamber Gascoigne?
5 What did you Thank in the ITV Saturday-evening pop show?
6 Which Doctor arrived on our screens in the Tardis in 1963?
7 Whose Casebook was based in a Scottish village surgery?
8 Which cartoon series had a Stone Age setting with Fred and Wilma?
9 Which Birds were flatmates in Liverpool?
10 Which Roundabout was about Dougal, Florence and Zebedee?
11 How was the the Man from the United Network Command for Law and Enforcement better known?
12 Which show began broadcasting highlights of the day's football?
13 What kind of animal was Mr Ed who was able to talk?
14 What was the first name of sci-fi adventurer Adamant?
15 Which series included Emma Peel and Steed?
16 Where was Cathy told to Come in the 1966 play about homelessness?
17 Which satirical programme was abbreviated to TW3?
18 What was the surname of Los Angeles defence lawyer Perry?
19 Which Place was the setting for the early soap with Mia Farrow and Ryan O'Neal?
20 What was the nickname of amateur sleuth Simon Templar?
21 Which long-running hymn singing programme began in 1961?
22 Which programme saw the first adventures of the starship Enterprise?
23 Which series starred the controversial Alf Garnett?
24 Which World about new inventions and discoveries began in 1965?
25 Which chart music show started in 1964?
26 Which American Andy hosted a long-running easy music show?
27 Who played in the football match watched by 32 million in 1966?
28 Who starred with Peter Cook in "Not Only... But Also"?
29 What was the surname of comedy duo Mike and Bernie?
30 In 1963 which Fab Four were all four panellists on "Juke Box Jury"?

Answers	Sport: The 60s *(see Quiz 26)*

1 Rome. 2 British. 3 Sonny. 4 Liverpool. 5 Trueman. 6 Australian.
7 Motor. 8 Matthews. 9 England. 10 Celtic. 11 Golf. 12 Clay. 13 Ann. 14 Arnold.
15 Cooper. 16 Graham Hill. 17 King. 18 Scotland. 19 Best. 20 Swimming. 21
South Africa. 22 Long. 23 Charlton. 24 World Cup. 25 Tennis. 26 West Germany. 27
Motor racing. 28 Ramsey. 29 Wimbledon. 30 Manchester United.

1 Red, yellow and blue are what type of colour?
2 Which Sharon was voted best expert at the 2005 National TV awards?
3 Which John was Labour leader before Tony Blair?
4 Which soccer side has Alexandra in its name?
5 The Acol system is used in which game?
6 How many years are celebrated by a ruby anniversary?
7 What three colours are in the flag of Belgium?
8 Whom did Ashley Peacock marry after Maxine's death in "Coronation Street"?
9 What number does the Roman numeral C stand for?
10 What was the name of Miss Rigby in the song by the Beatles?
11 In which month is Valentine's Day?
12 Which Ron played Fagin on film?
13 Roberta Flack had a No 1 with a song about the First Time I Saw Your what?
14 What are the initials of the poet Eliot?
15 What did Polly Flinders do?
16 Which Frederick wrote "The Day of the Jackal"?
17 Which term means related to the moon?
18 Which star actor links "Ocean's Eleven" and "The Brothers Grimm"?
19 Olympiakos have won the soccer league most times in which country?
20 On what part of your body would you wear a muff?
21 Which Wendy starred in "Butterflies"?
22 In which city is the Oval cricket ground?
23 Which Florence was known as the lady with the lamp?
24 What is a young fox called?
25 On which course is the Derby run?
26 Which special name is given to a group of ravens?
27 Who recorded the album "Thriller"?
28 On TV, is "Brookside" a close, an avenue or a drive?
29 Grandfather, cuckoo and carriage are types of what?
30 RoSPA is the Royal Society for the Prevention of what?

Answers	**Pot-Luck 16** *(see Quiz 31)*

1 Flying. 2 Florence Nightingale. 3 Germany. 4 Dr Doolittle. 5 Tony Blair. 6 HMV – His Master's Voice. 7 Carbon. 8 Popeye. 9 Red and white. 10 November. 11 Martin Bashir. 12 Arnold Layne. 13 Poker. 14 Geometry. 15 Simple Minds. 16 13. 17 Five. 18 Limbo. 19 Eight. 20 Grimm. 21 Heidi. 22 Temple. 23 Heifer. 24 Natalie. 25 Godiva. 26 Midas. 27 Domesday. 28 Paris. 29 Eye. 30 Briers.

Quiz 30 | 60s Films

1 On which Side of New York was the musical Story about rival gangs?
2 Who starred as Cleopatra and married co-star Richard Burton?
3 With which country is Lawrence associated in the film with Peter O'Toole?
4 Which role did Warren Beatty play to Faye Dunaway's Bonnie?
5 What type of Cowboy was Jon Voight in the 1969 film?
6 Who was The Graduate in the film of the same name?
7 Who won an Oscar as Professor Higgins in "My Fair Lady"?
8 Which musical by Lionel Bart was based on a Dickens novel?
9 Which western actor won his only Oscar for "True Grit"?
10 Which actress Mia starred in the controversial "Rosemary's Baby"?
11 What were the hills alive with in the musical set in Austria?
12 What was the nationality of Zorba in the film with Anthony Quinn?
13 Guess Who's Coming to which meal in the Katharine Hepburn film?
14 Which nanny did Julie Andrews win an Oscar for playing?
15 Who played Alfie?
16 Which blonde Julie was a Darling?
17 Who played Fanny Brice in "Funny Girl"?
18 Which Doctor did Omar Sharif play in the film set in the USSR?
19 Which Gregory won an Oscar for "To Kill a Mockingbird"?
20 Which Miss was Maggie Smith whose Prime won an Oscar in '69?
21 Which actor Paul played Thomas More in "A Man for All Seasons"?
22 How many Dalmatians starred in the 1961 Disney film?
23 Who was Butch Cassidy's partner?
24 In the 1968 film when was "The Space Odyssey"?
25 Which 1960 Hitchcock film has the most famous shower scene ever?
26 Which meal was taken at Tiffany's in the film with Audrey Hepburn?
27 Who played James Bond in "Dr No"?
28 What accompanied the Bad and the Ugly in the Clint Eastwood film?
29 Which Sweet girl was played by Shirley Maclaine in the 1968 musical?
30 Which film with Vanessa Redgrave was about King Arthur's court?

Answers | Transport (see Quiz 32)

1 M1. 2 Right. 3 Essex. 4 Ford. 5 Hot-air balloon. 6 Wright. 7 Queen Elizabeth II. 8 France. 9 Rolls Royce. 10 Atlantic. 11 Train. 12 English Channel. 13 Jet. 14 Concorde. 15 Black. 16 M25. 17 Manchester. 18 Jaguar. 19 Queen Mary. 20 M11. 21 Waterloo. 22 Germany. 23 Underground. 24 Paris. 25 Lorry. 26 Railway. 27 Folkestone. 28 London. 29 Moscow. 30 Dartford.

1 Dennis Bergkamp has a phobia about which form of travel?
2 In 1907, who was the first woman to receive the Order of Merit?
3 Which country does a car come from if it has the international registration letter D?
4 Which doctor had a pet chimp called Chee Chee?
5 Who was the youngest British PM of the 20th century?
6 Which company had Nipper the dog as its trademark?
7 C is the symbol of which chemical element ?
8 Which cartoon character has Bluto as his arch rival?
9 Which two colours appear on the flag of Denmark?
10 What is the last month of the year to have exactly 30 days?
11 The "Living with Michael Jackson" documentary was made by which British journalist?
12 In a Pink Floyd song who had the strange hobby of collecting clothes?
13 If you are playing Southern Cross you are playing a form of which game?
14 Euclid is associated with which branch of mathematics?
15 Which group had a No 1 with "Belfast Child"?
16 How many players are in a Rugby League team?
17 In the UK what is the maximum number of years between General Elections?
18 What type of dance involves moving under a low horizontal pole?
19 How many pints in a gallon?
20 Which brothers, Jacob and Wilhelm, wrote fairy tales?
21 Johanna Spyri created which little girl?
22 Which child star Shirley won an Oscar at the age of six?
23 What name is given to a cow that has not had a calf?
24 What is the first name of Nat King Cole's singing daughter?
25 Which Lady rode naked through the streets of Coventry?
26 In legend, which king turned everything he touched into gold?
27 William the Conqueror ordered which Book to be compiled?
28 Which Hilton heiress is named after a European capital city?
29 REM stands for rapid movement of what?
30 Which Richard starred in "Ever Decreasing Circles"?

Answers	Pot-Luck 15 *(see Quiz 29)*

1 Primary. 2 Sharon Osbourne. 3 Smith. 4 Crewe. 5 Bridge. 6 40. 7 Black, red and yellow. 8 Claire. 9 100. 10 Eleanor. 11 February. 12 Moody. 13 Face. 14 T. S. 15 Sat among the cinders. 16 Forsyth. 17 Lunar. 18 Matt Damon. 19 Greece. 20 Hands. 21 Craig. 22 London. 23 Nightingale. 24 Cub. 25 Epsom. 26 Unkindness. 27 Michael Jackson. 28 Close. 29 Clock. 30 Accidents.

1 Which motorway runs from London to Leeds?
2 Do more countries drive on the left or on the right?
3 In which county is Stansted airport?
4 Which company made the first production-line car, the Model T?
5 What did the Mongolfier brothers fly in in 1783?
6 What was the surname of aviation pioneers Orville and Wilbur?
7 What is the full name of the QE2?
8 Which country do Renault cars come from?
9 Who produced the luxury Silver Ghost?
10 Over which ocean did Alcock and Brown fly in 1919?
11 What would you be travelling in if you were in a Pullman?
12 Under which stretch of water would you be if you were on Le Shuttle?
13 Which engine for aircraft was patented by Frank Whittle in 1930?
14 Which Anglo-French supersonic aircraft made its first flight in 1969?
15 What is the traditional colour for a London taxi?
16 Which motorway circles London?
17 Which city is served by Ringway airport?
18 Which type of sports car is also the name of a big cat?
19 What was the Queen Elizabeth's luxury sister ship?
20 Which motorway runs from London to Cambridge?
21 Which London railway station is named after a battle with Napoleon?
22 Which country do Volkswagen cars originate in?
23 How would you be travelling if you were taking the Jubilee line?
24 In which city is Charles de Gaulle airport?
25 What type of vehicle is a juggernaut?
26 Which type of transport is George Stephenson famous for?
27 Near which Kent port is the English opening of the Channel Tunnel?
28 In which English city was the traffic system virtually shut down following terrorist bombs in 2005?
29 The Trans-Siberian railway runs from Vladivostock to which Russian city?
30 At which Thames crossing is there a tunnel and the Queen Elizabeth Bridge?

Answers	60s Films *(see Quiz 30)*

1 West. 2 Elizabeth Taylor. 3 Arabia. 4 Clyde. 5 Midnight. 6 Dustin Hoffman. 7 Rex Harrison. 8 Oliver! 9 John Wayne. 10 Farrow. 11 The Sound of Music. 12 Greek. 13 Dinner. 14 Mary Poppins. 15 Michael Caine. 16 Christie. 17 Barbra Streisand. 18 Zhivago. 19 Peck. 20 Jean Brodie. 21 Scofield. 22 101. 23 The Sundance Kid. 24 2001. 25 Psycho. 26 Breakfast. 27 Sean Connery. 28 The Good. 29 Charity. 30 Camelot.

1 2005 marked which anniversary of the Gunpowder Plot?
2 What is the zodiac sign of the Bull?
3 On a dart board, which number is bottom centre?
4 Who had a No 1 hit with the song "Dancing Queen"?
5 Born Arthur Jefferson in 1890, what was this comic better known as?
6 What profession did Hillary Clinton previously practise?
7 Who partnered Robbie Williams on the hit single "Kids"?
8 In which sport are there madisons and pursuits?
9 Who is the only singer to have No 1 hits in the 50s, 60s, 70s, 80s and 90s?
10 According to proverb, what does the hand that rocks the cradle do?
11 What was founded in 859 at Fez, Morocco, that is reckoned to be the oldest of its type in the world?
12 Which writer established the Three Laws of Robotics?
13 Called hood in America, what's this part of the car called in the UK?
14 Titan is a moon of which planet?
15 What is hydrophobia the fear of?
16 How many furlongs in a mile?
17 Which Terry created the 2005 movie "The Brothers Grimm"?
18 Which annual race was first held in 1829?
19 What type of animal is a Lhasa Apso?
20 Garibaldi, Nice and Ginger Nut are all types of what?
21 In the USA, which are the two main political parties?
22 Which Noel said, "Television is something you appear on: you don't watch it"?
23 What was the trade of Thomas Wolsey's father?
24 What did Siam change its name to?
25 Which Colin played the title role in Oliver Stone's movie "Alexander"?
26 Which Bay housed the island prison Alcatraz?
27 What colours are on the flag of Argentina?
28 In which town did Jesus grow up?
29 Who set up Biba?
30 If a triangle has an angle of 58 degrees and an angle of 77 degrees, what is the third angle?

Answers	**Pot-Luck 18** *(see Quiz 35)*

1 Captain Jack Sparrow. 2 Katherine Jenkins. 3 Altimeter. 4 George Michael. 5 Burt Reynolds. 6 Edward VIII. 7 Talk. 8 Fred Astaire. 9 Six. 10 Leviticus. 11 Housemaid's knee. 12 Milan. 13 Captain. 14 Black. 15 The Kabin. 16 Seven. 17 Fish. 18 On the face. It's a nose. 19 Mersey. 20 Dana. 21 Osama Bin Laden. 22 Hillary Clinton. 23 Prue. 24 Thompson Twins. 25 School. 26 Cairo. 27 Porridge. 28 Cricket. 29 Aubergine. 30 Ronald Reagan.

1 Which tough guy star of "Casablanca" married Lauren Bacall?

2 Who co-starred with Bob Hope in the Road films and died playing golf?

3 Which actress was shunned by Hollywood when she left her husband and children for director Roberto Rossellini?

4 What is the first name of actor Curtis, father of Jamie Lee?

5 Which Officer and a Gentleman married supermodel Cindy Crawford?

6 How was Ruth Elizabeth Davis better known?

7 Which director Cecil B. was famous for epic movies?

8 Which Kops were the creation of director Mack Sennett?

9 Which daughter of Judy Garland won an Oscar for "Cabaret"?

10 Who is Kirk Douglas's famous son?

11 Which actress Ava was Frank Sinatra's second wife?

12 What relation is Shirley Maclaine to fellow star Warren Beatty?

13 Which Katharine had a long relationship with Spencer Tracy?

14 Which actress Grace became Princess of Monaco?

15 Which British suspense film director worked in Hollywood from 1939?

16 Which actress daughter of Henry was known as Hanoi Jane because of her anti-Vietnam War activities in the 1970s?

17 Who co-starred with Vivien Leigh in "Gone with the Wind"?

18 How is Jack Lemmon's co-star in "The Odd Couple", Walter Matasschanskavasky better known?

19 Who was Fred Astaire's most frequent dancing partner?

20 Which child star Shirley went on to be a US Ambassador?

21 Which silent movie star Rudolph died at an early age?

22 Hollywood legends Lionel, Ethel and John share what surname?

23 Which actor Paul is the husband of actress Joanne Woodward?

24 Who was married to Sean Penn and was chosen for the role of Evita?

25 Who was born Doris Kappelhoff and co-starred with Rock Hudson?

26 Which star of "Top Gun" married Nicole Kidman?

27 Which actor James, famous for gangster roles, is credited with the catchphrase "You dirty rat!"?

28 Why was Jimmy Durante nicknamed Schnozzle?

29 Who married Richard Burton twice?

30 Which actress Demi married Bruce Willis?

Answers	Around Scotland *(see Quiz 36)*

1 East. 2 John o' Groat's. 3 Edinburgh. 4 Yes. 5 Hadrian. 6 St Andrews. 7 Whisky. 8 Balmoral. 9 Highland Games. 10 Skiing. 11 Mountains. 12 Aberdeen. 13 Shetland. 14 Ness. 15 Skye. 16 Kintyre. 17 Clyde. 18 Edinburgh. 19 Haggis. 20 Gretna Green. 21 Lake. 22 Ben Nevis. 23 Dundee. 24 Perth. 25 Tweed. 26 North Sea. 27 Valley. 28 Glasgow. 29 Dundee. 30 St Andrew.

1 Which character did Johnny Depp play in the movie "Pirates of the Caribbean"?
2 Which classical singer's second album was called "Second Nature"?
3 Which instrument measures a plane's height above sea level?
4 Who recorded the album "Listen without Prejudice"?
5 Who played the Bandit in "Smokey and the Bandit"?
6 Which king of England abdicated and was succeeded by his younger brother?
7 In rhyming slang what is meant by rabbit and pork?
8 How was Frederick Austerlitz better known?
9 How many players are there in a volleyball team?
10 What is the third book of the Old Testament?
11 What is the common name for the complaint bursitis?
12 In which city is La Scala opera house?
13 In the British army which rank comes between Lieutenant and Major?
14 What colour is the gem jet?
15 What is the name of the newsagent's in "Coronation Street"?
16 How many sides has a heptagon?
17 What type of creature is used for the dish Bombay duck?
18 Where on your body is your olfactory organ?
19 Which major river flows through Liverpool?
20 Which singer had a No 1 with "All Kinds of Everything"?
21 Who founded Al Qaeda in the 1980s?
22 Who was the first wife of a President in office to appear before a Grand Jury?
23 What is the first name of TV cook Leith?
24 Which trio took their name from characters in the Tintin cartoons?
25 What can be a group of fish or a place of education?
26 What is the capital of Egypt?
27 Which Ronnie Barker comedy was set inside a prison?
28 In which sport might you see a Chinaman and a maiden?
29 Which vegetable is also known as the egg plant?
30 Jane Wyman was the first wife of which famous American?

Answers	**Pot-Luck 17** *(see Quiz 33)*

1 400th. **2** Taurus. **3** 3. **4** Abba. **5** Stan Laurel. **6** Lawyer. **7** Kylie Minogue. **8** Cycling. **9** Cliff Richard. **10** Rule the world. **11** University. **12** Isaac Asimov. **13** Bonnet. **14** Saturn. **15** Water. **16** Eight. **17** Terry Gilliam. **18** Oxford and Cambridge boat race. **19** Dog. **20** Biscuit. **21** Democrats and Republicans. **22** Coward. **23** Butcher. **24** Thailand. **25** Colin Farrell. **26** San Francisco. **27** Blue and white. **28** Nazareth. **29** Barbara Hulanicki. **30** 45 degrees.

1 Is Dundee on the east or west coast of Scotland?
2 Which is the most northerly point on the British mainland?
3 Which city is Scotland's capital?
4 Are Scottish banknotes legal tender in England?
5 Who built a wall to divide Scotland from England?
6 Where is the Royal and Ancient Golf Club?
7 The name of which Scottish product means "water of life"?
8 Where is the Queen's Scottish residence?
9 What is the name of the Games held at Braemar?
10 Which sport is Aviemore particularly famous for?
11 What are the Cairngorms?
12 Which east coast port is known as the Granite City?
13 Which islands give their name to ponies and wool?
14 In which Loch is there said to be a monster?
15 Which Isle was linked to the mainland by a bridge in 1995?
16 Which Mull was the title of a song by Paul McCartney?
17 Which river flows through Glasgow?
18 Which city holds an annual Arts Festival?
19 Which speciality's ingredients include sheep's stomach and oatmeal?
20 Which village was a popular destination for runaway couples?
21 What does the word "loch" mean?
22 What is Scotland's highest mountain?
23 Which city gives its name to a rich fruit cake?
24 Which city shares its name with a city in Australia?
25 Which river in the Borders gives its name to a woollen fabric?
26 Which sea is to the east of the Scottish mainland?
27 What is a glen?
28 In which city is Hampden Park Stadium?
29 Which is further north, Edinburgh or Dundee?
30 Who is Scotland's patron saint?

Answers	Hollywood *(see Quiz 34)*

1 Humphrey Bogart. 2 Bing Crosby. 3 Ingrid Bergman. 4 Tony. 5 Richard Gere. 6 Bette. 7 De Mille. 8 Keystone. 9 Liza Minnelli. 10 Michael Douglas. 11 Gardner. 12 Sister. 13 Hepburn. 14 Kelly. 15 Alfred Hitchcock. 16 Jane Fonda. 17 Clark Gable. 18 Walter Matthau. 19 Ginger Rogers. 20 Temple. 21 Valentino. 22 Barrymore. 23 Newman. 24 Madonna. 25 Doris Day. 26 Tom Cruise. 27 Cagney. 28 Nose. 29 Elizabeth Taylor. 30 Moore.

1 Dr John Pemberton invented which drink in 1886?
2 Which Harry Potter film was released in November 2005?
3 What was the surname of the 41st and 43rd Presidents of the USA?
4 Victor Barna was five times world champion in which sport?
5 What is the Welsh name for Wales?
6 How many years are celebrated by an emerald anniversary?
7 In which village is "Emmerdale" set?
8 What three colours are on the flag of Australia?
9 What number does the Roman numeral L stand for?
10 Who recorded the album "Everything Changes"?
11 In cartoons, who "kept on walking"?
12 What do you suffer from if you have coryza?
13 What is the first name of TV cook Tovey?
14 What are the initials of comic writer Wodehouse?
15 Who directed the film "Tommy"?
16 The Haka is a dance performed by which rugby union team?
17 Which George wrote "Porgy and Bess"?
18 Snooker's Eddie Charlton comes from which country?
19 In which year were women first given the vote?
20 On what part of your body would you wear espadrilles?
21 Which of the following can vote in a general election: the mentally ill, criminals, people under 18?
22 In which country is the Curragh racecourse?
23 Which element is used in computer chips?
24 To five years either way, when was the GLC formed?
25 Which planet is 4,500 million years old?
26 What does the French word "pomme" mean?
27 What trees belong to the genus Quercus?
28 What was the last movie that Marlon Brando ever made?
29 Who wrote the poem "Anthem for Doomed Youth"?
30 The musical "The Woman in White" was based on a novel by which writer?

Answers | Pot-Luck 20 *(see Quiz 39)*

1 Darkness. 2 David Dimbleby. 3 John Joseph. 4 Bryan Robson. 5 Macmillan. 6 Devil Woman. 7 Bram Stoker. 8 Forget-me-not. 9 Cancer. 10 1855. 11 Nell Gwyn. 12 Enya. 13 Pack. 14 Orienteering. 15 Lee Marvin. 16 8. 17 Stave. 18 Robert Frost. 19 Peer Gynt. 20 General Custer. 21 Power boat racing. 22 Le Métro. 23 Gorilla. 24 Des O'Connor. 25 Wainwright. 26 St Francis. 27 John Prescott. 28 Krypton. 29 Toto. 30 Bull.

1 Where does a kangaroo keep its young?
2 Which black and white mammal lives in China's bamboo forests?
3 Where do koalas live?
4 How many legs does an adult insect have?
5 What type of creature is a black widow?
6 Which animal's nickname is "ship of the desert"?
7 Which breed of spaniel shares its name with a king?
8 Which sea creature is known as a Portuguese man-of-war?
9 What is a female sheep called?
10 What do carnivorous animals live on?
11 Which animals are described as canine?
12 What is a fox's tail called?
13 Which saint is the heaviest breed of dog named after?
14 What is special about a guinea pig's tail?
15 What are pigs' feet called?
16 Which elephants have the smaller ears, African or Indian?
17 What are edible sturgeon eggs called?
18 What name is given to the period of winter sleep by some animals?
19 What is Britain's hardiest and shaggiest bovine breed?
20 What would a billy and a nanny produce?
21 Which black and white mammal sprays a foul smelling liquid when attacked?
22 How does a boa constrictor kill its prey?
23 Why does a fish need gills?
24 What does a scorpion have at the end of its tail?
25 What does a chameleon change to camouflage itself?
26 What does an Isle of Man Manx cat not have?
27 What type of insect is a Red Admiral?
28 What is another name for an Alsatian dog?
29 What kind of animal is a Suffolk Punch?
30 A lynx is a member of which family group?

Answers | **Sport: Cricket** *(see Quiz 40)*

1 Australia and England. 2 Manchester. 3 Before. 4 Cork. 5 Andrew Flintoff. 6 Jack Russell. 7 Lord's. 8 Randall. 9 Jerusalem. 10 England. 11 Two. 12 Yorkshire. 13 Wicket keeper. 14 Nottingham. 15 None. 16 India. 17 W. G. 18 Yorkshire. 19 Stewart. 20 Caught and bowled. 21 Left. 22 Lancashire. 23 Sunday. 24 Six. 25 Brian Johnson. 26 Terence. 27 Australia. 28 Six. 29 Middlesex. 30 None.

Quiz 39 Pot-Luck 20

Answers – page 47

1 Which band's first album was called "Permission to Land"?
2 Who has presented the BBC's "Question Time" since 1994?
3 What are the real first names of racehorse trainer Jonjo O'Neill?
4 Which England soccer skipper was injured in both the 1986 and 1990 World Cup final stages?
5 Which Harold said, "Most of our people have never had it so good."
6 Cliff Richard and Marty Robbins had different songs that shared which title?
7 Which writer featured Jonathan Harker in his most famous novel?
8 Myosotis is more commonly known as which flower?
9 Which Tropic is further north, Capricorn or Cancer?
10 To ten years either way, when did Thomas Cook organize his first continental holiday?
11 Which orange seller became mistress of Charles II?
12 Who recorded the album "Shepherd Moons"?
13 What is the word for a group of hounds?
14 Which sport is a mixture of map reading and cross-country running?
15 Which actor recorded that he "was born under a wand'rin' star"?
16 How many legs has a spider?
17 In music, name the horizontal lines around which notes are written.
18 Which New England poet had "miles to go before I sleep"?
19 Which work does Anitra's Dance come from?
20 Who made his last stand at Little Bighorn?
21 Which sport awards the Harmsworth Trophy?
22 What is the Paris underground called?
23 Which is the largest of the apes?
24 Who did Morecambe and Wise not want to sing on their show?
25 Which Alfred mapped out moorland routes in northern England?
26 Which Italian saint was born at the town of Assisi?
27 Who became Deputy Prime Minister after Labour's election victory of 1997?
28 Which planet does Superman come from?
29 Who took "Africa" into the record charts?
30 What name is given to an adult male seal?

Answers | Pot-Luck 19 (see Quiz 37)

1 Coca Cola. 2 Harry Potter and the Goblet of Fire. 3 Bush. 4 Table tennis. 5 Cymru. 6 55. 7 Beckindale. 8 Blue, red and white. 9 50. 10 Take That. 11 Felix the Cat. 12 Common cold. 13 John. 14 P. G. 15 Ken Russell. 16 All Blacks. 17 Gershwin. 18 Australia. 19 1918. 20 Feet. 21 None. 22 Ireland. 23 Silicon. 24 1965. 25 Earth. 26 Apple. 27 Oaks. 28 The Brave. 29 Wilfred Owen. 30 Wilkie Collins.

1 Which international teams contest the Ashes?
2 In which city is the ground Old Trafford?
3 In LBW what does the B stand for?
4 Which bowler Dominic took a Test hat-trick in 1995?
5 Which cricketer was voted BBC Sports Personality for 2005?
6 Which English wicket keeper shares his name with a breed of dog?
7 The Nursery End, the Pavilion End and St John's Wood Road are all linked with which ground?
8 Which former England batsman Derek was known as "Rags"?
9 Which patriotic song was adopted by England in the 2005 Ashes?
10 Robin Smith is an international for which country?
11 How many bails are there on a set of wickets?
12 Which county does Geoff Boycott come from?
13 What was the specialist position of Australia's Rodney Marsh?
14 Trent Bridge is in which English city?
15 How many runs are scored in a maiden over?
16 Which country was captained by Kapil Dev?
17 What were the initials of legendary Victorian cricketer Dr Grace?
18 Which county does Michael Vaughan play for?
19 In the 1990s, which Alec has opened and kept wicket for England?
20 In scoring, what does c & b stand for?
21 Was David Gower a left- or right-handed batsman?
22 Which English county did West Indies skipper Clive Lloyd play for?
23 On which day of the week were John Player League games played?
24 How many valid deliveries are sent down in a Test cricket over?
25 Which cricket commentator on radio was known as "Johnners"?
26 What does the initial T stand for in I. T. Botham's name?
27 In which country do Sheffield Shield games take place?
28 What does the batsman score for a shot that sends the ball over the boundary without touching the ground?
29 England skippers Brearley and Gatting have both captained which county?
30 How many Tests did England win on the tour of Pakistan late in 2005?

Answers	Nature: Animals *(see Quiz 38)*

1 In a pouch. 2 Panda. 3 Australia. 4 Six. 5 Spider. 6 Camel. 7 King Charles. 8 Jellyfish. 9 Ewe. 10 Meat. 11 Dogs. 12 Brush. 13 St Bernard. 14 It doesn't have one. 15 Trotters. 16 Indian. 17 Caviar. 18 Hibernation. 19 Highland cattle. 20 Kids. 21 Skunk. 22 Squeezing. 23 To breathe. 24 Sting. 25 Colour. 26 A tail. 27 Butterfly. 28 German Shepherd. 29 Horse. 30 Cat.

Quiz 41 | Pot-Luck 21

Answers – page 53

LEVEL 1

1 What is the name of the computer game hedgehog?
2 What is the zodiac sign of the Crab?
3 Which gardener Alan wrote the novels "Mr MacGregor" and "Only Dad"?
4 Who had a No 1 hit with the song "Maggie May"?
5 In golf what is the term for two over par?
6 The initials TC stand for which cartoon character?
7 What were followers of John Wycliffe called?
8 Which country's national flag is a green rectangle?
9 Which subject does Simon Schama specialize in when making television programmes?
10 Who said – though not in English – "I think therefore I am"?
11 In education, what does GCSE stand for?
12 Which rock superstar is a former chairman of Watford football club?
13 Called a trailer in America, what's the name of this vehicle in the UK?
14 In which month is Royal Ascot horse-racing season?
15 What is agoraphobia a fear of?
16 What do the initials RAM stand for in computing?
17 Which village does Jane Marple live in?
18 How many kilogrammes make one metric ton?
19 Which comedian used the catchphrase, "Rock on, Tommy"?
20 What type of food is dill?
21 Which Scottish soccer team are known as "The Dons"?
22 Whom was Michael Schumacher driving for when he won his first Grand Prix?
23 Which day of the week is named after the Anglo-Saxon god Tiw?
24 On what date is American Independence Day?
25 What kind of animal is a seahorse?
26 The failure to produce enough insulin leads to which medical condition?
27 Which soccer side play at a Cottage?
28 Which insect transmits malaria?
29 In the fable, what did the boy cry to trick the villagers?
30 Which Colin was appointed George W. Bush's Secretary of State in 2001?

Answers	Pot-Luck 22 (see Quiz 43)

1 Germany. 2 Roman Abramovich. 3 Mother of pearl. 4 Simply Red. 5 The Corpse Bride. 6 O. 7 Eyes. 8 Judy Garland. 9 Terms at Oxford. 10 Samson. 11 Music. 12 Zither. 13 Blue whale. 14 Red. 15 Brian Jones. 16 Ten. 17 Numbers. 18 Walpurgis. 19 Peter Wright. 20 Swan. 21 Interpol. 22 Milligan. 23 Black Beauty. 24 Sturgeon. 25 Desmond Lynam. 26 Brussels. 27 Blue. 28 Olympus. 29 Squash. 30 Very High Frequency.

1 What is the first name of Mrs Bucket of "Keeping Up Appearances"?
2 Which actress Joanna played Patsy in "Absolutely Fabulous"?
3 Who was the café owner, played by Gorden Kaye, in "Allo Allo"?
4 In which sitcom does grumpy Victor Meldrew appear?
5 What is the surname of Del Boy and Rodney of "Only Fools and Horses"?
6 Was Ally McBeal a lawyer or an advertising executive?
7 What kind of Life did Jerry and Margo's neighbours Tom and Barbara lead?
8 What was the profession of Steptoe and Son?
9 In the sitcom title how many Children did Bill and Ben Porter have?
10 Which of Nora Batty's wrinkled garments turned on Compo?
11 Which two characters were "Just Good Friends"?
12 During which war was "Dad's Army" set?
13 Which senior political position did James Hacker MP reach?
14 In what type of establishment was "Are You Being Served?" set?
15 In which northeast city was "Auf Wiedersehen Pet" set?
16 Who is Tracey's sister in "Birds of a Feather"?
17 Whose servant was Baldrick?
18 Which sitcom was about the Boswell family from Liverpool?
19 At which hotel was Manuel the waiter?
20 In which series would you meet the Yellowcoats from Maplin's?
21 How were the Lads Terry Collier and Bob Ferris known?
22 Who shares an apartment with Grace?
23 Which clerical caper was set on Craggy Island?
24 How were the Men Behaving in the series about Gary and Tony ?
25 Which sitcom was set in a bar in Boston?
26 Who were Tom and Diana Waiting for at the Bayview Retirement Home?
27 What sort of Statesman was Alan B'Stard MP?
28 Where were the characters in "Porridge"?
29 Which Ricky created and starred in "The Office"?
30 Which series gave us the catchprase, "I don't believe it!"?

Answers | 60s Newsround (see Quiz 44)

1 John F. Kennedy. 2 6. 3 Berlin. 4 Eichmann. 5 Marilyn Monroe. 6 Wilson. 7 Beeching. 8 Martin Luther King. 9 Harold Macmillan. 10 Shrimpton. 11 Eagle. 12 India. 13 Moors. 14 Smith. 15 Wight. 16 USSR. 17 Manson. 18 West Germany. 19 Garland. 20 Edward. 21 Prince Charles. 22 The Moon. 23 Kray. 24 Israel. 25 Economics. 26 Flower. 27 Campbell. 28 Mini. 29 Czechoslovakia. 30 Brian Epstein.

Quiz 43 | Pot-Luck 22

Answers – page 51

1 Which country is Lufthansa from?
2 Who was the owner of Chelsea FC when they won the 2005 Championship?
3 What is another word for nacre?
4 Who recorded the album "Stars"?
5 In 2005 Tim Burton's directed a movie based on folk tale about what type of "Bride"?
6 In Morse Code what letter is represented by three dashes?
7 In rhyming slang what are mince pies?
8 How is Frances Gumm better known?
9 What are Trinity and Hilary?
10 In the Bible, who was betrayed by Delilah?
11 In which branch of the arts is the metronome used?
12 Which musical instrument featured in the theme of "The Third Man"?
13 What type of whale is the largest?
14 What colour is vermilion?
15 Which member of the Rolling Stones is the movie "Stoned" about?
16 How many sides has a decagon?
17 What is the fourth book of the Old Testament ?
18 Which night is April 30th?
19 "Spycatcher" was the controversial memoirs of which former intelligence officer?
20 A cob is a male of which creature?
21 Hello, hello, hello, what was founded in Vienna in 1923?
22 Which Spike said, "Money can't buy friends, but you can get a better class of enemy"?
23 What was the horse in the title of Anna Sewell's novel?
24 From which fish is caviar obtained?
25 Who took over from Richard Whiteley as the host of "Countdown"?
26 What is the capital of Belgium?
27 What colour is the dye obtained from the plant woad?
28 Which mountain was said to be home of the Greek gods?
29 Which game is played in an enclosed space with both players hitting the ball in the same direction?
30 What does VHF stand for?

Answers | Pot-Luck 21 (see Quiz 41)

1 Sonic. 2 Cancer. 3 Alan Titchmarsh. 4 Rod Stewart. 5 Double bogey. 6 Top Cat. 7 Lollards. 8 Libya. 9 History. 10 René Descartes. 11 General Certificate of Secondary Education. 12 Elton John. 13 Caravan. 14 June. 15 Open spaces. 16 Random Access Memory. 17 St Mary Mead. 18 One thousand. 19 Bobby Ball. 20 Herb. 21 Aberdeen. 22 Benetton. 23 Tuesday. 24 4th July. 25 Fish. 26 Diabetes. 27 Fulham. 28 Mosquito. 29 Wolf. 30 Colin Powell.

1 Who defeated Richard Nixon to become US president in 1960?
2 James Hanratty was charged with a murder on which A road?
3 Which European city was divided into East and West by a Wall?
4 Which Adolf was executed in May 1962 for his part in the Holocaust?
5 Which screen sex symbol was found dead in a bungalow near Hollywood in August 1962?
6 Which Harold became leader of the Labour Party in 1963?
7 Which Doctor wielded his axe on the railway network?
8 Who made a speech proclaiming, "I have a dream"?
9 Which Conservative resigned as prime minister in 1963?
10 Which model Jean was known as "The Shrimp"?
11 What type of creature was Goldie who made the headlines by escaping from London Zoo?
12 Mrs Indira Gandhi was appointed prime minister of which country?
13 Which notorious Murders involved Myra Hindley and Ian Brady?
14 Which Ian declared independence for Rhodesia?
15 On which Isle was there a 1969 rock festival featuring Bob Dylan?
16 Leonid Brezhnev became leader of which country?
17 Which Charles led "The Family" in the Sharon Tate murder?
18 Willi Brandt became chancellor of which country?
19 In 1969 which actress and singer Judy died at the age of 47?
20 Which Kennedy was involved in the car accident at Chappaquiddick?
21 Which member of the royal family was invested as Prince of Wales?
22 Neil Armstrong became the first man to set foot where?
23 Which gangland twins Ronald and Reginald were jailed?
24 Golda Meir became the first woman prime minister of which country?
25 LSE, the scene of student protest, was the London School of what?
26 What type of Power symbolized the 1967 peace and love festivals?
27 Which Donald was killed trying to break the world water speed record?
28 Which type of skirt was the main fashion of the 1960s?
29 Soviet tanks moved to crush the Dubcek reforms in which country?
30 Who was manager of the Beatles by the time they made the charts?

Answers	TV: Sitcoms *(see Quiz 42)*

1 Hyacinth. 2 Lumley. 3 René. 4 One Foot in the Grave. 5 Trotter. 6 Lawyer. 7 The Good Life. 8 Rag and bone men. 9 2 Point 4. 10 Stockings. 11 Vince and Penny. 12 Second World War. 13 Prime Minister. 14 Department store. 15 Newcastle. 16 Sharon. 17 Blackadder. 18 Bread. 19 Fawlty Towers. 20 Hi de Hi! 21 Likely Lads. 22 Will. 23 Father Ted. 24 Badly. 25 Cheers. 26 God. 27 New. 28 Prison. 29 Gervais. 30 One Foot in the Grave.

Quiz 45 — Pot-Luck 23

1 If it rains on St Swithin's Day, how many more days is it supposed to rain?
2 By which name of one word is Katie Price better known?
3 Released in 2005, the album "Tissues and Issues" was a success for which star?
4 Which composer wrote "The Marriage of Figaro"?
5 What is a low, shallow basket used by gardeners called?
6 How many years are celebrated by a golden anniversary?
7 In "David Copperfield" what was the surname of Uriah?
8 What is the first name of the main detective in "A Touch of Frost"?
9 What number does the Roman numeral M stand for?
10 What sort of creature is a capercaillie?
11 In which month is Remembrance Day?
12 Which TV drama was set in the delightfully named Glenbogle?
13 How many faces has an icosahedron?
14 What are the initials of "Lady Chatterley" author Lawrence?
15 What name is given to a litter of piglets?
16 What type of dancing is associated with Margot Fonteyn?
17 Which soap pub sells Churchill Strong?
18 Who recorded the album "Both Sides"?
19 How many children did Queen Victoria have?
20 Who is the resident Lord in "Private Eye"?
21 What are paper measures called equal to 500 sheets?
22 In which country is Flushing Meadow tennis stadium?
23 What is the domed recess at the east end of a church called?
24 What is a young goat called?
25 How did master escapologist Harry Houdini die?
26 After which George was the American state of Georgia named?
27 Which viral disease is also called grippe?
28 Who said, "Anyone can get old. All you have to do is live long enough"?
29 In what game do you peg, and score for pairs and fifteens?
30 What does PYO stand for?

Answers | Pot-Luck 24 (see Quiz 47)

1 Scapegoat. 2 300. 3 Norah Jones. 4 France. 5 Warhol. 6 Seven. 7 Lead. 8 Slade. 9 Intestate. 10 A pig. 11 Annie Oakley. 12 Meatloaf. 13 Swarm. 14 Clarinet. 15 Coyote. 16 Seven. 17 Natural. 18 Susan. 19 72. 20 Grape. 21 2 Point 4 Children. 22 Liverpool. 23 Will Young. 24 Flute. 25 Mrs Hudson. 26 Beaufort. 27 Paris. 28 Pictionary. 29 The Red Crescent. 30 Six.

1 In which Swiss mountain range is the Jungfrau?
2 Which is the next largest island in the world after Australia?
3 Which seaside resort is Super-Mare?
4 On which continent is the Kariba Dam?
5 What are Lakes Michigan, Superior, Huron, Erie and Ontario known as collectively?
6 If the southern limit of the tropics is Capricorn what is the northern limit called?
7 Which island is to the south of Australia?
8 In the south of which country was Saigon?
9 If you were in Benidorm in which country would you be?
10 Which London palace has a maze?
11 Which isle off the west coast of England has three legs as its symbol?
12 Which country is connected to Wales by the Severn Bridge?
13 Which US state is a collection of islands in the Pacific?
14 Which language do natives of Hamburg speak?
15 Which county has a red rose as its symbol?
16 Which Queen gave her name to the capital of Hong Kong?
17 Which Bank is made of sand in the North Sea?
18 In which county is Penzance?
19 Which islands are Sark and Alderney part of?
20 Greece is in which continent?
21 What are the counties of Essex, Suffolk, Norfolk and Cambridgeshire collectively known as?
22 Is Japan in the northern or the southern hemisphere?
23 What is the name of the biggest Canyon in Arizona?
24 The London Eye was built by which river?
25 Is the Arctic Circle near the north or the south pole?
26 On the south of which continent are the Andes?
27 If you were looking at the Ganges which country would you be in?
28 Which country do the Scilly Isles belong to?
29 Which country originally produced Fiat cars?
30 What is the most westerly point of England?

| **Answers** | **Pop: Sounds of the 70s** *(see Quiz 48)* |

1 The Brotherhood of Man. 2 Lee. 3 Glitter. 4 Bay. 5 Sweet. 6 Tyrannosaurus. 7 Slade. 8 Rod Stewart. 9 Kiki Dee. 10 Queen. 11 The Pips. 12 The Rubettes. 13 10 cc 14 5. 15 Sing. 16 Blondie. 17 Survive. 18 Nilsson. 19 Abba. 20 Genesis. 21 Electric Light Orchestra. 22 Fire. 23 Eagles. 24 Tiger. 25 Love. 26 Garfunkel. 27 Soul. 28 The Bee Gees. 29 Mungo Jerry. 30 Mondays.

1 What animal-linked name describes someone who always gets blamed?
2 How many seconds in five minutes?
3 "Come Away with Me" was the first No 1 album for which female artist?
4 Which country hosted the last World Cup of the 20th century?
5 Which Andy said, "In the future everyone will be famous for 15 minutes?"
6 In snooker what is the score for potting a black?
7 Pb is the symbol of which chemical element?
8 Who recorded the seasonal song "Merry Xmas Everybody"?
9 Which term means dying without having made a will?
10 Who or what was the Empress of Blandings?
11 Who was Little Sure Shot according to Sitting Bull?
12 Who recorded the album "Bat Out of Hell"?
13 What is the word for a group of bees?
14 Which musical instrument is played by Acker Bilk?
15 What is another name for the prairie wolf?
16 How many colours are there in the rainbow?
17 In music, what is a note if it is neither sharp nor flat?
18 Whom was Madonna desperately seeking in her first feature film?
19 How many inches in two yards?
20 What type of fruit is dried to produce a sultana?
21 Apart from "The Flowerpot Men" in which show do Bill and Ben appear?
22 Robbie Fowler started his career with which club?
23 Which Will advised "Leave Right Now" in 2003?
24 What instrument does James Galway play?
25 What is the name of Sherlock Holmes's housekeeper?
26 Which Admiral gave his name to a weather measurement scale?
27 Where was Glenn Miller flying to when his plane disappeared?
28 In which game do players have to guess a word from a drawing?
29 What is the Muslim equivalent of the Red Cross?
30 How many squares on a Rubik Cube never move?

Answers | Pot-Luck 23 *(see Quiz 45)*

1 40. **2** Jordan. **3** Charlotte Church. **4** Mozart. **5** Trug. **6** 50. **7** Heap. **8** Jack. **9** 1,000. **10** A bird. **11** November. **12** Monarch of the Glen. **13** 20. **14** D. H. **15** A farrow. **16** Ballet. **17** Queen Vic (EastEnders). **18** Phil Collins. **19** Nine. **20** Lord Gnome. **21** Ream. **22** USA. **23** Apse. **24** Kid. **25** A blow to his stomach. **26** King George II. **27** Influenza. **28** Groucho Marx. **29** Cribbage. **30** Pick Your Own.

1 Which Brotherhood had a Eurovision winner in 1976?
2 Peters and who said "Welcome Home" in 1973?
3 Which Gary was Leader of the Gang?
4 Which City Rollers had a hit with "Bye Bye Baby"?
5 A "Ballroom Blitz" came from which sugary-sounding group?
6 What had the T originally stood for in T Rex?
7 Which group led by Noddy Holder sang "Weer All Crazee Now"?
8 Who sang "Do Ya Think I'm Sexy"?
9 Who sang with Elton John on "Don't Go Breaking My Heart"?
10 "Bohemian Rhapsody" was recorded by which group?
11 Who helped Gladys Knight "make it through the night" in 1972?
12 "Sugar Baby Love" and "Jukebox Jive" were hits for which group?
13 What was the capacity of the group who said "I'm Not in Love"?
14 How many Jacksons were there when they sang "I Want You Back"?
15 What did the New Seekers say they would like to teach the world to do?
16 Fair-haired Debbie Harry sang with which group?
17 What did Gloria Gaynor say she would do in 1979?
18 Which Harry was "Without You" in 1972?
19 Which Swedish group met their Waterloo in 1974?
20 Which band has the same name as the first book in the Bible?
21 What does ELO stand for?
22 What joins Earth and Wind in a group's name?
23 Which birds of prey sang about the Hotel California?
24 What sort of feet did Mud sing about?
25 Showaddywaddy were Under the Moon of what in 1976?
26 Which singer Art had a solo No 1 after duo success with Paul Simon?
27 Which David of "Starsky & Hutch" fame charted with his ballads?
28 Who were "Stayin' Alive" with "Night Fever" in 1978?
29 Which Jerry sang "In the Summertime"?
30 What day did the Boomtown Rats not like?

Answers	Geography *(see Quiz 46)*

1 Alps. 2 Greenland. 3 Weston. 4 Africa. 5 Great Lakes. 6 Tropic of Cancer. 7 Tasmania. 8 Vietnam. 9 Spain. 10 Hampton Court. 11 Isle of Man. 12 England. 13 Hawaii. 14 German. 15 Lancashire. 16 Victoria. 17 Dogger Bank. 18 Cornwall. 19 Channel Islands. 20 Europe. 21 East Anglia. 22 Northern. 23 Grand Canyon. 24 River Thames. 25 North. 26 America. 27 India. 28 United Kingdom. 29 Italy. 30 Land's End.

Quiz 49 | Pot-Luck 25

1 What colour is a peridot stone?
2 What is the zodiac sign of the Twins?
3 In which part of the body is the patella?
4 Who had a No 1 hit with the song "Bachelor Boy"?
5 What is the second letter of the Greek alphabet?
6 What is the nest of an eagle called?
7 Which film star has a statue in Leicester Square?
8 Who wrote the screenplay and starred in the movie "Nanny McPhee"?
9 What was the name of David and Victoria Beckham's first child born in Spain?
10 What did the Rochdale Pioneers pioneer?
11 Which 1995 movie starred a wet Kevin Costner?
12 Which board game involves moving through rooms to solve a murder?
13 Called a tuxedo in America, what's this garment called in the UK?
14 What type of jewels are traditionally associated with Amsterdam?
15 What is zoophobia a fear of?
16 Which Irish boy band took their first seven singles to No 1?
17 What was Charon's job?
18 Which Edith sang "Je ne regrette rien" (No Regrets)?
19 What colour is the Central Line on a London Underground map?
20 What type of food is a bagel?
21 What sits on a dolly in a television studio?
22 Who says, "You'll like this – not a lot!"?
23 Which day of the week is named after the god Woden?
24 Who recorded the album "From the Cradle"?
25 Which "Coronation Street" supermarket employed Reg and Vera?
26 What is the claw of a bird of prey called?
27 Which colour features on the kit of both Blackburn Rovers and Newcastle United?
28 Dr Stephen Hawking wrote a brief history of what?
29 Which Club is concerned with pedigree in the dog world?
30 Which English king was painted by Hans Holbein?

Answers | Pot-Luck 26 *(see Quiz 51)*

1 Dan Brown. 2 Rupee. 3 Mark, Martin. 4 64. 5 Stuarts. 6 Eight. 7 Joey. 8 Sting. 9 Bush. 10 Solomon. 11 Gestapo. 12 Netherlands. 13 Holland. 14 Mauve. 15 Acer. 16 12. 17 St Valentine's Day. 18 Lodge. 19 John Keats. 20 Apron. 21 Israel. 22 Madness. 23 Jack Russell. 24 Cabbage. 25 Christina Aguilera. 26 Hydrogen. 27 Alan. 28 Ngaio Marsh. 29 Six. 30 Visual Display Unit.

1 Bobby Moore captained which country in the 1970 World Cup?

2 Which British golfer Tony won the US Open Championship?

3 In 1970 Margaret Court won four major tournaments in which sport?

4 Which horse-riding princess was voted Sportswoman of the Year?

5 At which Scottish stadium was there a crowd disaster in 1971?

6 Which Sebastian completed a hat-trick of running records in 1979?

7 John Conteh became a champion in which sport?

8 Which London team won the League and FA Cup double in 1971?

9 What was the sport of Britain's David Wilkie?

10 In 1976 which cricketer Viv hit 291 runs in an innings against England?

11 Which 19-year-old Evonne triumphed at Wimbledon in 1971?

12 Which Ray was the most successful snooker player of the 70s?

13 Which soccer team won the Scottish League every season from 1970 to 1974?

14 Which horse won the Grand National three times?

15 Who was manager of Nottingham Forest when they won the European Cup?

16 Which Brendan won the only British track and field medal of the 1976 Olympic Games?

17 Bjorn Borg comes from which country?

18 Which Barry became world 500cc motor-cycling champion?

19 Which Daley became the youngest ever athlete to represent Britain in the decathlon?

20 Which British player won the 1977 women's singles at Wimbledon?

21 Which English soccer side twice won the European Cup?

22 In which sport was Mike Brearley an England captain?

23 Which country outside the UK won the Grand Slam in 1977?

24 Which Suffolk soccer side won the FA Cup in 1978?

25 Which team won the 1978 soccer World Cup staged in Argentina?

26 In 1978–9 Hull Kingston Rovers were champions in which sport?

27 Which Niki was badly burnt in the 1976 German Grand Prix?

28 Which TV mogul started his own cricket unofficial Test series?

29 Which Jackie was world champion motor racing driver in 1971 and 1973?

30 Ally MacLeod was manager of which national soccer side?

Answers	70s Films *(see Quiz 52)*

1 Star Wars. 2 The Godfather. 3 A car. 4 A shark. 5 Saturday. 6 Kramer. 7 Superman. 8 Cuckoo's. 9 Grease. 10 Third. 11 Nile. 12 Rocky. 13 Kermit. 14 Eagle. 15 King Kong. 16 Towering Inferno. 17 M*A*S*H. 18 Orange. 19 Jackal. 20 Bugsy. 21 Clint Eastwood. 22 Diamonds. 23 Deer. 24 Beverly Hills. 25 Dog. 26 Robert Redford. 27 Great and Small. 28 Now. 29 Moon. 30 Poseidon.

1 Who wrote the mega-selling book "The Da Vinci Code"?
2 What is the currency of India?
3 On TV, what are the names of Pauline Fowler's two sons?
4 How many squares are there on a chess board?
5 James I and Charles I were members of which royal dynasty?
6 How many lanes are there in an Olympic swimming pool?
7 What was the name of the "Friends" spin-off starring Matt LeBlanc?
8 How is Gordon Sumner better known?
9 What name links singer Kate and former USA President George?
10 In the Bible, who was famous for his wisdom?
11 What was the secret state police of Nazi Germany called?
12 In which country is Schiphol airport?
13 Which Republic of Ireland player Matt shares his surname with a country?
14 What colour is heliotrope?
15 Which tree family includes the sycamore and maple?
16 How many sides has a dodecagon?
17 Which event did the first popular greeting card celebrate?
18 What is the home of a beaver called?
19 Who wrote of "Season of mists and mellow fruitfulness"?
20 What name is given to an extension of a stage in front of a curtain?
21 Of which country was Golda Meir prime minister?
22 Who recorded the album "Divine Madness"?
23 Which short-legged dog is named after the 18th-century parson who bred them?
24 Which vegetable is the main ingredient in coleslaw?
25 Who had a US and UK No 1 with "Genie in a Bottle"?
26 Which element has the atomic number 1 in the periodic table?
27 What is the first name of gardener and presenter Titchmarsh?
28 Who created Chief Inspector Alleyn?
29 How many legs has a daddy-long-legs?
30 What does VDU stand for?

Answers | Pot-Luck 25 *(see Quiz 49)*

1 Green. 2 Gemini. 3 Knee. 4 Cliff Richard. 5 Beta. 6 Eyrie. 7 Charlie Chaplin.
8 Emma Thompson. 9 Cruz. 10 The Co-op. 11 Waterworld. 12 Cluedo. 13 Dinner
jacket. 14 Diamonds. 15 Animals. 16 Westlife. 17 Ferryman who, in Greek mythology,
takes the dead to the underworld. 18 Piaf. 19 Red. 20 Bread roll. 21 A camera. 22
Paul Daniels. 23 Wednesday. 24 Eric Clapton. 25 Bettabuys. 26 Talon. 27 White. 28
Time. 29 Kennel. 30 Henry VIII.

1 Which Wars were there in 1977?
2 Which 1972 film, with Marlon Brando, was about the Mafia?
3 What was Herbie?
4 Which creature took a starring role in "Jaws"?
5 What Night was there Fever in the movie with John Travolta?
6 Who was versus Kramer in the Dustin Hoffman film?
7 Who is Clark Kent better known as?
8 Which bird's Nest did One fly over in 1975?
9 In which film did John Travolta and Olivia Newton-John sing "You're the One That I Want"?
10 What Kind of Close Encounters were there in 1977?
11 On which Egyptian river was there Death in the Agatha Christie film?
12 Which boxer did Sylvester Stallone play?
13 Name the frog in "The Muppet Movie".
14 Which bird of prey Landed in the war movie based on Jack Higgins' novel?
15 Which 1970s film about a giant ape was a remake of a 1933 movie?
16 Which disaster movie was about a fire in the world's tallest building?
17 Which film told of a mobile hospital in the Korean War?
18 Which fruit was Clockwork in the Stanley Kubrick film?
19 Which animal's Day was it in the film about an assassin based on the Frederick Forsyth novel?
20 What was the first name of gangster Malone?
21 Who starred in the western "Every Which Way but Loose"?
22 What were Forever in the James Bond movie?
23 What sort of Hunter was Robert de Niro in the film with Meryl Streep?
24 Where was Eddie Murphy a Cop in the film series?
25 Digby was the biggest what in the world?
26 Who starred with Paul Newman in "The Sting"?
27 How were All Creatures described in the 1974 film about a vet?
28 When was Apocalypse in the 1979 film?
29 Which planet features in the title of a 1979 Bond movie?
30 Which Adventure was about a disaster on a luxury liner?

Answers	**Sport: The 70s** *(see Quiz 50)*

1 England. 2 Jacklin. 3 Tennis. 4 Princess Anne. 5 Ibrox Park. 6 Coe. 7 Boxing. 8 Arsenal. 9 Swimming. 10 Richards. 11 Goolagong. 12 Reardon. 13 Celtic. 14 Red Rum. 15 Brian Clough. 16 Foster. 17 Sweden. 18 Sheene. 19 Thompson. 20 Virginia Wade. 21 Liverpool. 22 Cricket. 23 France. 24 Ipswich. 25 Argentina. 26 Rugby League. 27 Lauda. 28 Kerry Packer. 29 Stewart. 30 Scotland.

1 Catherine Parr survived which royal husband?
2 Whom did Roger Federer beat in the final of the 2005 US Open?
3 What is meant by the Latin phrase caveat emptor?
4 Which English club did soccer TV pundit Alan Hansen play for?
5 What spirit is made from fermented sugar cane?
6 How many years are celebrated by a silver anniversary?
7 Which actress played opposite Jim Carrey in "Eternal Sunshine Of The Spotless Mind"?
8 What is the capital of the Isle of Man?
9 How did Yetta Feldman die in "So Haunt Me"?
10 Which Tom starred in "Magnum"?
11 Which word meaning letter is in titles of books of the Bible?
12 Who recorded the album "Simply the Best"?
13 What paper is used to test acid and alkali?
14 What are the initials of English writer Priestley?
15 Who presented the first ever edition of "Mastermind"?
16 How many seconds in quarter of an hour?
17 Which special day follows Shrove Tuesday?
18 Who came first as US President, Washington or Lincoln?
19 Diana Ross, Florence Ballard and Mary Wilson formed what?
20 How is the UK golfing term albatross known in America?
21 Which social security benefit was introduced in 1909?
22 What name is adopted by Don Diego de la Vega?
23 What were the first three Eddystone lighthouses lit by?
24 What is a young hare called?
25 At what degree celsius does water freeze?
26 Which animal's name means river horse?
27 What is the first name of TV cook Carrier?
28 Which day of the week is dimanche in French?
29 Which actor George directed the movie "Good Night and Good Luck"?
30 Which actress does Orlando Bloom try to save in the movie "Pirates of the Caribbean"?

Answers	Food and Drink (see Quiz 55)

1 Eggs. 2 Deer. 3 Mint. 4 France. 5 Pancakes. 6 Chips. 7 Rasher. 8 Honey. 9 Smoked. 10 Potato. 11 Holland. 12 Oats. 13 Soup. 14 Ketchup. 15 Colourless. 16 Spain. 17 Apples. 18 Almonds. 19 Hot. 20 Sausage. 21 Yorkshire. 22 Beans. 23 Yellow. 24 Fish. 25 Brown. 26 Cheese. 27 Peas. 28 Italy. 29 Beer and lemonade. 30 Isle of Islay.

Quiz 54 | Pot-Luck 28

Answers – page 66

LEVEL 1

1 Which soap has the pub the Malt Shovel?
2 How many minutes in two and a half hours?
3 Which country is a car from if it has the international registration letters CH?
4 Who created and starred in the TV series "Extras"?
5 Which actor played Legolas Greenleaf in the "Lord of the Rings" trilogy?
6 In darts, what is the lowest score for three trebles?
7 N is the symbol of which chemical element ?
8 Who recorded the album "Parklife"?
9 Which member of the famous Arquette family was married to Nicolas Cage?
10 What is the last month of the year to have exactly 31 days?
11 Which Australian bird does not fly?
12 Which veteran DJ Tony was the first voice on Radio 1?
13 In geometry, how many minutes are there in a degree?
14 What is a segment of garlic called?
15 Which Barbra sang "A Woman in Love"?
16 What is the first letter on the bottom line of a keyboard?
17 Where is the veterinary surgery of Alistair Hebden Lloyd?
18 What is "black gold"?
19 How many feet are there in ten yards?
20 What is Edward Woodward's only hit single?
21 Which Henry started the Promenade Concerts?
22 Which composer wrote the Water Music?
23 What word means dry on a bottle of Italian wine?
24 Which garden shrub is known as the butterfly bush?
25 Whom is Debbie McGee married to?
26 Which types of programme does Hazel Irvine most usually present?
27 Which Dustin starred in "The Graduate"?
28 In the 1850s a Singer sewing machine became the first item to be sold under which trading terms?
29 Starting in March, in which month does the coarse fishing close season end in British rivers?
30 Which word can be someone in an army or a piece of toast?

Answers | Pot-Luck 29 (see Quiz 56)

1 John Peel. 2 Leo. 3 Chris de Burgh. 4 Marks and Gran. 5 Head. 6 Harry Enfield. 7 The Goon Show. 8 Ronnie Barker, Ronnie Corbett. 9 Baldrick. 10 Deep. 11 Independent Television News. 12 Flamingo. 13 Music hall. 14 Edward. 15 Horses. 16 Sweet Charity. 17 Dane. 18 Ruth. 19 Family Affairs. 20 Loaf of bread. 21 Polo. 22 Michael Barrymore. 23 Friday. 24 Frank. 25 Sri Lanka. 26 Tim Burton. 27 Spector. 28 Japanese flower arranging. 29 Andrew Flintoff. 30 London.

1 What is the main ingredient in an omelette?
2 Which animal does venison come from?
3 Which garden herb is made into a sauce often eaten with lamb?
4 In which country did the word biscuit originate?
5 What is traditionally eaten on Shrove Tuesday?
6 What is another name for French fries?
7 What is a slice of bacon called?
8 Which edible sugary substance do bees make?
9 What is done to a herring to make it into a kipper?
10 Which vegetable can be King Edward or Desirée?
11 Which country does Edam cheese originate from?
12 What do you add to milk to make porridge?
13 What is minestrone?
14 What is bottled tomato sauce called?
15 What colour is vodka?
16 Where did the dish paella originate?
17 Which fruit is covered with toffee at a fairground?
18 Which nuts are used to make marzipan?
19 Is a Spotted Dick usually eaten hot or cold?
20 What meat dish is Cumberland famous for?
21 Which pudding is eaten with roast beef?
22 Which vegetables can be French, runner or baked?
23 What colour is piccalilli?
24 What sort of food is a rollmop?
25 Is wholemeal bread brown or white?
26 If something is cooked "au gratin" what must it contain?
27 Petits pois are small what?
28 In which country is Peroni beer bottled?
29 What are the two main ingredients of a shandy?
30 Which Scottish island has seven working whisky distilleries on it?

Answers | Pot-Luck 27 *(see Quiz 53)*

1 Henry VIII. 2 Andre Agassi. 3 Buyer beware. 4 Liverpool. 5 Rum. 6 25. 7 Kate Winslet. 8 Douglas. 9 Choked on a chicken bone. 10 Selleck. 11 Epistle. 12 Tina Turner. 13 Litmus. 14 J. B. 15 Magnus Magnusson. 16 900. 17 Ash Wednesday. 18 Washington. 19 The Supremes. 20 Double eagle. 21 Old age pension. 22 Zorro. 23 Candles. 24 Leveret. 25 0. 26 Hippopotamus. 27 Robert. 28 Sunday. 29 George Clooney. 30 Keira Knightley.

1 "Margrave of the Marshes" is a memoir to which late DJ?

2 What is the zodiac sign of the Lion?

3 Who recorded the album "Spark to a Flame"?

4 Which duo created "Birds of a Feather"?

5 In the Bible, what part of John the Baptist's anatomy did Salome demand as a reward for her dancing?

6 Which comedian talked about "Loadsamoney"?

7 Which radio show was originally called "Crazy People"?

8 Which two TV comedians say "It's goodnight from me..." "...And it's goodnight from him"?

9 Who did Tony Robinson play in the "Blackadder" series?

10 According to proverb, how do still waters run?

11 In the broadcasting sector, what does ITN stand for?

12 Which exotic bird stands on one leg?

13 The Americans call it vaudeville, what is it called in Britain?

14 At the beginning of 2005 which was the only son of the Queen who was married?

15 What is hippophobia a fear of?

16 Which musical does "Hey Big Spender" come from?

17 Which Great breed of dog sounds as if it comes from Scandinavia?

18 What is the first name of TV cook Mott?

19 In which soap was Gary Costello played by Gary Webster?

20 What type of food is a bloomer?

21 Chukkas are the playing periods in which sport?

22 Who says, "All wight?"?

23 Which day of the week is named after the goddess Frigg?

24 Which Anne kept a diary while in hiding during the Second World War?

25 What was Ceylon renamed as?

26 Which Tim was director of the 2005 version of "Charlie and the Chocolate Factory"?

27 Which record producer Phil produced a "wall of sound" in the 1960s?

28 What is ikebana?

29 Which sportsman wrote an autobiography called "Being Freddie"?

30 Where will the 2012 Olympics be held?

Answers	Pot-Luck 28 *(see Quiz 54)*

1 Emmerdale. 2 150. 3 Switzerland. 4 Ricky Gervais. 5 Orlando Bloom. 6 Nine. 7 Nitrogen. 8 Blur. 9 Patricia. 10 December. 11 Emu. 12 Tony Blackburn. 13 60. 14 Clove. 15 Streisand. 16 Z. 17 Ambridge (in the Archers). 18 Oil. 19 30. 20 The Way You Look Tonight. 21 Wood. 22 Handel. 23 Secco. 24 Buddleia. 25 Paul Daniels. 26 Sport. 27 Hoffman. 28 Hire Purchase. 29 June. 30 Soldier.

Quiz 57 | TV: The 70s

Answers – page 69

1 Which Irish comedian held a cigarette, sat on a bar stool and chatted?
2 What was the profession of the Angels?
3 Which poetess Pam won "Opportunity Knocks" in 1975?
4 What made up the Bouquet in the series with Susan Penhaligon?
5 Whose Angels were undercover detectives?
6 The Duchess of which street was part of a 1970s drama series?
7 Which king and son of Queen Victoria was the subject of a TV serial?
8 Which Tudor queen was played by Glenda Jackson?
9 The Fall and Rise of which Perrin was played by Leonard Rossiter?
10 What was the first name of Basil Fawlty's wife?
11 How were Bill Oddie, Tim Brooke-Taylor and Graeme Garden known?
12 Which children's series told of life in a London comprehensive?
13 In which series did The Fonz appear?
14 Who was told It Ain't Half Hot in the sit com set in India?
15 When will it be Alright in the Denis Norden series begun in 1977?
16 Which Jim fixed it?
17 Which series about three delinquent OAPs began in the 1970s?
18 Whose Flying Circus was a big 1970s hit?
19 Which early-evening news magazine was transmitted throughout the country?
20 Which series about sheep dog trials began in the 1970s?
21 What was the nationality of detective Van Der Valk?
22 Which Liverpool shipping Line was an extremely popular long-running series?
23 In which part of the country was the Poldark series set?
24 Which building moisture problem was the title of the series about Rigsby and Miss Jones?
25 Who was Starsky's police partner?
26 Who started presenting "That's Life" in 1974?
27 Who starred in their Christmas Show watched by 28 million in 1977?
28 To what was Audrey Fforbes-Hamilton born?
29 If Lord Bellamy was Upstairs, where were Hudson and Mrs Bridges?
30 In which part of England was "When the Boat Comes In" set?

Answers	Literature *(see Quiz 59)*

1 Harry Potter novels. 2 Agatha Christie. 3 Brontë. 4 Wodehouse. 5 Adrian Mole. 6 Vet. 7 Cartland. 8 Rumpole. 9 Lady Chatterley. 10 Horse racing. 11 Archer. 12 Collins. 13 Rendell. 14 Peace. 15 Treasure. 16 Twist. 17 Pan. 18 Eagle. 19 Catherine. 20 James. 21 Alice. 22 Three. 23 Crusoe. 24 The Willows. 25 Scrooge. 26 Da Vinci. 27 Daffodils. 28 Poetry. 29 Belgian. 30 Monk.

1 Who wrote the travel book "Himalaya" and starred in the TV series with the same name?
2 What is the currency of the Netherlands?
3 What is the first name of TV cook Dimbleby?
4 Which birds congregate in a gaggle?
5 Who recorded the million-selling album "Be Here Now"?
6 Which veteran cricket commentator retired after the 2005 Ashes series?
7 In rhyming slang what is the Sweeney Todd?
8 How is Robert Zimmermann better known?
9 Which university did Prince William graduate from in 2005?
10 In the Bible, what was the name of the first garden?
11 How many minutes in four and three quarter hours?
12 What is the name of "She Who Must be Obeyed"?
13 Which cartoon character says, "Smarter than the average bear"?
14 What colour do you get if you mix red and yellow?
15 Which sport does Sam Torrance play?
16 How many sides has a rhombus?
17 In which children's TV show did Bungle, George and Zippy appear?
18 What colour was the Pimpernel in Baroness Orczy's novel?
19 Which major river flows through Vienna?
20 Which song was a hit for both Buddy Holly and Mud?
21 What can dogs do that wolves cannot?
22 In the film "Free Willy" what was Willy?
23 Where in the body is the cranium?
24 Which rock guitarist had a band called the Experience?
25 What can be planes or sprays of water?
26 What is the capital of Norway?
27 Grant and Truman have been presidents of which country?
28 Which name is shared by model Cindy and actor/singer Michael?
29 Who recorded the album "A Night at the Opera"?
30 What does VCR stand for?

Answers	Pot-Luck 31 *(see Quiz 60)*

1 Tuesday. 2 Sharon Osbourne. 3 Paddington. 4 Gary Rhodes. 5 Alaska. 6 30.
7 Endive. 8 Tank. 9 Simon Preston. 10 Tracy. 11 December. 12 Madness. 13
Badminton. 14 1878. 15 Wizzard. 16 Puffin. 17 Lenin. 18 Seafood/Fish. 19 T. Rex.
20 By sense of smell. 21 Suez. (The opera was Aida.) 22 Chestnut. 23 Kissin' Cousins.
24 Foal. 25 Jimmy Nail. 26 The Queen Mother. 27 Roger Federer. 28 Pepys. 29
Fish. 30 Open University.

1 Which best-selling novels centre round Hogwarts School?
2 Who created the character of Miss Marple?
3 Which Emily wrote "Wuthering Heights"?
4 Which creator of Jeeves and Wooster is known by his initials P. G.?
5 Whose first Secret Diary was written when he was 13 3/4?
6 What was the profession of James Herriot?
7 What was the surname of romantic novelist Dame Barbara?
8 Which London barrister was created by John Mortimer?
9 Whose Lover was the subject of a book by D. H. Lawrence?
10 Which sport are Dick Francis' novels about?
11 Which politician Jeffrey wrote "Kane and Abel"?
12 Which novelist Jackie has an actress sister called Joan?
13 Which Ruth created Inspector Wexford?
14 What did Tolstoy write about together with War?
15 What was on the Island Robert Louis Stevenson wrote about?
16 What was the surname of the Dickens character Oliver?
17 Which Peter took the Darling children to Never Never Land?
18 Which bird of prey Has Landed, in the book by Jack Higgins?
19 What was the first name of novelist Miss Cookson?
20 Which detective novelist is known by her initials P. D.?
21 Which little girl had Adventures Through the Looking Glass?
22 How many Musketeers were there in the title of the book by Dumas?
23 Which Robinson was shipwrecked on a desert island?
24 Where is the Wind in the story about Toad and Badger?
25 What was the surname of Ebenezer in "A Christmas Carol"?
26 Which artist's name features in the title of Dan Brown's best-selling book?
27 Which popular yellow spring flower did Wordsworth write about?
28 What type of writing is John Betjeman famous for?
29 What is the nationality of Agatha Christie's detective Poirot?
30 What is the religious occupation of medieval detective Cadfael?

Answers	TV: The 70s *(see Quiz 57)*

1 Dave Allen. 2 Nurses. 3 Ayres. 4 Barbed Wire. 5 Charlie's. 6 Duke Street. 7 Edward VII. 8 Elizabeth I. 9 Reginald. 10 Sybil. 11 The Goodies. 12 Grange Hill. 13 Happy Days. 14 Mum. 15 On the Night. 16 Savile. 17 Last of the Summer Wine. 18 Monty Python's. 19 Nationwide. 20 One Man and His Dog. 21 Dutch. 22 Onedin Line. 23 Cornwall. 24 Rising Damp. 25 Hutch. 26 Esther Rantzen. 27 Morecambe and Wise. 28 The Manor. 29 Downstairs. 30 North East.

1 On which day of the week is the Budget usually presented?
2 Which feisty female's autobiography was called "Extreme"?
3 Which fictional bear is named after a London station?
4 Who wrote a cookery book called "Keeping It Simple"?
5 What is the largest state of the USA?
6 How many years are celebrated by a pearl anniversary?
7 Which curly-leaved salad plant is a member of the chicory family?
8 Which armoured combat vehicle was first used in World War I?
9 Which doctor did Simon Shepherd play in "Peak Practice"?
10 In "Coronation Street" what is the name of Deirdre's daughter?
11 In which month is the shortest day?
12 Who recorded "Michael Caine"?
13 In which sport is the Thomas Cup awarded?
14 To ten years either way, when were women first allowed to take degrees at British universities?
15 Which group had a No 1 with "See My Baby Jive"?
16 Which bird is associated with Lundy Island?
17 How is Russian revolutionary Vladimir Ilyich Ulyanov better known?
18 Rick Stein's Cornish restaurant specializes in what type of food?
19 What were Marc Bolan and Micky Finn better known as?
20 How do male moths find female moths in the dark?
21 Which canal had an opera written especially for its opening?
22 What type of nut is a marron glacé?
23 In which film did Elvis Presley play a double role?
24 What is a young horse called?
25 Who recorded the album "Crocodile Shoes"?
26 Who became Lord Warden of the Cinque ports in 1978?
27 Who beat Andrew Murray in the final of the 2005 Thai Open?
28 Which Samuel kept a famous diary in the seventeenth century?
29 What is a coley?
30 In education, what does OU stand for?

Answers | Pot-Luck 30 *(see Quiz 58)*

1 Michael Palin. 2 Guilder. 3 Josceline. 4 Geese. 5 Oasis. 6 Richie Benaud. 7 Flying Squad. 8 Bob Dylan. 9 St Andrews. 10 Eden. 11 285. 12 Hilda Rumpole. 13 Yogi Bear. 14 Orange. 15 Golf. 16 Four. 17 Rainbow. 18 Scarlet. 19 Danube. 20 Oh Boy. 21 Bark. 22 A whale. 23 The head. 24 Jimi Hendrix. 25 Jets. 26 Oslo. 27 USA. 28 Crawford. 29 Queen. 30 Video Cassette Recorder.

1 What is Wales' highest mountain?
2 Which Welshman wrote "Portrait of the Artist as a Young Dog"?
3 Which Sea is to the north of Wales?
4 What are the Brecon Beacons?
5 Which island lies off the north west coast of Wales?
6 Which spring flower is a Welsh emblem?
7 What is the capital of Wales?
8 Which Channel is to the south of Wales?
9 Is Caernarvon Castle in the north or south of Wales?
10 Caerphilly is a town and also what type of food?
11 Which creature of legend is seen on the Welsh flag?
12 Which city in the south of the country is its second largest?
13 Which sport is played at Cardiff Arms Park?
14 Which wild cat gives its name to a Bay on Cardiff's quayside?
15 The production of which fuel affected the Welsh landscape until its decline in recent years?
16 Who was invested as Prince of Wales in 1969 at Caernarvon Castle?
17 Which vegetable is a Welsh emblem?
18 Which country lies to the east of Wales?
19 Who is the patron saint of Wales?
20 What is the mountainous area around Snowdon called?
21 Which Welsh Bay shares its name with a woollen jacket?
22 Which is the only Welsh county to have a first-class cricket team?
23 What is the currency of Wales?
24 Wales has the highest density in the world of which farm animal?
25 Which Welsh Secretary challenged John Major for the Tory Party leadership in the summer of 1995?
26 Which county is further north, Clwyd or Gwent?
27 Which Strait separates Anglesey from the mainland?
28 Which North Wales university town shares its name with a resort of Northern Ireland?
29 The UK's longest river rises in Wales. What is it called?
30 Which town is further south, Aberystwyth or Swansea?

Answers	Sport: Football (see Quiz 63)

1 Newcastle. 2 Vieira. 3 Blue and white. 4 Houllier. 5 USA. 6 Bristol. 7 Goal.
8 Newcastle. 9 Cole. 10 Blackpool. 11 Schmeichel. 12 Spain. 13 Rangers. 14
Manchester United. 15 Northern Ireland. 16 Red. 17 France. 18 Tottenham. 19
Bolton. 20 As hosts they automatically qualified. 21 Pleat. 22 Own goal. 23 2005.
24 Keegan. 25 Bramall. 26 Liverpool. 27 3.00pm. 28 Man Utd. 29 Everton. 30
Chelsea.

1 How did Van Gogh commit suicide?
2 What is the upper age limit for being an MP in the UK?
3 Who recorded the album "Time to Grow"?
4 Who was the first reigning British monarch to visit a Communist country?
5 Which opera features the song "Take a Pair of Sparkling Eyes"?
6 In snooker, how many points are scored for potting the green ball?
7 S is the symbol of which chemical element?
8 Who recorded the album "Music Box"?
9 Which card game is another name for a prison van?
10 What is the second month of the year to have exactly 31 days?
11 In the Bible, who led the children of Israel to the Promised Land?
12 What goes before "mantle", "slipper" and "smock" in flower names?
13 Which famous Welsh opera star celebrated his 40th birthday in 2005?
14 Which movie started out as a TV series about good ol' boys Bo and Luke Duke?
15 Which horse won the English Triple Crown in 1970?
16 Timperley Early and Cawood Castle are types of what?
17 In the solar system which is the third planet from the sun?
18 What has subdivisions comprising 12, 52 and 365 units?
19 How many sides in four oblongs?
20 According to proverb, a little what is a dangerous thing?
21 What would you be playing if you were talking about spares and strikes?
22 In rugby, what name is given to a forward on either end of the front row of a scrum?
23 Whose catchphrase was, "Heavens to Murgatroyd"?
24 What is the first name of TV cook Harriott?
25 What is the least valuable piece on a chessboard?
26 What was the name of Barnum's famous giant elephant?
27 Which Mr Clarkson wrote "The World According to Clarkson"?
28 How many pieces of silver did Judas get for betraying Christ?
29 Which food is made from the lining of a cow's stomach?
30 What collective name is used for items made from precious gems?

Answers	**Pot-Luck 33** *(see Quiz 64)*

1 Two. 2 Virgo. 3 Han Solo. 4 Clog. 5 Microsoft. 6 Kent. 7 Table Mountain. 8 Willy Wonka. 9 Holby City. 10 Simple Minds. 11 Robert Kennedy. 12 Scotland. 13 Monaco. 14 Ocean's Twelve. 15 Vodka and tomato juice. 16 Sparrow. 17 Squash. 18 Celine Dion. 19 Billy Joe McAllister. 20 Soup. 21 Rolls Royce. 22 Michael Caine. 23 Saturday. 24 As Time Goes By. 25 Outside. 26 Marilyn Monroe. 27 Blue. 28 Light flyweight. 29 500. 30 Cher.

1 Which team is known as the Magpies?
2 Which Patrick was Arsenal skipper when they went a season unbeaten in the Premiership?
3 What two colours are in Blackburn's home strip?
4 Which Gerard was the first Frenchman to manage Liverpool?
5 In which country were the 1994 World Cup finals held?
6 Which city has teams called Rovers and City?
7 What position did Peter Shilton play?
8 At which club did Shearer and Owen line up in the same side?
9 Which surname is shared by England players Ashley and Joe?
10 Which club is linked with the playing career of Jimmy Armfield?
11 Which Peter kept goal for both Man Utd and Man City?
12 Which country do Real Madrid come from?
13 In QPR what does the letter R stand for?
14 Which club did Steve Bruce play for in a Premiership-winning season?
15 Which country did George Best play for?
16 What is the home colour of Nottingham Forest?
17 Which country does David Ginola come from?
18 At which club did Terry Venables and Alan Sugar clash?
19 Which club appointed former player Sam Allardyce as manager in October 1999?
20 Why did France not play in qualifying games for the '98 World Cup?
21 Which David has managed Spurs, Luton and Sheffield Wednesday?
22 What do the letters o.g. stand for?
23 In which year did Roy Keane end his playing days with Man Utd?
24 Which Kevin has managed Newcastle, Fulham, Man City and England?
25 Which Lane do Sheffield United play at?
26 Which club is associated with the song "You'll Never Walk Alone"?
27 What is the traditional kick-off time for Saturday League games?
28 Edwin Van der Sar left Fulham to join which other Premiership club?
29 David Moyes first managed in the Premiership at which club?
30 Which London side did Ruud Gullit join in 1995?

Answers | **Around Wales** *(see Quiz 61)*

1 Snowdon. 2 Dylan Thomas. 3 Irish Sea. 4 Mountains. 5 Anglesey. 6 Daffodil. 7 Cardiff. 8 Bristol Channel. 9 North. 10 Cheese. 11 Dragon. 12 Swansea. 13 Rugby. 14 Tiger. 15 Coal. 16 Prince Charles. 17 Leek. 18 England. 19 St David. 20 Snowdonia. 21 Cardigan. 22 Glamorgan. 23 Pound sterling. 24 Sheep. 25 John Redwood. 26 Clwyd. 27 Menai Strait. 28 Bangor. 29 Severn. 30 Swansea.

1 How many packs of cards are needed for a game of Canasta?

2 What is the zodiac sign of the Virgin?

3 Which character did Harrison Ford play in "Star Wars"?

4 What is a sabot?

5 Bill Gates founded which computer corporation?

6 Which Clark was a journalist on "The Daily Planet"?

7 Where would you see fog called the Tablecloth?

8 Whom did Johnny Depp play in the 2005 version of "Charlie and the Chocolate Factory"?

9 In which TV drama series did the character Mubbs Hussein appear for four years?

10 Who recorded the album "Once Upon a Time"?

11 Whom did Sirhan Sirhan assassinate?

12 In which country was the 2005 G8 summit held?

13 What is ruled by the House of Grimaldi?

14 What was the sequel to "Ocean's Eleven" called?

15 What are the two main ingredients of a Bloody Mary?

16 In the rhyme, who killed Cock Robin?

17 What is a world sport, an American vegetable and a British soft drink?

18 Who recorded the album "The Colour of My Love"?

19 Who jumped off the Tallahatchee Bridge?

20 What type of food is consommé?

21 The "Silver Ghost" was what type of car?

22 Who says, "Not many people know that!"?

23 Which day of the week is named after the god Saturn?

24 What was Sam asked to play by Rick in "Casablanca"?

25 Where would you eat if you were eating al fresco?

26 How is Norma Jean Baker better known?

27 What colour features in the title of George Gershwin's Rhapsody?

28 What is the lowest weight in boxing?

29 How many sheets of paper are there in a ream?

30 Who was Sonny's singing partner?

Answers | Pot-Luck 32 *(see Quiz 62)*

1 He shot himself. 2 There isn't one. 3 Lemar. 4 Elizabeth II (1972 Yugoslavia). 5 The Gondoliers. 6 Three. 7 Sulphur. 8 Mariah Carey. 9 Black Maria. 10 March. 11 Moses. 12 Lady's. 13 Bryn Terfel. 14 The Dukes of Hazzard. 15 Nijinsky. 16 Rhubarb. 17 Earth. 18 A year. 19 16. 20 Knowledge. 21 Ten-pin bowling. 22 Prop. 23 Snagglepuss. 24 Ainsley. 25 Pawn. 26 Jumbo. 27 Jeremy Clarkson. 28 30. 29 Tripe. 30 Jewellery.

1 Which country are Qantas airlines from?
2 What is the currency of Russia?
3 What type of plant grows from seed, flowers and dies in a year?
4 Helen Sharman was the first Briton to go where?
5 What is Andy Capp's wife called?
6 Which two members of Bremner, Bird & Fortune share the same first name?
7 In rhyming slang what is Barnet Fair?
8 How is Declan McManus better known?
9 What animal is shown in the painting "The Monarch of the Glen"?
10 Where would you look to discover the Mount of the Moon and the Girdle of Venus?
11 Which insect might be used by a snooker player?
12 In Roman numerals what is MD + MD?
13 What is the first name of Polish film director Polanski?
14 What colour is saffron?
15 What was Al short for in Al Capone's name?
16 How many sides has a trapezium?
17 In which Olympic event would the competitor use ribbons and hoops?
18 Which metal is an alloy of copper and zinc?
19 Which major river flows through Cairo?
20 What is a Blenheim Orange?
21 Which country did Prime Minister Bhutto rule?
22 In which film did John Travolta play Vincent Vega?
23 What number is opposite a one on a dice?
24 Who recorded the album "Made in England"?
25 Which sporting captain called his autobiography "Calling the Shots"?
26 What is the capital of Sweden?
27 Which title gave hits to both Jennifer Rush and Frankie Goes to Hollywood?
28 What is Roget's word book known as?
29 Which Daniel succeeded Pierce Brosnan as 007?
30 Which band took "Crashed the Wedding" to No 1 in 2003?

Answers	**Pot-Luck 35** *(see Quiz 67)*

1 Basil Spence 2 Emily. 3 Nudist. 4 Niven. 5 Weathering. 6 Mario Lanza. 7 Wolves. 8 Mexico. 9 500. 10 Elly May. 11 March. 12 Paul McCartney. 13 Exit. 14 C. S. 15 Jacqueline Wilson. 16 Garden School. 17 Calcium. 18 Jethro Tull. 19 Take That. 20 Sleeve. 21 Beaufort. 22 South Africa. 23 20th. 24 Colt. 25 Aer Lingus. 26 Holidays. 27 Anton. 28 Deuce. 29 Shark. 30 Mineworkers.

1 Which Edward became prime minister in 1970?
2 What type of currency was introduced to Britain in 1971?
3 Idi Amin seized power in which country?
4 Henry Cooper retired from which sport?
5 What type of short pants became the fashion craze for women?
6 Bangladesh was formed from the eastern part of which country?
7 Which Sir Anthony was declared to be a Russian spy?
8 Which Mother won a Nobel Peace Prize?
9 Which Conservative leader became prime minister in 1979?
10 The Shah of which country was forced into exile?
11 The strike-bound months of 1978 and 1979 became known as the Winter of what?
12 Which Liberal leader resigned after allegations about his private life?
13 Which princess sought a divorce from the Earl of Snowdon?
14 In which sea off the British coastline was oil discovered?
15 Under Patrick Steptoe's guidance what was produced from a test tube for the first time in July 1978?
16 Whose shroud went on display at St John's Cathedral in Turin?
17 Steve Biko died in a cell in which country?
18 What sport did Kerry Packer try to take over with his cash offers?
19 Which king of rock died in Tennessee in 1977?
20 Freddie Laker brought cut-price travel in what type of transport?
21 Which Jubilee did Queen Elizabeth II celebrate in 1977?
22 The Sex Pistols were the leaders of the movement known as what kind of rock?
23 Which leader of Communist China died in 1976?
24 Which "Lucky" Lord vanished after the murder of his child's nanny?
25 Which scandal forced Richard Nixon to resign as US President?
26 Which countries fought in the 1973 Yom Kippur War?
27 What did the Amoco Cadiz spill off the Brittany coastline?
28 How many days were in a working week during the 1974 power shortage?
29 Which earl was murdered by the IRA in 1979?
30 Which Labour MP James became prime minister?

Answers | Geography *(see Quiz 68)*

1 Spain. 2 India and Pakistan. 3 Northumberland. 4 Peking. 5 Buckingham Palace. 6 Austria. 7 Devon. 8 Red. 9 Derbyshire. 10 Italy. 11 Africa. 12 West. 13 Argentina. 14 Paris. 15 Portugal. 16 Algeria. 17 Scafell Pike. 18 Scotland. 19 Oslo. 20 Africa. 21 Netherlands. 22 Florida. 23 France. 24 Birmingham. 25 Washington. 26 Pacific. 27 Brazil. 28 Europe. 29 Sweden. 30 Belgium.

Quiz 67 | Pot-Luck 35

Answers – page 75

LEVEL 1

1 Who designed Coventry cathedral?
2 What is the name of Florence's lay-dee companion in "Little Britain"?
3 In 1979, Brighton Council decided to allow what type of beach?
4 Which David told his life story in "The Moon's a Balloon"?
5 Rocks are broken down by the elements by what gradual process?
6 Which tenor took the title role in "The Great Caruso"?
7 The word lupine relates to which animals?
8 In which country is the volcano Popocatépetl?
9 What number does the Roman numeral D stand for?
10 What was Jed Clampett's daughter called in "The Beverley Hillbillies"?
11 In which month is the first day of spring?
12 Who co-wrote a "Liverpool Oratorio" with Carl Davis?
13 Which stage direction means to go off stage?
14 What are the two initials of Narnia creator Lewis?
15 Which best-selling children's writer penned "Diamond Girls" and "Love Lessons"?
16 What type of school did Diarmuid Gavin present on TV?
17 Which element is found in bones, shells and teeth?
18 In the early 1700s who invented a seed drill?
19 What are Gary Barlow, Howard Donald, Jason Orange and Mark Owen better known as?
20 What part of a garment is a raglan?
21 What scale is used to measure wind velocity?
22 In which country is the Table Mountain?
23 Which anniversary on UK screens did Aussie soap "Neighbours" celebrate in 2005?
24 What is a young stallion called?
25 What is the Republic of Ireland's airline called?
26 What does the French word vacances mean?
27 What is the first name of TV cook Mosimann?
28 In tennis, what is a score of 40 all called?
29 Threshers and hammerheads are types of what?
30 The NUM is the National Union of what?

Answers | Pot-Luck 34 *(see Quiz 65)*

1 Australia. 2 Rouble. 3 Annual. 4 Space. 5 Flo. 6 Bird & Fortune (John). 7 Hair. 8 Elvis Costello. 9 A red deer stag. 10 In the palm of your hand. 11 Spider. 12 MMM. 13 Roman. 14 Yellow. 15 Alphonse. 16 Four. 17 Rhythmic gymnastics. 18 Brass. 19 Nile. 20 An apple. 21 Pakistan. 22 Pulp Fiction. 23 A six. 24 Elton John. 25 Michael Vaughan. 26 Stockholm. 27 The Power of Love. 28 Thesaurus. 29 Daniel Craig. 30 Busted.

Quiz 68 | Geography

Answers – page 76

1 Which country can you easily walk to from Gibraltar?
2 Urdu is an important language in which two Asian countries?
3 Which is England's most northerly county?
4 What did Bejing used to be called?
5 Which is the Queen's London home?
6 In which European country is Salzburg?
7 Which county divides Cornwall from Somerset?
8 What "colour" is the Sea between Egypt and Saudi Arabia?
9 In which county is the Peak District?
10 In which country is the resort of Rimini?
11 Madagascar is to the east of which continent?
12 Is California on the east or west coast of the USA?
13 Which is the nearest country to the Falkland Islands?
14 Near which French city is the Disney Theme Park?
15 In which country is the Algarve?
16 Which is further west, Algeria or Ethiopia?
17 What is the highest point in England?
18 In which country is the county of Tayside?
19 Which Scandinavian capital begins and ends with the same letter?
20 Chad is in which continent?
21 What is Holland also known as?
22 In which US holiday state is Miami?
23 Which country is divided from Spain by the Pyrenees?
24 What is the largest city in the West Midlands?
25 Which town of Tyne and Wear shares its name with the US capital?
26 The Philippines are in which Ocean?
27 What is the largest country of South America?
28 In which continent is Slovenia?
29 Which country originally produced Volvo cars?
30 In which country do most Flemish speakers live?

Answers | **70s Newsround** *(see Quiz 66)*

1 Heath. 2 Decimal. 3 Uganda. 4 Boxing. 5 Hot. 6 Pakistan. 7 Blunt. 8 Teresa.
9 Margaret Thatcher. 10 Iran. 11 Discontent. 12 Jeremy Thorpe. 13 Margaret. 14
North Sea. 15 A baby. 16 Jesus Christ. 17 South Africa. 18 Cricket. 19 Elvis Presley.
20 Aircraft. 21 Silver. 22 Punk. 23 Mao Tse-tung. 24 Lucan. 25 Watergate. 26
Egypt, Syria and Israel. 27 Oil. 28 Three. 29 Mountbatten. 30 Callaghan.

1 Which extra title was given to Catherine II of Russia?
2 Which Fiona was Eamonn Holmes' long-running co-presenter on GMTV?
3 Which country is a car from if it has the international registration letter H?
4 Which came first, the House of Tudor or the House of Stuart?
5 Which Norman said, "He got on his bike and looked for work."
6 What was the name of the witch played by Agnes Moorhead in "Bewitched"?
7 Zn is the symbol of which chemical element?
8 In "Coronation Street" what is Ken Barlow's job?
9 According to proverb, one man's meat is another man's what?
10 Which actress played the title role in the movie "Domino"?
11 Williams and Conference are types of what?
12 Who recorded the album "Medusa"?
13 How many times did Will Carling skipper England before giving up the captaincy in '96?
14 What is the capital of Afghanistan?
15 Who was the female lead in the TV sitcom "Terry and June?"
16 Frank Lampard joined Chelsea from which club?
17 Who released the 2005 album "A Time to Live"?
18 Which Irish entertainer Val used to sing in a rocking chair?
19 How many yards in a mile?
20 Who was the only British female singer to have three UK No 1s in the 60s?
21 What was the name of the Ewing ranch in "Dallas"?
22 The USA government is nicknamed which relative?
23 What name is given to poisonous fluid from a snake?
24 Which Biblical town was destroyed with Gomorrah?
25 On what type of farm are horses bred?
26 What famous first in TV advertising is held by Bird's Eye frozen peas?
27 What number is Beethoven's concerto known as the "Emperor"?
28 Which US playwright wrote "The Price"?
29 What name is given to a baby elephant?
30 What colour pottery is Josiah Wedgwood noted for?

Answers | Pot-Luck 37 *(see Quiz 71)*

1 Spring. 2 Libra. 3 Madagascar. 4 Rolling Stones. 5 Flat. 6 Walt Disney. 7 Plum. 8 Carburettor. 9 Tongue. 10 A rest. 11 Greenwich Mean Time. 12 The Moon. 13 Waistcoat. 14 May. 15 Badminton. 16 An ear. 17 Miser. 18 Les Misérables. 19 Orwell. 20 Only Fools and Horses. 21 Jenny. 22 Fred Flintstone. 23 January. 24 Fleetwood Mac. 25 Lincoln. 26 Labour. 27 Friar. 28 Wall Street. 29 Australia. 30 Ronnie Corbett.

1 What was invented by Lazlo and Georg Biro?
2 Which fashion item is Oscar Levi Strauss responsible for?
3 What nationality was motor vehicle pioneer Gottlieb Daimler?
4 What was developed by André and Edouard Michelin?
5 What type of pen did Lewis Waterman invent?
6 Which air cushion vehicle was invented by Christopher Cockerell?
7 Which engine used in aircraft was invented by Sir Frank Whittle?
8 What did John Logie Baird invent, first called "seeing by wireless"?
9 Which communication system is Alexander Graham Bell famous for?
10 Who invented a code made up of dots and dashes?
11 For whom did Louis Braille develop his writing system?
12 Which method of food preservation did Clarence Birdseye invent?
13 What type of lamp is Humphry Davy famous for?
14 Which predecessor of the CD player did Thomas Edison create?
15 Which breakfast food was developed by Will Keith Kellogg in 1898?
16 Which invention is Marconi known for?
17 Which company, motto "Small is beautiful", was founded in the late 1940s and developed the Walkman?
18 Which explosive was invented by Alfred Nobel?
19 What type of milk did Louis Pasteur give his name to, because of the treatment it undergoes?
20 In which source of power were Volta and Ampère pioneers?
21 What powered James Watt's engine in 1765?
22 What would you use Isaac Singer's invention for?
23 In which room would you be most likely to use the inventions of Kenneth Wood – known to his friends as Ken?
24 At what sort of party might you see the invention of Earl W. Tupper?
25 Which frozen confection was originally called Eskimo pie?
26 Which Earl invented a snack of meat between two slices of bread?
27 What was special about the fabric Charles Macintosh invented?
28 Which essential for foreign tourists was invented by American Express?
29 George Eastman developed an easy to use hand-held what?
30 What type of aircraft is Sikorsky famous for?

Answers	TV: The 80s *(see Quiz 72)*

1 All Creatures Great and Small. 2 Allo Allo. 3 Jersey. 4 Boys from the Blackstuff. 5 Brideshead. 6 Lacey. 7 Fame. 8 French. 9 A Laugh. 10 Grant. 11 Highway. 12 The Galaxy. 13 Boats. 14 Oxford. 15 India. 16 Fire Brigade. 17 Lovejoy. 18 Miami. 19 Not the Nine o'Clock News. 20 All Hours. 21 Spitting Image. 22 Michael Aspel. 23 Dogs. 24 Roland. 25 Holland. 26 Barrister. 27 Japanese. 28 J.R. 29 Watchdog. 30 Sir Humphrey Appleby.

1 Which season does the word vernal relate to?
2 What is the zodiac sign of the Balance?
3 On which island are most lemurs found?
4 Who had a No 1 hit with the song "(I Can't Get No) Satisfaction"?
5 What type of horse racing does not include fences and obstacles?
6 Who created Mickey Mouse?
7 In nursery rhyme, what did Little Jack Horner pull out of a pie?
8 Which device produces the mix of air and petrol in internal combustion engines?
9 What is a butterfly's proboscis?
10 According to proverb, what is a change as good as?
11 What does GMT stand for?
12 Where did Wallace and Gromit visit in "A Grand Day Out"?
13 Called a vest in America, what's the name of this garment in the UK?
14 Hawthorn traditionally blooms in which month?
15 Which game is played with rackets and shuttlecocks?
16 Which part of his anatomy did Van Gogh cut off?
17 What word describes someone mean with money, like Scrooge?
18 In 2005, which musical celebrated 20 years in London's West End?
19 Which George wrote "Animal Farm"?
20 "The Green Green Grass" was a 2005 spin-off from which long-running TV sitcom?
21 What name is given to a female donkey?
22 Who says, "Yabbadabba Doo!"?
23 Which month is named after the god Janus?
24 Who recorded the album "Rumours"?
25 Which city of central England gave its name to a shade of green?
26 Was Clement Attlee a Conservative or Labour politician?
27 What was the profession or calling of Tuck in Sherwood Forest?
28 Where is the New York Stock Exchange?
29 In which country would you see wild wombats?
30 Who was Ronnie Barker's comic partner?

Answers	**Pot-Luck 36** *(see Quiz 69)*

1 The Great. 2 Fiona Phillips. 3 Hungary. 4 The House of Tudor. 5 Tebbit. 6 Endora. 7 Zinc. 8 Teacher. 9 Poison. 10 Keira Knightley. 11 Pear. 12 Annie Lennox. 13 57. 14 Kabul. 15 June Whitfield. 16 West Ham. 17 Stevie Wonder. 18 Doonican. 19 1,760. 20 Sandie Shaw. 21 South Fork. 22 Uncle Sam. 23 Venom. 24 Sodom. 25 Stud. 26 First product advertised in colour. 27 Fifth. 28 Arthur Miller. 29 Calf. 30 Blue.

1 Which series was about Yorkshire vet James Herriot?
2 In which series would you find the Fallen Madonna with the Big Boobies?
3 On which island was "Bergerac" set?
4 Which programme gave the catchphrase "Gissa job"?
5 What was Revisited in the series with Jeremy Irons?
6 Who was Cagney's police partner?
7 What were students at the New York High School of Performing Arts seeking?
8 Which Fields did Hester and William go to after "Fresh Fields"?
9 What was Jeremy Beadle Game for?
10 Which Russell was astrologer on "Breakfast Time"?
11 Which religious programme did Harry Secombe start to present?
12 What was the Hitch Hiker's Guide to?
13 What was being built in the yards in "Howard's Way"?
14 In which university city was Inspector Morse based?
15 In which eastern country was "The Jewel in the Crown" set?
16 Which emergency service is featured in "London's Burning"?
17 Which series featured Ian McShane as an antiques dealer?
18 In which city did Sonny Crockett investigate Vice?
19 What wasn't a news bulletin but did feature Pamela Stephenson and Rowan Atkinson?
20 When was the shop with David Jason and Ronnie Barker Open?
21 Which satirical programme featured latex puppets?
22 Who began presenting "This is Your Life" in 1987?
23 Which pets featured on the programmes with Barbara Woodhouse?
24 Which Rat revived the flagging fortunes of TV-am?
25 Which Jools presented "The Tube"?
26 What was the profession of claret-swigging Horace Rumpole?
27 Whom were the women prisoners of in "Tenko"?
28 Whose shooting in November 1980 was watched by 27 million?
29 What sort of dog became a consumer's champion in the 1980s?
30 Who was MP Jim Hacker's Permanent Under Secretary?

Answers	Inventors and Inventions (see Quiz 70)

1 Ball-point pen. 2 Jeans. 3 German. 4 Tyres. 5 Fountain pen. 6 Hovercraft. 7 Jet. 8 Television. 9 Telephone. 10 Morse. 11 Blind. 12 Deep freezing. 13 Safety lamp. 14 Gramophone. 15 Cornflakes. 16 Wireless. 17 Sony. 18 Dynamite. 19 Pasteurized. 20 Electricity. 21 Steam. 22 Sewing. 23 Kitchen. 24 Tupperware. 25 Choc ice. 26 Sandwich. 27 Waterproof. 28 Traveller's cheque. 29 Camera. 30 Helicopters.

1 Which country does the airline Iberia come from?
2 What is the currency of South Africa?
3 Who was the youngest leadership contender in the 2005 race for the Tory leadership?
4 Who wrote the Aldwych farces, including "Rookery Nook"?
5 What year is included in the name of the group who recorded "Simon Says"?
6 Which school did Queen Elizabeth II attend as a youngster?
7 In rhyming slang what is dog and bone?
8 What was Frederick Bulsara better known as?
9 The movie "Calendar Girls" was about members of which organization?
10 In the Bible, which book follows Matthew?
11 What famous first did Edward White achieve for America?
12 In which country is the Matterhorn?
13 Who was the first female DJ on Radio 1?
14 What colour is associated with an Oxford or Cambridge sports award?
15 Which rock forms the greater part of the White Cliffs of Dover?
16 Which Coronation Street couple remarried during the week of Charles and Camilla's wedding?
17 In tennis, what name is given to a serve that cannot be returned?
18 Who recorded the album "Bad"?
19 Which major river flows through Gloucester?
20 Who created "Dalziel and Pascoe"?
21 According to Rhoda, in which year was she born in the Bronx, New York?
22 Which card game has the same name as a horse-racing town?
23 Who founded the Rocket record label?
24 What was the first name of Burgess, the spy who defected to Russia?
25 How was Eric Bartholomew better known?
26 What is the capital of Denmark?
27 Who played M in "Die Another Day"?
28 "Just when you thought it was safe to go back in the water..." was the advertising line for which film?
29 In which street is the Bank of England?
30 What does TUC stand for?

Answers | Pot-Luck 39 *(see Quiz 75)*

1 Keystone. 2 Are You Being Served? 3 Salamander. 4 The Dail. 5 REM.
6 Kuwait City. 7 John Masefield. 8 Susan Hampshire. 9 Wallace and Gromit. 10 Parcel. 11 October. 12 Enya. 13 Matinee. 14 W. B. 15 Heather. 16 Dodd. 17 Bongos. 18 The Bar. 19 Shadows. 20 Head. 21 Dick Dastardly. 22 Andrew. 23 Hamburg. 24 Filly. 25 Status Quo. 26 New Orleans. 27 Whitelaw. 28 Slob. 29 Fiddler on the Roof. 30 Daniel Radcliffe.

1 What is the first name of supermodel Evangelista?
2 Which veteran Scottish rock star is married to model Rachel Hunter?
3 Princess Caroline is a member of which royal family?
4 What was the surname of Jackie Onassis's first husband?
5 What is the first name of actress/presenter Ms de Cadenet?
6 Lady Helen, daughter of the Duke and Duchess of Kent, named her son after which famous explorer?
7 What was the first name of tycoon Donald Trump's former wife?
8 What is the first name of actress and model Miss Hurley?
9 Who is the magician partner of model Claudia Schiffer?
10 Which Texan model married Mick Jagger?
11 Which Swedish actress is a former wife of the late Peter Sellers?
12 What is the surname of eight-times married actress Zsa Zsa?
13 What is the first name of celebrity photographer Bailey?
14 Which LA Hills are the home of many of the rich and famous?
15 What is the first name of kilt-wearing designer Gaultier?
16 How is skinny 1960s model Lesley Hornby better known?
17 In which city was George Best's funeral held?
18 What is the first name of actress/model Miss Seymour?
19 Who is the head of the Virgin group?
20 What is the first name of gossip columnist Dempster?
21 Which ski resort is a favourite for Prince Charles for his Xmas break?
22 What is the nationality of Sophia Loren?
23 Which TV show made Pamela Anderson famous?
24 Which princess is known by her husband's first name?
25 Which Lord and celebrity photographer passed away in the autumn of 2005?
26 What is the first name of fashion designer Westwood?
27 Of which country is Juan Carlos king?
28 What was the profession of the Queen's cousin Lord Lichfield ?
29 Which Pakistani cricketer married heiress Jemima Goldsmith?
30 Which fuel did the Getty family make their fortune from?

Answers | **Sport: The 80s** *(see Quiz 76)*

1 Lineker. 2 Bob Champion. 3 Geoff Boycott. 4 Ovett. 5 Liverpool. 6 Davis. 7 Australia. 8 Hailwood. 9 Watson. 10 Everton. 11 Navratilova. 12 Bolero. 13 Italy. 14 Zola Budd. 15 Los Angeles. 16 Lyle. 17 Brazil. 18 Dennis Taylor. 19 Belgium. 20 Javelin. 21 Boxing. 22 Boris Becker. 23 Maradona. 24 Flo Jo. 25 Bryan Robson. 26 Somerset. 27 France. 28 Czechoslovakia. 29 Rangers. 30 Jack Charlton.

Answers – page 83

1 Which knockabout Kops were created by Mack Sennett?
2 In which TV programme did the staff of Grace Brothers appear?
3 What is another name for the creature the axolotl?
4 What is the name of the Irish Parliament?
5 Which band features the lyrics of Michael Stipe?
6 What city is the capital of Kuwait?
7 Who wrote the poem "Sea Fever"?
8 Which Susan of "Monarch of the Glen" first found TV fame in the early 1960s?
9 Which duo were the stars of "The Curse of the Were-Rabbit"?
10 In the children's party game, what is passed around and unwrapped?
11 In which month is Halloween?
12 Who recorded the album "Watermark"?
13 What word taken from the French describes an afternoon show?
14 What are the initials of Irish poet Yeats?
15 Which moorland shrub is said to bring good luck?
16 Which comic Ken says, "How tickled I am"?
17 Which instrument is traditionally held between the knees?
18 What name is given to barristers collectively?
19 What are Hank Marvin, Brian Bennett and Bruce Welch better known as?
20 On what part of your body would you wear a homburg?
21 Which cartoon villain exclaimed, "Drat and double drat!"?
22 What is Freddie Flintoff's real first name?
23 In which city did the hamburger originate?
24 What is a young mare called?
25 Which rock group's name is the Latin for the existing state of things?
26 In the song, the House of the Rising Sun is in which city?
27 Which Conservative politician William spoke of a "short, sharp, shock"?
28 What is the surname of the decidedly anti-social TV characters Wayne and Waynetta?
29 The village of Anatevka appears in which musical?
30 Which Daniel played Harry in the Harry Potter films?

Answers	**Pot-Luck 38** *(see Quiz 73)*

1 Spain. 2 Rand. 3 David Cameron. 4 Ben Travers. 5 1910 (Fruitgum Co.) 6 None at all. 7 Phone. 8 Freddie Mercury. 9 The WI. 10 Mark. 11 First to walk in space. 12 Switzerland. 13 Annie Nightingale. 14 Blue. 15 Chalk. 16 Ken and Deidre. 17 Ace. 18 Michael Jackson. 19 Severn. 20 Reginald Hill. 21 1941. 22 Newmarket. 23 Elton John. 24 Guy. 25 Eric Morecambe. 26 Copenhagen. 27 Judi Dench. 28 Jaws II. 29 Threadneedle Street. 30 Trades Union Congress.

1 Which Gary was England's top soccer marksman of the 1980s?
2 Who fought back from cancer to win the Grand National?
3 Which English batsman became the highest run getter in Test history?
4 Which Steve was Sebastian Coe's great rival in mid-distance races?
5 Which club were English soccer champions six times in the 80s?
6 Which Steve became snooker World Champion in 1981?
7 The America's Cup left home for the first time ever to go to where?
8 Which motor-cycle legend Mike was killed in a motor accident in 1981?
9 Which Tom won both the US and British Opens in the same year?
10 Which team were English soccer champions under Howard Kendall?
11 Which Martina dominated Wimbledon in the 1980s?
12 Which piece of music by Ravel did Torvill and Dean use in winning an Olympic gold for ice dancing?
13 Which country beat West Germany to win the 1982 soccer World Cup?
14 The Daily Mail ran a campaign to get which South African athlete to receive a British passport?
15 Where in the USA was the centre for the 1984 Olympic Games?
16 In golf, which Sandy won the 1988 US Masters?
17 Which country is motor racing's Nelson Piquet from?
18 Who became a world snooker champion wearing "upside-down" glasses?
19 In which country was the 1985 Heysel Stadium soccer tragedy?
20 In which event did Tessa Sanderson win Olympic gold?
21 What was Barry McGuigan's sport ?
22 Which 17-year-old German won the Wimbledon men's singles?
23 Which Diego benefited from "The hand of God"?
24 What was the nickname of sprinter Florence Griffith-Joyner?
25 Who in soccer was known as "Captain Marvel"?
26 Viv Richards and Ian Botham played together for which county?
27 Which team won the Five Nations tournament from 1986 to 1989?
28 Which country does Ivan Lendl originate from?
29 Which Scottish soccer team was managed by Graeme Souness?
30 Which Englishman became soccer boss of the Republic of Ireland?

Answers | Jet Setters (see Quiz 74)

1 Linda. 2 Rod Stewart. 3 Monaco. 4 Kennedy. 5 Amanda. 6 Columbus. 7 Ivana. 8 Elizabeth. 9 David Copperfield. 10 Jerry Hall. 11 Britt Ekland. 12 Gabor. 13 David. 14 Beverly Hills. 15 Jean-Paul. 16 Twiggy. 17 Belfast. 18 Jane. 19 Richard Branson. 20 Nigel. 21 Klosters. 22 Italian. 23 Baywatch. 24 Michael. 25 Lord Lichfield. 26 Vivienne. 27 Spain. 28 Photographer. 29 Imran Khan. 30 Oil.

Quiz 77 | Pot-Luck 40

Answers – page 89

1 What is another name for the rowan tree?
2 How many hours in four days?
3 Which country is a car from if it has the international registration letter J?
4 Which musical was inspired by the songs of Abba?
5 Which Oscar said, "I have nothing to declare except my genius."
6 In darts, what is the lowest score from three different trebles?
7 Au is the symbol of which chemical element?
8 Which soap features the Woolpack pub?
9 Does Bryn Terfel have a bass/baritone or a tenor singing voice?
10 What name is given to the vast grassy plains of Russia?
11 Who has been married to Gemma Craven and Liz Hobbs?
12 Who recorded the album "Steam"?
13 Bovine relates to which kind of animals?
14 What is the chief ingredient in the production of glass?
15 Which creatures sang, "We All Stand Together"?
16 Which composer had the Christian names Johann Sebastian?
17 Which creature of the horror genre was created by Mary Shelley?
18 Which middle-distance runner became a Dame following the 2004 Olympics?
19 How many sides in three rectangles?
20 On which river does Stoke stand?
21 Which word could go before cab, skirt and van?
22 Six is the lowest of what type of number?
23 Which month is said to come in like a lion and go out like a lamb?
24 What is the name of Bill Clinton's daughter?
25 What did the navigator Amerigo Vespucci give his name to?
26 "Have I Got News for You" is the TV version of which radio show?
27 Who wrote "A Brief History of Time"?
28 How many cards are there in each suit?
29 In "EastEnders" what was Sam's surname before she married Ricky?
30 Which John captained Chelsea to the 2004/5 Premiership title?

Answers | Pot-Luck 41 (see Quiz 79)

1 Mark Spitz. 2 Chris Martin. 3 Chef. 4 John Lennon. 5 Cornet. 6 Honeysuckle. 7 Alfie Moon. 8 Hen party. 9 Tightrope. 10 Small bat. 11 Cannonball. 12 Carla Laine. 13 Rear light. 14 Joseph Conrad. 15 War of the Roses. 16 Age Concern. 17 Blackburn Rovers. 18 The Bonzo Dog Doo-Dah Band. 19 Black Forest. 20 Pasta. 21 Four. 22 Ten. 23 The Munsters. 24 Twickenham. 25 Captain Hook. 26 Walking in the Air. 27 Wren. 28 Roy Hudd. 29 Judo. 30 Julie Walters.

LEVEL 1

1 What relation was Danny de Vito to Arnold Schwarzenegger in their 1988 film?
2 Which Bruce starred in "Die Hard"?
3 Which singer won an Oscar for "Moonstruck"?
4 Out of which continent were Meryl Streep and Robert Redford in 1985?
5 In which film did Dustin Hoffman dress up as a woman to get a job as a soap star?
6 What was Richard Gere in the film with Debra Winger?
7 What does an inventor tell Honey he has Shrunk in the 1989 movie?
8 What does ET stand for in the 1982 film?
9 What sort of Attraction was there between Michael Douglas and Glenn Close?
10 Which bored housewife Shirley had an unforgettable Greek holiday?
11 Which disfigured Man did John Hurt portray in the 1980 film?
12 Which film told the story of two athletes in the 1924 Olympics?
13 What is Australian adventurer Mick Dundee's nickname?
14 Which adventurer Indiana was played by Harrison Ford?
15 Which Indian leader was played by Ben Kingsley?
16 What sort of Busters were Dan Aykroyd and Sigourney Weaver?
17 Which composer did Tom Hulse play in "Amadeus"?
18 Which film with Bob Hoskins is also the name of a painting?
19 Which former actor became president of the USA in 1980?
20 What was the Fish Called in the 1988 movie?
21 Which Naked film was the first in the series with Leslie Nielsen?
22 Who played James Bond in "For Your Eyes Only"?
23 What Strikes Back in the 1980 film?
24 Where was Eddie Murphy a Cop in the film series?
25 Where was Michael J. Fox Back to in 1985?
26 The Return of what in 1983 was the sixth film in the "Star Wars" series?
27 Which US pop superstar starred in "Moonwalker"?
28 Which cartoon Rabbit was Framed in 1988?
29 Which famous ship did they try to Raise in the 1980 film?
30 How many Men looked after Baby in 1987?

Answers	Pop: Sounds of the 80s *(see Quiz 80)*

1 Bermuda. 2 The Jam. 3 Eileen. 4 Twins. 5 Bucks Fizz. 6 Wham! 7 Madonna. 8 Red. 9 Ballet. 10 Police. 11 UB40. 12 Bryan Ferry. 13 Uptown. 14 Phil Collins. 15 Miami. 16 Easton. 17 Duran Duran. 18 Stevie Wonder. 19 Elaine Paige. 20 Love. 21 My Car. 22 Dire Straits. 23 Christmas. 24 Fun. 25 Ultra Vox. 26 In the Street. 27 Nick Berry. 28 Stevens. 29 The Mersey. 30 Kylie Minogue and Jason Donovan.

1 Which swimmer won seven gold medals at the 1972 Olympics?
2 Which Chris from Coldplay married Gwyneth Paltrow?
3 What is the profession of Antony Worrall Thompson?
4 Who had a No 1 hit with the song "Imagine"?
5 Which brass musical instrument shares its name with an ice-cream?
6 What is another name for the plant woodbine?
7 Which character in EastEnders did Kat Slater marry?
8 What type of pre-wedding party is for women only?
9 What is the cord high above the ground which acrobats perform on?
10 What are pipistrelles?
11 Which nickname did saxophonist Julian Adderley acquire?
12 Who wrote "Solo", "Butterflies" and "Luv"?
13 It's a tail lamp in the USA; what's this part of the car called in the UK?
14 Who wrote "Lord Jim"?
15 St Albans started and Bosworth finished which hostilities?
16 Which Concern is a charity about the needs of the elderly?
17 Which club did Chelsea sign Damien Duff from?
18 Which group recorded "I'm the Urban Spaceman"?
19 In which part of Germany might you find a chocolate gâteau with cream and cherries?
20 What type of food is canneloni?
21 How many laps are completed in a speedway race?
22 What was the title of Pearl Jam's first album?
23 In which TV series did Marilyn have an Uncle Herman?
24 Where are the headquarters of the Rugby Union?
25 Which fictional pirate had a bosun named Smee?
26 What is the theme song in the cartoon "The Snowman"?
27 Which bird has the Latin name Troglodytes troglodytes?
28 Who gives his name to Radio 2's "News Huddlines"?
29 In which sport did Neal Adams win Olympic medals?
30 Who is Victoria Wood's comic partner?

Answers | Pot-Luck 40 (see Quiz 77)

1 Mountain ash. 2 96. 3 Japan. 4 Mamma Mia!. 5 Wilde. 6 18. 7 Gold. 8 Emmerdale. 9 Bass/baritone. 10 Steppes. 11 Frazer Hines. 12 East 17. 13 Oxen. 14 Sand. 15 Frogs. 16 Bach. 17 Frankenstein's monster. 18 Kelly Holmes. 19 12. 20 Trent. 21 Mini. 22 Perfect number. (It is equal to the sum of its divisions.) 23 March. 24 Chelsea. 25 America. 26 The News Quiz. 27 Stephen Hawking. 28 13. 29 Mitchell. 30 John Terry.

1 Which Triangle did Barry Manilow sing about in 1981?

2 Which "well preserved" group had a hit with "Going Underground"?

3 Who did Dexy's Midnight Runners tell to Come On?

4 What relation were the Thompsons who had hits with "Love on Your Side" and "We are Detective"?

5 Which orange juice/champagne mix were Eurovision winners in 1981?

6 Andrew Ridgeley and George Michael were which group?

7 Who was Like a Virgin in 1984?

8 What colour was Chris de Burgh's Lady in, in 1986?

9 Which type of dance completes the Spandau group's name?

10 Which law enforcers sent a Message in a Bottle?

11 Which band shares its name with a form for the unemployed?

12 Who was a Jealous Guy with Roxy Music in 1981?

13 Where was Billy Joel's Girl in his 1983 Number 1?

14 Which Genesis drummer had three No 1 vocal hits in the 1980s?

15 Where does Gloria Estefan's Sound Machine come from?

16 Which Scottish Modern Girl Sheena had a hit with US singer Prince?

17 Which group did Simon Le Bon sing with?

18 Who Just Called to Say I Love You in 1984?

19 Who sang with Barbara Dickson on the hit "I Know Him So Well"?

20 What did Jennifer Rush sing about The Power of in 1985?

21 Where did Madness say they were Driving in 1982?

22 Which band headed by Mark Knopfler wanted "Money for Nothing"?

23 Band Aid asked Do They Know It's what?

24 What did Cyndi Lauper say Girls wanted to have more of?

25 Which group was Midge Ure chiefly associated with in the 80s?

26 Where were David Bowie and Mick Jagger Dancing in 1985?

27 Which former "EastEnders" and "Heartbeat" star had a hit with "Every Loser Wins" in 1986?

28 Which Shakin' star recorded "This Ole House"?

29 Where was the Ferry going across on the charity record in 1989?

30 Which two stars went from Ramsay Street to the top of the charts?

| **Answers** | 80s Films (see Quiz 78) |

1 Twin. 2 Willis. 3 Cher. 4 Africa. 5 Tootsie. 6 An Officer and a Gentleman. 7 The Kids. 8 Extra Terrestrial. 9 Fatal. 10 Valentine. 11 Elephant Man. 12 Chariots of Fire. 13 Crocodile. 14 Jones. 15 Gandhi. 16 Ghost. 17 Mozart. 18 Mona Lisa. 19 Ronald Reagan. 20 Wanda. 21 Naked Gun. 22 Roger Moore. 23 The Empire. 24 Beverly Hills. 25 The Future. 26 The Jedi. 27 Michael Jackson. 28 Roger. 29 The Titanic. 30 Three.

1 "I Got Plenty of Nuthin'" comes from which Gershwin work?
2 Who answers the phone by saying, "the lady of the house speaking"?
3 What would you find in an arboretum?
4 Which Tess co-hosted "Strictly Come Dancing" with Bruce Forsyth?
5 Which record label turned down the Beatles?
6 In which country is the dong used as currency?
7 What line goes before the line, "In the windmills of you mind"?
8 What is the antirrhinum more commonly known as?
9 Who was Queen of England for nine days before she was beheaded?
10 Which country has had two kings called Carol on the throne this century?
11 What did Madonna fall off to sustain broken bones in the autumn of 2005?
12 Who created the series "Prime Suspect"?
13 What's the surname of cartoon hero Quick Draw?
14 What colour is muscovado sugar?
15 In which unusual way does Yorick first appear on stage in "Hamlet"?
16 How many sides has a cube?
17 What is the currency of Israel?
18 Who was England's first-choice keeper in the 2002 World Cup?
19 Which major river flows through Bristol?
20 What is the surname of rugby players Tony and Rory?
21 Which character has been played by Albert Finney, Peter Ustinov and David Suchet?
22 What is the nationality of Chris de Burgh?
23 Which term means that material can be decomposed by natural means?
24 What sort of vehicle is a limousine?
25 Which veteran male broadcaster has been a long-term presenter of TV's "Children in Need"?
26 Who fronted the Tijuana Brass?
27 What is the largest wild member of the dog family?
28 Who is Magnus Magnusson's TV presenter daughter?
29 Ed Koch was the mayor of which town?
30 What does SNP stand for?

Answers	**Pot-Luck 43** *(see Quiz 83)*

1 Edelweiss. 2 Wayne Rooney. 3 Morecambe and Wise. 4 Cape Kennedy. 5 Colin Firth. 6 Henry VIII. 7 Live 8. 8 Holly. 9 240. 10 The Saint. 11 March. 12 Vincent Van Gogh (by Don McLean). 13 Ha'penny. 14 Hertfordshire. 15 Fuchsia. 16 West Indies. 17 Taylor. 18 Shorthand. 19 Wet Wet Wet. 20 Be prepared. Motto of the Boy Scouts, song of Scar. 21 Hops. 22 Kaiser Chiefs. 23 Colin Cowdrey. 24 Joey. 25 British Open. 26 The Outer Limits. 27 Samurai. 28 Cycling. 29 Kylie Minogue. 30 Dungeons and Dragons.

1 Which bird has a red breast?
2 Which birds can be barn, tawny or snowy?
3 What two colours is a magpie?
4 Which birds are associated with the Tower of London?
5 What colour is a female blackbird?
6 The teal belongs to which family group?
7 What word can go in front of sparrow or martin to name a bird?
8 Which bird lays its eggs in the nests of others?
9 Which bird has the same name as a chess piece?
10 Which bird featured in the film "Kes"?
11 Which part of the golden eagle is gold?
12 Which part of a bird was used as a pen?
13 An early riser is said to be up before which bird?
14 What colour is the plumage on the head of a male mallard?
15 What is special about a swallow's tail?
16 Which bird starts its name with the word "Bull"?
17 The jay is a member of which family?
18 Which seashore bird has a colourful triangular bill?
19 Which reddish-brown songbird sings just before dawn or after dusk?
20 What colour is a tufted duck?
21 Which game bird is a word meaning grumble?
22 Which bird is the symbol of peace?
23 Which bird was said to deliver babies?
24 Which bird is so called because of its fast flight?
25 What is the largest bird in the world?
26 Which flying toy shares its name with a bird?
27 What is a baby swan called?
28 Which letter of the alphabet sounds like a bird's name?
29 What is Britain's smallest bird?
30 Is a fledgling a young or old bird?

Answers	80s Newsround (see Quiz 84)

1 Hitchcock. 2 Zimbabwe. 3 SAS. 4 Poland. 5 John Lennon. 6 Yorkshire Ripper. 7 Ronald Reagan. 8 Edwina Currie. 9 Lockerbie. 10 Paying income tax. 11 Earthquake. 12 Unemployment. 13 Lady Diana Spencer. 14 London. 15 Falkland. 16 Queen Elizabeth II's. 17 A ship. 18 Kinnock. 19 France. 20 Yuppies. 21 North. 22 Two. 23 Car ferry. 24 Guinness. 25 Haiti. 26 Gorbachev. 27 Ethiopia. 28 Oil rig. 29 Bush. 30 Parkinson.

1 What is the national flower of Austria?
2 Coleen McLoughlin found fame as the fiancée of which football star?
3 The theatre show "The Play What I Wrote" is about which comedy duo?
4 What was the earlier name of Cape Canaveral?
5 Which actor played the children's father in the movie "Nanny McPhee"?
6 Which monarch is credited with writing "Greensleeves"?
7 Which 2005 pop charity concert took place to coincide with the G8 summit?
8 Which spiky tree has the scientific name Ilex aquifolium?
9 How many old pence were there in £1?
10 Which TV sleuth has the car registration number ST1?
11 In which month is St Patrick's Day?
12 The song starting, "Starry, starry night" is about whom?
13 Which pre-decimal coin do you shove in a table game?
14 In which county was the oil depot explosion in Dec 2005?
15 What did German botanist Leonhard Fuchs give his name to?
16 Curtly Ambrose played international cricket for which team?
17 Which name is shared by actress Elizabeth and snooker star Dennis?
18 What sort of quick writing did Pitman invent?
19 What were Marty Pellow, Graeme Clark, Tom Cunningham and Neil Mitchell better known as?
20 What's the link between the Boy Scouts and Uncle Scar?
21 What is dried in an oast house?
22 Who sang "I Predict a Riot" in 2005?
23 Which great English batsmen had the initials M.C.C.?
24 What is a young kangaroo called?
25 Which major golf championship is decided by a four-hole playoff?
26 Which programme started with the words, "There is nothing wrong with your television set...."?
27 Historically, what is the name of Japan's warrior class?
28 Which sport is Chris Boardman famous for?
29 Which Australian had a hit with "I Should be So Lucky"?
30 Which fantasy game has its name made up of places of imprisonment and legendary creatures?

Answers | Pot-Luck 42 (see Quiz 81)

1 Porgy and Bess. 2 Hyacinth Bucket. 3 Trees. 4 Tess Daly. 5 Decca. 6 Vietnam. 7 Like the circles that you find. 8 Snapdragon. 9 Lady Jane Grey. 10 Romania. 11 A horse. 12 Lynda La Plante. 13 McGraw. 14 Brown. 15 Appears as a skull picked up by Hamlet. 16 Six. 17 Shekel. 18 David Seaman. 19 Avon. 20 Underwood. 21 Hercule Poirot. 22 Irish. 23 Biodegradable. 24 A car. 25 Terry Wogan. 26 Herb Alpert. 27 Wolf. 28 Sally Magnusson. 29 New York. 30 Scottish National Party.

1 Which Alfred, a master film-maker, died in 1980?

2 What was Southern Rhodesia renamed?

3 Which crack force stormed the Iranian Embassy in London in 1980?

4 Lech Walesa led strikers in which country?

5 Which Beatle was shot dead in New York?

6 What name was given to murderer Peter Sutcliffe?

7 Which former Hollywood actor became US President?

8 Which MP Edwina became "Eggwina" after a salmonella scare?

9 Over 250 people died in an air crash at which Scottish border town?

10 What was Lester Piggott sent to jail for avoiding?

11 What natural disaster hit Armenia in 1988?

12 What topped 3,000,000 in Britain for the first time since the 1930s?

13 Who became a princess by marrying Prince Charles?

14 In which city did the Barbican arts centre open?

15 Which Islands were the cause of a war between Britain and Argentina?

16 Whose London bedroom did Michael Fagin break into?

17 What was "The Mary Rose" which saw sunlight after 400 years?

18 Which Neil became leader of the Labour Party in 1983?

19 In 1988 François Mitterrand was re-elected president of which country?

20 What name was given to young upwardly mobile persons?

21 Which Colonel Oliver starred in the US "Irongate" court hearing?

22 How many general elections did Margaret Thatcher win in the 1980s?

23 What was the "The Herald of Free Enterprise" which met disaster in 1987?

24 Which company, famed for stout, was implicated in a share scandal?

25 President "Baby Doc" fled from which country?

26 Which Mikhail became Soviet leader in 1985?

27 Bob Geldof organized Live Aid to provide food for which country?

28 What was Piper Alpha, scene of a deadly fire?

29 Which George was elected US president?

30 Which cabinet minister Cecil was forced to resign after his jilted mistress told her side of events to the press?

| **Answers** | **Nature: Bird Brains** *(see Quiz 82)* |

1 Robin. 2 Owls. 3 Black and white. 4 Ravens. 5 Brown. 6 Duck. 7 House. 8 Cuckoo. 9 Rook. 10 Kestrel. 11 Neck feathers. 12 Feather. 13 Lark. 14 Green. 15 Forked. 16 Bullfinch. 17 Crow. 18 Puffin. 19 Nightingale. 20 Black and white. 21 Grouse. 22 Dove. 23 Stork. 24 Swift. 25 Ostrich. 26 Kite. 27 Cygnet. 28 Jay. 29 Wren. 30 Young.

1 What is a smolt?

2 Which song contains the words,"If you lose your teeth when you're out to dine borrow mine!"

3 Which country is a car from if it has the international registration letters MEX?

4 Who came first as monarch, Queen Elizabeth I or Henry II?

5 The Charge of the Light Brigade took place during which battle?

6 In snooker, how many points are scored by potting the yellow ball?

7 Cu is the symbol of which chemical element?

8 Which soap pub sells Newton and Ridley?

9 What is the first month of the year to have exactly 31 days and follow a month of 31 days?

10 What are dried plums called?

11 In the past, which animal did doctors use to drain blood from the sick?

12 Who recorded the album "Post"?

13 What is the word for a group of porpoises?

14 What are the two main flavours in a banoffee pie?

15 Which first name was shared by two of the Tory leadership candidates in 2005?

16 What is the medical name for dizziness due to heights?

17 Which county shares its name with a make-up-selling lady?

18 On a map, what are lines called that join places of equal height above sea level?

19 How many pints in three quarts?

20 What is the name of TV cook Floyd?

21 What is a male goose called?

22 In which county is Land's End?

23 Which company created the IPod?

24 "Phiz" illustrated works by which famous writer?

25 What sort of Pie provided a classic hit for Don McLean?

26 Who played the title role of Ray Charles in the movie "Ray"?

27 How many do you get if you add a baker's dozen to a score?

28 Was 1994 a leap year?

29 Who partnered Robbie Williams on the No 1 hit single "Something Stupid"?

30 From which plant is linen obtained?

Answers | Pot-Luck 45 *(see Quiz 87)*

1 Tiny. 2 Capricorn. 3 Fish. 4 Chris de Burgh. 5 Scar. 6 Black and white. 7 School. 8 Leonardo DiCaprio. 9 Jerome. 10 Popes. 11 Member of the European Parliament. 12 Andrew Murray. 13 Turkey. 14 John Wesley. 15 Blocks. 16 Elizabeth I. 17 Hands. 18 Idle hands. 19 South Africa. 20 Fruit. 21 Guinea pig. 22 John McEnroe. 23 Newcastle United. 24 Diving. 25 Led Zeppelin. 26 Ascot. 27 D. 28 Soup. 29 John Wayne. 30 Mel Hutchwright.

1 Who wrote "Jamie's Italy"?

2 Which chef presented "The F Word"?

3 Who wrote the best-selling "How to be a Domestic Goddess"?

4 What type of "Talk" do Gregg Wallace and Charlie Hicks engage in?

5 Nick Nairn hails from which part of the UK?

6 What was the revamped "Masterchef" programme called?

7 Which TV chef broadcasts from River Cottage?

8 What is Jamie Oliver's wife called?

9 Which country does TV chef Bill Granger come from?

10 "How to Cheat at Cooking" was the first cookery book of which chef?

11 Was Ken Hom born in China or the USA?

12 Madhur Jaffrey writes chiefly about the cuisine of which country?

13 Which Manchester football team does Gary Rhodes famously support?

14 Was it Gordon Ramsay or Ainsley Harriott who was on Glasgow Rangers' books as a teenager?

15 Which Antony has presented "Saturday Kitchen"?

16 In 2005 did Jamie Oliver campaign about meals in schools or hospitals?

17 Which cookery programme saw Gary Rhodes doing battle with Jean Christophe Novelli?

18 Which Australian's cookery book was called "Simply Bill"?

19 On his "French Odyssey" did Rick Stein travel by barge or bicycle?

20 Le Gavroche was opened by which French brothers?

21 The third series of "Strictly Come Dancing" featured which chef?

22 Whose 2000 autobiography was called "Out of the Frying Pan"?

23 Which cook from the early days of TV was born Phyllis Primrose-Pechey?

24 Which TV cook's father was Chancellor of the Exchequer?

25 Was Mrs Beeton 21, 31 or 51 when she wrote her famous book of Household Management?

26 Which TV chef has a dog called Chalky?

27 Which TV cook said "Let's be having you" to a football crowd?

28 Was Ross Burden a success on "Masterchef" or "Mastermind"?

29 Has Lesley Waters or Sophie Grigson been a regular on "Ready Steady Cook"?

30 Which county does James Martin hail from?

Answers	Sport: Cricket (see Quiz 88)

1 1987. 2 Surrey. 3 Duck. 4 Devon Malcolm. 5 Lancashire. 6 Bradman. 7 40. 8 Ian Botham. 9 Wide. 10 Wicket keeper. 11 Three. 12 Shane Warne. 13 Slips. 14 Leicestershire. 15 A finger. 16 New Zealand. 17 Chappell. 18 Yorkshire. 19 Lara. 20 Extras. 21 Stumped. 22 Pakistan. 23 A six. 24 A pair. 25 Jonathan Agnew. 26 Edgbaston. 27 Australia. 28 Yes. 29 Glenn McGrath. 30 Simon Jones.

1 What size was Tim in "A Christmas Carol"?
2 What is the zodiac sign of the Goat?
3 What is held in a creel?
4 Who had a No 1 hit with the song "Lady in Red"?
5 What did Al Capone have on his face that gave him his nickname?
6 What two colours are on the flag waved at the end of a motor race?
7 In nursery rhyme, where did Mary's little lamb follow her to?
8 Which actor played the title role in the movie "The Aviator"?
9 Which half of Robson and Jerome played the part of Paddy Garvey?
10 What were Liberius, Sissinius and Constantine?
11 In the political sector, what does MEP stand for?
12 Which Briton entered the tennis top 100 for the first time in 2005?
13 The ancient city of Troy is in which modern country?
14 Who founded the Methodist movement?
15 What do sprinters start from in a track race?
16 Who ordered the execution of Mary Queen of Scots?
17 What do volleyball players hit the ball with?
18 According to the proverb, what does the devil make work for?
19 Which rugby nation was readmitted to international competition in 1993?
20 What type of food is a pomelo?
21 What is another name for a cavy?
22 Who said, "You cannot be serious!"?
23 Which English team did Michael Owen join on his return from Spain?
24 Which Olympic water sport includes twists, tucks and pikes?
25 Who recorded the original track "Stairway to Heaven"?
26 Which race meeting is as famous for its hats as for its horses?
27 What letter features on a snooker table?
28 What type of food is gazpacho?
29 How is Western actor Marion Morrison better known?
30 What was the name of the novelist played by Ian McKellen in "Coronation Street"?

| **Answers** | **Pot-Luck 44** *(see Quiz 85)* |

1 A young salmon. 2 Friendship (from Anything Goes). 3 Mexico. 4 Henry II. 5 Balaclava. 6 Two. 7 Copper. 8 Rovers' Return. 9 August. 10 Prunes. 11 Leech. 12 Björk. 13 School. 14 Banana and toffee. 15 David (Davies and Cameron). 16 Vertigo. 17 Avon. 18 Contour lines. 19 Six. 20 Keith. 21 Gander. 22 Cornwall. 23 Apple. 24 Charles Dickens. 25 American. 26 Jamie Foxx. 27 33. 28 No. 29 Nicole Kidman. 30 Flax.

1 When did England last win the Ashes before 2005 – was it 1967, 1977 or 1987?
2 The Oval is the home of which county?
3 What bird is linked to a score of nought?
4 Which 1990s English Test pace bowler has the same first name as an English county?
5 Which county has been captained by Mike Atherton?
6 Which Donald became the first Australian to score 300 test runs in a day?
7 At most, how many wickets can fall in a two-innings game?
8 Which former England all-rounder earned the nickname "Beefy"?
9 Which term describes a ball bowled out of the striker's reach?
10 Which specialist position does Adam Gilchrist take when fielding?
11 How many stumps are there on a set of wickets?
12 Which Aussie player is known – among other things – as Shanie?
13 What term describes fielders positioned closely behind the batsmen?
14 Grace Road is the ground of which county?
15 What must an umpire raise to show that a player is out?
16 Which country did all rounder Richard Hadlee play for?
17 What is the surname of Australian brothers Gregg and Ian?
18 Which county side did Fred Trueman play most of his cricket for?
19 Which West Indian batsman Brian started rewriting the record books in 1994?
20 What is added to the scores of the batsmen to make the total?
21 What does the abbreviation "st" stand for?
22 Which country did Abdul Qadir play for?
23 If the umpire raises both arms above his head what is he signalling?
24 What is a batsman said to collect if he scores 0 twice in a match?
25 Which radio commentator is known as "Aggers"?
26 Which Warwickshire ground hosts Test cricket?
27 Lillee and Thomson formed a deadly pace attack for which country?
28 Can a Test Match end in a tie?
29 Which world-class fast bowler made his last visit to England for the 2005 Ashes?
30 In 2005 which Welsh bowler Simon was injured and missed the final Ashes Test?

Answers	Celebrity Chefs (see Quiz 86)

1 Jamie Oliver. 2 Gordon Ramsay. 3 Nigella Lawson. 4 Veg Talk. 5 Scotland. 6 Masterchef Goes Large. 7 Hugh Fearnley-Whittingstall. 8 Jools. 9 Australia. 10 Delia Smith. 11 USA. 12 India. 13 United. 14 Gordon Ramsay. 15 Worrall Thompson. 16 Schools. 17 Hell's Kitchen. 18 Bill Granger. 19 Barge. 20 Roux brothers. 21 James Martin. 22 Keith Floyd. 23 Fanny Cradock. 24 Nigella Lawson. 25 21. 26 Rick Stein. 27 Delia Smith. 28 Masterchef. 29 Lesley Waters. 30 Yorkshire.

1 Which special birthday did "The Muppets" celebrate in the year 2005?
2 How many Desperate Housewives were there?
3 What is another name for the wildebeeste?
4 What word goes before glove, hound and trot?
5 What is Ryan O'Neal's actress daughter called?
6 Which English queen never married?
7 In rhyming slang what is a north and south?
8 Which PR man Max called his Memoirs "Read All About It"?
9 What was the name of the Elephant Man?
10 To ten years either way, when was the Automobile Association formed?
11 In the plant world, what do the letters RHS stand for ?
12 Between which two African countries are the Victoria Falls?
13 Which country is golfer Ian Woosnam from?
14 Which Mike was the name of the England manager, played by Ricky Tomlinson?
15 What does the word hirsute mean?
16 What word relates to Enya, the Wombles and Venezuela?
17 In feet how wide is a hockey goal?
18 Who wrote "Little Men"?
19 Which major river flows through New Orleans?
20 Whose last words were, "Thank God I have done my duty"?
21 Which country did General Franco rule?
22 Which sisters recorded "I'm in the Mood for Dancing"?
23 Which Hertfordshire town was Britain's first Garden City?
24 What can be HT, floribunda or a rambler?
25 Which word can mean suspicious or to do with seafood?
26 Where is the Sea of Showers?
27 Which king would have been blown up if the Gunpowder Plot had succeeded?
28 For which sport is Lennox Lewis famous?
29 Which purple precious gem is the birthstone for February?
30 Which game is connected with Boris Schapiro?

Answers	**Pot-Luck 47** *(see Quiz 91)*

1 Will Smith. 2 Zoe Salmon. 3 Prescott. 4 Rabbit. 5 Rose. 6 Banjos. 7 ET. 8 Sylvia's Mother. 9 Four. 10 Pressure of gases. 11 March. 12 Toad. 13 Flora. 14 J. R. R. 15 Spiderman. 16 Boxing. 17 Birmingham. 18 Supernanny. 19 Police. 20 Shoulders. 21 Emperor. 22 12. 23 Tin Pan Alley. 24 Three. 25 The clubhouse. 26 The first dog in space. 27 Billy Elliott. 28 Fireball XL5. 29 Wembley. 30 Heavy Goods Vehicle.

1 The Bay of Biscay lies to the north of which country?
2 Which Gulf lies between Iran and Saudi Arabia?
3 Brittany is part of which country?
4 Which US city is known by its initials LA?
5 Which South American country shares its name with a nut?
6 Near which large city is the Wirral?
7 Which is Britain's most southerly point on the mainland?
8 In which country is Shanghai?
9 In which county is Lake Windermere?
10 To which country does the island of Bermuda belong?
11 What is the northernmost town in England?
12 Is San Francisco on the east or west coast of the USA?
13 Which Union was Ukraine once part of?
14 In which country is Zurich?
15 In which country is the holiday destination of Bali?
16 Which island lies to the south of India?
17 In which country would you hear the language Afrikaans?
18 Which group of islands does Gran Canaria belong to?
19 Where would you be if you had climbed Mount Olympus?
20 In which US state is Orlando?
21 Which Ocean is to the west of Portugal?
22 In which country is The Hague?
23 Monte Carlo is in which principality?
24 Which US state has the Arctic Circle running through it?
25 Which Land in Denmark is made up of bricks?
26 Which Falls are on the Canadian/US border?
27 Which country's women might wear a kimono?
28 Which Ocean's name means peaceful?
29 Which country originally produced Peugeot cars?
30 What is the English for what the French call an autoroute?

Answers	**Scientists and Inventors** *(see Quiz 92)*

1 Penicillin. 2 X-rays. 3 Greek. 4 Bunsen burner. 5 Curie. 6 Albert. 7 Temperature.
8 Halley. 9 Stephen. 10 Newton. 11 Italian. 12 The atom. 13 Nicotine. 14
Darwin. 15 Microscope. 16 Rutherford. 17 Temperature. 18 Leonardo Da Vinci. 19
Edison. 20 Grass. 21 Attenborough. 22 Atom. 23 Antiseptic. 24 Morris. 25 Blood.
26 Weaving. 27 Pea. 28 Africa. 29 Steam. 30 Spinning Jenny.

1 Who played Muhammad Ali in the movie about the great boxer?
2 Which presenter of "Blue Peter" was Miss Northern Ireland 1999?
3 Which John became deputy Labour leader under Tony Blair?
4 What kind of animal features in the book "Watership Down"?
5 What flower is the emblem of the Labour Party?
6 Which instruments were featured in the hit single that came from the film "Deliverance"?
7 Who used a children's computer to "phone home"?
8 Who did Dr Hook speak to when trying to get through to Sylvia?
9 What number does the Roman numeral IV stand for?
10 What is measured by a manometer?
11 In which month is St David's Day?
12 What type of animal is a natterjack?
13 Which Roman goddess of flowers is the name of a brand of margarine?
14 What are the initials of writer Tolkien?
15 What superhero can Peter Parker turn into?
16 Clint Eastwood's movie "Million Dollar Baby" features which sport?
17 Which city do Aston Villa come from?
18 Jo Frost found TV fame as what?
19 What are Sting, Stewart Copeland and Andy Summers better known as?
20 On what part of your body would you wear a stole?
21 What is the world's largest species of penguin called?
22 In a pack of cards how many jacks' eyes can be seen?
23 London's Denmark Street acquired which nickname?
24 In "Fifteen to One" how many contestants take part in the final round?
25 Where is the 19th hole on an 18-hole golf course?
26 Who or what was Laika?
27 Which story of a boy dancer became a film then a West End musical?
28 Which spacecraft was commanded by Steve Zodiac?
29 In which stadium did England win the 1966 World Cup Final?
30 What do the initials HGV stand for?

Answers | Pot-Luck 46 (see Quiz 89)

1 50th. 2 Five. 3 Gnu. 4 Fox. 5 Tatum. 6 Elizabeth I. 7 Mouth. 8 Max Clifford.
9 John Merrick. 10 1905. 11 Royal Horticultural Society. 12 Zimbabwe and Zambia.
13 Wales. 14 Mike Bassett. 15 Hairy. 16 Orinoco. 17 12. 18 Louisa M. Alcott. 19
Mississippi. 20 Horatio Nelson. 21 Spain. 22 Nolan. 23 Welwyn. 24 A rose. 25
Fishy. 26 On the moon. 27 James I. 28 Boxing. 29 Amethyst. 30 Bridge.

1 Which drug is Alexander Fleming famous for discovering?
2 Which rays for examining the inside of the body did Röntgen discover?
3 What nationality was philosopher and scientist Aristotle?
4 What was Robert Bunsen famous for?
5 Which Pierre and Marie discovered radium?
6 What was the first name of German scientist Einstein?
7 Fahrenheit is associated with the measurement of what?
8 Which astronomer gave his name to the comet seen every 76 years?
9 What is the first name of physicist Hawking?
10 Which Sir Isaac discovered the law of gravity?
11 What was the nationality of astronomer Galileo?
12 What was Ernest Rutherford the first man to split?
13 Which juice did Jean Nicot extract from tobacco?
14 Which biologist Charles studied the evolution of the species?
15 Which instrument to magnify small objects was invented by Jansen?
16 Which Ernest discovered alpha, beta and gamma rays?
17 What does the scale named after Anders Celsius measure?
18 Which Italian painter drew early ideas for a helicopter?
19 Which American Thomas developed the light bulb?
20 Flymo developed a machine based on the hovercraft for cutting what?
21 Which naturalist Sir David has a film director brother Richard?
22 What did John Dalton define as the smallest particle of substance?
23 What did Lister discover which stopped wounds becoming septic?
24 Which zoologist Desmond broadcast discoveries about man in "The Naked Ape" and "The Human Zoo"?
25 What did Harvey discover is pumped round the body?
26 What was Kay's Flying Shuttle used for in 1733?
27 What is a common vegetable and flower used by Mendel in his theories on genetics?
28 On which continent have the Leakey family made discoveries about man's evolution?
29 What type of engines did George Stephenson develop?
30 What Spinning invention was named after its creator's daughter?

Answers | **Geography** (see Quiz 90)

1 Spain. 2 Persian Gulf. 3 France. 4 Los Angeles. 5 Brazil. 6 Liverpool. 7 Lizard.
8 China. 9 Cumbria. 10 Britain. 11 Berwick-upon-Tweed. 12 West. 13 Soviet. 14
Switzerland. 15 Indonesia. 16 Sri Lanka. 17 South Africa. 18 Canary Islands. 19
Greece. 20 Florida. 21 Atlantic. 22 Holland. 23 Monaco. 24 Alaska. 25 Legoland.
26 Niagara. 27 Japan. 28 Pacific. 29 France. 30 Motorway.

1 What name is given to the art of clipping hedges into shapes?
2 How many days in two non-leap years?
3 Which country is a car from if it has the international registration letter P?
4 Which Ben played the part of Fagin in Roman Polanski's movie "Oliver Twist"?
5 Which fruit is used to make the drink kirsch?
6 In darts, what is the highest score from three different trebles?
7 U is the symbol of which chemical element?
8 Which former wife of Chris Evans appeared as Dr Who's assistant on TV?
9 What kind of creature is a flying fox?
10 How many miles are there in eight kilometres?
11 What type of canoe is spelt the same backwards and forwards?
12 Who recorded the album "So Far So Good"?
13 What is the word for a squirrel's nest?
14 Which pop star began legal preceedings against Sony in 1993?
15 Which woodland area of Hampshire is noted for its ponies?
16 What is the name of Sharon and Ozzy Osbourne's eldest daughter?
17 Which German philosopher Karl wrote "Das Kapital"?
18 Who was Hare's grave-robbing partner in the 19th century?
19 How many sides in 15 triangles?
20 What is the name of TV cook Berry?
21 What is a male rabbit called?
22 Which Peter, an Australian singer, married Jordan in 2005?
23 What sort of food is Bel Paese?
24 How many athletes are there in an Olympic relay team?
25 What is the opposite of alkali?
26 What traditionally did a fletcher make?
27 What is the first word in the original TV theme song for "Neighbours"?
28 Who rolled down the hill last, Jack or Jill?
29 Who is chat show host Alan Partridge?
30 What part of the human body is treated by a dermatologist?

Answers	**Around Ireland** *(see Quiz 97)*

1 Liffey. 2 County Down. 3 Irish Sea. 4 Belfast. 5 Emerald Isle. 6 Shamrock. 7 Dublin. 8 Belfast. 9 Limerick. 10 Whiskey. 11 Atlantic. 12 Irish and English. 13 Crystal. 14 Galway. 15 Blarney Stone. 16 Kildare. 17 Horse racing. 18 Linen. 19 Patrick. 20 Whiskey and cream. 21 Tweed. 22 East. 23 Ferry ports. 24 Dublin. 25 Air. 26 Londonderry. 27 Cork. 28 Giant's Causeway. 29 Guinness. 30 IRL.

1 Which John painted "The Haywain"?
2 What was the surname of outrageous artist Salvador?
3 Which city, famous for its canals, did Canaletto paint?
4 What was the first name of Impressionist painter Cézanne?
5 Which Leonardo painted Mona Lisa?
6 Which parts of the Venus de Milo are missing?
7 Which animals is George Stubbs famous for painting?
8 Which Paul was famous for paintings of the South Seas?
9 Which Vincent lost an ear?
10 What was the first name of pop artist Warhol?
11 How is Francisco de Goya y Lucientes more simply known?
12 Which Greek artist's name means "The Greek"?
13 Which Spanish painter Pablo was the founder of Cubism?
14 Who was famous for his posters of French dance halls and cabarets?
15 What was the nationality of Rembrandt?
16 Edouard and Claude were Manet and Monet. Which was which?
17 Which items useful on a rainy day did Renoir paint?
18 Which branch of the arts was Barbara Hepworth famous for?
19 What was the nationality of Albrecht Dürer?
20 Which art gallery is in Trafalgar Square?
21 Who painted the ceiling of the Sistine Chapel?
22 In late 1995 the painting of which Royal caused controversy?
23 What is the first name of pop artist Hockney?
24 Which Tudor king is Hans Holbein famous for painting?
25 Which metal is sculptress Elisabeth Frink famous for using?
26 What was the nationality of portrait painter Millais?
27 Which member of the royal family has had his paintings reproduced on a set of stamps?
28 Which London art gallery was founded with the financial support of a sugar merchant?
29 What is the first name of sculptor Moore?
30 Which English artist is famous for his matchstalk men pictures?

Answers | Pot-Luck 50 *(see Quiz 96)*

1 Paris. 2 Peseta. 3 Charles Dickens. 4 USA. 5 Boris Becker. 6 Bolton. 7 Piano. 8 Lulu. 9 David Cornwell. 10 Pig. 11 Earth. 12 Dan Dare. 13 A hurricane. 14 New York Herald. 15 Jason Donovan. 16 Six. 17 Ardiles and Villa. 18 Suicide is Painless. 19 Potomac. 20 Horse. 21 Vietnam. 22 Cash on delivery. 23 Trumpet. 24 White. 25 Nigel Hawthorne. 26 Sunday. 27 Supersonic. 28 Chris Evert. 29 Cologne. 30 Stone.

1 Which cartoon mouse was Pixie's friend?
2 What is the zodiac sign of Aquarius?
3 "An Unearthly Child" was the first episode of which long-running TV series?
4 Who had a No 1 hit with the song "Bridge Over Troubled Water"?
5 What name is given to a person who makes and sells spectacles?
6 In printing and editing what do the letters UC signify?
7 In nursery rhyme, during which season did the Queen of Hearts make the tarts?
8 Which land does Peter Pan come from?
9 What is a young swan called?
10 Which man won both Wimbledon and the US Open in 2005?
11 What life-threatening thing appeared in London for the last time in 1962?
12 At which ground was the first match of the 2005 Ashes series held?
13 Called cotton candy in America, what's this sweet named in the UK?
14 At which famous Hall is the Royal British Legion Festival of Remembrance held?
15 Which Christmas decoration is a parasite of the apple tree?
16 What is the name of the disc used in ice hockey?
17 What vehicles race in the Indianapolis 500?
18 In the Nintendo game what is Mario's job?
19 What is the profession of Paul Rankin?
20 What colour did all lupins used to be?
21 In conservation, what do the letters FOE stand for?
22 Who says, "It's the way I tell 'em!"?
23 What was the ninth month of the Roman calendar?
24 On which day of the week does the Queen distribute Maundy Money?
25 Which part of the foot is between the sole and the heel?
26 What is the wife of an Earl called?
27 What was the first name of Admiral Lord Nelson?
28 Which UK soap staged a murder trial in May 1995?
29 What kind of rays cause a suntan?
30 Who is Steve Punt's comic partner?

Answers | Pot-Luck 48 *(see Quiz 93)*

1 Topiary. 2 730. 3 Portugal. 4 Ben Kingsley. 5 The cherry. 6 171. 7 Uranium. 8 Billie Piper. 9 A bat. 10 Five. 11 Kayak. 12 Bryan Adams. 13 Drey. 14 George Michael. 15 New Forest. 16 Aimee. 17 Marx. 18 Burke. 19 45. 20 Mary. 21 A buck. 22 Peter Andre. 23 Cheese. 24 Four. 25 Acid. 26 Arrows. 27 Neighbours. 28 Jill. 29 Steve Coogan. 30 Skin.

1 In which city is Orly airport?
2 What is the currency of Spain?
3 Back in the West End in 2005, the musical "Scrooge" was based on a novel by which author?
4 The Kentucky Derby is a horse race in which country?
5 Which former tennis champion became a regular on "They Think It's All Over"?
6 Which soccer team moved to the Reebok Stadium in the 1990s?
7 In rhyming slang what is a Joanna?
8 How is Marie McDonald McLaughlin Lawrie better known?
9 What is the real name of John Le Carré?
10 What is a Tamworth a type of?
11 What does the prefix geo mean?
12 With which pilot did Jocelyn Peabody explore space?
13 What destroyed millions of British trees in October 1987?
14 Which newspaper sent Stanley to find Livingstone?
15 Who had a No 1 with "Any Dream Will Do"?
16 How many sides has a cuboid?
17 Which two Argentinian footballers were bought by Spurs after the '78 World Cup?
18 What's the theme song of M*A*S*H?
19 Which major river flows through Washington DC?
20 What do you ride on if you take part in three-day eventing?
21 Which country did Ho Chi Minh rule?
22 What do the initials COD mean?
23 What instrument does Kenny Ball play?
24 What colour gloves does a snooker referee wear?
25 In "The Madness of King George" who played King George?
26 On which day of the week did "EastEnders" first screen an omnibus edition?
27 Which word means faster than the speed of sound?
28 Who was the first woman to win four consecutive US Open tennis titles?
29 Which word is a German city and a light perfume?
30 The first Harry Potter novel concerned the Philospher's what?

Answers | **Painters and Sculptors** *(see Quiz 94)*

1 Constable. 2 Dali. 3 Venice. 4 Paul. 5 Da Vinci. 6 Arms. 7 Horses. 8 Gauguin.
9 Van Gogh. 10 Andy. 11 Goya. 12 El Greco. 13 Picasso. 14 Toulouse-Lautrec. 15 Dutch. 16 Edouard Manet, Claude Monet. 17 Umbrellas. 18 Sculpture. 19 German.
20 National Gallery. 21 Michelangelo. 22 Princess of Wales. 23 David. 24 Henry VIII.
25 Bronze. 26 English. 27 Prince Charles. 28 Tate. 29 Henry. 30 L. S. Lowry.

1 Which river runs through through Dublin?
2 In which Irish county are the Mountains of Morne?
3 Which Sea is to the east of the Island of Ireland?
4 What is the capital city of Northern Ireland?
5 What sort of jewelled Isle is Ireland often called?
6 Which plant is the Irish emblem?
7 What is the capital of the Republic of Ireland?
8 In which Irish city is Queens University?
9 Which Irish town gives its name to a saucy rhyme?
10 Spell the Irish version of the drink the Scots call whisky.
11 Which Ocean is to the west of Ireland?
12 What are Ireland's two official languages?
13 Which type of glass is Waterford famous for?
14 Which Irish flute player James shares his name with a Bay ?
15 Which stone is kissed to receive the gift of smooth talking?
16 Which county shares its name with a fictional TV doctor?
17 Which sport is the Curragh famous for?
18 Which fabric made from flax is Ireland famous for?
19 Who is the patron saint of Ireland?
20 What do you put into Gaelic coffee apart from coffee?
21 Which fabric is Donegal famous for?
22 Is Belfast on the east or the west of the province?
23 What do the towns of Dun Laoghaire and Rosslare have in common?
24 O'Connell Street is which Irish city's main street?
25 How would you be travelling if you arrived at Shannon from abroad?
26 Which is further north, Belfast or Londonderry?
27 Which Irish town sounds like something in a wine bottle neck?
28 Which Causeway is said to have been built as a bridge from Ireland to Scotland?
29 Which stout is Dublin world-famous for?
30 What are the international registration letters for Ireland?

Answers	Pot-Luck 49 *(see Quiz 95)*

1 Dixie. 2 Water carrier. 3 Dr Who. 4 Simon and Garfunkel. 5 Optician. 6 Upper case or capital letter. 7 Summer. 8 Never Never Land. 9 Cygnet. 10 Roger Federer. 11 Smog. 12 Lord's. 13 Candy floss. 14 Royal Albert Hall. 15 Mistletoe. 16 Puck. 17 Cars. 18 Plumber. 19 Chef. 20 Blue. 21 Friends of the Earth. 22 Frank Carson. 23 November. 24 Thursday. 25 Instep. 26 Countess. 27 Horatio. 28 Brookside. 29 Ultra violet. 30 Hugh Dennis.

1 In "Little Britain" is it Lou or Andy who has to push the wheelchair?
2 In which TV hospital are Mark and Tricia Williams nurses?
3 The song "I Dreamed a Dream" comes from which musical?
4 Who was the last Viceroy of India?
5 On TV, who played Ryder, the narrator in "Brideshead Revisited"?
6 Which colourless, odourless light gas is used to lift airships?
7 Where in London is the Central Criminal Court?
8 In boxing what do the letters TKO stand for?
9 To a year each way, when was "The Generation Game" first shown?
10 Who created "The Flintstones"?
11 In which month is the Spring Bank Holiday?
12 Which Comic charity promoted National Red Nose Day?
13 How is Marian Fitzwalter more usually known?
14 What are the initials of Victorian writer Mr Gilbert?
15 What is the oldest university in the USA?
16 What was the "profession" of Captain Kidd?
17 What is the main colour of Nigeria's strip?
18 In which game do the players need glass balls?
19 Who wrote "Filthy, Rich and Catflap"?
20 What was Kat Moon's surname before she married Alfie?
21 Sid Vicious was a member of which punk band?
22 Which magazine did Hugh Hefner found?
23 Which sport did Bill Beaumont play?
24 What is a young badger called?
25 Which character did Harry Enfield play in the first series of "Men Behaving Badly"?
26 Which type of headgear did Procol Harum sing about?
27 What type of party or social gathering is for women only?
28 What was the nickname of TV cook Graham Kerr?
29 In boxing which weight is between fly and feather?
30 Which two numbers are missing from this row in Sudoku – 9, 2, 6, 5, 3, 7, 4?

Answers | Pot-Luck 52 *(see Quiz 100)*

1 Aggie. 2 720. 3 Noel Coward. 4 Edward II. 5 Umpire. 6 Ken Livingstone. 7 Silver. 8 Daniel. 9 Reginald Perrin. 10 Van Morrison. 11 Leanne. 12 Bryan Adams. 13 Birds. 14 Pete Best. 15 Neil Diamond. 16 Nancy Sinatra. 17 The Balkan Trilogy. 18 Mowgli. 19 Scaffold. 20 Sophie. 21 Square. 22 The conundrum. 23 Opera singer. 24 Golf. 25 Ealing comedies. 26 Elton John. 27 All Blacks. 28 Crowther. 29 Six. 30 The Shadows.

1 Where was Love in the 1994 record-breaking hit by Wet Wet Wet?
2 Who had a No 1 hit with "Ice Ice Baby"?
3 Who had a hit with the old Osmonds hit "Love Me for a Reason"?
4 Who had a hit in 1992 with "I Will Always Love You", the theme from "The Bodyguard"?
5 Which part of East London sang "Stay Another Day" in 1994?
6 Quite simply, what colour is Mick Hucknall's group?
7 Which two squaddies had new hits with old songs?
8 What sort of Hymns gave Verve a massive No 1 album?
9 Which 50-plus female took "Believe" to the top of the charts?
10 Who said Any Dream Will Do in his Technicolor Dreamcoat?
11 Whose Sister asked you to Stay in 1992?
12 Who wore Crocodile Shoes in 1994?
13 Who took a Stairway to Heaven before going to Animal Hospital?
14 Who joined George Michael on "Don't Let the Sun Go Down on Me"?
15 "Everything I Do (I Do It for You)" came from a film about which hero?
16 During which conflict was the record "Get Here" a UK Forces favourite?
17 Where were Eternal just a step from in 1994?
18 Which Streets did Bruce Springsteen sing about in 1994?
19 What was the name of the dance production Brothers who had a No 1 with "Setting Sun"?
20 Which disbanded group from the 1970s had a chart-topping greatest hits album called "Gold"?
21 Which seven-strong act first hit No 1 with "Bring It All Back"?
22 What nationality is Björk?
23 Who had a No 1 with the "Shoop Shoop Song"?
24 Which cartoon group had a No 1 with "Do the Bartman"?
25 Which Ebenezer was in the tile of the song by the Shamen?
26 Which rock star did Elvis Presley's daughter marry?
27 Which band had a top hit with "Country House"?
28 Which night did Whigfield sing about ?
29 Which Tom, a 1960s veteran, had his biggest ever album success with "Reload" in 1999?
30 How many people made up Steps – three, five or eight?

Answers	**Sport: The 90s** *(see Quiz 101)*

1 Damon Hill. 2 France. 3 Lancashire. 4 Faldo. 5 Monica Seles. 6 Hastings.
7 Rangers. 8 Phil Taylor. 9 South Africa. 10 Graham Taylor. 11 Grand National.
12 Wigan. 13 Gunnell. 14 George Graham. 15 It was cancelled. 16 Kriss. 17
Swimming. 18 Ireland. 19 Platt. 20 Skis. 21 France. 22 Scotland. 23 Dalglish. 24
John. 25 Conchita. 26 Alex Ferguson. 27 Hingis. 28 Triple Jump. 29 Javelin. 30
David Beckham.

1 Who co-presented "How Clean is Your House" along with Kim?
2 How many minutes in half a day?
3 Who wrote "Don't Let's be Beastly to the Germans"?
4 Who came first, Edward II or George II?
5 How was Rudi Koertzen involved in the 2005 Ashes tour?
6 Who was London's first directly elected Mayor?
7 Ag is the symbol of which chemical element ?
8 In "Coronation Street" what is Ken and Denise's little boy called?
9 David Nobbs created which character made famous by Leonard Rossiter?
10 Who was lead singer with Them?
11 Which Battersby girl returned to "Coronation Street" and had affairs with dad and son Danny and Jamie?
12 Who recorded the album "So Far So Good"?
13 Avian relates to which kind of creatures?
14 Whom did Ringo Starr replace as drummer with the Beatles?
15 How is Noah Kominsky better known?
16 Who sang with Frank Sinatra on the No 1 "Something Stupid"?
17 Which Trilogy was written by Olivia Manning?
18 What was the name of the boy in Disney's "The Jungle Book"?
19 How were Roger McGough, Mike McGear and John Gorman collectively known?
20 What is the first name of TV cook Grigson?
21 What shape is a boxing ring?
22 What is the final round of "Countdown" called?
23 How did Cecilia Bartoli find fame?
24 What game is played at St Andrews?
25 "Passport to Pimlico" was the first in the series of which British-made films?
26 Which legendary pop star wrote the music for the stage show "Billy Elliott"?
27 What is the nickname of the New Zealand rugby team?
28 Which Leslie introduced "The Price is Right" on UK TV?
29 How many time zones does Canada have?
30 Which group backed Cliff Richard in the 1960s?

Answers	**Pot-Luck 51** *(see Quiz 98)*

1 Lou. 2 Holby City. 3 Les Misérables. 4 Lord Mountbatten. 5 Jeremy Irons. 6 Helium. 7 Old Bailey. 8 Technical Knock Out. 9 1971. 10 Hanna-Barbera. 11 May. 12 Relief. 13 Maid Marian. 14 W. S. 15 Harvard. 16 Pirate. 17 Green. 18 Marbles. 19 Ben Elton. 20 Slater. 21 The Sex Pistols. 22 Playboy. 23 Rugby. 24 Cub. 25 Dermot. 26 Homburg. 27 Hen. 28 The Galloping Gourmet. 29 Bantam. 30 1 and 8.

1 Nigel Mansell was the first F1 Champion in the 1990s, who was the second?
2 Barthez, Dugarry and Thuram played for which FIFA World Cup-winning side?
3 England's cricket skipper played for which county side?
4 Which Nick won the British Open in 1990 and 1992?
5 Which tennis player was stabbed while on court?
6 In 1994 which rugby-playing Gavin was made an OBE?
7 Which Scottish team were champions every season in the 90s except 1997/8?
8 Who dominated world darts throughout the 1990s?
9 Which country returned to playing international sport in the 90s?
10 Which England soccer manager became known as a turnip?
11 Which steeplechase did Party Politics win in election year 1992?
12 Which rugby league team won the Challenge Cup every year for the first half of the 1990s?
13 Which Sally won Olympic gold in the 400-metre hurdles?
14 Which manager left Arsenal after taking a "bung"?
15 Why did no horse win the 1993 Grand National?
16 What is the first name of athlete Akabusi?
17 At which sport did Karen Pickering excel?
18 Which country did Sonia O'Sullivan race for?
19 Which former Villa player David became England's soccer captain?
20 What does Alberto Tomba wear on his feet when he competes?
21 Whom does Mary Pierce play tennis for?
22 Which country is snooker star Stephen Hendry from?
23 Which Kenny took Blackburn to the Premiership championship?
24 What is the first name of athlete Regis?
25 Which Miss Martinez beat Martina in a Wimbledon final?
26 Who managed Man Utd in their 1999 triple-winning season?
27 Which teenager Martina won Wimbledon, the US Open and Australian Open in 1997?
28 In which event was Jonathan Edwards world champion in 1995?
29 What does Steve Backley throw?
30 Which English player was hammered by the press after his 1998 World Cup red card?

Answers | Pop: Sounds of the 90s *(see Quiz 99)*

1 All Around. 2 Vanilla Ice. 3 Boyzone. 4 Whitney Houston. 5 East 17. 6 Red. 7 Robson and Jerome. 8 Urban Hymns. 9 Cher. 10 Jason Donovan. 11 Shakespear's. 12 Jimmy Nail. 13 Rolf Harris. 14 Elton John. 15 Robin Hood. 16 Gulf War. 17 Heaven. 18 Philadelphia. 19 Chemical Brothers. 20 Abba. 21 S Club. 22 Icelandic. 23 Cher. 24 The Simpsons. 25 Goode. 26 Michael Jackson. 27 Blur. 28 Saturday. 29 Tom Jones. 30 Five.

Quiz 102 | Pot-Luck 53

Answers – page 114

1 Which Kimberley was involved with David Blunkett when he resigned in 2004?
2 Rio Ferdinand and Alan Smith have both played for which two Uniteds?
3 How much does it cost to buy a station on a British Monopoly board?
4 Who had a No 1 hit with the song "Bohemian Rhapsody"?
5 In 2005 which Sean was nominated for a lifetime achievement award by the American Film Institute?
6 How many strings are there on a Spanish guitar?
7 How did the notorious witchfinder Matthew Hopkins die?
8 Which country did England cricketers tour after their Ashes win in 2005?
9 Where would you travel to find the Sea of Tranquillity?
10 On which special day in 1964 was "Top of the Pops" first transmitted?
11 In the military sector, what does TA stand for?
12 In which sport does the scoring begin at 15?
13 Called thumbtack in America, what's the name of this in the UK?
14 What game have Spassky, Fischer and Karpov played?
15 What type of hat was worn by Sherlock Holmes?
16 Which sisters had snakes on their heads in place of hair?
17 What was the "Flying Scotsman"?
18 What are you interested in if you study calligraphy?
19 In sailing, what is a warp?
20 What type of food is a profiterole?
21 In which country was Shergar kidnapped?
22 Who said, "Just like that!"?
23 What was the seventh month of the Roman calendar?
24 Which Russian ruler was known as "the Terrible"?
25 Which "copper" tree has reddish brown leaves?
26 What was the surname of landscape gardener Capability?
27 Which musical instrument was played by Larry Adler?
28 Who recorded "Sultans of Swing"?
29 In mythology what is Neptune the god of?
30 Prince William was accepted at which military school after he left university?

Answers | TV: The 90s *(see Quiz 104)*

1 Jennifer Saunders. 2 Soldier Soldier. 3 Time. 4 Baywatch. 5 The Big Breakfast. 6 Leisure Centre. 7 Lenny Henry. 8 Cracker 9 Of May. 10 Dead Donkey. 11 Spain. 12 Goodnight. 13 Police officer. 14 Cards. 15 Eliott. 16 Hurts. 17 Atkinson. 18 Noel Edmonds. 19 Doctors. 20 Nesbitt. 21 Horses. 22 Twin. 23 Year. 24 Hetty. 25 Yes. 26 Stars. 27 Dibley. 28 Panorama. 29 Jill Dando. 30 Rolf Harris.

1 Which English county did ex-Australian captain Allan Border play for?
2 In Parliament what was known as DORA?
3 In sport, who are the Blades?
4 In which musical does the song "Somewhere" appear?
5 Which steam bath originated in Finland?
6 What are protective eyeglasses called?
7 Which comedian created Monsieur Hulot?
8 Which MP Boris has edited the Spectator magazine?
9 What was the original theme song for "Absolutely Fabulous"?
10 Which dance goes, one-two-three-hop?
11 What is the prompting device used by TV presenters called?
12 Which Justin released the chart topping album "Justified"?
13 Who won the world professional snooker championship for the first time back in 1972?
14 In which House was James Herriot's veterinary practice?
15 Which MP has won two Oscars?
16 Who wrote "The History of Mr Polly"?
17 To five years either way, when was the first LP released commercially in Britain?
18 Which political leader appointed in 2005 went to Eton and Oxford?
19 Robin Cousins won an Olympic gold medal in which artistic sport?
20 Who created the Muppets?
21 Which piece of furniture is Benjamin Franklin credited with creating?
22 Which sit com shared its name with a food called the staff of life?
23 The Diamond Sculls takes place at which sporting event?
24 What is a group of five performers called?
25 Which sport do the Harlem Globetrotters play?
26 In soccer, which country did Eusebio play for?
27 Which city devastated in 2005 was a major influence on jazz music?
28 What is the nationality of Tom Conti?
29 If Redknapp was Harry, who was Jim in the Harry and Jim soccer management duo?
30 Which family featured with Gareth Gates on the No 1 single "Spirit in the Sky"?

| **Answers** | Pot-Luck 55 *(see Quiz 105)* |

1 Louis Walsh. 2 Dave. 3 Two. 4 Gladioli. 5 Mae West. 6 England. 7 John Bunyan. 8 Albatross. 9 South Pacific. 10 Pastry. 11 The Beach Boys. 12 Marie Curie. 13 Panorama. 14 Patriots. 15 Miss Marple. 16 Michael Fish. 17 Boom Bang-a-Bang. 18 Wisden Cricketers Almanack. 19 Phil Redmond. 20 Northern Ireland. 21 David Cassidy. 22 Canada. 23 Canada. 24 Baseball. 25 R. Kelly. 26 Dollar. 27 Two. 28 Tobacco smoke. 29 Maria. 30 Eddie Fitzgerald.

1 Who plays Edina in "Absolutely Fabulous"?
2 In which series did Robson and Jerome star?
3 What Goes By in the sit com with Jean and Lionel?
4 What is the series about LA lifeguards called?
5 What is the Channel 4 Breakfast programme called?
6 In "The Brittas Empire" what is Gordon manager of?
7 Who is the comedian husband of Dawn French who stars in "Chef!"?
8 Which series starred Robbie Coltrane as a police psychologist?
9 Which Darling Buds starred David Jason and Pam Ferris?
10 What did you Drop in the series about a newsroom?
11 In which country was "Eldorado" set?
12 What was said to Sweetheart in the series with Nicholas Lyndhurst?
13 What is Nick's job in "Heartbeat"?
14 What was the House made of in the political drama?
15 Which fashion House did Beatrice and Evangeline head?
16 What does Love do in the drama with Adam Faith and Zoë Wanamaker?
17 Which Rowan played the bumbling Mr Bean?
18 Who hosted a crazy Saturday-night House Party?
19 What was the profession of Jack and Beth in "Peak Practice"?
20 Which Rab C. was a Glasgow street philosopher?
21 Which animals was the series "Trainer" about?
22 Which Peaks provided a mysterious soap series in 1990–91?
23 How long did Peter Mayle spend in Provence?
24 What was the first name of private detective Mrs Wainthropp?
25 Did summer precede winter in Delia Smith's cookery collections?
26 What did contestants have In Their Eyes in the impersonation show?
27 Dawn French played the vicar of which parish?
28 On which long-running current affairs programme did the Princess of Wales give her first solo interview in 1995?
29 Which Breakfast News presenter took over the Holiday programme?
30 Which Australian presented "Animal Hospital"?

Answers	Pot-Luck 53 *(see Quiz 102)*

1 Quinn. 2 Leeds Utd and Man Utd. 3 £200. 4 Queen. 5 Sean Connery. 6 Six. 7 He was hanged as a wizard. 8 Pakistan. 9 The Moon. 10 New Year's Day. 11 Territorial Army. 12 Tennis. 13 Drawing pin. 14 Chess. 15 Deerstalker. 16 The Gorgons. 17 A train. 18 Handwriting. 19 Mooring rope. 20 Cake. 21 Ireland. 22 Tommy Cooper. 23 September. 24 Ivan. 25 Beech. 26 Brown. 27 Mouth organ. 28 Dire Straits. 29 The sea. 30 Sandhurst.

Answers – page 113

1 Who made up the "X Factor" jury with Simon Cowell and Sharon Osbourne?

2 Who is Cockney Chas's singing partner?

3 How many heads did Dr Doolittle's llama have?

4 What are Dame Edna Everage's favourite flowers?

5 Which blonde sex symbol used the pseudonym Jane Mast?

6 Which is the largest country in Great Britain?

7 Who wrote "Pilgrim's Progress"?

8 Which is the only bird capable of flying all day without flapping its wings?

9 "There is Nothing Like a Dame" comes from which musical?

10 What is something wrapped in if it is served "en croûte"?

11 Which 60s group was formed by the Wilson brothers?

12 Who was the first person known to have died from radiation poisoning?

13 Which word for a wide view is the name of a TV news programme?

14 Which New England team won the Super Bowl in 2002 and 2004?

15 Which character has been played by Margaret Rutherford and Joan Hickson?

16 Who assured viewers there were no hurricanes on the way in 1987?

17 Which song did Lulu sing in the Eurovision Song Contest?

18 What sporting publication is nicknamed "The Primrose Bible"?

19 Who created "Brookside"?

20 Which country does Roy Carroll play for?

21 Who shot to fame in the 70s as Keith Partridge?

22 In which country is the Jasper National Park?

23 Which country does snooker star Cliff Thorburn come from?

24 Which sport do the Pittsburgh Pirates play?

25 "Ignition" was a 2003 UK No 1 for which artist?

26 What is the currency of Australia?

27 How many times did Barry Sheene win the 500cc world motor cycle racing championship?

28 What do you dislike if you are misocapnic?

29 What is Mia short for in Mia Farrow's name?

30 What is the full name of the Coltrane character in "Cracker"?

| **Answers** | **Pot-Luck 54** *(see Quiz 103)* |

1 Essex. 2 Defence Of the Realm Act. 3 Sheffield United. 4 West Side Story. 5 Sauna. 6 Goggles. 7 Jacques Tati. 8 Boris Johnson. 9 This Wheel's on Fire. 10 Polka. 11 Autocue. 12 Justin Timberlake. 13 Alex Higgins. 14 Skeldale House. 15 Glenda Jackson. 16 H. G. Wells. 17 1950. 18 David Cameron. 19 Ice skating. 20 Jim Henson. 21 Rocking chair. 22 Bread. 23 Henley Regatta. 24 Quintet. 25 Basketball. 26 Portugal. 27 New Orleans. 28 Scottish. 29 Jim Smith. 30 The Kumars.

1 Which party won a fourth consecutive term of office in the UK in 1992?
2 Which Middle Eastern country was defeated in the Gulf War?
3 Which country was reunified in 1990?
4 Who became Deputy Prime Minister of the UK in 1995?
5 Which Manchester jail was the scene of rioting in 1990?
6 Which envoy of the Archbishop of Canterbury was released from the Lebanon?
7 Which three-times winner of the Grand National died?
8 Which rock legend's daughter did Michael Jackson marry?
9 Who succeeded Barbara Bush as the USA's First Lady?
10 Which Dimbleby interviewed the Prince of Wales on TV?
11 Who was the first female presenter of the National Lottery Live?
12 Which member of the royal family divorced and remarried?
13 Which Labour leader resigned after the 1992 General Election?
14 Assassinated Prime Minister Rabin was from which country?
15 Which tax was abandoned in favour of the Council Tax?
16 Which country won the Eurovision Contest in consecutive years in the first half of the decade?
17 Who described 1992 as an annus horribilis?
18 Which heavyweight boxing champion served a prison sentence?
19 Which media magnate drowned in mysterious circumstances?
20 George Carey succeeded Robert Runcie in which post?
21 Jill Morrell conducted a campaign to free which Beirut hostage?
22 Who became president of South Africa in 1994?
23 Which US singer celebrated his 80th birthday in December 1995?
24 Benazir Bhutto returned as prime minister of which Asian country?
25 Which Boris became president of the Russian Federation in 1991?
26 Which meat was at the heart of a scare about BSE?
27 Which link between England and France was opened?
28 Which American football star was acquitted of his wife's murder?
29 The imprisonment of Nick Leeson followed the collapse of which bank?
30 What replaced TV am as ITV's weekly breakfast programme?

Answers	90s Films *(see Quiz 108)*

1 Hugh Grant. 2 Braveheart. 3 Columbus. 4 Mrs Doubtfire. 5 Hook. 6 Sister Act. 7 Jack Lemmon. 8 List. 9 A dog. 10 A ghost. 11 Tom Hanks. 12 Patrick Swayze. 13 Kevin Costner. 14 The Silence of the Lambs. 15 Alone. 16 The Lion King. 17 Indecent. 18 Trousers. 19 Julia Roberts. 20 Sally. 21 Jurassic. 22 Seattle. 23 Pocahontas. 24 Batman. 25 Mohicans. 26 Aladdin. 27 Tom Cruise. 28 Dredd. 29 34th. 30 Golden.

1 Which Glasgow comedian is married to actress Pamela Stephenson?
2 Who were the parents of Cain, Able and Seth?
3 Which was the first British soccer side to win the European Cup?
4 What is the flavour of Tia Maria?
5 Which Joyce said, "George, don't do that!"
6 In snooker, what is the score from potting the pink?
7 N is the symbol of which chemical element ?
8 In "EastEnders" who is Kathy Mitchell's son by Pete Beale?
9 What is the second month of the year to have exactly 30 days?
10 Which Rupert played Ron in the Harry Potter films?
11 In England, where is the National Water Sports Centre?
12 In which US state is Jack Daniel's whiskey distilled?
13 How much was a groat worth?
14 Who hosted "The Last Resort"?
15 What was special about the size of the disc developed by Philips and Sony in the late 1970s?
16 Which two fruits were crossed to produce a nectarine?
17 In which country did judo develop?
18 Which rapper featured on The Pussycat Dolls' No 1 hit "Don't 'Cha"?
19 Which pop star was Jeff Banks married to?
20 What is the first name of TV cook Harris?
21 Who is the patron saint of travellers?
22 A caravan is a group of which animals?
23 In the pop song, who wore a "crimson dress that clings so tight"?
24 Which striker Andy has played for both City and United in Manchester?
25 Who picked up the nickname the "Louisville Lip"?
26 From which film did Duran Duran get their name?
27 Whose summer residence is at Castel Gandolfo?
28 In which city did the charity Oxfam originate?
29 How many games did Arsenal lose in winning the 2003/4 Premiership?
30 Which fashion item was Imelda Marcos famous for collecting?

Answers	**Pot-Luck 57** *(see Quiz 109)*

1 Coldplay. 2 Japan. 3 USA. 4 Ram. 5 Deputy Dawg. 6 Bobby Robson. 7 Smoked cod's roe. 8 Campion. 9 Gene Roddenberry. 10 One horse power. 11 Greenland. 12 Sari. 13 Rubella. 14 April Fool's Day. 15 Metro Goldwyn Mayer. 16 An anchor. 17 Derbyshire. 18 Smoke. 19 Barbie. 20 Rudolph Valentino. 21 Antiques. 22 Nettle. 23 The Olympic Games. 24 Sahara. 25 FBI. 26 Outside. 27 Snap. 28 Gascoigne. 29 Gimme! Gimme! Gimme! (A Man After Midnight). 30 Plums.

1 Which male star shot to fame in "Four Weddings and a Funeral"?
2 In which film shot in Ireland did Australian Mel Gibson play a Scot?
3 Who had to "Carry On" 500 years after the discovery of America?
4 In which film did Robin Williams dress up as a Scottish nanny?
5 What was the name of the Dustin Hoffman film about Peter Pan?
6 In which film did Whoopi Golberg first get into the habit?
7 Who joined Walter Matthau in the film "Grumpy Old Men"?
8 What did Schindler draw up in the Spielberg film?
9 What is Beethoven in the 1992 film?
10 What is Casper?
11 Who won an Oscar for "Forrest Gump" and "Philadelphia"?
12 Who starred with Demi Moore in "Ghost"?
13 Who was Whitney Houston's Bodyguard?
14 In which film did Anthony Hopkins play the role of Hannibal Lecter?
15 How was Macaulay Culkin left at Home in 1990?
16 What did the cub Simba become in the 1994 Disney film?
17 What kind of Proposal did Robert Redford make concerning Demi Moore?
18 What was Wrong in the Wallace and Gromit Oscar-winning film?
19 Who was the Pretty Woman in the 1990 film?
20 Whom did Harry meet in the film with Billy Crystal?
21 Which Park was the Spielberg film about dinosaurs?
22 Where was someone Sleepless in the film with Meg Ryan?
23 Which Disney release told the story of an American Indian heroine?
24 In which series of films would you find Robin and the Joker?
25 Daniel Day-Lewis starred in the Last of what in 1992?
26 In which film was Robin Williams the voice of the genie?
27 Who was Nicole Kidman's co star in "Far and Away" whom she later married?
28 Which Judge does Sylvester Stallone play in the comic cult movie?
29 On which street was there A Miracle in the Xmas movie with Richard Attenborough?
30 What colour is the Eye in the 007 film?

Answers | **90s Newsround** *(see Quiz 106)*

1 Conservatives. 2 Iraq. 3 Germany. 4 Michael Heseltine. 5 Strangeways. 6 Terry Waite. 7 Red Rum. 8 Elvis. 9 Hillary Clinton. 10 Jonathan. 11 Anthea Turner. 12 Princess Royal. 13 Neil Kinnock. 14 Israel. 15 Poll tax. 16 Ireland. 17 The Queen. 18 Mike Tyson. 19 Robert Maxwell. 20 Archbishop of Canterbury. 21 John McCarthy. 22 Nelson Mandela. 23 Frank Sinatra. 24 Pakistan. 25 Yeltsin. 26 Beef. 27 Channel Tunnel. 28 OJ Simpson. 29 Barings. 30 GMTV.

1 "X&Y" is the third album from which group?
2 Which country co-hosted the 2002 World Cup with South Korea?
3 Which country does tennis player Pete Sampras come from?
4 What is a male sheep called?
5 Who exclaims "Dagnabit!"?
6 Who was manager of Ipswich when they first won the FA Cup in '78?
7 What is taramasalata made from?
8 Which sleuth drove round East Anglia in a vintage Lagonda?
9 Who created "Star Trek"?
10 What is 1 Cheval-Vapeur equivalent to?
11 From which country's language does anorak come from?
12 What is a traditional Indian dress called?
13 The MMR vaccine covers measles, mumps and what else?
14 Boob Day is the Spanish equivalent of what in Britain?
15 In cinema, what does MGM stand for?
16 What is tattooed on Popeye's arm?
17 Which county did England's wicket keeper Bob Taylor play for?
18 If a sign in Germany announced Rauchen Verboten, what could you not do?
19 In the toy world, who is Ken's girlfriend?
20 Which film star's funeral in 1926 was attended by more than 100,000 mourners?
21 What did Lovejoy deal in?
22 Which stinging weed can be used to make a kind of beer?
23 What was held in Britain in 1908 and 1948?
24 In which desert did Mark Thatcher go missing?
25 Which organization's motto is "Fidelity, Bravery, Integrity"?
26 Would a Scotsman wear a sporran under or outside the kilt?
27 Which card game involves quickly spotting matching pairs?
28 Which ex-England soccer great Paul got the push as boss of Kettering in 2005?
29 Which ABBA hit did Madonna sample for her single "Hung Up"?
30 What is the drink slivovitz made from?

Answers | **Pot-Luck 56** *(see Quiz 107)*

1 Billy Connolly. 2 Adam and Eve. 3 Celtic. 4 Coffee. 5 Grenfell. 6 Six. 7 Nitrogen. 8 Ian. 9 June. 10 Rupert Grint. 11 Nottingham. 12 Tennessee. 13 4d (four old pence). 14 Jonathan Ross. 15 Compact. 16 Peach and plum. 17 Japan. 18 Busta Rhymes. 19 Sandie Shaw. 20 Valentina. 21 St Christopher. 22 Camels. 23 Pretty Flamingo. 24 Andy Cole. 25 Muhammad Ali. 26 Barbarella. 27 The Pope. 28 Oxford. 29 None. 30 Shoes.

Quiz 110 | Hollywood

1 Which singer starred in "The Bodyguard"?
2 Which actress Keaton starred in "Father of the Bride II"?
3 "Walk the Line" was a biopic of which country music legend?
4 Which Holly won an Oscar for a silent role in "The Piano"?
5 Which silent movie star was played by Robert Downey Jr in 1992?
6 Which Welsh actor starred with Jodie Foster in "The Silence of the Lambs"?
7 Which Bob starred in "Mona Lisa" before finding it "good to talk"?
8 Which Steven directed "Schindler's List"?
9 Which actor Sylvester has the nickname Sly?
10 Who is Donald Sutherland's actor son?
11 What is the first name of "Pulp Fiction" director Tarantino?
12 Which actress Melanie married Don Johnson – twice?
13 Which Nick co-starred with Barbra Streisand in "The Prince of Tides"?
14 What is the first name of actress Sarandon ?
15 Which Johnny starred as Edward Scissorhands?
16 Which Scottish actor Sean has an actor son Jason?
17 Which Emilio starred in "Young Guns" I and II?
18 Which Macaulay became one of the highest-paid child stars ever?
19 Which actress Glenn had a "Fatal Attraction"?
20 Which Al starred in "The Godfather" and "Scent of a Woman"?
21 Which actor Mel was born in the US but brought up in Australia?
22 What is the surname of father and daughter Peter and Bridget?
23 Which Robin became Mrs Doubtfire?
24 Which blond Daryl had adventures with the Invisible Man?
25 Who was Alec Baldwin's real and screen wife in "The Getaway"?
26 What is the first name of Joanne Whalley-Kilmer's husband?
27 Liza Minnelli and Lorna Luft are daughters of which Hollywood great?
28 Which actor succeeded Timothy Dalton as James Bond?
29 Which film director's real name is Allen Stewart Konigsberg?
30 Which actor won an Oscar as director of "Dances with Wolves"?

Answers | Pot-Luck 60 *(see Quiz 114)*

1 Somerset. 2 Jessica Fletcher. 3 Piccadilly. 4 Nancy. 5 Grant. 6 Casino Royale. 7 Bruce Forsyth. 8 Circus. 9 1963. 10 Two. 11 None. 12 Sixpence. 13 Peter Davison. 14 Casino Royale. 15 George VI. 16 Jack. 17 Manchester. 18 James Blunt. 19 Balmoral. 20 Clive Dunn. 21 Bridge. 22 UB40. 23 Roll call. 24 Poet Laureate. 25 Armstrong. 26 Wall Street. 27 Eight. 28 Jeremy Isaacs. 29 Wear. 30 ASLEF.

Quiz 111 | Pot-Luck 58

Answers – page 123

1 What is the seventh commandment?
2 What sport takes place in a velodrome?
3 Who had UK No 1s with "Independent Women" and "Survivor"?
4 Who sang the theme song for "The Man with the Golden Gun"?
5 Who said, "I shall hear in heaven"?
6 In which card game do you "peg out"?
7 Which bingo number is clickety click?
8 What was Ivan Lendl's first Wimbledon tournament win?
9 What is another name for Lady's Fingers?
10 Which member of the Monkees appeared in "Coronation Street"?
11 What colour is ebony?
12 What do you have at the bottom of a colander?
13 Who wrote the TV musical drama "Lipstick on Your Collar"?
14 Who was England's captain in the 2002 World Cup?
15 In which track event do you get wet even when it's not raining?
16 On which track at Pennsylvania Station did the Chattanooga Choo Choo leave?
17 What colour are French post boxes?
18 What does the letter U stand for in URL?
19 Who played Len Fairclough?
20 When during a meal would you have an hors d'oeuvre?
21 Which team did Alf Garnett support?
22 What is the US military academy called?
23 Over what type of food did Edwina Currie resign a ministerial post?
24 Which classical composer did Richard Chamberlain play in "The Music Lovers"?
25 What is the name of the cat which dips its paw in the food tin?
26 Who coached England's 2003 rugby World Cup-winning team?
27 What name is given to the style of riding when both the rider's legs are on the same side of the horse?
28 Who tragically died while appearing on Live at Her Majesty's?
29 Where might you find a breeze block?
30 Whose motto is "Nation shall speak unto nation"?

Answers | **Pot-Luck 61** *(see Quiz 115)*

1 Honolulu. **2** Mozart. **3** Gondola. **4** A hater of mankind. **5** Israel. **6** Somerset. **7** Donna Karan New York. **8** Arsenal. **9** Sharon Stone. **10** Demi Moore. **11** Bill Gates. **12** Irvine Welsh. **13** Gareth Gates. **14** Anfield, Liverpool. **15** Dublin. **16** Sett. **17** Centrepoint. **18** Gaggle. **19** Brian Lara. **20** They are all royal boroughs. **21** Emma Hamilton. **22** Amadeus. **23** Charles. **24** Sergeant Uhuru. **25** Andrew Flintoff. **26** King Harold. **27** Sancho Panza. **28** Myxamatosis. **29** A. A. Milne. **30** York.

1 What did Iran used to be called?
2 In which World are underdeveloped countries said to be?
3 Normandy is part of which country?
4 In which Sea is the island of Majorca?
5 Which country does the island of Rhodes belong to?
6 In which US state is Disney World?
7 Which county is abbreviated to Oxon?
8 In which country is the Costa del Sol?
9 Which is further south, Great Yarmouth or Brighton?
10 Is Torremolinos on the coast or inland?
11 Which sea lies between Italy and the former Yugoslavia?
12 On which coast of France are Cannes and St Tropez?
13 If you took a holiday in Gstaad what sport would you practise?
14 In which country is Buenos Aires?
15 In which continent is the holiday destination of Ibiza?
16 Where would you speak English and Maltese?
17 Which island lies at the eastern end of the Mediterranean?
18 Which group of islands does Tenerife belong to?
19 What is the Matterhorn?
20 What is the continent around the South Pole called?
21 Which country does the Loire flow through?
22 What is the world's second highest mountain?
23 In which Ocean is Greenland?
24 On which continent is the Kalahari desert?
25 What is the chief official language of Israel?
26 The Arctic Ocean is not covered mainly by water but by what?
27 Which tiny princedom is situated between France and Spain?
28 In which Sea is Cuba?
29 Which Falls are on the border between Zimbabwe and Zambia?
30 On which continent is the Amazon river?

| **Answers** | **Hollywood** *(see Quiz 110)* |

1 Whitney Houston. 2 Diane. 3 Johnny Cash. 4 Hunter. 5 Charlie Chaplin. 6 Anthony Hopkins. 7 Hoskins. 8 Spielberg. 9 Stallone. 10 Kiefer. 11 Quentin. 12 Griffith. 13 Nolte. 14 Susan. 15 Depp. 16 Connery. 17 Estevez. 18 Culkin. 19 Close. 20 Pacino. 21 Gibson. 22 Fonda. 23 Williams. 24 Hannah. 25 Kim Basinger. 26 Val. 27 Judy Garland. 28 Pierce Brosnan. 29 Woody Allen. 30 Kevin Costner.

1 What sort of Circle do conjurers join?
2 The biopic movie "The Aviator" was about which person?
3 Which city hosted the 2004 Olympic Games?
4 Which musical includes the characters Sky Masterson and Nathan Detroit?
5 What can be the name of a hat and a member of a cricket team?
6 Which sign of the zodiac follows Capricorn?
7 Which game might you be watching if you were at the Belfry?
8 Variola is more commonly called what?
9 Who wrote the play "An Inspector Calls"?
10 What is Diana Prince's other identity?
11 Which Scottish group took their name from a Scritti Politti lyric?
12 Which section do you look for in the newspaper to read what the stars have in store for you?
13 Which musical instrument does Nigel Kennedy play ?
14 Which residence of the Queen's was opened to the public in 1993?
15 In which month is the Le Mans 24-hour race held?
16 Who wrote the theme song to "Harry's Game"?
17 After what is London's Fleet Street named?
18 Which "Knight Rider" travelled to "Baywatch"?
19 Whom did Frank Bruno beat to become WBC heavyweight champion in 1995?
20 What is a cassoulet?
21 In which sport would you have an Eskimo roll?
22 What is another name for a Chinese gooseberry?
23 What is a 200th anniversary called?
24 How many players are there in a basketball team?
25 In ads, what was BT's bird called?
26 Which striker Jimmy has played soccer for Leeds, Chelsea and Middlesbrough?
27 What was the name of Hamlet's father?
28 On which day of the week did "The Archers" first have an omnibus edition?
29 What is the English name for Firenze?
30 To five years either way, when was the Royal Variety show first televised?

Answers | **Pot-Luck 58** *(see Quiz 111)*

1 Thou shalt not commit adultery. 2 Cycling. 3 Destiny's Child. 4 Lulu. 5 Beethoven.
6 Cribbage. 7 66. 8 Junior Wimbledon. 9 Okra. 10 Davy Jones. 11 Black. 12 Holes.
13 Dennis Potter. 14 David Beckham. 15 Steeplechase. 16 Track 29. 17 Yellow.
18 Uniform. 19 Peter Adamson. 20 Beginning. 21 West Ham. 22 West Point. 23
Eggs. 24 Tchaikovsky. 25 Arthur. 26 Sir Clive Woodward. 27 Side saddle. 28 Tommy
Cooper. 29 In a wall. 30 The BBC.

1 In which English county are Taunton and Wells?
2 Which fictional detective wrote "The Corpse Danced at Midnight"?
3 On the London Underground, on which line is Knightsbridge station?
4 What is the name of Frank Sinatra's daughter?
5 What is the name of Phil's brother in "EastEnders"?
6 In which Ian Fleming novel did James Bond first appear?
7 Whom did 1975 Miss World Wilnelia Merced marry in the 1980s?
8 What type of entertainment is the musical "Barnum" about?
9 In which year did "Dr Who" first appear on BBC?
10 Over how many days is an Olympic decathlon held?
11 How many World Cup final stages has Ryan Giggs played in?
12 In June 1980, which coin ceased to be legal tender?
13 Whom is actress Sandra Dickinson married to?
14 What was the title of the first movie in which Daniel Craig played James Bond?
15 Who was the first British monarch to visit America?
16 What is the first name of comedian Dee?
17 0161 is the dialling code for which city?
18 "Back to Bedlam" is the debut album by which singer?
19 At which Scottish home of the Queen did Charles and Camilla spend their honeymoon?
20 Which member of "Dad's Army" had a chart-topping hit?
21 At which game has Omar Sharif represented his country?
22 Which group features the children of 50s and 60s folk singer Ian Campbell?
23 What does Tenko mean in English?
24 C. Day Lewis and John Betjeman have both held which title?
25 Which Lance monopolized the Tour de France in the first years of the new millennium?
26 On which Street is the New York Stock Exchange?
27 How many times do you sing "Happy Birthday" if you sing two verses of the song?
28 Who left Channel 4 to become Director of the Royal Opera House?
29 Sunderland lies at the mouth of which river?
30 Of which union was Ray Buckton once a leader?

Answers	Geography (see Quiz 112)

1 Persia. 2 Third World. 3 France. 4 Mediterranean. 5 Greece. 6 Florida. 7 Oxfordshire. 8 Spain. 9 Brighton. 10 On the coast. 11 Adriatic. 12 South. 13 Skiing. 14 Argentina. 15 Europe. 16 Malta. 17 Cyprus. 18 Canary Islands. 19 Mountain. 20 Antarctica. 21 France. 22 K2. 23 Arctic. 24 Africa. 25 Hebrew. 26 Ice. 27 Andorra. 28 Caribbean. 29 Victoria. 30 South America.

1 What is the capital city of Hawaii?
2 The birth of which musical genius was celebrated in 2006?
3 What boat is found on the canals of Venice?
4 What is a misanthrope?
5 Where would you find a kibbutz?
6 Where are the Quantocks?
7 What do the initials DKNY stand for?
8 Which London underground station was named after a football club?
9 Who uncrossed their legs to much ado in "Basic Instinct"?
10 Who was the female lead in a harassment case in the film "Disclosure"?
11 Who founded the Microsoft Corporation?
12 Who wrote the novel "Trainspotting"?
13 Who had a No 1 with "The Long and Winding Road" coupled with "Suspicious Minds"?
14 Where are the Shankly Gates ?
15 In which city did Molly Malone wheel her wheelbarrow?
16 What is the name of the badger's residence?
17 Which office block is located at the junction of Charing Cross Road and Tottenham Court Road?
18 What is the collective noun for geese?
19 Who is the only cricketer to score 501 in first-class cricket?
20 What have Tunbridge Wells, Windsor and Kensington & Chelsea got in common?
21 Who was Admiral Lord Nelson's lover?
22 What was Mozart's middle name?
23 Which Prince moved into Clarence House after the Queen Mother died?
24 Who was the principal communications officer on the Starship Enterprise?
25 Who was voted Professional Cricketers' Association Player of the Year in 2004 and 2005?
26 Who got one in the eye at the Battle of Hastings?
27 Who was Don Quixote's sidekick?
28 What is the viral disease of rabbits?
29 Who wrote Winnie the Pooh?
30 Where is the Jorvik centre?

Answers | **Pot-Luck 59** *(see Quiz 113)*

1 Magic. 2 Howard Hughes. 3 Athens. 4 Guys and Dolls. 5 Bowler. 6 Aquarius. 7 Golf. 8 Smallpox. 9 J. B. Priestley. 10 Wonderwoman. 11 Wet Wet Wet. 12 Horoscope. 13 Violin. 14 Buckingham Palace. 15 June. 16 Clannad. 17 The river Fleet. 18 David Hasselhoff. 19 Oliver McCall. 20 A French stew. 21 Canoeing. 22 Kiwi fruit. 23 Bicentenary. 24 5. 25 Buzby. 26 Jimmy Floyd Hasselbaink. 27 Hamlet. 28 Sunday. 29 Florence. 30 1960.

1 Who married Patsy Kensit in April 1997?
2 Which singer's daughter is called Lourdes Maria?
3 Who has a backing group called the Waves?
4 Who took "Wannabe" to No. 1 in 1996?
5 Who was lead singer with Wet Wet Wet?
6 "Complicated" and "Sk8er Boi" are singles by which Canadian singer?
7 Who sang "Strangers in the Night"?
8 Who is the brother of the late Karen Carpenter?
9 Who wrote "Words", a 90s hit for Boyzone?
10 "PCD" was which group's debut album?
11 Who was Bernie Taupin's most famous songwriting partner?
12 Peter Kay resurrected the chart career of which vocalist Tony?
13 Who changed his name from Gordon Sumner to top the charts?
14 Which band's albums include "American Idiot" and "Nimrod"?
15 Who was the female vocalist with the Pretenders?
16 Who co-starred with Whitney Houston in "The Bodyguard"?
17 Who wrote the music for "Jesus Christ Superstar"?
18 Who were known on TV as Dave Tucker and Paddy Garvey?
19 Who sang that they were "Back for Good" in 1995?
20 Whose "new" single, "Free as a Bird", charted in 1995?
21 The title from which TV drama gave Jimmy Nail a hit in 1994?
22 Who was the subject of the biopic "What's Love Got to Do with It?"?
23 Whose first solo No. 1 was "Sacrifice/Healing Hands"?
24 Who was the British Monkee?
25 Which band released the single "I Believe in a Thing Called Love" in 2003?
26 Who had a hit with "Radio Ga Ga"?
27 Who was the father of the former Mrs Lisa Marie Jackson?
28 Which 80s duo included Andrew Ridgeley?
29 Who had his first UK solo No. 1 with "I Just Called to Say I Love You"?
30 Who was lead singer with Culture Club?

Answers | TV: Soaps *(see Quiz 118)*

1 Den & Dennis. 2 Rickman. 3 Fred Elliott. 4 "Emmerdale". 5 Steve. 6 Anita.
7 Mac. 8 Christopher Timothy. 9 Mitchells. 10 Robinson. 11 Branning. 12
Terry. 13 Battersby-Brown. 14 Patsy Kensit. 15 Leanne. 16 Peggy Mitchell. 17
"Coronation Street". 18 Malaysia. 19 Chester. 20 The Rover's Return. 21 Sydney.
22 "Neighbours". 23 Phil. 24 Sunday. 25 "Neighbours". 26 Alexis. 27 "Coronation
Street" (Manchester). 28 "Dallas". 29 "The Archers". 30 Hotpot.

Quiz 117 | Pot Luck 62

Answers – page 129

1 On which day are hot cross buns traditionally eaten?
2 How many signs of the zodiac are there?
3 In which decade of the 20th century was Muhammad Ali born?
4 In the 2005 Ashes, which England player featured in only the final test match?
5 Which Monica got involved with the US President in the 1990s?
6 Which soccer club has had Royal and Woolwich as part of its name?
7 Who wrote the novel "Lucky Jim"?
8 On a Monopoly board, what colour is Old Kent Road?
9 Who invented Braille?
10 In song, who was born "on a mountain top in Tennessee"?
11 What is Kampuchea now called?
12 Which Richard starred in "The Good Life"?
13 Lance Cairns played cricket for which country?
14 What word can go before "draft", "flow" and "shadow"?
15 Traditionally, what colour is willow pattern?
16 In which country is the city of Addis Ababa?
17 Which Boys recorded "Barbara Ann" in the 60s?
18 Which cartoon character has an anchor tattooed on his arm?
19 What is the square root of 4?
20 Iceberg and Dorothy Perkins are examples of what?
21 Which ex-Take That member won a Brit Award for the song "She's The One"?
22 Which film ends with "tomorrow is another day"?
23 A revolving firework is named after which saint?
24 Who murdered Abel?
25 Which international soccer boss met the "fake sheikh"?
26 Which Italian phrase used in English means in the fresh or cool air?
27 In which TV series did the characters Edina and Saffron appear?
28 Which Ben won an Oscar for Best Actor in "Gandhi"?
29 How many degrees in a right angle?
30 Which group had a No. 1 with "Hey Jude"?

Answers | Around the UK *(see Quiz 119)*

1 Strathclyde. 2 Leeds. 3 Clwyd. 4 M1. 5 Anglesey. 6 Northern Ireland. 7 One – Devon. 8 Lake District. 9 Scarborough. 10 Scotland. 11 Humber. 12 Birmingham. 13 Edinburgh. 14 East. 15 M11. 16 Regent's Park. 17 M4. 18 Isle of Wight. 19 Bognor, Lyme. 20 Ealing, Enfield. 21 Liverpool. 22 Guernsey. 23 The Mall. 24 Blackpool. 25 Fife. 26 Dartford. 27 M6. 28 Suffolk. 29 Glasgow. 30 North.

1 Which father and son both came to a sticky end in "EastEnders" in 2005?
2 What was Sharon's surname after she married Dennis?
3 Who is the Street's repetitive butcher?
4 In which soap did Dave Glover perish in a fire?
5 Which "Coronation Street" MacDonald twin went to prison?
6 Sunita of "Coronation Street" played which similar-sounding character in "Dinnerladies"?
7 What is Dr Brendan McGuire's nickname in "Doctors"?
8 Who was a vet in "All Creatures Great and Small" and a doctor in "Doctors"?
9 Which brothers returned to "EastEnders" in 2005?
10 In "Neighbours" what was the surname of Scott, Paul, Lucy and Julie?
11 In "EastEnders", which Jim married Dot?
12 What is the name of Jack and Vera Duckworth's wayward son?
13 In "Corrie", which double-barrelled name did Les and Cilla have?
14 Which former Mrs Liam Gallagher appeared in "Emmerdale"?
15 Which Battersby sister returned to "Corrie" in 2004?
16 What is the name of the Barbara Windsor character in "EastEnders"?
17 Which soap has an underwear factory called Underworld?
18 Where was Curly's wife Raquel heading for on leaving Weatherfield?
19 Which C is the setting for "Hollyoaks"?
20 Which soap pub is famous for its Newton & Ridley beer?
21 "Home and Away" is set near which Australian city?
22 Which soap's 20th anniversary storyline was about a Ramsay Street documentary?
23 Who is the most senior of the Archer family?
24 Which is the only day of the week Radio 4's "The Archers" is broadcast in the morning?
25 Which soap is set in Erinsborough?
26 What was the name of Joan Collins's character in "Dynasty"?
27 Which soap is set in the city that hosted the 2002 Commonwealth Games?
28 Which soap is "Knot's Landing" a spin-off from?
29 Which soap is set in Borsetshire?
30 Which dish is the Rover's Return's Betty Williams famous for?

Answers | Pop: Who's Who? *(see Quiz 116)*

1 Liam Gallagher. 2 Madonna. 3 Katrina. 4 The Spice Girls. 5 Marti Pellow. 6 Avril Lavigne. 7 Frank Sinatra. 8 Richard. 9 The Bee Gees. 10 The Pussycat Dolls. 11 Elton John. 12 Tony Christie. 13 Sting. 14 Green Day. 15 Chrissie Hynde. 16 Kevin Costner. 17 Andrew Lloyd Webber. 18 Robson and Jerome. 19 Take That. 20 The Beatles. 21 "Crocodile Shoes". 22 Tina Turner. 23 Elton John. 24 Davy Jones. 25 The Darkness. 26 Queen. 27 Elvis Presley. 28 Wham! 29 Stevie Wonder. 30 Boy George.

1 Glasgow is the administrative centre of which Scottish region?
2 Which is further north, Liverpool or Leeds?
3 What before the 1996 reorganization was the only Welsh county to begin with C?
4 Which motorway would you travel on from London to Leeds?
5 How is the Welsh island Ynys Mon also known?
6 In which part of the UK is Newry?
7 How many counties have a border with Cornwall?
8 In which District are Ullswater and Bassenthwaite?
9 Which resort beginning with S lies between Whitby and Bridlington?
10 In which country is Prestwick Airport?
11 On which river does Hull lie?
12 Which city's major station is New Street?
13 In which city is Princes Street a major shopping thoroughfare?
14 On which coast of Scotland is Dundee?
15 Which motorway would you travel on from London to Cambridge?
16 London Zoo is in which Park?
17 Which motorway stretches from the outskirts of London into Wales?
18 On which island are Shanklin and Sandown?
19 Which two south-coast resorts include the name Regis?
20 Which two London Boroughs begin with E?
21 In which city is Lime Street station and the Albert Dock?
22 On which Channel Island is St Peter Port?
23 Which road leads from Trafalgar Square up to Buckingham Palace?
24 St Annes lies to the south of which major seaside resort?
25 Which is the only Scottish region beginning with F?
26 Which tunnel is a major link around the M25?
27 Which motorway would you travel on from Birmingham to Lancaster?
28 Which county lies between Norfolk and Essex?
29 In which city is Sauciehall Street?
30 Does London's Euston station serve the north, south, east or west of the country?

Answers	**Pot Luck 62** *(see Quiz 117)*

1 Good Friday. 2 12. 3 40s. 4 Paul Collingwood. 5 Monica Lewinsky. 6 Arsenal. 7 Kingsley Amis. 8 Brown. 9 Louis Braille. 10 Davy Crockett. 11 Cambodia. 12 Briers. 13 New Zealand. 14 "Over". 15 Blue. 16 Ethiopia. 17 The Beach Boys. 18 Popeye. 19 2. 20 Rose. 21 Robbie Williams. 22 Gone with the Wind. 23 Catherine. 24 Cain. 25 Sven-Goran Eriksson. 26 Al fresco. 27 "Absolutely Fabulous". 28 Kingsley. 29 90. 30 The Beatles.

1 In the 1990s which Oscar-winning movie had the word English in the title?
2 Which Welsh comedian was a member of the Goons?
3 How many boys are there in Destiny's Child?
4 Which country has the internet code .ee?
5 In which country is the city of Acapulco?
6 How many millimetres in three centimetres?
7 Who wrote the novel "Jane Eyre"?
8 The character Elsie Tanner appeared in which TV soap?
9 Who had an 80s No. 1 with "You Win Again"?
10 In which decade of the 20th century was Woody Allen born?
11 Al is the chemical symbol for which element?
12 In which TV series did the characters James, Siegfried and Tristan appear?
13 What title did the eldest son of the king of France hold?
14 Ben Gurion airport is in which country?
15 What is the surname of athlete Dame Kelly?
16 Which Tim became Britain's most expensive soccer keeper in 1993?
17 Bob Cratchit appears in which Charles Dickens novel?
18 What does the C stand for in ACAS?
19 What is the administrative centre for the county of Avon?
20 Who painted HM the Queen to mark her 80th birthday?
21 What colour appears along with white on the Polish flag?
22 Which Glenda starred in "Elizabeth R"?
23 What is 3 cubed?
24 DEAR CASH is an anagram of which indoor game?
25 What is measured in amperes?
26 What is the study of the earth's crust and rocks called?
27 What term describes instruments that produce sound when struck?
28 Which Tony had a 50s hit with "Stranger in Paradise"?
29 In which city did Woody Allen make the film "Match Point"?
30 How many sides does a trapezium have?

Answers | **Pot Luck 64** *(see Quiz 122)*

1 Avril Lavigne. 2 Logie. 3 Storm. 4 "Cracker". 5 Five. 6 "Coast". 7 Agatha Christie. 8 Bill Clinton. 9 Queen Elizabeth I. 10 "Hound Dog". 11 Caffeine. 12 Dennis the Menace. 13 Rossiter. 14 "Show". 15 Rouge. 16 Stephen Sondheim. 17 Déjà vu. 18 1,000. 19 Canada. 20 "'Allo 'Allo". 21 Tuesday. 22 Hanks. 23 Grey and red. 24 Salvation Army. 25 Fred Flintstone. 26 Eyes. 27 Police. 28 Egypt. 29 Lent. 30 Dark blue.

1 How many different coloured squares are there on a chessboard?
2 What would you buy from a Gibbons' catalogue?
3 Whose three-dimensional cube became a 70s and 80s craze?
4 If 3 is on the top side of a dice, what number is on the hidden side?
5 What does a snorkel help you do?
6 What is the art of knotting cord or string in patterns?
7 In Scrabble what is the value of the blank tile?
8 What does the musical term largo mean?
9 What fairground attraction did George Ferris construct in the 1890s?
10 Jokers apart, how many red cards are there in a standard pack?
11 What does a twitcher look for?
12 Which game features Miss Scarlet and the Reverend Green?
13 What do we call the art of paper-folding, which originated in Japan?
14 How many discs does each player have to start with in draughts?
15 What type of dancing was originally only performed by men, usually dressed in white, with bells and garlands?
16 If you practise calligraphy what do you do?
17 If you're involved in firing, throwing and glazing what do you do?
18 Which game has a board, cards and wedges?
19 In which leisure pursuit might you do a Turkey Trot or a Bunny Hug?
20 How many people can you normally fit in a go-kart?
21 What is a John Innes No. 1?
22 If you combined k and p to make cables what would your hobby be?
23 What was developed to experience the excitement of surfing on land?
24 Which exercises are designed to increase oxygen consumption and speed blood circulation?
25 What is a whist competition or tournament called?
26 A Royal Flush is the best hand you can get in which card game?
27 Which British game is known as checkers in the USA?
28 Which card game has a pegboard used for scoring?
29 Where on your body would you wear flippers?
30 Which playing card is the Black Lady?

Answers	**Living World** *(see Quiz 123)*

1 Elm. 2 Fish. 3 Constriction. 4 Eagle. 5 Two. 6 Breed of terrier. 7 Snake. 8 Below. 9 Its colour. 10 Tree. 11 Southern. 12 Beaver. 13 Vixen. 14 Its tail. 15 Caterpillar. 16 Canada. 17 Deer. 18 Fungus. 19 America. 20 Skunk. 21 Shark. 22 White. 23 Liver. 24 Red. 25 Venom. 26 Fish. 27 Two. 28 Kangaroo. 29 Swim – type of tuna fish. 30 Australia.

1 In 2003, who had released the successful album "Let Go"?
2 What was the television pioneer John Baird's middle name?
3 What was Perfect in the 2000 movie with George Clooney?
4 What word can go after "nut" and before "jack"?
5 How many members of Westlife are there?
6 What was the name of the 2005 TV series about Britain's borders with the sea?
7 Who wrote the novel "The Murder of Roger Ackroyd"?
8 Which ex-US President saw areas affected by the 2004 tsunami with George Bush Snr?
9 Whom is the US state of Virginia named after?
10 Which Elvis song has the words "you ain't never caught a rabbit"?
11 Which stimulant is found in tea and coffee?
12 Who has a dog called Gnasher?
13 Which Leonard starred in "The Rise and Fall of Reginald Perrin"?
14 What word can go before "down", "jumping" and "off"?
15 Which make-up item is the French word for red?
16 Who wrote "Send in the Clowns"?
17 Which French phrase used in English means already seen?
18 What number is represented by the Roman numeral M?
19 The airline Labrador Airways is from which country?
20 In which TV series did the character René Artois appear?
21 Which day of the week is Shrove once a year?
22 Which Tom won an Oscar for Best Actor in "Forrest Gump"?
23 What two colours of squirrel are found in Britain?
24 The "War Cry" is the magazine of which organization?
25 Whose catchphrase is "Yabba-dabba-doo!"?
26 In Cockney rhyming slang what are mince pies?
27 Who had a 70s No. 1 with "Message in a Bottle"?
28 In which country is the city of Alexandria?
29 Ash Wednesday is the first day of which period of fasting?
30 On a Monopoly board, what colour is Mayfair?

| **Answers** | **Pot Luck 63** *(see Quiz 120)* |

1 The English Patient. 2 Harry Secombe. 3 None. 4 Estonia. 5 Mexico. 6 30. 7 Charlotte Brontë. 8 "Coronation Street". 9 Bee Gees. 10 30s. 11 Aluminium. 12 "All Creatures Great and Small". 13 Dauphin. 14 Israel. 15 Holmes. 16 Tim Flowers. 17 A Christmas Carol. 18 Conciliation. 19 Bristol. 20 Rolf Harris. 21 Red. 22 Jackson. 23 27. 24 Charades. 25 Electric current. 26 Geology. 27 Percussion. 28 Bennett. 29 London. 30 Four.

1 Which tree can be Dutch, English or wych?
2 What type of creature is a stingray?
3 How does a boa kill?
4 Which bird can be bald, golden or harpy?
5 How many humps does a Bactrian camel have?
6 What sort of animal is a Dandie Dinmont?
7 What is a mamba?
8 Would a tuber grow above or below the ground?
9 What is a chameleon famous for being capable of changing?
10 What is a monkey puzzle?
11 To which hemisphere do penguins belong?
12 Which creature constructs dams and lodges?
13 What is a female fox called?
14 What does a rattlesnake rattle when it is disturbed?
15 What is the larva of a butterfly or moth called?
16 Which country were Newfoundland dogs originally from?
17 The moose or elk are species of which creature?
18 What sort of plant is a common puffball?
19 On which continent is the opossum found in its natural habitat?
20 Which American creature is renowned for its foul-smelling defence mechanism?
21 What can be great white, tiger or whale?
22 What colour is a West Highland terrier?
23 Bile is a secretion of which organ of the body?
24 What colour are the bracts of a poinsettia?
25 What is snake poison called?
26 A shoal is a group of what type of creatures?
27 How many sets of teeth do most mammals have?
28 Which is larger, the wallaby or the kangaroo?
29 Does a skipjack jump, skip or swim?
30 Where are emus found in their natural habitat?

Answers	Hobbies & Leisure 1 *(see Quiz 121)*

1 Two. 2 Stamps. 3 Rubik's. 4 4. 5 Breathe under water. 6 Macramé. 7 Nil. 8 Slowly. 9 Ferris Wheel. 10 26. 11 Birds. 12 Cluedo. 13 Origami. 14 12. 15 Morris. 16 Handwriting. 17 Pottery. 18 Trivial Pursuit. 19 Ballroom dancing. 20 One. 21 Garden compost. 22 Knitting. 23 Skateboard. 24 Aerobics. 25 Whist drive. 26 Poker. 27 Draughts. 28 Cribbage. 29 Feet. 30 Queen of Spades.

1 In which month is Epiphany?
2 Who went with Christopher Robin to Buckingham Palace?
3 In which TV series did Mrs Slocombe and Mr Humphries first appear?
4 What word can go after "sand" and before "account"?
5 In which country is the city of Amritsar?
6 Which Amateur Association has the abbreviation AAA?
7 Who wrote the novel "Rebecca"?
8 The characters Jason and Sable appeared in which TV soap?
9 Moving clockwise on a dartboard what number is next to 1?
10 In which age group was Cher when she hit No. 1 with "Believe"?
11 What is the name of Del Trotter's local?
12 How many yards in a chain?
13 The zodiac sign Pisces covers which two calendar months?
14 Steve Backley is associated with which branch of athletics?
15 Which puzzle is made up of nine squares of nine squares and the digits one to nine?
16 Who was the first German to be Football Writers' Player of the Year?
17 In the Bible, which Book immediately follows Genesis?
18 What is 80 per cent of 400?
19 Frigophobia is the fear of what?
20 In the 80s, who had a No. 1 with "Eternal Flame"?
21 Charles de Gaulle airport is in which country?
22 Which Andrew starred in "Fawlty Towers"?
23 What device goes across a guitar fretboard to raise the pitch?
24 In printing, uppercase are what type of letters?
25 Beta is the second letter of which alphabet?
26 In which game would you find a night watchman?
27 Which Italian dictator was the founder of Fascism?
28 Mangetout and sugar snaps are types of what?
29 Which sporting event did Kylie Minogue close in 2000?
30 In song, in which Row was Mother Kelly's doorstep?

Answers | Pot Luck 66 (see Quiz 126)

1 Grandma. 2 Sepia. 3 Big Brother. 4 "Cup". 5 The WI. 6 Spurs. 7 Charles Kingsley. 8 Brown. 9 Victory in Europe. 10 Choux. 11 Doo-Dah Band. 12 Lyndhurst. 13 Belgium. 14 180. 15 Whitney Houston. 16 Geoff Hamilton. 17 Monday. 18 Pacino. 19 Countess. 20 "House". 21 Bell. 22 Jamboree. 23 20th. 24 Cricket. 25 Gold. 26 Familiarity. 27 Faux pas. 28 Barbara. 29 3. 30 Confederation.

1 At which club did Niall Quinn and Kevin Phillips form a strike force?
2 Who scored England's goal against Brazil in the 2002 World Cup?
3 Gilberto Silva won the World Cup with which country?
4 Who was Arsenal's regular keeper in the 1970–71 double season?
5 Which player was nicknamed "The Divine Ponytail"?
6 Which was the first English club to instal an artificial pitch?
7 Who was Blackburn's benefactor of the 90s?
8 Robins, Valiants and Addicks are all nicknames of which team?
9 Who took Wigan into the Premiership for the first time?
10 What colour are Colombian international shirts?
11 At which Premiership club did Dunn and Duff play in the same side?
12 David James played in goal for which London club?
13 At which club did Steve Bruce take over from Trevor Francis?
14 Keeper Chris Woods set a British record for clean sheets at which club?
15 Who became the first female football club managing director?
16 Who was manager when Ipswich first won the FA Cup?
17 Stan Collymore won his first England cap while at which club?
18 Which former Manchester United star also turned out for Fulham and Hibs?
19 Peter Schmeichel plays for which country?
20 What was Gazza's first London club?
21 Which Marco was three times European Footballer of the Year?
22 Tony Parkes was caretaker manager of which Premiership club?
23 At which Midland club did England striker Darius Vassell begin his career?
24 What was Bolton's home ground for most of the 20th century?
25 Vinny Jones has played for which country?
26 At which club did Alan Shearer start his league career?
27 Who was Celtic's boss when they first won the European Cup?
28 Which Italian side did Gazza play for?
29 Which club did Alex Ferguson leave to go to Manchester United?
30 Which Spurs keeper scored in a 60s Charity Shield game?

Answers	**50s Films** *(see Quiz 127)*

1 The Ten Commandments. 2 Charlton Heston. 3 Dog. 4 Peter Pan. 5 Ben Hur. 6 David Niven. 7 Walt Disney. 8 World War II. 9 Burton. 10 The Bridge on the River Kwai. 11 Elvis Presley. 12 Seatbelts. 13 Zanuck. 14 Chevalier. 15 Frank Sinatra. 16 Deborah Kerr. 17 Marlon Brando. 18 Rebel without a Cause. 19 Brigitte Bardot. 20 Gene Kelly. 21 Circus. 22 Lavender Hill. 23 Grace (Kelly). 24 Vertigo. 25 Humphrey Bogart. 26 Dirk Bogarde. 27 Annie Get Your Gun. 28 Doris Day. 29 Carousel. 30 None.

1 St Winifred's School Choir sang about which relative?
2 Which colour describes Victorian photographs?
3 Craig Phillips charted after winning on which Big TV show?
4 What word can go after "egg" and before "board"?
5 The movie "Calendar Girls" was about members of which organization?
6 In the 90s, which London club had the "Famous Five" strike force?
7 Who wrote the novel "The Water Babies"?
8 What colour is a female blackbird?
9 What does VE stand for in VE Day?
10 What type of pastry is used to make profiteroles?
11 In the group's name, what comes after Bonzo Dog?
12 Which Nicholas starred in "Goodnight Sweetheart"?
13 In which country is the city of Antwerp?
14 How many degrees in a semicircle?
15 In the 80s, who had a No. 1 with "One Moment in Time"?
16 Which BBC TV gardener died suddenly of a heart attack in 1996?
17 If Boxing Day is a Friday what day is December 1?
18 Which Al won an Oscar for Best Actor in "Scent of a Woman"?
19 What is the female equivalent of the rank of Earl?
20 What word can follow "light", "green" and "slaughter"?
21 Which former newsreader Martin Bell replaced Neil Hamilton as an MP?
22 What is a scout rally called?
23 Puccini died in which century?
24 Which sport includes the Frizzell County Championship?
25 Au is the chemical symbol for which element?
26 What, according to proverb, breeds contempt?
27 Which French phrase used in English means a false step or mistake?
28 What is Frank Sinatra's widow's first name?
29 What is the square root of 9?
30 What does the C stand for in the business organization the CBI?

Answers | **Pot Luck 65** *(see Quiz 124)*

1 January. 2 Alice. 3 "Are You Being Served". 4 "Bank". 5 India. 6 Athletics. 7 Daphne du Maurier. 8 "The Colbys". 9 18. 10 50s. 11 The Nag's Head. 12 22. 13 February, March. 14 Javelin. 15 Sudoku. 16 Jurgen Klinsmann. 17 Exodus. 18 320. 19 Being cold. 20 The Bangles. 21 France. 22 Sachs. 23 Capo. 24 Capitals. 25 Greek. 26 Cricket. 27 Mussolini. 28 Peas. 29 Olympic Games. 30 Paradise.

1 Which film told of Moses leading the Israelites to the Promised Land?
2 Who starred as Moses in the film?
3 What or who is Lady in "Lady and the Tramp"?
4 Which film of J. M. Barrie's book was described as "a painful travesty"?
5 Which 11-Oscar-winning film of 1959 cost four million dollars?
6 Who was the star of "Around the World in Eighty Days"?
7 Which film company released "Sleeping Beauty"?
8 The action of "South Pacific" takes place during which war?
9 Which Welsh actor Richard starred in "The Robe"?
10 Which 1957 film had the whistled "Colonel Bogey" as its theme?
11 Who played the pop star in "Jailhouse Rock"?
12 What completes the line from "All About Eve", "Fasten your _____, it's going to be a bumpy night"?
13 What was the surname of film the director Darryl F?
14 Which Maurice starred in "Gigi"?
15 Which US singer had an acting role in "From Here to Eternity"?
16 Which actress starred in "From Here to Eternity" and "The King and I"?
17 Who played the starring role of Terry in "On the Waterfront"?
18 Which film catapulted James Dean to stardom?
19 Which French star appeared in "And God Created Woman" set in St Tropez?
20 Which dancer/singer was the "American in Paris"?
21 Which entertainment features in "The Greatest Show on Earth"?
22 Which Ealing comedy Mob organized a bullion robbery?
23 Which future Princess starred in Hitchcock's "Rear Window"?
24 Which Hitchcock film features a detective who was afraid of heights?
25 Who played the boozy Charlie Allnut in "The African Queen"?
26 Which British actor was Simon Sparrow in the Doctor films?
27 Which musical told of the life of Annie Oakley?
28 Which singer/actress starred opposite Rock Hudson in "Pillow Talk"?
29 Which film featured "You'll Never Walk Alone"?
30 How many Oscars did "High Society" win?

Answers	UK Football *(see Quiz 125)*

1 Sunderland. 2 Michael Owen. 3 Brazil. 4 Bob Wilson. 5 Roberto Baggio. 6 QPR. 7 Jack Walker. 8 Charlton. 9 Paul Jewell. 10 Yellow. 11 Blackburn Rovers. 12 West Ham. 13 Birmingham. 14 Rangers. 15 Karen Brady. 16 Bobby Robson. 17 Nottingham Forest. 18 George Best. 19 Denmark. 20 Spurs. 21 Van Basten. 22 Blackburn. 23 Aston Villa. 24 Burnden Park. 25 Wales. 26 Southampton. 27 Jock Stein. 28 Lazio. 29 Aberdeen. 30 Pat Jennings.

1 Which motor racing star became Sir Jackie in the new millennium?
2 Which two colours are most frequently confused in colour blindness?
3 Which teen queen charted with "Born to Make You Happy"?
4 Who played Muhammad Ali in the movie Ali?
5 In the 90s, who had a No. 1 with "Always on My Mind"?
6 Moving anticlockwise on a dartboard, what number is next to 4?
7 Who wrote the novel "Lady Chatterley's Lover"?
8 Dennis Andries is associated with which sport?
9 In which country is the city of Bulawayo?
10 In which TV series did Sharon, Tracey and Dorian appear?
11 How many pints in a gallon?
12 What was the name of Dick Turpin's horse?
13 In which decade did Radio 1 start?
14 Wilkins Micawber appears in which Charles Dickens novel?
15 How is Allen Konigsberg better known?
16 Which girl band had a hit single with "Independent Woman"?
17 Which group of workers does ABTA represent?
18 Which actor died during the making of the Oscar-winning "Gladiator"?
19 What can be cardinal or ordinal?
20 In "Cinderella", what was the pumpkin turned in to?
21 What is the administrative centre for the county of Cornwall?
22 Which Henry starred in "Happy Days"?
23 The airline Luxair is from which country?
24 How does 7.20 p.m. appear on a 24-hour clock?
25 Which Frank created Billy Bunter?
26 In pre-decimal money how many farthings were in a penny?
27 The film "The Great Rock 'n' Roll Swindle" was about which group?
28 Whose catchphrase is "It's the way I tell 'em!"?
29 Which military tune is sounded at the start of the day?
30 How many sides has a rhombus?

Answers | **Pop: The 60s** *(see Quiz 130)*

1 The Beach Boys. 2 Monkees. 3 Elvis Presley. 4 Paperback Writer. 5 The Bee Gees.
6 The Kinks. 7 Supremes. 8 The Hollies. 9 Her feet. 10 Helen Shapiro. 11 Yes. 12
Springfield. 13 Matchstick. 14 Jim Reeves. 15 The Tremeloes. 16 Liverpool. 17 Frank
Ifield. 18 Dozy. 19 Proby. 20 San Francisco. 21 Dave Clark. 22 Bob Dylan. 23
Faithfull. 24 US. 25 Martin. 26 Move. 27 Herman. 28 Lonnie Donegan. 29 John
Lennon. 30 The Twist.

1 How many gold medals did Kelly Holmes win in Athens?
2 Where is the venue for the Olympics between the Athens and London Games?
3 Which Lord and former athlete led the UK bid for the 2012 Olympics?
4 Where were the Olympics when a kookaburra and a platypus were mascots?
5 What is Lord Coe's first name?
6 How often are the summer Olympics held?
7 What is the title of the Steven Spielberg movie about the 1972 Munich Olympics?
8 Which serving British PM was present at the opening of the Athens Olympics?
9 Which Matthew won a fourth consecutive gold medal for rowing in Athens?
10 In Athens, Amir Khan was the sole British representative in which sport?
11 What shape are the five symbols on the Olympic flag?
12 Which boxing legend lit the Olympic torch in Atlanta in 1996, despite his poor health?
13 Amir Khan won which colour medal in 2004?
14 Which future Dame carried the flag at the closing ceremony in Athens?
15 Which host for the 2008 Olympics came second in the 2004 medals table?
16 What colour is the background of the Olympic flag?
17 When the winners' flags are raised at the award ceremony, whose flag is in the middle?
18 In which London Square were the main celebrations after the UK's winning 2012 bid?
19 Which serving US President opened the Winter Olympics in the US in 2002?
20 How many Olympic gold medals did Colin Jackson win?
21 Kelly Holmes was once in which branch of the armed services?
22 Steve Backley took silver in the 1996 and 2000 in which field sport?
23 Sonia O'Sullivan took part in the Olympics representing which country?
24 Which Paula collapsed in Athens and returned home without a medal?
25 Which gold medallists were coaches on TV's pro/celeb "Dancing on Ice"?
26 Justine Henin Hardenne won tennis gold for which country in 2004?
27 For which racket sport did Emms & Robertson win silver in Athens?
28 How many men were in the boat when Matthew Pinsent won his fourth gold?
29 In which country were the Winter Olympics at Nagano held?
30 Did 102, 202 or 302 countries compete in the Athens Olympics?

Answers	**Pot Luck 68** *(see Quiz 131)*

1 Spanish. 2 Hair loss. 3 Tennis. 4 "Corporal". 5 Blonde. 6 German. 7 John Le Carré. 8 Coniston. 9 Apples. 10 Ali G. 11 Achilles. 12 Berry. 13 Ringo. 14 "Dutch". 15 Sebastian. 16 Plane crash. 17 St Paul's. 18 Bob Holness. 19 Banbury Cross. 20 Indian. 21 Red. 22 Passion. 23 Mars. 24 A la carte. 25 Pulp. 26 Elton John. 27 Hopkins. 28 Apex. 29 Morocco. 30 Postman Pat.

1 Who went "Surfin' USA"?
2 Micky Dolenz found fame in which simian-sounding group?
3 Who was Crying in the Chapel?
4 Which Beatles hit starts "Dear Sir or Madam, will you read my book"?
5 Brothers Barry, Maurice and Robin formed which group?
6 Who mocked the clothes conscious with "Dedicated Follower of Fashion"?
7 Diana Ross fronted which Tamla group?
8 Which group loved Jennifer Eccles?
9 Which part of her body did Sandie Shaw bare on stage?
10 Who sang "Don't Treat Me Like a Child" while still at school?
11 Were the Everley brothers actually brothers?
12 Which Dusty was Going Back?
13 Status Quo first charted with Pictures of what type of Men?
14 Which country-style singer was known as Gentleman Jim?
15 Who backed Brian Poole?
16 Which city did the Searchers come from?
17 Which Australian yodelled "I Remember You"?
18 Who completed the line-up with Dave Dee, Beaky, Mick and Tich?
19 Which trouser-splitting singer had the initials PJ?
20 Which city did the Flowerpot Men want to go to?
21 Whose Five were in Bits and Pieces?
22 Critics said Donovan was a British copy of which US performer?
23 Which Marianne was linked with Mick Jagger?
24 Which country did Roy Orbison come from?
25 Which George produced the Beatles' records?
26 Which group recorded "Flowers in the Rain"?
27 Who was backed by Hermits?
28 Who managed to get to No. 1 with a song about a dustman?
29 Which John wanted to Give Peace a Chance at the end of the 60s?
30 Which dance was Chubby Checker doing at the start of the 60s?

Answers	**Pot Luck 67** (see Quiz 128)

1 Stewart. 2 Red and green. 3 Britney Spears. 4 Will Smith. 5 Pet Shop Boys. 6 18.
7 D. H. Lawrence. 8 Boxing. 9 Zimbabwe. 10 "Birds of a Feather". 11 Eight. 12
Black Bess. 13 1960s. 14 David Copperfield. 15 Woody Allen. 16 Destiny's Child. 17
Travel agents. 18 Oliver Reed. 19 Numbers. 20 A coach. 21 Truro. 22 Winkler. 23
Luxembourg. 24 19.20. 25 Richards. 26 Four. 27 The Sex Pistols. 28 Frank Carson.
29 Reveille. 30 Four.

1 What nationality was Herb Alpert's Flea?
2 What is alopecia?
3 Sue Barker played which sport?
4 What word can go after "lance" and before "punishment"?
5 What colour is Lily Savage's hair?
6 What is the nationality of the Pope who succeeded Pope John Paul II?
7 Who wrote the novel "Tinker, Tailor, Soldier, Spy"?
8 On which lake was Donald Campbell killed?
9 Beauty of Bath and Discovery are types of what?
10 Which Ali is the alter ego of Sacha Baron Cohen?
11 Who died after being wounded in the heel by an arrow from Paris?
12 Which Nick starred in "Heartbeat"?
13 Which of the Beatles was the shortest?
14 What word can go before "auction", "courage" and "uncle"?
15 Which Coe led the efforts to get the 2008 Olympics in London?
16 The band leader Glenn Miller died in what type of tragedy?
17 In which British cathedral is the Whispering Gallery?
18 Who was the first presenter of "Blockbusters"?
19 In rhyme, where do you go to see a fine lady on a white horse?
20 Warm weather in autumn is described as what type of summer?
21 On a Monopoly board, what colour is Trafalgar Square?
22 What type of play is performed at Oberammergau?
23 In the song "Aquarius" which planet does Jupiter align with?
24 Which French phrase used in English means each dish individually priced?
25 Which band's singles include "Common People" and "Disco 2000"?
26 In the 90s, who had a No. 1 with "Sacrifice"?
27 Which Anthony won an Oscar for Best Actor in "The Silence of the Lambs"?
28 What term describes the highest point of a triangle?
29 In which country is the city of Casablanca?
30 Who loads his van "Early in the morning, Just as day is dawning"?

Answers	**The Olympics** *(see Quiz 129)*

1 Two. 2 Beijing. 3 Lord Coe. 4 Australia. 5 Sebastian. 6 Every four years. 7 Munich. 8 Tony Blair. 9 Pinsent. 10 Boxing. 11 Rings/Circles. 12 Muhammad Ali. 13 Silver. 14 Kelly Holmes. 15 China. 16 White. 17 Gold medallist's. 18 Trafalgar Square. 19 George W. Bush. 20 None. 21 Army. 22 Javelin. 23 Ireland. 24 Radcliffe. 25 Torvill & Dean. 26 Belgium. 27 Badminton. 28 Four. 29 Japan. 30 202.

1 What colour is crème de menthe?
2 Which county does Wensleydale cheese traditionally come from?
3 What type of vegetable is a Maris Piper?
4 What are the two main ingredients of a vinaigrette dressing?
5 What is the fruit flavour of Cointreau?
6 What type of food is coley?
7 What is basmati?
8 Which food accompaniment is Dijon famous for?
9 What is a small segment of garlic called?
10 What is the main ingredient of a traditional fondue?
11 What type of food is pitta?
12 Which shellfish are in Moules Marinière?
13 What is the top layer of a Queen of Puddings made from?
14 What type of meat is brisket?
15 What colour is paprika?
16 What is the chief vegetable ingredient of coleslaw?
17 At which stage of a meal would you have an hors d'oeuvre?
18 What type of drink is Darjeeling?
19 If a coffee was drunk au lait, what would it have added to it?
20 What is a tortilla?
21 What is a vol-au-vent made from?
22 Is a schnitzel sweet or savoury?
23 What colour is the flesh of an avocado?
24 Which red jelly is a traditional accompaniment to lamb?
25 What type of drink is Perrier?
26 What is mulligatawny?
27 What is filo?
28 What sort of fish is a kipper?
29 If a drink was served "on the rocks" what would it have in the glass?
30 What colour is the sauce served over a prawn cocktail?

Answers	The Royals (see Quiz 134)

1 1980s. 2 Fifty. 3 Kent. 4 Beatrice. 5 Peter. 6 None. 7 Photographer. 8 Edward (VIII). 9 Simpson. 10 Victoria. 11 Kent. 12 Rhys-Jones. 13 Sandringham. 14 Eton. 15 Prince Harry. 16 Princess Margaret. 17 George (VI). 18 Princess Anne. 19 The Queen and Prince Philip. 20 Diana, Princess of Wales. 21 Prince Philip. 22 St Paul's. 23 1950s. 24 Two. 25 Prince Charles. 26 96th. 27 Princess Anne. 28 Prince Edward. 29 Alexandra. 30 Louis.

1 In the 90s, who had a No. 1 with "Pray"?
2 In the Bible, which Book immediately follows Matthew?
3 What was the day job of the notorious mass murderer Harold Shipman?
4 What word can go after "pad" and before "smith"?
5 In which country is the city of Crakow (or Kraków)?
6 In which TV series did the character Margaret Meldrew appear?
7 What was the surname of the sisters in All Saints?
8 In which month is St David's Day?
9 "Bush bush!" are the last words of which song?
10 What colour is the wax covering Edam cheese?
11 How did Marc Bolan die?
12 At the rate of 17·5 per cent, what VAT would be added to a £100 item?
13 Thermophobia is the fear of what?
14 Trevor Bailey is associated with which sport?
15 How is John Barry Prendergast better known?
16 In the UK's first million-pound soccer deal, which club bought Trevor Francis?
17 In South Africa what does ANC stand for?
18 What part of the body did Adam not have that all other men do?
19 In which decade did Channel 4 start?
20 C is the chemical symbol for which element?
21 Which UK car manufacturer produced the Imp?
22 Which Su starred in "Hi-De-Hi"?
23 Which Mr Campbell was once Tony Blair's press secretary?
24 RED ANGER is an anagram of which job?
25 How many ounces in a pound?
26 Who produced Ike and Tina Turner's "River Deep, Mountain High"?
27 Which country was Nerys Hughes born in?
28 Moving clockwise on a dartboard what number is next to 5?
29 Who is the oldest Gallagher brother?
30 What is a Pontefract cake made of?

1 Conservative. 2 Campbell. 3 George VI. 4 Agatha Christie. 5 Suez. 6 Miss World.
7 Graham. 8 Winston Churchill. 9 Richards. 10 Eden. 11 Golding. 12 Car crash. 13
Eva Péron (Evita). 14 Reaching Everest's summit. 15 X certificate. 16 Marciano. 17
Dan Dare. 18 Australia. 19 Cuba. 20 Diamonds. 21 Smog. 22 London. 23 Anne
Frank. 24 "The Goon Show". 25 Hutton. 26 Liberace. 27 Munich. 28 Gaitskell. 29
Kelly. 30 Wright.

1 In which decade did Prince Charles marry Lady Diana Spencer?
2 In 2002 the Queen celebrated how many years as monarch?
3 Prince Michael's title is of which county?
4 Who is the elder of Prince Andrew's daughters, Beatrice or Eugenie?
5 What is Princess Anne's son's first name?
6 Which royal title do Princess Anne's children have?
7 What was the occupation of the late Princess Margaret's first husband?
8 What was the name of the king who abdicated in 1936?
9 What was the surname of the woman he married a year later?
10 What was the name of the first monarch of the 20th century?
11 Which Duchess comforted a weeping Jana Novotna at Wimbledon?
12 What was the maiden name of Sophie, Countess of Wessex?
13 What is the Queen's residence in Norfolk called?
14 Which school did Prince William attend in his teens?
15 Who is next in line to the throne after Prince William?
16 With which royal did Captain Peter Townsend have a romance?
17 What was the name of the king immediately before Elizabeth II?
18 Which royal has a daughter called Zara?
19 Which royal couple organized a large golden-wedding anniversary celebration in 1997?
20 Which royal highlighted the problems of landmines in Angola?
21 Who had a father called Prince Andrew and has a son called Prince Andrew?
22 In which cathedral did Charles and Diana marry?
23 In which decade did Elizabeth II come to the throne?
24 How many children did she have when she became Queen?
25 Whose country home is at Highgrove?
26 Which birthday did the Queen Mother celebrate in 1996?
27 Rear Admiral Timothy Laurence is married to which of the Queen's children?
28 Which of the Queen's children is Earl of Wessex?
29 Which Princess is married to Angus Ogilvy?
30 What was Lord Mountbatten's first name?

Answers	**Food & Drink 1** *(see Quiz 132)*

1 Green. **2** Yorkshire. **3** Potato. **4** Oil, vinegar. **5** Orange. **6** Fish. **7** Rice. **8** Mustard. **9** Clove. **10** Cheese. **11** Bread. **12** Mussels. **13** Meringue. **14** Beef. **15** Red. **16** Cabbage. **17** Beginning. **18** Tea. **19** Milk. **20** Pancake. **21** Pastry. **22** Savoury. **23** Green. **24** Redcurrant. **25** Mineral water. **26** Soup. **27** Pastry. **28** Herring. **29** Ice cubes. **30** Pink.

1 In 1959, which party was elected for the third time in a row in Britain?
2 Which Donald set a world water speed record in the Lake District?
3 Which monarch died at Sandringham in 1952?
4 "The Mousetrap" opened its London stage run, but who wrote it?
5 Colonel Nasser nationalized which canal?
6 The first of which contest was won by a woman from Sweden in 1951?
7 Which American evangelist Billy led a London crusade?
8 Which 77-year-old was returned as British Prime Minister?
9 Which Sir Gordon won the Derby for the first time?
10 Which Anthony became British Prime Minister in the 50s?
11 "Lord of the Flies" was written by which author William?
12 How did James Dean die?
13 Who died in the 50s and was played on film by Madonna in the 90s?
14 What was the peak of Edmund Hilary's achievements in 1953?
15 Which film classification was introduced to show films were unsuitable for the under 16s?
16 Which Rocky retired undefeated as a professional boxer?
17 Which character in children's comics was the "Pilot of the Future"?
18 Robert Menzies was PM of which country throughout the 50s?
19 Fidel Castro seized power in which country?
20 What, according to Marilyn Monroe, were a girl's best friend?
21 What was a London pea-souper?
22 The 1951 Festival of Britain was centred on which city?
23 The diary of which young girl hiding from the Germans was published?
24 Which radio show featured Bluebottle and Eccles?
25 Which Len captained England as they won the Ashes?
26 Which entertainer said, "I cried all the way to the bank"?
27 Manchester United's Bobby Charlton survived a plane crash in which city?
28 Which Hugh became leader of the Labour Party?
29 Which Grace married Prince Rainier of Monaco?
30 Which Billy became the first English soccer player to win 100 caps?

| **Answers** | **Pot Luck 69** *(see Quiz 133)* |

1 Take That. 2 Mark. 3 Doctor. 4 "Lock". 5 Poland. 6 "One Foot in the Grave". 7 Appleton. 8 March. 9 "Down at the Old Bull and Bush". 10 Red. 11 Involved in a car crash. 12 £17.50. 13 Heat. 14 Cricket. 15 John Barry. 16 Nottingham Forest. 17 African National Congress. 18 Navel. 19 1980s. 20 Carbon. 21 Hillman. 22 Pollard. 23 Alistair. 24 Gardener. 25 16. 26 Phil Spector. 27 Wales. 28 20. 29 Noel. 30 Liquorice.

1 How many zeros in a million written in digits?
2 Which TV series featured the characters Raquel and Uncle Albert?
3 Packham's Triumph and Conference are types of what?
4 What word can go after "bottle" and before "manager"?
5 How is George Ivan Morrison better known?
6 Which footballing Jack was nicknamed the Giraffe?
7 Who wrote the novel "Rumpole of the Bailey"?
8 What is East Pakistan now called?
9 On which hill did Fats Domino find his thrill?
10 In which decade of the 20th century was Ian Botham born?
11 In which country is the city of Durban?
12 Which band's singles include "2 Become 1" and "Too Much"?
13 What note is written in the space above the bottom line of the treble clef?
14 What word can go before "brother", "orange" and "thirsty"?
15 In which country was the 2005 G8 summit held?
16 Which is greater, 2/3 or 1/2?
17 The character Sheila Grant appeared in which TV soap?
18 Who played George in the TV family drama "All About George"?
19 Which French phrase used in English means have a good journey?
20 In 1974 parts of Durham and Yorkshire made which new county?
21 Bob Woolmer played cricket for which country?
22 Whose Best of 1990s album was "Cross Road"?
23 Which British film won nine Oscars in 1997?
24 Which planet in our solar system has the fewest letters in its name?
25 Which Daniel won an Oscar for Best Actor in "My Left Foot"?
26 What is the square root of 16?
27 In which activity do you purl and cast off?
28 In the Bible, who was paid 30 pieces of silver?
29 In politics, which Jack replaced Robin Cook as Foreign Secretary?
30 In the 60s, who had a No. 1 with "House of the Rising Sun"?

Answers	**Pot Luck 71** *(see Quiz 138)*

1 Glenda Jackson. 2 Sydney. 3 40s. 4 April and May. 5 Second book of Samuel.
6 Blur. 7 Robert Louis Stevenson. 8 "Glove". 9 Smoking and Health. 10 "Prime Suspect". 11 700. 12 Madonna. 13 "Neighbours". 14 Morocco. 15 Southampton.
16 Gardener. 17 Light blue. 18 Lotus. 19 St Stephen's. 20 Buffalo Bills. 21 Bedford.
22 Hayes. 23 Isosceles. 24 The Doors. 25 Uganda. 26 Sheffield. 27 1990s. 28 3.
29 Tom Hanks. 30 Yellow.

1 What name is given to a small, portable computer?
2 COBOL is common business-orientated what?
3 A molecule of water contains how many atoms of oxygen?
4 The study of fluids moving in pipes is known as what?
5 What is the process by which plants make food using light?
6 In a three-pronged plug what is the colour of the live wire?
7 Which small portable tape players were introduced by Sony?
8 Frank Whittle first produced what type of engine?
9 What is the chemical symbol for lead?
10 What do the initials LCD stand for?
11 Gouache is a type of what?
12 In the 1930s the Biro brothers produced the first low-cost what?
13 What device produces the air/petrol mix used in internal combustion engines?
14 Which Alfred invented dynamite and gelignite?
15 Sellafield is in which county in England?
16 What name is given to a screen picture that represents a standard computer function?
17 Which vehicle did J. C. Bamford give his name to?
18 What fuel is used by a Bunsen burner?
19 Which Michael invented the dynamo and the transformer?
20 What sort of pressure does a barometer measure?
21 In which decade did colour programmes first go out on British TV?
22 Which Chicago tower built in the 70s became the world's tallest building?
23 Clarence Birdseye developed processes for doing what to food?
24 Where in the Ukraine did a nuclear reactor explode in 1986?
25 Coal is composed of which element?
26 Watt, a unit of power, is named after which scientist?
27 In computing, WYSIWYG stands for "what you see is ..." what?
28 Which Bill founded Microsoft?
29 Which Sir Francis gave his name to a scale of wind force?
30 What does a Geiger counter measure?

Answers	**Movies: Superstars** *(see Quiz 139)*

1 Marlon Brando. 2 Anthony Hopkins. 3 Harrison Ford. 4 Nicholson. 5 Kate Winslet. 6 Caine. 7 Lemmon. 8 Demi Moore. 9 Hepburn. 10 Barbra Streisand. 11 Beatty. 12 Newman. 13 Australia. 14 Tom Hanks. 15 Meryl Streep. 16 80s. 17 Scotland. 18 Pacino. 19 Tom Cruise. 20 Purple. 21 Nolte. 22 Julia Roberts. 23 Clint Eastwood. 24 Dustin Hoffman. 25 Elizabeth Taylor. 26 Costner. 27 Shrek. 28 Jodie Foster. 29 Redford. 30 Pfeiffer.

1 In the 70s, which future MP had a shaved head to play a Tudor monarch?
2 In which city were the 2000 Olympics held?
3 In which decade of the 20th century was Cliff Richard born?
4 The zodiac sign Taurus covers which two calendar months?
5 In the Bible, which book immediately follows the first book of Samuel?
6 Which Brit pop band were formed in Colchester?
7 Who wrote the novel "Kidnapped"?
8 What word can go after "boxing" and before "puppet"?
9 The campaign ASH stands for Action on what?
10 In which TV series did Superintendent Jane Tennison appear?
11 How many centimetres in seven metres?
12 In the 80s, who had a No. 1 with "Who's That Girl"?
13 The character Scott Robinson appeared in which TV soap?
14 In which country is the city of Fez?
15 Theo Walcott joined Arsenal from which club?
16 On TV, Chris Beardshaw was known as the Flying what?
17 On a Monopoly board, what colour is the Angel, Islington?
18 Which UK car manufacturer produced the Elan?
19 Which saint's day follows Christmas Day?
20 In the 1990s, which team were Super Bowl runners-up four years in a row?
21 What is the administrative centre for the county of Bedfordshire?
22 Which Melvyn starred in "It ain't Half Hot, Mum"?
23 What term describes a triangle with two equal sides?
24 Who originally recorded "Light My Fire"?
25 Entebbe airport is in which country?
26 Which rugby league team are the Eagles?
27 In which decade did the writer Laurie Lee die?
28 Moving anticlockwise on a dartboard what number is next to 19?
29 Which Tom played the FBI agent in Spielberg's "Catch Me If You Can"?
30 What colour is quartz citrine?

Answers | Pot Luck 70 *(see Quiz 136)*

1 Six. 2 "Only Fools and Horses". 3 Pears. 4 "Bank". 5 Van Morrison. 6 Charlton.
7 John Mortimer. 8 Bangladesh. 9 Blueberry. 10 50s. 11 South Africa. 12 Spice
Girls. 13 F. 14 "Blood". 15 Scotland. 16 2/3. 17 "Brookside". 18 Rik Mayall.
19 Bon voyage. 20 Cleveland. 21 England. 22 Bon Jovi. 23 The English Patient.
24 Mars. 25 Day-Lewis. 26 4. 27 Knitting. 28 Judas Iscariot. 29 Straw. 30 The
Animals.

1 Who played the head of the Corleone family in "The Godfather"?
2 Which Welsh actor starred opposite Debra Winger in "Shadowlands"?
3 Who played Han Solo in "Star Wars"?
4 Which Jack starred with Shirley Maclaine in "Terms of Endearment"?
5 Which British actress has starred in "Titanic", "Enigma" and "Finding Neverland"?
6 Which British Michael won an Oscar for "Hannah and Her Sisters"?
7 Which Jack's films vary from "Some Like It Hot" to "The Odd Couple"?
8 Which Mrs Bruce Willis starred in "Ghost"?
9 Which Katharine has received a record 12 Oscar nominations?
10 Who starred in and wrote the song "Evergreen" for "A Star is Born"?
11 Which Warren starred in "Dick Tracy" and "Bugsy Malone"?
12 Which Paul was in "The Sting" and "The Color of Money"?
13 Although born in the US, where was Mel Gibson brought up?
14 Who won Oscars for "Philadelphia" in '93 and "Forrest Gump" in '94?
15 Who was the female Kramer in "Kramer v Kramer"?
16 In which decade did Sylvester Stallone first play Rambo?
17 Which country was Sean Connery born in?
18 Which Al won an Oscar for his role in "Scent of a Woman"?
19 Who was in "Rain Man" and was one of Four Good Men?
20 What "Color" is in the title of Whoopi Goldberg's first major film?
21 Which Nick starred in "The Prince of Tides"?
22 Which Julia won an Oscar for her portrayal of Erin Brokovich?
23 Who starred in "Every Which Way but Loose" and "The Outlaw Josey Wales"?
24 Which superstar played the title role in "Hook"?
25 Who married her seventh husband in Michael Jackson's garden?
26 Which Kevin played the President in "JFK"?
27 Mike Myers is the voice of which green ogre?
28 Who was in "Bugsy Malone" and "Taxi Driver" as a child and went on to "The Accused"?
29 Which Robert starred with Dustin Hoffman in "All the President's Men"?
30 Which Michelle played Catwoman in "Batman Returns"?

1 Which TV show has an anagram puzzle called the Conundrum?
2 Who were the first team to win the FA Premiership?
3 In which decade of the 20th century was Elton John born?
4 In which country is the city of Kathmandu?
5 In which TV programme did Florence and Zebedee appear?
6 Ca is the chemical symbol for which element?
7 Who wrote the novel "Dracula"?
8 What is 1/3 as a percentage to two decimal places?
9 The character Len Fairclough appeared in which TV soap?
10 Which song features "the girl with kaleidoscope eyes"?
11 Which fruit do Macintosh computers use as a logo?
12 Which man won Wimbledon and the US Open in 2005?
13 The late John Diamond was married to which cookery expert?
14 What word can go before "thorn", "sand" and "silver"?
15 Miss Havisham appears in which Charles Dickens novel?
16 Which instrument was Nat King Cole famous for playing?
17 Who won an Oscar for Best Actor in "Rain Man" in 1989?
18 Who sang "On the Good Ship Lollipop"?
19 Which present-day country do we associate with the Magyars?
20 Which song from "Bridget Jones's Diary" gave Geri Halliwell a 2001 hit?
21 Chris Patten was the last British Governor of where?
22 What make of car was the 1906 Silver Ghost?
23 In which month is St Swithin's Day?
24 What word can go after "slip" and before "rage"?
25 How is the actor Michel Shalhoub better known?
26 What colour was Gazza's hair during Euro 96?
27 In the 70s, who had a No. 1 with "We Don't Talk Anymore"?
28 The Kalahari desert is in which continent?
29 Which magician hosted "Every Second Counts"?
30 Which duke is associated with Arundel Castle?

Answers	Pot Luck 73 (see Quiz 142)

1 Feet. 2 "EastEnders". 3 Ahead. 4 "First". 5 Wide receiver. 6 Matt Busby. 7 J.R.R. Tolkein. 8 Rugby (Union). 9 Commander. 10 First decade. 11 Lord's. 12 72. 13 Yvon Petra. 14 1996. 15 March. 16 Hamlet. 17 In a while. 18 Port Stanley. 19 Palmer. 20 2. 21 Ukraine. 22 Owen. 23 Fears. 24 MG. 25 Eddie Cochran. 26 Lancashire. 27 Ethelred. 28 Peter Andre. 29 "One Man and His Dog". 30 The Cider House Rules.

1 Which Spaniard was Formula 1 Word Champion in 2005?
2 Was Geoff Boycott left- or right-handed as a batsman?
3 Which Spaniard won the Tour de France from 1991 to 1995?
4 Which Chris was WBO super middleweight champion in 1991?
5 Who was the first jockey to go through a seven-race card?
6 Who is the Crafty Cockney?
7 Whom did David Moyes replace as Everton manager?
8 Which Nigel was Formula 1 world champion in the 80s?
9 Which country does Greg Norman come from?
10 Which Australian tycoon was responsible for World Series Cricket?
11 Which cricketer Darren won "Strictly Come Dancing" in 2005?
12 Who was the National Hunt champion jockey from 1986 to 1992?
13 Who was Smokin' Joe?
14 Kelly Sotherton is a competitor in which multi-disciplined athletics event?
15 Woodforde and Woodbridge are partners in which sport?
16 Which snooker star was born on 22 August 1957 in Plumstead?
17 Which golfer Sandy won the British Open in the 80s?
18 Who was the jockey who rode Aldaniti to Grand National success?
19 Who succeeded Jack Charlton as soccer boss of the Republic of Ireland?
20 Golfer Annika Sorenstam is from which country?
21 Who announced in September '96 that he would race for the TWR Arrows?
22 Who was the first male Brit to make Wimbledon's last eight in the 90s?
23 Who retired aged 30 after winning the Premiership with Man. Utd?
24 Which Jo played Wightman Cup tennis for Britain through the 80s?
25 Who was manager of Nottingham Forest throughout the 80s?
26 Who won her third London marathon in 2005?
27 Which unseeded MaliVai reached the 1996 Wimbledon men's final?
28 What colour medal did the men's 4x100m. relay team win at the 2004 Olympics?
29 Who was the England cricket skipper in the ball-tampering claims of 1994?
30 Which scrum-half Gareth forged a partnership with Barry John for Cardiff and Wales?

Answers | TV Times 1 *(see Quiz 143)*

1 "The Sopranos". 2 "Strictly Come Dancing". 3 Cookery. 4 Detective. 5 "Songs of Praise". 6 "The X Files". 7 Doctor. 8 Feltz. 9 "Dinnerladies". 10 David. 11 Motoring. 12 Four. 13 Hamilton. 14 David Coleman. 15 "Peak Practice". 16 Pathologist. 17 Oxford. 18 Hospital. 19 "Rosemary and Thyme". 20 "Absolutely Fabulous". 21 "Newsnight". 22 Bean. 23 "Casualty". 24 Victor Meldrew. 25 "Ballykissangel". 26 Lisa. 27 Norden. 28 After. 29 Thaw. 30 Yorkshire.

1 In Cockney rhyming slang, what are "plates of meat"?
2 The character Michelle Fowler appeared in which TV soap?
3 Is France ahead of or behind Greenwich Mean Time?
4 What word can go after "safety" and before "aid"?
5 What position did American football's record-breaking Jerry Rice play?
6 Who managed the first English side to win soccer's European Cup?
7 Who wrote the novel "The Hobbit"?
8 Bill Beaumont is associated with which sport?
9 What does the C stand for in CBE?
10 In which decade of the 20th century was Barbara Cartland born?
11 Where was the first match of the 2005 Ashes series held?
12 How many inches in six feet?
13 Who was France's last Wimbledon Men's Singles winner of the 20th century?
14 When did the Super League begin in rugby league?
15 In which month does the Oscars ceremony usually take place?
16 In which play does the skull of Yorick appear?
17 In Bill Hayley's "See You Later, Alligator" what three words come before crocodile?
18 What is the capital of the Falkland Islands?
19 Who made up the trio with Emerson and Lake?
20 What number is cubed to give the answer 8?
21 In which country is the city of Kiev?
22 Which Bill starred in "Last of the Summer Wine"?
23 Phobophobia is the fear of what?
24 Which UK car manufacturer produced the Midget?
25 Who had a No. 1 with "Three Steps to Heaven" after his death?
26 Which county have Gallian and Fairbrother played cricket for?
27 Which English king was known as the Unready?
28 Which Australian singer did Jordan marry in 2005?
29 Which BBC programme features Sheepdog Championships?
30 For which movie did Michael Caine win his second Oscar?

| **Answers** | Pot Luck 72 *(see Quiz 140)* |

1 "Countdown". 2 Man. Utd. 3 40s. 4 Nepal. 5 "The Magic Roundabout". 6 Calcium. 7 Bram Stoker. 8 33.33. 9 "Coronation Street". 10 "Lucy in the Sky with Diamonds". 11 Apple. 12 Roger Federer. 13 Nigella Lawson. 14 "Quick". 15 Great Expectations. 16 Piano. 17 Dustin Hoffman. 18 Shirley Temple. 19 Hungary. 20 "It's Raining Men". 21 Hong Kong. 22 Rolls-Royce. 23 July. 24 "Road". 25 Omar Sharif. 26 Blond. 27 Cliff Richard. 28 Africa. 29 Paul Daniels. 30 Duke of Norfolk.

1 Tony, Carmela, Meadow and Anthony Jnr belong to which TV family?
2 "Dancing with the Stars" is the US version of which entertainment show?
3 What sort of TV programmes does Sophie Grigson present?
4 What is the profession of Frost in "A Touch of Frost"?
5 What is the BBC's long-running hymn-singing programme called?
6 In which programme do Mulder and Scully appear?
7 What is the occupation of Bramwell?
8 What is the surname of a presenter called Vanessa?
9 Bren, Twinkle and Dolly appeared in which Victoria Wood comedy?
10 Which Dimbleby presents the BBC's "Question Time"?
11 What is the programme "Top Gear" about?
12 In 1997, how many episodes of "Coronation Street" were there each week?
13 Which Geoff presented "Gardener's World" until his death in 1996?
14 Which chairman of "A Question of Sport" retired in 1997?
15 Which programme features the doctors of Cardale?
16 What is the profession of Sam Ryan in "Silent Witness"?
17 In which city does "Inspector Morse" take place?
18 What is the setting for "ER"?
19 Which programme has Felicity Kendal and Pam Ferris as green-fingered sleuths?
20 In which sitcom did Saffron and Bubble appear?
21 Which late-evening current-affairs programme does Jeremy Paxman often present?
22 Which Sean starred on TV as Sharpe?
23 Characters Josh Griffiths, Tess Bateman and Tina Seabrook were in which medical drama?
24 Whose famous catchphrase is "I don't believe it!"?
25 Which comedy series was about an English priest in Ireland?
26 Which member of the Simpson family is a vegetarian?
27 Which Denis presents "It'll Be Alright on the Night"?
28 Is the weather forecast immediately before or after "News at Ten"?
29 Which John played Kavanagh QC?
30 In which county does "Heartbeat" take place?

| **Answers** | **Sport: Who's Who?** *(see Quiz 141)* |

1 Fernando Alonso. 2 Right. 3 Miguel Indurain. 4 Eubank. 5 Frankie Dettori. 6 Eric Bristow. 7 Walter Smith. 8 Mansell. 9 Australia. 10 Kerry Packer. 11 Gough. 12 Peter Scudamore. 13 Joe Frazier. 14 Heptathlon. 15 Tennis (doubles). 16 Steve Davis. 17 Lyle. 18 Bob Champion. 19 Mick McCarthy. 20 Sweden. 21 Damon Hill. 22 Tim Henman. 23 Eric Cantona. 24 Durie. 25 Brian Clough. 26 Paula Radcliffe. 27 Washington. 28 Gold. 29 Michael Atherton. 30 Edwards.

Quiz 144 Pot Luck 74

Answers – page 156

LEVEL 1

1 Which Michael won an Oscar for Best Actor in "Wall Street"?
2 Which team did Michael Owen leave to go and play soccer in Spain?
3 In which decade of the 20th century was Jose Carreras born?
4 What word can go after "monk" and before "cake"?
5 In the 90s, who had a No. 1 with "Think Twice"?
6 How would 14 be written in Roman numerals?
7 Who wrote the novel "War and Peace"?
8 Who plays rugby union at the Recreation Ground, London Road?
9 In which UK No. 1 did Elvis Presley sing in German?
10 Whom did Margaret Thatcher follow as Conservative Party leader?
11 Quicksilver is another name for which element?
12 When Billie first topped the charts what was her surname?
13 Are the North Downs north of London?
14 In which country is the city of Kualalumpur?
15 How is Edward Stewart Mainwaring better known?
16 What colour are the shorts of Germany's international soccer side?
17 Dave Bedford is associated with which sport?
18 In the Bible, which book immediately follows St John's Gospel?
19 What word can follow "fruit", "rabbit" and "Suffolk"?
20 Where on the body could a cataract form?
21 Private Pike appeared in which TV series?
22 The airline Aeroflot is from which country?
23 Who wrote the Messiah?
24 What is the square root of 25?
25 Which planet is named after the Roman god of war?
26 Which scandal made US President Richard Nixon resign?
27 On a Monopoly board, what colour is Bond Street?
28 Which director is the subject of the movie "Gods and Monsters"?
29 Kurt Cobain was in which grunge group?
30 The character Cliff Barnes appeared in which TV soap?

Answers | Pot Luck 75 *(see Quiz 146)*

1 Ethiopia. 2 "The Good Life". 3 60s. 4 "Blood". 5 Boxing. 6 France. 7 Quatro.
8 Morris. 9 Nitrogen. 10 1,760. 11 Copper. 12 Abba. 13 Bamber Gascoigne. 14
Agency. 15 Genetically. 16 Ryan Giggs. 17 Potato. 18 Salome. 19 Your troubles. 20
The monster. 21 Acute. 22 Manic Street Preachers. 23 Guinevere. 24 Paul McCartney.
25 Tim Rice. 26 Decibels. 27 Topiary. 28 Carpenters. 29 "Countdown". 30 2.

1 Reykjavik is the capital of which country?
2 Which is farther south – Corsica or Sardinia?
3 Which river runs through Belgrade, Budapest and Vienna?
4 Which Peter spent a Year in Provence?
5 The Acropolis overlooks which capital city?
6 Which is the highest mountain in the Alps?
7 Do the stripes go horizontally or vertically on the Austrian flag?
8 Belgium's coast touches which sea?
9 What is the currency of Greece?
10 Which capital takes its name from a prince of Troy?
11 Which ocean is Europe's northern boundary?
12 Which mountains divide Spain from France?
13 Ankara is the capital of which country?
14 What is the currency of Denmark?
15 Which tiny European country has the European Court of Justice?
16 Which two colours make up the Greek flag?
17 Nero fiddled while which city burned?
18 Which of the three Baltic states of the former USSR does not begin with L?
19 What is the tourist area of southern Portugal called?
20 What is the capital of Malta?
21 Which mountains are Europe's eastern boundary?
22 What is the currency of Austria?
23 The Black Forest is a mountain range in which country?
24 Which country has the regions Lazio and Calabria?
25 What is the colour of the middle of the French flag?
26 Which Sea is Europe's southern boundary?
27 Which two major European rivers begin with R?
28 What would an English-speaking person call Bretagne?
29 Sofia is the capital of which country?
30 Which country has the markka or finnmark as its currency?

| **Answers** | **Pop: No. 1s** *(see Quiz 147)* |

1 Girls Aloud. 2 "Love is All Around". 3 1950s. 4 Black Eyed Peas. 5 Brother. 6 "White Cliffs of Dover". 7 Freddie Mercury. 8 Your Daughter. 9 "Mr Blobby". 10 Kate Bush. 11 Man. Utd. 12 Blondie. 13 Elton John. 14 "Without You". 15 Cliff Richard. 16 Gabrielle. 17 Massachusetts. 18 Take That. 19 "Yellow Submarine". 20 Abba. 21 Paul Simon. 22 Country. 23 Wham!. 24 Scaffold. 25 Village People. 26 The Shadows. 27 Waltz. 28 David Bowie. 29 Rednex. 30 Ricky Martin.

1 Live Aid raised money for famine relief in which country?
2 Margo and Jerry Leadbetter appeared in which TV series?
3 In which decade of the 20th century was Kenneth Branagh born?
4 What word can go after "blue" and before "hound"?
5 Nigel Benn is associated with which sport?
6 In which country is the city of Nice?
7 In the 70s, which Suzi had a No. 1 with "Devil Gate Drive"?
8 Which UK car manufacturer produced the Oxford?
9 80 per cent of Earth's atmosphere is formed by which gas?
10 How many yards in a mile?
11 Cu is the chemical symbol for which element?
12 Agnetha Faltskog was a singer with which group?
13 Who first presented BBC 2's "University Challenge"?
14 What does the A stand for in CIA?
15 What does the G stand for in the GM referring to crops?
16 Who in 1991 became the youngest ever Welsh soccer international?
17 Romano and Desiree are types of what?
18 Who wanted the head of John the Baptist?
19 In song, what do you pack up in your old kit bag?
20 What part did Boris Karloff play in the 30s film "Frankenstein"?
21 What name is given to angles of less than 90 degrees?
22 Which British band had the first No. 1 of the new millennium?
23 In legend, who was the wife of King Arthur?
24 Which Beatle played guitar left-handed?
25 Which lyricist has Miles Bindon as middle names?
26 Which units are used to measure sound intensity?
27 What name is given to trimming hedges into shapes?
28 "(They Long to be) Close to You" was the first hit for which group?
29 What was the first quiz to be seen on Channel 4?
30 Moving anticlockwise on a dartboard what number is next to 17?

Answers	**Pot Luck 74** *(see Quiz 144)*

1 Douglas. 2 Liverpool. 3 40s. 4 "Fish". 5 Celine Dion. 6 XIV. 7 Leo Tolstoy. 8 Bath. 9 Wooden Heart. 10 Edward Heath. 11 Mercury. 12 Piper. 13 No. 14 Malaysia. 15 Ed Stewart. 16 Black. 17 Athletics. 18 The Acts of the Apostles. 19 "Punch". 20 The eye. 21 "Dad's Army". 22 Russia. 23 Handel. 24 5. 25 Mars. 26 Watergate. 27 Green. 28 James Whale. 29 Nirvana. 30 "Dallas".

1 "Sound of the Underground" was the first No. 1 for which group?
2 "Four Weddings and a Funeral" made which song a No. 1?
3 In which decade did Elvis have his first UK No. 1?
4 "Where is the Love?" was the first No. 1 for which collective?
5 Which relative features in a Hollies song title?
6 Which other song was on Robson and Jerome's "Unchained Melody"?
7 Whose death gave "Bohemian Rhapsody" a second visit to No. 1?
8 Whom should you bring to the slaughter, according to Iron Maiden?
9 What was the imaginative title of Mr Blobby's first No. 1?
10 Who charted with a song about Heathcliff and Cathy?
11 Which soccer team were involved in "Come On You Reds"?
12 Who had No. 1s with "Call Me" and "Atomic"?
13 Who sang with Kiki Dee on "Don't Go Breaking My Heart"?
14 Which song was a No. 1 for both Nilsson and Mariah Carey?
15 Which English Sir has had No. 1s in the 50s, 60s, 70s, 80s and 90s?
16 Who had Dreams in 1993?
17 Which US state was the title of a Bee Gees No. 1?
18 Which band were Back for Good in 1995?
19 Which Beatle No. 1 featured the word Yellow in the title?
20 "The Winner Takes It All" was yet another No. 1 for which group?
21 Who wrote Simon and Garfunkel's "Bridge Over Troubled Water"?
22 What type of House did Blur take to the top of the charts?
23 George Michael first hit No. 1 as a member of which duo?
24 Who took "Lily the Pink" to No. 1?
25 Who thought it was fun to stay in the YMCA?
26 Whose first UK No. 1 was "Apache"?
27 In psychedelic '67, which old-time dance gave Engelbert Humperdinck a huge hit?
28 Who teamed up with Queen for "Under Pressure"?
29 Who had a No. 1 with "Cotton Eye Joe"?
30 Which singer first made No. 1 with "Livin' La Vida Loca"?

| **Answers** | **Euro Tour** (see Quiz 145) |

1 Iceland. 2 Sardinia. 3 Danube. 4 Mayle. 5 Athens. 6 Mont Blanc. 7 Horizontally. 8 North Sea. 9 Drachma. 10 Paris. 11 Arctic. 12 Pyrenees. 13 Turkey. 14 Krone. 15 Luxembourg. 16 Blue and white. 17 Rome. 18 Estonia. 19 The Algarve. 20 Valetta. 21 Urals. 22 Schilling. 23 Germany. 24 Italy. 25 White. 26 Mediterranean. 27 Rhine, Rhone. 28 Brittany. 29 Bulgaria. 30 Finland.

Quiz 148 Pot Luck 76

Answers – page 160

LEVEL 1

1 Which vitamin deficiency was responsible for scurvy?
2 Which Doctor had a dog called K9?
3 Which meat could not be eaten on the bone during the BSE crisis?
4 What word can go after "honey" and before "wax"?
5 How is the comedian Thomas Derbyshire better known?
6 Which Hilary won best Supporting Actress for "Boys Don't Cry"?
7 Who wrote the novel "Pride and Prejudice"?
8 Roger Black is associated with which sport?
9 How many seconds in one hour?
10 In which decade of the 20th century was Prince Charles born?
11 Who tried to mend his head with vinegar and brown paper?
12 In which decade did Mountain Biking become an Olympic event?
13 Where does an arboreal creature live?
14 Which descriptive word is linked with the singer John Baldry?
15 Which Henry won an Oscar for Best Actor in "On Golden Pond"?
16 What kind of bomb contains hydrogen sulphide?
17 What is the flavour of Pernod?
18 Little Nell appears in which Charles Dickens novel?
19 What word can go before "leader", "main" and "master"?
20 In which month is Hallowe'en?
21 What was Spice Girl Mel B called during her brief first marriage?
22 Which is smaller – 5/10 or 3/4?
23 What is a hora?
24 Who sang the theme from "Goldfinger"?
25 Which Nobel Prize did Nelson Mandela win?
26 In boxing, what is the maximum number of rounds in a contest?
27 The letter S is on which row of a keyboard?
28 In the 70s, who had a No. 1 with "Mama Weer All Crazee Now"?
29 In which country is the city of Palermo?
30 Which cartoon series features Pebbles and Bam Bam?

Answers | Pot Luck 77 *(see Quiz 150)*

1 Black. 2 A friend. 3 60s. 4 Purple. 5 July and August. 6 Cumbria. 7 H.E. Bates.
8 Black. 9 10. 10 The Beach Boys. 11 Nine. 12 Sleepy. 13 1960s. 14 Cocktail. 15
Pluto. 16 Ian McKellen. 17 Germany. 18 14. 19 The Beatles. 20 Rural England. 21
Majorca. 22 Her children. 23 Two. 24 Creedence Clearwater Revival. 25 Kiwi fruit.
26 "Neighbours". 27 Johnny Dankworth. 28 Reliant. 29 Makepeace. 30 Jones.

Answers – page 161

1 Charles Dodgson wrote his classic children's story under what name?
2 Which Frederick wrote "The Day of the Jackal"?
3 Fitzwilliam Darcy appears in which novel?
4 Whom did Bertie Wooster have as his manservant?
5 Which Irving Welsh novel was about Scottish heroin addicts?
6 Which county in England did Laurie Lee come from?
7 Which Arthur wrote the children's classic "Swallows and Amazons"?
8 Which James became Britain's most read vet?
9 Who created Thomas the Tank Engine?
10 Which French detective was created by Georges Simenon?
11 What was the first name of the girl who went to live at Green Gables?
12 Who created the Discworld books?
13 Which Ian created James Bond?
14 Which creatures are the central characters in "Watership Down"?
15 Who wrote "Rebecca"?
16 What was the name of the boy in "The Jungle Book"?
17 What term is used for writing a novel that will go out under someone else's name?
18 Which novelist born in 1886 had the initials H.G.?
19 What is Joseph Heller's novel with a number in its catchy title?
20 Which children's publisher has a black-and-red insect as its logo?
21 Who created Inspector Adam Dalgleish?
22 Which Douglas wrote "The Hitch Hiker's Guide to the Galaxy"?
23 Brother Cadfael belonged to which order of monks?
24 What sex was Richmal Crompton, author of the William books?
25 Which fictional barrister referred to his wife as "she who must be obeyed"?
26 Which country was Stephen King born in?
27 Which Victor wrote the novel "Les Misérables"?
28 Which Tory fundraiser wrote "Not a Penny More not a Penny Less"?
29 Who wrote "Murder on the Orient Express"?
30 John Grisham's novels centre on which profession?

Answers | Movies: Who's Who? *(see Quiz 151)*

1 Brooke Shields. 2 Agutter. 3 Austria. 4 Stone. 5 Sigourney. 6 Nielsen. 7 Jennifer Aniston. 8 France. 9 Kiefer. 10 Keira Knightley. 11 Alfred Hitchcock. 12 Kirk. 13 Rosanna. 14 Barrymore. 15 Cher. 16 The Doors. 17 Madonna. 18 King Kong. 19 Sissy. 20 Curtis. 21 Reese Witherspoon. 22 Bridges. 23 Schindler. 24 Tatum. 25 Keanu. 26 Basinger. 27 Jane. 28 Omar Sharif. 29 Bacall. 30 Gere.

1 What colour was the contestant's chair in "Mastermind"?
2 Whom can you phone on "Who Wants to be a Millionaire"?
3 In which decade of the 20th century was Diana, Princess of Wales born?
4 On a Monopoly board, what colour is Pall Mall?
5 The zodiac sign Leo covers which two calendar months?
6 In 1974 parts of Cumberland and Westmorland made which new county?
7 Who wrote the novel "The Darling Buds of May"?
8 What type of Coffee was a chart topper for All Saints?
9 How many sides does a decagon have?
10 Which group featured Brian Wilson?
11 How many spaces in a noughts-and-crosses frame?
12 Which of the Seven Dwarfs was always feeling tired?
13 In which decade did man first land on the moon?
14 What word can go after "prawn" and before "dress"?
15 Which was the first planet to be discovered in the last century?
16 Who played the novelist Mel Hutchwright in "Coronation Street"?
17 The airline Lufthansa is from which country?
18 Moving clockwise on a dartboard what number is next to 11?
19 In the 60s, who had a No. 1 with "Can't Buy Me Love"?
20 The CPRE is the Council for the Preservation of what?
21 In which country is the city of Palma?
22 Whom did Princess Diana leave most of her money to?
23 How many pints in a quart?
24 Which group had Clearwater as their middle name?
25 What is another name for Chinese gooseberries?
26 Madge and Harold Bishop appeared in which TV soap?
27 Which jazz musician Johnny was knighted in 2006?
28 Which UK car manufacturer produced the Robin?
29 Who was the female half of Dempsey and Makepeace?
30 Which Tom led the most weeks in the singles chart list for 1968?

Answers	**Pot Luck 76** *(see Quiz 148)*

1 C. 2 Doctor Who. 3 Beef. 4 "Bees". 5 Tommy Cannon. 6 Swank. 7 Jane Austen.
8 Athletics. 9 3,600. 10 40s. 11 Jack (in "Jack and Jill"). 12 1990s. 13 In a tree.
14 Long. 15 Fonda. 16 Stink bomb. 17 Aniseed. 18 The Old Curiosity Shop. 19
"Ring". 20 October. 21 Mel G. 22 5/10. 23 Dance (Jewish). 24 Shirley Bassey. 25
Peace. 26 15. 27 Middle. 28 Slade. 29 Italy. 30 "The Flintstones".

1 Which actress married André Agassi in 1997?
2 Which Jenny played Roberta in "The Railway Children"?
3 In which country was Arnold Schwarzenegger born?
4 Which Sharon played opposite Michael Douglas in "Basic Instinct"?
5 What did Susan Weaver change her first name to?
6 Which Leslie stars in "The Naked Gun" series of films?
7 Who divorced Brad Pitt in 2005?
8 In which country was Gerard Dépardieu born?
9 Who is Donald Sutherland's actor son?
10 Who played Elizabeth Bennet in the 2005 film version of "Pride and Prejudice"?
11 Who directed "Psycho" and "The Birds"?
12 What is the first name of Michael Douglas's father?
13 What is the first name of Ms Arquette, star of "Desperately Seeking Susan"?
14 Which Drew was in "E.T." and "Batman Forever"?
15 Which chart-topper was in "Silkwood" and "Moonstruck"?
16 In which film did Val Kilmer play the rock star Jim Morrison?
17 Which star of "Evita" was the first wife of the actor Sean Penn?
18 Which King did Peter Jackson direct in 2005?
19 How is Mary Elizabeth Spacek better known?
20 Which Tony is the father of Jamie Lee?
21 Who won an Oscar for her role in "Walk the Line"?
22 What is the surname of the father and son actors Lloyd, Jeff and Beau?
23 Which character did Liam Neeson play in "Schindler's List"?
24 Who is the Oscar-winning daughter of Ryan O'Neal?
25 Which actor Reeves starred in "Bram Stoker's Dracula"?
26 Which Kim was the Bond girl in "Never Say Never Again"?
27 Who is Bridget Fonda's actress/fitness fanatic aunt?
28 Which talented bridge player played the title role in "Doctor Zhivago"?
29 Which Lauren was married to Humphrey Bogart?
30 Which Richard starred opposite Julia Roberts in "Pretty Woman"?

Answers	Books (see Quiz 149)

1 Lewis Carroll. 2 Forsyth. 3 Pride and Prejudice. 4 Jeeves. 5 Trainspotting. 6 Gloucestershire. 7 Rackham. 8 Herriot. 9 Rev. Awdry. 10 Maigret. 11 Anne. 12 Terry Pratchett. 13 Fleming. 14 Rabbits. 15 Daphne Du Maurier. 16 Mowgli. 17 Ghosting. 18 Wells. 19 Catch-22. 20 Ladybird. 21 P. D. James. 22 Adams. 23 Benedictine. 24 Female. 25 Horace Rumpole. 26 US. 27 Hugo. 28 Jeffrey Archer. 29 Agatha Christie. 30 Legal profession.

Quiz 152 | Pot Luck 78

Answers – page 164

LEVEL 1

1 Which soccer club moved to the Riverside Stadium?
2 Ted Bovis and Gladys Pugh appeared in which TV series?
3 In which decade of the 20th century was Bobby Charlton born?
4 What word can go after "bowling" and before "house"?
5 In which TV show might tubby toast appear?
6 In which country is the city of Saragossa?
7 Who wrote the novel "Wuthering Heights"?
8 H is the chemical symbol for which element?
9 Which Joan had a 60s hit with "There but for Fortune"?
10 The letter W is on which row of a typewriter or computer keyboard?
11 In cooking, Florentine means garnished with which vegetable?
12 Which Edward starred in "Callan"?
13 What is the square root of 36?
14 Who had a little buddy called Boo Boo?
15 The character Reg Holdsworth appeared in which TV soap?
16 Nelson Mandela became South African president in which decade of last century?
17 What is the administrative centre for the county of Devon?
18 What word can go before "ball", "drunk" and "line?"
19 How is Dora Broadbent better known?
20 Who cried through her Oscar acceptance speech for "Shakespeare in Love"?
21 Who first hosted a "Supermarket Sweep" on daytime TV?
22 At 17·5 per cent, how much VAT is added to an item priced at £300?
23 Who was singer/songwriter with the Boomtown Rats?
24 Which Robert won an Oscar for Best Actor in "Raging Bull"?
25 What is the only English anagram of WRONG?
26 Which major battle took place between July and November 1916?
27 What is the term for written or recorded defamation?
28 What are the two colours of a standard "Blue Peter" badge?
29 What is 5/8 minus 1/4?
30 Who partnered Jennifer Warnes on "Up Where We Belong"?

Answers | **Sporting Chance 1** *(see Quiz 154)*

1 Denmark. 2 15. 3 British Darts Association. 4 American Football. 5 Cycling. 6 Biathlon. 7 Buster. 8 Oldham. 9 Annually. 10 Leicestershire. 11 15. 12 Gymnastics. 13 Birdie. 14 Jose Mourinho. 15 Golf. 16 Tony Greig. 17 Cheltenham. 18 England. 19 Middlesbrough. 20 Martina Hingis. 21 Rugby Union. 22 Surrey. 23 News of the World. 24 Black. 25 Boundary for six runs. 26 Sunday. 27 Self-defence. 28 Leicestershire. 29 Horse. 30 1970s.

1 What is the first name of Madonna's husband Mr Ritchie?
2 Has Madonna ever written any of her own hits?
3 Which word completes her documentary movie title, "I Want to Tell You a ..."?
4 Is Madonna's husband a car salesman or a movie director?
5 In which movie did she play Eva Peron?
6 Is Maverick the name of her recording company or her son?
7 Which album came first, "Music" or "Like a Virgin"?
8 Which True album was No. 1 when the single "Papa Don't Preach" was No. 1?
9 In 1998 Madonna had album success with Ray of what?
10 Was she in her 30s or 40s when she had success with the album "Music" in 2000?
11 Madonna was the most performed look and sound alike on which show?
12 Which Pie gave Madonna a 2000 No. 1 in the UK?
13 Which country follows "Don't Cry For Me" in her 1996 hit?
14 Which home of the US movie industry was the title of a 2003 hit?
15 Which Life was the name of a US No. 1?
16 Which 2002 Bond movie song gave Madonna a hit?
17 Which young singer joined her on "Me Against the Music"?
18 Did Madonna have her first hit albums in the 1980s or 1990s?
19 What type of stranger was the name of a 1999 hit?
20 What was the abbreviation of her Greatest Hits Volume 2 album?
21 Which single was No. 1 when the album "Like a Prayer" was No. 1?
22 In which part of the UK did Madonna marry Guy Ritchie?
23 Which actor Sean was Madonna's first husband?
24 The single "Ray of Light" came from which album?
25 Who is older, her first son or daughter?
26 What had she fallen from when she suffered broken bones in 2005?
27 Which Stranger was the song from a Mike Myers Austin Powers film?
28 Was "Hung Up" the title of a single or album?
29 What was her debut album Madonna imaginatively retitled as in 1985?
30 Which chart topper came first, "Hung Up" or "Frozen"?

Answers | Pot Luck 79 (see Quiz 155)

1 William Tell Overture. 2 Ceefax. 3 40s. 4 "Clip". 5 Boxing. 6 David. 7 Daniel Defoe. 8 As You Like It. 9 Exchange Rate Mechanism. 10 "Just Good Friends". 11 Triumph. 12 Birmingham. 13 Open spaces. 14 London. 15 20. 16 "EastEnders". 17 Doncaster. 18 Mendel. 19 "Amazing Grace". 20 Circumference. 21 Germany. 22 Lindsay. 23 The Three Musketeers. 24 Stars. 25 First and fifth (the last). 26 Six. 27 Crosby. 28 1,000. 29 Nancy. 30 D.

1 Which country does Thomas Gravesen play for?
2 How many reds are there at the start of a snooker game?
3 What does BDA stand for?
4 What sport do the Buffalo Bills play?
5 In which sport is the Giro D'Italia – the Tour of Italy?
6 Which sport combines cross-country skiing and rifle shooting?
7 What is the nickname of the heavyweight James Douglas?
8 Which rugby league team are the Bears?
9 How often is golf's US Masters held?
10 James Whittaker captained which side to the County Championship?
11 How many people are there in a hurling team?
12 Shannon Miler is famous for which sport?
13 In golf, what is the term for one under par for a hole?
14 Who became manager of Chelsea Football Club in 2004?
15 Hale Irwin is famous for which sport?
16 Which England captain helped set up Kerry Packer's cricket "circus"?
17 The Mackeson Gold Cup is run at which course?
18 Dave Whitcombe played darts for which country?
19 In the 90s, who lost the two major English finals and were relegated?
20 Which former Wimbledon champion came out of retirement in early 2006?
21 Are Sale, Wasps and Bath Rugby Union or Rugby League clubs?
22 Wentworth golf course is in which county?
23 Which newspaper supported a darts tournament from 1948 to 1990?
24 Which ball in snooker is worth seven points?
25 A cricket umpire raises both arms above his head to signal what?
26 On what day of the week is the Prix de L'Arc de Triomphe race held?
27 Aikido is the ancient Japanese art of what?
28 Which county cricket club has its home at Grace Road?
29 Was Bertie Blunt the name of the rider or the horse that won the 1996 Badminton Horse Trials?
30 In what decade did David Gower first play cricket for England?

Answers	Pot Luck 78 *(see Quiz 152)*

1 Middlesbrough. 2 "Hi-Di-Hi!". 3 30s. 4 "Green". 5 Teletubbies. 6 Spain. 7 Emily Brontë. 8 Hydrogen. 9 Baez. 10 Top letters row. 11 Spinach. 12 Woodward. 13 Six. 14 Yogi Bear. 15 "Coronation Street". 16 1990s. 17 Exeter. 18 Punch. 19 Dora Bryan. 20 Gwyneth Paltrow. 21 Dale Winton. 22 £52.50. 23 Bob Geldof. 24 de Niro. 25 Grown. 26 Somme. 27 Libel. 28 Blue and white. 29 3/8. 30 Joe Cocker.

1 Which classical overture became the "Lone Ranger" theme?
2 What is the BBC's teletext service called?
3 In which decade of the 20th century was Bill Clinton born?
4 What word can go after "paper" and before "board"?
5 Which sport features in the movie "Million Dollar Baby"?
6 Which Attenborough presented "The Blue Planet" about life beneath the sea?
7 Who wrote the novel "Robinson Crusoe"?
8 Sienna Miller appeared in which Shakespeare play, in the West End, 2005?
9 In monetary terms, what does ERM stand for?
10 The characters Vince and Penny appeared in which TV series?
11 Which UK car manufacturer produced the Herald?
12 What is the administrative centre for the county of West Midlands?
13 Agoraphobia is the fear of what?
14 In which UK city did the ill-fated Millennium Dome open?
15 Moving anticlockwise on a dartboard what number is next to 1?
16 The character Frank Butcher appeared in which TV soap?
17 Which rugby league team added Dragons to their name in the 90s?
18 Which Gregor was noted for experiments in genetics?
19 In song, which two words go before, "how sweet the sound, That saved a wretch like me"?
20 What is the boundary of a circle called?
21 In which country is the city of Stuttgart?
22 Which Robert starred in "Citizen Smith"?
23 Which book includes the words "All for one and one for all"?
24 Which are there more of on the USA flag stars or stripes?
25 In a limerick, which lines should rhyme with the second line?
26 How many pockets does a snooker table have?
27 Who sang with Stills, Nash and Young?
28 How many milligrams in a gram?
29 Annunziata Dell'Olio is usually known by which first name?
30 In music, what note is written on the line above the middle line of the treble clef?

Answers	Madonna *(see Quiz 153)*

1 Guy. 2 Yes. 3 Secret. 4 Movie director. 5 Evita. 6 Recording company. 7 Music.
8 True Blue. 9 Ray of Light. 10 40s. 11 "Stars in Their Eyes". 12 American Pie. 13
Argentina. 14 Hollywood. 15 "American Life". 16 "Die Another Day". 17 Britney
Spears. 18 1980s. 19 Beautiful. 20 GHV2. 21 "Like a Prayer". 22 Scotland. 23
Penn. 24 Ray of Light. 25 Her daughter. 26 Horse. 27 "Beautiful Stranger". 28
Single. 29 The First Album. 30 "Frozen".

1 Who made the "wind of change" speech?
2 George Cohen was a member of the world's winners at which sport?
3 Which call-girl Christine was involved in a government scandal?
4 Which future Princess of Wales was born in the 60s?
5 Edwin Aldrin became the second person to walk where?
6 Who played piano while Peter Cook sang?
7 Whom did Anthony Armstrong-Jones marry in 1960?
8 How did the English comic Tony Hancock die?
9 Whom did Richard Burton marry in Canada in 1964?
10 Gaddafi seized power in which country?
11 Which D. H. Lawrence book from the 20s featured in an Old Bailey obscenity trial?
12 Bob Dylan starred at a 1969 rock Festival on which British isle?
13 Which doctor's report led to the cutting of the railway network?
14 George Blake gained notoriety as what?
15 Which Francis sailed solo round the world?
16 Who became the youngest ever USA President?
17 Who was involved with John Lennon in a "bed-in" for peace?
18 Which President originally blocked Britain's entry into the EEC?
19 Which country banned a tour by England's cricketers?
20 Which country made the first manned space flight?
21 The Torrey Canyon was what type of transporter?
22 George Brown was a prominent MP for which party?
23 Which Private magazine signalled the satire boom?
24 Which theatre that "never closed" finally did close?
25 US President Johnson was known by which three initials?
26 Nuclear war threatened in 1962 over Soviet missiles in which country?
27 Which English footballer retired in 1965 at the age of 50?
28 Which Anglo-French supersonic airliner took to the skies?
29 Who was manager of the Beatles until his death in 1967?
30 Which ex-Nazi leader Adolf was tried and hanged?

Answers | Time & Space (see Quiz 158)

1 Mercury. 2 Big Bang. 3 Ursa Major (the Great Bear). 4 Sharman. 5 Galaxy. 6 Space Shuttle. 7 Star. 8 Jupiter. 9 Comet. 10 It exploded. 11 Kennedy. 12 The Moon. 13 Gravity. 14 Satellites. 15 Cosmology. 16 Glenn. 17 Apollo. 18 Uranus. 19 First man in space. 20 A year. 21 Halley's comet. 22 USA. 23 The Dog Star. 24 Quasars. 25 Patrick Moore. 26 Shakespeare. 27 Cheshire. 28 Light years. 29 A dog. 30 The Milky Way.

1 Elvis Costello was born in which country?
2 What word can go before "ground", "pedal" and "water"?
3 Two US cops, Christine and Mary Beth, appeared in which TV series?
4 What is Abyssinia now called?
5 For how long had David Cameron been an MP before he became Tory leader?
6 In which country did the final vote about hosting the 2012 Olympics take place?
7 Who wrote the novel "Middlemarch"?
8 Cambridge Gage and Victoria are types of what?
9 Which French phrase in English means a road closed at one end?
10 Which Irishman did Pele describe as the "greatest footballer in the world"?
11 Which is greater – 1/3 or 4/8?
12 Which Clive starred in "Dad's Army"?
13 In which decade of the 20th century was Eric Clapton born?
14 What word can go after "fish" and before "print"?
15 Chris Brasher is associated with which sport?
16 On a Monopoly board, what colour is Bow Street?
17 In schools, what do the initials GCSE stand for?
18 In which country is the city of Tangier?
19 Which US civil rights campaigner Rosa died in 2005 aged 92?
20 Who recorded the album "Money for Nothing"?
21 Geoff Miller played cricket for which country?
22 Ornithophobia is the fear of what?
23 What is 4 cubed?
24 What note is written in the space below the middle line of the treble clef?
25 Which Jack won an Oscar for Best Actor in "One Flew Over the Cuckoo's Nest"?
26 Is Barbados ahead of or behind Greenwich Mean Time?
27 Pearl celebrates which wedding anniversary?
28 Who "died" for the second time as "EastEnders" marked its 20th anniversary?
29 Which Alice declared: School's Out?
30 The character Charlene Mitchell appeared in which TV soap?

Answers	Pop: Singers (see Quiz 159)

1 Madonna. 2 Donny. 3 Sugababes. 4 Dana. 5 Stansfield. 6 Holder. 7 Enya. 8 Kenny Rogers. 9 Marc Bolan. 10 Smokey Robinson. 11 Pretenders. 12 John Denver. 13 Bryan Adams. 14 Phil Collins. 15 Cliff Richard. 16 K. T. Tunstall. 17 Nick Berry. 18 "Reet Petite". 19 Chris de Burgh. 20 Sting. 21 Jason Donovan. 22 Beyoncé. 23 Christina Aguilera. 24 Kylie Minogue. 25 Katie Melua. 26 M. 27 Engelbert Humperdinck. 28 Bob Marley. 29 UB40. 30 Craig David.

1 Which planet is closest to the sun?

2 Which Big theory explains the formation of the universe?

3 What is another name for the star constellation the Plough?

4 Which Helen became the first Briton in space?

5 What is the term for a giant group of stars held together by gravity?

6 In 1981, *Columbia I* was the first flight of which distinctive craft?

7 What can be a red dwarf or a white dwarf?

8 Which planet is the largest in our solar system?

9 Who or what was Hale-Bopp?

10 In 1986, what happened to Challenger 52 after take-off?

11 Cape Canaveral took on board the name of which US President?

12 Where is the Sea of Tranquillity?

13 What is the name of the force that keeps planets moving round the sun?

14 Tiros, Echo and Sputnik were types of what?

15 What is the name for the study of the structure of the universe?

16 Which John was the first American to orbit Earth?

17 What was the name of the project that first put man on the moon?

18 Alphabetically, which is last in the list of planets in our solar system?

19 What is Yuri Gagarin's famous first?

20 Approximately how long does it take the Earth to travel round the sun?

21 Which bright comet visits Earth every 76 years?

22 Which country launched the Pioneer space probes?

23 What is the popular name for the star Sirius?

24 Quasi-stellar sources are in short usually known as what?

25 Who is the long-time presenter of "The Sky at Night"?

26 The moons of Uranus are named after which playwright's characters?

27 Jodrell Bank is in which English county?

28 What units are used for measuring distance in space?

29 What was the first animal in space?

30 Our solar system lies in which galaxy?

Answers | The 60s *(see Quiz 156)*

1 Harold Macmillan. 2 Football. 3 Keeler. 4 Lady Diana Spencer. 5 On the moon.
6 Dudley Moore. 7 Princess Margaret. 8 Committed suicide. 9 Elizabeth Taylor. 10
Libya. 11 Lady Chatterley's Lover. 12 Isle of Wight. 13 Beeching. 14 A spy. 15
Chichester. 16 John Kennedy. 17 Yoko Ono. 18 De Gaulle. 19 South Africa. 20
USSR. 21 Oil tanker. 22 Labour. 23 Private Eye. 24 Windmill. 25 LBJ. 26 Cuba. 27
Stanley Matthews. 28 Concorde. 29 Brian Epstein. 30 Eichmann.

1 Who sang "Like a Virgin"?
2 Which Osmond sang "Puppy Love" and "Young Love"?
3 Mutya Buena left which group in December 2005?
4 Which Irish singer won Eurovision with "All Kinds of Everything"?
5 Which Lisa sang on the "Five Live EP"?
6 Which Noddy sang lead with Slade?
7 Which female singer went solo from Clannad?
8 Who sang "Coward of the County"?
9 Who sang lead with T. Rex?
10 Under what name did high-voiced William Robinson Jnr sing?
11 Chrissie Hynde was lead singer with which group?
12 Which writer and guitarist sang "Annie's Song"?
13 "(Everything I Do) I Do It for You" was a monster hit for whom?
14 Who had a No. 1 with "A Groovy Kind of Love"?
15 Who had a Christmas No. 1 with "Saviour's Day"?
16 Who won the Best British Female Solo Artist award at the Brits 2006?
17 Who sang "Every Loser Wins"?
18 Which song gave Jackie Wilson a No. 1 years after his death?
19 Who sang "The Lady in Red"?
20 Who was lead singer with the Police?
21 Who hit No. 1 with "Any Dream Will Do"?
22 "Crazy in Love" was the first solo No. 1 for which singer?
23 Which singer's second album was called "Stripped"?
24 Who released the album "Fever" in 2001?
25 The album "Call Off the Search" was released by which artist?
26 Heather Small sang lead with which people?
27 Who had a huge 60s hit with "Release Me"?
28 Who sang with the Wailers?
29 Ali Campbell sings lead with which group?
30 Who released the album "The Story Goes" in 2005?

Answers | Pot Luck 80 *(see Quiz 157)*

1 UK. 2 "Back". 3 "Cagney and Lacey". 4 Ethiopia. 5 Four years. 6 Singapore. 7 George Eliot. 8 Plum. 9 Cul-de-sac. 10 George Best. 11 4/8. 12 Dunn. 13 40s. 14 "Finger". 15 Athletics. 16 Orange. 17 General Certificate of Secondary Education. 18 Morocco. 19 Rosa Parks. 20 Dire Straits. 21 England. 22 Birds. 23 64. 24 A. 25 Nicholson. 26 Behind. 27 Thirtieth. 28 Dirty Den. 29 Cooper. 30 "Neighbours".

1 Eric Clapton, Ginger Baker and Jack Bruce formed which group?
2 What is the first name of the builder on "Ground Force"?
3 How many square feet in a square yard?
4 What word can go after "free" and before "corporal"?
5 In 1974 parts of Yorkshire and Lincolnshire made which new county?
6 He is the chemical symbol for which element?
7 Who wrote the novel "Dead Cert"?
8 Moving clockwise on a dartboard what number is next to 15?
9 Which cosmetic company had an ad which featured a distinctive doorbell?
10 Which rugby league team are the Blue Sox?
11 In the 80s, who had a No. 1 with "Karma Chameleon"?
12 Galileo Galilei airport is in which country?
13 In which decade of the 20th century was Steve Davis born?
14 David Broome is associated with which sport?
15 Which Irish boy band made the album "By Request"?
16 Who was Liverpool's regular soccer keeper throughout the 80s?
17 The letter E is on which row of a typewriter or computer keyboard?
18 Which Linford was BBC Sports Personality of the Year in 1993?
19 Mr Bumble appears in which Charles Dickens novel?
20 Which UK car manufacturer produced the Victor?
21 In which country is the city of Toulouse?
22 Which Carol presented "Changing Rooms" on TV?
23 What is the administrative centre for the county of Berkshire?
24 How many degrees in a circle?
25 The zodiac sign Aquarius covers which two calendar months?
26 In which US state was Condoleezza Rice born?
27 What term describes vegetables cut thinly and slowly cooked in butter?
28 In 2005, which continent was the only one where there were fatalities due to bird flu?
29 The character Clayton Farlow appeared in which TV soap?
30 Which Holly was in Frankie Goes to Hollywood?

Answers | **Pot Luck 82** *(see Quiz 162)*

1 Farrow. 2 St Paul's. 3 Bowls. 4 "Ball". 5 Bangkok. 6 Wolves. 7 Arthur C. Clarke.
8 November. 9 Frank Zappa. 10 Wayne. 11 90. 12 French. 13 30s. 14 Greenwich
Mean Time. 15 Two. 16 Pasta shapes. 17 Acker Bilk. 18 Canada. 19 "Box". 20
Paul McCartney. 21 Conservative. 22 7. 23 Toby. 24 Tenth. 25 "Knots Landing". 26
U2. 27 April 23. 28 Three. 29 MG Rover. 30 Threat.

1 Jack the Ripper operated in which city?
2 What nationality was the fictional sleuth Hercule Poirot?
3 Who was Burke's body-snatching partner?
4 Who wrote the comic opera "Trial by Jury"?
5 What is the name of a secret crime society based in Hong Kong?
6 Al Capone was imprisoned in the 30s for what offence?
7 Which notorious American island prison closed in March, 1963?
8 How were the US outlaws Parker and Barrow better known?
9 Which criminal was released by Pontius Pilate instead of Jesus?
10 Which Myra was involved in the Moors Murders?
11 Policemen got the nickname Peelers from whom?
12 How did Frederick West take his life?
13 When did the Knave of Hearts steal the tarts?
14 In which city was John Lennon murdered?
15 Which Kray twin was the first to die?
16 What is the Flying Squad in cockney rhyming slang?
17 What name is given to the crime of deliberately burning someone else's property?
18 Which Nick got nicked for the Barings Bank scam?
19 In which decade was the Great Train Robbery?
20 Whom did Dr Crippen murder?
21 In the US, which Charles led his "family" in ritual killings?
22 Which Arsenal boss got the boot after a bung?
23 Why does Ruth Ellis have her place assured in British crime history?
24 Lee Harvey Oswald was accused of murdering which famous American?
25 Klaus Barbie became known as the Butcher of where?
26 In England and Wales how many people sit on a jury?
27 Peter Sutcliffe became known as what?
28 Ernest Saunders was involved with the fraud trial at which drinks company?
29 Rudolf Hess spent the last years of his life at which prison?
30 Sweeney Todd operated in which London Street?

Answers | TV Gold *(see Quiz 163)*

1 "Casualty". 2 Percy Thrower. 3 The Lone Ranger. 4 The clergy. 5 Mindy. 6 Joanna Lumley. 7 Stephenson. 8 "Panorama". 9 "Please Sir". 10 18th. 11 Henry VIII. 12 Starsky. 13 "Bonanza". 14 "The Beverly Hillbillies". 15 "Neighbours". 16 "The Good Old Days". 17 "The Forsyte Saga". 18 Scott, Whitfield. 19 Pub. 20 Alsatian. 21 Cookery. 22 Hancock. 23 Roger Moore. 24 Eamonn Andrews. 25 Jacques. 26 Three. 27 Dave Allen. 28 The winners were all women. 29 "I Love Lucy". 30 "The Simpsons".

1 Which Mia married André Previn?
2 Which church appeared on the Thames TV logo?
3 David Bryant is associated with which sport?
4 What word can go after "beach" and before "gown"?
5 In which city is the Seacon Square shopping centre?
6 Stan Cullis took which English soccer club to the championship?
7 Who wrote the novel "2001: A Space Odyssey"?
8 In which month is St Andrew's Day?
9 Who was the long-time leader of the Mothers of Invention?
10 Which John won an Oscar for Best Actor in "True Grit"?
11 What number is represented by the Roman numerals XC?
12 Which was the only Grand Slam title Pete Sampras did not win?
13 In which decade of the 20th century was Sophia Loren born?
14 What does the abbreviation GMT stand for?
15 How many people compete against each other in Countdown?
16 What are farfalle, pansotti and rigati?
17 Which musician wrote and recorded "Stranger on the Shore"?
18 In which country is the city of Vancouver?
19 What word can follow "letter", "tool" and "witness"?
20 Who was the first Beatle to become engaged this century?
21 Jailed peer Lord Archer was Deputy Chairman of which political party?
22 What is the square root of 49?
23 What is the dog called in a Punch and Judy show?
24 Tin denotes which wedding anniversary?
25 The character Karen Fairgate appeared in which TV soap?
26 Which group made the album "The Joshua Tree"?
27 What date is St George's Day?
28 In song, how many times is Happy Birthday referred to before naming the person?
29 Which motor company went into receivership in England in May 2005?
30 What is the only English anagram of HATTER?

Answers | Pot Luck 81 *(see Quiz 160)*

1 Cream. 2 Tommy. 3 Nine. 4 "Lance". 5 Humberside. 6 Helium. 7 Dick Francis.
8 2. 9 Avon. 10 Halifax. 11 Culture Club. 12 Italy. 13 50s. 14 Equestrianism. 15
Boyzone. 16 Bruce Grobbelaar. 17 Top letters row. 18 Christie. 19 Oliver Twist. 20
Vauxhall. 21 France. 22 Smillie. 23 Reading. 24 360. 25 January and February. 26
Alabama. 27 Julienne. 28 Asia. 29 "Dallas". 30 Johnson.

1 "Holby City" is a spin-off from which medical drama?
2 Which veteran presented "Gardening Club" in the 50s and 60s?
3 Who had a sidekick called Tonto?
4 "All Gas and Gaiters" was one of the first sitcoms to poke fun at whom?
5 Who was the female half of Mork and Mindy?
6 Which blonde actress played Purdey in "The New Avengers"?
7 Which Pamela was a regular on "Not the Nine O'Clock News"?
8 What is the world's longest-running current-affairs programme?
9 Which sitcom featured Bernard Hedges of Fenn Street School?
10 In which century was "Poldark" set?
11 Which king was played by Keith Michell in 1970?
12 Was it Starsky or Hutch who started a trend for chunky cardigans?
13 Which series featured the Cartwrights of the Ponderosa?
14 Which 60s sitcom was about the oil-rich Clampett family?
15 The Bishops, the Robinsons and the Timminses are families in which Australian soap?
16 Which show re-created the era of music hall?
17 Which Saga was the last the BBC produced in black and white?
18 What were the real-life surnames of Terry and June?
19 What are the Woolpack, the Queen Victoria and the Rover's Return?
20 What breed of dog was Rin-Tin-Tin?
21 What type of programme did Fanny Cradock present?
22 Whose Half Hour featured "the lad himself"?
23 Which future James Bond starred as Ivanhoe in the 50s?
24 Which Irishman presented "This is Your Life" from the 1950s?
25 Which Hattie starred in sitcoms with Eric Sykes?
26 How many Goodies were there?
27 Which Irish comic finished his act with "May your God go with you"?
28 Why was "Mastermind" an incongruous title for the first three series?
29 In which sitcom did Lucille Ball and her husband Desi Arnaz play Lucy and Ricky Ricardo?
30 Which yellow cartoon family live in Springfield?

Answers | Crime & Punishment *(see Quiz 161)*

1 London. 2 Belgian. 3 Hare. 4 Gilbert and Sullivan. 5 Triad. 6 Tax evasion. 7 Alcatraz. 8 Bonnie and Clyde. 9 Barabbas. 10 Hindley. 11 Sir Robert Peel. 12 Hanged himself. 13 On a summer's day. 14 New York. 15 Ronnie. 16 Sweeney Todd. 17 Arson. 18 Leeson. 19 1960s. 20 His wife. 21 Manson. 22 George Graham. 23 Last woman to be executed. 24 J. F. Kennedy. 25 Lyons. 26 12. 27 The Yorkshire Ripper. 28 Guinness. 29 Spandau. 30 Fleet Street.

1 How many square yards in an acre?

2 Which TV drama was set in Glenbogle?

3 In which decade of the 20th century was Margaret Thatcher born?

4 Which pop charity concert took place in 2005 to coincide with the G8 summit?

5 Who plays rugby union at Welford Road?

6 In the Bible, which book immediately follows Exodus?

7 Who wrote the novel "The Runaway Jury"?

8 In which country is the city of São Paulo?

9 Joe and Annie Sugden appeared in which TV series?

10 Moving anticlockwise on a dartboard, what number is next to 5?

11 Who sang with Dolly Parton on "Islands in the Stream"?

12 On a Monopoly board, what colour is Park Lane?

13 Who directed the 2005 movie "Charlie and the Chocolate Factory"?

14 What word can go after "double" and before "section"?

15 What name is given to a yacht with two hulls?

16 In song, which road is taken to get to Scotland "afore ye"?

17 In theatre, what is traditionally the main colour in a Pierrot costume?

18 Which UK car manufacturer produced the Princess?

19 How is actor Ronald Moodnick better known?

20 Which Scottish club did defender Alan Stubbs play for?

21 Who in the 50s had "Rock Island Line" as his first million-seller?

22 In which country was Pope John Paul II's funeral held?

23 The airline Qantas is from which country?

24 What is 75 per cent of 200?

25 What name is given to a thin Mexican pancake?

26 Which English city has Oxford Road, Victoria and Piccadilly railway stations?

27 What is the former Prime Minister John Major's constituency?

28 Who called his autobiography "From Drags to Riches"?

29 Which Cat sang "I Love My Dog"?

30 Which former Prime Minister James died in 2005?

Answers	Pot Luck 84 *(see Quiz 166)*

1 George Bush. 2 "Paper." 3 "Fawlty Towers". 4 Tomato. 5 Edith Piaf. 6 Glasgow. 7 "EastEnders". 8 Liverpool. 9 Status Quo. 10 30s. 11 1/3. 12 Johnson. 13 March and April. 14 "Yard". 15 Boxing. 16 Stationery Office. 17 Switzerland. 18 Tom Jones. 19 Knight. 20 "Jim fixed it for me". 21 Meteors. 22 Lawrie Sanchez. 23 Scofield. 24 Hypotenuse. 25 Nickel. 26 "Brookside". 27 US. 28 Two turtle doves. 29 "Dad's Army". 30 Kelly Clarkson.

1 Who won a BAFTA for his role in "Lawrence of Arabia" but not an Oscar?
2 Who starred in "Funny Girl" and "Lawrence of Arabia"?
3 Who starred in "Mary Poppins" and "The Sound of Music"?
4 What is the job of Bert, alias Dick Van Dyke, in "Mary Poppins"?
5 In which Disney film does "The Bare Necessities" appear?
6 Which daughter of Charlie Chaplin appeared in "Doctor Zhivago"?
7 Who was Butch Cassidy in "Butch Cassidy and the Sundance Kid"?
8 Which classic had the line "This is Benjamin. He's a little worried about his future"?
9 Who played Eliza Doolittle in "My Fair Lady"?
10 In which city does "One Hundred and One Dalmatians" take place?
11 Which 1963 BAFTA winner shared its name with a 60s Welsh singer?
12 How many "years BC" were in the title of the 1966 Raquel Welch film?
13 Which "The Upper Hand" actress starred in "Goldfinger"?
14 In which film does 007 seek a diamond smuggler?
15 How many were there in the Dirty band led by Charles Bronson?
16 Which Romeo and Juliet type of musical won most Oscars in the 60s?
17 In which 1968 musical did Bill Sikes murder Nancy?
18 What was Paul Scofield A Man for in 1966?
19 Who co-starred with Jon Voight as Ratso Rizzo in "Midnight Cowboy"?
20 Who is the incompetent Inspector in the "Pink Panther" films?
21 Which "Carry On" film tells of the all-female Glamcabs firm?
22 Who starred in "The Alamo" and "True Grit"?
23 In "Easy Rider" what are the riders riding?
24 In which 60s film did the deranged character Norman Bates appear?
25 Which Mrs Richard Burton starred in "Who's Afraid of Virginia Woolf"?
26 Which Goon starred in "Dr Strangelove"?
27 Who co-starred with Walter Matthau in "The Odd Couple"?
28 Tommy Steele sang the title song in Half a what in 1967?
29 Who was a GI and was the star of a film with that in the title?
30 Which blonde's last film was "The Misfits" in 1960?

Answers | **The Media 1** *(see Quiz 167)*

1 The Sun. 2 Anglia Television. 3 Channel 5. 4 Central. 5 Associated Television. 6 Radio 4. 7 The Mail on Sunday. 8 British Broadcasting Corporation. 9 1930s. 10 BBC 2. 11 Prime Minister. 12 Welsh. 13 Channel 4. 14 British Sky Broadcasting. 15 Camcorder. 16 Sunday. 17 News. 18 Adverts. 19 Drama-documentary. 20 Today. 21 Football. 22 BBC 2. 23 London Weekend Television. 24 GMTV. 25 "Today". 26 Granada. 27 HTV. 28 "News at Ten". 29 Independent. 30 BBC 1 and BBC 2.

Quiz 166 Pot Luck 84

Answers – page 174

LEVEL 1

1 Who was the outgoing American President when Bill Clinton took office?
2 What word can go before "bag", "clip" and "tiger"?
3 Manuel and Sybil appeared in which TV series?
4 Love apple is an old-fashioned name for what?
5 How was the singer Edith Giovanna Gassion better known?
6 In which city was Kenny Dalglish born?
7 Before "Guys and Dolls" in the West End, Nigel Harman found fame in which TV soap?
8 What is the administrative centre for the county of Merseyside?
9 Veteran rockers Rossi and Parfitt are in which group?
10 In which decade of the 20th century was Mary Quant born?
11 Which is smaller – 3/8 or 1/3?
12 Which Don starred in "Miami Vice"?
13 The zodiac sign Aries covers which two calendar months?
14 What word can go after "farm" and before "stick"?
15 Joe Bugner is associated with which sport?
16 In HMSO what does SO stand for?
17 In which country is the city of Zürich?
18 "It's Not Unusual" was the first No. 1 for which singer?
19 Which chess piece can change direction in a normal move?
20 What is the inscription on a "Jim'll Fix It" medal?
21 Meteorophobia is the fear of what?
22 Who was Northern Ireland's boss in their famous victory over England in Belfast, September 2005?
23 Which Paul won an Oscar for Best Actor in "A Man for All Seasons"?
24 What name is given to the longest side of a right-angled triangle?
25 Ni is the chemical symbol for which element?
26 The character Beth Jordache appeared in which TV soap?
27 Which country did the Righteous Brothers come from?
28 In song, what did my true love send me on the second day of Christmas?
29 Which sitcom was set in Walmington-on-Sea?
30 "Breakaway" was the second album by which American Idol?

Answers | Pot Luck 83 *(see Quiz 164)*

1 4,840. 2 "Monarch of the Glen". 3 20s. 4 Live 8. 5 Leicester. 6 Leviticus. 7 John Grisham. 8 Brazil. 9 "Emmerdale". 10 12. 11 Kenny Rogers. 12 Dark blue. 13 Tim Burton. 14 "Cross". 15 Catamaran. 16 Low Road. 17 White. 18 Austin. 19 Ron Moody. 20 Celtic. 21 Lonnie Donegan. 22 The Vatican, Italy. 23 Australia. 24 150. 25 Tortilla. 26 Manchester. 27 Huntingdon. 28 Danny La Rue. 29 Stevens. 30 James Callaghan.

1 Which British daily paper was founded in the 1960s?
2 Which independent TV company serves East Anglia?
3 Which channel began broadcasting in March 1997?
4 Which company took over ATV's Midlands broadcasting?
5 What did ATV stand for?
6 On which Radio station is "The Archers" broadcast?
7 What is the Daily Mail's sister Sunday paper called?
8 What does BBC stand for?
9 In which decade did the BBC begin a TV broadcasting service?
10 Which channel was the third UK terrestrial channel?
11 Which political role did the Italian TV magnate Silvio Berlusconi have in 1994?
12 S4C broadcasts in which minority UK language?
13 On which channel was "Brookside" broadcast?
14 What is BSkyB an abbreviation of?
15 What is a video recorder and a recording device in one unit called?
16 Which day of the week is the Observer published?
17 What type of information does CNN broadcast?
18 In early ITV what was shown in a "natural break"?
19 What kind of programme is a drama-doc?
20 Which daily UK paper was founded in the 80s and ceased in the 90s?
21 What subject is catered for by the magazine Four Four Two?
22 On which channel were colour broadcasts first seen in the UK?
23 In broadcasting what did LWT stand for?
24 Which 90s breakfast TV station was originally known as Sunrise TV?
25 What is Radio 4's early-morning news programme called?
26 Which TV company was named after a Spanish city loved by its founder?
27 Harlech Television's name was shortened to what?
28 What was the UK's first 30-minute TV news programme begun in '67?
29 What did I stand for in IBA before 1991?
30 Which TV channels does the TV licence fund?

| **Answers** | 60s Films *(see Quiz 165)* |

1 Peter O'Toole. 2 Omar Sharif. 3 Julie Andrews. 4 Chimney sweep. 5 The Jungle Book. 6 Geraldine. 7 Paul Newman. 8 The Graduate. 9 Audrey Hepburn. 10 London. 11 Tom Jones. 12 One Million. 13 Honor Blackman. 14 Diamonds are Forever. 15 Dozen. 16 West Side Story. 17 Oliver!. 18 All Seasons. 19 Dustin Hoffman. 20 Clouseau. 21 Cabby. 22 John Wayne. 23 Motorbikes. 24 Psycho. 25 Elizabeth Taylor. 26 Peter Sellers. 27 Jack Lemmon. 28 Sixpence. 29 Elvis Presley. 30 Marilyn Monroe.

1 Michael Hutchence dated which model Helena before Paula Yates?
2 What was Peter Andre and Jordan's baby son called?
3 Which Johnny's name was once linked to the model Kate Moss?
4 What was Stella McCartney's first baby son called?
5 Which former Pakistan cricket captain married Jemima Goldsmith?
6 Which soul singer was the dad of Mandla Kadjaly Carl Stevland Morris?
7 How is Katie Price better known?
8 What is the first name of the TV presenter Ms Frostrup?
9 What is Mrs Michael Jackson II's first name?
10 Carys and Dylan are the children of Michael Douglas and which actress?
11 What is the profession of Claudia Shiffer's ex, David Copperfield?
12 Which actress married Richard Burton twice?
13 Which star of "Evita" married the actress Melanie Griffith?
14 Which Royal Prince's name was linked with photographer Koo Stark?
15 Which former son-in-law of the Queen remarried in 1997?
16 Which tenor left his wife for a Miss Mantovani?
17 Which TV newsman Michael said men were now no more than "sperm donors"?
18 Which comedian Paul split with wife Caroline Quentin in 1997?
19 Which singer was the second Mrs Andrew Lloyd Webber?
20 What is the first name of David Emanuel's fashion designer ex-wife?
21 Nicky Clarke's name is famous in which fashion field?
22 Trudie Styler married which singer/rainforest conservationist in 1992?
23 Which star of "Minder" has been married to the actress Rula Lenska?
24 Which model Elle is an ex-flame of the actor Kevin Costner?
25 What is the first name of Tony Blair's wife?
26 Which Francesca partnered Robson Green on TV and Ralph Fiennes in real life?
27 Who has been the husband of Rachel Hunter and Alana Hamilton?
28 Who is the wife of Derek Redmond and mother of Elliot?
29 What is the first name of Chelsea Clinton's mother?
30 Which actress, a.k.a. Dorien, had a rose named after her at the 1997 Chelsea Flower Show?

Answers | Record Breakers *(see Quiz 170)*

1 Somerset. **2** Cycling. **3** Faldo. **4** Alan Shearer. **5** Hingis. **6** Wigan. **7** Swimming. **8** Javelin. **9** Clive Lloyd. **10** Glenn Hoddle. **11** Underwood. **12** Man. Utd. **13** Joe Davis. **14** Badminton. **15** United States of America. **16** Shriver. **17** Rhodes. **18** Connors. **19** Andrew. **20** Offiah. **21** Brazil. **22** 147. **23** Brian Lara. **24** Hastings. **25** English Channel. **26** Nicklaus. **27** Mark and Steve. **28** Scotland. **29** All Blacks. **30** Wales.

1 Who was the first female presenter of "Desert Island Discs"?
2 Which UK car manufacturer produced the Zodiac?
3 What is Formosa now called?
4 What word can go after "sea" and before "heart"?
5 In "The Simpsons" who or what is Duff?
6 The letter M is on which row of a typewriter or computer keyboard?
7 Who wrote the novel "Lord Of The Flies"?
8 What is a third of 1,200?
9 Which country does midfielder Tugay play for?
10 In which decade of the 20th century was Jimmy Connors born?
11 Which Noel wrote the play "Hay Fever"?
12 Who formed a trio with Paul and Mary?
13 The character Annie Walker appeared in which TV soap?
14 Who created the detective Miss Marple?
15 Which prime minister held office first – Wilson or Heath?
16 What is 1/2 plus 2/8?
17 What is the administrative centre for the county of Dorset?
18 With which event in athletics was Geoff Capes associated?
19 In the US, who presented "The Tonight Show" for 30 years?
20 Which Bob invented the Moog Synthesiser?
21 How many metres in four kilometres?
22 Which George starred in "Minder"?
23 What was the movie sequel to "Silence of the Lambs" called?
24 Adnams brewery is located in which county?
25 Which Liverpudlian grandfather told "Thomas the Tank Engine" tales on TV?
26 In which country is South America's highest mountain?
27 Moving clockwise on a dartboard what number is next to 9?
28 In which country is the city of Istanbul?
29 Who has presented "Through the Keyhole" with Loyd Grossman?
30 Which standard begins, "They asked me how I knew, my true love was true"?

Answers | **Pot Luck 86** *(see Quiz 171)*

1 USA. 2 "Half". 3 20s. 4 Blue. 5 Paula Radcliffe. 6 Gordon Brown. 7 Thomas Hardy. 8 Little Jimmy Osmond. 9 Marlon Brando. 10 Huddersfield. 11 Orwell. 12 Willis. 13 Le Bon. 14 "Weight". 15 Horse racing. 16 Imperial. 17 Sheila Hancock. 18 F. 19 Sahara. 20 8. 21 Bryan Ferry. 22 "Porridge". 23 Custer. 24 Spain. 25 Red. 26 Katrina. 27 Cloud. 28 Square. 29 Bruce Forsyth. 30 David Cameron.

1 Ian Botham first played for which county?
2 Eddie Merckx was a record breaker in which sport?
3 In 1977, which Nick became the youngest ever Ryder Cup player?
4 Who set a new transfer record when he was bought and sold by Blackburn?
5 In the 90s which Martina became Wimbledon's youngest ever senior champ?
6 Which team set a record run as rugby league champs in the 90s?
7 In which sport was Mark Spitz a record breaker?
8 In which event did Fatima Whitbread set a 1986 world record?
9 Who holds the record for most games as West Indian cricket captain?
10 In 1996, who became England's youngest ever soccer boss?
11 Which Rory played rugby union 85 times for England?
12 Which club won a hat-trick of championships from 1999 to 2001?
13 Who won the first 15 World Pro Snooker championships?
14 Gillian Clark made record England appearances in which sport?
15 Record-breaking sprinter Tim Montgomery is from which country?
16 Which Pam was Martina Navratilova's doubles partner in the 80s?
17 Which Wilfred set a record as England's oldest player of Test cricket?
18 Which Jimmy was first to 100 tennis singles titles in a career?
19 In 1994, which Rob scored a record 27 points in a rugby union game for England?
20 Which Martin left Widnes for Wigan in a record rugby transfer?
21 Which team won soccer's World Cup for a record fourth time in 1994?
22 What is the maximum break in snooker?
23 Who became the first player to score over 500 in first-class cricket?
24 Which Gavin became Scotland's most capped rugby union player?
25 Matthew Webb was the first person to swim what?
26 Which Jack was first to six triumphs in golf's US Masters?
27 What is the name of cricket's Aussie Waugh brothers?
28 Which country is Stephen Hendry from?
29 Sean Fitzpatrick played for which international team?
30 Billy Meredith was playing soccer for which country when aged 45?

Answers	**Famous Names** *(see Quiz 168)*

1 Christiansen. 2 Junior. 3 Depp. 4 Miller. 5 Imran Khan. 6 Stevie Wonder. 7 Jordan. 8 Mariella. 9 Debbie. 10 Catherine Zeta-Jones. 11 Magician. 12 Elizabeth Taylor. 13 Antonio Banderas. 14 Andrew. 15 Mark Phillips. 16 Pavarotti. 17 Michael Buerk. 18 Merton. 19 Sarah Brightman. 20 Elizabeth. 21 Hairdressing. 22 Sting. 23 Dennis Waterman. 24 Macpherson. 25 Cherie. 26 Annis. 27 Rod Stewart. 28 Sharron Davies. 29 Hillary. 30 Lesley Joseph.

1 In which country is the city of Albuquerque?
2 What word can go before "baked", "measures" and "time"?
3 In which decade of the 20th century was Doris Day born?
4 What colour is Noddy's hat?
5 Who won the Women's Marathon gold medal at the 2005 World Championships?
6 Which Chancellor presented the first Budget of this new millennium?
7 Who wrote the novel "Tess of the D'Urbervilles"?
8 In the 70s, who had a No. 1 with "Long-Haired Lover from Liverpool"?
9 Who won an Oscar for Best Actor in "The Godfather"?
10 Which rugby league side added Giants to their name in the 90s?
11 Which 20th-century novelist used a Suffolk river as a pen name?
12 Which Bruce starred in "Moonlighting"?
13 Which Simon was vocalist with Duran Duran?
14 What word can go after "paper" and before "lifter"?
15 Henry Cecil is associated with which sport?
16 In the royal address HIH what does I stand for?
17 Whose autobiography about herself and her late husband was called "The Two of Us"?
18 In music, what note is written on the top line of the treble clef?
19 Timbuktu is on the edge of which desert?
20 What is the square root of 64?
21 Who was singer with Roxy Music?
22 The characters Fletcher and Godber appeared in which TV series?
23 Which general made a last stand at Little Big Horn?
24 The airline Iberia is from which country?
25 On a Monopoly board, what colour is Strand?
26 Which hurricane devastated New Orleans in September 2005?
27 What is the only English anagram of COULD?
28 What type of a rectangle has four equal sides and angles?
29 Who introduced "the eight who are going to generate"?
30 Who was the youngest leadership contender in the 2005 race for the Tory leadership?

| **Answers** | **Pot Luck 85** *(see Quiz 169)* |

1 Sue Lawley. 2 Ford. 3 Taiwan. 4 "Lion". 5 A brand of beer. 6 Bottom. 7 William Golding. 8 400. 9 Turkey. 10 50s. 11 Coward. 12 Peter. 13 "Coronation Street". 14 Agatha Christie. 15 Wilson. 16 3/4. 17 Dorchester. 18 Shot. 19 Johnny Carson. 20 Bob Moog. 21 4,000. 22 Cole. 23 Hannibal. 24 Suffolk. 25 Ringo Starr. 26 Argentina. 27 12. 28 Turkey. 29 David Frost. 30 "Smoke Gets in Your Eyes".

1 Which Spaniard won a British Open at golf?
2 Whom did Ted Heath replace as British PM?
3 The tennis superstar Bjorn Borg came from which country?
4 In the UK, the age of majority was lowered from 21 to what?
5 The song "Bright Eyes" was about what type of animal?
6 Haile Selassie was deposed in which country?
7 Which rock legend died at his mansion Graceland?
8 D-Day in 1971 introduced what to Britain?
9 Which athlete Sebastian broke three world records in six weeks?
10 Which art historian Sir Anthony was revealed to be a spy?
11 Idi Amin became President of which country?
12 Who vanished after the murder of Lady Lucan's nanny?
13 The Ayatollah Khomeini drove the Shah from which country?
14 Which Princess was named Sportswoman of the Year?
15 Which legendary artist Pablo died in 1973?
16 Which organization bombed pubs in Guildford and Birmingham?
17 In 1971, 200,000 people demonstrated in the US against which war?
18 Bobby Fischer became a world champion in which game?
19 Olga Korbut delighted the world in what?
20 Whose Silver Jubilee celebrations led to a week of festivities in 1977?
21 In 1976 Jeremy Thorpe resigned as leader of which party?
22 Which Richard was re-elected as President of the US?
23 Which James became motor racing's Formula 1 world champion?
24 Who became the first female leader of a British political party?
25 Which former British monarch passed away?
26 The monarchy returned to Spain after the death of which general?
27 Whom did Princess Anne marry in 1973?
28 Which author Aleksandr was expelled from the USSR?
29 Which commodity quadrupled in price after Israeli-Arab conflict?
30 Second Division Sunderland beat which soccer giants to win the FA Cup?

Answers	Pop: Charts (see Quiz 174)

1 Elton John. 2 Bowie. 3 "My Way". 4 Girls Aloud. 5 Stewart. 6 Westlife. 7 UB40.
8 Eminem. 9 Young. 10 Waterloo. 11 "Unchained Melody". 12 Bee Gees. 13 On
the Block. 14 Missy Elliott. 15 Destiny's Child. 16 80s. 17 Blondie. 18 David Bowie.
19 Newton-John. 20 "Stand by Me". 21 "Somethin' Stupid". 22 Abba. 23 "Amazing
Grace". 24 Beautiful South. 25 Lennon. 26 Aerosmith. 27 "Living Doll". 28 The Bee
Gees. 29 1960s. 30 1950s.

Quiz 173 | Pot Luck 87

1 Tony Blair is MP for which constituency?
2 What is sauerkraut?
3 The characters Rigsby and Miss Jones appeared in which TV series?
4 What word can go after "pine" and before "turnover"?
5 Jeremy Bates is associated with which sport?
6 What's the fruity link with the name of William III of England?
7 Who wrote the novel "For Whom the Bell Tolls"?
8 In the Bible, which book immediately follows Luke?
9 How many pounds in a stone?
10 In which decade of the 20th century was George Best born?
11 Which English side did Liverpool beat on their way to 2005's Champions League Final?
12 In history, which harbour in the US had a famous Tea Party?
13 Is Uruguay ahead of or behind Greenwich Mean Time?
14 "What I Go to School for" was the debut single by which band?
15 On a dartboard what number is opposite 20?
16 Which UK car manufacturer produced the Avenger?
17 In which country is the city of Auckland?
18 On a Monopoly board, what colour is Piccadilly?
19 What was Henri Paul's involvement in the crash in which Princess Diana died?
20 Glenn Hoddle finished his playing career with which club?
21 Sydney Carton appears in which Charles Dickens novel?
22 In which month is St Patrick's Day?
23 Which Annette starred in "One Foot in the Grave"?
24 What is a quarter of 180?
25 Dr Hook sang about whose mother?
26 In which series did a dog called Rowf play the piano?
27 Who was awarded a supper of brown bread and butter?
28 In which month is the London Marathon held?
29 On TV what sort of animal was Dylan?
30 In the 70s, who had a No. 1 with "Dancing Queen"?

Answers | Pot Luck 88 *(see Quiz 175)*

1 "Candle in the Wind". 2 Anne Bancroft. 3 Middle. 4 "Stand". 5 Chemical Brothers. 6 David Seaman. 7 Jeffrey Archer. 8 Olympic. 9 Carmichael. 10 Radius. 11 Osborne. 12 Barker. 13 70s. 14 "Stone." 15 David Trimble. 16 Iraq. 17 Oxygen. 18 "Yesterday". 19 Rex Harrison. 20 Cherry. 21 Four. 22 Mutley. 23 American. 24 Inspector Morse. 25 Nicholas Witchell. 26 Kylie Minogue. 27 "The Magic Roundabout". 28 "Emmerdale". 29 December and January. 30 Brown.

1 Whose first chart success was "Your Song"?

2 Which David has charted with both Bing Crosby and Mick Jagger?

3 Which Frank Sinatra hit has charted on more than ten occasions?

4 "The Show," "No Good Advice" and "Biology" are singles by which Popstars?

5 Which Rod has had over 50 chart hits?

6 "Swear It Again" was which record-breaking boy band's debut single?

7 "Red Red Wine" was the first No. 1 for which group?

8 Dido's song "Thank You" was sampled by which rapper on his song "Stan"?

9 In the 80s, which Paul first charted with "Wherever I Lay My Hat"?

10 Where in London did the Kinks watch the Sunset?

11 Which song was No. 1 for Jimmy Young and Robson and Jerome?

12 Who were Alone in the charts, 30 years after their first hit?

13 Which New Kids had seven singles in the charts in 1990?

14 "Work It" and "Get Ur Freak On" are singles by which artist?

15 "Independent Women Part 1" was the first No. 1 single for which group?

16 In which decade did Belinda Carlisle first hit the UK charts?

17 Debbie Harry fronted which chart busters in the late 70s early 80s?

18 Whose first chart entry was "Space Oddity"?

19 Which Olivia charted with John Travolta and ELO?

20 Which Ben E. King classic made No. 1 25 years after it was recorded?

21 Which song gave Robbie Williams and Nicole Kidman a No. 1 in 2001?

22 "Waterloo" was the first chart success for which group?

23 Which Judy Collins song amazingly charted eight times in the 70s?

24 "Song for Whoever" was the first hit for which Beautiful group?

25 Which John had three No. 1s following his murder?

26 "I Don't Want to Miss a Thing" was the first top ten hit for which group?

27 Which early hit did Cliff Richard rerecord with the Young Ones?

28 Boyzone charted with "Words" in the 90s, but who made the original?

29 In which decade did Stevie Wonder first hit the UK charts?

30 In which decade did charts start to be compiled in the UK?

Answers	**The 70s** (see Quiz 172)

1 Severiano Ballesteros. 2 Harold Wilson. 3 Sweden. 4 18. 5 Rabbit. 6 Ethiopia.
7 Elvis Presley. 8 Decimal coins. 9 Coe. 10 Blunt. 11 Uganda. 12 Lord Lucan.
13 Iran. 14 Anne. 15 Picasso. 16 IRA. 17 Vietnam. 18 Chess. 19 Gymnastics.
20 Queen Elizabeth II. 21 Liberal. 22 Nixon. 23 Hunt. 24 Margaret Thatcher. 25 Edward VIII. 26 Franco. 27 Captain Mark Phillips. 28 Solzhenitsyn. 29 Oil. 30 Leeds.

1 Which Elton John song includes the words "Goodbye Norma Jean"?
2 Which movie Mrs Robinson died in 2005?
3 The letter A is on which row of a keyboard?
4 What word can follow "band", "hat" and "grand"?
5 Who had the award-winning 1999 album "Surrender"?
6 Who was Arsenal's keeper throughout the 1990s?
7 Who wrote the novel "The Fourth Estate"?
8 Which International Committee has the initials IOC?
9 Which Hoagy penned "Stardust"?
10 What is the distance from any point on the circumference to the centre of a circle?
11 Which John wrote the play "Look Back In Anger"?
12 Which Ronnie starred in "Open All Hours"?
13 In which decade of the 20th century was Spice Girl Emma born?
14 What word can go after "sand" and before "mason"?
15 Which Good Friday agreement co-architect lost his Northern Ireland seat in May 2005?
16 In which country is the city of Baghdad?
17 O is the chemical symbol for which element?
18 In the song title what goes after "Yester-Me Yester-You"?
19 Who won an Oscar for Best Actor in "My Fair Lady"?
20 From which fruit is the drink kirsch made?
21 In ten-pin bowling, how many pins are there in the back row?
22 What is Dick Dastardly's dog called?
23 What nationality were the tycoons who bought Manchester United in 2005?
24 Who is Colin Dexter's most famous creation?
25 About which BBC journalist Nicholas did Prince Charles say, "I can't bear that man"?
26 Which Australian lady is the most successful ex-soap star in the UK charts?
27 In which series did Zebedee appear?
28 The character Dolly Skilbeck appeared in which TV soap?
29 The zodiac sign Capricorn covers which two calendar months?
30 On a Monopoly board, what colour is Whitechapel?

Answers | **Pot Luck 87** *(see Quiz 173)*

1 Sedgefield. 2 Pickled cabbage. 3 "Rising Damp". 4 Apple. 5 Tennis. 6 Orange. 7 Ernest Hemingway. 8 John. 9 14. 10 40s. 11 Chelsea. 12 Boston. 13 Behind. 14 Busted. 15 3. 16 Hillman. 17 New Zealand. 18 Yellow. 19 Driver of the car she was in. 20 Chelsea. 21 A Tale of Two Cities. 22 March. 23 Crosbie. 24 45. 25 Sylvia's. 26 "The Muppets". 27 Little Tommy Tucker. 28 April. 29 Rabbit. 30 Abba.

1 In "Dad's Army" who called Sgt Wilson Uncle Arthur?
2 What is the nationality of Margaret Meldrew?
3 Which family lived in Nelson Mandela House, Peckham?
4 In which show did Monica, Rachel, Phoebe, Chandler, Joey and Ross feature?
5 "Frasier" character Daphne Moon came from which country of the British Isles?
6 Which Felicity was the star of "Solo"?
7 Who plays Jean, husband of Lionel, in "As Time Goes By"?
8 Where did Hester and William Fields head for in the 80s/90s sitcom?
9 Which 70s character wore a knitted tanktop, long mac and a beret?
10 Which sitcom featured Mimi La Bonc and a painting by Van Clomp?
11 What was the occupation of Gladys Emmanuel in "Open All Hours"?
12 Chat show family the Kumars live at which number?
13 Where were Miss Tibbs, Miss Gatsby and Major Gowen permanent guests?
14 In the 80s how were Candice, Amanda, Jennifer and Shelley known?
15 On which birthday did Tom Good begin "The Good Life"?
16 Truman and Adler are the surnames of which sitcom flatmates?
17 Which 70s sitcom saw Wendy Richard as Miss Brahms?
18 Which Birmingham comic starred as Bob Louis in "The Detectives"?
19 What was the profession of Tom and Toby in "Don't Wait Up"?
20 How were the mature Dorothy, Blanche, Rose and Sophia known?
21 How was Bombadier Beaumont known in "It ain't Half Hot Mum"?
22 In which show did Paul Nicholas play Vince Pinner?
23 What is the first name of Mr Bucket in "Keeping Up Appearances"?
24 Which sitcom was set in HMP Slade?
25 Which blonde does Leslie Ash play in "Men Behaving Badly"?
26 "Drop the Dead Donkey" takes place in what type of office?
27 In which show did Baldrick first appear?
28 Which sitcom chronicled the life of Zoë and Alec Callender?
29 Which show's theme song was "Holiday Rock"?
30 Which sitcom was set on Craggy Island?

Answers	**On the Map** (see Quiz 178)

1 England. 2 Mountain. 3 Bath. 4 Suez Canal. 5 Downing Street. 6 America. 7 Canterbury. 8 They're not surrounded by water. 9 Norwich. 10 K2. 11 The Cenotaph. 12 Belgium. 13 Washington DC. 14 Ayers Rock. 15 Halifax. 16 Munich. 17 Hadrian's Wall. 18 Red. 19 The Queen Mother. 20 Antarctica. 21 New South Wales. 22 Japan. 23 Sicily. 24 Midlands. 25 Niagara. 26 Paris. 27 Arab. 28 Holland. 29 Sandwich. 30 Mediterranean.

1 Who is R2D2's robot companion in "Star Wars"?
2 In the "Street" what was Betty Williams's surname before she married Billy?
3 In which decade of the 20th century was Tim Henman born?
4 What word can go after "pike" and before "nurse"?
5 How is the rock guitarist William Perks better known?
6 Which Michael began his TV chat shows back in 1971?
7 Who wrote the novel "Three Men in a Boat"?
8 Arachnophobia is the fear of what?
9 The character Nick Cotton appeared in which TV soap?
10 What is Persia now called?
11 Finishing second in 2005, which Arsenal star was the Premiership's leading scorer?
12 Which comic got major stars to act in "a play what I wrote"?
13 How many grams in a kilogram?
14 Queen Anne Boleyn was said to possess an extra what on her body?
15 Who was Queen of the Greek Gods?
16 Which is greater – 6/8 or 2/3?
17 How many pence is the value of smallest silver-coloured UK coin?
18 Moving clockwise on a dartboard what number is next to 16?
19 Henry Cotton is associated with which sport?
20 What word can go before "hound", "pressure" and "vessel"?
21 Cambridge Favourite and Cambridge Vigour are types of what?
22 What was Elton John's first solo No. 1 in the US?
23 In which country is the city of Bangalore?
24 Wayne Daniel played cricket for which country?
25 What is 5 cubed?
26 What is the only English anagram of CLERIC?
27 What note is written in the space above the middle line of the treble clef?
28 Which UK car manufacturer produced the Cowley?
29 The character Frank Spencer appeared in which TV series?
30 Which number follows S Club in the band's title?

| **Answers** | 70s Films *(see Quiz 179)* |

1 Pink Panther. 2 Jack Nicholson. 3 Jaws. 4 Fifties. 5 The Godfather. 6 Superman. 7 Spielberg. 8 Chicago. 9 Gibb. 10 The Muppet Movie. 11 Jesus Christ Superstar. 12 Streisand. 13 Towering Inferno. 14 Airport. 15 Los Angeles. 16 King Kong. 17 Roger Moore. 18 M*A*S*H. 19 McQueen. 20 Last Tango in Paris. 21 Rocky. 22 Poseidon Adventure. 23 Hall. 24 Glenda Jackson. 25 Alice. 26 Cabaret. 27 Dudley. 28 Vietnam. 29 On the Roof. 30 Cop.

1 If you were in France and crossed La Manche, where would you be?
2 In Scotland what does Ben mean in a place name?
3 Which Somerset city has a Spa railway station?
4 Which Canal links the Mediterranean and the Red Sea?
5 In which London street is the Chancellor of the Exchequer's official residence?
6 In which continent is the Hoover Dam?
7 In which city is England's oldest cathedral?
8 What do the Isle of Ely and the Isle of Dogs have in common?
9 In which city is the University of East Anglia?
10 By which letter and number is Mount Godwin-Austen known?
11 Which war memorial is in Whitehall?
12 Which country has the international vehicle registration letter B?
13 Which capital city stands on the Potomac river?
14 Which Australian rock is sacred to the aborigines?
15 The capital of Nova Scotia shares its name with which Yorkshire town?
16 Which German city hosted the 1972 Olympics?
17 What was man-made and stretches from Tyne and Wear to Cumbria?
18 On the London Underground what colour is the Central Line?
19 Glamis Castle was the childhood home of which late royal?
20 Which continent is the iciest?
21 Which Australian state is made up of three words?
22 In which country is Mount Fuji?
23 On which island is the volcanic Mount Etna?
24 In which area of the UK is the Black Country?
25 On which river are the Niagara Falls?
26 In which city would you find the Champs Elysées?
27 What does A stand for in the Middle Eastern UAE?
28 In which country is the port of Rotterdam?
29 Which of the Cinque Ports shares its name with a snack food?
30 Which European Sea's name means "Middle of the earth"?

Answers | TV: Sitcoms *(see Quiz 176)*

1 Pike. 2 Scottish. 3 The Trotters. 4 "Friends". 5 England. 6 Kendal. 7 Judi Dench. 8 France. 9 Frank Spencer. 10 "'Allo 'Allo". 11 Nurse. 12 Number 42. 13 Fawlty Towers. 14 "Girls on Top". 15 40th. 16 "Will and Grace". 17 "Are You Being Served?". 18 Jasper Carrott. 19 Doctors. 20 The Golden Girls. 21 Gloria. 22 "Just Good Friends". 23 Richard. 24 "Porridge". 25 Deborah. 26 TV newsroom. 27 "Blackadder". 28 "May to December". 29 "Hi-De-Hi". 30 "Father Ted".

1 Which Pink character appeared in three top films of the 70s?
2 Which Jack won an Oscar in 1975 for "One Flew Over the Cuckoo's Nest"?
3 Which film was described as 'shark stew for the stupefied'?
4 In which decade does the action of "Grease" take place?
5 Which 1972 movie detailed the career of the Corleone family?
6 In which film did Clark Kent combat the Spider Lady?
7 Which Steven directed "Close Encounters of the Third Kind"?
8 In which gangster city does the action of "The Sting" take place?
9 Which brothers wrote most of the songs for "Saturday Night Fever"?
10 Which 1977 Movie had a frog as one of its main stars?
11 Which was the first Rice/Lloyd Webber musical made into a film?
12 Which Barbra starred in "A Star is Born"?
13 Which film was based on "The Tower" and "The Glass Inferno"?
14 Which disaster movie was described as "Grand Hotel in the sky ..."?
15 In which Californian city did "Earthquake" take place?
16 Which gorilla was the star of a 1976 remake of a 30s classic?
17 Who played James Bond in "Moonraker"?
18 Which 1970 war film led to a long-running TV spin-off with Alan Alda?
19 Which Steve starred in "Papillon"?
20 Which 1972 film has Marlon Brando and Maria Schneider in the lead roles?
21 Which boxer did Sylvester Stallone create on the big screen?
22 Which disaster movie tells of a capsized luxury liner?
23 Which Annie was an Oscar winner for Woody Allen?
24 Which future British MP won an Oscar for "Women in Love" in 1970?
25 Who Doesn't Live Here Any More in the 1974 movie?
26 Which Liza Minnelli Oscar-winning film was set in pre-war Germany?
27 Which Mr Moore starred opposite Bo Derek in "10"?
28 Which Asian war was "The Deer Hunter" about?
29 Where was the Fiddler in the 1971 film?
30 What was the profession of "hero" Doyle in "The French Connection"?

Answers | **Pot Luck 89** *(see Quiz 177)*

1 C3PO. 2 Turpin. 3 70s. 4 "Staff". 5 Bill Wyman. 6 Parkinson. 7 Jerome K. Jerome. 8 Spiders. 9 "EastEnders". 10 Iran. 11 Thierry Henry. 12 Ernie Wise. 13 1,000. 14 Finger. 15 Hera. 16 6/8. 17 5 pence. 18 8. 19 Golf. 20 "Blood". 21 Strawberry. 22 Crocodile Rock. 23 India. 24 West Indies. 25 125. 26 Circle. 27 C. 28 Morris. 29 "Some Mothers Do 'Ave 'Em". 30 7.

1 Which Ken starred as Rebus in the 2006 series based on Ian Rankin's novels?
2 Which major landmark is seen at the start of "News at Ten"?
3 In the 90s, who had a No. 1 with "Vogue"?
4 Who was the first British PM in this new millennium?
5 Prince Michael of Moldavia appeared in which TV soap?
6 In which country is the city of Berne?
7 Who wrote the novel "Cider With Rosie"?
8 The zodiac sign Gemini covers which two calendar months?
9 What does the Q stand for in IQ?
10 In which decade of the 20th century was Bob Dylan born?
11 Which famous chef has a wife known as Jules?
12 Which Helen starred in "Prime Suspect"?
13 Indira Gandhi International airport is in which country?
14 What word can go after "top" and before "trick"?
15 Which Mike directed Imelda Staunton in the movie "Vera Drake"?
16 What colour are Holland's international soccer shirts?
17 Whose No. 1 follow up to their first No. 1 was "Say You'll be There"?
18 What did Wigan's name become for the 1997 rugby league season?
19 What is the administrative centre for the county of Buckinghamshire?
20 The character Captain Kirk appeared in which TV series?
21 Is Turkey ahead of or behind Greenwich Mean Time?
22 What were the two colours of Andy Pandy's costume?
23 Who backed Buddy Holly?
24 What does 1/2 x 1/2 equal?
25 On a Monopoly board, what colour is Euston Road?
26 Which is closer to the sea – London or New York?
27 Who predicted that everyone would be famous for 15 minutes?
28 Who won an Oscar for Best Actor in "Ben Hur"?
29 What is the square root of 100?
30 Which unseeded player won the 2001 Wimbledon Men's Final?

Answers	Pot Luck 91 *(see Quiz 182)*

1 Top letters row. 2 Gaynor. 3 Magnesium. 4 "Pole". 5 Eric Morecambe. 6 Benfica. 7 James Herriot. 8 Greece. 9 Williams sisters. 10 36. 11 Saddam Hussein. 12 Merseyside. 13 Rail crash. 14 Golf. 15 "Coronation Street". 16 Alan Sugar. 17 60/100. 18 9. 19 Triumph. 20 "Room". 21 Spain. 22 90s ("Candle in the Wind '97"). 23 B. 24 Second. 25 The badger. 26 Norwich. 27 13. 28 Chelsea. 29 Books. 30 "Steptoe and Son".

1 If you practised callisthenics what type of activity would you be doing?
2 If you were watching someone on a PGA tour what would you be watching?
3 Which board game has a Genus Edition?
4 Which toy was Hornby most famous for?
5 What do you hit with a racket in badminton?
6 What was the traditional colour for Aran wool?
7 What sort of toy was a Cabbage Patch?
8 In which board game do you draw the meaning of a word?
9 Which game is also the name of a gourdlike vegetable?
10 How many balls are used in a game of billiards?
11 How many members make up a water polo team?
12 What type of food would you get at Harry Ramsden's?
13 Which game has lawn and crown green varieties?
14 In which sport would you wear blades or quads?
15 In DIY, which is shinier – emulsion or gloss?
16 Which is normally larger, a pool table or a billiards table?
17 In Scrabble what colour are the double-word-score squares?
18 In which county is Alton Towers?
19 Which London museum is named after a queen and her cousin?
20 In which sport would you use a sabre, foil or épée?
21 Which is the most versatile piece on a chessboard?
22 Which game is called the national pastime in the USA?
23 Which Lancashire seaside resort has a famous Pleasure Beach?
24 Which Manchester TV studio became a tourist attraction in the 80s?
25 Which actress Jane pioneered her workout plans for others to use?
26 What type of tourist attraction is at Whipsnade Park?
27 What is Barbie's boyfriend called?
28 Which city boasts the Jorvik Viking Centre?
29 Which total is aimed for in pegging in a game of cribbage?
30 In snooker what is the white ball called?

Answers | History: Who's Who? *(see Quiz 183)*

1 George VI. 2 Abraham Lincoln. 3 Julius Caesar. 4 No one. 5 Duke of Wellington. 6 Lady Jane Grey. 7 King John. 8 Joan of Arc. 9 Catherine of Aragon. 10 General Gordon. 11 II. 12 The Terrible. 13 James. 14 William Pitt. 15 George. 16 Tutankhamen. 17 Francis Drake. 18 Architect. 19 The McDonalds. 20 Edward. 21 Trafalgar. 22 Guy Fawkes. 23 Lionheart (Coeur de Lion). 24 Beheaded. 25 Prince Albert (Queen Victoria's husband). 26 Charles II. 27 The Conqueror (the First). 28 Antoinette. 29 Georgia. 30 Queen Victoria.

1 The letter R is on which row of a typewriter or computer keyboard?
2 Which Gloria recorded "I Will Survive"?
3 Mg is the chemical symbol for which element?
4 What word can go after "flag" and before "cat"?
5 How is Eric Bartholomew better known?
6 Eusebio played for which Portuguese club?
7 Who wrote the book "Vet in a Spin"?
8 The airline Olympic is from which country?
9 Which sisters have played each other in a Grand Slam singles final this century?
10 How many feet in a dozen yards?
11 Who was leader of Iraq during the 1991 Gulf War?
12 In 1974 parts of Lancashire and Cheshire made which new county?
13 What sort of crash at Hatfield meant travel problems for many months in England?
14 Laura Davies is associated with which sport?
15 The character Bet Gilroy appeared in which TV soap?
16 Which Alan starred in "The Apprentice" on TV?
17 Which is smaller – 60/100 or 8/10?
18 How many zeros in a billion written in digits?
19 Which UK car manufacturer produced the Dolomite?
20 What word can follow "box", "cloak" and "waiting"?
21 In which country is the city of Bilbao?
22 In which decade did Elton John have his best-ever-selling single?
23 In music, what note is written on the middle line of the treble clef?
24 Paper celebrates which wedding anniversary?
25 Which creature has been described as "the most ancient Briton of English beasts"?
26 What is the administrative centre for the county of Norfolk?
27 Moving anticlockwise on a dartboard what number is next to 6?
28 Graeme Le Saux had two spells with which London club?
29 Bibliophobia is the fear of what?
30 The father and son Albert and Harold appeared in which TV series?

Answers | Pot Luck 90 *(see Quiz 180)*

1 Ken Stott. 2 Big Ben. 3 Madonna. 4 Tony Blair. 5 "Dynasty". 6 Switzerland. 7 Laurie Lee. 8 May and June. 9 Quotient. 10 40s. 11 Jamie Oliver. 12 Mirren. 13 India. 14 "Hat". 15 Mike Leigh. 16 Orange. 17 Spice Girls. 18 Wigan Warriors. 19 Aylesbury. 20 "Star Trek". 21 Ahead. 22 Blue and white. 23 The Crickets. 24 1/4. 25 Light blue. 26 New York. 27 Andy Warhol. 28 Charlton Heston. 29 10. 30 Goran Ivanisevic.

1 Who was British monarch throughout the Second World War?
2 Which US President was assassinated at the theatre?
3 Which ruler was stabbed to death in Rome in March 44 BC?
4 Who was Queen Elizabeth I's husband?
5 Who led the British forces at the Battle of Waterloo?
6 Who was Queen of England for nine days?
7 Which monarch was forced to sign the Magna Carta?
8 Which teenage girl led the French army against the English in the 15th century?
9 Who was Henry VIII's first wife?
10 Who was the famous General killed at Khartoum?
11 Which King Henry ordered the murder of Thomas Becket?
12 Which unpleasant-sounding Ivan was crowned first Tsar of Russia?
13 What was the name of the first King of England and Scotland?
14 Who was the Younger PM who introduced income tax?
15 From 1714 to 1830 all British monarchs were called what?
16 Who had his tomb in the Valley of Kings discovered in the 1920s?
17 Who was the famous captain of the ship the Golden Hind?
18 Inigo Jones followed which profession?
19 Who were massacred by the Campbells at Glencoe?
20 Of British monarchs, have more been called William or Edward?
21 In which battle was Admiral Horatio Nelson fatally wounded?
22 Who took the rap for the failed pot to blow up James I?
23 By what name was Richard I known?
24 How did Charles I die?
25 Whom does the Albert Hall in London commemorate?
26 To which monarch did Nell Gwyn display her oranges?
27 Which William ordered the building of the Tower of London?
28 Which Queen Marie lost her head in the French Revolution?
29 King George II gave his name to which American state?
30 Which monarch has ruled longest in the UK?

Answers	Hobbies & Leisure 2 *(see Quiz 181)*

1 Keep fit. 2 Golf. 3 Trivial Pursuit. 4 Train sets. 5 Shuttlecock. 6 Cream. 7 Doll. 8 Pictionary. 9 Squash. 10 Three. 11 Seven. 12 Fish and chips. 13 Bowls. 14 Roller skating. 15 Gloss. 16 Billiards table. 17 Pink. 18 Staffordshire. 19 Victoria and Albert. 20 Fencing. 21 Queen. 22 Baseball. 23 Blackpool. 24 Granada. 25 Fonda. 26 Zoo. 27 Ken. 28 York. 29 31. 30 Cue ball.

1 Which German player effectively created the sweeper role?
2 Which country does Patrick Berger play for?
3 What is the colour of the strip of the Welsh national team?
4 Which Billy was Northern Ireland manager throughout the 80s?
5 Boca Juniors come from which country?
6 Which striker's England goal tally was one short of Bobby Charlton's?
7 Franco Baresi played 450 plus games for which Italian club?
8 What was the Brazil v. Italy 1994 World Cup Final score at full time?
9 Jan Ceulemans played for which country?
10 At which Dutch club did Denis Bergkamp start his career?
11 In October 1995, who was the first Brazilian to sign for Middlesbrough?
12 Which country does Dwight Yorke play for?
13 Carlos Alberto was skipper of which World Cup-winning country?
14 George Weah plays for which country?
15 Which Lothar is Germany's most capped player?
16 Who followed Cruyff as coach at Barcelona?
17 Which country hosted the 1994 World Cup?
18 Which Republic star Liam played for Juventus and Sampdoria?
19 The Stadium of Light is home of which Portuguese club?
20 What was the "colour" of the type of goal that decided Euro 96's Final?
21 Which Scottish boss died of a heart attack during a game against Wales?
22 In which country did Pele wind down his playing career?
23 Who scored England's first and last goals in Euro 96?
24 Stephane Henchoz of Blackburn, Liverpool and Wigan plays for which country?
25 Angola, Argentina and Austria – which country did not make it to Germany 2006?
26 Which country hosted the 1966 World Cup?
27 Alfredo di Stefano was a regular European Cup Final scorer for which club?
28 Which Russian winger played for Man. Utd and Everton?
29 Who was the first person to have been in charge of England and Australia?
30 Gazza has played club football in which three European countries?

Answers	**Animal World** *(see Quiz 186)*

1 Life span. 2 Dog. 3 Colony. 4 Aardvark. 5 Camels. 6 Dog. 7 Four. 8 Adder. 9 Eucalyptus. 10 Scotland. 11 Toad. 12 Zoology. 13 Black and white. 14 Donkey. 15 Herd. 16 Mandrill. 17 Goat. 18 Badger. 19 Carnivore. 20 Joey. 21 Earthworm. 22 Bear. 23 Seal. 24 Ape. 25 Hare. 26 Squirrel. 27 Cheetah. 28 Elephant. 29 Pack. 30 Australia.

Quiz 185 | Pot Luck 92

Answers – page 197

1 Which prime minister held office first – Eden or Macmillan?
2 Which Don made the album "American Pie"?
3 Who won an Oscar for Best Actor in "The King and I"?
4 Who plays rugby union at Kingsholm Road?
5 The character Mrs Mangel appeared in which TV soap?
6 Sharron Davies is associated with which sport?
7 Who wrote the novel "Animal Farm"?
8 Which ex soap star recorded "Counting Down the Days" and "Left of the Middle"?
9 In the Bible, which book immediately follows the Acts of the Apostles?
10 Which Premiership boss completed 10 years at the same club in June 2005?
11 In which country is the city of Calgary?
12 Which Martin starred in "The Chief"?
13 In which decade of the 20th century was Sue Lawley born?
14 What word can go after "sign" and before "office"?
15 Which Marvin Heard It Through the Grapevine?
16 Which Virginia was BBC Sports Personality of The Year in 1977?
17 Which George wrote the play "Pygmalion"?
18 Uriah Heep appears in which Charles Dickens novel?
19 What colour is in Cilla Black's maiden name?
20 In which English Park was the 2005 Live8 Concert held?
21 How would 71 be shown in Roman numerals?
22 Jack Regan and George Carter appeared in which TV series?
23 Known as 9/11 in America how would the date be known in the UK?
24 In which month is St George's Day?
25 Which bird gave Fleetwood Mac their first No. 1?
26 What type of book links Bridget Jones and Samuel Pepys?
27 Which lumbering animals appear in the "Fantasia" ballet dance?
28 What instrument did Fats Waller play?
29 What is the only English anagram of CAUTION?
30 In which decade did Labour gain its biggest parliamentary majority?

Answers | Pot Luck 93 *(see Quiz 187)*

1 "Till Death Us Do Part". 2 Saddam Hussein. 3 Wolseley. 4 "Fisher". 5 Lynda La Plante. 6 Houllier. 7 Ben Elton. 8 M. 9 Four. 10 40s. 11 Democrat, Republican. 12 Battenberg. 13 Germany. 14 The Everly Brothers. 15 Cowardly Lion. 16 Watch. 17 Butterfly. 18 Gloria Estefan. 19 911. 20 "Public". 21 13. 22 Two. 23 Equilateral. 24 Decanters. 25 Venus. 26 Edinburgh. 27 Crudités. 28 Pole Vault. 29 Iceland. 30 Enclosed spaces.

1 In mammals, the Asian elephant is second but man has the longest – what?

2 A papillon is a breed of what?

3 What is the term for a group of beavers?

4 Alphabetically, which animal always comes first?

5 Dromedary and Bactrian are types of what?

6 What is a male fox called?

7 How many teats does a cow usually have?

8 In Britain, which is the only venomous snake?

9 What type of leaves does a koala feed on?

10 The cairn terrier was originally bred in which country?

11 What type of animal is a natterjack?

12 What type of "ology" is the study of animals?

13 What colour are the markings on a skunk?

14 A jenny is a female what?

15 What is the term for a group of elephants?

16 Which monkey has a blue and red face?

17 What type of animal is an ibex?

18 Which animal lives in an earth or sett?

19 What type of animal eats meat?

20 What name is given to a baby kangaroo?

21 Which creature provides a mole's main source of food?

22 What type of animal was Baloo in "The Jungle Book"?

23 The common and the grey are types of which creature that breed around the coast of Britain?

24 What kind of Naked creature did Desmond Morris write about?

25 A leveret is a young what?

26 Which animal's home is called a drey?

27 Which creature is the fastest land mammal?

28 Which is the largest land animal?

29 What is the term for a group of foxhounds?

30 The wild dog the dingo comes from which country?

| **Answers** | **World Soccer** *(see Quiz 184)* |

1 Franz Beckenbauer. 2 Czech Republic. 3 Red. 4 Bingham. 5 Argentina. 6 Gary Lineker. 7 AC Milan. 8 0-0. 9 Belgium. 10 Ajax. 11 Juninho. 12 Trinidad & Tobago. 13 Brazil. 14 Liberia. 15 Matthaus. 16 Bobby Robson. 17 USA. 18 Brady. 19 Benfica. 20 Golden. 21 Jock Stein. 22 USA. 23 Alan Shearer. 24 Switzerland. 25 Austria. 26 England. 27 Real Madrid. 28 Andrei Kanchelskis. 29 Terry Venables. 30 England, Italy, Scotland.

1 The characters Alf, Else and Rita appeared in which TV series?
2 Who was the first leader of Iraq in the 21st century?
3 Which UK car manufacturer produced the Hornet?
4 What word can go after "king" and before "man"?
5 How is the TV writer Lynda Titchmarsh better known?
6 Which Frenchman left Liverpool for Benitez to take over?
7 Who wrote the novel "Gridlock"?
8 What is the Roman numeral for one thousand?
9 How many gills in a pint?
10 In which decade of the 20th century was Mick Jagger born?
11 What are the two main parties in the US?
12 What name is given to a two-coloured oblong cake covered with almond paste?
13 In which country is the city of Dresden?
14 Which Brothers sang about the Price of Love?
15 Who wanted to ask the Wizard of Oz for courage?
16 In past times, what would a gentleman keep in his fob pocket?
17 What kind of creature is a cabbage white?
18 Who sang with the Miami Sound Machine?
19 Which US emergency phone number is also the name of a band to make No. 1?
20 What word can go before "holiday", "relations" and "school"?
21 Moving clockwise on a dartboard what number is next to 4?
22 How many Grand Slams did Roger Federer win in 2005 – one, two or three?
23 What type of triangle has equal sides and angles?
24 What is locked up in a tantalus?
25 Which planet is also referred to as the morning star?
26 Where is the HQ of the Scottish parliament?
27 What name is given to a starter dish of sliced raw vegetables?
28 Yelena Isinbayeva became the first woman to clear 5m. in which athletic discipline?
29 Which country does Eidur Gudjohnsen play for?
30 Claustrophobia is the fear of what?

Answers	**Pot Luck 92** *(see Quiz 185)*

1 Eden. 2 Maclean. 3 Yul Brynner. 4 Gloucester. 5 "Neighbours". 6 Swimming.
7 George Orwell. 8 Natalie Imbruglia. 9 Romans. 10 Alan Curbishley. 11 Canada.
12 Shaw. 13 40s. 14 "Post". 15 Gaye. 16 Wade. 17 Bernard Shaw. 18 David
Copperfield. 19 White. 20 Hyde Park. 21 LXXI. 22 "The Sweeney". 23 11th
September. 24 April. 25 Albatross. 26 Diary. 27 Hippos. 28 Piano. 29 Auction. 30
1990s.

1 Who recorded "Rubber Soul"?
2 What goes after "What's the Story" in the title of Oasis's album?
3 Which Phil recorded "No Jacket Required"?
4 Who recorded "Dark Side of the Moon"?
5 Which Rod had six consecutive No. 1 albums in the 70s?
6 Who recorded "Purple Rain"?
7 Which group had a Night at the Opera and a Day at the Races?
8 Who recorded "Blue Hawaii"?
9 Paul McCartney was in which group for "Band on the Run"?
10 Who called their greatest hits album "End of Part One"?
11 Which legendary guitarist recorded "From the Cradle"?
12 Who recorded "Off the Wall"?
13 Mike Oldfield presented what type of Bells?
14 Who recorded "The Colour of My Love"?
15 "The Breakthrough" is the seventh album by which artist?
16 Who recorded "Breakfast in America"?
17 Which Abba album had a French title?
18 Neil Diamond's film soundtrack album was about what type of singer?
19 What was the Kaiser Chiefs' debut album called?
20 Who recorded "Brothers in Arms"?
21 Which group were of a Different Class in 1995?
22 In the 90s, who broke out with "The Great Escape"?
23 Which Bruce spent most weeks in the album charts in 1985?
24 Who recorded "Bridge Over Troubled Water"?
25 In the 70s who recorded "Goodbye Yellow Brick Road"?
26 Which Simply Red album featured "For Your Babies" and "Stars"?
27 "Rumours" provided over 400 weeks on the album chart for whom ?
28 Who recorded "Bat out of Hell"?
29 Which Michael – not Jackson – spent most weeks in the 1991 charts?
30 What was Definitely the first No. 1 album from Oasis?

Answers | TV Times 2 *(see Quiz 190)*

1 Anderson. 2 "Boys from the Blackstuff". 3 Boston. 4 Finlay. 5 Stephen Fry. 6 Melbourne. 7 "Little Britain". 8 Alf and Else. 9 "To the Manor Born". 10 Dogs. 11 Gordon Ramsay. 12 A hospital. 13 Britain. 14 Joan Collins. 15 Aspel, Parkinson. 16 Helen. 17 Adie. 18 Charles Dickens. 19 Bobby Ewing. 20 Who. 21 Doctor Who. 22 Northern Ireland. 23 House of Commons. 24 "Heartbeat". 25 "Have I Got News for You". 26 Terry Wogan. 27 Smith and Jones. 28 Martin Bell. 29 Frank. 30 "Eldorado".

1 Which TV Doctor first appeared in the 1960s in a phone box?
2 What is Siam now called?
3 In which decade of the 20th century was Bonnie Langford born?
4 In which country is the city of Faisalabad?
5 Audrey Fforbes-Hamilton appeared in which TV series?
6 Alicante and Marmande are types of what?
7 Who wrote the novel "Black Beauty"?
8 In France, what is the abbreviation for Monsieur?
9 Which Michael declared "Love Changes Everything"?
10 Which Steve got the sack as Millwall boss in July 2005 before the season began?
11 What is the square root of 121?
12 Which John starred in "Bergerac"?
13 The airline Aer Lingus is from which country?
14 What word can go after "paper" and before "reaction"?
15 What is the administrative centre for the county of Essex?
16 Is Bermuda ahead of or behind Greenwich Mean Time?
17 In the 80s, who had a No. 1 with "Imagine"?
18 The zodiac sign Sagittarius covers which two calendar months?
19 Which country does racing driver Riccardo Patrese come from?
20 Which ex-PM became a guardian to Princes William and Harry after their mother's death?
21 On a Monopoly board, what colour is Regent Street?
22 The character Amy Turtle appeared in which TV soap?
23 Was Neptune a Roman or Greek god?
24 Who won an Oscar for Best Actress in "The Silence of the Lambs"?
25 What is the traditional accompaniment to haggis on Burns Night?
26 How many minutes in half a day?
27 Which trumpeter Kenny performed with his Jazzmen?
28 How many walls surround a squash court?
29 The resort of Morecambe is in which county?
30 A4 is a size of what?

Answers	**Performing Arts** *(see Quiz 191)*

1 Ballet. 2 Drury Lane. 3 Opera. 4 Moscow. 5 Gilbert and Sullivan. 6 French. 7 None. 8 The Proms. 9 Glenn Miller. 10 Opera. 11 Milan. 12 Violin. 13 Music Hall. 14 USA. 15 Circus. 16 Good luck. 17 Nashville. 18 Tom Stoppard. 19 Three. 20 Rudolph, Margot. 21 English. 22 Harmonica. 23 Ballet. 24 Brass. 25 New York. 26 Greece. 27 Tchaikovsky. 28 The Met. 29 Sydney. 30 Miller.

Answers – page 198

1 Which Clive chaired "Whose Line is It Anyway"?
2 Which 80s drama centred on Liverpudlian Yosser Hughes?
3 In which US city did the action of "Cheers" take place?
4 Which Doctor abandoned his Casebook in the 90s revival of the series?
5 Who played Jeeves to Hugh Laurie's Bertie Wooster?
6 In "Neighbours" Erinsborough is a suburb of which city?
7 David Walliams and Matt Lucas star in which "little" sketch show?
8 What were Rita Garnett's parents called?
9 In which series did Richard de Vere buy Grantleigh Manor?
10 Which animals did Barbara Woodhouse usually appear with?
11 Which TV chef regularly confronts "Kitchen Nightmares"?
12 What is "Jimmy's"?
13 In 2005 David Dimbleby presented "A Picture" of which country?
14 Which British actress played Alexis Carrington in "Dynasty"?
15 Which two Michaels have hosted "Give Us a Clue"?
16 What was James's wife called in "All Creatures Great and Small"?
17 Which Kate is famous for her news reports from Tiananmen Square?
18 The drama series "Bleak House" was based on a novel by which author?
19 In "Dallas" which character returned from the dead in the shower?
20 Which Doctor has had assistants called Vicki, Jo, Melanie and Ace?
21 "Who" did Christopher Eccleston and David Tennant play in 2005?
22 Where was "Harry's Game" set?
23 What is the House in TV's "House of Cards"?
24 Which drama features Claude Jeremiah Greengrass?
25 Which comedy show is TV's answer to radio's "News Quiz"?
26 Who is the male presenter of BBC TV's "Children in Need"?
27 Which two comedians were famous for their "head-to-head" scenes?
28 Which TV war reporter became an MP in 1997?
29 Who's the feckless father of the Gallaghers in "Shameless"?
30 Which soap was trailed as "sex, sun and sangria"?

Answers | Pop: Albums *(see Quiz 188)*

1 The Beatles. 2 "Morning Glory". 3 Collins. 4 Pink Floyd. 5 Stewart. 6 Prince.
7 Queen. 8 Elvis Presley. 9 Wings. 10 Wet Wet Wet. 11 Eric Clapton. 12 Michael
Jackson. 13 Tubular. 14 Celine Dion. 15 Mary J. Blige. 16 Supertramp. 17 Voulez-
Vous. 18 A jazz singer. 19 Employment. 20 Dire Straits. 21 Pulp. 22 Blur. 23
Springsteen. 24 Simon & Garfunkel. 25 Elton John. 26 Stars. 27 Fleetwood Mac. 28
Meat Loaf. 29 Bolton. 30 Definitely Maybe.

1 Diaghilev was associated with which branch of the arts?
2 In which London lane is the Theatre Royal?
3 Guiseppe Verdi is most famous for which type of musical work?
4 In which city is the Bolshoi Theatre?
5 Who wrote "HMS Pinafore"?
6 What was the nationality of the pianist and composer Claude Debussy?
7 How many symphonies did Beethoven write after the ninth?
8 Which series of concerts is held in late summer at the Albert Hall?
9 Which dance band leader disappeared during World War II?
10 In which branch of the arts did Joan Sutherland achieve fame?
11 In which Italian city is La Scala?
12 Which musical instrument did Stéphane Grappelli play?
13 What type of entertainment did the Americans call vaudeville?
14 If you receive a Tony you have been performing in which country?
15 What kind of entertainment did Barnum call "the Greatest Show on Earth"?
16 What do you wish a performer when you say "break a leg"?
17 What is the name of the music centre that is the capital of Tennessee?
18 Which playwright married the TV doctor, Miriam?
19 How many sisters were in the title of the play by Chekhov?
20 What were the first names of Nureyev and Fonteyn?
21 What was Elgar's nationality?
22 Which musical instrument did Larry Adler play?
23 Darcey Bussell is associated with which branch of the arts?
24 The cornet belongs to which family of musical instruments?
25 In which city is Broadway?
26 A balalaika originates from which country?
27 Which composer had the first names Peter Ilyich?
28 What is New York's Metropolitan Opera more popularly called?
29 Which Australian city has an imaginatively designed Opera House?
30 Which Arthur wrote "The Crucible"?

Answers | **Pot Luck 94** *(see Quiz 189)*

1 Dr Who. 2 Thailand. 3 60s. 4 Pakistan. 5 "To the Manor Born". 6 Tomato. 7 Anna Sewell. 8 M. 9 Ball. 10 Steve Claridge. 11 11. 12 Nettles. 13 Ireland. 14 "Chain". 15 Chelmsford. 16 Behind. 17 John Lennon. 18 November and December. 19 Italy. 20 John Major. 21 Green. 22 "Crossroads". 23 Roman. 24 Jodie Foster. 25 Mashed swede (neeps). 26 720. 27 Ball. 28 4. 29 Lancashire. 30 Paper.

1 In rugby, what did Keighley add to their name in the 90s?
2 Dipsophobia is the fear of what?
3 In which decade of the 20th century was John Thaw born?
4 What word can go after "soap" and before "office"?
5 Which quiz was presented by Bamber Gascoigne then Jeremy Paxman?
6 Kendall, Walker and Royle have all managed which club?
7 Who wrote the novel "Tom Sawyer"?
8 How many yards in a furlong?
9 Putin became head of state of which country?
10 In the 80s, who had a No. 1 with "Papa Don't Preach"?
11 What is the only English anagram of TEND?
12 Edwina Currie represented which political party?
13 Which country does the drink ouzo come from?
14 How many times do you sing "jingle" in a chorus of jingle bells?
15 In which year did Elizabeth II celebrate 50 years on the throne?
16 Moving anticlockwise on a dartboard what number is next to 15?
17 In which country is the city of Gothenburg?
18 What is Dec's first name as in Ant & Dec?
19 What word can follow "filter", "graph" and "rice"?
20 In which city did Tony Bennett leave his heart?
21 By what name is endive known in the US?
22 Which Nigel starred in "Yes Minister"?
23 Which UK car manufacturer produced the Prefect?
24 What is 60 per cent of 3,000?
25 Carlo Cudicini and Ed De Goey have both kept goal for which London club?
26 What is the sum of a century plus a gross?
27 A mazurka is a type of what?
28 On the Swedish flag what is the colour of the cross?
29 The soldier Robert Clive has his name linked with which country?
30 Who led the Family Stone?

| **Answers** | **Pot Luck 96** *(see Quiz 194)* |

1 Seaweed. 2 Jade Goody. 3 Obtuse. 4 Black. 5 Score nothing. 6 Boxing. 7 Douglas Adams. 8 A knot. 9 Honor Blackman. 10 Four. 11 Abba. 12 Defence. 13 30s. 14 "Blind". 15 Marat Safin. 16 Andrew. 17 Wilde. 18 Germany. 19 Charles Aznavour. 20 Paul Ince. 21 "Coronation Street". 22 Middle letters row. 23 "Crossroads". 24 Zirconium. 25 None. 26 The maiden all forlorn. 27 North Sea. 28 Ireland. 29 Mohammed Al Fayed. 30 Blur.

Quiz 193 | 80s Films

1 Which Attenborough brother directed "Gandhi"?
2 What is the nationality of the hero of "Crocodile Dundee"?
3 Which Raging animal is in the title of the 1980 Robert De Niro film?
4 The Return of what was the third of the "Star Wars" trilogy?
5 Whose Choice won Meryl Streep an Oscar in 1982?
6 Which British film was about the 1924 Olympics?
7 The Adventures of which Baron proved to be one of the greatest cinematic flops in history?
8 Which Crusade featured in the title of the 1989 "Indiana Jones" movie?
9 In which city does "Beverly Hills Cop" take place?
10 What sort of People were the stars of the 1980 Donald Sutherland film?
11 Which Henry and Katharine won Oscars for "On Golden Pond"?
12 In which film did Bob Hoskins play opposite a cartoon character?
13 Who renewed his battle against the Joker in 1989?
14 How many Men starred with a baby in the 1987 movie?
15 In which 1982 film did Dustin Hoffman appear in drag?
16 In which US state was the Best Little Whorehouse in 1982?
17 Which organization is "Married to the Mob" about?
18 Which country did the DJ say Good Morning to in the 1987 film?
19 Which continent featured in the Robert Redford/Meryl Streep film about Karen Blixen?
20 Whom was the chauffeur Driving in the 1989 film?
21 Which financial location was the subject of a Michael Douglas film?
22 Which Warren Beatty film of the 80s was set in communist Russia?
23 The Kiss of whom provided William Hurt with an Oscar?
24 Who and Her Sisters were the subject of a Woody Allen movie?
25 Which Kevin appeared in "A Fish Called Wanda"?
26 If Billy Crystal was Harry, who was Sally in 1989?
27 Where was the American Werewolf in the 1981 film?
28 "The Killing Fields" deals with events in which neighbour of Vietnam?
29 Which Helena starred in "A Room with a View"?
30 Where was the Last Exit to in 1989?

Answers | Celebs *(see Quiz 195)*

1 Sienna Miller's. 2 Doherty. 3 Swedish. 4 Gaby Roslin. 5 Monaco. 6 Andre. 7 Ekland. 8 Football Association. 9 Gazza. 10 None. 11 Max. 12 Boys – in a Wonderbra ad. 13 Ellen MacArthur. 14 Zandra. 15 Britney Spears. 16 The Spice Girls. 17 Tennis. 18 Japanese. 19 Versace. 20 Helvin. 21 Prince Rainier of Monaco. 22 California. 23 Laura Ashley. 24 Frost. 25 Laura. 26 Wayne Rooney. 27 Hugh Grant. 28 Jasper. 29 Catherine Zeta Jones. 30 Princess of Wales.

1 Agar-agar is a type of gelatine made from what?
2 In 2005, which former "Big Brother" contestant opened a beauty salon called "Ugly's" in Hertford?
3 What type of angles are greater than 90 but less than 180 degrees?
4 What colour goes before Sabbath and Box in group names?
5 In 2003, Jemini were the first UK act to do what in the Eurovision Song Contest?
6 Terry Downes is associated with which sport?
7 Who wrote the book "The Hitch Hiker's Guide to the Galaxy"?
8 What is a sheep-shank?
9 Who played Pussy Galore in "Goldfinger"?
10 How many portraits are carved into Mount Rushmore?
11 In the 70s, who had a No. 1 with "Knowing Me Knowing You"?
12 Which Ministry is the MoD?
13 In which decade of the 20th century was Paul Daniels born?
14 What word can go after "colour" and before "spot"?
15 Who won the Men's 2005 Australian Open?
16 Alphabetically, who is the first of the Apostles?
17 Which Oscar wrote the play "The Importance of Being Earnest"?
18 In which country is the city of Hanover?
19 How is Charles Aznavurjan better known?
20 Who was the first black soccer player to captain England?
21 The character Stan Ogden appeared in which TV soap?
22 The letter D is on which row of a typewriter or computer keyboard?
23 Which soap set in a motel was briefly revived by ITV in 2001?
24 Zr is the chemical symbol for which element?
25 How many Tory MPs were left in Scotland after the 1997 general election?
26 In "The House That Jack Built", who milked the cow with the crumpled horn?
27 The River Tay flows into which sea?
28 Which country did the late comedian Dave Allen come from?
29 Which entrepreneur was Fulham chairman when they went into the Premiership?
30 "There's No Other Way" was the first top ten hit for which group?

Answers | Pot Luck 95 *(see Quiz 192)*

1 Cougars. 2 Drinking. 3 40s. 4 "Box". 5 "University Challenge". 6 Everton. 7 Mark Twain. 8 220. 9 Russia. 10 Madonna. 11 Dent. 12 Conservative. 13 Greece. 14 Six. 15 2002. 16 10. 17 Sweden. 18 Declan. 19 "Paper". 20 San Francisco. 21 Chicory. 22 Hawthorne. 23 Ford. 24 1,800. 25 Chelsea. 26 244. 27 Dance. 28 Yellow. 29 India. 30 Sly.

1 Whose engagement to Jude Law was an on and off event in 2005?
2 Which Pete hit the headlines with Kate Moss in 2005?
3 Which language other than English does Ulrika Jonsson speak?
4 Who is the daughter of the veteran broadcaster Clive Roslin?
5 Royals Albert, Caroline and Stephanie are from which principality?
6 Which Peter did Jordan marry in 2005?
7 Which Swedish Britt was married to Peter Sellers?
8 Faria Alam's industrial tribunal re unfair dismissal involved which Association's HQ?
9 Which controversial footballer married Sheryl Failes?
10 Of Paula Yates and Bob Geldof's three children, how many are boys?
11 What is the first name of the publicist Mr Clifford?
12 To whom did Eva Herzigova most famously say hello?
13 Which Ellen was made the youngest ever Dame in February 2005?
14 What is the first name of the flamboyant fashion designer Ms Rhodes?
15 Who launched her perfume Fantasy days after the birth of first child Sean Preston?
16 Which quintet first advertised Pepsi in mid-1997?
17 Brooke Shields and Tatum O'Neal both married which type of sporting stars?
18 What is the nationality of the fashion designer Kenzo?
19 Who designed Liz Hurley's infamous "safety pin" dress?
20 Which model Marie was married to the photographer David Bailey?
21 Who was Europe's longest-serving monarch until his death in April 2005?
22 In which US state did Michael Jackson go on trial in 2005?
23 What was the designer Laura Mountney's married and business name?
24 Which political interviewer David is married to the daughter of the Duke of Norfolk?
25 What is the first name of Princes William and Harry's step sister?
26 Coleen McLoughlin's name has been linked to which Man. Utd soccer star?
27 Which English actor was arrested in Hollywood in a Divine situation?
28 What is Sir Terence Conran's designer son called?
29 Which Oscar-winning actress has children called Dylan and Carys?
30 Andrew Morton became a celeb. due to a biography of whom?

Answers | 80s Films *(see Quiz 193)*

1 Richard. 2 Australian. 3 Bull. 4 The Jedi. 5 Sophie's. 6 Chariots of Fire. 7 Munchhausen. 8 Last. 9 Los Angeles. 10 Ordinary. 11 Fonda, Hepburn. 12 Who Framed Roger Rabbit?. 13 Batman. 14 Three. 15 Tootsie. 16 Texas. 17 Mafia. 18 Vietnam. 19 Africa. 20 Miss Daisy. 21 Wall Street. 22 Reds. 23 The Spider Woman. 24 Hannah. 25 Kline. 26 Meg Ryan. 27 London. 28 Cambodia. 29 Bonham-Carter. 30 Brooklyn.

Quiz 196 | Pot Luck 97

Answers – page 208

LEVEL 1

1 Clive Rice played cricket for which country?
2 James Grieve and Lord Lambourne are types of what?
3 Which UK car manufacturer produced the Hunter?
4 In which month is All Saints' Day?
5 How is Francis Avallone better known?
6 Which team did Coventry beat in their 80s FA Cup Final triumph?
7 Who wrote the novel "A Clockwork Orange"?
8 In which country is Ho Chi Minh City?
9 What word describes a straight line crossing the centre of a circle?
10 In which decade of the 20th century was Jim Davidson born?
11 Which Bill topped the most weeks in the chart list for 1956?
12 Which ground hosted England's final home qualifier for the 2006 World Cup?
13 Richard Dunwoody is associated with which sport?
14 What word can go after "salad" and before "gown"?
15 How many square inches in a square foot?
16 In "Snow White", what do the dwarfs tell you to do while you work?
17 Who was queen of the Roman Gods?
18 If February 1 is a Thursday in a non-leap year, what day is March 1?
19 The butler Hudson appeared in which TV series?
20 Haematophobia is the fear of what?
21 On a Monopoly board, what colour is Vine Street?
22 In the 60s, who had a No. 1 with "Honky Tonk Women"?
23 Which is greater – 2/3 or 7/10?
24 What word can go before "all", "cast" and "take"?
25 What is South West Africa now called?
26 Which Michael links TV's "Some Mothers Do 'Ave 'Em" and "The Woman in White"?
27 Gazpacho is a type of what?
28 In which city does Batman operate?
29 Which Mike was the musical force behind the Wombles?
30 In ancient China, which precious green stone vase was buried with the dead?

Answers	Pot Luck 98 *(see Quiz 198)*

1 Italy. 2 Jerry Lee Lewis. 3 Harry Potter series. 4 "Cream". 5 Chester. 6 Equestrianism. 7 Raymond Chandler. 8 Tyne and Wear. 9 Ronni Ancona. 10 Wolves. 11 Bottom. 12 Beaver. 13 12. 14 South Africa. 15 Maria Callas. 16 The Republic of Ireland. 17 Nicholas Nickleby. 18 Mme. 19 September. 20 Bucks Fizz. 21 Edward Heath. 22 MacNee. 23 Sudan. 24 Citrus. 25 Altitude. 26 Liza Minnelli. 27 Jimmy Carter. 28 Sand. 29 Ahead. 30 Trumpet.

Quiz 197 | Sporting Chance 2

1 The green jacket is presented to the winner of which event?
2 Which Southampton soccer legend retired in 2002?
3 In boxing, what weight division is directly below heavyweight?
4 In horse racing, in which month is the Melbourne Cup held?
5 Tennis players Kim Clijsters and Justine Henin-Hardenne are from which country?
6 Who won the Wimbledon women's singles most times in the 80s?
7 The 2004 Summer Olympics took place in which country?
8 Wayne Rooney left Everton for which club in August 2004?
9 How often is cycling's Tour of Spain held?
10 The golfer Nick Price comes from which country?
11 A cricket umpire extends both arms horizontally to signal what?
12 The boxers Ray Leonard and Ray Robinson were both known as what?
13 In which sport did Michelle Smith find fame?
14 In golf, what is the term for two under par for a hole?
15 What sport do the Pittsburgh Steelers play?
16 The Harry Vardon Trophy is presented in which sport?
17 Which country won the 1996 cricket World Cup Final?
18 Which county cricket club has its home at Old Trafford?
19 What is the nickname of rugby union's William Henry Hare?
20 In horse racing, which of the five Classics is held at Doncaster?
21 In boxing, what do the initials WBA stand for?
22 Which sport is the 'T' in LTA?
23 At which French course is the Prix du Jockey-Club held?
24 In golf, who won the Masters in 2005?
25 LOVELY is an anagram of which tennis term?
26 Which sport takes place in a velodrome?
27 In equestrianism, which Nick won the Volvo World Cup in 1995?
28 Which country won their fifth Football World Cup in 2002?
29 The terms serve, dig and spike relate to which sport?
30 Which rugby league team are the Tigers?

Answers	The 80s (see Quiz 199)

1 Lester Piggott. 2 Argentina. 3 October. 4 Marathon. 5 Bob Geldof. 6 Poland. 7 Mike Gatting. 8 Shergar. 9 Ronald Reagan. 10 Brighton. 11 Whitbread. 12 Foot. 13 Yuppies. 14 London. 15 Steel. 16 Egypt. 17 McEnroe. 18 Terry Waite. 19 Madonna. 20 Grade. 21 Arthur Scargill. 22 Livingstone. 23 AIDS. 24 Greenham. 25 Extraterrestrial. 26 Lawson. 27 Conservative. 28 Mary Rose. 29 India. 30 William.

1 Gnocchi is a food from which country?
2 In the 50s, who had a No. 1 with "Great Balls of Fire"?
3 The Tri-Wizard games feature in which series of books and films?
4 What word can go after "ice" and before "cheese"?
5 What is the administrative centre for the county of Cheshire?
6 Liz Edgar is associated with which sport?
7 Who wrote the book "The Big Sleep"?
8 In 1974 parts of Northumberland and Durham made which new county?
9 Which Ronni featured as an impressionist along with Alistair McGowan?
10 In rugby league what did Warrington add to their name for 1997?
11 The letter X is on which row of a typewriter or computer keyboard?
12 Which gnawing Canadian animal has bright-orange teeth?
13 What is the square root of 144?
14 Jan Smuts airport is in which country?
15 How is the opera singer Maria Kalogeropoulos better known?
16 Frank Stapleton became highest scorer for which international side?
17 Wackford Squeers appears in which Charles Dickens novel?
18 In France, what is the abbreviation for Madame?
19 In which month of 2005 did Hurricane Katrina hit New Orleans?
20 "Making Your Mind Up" was the first No. 1 for which group?
21 Which former British Prime Minister Edward died in 2005?
22 Which Patrick starred in "The Avengers"?
23 In which country is the city of Khartoum?
24 What is the only English anagram of RUSTIC?
25 What term describes the measurement of height?
26 Who won an Oscar for Best Actress in "Cabaret"?
27 Who was the outgoing American President when Ronald Reagan took office?
28 What is the main ingredient in glass?
29 Is Zambia ahead of or behind Greenwich Mean Time?
30 What instrument did Eddie Calvert play?

Answers | **Pot Luck 97** *(see Quiz 196)*

1 South Africa. 2 Apple. 3 Hillman. 4 November. 5 Frankie Avalon. 6 Spurs. 7 Anthony Burgess. 8 Vietnam. 9 Diameter. 10 50s. 11 Haley. 12 Old Trafford. 13 Horse Racing. 14 "Dressing". 15 144. 16 Whistle. 17 Juno. 18 Thursday. 19 "Upstairs Downstairs". 20 Blood. 21 Orange. 22 Rolling Stones. 23 7/10. 24 "Over". 25 Namibia. 26 Michael Crawford. 27 Soup. 28 Gotham. 29 Batt. 30 Jade.

1 Which British jockey was jailed for tax evasion in 1987?
2 General Galtieri was ousted as president of which country?
3 In which month was the hurricane of 1987 that swept Britain?
4 Which London race was held for the first time?
5 Who was the founder of Band Aid?
6 The Solidarity movement opposed communists in which country?
7 Which England cricket captain rowed with a Pakistani umpire?
8 Which Derby-winning horse was kidnapped while in Ireland?
9 Which ex-movie actor became President of the US?
10 The IRA bombed a Tory Party conference at which seaside venue?
11 Which Fatima won Olympic gold for Britain in the javelin?
12 Which Michael became leader of the Labour Party?
13 Young upwardly mobile persons became known as what?
14 In which city were Prince Charles and Lady Diana Spencer married?
15 Which David stood down as Liberal leader in 1988?
16 Army officers assassinated President Sadat of which country?
17 Which John ended Borg's Wimbledon dominance?
18 Who was the special representative of the Archbishop of Canterbury taken hostage in Beirut?
19 Which female soloist has had six UK No. 1s including "In the Groove"?
20 Which Michael took over as head of Channel 4?
21 Who was leader of the NUM in the mid-80s strikes?
22 Which Ken emerged as leader of the Greater London Council?
23 "Don't Die of Ignorance" was a slogan linked with which disease?
24 Which Common witnessed protest against nuclear cruise missiles?
25 What does ET stand for in the Spielberg movie?
26 Which Nigel resigned as Mrs Thatcher's Chancellor ?
27 Which party had a landslide victory in Britain in the 1983 elections?
28 Which Tudor ship was raised from the seabed?
29 There was a chemical leak at Bhopal – in which country?
30 Which Prince was the first-born child of the Princess of Wales?

Answers	Sporting Chance 2 *(see Quiz 197)*

1 US Masters. 2 Matt Le Tissier. 3 Cruiserweight. 4 November. 5 Belgium. 6 Martina Navratilova. 7 Greece. 8 Manchester United. 9 Annually. 10 Zimbabwe. 11 A wide. 12 Sugar Ray. 13 Swimming. 14 Eagle. 15 American Football. 16 Golf. 17 Sri Lanka. 18 Lancashire. 19 Dusty. 20 St Leger. 21 World Boxing Association. 22 Tennis. 23 Chantilly. 24 Tiger Woods. 25 Volley. 26 Cycling. 27 Skelton. 28 Brazil. 29 Volleyball. 30 Castleford.

Answers – page 212

1 "You Can't Hurry Love" was the first No. 1 for which male singer?

2 Who is the Boss?

3 Stephen, Ronan, Mikey, Shane and Keith were which chart-topping boy band?

4 Who was a "Rocket Man" in the 70s?

5 Ziggy Stardust was the creation of which performer?

6 Whose autobiography was titled "Moonwalk"?

7 Which Welsh singer was knighted in the 2006 New Year Honours List?

8 The death of whose son inspired the song "Tears in Heaven"?

9 Which Peter was a founder member of Genesis?

10 Which supergroup took "Innuendo" to No. 1 in the UK?

11 Whose name had turned into a symbol for "Most Beautiful Girl in the World"?

12 Including membership of a group, which Paul has 20-plus UK No. 1s?

13 Which female star recorded "Chain Reaction"?

14 "Holiday" was the first hit in the UK for which solo performer?

15 Who created the fashion for wearing only one glove?

16 Which George sang "Careless Whisper"?

17 In the 80s, which Barbra was "A Woman in Love"?

18 Who was nicknamed the Pelvis in the 50s?

19 Who – after his death – had a No. 1 called "Living on My Own"?

20 Who was Tina Turner's first husband?

21 Who was Dancing in the Street with Dave Bowie for Live Aid ?

22 Who used to sing with the Faces?

23 Which country queen first hit the charts with "Jolene"?

24 Whose first UK Top Ten hit was "Dancing in the Dark" in 1985?

25 What was the Spice Girls' debut single?

26 In which film did Madonna sing "Another Suitcase in Another Hall"?

27 In the 90s, who sang "I've Got You Under My Skin" with Bono?

28 "Genie in a Bottle" and "Dirrty" have been No. 1s for which artist?

29 What was the 1990 duet hit single for Tina Turner and Rod Stewart?

30 "Cracklin' Rosie" was the first hit of which singer/writer?

Answers | TV: Cops & Robbers *(see Quiz 202)*

1 "EastEnders". 2 "Cracker". 3 Hill Street. 4 Adam. 5 Chef. 6 New York. 7 Poirot.
8 "Prime Suspect". 9 He was a ghost. 10 Sherlock Holmes. 11 Pierce Brosnan. 12
East Anglia. 13 Prison. 14 Jim. 15 "The Bill". 16 Kojak. 17 Hamish Macbeth.
18 Maigret. 19 Inspector Wexford. 20 "Miami Vice". 21 Bergerac. 22 Boon. 23
Ironside. 24 Red. 25 Miss Marple. 26 "New Tricks". 27 Roderick. 28 Singing. 29
"Z Cars". 30 Jimmy Nail.

1 Which Rik starred in "The New Statesman"?
2 What word can follow "clip", "dart" and "side"?
3 In which country is the city of Kingston?
4 Moving anticlockwise on a dartboard what number is next to 9?
5 Which blockbuster book features a murder of a curator at the Louvre?
6 CJD was the human form of which disease also known by three letters?
7 Who wrote the novel "Tilly Trotter"?
8 Hippophobia is the fear of what?
9 Glen Campbell sang about what type of Cowboy?
10 Zn is the chemical symbol for which element?
11 What nationality was the first non-British England soccer manager?
12 TV's "London's Burning" was about life in which emergency service?
13 In which decade of the 20th century was Anna Ford born?
14 What word can go after "Victoria" and before "tomato"?
15 How many cubic feet in a cubic yard?
16 "Vision of Love" was the first Top Ten hit for which Mariah?
17 What other fruit is crossed with a plum to produce a nectarine?
18 What do you have a pocket full of if you play ring-a-ring-o'-roses?
19 What note is written in the space below the top line of the treble clef?
20 Ruby denotes which wedding anniversary?
21 Which UK car manufacturer produced the Viva?
22 What is the name of Queen Victoria's house on the Isle of Wight?
23 Which Cockney duo sang "There ain't No Pleasing You"?
24 Chapatti is unleavened bread originally from which country?
25 What is three-eighths of 96?
26 Which old English coin was known as the tanner?
27 The River Mersey flows into which sea?
28 Alphabetically, which is the first of the days of the week?
29 In the 90s, who had a No. 1 with "I Will Always Love You"?
30 The character Derek Wilton appeared in which TV soap?

Answers | **Pot Luck 100** *(see Quiz 203)*

1 AC Milan. 2 June and July. 3 20s. 4 "Barrel". 5 "Yes [Prime] Minister". 6 The sea. 7 Conan Doyle. 8 Extras. 9 Reflex. 10 Ireland. 11 Vivien Leigh. 12 Scotland. 13 September. 14 Teaching. 15 Liberty X. 16 Elton John. 17 Deuteronomy. 18 Japan. 19 Newcastle United. 20 Nelson's. 21 Batman. 22 Sofia Coppola. 23 Scotland. 24 19th. 25 Conservative. 26 Australia. 27 1/4. 28 "EastEnders". 29 Petula Clark. 30 White.

1 Michael French left which soap to star as Slade in "Crime Traveller"?
2 Which series featured Eddie "Fitz" Fitzgerald?
3 Which police station's Blues were led by Captain Frank Furillo?
4 What is the first name of P. D. James's Commander Dalgliesh?
5 In "Pie in the Sky" which profession did Henry combine with policing?
6 In which city was "Cagney and Lacey" set?
7 Which European sleuth's assistant was Captain Hastings?
8 Which series about a woman detective was written by Lynda La Plante?
9 Why was Marty Hopkirk an unusual detective?
10 Which Victorian sleuth was portrayed on TV by Jeremy Brett?
11 Which future 007 played Remington Steele?
12 In which area of the UK was "The Chief" set?
13 Drama series "Bad Girls" is set in what type of establishment?
14 What was the first name of Rockford of "The Rockford Files"?
15 Roberta Taylor and Todd Carty have both featured in which long-running drama?
16 Which New York cop ate lollipops?
17 Which policeman had a West Highland terrier called Wee Jock?
18 Which French detective had a pipe, raincoat and trilby?
19 Which Ruth Rendell detective lived in Kingsmarkham?
20 Which Florida-based drama had a theme song by Jan Hammer?
21 In the 80s who was rooting out villains in Jersey?
22 Which Midlands troubleshooter had a sidekick called Rocky?
23 Which wheelchair-bound detective was played by Raymond Burr?
24 What colour is Inspector Morse's Jaguar?
25 Which elderly female sleuth was played by Joan Hickson from 1984?
26 As retired cops, Waterman, Bolam and Armstrong were up to "New" what?
27 What is the first name of Inspector Alleyn, created by Ngaio Marsh?
28 What was unusual about the detective in the Dennis Potter drama?
29 "Softly Softly" was the sequel to which TV police classic series?
30 Which Geordie actor starred as "Spender"?

Answers	**Pop: Superstars** *(see Quiz 200)*

1 Phil Collins. 2 Bruce Springsteen. 3 Boyzone. 4 Elton John. 5 David Bowie. 6 Michael Jackson. 7 Tom Jones. 8 Eric Clapton. 9 Gabriel. 10 Queen. 11 Prince. 12 McCartney. 13 Diana Ross. 14 Madonna. 15 Michael Jackson. 16 Michael. 17 Streisand. 18 Elvis Presley. 19 Freddie Mercury. 20 Ike Turner. 21 Mick Jagger. 22 Rod Stewart. 23 Dolly Parton. 24 Bruce Springsteen. 25 "Wannabe". 26 Evita. 27 Frank Sinatra. 28 Christina Aguilera. 29 "It Takes Two". 30 Neil Diamond.

1 Whom did Liverpool defeat in the Champions League final in 2005?
2 The zodiac sign Cancer covers which two calendar months?
3 In which decade of the 20th century was Bruce Forsyth born?
4 What word can go after "biscuit" and before "organ"?
5 The characters Jim and Annie Hacker appeared in which TV series?
6 Poseidon was the Greek god of what?
7 Who wrote "The Hound of the Baskervilles"?
8 Which 2005 TV comedy series had Kate Winslet dressed as a nun?
9 Which angles are more than 180 but less than 360 degrees?
10 Which country did Clannad come from?
11 Who won an Oscar for Best Actress in "Gone with the Wind"?
12 Shortbread is a speciality of which country?
13 Alphabetically, what is the last of the calendar months?
14 Which profession is represented by the NAS/UWT?
15 "Just a Little" was the first No. 1 for which group?
16 Who was the first rock star to become chairman of a soccer club?
17 What is the fifth book of the Old Testament?
18 In which country is the city of Kyoto?
19 Bellamy and Jenas were both PFA Young Player of the Year while at which club?
20 The Victory was whose flagship?
21 In comics, on TV and in film, how is Bruce Wayne better known?
22 "The Virgin Suicides" was the debut directorial movie of which Sofia?
23 Which country does TV presenter Lorraine Kelly come from?
24 In which century was the Manchester Ship Canal opened?
25 Prime Minister Stanley Baldwin represented which political party?
26 The airline Aus-air is from which country?
27 Which is smaller – 2/3 or 1/4?
28 The character David Wicks appeared in which TV soap?
29 Who took "Downtown" into the charts in the 60s and the 80s?
30 What is the middle colour of the Italian flag?

Answers | **Pot Luck 99** *(see Quiz 201)*

1 Mayall. 2 "Board". 3 Jamaica. 4 14. 5 Da Vinci Code. 6 BSE. 7 Catherine Cookson. 8 Horses. 9 Rhinestone. 10 Zinc. 11 Swedish. 12 Fire brigade. 13 40s. 14 "Plum". 15 27. 16 Carey. 17 Peach. 18 Posies. 19 E. 20 Fortieth. 21 Vauxhall. 22 Osborne House. 23 Chas and Dave. 24 India. 25 36. 26 Sixpence. 27 Irish Sea. 28 Friday. 29 Whitney Houston. 30 "Coronation Street".

1 What colour wine goes into sangria?
2 Which country does Calvados come from originally?
3 What is the outer layer of a baked Alaska made from?
4 What colour is usually associated with the liqueur Chartreuse?
5 What is the main ingredient of a caramel sauce?
6 What are the two main vegetable ingredients of bubble and squeak?
7 What are large tubes of pasta called, usually eaten stuffed?
8 What is espresso?
9 Is Greek yoghurt thick, or does it have a pouring consistency?
10 Mozzarella cheese is used on top of which snack-food favourite?
11 Rick Stein's TV programmes are chiefly about which food?
12 Which nuts are used in marzipan?
13 Which county is traditionally famous for its hotpot?
14 Chapatti is an item from which country's cuisine?
15 Italian egg-shaped tomatoes are named after which fruit?
16 What colour is demerara sugar?
17 What sort of fruit would go into a Dundee cake?
18 What colour is an extra-virgin olive oil?
19 A crown roast would be made up from which meat?
20 Morel and oyster are which types of vegetable?
21 What sort of drink would fino or oloroso be?
22 What is a crouton made from?
23 Is green bacon smoked or unsmoked?
24 What is a Blue Vinney?
25 Which spice would a steak au poivre have on its outside?
26 Would a brut champagne be sweet or dry?
27 Which herb is used in pesto sauce?
28 Would a three-star brandy be very good, average or rather inferior?
29 Does a raw apricot have equal, more or fewer calories than a fresh one?
30 Which fruit could be honeydew or cantaloupe?

Answers | **Pot Luck 101** (see Quiz 206)

1 St Martin's. 2 The US Open. 3 A-Ha. 4 "Room". 5 Tom Jones. 6 Camelot. 7 Gerald Durrell. 8 Eight. 9 Tin-Tin. 10 40s. 11 Nellie Dean. 12 Suchet. 13 Cook. 14 Middle letters row. 15 Pumpkin pie. 16 Two. 17 Newcastle. 18 "Do the Bartman". 19 22.45. 20 "Jack". 21 Horse racing. 22 Yellow. 23 Reliant. 24 Water. 25 Germany. 26 3. 27 Kylie Minogue. 28 Pippa Funnell. 29 Chore. 30 Barbary.

1 In which decade did the driving test introduce a written section?
2 What is an Eskimo canoe called?
3 Which is Germany's main airport?
4 What name is given to a cigar-shaped airship?
5 Which musical features a song about a "surrey with a fringe on top"?
6 The Montgolfier brothers flew in what type of craft?
7 Which motor company made the first production-line car?
8 What shape is the bottom of a punt?
9 E is the international vehicle registration letter of which country?
10 Whose 60s report axed many railway lines in Britain?
11 Orly airport is in which city?
12 In which country did the Toyota Motor Corporation originate?
13 Eurostar goes from which London station?
14 In song, "my old man said follow" which vehicle?
15 A Chinook is what type of vehicle?
16 What colour is the Circle Line on a London Underground map?
17 In which century was the Suez Canal opened?
18 What is the Boeing 747 usually known as?
19 What is the international vehicle registration letter of Germany?
20 The SNFC operates in which country?
21 What is the usual colour of an aeroplane's black box?
22 In the 1820s, who designed the locomotive the Rocket?
23 Which country does a sampan come from?
24 In which decade did Concorde enter commercial service?
25 What type of transporter was the ill-fated Herald of Free Enterprise?
26 The major cargo port of Felixstowe is in which county?
27 Which Sir Freddie saw his airways company collapse in 1982?
28 What type of cars did the de Lorean factory produce?
29 Which brothers pioneered the first powered flight?
30 S is the international vehicle registration letter of which country?

Answers | **Screen Greats** *(see Quiz 207)*

1 Fred Astaire. 2 Humphrey Bogart. 3 Charlie Chaplin. 4 Shirley Temple. 5 Hepburn. 6 Marilyn Monroe. 7 Clark Gable. 8 Dorothy Lamour. 9 Bette Davis. 10 Orson Welles. 11 John Wayne. 12 Rudolph Valentino. 13 Stanwyck. 14 Rooney. 15 Peck. 16 Bela Lugosi. 17 McQueen. 18 Leigh. 19 Laurel. 20 Rock Hudson. 21 England. 22 Garland. 23 Douglas. 24 Marlene Dietrich. 25 Bing Crosby. 26 Cagney. 27 Mitchum. 28 Stockholm. 29 Joan, Olivia. 30 Cooper.

1 In verse, which bells said "You owe me five farthings"?
2 Which Grand Slam did Kim Clijsters win in 2005?
3 Which 1980s chart band from Norway released the album "Analogue" in 2006?
4 What word can go after "board" and before "service"?
5 How is the singer Thomas Woodward better known?
6 Which word links King Arthur and the National Lottery?
7 Who wrote the novel "My Family and Other Animals"?
8 How many gallons in a bushel?
9 Who was Herge's most famous comic creation?
10 In which decade of the 20th century was Keith Floyd born?
11 In song what name follows "There's an old mill by a stream"?
12 Which David starred in "Poirot"?
13 Would you expect Antony Worrall Thompson to cook, decorate or value things on TV?
14 The letter K is on which row of a typewriter or computer keyboard?
15 In America, what is the traditional Thanksgiving Day dessert?
16 How many of Henry VIII's wives were executed?
17 "Byker Grove" was set in which city?
18 What was the name of the first UK hit single by The Simpsons?
19 How does 10.45 p.m. appear on a 24-hour clock?
20 What word can go before "frost", "knife" and "pot"?
21 Josh Gifford is associated with which sport?
22 On a Monopoly board, what colour is Leicester Square?
23 Which UK car manufacturer produced the Kitten?
24 Hydrophobia is the fear of what?
25 In which country is the city of Leipzig?
26 Moving clockwise on a dartboard what number is next to 17?
27 In the 80s, who had a No. 1 with "I Should be So Lucky"?
28 Which Pippa won the Badminton and Burghley Horse Trials in 2003?
29 What is the only English anagram of OCHRE?
30 What type of apes live on the rock of Gibraltar?

Answers | Food & Drink 2 *(see Quiz 204)*

1 Red. 2 France. 3 Meringue. 4 Green. 5 Sugar. 6 Potatoes, cabbage. 7 Cannelloni. 8 Coffee. 9 Thick. 10 Pizza. 11 Fish. 12 Almonds. 13 Lancashire. 14 India's. 15 Plum. 16 Brown. 17 Raisins, currants, sultanas. 18 Green. 19 Lamb. 20 Mushrooms. 21 Sherry. 22 Bread. 23 Unsmoked. 24 Cheese. 25 Peppers. 26 Dry. 27 Basil. 28 Very good. 29 Fewer. 30 Melon.

1 Who was Ginger Rogers's most famous screen partner?
2 Who played Rick Blaine in "Casablanca"?
3 Which tramp's hat and cane were sold for £55,000 in the early 90s?
4 Who won an Oscar in 1934 when she was six years old?
5 Which Katharine starred in many films with Spencer Tracy?
6 Which blonde starred as Lorelei Lee in "Gentlemen Prefer Blondes"?
7 Who starred in "It Happened One Night" and "Gone with the Wind"?
8 Who was the female member of the Road films trio?
9 Who acted with her fourth husband in "All About Eve"?
10 Who played the title role in "Citizen Kane"?
11 Whose real name was Marion and was most famous for his westerns?
12 Which silent-movie star was born Rodolpho Alphonso Guglielmi di Valentina d'Antonguolla?
13 Which Hollywood star Barbara was in "The Thorn Birds" and "The Colbys" on TV?
14 Which diminutive star Mickey played a cigar-smoking midget in his first film at the age of seven?
15 Which Gregory won an Oscar for "To Kill a Mockingbird"?
16 Which Dracula star was born Bela Ferenc Denszo Blasko?
17 Which Steve of "The Great Escape" did his own racing stunts?
18 Which Vivien was once Mrs Laurence Olivier?
19 Which half of Laurel and Hardy was born in the Lake District?
20 Which famous co-star of Doris Day died of AIDS in 1985?
21 In which country was Cary Grant born?
22 Which Judy started out as part of the Gumm Sisters Kiddie Act?
23 What was the first name of the father and son actors Fairbanks?
24 Which Berlin-born star's first major film was "The Blue Angel" in 1930?
25 Which actor/singer in "High Society" died on a golf course?
26 Which James is credited with the catchphrase "You dirty rat!"?
27 Which Robert is known for his languid, sleepy eyes?
28 In which European capital city was Greta Garbo born?
29 What were the first names of sisters Fontaine and De Havilland?
30 Which Gary, of "High Noon" was the archetypal strong silent type?

Answers | Travel & Transport (see Quiz 205)

1 1990s. 2 Kayak. 3 Frankfurt. 4 Zeppelin. 5 Oklahoma!. 6 Hot-air balloon. 7 Ford. 8 Flat. 9 Spain. 10 Dr Beeching. 11 Paris. 12 Japan. 13 Waterloo. 14 Van. 15 Helicopter. 16 Yellow. 17 19th. 18 Jumbo jet. 19 D. 20 France. 21 Orange. 22 George Stephenson. 23 China. 24 1970s. 25 Ferry. 26 Suffolk. 27 Laker. 28 Sports cars. 29 Wright Brothers. 30 Sweden.

1 Who played the title role in "Judge John Deed"?
2 The character Dave Glover appeared in which TV soap?
3 What was the sequel to the "human" version of 101 Dalmatians called?
4 Dusty Hare is associated with which sport?
5 Of which country is NBC a major broadcasting company?
6 What number is represented by the Roman numeral D?
7 Who wrote the novel "Dr No"?
8 What is the administrative centre for the county of Hampshire?
9 Who or what were Wilma, Katrina and Rita in 2005?
10 In the 90s, who had a No. 1 with "These are the Days of Our Lives"?
11 Who plays rugby union at the Franklins Garden, Weedon Road?
12 In mythology, was Aphrodite a Greek or Roman goddess?
13 In music, what note is written on the line below the middle line of the treble clef?
14 What word can go after "trade" and before "Jack"?
15 Which singer who found fame in her teens shares her surname with a religious building?
16 Who were runners-up in soccer's 1994 World Cup?
17 Which Sam Cooke song includes the words "draw back your bow"?
18 What name is given to small cubes of fried bread served with soup?
19 Balaclava was a battle in which war?
20 What is the square root of 169?
21 In which country is the city of Malaga?
22 Did Ernie Else first win the Open in 2000, 2002 or 2004?
23 Which group backed Steve Harley?
24 "This is 5" was the first programme shown on which channel?
25 Which constellation has three stars forming a "belt"?
26 What colour is umber?
27 Who won an Oscar for Best Actress in "Mary Poppins"?
28 What is 1/4 plus 1/8?
29 Which former Scottish skipper Gary enjoyed an Indian summer with Liverpool?
30 Which Elvis recorded "Oliver's Army"?

Answers | Pot Luck 103 *(see Quiz 210)*

1 Kiki Dee. 2 "Absolutely Fabulous". 3 Burma (Myanmar). 4 "Nap". 5 David Soul.
6 Alex Ferguson. 7 Arthur Hailey. 8 Uranium. 9 Kieren Fallon. 10 50s. 11 1. 12
Bolam. 13 Being alone. 14 Worcester. 15 Percentage. 16 Triumph. 17 November.
18 Cricket. 19 "Pudding". 20 1970s. 21 Dodd. 22 Rhinos. 23 Ahead. 24 Harold
Wilson. 25 112. 26 Denmark. 27 Vingt. 28 Air Commodore. 29 Silver. 30 Joss
Stone.

1 Which green plant is widely seen on St Patrick's Day?
2 Which term describes a plant crossed from different species?
3 Where in London are the Royal Botanical Gardens?
4 If a leaf is variegated it has two or more what?
5 What is the flower truss of a willow tree called?
6 Which flower became the emblem of the Labour Party in the 80s?
7 Which part of a tree is cork made from?
8 Which former Tory minister shares his name with a type of tree?
9 Which Busy plant is also called Impatiens walleriana?
10 Which part of a plant may be called tap?
11 Which word describes a plant which can withstand the cold and frost?
12 Which "trap" shares its name with a planet?
13 What name is given to a plant which completes its life cycle in less than a year?
14 Are conifers evergreen or deciduous?
15 Which London borough hosts an annual flower show?
16 The thistle may be a weed to some but it's the symbol of which country?
17 What does a fungicide do to fungi?
18 Which garden vegetable – often used as a fruit – has edible stems and poisonous leaves?
19 What is the study of plants called?
20 A type of crocus produces which yellow spice or flavouring?
21 What are the fruits of the wild rose called?
22 Which holly trees are the only ones to bear berries?
23 Which plant associated with the seaside is used to make laver bread?
24 The cone or flower cluster of which plant is used to make beer?
25 Which tree can be white or weeping?
26 Archers made their bows from which wood commonly found in churchyards?
27 Does a crocus grow from a bulb or a corm?
28 On which continent did potatoes originate?
29 The maple is the national emblem of which country?
30 Is the cocoa tree native to North or South America?

| **Answers** | Headlines *(see Quiz 211)* |

1 Galloway. 2 Warne. 3 Whale. 4 Kennedy. 5 Four. 6 Western. 7 Davies. 8 West Indies. 9 Gordon Ramsay. 10 Michael Vaughan. 11 King's Cross. 12 Kelly Holmes. 13 Sandhurst. 14 Richard Whiteley. 15 Rooney. 16 Pitt. 17 Jackson. 18 Oil depot. 19 Turkey. 20 Israel. 21 Blunkett. 22 Prince Charles. 23 Stewart. 24 Kelly. 25 Flintoff. 26 Rusedski. 27 Young. 28 Sienna Miller. 29 Boys. 30 Banks.

1 Who sang with Elton John on "True Love"?
2 The character Patsy Stone appeared in which TV series?
3 In which country is the city of Mandalay?
4 What word can go after "kid" and before "kin"?
5 How is David Soulberg better known?
6 Who was the first manager to win the English soccer double twice?
7 Who wrote the novel "Airport"?
8 U is the chemical symbol for which element?
9 Who has won the Derby on Kris Kin and North Light?
10 In which decade of the 20th century was Ruby Wax born?
11 On a dartboard what number is opposite 19?
12 Which James starred in "The Likely Lads"?
13 Monophobia is the fear of what?
14 What is the administrative centre for the county of Hereford and Worcester?
15 Which term describes a way of representing a number as a fraction of one hundred?
16 Which UK car manufacturer produced the Toledo?
17 In which month is Thanksgiving Day in the USA?
18 Rachel Heyhoe Flint is chiefly associated with which sport?
19 What word can follow "milk", "summer" and "Yorkshire"?
20 Did the Two Ronnies begin in the 1960s, 1970s or 1990s?
21 Which comedian Ken sang "Love is Like a Violin"?
22 In rugby league, what did Leeds add to their name in the 1990s?
23 Is Greece ahead of or behind Greenwich Mean Time?
24 Who was the outgoing PM when Edward Heath took office?
25 How many pounds in a hundredweight?
26 The airline Danair is from which country?
27 What is French for twenty?
28 Which RAF rank is the higher – Air Commodore or Group Captain?
29 In heraldry what is argent?
30 "Mind, Body and Soul" was the debut album by which artist?

| **Answers** | **Pot Luck 102** *(see Quiz 208)* |

1 Martin Shaw. 2 "Emmerdale". 3 102 Dalmatians. 4 Rugby (Union). 5 USA. 6 500.
7 Ian Fleming. 8 Winchester. 9 Hurricanes. 10 Queen. 11 Northampton. 12 Greek.
13 G. 14 "Union". 15 Charlotte Church. 16 Italy. 17 Cupid. 18 Croutons. 19
Crimean. 20 13. 21 Spain. 22 2002. 23 Cockney Rebel. 24 Channel 5. 25 Orion.
26 Brown. 27 Julie Andrews. 28 3/8. 29 McAllister. 30 Costello.

1 Which controversial MP George took part in "Celebrity Big Brother"?

2 In 2004 which Aussie bowler Shane reached 500 wickets?

3 What type of creature was very unusually washed up the Thames in January 2006?

4 Which Charles stood down as Lib Dem leader at the beginning of 2006?

5 Did three, four or five bombs explode in London on 7th July 2005?

6 Was 2006 Golden Globe winner "Brokeback Mountain" a western or a documentary?

7 Which David did David Cameron beat to become Tory leader?

8 Brian Lara scored the first 400 runs in a Test innings for which country?

9 Which outspoken TV chef received an OBE in the 2006 New Year's Honours?

10 Who led the England cricket team to Ashes glory in 2005?

11 Which major London station was the site of one of the bombs in July 2005?

12 In 2005, which double Olympic gold winner announced her retirement?

13 In 2006 Prince William started training at which military institution?

14 Which host of TV's "Countdown" died in 2005?

15 Which Wayne became the youngest England footballer in 2003?

16 Which Brad adopted partner Angelina Jolie's children in 2006?

17 Which sprint hurdler Colin quit international athletics in 2003?

18 What type of depot caught fire in Buncefield, Herts in December 2005?

19 In which country were there fatalities from bird flu in early 2006?

20 PM Sharon led which country when he suffered a stroke in early 2006?

21 Which ex-minister David was the subject of the play "A Very Social Secretary"?

22 Which Royal married in 2005?

23 Which rock star Rod became a father again in his sixties in 2005?

24 Which Ruth succeeded Charles Clarke as Education Secretary?

25 Which Freddie became the 2005 BBC "Sports Personality of the Year"?

26 Which British tennis player Greg was cleared of taking nandrolone in 2004?

27 Which Will shot to fame on "Pop Idol"?

28 Which actress had an on/off relationship with Jude Law in 2005?

29 Were David Beckham's first three children boys or girls?

30 Which former Sports Minister Tony died while on holiday in the US in 2006?

Answers	**Plant World** *(see Quiz 209)*

1 Shamrock. 2 Hybrid. 3 Kew. 4 Colours. 5 Catkin. 6 Red rose. 7 Bark. 8 Redwood. 9 Busy Lizzie. 10 Root. 11 Hardy. 12 Venus Flytrap. 13 Annual. 14 Evergreen. 15 Chelsea. 16 Scotland. 17 Kills them. 18 Rhubarb. 19 Botany. 20 Saffron. 21 Hips. 22 Females. 23 Seaweed. 24 Hop. 25 Willow. 26 Yew. 27 Corm. 28 America. 29 Canada. 30 South.

1 Kicking King won which major race at Cheltenham in 2005?
2 Mick the Miller was a champion in which sport?
3 Which Liz won the 1991 New York Marathon?
4 Which country did motor racing's Nelson Piquet come from?
5 Which Carl won Olympic 100m. gold in 1984 and 1988?
6 The quick bowler Shaun Pollock plays for which country?
7 Mike Hazelwood is associated with which sport?
8 Which athlete Diane was cleared of charges of drugs taking in March '96?
9 Which snooker player was known as Hurricane?
10 Which Graham was Formula 1 World Champion in the 60s?
11 Which speed race goes from Putney to Mortlake?
12 Steve Cram comes from which town in the north-east?
13 Sanath Jayasuriya raced to a 48-ball century in '96 for which country?
14 Which country is Jacques Villeneuve from?
15 Which Kriss broke a British 20-year record in the 400m. hurdles?
16 Where is the San Marino Grand Prix raced?
17 Which team scored in the first minute of the 1997 FA Cup Final?
18 In motor racing, who lost his place with the Williams team in the year he finished World Champion?
19 Which Barry was a 70s motorcycling world champion?
20 In what sport has Sarah Hardcastle won Olympic medals?
21 Which record-breaking athlete became a Tory MP in the 90s?
22 Which German won nine Grand Prix victories in 1995?
23 The Curragh race course is in which Irish county?
24 Which Zola controversially ran for Britain in the 80s ?
25 Which county does Sally Gunnell come from?
26 Which snooker player was nicknamed Whirlwind?
27 Which Ben was stripped of 100m. Olympic Gold after a drugs test?
28 Which country did motor racing's Ayrton Senna come from?
29 Which sport takes place on the Cresta Run?
30 Who won Olympic 100m. gold in 1992 for Britain?

| **Answers** | **Musicals** *(see Quiz 214)* |

1 Cats. 2 Travolta. 3 Crawford. 4 Barbara Dickson. 5 Chess. 6 Mary Poppins. 7 The Producers. 8 Madonna. 9 Joseph. 10 "Don't Cry for Me, Argentina". 11 Grease. 12 Abba. 13 Banderas. 14 Cliff Richard. 15 Andrew Lloyd Webber. 16 Townshend. 17 Tim Rice. 18 Technicolor. 19 Abba. 20 Les Misérables. 21 Phantom of the Opera. 22 Electric Light Orchestra. 23 Summer. 24 Sunset Boulevard. 25 Jason Donovan. 26 Paige. 27 Essex. 28 Cabaret. 29 Oliver!. 30 Ball.

1 The warmth rating of what is measured in togs?
2 The character Von Klinkerhoffen appeared in which TV series?
3 In which decade of the 20th century was Chris Tarrant born?
4 Which book is known as the NEB?
5 In the 60s, who had a No. 1 with "Eleanor Rigby"?
6 Gold denotes which wedding anniversary?
7 Who wrote the novel "Schindler's Ark"?
8 Totnes and Tiverton castles are both in which county?
9 In architecture, what is a water spout carved as a grotesque face?
10 In the US, whom was Senator McCarthy trying to identify in his "witch-hunts"?
11 In mythology, who had a face that launched a thousand ships?
12 Who was Chelsea's regular keeper in their 2004–5 Premiership-winning season?
13 Who has hosted his "House Party", and "Deal or No Deal"?
14 What word can go after "home" and before "house"?
15 How is the singer Paul Hewson better known?
16 What colour was the London bus ripped apart in the July 2005 bomb attack?
17 The zodiac sign Virgo covers which two calendar months?
18 Which Harry Potter novel was the first to feature the word Blood in the title?
19 In London what are Harlequins and Saracens?
20 In 1965, "Times They are A-Changin'" was whose first Top Ten hit?
21 In which country is the city of Marrakesh?
22 Which teen TV soap featured the Hunters and the Morgans?
23 In economics, what does the B stand for in PSBR?
24 Gouda cheese comes from which country?
25 Which Henry claimed that "History is bunk"?
26 Who won an Oscar for Best Actress in "Sophie's Choice"?
27 What is the only English anagram of INCH?
28 Which Rod topped the most weeks in the chart list for 1976?
29 Which veteran singer turned into a Sex Bomb with the Stereophonics?
30 Who presents "Film 2006" on TV?

| **Answers** | **Pot Luck 105** *(see Quiz 215)* |

1 6,080. 2 Japan. 3 Phil Mickelson. 4 "Pigeon". 5 Arsenal. 6 Keith Moon. 7 Bob the Builder. 8 Wednesday. 9 American Football. 10 Matthew. 11 1,440. 12 The Generation Game. 13 Green. 14 David Copperfield. 15 Vauxhall. 16 "Waltzing Matilda". 17 Top letters row. 18 Phoenix. 19 Access. 20 Aries. 21 Transom. 22 Darren Gough. 23 Monday. 24 Women. 25 New York. 26 7. 27 Cricket. 28 Foreigners. 29 "EastEnders". 30 Madonna.

1 The song "Memory" comes from which musical?
2 Which John starred in the film of "Grease"?
3 Which Michael had a hit with "Music of the Night"?
4 Who sang with Elaine Paige on the single "I Know Him So Well?"
5 Which musical did the song come from?
6 Which musical about a magical nanny is based on a film with Julie Andrews?
7 The song "Springtime for Hitler" comes from which musical?
8 In the film "Evita", who sang "You Must Love Me"?
9 Phillip Schofield and Jason Donovan have played which biblical character?
10 In which song are the words, "I kept my promise, Don't keep your distance"?
11 Which musical features Danny and Sandy in the rock 'n' roll 50s?
12 Tim Rice and writers from which supergroup wrote "Chess"?
13 Which Antonio featured in the film "Evita"?
14 Who starred in the 60s film "Summer Holiday"?
15 Who provided the music for "Cats"?
16 Which Pete wrote the rock opera "Tommy"?
17 Who wrote the lyrics for "Jesus Christ Superstar"?
18 What word describes Joseph's Dreamcoat?
19 The hit musical "Mamma Mia" is based on the music of which pop group?
20 Which Victor Hugo novel became a musical?
21 Which stage musical is set in the Paris Opera House?
22 Which Orchestra feature on the No. 1 hit "Xanadu"?
23 Which type of Nights are in the title of a No. 1 single from "Grease"?
24 In which musical does the character Norma Desmond appear?
25 Who had a UK No. 1 with "Any Dream Will Do"?
26 Which Elaine played Grizabella the Glamour Cat?
27 Which Cockney David played Che on stage in "Evita"?
28 Which musical does the song "Cabaret" come from?
29 "As Long as He Needs Me" comes from which musical?
30 Which Michael first starred in "Aspects of Love"?

Answers	**Speed Stars** (see Quiz 212)

1 Gold Cup. 2 Greyhound racing. 3 McColgan. 4 Brazil. 5 Lewis. 6 South Africa.
7 Water skiing. 8 Modahl. 9 Alex Higgins. 10 Hill. 11 University boat race. 12 Gateshead. 13 Sri Lanka. 14 Canada. 15 Akabusi. 16 Imola. 17 Chelsea. 18 Damon Hill. 19 Sheene. 20 Swimming. 21 Sebastian Coe. 22 Michael Schumacher. 23 Kildare. 24 Budd. 25 Essex. 26 Jimmy White. 27 Johnson. 28 Brazil. 29 Bobsleigh. 30 Linford Christie.

Quiz 215 | Pot Luck 105

Answers – page 223

1 How many feet in a nautical mile?
2 In which country is the city of Osaka?
3 Which Phil won the US PGA in 2005?
4 What word can go before "hole", "pie" and "post"?
5 Ray Parlour and Kanu were colleagues with which London club?
6 Who was the original drummer with the Who?
7 Which Bob added his occupation to his name to top the UK charts?
8 If the first of June is a Monday what day is the 1st of July?
9 What sport is played by the San Francisco 49ers?
10 In the Bible, what is the first bok of the new Testament?
11 How many minutes in a day?
12 Which game show links Jim Davidson, Bruce Forsyth and Larry Grayson?
13 On a Monopoly board, what colour is Oxford Street?
14 Peggotty appears in which Charles Dickens novel?
15 Which UK car manufacturer produced the Cresta?
16 Which song mentions a jolly swagman?
17 The letter U is on which row of a typewriter or computer keyboard?
18 In legend, which bird rises from its own ashes?
19 In computing, what does the A stand for in RAM?
20 Alphabetically, what is the first sign of the zodiac?
21 What name is given to the horizontal bar of a window?
22 Which England cricketer won "Strictly Come Dancing" in partnership with Lilia Kopylova?
23 What day of the week did the Boomtown Rats not like?
24 What does a misogynist hate?
25 In baseball which city can support the Mets or the Yankees?
26 Moving clockwise on a dartboard, what number is next to 19?
27 Chris Old is associated with which sport?
28 Xenophobia is the fear of what?
29 The character Dennis Watts appeared in which TV soap?
30 In the 80s, who had a No. 1 with "True Blue"?

Answers | Pot Luck 104 (see Quiz 213)

1 Duvets. 2 "'Allo 'Allo". 3 40s. 4 New English Bible. 5 The Beatles. 6 Fiftieth. 7 Thomas Keneally. 8 Devon. 9 Gargoyle. 10 Communists. 11 Helen of Troy. 12 Petr Cech. 13 Noel Edmonds. 14 "Work". 15 Bono. 16 Red. 17 August & September. 18 Harry Potter and the Half-Blood Prince. 19 Rugby union teams. 20 Bob Dylan. 21 Morocco. 22 "Hollyoaks". 23 Borrowing. 24 Holland. 25 Ford. 26 Meryl Streep. 27 Chin. 28 Stewart. 29 "Tom Jones". 30 Jonathan Ross.

1 Which series dealt with International Rescue and their super aircraft?
2 Where would you find a rabbit called Dylan and Ermintrude the cow?
3 In "The Muppets" what was Fozzie?
4 Which continent did Paddington Bear come from?
5 What sort of animals were Pinky and Perky?
6 Which programme began "Here is a house. Here is a door. Windows: one, two, three, four"?
7 What was the number plate on Postman Pat's van?
8 Which show featured Zippy, George plus Rod, Jane and Freddy?
9 Which show features the tallest, the fastest, the biggest of everything?
10 What sort of animal was Skippy?
11 Which Gerry and Sylvia pioneered supermarionation?
12 Miss Hoolie, PC Plum and Josie Jump feature on which programme?
13 Which podgy cartoon Captain's ship was the Black Pig?
14 Who delivers letters in Greendale?
15 Which Tank Engine is blue and has the number 1 on it?
16 Wendy, Dizzy and Scoop help which cartoon handyman?
17 Whose vocabulary was limited to words like "flobbalot"?
18 Whose friends were Teddy and Looby Loo?
19 Which show awarded cabbages to its losers?
20 Which school did Tucker, Zammo and Tegs attend?
21 Which country did Ivor the Engine come from?
22 Who lives in Fimble Valley?
23 What was ITV's answer to "Blue Peter" called ?
24 In which show did Uncle Bulgaria, Tomsk and Tobermory appear?
25 Who are Tinky-Winky, Dipsy, La-La and Po?
26 What was Worzel Gummidge?
27 Who lives in the Hoob Mobile?
28 Which show featured Dill the dog and Parsley the lion?
29 What sort of creature was Basil Brush?
30 What form of entertainment are Hanna-Barbera famous for?

Answers | The 90s *(see Quiz 218)*

1 The Queen. 2 Sri Lanka. 3 Margaret Thatcher. 4 Mel and Kim. 5 Channel tunnel.
6 John McCarthy. 7 George Bush Snr. 8 Hadlee. 9 The BBC. 10 Imran Khan. 11
Glasgow. 12 MPs. 13 Bobby Robson. 14 Comet. 15 David Mellor. 16 Michael
Heseltine. 17 Ireland. 18 Atlanta in 1996. 19 Laura Davies. 20 The Referendum Party.
21 John Smith. 22 Ladies' public toilets. 23 Tonya Harding. 24 Freddie Mercury. 25
O.J. Simpson. 26 Estée Lauder. 27 Carson. 28 Eric Cantona. 29 Windsor. 30 Camelot.

1 Which Bette won an Oscar for Best Actress in "Dangerous"?
2 What is 10 cubed?
3 What is the administrative centre for the county of Shropshire?
4 What word can go after "music" and before "mark"?
5 How is Marvin Lee Addy better known?
6 In which best-selling book are Opus Dei entwined in the plot?
7 Who wrote the novel "The Shining"?
8 Tom Thumb and Little Gem are types of what?
9 In France, what is the abbreviation for Mademoiselle?
10 Which clown is Bart Simpson's idol?
11 Brian Jacks is associated with which sport?
12 What does the Y stand for in NIMBY?
13 C. J. Parker and Lt Mitch Bucannon appeared in which TV series?
14 Alan Pardew moved as boss of Reading to take over at which London club?
15 What did Castleford's name become for the 1997 rugby league season?
16 The airline El Al is from which country?
17 Who was the outgoing American President when Jimmy Carter took office?
18 What is Ceylon now called?
19 What was the name of the tiny iPod launched in September 2005?
20 What word can follow "clay", "racing" and "wood"?
21 In which country is the city of Poana?
22 What happened to Victor Meldrew in the final episode of "One Foot in the Grave"?
23 Which Pink rock band reassembled at Live 8 in Hyde Park in 2005?
24 Shannon Lawson and Yasmin Salter are what type of TV Wives?
25 Diamond denotes which wedding anniversary?
26 Which army rank is the higher – colonel or brigadier?
27 The character Kim Tate appeared in which TV soap?
28 What is the only English anagram of ACHES?
29 What was Lot's wife turned into?
30 A merino is what kind of creature?

Answers	**World Tour** *(see Quiz 219)*

1 Perth. 2 Beijing. 3 Emus don't fly. 4 Mediterranean. 5 South Africa. 6 Bay of Biscay. 7 Bulgarian. 8 Italy. 9 East Germany. 10 Jerusalem. 11 South. 12 Seven. 13 Italy. 14 Casablanca. 15 Germany. 16 Cocaine. 17 Nile. 18 Barcelona. 19 Colchester. 20 Jodhpurs. 21 France and Spain. 22 Japan. 23 Africa. 24 Paris. 25 Victoria. 26 Arizona. 27 Estonia. 28 Qatar. 29 America. 30 Rupee.

1 Who described 1992 as an "annus horribilis"?
2 Which country beat Australia in the final of the 1996 Cricket World Cup?
3 Who became the first Prime Minister to be made a baroness?
4 Dying of cancer at 22, Mel Appleby had been part of which pop duo?
5 In which tunnel was there a major fire in autumn 1996?
6 Which former Beirut hostage wrote a book with Jill Morrell?
7 Who lost when Bill Clinton first became US President?
8 Which New Zealander Richard became the first to 400 Test wickets?
9 Before he was elected an MP in 1997, who was Martin Bell's employer?
10 Which Pakistan cricketer was named in the Botham/Lamb libel case?
11 Which Scottish city was the Cultural Capital of Europe in 1990–1?
12 Who voted themselves a 26-per-cent pay rise in 1996?
13 Who managed England's soccer team in Italia 90?
14 Hale-Bopp hit the headlines in the 90s, but who or what was it?
15 Which former "Minister of Fun" resigned over a scandal with an actress?
16 Who was John Major's Deputy Prime Minister?
17 Which country dominated the Eurovision Song Contest in the 90s?
18 Which Olympics were blighted by the Centennial Park bomb?
19 Which golfer became the first British woman in history to earn a million from her sport?
20 Which Party did Sir James Goldsmith found before the 1997 election?
21 Who immediately preceded Tony Blair as leader of the Labour Party?
22 In 1997 the WI campaigned for more private space in which public places?
23 In 1994 which ice skater was involved in a strange plot to cripple Nancy Kerrigan?
24 Which member of Queen died?
25 Which ex-footballer's trial was a long-running saga on US TV?
26 Which cosmetic house signed up Liz Hurley in 1995?
27 Which Willie announced his retirement from horse racing in 1997?
28 Which French footballer moved from Leeds to Man. Utd?
29 Which royal castle caught fire in 1992?
30 Which company won the contract for the National Lottery?

Answers	Children's TV *(see Quiz 216)*

1 "Thunderbirds". 2 "The Magic Roundabout". 3 A Bear. 4 (South) America. 5 Piglets.
6 "Playschool". 7 PAT 1. 8 "Rainbow". 9 "Record Breakers". 10 Kangaroo. 11
Anderson. 12 "Balamory". 13 Pugwash. 14 "Postman Pat". 15 Thomas. 16 "Bob the
Builder". 17 Bill and Ben the Flowerpot Men. 18 Andy Pandy. 19 "Crackerjack". 20
Grange Hill. 21 Wales. 22 "The Fimbles". 23 "Magpie". 24 "The Wombles". 25 "The
Teletubbies". 26 Scarecrow. 27 "The Hoobs". 28 "The Herbs". 29 Fox. 30 Cartoons.

1 The capital of Western Australia shares its name with which Scottish city?
2 How is Peking now more commonly known?
3 In which country would you see an emu fly?
4 Is French Provence nearer the Channel or the Mediterranean?
5 In which country do people speak Afrikaans?
6 Which bay to the west of France is notorious for its rough seas?
7 What is the principal language of Bulgaria?
8 If you were visiting the home of Parmesan cheese, in which country would you be?
9 Which country used to be called the DDR?
10 In which city is the Wailing Wall?
11 Is the Orinoco in North or South America?
12 How many consonants are there in Mississippi?
13 Which country has the international vehicle registration letter I?
14 Which major town of Morocco shares its name with a famous film?
15 In which country is Bavaria?
16 Which drug is Colombia's chief export?
17 On which long African river is the Aswan Dam?
18 Which Spanish city hosted the 1992 Olympics?
19 In which city is the University of Essex?
20 An Indian city gave its name to which style of riding breeches?
21 Andorra lies between which two countries?
22 Which country's national sport is Sumo wrestling?
23 The Cape of Good Hope is at the tip of which continent?
24 Which city has the cathedrals of Notre Dame and Sacre Coeur?
25 Which falls lie on the Zambesi river?
26 Which US state, capital Phoenix, is called the Grand Canyon state?
27 Which Baltic state has Tallinn as its capital?
28 Which is the only country in the world to begin with Q?
29 In which continent is Mount McKinley?
30 Which currency would you spend in Pakistan?

Answers	**Pot Luck 106** *(see Quiz 217)*

1 Davis. 2 1,000. 3 Shrewsbury. 4 "Hall". 5 Meat Loaf. 6 Da Vinci Code. 7 Stephen King. 8 Lettuce. 9 Mlle. 10 Krusty the Clown. 11 Judo. 12 Yard. 13 "Baywatch". 14 West Ham. 15 Castleford Tigers. 16 Israel. 17 Gerald Ford. 18 Sri Lanka. 19 Nano. 20 "Pigeon". 21 India. 22 Died. 23 Pink Floyd. 24 "Footballers' Wives". 25 Sixtieth. 26 Brigadier. 27 "Emmerdale". 28 Chase. 29 Pillar of salt. 30 Sheep.

1 In the 70s, who had a No. 1 with "Bright Eyes"?
2 What word can go before "ache", "ring" and "wig"?
3 Mark James is associated with which sport?
4 Blake and Krystle Carrington appeared in which TV series?
5 In tennis, what name is given to a score of 40-40?
6 Maastricht airport is in which country?
7 Who wrote the novel "The Invisible Man"?
8 What is 4/10 minus 2/5?
9 In Greek mythology, who was god of the sun?
10 In which decade of the 20th century was Phillip Schofield born?
11 Which UK car manufacturer produced the Capri?
12 Which Paul starred in "The Good Life"?
13 How would 42 be shown in Roman numerals?
14 What word can go after "special" and before "line"?
15 Shayne Ward and Steve Brookstein have both won which TV show?
16 Which club did Roy Keane play for before his move to Man. Utd?
17 What does E stand for in PEP?
18 In which country is the city of Port Elizabeth?
19 In which month is Christmas in Australia?
20 The zodiac sign Scorpio covers which two calendar months?
21 Which Englishman produced the highest individual innings of the 2005 Ashes series?
22 Ra is the chemical symbol for which element?
23 Which female singer went straight to No. 1 in the US with "Fantasy"?
24 In which movie did Keanu Reeves first appear as computer hacker Neo?
25 How many kilograms in seven tonnes?
26 Is Greenland ahead of or behind Greenwich Mean Time?
27 The letter Y is on which row of a typewriter or computer keyboard?
28 Who won ice figure skating gold for Britain in 1980?
29 What is the administrative centre for the county of Cleveland?
30 Moving anticlockwise on a dartboard what number is next to 11?

Answers | **Pot Luck 108** *(see Quiz 222)*

1 Chelsea. 2 "Dallas". 3 60s. 4 Trinidad. 5 Blue. 6 Federation. 7 Salman Rushdie.
8 Switzerland. 9 Billy Ocean. 10 Cobbler. 11 James Callaghan. 12 Brambell. 13
American Football. 14 Wednesday. 15 Their relatives. 16 Fish. 17 12.50. 18 Christie.
19 Sarah Lancashire. 20 A car. 21 Dumb. 22 Upper arm. 23 Rivet. 24 Italy. 25
Sheep. 26 Dougal. 27 Red. 28 Simply Red. 29 Saddam Hussein. 30 McGee.

1 In which film did Hannibal Lecter first appear?
2 Which Steven Spielberg film was described as "65 million years in the making"?
3 Which film gave Macaulay Culkin his first huge success?
4 Which English film swept the Oscar board in 1997?
5 In which film did Robin Williams dress as a Scottish housekeeper?
6 Which actor was the ghost in the film of the same name?
7 Whom did Kevin Costner protect in "The Bodyguard"?
8 Which musical instrument was the title of a 1993 Oscar winner?
9 Which comedy was described as "Five good reasons to stay single"?
10 In which film was Robin Williams the voice of the genie?
11 Which hero was Prince of Thieves in 1991?
12 Which creatures had the prefix Teenage Mutant Ninja?
13 In which film is Peter Pan a father and a lawyer?
14 Which Disney film was about the heroine who saved Captain Smith?
15 In which movie did Nigel Hawthorne play an English monarch?
16 Which 1990 Western had Kevin Costner as actor and director?
17 Which Disney film included "The Circle of Life" and "Hakuna Matata"?
18 Who played Eva Duarte in a 1996 musical?
19 In which film did Susan Sarandon play a nun who visits a prisoner on Death Row?
20 Which Disney Story was the first to be wholly computer-generated?
21 Which 1993 Spielberg film was largely shot in black and white?
22 In which film did Mel Gibson play the Scots hero William Wallace?
23 Which Whoopi Goldberg film was subtitled "Back in the Habit"?
24 Which western actor directed and starred in "Unforgiven"?
25 Which British actor Jeremy won an Oscar for "Reversal of Fortune"?
26 Which Tom was the star of "Forrest Gump"?
27 Which film had the song "Streets of Philadelphia"?
28 Which Jamie starred in "Fierce Creatures"?
29 Who played James Bond in "Goldeneye"?
30 Which US President did Anthony Hopkins play on film in 1995?

Answers	**Hobbies & Leisure** (see Quiz 223)

1 12. **2** Baseball. **3** 108. **4** Pontoon. **5** Sonic. **6** Hampton Court. **7** Tower of London. **8** Blue. **9** Pottery. **10** Birmingham. **11** Duplo. **12** Gretna Green. **13** Safari Park. **14** Conley. **15** Great Yarmouth. **16** Double-knitting. **17** Rook/castle. **18** Seven. **19** Red. **20** Breast stroke. **21** Equestrian. **22** Dwarf plants. **23** Dance. **24** Stamp collecting. **25** Water polo. **26** Bath. **27** Moths or butterflies. **28** Circular. **29** Paris. **30** Imperial War Museum.

1 Which club has fielded the strikers Crespo and Kesman?
2 J. R. Ewing and Miss Ellie appeared in which TV series?
3 In which decade of the 20th century was Rory Bremner born?
4 In which country is the city of Port of Spain?
5 What colour are the labels indicating who is the "weakest link" on the TV quiz show?
6 In the initials FIFA, what does the first F stand for?
7 Who wrote the controversial novel "The Satanic Verses"?
8 Which country's stamps have featured the word Helvetia?
9 In the 80s, who had a No. 1 with "When the Going Gets Tough, the Tough Get Going"?
10 What is the only English anagram of CLOBBER?
11 Who was the outgoing PM when Margaret Thatcher took office?
12 Which Wilfred starred in "Steptoe and Son"?
13 What sport is played by the Miami Dolphins?
14 Alphabetically, what is the last of the days of the week?
15 A nepotist favours what type of people?
16 Billingsgate Market was famous for what sort of food?
17 What is 1/8 as a percentage to two decimal points?
18 Which Julie won an Oscar for Best Actress in "Darling"?
19 Which ex-Corrie star Sarah starred on stage in "Guys and Dolls"?
20 Who or what was Genevieve in the classic film of the same name?
21 A lift for food in a restaurant is known as what kind of waiter?
22 The humerus is in what part of the body?
23 Countersunk, flat-headed and snap-head are common types of what?
24 Which country did Galileo come from?
25 In Australia what is a jumbuck?
26 What is the name of the "Magic Roundabout" dog?
27 On a Monopoly board, what colour is Fleet Street?
28 Which group were simply Holding Back the Years in the 1986 charts?
29 Which former leader went on trial in his own country in October 2005?
30 Which Debbie married Paul Daniels?

---

1 How many court cards are there in a standard pack?
2 In which game would you have a pitcher's mound and an outfield?
3 How many cards are needed for a game of canasta?
4 Which card game is also called vingt-et-un?
5 What is the name of the hedgehog in Sega's computer game?
6 Which London Palace has a famous maze?
7 Where are the Crown Jewels housed?
8 What colour flag is awarded by the EC to beaches of a certain standard?
9 What would you collect if you collected Clarice Cliff?
10 Near which city is Cadbury World?
11 What is the junior version of Lego called?
12 Where in Scotland is an Old Blacksmith's shop a tourist attraction?
13 What type of wildlife attraction is Longleat famous for?
14 Which Rosemary is famous for her keep-fit books and videos?
15 Which Norfolk seaside resort has a famous Pleasure Beach?
16 In knitting, which yarn is thicker, double-knitting or four-ply?
17 In chess, which piece can be called two different things?
18 How many cards do you deal to each player in rummy?
19 In Scrabble what colour are the triple-word score squares?
20 Which is the oldest swimming stroke?
21 What type of competition might you watch at a gymkhana?
22 If you like bonsai what would you be interested in?
23 Tango, waltz and tap are types of which pastime?
24 What would your hobby be if you bought a first-day cover?
25 Which sport was originally called "football in the water"?
26 Which UK city would you visit to see Roman Baths and a famous Pump Room?
27 If you collected lepidoptera what would you collect?
28 In ice hockey what shape is a puck?
29 Europe's first Disney theme park was built near which city?
30 What type of museum has Imperial in front of its name in London?

Answers	**90s Films** *(see Quiz 221)*

1 The Silence of the Lambs. 2 Jurassic Park. 3 Home Alone. 4 The English Patient. 5 Mrs Doubtfire. 6 Patrick Swayze. 7 Whitney Houston. 8 The Piano. 9 Four Weddings and a Funeral. 10 Aladdin. 11 Robin Hood. 12 Turtles. 13 Hook. 14 Pocahontas. 15 The Madness of King George. 16 Dances with Wolves. 17 The Lion King. 18 Madonna. 19 Dead Man Walking. 20 Toy Story. 21 Schindler's List. 22 Braveheart. 23 Sister Act 2. 24 Clint Eastwood. 25 Irons. 26 Hanks. 27 Philadelphia. 28 Lee Curtis. 29 Pierce Brosnan. 30 Nixon.

Quiz 224 | Pot Luck 109

Answers – page 236

LEVEL 1

1 The airline Finnair is from which country?
2 Where was the 2005 G8 summit held?
3 In which decade of the 20th century was Shane Richie born?
4 Colin Milburn is associated with which sport?
5 In which month is VE Day?
6 Moving anticlockwise on a dartboard, what number is next to 16?
7 Who wrote the novel "A Town Like Alice"?
8 In which country is the city of Salonika?
9 Which UK car manufacturer produced the Alpine?
10 The character Alan B'Stard appeared in which TV series?
11 Which former footballer won "Strictly Ice Dancing" in partnership with Zoia Birmingham in 2004?
12 How many acres in a square mile?
13 In billiards how many points are scored for a cannon?
14 A car must have its first MOT by what age?
15 Who is GP to the "The Simpsons"?
16 Who was team boss when WBA made their great relegation escape in 2004–05?
17 Jacob Marley appears in which Charles Dickens novel?
18 What is an ampersand used to mean?
19 Which liberation organization had the initials PLO?
20 A cricket umpire raises his index finger above his head to indicate what?
21 Zoophobia is the fear of what?
22 Which Arthur starred in "Dad's Army"?
23 In heraldry what is or?
24 Gorgonzola cheese comes from which country?
25 In computing, what does the O stand for in ROM?
26 Which American city was devastated by the earthquake of 1906?
27 What name is given to the vertical bar of a window?
28 What did former US President Jimmy Carter grow on his farm?
29 Which county have Boycott and Illingworth played cricket for?
30 Who got to No. 1 on both sides of the Atlantic with "Spinning Around"?

| **Answers** | Pot Luck 110 *(see Quiz 226)* |

1 Cooper. 2 Cricket. 3 Jesus wept. 4 Serene. 5 Steve Bell. 6 Finney. 7 Jules Verne. 8 Houston. 9 Mexico. 10 Abacus. 11 Ant. 12 September & October. 13 50s. 14 Snooker. 15 Nitrogen. 16 "Dad's Army". 17 D-Ream. 18 Hull. 19 Potter. 20 Queen Victoria. 21 Spain. 22 1/16. 23 11. 24 Cheating. 25 Sue Barker. 26 Barbra Streisand. 27 Gwen Stefani. 28 Tuesday. 29 Commodore. 30 First.

1 What does 'e' stand for in e-mail?
2 What was the world's first stamp called?
3 Which country has most first-language speakers of English?
4 What does the abbreviation BT stand for?
5 If A is for Alpha and B is for Bravo, what is C for ?
6 What did Samuel Morse design for communications?
7 When a number of computers are connected what are they called?
8 Which punctuation mark and letters indicate a UK Internet user?
9 What is the BBC's news channel called?
10 In speech how should you – officially, at least – address a pope?
11 The Braille alphabet is made up of raised what?
12 Oftel is an independent watchdog relating to which service?
13 What does Hon. mean in the form of address Right Hon.?
14 A physician is addressed as Doctor; how is a male surgeon addressed?
15 The Greek letter beta corresponds with which letter of our alphabet?
16 Sputnik 1 was the first artificial what?
17 Which country has Le Monde as a major national newspaper?
18 What is Reuters?
19 In communication terms what is the Washington Post?
20 What does the "I" stand for in ISP?
21 On inland phone calls when does the cheaper evening rate begin, Monday to Friday?
22 What is the third letter on the top row of a keyboard?
23 If a skull and crossbones is seen on a container what does it mean?
24 To use a French road called a "péage" what must you do?
25 Which BT number do you dial to find your last caller's number?
26 Is it possible for a fax and a phone line to have the same number?
27 On the Internet what does the abbreviation WWW stand for?
28 An autoroute in France and an autobahn in Germany is what?
29 In what mobile device would you find a SIM card?
30 What is the smallest denomination of postage stamp you can buy?

| **Answers** | TV Times 3 *(see Quiz 227)* |

1 Anne Robinson. 2 The A-Team. 3 Harriott. 4 Australia. 5 "A Question of Sport". 6 "Question Time". 7 Parkinson. 8 Rubber. 9 Saunders. 10 1940s. 11 Esther Rantzen. 12 Arthur Fowler. 13 Scotland. 14 Hughie Green. 15 "Rome". 16 Corbett. 17 Auf Wiedersehen Pet. 18 Fry. 19 1950s. 20 Picnic baskets. 21 "Yes Minister". 22 Family. 23 Sunday. 24 Desperate. 25 "Lost". 26 Delia Smith. 27 McCall. 28 Madeley, Finnigan. 29 "Countdown". 30 Australia.

1 Which boxer Henry was BBC Sports Personality of the Year in 1970?
2 In which sport was the Twenty20 Cup introduced?
3 What are the words in the shortest verse of the Bible?
4 In the royal address HSH what does S stand for?
5 Which cartoonist draws "If..." for the Guardian newspaper?
6 Which Tom was the first player to be twice Footballer of the Year?
7 Who wrote the novel "Around the World in Eighty Days"?
8 Which Whitney led the most weeks in the singles chart list for 1993?
9 In which country is the city of Tijuana?
10 Which ancient calculator used a frame and beads?
11 Which of Ant & Dec has the surname McPartlin?
12 The zodiac sign Libra covers which two calendar months?
13 In which decade of the 20th century was Jimmy Nail born?
14 Doug Mountjoy is associated with which sport?
15 N is the chemical symbol for which element?
16 The character ARP Warden Hodges appeared in which TV series?
17 In the 90s, who had a No. 1 with "Things Can Only Get Better"?
18 What is the administrative centre for the county of Humberside?
19 Which Dennis wrote "The Singing Detective"?
20 Who was the British monarch at the start of the 20th century?
21 In which country did the 1992 Olympics take place?
22 What does 1/4 x 1/4 equal?
23 How many players are there in a hockey team?
24 What is the only English anagram of TEACHING?
25 Who was the first female presenter of "A Question of Sport" on TV?
26 Who won an Oscar for Best Actress in "Funny Girl"?
27 "What You Waiting For?" and "Rich Girl" are singles by which artist?
28 If March 1 is a Saturday, what day is April 1?
29 In the Royal Navy which rank is higher – commander or commodore?
30 Cotton denotes which wedding anniversary?

Answers | Pot Luck 109 *(see Quiz 224)*

1 Finland. 2 Gleneagles. 3 60s. 4 Cricket. 5 May. 6 7. 7 Nevil Shute. 8 Greece. 9 Chrysler. 10 "The New Statesman". 11 David Seaman. 12 640. 13 Two. 14 Three years. 15 Dr Julius Hibbert. 16 Bryan Robson. 17 A Christmas Carol. 18 And. 19 Palestine. 20 Batsman is out. 21 Animals. 22 Lowe. 23 Gold. 24 Italy. 25 Only. 26 San Francisco. 27 Mullion. 28 Peanuts. 29 Yorkshire. 30 Kylie Minogue.

1 Who was the first permanent female presenter of "Points of View"?
2 Which Team heroically helped those in trouble in the 80s?
3 Which Ainsley replaced Fern Britton as presenter of "Ready Steady Cook"?
4 In which country is "Prisoner Cell Block H" set?
5 Which quiz features a picture board and "what happens next"?
6 Which political programme is based on radio's "Any Questions"?
7 Which Michael presents an eponymous chat show?
8 What were the "Spitting Image" puppets made from?
9 Which Jennifer partners Dawn French?
10 Which decade was the setting for "Tenko"?
11 Who was the main female presenter of "That's Life"?
12 Which "EastEnders" character died on his allotment?
13 Which country is Rab C. Nesbitt from?
14 Which former "Opportunity Knocks" presenter died in 1997?
15 Which 2005 drama told the story of the founding of the Roman Empire?
16 Who always embarked on a long monologue in "The Two Ronnies"?
17 What did Denis Neville and Oz say to those they left behind in the North-East in the 80s?
18 "QI" is presented by which Stephen?
19 In which decade did the action of "M*A*S*H" take place?
20 Which sort of containers are Yogi Bear's favourite?
21 In which sitcom did Private Secretary Bernard Woolley appear?
22 Robert Lindsay and Zoe Wanamaker starred in a sitcom about "My" what?
23 On which day of the week is "The Antiques Roadshow" broadcast?
24 What were the "Housewives" who lived on Wisteria Lane?
25 Which 2005 US drama followed the fortunes of survivors after a plane crash?
26 Which cook presented a Winter and Summer Collection in the 90s?
27 Which Davina presents "Big Brother"?
28 What are the surname of Richard and Judy?
29 Des Lynam began presenting which words and numbers quiz in October 2005?
30 "I'm A Celebrity … Get Me Out of Here!" is filmed in which country?

Answers	**Communications** (see Quiz 225)

1 Electronic. **2** Penny Black. **3** USA. **4** British Telecom. **5** Charlie. **6** Morse code. **7** Network. **8** .uk. **9** News. **10** Your Holiness. **11** Dots. **12** Telecommunications. **13** Honourable. **14** Mr. **15** B. **16** Satellite. **17** France. **18** A news agency. **19** Newspaper. **20** Internet. **21** 6 p.m. **22** E. **23** Poison or danger. **24** Pay a toll. **25** 1471. **26** Yes. **27** World Wide Web. **28** Motorway. **29** Mobile phone. **30** 1p.

1 Kelvedon Wonder and Little Marvel are types of what?
2 Which programme presented prizes on a conveyor belt?
3 In the 90s, who had a No. 1 with "I Believe"?
4 Which veteran comic Eric featured in the Harry Potter films?
5 On a Monopoly board, what colour is Pentonville Road?
6 The movie Munich is about which tragic event in this city?
7 Who wrote the novel "The Inimitable Jeeves"?
8 Which of Queen Elizabeth II's children was first to marry?
9 What is the administrative centre for the county of Suffolk?
10 In which decade of the 20th century was Joanna Lumley born?
11 Who went to sea with silver buckles on his knee?
12 How many fluid ounces in a pint?
13 Which band were formed from the "Popstars" TV show?
14 What is 1/6 as a percentage to two decimal places?
15 Would you expect Monty Don to cook, dance or garden on TV?
16 Who was England's manager for Gary Lineker's last international?
17 Which UK car manufacturer produced the Stag?
18 In music, what note is written on the bottom line of the treble clef?
19 On a dartboard what number is opposite 5?
20 RIBA is the Royal Institute of British what?
21 Which Prayer was a millennium chart topper for Sir Cliff Richard?
22 In which month is Independence Day in the USA?
23 Jason Wilcox played soccer for which country?
24 In which country is the city of Turin?
25 How are angles measured other than degrees?
26 The Battle of Waterloo was fought in which country?
27 The letter O is on which row of a typewriter or computer keyboard?
28 What colour is the centre of an archery target?
29 Pop and Ma Larkin appeared in which TV series?
30 Which kind of pear is usually served as a starter?

Answers	**Tour de France** *(see Quiz 230)*

1 Henri Desgrange. 2 Maurice Garin. 3 Jacques Anquetil. 4 Eddy Merckx. 5 Seven.
6 Tom Simpson. 7 Canterbury. 8 White jersey *(maillot blanc)*. 9 Polka dot *(maillot pois)*. 10 Miguel Indurain. 11 Louison Bobet. 12 Fauso Coppi. 13 1903. 14 Pyrenees.
15 François Faber (Luxembourg). 16 Floyd Landis. 17 Laurent Fignon. 18 Bidon.
19 1919. 20 Raymond Poulidor. 21 Green. 22 Red. 23 Bernard Hinault. 24 The Champs-Élysées. 25 Jacques Goddet. 26 Philippe Thys. 27 Richard Virenque. 28 Gino Bartali. 29 It's Not About the Bike. 30 Stephen Roche.

1 Who was in goal when Liverpool won the Champions League Final in 2005?
2 Who won the Ryder Cup in 2004?
3 What sport do the New York Yankees play?
4 Which Pete had a hat-trick of Wimbledon triumphs in the 90s?
5 What did Dionicio Ceron win in London in 1994, 95 and 96?
6 In which city did Linford Christie win Olympic 100m. gold?
7 What sport does Michael Jordan play?
8 The businessman Samuel Ryder initiated a cup in which sport?
9 Which rugby league team are the Bulls?
10 What do the initials WBC stand for?
11 Which Russian won the Ladies Singles title at Wimbledon in 2004?
12 Which major British racing event was postponed in 1997 after a bomb scare?
13 How often are showjumping World Championships held?
14 At which sport did Liz Hobbs find fame?
15 Duncan Fletcher was awarded what honour after England's 2005 Ashes victory?
16 Which Lloyd was undisputed welterweight world champion in 1986?
17 Shaun Wright-Phillips joined Chelsea from which club?
18 What sport do the Dallas Cowboys play?
19 Horse racing's Belmont Stakes is run in which country?
20 In golf, what is a double bogey?
21 How many players a side are there in basketball?
22 A cricket umpire waves an arm from side to side to signal what?
23 Who was the Brown Bomber?
24 What did Emerson Fittipaldi break at Michigan in 1996?
25 Which team said goodbye to their home Baseball Ground in 1997?
26 Which Dan was the BBC's voice of tennis from the 50s to the 90s?
27 Anita Lonsbrough is associated with which sport?
28 In which decade was cricket's first World Cup Final played?
29 Where is the Horse of the Year show staged?
30 Which county cricket club has its home at Edgbaston?

Answers	The Last Round (see Quiz 231)

1 Highbury. 2 Dan Brown. 3 Gold. 4 Acid. 5 The man in the moon. 6 Toblerone. 7 Pudding Lane. 8 Snooty. 9 Cricket. 10 The Hanging Gardens. 11 Ant & Dec. 12 A shilling (now 5p). 13 Pizza. 14 Green. 15 Harry Potter series. 16 Six. 17 Australian Open. 18 Oliver Twist. 19 German. 20 Boston. 21 Six. 22 Nothing. 23 A fish. 24 Palindromes. 25 Kiwi fruit. 26 Poncho. 27 Six. 28 Insects. 29 Five. 30 Bird.

Quiz 230 | Tour de France

Answers – page 238

1 Who devised the very first Tour de France as a publicity stunt for his newspaper?

2 Who won the first Tour de France?

3 Who was the first rider to win the Tour de France five times?

4 Which champion was nicknamed "The Cannibal"?

5 How many times did Lance Armstrong win the Tour de France?

6 Which cyclist died on the slopes of Mont Ventoux in 1967?

7 Where was the finish of the 2nd Stage of the 2007 Tour de France?

8 What jersey is awarded to the best-placed Tour de France rider aged 25 or under?

9 What jersey is worn by the King of the Mountains?

10 Which multiple winner of the Tour de France hailed from the Basque country?

11 Who was the first rider to win the Tour de France three times in succession?

12 In the post WW2 period, which Italian rider fought with his compatriot Gino Bartali for the honour of being the "campionissimo" – the champion of champions?

13 In what year was the first Tour de France held?

14 In which mountain range is the formidable Col du Galibier?

15 Who was the first non-Frenchman to win the Tour de France?

16 Which winner of the 2006 Tour de France failed a drugs test?

17 Which Tour de France champion was nicknamed "The Professor"?

18 Do the Tour de France riders drink from a musette or a bidon?

19 In which year was the overall winner of the Tour de France awarded a yellow jersey for the first time?

20 Which rider became popularly known as the "eternal second"?

21 What colour jersey is worn by the leading points winner?

22 What is the colour of the pennant that is used to indicate the last kilometre of the race?

23 Which Tour champion was nicknamed "The Badger"?

24 Since 1975 whereabouts in Paris does the race finish?

25 Who succeeded Henri Desgrange as Tour director?

26 Who was the first rider to win the Tour de France three times?

27 Which rider has won the "King of the Mountains" for a record seven times?

28 Which rider holds the record of the longest time span between victories?

29 What is the title of Lance Armstrong's autobiographical account of his battle with cancer?

30 Which Irishman won the Tour de France in 1987?

Answers | Pot Luck 111 *(see Quiz 228)*

1 Pea. 2 "Generation Game". 3 Robson and Jerome. 4 Eric Sykes. 5 Light blue. 6 Massacre at 1972 Olympics. 7 P. G. Wodehouse. 8 Princess Anne. 9 Ipswich. 10 40s. 11 Bobby Shaftoe. 12 20. 13 Hear'say. 14 16.66. 15 Garden. 16 Graham Taylor. 17 Triumph. 18 E. 19 17. 20 Architects. 21 Millennium Prayer. 22 July. 23 England. 24 Italy. 25 Radians. 26 Belgium. 27 Top letters row. 28 Gold. 29 "The Darling Buds of May". 30 Avocado.

1 The 2005–6 football season was the last that Arsenal played at which stadium?

2 The character Robert Langton is the hero of whose novels?

3 The discovery of what caused a rush to California in 1848?

4 What is the opposite of alkali?

5 In rhyme, who asked his way to Norwich when he came down too soon?

6 Which nutty chocolate is sold in triangular bars?

7 In which lane is the Great Fire of London said to have started?

8 Which lord was removed from the Beano in 1992?

9 In which game could an Australian's Chinaman beat an Englishman?

10 Which of the Wonders of the World was at Babylon?

11 Who presented a TV "Takeaway" on Saturday night?

12 A bob was the popular name of which old English coin?

13 What was the Teenage Mutant Turtles' favourite food?

14 What comes after red, orange and yellow in the rainbow's colours?

15 Which books and films featured Professor Dumbledore?

16 How many legs does a male insect have?

17 Which Grand Slam tournament did Andre Agassi win in 2000, 2001 and 2003?

18 Which workhouse boy asked for more?

19 Which language does the word kitsch come from?

20 What is the state capital of Massachusetts?

21 How many strings does a Spanish guitar have?

22 What did Old Mother Hubbard keep in her cupboard?

23 What kind of creature is an anchovy?

24 Dad, kayak and rotavator are examples of what type of words?

25 Which juicy green fruit is named after a New Zealand bird?

26 What is the name for a blanket-like cloak with a slit for the head?

27 Most snow crystals have how many sides?

28 What does an entomologist study?

29 In Britain a general election must be held after how many years?

30 What sort of creature is a treecreeper?

Answers	Sporting Chance 3 (see Quiz 229)

1 Jerzy Dudek. 2 Europe. 3 Baseball. 4 Sampras. 5 Marathon. 6 Barcelona. 7 Basketball. 8 Golf. 9 Bradford. 10 World Boxing Council. 11 Maria Sharapova. 12 Grand National. 13 Every four years. 14 Water Skiing. 15 OBE. 16 Honeyghan. 17 Man. City. 18 American football. 19 USA. 20 Two over par for a hole. 21 Five. 22 Boundary for 4 runs. 23 Joe Louis. 24 His neck. 25 Derby. 26 Maskell. 27 Swimming. 28 1970s. 29 Wembley Arena. 30 Warwickshire.

The Medium Questions

This next selection of questions is getting a little more like it. For an open entry quiz then you should have a high percentage of medium level questions – don't try to break people's spirits with the hard ones just make sure that people play to their ability.

Like all questions this level of question can be classed as either easy or impossible depending on whether you know the answer or not and although common knowledge is used as the basis for these questions there is a sting in the tail of quite a few. Also, if you have a serious drinking squad playing then they can more or less say goodbye to the winner's medals, but that isn't to say they will feel any worse about it.

Specialists are the people to watch out as those with a good knowledge of a particular subject will doubtless do well in these rounds so a liberal sprinkling of pot-luck questions are needed to flummox them.

1 The first book title was Harry Potter and what?
2 What do J. K. Rowling's initials stand for?
3 What is the most popular sport among wizards?
4 Which Harry Potter novel was first published in 2005?
5 What is the first name of the giant Hagrid?
6 Which Emma played Hermione in the Harry Potter films?
7 What is Ron's surname?
8 What is the third word of all the book titles?
9 In the US version what did "The Philosopher's Stone" become in the book title?
10 Who is "You know who" and "He Who Must not be Named"?
11 Which actor played Hagrid in the Harry Potter films?
12 Which company bought J. K. Rowling's first script and published the novel?
13 Cornelius Fudge is the Minister for what?
14 Which city is a favoured venue for midnight launches with J. K. Rowling present?
15 Which Chris directed the first Harry Potter movie?
16 What is the name of the Slytherin Student who keeps company with Draco Malfoy?
17 Which character did the late Richard Harris play on film?
18 Parselmouth is the name for a wizard that can do what special thing?
19 What type of transport appears on the cover of the children's edition of The Philosopher's Stone?
20 What is the name of Ron's pet rat?
21 In "The Half-Blood Prince" is Harry is in his fourth, fifth or sixth year at Hogwarts?
22 What was the second book to be published?
23 Which book has Ron inviting Harry to the Quidditch World Cup?
24 Which university did J. K. Rowling attend?
25 What did "DA" stand for?
26 What is the name of the soul-sucking guards from Azkaban?
27 Which Mike directed the movie The Goblet of Fire?
28 What is the name of the national wizarding newspaper?
29 Which book cover depicts a creature rising above some flames?
30 What has happened to Harry's parents?

Answers | Nature: Animals *(see Quiz 3)*

1 Starfish. 2 Adult. 3 Tadpole. 4 Colour. 5 Skin. 6 Venom. 7 Africa. 8 Bat. 9 Grizzly. 10 Caribou. 11 Seven. 12 Insects. 13 Grey, red. 14 Cheetah. 15 Scottish. 16 Blue. 17 Man. 18 Trees. 19 Chihuahua. 20 Yes. 21 Horn. 22 Tiger. 23 Goat. 24 Kangaroo. 25 Two. 26 Panther. 27 Earthworms. 28 China. 29 Elk. 30 Dams.

1 Which world leader's funeral took place the day Charles and Camilla were due to be married?
2 In which country is Baden-Baden?
3 Who captained England in the famous 5–1 victory in Germany in 2001?
4 Whom did Michael Howard succeed as Tory Party leader?
5 Which English king was nicknamed Rufus?
6 Which county gives its name to a horse known as a Punch?
7 The Angel of the North was erected next to which major road?
8 Obstetrics is the study of what?
9 Which bird gave Fleetwood Mac a No 1 instrumental?
10 In proverb speech is silver but what is golden?
11 Who became known as "The King of the Wild Frontier"?
12 What is the heavy rain of summer called in Asia ?
13 What is alopecia?
14 Which London station would you arrive at if you travelled from Ipswich?
15 What fruit are you said to be if you are accompanying a courting couple?
16 Frederick the Great was king of which country?
17 Before going solo Beyoncé Knowles fronted which female band?
18 Which city was built on seven hills?
19 What type of creature is a painted lady?
20 What is a lift for food in a restaurant known as?
21 Which Latin phrase means in good faith?
22 What does a misogynist hate?
23 Which American president had a wife known as Ladybird?
24 What name is given to animals that eat grass and plants?
25 What is Delft in Holland famous for?
26 In the Bible, which king had to decide which of two women was the mother of a child?
27 Fletcher Christian led a mutiny on which ship?
28 Who wrote "Under Milk Wood"?
29 What is the capital of Hawaii?
30 What is the post code known as in America?

Answers | Pot-Luck 2 *(see Quiz 4)*

1 Iris. 2 Mime. 3 Charles Kennedy. 4 Juventus. 5 Bristol. 6 Natasha Kaplinsky. 7 Mrs Brown. 8 Thomas More. 9 Kennedy. 10 Cuba. 11 Phoenix. 12 Marx Brothers. 13 Piebald. 14 Stoat. 15 Sea sickness. 16 Poland. 17 Thomas à Becket. 18 Animal Farm. 19 Cup and lip. 20 Rhesus. 21 Acute. 22 Isle of Wight. 23 Beethoven. 24 Testator. 25 Violin. 26 Black. 27 Coast. 28 Chlorophyll. 29 Louisiana. 30 Quicksilver.

1 What is a common name for the asteroidea which have five arms?
2 At what stage of development is the imago stage of an insect?
3 What is the aquatic larva of an amphibian more commonly called?
4 What is a chameleon capable of changing?
5 What does a reptile shed in the process of sloughing?
6 What is another name for snake poison?
7 The aardvark is a native of which continent?
8 Which is the only mammal able to fly?
9 Which type of dark-coloured bear is the largest?
10 What do Americans call reindeer?
11 Man has seven vertebrae in his neck. How many does a giraffe have?
12 What is the main diet of hedgehogs?
13 Which two colours are wolves?
14 What is the fastest land animal?
15 From which border do Border collies originate?
16 What colour is a chow chow's tongue?
17 What is the mammal homo sapiens better known as?
18 Where does an arboreal animal live?
19 What is the smallest breed of dog?
20 Do dolphins have teeth?
21 Which part of the rhino is regarded as an aphrodisiac?
22 Which is the largest of the cats?
23 The ibex is a member of which animal family?
24 Which is generally larger, a wallaby or a kangaroo?
25 How many sets of teeth do most mammals have?
26 What is the black leopard more commonly known as?
27 What do moles mainly feed on?
28 Which country does the breed of dog, shih tzu, come from?
29 What would the Europeans call what the Americans call a moose?
30 What do beavers build?

Answers	**Harry Potter** *(see Quiz 1)*

1 The Philosopher's Stone. **2** Joanne Kathleen. **3** Quidditch. **4** Harry Potter and the Half Blood Prince. **5** Rubeus. **6** Emma Watson. **7** Weasley. **8** And. **9** The Sorcerer's Stone. **10** Lord Voldemort. **11** Robbie Coltrane. **12** Bloomsbury. **13** Magic. **14** Edinburgh. **15** Chris Columbus. **16** Pansy Parkinson. **17** Dumbledore. **18** Talk to snakes. **19** Train. **20** Scabbers. **21** His sixth year. **22** Chamber of Secrets. **23** Goblet of Fire. **24** Exeter. **25** Dumbledore's Army. **26** Dementors. **27** Mike Newell. **28** The Daily Prophet. **29** Order of the Phoenix. **30** Killed (by Lord Voldemort).

1 What is the coloured part of the eye called?
2 With what type of entertainment is Marcel Marceau associated?
3 The wife of which party leader gave birth to a son during the 2005 election campaign?
4 Thierry Henry joined Arsenal from which club?
5 In which British city is the station Temple Meads?
6 Who was the first female winner of "Strictly Come Dancing"?
7 Judi Dench won a Golden Globe in 1998 for which film?
8 Which Tudor figure is the main character in "A Man for All Seasons"?
9 Which American president had the first names John Fitzgerald?
10 In which country is Havana?
11 In legend, which bird rose from its own ashes?
12 Which brothers starred in the film "Duck Soup"?
13 What term describes a black and white horse?
14 Which animal does ermine come from?
15 If you have "mal de mer" what are you suffering from?
16 The Solidarity movement began in which country?
17 In 1170, which Archbishop of Canterbury was murdered?
18 What kind of farm did George Orwell write about?
19 In proverb, there is "many a slip 'twixt" what and what?
20 Which monkey possesses a blood factor that is shared with humans?
21 What type of angle is less than 90 degrees?
22 On which Isle is Osborne House?
23 Who composed the piece of music known as the "Moonlight Sonata"?
24 What name is given in law to a person who makes a will?
25 Stéphane Grappelli is famous for playing which instrument?
26 What colour were the shirts of Mussolini's Italian Fascists?
27 What was the title of the 2005 TV series about Britain's borders with the sea?
28 What is the green colouring matter in plants known as?
29 Which American state does cajun music come from?
30 What is another name for mercury?

Answers	Pot-Luck 1 *(see Quiz 2)*

1 Pope John Paul II. 2 Germany. 3 David Beckham. 4 Iain Duncan Smith. 5 William II. 6 Suffolk. 7 A1. 8 Childbirth. 9 Albatross. 10 Silence. 11 Davy Crockett. 12 Monsoon. 13 Baldness. 14 Liverpool Street. 15 Gooseberry. 16 Prussia. 17 Destiny's Child. 18 Rome. 19 Butterfly. 20 A dumb waiter. 21 Bona fide. 22 Women. 23 Lyndon Johnson. 24 Herbivore. 25 Pottery. 26 Solomon. 27 HMS Bounty. 28 Dylan Thomas. 29 Honolulu. 30 Zip code.

1 What were the full first names of the founders of the House of Eliott?
2 Which was the then most expensive TV series ever when it was first broadcast in 2005?
3 Which family lived at 165 Eaton Place, London?
4 Which actress played wife No 1 in "The Six Wives of Henry VIII" and Mrs Victor Meldrew?
5 Whom did Demelza marry in the drama set in Cornwall?
6 Which 1970s series was based on novels by Anthony Trollope ?
7 Which shipping line did the "Charlotte Rhodes" belong to?
8 Which mistress of Edward VII was played by Francesca Annis?
9 Derek Jacobi played the title role as which Roman emperor?
10 Which saga was about Soames, Irene, Jolyon and their family?
11 In which country was "The Far Pavilions" set?
12 During which war was "By the Sword Divided" set?
13 In "Brideshead Revisited" what was Aloysius?
14 What is the profession of Eleanor Bramwell in the Victorian series?
15 Who played the title role in the series about Elizabeth I?
16 Which compass points formed the title of an American Civil War drama?
17 What was the profession of the Duchess of Duke Street?
18 Which James Bond once played Mr Rochester in a TV version of "Jane Eyre"?
19 Who links "Ab Fab" Saffron and "Pride and Prejudice" Lydia Bennet?
20 In "Upstairs, Downstairs" what was butler Hudson's first name?
21 The drama "Whatever Love Means" was about which love triangle?
22 Which daughter of Vanessa Redgrave played Mrs Simpson in the 2005 drama "Wallis and Edward"?
23 Which "Good Lifer" starred on TV as Edward VII's sister?
24 Which romantic hero was played by Colin Firth in 1995?
25 Which series was "Thomas and Sarah" a spin-off from?
26 Which movement was the series "Shoulder to Shoulder" about?
27 Which tyrannical Italian family was the subject of a series in 1981?
28 Which drama featured Peggy Ashcroft and Geraldine James in wartime India?
29 Who played Churchill in "The Wilderness Years"?
30 Who wrote "Middlemarch", the novel the TV serial was based on?

Answers	Theatre and Musicals *(see Quiz 7)*

1 Anthony Andrews. 2 Sarah Brightman. 3 David Essex. 4 Sunset Boulevard. 5 La Cage aux Folles. 6 The Sound of Music. 7 Tony. 8 Chicago. 9 Kiss Me, Kate. 10 Theatre Royal. 11 Michael Ball. 12 Don Black. 13 Tim Rice. 14 Show Boat. 15 Happy Talk. 16 Siam (now Thailand). 17 West Side Story. 18 Stripper. 19 Stephen Sondheim. 20 Carousel. 21 Michael Crawford. 22 Joyce Grenfell. 23 Gaston Leroux. 24 Mary Magdalen. 25 Chess. 26 Roger Moore. 27 Petula Clark. 28 Cats. 29 Hair. 30 A Chorus Line.

1 Which animal appears on the front of a British passport with a lion?
2 What does a theodolite measure?
3 Which poisonous gas is given off from a car exhaust?
4 In Scotland, what are Eigg, Muck and Rhum?
5 In Channel 4's 2005 historical drama about the life of Elizabeth I, who played Elizabeth?
6 Robert Menzies was prime minister of which country?
7 What is the currency of Poland?
8 "The Two of Us" was an autobiography about which actress and her late husband?
9 In maths, what is meant by three dots in a triangular formation?
10 Traditionally, what does a cooper make?
11 Which motorway goes from east to west across the Pennines?
12 What are workers and drones types of?
13 What is the middle name of Winston S. Churchill?
14 On what calendar date is Burns Night?
15 What is the home of a beaver called?
16 How many railway stations are there on a Monopoly board?
17 What was the title of the movie sequel to "The Mask of Zorro"?
18 What has the body of a lion and the head of a human?
19 Who invented the method by which the blind can read by touch?
20 Who sang the Bond theme "Goldfinger"?
21 What does a costermonger sell?
22 What did the Italian soldier Garibaldi give his name to?
23 How many Premiership sides did Millwall beat to reach the 2004 FA Cup Final?
24 Which sea is north of Turkey?
25 What colour are the flowers of St John's Wort?
26 Segovia is associated with which musical instrument?
27 Cold meat and cold potatoes can produce what dish?
28 Which king is supposed to have hidden in a tree after the Battle of Worcester?
29 Which brothers flew the first manned, powered aeroplane?
30 The Heriot-Watt university is in which city?

Answers | Pot-Luck 4 *(see Quiz 8)*

1 We Will Rock You – The Queen Musical. 2 Leeds United. 3 Sharp. 4 White and yellow. 5 24. 6 Bishop. 7 Animal. 8 South Africa. 9 Van Gogh. 10 Berkshire. 11 Radius. 12 Mont Blanc. 13 Six. 14 H. G. Wells. 15 Runnymede. 16 90 degrees. 17 Bakewell. 18 Yellow. 19 Bad breath. 20 Enid Blyton. 21 Mediterranean. 22 Pontoon. 23 Sue MacGregor. 24 Mexico and USA. 25 5. 26 20. 27 Three. 28 Princess Anne. 29 Raymond Chandler. 30 Geology.

1 Which Anthony has starred in "My Fair Lady" and "The Woman in White" on the West End stage?
2 Which musical star was Andrew Lloyd Webber's second wife?
3 Who played Che in the original stage production of "Evita"?
4 Which was Elaine Paige's first musical on Broadway?
5 Which musical does the song "I am What I am" come from?
6 In which musical is Maria von Trapp the heroine?
7 Which theatre award is named after actress Antoinette Perry?
8 The characters of Billy Flynn, Mama Morton and Velma Kelly appear in which musical?
9 Which musical is based on "The Taming of the Shrew"?
10 What is the name of the most famous theatre in London's Drury Lane?
11 Who originally played the role of Alex in "Aspects of Love"?
12 Who wrote the lyrics for "Tell Me on a Sunday" and "Sunset Boulevard"?
13 Who co-produced the revival of "Anything Goes" with Elaine Paige?
14 Which musical is the song "Ol' Man River" from?
15 Which song from "South Pacific" was recorded by Captain Sensible?
16 In which country is "The King and I" set?
17 Which musical are the songs "Tonight" and "Somewhere" from?
18 What was the profession of the heroine in "Gypsy"?
19 Who wrote "Into the Woods" and "A Little Night Music"?
20 In which musical does "You'll Never Walk Alone" appear?
21 Who played the title role in "Barnum" and "Billy"?
22 Which actress was Maureen Lipman's show "Re Joyce" about ?
23 Who wrote the novel that forms the basis of the musical "Phantom of the Opera"?
24 Which character sings "I Don't Know How to Love Him" in "Jesus Christ Superstar"?
25 Which musical is "I Know Him So Well" from?
26 Which former Saint turned down a musical role in "Aspects of Love"?
27 Who replaced Elaine Paige as Norma Desmond in the London production of "Sunset Boulevard"?
28 In which musical do they sing about a "Jellicle Ball"?
29 Which musical hailed the dawning of the age of Aquarius?
30 Which musical is the song "One" from?

Answers	TV: Costume Drama *(see Quiz 5)*

1 Beatrice and Evangeline. 2 Rome. 3 Bellamy family. 4 Annette Crosbie. 5 Ross Poldark. 6 The Pallisers. 7 Onedin Line. 8 Lillie Langtry. 9 Claudius. 10 Forsyte Saga. 11 India. 12 English Civil War. 13 A teddy. 14 Doctor. 15 Glenda Jackson. 16 North and South. 17 Cook. 18 Timothy Dalton. 19 Julia Sawalha. 20 Angus. 21 Charles, Diana and Camilla. 22 Joely Richardson. 23 Felicity Kendal. 24 Mr Darcy. 25 Upstairs, Downstairs. 26 The suffragettes. 27 The Borgias. 28 The Jewel in the Crown. 29 Robert Hardy. 30 George Eliot.

1 The characters Killer Queen and Scaramouche feature in which musical?
2 Jonathan Woodgate was first capped for England while at which club?
3 In music, a flat sign lowers a note but what sign raises a note?
4 What are the two main colours on the Vatican flag?
5 Chemically pure gold contains how many carats?
6 In chess, which piece always moves diagonally?
7 Are sea-urchins animal, vegetable or mineral?
8 In which country did the England team play Test cricket in January 2005?
9 Which artist painted "Sunflowers"?
10 In which county is Windsor Castle?
11 What term is given to the distance from the centre of a circle to the outer edge?
12 Which is the highest mountain in the Alps?
13 How many points are there on a snowflake?
14 Who wrote the story "The Invisible Man"?
15 On which island did King John set his seal to the Magna Carta?
16 How many degrees in a right angle?
17 Which Derbyshire town gives its name to a Tart?
18 Jonquil is a shade of which colour?
19 What is halitosis?
20 Who created the character Kiki the parrot?
21 Which sea does the River Rhone flow into?
22 In which card game can you stick and twist?
23 Which female presenter introduced Radio 4's "Today" programme from 1994 to 2002?
24 The Rio Grande separates which two countries?
25 What do 2 + 2 = according to Radiohead?
26 How many decades are there in two centuries?
27 How many stripes does a police sergeant have on his arm?
28 Which royal was quoted by the press as saying "Why don't you naff off"?
29 Which writer created Philip Marlowe, the private eye?
30 What is the name for the study of rocks and the earth's crust?

| **Answers** | **Pot-Luck 3** *(see Quiz 6)* |

1 Unicorn. 2 Angles. 3 Carbon monoxide. 4 Islands. 5 Helen Mirren. 6 Australia. 7 Zloty. 8 Sheila Hancock. 9 Therefore. 10 Barrels. 11 M62. 12 Bees. 13 Spencer. 14 25th January. 15 Lodge. 16 Four. 17 The Legend of Zorro. 18 The Sphinx. 19 Louis Braille. 20 Shirley Bassey. 21 Fruit and vegetables. 22 A biscuit. 23 None. 24 Black Sea. 25 Yellow. 26 Guitar. 27 Bubble and squeak. 28 Charles II. 29 Wright Brothers. 30 Edinburgh.

1 What team is known as The Baggies?
2 In which year did Arsène Wenger join Arsenal as manager?
3 What two colours are in Derby's home strip?
4 Who said, "When seagulls follow the trawler it is because they think the sardines will be thrown into the sea"?
5 In which country was the Final of the 2002 World Cup played?
6 Which city has a team of the same name and a United team?
7 Hernan Crespo joined Chelsea in 2003 from which club?
8 Bobby Gould and Phil Neal have both managed which club?
9 Who plays home games at the New Den?
10 Which club is linked with the playing career of Tom Finney?
11 Who managed Liverpool to the 1986 FA Cup and League double?
12 Which country do Brondby come from?
13 Which famous first will always be held by Keith Peacock?
14 Which club did Mark Atkins play for in a Premiership-winning season?
15 Which country did Mike England play for?
16 What is the home colour of Crystal Palace?
17 Which country does Craig Bellamy play for?
18 Which team had Radford and Kennedy as a strike force?
19 Which club broke the Auld Firm dominance to win the Scottish League Cup in 2004?
20 Michael Carrick joined Spurs from which other London club?
21 To two years, when did the late, great George Best leave Man Utd?
22 Who has managed both Southampton and Celtic?
23 Who was the manager when England won the 1966 World Cup?
24 Which country did Alan Brazil play for?
25 Who made comments implying some Man Utd fans were only there for the prawn sandwiches?
26 Which player was involved in Britain's first million-pound transfer?
27 David Murray has been an influential chairman of which Scottish club?
28 Which club has been managed by Bobby Robson, Kevin Keegan and Ruud Gullit?
29 Which Arsenal player followed Robert Pires as the Football Writers' Player of the Year?
30 Who went to Newcastle from Man Utd in the Andy Cole transfer deal?

Answers	Pot-Luck 5 *(see Quiz 11)*

1 Alice Cooper. 2 Colditz. 3 Iraq. 4 Decibels. 5 Egypt. 6 Yorkshire. 7 Shoes. 8 Golf. 9 Tchaikovsky. 10 60. 11 Sandringham House. 12 Batman. 13 Morocco. 14 Dublin. 15 Elysée Palace. 16 144. 17 Canoeing. 18 June. 19 Boats. 20 When it is about to leave port. 21 Comet. 22 Hansard. 23 Judaism. 24 Australia and New Zealand. 25 Vertical. 26 Five. 27 Four. 28 The eye. 29 Sheila. 30 H and N.

1 How long is a Member of Parliament elected for?
2 In which year in the 1970s were there two general elections?
3 Which party won Bethnal Green & Bow at the 2005 general election?
4 After the 2005 election had the Liberals got more or fewer parliamentary seats than before?
5 Which candidate stood down from the Lib Dem leadership election in 2006?
6 Who was Britain's first black woman MP?
7 Who was Tory leader at the time of the 2005 general election?
8 Who became Labour leader after the 1992 election defeat?
9 Which future PM failed to win Dartford for the Tories in 1950 and 1951?
10 Which two Davids headed the Alliance party in 1983?
11 Which prime minister's father was a trapeze artist?
12 The House of Commons consists of how many members?
13 Who replaced Alan Clark as MP for Kensington & Chelsea?
14 Who gave up the title of Viscount Stansgate to remain an MP?
15 Which MP is the son-in-law of Alf Garnett's son-in-law?
16 Who was the leader of the opposition at the time of the 2001 general election?
17 What was the first name of the wife of the leader of the opposition in the 2005 general election?
18 Who wrote the novel "A Parliamentary Affair"?
19 Who resigned as a government minister over the Sara Keays affair?
20 Which party won the general election in 1945?
21 Which former minister has presented "Six O Six" on Radio 5 Live?
22 Name the 1992 Tory party chairman who lost his Bath seat?
23 Which former deputy Labour leader, whose father was once a Catholic priest, stood down after the 1992 General Election?
24 What was Norman Tebbitt's job before entering Parliament?
25 Which party did Screaming Lord Sutch represent?
26 Who became deputy Labour leader after the 1992 General Election?
27 Which constituency did the late Mo Mowlam represent?
28 What did the Ecology Party change its name to in 1985?
29 What was Dennis Skinner's job before he entered Parliament?
30 Which MP won gold medals at the 1980 and 1984 Olympics?

Answers	Heavy Metal *(see Quiz 12)*

1 Yardbirds. 2 Black Night. 3 John. 4 Black Sabbath. 5 Iron Maiden. 6 Led Zeppelin III. 7 Metallica. 8 Def Leppard. 9 Birmingham. 10 Deep Purple. 11 AC/DC. 12 Ozzy Ozbourne. 13 Drums. 14 Sandy Denny. 15 Bat Out of Hell. 16 David Coverdale's Whitesnake. 17 Machine Head. 18 Dennis Wheatley. 19 Bass guitar. 20 Ian Gillan. 21 Jimmy Page. 22 Playing guitar solos. 23 An arm. 24 Rick Wakeman. 25 Pyromania. 26 Phil Collins. 27 But I Won't Do That. 28 Rainbow. 29 Iommi. 30 Iron Maiden.

1 Which gender-bender name did rock star Vincent Furnier adopt?
2 Which German prison camp did Pat Reid try to escape from?
3 Kurds, Shias and Sunnis were involved in elections in which country in 2005?
4 What measure is used for sound or noise?
5 Farouk was king of which country?
6 Which county used to be divided into Ridings?
7 Which item of clothing is linked with the name Jimmy Choo?
8 Which sport is played at Sunningdale?
9 Who composed the "1812 Overture"?
10 What is the mean of 40, 60 and 80?
11 Which royal residence is in Norfolk?
12 In comics, by what name is Bruce Wayne known?
13 Marrakesh is in which country?
14 In the traditional song, in which city did Molly Malone sell cockles and mussels?
15 What is the official residence of the French president?
16 How many square inches in a square foot?
17 In which sport are there wild water, sprint and slalom events?
18 In which month is the longest day in Britain?
19 Smack and sampan are types of what?
20 When is the Blue Peter flag raised on a ship?
21 What type of heavenly body is named after Edmund Halley?
22 Which book records debates in Parliament?
23 Which religion observes the Passover?
24 Anzac troops come from which two countries?
25 In aviation VTOL stands for what type of take-off and landing?
26 How many lines in a limerick?
27 How many years is the term of office of the American president?
28 In which part of the body is the cornea located?
29 What is the first name of John Peel's widow?
30 Which two letters of the alphabet identify the virus known as bird flu?

Answers	**Sport: Football** *(see Quiz 9)*

1 West Bromwich Albion. 2 1996. 3 Black and white. 4 Eric Cantona. 5 Japan. 6 Dundee. 7 Inter Milan. 8 Coventry. 9 Millwall. 10 Preston. 11 Kenny Dalglish. 12 Denmark. 13 First substitute in a League game. 14 Blackburn. 15 Wales. 16 Red and blue. 17 Wales. 18 Arsenal. 19 Livingston. 20 West Ham. 21 1974. 22 Gordon Strachan. 23 Alf Ramsey. 24 Scotland. 25 Roy Keane. 26 Trevor Francis. 27 Rangers. 28 Newcastle United. 29 Thierry Henry. 30 Keith Gillespie.

1 Which group was Jimmy Page in before forming Led Zeppelin?
2 What was Deep Purple's first hit in the singles charts?
3 What is Ozzy Ozbourne's actual first name?
4 Which group were "Paranoid" in the charts?
5 Which group took its name from a medieval instrument of torture?
6 They were known for imaginative cover designs, but what was the title of Led Zeppelin's third album?
7 Which band released the album "St Anger" that topped the US charts in 2003?
8 Which group founded the Bludgeon Riffola label?
9 Which city did Black Sabbath come from?
10 Ian Gillan, Graham Bonnet and David Coverdale sang for which group?
11 In which group did Angus Young wear short trousers?
12 Who recorded "Bark at the Moon"?
13 What instrument did Ian Paice play?
14 Which folk singer sang on Led Zep's "The Battle of Evermore"?
15 Which album from 1978 was reissued in 1991 and led to a 1993 sequel?
16 How were Whitesnake credited on their first recordings?
17 "Smoke on the Water" came from which album?
18 Terry Butler changed his group's name to Black Sabbath after reading a novel by which author?
19 What instrument does Iron Maiden founder Steve Harris play?
20 "Naked Thunder" was the first solo album by which singer?
21 Who wrote "Stairway to Heaven"?
22 On stage, Nugent, Kramer and Pinera indulged in what kind of duels?
23 What did Def Leppard drummer Rick Allen lose in a car accident?
24 Which Yes keyboard player was on "Sabbath Bloody Sabbath"?
25 "Rock of Rages" was on which Def Leppard album?
26 Who was guest drummer for Led Zeppelin at the Live Aid concert?
27 What words in brackets end the title "I Would Do Anything for Love?"
28 Which group did Ritchie Blackmore form on leaving Deep Purple?
29 Which guitarist Tony was an original member of Black Sabbath?
30 Which band released the album "Dance of Death" in 2003?

Answers | Election Fever (see Quiz 10)

1 Five years. 2 1974. 3 Respect – The Unity Coalition. 4 More. 5 Mark Oaten. 6 Diane Abbott. 7 Michael Howard. 8 John Smith. 9 Margaret Roberts (later Thatcher). 10 Owen and Steel. 11 John Major's. 12 651. 13 Michael Portillo. 14 Tony Benn. 15 Tony Blair. 16 William Hague. 17 Sandra. 18 Edwina Currie. 19 Cecil Parkinson. 20 Labour. 21 David Mellor. 22 Chris Patten. 23 Roy Hattersley. 24 Airline pilot. 25 Monster Raving Loony Party. 26 Margaret Beckett. 27 Redcar. 28 Green Party. 29 Miner. 30 Sebastian Coe.

1 Who had the first No 1 with "Unchained Melody"?
2 Which rogue trader brought about the downfall of Barings Bank?
3 Which jockey rode over 200 winners in both 1997 and 1998?
4 In which country is the Dordogne?
5 What kind of creature is a natterjack?
6 Which team were on the receiving end of Man Utd's 9–0 record Premier victory?
7 Which cricket team plays home county games at Edgbaston?
8 How is the letter S represented in morse code?
9 If something is Cantonese which country does it come from?
10 Whose murder conviction was overturned after 45 years in 1998?
11 What is the background colour of motorway signs?
12 In which resort was "Fawlty Towers" set?
13 Orthodontics involves what parts of the body?
14 In China what was the colour of Chairman Mao's "little book"?
15 In which film does Professor Higgins appear?
16 How many ribs does a human have?
17 Zen is a form of what type of religion?
18 What does a pathologist study?
19 In which European country is Malmö?
20 What name is given to a book in which a sea captain charts events on a voyage?
21 What type of pet animal can be Chinchilla or Dutch?
22 What is the longest word that appears in the film "Mary Poppins"?
23 On the road, what does a red circular sign with a white band across it mean?
24 In which city is the Doge's Palace?
25 In the past, what was an Iron Horse?
26 Buff Orpingtons and Plymouth Rocks are types of what?
27 Which city in North Wales has the name of a Welsh saint?
28 In which sport is the Curtis Cup awarded?
29 Which canal takes food through your body?
30 Who wrote the controversial "Satanic Verses"?

Answers	**Pot-Luck 7** *(see Quiz 15)*

1 20. 2 Valletta. 3 In the neck. 4 A hawk. 5 The Beatles. 6 Spanish. 7 Princess Margaret. 8 Rabbit. 9 Pontius Pilate. 10 Bootlegger. 11 Skye. 12 Caron Keating. 13 Golf. 14 Mullion. 15 A flower grows. 16 Ball. 17 Black. 18 Sheep. 19 Nepotism. 20 Neville Chamberlain. 21 Aurora Borealis. 22 James I. 23 Hippocratic Oath. 24 Susan. 25 AS Monaco. 26 Two. 27 Baloo. 28 Blue or violet. 29 Salisbury. 30 Maeve Binchy.

1 What country is Pecorino cheese from?
2 What type of pastry are profiteroles made from?
3 Which fruits are usually served "belle hélène"?
4 What is the main flavour of aïoli?
5 Which vegetable can be oyster, chestnut or shitaki?
6 What is wiener schnitzel?
7 How is steak tartare cooked?
8 Which drink is Worcester sauce traditionally added to?
9 Which fish is the main ingredient of Scotch Woodcock?
10 Which area of England are Singing Hinnies from?
11 What is beef fillet cooked in puff pastry called?
12 What gives Windsor Red cheese its colour and flavour?
13 What is a Worcester Pearmain?
14 Which meat is used in Glamorgan sausages?
15 Which vegetables can be Pentland Crown or Maris Bard?
16 What type of food is basmati?
17 What is Roquefort cheese made from?
18 What are the two main ingredients of angels on horseback?
19 Which fruit is a cross between a blackberry and a raspberry?
20 Which type of pasta's name means "little worms"?
21 What ingredient is included in food in a florentine style?
22 What is pancetta?
23 What is the main ingredient of a black pudding?
24 Which herb is in pesto sauce?
25 In Indian cookery what is naan?
26 What type of food is Cullen Skink?
27 What type of fish is in an Omelette Arnold Bennett?
28 What shape is the pasta called rigatoni?
29 What is couscous made from?
30 What does a Pomfret or Pontefract cake taste of?

Answers	Sci-Fi Movies *(see Quiz 16)*

1 Robocop. 2 Carrie Fisher. 3 Arthur C. Clarke. 4 Planet of the Apes. 5 Vulcan.
6 2000 A.D. 7 Steven Spielberg. 8 Barbarella. 9 451. 10 Superman. 11 Arnold
Schwarzenegger. 12 Queen. 13 The Death Star. 14 Peter Jackson. 15 Ants. 16 The
Invisible Man. 17 David Bowie. 18 The Omega Man. 19 Cars. 20 Logan's Run. 21
The Day the Earth. 22 Forbidden Planet. 23 Scream. 24 20,000. 25 Dr Strangelove.
26 Alec Guinness. 27 The Night of the Living Dead. 28 Keanu Reeves. 29 Dale Arden.
30 Spider.

1 In Sudoku, what is the total of the even numbers in a completed row?
2 What is the capital city of Malta?
3 Where in the body is the thyroid gland?
4 In politics what is the opposite of a dove?
5 Which group have had most British No 1 single hits?
6 What is the main language spoken in Mexico?
7 Which late Royal was the subject of a Channel 4 biopic broadcast in November 2005?
8 A cony is what sort of animal?
9 When Jesus was crucified, which Roman was governor of Jerusalem?
10 In the United States what name was given to a seller of illegal alcohol?
11 Which Scottish Isle became linked to the mainland by a bridge in 1995?
12 Who was Gloria Hunniford's daughter, subject of the book "Next to Me"?
13 Henry Cotton became famous in which sport?
14 What name is given to a vertical divide in a window?
15 In the song "I Believe", what happens for every drop of rain that falls?
16 Which word of four letters can go after beach and before gown to make new words?
17 What colour is the Northern Line on a London Underground map?
18 Astrakhan comes from which creature?
19 What is the name given to the practice of favouring your own relatives?
20 Which British prime minister spoke of "peace in our time"?
21 What is another name for the Northern Lights?
22 Who was monarch directly after Elizabeth I?
23 What is the name of the medical oath taken by doctors?
24 What is the name of the elder of the two girls in "The Lion, the Witch and the Wardrobe"?
25 Fabien Barthez joined Man Utd from which club?
26 How many packs of cards are needed to play bezique?
27 What is the name of the singing bear in Disney's "Jungle Book"?
28 What colour are the flowers of a periwinkle?
29 Which English city was once known as Sarum?
30 Who wrote the novel "The Glass Lake"?

Answers | Pot-Luck 6 (see Quiz 13)

1 Jimmy Young. 2 Nick Leeson. 3 Kieren Fallon. 4 France. 5 A toad. 6 Ipswich Town. 7 Warwickshire. 8 Dot dot dot. 9 China. 10 Derek Bentley. 11 Blue. 12 Torquay. 13 The teeth. 14 Red. 15 My Fair Lady. 16 24. 17 Buddhism. 18 Diseases. 19 Sweden. 20 Log. 21 Rabbit. 22 Supercalifragilisticexpialidocius. 23 No entry. 24 Venice. 25 Steam locomotive. 26 Chickens. 27 St Asaph. 28 Golf. 29 Alimentary. 30 Salman Rushdie.

1 Which character was described as "part man, part machine, all cop"?
2 Who played the part of the rebel princess in "Star Wars"?
3 "2001: A Space Odyssey" was based on a short story by whom?
4 What was the first in the five-film series of man and monkey conflict?
5 What planet did long-eared Mr Spock come from?
6 "Judge Dredd" was based on the character from which comic?
7 Which director said, "I'm embarrassed and ashamed that I get paid for doing this"?
8 In which film did Jane Fonda "do her own thing" in the 40th century?
9 What was the Fahrenheit reading in Truffaut's 1960s film?
10 Which hero has been portrayed by Christopher Reeve and Kirk Alyn?
11 Who was the star of "The Terminator" films?
12 Which rock band did the score for the 1970s romp "Flash"?
13 What was Darth Vader's spacecraft in "Star Wars"?
14 Who directed the 2005 version of "King Kong"?
15 Which creatures mutated in "Them"?
16 In which film did Claude Rains star as someone who was not seen?
17 Which rock star played Newton in "The Man Who Fell to Earth"?
18 In which film does Charlton Heston think he is Earth's last survivor?
19 Which vehicles set out to devour Paris?
20 In which film are people terminated at the age of 30?
21 In titles, which words go before "Stood Still" and "Caught Fire"?
22 Robbie the Robot and Dr Morbius appear in which film?
23 "Alien" posters said that "in space no one can hear you" do what?
24 In the 1953 film how many fathoms did the Beast come from?
25 "How I Learned to Stop Worrying and Love the Bomb" is known by what shorter title?
26 Which veteran actor played Ben (Obi-Wan) Kenobi?
27 In which 1960s film does rocket radiation activate flesh-eating zombies?
28 Who was the main star of "The Matrix" series of movies?
29 Who is the female companion of Flash Gordon?
30 In "The Incredible Shrinking Man" which creature does the man fight off with a needle?

Answers	**Food and Drink** *(see Quiz 14)*

1 Italy. 2 Choux pastry. 3 Pears. 4 Garlic. 5 Mushroom. 6 Veal. 7 It's served raw. 8 Tomato juice. 9 Anchovy. 10 North East. 11 Beef Wellington. 12 Red wine. 13 Apple. 14 None, they are made from cheese. 15 Potatoes and cabbage. 16 Rice. 17 Ewe's milk. 18 Oysters and bacon. 19 Tayberry. 20 Vermicelli. 21 Spinach. 22 Bacon. 23 Blood. 24 Basil. 25 Bread. 26 Soup. 27 Smoked haddock. 28 Tube-shaped. 29 Semolina. 30 Liquorice.

1 Which two countries agreed in November 2005 to field a joint team at the Beijing Olympics?
2 If two straight lines are always the same distance apart what are they said to be?
3 Kate Bush released the album "Aerial" in 2005 – how many years had gone by since her last album?
4 Nat Lofthouse was famous in which sport?
5 In the 14th century what was the bubonic plague called in England?
6 What is another word for a sleepwalker?
7 What do the initials WO stand for as a rank in the army?
8 Which Italian city was painted by Canaletto?
9 Who composed the "Enigma Variations"?
10 In politics, how many readings does a bill have in the House of Commons?
11 Yum Yum and Ko-Ko appear in which opera?
12 In which war was the Victoria Cross first awarded?
13 An ampersand is a sign for which word?
14 In Spanish, which word is used to address a young, or unmarried, lady?
15 The Suez Canal connects the Red Sea with which other Sea?
16 Which country did composer Aaron Copland come from?
17 Where did the Norse gods live?
18 In financial terms, what is the IMF?
19 Who was the first woman to edit the Sun newspaper?
20 Who composed the music for "West Side Story"?
21 "The City of Dreaming Spires" is which English city?
22 David Ben-Gurion was the first prime minister of which country?
23 What word means to gradually get louder and louder?
24 Troglodytes lived in what particular type of dwelling?
25 The borders of Turkey make up most of the land around which sea?
26 "Somewhere My Love" was the theme tune of which film?
27 How many players are there in a netball team?
28 If you are sinistral, what are you?
29 Mahmoud Ahmadinejad was Prime Minister of which country?
30 Mount Parnassus is in which country?

Answers | **Around England** *(see Quiz 19)*

1 Cambridgeshire. 2 Furniture. 3 Sellafield. 4 Ealing, Enfield. 5 Blackpool. 6 The Fens. 7 Chester. 8 Two. 9 York. 10 Lancashire. 11 Norwich. 12 Dorset. 13 Cowley. 14 Plymouth. 15 Shropshire. 16 Isle of Wight. 17 Bath. 18 East. 19 Gateshead. 20 Cambridge. 21 Worcestershire. 22 Greater Manchester. 23 Lake District. 24 North. 25 Bexhill-on-Sea. 26 Liverpool. 27 Essex. 28 Holy Island. 29 Northumberland. 30 Waterloo.

1 Little Rock is the capital of which US state?
2 On which granite cliff are the faces of four presidents carved?
3 Which language is the first language of 6% of the population?
4 Which natural disaster is the San Andreas Fault prone to?
5 What does DC stand for in Washington DC?
6 In which city is the University of Virginia located?
7 In which state is the Grand Canyon?
8 What are a group of six states on the northeast coast known as collectively?
9 Which Kander and Ebb musical was set in a city in Illinois?
10 Which was the first of the original 13 states of the United States?
11 Where is the main space exploration centre in Florida?
12 In which city is almost half of the population of Illinois to be found?
13 How long is the motor race which Indianapolis is famous for?
14 Which town is famous for its jazz music?
15 Which mountainous forest state has a settlement of Crow Indians?
16 What is traditionally easily available in Reno?
17 In which city is La Guardia airport?
18 Which US state has the highest population?
19 Which two New York boroughs begin with B?
20 Key West and Key Largo are off the coast of which state?
21 Which US state used to be called the Sandwich Islands?
22 Which New York street is famous for its fashion stores?
23 The name of which state has four letters, the first and last the same?
24 The discovery of what in 1848 led to the expansion of California?
25 Kansas is the United States' chief producer of which grain?
26 Which Michigan town is famous for the production of motor vehicles?
27 Which New York borough is noted for its skyscraper skyline?
28 Other than White Americans what is the largest racial group on Hawaii?
29 Which US state is the title of a musical by Rodgers and Hammerstein?
30 Which city, the capital of Tennessee, is famous for its music?

Answers	**Pot-Luck 9** *(see Quiz 20)*

1 Kirsten Dunst. **2** The Albatross. **3** The Dandie Dinmont. **4** The Moskva. **5** Mount Olympus. **6** Gene Kelly. **7** Michael and John. **8** The Moonstone. **9** Roses. **10** The Brave. **11** Biology. **12** Mercury. **13** The Crimean War. **14** Catherine Parr. **15** William Brown. **16** Officer of the Order of the British Empire. **17** Jason. **18** Peter Phillips. **19** German. **20** Destiny's Child. **21** Tchaikovsky. **22** Labrador Retriever. **23** William IV. **24** Helium. **25** Trinidad & Tobago. **26** China. **27** Anne Brontë. **28** St Mary Mead. **29** The Clock Tower. **30** His ear.

1 Which county did Huntingdonshire become part of in 1974?
2 What is High Wycombe famous for manufacturing?
3 Which atomic energy establishment used to be called Windscale?
4 Which two London boroughs begin with E?
5 Which seaside resort is on the Fylde?
6 What is the low-lying area of East Anglia called?
7 Which city was a Roman fortress called Deva and retains its medieval walls?
8 How many tunnels under the Mersey link Liverpool to the Wirral?
9 In which northern city is the National Railway Museum?
10 The Ribble is the chief river of which county?
11 In which city is the University of East Anglia?
12 Which county is Thomas Hardy associated with?
13 Which part of Oxford was famous for motor car manufacture?
14 Which Devon port has a famous Hoe?
15 Which county is also known as Salop?
16 Which Isle has Needles off its west coast?
17 Where would you find the 18th-century Assembly Rooms and Royal Crescent?
18 Which county does not exist: North, South, East or West Yorkshire?
19 In which town is the shopping complex, the Metro Centre?
20 Where would you find the Backs and the Bridge of Sighs?
21 Alphabetically what is the last county?
22 In which Metropolitan county are Trafford and Tameside?
23 In which National Park is Scafell Pike?
24 On which bank of the Thames is the City of London?
25 In which town is the modernist De La Warr Pavilion to be found?
26 Which city is served by John Lennon Airport?
27 Which county lies between the North Sea and Greater London?
28 What is Lindisfarne also known as?
29 In which county is Hadrian's Wall?
30 From which London station are there trains direct to the continent through the Channel Tunnel?

Answers | Pot-Luck 8 *(see Quiz 17)*

1 North & South Korea. 2 Parallel. 3 12 years. 4 Football. 5 The Black Death. 6 Somnambulist. 7 Warrant officer. 8 Venice. 9 Elgar. 10 Three. 11 Mikado. 12 Crimean. 13 And. 14 Señorita. 15 Mediterranean. 16 United States. 17 Valhalla. 18 International Monetary Fund. 19 Rebekah Wade. 20 Leonard Bernstein. 21 Oxford. 22 Israel. 23 Crescendo. 24 Caves. 25 Marmara. 26 Dr Zhivago. 27 Seven. 28 Left-handed. 29 Iran. 30 Greece.

1 Who was Orlando Bloom's female co-star in the movie "Elizabethtown"?
2 What was the nickname of German swimmer Michael Gross?
3 Which breed of dog is named after a character in a novel by Sir Walter Scott?
4 On which river does Moscow stand?
5 Where do the Greek gods live?
6 Which dancer sang in the rain?
7 What were the names of Wendy Darling's brothers in "Peter Pan"?
8 Which Wilkie Collins book is said to be the first detective story written in English?
9 Ena Sharples and Elizabeth of Glamis are types of what?
10 What was the title of the first movie that was directed by Johnny Depp?
11 Which "ology" is the study of human life?
12 Which planet is nearest to the sun?
13 In which war was the Charge of the Light Brigade?
14 Who was Henry VIII's last wife?
15 Which William led a gang called the Outlaws?
16 If you were awarded an OBE what would you be?
17 Who led the Argonauts in their quest for the Golden Fleece?
18 Who is the Queen's eldest grandchild?
19 What nationality was Richard Wagner?
20 "No, No, No" was the first UK top ten hit for which girl group?
21 Who wrote the music for "The Nutcracker"?
22 What is the most common breed of guide dog?
23 Which William did Queen Victoria succeed to the throne?
24 Which gas is used in modern airships?
25 Which country does footballer Dwight Yorke play for?
26 In which country were fireworks invented?
27 Who wrote "Agnes Grey"?
28 Where does Miss Marple live?
29 In which tower is Big Ben?
30 Which part of Captain Jenkins was cut off to start a war?

Answers	**Around the United States** *(see Quiz 18)*

1 Arkansas. 2 Mount Rushmore. 3 Spanish. 4 Earthquakes. 5 District of Columbia. 6 Charlottesville. 7 Arizona. 8 New England. 9 Chicago. 10 Delaware. 11 Cape Canaveral. 12 Chicago. 13 500 miles. 14 New Orleans. 15 Montana. 16 Divorce. 17 New York. 18 California. 19 Bronx, Brooklyn. 20 Florida. 21 Hawaii. 22 Fifth Avenue. 23 Ohio. 24 Gold. 25 Wheat. 26 Detroit. 27 Manhattan. 28 Japanese. 29 Oklahoma. 30 Nashville.

1 How many countries took part in the 2004 Olympic Games – 188, 202, 218?

2 What type of medal did boxer Amir Khan win at the 2004 Olympic Games?

3 How many gold medals did Mark Spitz win in Munich in 1972?

4 Which country is 1972 Pentathlon winner Mary Peters from?

5 What colour medal did Sharron Davies win in Moscow?

6 In which two successive Olympics did Daley Thompson win gold?

7 In which team game did Britain's men win gold in Seoul in 1988?

8 Which country has won most summer Olympic medals since 1896?

9 Whose long-jump record in the 1968 Olympics lasted for 24 years?

10 Which boxer won gold for Canada in Seoul in 1988?

11 Which country did athletes with FRG after their names represent?

12 Who won silver at 100 metres in '88 and gold in the same event in '92?

13 Which country won most gold medals in 2004?

14 Which gymnast scored the first perfect ten in Olympic history?

15 Which Cathy lit the cauldron at the start of the 2000 Sydney Olympics?

16 Who was disqualified after a drugs test in the Men's 100 metres in 1988?

17 Who collided with Zola Budd in the 3000 metres in 1984?

18 Who won Britain's first men's swimming gold for 68 years in 1976?

19 At which sport was Katarina Witt an Olympic champion?

20 In which city were the Winter Olympics held when Torvill and Dean won gold in 1984?

21 Which gold medal winner in 2004 was born in Pembury, Kent in 1970?

22 Which swimming event was introduced to the Olympics in 1984?

23 In which month was the Athens 2004 Olympics?

24 Which British skater won gold in 1980?

25 What are the five colours of the Olympic rings?

26 In 1984 who won gold in the Men's 800 metres and the 1500 metres?

27 In which country were the first modern Olympics held in 1896?

28 Who won the Women's 400-metre hurdles in Barcelona in 1992?

29 How many judges out of nine gave Torvill and Dean full marks for artistic impression in 1984?

30 Who was Britain's first-ever gold medallist in a throwing event in 1984?

Answers | Royals *(see Quiz 23)*

1 Twice. 2 Grand National. 3 Prince Harry. 4 Blue. 5 Timothy Lawrence. 6 Prince Andrew. 7 Gordonstoun. 8 Income tax. 9 Norman Hartnell. 10 Sophie. 11 John Bryan. 12 As the bride's mother. 13 Duke of Kent. 14 One. 15 Highgrove. 16 The Prince's Trust. 17 Zara Phillips. 18 HSBC. 19 Prince Charles. 20 Kiri Te Kanawa. 21 Elizabeth and David Emanuel. 22 Queen Mother. 23 Princess Alexandra. 24 Lord Mountbatten. 25 Princess Michael of Kent. 26 Louise. 27 Wales. 28 Ruby. 29 Queen Elizabeth II. 30 Royal Marines.

1 Which club became the first to win the FA Cup ten times?
2 St Stephen's Day is better known as which day?
3 Who recorded the original of "Love is All Around"?
4 Who became the first First Minister of the new Scottish Parliament?
5 A scallop sculpture on Aldeburgh beach in Suffolk is a tribute to which composer?
6 Which watch is from 8pm to midnight at sea?
7 Which two countries are divided by the Palk Strait?
8 Which Derbyshire town is noted for a church with a crooked spire?
9 In which field of writing is Simon Armitage mainly concerned?
10 What type of stone is the Koh-i-noor?
11 What is the study of family history called?
12 Which creature sends down share values on the stock exchange?
13 Which sport has its headquarters in St John's Wood, London?
14 Which language was invented for international use?
15 What was climbed "Because it is there"?
16 The Lutine bell is in which London institution?
17 The inspiration for which children's book character died in April 1996?
18 Which drug is obtained from foxglove leaves?
19 In which county is Romney Marsh?
20 Which magazine is the flagship of the Consumers Association?
21 Which four words follow "To be or not to be..."?
22 In France what title was given to the eldest son of the king?
23 What are the colours of the berries of the Mountain Ash?
24 What part of Cyrano de Bergerac's anatomy was particularly large?
25 In Japan what name is given to ritual sacrifice?
26 Whom did Flora Macdonald rescue?
27 Purchase tax was abolished in 1973, but what replaced it?
28 In the song, who regrets she is unable to lunch today?
29 Who was the god of war in Roman mythology?
30 The Gobi Desert is in which continent?

| **Answers** | **Pot-Luck 11** *(see Quiz 24)* |

1 Carbon. 2 Bryan McFadden. 3 Zeus. 4 The Volga. 5 Sir Isaac Newton. 6 Sonny.
7 Lisa Marie Presley. 8 Carmen. 9 Four. 10 Surbiton. 11 Fred Astaire. 12 Nagasaki.
13 Normandy. 14 Catch 22. 15 Brown. 16 Twentieth. 17 Light. 18 Black Sea.
19 Mandy Rice-Davis. 20 Simba. 21 Black Rod. 22 Astrologists. 23 Orchestra. 24
Skye Terrier. 25 John Dillinger. 26 Tosca. 27 The North Sea. 28 Butcher. 29 Die
Fledermaus. 30 West Germany.

1 How many times had Wallis Simpson been married before she married Edward VIII?

2 Which major sporting event took place on the same day that Charles and Camilla were married?

3 Which prince's last three names are Charles Albert David?

4 What colour was the suit Diana Spencer wore in her engagement photograph in 1981?

5 What is the name of the Princess Royal's second husband?

6 What was Prince Philip's father called?

7 Which Scottish school did Prince Charles go to?

8 What did the Queen agree to pay for the first time in 1992?

9 Who created Princess Elizabeth's wedding dress in 1947?

10 What is the Queen's youngest daughter-in-law called?

11 Who was the Duchess of York's financial adviser in 1992?

12 In what capacity was Mrs Susan Barrantes invited to the wedding of Prince Andrew and Sarah Ferguson?

13 Whom did Katharine Worsley marry in 1961?

14 How many official speeches did Camilla, Duchess of Cornwall, make on her first official visit to the US?

15 Where is the Prince of Wales' home in Gloucestershire?

16 Which organization did Prince Charles set up in 1976?

17 Who is the Queen's second eldest grandchild?

18 Which bank did Prince William work for on work experience in 2005?

19 Who is Earl of Chester?

20 Which opera singer sang at the wedding of Charles and Diana?

21 Who designed Diana Spencer's wedding dress?

22 Whose Christian names are Elizabeth Angela Marguerite?

23 Who is the Duke of Kent's sister?

24 Who was known as Uncle Dickie?

25 Which princess's first names are Marie Christine?

26 What is the Queen's youngest granddaughter-in-law called?

27 Royal wedding rings are made from gold from which country?

28 Which coloured stone was in Fergie's engagement ring?

29 Who as a child was known to her family as Lilibet?

30 Which branch of the armed forces did Prince Edward briefly join in 1986?

| **Answers** | The Olympics (see Quiz 21) |

1 202. 2 Silver. 3 Seven. 4 Northern Ireland. 5 Silver. 6 1980 and 1984. 7 Hockey. 8 United States. 9 Bob Beamon's. 10 Lennox Lewis. 11 West Germany. 12 Linford Christie. 13 United States. 14 Nadia Comaneci. 15 Cathy Freeman. 16 Ben Johnson. 17 Mary Decker. 18 David Wilkie. 19 Ice skating. 20 Sarajevo. 21 Kelly Holmes. 22 Synchronized swimming. 23 August. 24 Robin Cousins. 25 Black, yellow, red, green, blue. 26 Sebastian Coe. 27 Greece. 28 Sally Gunnell. 29 Nine. 30 Tessa Sanderson.

1 Coal is composed of which element?
2 Who left Westlife in March 2004?
3 Who was chief of the Greek gods?
4 What is the longest river in Russia?
5 Who formulated the law of gravity?
6 What was Sophie Ellis Bextor's first male child called?
7 Who has been married to Michael Jackson and Nicolas Cage?
8 In which opera does the heroine work in a cigarette factory?
9 When Steve Redgrave won his fifth Olympic gold how many rowers were there in the boat?
10 In which surburban district of London was the "Good Life" set?
11 Who was Ginger Rogers' most famous dancing partner?
12 Two Japanese cities were hit by atomic bombs in World War II. Hiroshima was one: what was the other?
13 William of where won the Battle of Hastings?
14 In which novel does the character Major Major Major Major appear?
15 What is the colour of the live wire in a three-pin plug?
16 In which century did Queen Victoria die?
17 Which word goes after lime and before house to make two new words?
18 What sea lies between Turkey and Russia?
19 Who said, "Well he would say that, wouldn't he?"
20 In Disney's "The Lion King" who is king at the end of the picture?
21 Whom does the monarch send to summon the Commons to her at the State Opening of Parliament?
22 Which 'ologists study the future through the movement of the planets?
23 What musical word is an anagram of cart-horse?
24 What breed of dog was Greyfriars Bobby?
25 Which 1930s US criminal was known as "Public Enemy No 1"?
26 Of which opera is Floria Tosca the heroine?
27 Which sea provides much of Britain's domestic gas?
28 To what trade had highwayman Dick Turpin been apprenticed?
29 Which Viennese opera title when translated is "The Bat"?
30 Which country were beaten finalists in the 2002 FIFA World Cup?

Answers	**Pot-Luck 10** *(see Quiz 22)*

1 Man Utd. 2 Boxing Day. 3 The Troggs. 4 Donald Dewar. 5 Benjamin Britten. 6 First watch. 7 India and Sri Lanka. 8 Chesterfield. 9 Poetry. 10 Diamond. 11 Genealogy. 12 Bear. 13 Cricket. 14 Esperanto. 15 Mount Everest. 16 Lloyds. 17 Christopher Robin. 18 Digitalis. 19 Kent. 20 Which? 21 That is the question. 22 Dauphin. 23 Red. 24 His nose. 25 Hara-kiri. 26 Bonnie Prince Charlie. 27 VAT – Value Added Tax. 28 Miss Otis. 29 Mars. 30 Asia.

1 Was bird flu first detected in America, Asia or Europe?

2 What species of kite breeds in Britain?

3 What is the study of birds' eggs called?

4 An exaltation is a group of which birds?

5 What would you see if there was a Turdus on your window sill?

6 What colour are wild budgerigars?

7 A scapular on a bird is a type of what?

8 Which bird song sounds like chiff-chaff chiff-chaff?

9 Which bird is sacred in Peru?

10 What is the smallest British bird?

11 What type of birds are ratites?

12 Which birds group to mate and are shot in braces?

13 What name is given to a flock or gathering of crows?

14 What is special about the bones of most birds?

15 Which family of birds does the robin belong to?

16 Golden and argus are varieties of which bird?

17 Which of the senses is poorly developed in most birds?

18 What is special about a palmiped?

19 Which bird lays the largest egg?

20 What is the oldest known fossil bird?

21 What is the main food of the oyster catcher?

22 What is the shaft of a feather called?

23 Which extinct bird was last sighted in Mauritius?

24 What does a syrinx help a bird to do?

25 Which three features distinguish birds from other creatures?

26 What name is given to a castrated cockerel?

27 What is the common name for all small birds of prey?

28 Which bird is the symbol of the RSPB?

29 What name is given to a flock or gathering of starlings?

30 What is the main group in the family Phasianidae?

| **Answers** | Karaoke (see Quiz 27) |

1 Is this just fantasy? 2 Unchained Melody. 3 My, my, my Delilah. 4 My Way. 5 Advertising Space. 6 In his kiss. 7 Your head. 8 Chris de Burgh. 9 The curtain. 10 In the wind. 11 She was a showgirl. 12 New York. 13 Eton Rifles. 14 Matchstalk cats and dogs. 15 I feel it in my fingers. 16 Ten. 17 Jolene. 18 All right. 19 Thought control. 20 Midnight. 21 Your lips. 22 This feeling inside. 23 Rosemary and thyme. 24 Guitar George. 25 Tell me more. 26 Hospital Food. 27 River deep mountain high. 28 Eleanor Rigby. 29 Make me cry. 30 A whiter shade of pale.

Quiz 26 | Pot-Luck 12

Answers – page 270

LEVEL 2

1 Which principality lies between France and Spain in the Pyrenees?
2 Canaan Banana was the first president of which country?
3 What was the name of the Queen of Faeries in "A Midsummer Night's Dream"?
4 Who was divorced from Mark Phillips?
5 What was the name of the girl who visited the Wizard of Oz?
6 Who came directly after Pope John Paul I?
7 Which team did Arsenal beat in the FA Cup Final in 2002 to complete the double?
8 Which "EastEnders" actress has a daughter named Tallulah Lilac?
9 Which stretch of water separates Alaska from the Russian mainland?
10 What did Sandie Shaw bare in the Eurovision Song Contest?
11 Who was the last chemist to be prime minister of Britain?
12 In 1979, who sang about "Walking on the Moon"?
13 Which Jane married Gerald Scarfe?
14 How many letters are there in the Greek alphabet?
15 Which camels have more humps, Dromedaries or Bactrians?
16 "If I were a Rich Man" comes from which stage show?
17 Which word follows "paper" and precedes "gammon" to make two new words?
18 Who was lead singer with the Boomtown Rats?
19 What was the name of Lady Penelope's puppet chauffeur?
20 What was St Luke's profession?
21 Which Michael Caine film was about the battle at Rorke's Drift?
22 In mythology, Minerva was the goddess of what?
23 What is exactly 26 miles and 385 yards long?
24 If you betray your country what crime do you commit?
25 Which politician was the subject of TV's "A Very Social Secretary"?
26 What in France is "Le Figaro"?
27 The musical "Blood Brothers" is based in which city?
28 What is the middle name of Cruz Beckham?
29 Who took over as England cricket captain from Graham Gooch?
30 The Lorelei rock is on which river?

Answers	TV: Police Serials *(see Quiz 28)*

1 Glasgow. 2 Frank. 3 Terry Venables. 4 Dixon of Dock Green. 5 Ruth Rendell. 6 Kojak. 7 Martin Shaw. 8 Jim. 9 Robert Lindsay. 10 Pierce Brosnan. 11 Metropolitan Police. 12 Pepper. 13 Jemima Shore. 14 Tubbs. 15 Juliet Bravo. 16 Dave and Ken. 17 Hawaii Five-O. 18 Morse Code. 19 Magnum. 20 The Avengers. 21 Poetry. 22 Sweeney Todd – Flying Squad. 23 Van de Valk. 24 Basset hound. 25 Cambridge. 26 Los Angeles. 27 Maigret. 28 Z Cars. 29 Radio presenter. 30 Cagney and Lacey.

1 What line follows "Is this the real life"?
2 "Time goes by so slowly, And time can do so much," comes from which song?
3 What line comes before "Why, why, why, Delilah?"?
4 "And so I face the final curtain" comes from which song?
5 Which Robbie Williams song names Marlon Brando?
6 Finish the line: "If you want to know if he loves you so, It's..."
7 What do you hold up high when you walk through a storm?
8 Who sang "Never seen you looking so gorgeous as you did tonight"?
9 Jason Donovan closed his eyes and drew back what?
10 "The answer, my friend, is blowing..." where?
11 What line comes after "Her name was Lola"?
12 Where are you if you "wake up in a city that never sleeps"?
13 In which song by the Jam is there "a row going on, down in Slough"?
14 What did he paint apart from "Matchstalk Men"?
15 What line comes before "I feel it in my toes"?
16 How many times do you sing "Yeah" in the chorus of "She Loves You"?
17 To whom did Dolly Parton beg "Please don't take my man"?
18 If tonight is the night how is Whitney Houston feeling?
19 According to Pink Floyd, "We don't need no education, We don't need no..." what?
20 What word comes before "Not a sound from the pavement"?
21 Finish the line: "You never close your eyes anymore when I kiss..."
22 Which Elton John line follows "It's a little bit funny"?
23 Which two herbs go with "parsley, sage"?
24 In "Sultans of Swing" who "knows all the chords"?
25 In "Grease", what line comes before "Did she put up a fight?"?
26 Which David Gray song features the line, "Tell me something I don't already know"?
27 What four words go after "Do I love you, My oh my"?
28 Who was "wearing a face that she keeps in a jar by the door"?
29 "Do you really want to hurt me? Do you really want to" do what?
30 "Her face at first just ghostly turned" what colour?

Answers	**Nature: Birds** *(see Quiz 25)*

1 Asia. 2 Red. 3 Oology. 4 Larks. 5 A thrush. 6 Green. 7 Feather. 8 Chiffchaff. 9 Condor. 10 Wren. 11 Flightless. 12 Pheasants. 13 Murder. 14 They are hollow. 15 Thrush. 16 The pheasant. 17 Smell. 18 It has webbed feet. 19 Ostrich. 20 Archaeopteryx. 21 Mussels. 22 Quill. 23 The dodo. 24 Sing. 25 Beaks, feathers and wings. 26 Capon. 27 Hawks. 28 Avocet. 29 A chattering. 30 Pheasants.

1 In which city is "Taggart" set?
2 What is "The Bill"'s DI Burnside's first name?
3 Who was co-creator of "Hazell" with Gordon Williams?
4 Which police series had the theme music "An Ordinary Copper"?
5 Who created the character of Chief Inspector Wexford?
6 Which detective called people "Pussycat"?
7 Which actor links "The Chief" and "The Professionals"?
8 What was Bergerac's first name?
9 Who played the part of Jericho in the 2005 series?
10 Who played the title role in "Remington Steele"?
11 Whom did Spender work for before being posted back to Newcastle?
12 In "Police Woman" what was Sgt Anderson's nickname?
13 Which series starred Patricia Hodge in the title role?
14 Who was Crockett's partner in "Miami Vice"?
15 In which series did Jean Darblay, then Kate Longton, appear?
16 What were Starsky and Hutch's first names?
17 In which series did Steve Garrett say "Book 'em Danno!"?
18 What sound was the theme music for "Inspector Morse" based on?
19 Which detective shares his name with a chocolate covered ice-cream bar?
20 Which long-running crime series was a spin-off from a programme called "Police Surgeon"?
21 What sort of literature does Commander Adam Dalgliesh write?
22 How did "The Sweeney" get its name?
23 Which series had the chart-topping "Eye Level" as its theme tune?
24 What breed of dog was Columbo's companion Fang?
25 In "Dempsey and Makepeace" which university had Lady Harriet graduated from?
26 In which city did "Burke's Law" take place?
27 Which detective has been played by Richard Harris and Michael Gambon?
28 Which series was set in Seaport and Newtown?
29 What was the occupation of Eddie Shoestring?
30 In which series did cops Petrie and Isbecki appear?

| **Answers** | Pot-Luck 12 (see Quiz 26) |

1 Andorra. 2 Zimbabwe. 3 Titania. 4 Princess Anne. 5 Dorothy. 6 John Paul II. 7 Chelsea. 8 Jessie Wallace. 9 Bering Strait. 10 Her feet. 11 Margaret Thatcher. 12 The Police. 13 Asher. 14 24. 15 Bactrian camels. 16 Fiddler on the Roof. 17 Back. 18 Bob Geldof. 19 Parker. 20 Doctor. 21 Zulu. 22 Wisdom. 23 The Marathon. 24 Treason. 25 David Blunkett. 26 Newspaper. 27 Liverpool. 28 David. 29 Mike Atherton. 30 Rhine.

1 Which gas shares its name with Superman's home planet?
2 In politics, to whom does the expression "Father of the House" refer?
3 On which island is Wall Street?
4 Who made the first full state visit to the UK by a US President?
5 What is the study of fluids moving in pipes?
6 What type of person studies the relationship between living organisms and their environment?
7 Who wrote the River Cottage cookery books?
8 Which English town is an anagram of ancestral?
9 Where, in Baker Street, did Sherlock Holmes live?
10 What does the word "Bolshoi" mean?
11 In mythology, who was banished by his son Jupiter?
12 Which London borough is the "G" in GMT?
13 Where in London is the Royal Opera House?
14 What is Eric Clapton's middle name?
15 How many dancers feature in a pas de deux?
16 Which William wrote a poem about daffodils?
17 What was the name of the World War I ace nicknamed "The Red Baron"?
18 Who produced the works of art "My Bed" and "Everyone I Have Ever Slept With"?
19 Who invented frozen food?
20 What unit is used to measure the gas we use in our homes?
21 What title did Harold Macmillan take?
22 In "Billy Elliot" what does Billy's father want him to train at instead of ballet?
23 Which Shakespeare play is in three parts?
24 What is a mordant?
25 Which "ology" is the art of ringing bells?
26 How was Achilles killed?
27 Matt Holland and Hermann Hreidarsson were together at Charlton and which other soccer club?
28 Which precinct does Ed McBain write about?
29 Who wrote the novel "Dr Zhivago"?
30 Who was prime minister of Britain at the outbreak of World War II?

Answers | Pot-Luck 14 *(see Quiz 31)*

1 Edward Heath. 2 Alan Sheppard. 3 Crufts. 4 Ireland. 5 Psychology. 6 Formic acid. 7 George III. 8 Fred Perry. 9 The Crimea. 10 Meal. 11 Richard Dunwoody. 12 Terpsichore. 13 Jimi Hendrix. 14 China. 15 Germany. 16 Red. 17 Man City. 18 The Times. 19 Flowers. 20 21. 21 Nitrous oxide. 22 Egypt. 23 1990s 24 Dermatology. 25 Sulphuric acid. 26 Plastering. 27 Edward Gibbon. 28 Poland. 29 Dorothy L. Sayers. 30 Children.

1 What is the plate connecting two lengths of railway track called?
2 What, according to tradition, takes four years to paint from end to end?
3 Which letter do post-war tanks all begin with?
4 Outside which London building were traffic lights first installed?
5 In World War II what was a McRobert's Reply?
6 What did LNER stand for?
7 Which Alistair was Secretary of State for Transport at the start of Labour's third term in office?
8 Which was the first true jet to enter passenger service?
9 What is the popular name for the Boeing 747 and the European airbus?
10 What links the Pacific Ocean with the Caribbean?
11 Who introduced the C5 in 1985?
12 Which motorway goes from London to Winchester?
13 Which nickname is given to aircraft such as the Harrier?
14 Who developed the Mini?
15 Which type of transport is Zeppelin associated with?
16 Where is O'Hare International airport?
17 What is the distress word for ships and aircraft?
18 Which four-wheel drive vehicle was launched in 1940?
19 Which word is used to describe the frame, wheels and machinery of a car?
20 The first motor car race was held to Bordeaux and back to where?
21 Which country has the international registration letter M?
22 Which US car manufacturer makes Astra, Corsa and Chevrolet?
23 What is the distance between two rails on a track called?
24 What colour is the District Line on a London Underground map?
25 From which two London stations could you travel to Scotland direct?
26 Which two classes of travel are there on Inter City trains?
27 In terms of tonnes of cargo handled, which is Europe's busiest port?
28 What does 'Volkswagen' mean?
29 On which side of the road do the Japanese drive?
30 In which city is Lime St Station?

Answers | **Religious Fervour** (see Quiz 32)

1 Jesus Christ's. 2 Brazil. 3 Ecumenical Movement. 4 Jehovah's Witnesses. 5 The Salvation Army. 6 Ramadan. 7 Jihad. 8 Buddhism. 9 Japan. 10 Russia. 11 Quakers. 12 Hinduism. 13 Mecca. 14 Hare Krishna. 15 Sikhs. 16 Scientology. 17 Chinese. 18 Mormons. 19 Transcendental Meditation. 20 Rastafarianism. 21 Temple. 22 Islam. 23 Kosher. 24 Eskimos. 25 Unitarians. 26 Church of Christ, Scientist. 27 John and Charles. 28 Immersion. 29 Moonies. 30 Sunday.

Quiz 31 | Pot-Luck 14

Answers – page 271

1 Whom did Margaret Thatcher replace as leader of the Tory Party?
2 Who hit a golf shot on the moon?
3 Which dog show was first held in Islington in 1891?
4 Darina Allen specializes in food that comes from which country?
5 In which "ology" were Freud and Jung active?
6 What acid gives nettles their sting?
7 Which king was nicknamed "Farmer George"?
8 Who was the last Briton to win the men's singles at Wimbledon?
9 On which peninsula is the city of Sevastopol situated?
10 Which word goes after piece and before times to make two new words?
11 Which jockey produced an autobiography titled "Obsessed"?
12 Who was the Greek muse of dance?
13 Which rock guitarist prophetically said, "When you're dead you're made for life"?
14 In which country is Puccini's "Turandot" set?
15 Which country did "Kaiser Bill" rule?
16 What colour of ballet shoes did Hans Christian Andersen write about?
17 Which club did David Seaman join on a free transfer after leaving Arsenal?
18 Which British newspaper is nicknamed "The Thunderer"?
19 What according to Scott McKenzie did you wear in your hair in San Francisco?
20 After 1928, women over what age were given the vote?
21 What is the correct name for laughing gas?
22 In which country was Harrods owner Mohamed al Fayed born?
23 In which decade of the last century did the Church of England vote for women priests?
24 Which "ology" is concerned with the human skin?
25 What is H_2SO_4?
26 Finish and browning are used in which building trade?
27 Who wrote the "Decline and Fall of the Roman Empire"?
28 In which country was Catherine the Great born?
29 Who chronicled the cases of Lord Peter Wimsey?
30 Whom is UNICEF responsible for?

Answers | Pot-Luck 13 (see Quiz 29)

1 Krypton. 2 The longest-serving MP. 3 Manhattan. 4 George W. Bush. 5 Hydraulics. 6 Ecologist. 7 Hugh Fearnley Whittingstall. 8 Lancaster. 9 221B. 10 Big. 11 Saturn. 12 Greenwich. 13 Covent Garden. 14 Patrick. 15 Two. 16 Wordsworth. 17 Baron von Richthofen. 18 Tracey Emin. 19 Clarence Birdseye. 20 Therms. 21 Earl of Stockton. 22 Boxing. 23 Henry VI. 24 A substance used to fix colours in dyeing. 25 Campanology. 26 By an arrow in his heel. 27 Ipswich Town. 28 The 86th Precinct. 29 Boris Pasternak. 30 Neville Chamberlain.

1 Whose birth shaped the calendar of the Western world?
2 Which country has the largest number of Roman Catholics?
3 Which movement promotes understanding between different branches of the Christian faith?
4 What are members of the Watchtower Movement better known as?
5 Whose newspaper is called "The Warcry"?
6 During which month do Muslims fast from before sunrise to sunset?
7 What term is used in Islam for "Holy War"?
8 Which religion is based on the teaching of Siddhartha Gautama?
9 Shintoism is the native religion of which country?
10 Which country has the largest Orthodox Church?
11 What are members of the Society of Friends called?
12 In which religion are Shiva and Vishnu major gods?
13 Where should Muslims make a pilgrimage to once in their lifetime?
14 How is the International Society for Krishna Consciousness known?
15 Who have uncut hair worn in a turban and uncut beards?
16 Which religion was founded by a science fiction author?
17 What nationality was Confucius?
18 What are members of the Church of Jesus Christ of Latter Day Saints better known as?
19 What does TM stand for in the movement founded by the Maharishi?
20 Dreadlocks in the hair and a musical style are hallmarks of which movement linked with Ethiopia?
21 In Hinduism what is a mandir?
22 Which religion has Sunnis and Shiites?
23 In Judaism treifa foods are forbidden. Which foods are allowed?
24 Shamanism is the dominant religion of which Arctic people?
25 Which Christian group deny the idea of the Trinity?
26 Which Church was founded by Mary Baker Eddy in the USA in 1879?
27 Which two Wesleys founded Methodism?
28 What sort of baptism does the Baptist Church practise?
29 What are members of the Unification Church better known as?
30 In Judaism what is the first day of the week?

Quiz 33   Pot-Luck 15

1 Who was elected Governor of California in 2003?
2 Which of the seven deadly sins begins with G?
3 What was Ghana's former name?
4 The Dutch royal family acquired its name from which French town?
5 Is the corncrake a bird, mammal or reptile?
6 What name is given to animals that do not hunt or eat meat?
7 Over which continent did the ozone hole form?
8 Which tanker suffered a severe oil spill in Alaska in 1989?
9 Where is the pituitary gland?
10 Which structural tissue is found in between the vertebral discs?
11 The five-year marriage of Ethan Hawke and which actress ended in August 2005?
12 In which country was former Tory leader Iain Duncan Smith born?
13 In which country would you find polders?
14 In which country are the Angel Falls?
15 After her "Strictly Come Dancing" triumph, Jill Halfpenny landed a role in which West End musical?
16 In which two cities would you find Cleopatra's Needles?
17 In which African country is Timbuktu?
18 Which BBC journalist was at the centre of the controversy over a weapons expert's report on the Iraq war?
19 Which English prime minister was known as "the Great Commoner"?
20 Who was the first person to notice that the Sun had spots?
21 Which metal is the best conductor of electricity?
22 Which actress's real name is Julia Wells?
23 Which secret society refers to God as "the great architect of the Universe"?
24 Which building is used for the election of a pope?
25 With whom did Bing Crosby sing "True Love" in the film "High Society"?
26 Which two colours appear on the UN flag?
27 What is the name of the Welsh Nationalist party?
28 What kind of stone is marble?
29 What name is given to the thousands of small bodies that orbit the Sun?
30 Which island was held by the Knights of St John from 1530 to 1798?

Answers | **Soul and Motown** (see Quiz 35)

1 Reach Out, I'll be There. 2 Berry Gordy. 3 Dave. 4 Aretha Franklin. 5 Holland. 6 Otis Redding. 7 The Broken Hearted. 8 Jackie Wilson. 9 The Isley Brothers. 10 James Brown. 11 The Supremes. 12 After the song Tammy by Debbie Reynolds. 13 You Keep Me Hangin' On. 14 Wilson Pickett. 15 The Vandellas. 16 Arthur Conley. 17 I'm Still Waiting. 18 Lionel Richie. 19 Gladys Knight. 20 Bobby Brown. 21 Stevie Wonder. 22 The Temptations. 23 Jimmy Mack. 24 William. 25 Midnight. 26 Reflections. 27 Marvin Gaye. 28 Atlantic. 29 Edwin Starr. 30 Junior Walker.

1 In darts, what is the maximum check-out score?
2 Who has won most international soccer caps for England?
3 Which country did boxer Lennox Lewis represent at the Olympics?
4 How many points did England score in the 2003 rugby union World Cup Final of 2003?
5 Which group were England in for the 2006 FIFA World Cup?
6 Which country turned Rugby Union's Five Nations into the Six Nations Championship in 2000?
7 Boxer Amir Khan comes from which north west town?
8 In 2005 Eddie Jones got sacked as rugby coach of which country?
9 For what sport is Ellery Hanley famous?
10 Is snooker's Jimmy White left-handed or right-handed?
11 What important role did Oliver McCall play in Frank Bruno's career?
12 At which Grand Prix circuit did Ayrton Senna lose his life?
13 Who was the first man to do the 100-metre breast stroke in under a minute?
14 The WDC is the World Darts Council, but what is the PDC?
15 Where was Barry Sheene involved in a 175 mph crash in 1975?
16 Which twisting circuit on the Grand Prix calendar is only 1.95 miles long?
17 Has croquet ever been a sport in the Olympics?
18 Which boxer used to enter the ring to Tina Turner's "Simply the Best"?
19 Whose shoulder was injured during Martin Johnson's 2005 testimonial?
20 In Rugby Union, who is Australia's record try scorer?
21 What make of car has made Michael Schumacher F1 World Champion in his triumphs this century?
22 In speedway racing, how many laps of the track does a race consist of?
23 Apart from England which European country took part in cricket's 1996 World Cup?
24 Which world heavyweight boxing champion died in an air-crash in 1969?
25 Who won a 100-metre breast stroke gold in the 1980 Olympics?
26 In badminton, how many points win a single game?
27 Which trainer is known as the "Queen of Aintree"?
28 Is an own goal allowed for in the rules of hockey?
29 Which two sports take place on a piste?
30 Which club side does Jonny Wilkinson play for?

Answers | Pot-Luck 16 *(see Quiz 36)*

1 Piano. 2 Southampton. 3 Ukraine. 4 1990. 5 Rome. 6 New Zealand. 7 Le Mans. 8 Brazil and Colombia. 9 Quito. 10 Inert gases. 11 Nucleus. 12 Peter Wright. 13 Samuel Beckett. 14 Adelaide. 15 Rainbow Warrior. 16 Sally Gunnell. 17 The Nag's Head. 18 Laurence Olivier. 19 You're So Vain. 20 Rembrandt. 21 The Brothers Grimm. 22 Danish. 23 Robert Baden-Powell. 24 Chuck Berry. 25 Alchemy. 26 William Bragg. 27 Imran Khan. 28 India. 29 Laura. 30 Paddy Ashdown.

1 The Four Tops had only one British No 1. What was it?
2 Who was the boss of Tamla Motown?
3 Who sang with Sam on the hit "Soul Man"?
4 Which female soul star has recorded with Elton John, George Michael and George Benson?
5 Who made up the songwriting trio with Holland and Dozier?
6 Who was sitting on the dock of the bay?
7 Who according to Jimmy Ruffin "had love that has now departed"?
8 Which soul singer died in 1984 after lying in a coma for eight years?
9 Rudolph, Ronald and O'Kelley were which singing Brothers?
10 Who is known as "The Godfather of Soul"?
11 Which group featured Cindy Birdsong?
12 The Motown label was nearly called Tammy. After which Tammy?
13 Which Tamla song starts, "Set me free, why don't you babe"?
14 In the 1960s who was known as "The Wicked Pickett"?
15 Which group backed Martha Reeves?
16 Who recorded the soul classic "Sweet Soul Music"?
17 What was Diana Ross's first solo British No 1?
18 Which singer went solo after performing with the Commodores?
19 Who was backed by the Pips?
20 Which soul singer married Whitney Houston in 1992?
21 Who sang "I Was Made to Love Her"?
22 Eddie Kendricks and David Ruffin were lead singers with which group?
23 Whom did Martha Reeves want to "hurry back"?
24 What was Smokey Robinson's real first name?
25 Which hour did Cropper and Pickett write about?
26 Which was the first single in which the Supremes were billed as Diana Ross and the Supremes?
27 Who originally heard it through the grapevine?
28 On which label did Aretha Franklin record in the 1960s?
29 Who had a Tamla hit with "War"?
30 Who fronted the All Stars?

| **Answers** | **Pot-Luck 15** *(see Quiz 33)* |

1 Arnold Schwarzenegger. 2 Gluttony. 3 Gold Coast. 4 Orange. 5 Bird. 6 Herbivore. 7 Antarctic. 8 Exxon Valdez. 9 In the brain. 10 Cartilage. 11 Uma Thurman. 12 Scotland. 13 Netherlands. 14 Venezuela. 15 Chicago. 16 London and New York. 17 Mali. 18 Andrew Gilligan. 19 William Pitt the Elder. 20 Galileo. 21 Silver. 22 Julie Andrews. 23 Freemasons. 24 Sistine Chapel. 25 Grace Kelly. 26 Blue and white. 27 Plaid Cymru. 28 Limestone. 29 Asteroids. 30 Malta.

1 Which instrument did Franz Liszt play?
2 Graeme Le Saux finished his soccer playing days with which club?
3 In which republic of the former USSR is Chernobyl?
4 In which year were East and West Germany unified?
5 Where was the treaty signed that established the EEC?
6 Who won the first Rugby Union World Cup, held in 1987?
7 On which circuit is motor racing's Grand Prix d'Endurance run?
8 Which two South American countries produce the most coffee?
9 What is the capital of Ecuador?
10 Helium belongs to which group of elements?
11 Where in the cell is DNA stored?
12 Who was the author of "Spycatcher" in 1987?
13 Who wrote the play "Waiting for Godot"?
14 Which Australian city is named after William IV's queen?
15 Which Greenpeace ship was sunk in Auckland harbour in 1985?
16 Who was the first female Brtish athlete to win world, Olympic, European and Commonwealth titles?
17 What is Del Boy's local?
18 Who was the first director of Britain's National Theatre Company?
19 Which song features the line "I bet you think this song is about you"?
20 Who painted "The Nightwatch?"
21 Which German brothers collected such stories as "Hansel and Gretel"?
22 What nationality was Hans Christian Andersen?
23 Who said, "A Scout smiles and whistles under all circumstances"?
24 Who first urged Beethoven to "roll over" in 1956?
25 What name was given to the practice that tried to turn lead into silver and gold?
26 Who shared a Nobel Prize for physics with his son?
27 Who entered Pakistani politics in 1995 after a successful career as a cricketer?
28 In which country was Rudyard Kipling born?
29 What is Prince Charles's step daughter called?
30 Who was Liberal Democrat leader immediately before Charles Kennedy?

Answers	**Sports Bag** *(see Quiz 34)*

1 170 – two treble 20s plus bull. 2 Peter Shilton. 3 Canada. 4 20. 5 Group B.
6 Italy. 7 Bolton. 8 Australia. 9 Rugby League. 10 Left-handed. 11 Bruno beat McCall to become the WBC Heavyweight champion. 12 San Marino, Italy. 13 Adrian Moorhouse in 1987. 14 Professional Darts Council. 15 Daytona. 16 Monaco. 17 Yes. 18 Chris Eubank. 19 Jonah Lomu. 20 David Campese. 21 Ferrari. 22 Four. 23 Netherlands. 24 Rocky Marciano. 25 Duncan Goodhew. 26 15 points. 27 Jenny Pitman. 28 Yes. 29 Fencing and skiing. 30 Newcastle.

1 About which conflict is the Sam Mendes film "Jarhead" about?
2 During which war was "Platoon" set?
3 Which Hollywood legend played Kurtz in "Apocalypse Now"?
4 Who played Hawkeye and Trapper John in "M*A*S*H"?
5 How was the film "Patton" known in the UK?
6 For which Robert de Niro film was "Cavatina" the theme music?
7 Who won an Oscar as the Colonel in "The Bridge on the River Kwai"?
8 In "The Colditz Story" what type of building was Colditz?
9 In which English county were the GIs billeted in "Yanks"?
10 What type of soldiers were the four Britons in "The Wild Geese"?
11 Which 1963 film about Allied POWs starred James Garner and Steve McQueen?
12 Hits from which decade were on the soundtrack of "Good Morning, Vietnam"?
13 Which George was the star of "Three Kings"?
14 How were the 12 convicts recruited for a suicide mission known in the 1967 movie?
15 Which novel was "Schindler's List" based on?
16 Which US singer played Von Ryan in "Von Ryan's Express"?
17 Whose café was a meeting place for war refugees in "Casablanca"?
18 Who wrote the novel on which "Where Eagles Dare" was based?
19 Which musical satire on war was directed by Richard Attenborough?
20 Where was it "All Quiet" in the classic film made in 1930?
21 At the time of which World War II event is "From Here to Eternity" set?
22 In "A Town Like Alice" what does "Alice" refer to?
23 Which anti-Vietnam War activist starred in "Coming Home"?
24 Who was the subject of the film "The Desert Fox"?
25 Which 1940 film starred Charlie Chaplin as despot Adenoid Hynkel?
26 Who directed "Born on the Fourth of July"?
27 Whose heroes were Clint Eastwood and Telly Savalas in 1970?
28 "The Eagle Has Landed" centres on a plot to kidnap whom?
29 Who won the Oscar for best actress in 1982 for "Sophie's Choice"?
30 In which country is "The Killing Fields" set?

Answers | Literature (see Quiz 39)

1 Serpent. 2 Hercule Poirot. 3 John Grisham. 4 The Prodigal Daughter. 5 Antonia.
6 10/6. 7 John McCarthy. 8 Australia. 9 Brian Keenan. 10 John Le Carré.
11 Shrewsbury. 12 Margaret Thatcher's. 13 Nancy Sinatra. 14 Ben Elton. 15 Gamekeeper. 16 Jack Higgins. 17 Maureen Lipman. 18 The Camomile Lawn. 19 Ian Fleming. 20 Sharpe. 21 Edwina Currie. 22 Georges Simenon. 23 Nelson Mandela. 24 Rudyard Kipling. 25 China. 26 Julian Fellowes. 27 Bunter. 28 Mercenaries. 29 Les Misérables. 30 Dan Brown.

1 What is Terry Wogan's real first name?
2 What name was given to the 19th-century group who wrecked machines?
3 What is the name of Orson Welles' first film, made when he was 26?
4 Which party did George Galloway belong to when he was elected to Parliament in 2005?
5 Which river runs through the Grand Canyon?
6 Name the geological fault that runs the length of California.
7 Which bandmaster composed "The Stars and Stripes Forever"?
8 Which drug is derived from the willow, Salix alba?
9 Where was Captain Cook killed?
10 Which star actor links "Charlie and the Chocolate Factory" and "The Libertine"?
11 Which hurricane threatened Texas shortly after hurricane Katrina struck in 2005?
12 What is the full name for DNA?
13 Other than the "Odyssey", which work is Homer famed for?
14 Name the art of making decorative lacework with knotted threads?
15 To which family does the chive belong?
16 Which indoor game was invented by British Army Officers in India in 1875?
17 Which microbe is the basis of the brewing and baking industry?
18 In 2005, which birthday did Thomas the Tank Engine celebrate?
19 In bluegrass music who is Flatt's partner?
20 Philip Glass wrote an opera about which scientist?
21 Who led the crew of the "Argo" in their search for the golden fleece?
22 What planet was home for the aliens in Wells's "The War of the Worlds"?
23 Who is credited with the invention of scat singing?
24 Which group consisted of Les, Eric, Woody, Alan and Derek?
25 Name Mary Quant's shop, which revolutionized fashion in the 1960s?
26 Which mountain was first climbed by Edward Whymper in 1865?
27 In fiction, Michael Henchard became mayor of which town?
28 Which Kray twin survived the other?
29 Who discovered that the universe is expanding?
30 In music, what is meant by pianissimo?

Answers | Pot-Luck 18 *(see Quiz 40)*

1 One. 2 Tea. 3 Pole or North Star. 4 Two. 5 Anton Chekhov. 6 Black Prince. 7 Bees. 8 Myxomatosis. 9 The inner ear. 10 Nuts. 11 Crete. 12 Katie Price. 13 Napoleon Bonaparte. 14 Anaemia. 15 Chelsea. 16 Saudi Arabia. 17 South Korea. 18 Aneurin Bevan. 19 Golden Gate. 20 Capability Brown. 21 Praying Mantis. 22 Yellowstone, Wyoming. 23 Trachea. 24 William Hague. 25 Istanbul. 26 Dinar. 27 Cadiz. 28 Joanne Harris. 29 Oxygen. 30 Nineteen Eighty-Four.

1 Which creature features on the adult edition of "The Chamber of Secrets"?
2 Which fictional detective is assisted by Captain Hastings?
3 Who wrote "The Firm" and "The Pelican Brief"?
4 What was Jeffrey Archer's sequel to "Kane and Abel" called?
5 What is the first name of the novelist A. S. Byatt?
6 In "Alice in Wonderland" what price did the Mad Hatter have on his hat?
7 Who co-wrote "Some Other Rainbow" with Jill Morrell?
8 In which country is the beginning of "The Thorn Birds" set?
9 Which former Beirut hostage wrote "An Evil Cradling"?
10 How is adventure writer David Cornwell better known?
11 Which town is the main setting for the Cadfael novels?
12 Part of whose life story is called "The Path to Power"?
13 Who wrote the biography "Frank Sinatra: An American Legend"?
14 Which alternative comedian wrote "Gridlock"?
15 What was the job of Mellors in "Lady Chatterley's Lover"?
16 Under which pseudonym does Harry Paterson also write?
17 Which comedy actress wrote "When's It Coming Out"?
18 Which Mary Wesley novel transferred to TV with Felicity Kendal and Paul Eddington?
19 Which suspense novelist was the cousin of horror movie actor Christopher Lee?
20 What is the name of Bernard Cornwell's hero, played on TV by Sean Bean?
21 Which politician wrote "A Woman's Place"?
22 Who created the detective Maigret?
23 Whose autobiography is called "Long Walk to Freedom"?
24 Who wrote the tales on which the film "The Jungle Book" was based?
25 In which country was the best-seller "Wild Swans" set?
26 Which Oscar-winning script writer wrote the novel "Snobs"?
27 What was the name of Lord Peter Wimsey's butler?
28 What were the "Dogs of War" in Frederick Forsyth's novel?
29 Which novel by Victor Hugo became a long-running musical?
30 Which mega-selling author wrote "Deception Point"?

Answers	**War Films** *(see Quiz 37)*

1 1991 Gulf War. **2** Vietnam War. **3** Marlon Brando. **4** Donald Sutherland and Elliott Gould. **5** Patton – Lust for Glory. **6** The Deer Hunter. **7** Alec Guinness. **8** A castle. **9** Lancashire. **10** Mercenaries. **11** The Great Escape. **12** The 1960s. **13** Clooney. **14** The Dirty Dozen. **15** Schindler's Ark. **16** Frank Sinatra. **17** Rick's Café. **18** Alistair MacLean. **19** Oh! What a Lovely War. **20** On the Western Front. **21** Pearl Harbor. **22** Alice Springs. **23** Jane Fonda. **24** Rommel. **25** The Great Dictator. **26** Oliver Stone. **27** Kelly's Heroes. **28** Winston Churchill. **29** Meryl Streep. **30** Cambodia.

1 The poster advertising "Mamma Mia" features how many people?
2 What popular drink was known in China as early as 2737 BC?
3 What is the other name for the star Polaris?
4 On how many stone tablets were the Ten Commandments engraved?
5 Who wrote "The Three Sisters"?
6 What was the nickname of Edward Prince of Wales, son of Edward III?
7 Which insects communicate with one another by dancing?
8 Which disease was deliberately introduced in rabbits in the UK?
9 Where are the semicircular canals in the body?
10 What part of a cola tree is used to flavour drinks?
11 Which is the largest Greek island?
12 Who wrote "Being Jordan"?
13 Who married Joséphine de Beauharnais and Princess Marie Louise?
14 Lack of iron in the diet may cause which disease?
15 Marcel Desailly joined which club after winning the World Cup with France?
16 Riyadh is the capital of which country?
17 In which Far Eastern country was the Unification Church (Moonies) founded in 1954?
18 Which minister of health inaugurated the National Health Service?
19 Which strait links San Francisco Bay with the Pacific?
20 Which famous gardener helped landscape Blenheim and Stowe?
21 Which insect sometimes eats its male mate during copulation?
22 What was the first national park established in the United States in 1872?
23 What is the scientific name for the windpipe?
24 Who became Tory party leader immediately after John Major?
25 In which city would you find the Blue Mosque?
26 What is the currency of Algeria?
27 In which port did Sir Francis Drake "singe the King of Spain's beard"?
28 Who wrote "Chocolat" and "Gentlemen and Players"?
29 What is the commonest element in the Earth's crust?
30 Which George Orwell novel showed the dangers of excessive state control?

| **Answers** | **Pot-Luck 17** *(see Quiz 38)* |

1 Michael. 2 Luddites. 3 Citizen Kane. 4 Respect. 5 Colorado. 6 San Andreas fault. 7. John Philip Sousa. 8 Aspirin. 9 Hawaii. 10 Johnny Depp. 11 Rita. 12 Deoxyribonucleic acid. 13 The Iliad. 14 Macramé. 15 Onion. 16 Snooker. 17 Yeast. 18 60th. 19 Scruggs. 20 Albert Einstein. 21 Jason. 22 Mars. 23 Louis Armstrong. 24 The Bay City Rollers. 25 Bazaar. 26 Matterhorn. 27 Casterbridge. 28 Reggie survived Ronnie. 29 Edwin Hubble. 30 Very softly.

1 Claret wine is produced in the region surrounding which French city?

2 What would be the term to describe a dry champagne?

3 In which country is the wine-growing Barossa Valley?

4 Which white wine grape variety is most widely planted in California?

5 In which country is the Marlborough wine region?

6 Retsina is native to which country?

7 Which wine has the varieties Malmsey and Sercial?

8 What is the normal capacity for a bottle of wine?

9 In which country is Rioja produced?

10 Along which river is most of France's Sauvignon Blanc cultivated?

11 What colour are most English wines?

12 Which scientist discovered that yeast causes fermentation?

13 What is a crate of twelve bottles of wine called?

14 Which country does Sukhindol wine come from?

15 In which part of the United States is the Zinfandel grape chiefly cultivated?

16 What is the first name of wine writer Ms Robinson?

17 In which country is the wine-making area of Stellenbosch?

18 How many normal-size wine bottles would you have in a Methuselah?

19 How are fizzy wines, other than champagnes, described?

20 In which area of Italy is Chianti Classico produced?

21 Would a French wine described as "doux" be medium sweet or medium dry?

22 What are the three styles of port?

23 What colour are most of the wines from France's Anjou region?

24 In which South American country is Casablanca Valley?

25 Which red wine is drunk when young and is called "nouveau"?

26 In which country was a vine variety called "vegetable dragon pearls"?

27 Which wine can be "fino" or "oloroso"?

28 What is Moët et Chandon?

29 Who is the female wine expert on the BBC's "Food and Drink" programme?

30 Along which river and its tributaries do the German vineyards lie?

| **Answers** | **Premiership Soccer** *(see Quiz 43)* |

1 Wayne Rooney. 2 Liverpool. 3 Wigan. 4 Charlton. 5 Eric Cantona. 6 Iceland. 7 Bryan Robson. 8 Dean Kiely. 9 Chelsea. 10 Ipswich. 11 Preston. 12 Facundo Sava. 13 Alan Shearer. 14 Laurent Blanc. 15 Spurs. 16 Leeds. 17 Liverpool. 18 Argentina. 19 Birmingham. 20 16 years old. 21 Anderton. 22 Denis Irwin. 23 Liverpool. 24 West Ham. 25 Glenn Hoddle. 26 Sunderland. 27 Lee Bowyer. 28 Graham Taylor. 29 James Beattie. 30 2002-03.

Quiz 42 | Pot-Luck 19

Answers – page 286

1 Who preceded Jose Mourinho as Chelsea manager?
2 Picardy is in the northeast of which country?
3 NUPE was the National Union of what?
4 Which cathedral has the highest spire in Britain?
5 Who sang "Hey, babe, take a walk on the wild side"?
6 The Brenner Pass links which two countries?
7 Which two fruits are anagrams of each other?
8 What is the chief member of a lifeboat crew called?
9 In geography, which term means the joining of two rivers?
10 Which musical note follows fah?
11 How many phases of the moon are there in a lunar month?
12 Which river flows through Cambridge?
13 In geometry what type of line bisects a circle?
14 Which university is based at Milton Keynes?
15 What on your body would a trichologist be concerned with?
16 Which former butler to the Princess of Wales was involved in a pending court case that collapsed in October 2002?
17 What was Gilbert White's field of work?
18 In the board game Cluedo what is the name of the Reverend?
19 Brussels, Honiton and Nottingham are all renowned for which product?
20 Which radio serial is "an everyday story of country folk"?
21 What was David Blunkett's government job when he resigned in 2004?
22 Who wrote that "The workers have nothing to lose but their chains"?
23 What have you done if you have committed patricide?
24 Which donkey is Winnie the Pooh's friend?
25 In which district are Hawes and Ullswater?
26 Which major art gallery was opened in London in 2000?
27 In the Bible, where was the traveller going to in the parable of the Good Samaritan?
28 To what kind of meeting was Mahatma Gandhi going when he was assassinated?
29 What colour are Aylesbury ducks?
30 Which stage musical, based on a Disney movie, opened in London's West End in December 2004?

Answers	Nature: Fish *(see Quiz 44)*

1 The tail. **2** Red/orange. **3** Tuna. **4** Herring. **5** Roe. **6** Tench. **7** Salmon. **8** Whale shark. **9** Sardine. **10** Blue/black. **11** Liver. **12** Carp. **13** Fish rearing. **14** Silver bream. **15** Whelk. **16** Small shark. **17** Rock salmon. **18** Hermit crab. **19** On its back. **20** Trout. **21** Ten. **22** Izaak Walton. **23** Flatfish. **24** Sprats. **25** Round its mouth. **26** A grain of sand. **27** Pike. **28** Red mullet. **29** Dover sole. **30** Clam.

1 Who scored Man Utd's first goal following the death of George Best?
2 Milan Baros first played in the Premiership with which club?
3 Which club enjoyed their first ever season in the top division in 2005–06?
4 Charlton, Man Utd, Spurs, West Ham – which club has Teddy Sheringham not played for?
5 Who was the first footballer to win the Premier League Championship with two different clubs?
6 Which country does Bolton's super shot stopper Jussi Jaaskelainen play for?
7 Which manager masterminded WBA's escape from relegation, 2004–05?
8 Which Dean of the Republic of Ireland has been a keeper for Charlton?
9 Joe Cole played for which club during their relegation season?
10 At which club did Richard Wright first play in the Premier League?
11 Which club did David Moyes manage before going to Everton?
12 Which Fulham player donned a Zorro mask after scoring?
13 Which striker has played for Southampton, Blackburn and Newcastle?
14 Which defender of the French World Cup-winning squad went to Man Utd?
15 Kasey Keller and Neil Sullivan have both kept goal for which club?
16 Which club had O'Leary, Venables and Reid as managers in this new millennium?
17 At which club did Henchoz and Hyypia form a defensive pairing?
18 Juan Veron had spells with Man Utd and Chelsea, but which country did he play for?
19 Frenchman Christophe Dugarry had a spell with which Midlands club?
20 How old was Wayne Rooney when he first played in the Premiership?
21 Which Darren earned the nickname "Sicknote" at Tottenham?
22 Which former Oldham defender played over 300 games for Man Utd?
23 Which club had a group of high-living players dubbed "The Spice Boys"?
24 Which club did Nigel Winterburn move to after 400-plus games for Arsenal?
25 Who was the last Englishman to manage Chelsea?
26 Reid, Wilkinson, Cotterill and McCarthy all managed which club in a relegation season?
27 Who was sent off for an on field fight with his Newcastle team-mate Kieron Dyer?
28 David O'Leary took over at Aston Villa from which manager?
29 Which England striker James went from Southampton to Everton?
30 In which season did Roy Keane last win the Premiership with Man Utd?

Answers	**Food and Drink: Wine** *(see Quiz 41)*

1 Bordeaux. 2 Brut. 3 Australia. 4 Chardonnay. 5 New Zealand. 6 Greece. 7 Madeira. 8 75 centilitres. 9 Spain. 10 Loire. 11 White. 12 Louis Pasteur. 13 Case. 14 Bulgaria. 15 California. 16 Jancis. 17 South Africa. 18 Eight. 19 Sparkling. 20 Tuscany. 21 Medium sweet. 22 Ruby, tawny and vintage. 23 Rosé. 24 Chile. 25 Beaujolais. 26 China. 27 Sherry. 28 Champagne. 29 Jilly Goolden. 30 Rhine.

1 Where is a fish's caudal fin?
2 What colour are the spots on a plaice?
3 What sort of fish is a skipjack?
4 Which family does the anchovy belong to?
5 Caviare is which part of the sturgeon?
6 Tinca tinca is the Latin name of which fish?
7 Alevin and parr are stages in the development of which fish?
8 What is the world's largest fish?
9 What is a young pilchard called?
10 What colour is a live lobster?
11 From which part of the cod is a beneficial oil produced?
12 The minnow is the smallest member of which family?
13 What is pisciculture?
14 Which fish has been nicknamed "tin plate"?
15 What is a buckie another name for?
16 What sort of fish is a dogfish?
17 What is a dogfish called when it is bought for food?
18 Which type of crab lives in hollow objects such as snail shells?
19 Where is a fish's dorsal fin?
20 Which fish has the varieties brown, sea or rainbow?
21 How many arms does a squid have?
22 Who wrote "The Compleat Angler"?
23 Flounder is a common name for which type of fish?
24 What are brisling also called?
25 Where would you find barbels on a fish?
26 What starts an oyster developing a pearl in its shell?
27 Which fish has the same name as an early infantry weapon?
28 Which fish is also called goatfish or surmullet?
29 What is another name for the common European sole?
30 What is a geoduck?

Answers	Pot-Luck 19 *(see Quiz 42)*

1 Claudio Ranieri. 2 France. 3 Public Employees. 4 Salisbury. 5 Lou Reed. 6 Austria and Italy. 7 Lemon and melon. 8 Coxswain. 9 Confluence. 10 Soh. 11 Four. 12 The Cam. 13 Diameter. 14 Open University. 15 Hair. 16 Paul Burrell. 17 Naturalist. 18 Green. 19 Lace. 20 The Archers. 21 Home Secretary. 22 Karl Marx. 23 Murdered your father. 24 Eeyore. 25 Lake District. 26 Tate Modern. 27 Jericho. 28 Prayer meeting. 29 White. 30 Mary Poppins.

1 In Sudoku, what is the total of a square containing each number used once?
2 Which device is used on a guitar fretboard to raise the pitch of the strings?
3 Which king was reigning in Britain at the start of the First World War?
4 In imperial measurement, how many yards are in a chain?
5 What kind of tree is an osier?
6 On TV, "who was feared by the bad, loved by the good"?
7 With what do you play a vibraphone?
8 On a ship what are the scuppers?
9 At which club did Stuart Pearce end his playing days?
10 Who became ruler of Spain after the Spanish Civil War?
11 In literature, how many Arabian Nights were there?
12 Which singer said, "You're not drunk if you can lie on the floor without holding on"?
13 Black, Italian and Lombardy are all types of which tree?
14 In which war was the Battle of Jutland?
15 What is the square root of 169?
16 Which star of the movie "Mr and Mrs Smith" is a Goodwill Ambassador to the UN?
17 What is the name given to the lowest layer of the atmosphere?
18 What was added to rum to make the drink grog?
19 In London where is Poet's Corner?
20 In which country did the former Foreign Secretary Robin Cook die?
21 For which of these games would you use dice: ludo, whist, hopscotch, snakes-and-ladders?
22 What instrument would you use to measure the diameter of a cylinder?
23 In which month is Michaelmas Day?
24 In which English county would you find the coastal resort of California?
25 Which former Spice Girl recorded the album "Beautiful Intentions"?
26 For what is Elizabeth Fry chiefly remembered?
27 What fruit do we get from a rose?
28 What was Cleo Laine's job before she was a singer?
29 Which ocean is crossed to sail from San Francisco to Sydney?
30 Who was the British member of the Monkees?

Answers	Pot-Luck 21 (see Quiz 47)

1 Yew. 2 Greece. 3 Maurice Gibb. 4 Portugal. 5 Gordon Strachan. 6 It had no toes.
7 Computer languages. 8 Five and a half. 9 Michael Ball. 10 Model T Ford. 11 Max
Wall. 12 Watt. 13 Straws. 14 A spy or informer. 15 The Gruffalo's Child. 16 Stitches.
17 The Merchant of Venice. 18 Bob Dylan. 19 Adam Ant. 20 By rubbing its legs
against its wings or together. 21 Massachusetts. 22 Stephen. 23 Tennis. 24 Wore
them. They are very wide trousers. 25 Paris. 26 Charles Edward Stuart. 27 Brendan
Cole. 28 Georgia. 29 George Clooney. 30 Thomas.

1 Which dance favourite became Kylie's first UK million-seller?

2 Which Village People chart hit was made up of initial letters?

3 Which boy's name took Sister Sledge to No 1 in 1985?

4 Cheryl Jones and Sandra Denton spiced up their names to what?

5 Who recorded the 2002 No 1 album "Come with Us"?

6 Which Doors song was given the disco treatment by Amii Stewart?

7 In which song does the line "Too Ra Loo Ra Loo Rye Aye" appear?

8 Which girl group backed Disco Tex?

9 Who was too sexy in 1991?

10 Whose name comes before the Mastermixers?

11 Which Richie Valens 1950s hit charted for Los Lobos in 1987?

12 Who was "Never Gonna Give You Up" in 1987?

13 Who did Madonna tell "don't preach" in the 1986 No 1?

14 Which country do Black Box come from?

15 Who recorded "Funky Stuff" and "Jungle Boogie"?

16 Which group found success in the 1970s with "Night Fever"?

17 Who teamed up with Take That in "Relight My Fire"?

18 Who recorded "Wham Rap"?

19 Who else was on "Keep On Pumpin' It" along with the Visionmasters and Tony Knight?

20 What was on the B side of Boney M's "Rivers of Babylon"?

21 Which disco hit singer thought that "Love's Unkind"?

22 What was a No 1 for The Simpsons?

23 Who had "A Night to Remember" in 1982?

24 While Tina Charles loved to love, what did her baby love to do?

25 In his baggy trousers, what name is rapper Stanley Burrell known as?

26 Who had "Heartache" in 1987?

27 Who had a 2001 dance hit with "Clint Eastwood"?

28 Who recorded the 1970s disco song "You're My First My Last My Everything"?

29 Who is credited on "Lady Marmalade" along with Christina Aguilera, Lil' Kim and Mya?

30 How is Robert Bell better known?

Answers	Around Europe (see Quiz 48)

1 Albania. 2 Oberammergau. 3 Yugoslavia. 4 Malta. 5 Austria's. 6 Spain and Portugal. 7 The Hague. 8 Strait, Turkey. 9 Munich. 10 Greece. 11 Italy. 12 Liechtenstein. 13 Baltic. 14 France, Italy, Switzerland and Austria. 15 Russia. 16 Cologne. 17 Iceland. 18 Denmark and Norway. 19 Moldova. 20 The Netherlands. 21 Belgium. 22 Lorraine and Nancy. 23 Denmark. 24 Mont Blanc. 25 Germany's. 26 Bulgaria. 27 Finnish and Swedish. 28 Red Cross. 29 The Algarve. 30 Ukraine.

1 From which wood were longbows made?
2 In which country is the Corinth Canal?
3 Which member of the Bee Gees died following a stomach operation in 2003?
4 Of which European country are Madeira and the Azores a part?
5 Who managed Southampton when they reached the 2003 FA Cup Final?
6 In a poem by Edward Lear, what was peculiar about the "Pobble"?
7 Pascal, Cobol and Basic are all types of what?
8 In yards, how long was a rod, pole, or perch?
9 Which musical theatre star released his "Love Changes Everything" album in 2004?
10 What is or was a tin lizzie?
11 Which comedian's catch phrase was, "Now there's a funny thing"?
12 What name is given to the unit of electrical power?
13 According to the proverb what do drowning men clutch?
14 What is a copper's nark?
15 What was the sequel to the popular children's picture book "The Gruffalo" called?
16 Back, blanket and buttonhole are all types of what?
17 In which Shakespeare play is Shylock introduced?
18 Which folk singer wrote the song "The Times They are A-Changin'"?
19 In pop, who was King of the wild frontier?
20 How does a grasshopper produce its distinctive sound?
21 Of which US state is Boston the capital?
22 Who came to the throne of England on the death of Henry I?
23 With which sport do you associate Rosemary Casals?
24 What did people do with Oxford bags?
25 In which city is Sacré Coeur?
26 Who assumed the guise of Betty Burke?
27 Whom did both Natasha Kaplinsky and Fiona Phillips partner on "Strictly Come Dancing"?
28 Which is the home state of former president Jimmy Carter?
29 Who co starred with Catherine Zeta Jones in the movie "Intolerable Cruelty"?
30 What is Sean Connery's real first name?

Answers | Pot-Luck 20 (see Quiz 45)

1 45 (Numbers 1 to 9). 2 Capo. 3 George V. 4 22. 5 Willow. 6 Robin Hood. 7 With small mallets. 8 Holes to allow water to run off the deck. 9 Man City. 10 General Franco. 11 1001. 12 Dean Martin. 13 Poplar. 14 First World War. 15 13. 16 Angelina Jolie. 17 The troposphere. 18 Water. 19 Westminster Abbey. 20 Scotland. 21 Ludo and snakes-and-ladders. 22 Callipers. 23 September (29th). 24 Norfolk. 25 Melanie C. 26 Prison reform. 27 Hips. 28 Hairdresser. 29 Pacific. 30 Davy Jones.

1 Which country's capital is Tirana?
2 Where is a passion play staged every ten years?
3 Which state was Macedonia part of from 1945 to 1991?
4 Which island holds the George Cross?
5 Which country's highest mountain is the Grossglockner?
6 Which countries are on the Iberian Peninsula?
7 Where is the Netherlands' seat of government and administration?
8 What are the Dardanelles and where are they?
9 Which southern German city is famous for its October beer festival?
10 Which country is called Elleniki Dimokratia or Hellenic Republic?
11 Which country's chief river is the Po?
12 Which country, whose capital is Vaduz, has no armed forces?
13 Which sea lies to the north of Poland?
14 In which four countries are the Alps?
15 Which country covers 10% of the globe's land surface?
16 By what English name is Köln known?
17 Which country's landscape is made up of volcanoes and geysers?
18 Between which countries does the Skagerrak lie?
19 What are Bessarabia, Moldavia and a former part of the USSR now known as?
20 Which country has had a prime minister called Wim Kok?
21 Albert II became king of which country in 1993?
22 A region of eastern France has a girl's name with another girl's name as its capital. What are they?
23 Which country do Greenland and the Faeroe Islands belong to?
24 What is France's highest point?
25 Whose upper house of Parliament is called the Bundesrat?
26 Which country's currency is the lev?
27 What are the two official languages of Finland?
28 Which aid organization's emblem is the Swiss flag with its colours reversed?
29 Which Portuguese province borders Spain and the Atlantic Ocean?
30 Which is Europe's largest country after Russia?

Answers	Pop: Dance and Disco *(see Quiz 46)*

1 Can't Get You Out of My Head. 2 YMCA. 3 Frankie. 4 Salt 'N' Pepa. 5 Chemical Brothers. 6 Light My Fire. 7 Come On Eileen by Dexy's Midnight Runners. 8 The Sex-O-Lettes. 9 Right Said Fred. 10 Jive Bunny. 11 La Bamba. 12 Rick Astley. 13 Papa. 14 Italy. 15 Kool and the Gang. 16 The Bee Gees. 17 Lulu. 18 Wham! 19 Kylie Minogue. 20 Brown Girl in the Ring. 21 Donna Summer. 22 Do the Bartman. 23 Shalamar. 24 Dance. 25 M. C. Hammer. 26 Pepsi and Shirlie. 27 Gorillaz. 28 Barry White. 29 Pink. 30 Kool, of Kool and the Gang.

1 What is the longest-running children's TV programme?
2 Who host Dick and Dom in "Da Bungalow"?
3 "Can We Fix It" relates to which handyman?
4 In which country is "Balamory" set?
5 Which village's postmistress is called Mrs Goggins?
6 What was "Fingermouse" made from?
7 Who fought against Bulk and Texas Pete?
8 Who presented his own "Cartoon Time" and "Cartoon Club"?
9 Which three singers from "Rainbow" were given their own series?
10 Which show ended ruefully with "Bye bye, everybody, bye bye"?
11 Which show was first presented by Emma Forbes and Andi Peters?
12 Was the 2005 show "Raven" a fantasy game show or a wildlife programme?
13 Which family had a daily help called Mrs Scrubbitt?
14 Which magazine programme had a mascot called Murgatroyd?
15 What sort of animal was Parsley in "The Herbs"?
16 Who had magical adventures and lived at 52 Festive Road?
17 Which pre-school programme was the first programme on BBC2?
18 The characters Bella and Milo appeared in which show?
19 Who were Andy Pandy's two best friends?
20 In which 1980s/1990s series did Robin of Islington and Little Ron appear?
21 In which show for the under fives did the Muppets first appear?
22 In "Rag, Tag and Bobtail" which was the hedgehog?
23 What was the registration number of Lady Penelope's pink Rolls?
24 Who is associated with the catchphrase "Get down, Shep"?
25 Which show was TV's answer to the Guinness Book of Records?
26 Where do the Hoobs come from?
27 Who took over from Phillip Schofield as presenter of Children's BBC?
28 In which county was Camberwick Green?
29 Who gave his name to the early bulletins of "Newsround"?
30 What is the logo on a Blue Peter badge?

| **Answers** | Around Ireland *(see Quiz 51)* |

1 Two. 2 Stone. 3 Oak or blackthorn. 4 Belfast. 5 Shannon. 6 Lough Neagh. 7 Lead-zinc. 8 Lava. 9 Enniskillen. 10 Mountains of Mourne. 11 Cork. 12 Abbey Theatre. 13 Macgillicuddy's Reeks. 14 Golden Vale. 15 Antrim, Armagh. 16 Queen's. 17 Mountain peaks. 18 St Brigit. 19 TV listings. 20 Smoking. 21 Waterford. 22 The Twelve Bens. 23 Hills. 24 Queen's County. 25 Leinster. 26 Bells. 27 Kerry, Kildare, Kilkenny. 28 Sligo. 29 University of Ulster. 30 Armagh, Belfast, Derry/Londonderry.

1 Which country staged the last FIFA World Cup Final of the 20th century outside Europe?

2 Who created a garden at Sissinghurst in Kent?

3 Who recorded the album "Odyssey"?

4 What is Prince William's second name?

5 What chicken dish is named after a battle of the Napoleonic Wars?

6 In 2005 at which ground did England beat Australia by two runs?

7 Which "Cutting It" star appeared in the movie "The Wedding Date"?

8 Which famous writer was married to archaeologist Sir Max Mallowan?

9 Who invented the Flying Shuttle in 1733?

10 What kind of gas was used in the trenches during World War I?

11 Who sang "Islands in the Stream"?

12 Which Sondheim musical tells the story of a murdering barber?

13 What breed of retriever takes its name from a North American bay?

14 What does a Geiger Counter measure?

15 In which "ology", founded in the early 1950s, is self-awareness paramount?

16 Which star of "The X Files" appeared in the 2005 UK TV drama "Bleak House"?

17 Who defeated Richard III at Bosworth in 1485?

18 Which Hollywood actress's real name was Lucille Le Sueur?

19 Beaumaris, Conway and Harlech are famous for what type of building?

20 Whom did the religious assassins known as Thugs worship?

21 If you were an LLD what profession would you be involved in?

22 Which famous brothers made a movie called "A Night at the Opera"?

23 What is a tine?

24 Who was the first regular female presenter of "Points of View"?

25 Which William featured in the title of a Benjamin Britten opera?

26 Which country was invaded during Operation Barbarossa?

27 Which famous children's author and artist lived and worked in the Lake District for much of her life?

28 How many of Henry VIII's wives were called Anne?

29 What did miners use to find out if there was gas in a pit?

30 Of which party were Bill Rodgers and Roy Jenkins founder members?

Answers | Pot-Luck 23 *(see Quiz 52)*

1 Henry Cooper. 2 Her father, King George VI. 3 Barium. 4 Sociology. 5 For the Good Times. 6 William III and Mary II. 7 New Zealander. 8 Greek Orthodox. 9 Leda. 10 Sealed with a loving kiss. 11 Alec Guinness. 12 The stamen. 13 The Prince of Wales. 14 William Wilberforce. 15 Marshal Blücher. 16 Lee Dixon. 17 Independent on Sunday. 18 Rare (noble or inert gases). 19 Canterbury. 20 The Acts of the Apostles, 1. 21 Laurence Dallaglio. 22 Nicole. 23 Physiologists. 24 Ombrophobia. 25 Dollywood. 26 Ewan McGregor. 27 Susan Coolidge. 28 Odin. 29 Delano. 30 Lieutenant Pinkerton.

1 How many wheels does a jaunting car have?
2 On what would you see Ogham writing?
3 Which of two kinds of wood can a shillelagh be made from?
4 In which city is the Maze Prison?
5 Which is Ireland's chief river?
6 Which lake is the British Isles' largest?
7 What is the mine at Navan famous for?
8 What are the columns of the Giant's Causeway made from?
9 What is the county town of Fermanagh?
10 Which mountains stretch from Carlingford Lough to Dundrum Bay?
11 Which county's Irish name is Corcaigh?
12 What is Dublin's most famous theatre called?
13 What are the highest uplands in Ireland?
14 What is the name of the fertile vale in Limerick?
15 Which two of the counties of Northern Ireland begin with A?
16 What is Belfast's university called?
17 What are Slieve Donard and Slieve Commedagh?
18 Whose Saint's day is celebrated on 2nd February?
19 If you bought the RTE Guide what information would you receive?
20 In the early years of this millennium what was banned from pubs in Ireland?
21 Which is further north, Waterford or Cork?
22 What are the quartzite mountains in Connemara called?
23 What are drumlins?
24 What did Laoighis used to be called?
25 Which province of southeast Ireland includes the counties of Wexford and Wicklow?
26 What is St Ann's Shaldon Church famous for?
27 Which three counties of the Republic of Ireland begin with K?
28 Which county do Westlife come from?
29 Which university is at Coleraine?
30 Which three places in Northern Ireland may officially use the title "city"?

Answers | Children's TV *(see Quiz 49)*

1 Blue Peter. 2 Richard McCourt & Dominic Wood. 3 Bob the Builder. 4 Scotland. 5 Greendale. 6 Paper. 7 SuperTed. 8 Rolf Harris. 9 Rod, Jane and Freddy. 10 Sooty. 11 Live and Kicking. 12 Fantasy game show. 13 The Woodentops. 14 Magpie. 15 Lion. 16 Mr Benn. 17 Play School. 18 The Tweenies. 19 Teddy and Looby Loo. 20 Maid Marian and Her Merry Men. 21 Sesame Street. 22 Rag. 23 FAB1. 24 John Noakes. 25 Record Breakers. 26 Hoobland. 27 Andy Crane. 28 Trumptonshire. 29 John Craven. 30 Ship.

1 Which English boxer had Muhammad Ali (Cassius Clay) on the floor?
2 Who bought Queen Elizabeth II her first corgi?
3 Which highly insoluble substance is opaque to X-rays?
4 What is the study and functioning of human societies called?
5 "Lay your head upon my pillow" appears in which Perry Como song?
6 Which king and queen ruled Britain jointly from 1689 to 1694?
7 What nationality was detective writer Ngaio Marsh?
8 What branch of Christianity still flourishes in Russia?
9 Whom did Zeus seduce when he assumed the guise of a swan?
10 What does "SWALK" stand for?
11 On TV, who played George Smiley in "Smiley's People"?
12 What is the male reproductive organ of a plant called?
13 In the song, "I danced with a man, who danced with a girl who danced with..." whom?
14 Which William was concerned with abolishing slavery?
15 Who commanded the Prussian troops at the Battle of Waterloo?
16 Which veteran full-back was part of Arsenal's 2002 double winning squad?
17 Which Sunday newspaper first featured extracts from Bridget Jones's Diary in the mid 1990s?
18 Krypton, neon, radon, xenon and helium are what kind of gases?
19 Mo Mowlam spent her final days in which city?
20 In the Bible, which book comes after Saint John?
21 Who resigned as England Rugby captain in 1999 following allegations concerning drugs?
22 Who is papa's daughter in the Renault ad?
23 The functioning of living organisms is the concern of which "ologists"?
24 What is fear of rain called?
25 What is Dolly Parton's theme park in Tennessee called?
26 Which star of "Star Wars" also starred in "Guys and Dolls" in the West End?
27 Who wrote the "What Katy Did Next"?
28 Who was Thor's father?
29 What did the "D" stand for in Franklin D. Roosevelt?
30 Which American told Madam Butterfly that he loved her?

| **Answers** | Pot-Luck 22 *(see Quiz 50)* |

1 USA. 2 Vita Sackville-West. 3 Hayley Westenra. 4 Arthur. 5 Chicken Marengo. 6 Edgbaston. 7 Sarah Parish. 8 Agatha Christie. 9 John Kay. 10 Mustard gas. 11 Kenny Rogers and Dolly Parton. 12 Sweeney Todd. 13 Chesapeake Bay Retriever. 14 Radioactivity. 15 Scientology. 16 Gillian Anderson. 17 Henry VII. 18 Joan Crawford. 19 Castles. 20 The goddess Kali. 21 The legal profession (Doctor of Law). 22 The Marx Brothers. 23 The prong of a fork. 24 Anne Robinson. 25 Billy Budd. 26 USSR. 27 Beatrix Potter. 28 Two. 29 Caged birds. 30 The Social Democratic Party.

1 Who was the first unseeded man to win Wimbledon?
2 Which tennis star married Tatum O'Neal?
3 How many times did Martina Navratilova win the Wimbledon singles?
4 What was Evonne Goolagong's married name?
5 Which Australian pair dominated the men's doubles in the late 1960s?
6 Who is the only black American to have won the men's singles at Wimbledon?
7 Who is Czech Cyril Suk's famous sister?
8 In which year did Ivan Lendl win Wimbledon?
9 Which British pair won the Wimbledon mixed doubles in 1987?
10 Roger Federer hails from which country?
11 Which woman French player won the Australian Open in 1995?
12 Who is the elder of the two tennis-playing Williams sisters?
13 Which cup for women was contested between the US and Britain?
14 Where is the final of the US Open played?
15 Which US champion was married to British player John Lloyd?
16 Who was the first male tennis player to win 100 tournaments?
17 Which two women competed in the all-British Wimbledon final in 1961?
18 What is the international team competition for men called?
19 What are the colours of the All England Lawn Tennis Club?
20 In 1996, 1997, 2003 and 2004 Tim Henman went out of Wimbledon at which stage?
21 What did line judge Dorothy Brown do in a 1964 Wimbledon match?
22 Whom did Virginia Wade beat in the final to win Wimbledon in 1977?
23 Which German won the Wimbledon men's singles in 1991?
24 Who won his first US Open title in 1990?
25 Which American won the ladies' singles and doubles at Wimbledon in 1999?
26 What is the surface of the courts at Roland Garros in Paris?
27 Why did Catherine McTavish make Wimbledon history in 1979?
28 Which Greek Cypriot lost the men's final at the Australian Open in 2006?
29 What is the score in tennis when the tie break is introduced?
30 Which sisters won Olympic gold in tennis in 2000?

Answers	**Pop: Duos** (see Quiz 55)

1 Chas and Dave. **2** Wake Up Little Suzie. **3** Husband. **4** Wham! **5** Sweet Dreams (are Made of This). **6** Donkey. **7** Simon and Garfunkel. **8** Lionel Richie. **9** Opportunity Knocks. **10** Kiki Dee. **11** Esther and Abi. **12** L. S. Lowry. **13** Gimme Dat Ding. **14** Love you. **15** Marvin Gaye. **16** Everly Brothers. **17** Mel and Kim. **18** One. **19** Charles and Eddie. **20** Soft Cell. **21** Phil Spector. **22** John Travolta and Olivia Newton-John. **23** The World. **24** Roger Whittaker, Des O'Connor. **25** Erasure. **26** Chemical Brothers. **27** Nomad. **28** One. **29** Homeward Bound. **30** Pet Shop Boys.

1 What kind of dancer was Mr Bojangles?
2 Who secretly married Kevin Federline in 2005?
3 Where did William III defeat a French and Irish army in 1690?
4 In the 1990s, which British manager won successive titles with PSV Eindhoven?
5 What was American inventor Thomas Edison's middle name?
6 What does hydrogen combine with to form water?
7 Where in the House of Lords do peers with no party loyalties sit?
8 What is the northernmost point of the British mainland?
9 Which cartoon cat is the creation of Jim Davis?
10 What is the process by which plants use light to make food?
11 Which branch of medical science is concerned with muscle?
12 Which actor's real name was Reginald Carey?
13 Prince George of Denmark was the husband of which English queen?
14 What was the true vocation of the detective in the stories by G. K. Chesterton?
15 In darts, who won the World Masters five times between 1977 and 1984?
16 Whom did Orpheus attempt to rescue from the underworld?
17 In the song, how many little girls were in the back seat a-kissin' and a-huggin' with Fred?
18 What does ENO stand for?
19 A plant produced by crossing different species is known as what?
20 What was the Birmingham Royal Ballet previously known as?
21 Who were the hosts of football's African Cup of Nations in 2006?
22 On what day in 1939 did Britain declare war on Germany?
23 Which French writer lived with the composer Chopin?
24 Which TV chef presented a "French Odyssey" in 2005?
25 What is the most abundant gas in the atmosphere?
26 Who was the first woman elected to the British Parliament?
27 Where on the human body is the skin the thinnest?
28 What nationality was the Pope who succeeded Pope John Paul II?
29 Which actress replaced Amanda Burton as the forensic scientist in "Silent Witness"?
30 Which "ology" is concerned with the study and treatment of crime?

Answers | Pot-Luck 25 *(see Quiz 56)*

1 Pythagoras. 2 Taxi driver. 3 Michael Foot. 4 She was her half-sister. 5 Jacqueline Wilson. 6 The Arctic Ocean. 7 Scandinavian. 8 Two. 9 Guy Ritchie. 10 Pampas grass. 11 Swan Lake. 12 Ewart. 13 Robert Baden-Powell. 14 Colleen McCullough. 15 The 1920s. 16 Hydrogen. 17 Glenn Hoddle. 18 Red. 19 Borzoi. 20 212 degrees. 21 Palaeontology. 22 Michael Buerk. 23 James VI of Scotland, who was James I of England. 24 Call for the Dead. 25 David and Victoria Beckham. 26 Diana. 27 M. 28 Mimi's (in La Bohème). 29 Lancelot. 30 Andrew Lloyd Webber.

1 How are Messrs Hodges and Peacock better known?
2 "It's four o'clock and we're in trouble deep" comes from which Everly Brothers song?
3 What relation was Sonny to Cher in their single-making days?
4 Pepsi and Shirlie provided backing vocals for which superstar group?
5 What was the first Eurythmics top ten single back in 1983?
6 What little animal did Nina and Frederick sing about?
7 Which duo were made up of Paul and Art?
8 Whom did Diano Ross duo with on "Endless Love"?
9 Which TV show gave Peters and Lee their first break?
10 Whom did Elton John sing with on his first British No 1?
11 What were the first names of the Ofarims?
12 Which artist did Brian and Michael sing about?
13 What was the Pipkins' only hit?
14 According to Peter and Gordon, to know you is to do what?
15 "It Takes Two" featured Tammi Terrell and who else?
16 Which duo has spent most weeks in the UK single charts?
17 Who were respectable in 1987?
18 How many of duo Miki and Griff were female?
19 Which duo had a No 1 with "Would I Lie to You"?
20 Which duo comprised Marc Almond and David Ball?
21 Who produced Ike and Tina Turner's "River Deep Mountain High"?
22 Which male/female singing duo had 16 weeks at No 1 in 1978?
23 According to "Tears for Fears", what did everyone want to rule?
24 Which duo charted with the "The Skye Boat Song"?
25 Which duo appeared in drag in an Abba tribute?
26 Tom Rowlands and Ed Simons make up which production dance duo?
27 Who charted with "(I Wanna Give You) Devotion"?
28 How many girls in the duo Everything but the Girl?
29 Which Simon and Garfunkel song starts "I'm sitting in a railway station"?
30 How are Christopher Lowe and Neil Tennant better known?

Answers	Tennis *(see Quiz 53)*

1 Boris Becker. **2** John McEnroe. **3** Nine. **4** Cawley. **5** Newcombe and Roche. **6** Arthur Ashe. **7** Helena Sukova. **8** He never won it. **9** Jeremy Bates & Jo Durie. **10** Switzerland. **11** Mary Pierce. **12** Venus. **13** Wightman Cup. **14** Flushing Meadow. **15** Chris Evert. **16** Jimmy Connors. **17** Christine Truman and Angela Mortimer. **18** Davis Cup. **19** Green and purple. **20** Quarter-finals. **21** Fell asleep. **22** Betty Stove. **23** Michael Stich. **24** Pete Sampras. **25** Lindsay Davenport. **26** Clay. **27** Its first woman umpire. **28** Marcos Baghdatis. **29** Six games all. **30** Venus and Serena Williams.

1 Whose famous theorem is concerned with the sums of the squares of the sides of right-angled triangles?
2 What was "Mastermind" winner Fred Housego's job?
3 Whom did Neil Kinnock succeed as leader of the Labour Party?
4 What relation was Mary I to Elizabeth I?
5 Which lady novelist was children's laureate in 2005?
6 Which ocean lies to the north of Russia?
7 In which mythology does Yggdrasil feature?
8 How many step children does Prince Charles have?
9 Who directed the 2005 movie "Revolver"?
10 What is Cortaderia selloana better known as?
11 Of which ballet is Prince Siegfried hero?
12 What was William Gladstone's middle name?
13 Who led the British forces during the Siege of Mafeking?
14 Who wrote "The Thorn Birds"?
15 In which decade did John Logie Baird invent television?
16 What gas is given off by pouring dilute sulphuric acid on to granulated zinc?
17 Who was England's coach in France 98?
18 What colour is the "This is Your Life" book?
19 What is another name for the Russian wolfhound?
20 What is the boiling point of water on the Fahrenheit Scale?
21 Which "ology" is concerned with fossils?
22 Which reporter fronted the film footage that sparked off Band Aid?
23 Whose nickname was "the Wisest Fool in Christendom"?
24 In which book did John le Carré's George Smiley first appear?
25 The aftershave Instinct was created by which married couple?
26 A temple to whom was sited at Ephesus?
27 Who was 007's boss?
28 In opera, whose tiny hand was frozen?
29 What was landscape gardener Capability Brown's real first name?
30 Which composer had a Broadway hit with "Song and Dance"?

Answers | **Pot-Luck 24** *(see Quiz 54)*

1 A tap dancer. 2 Britney Spears. 3 At the Battle of the Boyne. 4 Bobby Robson. 5 Alva. 6 Oxygen. 7 On the cross benches. 8 Dunnet Head. 9 Garfield. 10 Photosynthesis. 11 Myology. 12 Rex Harrison. 13 Queen Anne. 14 He was a Catholic priest. 15 Eric Bristow. 16 Eurydice. 17 Seven. 18 English National Opera. 19 A hybrid. 20 Sadlers Wells Opera Ballet. 21 Egypt. 22 3rd September. 23 George Sand. 24 Rick Stein. 25 Nitrogen. 26 Countess Markievicz. 27 On the eye. 28 German. 29 Emilia Fox. 30 Criminology.

1 In which month in 1914 did the First World War begin?
2 What were people told to "keep burning" in the hit song of 1914?
3 What was the occupation of Edith Cavell, who was shot by the Germans on a spying charge?
4 Who became Prime Minister of Britain in 1916?
5 What did George V ban in his household to encourage others to do the same, and help the war effort?
6 In the 1915 song where did you "Pack Up Your Troubles"?
7 How did Lord Kitchener die?
8 At which battle in 1916 were there said to be a million fatalities?
9 Which new weapon was introduced in battle in 1916?
10 What was the 1914–18 war known as until 1939?
11 What was the nationality of dancer Mata Hari, shot as a spy?
12 In which year did the United States enter the First World War?
13 Why were British soldiers called Tommies (short for Tommy Atkins)?
14 Which new British military force was established in 1918?
15 The German attack on which country caused Britain to enter the Second World War?
16 Which German word meaning "lightning war" entered the English language?
17 According to the World War II poster what did "Careless Talk" do?
18 What was the nickname of anti-British broadcaster, William Joyce?
19 According to Churchill he had nothing to offer in 1940 but what?
20 Which great evacuation of 1940 was called Operation Dynamo?
21 What was the German air force called?
22 What were the Local Defence Volunteers renamed?
23 Which fruit was no longer imported after 1940?
24 Which US bandleader went missing over the Channel in 1944?
25 Where did the Bevin Boys work?
26 What was the popular name for pilotless aircraft, V-1s?
27 What was snoek?
28 Who commanded the Allied forces that invaded Europe on D-Day?
29 Which scantily clad female had a daily strip in the "Daily Mirror"?
30 In which French city did Germany surrender in World War II?

Answers | Pot-Luck 26 *(see Quiz 59)*

1 France. 2 Car crash. 3 Boris Karloff. 4 Henry Morton Stanley discovered David Livingstone. 5 Hydrogen. 6 Mrs Malaprop in Sheridan's The Rivals. 7 The Gordon setter (after the Duke of Richmond and Gordon). 8 John Mortimer. 9 Borsetshire. 10 George IV. 11 Sheridan. 12 Helicopter. 13 Phrenologists. 14 Richmal Crompton. 15 St Petersburg. 16 Two. 17 Kilohertz. 18 Nigeria. 19 Ivy 20 Scottish country dancing. 21 Flanders and Swan. 22 Rik Mayall. 23 Iris Murdoch. 24 Uranus. 25 One. 26 The Return of the King. 27 Nanette Newman. 28 Estonia. 29 Menelaus. 30 Congress.

1 Which country is Kiri Te Kanawa from?
2 What are the Christian names of the three tenors?
3 Which German composer's only opera was "Fidelio"?
4 Which Gilbert and Sullivan opera is set in the Tower of London?
5 Which composer from East Anglia wrote the opera "Peter Grimes"?
6 What was the nationality of ballet composer Aaron Copland?
7 What was the name of Gounod's opera based on Doctor Faustus?
8 How did Lehár describe the Widow in his operetta?
9 Who wrote "Madame Butterfly" and "La Bohème"?
10 Which opera does "Nessun Dorma" come from?
11 Which work did the Who call a rock opera?
12 Where was the Barber from in the title of Rossini's opera?
13 How is Kurt Weill's "Die Dreigroschenoper" better known?
14 What does an operetta have which an opera usually doesn't?
15 Which Russian dancer gave his name to a famous racehorse?
16 Who wrote the ballets "Swan Lake" and "The Nutcracker"?
17 Which surname is shared by composers Johann and Richard?
18 What was the profession of Frederick Ashton?
19 Which controversial dancer died when her scarf caught in the wheels of her sports car?
20 What is the religious equivalent of opera without costumes and scenery?
21 Which Russian ballerina gave her name to a meringue dessert?
22 Who was Margot Fonteyn's most famous dancing partner?
23 Which 2005 ballet was based on a Tim Burton/Johnny Depp film?
24 What is the nationality of Alicia Markova?
25 For which sporting event was "Nessun Dorma" a TV theme tune?
26 What is Lesley Garrett's home county?
27 Which Italian composer's English name would be Joseph Green?
28 Which Russian-born composer wrote "The Rite of Spring"?
29 In ballet what is a jeté?
30 In 2005, which Royal Ballet production did not have matinees as it was deemed too shocking?

Answers | Movies: Comedies *(see Quiz 60)*

1 My Big Fat Greek Wedding. 2 Daniel. 3 (Bend It Like) Beckham. 4 Bruce Willis. 5 Arnold Schwarzenegger. 6 City Under Siege. 7 Ghostbusters. 8 Jessica Lange. 9 Julia Roberts. 10 Paul Newman and Robert Redford. 11 Manhattan. 12 Dolly Parton. 13 Disney. 14 Mel Gibson. 15 Michael Caine. 16 Meg Ryan and Billy Crystal. 17 Stockbroker. 18 Carry On Sergeant. 19 Clouseau. 20 Priscilla Presley. 21 Three Men and a Little Lady. 22 Butch Cassidy and the Sundance Kid. 23 Scottish. 24 Maggie Smith. 25 A pig. 26 The Mafia. 27 Big. 28 St Valentine's Day Massacre. 29 Woody Allen. 30 Harpo and Groucho (Marx).

1 Yasser Arafat died in November 2004 in which country?
2 How did Princess Grace of Monaco die?
3 Which horror movie actor's real name is William Pratt?
4 Who "discovered" whom at Ujiji in 1871?
5 Which gas has the chemical symbol H?
6 Which character says, "He is the very pineapple of politeness"?
7 Which breed of setter is named after a British duke?
8 Who wrote "Paradise Postponed"?
9 In which fictional county do the Archers live?
10 Which George did the Prince Regent become?
11 What is Hyacinth Bucket's absentee son called?
12 The poster advertising "Miss Saigon" featured what type of transport?
13 Which "ologists" study bumps on the human head?
14 Who wrote the book "William the Detective"?
15 Which Russian city used to be called Leningrad?
16 How many faces did the Romans believe Janus to have?
17 kHz is an abbreviation for what?
18 Kanu of Arsenal and WBA played international football for which country?
19 Hedera helix is better known as what?
20 What kind of dances are Hamilton House and Petronella?
21 Which duo wrote and first recorded "Mud Mud, Glorious Mud"?
22 Who played the part of George in the TV family drama "All About George"?
23 Who wrote the novel "The Bell"?
24 Which planet did Herschel discover in 1781?
25 How many atoms of oxygen are there in one molecule of water?
26 What was the title of the third "Lord of the Rings" movie?
27 Who is Emma Forbes's mother?
28 The USSR annexed three Baltic states in 1940. Latvia and Lithuania were two: what was the third?
29 Who was Helen of Troy's husband?
30 What does the "C" in TUC stand for?

| **Answers** | **World Wars** *(see Quiz 57)* |

1 August. 2 Home fires. 3 Nurse. 4 Lloyd George. 5 Alcohol. 6 In your old kit bag. 7 Lost at sea. 8 Somme. 9 Tank. 10 The Great War. 11 Dutch. 12 1917. 13 Sample name on recruitment form. 14 RAF. 15 Poland. 16 Blitzkrieg. 17 Costs Lives. 18 Lord Haw Haw. 19 Blood, toil, tears and sweat. 20 Dunkirk. 21 Luftwaffe. 22 Home Guard. 23 Bananas. 24 Glenn Miller. 25 Coalmines. 26 Doodle-bug or buzz bomb. 27 Fish. 28 Eisenhower. 29 Jane. 30 Reims.

1 In which 2002 movie did Nia Vardalos play a frumpy waitress in her Greek family's restaurant?
2 Who is Bridget Jones' boss in "Bridget Jones' Diary"?
3 In the 2001 movie directed by Gurinder Chadha, which footballer's surname is in the title?
4 Who was the baby's voice in "Look Who's Talking"?
5 Which tough guy was the star of "Kindergarten Cop"?
6 What was the subtitle of "Police Academy 6"?
7 Which film was about the activities of unemployed parapsychologists in New York?
8 Who won an Oscar for "Tootsie"?
9 Who was Richard Gere's co-star in "Pretty Woman"?
10 Which actors played the two revenging con men in "The Sting"?
11 In which area of New York is "Crocodile Dundee" set?
12 Which country singer starred in "Nine to Five"?
13 Which studios produced "Honey I Shrunk the Kids"?
14 Who plays the chauvinistic advertising executive in "What Women Want"?
15 Which English actor starred in "The Muppet Christmas Carol"?
16 Who played the title roles in "When Harry Met Sally"?
17 What was the profession of the Patrick Swayze character in "Ghost"?
18 Which was the first "Carry On" film?
19 Who is the police inspector in "The Pink Panther" films?
20 Which late superstar's wife stars in "The Naked Gun" films?
21 What was the sequel to "Three Men and a Baby"?
22 Which film included the song "Raindrops Keep Fallin' on My Head"?
23 What was the nationality of Mrs Doubtfire in the film of the same name?
24 Who played the role of Wendy in "Hook"?
25 In the film "Babe" who or what is "Babe"?
26 Who is Whoopi Goldberg hiding from in "Sister Act"?
27 In which film is Tom Hanks a small boy in a grown man's body?
28 Which historic event triggers the plot in "Some Like It Hot"?
29 Who directed "Annie Hall" and "Match Point"?
30 Who were Chico, Gummo and Zeppo's two brothers?

Answers	Opera and Ballet *(see Quiz 58)*

1 New Zealand. 2 Placido (Domingo), José (Carreras) and Luciano (Pavarotti). 3 Beethoven. 4 The Yeomen of the Guard. 5 Benjamin Britten. 6 American. 7 Faust. 8 Merry. 9 Puccini. 10 Turandot. 11 Tommy. 12 Seville. 13 The Threepenny Opera. 14 Spoken dialogue. 15 Nijinsky. 16 Tchaikovsky. 17 Strauss. 18 Choreographer. 19 Isadora Duncan. 20 Oratorio. 21 Pavlova. 22 Rudolf Nureyev. 23 Edward Scissorhands. 24 English. 25 1990 World Cup. 26 Yorkshire. 27 Giuseppe Verdi. 28 Stravinsky. 29 Jump. 30 The Lesson.

1 Who wrote the music for the "The Threepenny Opera"?
2 Which botanist gave his name to fuchsias?
3 What nationality was ballet star Rudolf Nureyev?
4 Who is known as "The Big Yin"?
5 Which two countries fought for supremacy in the Punic Wars?
6 Who left an unfinished novel called "Sanditon"?
7 In which country did broadcaster John Peel die?
8 Sara Paretsky is known for writing what type of novels?
9 Who carried the spirits of dead warriors to Valhalla?
10 The Soviet secret police were known by their initials: what were they?
11 Who succeeded George Carey as Archbishop of Canterbury?
12 In the children's fiction what type of creature is the ballerina Angelina?
13 Which William was married to Mary II?
14 Who said, "To err is human but it feels divine"?
15 In which TV programme did John Humphrys take over from Magnus Magnusson?
16 In Indian cuisine, what vegetable is referred to as "Aloo"?
17 If an elderly couple are happily married whom are they likened to?
18 Who's real name is Sofia Scicolone?
19 Which sport is played at Rosslyn Park?
20 What do we call a period of play in polo?
21 Which country's name means the Saviour?
22 How many cents are there in a US nickel?
23 With which country do you associate the drink pernod?
24 Rudi Voller took which team to the 2002 World Cup tournament?
25 What do we call what the Spaniards call an autopista?
26 Of which country is Tripoli the capital?
27 If you had an escutcheon, what would be shown on it?
28 Which city has given its name to a wheelchair and to a bun?
29 Which animal is associated with Paddy McGinty?
30 How much in old money was a tanner?

| **Answers** | **Pot-Luck 28** *(see Quiz 63)* |

1 Donald Campbell. 2 Jennifer Lopez. 3 Harold Shipman. 4 Hyde Park. 5 Canada. 6 William Golding. 7 Cowboy. 8 White or red. 9 Edgar Rice Burroughs. 10 Suffolk. 11 Caretaker. 12 Buzz Aldrin. 13 Spinning. 14 Chalk. 15 Tights. 16 One. 17 Farming, agriculture. 18 Ice. 19 Hamas. 20 Cynthia Lennon. 21 Jack and Annie Walker. 22 Louis XVI. 23 Made to measure. 24 Retract them. 25 The pot. 26 Busman's holiday. 27 Keira Knightly. 28 A wig. 29 Bayern Munich. 30 Matt Damon.

1 How many of the four majors did Tiger Woods win in 2003 and 2004?
2 Which European No 1 golfer won the Hong Kong Open in 2005?
3 Who is nicknamed "The Great White Shark"?
4 Which actress did Sam Torrance marry?
5 What is the women's equivalent of the Ryder Cup?
6 Which European Open gave Seve Ballesteros his first-ever European win back in 1976?
7 Where does Ernie Els hail from?
8 What does the D stand for in Arnold D. Palmer?
9 What is a bunker known as in the United States?
10 What is the maximum number of clubs permitted in a golf bag?
11 Which English player scored a hole in one on the final day of the 1995 Ryder Cup?
12 Who was the first German to win the German Open?
13 Where is the "home of golf"?
14 In which year did Tiger Woods win his first Open Championship?
15 Which country does Michael Campbell come from?
16 In stroke play, what is the penalty for playing the wrong ball?
17 What do the initials PGA stand for?
18 What is the amateur's equivalent of the Ryder Cup?
19 At which "appetizing" course did Sandy Lyle win the 1985 British Open?
20 Who is "The Golden Bear"?
21 Which is the oldest golf club in England?
22 At what age can a player join the Seniors' Tour?
23 Name Europe's 1997 Ryder Cup captain?
24 Which Henry won his first British Open in 1934?
25 What nationality is golfer Vijay Singh?
26 Which British golfer won the British Open in 1969?
27 Which famous American played his last British Open in 1995?
28 In which tournament does a player win a green jacket?
29 Which country does former Open winner Paul Lawrie come from?
30 Ernie Els had surgery on which part of his anatomy in 2005?

Answers	**Jazz and Blues** *(see Quiz 64)*

1 Satchmo. 2 The Yardbirds. 3 Harry Connick Jnr. 4 Moscow. 5 Bessie Smith. 6 Petite Fleur. 7 Dave Brubeck. 8 Twentysomething. 9 Bluesbreakers. 10 Piano. 11 Kenny G. 12 Ronnie Scott. 13 Diana Ross. 14 Benny Goodman. 15 John Lee Hooker. 16 Cleo Laine. 17 Humphrey Lyttelton. 18 Little Walter. 19 Saxophone. 20 Peggy Lee. 21 Muddy Waters. 22 Buddy Rich. 23 France. 24 Long John Baldry. 25 Paramount. 26 Piano. 27 Clarinet. 28 Gary Moore. 29 John Dankworth. 30 Cream.

1 Who was the last person to hold both water and land speed records?
2 Who starred opposite Richard Gere in "Shall We Dance"?
3 Which high-profile UK serial killer was found hanged in his prison cell in January 2004?
4 In which park is the Serpentine?
5 Of which country is Baffin Island a part?
6 Who wrote the novel "Lord of the Flies"?
7 In South America, what is a gaucho?
8 What colour are the flowers of the hawthorn?
9 Which US writer created Tarzan?
10 Ipswich is the administrative headquarters of which English county?
11 What job is done by a concierge?
12 Which astronaut was the second man to set foot on the moon?
13 With what industry is the inventor Richard Arkwright associated?
14 What is the common name for calcium carbonate?
15 What do we call what the Germans call "Strumpfhose"?
16 In chess, how many squares can the king move at a time?
17 With which industry is the Royal Smithfield Show concerned?
18 On what type of surface is the sport of curling played?
19 Which militant Islamic group won a landslide victory in the 2006 Palestinian elections?
20 Whose book about her ex-husband was simply called "John"?
21 Who were the first landlords of the Rovers' Return?
22 Which French king was husband to Marie Antoinette?
23 What are bespoke clothes?
24 What can cats do with their claws that dogs cannot do?
25 According to the proverb, what shouldn't call the kettle black?
26 What sort of a holiday is it if you do the same thing as in your job?
27 Who played Elizabeth Bennet in the 2005 film of "Pride and Prejudice"?
28 What is a peruke?
29 England's Owen Hargreaves first played in a European Cup final for which club?
30 Luciana Barroso married which Hollywood actor in December 2005?

| **Answers** | Pot-Luck 27 *(see Quiz 61)* |

1 Kurt Weill. 2 Leonhard Fuchs. 3 Russian. 4 Billy Connolly. 5 Rome and Carthage. 6 Jane Austen. 7 Peru. 8 Crime novels. 9 The Valkyries. 10 KGB. 11 Rowan Williams. 12 Mouse. 13 William III. 14 Mae West. 15 Mastermind. 16 Potatoes. 17 Darby and Joan. 18 Sophia Loren. 19 Rugby Union. 20 Chukka. 21 El Salvador. 22 Five. 23 France. 24 Germany. 25 Motorway. 26 Libya. 27 Your coat of arms. 28 Bath. 29 Goat. 30 Six pence.

Quiz 64   Jazz and Blues   Answers – page 304   **LEVEL 2**

1 What was Louis Armstrong's nickname?
2 Which 1960s band featured Eric Clapton and Jimmy Page?
3 Which singer recorded the "When Harry Met Sally" soundtrack?
4 In which city were Kenny Ball and his jazzmen at midnight?
5 Which 1920s blues singer recorded "Down Hearted Blues"?
6 What was Chris Barber's only hit single?
7 Whose quartet famously decided to "Take Five"?
8 What was Jamie Cullum's breakthrough album?
9 What was John Mayall's group known as?
10 What instrument did Earl Hines play?
11 Which jazz-funk saxophonist had a hit in 1987 with "Songbird"?
12 Which jazz musician opened a London club in 1959?
13 Who played Billie Holiday in the film "Lady Sings the Blues"?
14 Which clarinettist lived from 1909 to 1986 and had his "Story" told in a 1955 film?
15 Which veteran blues performer recorded "The Healer"?
16 How is singer Clementina Dinah Campbell better known?
17 Which trumpeter talks of Mornington Crescent in a radio panel game?
18 Under what name did Marion Walter Jacobs record?
19 What instrument is associated with Courtney Pine?
20 Who sang "He's a Tramp" in Disney's "Lady and the Tramp"?
21 Who recorded "Hoochie Coochie Man" and "Got My Mojo Working"?
22 Which virtuoso jazz drummer started out in a vaudeville act as Baby Trapps the Drum Wonder?
23 In which country was Alexis Korner born?
24 Which bluesman had a No 1 with "Let the Heartaches Begin"?
25 What was the name of Mr Acker Bilk's Jazz Band?
26 Which instrument does Jamie Cullum play?
27 What instrument is associated with Monty Sunshine?
28 Which guitarist released the album "Ballads and Blues"?
29 Who turned "Three Blind Mice" into "Experiments with Mice"?
30 Which group were formed by Bruce, Baker and Clapton?

Answers	**Sport: Golf** *(see Quiz 62)*

1 None. 2 Colin Montgomerie. 3 Greg Norman. 4 Suzanne Danielle. 5 Curtis Cup.
6 Dutch Open. 7 South Africa. 8 Daniel. 9 Trap. 10 14. 11 Howard Clark. 12
Bernhard Langer. 13 St Andrews. 14 2000. 15 New Zealand. 16 Two strokes. 17
Professional Golfers' Association. 18 Walker Cup. 19 Sandwich. 20 Jack Nicklaus. 21
Royal Blackheath, Kent. 22 50 years. 23 Seve Ballesteros. 24 Cotton. 25 Fijian. 26
Tony Jacklin. 27 Arnold Palmer. 28 US Masters. 29 Scotland. 30 Knee.

1 Which entertainer returned to London's West End as Scrooge in 2005?
2 Which ex-England soccer manager wrote "Farewell But Not Goodbye"?
3 By what name is Formosa now known?
4 What have Thistle, Brent and Ninian in common?
5 Who became queen of the Netherlands in 1980?
6 Who wrote the poem that begins, "Shall I compare thee to a summer's day"?
7 Singer Daniel Powter is from which country?
8 What is Al Pacino's full first name?
9 Provence and Brittany are both parts of which country?
10 Who played the scarecrow, Worzel Gummidge, on television?
11 Nowadays, who might wear a wimple?
12 Which country lies immediately south of Estonia?
13 In geography, what is a cataract?
14 Which English soccer team plays at home at Molyneux?
15 In America what is Airforce One?
16 With which sport do you associate Karen Pickering?
17 Who was the lead singer of the group, the Who?
18 What does the reference book, Crockfords, list?
19 What is Prince Charles' step son called?
20 Where in the body is the humerus?
21 In which country is the city of Jakarta?
22 As what did Grimaldi achieve fame?
23 In which US city is Grand Central Station?
24 Of which ancient empire was Nebuchadnezzar king?
25 In which art did Sir Henry Irving become famous?
26 When the sun is at its zenith, where is it?
27 The tears of which creatures are said to be a sign of insincere grief?
28 In which sport does the Harlequin Club compete?
29 For what achievement is Valentina Tereshkova famous?
30 In 2004, members of which organization attacked the PM with flour in the House of Commons?

| **Answers** | **Around Africa** *(see Quiz 67)* |

1 Zambia, Zimbabwe. 2 Sahara Desert. 3 Ethiopia. 4 Organization of African Unity. 5 Burkina Faso. 6 A wind. 7 Uganda. 8 Namibia. 9 Cocoa. 10 Victoria. 11 Kilimanjaro. 12 Portuguese. 13 Libya. 14 Nigeria. 15 Rwanda. 16 Dutch. 17 Victoria Falls. 18 Sahel. 19 Gold. 20 Casablanca. 21 Botswana. 22 Sudan. 23 Wildlife. 24 South Africa. 25 None, it is native to Asia not Africa. 26 Dams. 27 North. 28 Somalia. 29 A click, made in the throat. 30 Pretoria.

1 Which 2004 Oscar-winning actress was the face of L'Oréal in 2005?
2 Which former model is married to actor Leigh Lawson?
3 Which singer collaborated with Tommy Hilfiger on the "true star" series of perfumes?
4 Which model has been married to rock star Bill Wyman and footballer Pat Van Den Hauwe?
5 Which daughter of David Arquette and Courteney Cox shares a first name with a fashion legend?
6 Which supermodel's name was linked with Babyshambles front man Pete Doherty during a drugs scandal in 2005?
7 Who released a perfume called Stella in 2005?
8 Which cosmetic house did Liz Hurley become the face of in 1995?
9 Which famous photographer was Marie Helvin married to?
10 Which Oscar winner for "The Hours" advertised Chanel No 5?
11 Which designer is well known for her pink hair?
12 Which fruit gave its name to ex-model Debbie Moore's dance studio?
13 Which former model did Ringo Starr marry?
14 Who is the designer daughter of food critic Egon Ronay?
15 In what area of fashion is Barbara Daly famous?
16 Which famous hairdresser married Lulu?
17 Which garment is Jean-Paul Gaultier famous for wearing?
18 Who is the Frost half of the FrostFrench lingerie label?
19 Who said, "A woman is as young as her knees"?
20 Who designed Liz Hurley's famous "safety pin" dress?
21 Which model did Peter Andre marry in 2005?
22 What is the first name of designer St Laurent?
23 Which cosmetic house did Charles Revson found?
24 Which model has a daughter called Lila Grace?
25 Which pop singer was designer/TV presenter Jeff Banks married to?
26 Woodall and Constantine are the surnames of which fashion experts?
27 Which London street was famous for its 1960s boutiques?
28 Which hairdresser pioneered the geometric haircut in the 1960s?
29 Which Italian city is at the heart of the fashion industry?
30 Which Vivienne is famous for her outrageous designs?

Answers | **Pot-Luck 30** *(see Quiz 68)*

1 Half a loaf. 2 Cat. 3 Bizet. 4 A rope. 5 Worcestershire sauce. 6 Kensington Gardens. 7 Franz Ferdinand. 8 Having the same centre. 9 Pinocchio. 10 The Pickwick Papers. 11 Bread. 12 Terry Pratchett. 13 Orlando. 14 Wines. 15 Cheeses. 16 Gwen Stefani. 17 Fashion leader. 18 Scotland. 19 Bob Monkhouse. 20 Fish. 21 Theatres. 22 South Africa. 23 John Bunyan. 24 Dressing. 25 1605. 26 D. H. Lawrence. 27 Candles. 28 You Raise Me Up. 29 Swan. 30 Silvio Berlusconi.

1 The names of which two African countries begin with the letter Z?
2 What covers 85% of Algeria?
3 Famine in which country triggered the Band Aid Charity?
4 What do the initials OAU stand for?
5 Of which country is Ouagadougou the capital?
6 What is the Harmattan?
7 Which is further west, Uganda or Kenya?
8 Which country used to be called South West Africa?
9 Which substance, used to make a drink, is Ghana's main export?
10 Which lake lies between Kenya, Tanzania and Uganda?
11 What is Africa's highest mountain?
12 Which European language is an official language of Angola?
13 In which African country is El Alamein, scene of a World War II battle?
14 Which country is the main economic power in West Africa?
15 Which country is further north, Rwanda or Burundi?
16 Which language is Afrikaans derived from?
17 Near which major landmark is the Boiling Pot?
18 What is the area of savanna in West Africa called?
19 South Africa is the world's leading exporter of what?
20 Which Moroccan city is the name of a famous film?
21 The Kalahari Desert lies chiefly in which country?
22 What is the largest country in Africa?
23 What is the Okavango Swamp famous for?
24 In which country are the political parties ANC and Inkatha?
25 Which African country is the tiger native to?
26 Which man-made structures would you see at Aswan and Kariba?
27 Does most of Africa lie to the north or to the south of the Equator?
28 Which country occupies the Horn of Africa?
29 Which sound is unique to many African languages including Xhosa?
30 What is the administrative capital of South Africa?

Answers	Pot-Luck 29 *(see Quiz 65)*

1 Tommy Steele. 2 Bobby Robson. 3 Taiwan. 4 All are (North Sea) oilfields. 5 Beatrix. 6 Shakespeare. 7 Canada. 8 Alfredo. 9 France. 10 Jon Pertwee. 11 A nun. 12 Latvia. 13 Waterfall. 14 Wolverhampton Wanderers. 15 The president's plane. 16 Swimming. 17 Roger Daltry. 18 The clergy of the Church of England. 19 Tom. 20 Upper arm. 21 Indonesia. 22 Clown. 23 New York. 24 Babylonia. 25 Theatre. 26 Directly overhead. 27 Crocodile. 28 Rugby Union. 29 She was the first woman in space. 30 Fathers 4 Justice.

1 According to the proverb, what is better than no bread?
2 What kind of animal is a Persian Blue?
3 Who composed the opera "Carmen"?
4 On a ship or boat what is a painter?
5 What condiment is manufactured by Lea & Perrins?
6 Where in London is the statue of Peter Pan?
7 Alex Kapranos is the front man for which band?
8 In geometry, what is meant by concentric?
9 Which wooden puppet was first written about by Carlo Collodi?
10 In which of Dickens's novels does Sam Weller appear?
11 Which food, not rationed during World War II, was rationed after it?
12 Whose novels include "Going Postal" and "Thud!"?
13 What is the name of the marmalade cat created by Kathleen Hale?
14 For what is the Médoc area of France famous?
15 What are Cheshire, Gouda and Gorgonzola?
16 LAMB is the clothing line designed by which singer?
17 As what did Beau Brummel achieve fame?
18 Which country used to have a coin called a bawbee?
19 Who was the first presenter of "Family Fortunes"?
20 What do we call what the Italians call pesce?
21 In London, the Cambridge, the Lyric and the Adelphi are all what?
22 Of which country was Field-Marshal Smuts prime minister?
23 Which religious writer was born in Elstow, near Bedford?
24 What word can go after salad and before gown?
25 In which year was the Gunpowder Plot?
26 Who wrote the novels "Sons and Lovers" and "The Rainbow"?
27 What does a chandler make?
28 Westlife won the award of Britain's Record of the Year 2005 for which song?
29 Black, Whooper, and Bewick are all types of which bird?
30 Which Italian Prime Minister also had the distinction of being the country's richest man?

Answers	**Supermodels and Fashion** (see Quiz 66)

1 Charlize Theron. 2 Twiggy. 3 Beyoncé. 4 Mandy Smith. 5 Coco (Chanel). 6 Kate Moss. 7 Stella McCartney. 8 Estée Lauder. 9 David Bailey. 10 Nicole Kidman. 11 Zandra Rhodes. 12 Pineapple. 13 Barbara Bach. 14 Edina Ronay. 15 Make-up. 16 John Frieda. 17 Kilt. 18 Sadie Frost. 19 Mary Quant. 20 Versace. 21 Katie Price (Jordan). 22 Yves. 23 Revlon. 24 Kate Moss. 25 Sandie Shaw. 26 Trinny and Susannah. 27 Carnaby Street. 28 Vidal Sassoon. 29 Milan. 30 Westwood.

1 What do conifers have in their cones?
2 Which tree's leaves are the symbol of the National Trust?
3 Which three coniferous trees are native to Britain?
4 Which garden tree with yellow flowers has poisonous seeds?
5 What colour are the flowers of the horse chestnut tree?
6 In which country did the bonsai technique develop?
7 Which tree do we get turpentine from?
8 In which continent did the monkey-puzzle tree originate?
9 Which tree produces cobs and filberts?
10 Aspen is from which family of trees?
11 Is the wood of a coniferous tree hard or soft?
12 What is the more common name for the great maple?
13 What sort of environment do alder trees grow in?
14 Which tree is cork obtained from?
15 In which county is England's largest forest?
16 Which tree is sago obtained from?
17 Which beech tree has purplish leaves?
18 What is the Spanish chestnut also called?
19 Which tree can be English, American or Eurasian?
20 To which family does the umbrella tree belong?
21 The teak is native to which continent?
22 Which wood is used for piano keys?
23 Which maple's sap is used to make maple syrup?
24 To which family does the osier belong?
25 Which is thought to be the tallest tree in the world and one of the longest-lived?
26 Which tree produces "keys"?
27 What colour flowers does a jacaranda tree have?
28 Which tree produces the seeds from which cocoa is made?
29 To which group of trees do blue gum and red gum belong ?
30 What is the linden tree also called?

Answers	Sport: Cricket (see Quiz 71)

1 County. 2 2003. 3 Gary Sobers. 4 Ian Botham. 5 Keedie. 6 Richie Benaud.
7 All maidens – no runs conceded. 8 Brian Close. Played at 18 and finally at 45. 9 Inzamam ul-Haq. 10 11. 11 Somerset, Worcestershire and Durham. 12 Yorkshire. 13 Canterbury. 14 Middlesex. 15 Wilfred Rhodes. 16 Mark and Steve. 17 Lord's. 18 Jamaica. 19 Danish. 20 Warwickshire. 21 Harold Larwood. 22 Grace. 23 Colin and Christopher Cowdrey. 24 Jim Laker. 25 Malcolm Nash. 26 22. 27 Right arm raised in horizontal position. 28 Javed Miandad of Pakistan. 29 Durham. 30 Viv Richards.

1 In which country did the poets Keats and Shelley both die?
2 How many tusks does a warthog have?
3 What is the nearest star to the solar system?
4 Who wrote "Porgy and Bess"?
5 Who was king of France at the time of the French Revolution?
6 Which card game has two forms, called auction and contract?
7 In which country does the Amazon rise?
8 Graphite is composed of which element?
9 Who was the first English captain to lift the Webb Ellis Trophy?
10 What can be seen from Earth only once every 76 years?
11 Who was prime minister of Australia from 1983 to 1991?
12 Where was the Mount Pinatubo eruption?
13 What was notable about all the dancers in Matthew Bourne's version of Swan Lake?
14 What is the nationality of opera singer Renee Fleming?
15 Who became potter to King George III in 1806?
16 What does "m" stand for in Einstein's equation $E=mc^2$?
17 Which sign of the zodiac is represented as a man pouring water from a jug?
18 Who preferred "50,000 rifles to 50,000 votes"?
19 Who devised the modern system for naming and classifying plants and animals?
20 Whose fan did Oscar Wilde write about?
21 What name is given to the set of fans at the front of a jet engine?
22 How many gold medals did Michael Phelps win at the Athens Olympics in 2004?
23 On the shores of which lake does Toronto stand?
24 What is the scientific name for the lemon tree?
25 On which day in 1066 was William the Conqueror crowned king of England?
26 What is the currency of the British colony of Bermuda?
27 Sir Christopher Wren was a professor in which scientific field?
28 What is the first name of the second Mrs Paul McCartney?
29 Who was Pinocchio's father?
30 Where are the Tivoli Gardens?

Answers | Pot-Luck 32 *(see Quiz 72)*

1 XY. 2 Bernard Hill. 3 Atmospheric pressure. 4 Donovan. 5 Gamma. 6 Orange. 7 Indonesia's. 8 Thirty. 9 Ralph Fiennes. 10 Miles Davis's. 11 James Chadwick. 12 Emporio. 13 Opera. 14 Lyle Lovett. 15 Edward Heath. 16 Solomon Grundy. 17 Dr No. 18 Pink Floyd. 19 The binary system. 20 1995–96. 21 Tuna fishing. 22 Pancreas. 23 17th century. 24 Victoria. 25 Crystal Palace. 26 Atlas Mountains. 27 American Civil War. 28 Della Street. 29 Periodic table. 30 Osiris.

1 What does the first C stand for in TCCB?
2 In which year did Michael Vaughan take over as England captain?
3 Which West Indies star with bat and ball scored over 8,000 Test runs?
4 Who was the last cricketer to be named BBC Sports Personality of the Year before Freddie Flintoff?
5 Which lady sang on the 2005 England squad's version of "Jerusalem"?
6 Which popular figure wrote "My Spin on Cricket"?
7 What was remarkable about the 16 overs that South Africa's Hugh Tayfield bowled against England at Durban in 1957?
8 Who was England's youngest and later oldest post-war Test player?
9 Who skippered Pakistan in the 2005 series victory over England?
10 In 1995, Jack Russell took how many catches in a Test to create a new world record?
11 Which three counties did Ian Botham play for?
12 Which county have won the championship most times?
13 Where is Kent's cricket ground headquarters?
14 Edmonds and Emburey were the spinning duo for which county?
15 Which all-rounder took 100 wickets and scored 1000 runs in 16 seasons between 1903 and 1926?
16 What are the Christian names of Australia's Waugh brothers?
17 Where do Middlesex play home matches?
18 On which West Indian island is Sabina Park?
19 Which name of Pakistani wrist spinner Kaneria suggests he comes from Scandinavia?
20 Which English county has Brian Lara played for?
21 Who was the "bodyline" bowler?
22 Gloucestershire cricketers of the 1870s W. G. and E. M. had what surname?
23 Who are the only father and son to captain England?
24 Which Englishman took 19 wickets in a 1956 Test against Australia?
25 Who was bowling for Glamorgan when Sobers hit six sixes in an over?
26 How many Test centuries did Geoff Boycott score for England?
27 What is the umpire's signal for a no-ball?
28 Who was selected for all World Cups from 1975 to 1995?
29 Which was the first new county to join the championship in the 1990s?
30 Who was West Indian captain before Richie Richardson?

Answers | Nature: Trees *(see Quiz 69)*

1 Seeds. 2 Oak. 3 Yew, Scots Pine, Juniper. 4 Laburnum. 5 White/cream. 6 Japan. 7 Pine. 8 South America. 9 Hazel. 10 Poplar. 11 Soft. 12 Sycamore. 13 Wet. 14 Cork oak. 15 Northumberland. 16 Palm. 17 Copper beech. 18 Sweet chestnut. 19 Elm. 20 Magnolia. 21 Asia. 22 Ebony. 23 Sugar maple. 24 Willow. 25 Redwood. 26 Ash. 27 Blue/violet. 28 Cacao. 29 Eucalyptus. 30 Lime.

1 Which sex chromosomes are possessed by a human male?
2 Who played King Theoden of Rohan in the last two parts of the "Lord of the Rings" trilogy?
3 What does a barometer measure?
4 Which pop star from the 1960s called his autobiography "The Hurdy Gurdy Man"?
5 What is the third letter of the Greek alphabet?
6 What is the flavour of Grand Marnier?
7 Whose national airline is called Garuda?
8 How many counters are on a backgammon board at start of play?
9 Who voiced Victor Quartermaine in "Wallace and Gromit: The Curse of the Were-Rabbit"?
10 In the 1950s whose quintet did John Coltrane play with?
11 Who discovered the neutron?
12 Under what label did Giorgio Armani design clothes?
13 What word can go after soap and before house?
14 Which country singer married Julia Roberts in 1993?
15 Which prime minister brought in a 10.30pm TV curfew in 1973?
16 In the nursery rhyme who was married on a Wednesday?
17 Which Bond movie featured the partially dressed Ursula Andress?
18 Which British rock band had Syd Barrett among its founders?
19 Which number code system is based on the digits 1 and 0?
20 David Beckham first won the Premiership with Man Utd in which season?
21 What type of driftnet fishing caused the deaths of hundreds of dolphins in the 1980s?
22 Which organ of the body secretes insulin?
23 In which century was tea first brought to Europe?
24 Of which Australian state is Melbourne the capital?
25 What was built in Hyde Park for the Great Exhibition of 1851?
26 Mount Toubkal is the highest peak of which mountain range?
27 Which war started with the bombardment of Fort Sumter?
28 Who was Perry Mason's secretary?
29 What name is given to the most used table of the elements?
30 Who was the Egyptian god of the underworld?

Answers | Pot-Luck 31 *(see Quiz 70)*

1 Italy. 2 Four. 3 Alpha Centauri. 4 George Gershwin. 5 Louis XVI. 6 Bridge. 7 Peru. 8 Carbon. 9 Martin Johnson. 10 Halley's Comet. 11 Bob Hawke. 12 The Philippines. 13 They were all men. 14 American. 15 Josiah Spode. 16 Mass. 17 Aquarius. 18 Benito Mussolini. 19 Linnaeus. 20 Lady Windermere's. 21 Compressor. 22 Six. 23 Lake Ontario. 24 Citrus limon. 25 Christmas Day. 26 Bermuda dollar. 27 Astronomy. 28 Heather. 29 Geppetto. 30 Copenhagen.

1 Which method of fast writing did Isaac Pitman develop?
2 Which two major electronics companies developed the compact disc in 1979?
3 What was invented by US students using aluminium flan cases?
4 In which country was the first modern motorway created?
5 Who registered the first patents for the railway sleeping car?
6 Which Swiss company developed the first widely used instant coffee?
7 Which rubber-based product was patented in the United States in 1869?
8 Why was the invention of the electric iron useless in America in 1882?
9 What was American Mr Bissel's dust-collecting invention?
10 What was the surname of King Camp who invented the safety razor?
11 What was the occupation of Dom Pierre Perignon who developed the champagne process?
12 What type of pens did Pentel invent?
13 Which building toy was designed by a Dane, Ole Kirk Christiansen?
14 What is unusual about Mark Button's invention, the Koosh ball?
15 Which Kimberley Clark Co invention was first called Celluwipes?
16 Which form of precautionary medicine was discovered by Edward Jenner?
17 What was the nationality of saxophone inventor Adolphe Sax?
18 Which type of transport did John Outram invent in 1775?
19 Which sauce did Henry Heinz invent in 1876?
20 JVC launched VHS format in 1976, but what does VHS stand for?
21 Which drink was created when Indian army officers added quinine to soda water to help fight malaria?
22 In which country were cultured pearls first obtained?
23 What was Alka-Seltzer first marketed as?
24 The Penny Black was the first adhesive stamp, how was the Penny Red a first?
25 In which country were banknotes first used?
26 Which weapon did Samuel Colt develop and popularize?
27 Which musical instrument did American Rickenbacher create?
28 What was based on the Victorian game called Magic Square?
29 What did the owner of the Humpty Dumpty store in Oklahoma invent?
30 Which type of fastening was first used on snow boots?

Answers	Pop: Solo Stars *(see Quiz 75)*

1 No. 2 The Day I Met Marie. 3 Elvis Presley. 4 Holiday. 5 Rod Stewart. 6 Bryan Hyland. 7 Perry Como. 8 Bonnie Tyler. 9 Green Door. 10 Bobby Brown. 11 Christina Aguilera. 12 RSVP. 13 Thunderball. 14 Gene Pitney. 15 Marti Webb. 16 Will Young. 17 Maggie May. 18 Frank Ifield. 19 Careless Whisper. 20 Sam Cooke. 21 In Dreams. 22 They Call the Wind Mariah. 23 Seal. 24 Elton John. 25 Belinda Carlisle. 26 Tamla Motown. 27 25 mph. 28 Bruce Springsteen. 29 Cher – Gypsies, Tramps and Thieves. 30 Georgia.

1 What is the Aurora Australis also called?

2 Which three South American countries does the Equator cross?

3 What was the first X-rated film to win an Oscar?

4 What is the name of the national airline of Israel?

5 Which pop star earned his bus pass and became an official OAP on 14 October 2005?

6 Which female cookery writer wrote "Climbing the Mango Trees"?

7 What did Little Polly Flinders spoil?

8 Who wrote "Anna Karenina"?

9 What metallic element is mixed with tin to form the alloy bronze?

10 Who was the founder of the Christian Science movement?

11 Made this millennium, in which decade was the detective series "Jericho" set?

12 In which city did Karl Marx write "Das Kapital"?

13 How is the Caribbean island of St Christopher more familiarly known?

14 Which planet has a pink appearance?

15 Who was world professional billiards champion from 1968 to 1980?

16 Which is the most northerly capital city in Europe?

17 Which New York baseball player who married Marilyn Monroe?

18 Which country is the world's leading producer of copper?

19 Which acid builds up in the muscles during severe exercise?

20 Who circumnavigated the world solo in "Gipsy Moth IV" in 1966–67?

21 Which Australian city stands near the mouth of the Yarra river?

22 What common mineral is formed by the fossilization of vegetation?

23 Which stand-up comedian created the character the Pub Landlord?

24 Which comic playwright wrote the trilogy "The Norman Conquests"?

25 Who took over the movie role of Clarice Starling from Jodie Foster?

26 Who was George Logan better known as?

27 What form of energy is produced by an electric motor?

28 Which beautiful youth did the Greek goddess Aphrodite love?

29 Who said "When you are as great as I am, it's hard to be humble"?

30 Which country's flag shows a green star on a red background?

Answers	Painting and Scupture *(see Quiz 76)*

1 Gainsborough. 2 Renoir. 3 Mona Lisa. 4 Jack Russell. 5 The Rake's. 6 The Laughing Cavalier. 7 Sphinx. 8 Op Art. 9 Wet plaster. 10 Statue of Liberty. 11 Nude. 12 Engravings. 13 Mount Rushmore. 14 Sculpture. 15 Millais. 16 Henry Moore. 17 Salvador Dali. 18 Rembrandt. 19 Andy Warhol. 20 Portraits. 21 Buddha. 22 Van Gogh. 23 Glue. 24 Picasso. 25 Impressionist. 26 Pop Art. 27 Dancers. 28 Russia. 29 Suffolk. 30 Jacob.

1 Did John Lennon have a solo single No 1 in his lifetime?
2 Which Cliff Richard hit starts "Imagine a still summer's day"?
3 Colonel Tom Parker launched which star?
4 Which was Madonna's first UK top ten hit?
5 Which singer recorded "Every Picture Tells a Story"?
6 Who had a hit with the original version of "Sealed with a Kiss"?
7 Which former barber charted from 1953 to 1973?
8 Which lady was "Lost in France"?
9 What was a hit for both Frankie Vaughan and Shakin' Stevens?
10 Britney Spears had a hit with "My Prerogative", but who had the original hit?
11 Who had No 1s with both "Dirrty" and "Beautiful"?
12 Which Jason Donovan single is made up of initials?
13 Tom Jones sang for which Bond film?
14 Which solo star had his first No 1 in a duo with Marc Almond in 1989?
15 Apart from Michael Jackson, which female singer charted with "Ben"?
16 Who had a No 1 in 2003 with "Friday's Child"?
17 Which Rod Stewart hit starts "Wake up, Maggie..."?
18 Can you remember who sang "I Remember You"?
19 What was George Michael's first solo No 1?
20 Whose "Wonderful World" was a bigger hit as a reissue 26 years after the original?
21 Which Roy Orbison hit begins, "A candy-coloured clown they call the sandman"?
22 Mariah Carey was named after which song in "Paint Your Wagon"?
23 Which singer was "Crazy" with his first single success?
24 Which superstar has been chairman of Watford football club?
25 Which female singer recorded "Heaven is a Place on Earth"?
26 Which label did Michael Jackson first record on?
27 According to Tina Turner, what was the speed limit in Nutbush?
28 Who was born in the United States of Irish-Italian parents and with the middle names Frederick Joseph ?
29 Who sang that she was "born in the wagon of a travelling show"?
30 Which country does Katie Melua come from?

Answers	**Hi-Tech: Inventions** *(see Quiz 73)*

1 Shorthand. 2 Sony and Philips. 3 Frisbee. 4 Italy. 5 Pullman. 6 Nestlé. 7 Chewing gum. 8 Homes did not have electricity. 9 Carpet sweeper. 10 Gillette. 11 Monk. 12 Felt tips. 13 Lego. 14 It doesn't bounce. 15 Paper handkerchiefs. 16 Vaccination. 17 Belgian. 18 Tram. 19 Tomato ketchup. 20 Video Home System. 21 Tonic water. 22 Japan. 23 Cold cure. 24 Perforated. 25 Sweden. 26 Revolver. 27 Electric guitar. 28 Crossword puzzles. 29 Supermarket trolley. 30 Zip.

1 Who painted "The Blue Boy" and "Mr and Mrs Andrews"?
2 Which Pierre-Auguste painted "Umbrellas" and "The Bathers"?
3 What is Leonardo da Vinci's "La Gioconda" also known as?
4 Which English cricketer is a keen amateur watercolour artist?
5 Whose Progress did William Hogarth paint?
6 What is arguably the most famous painting by Dutchman Frans Hals?
7 Which Egyptian sculpture is more than 73 metres long?
8 Which 1960s art vogue was based on optical illusion?
9 What is paint applied to in a fresco?
10 Which sculpture did Auguste Bartholdi give to the United States?
11 What is notable about the woman in Ingres' "Valpinçon Bather"?
12 What type of work is Albrecht Dürer famous for?
13 Where in the United States would you find Washington's head 18 metres high?
14 What art form is a Japanese netsuke?
15 Who painted "Bubbles", which has been used in a soap ad?
16 Which English sculptor produced rounded forms such as "Reclining Figure"?
17 Which Spaniard is known for his hallucinatory paintings?
18 Which Dutch painter is well known for his self-portraits?
19 Who painted Campbell soup tins and Marilyn Monroe?
20 What type of paintings is Joshua Reynolds famous for?
21 A statue in Afghanistan of which religious teacher standing 53 metres high was destroyed by the Taliban in 2001?
22 Whose "Irises" and "Sunflowers" were two of the world's most expensive paintings at auction?
23 What is the binding medium in gouache technique?
24 Which Spaniard founded the Cubist movement?
25 Of which school of painting was Claude Monet a leading exponent?
26 For which art style is David Hockney famous?
27 Which performers were a favourite subject for painter/sculptor Degas?
28 In which country was the French painter Marc Chagall born?
29 In which county is "Constable country", named after its famous son?
30 What was the first name of sculptor Epstein?

Answers	**Pot-Luck 33** *(see Quiz 74)*

1 The Southern Lights. 2 Brazil, Colombia and Ecuador. 3 Midnight Cowboy. 4 El-Al.
5 Cliff Richard. 6 Madhur Jaffrey. 7 Her nice new clothes. 8 Leo Tolstoy. 9 Copper.
10 Mary Baker Eddy. 11 1950s. 12 London. 13 St Kitts. 14 Mars. 15 Rex Williams.
16 Helsinki. 17 Joe DiMaggio. 18 Chile. 19 Lactic acid. 20 Francis Chichester.
21 Melbourne. 22 Coal. 23 Al Murray. 24 Alan Ayckbourn. 25 Julianne Moore.
26 Evadne Hinge (of Hinge and Brackett). 27 Mechanical energy. 28 Adonis. 29
Muhammad Ali. 30 Morocco.

1 The year 2006 marks which anniversary of Mozart's birth?
2 Goalkeeper Richard Wright joined Everton from which club?
3 In which movie did Nicolas Cage play the character Yuri Orlov?
4 What source of light is used in producing a hologram?
5 Which Bond movie was a hit for Sheena Easton?
6 Which instrument does the musician Einaudi play?
7 Where in Canada is the world's second-largest French-speaking city?
8 Which character did Clark Gable play in "Gone with the Wind"?
9 Which tsar conquered Kazan and Siberia in the 16th century?
10 What was the subtitle of the movie "Miss Congeniality 2"?
11 In which year did Britain abandon the gold standard?
12 Which Italian artist included Halley's comet in a fresco of the Nativity?
13 Which object took almost seven hours to rise from the Solent in 1982?
14 Which "Dad's Army" actor was married to Hattie Jacques?
15 What name is given to the genetic make-up of an individual?
16 Where did chess originate in the second century AD?
17 What happened to the main character in Kafka's "Metamorphosis"?
18 What style of music was pioneered by jazzmen Charlie Parker and Dizzy Gillespie?
19 Which 18th-century priest discovered that plants absorb air?
20 Cecil Beaton won Oscars for his designs for which two films?
21 In the rhyme, what is Friday's child?
22 What is the name given to the chief religious leader of a synagogue?
23 What were the surnames of the tennis doubles stars known as the Woodies?
24 What did Mahatma Gandhi train to become?
25 Where would you find an avenue of sphinxes?
26 Which instrument did Lionel Hampton introduce to jazz?
27 Who played the Riddler in "Batman Forever"?
28 Who was the last prisoner to be held at Spandau?
29 Which rock star, known as "Slowhand", received an OBE in 1995?
30 Which theme from a film did the BBC use for the 1984 Olympics?

Answers	**Pot-Luck 35** *(see Quiz 79)*

1 Spanish. 2 Hamlet. 3 Hindu. 4 Madeleine Albright. 5 Squirrel. 6 Zimbabwe. 7 The Medway. 8 Nigella Lawson. 9 November. 10 Keith Richard. 11 Isaac. 12 James II. 13 Canary. 14 Manitoba. 15 Italy. 16 Battle of Bosworth. 17 Noel Coward. 18 Bench. 19 Canada. 20 Eyes. 21 Tea. 22 Anne Boleyn. 23 Etna. 24 The Seagull. 25 Salome. 26 Magyar. 27 On its tail. 28 Gerald Ford. 29 Steffi Graf. 30 Suez Canal.

1 In "Doctor Who" what does TARDIS stand for?
2 Which film starts with a telephone conversation between Cypher and Trinity?
3 In which series did scientist Dr Sam Beckett appear?
4 What was the Six Million Dollar Man's previous occupation?
5 In which sci-fi series did Joanna Lumley and David McCallum star?
6 What was unusual about Dr Peter Brady and Dr Daniel Westin?
7 What was the name of Dr Who's assistant as played by Billie Piper?
8 Which Edwardian adventurer, trapped in ice, thawed out in 1966?
9 What was Steve Zodiac's spacecraft?
10 Where were the Robinson family lost in the 1960s series?
11 What is Doctor Who always called in the series?
12 Which series has had Eartha Kitt in the role of Catwoman?
13 Who played Jamie in "Doctor Who" and Joe Sugden in "Emmerdale"?
14 What were Captain Kirk's two Christian names?
15 How was Diana Prince better known?
16 What did "A" stand for in the name of the 1960s series?
17 What was special about the Man from Atlantis, Mark Harris?
18 Which 11th-century wizard became trapped in the 20th century?
19 In "Doomwatch" what was Doomwatch?
20 Who travelled in "The Liberator" fighting the Federation?
21 What was the surname of Professor Bernard whose name has become synonymous with early TV sci-fi?
22 What was the title of the Star Trek series that resumed in 1990?
23 Which series preceded "Galactica 80"?
24 In "Doctor Who" what was the Daleks' most famous command?
25 In "Star Trek" what colour was Mr Spock's blood?
26 Which children's series featured Spectrum and Colonel White?
27 Which series is remembered for Diana seeming to swallow a mouse?
28 What was the surname of global rescuers Jeff, Scott and Virgil?
29 In which 1970s series had 95% of the world's population been wiped out by a killer virus?
30 What sort of vehicle was Stingray?

Answers	New Millennium Milestones (see Quiz 80)

1 Arnold Schwarzenegger. 2 Tate Modern. 3 Millennium Bridge. 4 Hillary Clinton. 5 Submarine. 6 The Guardian. 7 Indonesia. 8 Routemaster bus. 9 101. 10 December. 11 Ukraine. 12 Angela Merkel. 13 Buncefield. 14 Mars. 15 Yasser Arafat. 16 Two. 17 Shed (Shed-Boat-Shed). 18 Rudolph Giuliani. 19 Bali. 20 Nepalese. 21 Kelly Holmes. 22 Three. 23 Pete Sampras. 24 Martin Johnson. 25 George Best. 26 Cats. 27 Israel. 28 Fountain. 29 M25. 30 The Mousetrap.

1 What is the main language spoken in Chile?
2 In which Shakespeare play do we meet two grave diggers?
3 Which Eastern religion includes the caste system?
4 Which prominent US politician was born Madeleine Korbel in Czechoslovakia in the 1930s?
5 What animal lives in a drey?
6 In which African country is the city of Bulawayo?
7 On which river do Rochester, Chatham and Gillingham stand?
8 Who wrote the cookery book "Feast", which featured two large cooking pots on its cover?
9 In which month in 2003 did England triumph to win the Rugby World Cup?
10 Who said, "I never had any problems with drugs, only with policemen"?
11 In the Bible, name the son whom Abraham was asked to sacrifice?
12 Who was the last Roman Catholic king of England?
13 What sort of bird is a Cinnamon Norwich?
14 Winnipeg is the capital of which Canadian province?
15 Of which country was Aldo Moro prime minister?
16 At which battle was Richard III killed?
17 Who wrote the operetta "Bitter Sweet" and the play "Private Lives"?
18 What do we call a group of bishops?
19 Which country does a car come from if it shows CDN as the international registration letters?
20 What part of the body would be affected if you suffered from myopia?
21 What cargo did the ship "Cutty Sark" carry?
22 Who was the mother of the first Queen Elizabeth?
23 What is the name of the famous active volcano on the island of Sicily?
24 Which bird is also the name of a play by Chekhov?
25 Who asked for the head of John the Baptist?
26 Which is the main language spoken in Hungary?
27 Whereabouts on a whale are its flukes?
28 Who succeeded Richard Nixon as president of the United States in 1974?
29 Who is Jaz Elle Agassi's mum?
30 Which important ship canal was built by Ferdinand de Lesseps?

Answers | Pot-Luck 34 *(see Quiz 77)*

1 250th. 2 Arsenal. 3 Lord of War. 4 Laser. 5 For Your Eyes Only. 6 Piano. 7 Montreal. 8 Rhett Butler. 9 Ivan the Terrible. 10 Armed & Fabulous. 11 1931. 12 Giotto. 13 The Mary Rose. 14 John Le Mesurier. 15 Genotype. 16 India. 17 Turned into an insect. 18 Bebop. 19 Stephen Hales. 20 Gigi and My Fair Lady. 21 Loving and giving. 22 Rabbi. 23 Woodford and Woodbridge. 24 Lawyer. 25 Luxor, Egypt. 26 Vibraphone. 27 Jim Carrey. 28 Rudolf Hess. 29 Eric Clapton. 30 Chariots of Fire.

1 Who became Governor of California in 2003?

2 What was the name of the then largest modern art gallery opened by the Queen in 2000?

3 Which was London's first new river crossing for 100 years, opened in 2000?

4 In 2000 who became the first First Lady to join the US Senate?

5 What type of vessel was the Kursk, involved in an accident in 2002?

6 Which broadsheet British newspaper changed to Berliner format in 2005?

7 In which country is Aceh, a region badly devastated by the 2004 tsunami?

8 Which form of London Transport ceased in December 2005?

9 How old was the Queen Mother when she died in 2002?

10 In what month in 2005 were gay 'marriages' allowed through civil partnership registrations?

11 In 2004, which part of the former USSR witnessed an Orange Revolution?

12 Who became Germany's first Chancellor from the former Eastern bloc?

13 An explosion at which oil depot caused the biggest peace time blaze seen in England?

14 Beagle 2 was launched to probe which planet?

15 Mahmoud Abbas replaced whom as leader of the PLO in 2005?

16 How many Popes were there in 2005?

17 The "shed" that won the Turner Prize in 2005 started life as a what?

18 Michael Bloomberg replaced whom as mayor of New York?

19 Which island was the scene of a terrorist attack in 2002?

20 Which Royal Family suffered a mass massacre of its members in June 2001?

21 In May 2005 which record breaker was crowned Laureus World Sportswoman of the Year in Portugal?

22 How many airliners attacked the Pentagon on 11 September 2001?

23 Which tennis star became the man with most Grand Slam tournament titles?

24 Who was the captain of the 2003 Rugby World Cup winners?

25 Which former Northern Ireland and Man United legend died in 2005?

26 Which musical became the first to establish a 20-year West End run?

27 In September 2005 which country pulled out of the Gaza Strip?

28 What type of memorial to Princess Diana was built in Hyde Park?

29 Which road carried Britain's first 12-lane stretch of motorway?

30 Which stage show clocked up a 50-year run in London's West End?

| **Answers** | TV: Sci Fi *(see Quiz 78)* |

1 Time And Relative Dimensions In Space. 2 The Matrix. 3 Quantum Leap. 4 Astronaut. 5 Sapphire and Steel. 6 Invisible. 7 Rose. 8 Adam Adamant. 9 Fireball XL5. 10 Space. 11 The Doctor. 12 Batman. 13 Frazer Hines. 14 James Tiberius. 15 Wonder Woman. 16 Andromeda. 17 Half man, half fish. 18 Catweazle. 19 Government department. 20 Blake's Seven. 21 Quatermass. 22 The Next Generation. 23 Battlestar Galactica. 24 Exterminate. 25 Green. 26 Captain Scarlet and the Mysterons. 27 V. 28 Tracy. 29 Survivors. 30 Submarine.

1 When a cow stands up, which legs does it get up on first?
2 Who sang "On the good ship Lollipop"?
3 According to the proverb, what is the better part of valour?
4 How many teams started the Euro 2004 tournament in Portugal?
5 The oil storage terminal at Buncefield, scene of a major explosion, was near which English town?
6 From which London railway station do you normally travel to Bristol?
7 In which film is the Harry Lime theme?
8 Which American city is named after a British prime minister?
9 Where would you find a dead man's handle?
10 Who wrote the Orange Prize-winning book "Small Island"?
11 On which river does swan-upping take place?
12 Which country lies immediately east of Iraq?
13 Which London building is nicknamed "Ally Pally"?
14 Who claimed that "History is Bunk"?
15 In which English city is the cathedral known as "Paddy's Wigwam"?
16 From which port was the bulk of the British Expeditionary Force in France evacuated in 1940?
17 Which architect designed New York's Guggenheim Museum?
18 Who wrote "Gulliver's Travels"?
19 In which city was General Gordon put to death?
20 What kind of animal is a pipistrelle?
21 According to the proverb which fruit tastes sweetest?
22 What was the name for the ancient Egyptian good luck charm in the shape of a beetle?
23 Who was Spain's first ever F1 World Champion?
24 Who said "Father, I cannot tell a lie"?
25 Nitrous oxide is more commonly known as which gas?
26 In German fable who sold his soul to Mephistopheles?
27 What do Bluebell, the Watercress, and the Severn Valley all have in common?
28 What is Freddie Starr's real name?
29 Which sport did David Duckham play?
30 Which major political figure became MP for Witney in 2001?

Answers	**Pot-Luck 37** *(see Quiz 83)*

1 Slander. 2 July. 3 Jet. 4 The Crusades. 5 1961. 6 Newfoundland. 7 Aardvark.
8 Dr Crippen. 9 Tom & Jerry. 10 Can-can. 11 Susan Hill. 12 All work and no play.
13 Daisy. 14 House of Lords. 15 Bulgaria. 16 Sikh. 17 Mushrooms or toadstools.
18 Canada. 19 Equipment. 20 Marchioness. 21 Tunisia. 22 The Salvation Army. 23 Joshua. 24 Coldplay. 25 Tasman Sea. 26 Limited. 27 Grapefruit. 28 Heart surgery.
29 Ernest. 30 The Dam Busters.

1 Which Rio-based club is named after a Portuguese navigator?
2 Which Japanese city is home to Grampus Eight?
3 Who was dubbed "El Beatle" by fans in Portugal?
4 On which day of the week do the Spanish usually play football?
5 Former Celtic favourite Henrik Larsson represented which country?
6 Which Dutch side play their games in the Philips Stadium?
7 Which country does Michael Essien play for?
8 Which country was in three of the first four European finals?
9 Which city is home to Racing Club and River Plate?
10 At which ground do the Republic of Ireland play home games?
11 Which former goalie coached both Juventus and Lazio?
12 In which European country are the headquarters of UEFA?
13 Who did England play in their final 2006 World Cup Group qualifier?
14 Where did Aston Villa win the European Cup in 1982?
15 Where in France is the ground known as Le Stadium?
16 Who scored two goals in the 2002 Final of the World Cup?
17 Who was FIFA World Footballer of the Year in 1998, 2000 and 2003?
18 In what year was the first ever European Cup match played?
19 Who was the first manager to coach both Australia and England?
20 Independiente are a leading club in which country?
21 Which side beat Arsenal in the 1995 European Cup Winners' Cup with a goal in the last minute of extra time?
22 In which country was the 1992 European Championship staged?
23 Name the the beaten finalists in the 1994 World Cup final?
24 2003 was the year that which English ground first hosted a European Champion Clubs' Cup Final?
25 Figo, Raul and Zidane played together at which club?
26 Who won the Club World Championship final in 2005?
27 Which was the first British team to lift the European Cup after a penalty shoot-out?
28 Alfredo di Stefano played international football for three countries – Argentina, Spain and which other country?
29 Which item of kit was made compulsory by FIFA in 1990?
30 Who is the only player to score a hat-trick in a World Cup final?

| **Answers** | **Trouble Spots** (see Quiz 84) |

1 Shah of Iran. **2** Afghanistan. **3** Kenya. **4** Six Days. **5** Jackie Mann. **6** General Belgrano. **7** Hungary. **8** Nicaragua. **9** Nasser. **10** Bay of Pigs. **11** Algeria. **12** Canary Wharf. **13** Palestine Liberation Organization. **14** Zimbabwe (Southern Rhodesia). **15** Corazón Aquino. **16** Gulf War. **17** Cyprus. **18** Iraq. **19** Korean War. **20** Martin Luther King, Robert Kennedy. **21** China. **22** Vietnam. **23** Galtieri. **24** Nigeria. **25** South Africa. **26** Prague's. **27** France. **28** Entebbe airport. **29** Yugoslavia. **30** Tiananmen.

1 If libel is a written defamation, what is oral defamation?
2 On which month in 2005 was it announced that London had won its bid to host the 2012 Olympics?
3 Which word can go after jumbo and before black?
4 What name was given to the mediaeval warlike expeditions to the Holy Land?
5 In which year was the first manned space flight?
6 In Canada, of which province is St John's the capital?
7 Which animal's name literally means "earth pig"?
8 Who was the first major criminal to be arrested as a result of the use of radio?
9 Who made their screen debut in "Puss in Boots"?
10 Which dance is usually performed to "Orpheus in the Underworld"?
11 Who wrote the novel which formed the basis for the play "The Woman in Black"?
12 According to the proverb what makes Jack a dull boy?
13 Of which flower is ox-eye a type?
14 In Britain which is the ultimate court of appeal?
15 Which country did tennis-playing sisters Katerina and Manuela Maleeva come from?
16 Amritsar is a holy city for the followers of which religion?
17 What are ink-caps, death caps and puffballs all types of?
18 Which country was once called New France?
19 What does the second E in the acronym ERNIE stand for?
20 What is the wife of a marquis called?
21 In which country is the ruined city of Carthage?
22 Which religious body publishes a magazine called "The War Cry"?
23 In the Bible, who led the Israelites to the Battle of Jericho?
24 Who won the Best UK and Ireland award at the 2005 MTV Awards?
25 Which sea lies between New Zealand and Australia?
26 The initials plc stand for what type of public company?
27 What is the common name for the fruit Citrus grandis?
28 Sir Magdi Yacoub is an expert in which field?
29 What was Sergeant Bilko's first name?
30 What daring raid was led by Guy Gibson?

Answers Pot-Luck 36 (see Quiz 81)

1 Back. 2 Shirley Temple. 3 Discretion. 4 16. 5 Hemel Hempstead. 6 Paddington. 7 The Third Man. 8 Pittsburgh. 9 In an electric train, tube train. 10 Andrea Levy. 11 The Thames. 12 Iran. 13 Alexandra Palace. 14 Henry Ford. 15 Liverpool. 16 Dunkirk. 17 Frank Lloyd Wright. 18 Jonathan Swift. 19 Khartoum. 20 A bat. 21 Forbidden fruit. 22 The scarab. 23 Fernando Alonso. 24 George Washington. 25 Laughing gas. 26 Faust. 27 Railways. 28 Freddie Starr. 29 Rugby Union. 30 David Cameron.

1 Who fled his "Peacock Throne" into exile in 1979?
2 Where did the mujahideen resist Soviet attack?
3 Which country was the scene of the Mau Mau rebellion in the 1950s?
4 How long did the Arab-Israeli War of 1967 last?
5 Which English World War II veteran was a Beirut kidnap victim?
6 Which Argentinian cruiser was sunk outside an exclusion zone during the Falklands War?
7 Where did Russian troops crush an anti-Soviet uprising in 1956?
8 Where did the Sandinistas overthrow the government in 1979?
9 Who was president of Egypt during the Suez Crisis in 1956?
10 In which Bay was there a failed attempt by exiled Cubans to invade Cuba?
11 Where in North Africa did a war for independence take place between 1954 and 1962?
12 In 1996, where in London was an IRA bomb planted to end a ceasefire?
13 In the Middle East conflict what does PLO stand for?
14 Where did ZANU and ZAPU fight for independence?
15 Who ousted Ferdinand Marcos as president of the Philippines?
16 In which war was Operation Desert Storm?
17 Where did Greeks and Turks clash in major unrest in 1964?
18 Who fought against Iran in the 1980–88 conflict?
19 Which war was fought along the 38th parallel?
20 Which two public figures were assassinated in the United States in 1968?
21 Where in the 1960s was there a Cultural Revolution?
22 In which country did the My Lai massacre take place?
23 Who was the Argentinian president during the Falklands conflict?
24 Biafra was a breakaway state from which African country?
25 In which country did Steve Biko die in detention ?
26 Which city's "Spring" was ended by a Soviet invasion in 1968?
27 Whom did Vietnam gain independence from in 1954?
28 Where in Uganda was a hijacked Air France plane stormed in 1976?
29 Which country disintegrated following the outbreak of civil war in 1992?
30 In which Peking square were pro-democracy demos violently suppressed?

Answers | **World Soccer** *(see Quiz 82)*

1 Vasco da Gama. 2 Nagoya. 3 George Best. 4 Sunday. 5 Sweden. 6 PSV Eindhoven. 7 Ghana. 8 USSR. 9 Buenos Aires. 10 Lansdowne Road. 11 Dino Zoff. 12 Switzerland. 13 Poland. 14 Rotterdam. 15 Toulouse. 16 Ronaldo. 17 Zinedine Zidane. 18 1955. 19 Terry Venables. 20 Argentina. 21 Zaragoza. 22 Sweden. 23 Italy. 24 Old Trafford. 25 Real Madrid. 26 Sao Paulo (Brazil). 27 Liverpool. 28 Colombia. 29 Shin guard. 30 Geoff Hurst.

1 Which novel is about a boy called Billy Casper who trains a hawk?
2 Martina Navratilova won most doubles trophies with which partner?
3 With what is Threadneedle Street associated?
4 In which art has Beryl Grey achieved fame?
5 Who lives in a kraal?
6 Who was the first female to get the top job of director general of MI5?
7 What colour is angelica?
8 With which country is the famous soldier Robert Clive associated?
9 What happens in a vortex?
10 To which section of the orchestra does the tuba belong?
11 In the song, who stuck a feather in his hat called macaroni?
12 What was the first Ealing Comedy?
13 Whom did George W. Bush appoint as Secretary of Defence in 2001?
14 In which sporting event does the winning team move backwards?
15 What is a fandango?
16 Eau-de-nil is a shade of what colour?
17 Which revolution began in 1917?
18 Who is said to have introduced the habit of smoking into this country?
19 After seven which is the next highest prime number?
20 In boxing at what weight do you fight if you weigh over 12 stone 7 pounds?
21 Who wrote the novel "Jane Eyre"?
22 In 1990 and 1991 Matthew Pinsent rowed for which winning Boat Race crews?
23 Which author wrote "The Flood" and "Mortal Causes"?
24 In which country were turkeys first found?
25 What is a carillon?
26 How many moves are there in a chess game in which White opens and wins with Fool's Mate?
27 In which month each year is Battle of Britain week?
28 In a bullfight who kills the bull?
29 What size of bottle is a magnum?
30 What is David Frost's middle name?

| **Answers** | **Pot-Luck 39** *(see Quiz 87)* |

1 Genesis. 2 A space. 3 Crab. 4 Richard Burton. 5 Belgium. 6 The Importance of Being Earnest. 7 In your foot. 8 Renee Zellwegger. 9 Places of the same height. 10 The parson. 11 Beauty. 12 Laurel and Hardy. 13 Swan. 14 B. 15 Joe Louis. 16 China. 17 British admirals. 18 Long-distance running. 19 Charles. 20 The Merchant of Venice. 21 At the base of the neck. 22 Spain. 23 Sahara. 24 P. D. James. 25 To smell. 26 Ronnie Barker. 27 72 (accept 65–79). 28 Wimbledon. 29 Toyota. 30 New Year's Eve.

1 Who was known as "Gentleman Jim"?
2 Which country anthem starts "Sometimes it's hard to be a woman"?
3 Which John Denver song did Peter, Paul and Mary take into the charts?
4 Which Dolly Parton song was a chart hit for Whitney Houston?
5 Which country music legend died in 2003 at the age of 71?
6 Which country star had a hit with "Kiss an Angel Good Morning"?
7 Which singer/songwriter penned "The Last Thing on My Mind"?
8 Which country star has had five husbands, including George Jones, and been kidnapped?
9 Which group was fronted by singer/songwriter Dave Cousins?
10 Which folk singer was called "Judas" for going electric?
11 Which city in eastern England has been the venue for a long-standing folk festival?
12 Who wrote "Your Cheatin' Heart"?
13 Which Rochdale Cowboy was a 1970s folk club favourite?
14 Who recorded the album "No Fences"?
15 Who is the long-time lead singer with Steeleye Span?
16 Who declared "Thank God I'm a Country Boy"?
17 In what language was Fairport Convention's only English hit sung?
18 Which guitarist teamed up with Mark Knopfler on "Neck and Neck"?
19 Who wrote US dust-bowl songs and "This Land is Your Land"?
20 How did Patsy Cline die?
21 Who took "There But for Fortune" into the UK single charts?
22 Under what name did Brenda Gail Webb become famous?
23 Who wrote the folk club classic "Streets Of London"?
24 Who wrote "Where Have All the Flowers Gone"?
25 How is Alexandra Denny better known?
26 Who recorded the album "Shotgun Willie"?
27 How are the trio of Yarrow, Stookey and Travers better known?
28 Who was on "Honky Tonk Angels" with Dolly Parton and Tammy Wynette?
29 Which Latin carol gave Steeleye Span a chart hit?
30 Which boy with a girl's name did Johnny Cash sing about?

Answers	**Action Movies** *(see Quiz 88)*

1 Long Island. 2 Sean Connery. 3 Bruce Willis. 4 The Godfather. 5 Superman. 6 The Philosopher's Stone. 7 The architect. 8 Dr No. 9 The Return of the King. 10 Lee Van Cleef. 11 Raiders of the Lost Ark. 12 William Wallace. 13 Chicago. 14 Stallone. 15 Live and Let Die. 16 Daniel Day-Lewis. 17 David Lean. 18 Patriot Games. 19 Directing. 20 On Her Majesty's Secret Service. 21 Robert De Niro. 22 Unforgiven. 23 Faye Dunaway. 24 Kathleen Turner. 25 Car chase. 26 The Spy Who Loved Me. 27 True Grit. 28 Dirty Harry. 29 Liam Neeson. 30 Lois Maxwell.

1 Which book of the Bible tells us about the creation of the world?
2 What is a lacuna?
3 Edible, blue and hermit are all types of which creature?
4 Who played Thomas à Becket to Peter O'Toole's Henry II?
5 In which country is Waterloo, site of the Napoleonic battlefield?
6 In which play does Miss Prism appear?
7 Where is the metatarsal arch?
8 Which actress played opposite Russell Crowe in the movie "Cinderella Man"?
9 On a map, which places are joined by a contour?
10 In the song, which official is waiting "for me and my gal"?
11 What is pulchritude?
12 Which film comedians are associated with the phrase, "That's another fine mess you got me in"?
13 Which creature's song refers to a final speech or performance?
14 Which letter of the alphabet is used to describe a soft lead pencil?
15 Who was nicknamed the Brown Bomber?
16 In which country were there originally mandarins?
17 Who or what are Effingham, Grenville, Benbow and Collingwood?
18 For which sport is Gordon Pirie remembered?
19 What was Buddy Holly's real first name?
20 Which of Shakespeare's plays involves a pound of flesh?
21 Where are your clavicles?
22 A lady would wear a mantilla in which country?
23 In area, which is the world's largest desert?
24 First published in October 2005, who wrote the novel "The Lighthouse"?
25 What do your olfactory organs help you do?
26 Which comic actor who died in 2005 used the pseudonym Gerald Wiley as a writer?
27 To within a margin of seven more or less, what is a grown man's normal pulse rate in beats per minute?
28 What was Venus Williams' first tennis Grand Slam title?
29 Which motor company developed the Pivo, which can swivel to assist when parking?
30 Which festival is called Saint Sylvestre or San Silvestro in certain countries?

Answers | Pot-Luck 38 (see Quiz 85)

1 Kestrel for a Knave, by Barry Hines (Kes). 2 Pam Shriver. 3 Bank of England. 4 Ballet (dance). 5 A Zulu. 6 Stella Rimington. 7 Green. 8 India. 9 Everything swirls around. 10 Brass. 11 Yankee Doodle. 12 Passport to Pimlico. 13 Donald Rumsfeld. 14 Tug of war. 15 Dance. 16 Green/blue-green. 17 Russian Revolution. 18 Sir Walter Raleigh. 19 Eleven. 20 Heavyweight. 21 Charlotte Brontë. 22 Oxford. 23 Ian Rankin. 24 North America. 25 Set of bells. 26 7. 27 September. 28 Matador. 29 Holds two ordinary bottles. 30 Paradine.

1 Off which island is "Jaws" set?
2 Who played Harrison Ford's father in "Indiana Jones and the Last Crusade"?
3 Who is the cop battling with terrorists in "Die Hard"?
4 Which films are about the Corleone family?
5 What is Christopher Reeve's most famous role?
6 What is the name of the gem Harry Potter is looking for in the first Harry Potter movie?
7 In "Towering Inferno" Steve McQueen was the fireman: what was Paul Newman?
8 Which was the first Bond movie?
9 What was the final Lord of the Rings movie called?
10 Who was Bad in Spaghetti Westerns?
11 Which was the first of the "Indiana Jones" films to be released?
12 Which hero did Mel Gibson play in "Braveheart"?
13 In which city is "The Untouchables" set?
14 Who was involved in the writing of the "Rocky" and "Rambo" films?
15 Which was the first Bond film with Roger Moore?
16 Who played the starring role in "Last of the Mohicans"?
17 Who directed "Lawrence of Arabia"?
18 Which film starred Harrison Ford as an ex-CIA man?
19 For what did Kevin Costner win an Oscar in "Dances with Wolves"?
20 Which was George Lazenby's only Bond film?
21 Who starred as Jake La Motta in "Raging Bull"?
22 Which Clint Eastwood film won an Oscar for Gene Hackman as the sheriff of Big Whiskey?
23 Who played Bonnie to Warren Beatty's Clyde?
24 Who co-starred with Michael Douglas in "Romancing the Stone"?
25 What was the memorable, and at that time innovative, scene in "Bullitt"?
26 Which Bond film had the song "Nobody Does It Better"?
27 In which film did John Wayne win his only Oscar?
28 Which movie preceded "Magnum Force" and "The Enforcer"?
29 Who plays the title role in "Rob Roy"?
30 Who plays Miss Moneypenny in the early Bond films?

Answers	**Folk and Country** *(see Quiz 86)*

1 Jim Reeves. 2 Stand by Your Man. 3 Leaving on a Jet Plane. 4 I Will Always Love You. 5 Johnny Cash. 6 Charlie Pride. 7 Tom Paxton. 8 Tammy Wynette. 9 The Strawbs. 10 Bob Dylan. 11 Cambridge. 12 Hank Williams. 13 Mike Harding. 14 Garth Brooks. 15 Maddy Prior. 16 John Denver. 17 French. 18 Chet Atkins. 19 Woody Guthrie. 20 In an air crash. 21 Joan Baez. 22 Crystal Gayle. 23 Ralph McTell. 24 Pete Seeger. 25 Sandy Denny. 26 Willie Nelson. 27 Peter, Paul, Mary. 28 Loretta Lynn. 29 Gaudete. 30 Sue.

1 Which country has been officially called Myanmar since 1989?
2 Which country is made up of over 800 islands including Viti Levu?
3 Which desert covers part of China and Mongolia?
4 What title does the head of state of Nepal have?
5 Which 7000-island country lies in the Pacific, northeast of the South China Sea?
6 How is the Republic of China better known?
7 To which country does East Timor belong?
8 Which neighbouring countries' currency is the won?
9 What was the name of Bangladesh between 1947 and 1972?
10 In which country are the Cameron Highlands?
11 What are the majority of the islands of Micronesia composed of?
12 Which country is bordered by Laos, Vietnam and Thailand?
13 Which sea lies to the north of Iran?
14 What is Japan's highest mountain?
15 How many vowels are there in Kyrgyzstan?
16 Which country's official name in Hindi is Bharat?
17 What are China's famous "warriors" made from?
18 Which country's capital is Ulan Bator?
19 In which two countries is the Thar desert?
20 Which social system is divided into brahmins, ksatriyas vaisyas and sundras?
21 Where were Gurkhas originally from?
22 Which area of Russia has had the lowest temperatures in the world recorded there?
23 When "The Sound of Music" was shown in Korea what was missing?
24 What are the Seychelles' three official languages?
25 What is the capital of Singapore?
26 Which country's flag is a red circle on a green background?
27 Which Pacific islands share their name with a wise man in the Bible?
28 What did Ho Chi Minh City used to be called?
29 Which country has designated Chachoengsao as its new capital?
30 How many rivers does Tonga have?

Answers	**Around Scotland** *(see Quiz 91)*

1 Distillery. 2 Sir Walter Scott. 3 Southwest. 4 Extinct volcano. 5 Bird sanctuary. 6 St Giles Cathedral. 7 Bute. 8 Holyrood House. 9 Aberdeen. 10 Nuclear power. 11 Two. 12 Princes Street. 13 Glamis Castle. 14 Silicon Glen. 15 Caledonian Canal. 16 Iona. 17 Meadowbank. 18 Tay Bridge. 19 Bell's. 20 Blair Castle. 21 Fingal's Cave. 22 Scone Palace. 23 Loch Ness. 24 Perth. 25 Culloden. 26 Dee. 27 Abbeys. 28 Stone Age. 29 Loch Lomond. 30 Tomatin.

1 Of which country is Freetown the capital?
2 What is the term for a group of partridges?
3 What was the occupation of the legendary "Casey Jones"?
4 According to the proverb what is the mother of invention?
5 What is an area of water separated from the open sea by a coral reef?
6 How many countries starting with a letter J reached Euro 2004 in Portugal?
7 In the London theatre what is the longest-running play ever?
8 Which actor played Nicole Kidman's husband in the movie "The Stepford Wives"?
9 In astronomy what are falling stars properly called?
10 What are Hickling, Barton, and Breydon Water?
11 In 1989, which electronic giant bought Columbia Pictures?
12 What is meant by the Italian phrase "che sara sara"?
13 What does an American mean when he talks of a check in a restaurant?
14 Whom might you expect to see working in a dig?
15 If a ship runs up a yellow flag what does it mean?
16 Which is the smallest bird in the world?
17 Which Saint's day falls on 30 November?
18 In fiction who lived in the stables at Birtwick Hall?
19 Who was Oberon?
20 Which name is shared by David Beckham and Kevin Keegan?
21 In cookery, what is meant by coddling?
22 Which trade is especially likely to use an awl?
23 Who played President Bartlet in "West Wing"?
24 In World War II on what were we "going to hang out the washing"?
25 In which city was there formerly a parliament building called the Reichstag?
26 In which London building is the Whispering Gallery?
27 Which duo have produced songs for Tottenham Hotspur?
28 Who became President of Ireland in 1997?
29 What name was given to an airship that could be steered?
30 What was Darkness's follow up album to "Permission to Land"?

Answers | Pot-Luck 41 *(see Quiz 92)*

1 35p. 2 Powys. 3 Arsenal. 4 On a staircase. 5 Naturalist, entomologist. 6 Archbishop of Canterbury. 7 81. 8 Loudspeakers. 9 Bury St Edmunds, Suffolk. 10 In a low voice. 11 Atlantic. 12 Wagons, carts. 13 Rosary. 14 Leonardo. 15 Postage stamps. 16 It turns blue. 17 Margaret Mitchell. 18 Gerald Durrell. 19 Anatomy. 20 Seizure of power. 21 Clown (mime). 22 Revelation. 23 Anna Ford. 24 At right angles. 25 Venezuela. 26 Birmingham. 27 Brussels. 28 Channel Islands. 29 Michael Caine. 30 Teacher.

1 Edradour is the smallest what in Scotland?
2 Which famous Scottish writer lived at Abbotsford by the Tweed?
3 In which direction from Edinburgh do the Pentland Hills lie?
4 What is Berwick Law?
5 What is the Bass Rock famous as?
6 Which cathedral is also known as the High Kirk of Edinburgh?
7 Rothesay is the chief town of which island?
8 What is at the foot of the Royal Mile in Edinburgh?
9 Which city is at the mouth of the rivers Don and Dee?
10 What is produced at Torness?
11 How many bridges are there over the Firth of Forth?
12 What lies between Charlotte Square and St Andrew's Square?
13 Where was the childhood home of the Queen Mother?
14 What is the industrial area in and around Livingston nicknamed?
15 Which canal links the lochs of the Great Glen?
16 Which historic island is off the southwest tip of the Isle of Mull?
17 What is the name of Edinburgh's stadium where the Commonwealth Games have been held?
18 Which rail bridge is the longest in Europe?
19 Which famous whisky is made at Blair Athol?
20 Which baronial castle is the seat of the only British subject allowed to maintain his own private army?
21 What is the most famous cave on Staffa?
22 Which palace was once the site of a famous coronation stone?
23 Which loch contains the largest volume of fresh water in the British Isles?
24 Which city is often called the Fair City?
25 Leanach farmhouse can be seen on which moorland field of battle?
26 On which river does Balmoral stand?
27 Remains of what type of building are at Kelso and Jedburgh?
28 What type of village can be seen at Skara Brae?
29 Which loch is the largest stretch of inland water in Britain?
30 Where is Scotland's largest malt whisky distillery?

Answers	**Around Asia** *(see Quiz 89)*

1 Burma. 2 Fiji. 3 Gobi. 4 King. 5 Philippines. 6 Taiwan. 7 Indonesia.
8 North and South Korea. 9 East Pakistan. 10 Malaysia. 11 Coral. 12 Cambodia. 13 Caspian. 14 Mount Fujiyama. 15 One. 16 India. 17 Terracotta. 18 Mongolia's. 19 India and Pakistan. 20 Caste system. 21 Nepal. 22 Siberia. 23 Music. 24 English, French and Creole. 25 Singapore. 26 Bangladesh. 27 Solomon Islands. 28 Saigon. 29 Thailand. 30 None.

1 If VAT is 17.5% what is the VAT on an item costing £2?
2 In which county are the Brecon Beacons?
3 Emmanuel Petit was at which English club when he scored in a World Cup final?
4 Where would you find treads and risers close together?
5 As what did Henri Fabre achieve fame?
6 Whose official residence is Lambeth Palace?
7 How many individual squares are there in a standard Sudoku puzzle?
8 What are woofers and tweeters?
9 Restored in the 21st century, in which town is St Edmundsbury Cathedral?
10 What is meant by "sotto voce"?
11 In which ocean is the Sargasso Sea?
12 What are made by wainwrights?
13 What do Catholics call the string of beads they use when praying?
14 Who painted the most famous version of "The Last Supper"?
15 What is the subject matter covered by a Gibbons's catalogue?
16 What happens when red litmus paper is put in an alkaline solution?
17 Who wrote the novel "Gone with the Wind"?
18 Which naturalist is the author of "My Family and Other Animals"?
19 What word is used for the science dealing with the body structure?
20 What is a coup d'état?
21 As what kind of entertainer did Grock achieve fame?
22 Which is the last book of the Bible?
23 Which TV newsreader was married to cartoonist Mark Boxer?
24 How do bevel gears engage with one another?
25 Of which country is Caracas the capital?
26 Which soccer side plays at St Andrews?
27 In which capital is the statue of a small boy, the Mannekin Pis?
28 Where, today, would you find a bailiwick?
29 Which actor played Dr Larch in "The Cider House Rules"?
30 Before becoming famous, what was opera star Katherine Jenkins' profession?

Answers | Pot-Luck 40 *(see Quiz 90)*

1 Sierra Leone. 2 A covey. 3 Railroad engineer. 4 Necessity. 5 Lagoon. 6 None.
7 The Mousetrap. 8 Matthew Broderick. 9 Meteors. 10 Norfolk Broads. 11 Sony.
12 What ever will be, will be. 13 The bill. 14 Archaeologist. 15 No disease aboard, and it needs clearance. 16 Hummingbird. 17 St Andrew. 18 Black Beauty. 19 King of the fairies. 20 Joseph. 21 Simmering briefly. 22 Leather worker/shoemaker. 23 Martin Sheen. 24 Siegfried Line. 25 Berlin. 26 St Paul's. 27 Chas & Dave. 28 Mary McAleese. 29 Dirigible. 30 One Way Ticket to Hell... and Back.

1 What is the common name for the antirrhinum?
2 Which hanging basket favourite is also called pelargonium?
3 What qualities do the flowers helichrysum and acroclinium have?
4 By what name is Solidago known?
5 What type of bell is a campanula?
6 Which yellow, pink-flushed rose was bred by Meilland in 1945?
7 Which wild flower is also known as the knapweed?
8 Which flower has rung-like leaflets?
9 What would you find in an anther on a stamen?
10 What is the common name for the plant Impatiens?
11 Which flowers are said to symbolize the Crucifixion?
12 Which flower, also called chalk plant or baby's breath, is a favourite with flower arrangers ?
13 Bachelor's buttons are a variety of which yellow wild flower?
14 Which flower's seeds are pickled to make capers?
15 Which animals love nepeta, giving the latter its common name?
16 What sort of hyacinth is a muscari?
17 Which flower – Lychnis – shares its name with a fictional detective?
18 Which two flowers would you find in an orchestra?
19 Which flower gets its name from a Persian or Turkish word for turban?
20 Which plant is grown not for its flowers but for its silvery seed pods?
21 Which family do azaleas belong to?
22 Jonquils are members of which family?
23 Which plant is also called the torch lily?
24 Which climbing plant has the variety Nelly Moser?
25 Which flower's foundation varieties are alba, gallica and damascena?
26 Which plant was named after the Greek goddess of the rainbow?
27 What sort of purplish-blue daisies are types of aster?
28 Which bloom's name means golden flower, although it can be many different colours?
29 What colour is the rose Silver Jubilee?
30 Which country sent the first dahlia seeds to Europe?

Answers	Pop: Worldwide *(see Quiz 96)*

1 Switzerland. 2 Greece. 3 Germany. 4 Italy. 5 Norway. 6 Germany. 7 José Carreras. 8 Dannii. 9 Montserrat Caballé. 10 Denmark. 11 Jason Donovan. 12 Ireland. 13 Jamaica. 14 France. 15 Two Little Boys. 16 Eddy Grant. 17 Chariots of Fire. 18 Chris de Burgh. 19 Perez Prado. 20 Boyzone. 21 Riverdance. 22 Yoko Ono. 23 West Indies. 24 Boogie. 25 Placido Domingo. 26 Sweden. 27 Maurice, Jean-Michel. 28 Sinead O'Connor. 29 Je t'aime. 30 España.

1 ICBM stands for Inter-Continental what?
2 What was a matchlock?
3 In which TV show did creatures cry "Exterminate!"?
4 What is the male equivalent of a ranee?
5 In chemistry, what is a substance which cannot be split into simpler substances?
6 According to the Germans, who were the 'Ladies from Hell'?
7 Who created "Till Death Us Do Part"?
8 In "Two Little Boys", what did each boy have that was wooden?
9 Which American rodent builds dams and fells trees?
10 In which river was Jesus Christ baptized?
11 In which Shakespeare play does a forest apparently move?
12 What do Americans call a pack of cards?
13 Who were the beaten finalists when France first won the World Cup?
14 What was the name of the first nuclear-powered submarine?
15 Who played Tony Blair on television in "A Very Social Secretary"?
16 Which word can go after funny and before china?
17 If you were driving at 50 miles per hour, at how many kilometres per hour would you be going (approximately)?
18 Which English king died at the age of 15?
19 In which sport are stones and a broom used?
20 Which surname links a Spice Girl and the first US Vice President?
21 Of which country was John George Diefenbaker prime minister?
22 In which language did Aristophanes write his plays?
23 Of which country was Archbishop Makarios prime minister?
24 Which member of U2 has the real name of Paul Hewson?
25 Of which US state is Little Rock the capital?
26 Which part of the body is described by the word labial?
27 In which West Country city is the railway station St David's?
28 For which country did Dennis Law play soccer?
29 Who created the Rebus novels?
30 Who was the youngest member of England's Rugby World Cup-winning squad in 2003?

Answers | Pot-Luck 43 (see Quiz 97)

1 Eros. 2 Green. 3 Friday. 4 Sailing/yachting. 5 Flyweight. 6 Sheep. 7 David Lloyd George. 8 Christine Keeler. 9 Sean Penn. 10 Yellow. 11 Karl Jenkins. 12 El Dorado. 13 Bank manager. 14 Dark blue. 15 La Paz. 16 Sculpture. 17 Ireland. 18 Hymn book. 19 Raven. 20 Astro. 21 Netherlands. 22 Colorado river. 23 Archery. 24 Femur. 25 Atlantic. 26 Kookaburra. 27 Greyfriars. 28 Calvary or Golgotha. 29 Colin Montgomerie. 30 Polo.

1 Which is the oldest British flat classic race?
2 Which jockey won the Derby, Oaks and St Leger in 2001?
3 Which jockey riding Shergar in 1981 won in his first Derby ride?
4 Which jockey won the Prix de l'Arc de Triomphe from 1985 to 1987 on three different horses?
5 Where did Britain's first evening meeting take place?
6 Who rode Henbit, Nashwan and Erhaab to Derby victories?
7 Which horse, in 1977, became the first to win the Mackeson and Hennessy in the same season?
8 Which horse had a hat-trick of wins in the Cheltenham Gold Cup from 2002 to 2004?
9 Who was the first woman to ride a winner over fences in Britain?
10 In 1925 at Windsor, bookmakers went on strike. Against what?
11 Where was the Derby held during the two World Wars?
12 On which course in Australia is the Melbourne Cup run?
13 Which jockey had most Classic wins before Lester Piggott?
14 Which was the first racecourse equipped with a photo-finish camera?
15 On which horse did Princess Anne win her first flat race?
16 Diomed was the first winner of which great race?
17 Which race came first, the 1000 Guineas or 2000 Guineas?
18 What is Dick Hern's real first name?
19 Who was Champion National Hunt jockey for four years before the new millennium and four after it?
20 Where is the Happy Valley racecourse?
21 What is the first name of Peter Scudamore's father?
22 In betting, how much is a monkey?
23 In which Surrey town is Sandown racecourse?
24 Lester Piggott shares his birthday with which annual event?
25 In which country did Steve Donoghue ride his first winner?
26 What is the real first name of Richard Dunwoody?
27 Son of a famous father, who had his first winner at Kempton in 1978?
28 Who won the Derby on Kris Kin in 2003 and North Light in 2004?
29 How many individual bets make up a Yankee?
30 How many Grand Nationals did Desert Orchid win?

Answers	**Nature: Flowers** *(see Quiz 93)*

1 Snapdragon. 2 Geranium. 3 Everlasting. 4 Golden Rod. 5 Canterbury bell. 6 Peace. 7 Cornflower. 8 Jacob's ladder. 9 Pollen. 10 Busy Lizzie. 11 Passion flower. 12 Gypsophila. 13 Buttercups. 14 Nasturtium. 15 Cats (Catmint). 16 Grape hyacinth. 17 Campion. 18 Viola, Bugle. 19 Tulip (tuliban). 20 Honesty. 21 Rhododendron. 22 Narcissus. 23 Red hot poker. 24 Clematis. 25 Rose. 26 Iris. 27 Michaelmas daisy. 28 Chrysanthemum. 29 Pink. 30 Mexico.

1 Whom did Celine Dion represent in the 1988 Eurovision Song Contest?
2 What is Demis Roussos' home country?
3 Which country does James Last come from?
4 U Got 2 Know where Cappella are from, do you?
5 Their first No 1 was "The Sun Always Shines on TV". Where were they from?
6 Members of Los Bravos were from Spain and from where else?
7 Which opera singer had a hit with "Amigos Para Siempre" (Friends for Life) in 1992?
8 Which Minogue sister had a hit with "Love and Kisses"?
9 Who duetted with Freddie Mercury on "Barcelona"?
10 Where does Whigfield hail from?
11 Which Australian had three consecutive No 1s between December 1988 and June 1989?
12 Which country won the Eurovision Song Contest in 1992, 1993 and 1994?
13 Which country are Bob and Ziggy Marley associated with?
14 Where is 70s chart topper Charles Aznavour from?
15 Which Rolf Harris record went to No 1 in 1969?
16 Who said "I Don't Wanna Dance" in 1982?
17 Which film theme gave Vangelis a hit in 1981?
18 Who was "Missing You" in 1988?
19 Who had a hit with "Guaglione" nearly 40 years after his first No 1?
20 Which Irish group sang "Love Me for a Reason" in 1994?
21 Which song and show started as a Eurovision interval filler?
22 Which famous widow was "Walking on Thin Ice" in 1981?
23 From which island group did Boney M hail?
24 In 1977 Baccara said "Yes, Sir, I Can..." what?
25 Who sang "Perhaps Love" with John Denver?
26 Whom did Abba win Eurovision for in 1974?
27 What are the first names of father and son musicians Jarre?
28 Whose first No 1 was "Nothing Compares 2 U"?
29 What was Jane Birkin and Serge Gainsbourg's famous recording?
30 Swedish Sylvia sang "Y Viva" where?

Answers | Pot-Luck 42 *(see Quiz 94)*

1 Ballistic missile. 2 Gun. 3 Dr Who. 4 Rajah. 5 Element. 6 Scottish Highland soldiers in kilts. 7 Johnny Speight. 8 Horse. 9 Beaver. 10 The Jordan. 11 Macbeth. 12 A deck. 13 Brazil. 14 Nautilus (in 1955). 15 Robert Lindsay. 16 Bone. 17 80 kilometres per hour. 18 Edward VI. 19 Curling. 20 Adams (Victoria and John). 21 Canada. 22 Greek. 23 Cyprus. 24 Bono. 25 Arkansas. 26 The lips. 27 Exeter. 28 Scotland. 29 Ian Rankin. 30 Jonny Wilkinson.

1 In Greek mythology, who is the god of love?
2 At night what colour light is shown on the starboard side of a ship?
3 Which day of the week is the Muslim holy day?
4 If you were using a spinnaker, what would you be doing?
5 What is the lightest weight in boxing?
6 What kind of animal is a merino?
7 Who was the first prime minister to make use of Chequers?
8 In a political scandal, who said, "Discretion is a polite word for hypocrisy"?
9 Who was Nicole Kidman's co star in the movie "The Interpreter"?
10 What colour jersey is worn by the leader in the Tour de France?
11 Who composed the choral work "The Armed Man"?
12 What was the name of the mythical South American city of gold?
13 In "Dad's Army" what was Captain Mainwaring's day job?
14 On a London Underground map, what colour is the Piccadilly line?
15 What is the capital of Bolivia?
16 In which art has Barbara Hepworth become famous?
17 Which country shares its name with the daughter of Alex Baldwin and Kim Basinger?
18 What sort of book was compiled by Moody and Sankey?
19 Which bird did Noah first send out of the ark?
20 How is Terence Williams of UB40 better known?
21 Of which country is Ajax a famous football team?
22 Which river flows through the Grand Canyon in the United States?
23 What sport would you practise if you were a toxophilite?
24 What is the name of the bone in your thigh?
25 In which ocean are the Azores?
26 Which Australian bird is famous for laughing?
27 Which school did Billy Bunter go to?
28 What is the name of the hill where Jesus Christ was crucified?
29 Who was runner up to Tiger Woods in the Open of 2005?
30 Which royal sport would you see at Cowdray Park and Hurlingham?

Answers	**Sport: Horse Racing** *(see Quiz 95)*

1 St Leger. 2 Michael Kinane. 3 Walter Swinburn. 4 Pat Eddery. 5 Hamilton. 6 Willie Carson. 7 Bachelor's Hall. 8 Best Mate. 9 Jane Thorne. 10 Betting tax. 11 Newmarket. 12 Flemington Park. 13 Frank Buckle. 14 Epsom. 15 Gulfland. 16 Derby. 17 2000 Guineas in 1809. 18 William. 19 Tony McCoy. 20 Hong Kong. 21 Michael. 22 £500. 23 Esher. 24 Guy Fawkes Night. 25 France. 26 Thomas. 27 Walter Swinburn, Jnr. 28 Kieren Fallon. 29 11. 30 One.

1 Which Oscar-winning actress adopted children Maddox and Zahara?
2 Which Welsh singer's name was linked with rugby's Gavin Henson in 2005?
3 Which rock star became dad to Alistair at the age of 60 in 2005?
4 Which French actor announced his retirement in 2005?
5 What is the first name of the crown prince of Spain?
6 Before their resignations in 1996 whom did Patrick Jephson and Steve Davies work for?
7 What were George Best's two wives called?
8 Which "Baywatch" star married Tommy Lee?
9 What were the two married names of the late Jacqueline Bouvier?
10 Whom did actress Jennifer Garner marry in 2005?
11 At the start of his career, which footballer's name was linked to Coleen McLoughlin?
12 What nickname was given to the group of artists which included Dean Martin, Frank Sinatra and Peter Lawford ?
13 Which superstar and former playboy is Annette Bening married to?
14 Which one-time Hollywood pair have a daughter called Dakota ?
15 Which film actress did Ashton Kutcher marry in 2005?
16 Which actress is the wife of Simon MacCorkindale?
17 Which heiress to a hotel chain appeared in the TV series "The Simple Life"?
18 Who got engaged to Jude Law on Christmas Day 2004?
19 Who was Athina Roussel's multi-millionairess mother?
20 What is the first name of Michael Caine's wife?
21 From which US state does model Jerry Hall come?
22 Who was Mrs Larry Fortensky until early 1996?
23 Who is Lady Helen Taylor's mother?
24 Who was widowed in 1990 when her husband's boat went out of control?
25 Who was married to and also separated from country singer Kenny Chesney in 2005?
26 Which southern French resort holds a yearly film festival?
27 Which film star is Mrs Carlo Ponti?
28 Which singer made a documentary called "I Want to Tell You a Secret"?
29 Which supermodel married British film producer Matthew Vaughn?
30 Which husband of Sarah Jessica Parker appeared in the 2005 movie version of "The Producers"?

Answers | **Popular Classics** (see Quiz 100)

1 Handel. 2 Enigma Variations. 3 Beethoven. 4 Finlandia. 5 The Pearl Fishers. 6 Iolanthe. 7 Washington Post. 8 Air on a G String. 9 Pachelbel. 10 From the New World. 11 The Four Seasons. 12 Frederick Delius. 13 Guitar. 14 Elijah. 15 Eine Kleine Nachtmusik (A Little Night Music). 16 Ravel. 17 Animals. 18 Purcell. 19 The Thieving Magpie. 20 The Planets. 21 Choral Symphony. 22 Violin. 23 Peter and the Wolf. 24 Ballet. 25 The Ring. 26 Computer. 27 Land of Hope and Glory. 28 Danube. 29 Britannia rules the waves. 30 France.

1 The River Ganges is a holy place for the followers of which religion?
2 What is the name for the home of an eagle?
3 Where was Robbie Burns born in Ayrshire?
4 Which Shakespearian play takes place in Illyria?
5 Which two leaders had a meeting in the Brenner Pass in World War II?
6 Tom Thumb, Tennis Ball and Winter Density are all types of what?
7 Which flower is particularly associated with Mary, the Madonna?
8 On which Yorkshire moor was a battle fought on July 2nd, 1644?
9 Which music hall comedian was known as the "Cheeky Chappie"?
10 In which industry was Lord Nuffield a pioneer?
11 Which word describes architecture dating from the time of James I?
12 What word describes the minimum number of members on a committee in attendance for it to reach valid decisions?
13 Who composed the "Thunder and Lightning" Polka?
14 Which war was fought in the Far East from 1950 to 1953?
15 What type of animal is a Kerry Blue?
16 In which year was the evacuation of Dunkirk?
17 Who won the Best Male Performer award at the 2005 MTV Awards?
18 What does an anemometer measure?
19 What is a filbert?
20 Which strait links the Black Sea and the Sea of Marmara?
21 What does a lexicographer write or make?
22 What was the name of the prison in "Porridge"?
23 Who or what live in a holt?
24 Which city was once known as Eboracum?
25 Which country's Royal family include Crown Prince Frederik and Crown Princess Mary?
26 What is the name of the largest art gallery in Russia, situated in St Petersburg?
27 By what name is mid-Lent Sunday popularly known?
28 What was the name of Britney Spears' first son?
29 Of the Seven Wonders of the World, where was the Colossus?
30 Which gorge is crossed by the Clifton suspension bridge?

Answers | **Pot-Luck 45** *(see Quiz 101)*

1 Ways of ringing church bells. 2 Goat. 3 Nigeria. 4 Eye. 5 Its passion play (held every ten years). 6 Carlisle. 7 Jay Leno. 8 Forehead. 9 Palm Sunday. 10 Spain. 11 Ivor Novello. 12 A watch. 13 Jerusalem. 14 Lemmings. 15 Tax collector. 16 Nicolas Cage. 17 Dr Samuel Johnson. 18 Hamlet. 19 Evening. 20 Sheep. 21 Journalists, the press. 22 Edinburgh. 23 A wreath. 24 Sparking plug. 25 Norwegian. 26 Anthea Redfern. 27 Composer. 28 Bernard Montgomery. 29 Zidane. 30 Stephen Daldry.

1 Who wrote "The Hallelujah Chorus"?
2 From which work does the piece "Nimrod" come from?
3 Who wrote the concerto called "The Emperor"?
4 Which work by Sibelius represented the defiance of the Finns?
5 Which Bizet opera features the duet "Au Fond du Temple Saint"?
6 In which Gilbert and Sullivan opera do fairies take over Parliament?
7 Which US newspaper shares its name with a march by Sousa?
8 Which work by Bach became famous in a cigar advertisement?
9 Who wrote Pachelbel's Kanon?
10 What is Dvorak's 9th Symphony, written in the US, often called?
11 Which Vivaldi composition did Nigel Kennedy popularize?
12 Who wrote "On Hearing the First Cuckoo in Spring"?
13 For which instrument is Joaquín Rodrigo most famous?
14 Which Old Testament prophet was the subject of an oratorio by Mendelssohn?
15 Which title of a composition by Mozart was translated by Stephen Sondheim into the name of a musical?
16 Who wrote the Bolero Torvill and Dean danced to?
17 What was in the Carnival in the Saint-Saëns composition?
18 Which English composer's 300th anniversary took place in 1995?
19 What is the English title of "La gazza ladra" by Rossini?
20 Which suite is Gustav Holst's most famous composition ?
21 What is Beethoven's 9th Symphony known as?
22 For which instrument did Paganini chiefly compose?
23 Which famous piece by Prokofiev is for orchestra and narrator?
24 What type of performance was "The Rite of Spring" written for?
25 What is the Wagner opera cycle which includes "Siegfried" and "Die Walküre"?
26 What are pieces by Iannis Xenakis written with the aid of?
27 How is the "Pomp and Circumstance March" better known?
28 Which river is celebrated in Johann Strauss's most famous waltz?
29 Which line follows "Rule Britannia" in the chorus of the song?
30 Who is Russia's opponent in the campaign commemorated in the "1812 Overture"?

Answers | Celebs: Jet Setters *(see Quiz 98)*

1 Angelina Jolie, 2 Charlotte Church. 3 Rod Stewart. 4 Gérard Dépardieu. 5 Felipe. 6 The Princess of Wales. 7 Angie and Alex. 8 Pamela Anderson. 9 Kennedy, Onassis. 10 Ben Affleck. 11 Wayne Rooney. 12 Rat Pack. 13 Warren Beatty. 14 Don Johnson and Melanie Griffith. 15 Demi Moore. 16 Susan George. 17 Paris Hilton. 18 Sienna Miller. 19 Christina Onassis. 20 Shakira. 21 Texas. 22 Elizabeth Taylor. 23 The Duchess of Kent. 24 Princess Caroline of Monaco. 25 Renee Zellweger. 26 Cannes. 27 Sophia Loren. 28 Madonna. 29 Claudia Schiffer. 30 Matthew Broderick.

1 What are Steadman triples, Plain Bob Caters and Gransire triples?
2 What kind of animal is a chamois?
3 In which African country is the city of Ibadan?
4 Which part of the body would be affected by astigmatism?
5 For what is Oberammergau famous?
6 Which city is the administrative headquarters of Cumbria?
7 Which Jay has hosted "The Tonight Show" in the US?
8 Where in your body is the frontal bone?
9 On which day does the Church celebrate Jesus entering Jerusalem?
10 This century, Prince Felipe has been heir to which throne?
11 Who wrote "The Dancing Years" and "King's Rhapsody"?
12 What is the collective noun to describe a number of nightingales?
13 With which holy city is the name Zion associated?
14 Which Scandinavian animals are famous for running over cliff tops?
15 Before he became a disciple of Jesus, what was Matthew's job?
16 Which actor co stars with Ethan Hawke in the movie "Lord of War"?
17 Boswell wrote the biography of which famous writer?
18 Ophelia appears in which Shakespeare play?
19 To what does the adjective crepuscular refer?
20 In Australia, what animal is a jumbuck?
21 Who or what is meant the Fourth Estate?
22 Which city has or had the nickname Auld Reekie?
23 What was awarded to winners in the original Olympic Games?
24 In a car what is the device called that secures electrical ignition?
25 What nationality was the playwright Ibsen?
26 Who was Bruce Forsyth's second wife?
27 As what did Bela Bartók achieve fame?
28 Who commanded the Allied ground forces in the Normandy invasion of 1944?
29 Which player hit two goals in the 1998 World Cup final?
30 Which theatre director was Oscar nominated for the movie "Billy Elliot"?

| **Answers** | **Pot-Luck 44** *(see Quiz 99)* |

1 Hinduism. 2 Eyrie. 3 Alloway. 4 Twelfth Night. 5 Hitler and Mussolini. 6 Lettuce.
7 Lilies. 8 Marston Moor. 9 Max Miller. 10 Motor car manufacturing. 11 Jacobean.
12 Quorum. 13 Johann Strauss the Younger. 14 Korean War. 15 Dog. 16 1940. 17
Robbie Williams. 18 Wind speed. 19 A hazelnut. 20 The Bosporus. 21 Dictionaries.
22 HMP Slade. 23 Otters. 24 York. 25 Denmark. 26 The Hermitage. 27 Mothering
Sunday. 28 Sean Preston. 29 Rhodes. 30 The Avon Gorge.

1 Nancy Spungeon was the girlfriend of which punk performer?

2 Which grunge purveyor blew his brains out in 1994?

3 Which glam rocker proclaimed himself the "Godfather of Punk"?

4 Who was murdered by his father on his birthday in 1984?

5 Who had No1 albums in 1982 with "Number of the Beast" and "Seventh Son of a Seventh Son" in 1988?

6 Which interviewer challenged the Sex Pistols to swear on TV?

7 Which 1960s hit singer was famous for his trousers splitting on stage?

8 Which group made the top ten in 1991 after 20 minor hits over 15 years?

9 Which rock superstar did Mark Chapman gun down?

10 "Aquarius" came from which show that shocked 1960s audiences?

11 Who started life as John Lydon?

12 Who recorded "Grimly Fiendish" with the record number GRIM 1?

13 Who recorded – and set himself on – "Fire"?

14 Which group recorded the album "Nevermind"?

15 In 1993 what was Snoop Doggy Dogg arrested for?

16 Which Frankie Goes to Hollywood hit was banned by the BBC?

17 Which group was formed by Jello Biafra in the late 1970s?

18 Who was manager of the Sex Pistols?

19 The film "The Rose" was loosely based on whose life?

20 Which actress should have partnered Serge Gainsbourg on "Je t'aime" but withdrew from the project?

21 Which Sinatra song did Sid Vicious record?

22 Who were the "Hersham Boys"?

23 What is Boy George's real name?

24 Whose stage act included simulated "killings" of a doll and a chicken?

25 Reg Presley was said to be "too suggestive" with which group?

26 Which cult hero did Val Kilmer play in a 1991 Oliver Stone movie?

27 Who in 1966 spoke of being "more popular than Jesus'"?

28 Who released the solo album "Blaze of Glory" which included tracks from "Young Guns II"?

29 Which Australasian rock band included singer Michael Hutchence?

30 Who released the then extremely controversial "Let's Spend the Night Together" in 1967?

| **Answers** | Around Australia *(see Quiz 104)* |

1 Sydney. 2 Great Barrier Reef. 3 Ayers Rock or Uluru. 4 Canberra. 5 Pacific and Indian. 6 Bondi Beach. 7 The Northern Territory. 8 Botany Bay. 9 Brisbane river. 10 Queensland. 11 Western Australia. 12 The Blue Mountains. 13 Alice Springs. 14 Melbourne. 15 Wave Rock. 16 The Gold Coast. 17 Kakadu National Park. 18 Kuranda, Queensland. 19 Fraser Island. 20 Cairns. 21 Great Dividing Range. 22 Surfers' Paradise. 23 Cape Tribulation. 24 Perth. 25 The Bungle Bungle Range. 26 The Twelve Apostles. 27 Mount Bartle Frere. 28 Adelaide. 29 The Pinnacles. 30 Cape York.

Quiz 103 | Pot-Luck 46 | Answers – page 347 | LEVEL 2

1 Who said, "Anyone who hates children and dogs can't be all bad"?
2 In our solar system which planet takes the least time to orbit the sun?
3 What is the name of René's wife in "Allo Allo"?
4 Whose cave inspired Mendelssohn to compose his Hebrides overture?
5 Who wrote the Waverley novels?
6 Which word can go after blue and before neck?
7 Who was George W. Bush's first Vice President?
8 Is an okapi animal or vegetable or mineral?
9 Which musical was voted Britain's favourite in a 2005 Radio 2 poll?
10 On which country's stamps would you find the words Magyar Posta?
11 Whom did Joe Bugner defeat in his comeback fight in Sydney, in 1986?
12 Where was Marat when Charlotte Corday murdered him?
13 Nickelodeon was a name given to a juke box. What was it originally?
14 At what did Antonio Stradivari achieve fame?
15 To one place of decimals, how many centimetres equal one inch?
16 By what English name is the mountain Yr Wyddfa known?
17 Is the suburb of Southgate in the north, south, east or west of London?
18 Which famous British film company was associated with the symbol of a man striking a gong?
19 In Greek tragedy, which king married his own mother?
20 Which star sign is shared by Pat Cash and Steffi Graf?
21 Whose real name is Steveland Judkins?
22 In geometry, how many degrees are there in a complete circle?
23 In which kind of building is there a transept?
24 In London, which road runs from Charing Cross to Fleet Street?
25 Which alloy of tin and lead is used for making tankards and mugs?
26 What Egyptian obelisk stands on the Thames Embankment?
27 In which country did Boavista win their first league title in 2001?
28 What was Serena Williams' first tennis Grand Slam title?
29 What does a Frenchman mean when he says "Quel dommage"?
30 Who was the second wife of Tom Cruise?

Answers | **American Sport** *(see Quiz 105)*

1 National Football League. 2 Ice hockey. 3 Pittsburgh Stealers. 4 Baseball. 5 No-one. It was cancelled because of a strike by players. 6 Ice hockey. 7 Houston. 8 Washington. 9 Georgman Herman Ruth. 10 Florida. 11 Brad Friedel. 12 London Ravens. 13 American football. 14 Boston Red Sox. 15 1970. 16 Six. 17 Basketball. 18 Yogi. 19 New York. 20 Basketball. 21 The visiting team. 22 1994. 23 American football. 24 Canada. 25 Scott Hamilton and Brian Boitano. 26 The Pro Bowl. 27 LA Lakers. 28 Green Bay Packers. 29 Baseball. 30 Nine.

1 Which city with 3 million inhabitants is Australia's largest?
2 What is the name of the world's longest reef?
3 Which sacred rock is the world's largest monolith?
4 What is the capital of Australia?
5 Which two oceans are to the east and west of Australia?
6 What is the name of the surfing beach on the outskirts of Sydney?
7 Darwin is the capital of which state?
8 At which famous east coast bay did James Cook arrive in April 1770?
9 Which meandering river is Brisbane built around?
10 Which state is commonly called the Sunshine State?
11 Perth is the capital of which Australian state?
12 Which mountain range to the west of Sydney was partly destroyed by bush fires in December 1993?
13 Which is the nearest major town to the southwest of Ayers Rock?
14 What is the capital of the state of Victoria?
15 Which granite formation, formed by the wind, is to the east of Perth?
16 What is the coastline to the south of Brisbane called?
17 Which national park, known for its Aboriginal rock paintings and wildlife, lies to the east of Darwin?
18 Which "village in the rainforest" at the highest end of the Barron Gorge is the home to the only permanent Aboriginal theatre in Australia?
19 What is the world's largest sand island northeast of Brisbane?
20 What is Queensland's most northerly city?
21 Which mountain range runs parallel to the east coast for 4000 kilometres?
22 Which famous surfing beach is to the south of Brisbane?
23 Where does the rainforest meet the sea in northern Queensland?
24 Which state capital lies on the Swan River?
25 Which range of domed mountains lies in Purnululu National Park?
26 Along the Great Ocean Road in Victoria what 12 off-coast formations would you discover?
27 Which mountain, at 1611 metres, is the highest in Queensland?
28 Which Australian city hosted its final Formula 1 race in 1995?
29 Which fossilized remains of an ancient forest are found in the Nambung?
30 Which cape is at the northernmost tip of Australia in Queensland?

Answers | Pop: Shock Rock (see Quiz 102)

1 Sid Vicious. 2 Kurt Cobain. 3 Marc Bolan. 4 Marvin Gaye. 5 Iron Maiden. 6 Bill Grundy. 7 P. J. Proby. 8 Clash. 9 John Lennon. 10 Hair. 11 Johnny Rotten. 12 Damned. 13 Arthur Brown. 14 Nirvana. 15 A charge of murder. 16 Relax. 17 Dead Kennedys. 18 Malcolm McLaren. 19 Janis Joplin. 20 Brigitte Bardot. 21 My Way. 22 Sham 69. 23 George Alan O'Dowd. 24 Alice Cooper. 25 The Troggs. 26 Jim Morrison. 27 John Lennon – about the Beatles. 28 Jon Bon Jovi. 29 INXS. 30 The Rolling Stones.

1 In American football was does NFL stand for?
2 Which sport do the Buffalo Sabres play?
3 Which club was the first to win the Super Bowl two years in succession on two occasions?
4 Which sport has a Hall of Fame at Cooperstown, New York?
5 Who won the Baseball World Series in 1994?
6 In which sport is the Stanley Cup awarded?
7 Where are the Astros baseball team from?
8 Which city do the Redskins American football team come from?
9 What were "Babe" Ruth's real first names?
10 Where do World Series winners in 1997 and 2003 the Marlins come from?
11 Which Blackburn Rovers keeper played for the United States in the 2002 FIFA World Cup?
12 The first Budweiser Bowl in the UK in 1986 was won by which team?
13 The Princetown College rules drawn up in 1867 affect which sport?
14 Who lifted "The Curse of the Bambino" in 2004?
15 In American football in which year did the AFL and the NFL merge?
16 How many people are there in an ice hockey team?
17 What game is played by the Detroit Pistons?
18 What was the nickname of baseball's Lawrence Peter Berra?
19 Giants and Jets have triumphed in the Super Bowl for which city?
20 The invention of which sport is credited to Dr J. A. Naismith?
21 In baseball, which team bats first?
22 Which year were American professionals first allowed to enter the World Basketball Championships?
23 Which sport do the Miami Dolphins play?
24 In which country were the rules for modern ice hockey formulated?
25 Which two American men won ice skating Olympic gold in the 1980s?
26 Which trophy do teams from AFC and NFC players contest?
27 Which LA team had a 2000 to 2002 hat-trick of triumphs in basketball's NBA Championship?
28 Which team won the first Super Bowl?
29 Which sport do the Atlanta Braves play?
30 How many players are there in a baseball team?

| **Answers** | Pot-Luck 46 *(see Quiz 103)* |

1 W. C. Fields. 2 Mercury. 3 Edith. 4 Fingal's. 5 Sir Walter Scott. 6 Bottle. 7 Dick Cheney. 8 Animal. 9 Les Misérables. 10 Hungary's. 11 James Tillis. 12 In his bath. 13 US cinema (admission was a nickel). 14 Violin maker. 15 2.5. 16 Snowdon. 17 North. 18 The Rank Organization. 19 Oedipus. 20 Gemini. 21 Stevie Wonder. 22 360. 23 Church (or cathedral). 24 The Strand. 25 Pewter. 26 Cleopatra's Needle. 27 Portugal. 28 US Open. 29 "What a pity". 30 Nicole Kidman.

Quiz 106 | Pot-Luck 47

1 Who composed the opera "The Tales of Hoffman"?
2 Which letters could David Beckham add to his name following a presentation in 2003?
3 For what is Frank Lloyd Wright famous?
4 Who wrote a novel about Kenilworth in Warwickshire?
5 What are the Howard League concerned with?
6 Mount Ararat is the traditional resting place of which ship or boat?
7 In "Treasure Island", which sailor dreamed of toasted cheese?
8 In South America what kind of building is a hacienda?
9 Which country won the Battle of Flodden?
10 In a fairy story a queen had to guess the name of a little man or lose her baby. What was his name?
11 In which book would you find Mrs Do-as-you-would-be-done-by?
12 What did the M stand for in the name of writer Louisa M. Alcott ?
13 The play "And Then There were None" is based on a book by which author?
14 What term is given to the making of patterns by inlaying different coloured pieces of wood?
15 In which art did John and Ethel Barrymore achieve fame?
16 Which Oscar winner, for "Fargo", married director Joel Coen?
17 In the United States what item of clothing do they call suspenders?
18 Fashion designer Giorgio Armani studied for which profession in Milan?
19 Which is these is not a freshwater fish: cod, pike, carp, roach?
20 In 2001, which individual won the Nobel Peace Prize jointly with the UN?
21 Who wrote the Inspector Morse novels?
22 What is a mazuka?
23 In which Libyan seaport did Australian forces endure a long siege in World War II?
24 What is the common name for solidified carbon dioxide?
25 Nowadays, which is the largest British bird?
26 With which composer is the German town of Bayreuth associated?
27 Which university is situated at Uxbridge in Middlesex?
28 Which is the highest female voice?
29 What kind of material is cheesecloth?
30 Under Hitler, who was Nazi minister of propaganda?

| **Answers** | **Pot-Luck 48** *(see Quiz 108)* |

1 Katherine Jenkins. 2 Cinque Ports (the original five). 3 Colgate. 4 Its stomach. 5 First female taxi driver. 6 Jerusalem (Christian, Jewish and Muslim). 7 Tartan. 8 Asia. 9 Denmark. 10 Music hall. 11 John Lowe. 12 Shooting. 13 A bevy. 14 Lindsay Davenport. 15 Two. 16 Euston. 17 Othello. 18 Jodie Marsh. 19 Purgatory. 20 Dead Cert. 21 Roman. 22 The Worst Witch books. 23 Fern. 24 Dr Kildare. 25 1961. 26 Job. 27 Jeremy Paxman. 28 Mars. 29 Bayern Munich. 30 Strong, warrior women.

1 In which film does Robert De Niro ask "are you talkin' to me?"?
2 Who wrote the book on which "The Russia House" was based?
3 Whom was the Jackal trying to assassinate in "The Day of the Jackal"?
4 Which president is being referred to in "All the President's Men"?
5 Who won an Oscar for "The Accused"?
6 Which movie was the first collaboration between Steven Spielberg and Tom Cruise?
7 What is Hitchcock said to have used for the blood in "Psycho"?
8 Which three actors have each played Richard Hannay in "The 39 Steps"?
9 Who played the role of South African Donald Woods in "Cry Freedom"?
10 What sort of establishment is the setting for "The China Syndrome"?
11 For which film did the reviewer write "Enough to make you kick the next pigeon you come across"?
12 What relation is Carter to Cain in "Raising Cain"?
13 On whose novel is the Sissy Spacek film "Carrie" based?
14 Who play the getaways in the remake of "The Getaway"?
15 What is the relationship between Tippi Hedren of Hitchcock's "Marnie" and Melanie Griffith of "A Stranger Among Us"?
16 What was the nationality of Alfonso Cuaron, who directed the third Harry Potter movie?
17 In which classic film do Mrs Danvers and Maxim de Winter appear?
18 Whose "Fatal Attraction" to Glenn Close cost him dear?
19 For which film did Steven Spielberg win his first Oscar as Director?
20 Who were the first performers to win the Best Actor and Actress Oscars in the same film after Henry Fonda and Katharine Hepburn in 1981?
21 Who starred in Hitchcock's "Dial M For Murder" and "Rear Window"?
22 Where was Jack Lemmon's son "Missing"?
23 In which classic film is "Rosebud..."a piece in the jigsaw puzzle?
24 In Hitchcock's "Frenzy" what are the victims strangled with?
25 Who costarred with Oscar-winner Jane Fonda in "Klute"?
26 In "The Crying Game" to which organization does the gunman belong?
27 Which filmed Anthony Shaffer play starred Michael Caine and Laurence Olivier?
28 Which Apollo mission was the subject of a film with Tom Hanks?
29 What was described as "Five criminals. One line up. No coincidence"?
30 Who causes terror in "The Hand That Rocks the Cradle"?

Answers | Hi-Tech: Scientists *(see Quiz 109)*

1 Hertz. 2 Becquerel. 3 Copernicus. 4 Stephen Hawking. 5 Nuclear fission. 6 Trigonometry. 7 Kelvin. 8 Atomic particles. 9 Bessemer. 10 Radar. 11 DNA. 12 Ampère. 13 Descartes. 14 Davy. 15 HIV. 16 Chadwick. 17 Hydrogen bomb. 18 Cathode ray tube. 19 Boyle. 20 Faraday. 21 First woman. First person to receive it twice. 22 Andrei Sakharov. 23 Werner von Braun. 24 Logarithms. 25 Polonium, radium. 26 Multiply. 27 Taxonomy. 28 Metric. 29 Galapagos. 30 Explosion of the atomic bomb.

Quiz 108 | Pot-Luck 48

1 "Living The Dream" was the third album released by which singer?
2 What name links Hastings, New Romney, Hythe, Dover and Sandwich?
3 In ads, which toothpaste gave you a ring of confidence?
4 According to Napoleon, what does an army march on?
5 In April 1967, what famous first did Shirley Preston achieve in London?
6 Which city is a holy one for three religions?
7 In Scotland what style of cloth was illegal from 1745 to 1782?
8 In land area which is the world's largest continent?
9 Of which country is Jutland a part?
10 In what kind of theatre did Vesta Tilley become famous?
11 Who in 1984 scored the first nine-dart 501 finish in a major event?
12 In the Wild West, for what was Annie Oakley famous?
13 Which word is used for a group of quails?
14 Which female tennis player finished 2004 ranked as World No 1?
15 How many Bond films did Timothy Dalton star in?
16 From which London station would you leave if travelling to Carlisle?
17 In a Shakespeare play who kills Desdemona?
18 Which glamour model wrote an autobiography entitled "Keeping It Real"?
19 What do Roman Catholics call the state or place where souls are purified after death?
20 What was the title of Dick Francis's first horse-racing thriller?
21 Which empire was ruled by Titus?
22 Which series of children's books are set in Miss Cackle's Academy for Witches and Wizards?
23 What kind of plant is maidenhair?
24 On TV, whose boss was Dr Gillespie?
25 Which was the last year which looked the same when the figures were looked at upside down?
26 Which Old Testament book is about the sufferings of one man?
27 Who has presented both "Newsnight" and "University Challenge"?
28 Which planet is also known as the Red Planet?
29 Which German team was first to win the European Cup?
30 In mythology who were the Amazons?

Answers | Pot-Luck 47 *(see Quiz 106)*

1 Offenbach. 2 OBE. 3 Architecture. 4 Sir Walter Scott. 5 Prison reform. 6 Noah's Ark. 7 Ben Gunn. 8 (Large) estate/farmhouse. 9 England. 10 Rumpelstiltskin. 11 The Water Babies (by Charles Kingsley). 12 May. 13 Agatha Christie. 14 Marquetry. 15 Acting. 16 Frances McDormand. 17 Braces. 18 Medicine. 19 Cod. 20 Kofi Annan. 21 Colin Dexter. 22 A dance. 23 Tobruk. 24 Dry ice. 25 Mute swan. 26 Wagner. 27 Brunel University. 28 Soprano. 29 Muslin. 30 Goebbels.

1 Who discovered radio waves?

2 Who gave his name to a unit of radioactivity?

3 Which 16th-century scientist proposed that the Earth orbited the Sun?

4 Who is best known for his theory of black holes?

5 On what did Otto Hahn, Lise Meitner and Fritz Strassman work?

6 In which branch of mathematics was Hipparchus a pioneer?

7 Which Baron of Largs gave his name to the degrees on the absolute scale?

8 What does Hans Geiger's Geiger counter detect?

9 Whose process decarbonized iron?

10 Which tracking device did Sir Robert Watson-Watt develop?

11 What did Crick, Watson and Wilkins determine the structure of?

12 Who formulated a law of electromagnetism and pioneered techniques in measuring electricity?

13 Which French philosopher created analytical geometry?

14 Which English chemist discovered the most elements?

15 Which virus was Robert Gallo one of the first to identify?

16 Which English physicist discovered the neutron?

17 What type of bomb did Edward Teller develop?

18 What sort of tube did William Crookes invent?

19 Who gave his name to the law that states that the pressure of gas is proportional to its volume?

20 Which physicist and chemist gave his name to the law of induction?

21 In terms of Nobel prizes how did Marie Curie achieve two "firsts"?

22 Which physicist who contributed to the development of Soviet nuclear weapons was also a civil rights campaigner?

23 Which German-born rocket engineer worked on the space programme?

24 Which aids to calculation did John Napier devise?

25 Which two elements did the Curies discover?

26 Leibniz's calculating machine was the first to perform which function?

27 Which word was Candolle the first to use in the classification of plants?

28 For which measuring system did Joseph Louis Lagrange lay the foundations?

29 Which Islands inspired Darwin write "The Origin of Species"?

30 For which Soviet development was Igor Kurchatov team leader?

Answers | Movies: Thrillers *(see Quiz 107)*

1 Taxi Diver. 2 John Le Carré. 3 Charles de Gaulle. 4 Richard Nixon. 5 Jodie Foster. 6 Minority Report. 7 Chocolate sauce. 8 Robert Donat, Kenneth More, Robert Powell. 9 Kevin Kline. 10 Nuclear power plant. 11 The Birds. 12 Twin brother. 13 Stephen King's. 14 Alec Baldwin and Kim Basinger. 15 Mother and daughter. 16 Mexican. 17 Rebecca. 18 Michael Douglas. 19 Schindler's List. 20 Anthony Hopkins and Jodie Foster. 21 Grace Kelly. 22 Chile. 23 Citizen Kane. 24 Necktie. 25 Donald Sutherland. 26 IRA. 27 Sleuth. 28 13. 29 The Usual Suspects. 30 The nanny.

1 When it is made in Europe, what are the three main ingredients of a kedgeree?
2 If a violinist is playing pizzicato, what is he doing?
3 For what kind of building is Rievaulx in North Yorkshire famous?
4 Which alcoholic drink is flavoured with juniper?
5 What is the legal term for telling lies under oath?
6 In which town in 1914 was an archduke assassinated?
7 What was a Sopwith Camel?
8 In which London park would you find Birdcage Walk?
9 What was the trade of the famous Russian Fabergé?
10 Who composed "Finlandia"?
11 In which country did David Coulthard win his first F1 Grand Prix?
12 What is a dactylogram?
13 Which group of islands are you going to if you are sailing to Skye?
14 Whom did Edward VII marry?
15 Which striker John has played for Luton, Arsenal, West Ham, Wimbledon and Celtic?
16 From the fibres of which plant is linen made?
17 What does the letters I stand for in AIDS stand for?
18 Which king was responsible for building the Tower of London?
19 What instrument is Larry Adler famed for?
20 How many equal angles are there in an isosceles triangle?
21 What marine mammals include belugas, blues and sperms?
22 In which city is Sauchiehall Street?
23 On an American Monopoly board, what are B & O, Reading, Short Line and Pennsylvania?
24 For what are the letters OM an abbreviation?
25 What is shepherd's purse?
26 Which day of the week is the Jewish sabbath?
27 Whose official residence is the Mansion House in London?
28 Over which country did the Ptolemies once rule?
29 Which Shirley co starred with Cameron Diaz in "In Her Shoes"?
30 Which football manager modestly called his autobiography "Anatomy of a Winner"?

Answers	Pop Groups *(see Quiz 114)*

1 Paul Weller. 2 Dozy. 3 Busted. 4 I Believe in a Thing Called Love. 5 Pink Floyd. 6 Monday. 7 Pray. 8 U2. 9 Keith Moon. 10 UB40. 11 The Osmonds. 12 Supertramp. 13 Waterloo Sunset. 14 Thin Lizzy. 15 Manfred Mann. 16 The Moody Blues. 17 Status Quo. 18 Scotland. 19 Electric Light Orchestra. 20 Jackson Five. 21 Jam. 22 Leeds. 23 Stars. 24 T. Rex. 25 The Eagles. 26 The Troggs. 27 10cc. 28 Spandau Ballet. 29 Culture Club. 30 Seven Seas of Rye.

1 Which Ashley was named best Comedy Actress in the 2005 British Comedy Awards?

2 Who created the series "Extras" with Ricky Gervais?

3 Which show had the Enid Blyton spoof "Five Go Mad in Dorset"?

4 Name the first two regular team captains in "Have I Got News for You?".

5 Who created Algernon the Rasta and the Reverend Nat West?

6 Which writer hosts the ITV predecessor of "Auntie's Bloomers"?

7 Who created Lauren, the schoolgirl from hell?

8 What was Peter Cook and Dudley Moore's revue show called?

9 What is the surname of the family in "My Family"?

10 Who was the resident vocalist on "That Was the Week That was"?

11 Who impersonated Angela Rippon in "Not the Nine O'Clock News"?

12 Who closed his show with the phrase "May your god go with you"?

13 Who came to fame in "The Comedians" before heading for Walford?

14 Which "Only Fools and Horses" characters were the chief couple in the spinoff "The Green Green Grass"?

15 Which sitcom featured Jean and Lionel?

16 Who joined French and Saunders in the writing of "Girls on Top"?

17 In "The Frost Report" John Cleese was upper class and Ronnie Barker middle class: who was working class?

18 In which show would you find "The Argument Clinic" and the game show "Blackmail"?

19 Which 90s show featured "Jessie's Diets"?

20 In which comedy show did Sanjeev ask various celebrities into his home to be quizzed by his family?

21 Which Chris features in "Hello" and "The Thick of It"?

22 Who was Captain Fantastic in "Do Not Adjust Your Set"?

23 Who created the "Spitting Image" puppets?

24 Who is sports commentator Alan Partridge's true alter ego?

25 In "My Family" what is father Ben's profession?

26 Who has his own series "...Who Else"?

27 Who created Stavros, the kebab shop owner?

28 Who was the dumb, giggly blonde on "Rowan and Martin's Laugh In"?

29 Who is Jennifer Saunders' "alternative" comedian husband?

30 Who plays the character of Lou in "Little Britain"?

Answers | Pot-Luck 51 (see Quiz 115)

1 Fullers. 2 Athos, Porthos and Aramis. 3 Gary Trudeau. 4 Harold Wilson. 5 Amstel. 6 Jarvis Cocker. 7 NW6. 8 Basque. 9 Oakham. 10 Charles Clarke. 11 The Rand. 12 The Bay of Bengal. 13 World War I. 14 Moonlight Serenade. 15 William Wordsworth. 16 Pluto. 17 Akala. 18 Peter Schmeichel. 19 Alfred Lord Tennyson. 20 Resource. 21 Central. 22 Matthew MacFadyen. 23 The Bahamas. 24 Rocky Marciano. 25 Elizabeth Bennet. 26 The Mountains of Mourne. 27 France. 28 Colin Baker. 29 The Italian Job. 30 Jerry Garcia.

1 What does GATT stand for?
2 Where would you see the Dow Jones index?
3 What is a group of producers acting together to fix prices called?
4 Why is Yemen unique in terms of currencies?
5 Which body assesses whether a takeover is in the public interest?
6 The Channel Islands, Gibraltar and the Isle of Man use British currency but, economically, what else do they have in common?
7 What is the chancellor of the exchequer's official London address?
8 Other than in Denmark where is the Danish krone used?
9 What name is given to economic activities which are unrecorded?
10 In which continent is the CFA franc a widespread currency?
11 In which country is the multinational Samsung based?
12 What is a country's GNP?
13 In which country was OPEC founded?
14 Which common market area does CARICOM deal with?
15 The European Union came into being in 1993 after which treaty?
16 In which country is the multinational Nestlé based?
17 Which area of the economy is the CAP concerned with?
18 What is the Japanese share index called?
19 What does ERM stand for?
20 Which states are referred to as the Visegrad Group or CEFTA states?
21 Who were the first two countries to withdraw from the ERM?
22 Which country is the world's largest coffee exporter?
23 Where is the headquarters of the International Monetary Fund ?
24 What name is given to the leading Western economic powers?
25 APEC encourages trade between countries bordering which ocean?
26 Where would you see the FT-SE share index?
27 What position did John Major hold immediately before becoming prime minister in 1990?
28 What does ECU stand for in terms of European Monetary Union?
29 What is the OFT?
30 Where is the headquarters of the Organization for Economic Cooperation and Development?

Answers	Pot-Luck 49 *(see Quiz 110)*

1 Fish/eggs/rice. 2 Plucking the strings. 3 Its abbey. 4 Gin. 5 Perjury. 6 Sarajevo.
7 Aeroplane. 8 St James's Park. 9 Goldsmith. 10 Sibelius. 11 Portugal. 12 A fingerprint. 13 Inner Hebrides. 14 Princess Alexandra of Denmark. 15 Hartson. 16 Flax. 17 Immune (Acquired Immune Deficiency Syndrome). 18 William the Conqueror. 19 Harmonica. 20 Two. 21 Whales. 22 Glasgow. 23 Stations. 24 Order of Merit. 25 A wild flower. 26 Saturday. 27 Lord Mayor of London. 28 Egypt. 29 Shirley MacLaine. 30 Jose Mourinho.

Answers – page 357

1 Which 2005 TV series saw celebrities trying to discover their family tree?
2 Tsar Kolokol is the biggest what in the world?
3 In which fictitious Hampshire town does Chief Inspector Wexford work?
4 Which politician's memoirs appeared in the book "Upwardly Mobile"?
5 In the Victorian age what did Mary Ann Cotton gain notoriety as?
6 What instrument did Nat King Cole play?
7 Cleopatra supposedly bathed in the milk of which animal?
8 Who was the first Eliza Doolittle in the stage version of "My Fair Lady"?
9 What was tested at Bikini Atoll in 1954?
10 The Boat Race course is situated between Putney and where?
11 Charles II gives his name to which type of animal?
12 Who played the monster in the 1931 movie "Frankenstein"?
13 Who sang about Mr Woo?
14 Who had a flagship called "Victory"?
15 What toy is named after US president Theodore Roosevelt?
16 David Beckham scored his first senior goal for which club?
17 Which famous person did John Wilkes Booth shoot?
18 What is the pigment inside red blood cells?
19 In which London art gallery did an exhibition of Henri Rousseau's paintings open in 2005?
20 Who is the patron saint of mountaineers?
21 Who played Ma Larkin to David Jason's Pa?
22 Which ocean is the world's deepest?
23 Who was the author of the best-selling "Country Diary of an Edwardian Lady"?
24 Which bandleader shared his name with a British prime minister?
25 Which star from "Friends" appeared in London's West End in "Some Girls"?
26 In geography what is a shoal?
27 What is a ban on international trade with a country called?
28 In broadcasting what does CNN stand for?
29 Which Irish singer recorded the album "Day without Rain"?
30 What is Rumpole's first name in the character created by John Mortimer?

Answers | TV: Comedy *(see Quiz 111)*

1 Ashley Jensen. 2 Stephen Merchant. 3 The Comic Strip Presents. 4 Paul Merton, Ian Hislop. 5 Lenny Henry. 6 Denis Norden. 7 Catherine Tate. 8 Not Only ... But Also. 9 Harper. 10 Millicent Martin. 11 Pamela Stephenson. 12 Dave Allen. 13 Mike Reid. 14 Boycie and Marlene. 15 As Time Goes By. 16 Ruby Wax. 17 Ronnie Corbett. 18 Monty Python's Flying Circus. 19 The Fast Show. 20 The Kumars at No 42. 21 Chris Langham. 22 David Jason. 23 Fluck and Law. 24 Steve Coogan. 25 Dentist. 26 Rory Bremner. 27 Harry Enfield. 28 Goldie Hawn. 29 Adrian Edmondson. 30 David Walliams.

1 Who was lead singer with Style Council?
2 Who sang with Dave Dee, Beaky, Mick and Tich?
3 Who brought out the album "A Present for Everyone" in 2003?
4 What was the first top ten hit single for the Darkness?
5 Which group featured Dave Gilmour and Roger Waters?
6 Which day did the Boomtown Rats not like?
7 What was Take That's first No 1?
8 Which Irish supergroup started life known as Feedback?
9 Who was the Who's original drummer?
10 Which group formed their own label Dep International?
11 Merrill, Jay, Wayne, Jimmy and Donny made up which group?
12 Which group made the album "Crisis? What Crisis"?
13 Which Kinks hit starts, "Dirty old river, must you keep rolling..."?
14 Which group was led by Phil Lynott?
15 Paul Jones and Mike D'Abo both sang lead with which group?
16 Justin Hayward and Denny Laine were members of which group?
17 Which group opened the Wembley Stadium section of Live Aid?
18 Wet, Wet, Wet come from which country?
19 Which group sang about Horace Wimp?
20 How were the Jacksons credited on their early hits?
21 Whose first top ten single was "The Eton Rifles" in 1979?
22 Which city do the Kaiser Chiefs come from?
23 Which Simply Red album contained "For Your Babies"?
24 Which glam group asked "Metal guru, is it you?"?
25 Which group wanted to "Take It to the Limit"?
26 Which group had the original hit with "Love is All Around"?
27 Who thought that "Life is a Minestrone"?
28 Gary and Martin Kemp were members of which group?
29 Which group had seven consecutive top four hits until the release of "The Medal Song"?
30 What was Queen's first hit?

| **Answers** | **Modern History: Boom and Bust** *(see Quiz 112)* |

1 General Agreement on Tariffs and Trade. 2 Wall Street. 3 Cartel. 4 Two. 5 Monopolies & Mergers Commission. 6 Issue their own bank notes. 7 11 Downing Street. 8 Greenland, Faeroe Islands. 9 Black economy. 10 Africa. 11 South Korea. 12 Gross national product. 13 Iraq. 14 Caribbean. 15 Maastricht. 16 Switzerland. 17 Agriculture. 18 Nikkei. 19 Exchange Rate Mechanism. 20 Czech Republic, Hungary, Poland, Slovakia. 21 UK, Italy. 22 Brazil. 23 Washington. 24 G7. 25 Pacific. 26 London. 27 Chancellor of the exchequer. 28 European Currency Unit. 29 Office of Fair Trading. 30 Paris.

1 Who brews London Pride?
2 Name the three Musketeers?
3 Which cartoonist draws the Doonesbury strip?
4 Which premier was Huddersfield's most famous son?
5 Which Dutch river is also the name of a beer?
6 Who executed a one-man stage invasion to disrupt Michael Jackson's appearance at the 1996 Brit Awards?
7 What is the postal code for Kilburn?
8 Which item of lingerie is also the language of the inhabitants of the Western Pyrenees?
9 What was the county town of Rutland?
10 Who took over from David Blunkett as Home Secretary?
11 What is the currency of South Africa?
12 What is the largest bay in the world?
13 The play "Journey's End" is set against the background of which conflict?
14 What was Glenn Miller's signature tune?
15 Which famous poet lived in Dove Cottage?
16 Which is the most distant planet in the solar system?
17 Who was the leader of the wolfpack in "The Jungle Book"?
18 Who was Man Utd's captain in the 1999 European Champions' Cup Final?
19 Who wrote the poem "The Lady of Shallot"?
20 What does the letter R stand for in URL?
21 Which Underground line is Marble Arch station on?
22 Who played the role made famous by Colin Firth in the 2005 remake of "Pride and Prejudice"?
23 Where did Edward VIII spend most of WWII?
24 Who retired as undefeated heavyweight boxing champion of the world?
25 What is the name of the heroine of Jane Austen's novel "Pride and Prejudice"?
26 Which Irish mountains sweep down to the sea?
27 Which country was selected to host the Rugby World Cup of 2007?
28 Who was the sixth TV Doctor Who?
29 Which 1969 film featured cockney ram-raiders in Turin?
30 Which member of the Grateful Dead died in 1995?

Answers	Pot-Luck 50 *(see Quiz 113)*

1 Who Do You Think You are?. 2 Bell. 3 Kingsmarkham. 4 Norman Tebbit. 5 A mass murderer. 6 Piano. 7 Ass. 8 Julie Andrews. 9 Hydrogen bomb. 10 Mortlake. 11 Dog. King Charles Spaniel. 12 Boris Karloff. 13 George Formby. 14 Lord Nelson. 15 Teddy bear. 16 Preston North End. 17 Abraham Lincoln. 18 Haemoglobin. 19 Tate Modern. 20 Saint Bernard. 21 Pam Ferris. 22 Pacific. 23 Edith Holden. 24 Ted Heath. 25 David Schwimmer. 26 An area of sandbanks. 27 Embargo. 28 Cable News Network. 29 Enya. 30 Horace.

1 Who had a 70s hit with "Feelings"?
2 Who duetted with Beyoncé Knowles on the top ten hit "Baby Boy"?
3 Which Irish singer has made records with Clannad and Sinatra?
4 Who were the first Russian act to top the UK chart?
5 Who was lead singer with the Animals?
6 Who did Nick Berry play in "EastEnders" at the time of his first No. 1?
7 Whom did Marc Almond sing with for his first No. 1?
8 Who – in song – lived high on a mountain in Mexico?
9 The Sugababes' hit "Too Lost in You" came from the soundtrack to which 2003 film?
10 Who has recorded with Cliff Richard, Steve Harley and Jose Carreras?
11 Who was the "Wichita Lineman"?
12 What word added to Bells, Mink and Pearl completes group names?
13 Who was lead singer with the Bay City Rollers?
14 Which country did Aneka – who sang "Japanese Boy" – come from?
15 Who sang "Private Number" with William Bell?
16 Who was responsible for the English lyrics of "My Way"?
17 Who were Bobby, Mike, Cheryl and Jay?
18 Whom did Chubby Checker sing with on the 80s twist revival single?
19 What was Norman Cook's first number one as Fatboy Slim?
20 "Innocent Eyes" was the debut album of which "Neighbours" actress?
21 Who was the Geno referred to in Dexy's Midnight Runners' No. 1?
22 Which Spice Girl comes from Leeds?
23 Who wrote and sang the original "Spirit in the Sky"?
24 Who took "Wonderwall" into the charts for the second time in 1995?
25 Who was the first female artist to have a No. 1 and wear an eye patch?
26 Who wrote "All by Myself"?
27 What was the first No. 1 for the Corrs?
28 Who sang with Peabo Bryson on "A Whole New World"?
29 Our Cilla's "Anyone Who Had a Heart" was a cover of which singer's song?
30 Who was the guitar virtuoso who wrote "Albatross"?

Answers	**Narnia** *(see Quiz 118)*

1 Seven. 2 Liam Neeson. 3 Cair Paravel. 4 The Magician's Nephew. 5 Winter. 6 Talking mouse. 7 The Professor. 8 Ship. 9 Jadis. 10 Peter. 11 At a train station. 12 The Voyage of the Dawn Treader. 13 The Lion, the Witch and the Wardrobe. 14 Bree. 15 Maugrim. 16 Cousin. 17 Marsh-wiggle. 18 Susan. 19 The Last Battle. 20 Charn. 21 Turkish Delight. 22 Tirian. 23 Calormen. 24 The First King and Queen. 25 His goddaughter (Lucy Barfield). 26 Hedgehog. 27 The Horse and His Boy. 28 Jill Pole. 29 Jewel. 30 1956.

1 Which moor is named after the county town of Cornwall?
2 Who laid the foundation stone at Coventry Cathedral?
3 In which city was Stéphane Grappelli born?
4 Who had a No. 1 in the 60s with "Everlasting Love"?
5 Which tennis player was given the name "Ice Man" by the press?
6 Who played Cherie Blair in TV's "A Very Social Secretary"?
7 Which does fibrin cause the blood to do?
8 In 2006's World Cup, who was in Group F with Australia, Brazil and Japan?
9 In which county are England's highest cliffs?
10 What is the Russian word for citadel?
11 In which century was George Frederick Handel born?
12 Which sportsman wrote the autobiography "Unleashed"?
13 Which rail company was convicted of breaking safety rules over the Hatfield crash?
14 Who was the creator of TV sleuth Jonathan Creek?
15 What is the Pentateuch?
16 In which sitcom did Sandra Hennessey appear?
17 What was the name of the first cloned sheep?
18 Which school did Billy Bunter go to?
19 Who wrote the books on which "The Jewel in the Crown" was based?
20 What is the name of Lisa Simpson's teacher?
21 Allurophobia is a fear of what?
22 What do the letters P.S. stand for at the end of a letter?
23 Whose last words were "That was a great game of golf, fellas"?
24 In the Chinese calendar which year follows the year of the tiger?
25 Who was the first person to captain, coach and manage England at cricket?
26 Who was King of the Huns from 406 to 453?
27 What word can go after "tar" and before "gent"?
28 What was the fine for a late self-assessment tax return in Jan 2006?
29 In which decade of the 20th century was Eric Clapton born?
30 Which actor played the only Dirty Dozen member to survive?

Answers | **Around the UK** *(see Quiz 119)*

1 Four. 2 Portsmouth. 3 The Guild Hall. 4 Tobermory. 5 Sark. 6 Anglesey. 7 Cambridge. 8 Lloyd's of London. 9 Scillies. 10 Cheviots. 11 Glasgow. 12 Irish Sea. 13 Buckinghamshire. 14 York Minster. 15 Solway Firth. 16 Coventry. 17 Melton Mowbray. 18 The Backs. 19 Derbyshire. 20 Ermine Street. 21 Lytham St Annes. 22 Parkhurst. 23 Grosvenor Square. 24 The Great Fire of London. 25 The Solent. 26 Windsor. 27 Southend. 28 Downing Street. 29 Mermaid. 30 Northumberland.

1 How many Chronicles of Narnia are there?
2 Who voiced Aslan in the 2005 film "The Lion, the Witch and the Wardrobe"?
3 What is the name of the Narnian castle housing the four thrones?
4 Digory and Polly appear in which book?
5 Which season is Narnia in at the start of "The Lion, the Witch and the Wardrobe"?
6 What sort of animal is Reepicheep?
7 In the later Chronicles how is Digory better known?
8 What mode of transport is the *Dawn Treader*?
9 What is the real name of the White Witch?
10 Who is the eldest of the Pevensie children?
11 Where are the Pevensie children at the start of "Prince Caspian"?
12 Which is the fifth book of the Chronicles of Narnia?
13 Which book was written first?
14 What is the name of the horse in "The Horse and His Boy"?
15 Who is the chief of the White Witch's secret police?
16 What relation is Eustace Scrubb to the four Pevensie children?
17 In "The Silver Chair" what sort of creature is Puddleglum?
18 Which of the children is called "The Gentle" after the coronation?
19 The evil Tash appears in which book?
20 In "The Magician's Nephew" Jadis is woken in which land?
21 What does the White Witch tempt Edmund with?
22 Who was the last King of Narnia?
23 In which land does "The Horse and His Boy" begin?
24 In "The Magician's Nephew" what did the Cabbie and his wife become in Narnia?
25 Whom did C. S. Lewis dedicate "The Lion, the Witch and the Wardrobe" to?
26 In "Prince Caspian" what sort of animal is Hogglestock?
27 Shasta, Hwin and Aravis appear in which book?
28 Which of Eustace's school friends travels to Narnia with him?
29 What is the name of the Unicorn in "The Last Battle"?
30 In which year was "The Last Battle" originally published?

| **Answers** | Pop: Who's Who? *(see Quiz 116)* |

1 Morris Albert. 2 Sean Paul. 3 Bono. 4 t.A.T.u. 5 Eric Burdon. 6 Simon Wicks. 7 Gene Pitney. 8 Angelo (Brotherhood of Man). 9 Love Actually. 10 Sarah Brightman. 11 Glen Campbell. 12 Blue. 13 Les McKeown. 14 Scotland. 15 Judy Clay. 16 Paul Anka. 17 Bucks Fizz. 18 Fat Boys. 19 "Praise You". 20 Delta Goodrem. 21 Geno Washington. 22 Mel B (Scary). 23 Norman Greenbaum. 24 Mike Flowers Pops. 25 Gabrielle. 26 Eric Carmen. 27 "Breathless". 28 Regina Belle. 29 Dionne Warwick. 30 Peter Green.

1 How many faces has the clock on Big Ben's tower?
2 In which port were Dickens and Brunel both born?
3 In which London building is the Lord Mayor's banquet held?
4 Which Womble was named after the town on the Isle of Mull?
5 Which Channel Island is famous for having no cars?
6 Where is Beaumaris Castle?
7 Girton and Newnham are colleges of which university?
8 Where in London is the Lutine Bell?
9 Bryher is part of which islands?
10 Which Hills divide England and Scotland?
11 Cumbernauld is near which British city?
12 Which Sea joins the St George's Channel and the North Channel?
13 In which county is Chequers, the Prime Minister's country residence?
14 What is England's second largest cathedral?
15 Which Firth lies between south-west Scotland and north-west England?
16 Where is The Cathedral Church of St Michael, consecrated in 1962?
17 Which Leicestershire town is famous for its pork pies?
18 What are the canals in Cambridge called?
19 In which county is the southern end of the Pennine Way?
20 Which Roman road shares its name with a type of fur?
21 What is ERNIE's original home town?
22 What is the high-security prison on the Isle of Wight called?
23 In which London Square is the US Embassy?
24 Which disaster does London's Monument commemorate?
25 Which waterway divides the Isle of Wight from the mainland?
26 Which castle has St George's Chapel?
27 What is the nearest seaside resort to London?
28 Where in London are there gates named after Margaret Thatcher?
29 Which theatre was founded in 1959 at Blackfriars in London?
30 Dogger Bank is off which English county?

Answers	**Pot Luck 52** *(see Quiz 117)*

1 Bodmin Moor. **2** Queen Elizabeth II. **3** Paris. **4** Love Affair. **5** Bjorn Borg. **6** Doon MacKichan. **7** Clot. **8** Croatia. **9** Devon. **10** Kremlin. **11** 17th. **12** Jack Russell. **13** Network Rail. **14** David Renwick. **15** First five books of the Old Testament. **16** "The Liver Birds". **17** Dolly. **18** Greyfriars. **19** Paul Scott. **20** Miss Hoover. **21** Cats. **22** Postscript. **23** Bing Crosby. **24** Rabbit. **25** Ray Illingworth. **26** Attila. **27** "Tan". **28** £100. **29** 40s. **30** Charles Bronson.

1 In medical terms, what are you if you are "DOA"?
2 In which crisis, in 1956, did England become involved?
3 What does Anno Domini mean?
4 Which Neil Diamond song was a No. 1 for UB40?
5 In which city is the area of Toxteth?
6 John Sentamu was Bishop of where, before becoming Archbishop of York?
7 In the farce, where did Charley's Aunt come from?
8 Over which sea was Glenn Miller lost?
9 Where is Britain's most southerly mainland point?
10 Andy Todd joined Blackburn from which Premiership club?
11 What do W and S stand for in W. S. Gilbert's name?
12 In "EastEnders", who was the child of Phil and Kathy?
13 In which century was Leonardo da Vinci born?
14 What was invented by Lewis E. Waterman?
15 Who wrote the novel "Emma"?
16 In which German town was "Auf Wiedersehen Pet" set?
17 Which birthstone is linked to January?
18 In which decade was the series "Agony" screened for the first time?
19 How is the General Purpose (GP) Vehicle commonly known?
20 Which poem begins, "Is there anybody there? said the Traveller"?
21 Whom did George Bush defeat to become US President in 1988?
22 "The Town of Titipu" is the subtitle of which light opera?
23 Who was the first person to fly solo non-stop around the world?
24 Which Japanese word means "divine wind"?
25 What did Fred Quimby produce so that his name is still seen today?
26 What was the live cargo on the Mayflower on its second trip to America?
27 Who played the title role in "Edward Scissorhands"?
28 Who wrote the musical "Spamalot"?
29 Who played Ulla in the 2005 movie remake of "The Producers"?
30 In which county is Stonehenge?

Answers | **Pot Luck 54** *(see Quiz 122)*

1 County of Swansea (was West Glamorgan till 1996). 2 Metal strips. 3 Brazil. 4 Abraham Lincoln. 5 Damascus. 6 Greater London. 7 A chef. 8 Eagle. 9 Olivia Newton-John. 10 Seville. 11 19th. 12 J. G. Ballard. 13 "Ring-a-ring-a Roses". 14 Benny Goodman. 15 Belgian. 16 1986. 17 Peter. 18 Born same year (1935). 19 Died of syphilis. 20 Siamese. 21 Prima facie. 22 17. 23 Queen Elizabeth II. 24 Publishing (Writing). 25 Baz Luhrmann. 26 Oldham. 27 30s. 28 Lady Chatterley. 29 Tropic of Cancer. 30 Indonesia.

1 Fountains Abbey is in which county?
2 In which museum would you see Constable's "Haywain"?
3 In what activity would you make a banjo cable or a leaf rib?
4 What moves when a chess player moves two pieces in one move?
5 Where would you go to see the Battle of the Flowers?
6 What would you have if you were a collector of Coalport?
7 How many tricks make up a grand slam in bridge?
8 What is the Viking Centre in York called?
9 What is the national game of the Basques?
10 In which seaside resort was Frontierland built?
11 What is the value of the ace in baccarat?
12 What is the practice of creating replicas of animals from their dead skins called?
13 Which Cluedo weapon is nearest the beginning of the alphabet?
14 What is the minimum number of players in a game of bezique?
15 The aim is to knock down how many pins in a game of skittles?
16 What was the name of the first Rolls-Royce?
17 What is Brighton Pier called?
18 Which Essex town is famous for its Oyster Festival?
19 The Eurotunnel Exhibition Centre was built near which port?
20 In pottery what is slip?
21 What is numismatics?
22 Alfred Wainwright wrote books on which leisure activity?
23 How many wheels are there normally on a skateboard?
24 In which month is the London-to-Brighton Veteran Car Run?
25 Where did bonsai gardens originate?
26 What would you be doing if you practised a strathspey and a pas de basque?
27 What is the practice of formal handwriting called?
28 In knitting what does psso mean?
29 In which city would you be if you went to the Fitzwilliam Museum?
30 What do British stamps not have on them which most other stamps do?

Answers	**Living World** *(see Quiz 123)*

1 Drone. 2 Crab. 3 Antennae. 4 Host. 5 Five. 6 Scarab. 7 Moulting. 8 Fish. 9 Puffin. 10 Shell or shellfish. 11 Dog. 12 Smell. 13 Change of shape. 14 Beating its wings. 15 Raven. 16 Bird sanctuary in Suffolk. 17 Thrips. 18 Three. 19 Sand or mud. 20 Bird (hedge sparrow). 21 Nervous system. 22 Aboriginal Australian. 23 Ladybug. 24 None. 25 Grouse – it is the start of the grouse shooting season. 26 Gristle. 27 Its coat turns white. 28 Song thrush. 29 Cell. 30 Horns.

1 In which Welsh county is the Gower Peninsula?
2 What was first put into £1 notes in 1940?
3 Who were defending champions at the 1966 football World Cup?
4 Who was the first American president to be assassinated?
5 Which city in the book of Genesis is still in existence?
6 What did the City of London and 32 metropolitan boroughs become in 1965?
7 What did Ian Beale train to be in the early "EastEnders" episodes?
8 What bird is depicted over the door of the US Embassy in London?
9 Who has had hits with ELO, Cliff Richard and John Travolta?
10 In which city is Bizet's "Carmen" set?
11 In which century was Abraham Lincoln born?
12 Who wrote "Empire Of The Sun"?
13 Which children's rhyme was associated with the Black Death?
14 Who was known as the King of Swing?
15 What nationality was the winner of the 2005 women's French Open final?
16 In which year did Margaret Thatcher open the M25?
17 What is Pascoe's first name in "Dalziel & Pascoe"?
18 What do Johnny Mathis, Elvis Presley and Little Richard all share?
19 How did Al Capone meet his death?
20 Blue and seal-points are types of which cat?
21 Which Latin term – usually applied to legal evidence – means at first sight?
22 What is the next highest prime number above 13?
23 Who is the famous president of Sandringham WI?
24 What is Victor Gollancz particularly associated with?
25 Who directed the movie "Moulin Rogue"?
26 Where in England was a railway station called Mumps?
27 In which decade of the 20th century was Sean Connery born?
28 Who had a lover called Mellors?
29 Which Tropic line goes through Taiwan?
30 In which country is Aceh province, scene of the 2004 tsunami?

Answers	**Pot Luck 53** *(see Quiz 120)*

1 Dead On Arrival. 2 The Suez Crisis. 3 In the year of our Lord. 4 "Red Red Wine". 5 Liverpool. 6 Birmingham. 7 Brazil. 8 English Channel. 9 Lizard Point. 10 Charlton. 11 William Schwenck. 12 Ben. 13 15th. 14 Fountain Pen. 15 Jane Austen. 16 Dusseldorf. 17 Garnet. 18 1970s. 19 Jeep. 20 "The Listeners". 21 Michael Dukakis. 22 The Mikado. 23 Steve Fossett. 24 Kamikaze. 25 Tom and Jerry cartoons. 26 Slaves. 27 Johnny Depp. 28 Eric Idle. 29 Uma Thurman. 30 Wiltshire.

1 What is the male honey bee known as?
2 Hermit and spider are types of what?
3 What is another name for an insect's feelers?
4 What name is given to the body a parasite feeds on?
5 How many eyes does a bee have?
6 Which beetle was sacred to the Egyptians?
7 What is the process of casting skin, hair or feathers called?
8 What is a gurnard?
9 Which bird is associated with Lundy Island?
10 What is a conch?
11 What sort of animal is a papillon?
12 What is the olfactory sense?
13 What does the term metamorphosis mean?
14 What is a hummingbird's hum caused by?
15 Which is the largest member of the crow family?
16 What and where is Minsmere?
17 What is another name for thunderflies or thunderbugs?
18 How many parts are there to an insect's body?
19 What do lugworms live in?
20 What is a dunnock?
21 Which system controls touch, sight and hearing?
22 From which language does the word budgerigar come?
23 What do the Americans call what the British call a ladybird?
24 How many wings does a flea have?
25 For whom is the Glorious Twelfth not glorious?
26 What is another name for cartilage?
27 How does a stoat's appearance change in the winter?
28 What is a mavis?
29 What is the smallest living unit called?
30 What do polled cattle not have?

Answers	Hobbies & Leisure 1 *(see Quiz 121)*

1 North Yorkshire. 2 National Gallery. 3 Knitting. 4 Castle, King. 5 Jersey. 6 China.
7 13. 8 Jorvik. 9 Pelota. 10 Morecambe. 11 One. 12 Taxidermy. 13 Candlestick.
14 Two. 15 Nine. 16 Silver Ghost. 17 Palace Pier. 18 Colchester. 19 Folkestone. 20
Liquid clay. 21 Study and collection of coins. 22 Fell walking. 23 Four. 24 November.
25 China. 26 Scottish dancing. 27 Calligraphy. 28 Pass slipped stitch over. 29
Cambridge. 30 The name of the country.

1 Which London hospital took its first infant patient in 1852?
2 Which Cornish village claims to be the birthplace of King Arthur?
3 Which is the main river to flow through Hamburg?
4 Which band had a lead singer called Morrissey?
5 Who was jilted on her wedding day in "Great Expectations"?
6 What patent did Graham Bell file three hours before Elisha Gray?
7 What was the nickname given to V1 Flying bombs in World War II?
8 Which common British garden creature belongs to the locust family?
9 What damaged Alexandra Palace in both 1873 and 1980?
10 Which motel provides the setting in "Psycho"?
11 In which century was David Livingstone born?
12 Which character was the transvestite in "M*A*S*H"?
13 Who was the first female presenter of "Blue Peter"?
14 What does Genghis Khan mean?
15 Who wrote the book "Clayhanger"?
16 Which ocean liner, retired in 1967, became a hotel in Long Beach?
17 Paper sized 210mm x 297mm is known by which A number?
18 If it's 12 noon GMT what time is it in Berlin?
19 C.M.B. are the initials of which Simpsons character?
20 Preston is on which river?
21 What colour was the Three Lions logo on England's shirts in the 2005 Ashes?
22 Which was the last Oxford University college to be made up of all female students?
23 Alan Minter was undisputed world boxing champion at which weight?
24 Who plays the American love interest in "Match Point"?
25 On a World War II battleship, what was called a Mae West ?
26 On record, who was the child with the talking magic piano?
27 Who had the only speaking part in Marcel Marceau's "Silent Movie"?
28 Charles Ross and Epicure are types of which fruit?
29 What time is it when Wee Willie Winkie runs through the town?
30 Who founded the Jesuits?

Answers | Pot Luck 56 *(see Quiz 126)*

1 Greater Manchester. 2 The Pope. 3 The Pickwick Papers. 4 Miami Beach. 5 Sinn Fein. 6 The Cresta Run. 7 Mandrills. 8 Sami Hyypia. 9 12. 10 "Miss Independent". 11 William Ewart. 12 The gherkin. 13 Sir James Goldsmith. 14 God. 15 London Marathon. 16 Malcolm Bradbury. 17 Cribbage. 18 Comma. 19 15th. 20 Dandy. 21 Minnie Driver. 22 "Bar". 23 Androcles. 24 A contour line. 25 20s. 26 Chigwell. 27 None. 28 Ruby. 29 Henry II. 30 Aardwolf.

1 Who was the first boss to win the championship with separate English clubs?
2 How many FA Cup Finals did George Best play in?
3 How old was Roy Keane when he moved to Celtic?
4 Which Scottish team are known as the Wee Rovers?
5 Which club's ground has the Darwen End?
6 Which newspaper involved Sven Goran Eriksson with the "fake sheikh"?
7 Which country did Dennis Tuert play for?
8 John Collins made his debut at which Scottish club?
9 Where was John Barnes born?
10 Who was the first keeper to captain an FA Cup-winning side?
11 Which Yorkshire club has its ground in Grove Street?
12 Which club did Dean Ashton leave to join Norwich?
13 Which Athletic side are known as the Wasps?
14 Which London team won the first Full Members' Cup in 1986?
15 Which footballing Danny refused to go on "This is Your Life"?
16 Which Gary was crocked by Gazza's wild 1991 FA Cup Final tackle?
17 Who was the first black player/manager of an English league side?
18 Muzzy Izzet represented which country in the 2002 World Cup?
19 Rafael Benitez took which club to triumph in La Liga?
20 What did Bolton, Derby and Stoke all do in the summer of 1997?
21 In which decade did Wales first reach the final stages of the World Cup?
22 Which was the first Belgian club to win a major European trophy?
23 Which England manager was born in Sacriston, Co. Durham?
24 Which country does the club Flamengo come from?
25 What was Stirling Albion's famous Scottish first for their ground?
26 In the 90s which player has played against and for Chelsea in FA Cup Finals?
27 Who were the only British team to win the UEFA Cup in the 1980s?
28 Who was Portsmouth boss in between the Harry Redknapp tenures?
29 David James joined Liverpool from which team?
30 Who play at Brockville Park?

Answers | **Action Movies** *(see Quiz 127)*

1 Blofeld. 2 Robert Aldrich. 3 From Russia with Love. 4 The Riddler. 5 Dante's Peak. 6 Bruce Lee. 7 Beer. 8 Boxing. 9 Doctor. 10 Bus. 11 Donnie Brasco. 12 San Francisco. 13 Tomorrow Never Dies. 14 Die Hard with a Vengeance. 15 Jane Seymour. 16 1930s. 17 Heaven and Earth. 18 Submarine. 19 Vietnam. 20 Frank Sinatra. 21 Sylvester Stallone. 22 Terminator 2. 23 Michelle Pfeiffer. 24 Barry Norman. 25 Francis Ford Coppola. 26 Waterworld. 27 Tina Turner. 28 Marseilles. 29 Apollo 13. 30 Sean Connery.

1 In which county is Wigan?
2 Who sends encyclical letters?
3 Mr Wardle of Dingley Dell appeared in which Dickens book?
4 Where was the "Police Academy 5" movie set?
5 Which Party was introduced to Ireland in 1902 by Arthur Griffin?
6 Which world-famous European sporting track is rebuilt every year?
7 What name is given to the monkeys with red and blue bottoms?
8 Which footballer went from MyPa 47 to Willem II to Liverpool?
9 What is the highest number on the Richter scale?
10 What was Kelly Clarkson's 2003 debut single?
11 What do W and E stand for in W. E. Gladstone's name?
12 How is the Swiss Re headquarters building more commonly known?
13 Who led the Referendum Party in 1997?
14 Theophobia is a fear of what?
15 Katrin Dorre had a hat-trick of wins in the 90s in which event?
16 Who wrote "The History Man"?
17 What card game can you peg out in?
18 Which punctuation mark has the same name as a butterfly?
19 In which century was Michelangelo born?
20 In which comic did Korky the Cat first appear?
21 Who played John Cleese's daughter in "Will & Grace"?
22 What word can go before "gain", "row" and "tender"?
23 In legend, who removed the thorn from the lion's paw?
24 What line on a map connects points of the same height?
25 In which decade of the 20th century was Doris Day born?
26 In which suburb was "Birds of a Feather" set?
27 How many professional fights did Rocky Marciano lose?
28 Which birthstone is linked to July?
29 What was the answer that won the first "Who Wants to be a Millionaire" million?
30 Alphabetically, which is the second creature in the dictionary?

Answers | Pot Luck 55 (see Quiz 124)

1 The Great Ormond Street Children's Hospital. 2 Tintagel. 3 The Elbe. 4 The Smiths. 5 Miss Havisham. 6 Telephone. 7 Doodlebugs. 8 The grasshopper. 9 Fire. 10 The Bates Motel. 11 19th. 12 Corporal Klinger. 13 Leila Williams. 14 Universal ruler. 15 Arnold Bennett. 16 Queen Mary. 17 A4. 18 1 p.m. 19 Mr Burns. 20 Ribble. 21 Blue. 22 St Hilda's College. 23 Middleweight. 24 Scarlett Johansson. 25 A life jacket. 26 Sparky. 27 Marcel Marceau. 28 Apples. 29 Past 8 o'clock. 30 Ignatius Loyola.

1 Which Bond villain has been played by Telly Savalas and Donald Pleasence?
2 Who directed "Hustle" and "The Dirty Dozen"?
3 What was the second Bond film?
4 Which role did Jim Carrey play in "Batman Forever"?
5 In which 1997 film does Pierce Brosnan play a vulcanologist?
6 Whose film biography was called "Dragon"?
7 What does "Ice Cold" refer to in the John Mills film "Ice Cold in Alex"?
8 Which sport features in "Million Dollar Baby"?
9 What was the occupation of the Fugitive?
10 Which means of transport dominates in "Speed"?
11 Which 1997 Mafia film starred Al Pacino and Johnny Depp?
12 In which US city is "Metro" set?
13 What was Pierce Brosnan's second film as James Bond?
14 What was the third "Die Hard" film called?
15 Who played Bond girl Solitaire in "Live and Let Die"?
16 In which decade does the action of "Raiders of the Lost Ark" take place?
17 What was Oliver Stone's final Vietnam Trilogy film?
18 Which means of transport features in "The Hunt for Red October"?
19 Which country is the setting for Oliver Stone's "Platoon"?
20 Who plays the US captain escaping an Italian POW camp in "Von Ryan's Express"?
21 Who co-wrote and starred in "Cliffhanger" in 1993?
22 Which action movie is subtitled "Judgment Day"?
23 Who is the actress caught between an undercover cop and a drug dealer in "Tequila Sunrise"?
24 Which film critic's father produced "The Cruel Sea"?
25 Who directed the first three "Godfather" films?
26 Which 1995 film allegedly cost £1.3 million per minute screen time?
27 Which singer joined Mel Gibson for "Mad Max Beyond Thunderdome"?
28 Which city is the setting for "French Connection II"?
29 Which film's action begins with "Houston, we have a problem"?
30 Who played 007 in 1984 in "Never Say Never Again"?

Answers	Football (see Quiz 125)

1 Herbert Chapman. 2 None. 3 34. 4 Albion Rovers. 5 Blackburn Rovers. 6 News Of the World. 7 England. 8 Hibs. 9 Jamaica. 10 Dave Beasant. 11 Barnsley. 12 Crewe. 13 Alloa. 14 Chelsea. 15 Blanchflower. 16 Charles. 17 Viv Anderson. 18 Turkey. 19 Valencia. 20 Moved grounds. 21 50s. 22 Anderlecht. 23 Bobby Robson. 24 Brazil. 25 First artificial pitch. 26 Mark Hughes. 27 Ipswich. 28 Alain Perrin. 29 Watford. 30 Falkirk.

1 What was a hit for Bobby "Boris" Pickett and the Crypt-Kickers?
2 What was the first name of Woody Allen's third wife?
3 Which former US president was born in Tampico, Illinois?
4 Which country signed the Waitangi Treaty with Britain?
5 What was the sequel to "Winnie the Pooh"?
6 What is the common name for inflamed sebaceous glands?
7 What kind of creature is a Queen Alexandra's Birdwing?
8 What returned to Piccadilly Circus in 1947 after being in hiding during the war?
9 What is the subject of Landseer's painting "The Monarch of the Glen"?
10 Which member of Queen wrote "Radio Ga Ga"?
11 What is the only English anagram of CROUTON?
12 Which English county was the home to the world's first iron bridge?
13 The Thomas Cup is awarded in which sport?
14 In woodwork, what does a tenon fit to form a joint?
15 Who was the hero of "The Camels are Coming", published in 1932?
16 What was Tonto's horse called?
17 What is the capital of Angola?
18 Who wrote the novel "The Tenant of Wildfell Hall"?
19 What type of skate was invented in 1760 by Joseph Merlin?
20 Which Indian cricketer was nicknamed "Little Master"?
21 In fiction, where did Tom Brown graduate to?
22 In which century was Mozart born?
23 Which character did Laurence Olivier play in "Brideshead Revisited"?
24 What revolutionary fought with Castro and eventually died in Bolivia?
25 Who wrote the First World War poem "Anthem for Doomed Youth"?
26 In Scrabble, how many points is the letter R worth?
27 Which city was described as a "window on Europe" by Peter the Great?
28 Who was Inspector Clouseau's manservant?
29 In which Dickens novel does John Jarndyce appear?
30 Which US city felt an earthquake for 47 seconds on April 18 1906?

Answers	Pop: Groups *(see Quiz 130)*

1 Bangles. 2 Norway. 3 Manfred Mann. 4 Feeder. 5 "Heart of Glass". 6 Art of Noise. 7 Applejacks. 8 Goss. 9 Bananarama. 10 Andy Fairweather-Low. 11 Catatonia. 12 The Bay City Rollers. 13 Pink Floyd. 14 The Byrds. 15 "With a Little Help from My Friends". 16 Aphrodite's Child. 17 Ireland. 18 The Small Faces. 19 Middle of the Road. 20 Adam Faith. 21 The Jam. 22 The Band. 23 The Bluebells. 24 Hot Chocolate. 25 The Bachelors. 26 Texas. 27 The Wombles. 28 Beautiful South. 29 Colchester. 30 Hull.

1 Who presented "Crimewatch UK" with Nick Ross prior to Jill Dando?
2 Which "EastEnders" character was played by veteran actor Ray Brooks?
3 Who is the priest played by Stephen Tomkinson in "Ballykissangel"?
4 Who replaced Botham and Beaumont on "A Question of Sport"?
5 Which Martin played Judge John Deed?
6 Who left "Blue Peter" to join the "Clothes Show" team?
7 Who is known as "Mr Trick Shot"?
8 Who starred as Blanco in "Porridge"?
9 Which TV star's first record release was "Extremis"?
10 Who won "Celebrity Big Brother" at the start of 2006?
11 Who were the stars of "A Close Shave"?
12 Who wrote "The Singing Detective" and "Pennies from Heaven"?
13 Which Agatha Christie sleuth was played by Geraldine McEwan?
14 Who co-starred with Adam Faith in "Love Hurts"?
15 Who is Anthea Turner's TV presenter sister?
16 Who left "Peak Practice" for "Bliss"?
17 Which female replaced Matthew Kelly as host of "Stars in Their Eyes"?
18 Who was known as the Green Goddess?
19 Who first presented the weather on BBC's "Breakfast Time"?
20 Who was known as the Galloping Gourmet?
21 Who became resident cook on GMTV in spring 1997?
22 Who first presented "The Antiques Roadshow" in 1981?
23 Who first presented Channel 4's game show "Deal or No Deal"?
24 Who hosted the retrospective quiz show "Backdate"?
25 Which TV star was flown in from the US to introduce the Spice Girls' first live UK performance?
26 Who is dubbed the King of Swing during election campaigns?
27 Who replaced Anthea Turner on GMTV's breakfast couch?
28 Who is Beverley Callard's actress daughter?
29 Who first presented "Nine O'Clock Live" on GMTV?
30 Who first presented "Sunday AM", which replaced "Breakfast with Frost"?

| **Answers** | **Pot Luck 58** *(see Quiz 131)* |

1 Light blue. 2 Four years. 3 Winchester. 4 Lake Superior. 5 Darts. 6 Ermine Street. 7 Japan. 8 Unforgiven. 9 Andy Johnson (Crystal Palace). 10 It turns to stone. 11 16th. 12 Prince Philip. 13 LeAnn Rimes. 14 Andante. 15 Atlantic. 16 Japanese. 17 Anthony Burgess. 18 Kansas. 19 Booth. 20 Edinburgh. 21 Hooves. 22 An Oscar. 23 Moon River. 24 Benjamin Jonson. 25 40s. 26 Jimmy Young. 27 "Feel Good Time". 28 Haile Selassie. 29 Ruth. 30 Bashful.

1 Which all-girl group included Michael Steele?
2 Which country did A-Ha come from?
3 Mike D'Abo and Paul Jones sang with which group?
4 "Buck Rogers" was the first top ten hit for which band?
5 What was Blondie's first No. 1?
6 Who has had hits featuring Duane Eddy, Max Headroom and Tom Jones?
7 Which 60s group charted with "Tell Me When"?
8 What was the surname of Luke and Matt of Bros?
9 Who were Sarah Dullin, Siobhan Fahey and Keren Woodward?
10 Who was lead singer with Amen Corner?
11 "International Velvet" and "Paper Scissors Stone" are albums by which group?
12 Which group featured Stewart "Woody" Wood?
13 Which group made records about an Arnold and an Emily?
14 Roger McGuinn and David Crosby were in which 60s band?
15 What was Wet Wet Wet's first No. 1?
16 Which 60s group featured Demis Roussos and Vangelis?
17 Thin Lizzy came from which country?
18 Steve Marriott and Ronnie Lane were in which band?
19 Which group were responsible for "Chirpy Chirpy Cheep Cheep"?
20 In the 60s whom did the Roulettes back?
21 Who were "Going Underground" in 1980?
22 Who backed Bob Dylan on his late 60s and 70s tour?
23 Which Scottish group hit No. 1 after splitting up thanks to airplay from a Volkswagen ad in 1993?
24 Errol Browne is lead singer with which long-standing group?
25 Which group first charted with the Paul Simon classic "The Sound of Silence"?
26 Whose hits include "Halo", "Say What You Want" and "Carnival Girl"?
27 Which furry group were put together by Mike Batt?
28 Jacqueline Abbott and Briana Corrigan have sung with which group?
29 What is Blur's hometown?
30 Where were the Housemartins based?

| **Answers** | **Pot Luck 57** *(see Quiz 128)* |

1 "The Monster Mash". 2 Soon-Yi. 3 Ronald Reagan. 4 New Zealand. 5 The House at Pooh Corner. 6 Acne. 7 A butterfly. 8 Eros. 9 A stag. 10 Roger Taylor. 11 Contour. 12 Shropshire. 13 Badminton. 14 Mortise. 15 Biggles. 16 Scout. 17 Luanda. 18 Anne Brontë. 19 Roller skate. 20 Sunil Gavaskar. 21 Oxford. 22 18th. 23 Lord Marchmain. 24 Che Guevara. 25 Wilfred Owen. 26 1. 27 St Petersburg. 28 Cato. 29 Bleak House. 30 San Francisco.

1 What is the background colour of the United Nations flag?
2 How old is a horse when it changes to a mare from a filly?
3 Which city is home to Britain's longest cathedral?
4 Which of the Great Lakes is the largest freshwater lake in the world?
5 The BDO is the UK governing body of which sport?
6 Which Roman road linked London to York?
7 What country are chrysanthemums native to?
8 Clint Eastwood won his first Best Director Oscar for which film?
9 Who was the Premiership's second top scorer as his club went down in 2005?
10 What happens to something if it is – literally – petrified?
11 In which century was William Shakespeare born?
12 Which Royal celebrates his birthday on June 10?
13 "Can't Fight the Moonlight" was the first No. 1 for which singer?
14 Which musical term means at a walking pace?
15 What does the A stand for in NATO?
16 The word tsunami originated from which language?
17 Who wrote the novel "A Clockwork Orange"?
18 Which American state is home to Dodge City?
19 What was Cherie Blair's surname before her wedding to Tony?
20 Which city hosted rugby union's Heineken Cup final of 2005?
21 What does an ungulate animal have?
22 What is 10 inches tall, gold-plated and weighs seven pounds?
23 In song, what river is wider than a mile?
24 In 1616, who became the first Poet Laureate?
25 In which decade of the 20th century was Robert de Niro born?
26 Which Radio 2 DJ used to finish his show with "TTFN" or "BFN"?
27 Which Pink song features in the film "Charlie's Angels: Full Throttle"?
28 How was Ras Tafari Makonnen better known?
29 In the Old Testament, the book of which woman directly follows Judges?
30 Alphabetically, who is the first of Snow White's Seven Dwarfs?

| **Answers** | TV: Who's Who *(see Quiz 129)* |

1 Sue Cook. 2 Joe. 3 Peter Clifford. 4 Ally McCoist, John Parrott. 5 Shaw. 6 Tim Vincent. 7 John Virgo. 8 David Jason. 9 Gillian Anderson. 10 Chantelle Houghton. 11 Wallace and Gromit. 12 Dennis Potter. 13 Miss Marple. 14 Zoë Wanamaker. 15 Wendy Turner. 16 Simon Shepherd. 17 Cat Deeley. 18 Diana Moran. 19 Francis Wilson. 20 Graham Kerr. 21 Ross Burden. 22 Hugh Scully. 23 Noel Edmonds. 24 Valerie Singleton. 25 Jennifer Aniston. 26 Peter Snow. 27 Fiona Phillips. 28 Rebecca Callard. 29 Lorraine Kelly. 30 Andrew Marr.

1 Which type of wheat is used in gnocchi?
2 What type of meat is used in osso bucco?
3 What is the flavour of kummel?
4 Which cream has more fat, clotted cream or double cream?
5 What are suntinas?
6 What is special about porcini mushrooms?
7 How is Parmigiano Reggiano usually known in the UK?
8 Burtonwood Ales were originally based near which town?
9 What sort of meat is silverside?
10 What is the Italian equivalent of a French vin de table?
11 Which spirit is used in a Manhattan?
12 Which fruit flavour is used in crêpes suzette?
13 What are the two main ingredients of a coulibiac?
14 What is sake wine made from?
15 Which flavoured liqueur is used to make Kir?
16 What are the two main ingredients of kedgeree?
17 Which breeds of cow produce so-called gold-top milk?
18 Which liqueur is used in a sidecar?
19 Which type of pastry is usually bought frozen in wafer-thin slices?
20 Which two cheeses are layered in a Huntsman cheese?
21 How many standard bottles of wine are equivalent to a methuselah?
22 What is pancetta?
23 What type of flour is traditionally used in blinis?
24 What are flageolet and cannellini?
25 Which country does chorizo sausage come from?
26 From which part of France does Calvados originate?
27 What is focaccia?
28 Which two main ingredients would you add to spaghetti to make spaghetti alla carbonara?
29 What type of milk has a bottle with a blue-and-silver-checked cap?
30 What is arborio?

Answers | **The Royals** *(see Quiz 134)*

1 Scotland. 2 Princess Beatrice. 3 George III. 4 Duke and Duchess of Kent. 5 Billy Connolly.
6 Martin Bashir. 7 James Hewitt. 8 Lady Sarah Armstrong-Jones. 9 Princess Margaret. 10
79. 11 The Hon. Frances Shand Kydd. 12 Stephanie of Monaco. 13 George V. 14 Angola.
15 Her pet corgi. 16 Princess Anne. 17 HMY. 18 The Yeomen of the Guard. 19 £15 million.
20 Princess Anne. 21 White with cream centre. 22 Winston Churchill. 23 Crathie, outside
Balmoral. 24 Queen Mother (as George VI's consort). 25 Roddy Llewellyn. 26 June. 27
William, Philip. 28 Viscount Linley – garden furniture. 29 Prince Harry. 30 Queen Elizabeth
II's 80th birthday (party for children).

1 What was Disney's second animated feature film?
2 What is a glow worm, as it is not a worm?
3 Where are the world headquarters of the Mormon Church?
4 Which Motown group featured Lionel Richie before he went solo?
5 What was the nickname of boxer Dave Green?
6 Which animal's name is Aboriginal and means "No drink"?
7 Which role did Phil Collins play in a stage version of "Oliver!"?
8 Which flowering plant family includes asparagus?
9 Which Irish county would you be in if you were in Tipperary?
10 Who was Muhammad Ali's first professional opponent outside the US?
11 Who wrote the children's classic "The Secret Garden"?
12 What was the nickname of Sir Arthur Travers Harris?
13 What genus and species is man classified as?
14 Which imaginary island was created in 1516 by Sir Thomas More?
15 Who had a 50s No. 1 with "The Story of My Life"?
16 In which state was "Dynasty" set?
17 Which British school did Kurt Hahn found in the 1930s?
18 In which decade was the series "'Allo 'Allo" screened for the first time?
19 What word can go after "port" and before "seaman"?
20 In which continent is Lake Titicaca?
21 Launched in July 2005, what became the fastest-selling book in history?
22 The "fake sheikh' story mentioned Sven replacing which club manager?
23 In which century was Charles Perrault collecting his fairy stories?
24 If the weather is calm what is wind force on the Beaufort scale?
25 What is the capital of Libya?
26 What was the name of the chess-playing computer that beat Kasparov?
27 Concorde and Louise Bonne are types of which fruit?
28 Which former member of S Club 7 released the 2005 album "Relentless"?
29 Lynette Scavo had how many children in "Desperate Housewives"?
30 What type of quadrilateral has all sides the same length but contains no right angles?

Answers | **World Leaders** *(see Quiz 135)*

1 Bolivia. 2 Milton Obote. 3 Hirohito. 4 Raisa. 5 Anwar Sadat. 6 Arkansas. 7 Sirimavo Bandaranike. 8 1970s. 9 Zimbabwe. 10 Mary Robinson. 11 Juan Peron. 12 Makarios. 13 Charles de Gaulle. 14 Haiti. 15 Menachem Begin. 16 The Red Brigade. 17 1960s. 18 Firing squad. 19 Benazir Bhutto. 20 Canada. 21 Cardiff. 22 Iraq. 23 Leonid Brezhnev. 24 Zimbabwe. 25 Gerald Ford. 26 Pieter Botha. 27 Philippines. 28 Egypt. 29 General de Gaulle. 30 Albania.

1 In which country did Charles and Camilla spend their honeymoon?
2 Who is the first female in line to the throne?
3 Which King (name and number) was the subject of a 1995 film?
4 Who are the parents of Lady Helen Taylor?
5 Who played John Brown when Judi Dench was Victoria on TV?
6 Who interviewed Princess Diana for "Panorama" in 1995?
7 Princess Diana confessed to having had an affair with whom?
8 Who was Princess Anne's bridesmaid when she married Mark Phillips?
9 Who was Serena Linley's mother-in-law?
10 How many lots were there in the Christie's sale of Diana's dresses?
11 Who was Prince Charles's mother-in-law for 14 years?
12 Which Princess was married to the bodyguard Daniel Ducruet?
13 Emily Davison died under the hooves of which king's horse?
14 Which country did Princess Diana visit to publicize the dangers of landmines?
15 Who was Susan who accompanied Princess Elizabeth on her honeymoon?
16 Who was the first royal after Henry VIII to marry after a divorce?
17 Which letters did Britannia have before its name?
18 Who are the oldest royal bodyguards?
19 Reputedly how much was the Princess of Wales's divorce settlement?
20 Who presented the trophy at the 1997 Grand National?
21 What colour are "Princess of Wales" roses?
22 Who was Queen Elizabeth II's first prime minister?
23 In which church did Princess Anne's second marriage take place?
24 Who was the last Empress of India?
25 Which gardener's name was linked with Princess Margaret in the 70s?
26 In which month of the year is the Garter Service?
27 Which two Princes have birthdays in June?
28 Which Royal was an exhibitor at the 1997 Chelsea Flower Show?
29 Which prince ill-advisedly went to a fancy-dress party in a Nazi uniform?
30 Bob the Builder and Postman Pat were involved in which royal function?

Answers	**Food & Drink 1** *(see Quiz 132)*

1 Semolina. 2 Veal. 3 Caraway. 4 Clotted cream. 5 Citrus fruits. 6 Dried. 7 Parmesan cheese. 8 Warrington. 9 Beef. 10 Vino da tavola. 11 Whiskey or Bourbon. 12 Orange. 13 Fish, pastry. 14 Rice. 15 Blackcurrant. 16 Smoked fish, rice. 17 Guernseys and Jerseys. 18 Cointreau. 19 Filo. 20 Double Gloucester and Stilton. 21 Eight. 22 Bacon. 23 Buckwheat. 24 Dried beans. 25 Spain. 26 Normandy. 27 An Italian bread. 28 Bacon and eggs. 29 Skimmed. 30 Italian rice.

1 In February 2006 Evo Morales became president of which country?
2 In the 70s whom did Idi Amin oust from power in Uganda?
3 Which Emperor of Japan ruled for over 60 years in the 20th century?
4 What was the first name of Mrs Gorbachev?
5 Who succeeded President Nasser in Egypt?
6 Bill Clinton has been governor of which state?
7 Who was the world's first woman prime minister?
8 In which decade did Juan Carlos I become King of Spain?
9 Robert Mugabe was prime minister and president of which country?
10 Who became Ireland's first woman president?
11 Who was president of Argentina from 1946 to 1955?
12 Which archbishop became the first president of an independent Cyprus?
13 Who was French president during the Paris student riots of the 60s?
14 In which country did Baby succeed Papa?
15 Which Israeli leader won the Nobel Peace Prize in 1978?
16 Which terrorist group murdered Italy's Aldo Moro?
17 In which decade did Indira Gandhi first become Indian prime minister?
18 How was Romanian dictator Ceaucescu executed?
19 Who was the first prime minister to give birth while in office?
20 Paul Martin was prime minister of which country?
21 The former British PM James Callaghan became Baron Callaghan of where?
22 Ibrahim Jaafari served as prime minister of which conflict-torn country?
23 Who ousted Khrushchev in the Kremlin coup of the 60s?
24 Canan Banana was the first president of which country?
25 Nelson Rockefeller was vice-president to which USA president?
26 Who was president of South Africa before F. W. de Klerk?
27 Corazon Aquino was president of which country?
28 In which country did King Farouk abdicate after a military coup?
29 Who was the first president of the Fifth French Republic?
30 The splendidly named King Zog ruled which East European country?

Answers	**Pot Luck 59** *(see Quiz 133)*

1 Pinocchio. 2 A beetle. 3 Salt Lake City. 4 The Commodores. 5 Boy. 6 Koala. 7 The Artful Dodger. 8 Lily. 9 County Tipperary. 10 Henry Cooper. 11 Frances Hodgson Burnett. 12 "Bomber". 13 Homo sapiens. 14 Utopia. 15 Michael Holliday. 16 Colorado. 17 Gordonstoun. 18 1980s. 19 "Able". 20 South America. 21 Harry Potter and the Half-Blood Prince. 22 David O'Leary. 23 17th. 24 0. 25 Tripoli. 26 Deep Blue. 27 Pears. 28 Jo O'Meara. 29 Four. 30 Rhombus.

1 Which is the third film of the "Star Wars" trilogy?
2 What is the diameter in inches of a standard competition dartboard?
3 "Out of Nothing" was a 2004 album by which band?
4 A beluga is a type of what?
5 Lent always begins on which day of the week?
6 Which royal told the press to "naff off" at the Badminton Horse Trials?
7 David Wagstaffe was the first British footballer to be shown what?
8 Which language does the word "anorak" come from?
9 Why did the catfish get its name?
10 In which city did Liverpool win the 2005 Champions League Final?
11 Who wrote the novel "The Woman In White"?
12 What was the nickname of Arthur Marx?
13 In which century was Richard the Lionheart born?
14 Which US state is renowned for its Black Hills?
15 What kind of school was run by Pussy Galore?
16 Photophobia is a fear of what?
17 What relation, if any, was Pitt the Elder to Pitt the Younger?
18 Catherine Zeta Jones won the Supporting Oscar for which film?
19 Which character did Emma Samms play in "Dynasty"?
20 Which countries share the world's longest frontier?
21 Which country did the Cheeky Girls come from?
22 On what part of the body are mukluks worn?
23 Which film from 1970 tells of a relationship of a boy and a kestrel?
24 What is the first name of the girl who dies in "Love Story"?
25 In economics, who in the 90s was "Steady Eddie"?
26 What is the Royal Navy equivalent of the army rank of major general?
27 Which birthstone is linked to February?
28 Chapter II was the second album from which artist?
29 In which decade of the 20th century was Placido Domingo born?
30 What is the name of the Vatican's army?

Answers | **Pot Luck 61** *(see Quiz 138)*

1 Busy Lizzy. 2 Xian. 3 Royal Canadian Mounted Police. 4 The Railway Children. 5 Coffee. 6 June Brown. 7 The decimal halfpenny. 8 Powys. 9 Richard I. 10 Snowdon. 11 19th. 12 Fyodor Dostoevsky. 13 Malcolm X. 14 Take That. 15 Coca-Cola. 16 Iraq. 17 Kim Philby. 18 "The Paradise Club". 19 India. 20 David Gray. 21 "Rain". 22 Slate. 23 Purple. 24 Stephen Fleming. 25 50s. 26 Paula Radcliffe. 27 Napoleon. 28 Pandora's. 29 Peter. 30 Norwich City's.

1 Which country was the first to legalize trade unions?
2 What does the letter A stand for in AOL?
3 Which revolutionary product did Proctor & Gamble launch in 1969?
4 What does the letter I stand for in CBI?
5 Along with Corn Flakes which cereal did Kellogg's export to the UK in 1922?
6 What name is given to an alloy that joins surfaces together?
7 Which company's first computer, the 701, was produced in 1953?
8 Which company's red-triangle trademark was the first to be registered?
9 Which industrialist became first Lord Mayor of Dublin in 1851?
10 Who invented and marketed a vehicle powered by a washing-machine motor?
11 Which company did Israel Moses Sieff develop?
12 The jelly Vaseline was a by-product from which industry?
13 Which convenience product was launched from its factory in St Andrews Road, Walthamstow, in 1945?
14 Which London retailer sold the first Heinz products in the UK in 1895?
15 Who formed the Electric Suction Sweeper Co. in 1908?
16 How is a complex electronic circuit built on a small piece of silicon more commonly known?
17 Which two companies first developed the compact disc?
18 Who founded the British and North American Royal Mail Steam Packet Company which later bore his name?
19 Fred Dibnah was famous in which industry?
20 Which company introduced travellers' cheques?
21 Lord Nuffield was the first British mass producer of what?
22 Which of his names did Woolworth use as a brand name in stores?
23 Which business did Howard Hughes finance from his oil profits?
24 In which century was the first English patent granted?
25 Which Swiss company first developed waterproof watches?
26 How would polyvinyl chloride be relevant to a double-glazing salesman?
27 What was the first-ever household detergent?
28 What was founded as Fabbrica Italiana Automobili Torino in 1899?
29 Who gave his name to his invention the whirlpool bath?
30 Which company did Terence Conran found in 1971?

Answers | Movies: Superstars (see Quiz 139)

1 Jack Nicholson. 2 Harrison Ford. 3 Meg Ryan. 4 Clint Eastwood. 5 Sean Connery. 6 Clark Gable. 7 Katharine Hepburn. 8 Fletcher Christian. 9 Cary Grant. 10 Lawyer. 11 Tom Cruise. 12 Michael Douglas. 13 Michelle Pfeiffer. 14 Humphrey Bogart. 15 Scent of a Woman. 16 Spencer Tracy. 17 "Thanks for the Memory". 18 Fred Astaire and Ginger Rogers. 19 Joan Crawford. 20 Arnold Schwarzenegger. 21 Waterworld. 22 Anthony Hopkins. 23 Robert Redford. 24 Tony Curtis. 25 Demi Moore. 26 Dustin Hoffman. 27 Meryl Streep. 28 Bette Davis. 29 Sylvester Stallone. 30 Duke.

1 Which plant's scientific name is *Impatiens*?
2 Which Chinese city is home to the Terracotta Army?
3 What did the North West Mounted Police become in 1920?
4 Who were Roberta, Phyllis and Peter collectively known as?
5 Which drink is named after the Ethiopian city of Kaffa?
6 Who played Dot Cotton in "EastEnders"?
7 What coin was made compulsory in 1971 and illegal in 1985?
8 Which county is home to the Brecon Beacons?
9 Which King received the support of Robin Hood?
10 What is the highest UK peak south of the Scottish border?
11 In which century was Fred Astaire born?
12 Who wrote the novel "Crime and Punishment"?
13 How was Malcolm Little better known?
14 Who had a 90s No. 1 with "Pray"?
15 Which drink has "7X" as a secret formula?
16 Ayad Allawi served as interim prime minister of which country in 2004?
17 Who published "My Silent War" in the USSR in 1968?
18 In which series did Frank and Danny Kane appear?
19 Which country was the setting for "Carry On up the Khyber"?
20 "Life in Slow Motion" and "White Ladder" are albums by which singer?
21 What word can go after "rest" and before "hood"?
22 Which stone is used in snooker tables?
23 In "The Simpsons", what colour is Waylon Smithers's bow tie?
24 Which Stephen captained Notts to cricket's 2005 County Championship?
25 In which decade did Minnie the Minx first appear in the Beano?
26 Which Brit won an individual medal in 2005 World Athletics Championship?
27 Which well-known Frenchman designed Italy's flag?
28 Whose box was opened by Epimethius?
29 Which name derived from Greek means stone or rock?
30 Which team's football kit was designed by Bruce Oldfield in 1997?

Answers | **Pot Luck 60** *(see Quiz 136)*

1 Return of the Jedi. 2 18. 3 Embrace. 4 Whale. 5 Wednesday. 6 The Princess Royal. 7 A red card. 8 Eskimo. 9 It has whiskers. 10 Istanbul. 11 Wilkie Collins. 12 "Harpo". 13 12th. 14 South Dakota. 15 A flying school. 16 Strong light. 17 Father. 18 Chicago. 19 Fallon Carrington-Colby. 20 Canada and USA. 21 Romania. 22 Feet. 23 Kes. 24 Jenny. 25 Eddie George. 26 Rear admiral. 27 Amethyst. 28 Ashanti. 29 40s. 30 The Swiss Guard.

1 Who played Garrett Breedlove in "Terms of Endearment"?
2 Who was the male co-star with Sigourney Weaver and Melanie Griffith in "Working Girl"?
3 How is Margaret Mary Emily Anne Hyra better known?
4 Which superstar was mayor of his home town Carmel, California?
5 Who was contestant No. 24 in the 1950 Mr Universe contest?
6 Whose most famous line was "Frankly, my dear, I don't give a damn"?
7 Who used Eleanor Roosevelt as her inspiration for her role in "The African Queen"?
8 Clark Gable, Marlon Brando and Mel Gibson have all played which sailor on film?
9 On film who did Mae West invite to "come up some time an' see me"?
10 What was Tom Hanks's profession in "Philadelphia"?
11 Who co-starred with Paul Newman in "The Color of Money"?
12 Which actor had the line "Greed is good" in "Wall Street" in 1987?
13 Who sang "Makin' Whoopee" on Jeff Bridges's piano in "The Fabulous Baker Boys"?
14 Who won an Oscar as Charlie Allnut in "The African Queen"?
15 For which film did Al Pacino win his first Oscar?
16 Who received an Oscar nomination for his last film "Guess Who's Coming to Dinner"?
17 What is Bob Hope's signature tune?
18 Who were first paired on screen in "Flying Down to Rio"?
19 Which actress was the subject of the film "Mommie Dearest"?
20 Who married the journalist Maria Shriver, a niece of President Kennedy?
21 Which Kevin Costner film was one of the most expensive flops ever?
22 Who played the doctor in "The Elephant Man"?
23 Who founded the the Sundance Institute for new film-makers?
24 Who parodied his hero Cary Grant in "Some Like It Hot"?
25 How is Demetria Guynes better known?
26 Who played Carl Bernstein in "All the President's Men"?
27 Which actress sounded Polish in 1982, Danish in 1985 and Australian in 1988?
28 Who had six Best Actress Oscar nominations between 1938 and 1942?
29 Who wrote the script for "Rocky"?
30 What was John Wayne's nickname?

Answers | Technology & Industry *(see Quiz 137)*

1 Britain. 2 America. 3 Ariel. 4 Industries. 5 All Bran. 6 Solder. 7 IBM. 8 Bass brewery. 9 Guinness. 10 Clive Sinclair. 11 Marks and Spencer. 12 Petroleum. 13 Andrex toilet roll. 14 Fortnum & Mason. 15 William Hoover. 16 Microchip. 17 Philips and Sony. 18 Cunard. 19 Steeplejack. 20 American Express. 21 Cars – William Morris. 22 Winfield. 23 Film. 24 15th. 25 Rolex. 26 uPVC – used for window frames. 27 Persil. 28 Fiat. 29 Candido Jacuzzi. 30 Habitat.

1 Which singer who died in 2006 formed the Wicked record company?
2 What kind of plants is the name Harry Wheatcroft linked with?
3 Which ocean are the Seychelles in?
4 What expense became compulsory for cars in 1921?
5 Which country has the internet code .gl?
6 Which decade saw the first FA Cup Final at Wembley?
7 What kind of reference book was Bradshaw's?
8 What is a butterfly larva more commonly called?
9 Which actress appeared in Woody Allen's "The Purple Rose of Cairo"?
10 Which fictional doctor lived in Puddleby-on-Marsh?
11 In which decade of the 20th century was Mikhail Gorbachev born?
12 What was Bob Marley's middle name?
13 What is the only English anagram of TOENAIL?
14 If it's 12 noon GMT what time is it in Athens?
15 Who wrote "Journey to the Centre of the Earth"?
16 Alan Hansen joined Liverpool from which club?
17 Which club did Duncan Ferguson play for in between spells at Everton?
18 Which is the only active volcano in mainland Europe?
19 In which century was Jane Austen born?
20 On which ranch was "Bonanza" set?
21 How many counters does backgammon have of each colour?
22 Who co-founded the Aldeburgh Festival in 1948?
23 What is the capital of Morocco?
24 Who authorized the authorized version of the Bible?
25 "I am a Bird Now" is the second album by which group?
26 What is the next highest prime number above 23?
27 Who won the decathlon in the 1980 Olympics?
28 "The Lass That Loved a Sailor" is the subtitle of which light opera?
29 What is the name of Tony Blair's first-born son?
30 Careless and Invictor are types of which fruit?

Answers | Pot Luck 63 *(see Quiz 142)*

1 Right breast. 2 The discus. 3 Osborne House. 4 "No Woman No Cry". 5 Nicholas Nickleby. 6 Lungs. 7 Thomas. 8 A type of beetle. 9 Justin Gatlin. 10 The Cadburys. 11 Daniel Defoe. 12 William Joyce. 13 Mongooses. 14 Alvin Stardust. 15 19th. 16 Post meridiem. 17 Private Charles Godfrey. 18 Latin. 19 Stagnation. 20 Nana. 21 Fire. 22 Quito. 23 One. 24 The MGs. 25 Notting Hill. 26 "Iron". 27 BBC. 28 Nepal. 29 Number two. 30 Leicester.

1 Who fought Muhammad Ali in the Rumble in the Jungle?
2 Jennifer Susan Harvey is better known by what name?
3 In which city did George Best pass away?
4 Which Italian said he could not "understand a word Dennis Wise is saying"?
5 What was the first Grand Slam title won by Kim Clijsters?
6 Who was skipper of Middlesbrough's 1997 FA Cup Final team?
7 Who was the female competitor excused a sex test at the 1976 Olympics?
8 Who was the first Swede to win Wimbledon's Men's Singles?
9 Who was Marvellous Marvin?
10 Liverpool signed Fernando Morientz from which club?
11 Mark Dudbridge is associated with which sport?
12 Who won the 125th Open at Lytham?
13 Who was the first black athlete to captain Great Britain men's team?
14 Who retired in the 90s after 15 years as chairman of the FA?
15 Who is Michael Schumacher's younger racing driver brother?
16 Which Spanish player interrupted Graf's reign as women's singles champion at Wimbledon?
17 Who was the English captain of the 1980 British Lions tour?
18 Which boxer was born in Bellingham, London, on May 3 1934?
19 Which left-handed batsman has scored most test runs for England?
20 Who was Leeds's manager before George Graham?
21 Who is the first person to manage Everton three times?
22 Who was first to win the US Masters five times?
23 Which country does Chelsea star Didier Drogba play for?
24 Who was first to ride seven Derby winners?
25 Is England cricketer Andrew Strauss a left- or right-handed batsman?
26 Who partnered Hingis to win Wimbledon's 1996 women's doubles?
27 Who won the US Tennis Open while her father was in a legal court?
28 Who had a set to with umpire Shakoor Rana at Faisalabad in 1987?
29 Who managed Frank Bruno?
30 Who scored Southampton's FA Cup Final winner in the 70s?

Answers | TV Times 1 *(see Quiz 143)*

1 James. 2 "Who Do You Think You are?". 3 Xylophone. 4 Yorkshire. 5 "Desperate Housewives". 6 Courtney. 7 The Flintstones. 8 The Thrift. 9 Prunella Scales. 10 Erica Matthews. 11 Aidensfield. 12 Lawyers. 13 Jack Davenport. 14 Dermot. 15 Napoleon. 16 Fireman Sam. 17 Tin Tin. 18 June Whitfield. 19 1950s. 20 Harry Worth. 21 Gravesend. 22 Ulrika Jonsson. 23 CJ. 24 Gus Hedges. 25 Jane Seymour. 26 "The Thin Blue Line". 27 Blanche. 28 "Flog It". 29 "Paradise Gardens". 30 Diane-Louise Jordan.

1 Which of Janet Jackson's breasts appeared briefly at the 2004 Super Bowl?
2 What is thrown in the Olympics weighing 4lb 6oz?
3 Which house on the Isle of Wight was home to Queen Victoria?
4 Which Bob Marley song got to 22 in 1975 then the top ten in 1981?
5 Which Dickens character had a friend called Smike?
6 What name is given to a whale's breathing organs?
7 Alphabetically, who was last of the Twelve Apostles?
8 What is a devil's coachhorse?
9 Which man won Olympic 100m. gold in 2004?
10 Which family built the town called Bourneville?
11 Who wrote the novel "Moll Flanders"?
12 Whose nickname was "Lord Haw Haw"?
13 What is the plural of mongoose?
14 Who had a 70s No. 1 with "Jealous Mind"?
15 In which century was Al Capone born?
16 What does the time abbreviation p.m. stand for?
17 Which character did Arnold Ridley play in "Dad's Army"?
18 In which language did St Patrick write his autobiography?
19 What is the only English anagram of ANTAGONIST?
20 What is the name of the dog in "Peter Pan"?
21 Pyrophobia is a fear of what?
22 What is the capital of Ecuador?
23 In Scrabble, how many points is the letter S worth?
24 Who were Booker T's backing group?
25 Julia Roberts and Hugh Grant starred in a film about which area of London?
26 What word can follow "cast", "pig" and "steam"?
27 In 2004, where did Mark Thompson replace Greg Dyke?
28 Which country is Mount Everest in?
29 What was the highest chart position held by Coldplay single "In My Place"?
30 Engelbert Humperdinck is from which English city?

| **Answers** | **Pot Luck 62** (see Quiz 140) |

1 Wilson Pickett. 2 Roses. 3 The Indian Ocean. 4 Tax discs. 5 Greenland. 6 1920s.
7 Railway timetable. 8 Caterpillar. 9 Mia Farrow. 10 Dr Doolittle. 11 30s. 12 Nesta.
13 Elation. 14 2 p.m. 15 Jules Verne. 16 Partick Thistle. 17 Newcastle Utd. 18
Mount Vesuvius. 19 18th. 20 The Ponderosa. 21 15. 22 Benjamin Britten, Peter Pears.
23 Rabat. 24 James I. 25 Anthony and the Johnsons. 26 29. 27 Daley Thompson.
28 HMS Pinafore. 29 Euan. 30 Gooseberry.

1 What is the first name of Kavanagh QC?
2 What was the BBC celebrity family history programme called?
3 Patrick Moore is famous for playing which musical instrument?
4 In which county was "Where the Heart Is" set?
5 Which TV show chronicled life in Wisteria Lane?
6 In "EastEnders", who was the child of Grant and Tiffany?
7 Whom did the Simpsons replace as TV's longest-running cartoon family in 1997?
8 What is the name of the infirmary in "Bramwell"?
9 Who played Jane Horrocks's bossy mum in the Tesco ads?
10 Which female doctor succeeded Beth Glover in "Peak Practice"?
11 What is the fictional village where "Heartbeat" is set?
12 What is the profession of the chief characters in "This Life"?
13 Which actor is the son of Nigel Davenport and Maria Aitken?
14 Which role did Harry Enfield play in "Men Behaving Badly"?
15 What did the ARP warden call Mainwaring in "Dad's Army"?
16 Which children's TV character lives in Pontypandy?
17 Which detective has a dog called Snowy?
18 Who is the comedienne mother of the actress Suzy Aitchison?
19 In which decade was "Hi-De-Hi" first set?
20 Which comedian began his show with a shop-window illusion?
21 Where was Dot Cotton living before she returned to Walford in 1997?
22 Who was the blondest person on "Shooting Stars"?
23 Who was Reginald Perrin's boss?
24 Whose catchphrase in "Drop the Dead Donkey" was "I'm not here"?
25 Who plays the title role in "Dr Quinn: Medicine Woman"?
26 In which show would you find PC Goody?
27 What is the first name of Tracy's grandmother in "Coronation Street"?
28 Which antiques auction show was hosted by Paul Martin?
29 Which Geoff Hamilton series was first shown after his death?
30 Who left "Blue Peter" in 1996 and presented "Songs of Praise"?

Answers	Sport: Who's Who? (see Quiz 141)

1 George Foreman. 2 Jenny Pitman. 3 London. 4 Gianfranco Zola. 5 US Open. 6 Nigel Pearson. 7 Princess Anne. 8 Bjorn Borg. 9 Marvin Hagler. 10 Real Madrid. 11 Darts. 12 Tom Lehman. 13 Kris Akabusi. 14 Sir Bert Millichip. 15 Ralf. 16 Conchita Martinez. 17 Bill Beaumont. 18 Henry Cooper. 19 David Gower. 20 Howard Wilkinson. 21 Howard Kendall. 22 Jack Nicklaus. 23 Ivory Coast. 24 Lester Piggott. 25 Left-handed. 26 Helena Sukova. 27 Steffi Graf. 28 Mike Gatting. 29 Terry Lawless. 30 Bobby Stokes.

1 Which part of London is famous for its diamond trade?
2 What was first broadcast from Greenwich by the BBC in February 1924?
3 Who was the longest-reigning British king?
4 Which sport was the subject of the Popplewell Report in 1985?
5 Which building was Prime Minister Lloyd George the first to use?
6 Which group of islands includes Aran?
7 What is the Swiss author Johanna Spyri's best-known children's novel?
8 In sporting terms, what does the BBBC stand for?
9 On which river does New Orleans stand?
10 What was first published in The Times on February 1 1930?
11 In which century was Johann Sebastian Bach born?
12 Who wrote the novel "The Count of Monte Cristo"?
13 Who was the first presenter of "Grandstand"?
14 The "Cat and Mouse Act" was to counter activities of which movement?
15 Which actor linked with the role of Superman passed away in 2004?
16 What was Kojak's first name?
17 Which country has San Salvador as its capital?
18 Who had a 60s No. 1 with "I've Gotta Get a Message to You"?
19 Laurence Olivier took the title Baron Olivier of where?
20 Goldie Hawn is mum to which well-known actress?
21 How many laps are there in a single speedway race?
22 Which inflamed part of your body suffers from encephalitis?
23 In which decade of the 20th century was Che Guevara born?
24 What word can go after "race" and before "fly"?
25 Who ended his Liverpool days with a goal in a 2005 European Final?
26 What is a Dorset Blue Vinney?
27 Where is the University of Strathclyde based?
28 Who is Melchester Rovers' most famous striker?
29 "Breathe" was a number one for Sean Paul and which singer?
30 Which bird was on the old coin the farthing?

Answers | **Pot Luck 65** *(see Quiz 146)*

1 Tower Bridge. 2 Idi Amin. 3 Personal best. 4 The ring. 5 Melbourne. 6 Lola. 7 Charlie Brown. 8 Columbia. 9 May Day. 10 London. 11 David Herbert. 12 Boxing Day – 26th December. 13 Chronos. 14 Violin. 15 17th. 16 Bodies from graves. 17 E. 18 Sardonyx. 19 Skiing. 20 American Independence. 21 Spain. 22 Piltdown Man. 23 The Goons. 24 Dublin. 25 Without an orchestra. 26 1970s. 27 Leskanich. 28 New York. 29 Daphne du Maurier. 30 Glasgow.

1 In which city is the largest Christian church in the world?
2 What is the official home of the French President?
3 On which island is Ajaccio?
4 What is the French town of Limoges famous for?
5 Which part of Paris is famous as the artists' quarter?
6 Where is the European Court of Justice?
7 Ibiza and Majorca are part of which island group?
8 The Oise and the Marne are tributaries of which river?
9 Where is the Abbey Theatre?
10 What is Germany's highest mountain?
11 On which river does Florence stand?
12 Which Mediterranean island was the HQ of the Knights of St John?
13 Which country has most European neighbours?
14 The RER is part of which city's underground system?
15 The Azores belong to which European country?
16 How many Benelux countries are there?
17 Andorra is among which mountains?
18 Piraeus is the port of which city?
19 In which country is Lake Garda?
20 Where does the river Loire flow into the Atlantic?
21 In which central European country is Lake Balaton?
22 Which country do the Faeroe Islands belong to?
23 The Skagerrak links the Kattegat with which Sea?
24 Which country's official name is Konungariket Sverige?
25 The parliament of which country is called the Cortes?
26 Ljubljana is the capital of which country of the former Yugoslavia?
27 Which Republic lies between Poland and Hungary?
28 Utrecht is in which European country?
29 Where is Monegasque spoken?
30 Which is the southernmost and largest of Greece's many islands?

| **Answers** | Pop: No. 1s *(see Quiz 147)* |

1 Partners in Kryme. 2 The Aces. 3 Chrissie Hynde. 4 "If You're not the One". 5 "Tiger Feet". 6 "What Makes a Man". 7 Los Lobos. 8 Evanescence. 9 "Free." 10 90s. 11 "(Come Up and See Me)". 12 Blur. 13 "Dancing Queen". 14 David Soul. 15 "Saving All My Love for You". 16 Gary Brooker. 17 "Vogue". 18 Jazzy Jeff. 19 "Day Tripper". 20 Reg Presley. 21 Kiki Dee. 22 Terry Jacks. 23 "Mr Blobby". 24 "The Legend of Xanadu". 25 "Baby Come Back". 26 "Super Trouper". 27 Geri Halliwell. 28 "Fairground". 29 "Let It be". 30 "What's Another Year?".

1 Which bridge on the Thames is closest to the Tower of London?
2 Who seized power in Uganda in 1971?
3 What does "PB" against a runner's name indicate?
4 What was made by Sauron in a J. R. R. Tolkien book?
5 On TV, in which city is Ramsay Street?
6 Who is Charlie's sister in the CBeebies series based on Lauren Child's books?
7 Which character loves the little red-haired girl in "Peanuts"?
8 Which US space shuttle was the first to gain orbit into space?
9 Which annual holiday did the 1992 government want to move?
10 Which city provides the setting for "Nineteen Eighty-Four"?
11 What do the D and H stand for in D. H. Lawrence's name?
12 Which holiday date saw Michael Owen's first return to Anfield after his spell in Europe?
13 Who was the Greek god of time?
14 What musical instrument was played by Sherlock Holmes?
15 In which century was Sir Isaac Newton born?
16 If you were a resurrectionist, what would you steal?
17 In Morse code what letter is represented by one dot?
18 Which birthstone is linked to August?
19 Albert Tomba has been a world champion in which sport?
20 In which war was the Battle of Bunker Hill?
21 In which country did the fandango originate?
22 Which Man was discovered in East Sussex in 1912?
23 Which comic team included a Welshman, an Indian-born Anglo-Irishman and an Anglo-Peruvian?
24 Handel's "Messiah" was first put on for the public in which city?
25 What does karaoke mean?
26 In which decade was "The Antiques Roadshow" first screened?
27 What is the surname of the Eurovision Song Contest winner Katrina?
28 In which city was "Fame" set?
29 Who wrote the novel "Jamaica Inn"?
30 Which Scottish city has Saint Mungo as its patron saint?

Answers	**Pot Luck 64** *(see Quiz 144)*

1 Hatton Garden. 2 The time signal. 3 George III. 4 Football. 5 Chequers. 6 The Hebrides. 7 Heidi. 8 The British Boxing Board of Control. 9 The Mississippi. 10 A crossword. 11 17th. 12 Alexandre Dumas. 13 Peter Dimmock 14 Suffragettes. 15 Christopher Reeve. 16 Theo. 17 El Salvador. 18 Bee Gees. 19 Brighton. 20 Kate Hudson. 21 Four. 22 Brain. 23 20s. 24 "Horse". 25 Vladimir Smicer. 26 A cheese. 27 Glasgow. 28 Roy Race. 29 Blu Cantrell. 30 The wren.

1 Who had a 90s No. 1 with "Turtle Power"?
2 Who backed Desmond Dekker on "The Israelites"?
3 Who had a No. 1 with Cher, Neneh Cherry and Eric Clapton?
4 What was Daniel Bedingfield's second No. 1?
5 What was Mud's first No. 1?
6 What was the first Westlife single not to reach No. 1?
7 Who had a 80s No. 1 with "La Bamba"?
8 "Bring Me to Life" was a No. 1 in 2003 for which group?
9 What was the title of Deniece Williams's 1977 No. 1?
10 In which decade did Lulu first top the UK charts?
11 What in brackets is added to the title "Make Me Smile"?
12 Who had the first No. 1 on the Food label?
13 Which No. 1 contains the words "hear the beat of the tambourine"?
14 Who had a 70s No. 1 with "Silver Lady"?
15 What was Whitney Houston's first UK No. 1?
16 Who was Procol Harum's "Whiter Shade of Pale" vocalist?
17 Which was No. 1 first for Madonna – "Vogue" or "Frozen"?
18 Who had a No. 1 with the Fresh Prince?
19 What was on the other side of the Beatles' "We Can Work It Out"?
20 Who wrote "Love is All Around"?
21 Who partnered Elton John on his first UK No. 1?
22 Who had a 70s No. 1 with "Seasons in the Sun"?
23 In the 90s, which single bounced back to No. 1 a week after losing the top spot?
24 What was the only No. 1 for Dave Dee, Dozy, Beaky, Mick and Tich?
25 Which song gave a No. 1 for both the Equals and Pato Branton?
26 What was Abba's last No. 1?
27 "Mi Chico Latino" was the first No. 1 for which former Spice Girl?
28 What was Simply Red's first No. 1?
29 The Zebrugge ferry disaster led to which song topping the charts?
30 Which Eurovision Song Contest winner gave Johnny Logan a No. 1?

Answers	**Euro Tour** *(see Quiz 145)*

1 Rome. 2 Elysée Palace. 3 Corsica. 4 Porcelain. 5 Montmartre. 6 Luxembourg. 7 Balearics. 8 Seine. 9 Dublin. 10 Zugspitze. 11 Arno. 12 Malta. 13 Germany (six). 14 Paris. 15 Portugal. 16 Three. 17 Pyrenees. 18 Athens. 19 Italy. 20 Nantes. 21 Hungary. 22 Denmark. 23 North Sea. 24 Sweden. 25 Spain. 26 Slovenia. 27 Czech Republic. 28 The Netherlands. 29 Monaco. 30 Crete.

1 Which group of islands were the first discovery for Columbus in 1492?
2 Which actor from "The A-Team" appeared in "Rocky III"?
3 What is the inscription on the Victoria Cross?
4 Where is Frogmore?
5 What does an ice hockey match begin with?
6 Which family of birds includes the robin?
7 Who played Norman Bates in "Psycho"?
8 What did Steven Nice of Cockney Rebel change his name to?
9 What is Canada's largest port on the Pacific?
10 Which "Simpsons" character opened the Leftorium?
11 From 2000–5, players from how many countries made the Wimbledon women's final?
12 In which decade was Cadbury's Wispa bar launched?
13 Mark Thatcher pleaded guilty to charges relating to a coup in which country?
14 What is the capital of Latvia?
15 What colour was Moby Dick?
16 In which century was Walter Raleigh born?
17 What is another name for a natatorium?
18 Who wrote the novel "Silas Marner"?
19 Whose name is now used for a collaborator with the enemy?
20 In which country was Sir Alexander Fleming born?
21 Who introduced the "New Look" in 1947?
22 Tom Thumb, Tennis Ball and Winter Density are types of what?
23 What does "poly" mean as in "polygon" or "polyglot"?
24 In music, there must be at least how many flats if the D is played flat?
25 Which large bird is sacred in Peru?
26 In which decade of the 20th century was Prince Philip born?
27 Which type of course fishing uses a gag and gaff?
28 Which character did Catherine Zeta Jones play in "The Darling Buds of May"?
29 Euclid established the foundations of which branch of study?
30 How many were present at the Last Supper?

Answers | **Pot Luck 67** *(see Quiz 150)*

1 Lily. 2 Spain. 3 3 points. 4 Meg. 5 Annie Walker. 6 Tear gas. 7 Berkshire. 8 Square. 9 Dr Zhivago. 10 The USA. 11 Henry Fielding. 12 Estonia. 13 Maurice Greene. 14 Bryan McFadden. 15 Coagulate. 16 Polish. 17 Single. 18 13. 19 Dumbledore. 20 Proverbs. 21 Macmillan (Lord Stockton). 22 Fish. 23 Romania. 24 England. 25 16th. 26 Indianapolis. 27 C5. 28 Georgia. 29 Sylvia Plath. 30 Air marshal.

1 What was the first book in English to be printed in England?
2 Which books do castaways automatically receive on "Desert Island Discs"?
3 Who was responsible for "The Complete Hip and Thigh Diet"?
4 In which century was the "Oxford English Dictionary" started in earnest?
5 Which book had to be owned compulsorily by every member of his country's adult population?
6 Which religious sect published "The Truth That Leads to Eternal Life"?
7 Whose third novel was entitled "Beyond Beauty"?
8 Which British publisher launched Penguin titles in 1935?
9 In which decade did Guinness start to publish their "Book of Records" annually?
10 Who began publishing Beatrix Potter's books in 1902?
11 Who wrote "The Thorn Birds"?
12 What was Jeffrey Archer's first successful novel?
13 Which Harry Potter book was published next after "Chamber of Secrets"?
14 What was Jeffrey Archer's sequel to "Kane and Abel"?
15 Who wrote The "Downing Street Years"?
16 Who created the character Emma Harte?
17 Which French novelist wrote "Gigi?
18 Who wrote "Girls in Love", a top seller for children and teens?
19 Who wrote "The Female Eunuch"?
20 Which book title links Jules Verne and Michael Palin?
21 Which Roddy Doyle best-seller won the Booker Prize in 1993?
22 What was Audrey Eyton's best-selling book of the 1980s?
23 In which county was Jane Austen born?
24 What is a bibliophile?
25 Which author created the Bridget Jones novels?
26 Who wrote "The Godfather"?
27 Who wrote "Possession"?
28 What was the name of "Poirot's Last Case"?
29 Who also writes as Barbara Vine?
30 In which county was Catherine Cookson born?

| **Answers** | **Movies: Who's Who?** *(see Quiz 151)* |

1 Renee Zellweger. 2 Glenn Close. 3 The Aviator. 4 Miriam Margolyes, Joanna Lumley. 5 Oliver Stone. 6 Val Kilmer. 7 Ralph Fiennes. 8 John Cleese. 9 John Hurt. 10 Ava Gardner. 11 20th Century Fox, Betty Grable. 12 Fay Wray. 13 Cher. 14 Sheriff of Nottingham. 15 Cameron Diaz. 16 Mick Jagger. 17 George Clooney. 18 Grace Kelly. 19 Tina Turner. 20 Richard Gere. 21 Arthur Miller. 22 The Odd Couple (Walter Matthau and Jack Lemmon). 23 Sally Field. 24 Quentin Tarantino. 25 John Travolta. 26 Sean Connery. 27 Johnny Depp. 28 Barbra Streisand. 29 Sam. 30 Liz Hurley.

1 Which family of plants does garlic belong to?
2 Which is the largest country on the Iberian peninsula?
3 What was the value of a rugby union try prior to 1971?
4 Who is the eldest of the March girls in "Little Women"?
5 Which character was played by Doris Speed in "Coronation Street"?
6 Which gas was first used by the Germans in 1915 against Russia?
7 Which county formerly had Abingdon as its county town?
8 What shape is the trunk of a cottonwood tree?
9 Which doctor was in love with Lara Antipova?
10 Which country is the largest producer of meat in the world?
11 Who wrote the novel "Tom Jones"?
12 Which country has the internet code .ee?
13 In 100m. who won bronze in the 2004 and gold in the 2000 Olympics?
14 Who left Westlife in 2004?
15 What is the only English anagram of CATALOGUE?
16 What nationality was Marie Curie?
17 What does "mono" mean as in the words "monocle" or "monorail"?
18 How many people are portrayed in da Vinci's "The Last Supper"?
19 The late Richard Harris played which character in Harry Potter?
20 In the Old Testament which book directly follows Psalms?
21 Which member of the Lords denounced privatization as "selling the family silver"?
22 Ichthyophobia is a fear of what?
23 Which country was the birthplace of the tennis player Ilie Nastase?
24 In which country was the composer Gustav Holst born?
25 In which century was Elizabeth I born?
26 What is the state capital of Indiana, USA?
27 What name was given to Sinclair's electric, three-wheeled car?
28 In which American state was Ray Charles born?
29 Who wrote a semi-autobiographical novel called "The Bell Jar"?
30 What is the RAF equivalent of the Royal Navy rank of vice-admiral?

Answers	**Pot Luck 66** *(see Quiz 148)*

1 The Bahamas. **2** Mr T. **3** "For valour". **4** Windsor (Castle grounds). **5** A face-off. **6** Thrush. **7** Anthony Perkins. **8** Steve Harley. **9** Vancouver. **10** Ned Flanders. **11** Three (USA, Russia and Belgium). **12** 1980s. **13** Equatorial Guinea. **14** Riga. **15** White. **16** 16th. **17** A swimming pool. **18** George Eliot. **19** Quisling. **20** Scotland. **21** Dior. **22** Lettuce. **23** Many. **24** Four. **25** Condor. **26** 20s. **27** Pike Fishing. **28** Mariette. **29** Geometry. **30** 13.

1 Who played opposite Ewan McGregor in the comedy "Down with Love"?
2 Who played Cruella de Vil in the "real" version of "101 Dalmatians"?
3 Which Martin Scorsese film was about the life of Howard Hughes?
4 Who played the aunts in "James and the Giant Peach"?
5 Who directed "Born on the Fourth of July" and "Natural Born Killers"?
6 Who played the Saint in the 90s movie?
7 Who was chosen to play Heathcliff in the 90s "Wuthering Heights"?
8 Who was the British star of "Fierce Creatures"?
9 Who starred as the Elephant Man?
10 Who married Mickey Rooney and Frank Sinatra?
11 Who insured whose legs for a million dollars with Lloyd's of London?
12 Who was the heroine in the 30s version of "King Kong"?
13 Who played the mother in "Mermaids"?
14 Whom did Alan Rickman play in "Robin Hood, Prince of Thieves"?
15 Who played opposite Leonardo DiCaprio in "The Gangs of New York"?
16 Whose film production company is called Jagged Films?
17 Who played Batman in the 1997 "Batman and Robin"?
18 Which blonde screen legend made only 11 films, three for Hitchcock?
19 Which rock star did Angela Bassett play in a 1993 biopic?
20 Who was Jack Somersby in "Somersby"?
21 Who wrote the screenplay of "The Crucible"?
22 How are Felix Ungar and Oscar Madison better known?
23 Who played Robin Williams's estranged wife in "Mrs Doubtfire"?
24 Who directed "Pulp Fiction" and "Reservoir Dogs"?
25 Who played Vince Vega in "Pulp Fiction"?
26 Which ex-007 appeared for two minutes at the end of "Robin Hood: Prince of Thieves"?
27 Which star actor Johnny had his name linked with Winona Ryder?
28 Which actress directed "Prince of Tides" and "Yentl"?
29 Which role did Dooley Wilson play in "Casablanca"?
30 Who produced the Hugh Grant movie "Extreme Measures"?

Answers	**Books** (see Quiz 149)

1 The Canterbury Tales. 2 The Bible and the complete works of Shakespeare. 3 Rosemary Conley. 4 19th. 5 Chairman Mao's Little Red Book. 6 Jehovah's Witnesses. 7 Zadie Smith. 8 Allen Lane. 9 1960s. 10 Frederick Warne. 11 Colleen McCullough. 12 Not a Penny More, not a Penny Less. 13 Prisoner of Azkaban. 14 The Prodigal Daughter. 15 Margaret Thatcher. 16 Barbara Taylor Bradford. 17 Colette. 18 Jacqueline Wilson. 19 Germaine Greer. 20 Around the World in Eighty Days. 21 Paddy Clarke Ha Ha Ha. 22 The F-Plan Diet. 23 Hampshire. 24 A book lover. 25 Helen Fielding. 26 Mario Puzo. 27 A. S. Byatt. 28 Curtain. 29 Ruth Rendell. 30 County Durham.

1 Who scored the only goal in N. Ireland's 2005 victory over England?
2 Which US president won a Nobel Prize in 1906?
3 Which national holiday was first celebrated in England in 1974?
4 What was Fletcher's first name in "Porridge"?
5 Which city is the capital of the Andalusia region of Spain?
6 What name is given to a coffin by Americans?
7 Which musical's characters include Danny Zucco and Sandy Olsson?
8 Which area of Spain did Don Quixote come from?
9 Which British birds are shot in braces and form a nye?
10 Who was England's 1980 rugby union Grand Slam winners' captain?
11 Who wrote the novel "The Great Gatsby"?
12 In which decade of the 20th century was Paul Newman born?
13 What was the name of the chef in "Fawlty Towers"?
14 What was Margaret Thatcher's maiden name?
15 What word can go before "beans", "quartet" and "vest"?
16 Who succeeded Wordsworth as Poet Laureate?
17 What is the capital of Venezuela?
18 Who had a 70s No. 1 with "Don't Cry for Me, Argentina"?
19 Giles, Jak and Trog are all examples of what?
20 Which country has the football team Anderlecht?
21 What is dowsing?
22 Other than Austria, what other country do Tyroleans come from?
23 The artist Roy Lichtenstein comes from which country?
24 The song "Three Coins in a Fountain" came from which 50s film?
25 Who is the clown in Shakespeare's "Henry IV"?
26 Nitrous oxide is also known as what ?
27 What was Richard Nixon's middle name?
28 If it's 12 noon GMT what time is it in Jerusalem?
29 In which century was Charles Dickens born?
30 In which county is Ambridge?

Answers | Cricket *(see Quiz 154)*

1 Durham. 2 Shane Warne. 3 Andrew Strauss. 4 "Tich". 5 Glamorgan. 6 Warwickshire. 7 Dragon. 8 Phil Edmonds, John Emburey. 9 New Zealand. 10 Yellow. 11 Derbyshire. 12 Bangladesh. 13 Australia. 14 David Lloyd. 15 Mike Denness. 16 Jim Laker. 17 Worcestershire. 18 Left-handed. 19 Tree on the playing area (blown over in a gale). 20 Bob Willis. 21 25. 22 Dominic Cork. 23 Victoria. 24 Essex. 25 1981. 26 Hampshire. 27 1870s. 28 Matthew Hoggard. 29 Australia. 30 Yes.

1 Which 1979 hit was a remixed 2003 No. 1 for Elton?
2 Who collaborated with Elton on the score of "Aida"?
3 Which song has the line, "I sat on the roof and kicked off the moss"?
4 Elton went through a civil "marriage" ceremony with which long-time partner?
5 What was the name of the record label Elton John started?
6 Elton teamed up with Blue for which No. 1 single?
7 Which club made an F.A. Cup Final when Elton was Chairman?
8 Who duetted with Elton on the 2002 version of "Your Song"?
9 Which controversial artist did Elton partner at the US Grammy 2001 awards?
10 Which song contains the words, "and all this science I don't understand"?
11 Which year was the first since 1971 that Elton didn't have a single on the charts?
12 How old was Elton at the time of his civil partnership "marriage"?
13 Which hit starts, "You could never know what it's like"?
14 Which TV personality was compere at Elton's 2005 stag night cabaret?
15 Elton worked on which musical about a ballet-dancing boy?
16 Who duetted with Elton on "True Love"?
17 Which hit spent an incredible 45 weeks at No. 1 in Canada?
18 Which album includes singles "I Want Love" and "Original Sin"?
19 Was it in 1992, 1998 or 2003 that he became Sir Elton?
20 What was the nationality of Elton's wife of the 1980s Renate Blauel?
21 Which single was a hit recorded with Luciano Pavarotti?
22 What is the first word of "Candle in the Wind"?
23 Which creature was the title of a 1970 No. 1 album?
24 Which 1973 album was reissued in 2001?
25 Who was his co-writer on the classic "Crocodile Rock"?
26 Elton is godfather to which member of the Lennon family?
27 In song, what type of transport was Daniel travelling on?
28 Who is credited writing "Don't Go Breaking My Heart" with Ann Orson?
29 Where was the Elton's 2005 civil "marriage" ceremony held?
30 Elton wrote the music to which 2006 vampire musical?

Answers | Pot Luck 69 *(see Quiz 155)*

1 The Sun. 2 A butcher. 3 Severn. 4 Nigel Mansell. 5 The United Nations. 6 Telephone directory. 7 Gladioli. 8 Mary Pierce. 9 "What Took You So Long". 10 Raglan. 11 E. M. Forster. 12 Duarte. 13 16th. 14 3. 15 Minnehaha. 16 Eight. 17 Lily Savage. 18 Neville Chamberlain. 19 Ian McKellen. 20 18. 21 Cherry. 22 Edinburgh. 23 Lions. 24 Roger Hargreaves. 25 Seventh. 26 June. 27 Rose Petals. 28 Denmark. 29 Cruz. 30 John Kerry.

1 Which county were admitted to the County Championship in 1992?
2 Who was Australia's Man of the Series in the 2005 Ashes?
3 In 2005, who became the fourth quickest England player to 1,000 Test runs?
4 What was Alfred Freeman's nickname?
5 Which county has its HQ at Sophia Gardens?
6 Which county did Dermot Reeve take to the championship?
7 What creature is on the Somerset badge?
8 Which pair of spinners – both with surnames beginning with an E – dominated the 80s at Middlesex?
9 Which country did Martin Crowe play for?
10 What is the colour of the "Wisden Cricketers' Almanac"?
11 Which county has its headquarters in Nottingham Road?
12 Which country won their first ever Test in January 2005?
13 Which country was first to win a Test in the 2005 Ashes series?
14 Which cricket personality is known as Bumble?
15 Who was the first Scotsman to captain England?
16 Who became the first Test bowler to take 19 wickets in a game?
17 Which county did Ian Botham join on leaving Somerset?
18 Is Brian Lara a right- or left-handed batsman?
19 What did the St Lawrence Ground in Canterbury lose in Jan. 2005?
20 Which England fast bowler took Dylan as a middle name in honour of Bob Dylan?
21 How old was Mike Atherton when he was made England captain?
22 In 1995, which Englishman took a Test hat-trick against the West Indies?
23 Shane Warne first captained which Australian state side?
24 Which county did Nasser Hussain play for?
25 In what year was the series that became known as Botham's Ashes?
26 Which county did Malcolm Marshall and Gordon Greenidge play for?
27 In which decade did the first Australia v. England Test take place?
28 Which English bowler took 12 for 205 against South Africa in 2005?
29 Which country did Ian Redpath play for?
30 Did Geoff Boycott ever captain England?

Answers	**Pot Luck 68** *(see Quiz 152)*

1 David Healey. 2 Theodore Roosevelt. 3 January 1. 4 Norman. 5 Seville. 6 A casket.
7 Grease. 8 La Mancha. 9 Pheasants. 10 Bill Beaumont. 11 F. Scott Fitzgerald.
12 20s. 13 Terry. 14 Roberts. 15 "String". 16 Tennyson. 17 Caracas. 18 Julie
Covington. 19 Newspaper cartoonists. 20 Belgium. 21 Water divining. 22 Italy. 23
America. 24 Three Coins in a Fountain. 25 Falstaff. 26 Laughing gas. 27 Milhous. 28
2 p.m. 29 19th. 30 Borsetshire.

1 Which is the only star in our solar system?
2 What was Mr Jones's job other than a Corporal in "Dad's Army"?
3 Which river flows from the Cambrian Mountains to the Bristol Channel?
4 Which World Champion appeared on Isle of Man stamps in 1992?
5 Which organization replaced the League of Nations?
6 What was first produced listing 255 names in London in 1880?
7 What is the plural of gladiolus?
8 Which woman lost two Grand Slam finals during 2005?
9 What was the first No. 1 for former Spice Girl Emma Bunton?
10 Which Welsh town gave its name to a style of sleeve?
11 Who wrote the novel "Howards End"?
12 What was Eva Peron's maiden name?
13 In which century was Francis Drake born?
14 How many pedals does a grand piano have?
15 Who was Hiawatha's wife?
16 In Scrabble, how many points is the letter X worth?
17 How is Paul O'Grady better known?
18 Who was proved wrong when he said, "I believe it is peace for our time"?
19 Who played Gandalf the Grey in the first "Lord of the Rings" film?
20 What is the diameter in inches of a basketball hoop?
21 Merton Glory and Napoleon Bigarreau are types of which fruit?
22 The Napier University is located in which city?
23 In American football which creatures come from Detroit?
24 Who wrote about the Mr Men?
25 Which of the Ten Commandments deals with adultery?
26 In which month does Prince William have his birthday?
27 Which petals are used by the royal family as confetti?
28 Controversial cartoons about Muhammad in 2006 came from which country?
29 Which was the first of the Beckham children to be born in Spain?
30 Whom did George W. Bush defeat when he became President for the second term?

Answers	**Elton John** *(see Quiz 153)*

1 "Are You Ready for Love". 2 Tim Rice. 3 "Your Song". 4 David Furnish. 5 Rocket.
6 "Sorry Seems to be the Hardest Word". 7 Watford. 8 Alessandro Safina. 9 Eminem.
10 "Rocket Man". 11 2000. 12 58 years old. 13 "I'm Still Standing". 14 Paul O'Grady. 15 Billy Elliot. 16 Kiki Dee. 17 "Candle in the Wind" 1997. 18 Songs from the West Coast. 19 1998. 20 German. 21 "Live Like Horses". 22 Goodbye. 23 Caribou. 24 Goodbye Yellow Brick Road. 25 Bernie Taupin. 26 Sean Lennon. 27 A plane. 28 Carte Blanche. 29 Windsor Guildhall. 30 Lestat.

1 What did widow Jackie K. become?
2 What was ITV's first live pop programme?
3 Where did the world-record-breaking runner Peter Snell come from?
4 Who was premier of Rhodesia when UDI was declared?
5 In what year was the death penalty abolished in Britain?
6 What did the L stand for in Mary Whitehouse's NVLA?
7 Who was best man at the wedding of David Bailey and Catherine Deneuve?
8 Which No. 1 started "The taxman's taken all my dough"?
9 Which group did away with the "magic circle" process of choosing a leader?
10 Which former boxing world champion was found shot dead in Soho?
11 Jan Palach set himself alight to protest against the Russian invasion of which country?
12 Whom did Lulu marry on February 18 1969?
13 What was the nickname of the East End murder victim Jack McVitie?
14 What was the BBC's longest-running radio show, which ended in 1969?
15 Which line on the Underground was opened in 1969?
16 In which city did John and Yoko hold their honeymoon bed-in?
17 Which senator was involved in the car crash at Chappaquiddick?
18 Whom did Ann Jones beat in the 1969 Wimbledon women's singles?
19 Where did the Stones gave a free, open-air concert, after Brian Jones's death?
20 The Queen dedicated an acre of land in Runnymede to whom?
21 What did Dr Michael Ramsay become in June 1961?
22 Who phoned Neil Armstrong on his first moon walk?
23 Barbara Hulanicki founded which store?
24 How old was Prince Charles when he was invested as Prince of Wales?
25 On which course did Tony Jacklin win the British Open in 1969?
26 Where was the home town of round-the-world sailor Alec Rose?
27 Who designed the new cathedral at Coventry?
28 Whom did Sharon Tate marry in 1968?
29 In which city did the first heart transplant operation take place?
30 Who was linked with the phrase "Turn on, tune in and drop out"?

Answers	Time & Space *(see Quiz 158)*

1 Venus. 2 Mice. 3 First human fatality. 4 Halley. 5 Hawaii. 6 Uranus. 7 Southern Crown and Northern Crown. 8 Six. 9 Eclipse. 10 Gemini. 11 Manchester. 12 Neptune. 13 Order of discovery. 14 Mr Spock. 15 Valentina Tereshkova. 16 Extra Vehicular Activity. 17 Earth. 18 One. 19 Aurora Borealis. 20 Jupiter. 21 27.3 days. 22 Pluto. 23 Saturn. 24 Big Bang Theory. 25 Light year. 26 Mars. 27 Away from it. 28 Venus. 29 Proxima Centauri. 30 The Sun.

1 What is the capital of County Antrim in Ireland?
2 What was Roy Orbison's first UK No. 1 single?
3 What was banned by Napoleon which led to the development of sugar beet?
4 What was the fictional village in "All Creatures Great and Small"?
5 Which motorway goes across the Pennines west to east?
6 How many points win a game of badminton?
7 Who cut off Van Gogh's ear?
8 What musical invention was developed by David Rockola?
9 How many lines in a sonnet?
10 Which fruit is Spain's national symbol?
11 Who wrote stories about Kirrin Island?
12 Which "Ally McBeal" star was in "Guys and Dolls" in the West End, 2005?
13 Who was the Met Police Commissioner at the time of the 2005 bombings?
14 Which birthstone is linked to March?
15 Which star actor links "Father Ted" and "My Hero"?
16 Which story was "West Side Story" based on?
17 In which century was John Constable born?
18 Who was joint manager at Charlton with Alan Curbishley in the 1990s?
19 What is special about the feet of a palmiped?
20 What was Lady Churchill's reaction to Graham Sutherland's portrait of her husband?
21 Which US general was nicknamed Old Blood and Guts?
22 What word can go after "leg" and before "ear"?
23 The Aldeburgh Festival is held in which county?
24 In which decade of the 20th century was Jack Nicklaus born?
25 Carnophobia is a fear of what?
26 "Everything", "As", and "No More Drama" are top ten hits for which artist?
27 Where were the 2005 World Athletics Championship held?
28 Who is the mother of Liam Gallagher's son Lennon?
29 How many different UK Prime Ministers were there in the 1990s?
30 What is the deepest land gorge in the world?

Answers | Pop: Superstars *(see Quiz 159)*

1 Britney Spears. 2 "Reason to Believe". 3 Robbie Williams and Kylie Minogue. 4 Pink Floyd. 5 Mississippi. 6 Aladdin Sane. 7 "Rocket Man". 8 Celine Dion. 9 Prince. 10 George Michael. 11 "Chain Reaction". 12 Breathless Mahoney. 13 Left. 14 Eric Clapton. 15 The Jordanaires. 16 Tina Turner. 17 Queen. 18 Bob Marley. 19 Off the Wall. 20 Prince. 21 Jade. 22 Dolly Parton. 23 Voulez-Vous. 24 George Michael. 25 Never a Dull Moment. 26 Madonna. 27 Mariah Carey. 28 Neil Diamond. 29 Elvis Presley. 30 Elton John.

1 Which planet appears brightest to the naked eye?
2 What creatures were Laska and Beny, who went into space in 1958?
3 Which space first was Vladimir Komarov in 1967?
4 Who first predicted correctly the intermittent return of a famous comet?
5 In which US state is the Keck Telescope?
6 Which planet's moons have names of Shakespearean characters?
7 How are Corona Australis and Corona Borealis also known?
8 How many Apollo missions resulted in successful moon landings?
9 When the Earth or the moon enters the other's shadow what is it called?
10 Which is the only sign of the zodiac named after two living things?
11 Jodrell Bank is the observatory of which university?
12 Which planet did Johann Galle discover in 1846?
13 What is the system of numbering asteroids?
14 Which "Star Trek" character is asteroid No. 2309 named after?
15 Whose spacecraft was called Vostok VI?
16 In moon exploration what was EVA?
17 Which planet lies between Venus and Mars?
18 How many orbits of the Earth did Gagarin make in Vostok I?
19 What are the Northern Lights also known as?
20 Ganymede and Io are moons of which planet?
21 How long does it take the moon to complete a revolution of Earth?
22 Which planet did Clyde Tombaugh discover in 1930?
23 Which planet's rings and moons were photographed by Voyager 1 in 1980?
24 Which theory states that the universe came into being as a result of an explosion?
25 What does the abbreviation "ly" stand for?
26 Which planet has two moons called Phobos and Demos?
27 In relation to the sun in which direction does a comet's tail point?
28 Which planet in our solar system is only slightly smaller than Earth?
29 What is the nearest star to our sun?
30 The sidereal period is the time it takes a planet to orbit what?

| **Answers** | The 60s (see Quiz 156) |

1 Jackie O. (Onassis). 2 "Ready, Steady, Go!". 3 New Zealand. 4 Ian Smith. 5 1965.
6 Listeners. 7 Mick Jagger. 8 "Sunny Afternoon" (The Kinks). 9 Conservatives. 10
Freddie Mills. 11 Czechoslovakia. 12 Maurice Gibb. 13 "The Hat". 14 "The Dales".
15 The Victoria Line. 16 Amsterdam. 17 Edward Kennedy. 18 Billie Jean King. 19
Hyde Park. 20 President Kennedy. 21 Archbishop of Canterbury. 22 Richard Nixon. 23
Biba. 24 20. 25 Lytham St Annes. 26 Portsmouth. 27 Sir Basil Spence. 28 Roman
Polanski. 29 Cape Town. 30 Timothy Leary.

1 "Lucky", "Boys" and "Sometimes" were all top ten hits for which artist?
2 What was coupled with "Maggie May" on Rod Stewart's single?
3 Which solo singers paired up to release "Kids" in 2000?
4 Reclusive Syd Barrett was a founder of which supergroup?
5 In which state was Elvis Presley born?
6 Which album has Bowie with a red lightning flash design on his face?
7 Which Elton John song starts "She packed my bags last night pre-flight"?
8 "A New Day Has Come" was the first top ten of this century for which star?
9 Whose albums include "Diamonds and Pearls" and "Symbol"?
10 In the 90s who got into legal battle with Sony over his contract?
11 Which Gibb brother's song gave Diana Ross a No. 1?
12 What role did Madonna portray in the film "Dick Tracy"?
13 On the cover of "Thriller" Jackson is leaning on which elbow?
14 Which guitarist was "Unplugged" in 1992?
15 Which vocal harmony group backed Elvis from the mid-50s?
16 Who appeared as the Acid Queen in the film "Tommy"?
17 Roger Taylor was a member of which supergroup?
18 Which reggae superstar was given a state funeral in Jamaica?
19 Which Michael Jackson album first included "Don't Stop 'Til You Get Enough"?
20 Which superstar produced music for the 1989 "Batman" film?
21 What is the name of Mick Jagger's daughter by Bianca?
22 Which female singer wrote "I Will Always Love You"?
23 Which Abba album had a French title?
24 Who was "In a Different Corner" in 1986?
25 Which album sleeve featured Rod Stewart sitting in an armchair?
26 A fly-on-the-wall 90s documentary invited the public to be in bed with who?
27 Which artist released "The Emancipation of Mimi" album in 2005?
28 Who duetted with Streisand on "You Don't Bring Me Flowers"?
29 Who won a talent show, aged ten, singing "Old Shep"?
30 Who recorded the album "Sleeping with the Past"?

Answers | Pot Luck 70 *(see Quiz 157)*

1 Antrim. 2 "Only the Lonely". 3 Imported sugar. 4 Darrowby. 5 M62. 6 15. 7 Himself. 8 The jukebox. 9 14. 10 Pomegranate. 11 Enid Blyton. 12 Jane Krakowski. 13 Sir Ian Blair. 14 Aquamarine (bloodstone). 15 Ardal O'Hanlon. 16 Romeo & Juliet. 17 18th. 18 Steve Gritt. 19 They're webbed. 20 She destroyed it. 21 George Patton. 22 "End". 23 Suffolk. 24 40s. 25 Meat. 26 Mary J. Blige. 27 Helsinki. 28 Patsy Kensit. 29 Three. 30 The Grand Canyon.

1 What is a compote?
2 Which of Boeing's jets were launched in 1958, seating 189?
3 Who sang the theme song to the Bond film "Octopussy"?
4 Which mining town is named Berneslai in the Domesday Book?
5 What is the main edible export of Argentina?
6 Who was assassinated by Satwant and Beant Singh?
7 In "The Simpsons" who is reverend of Springfield?
8 Which family of fruit does the kumquat belong to?
9 Which Soviet football team was the first to make a European final?
10 Michael Henchard was the mayor of which fictional town?
11 Which character did Nicole Kidman play in "Moulin Rouge"?
12 What is the only English anagram of FIENDISH?
13 Which desert spreads into South West Africa from Botswana?
14 "The King of Barataria" is the subtitle of which light opera?
15 In which suburb was "The Good Life" set?
16 Hakan Sukor played soccer for which country?
17 Which play by George Bernard Shaw inspired "My Fair Lady"?
18 Which letter and number follow Albert Square, Walford?
19 Which England soccer keeper had the first names Raymond Neal?
20 Who wrote the novel "The French Lieutenant's Woman"?
21 Who sits on the Woolsack?
22 Athene is the Greek goddess of wisdom. Who is the Roman?
23 Who wrote "Hark, the Herald Angels Sing"?
24 Which state became the 50th American state?
25 Who created Perry Mason?
26 Which former film star was US Ambassador to Ghana in the 70s?
27 Who got the sack from the Beatles before they hit the big time?
28 What do H and G stand for in H. G. Wells's name?
29 What was called the Pluto Platter when it was originally sold?
30 In which century was Captain James Cook born?

Answers	**Pot Luck 72** *(see Quiz 162)*

1 A lake. 2 Suspenders. 3 "Life on Mars". 4 Matt Monro. 5 Windsor (St George's Chapel). 6 Hurricanes. 7 Sand. 8 Margaret Thatcher. 9 Cloves. 10 Wednesday. 11 Graham Greene. 12 Erwin (Rommel). 13 David Walliams. 14 Andy. 15 Ten. 16 Teeth. 17 19th. 18 Enforcement. 19 Hockey. 20 "Hey Ya!". 21 North. 22 Turkey. 23 47. 24 Narcissus. 25 50s. 26 Rhubarb. 27 Red with a white flash. 28 Purple. 29 Brad Pitt. 30 Electrician.

1 In which sensational case was wireless telegraphy first used to apprehend a murderer?

2 At what number in Rillington Place did John Christie live?

3 In the 60s whom did James Earl Ray assassinate?

4 What treasure trove did Colonel Thomas Blood try to steal in the 17th century?

5 To two years, when was the last hanging in Britain?

6 In 1981, which leading figure was wounded by John Hinckley?

7 Which parts of the body went into a pillory?

8 Albert de Salvo was better known as what?

9 In which city did Burke and Hare operate?

10 In light opera who wanted "to let the punishment fit the crime"?

11 To ten years each way, when was Dick Turpin hanged?

12 In which month was President Kennedy assassinated?

13 Mary Ann Nicholas and Mary Kelly were victims of whom?

14 In which Gloucester street was the Wests' House of Horrors?

15 The Old Bailey figure of justice holds a sword and what else?

16 What was the the profession of Mary Ann Cotton, hanged in 1873?

17 Who was Britain's last chief hangman?

18 Alphonse Bertillon and Sir Francis Galton were concerned with which aid to criminal detection?

19 George Cornell was shot in which East End pub?

20 In the 70s who was accused of stealing a fur coat and passport from Miss World?

21 In the 17th century which judge sat for the so-called Bloody Assizes?

22 Hawley Harvey were the first names of which murderer?

23 On August 6 1890, Auburn Prison, New York, had the first what?

24 In what decade was flogging finally abolished in Britain?

25 What weapon was used to murder the Bulgarian defector Georgi Markov in London in the 70s?

26 In the 90s which Kray brother was found guilty of drug trafficking?

27 Who shot the person believed to have shot President Kennedy?

28 Who was the first British PM murdered while in office?

29 Edgar Ray Allan was jailed in 2005 for crimes while leading which group?

30 Which doctor was at the centre of the Profumo affair?

Answers | **TV Gold** *(see Quiz 163)*

1 Rat. 2 Daniel Craig. 3 Audrey. 4 Grange Hill. 5 Victoria. 6 Old people's home.
7 Jim Davidson. 8 Sister. 9 "You dirty old man". 10 Terry Wogan. 11 "Robin's Nest". 12 1950s. 13 "The Jewel in the Crown". 14 "Nearest and Dearest". 15 The Munsters. 16 Thora Hird. 17 "Porridge". 18 Privet. 19 Richard Briers, Prunella Scales. 20 Roper. 21 Mobile Army Surgical Hospital. 22 "The Liver Birds". 23 A talking horse. 24 "Brideshead Revisited". 25 Morris Minor. 26 "On the Buses". 27 Tom Baker. 28 Samantha. 29 "Only When I Laugh". 30 Rock 'n' Roll.

1 What is the Caspian Sea, as it is not a sea?
2 What do Americans call braces?
3 Which cop show featured the character Sam Tyler?
4 Who sang the Bond theme "From Russia with Love"?
5 Where is the tomb of King Henry VIII?
6 Active in 2004, who or what were Charley, Frances and Ivan?
7 What accounts for only 28 per cent of the Sahara Desert ?
8 Who was the youngest female Conservative candidate in the 1951 General Election?
9 Which spice is the most produced in Zanzibar?
10 If April Fools' Day is a Tuesday what day is St George's Day?
11 Who wrote the novel "The Power and the Glory"?
12 What was the first name of the man known as the Desert Fox?
13 Who is the taller of the creators of Little Britain?
14 What is Dalziel's first name in "Dalziel & Pascoe"?
15 In Scrabble, how many points is the letter Q worth?
16 What do frogs have that toads do not in their mouths?
17 In which century was T. S. Eliot born?
18 In "The Man from UNCLE", what did the E stand for?
19 In 1971 Pakistan won the first World Cup in which sport?
20 What was Outkast's second top ten hit?
21 Which direction does the Nile River flow?
22 Which country made a 2005 debut as a Formula One venue?
23 What is the next-highest prime number above 43?
24 Who pined for the love of his reflection?
25 In which decade of the 20th century was Bjorn Borg born?
26 Hawk's Champagne and Prince Albert are types of which fruit?
27 What colour was Starsky and Hutch's car?
28 What is the most common colour of amethyst?
29 While making "Friends", whom did Jennifer Aniston marry in real life?
30 What was Lech Walesa's job in the Gdansk shipyards?

Answers	**Pot Luck 71** *(see Quiz 160)*

1 Stewed fruit. 2 The 707. 3 Rita Coolidge. 4 Barnsley. 5 Beef. 6 Mrs Indira Gandhi. 7 Reverend Lovejoy. 8 Citrus. 9 Moscow Dynamo. 10 Casterbridge. 11 Satine. 12 Finished. 13 Kalahari. 14 The Gondoliers. 15 Surbiton. 16 Turkey. 17 Pygmalion. 18 E20. 19 Clemence. 20 John Fowles. 21 Lord Chancellor. 22 Minerva. 23 Charles Wesley. 24 Hawaii. 25 Erle Stanley Gardner. 26 Shirley Temple Black. 27 Pete Best. 28 Herbert George. 29 The Frisbee. 30 18th.

1 What type of pet did Manuel adopt in "Fawlty Towers"?
2 Which future James Bond starred in "Our Friends in the North"?
3 What was Terry's sister called in "The Likely Lads"?
4 Which series featured Benny, Judy, Trisha and Tucker when it began?
5 Who was the third of "Take Three Girls" with Kate and Avril?
6 In what type of place was "Waiting for God" set?
7 Who was Jim London in "Up the Elephant and Round the Castle"?
8 What relation was Hattie Jacques to Eric in their "Sykes and ..." series?
9 What did Harold Steptoe always call his father?
10 Which chat show was the "togmeister"?
11 What was the Richard O'Sullivan spin-off from "Man About the House"?
12 In which decade were weather forecasters seen, rather than just heard on TV?
13 Daphne Manners and Hari Kumar were characters in which series?
14 Jimmy Jewel and Hylda Baker were Eli and Nellie Pledge in which show?
15 Which TV family were headed by Herman and Lily?
16 Which veteran actress played the wife in "Meet the Wife"?
17 In which classic did you find Blanco, Lukewarm and Gay Gordon?
18 What was Bernard Hedges's nickname in "Please Sir"?
19 Who were the two stars of "Marriage Lines"?
20 What was the surname of George and Mildred?
21 What does M*A*S*H* stand for?
22 Which flatmates originally lived in Huskisson Road, Liverpool?
23 Who or what was Mr Ed?
24 Which classic drama centred on the Marchmain family?
25 What make of car did Nurse Emmanuel drive in "Open All Hours"?
26 In which show did Reg Varney play Stan Butler?
27 Who was the fourth Doctor Who?
28 What was the name of the young blonde witch in "Bewitched"?
29 In which series were Figgis, Glover and Norman hospital patients?
30 What completes the title of Debbie Horsfield's series, "Sex, Chips and..."?

Answers	**Crime & Punishment** *(see Quiz 161)*

1 Dr Crippen. 2 10. 3 Martin Luther King. 4 The Crown Jewels. 5 1964. 6 President Reagan. 7 Neck and wrists. 8 The Boston Strangler. 9 Edinburgh. 10 The Mikado. 11 1739. 12 November. 13 Jack the Ripper. 14 Cromwell Street. 15 Scales. 16 Nurse. 17 Harry Allen. 18 Fingerprints. 19 The Blind Beggar. 20 George Best. 21 Judge Jeffreys. 22 Dr Crippen. 23 Death by electrocution. 24 1940s. 25 An umbrella (injected him with poison). 26 Charlie. 27 Jack Ruby. 28 Spencer Percival. 29 Ku-Klux Klan. 30 Stephen Ward.

Answers – page 408

1 Which TV comedy featured the PR man Malcolm Tucker?
2 What name is given to a hill in the centre of any Greek city?
3 What canal was closed from 1967 to 1975?
4 What was the second No. 1 for boy band Blue?
5 Which Olympic sport needs a planting box?
6 Which popular tourist area is Northern Africa's smallest country?
7 Who was the leader of Cuba's rebel July 26 faction?
8 In 2005, who won the World Rally Championship for a second time?
9 What animal was the first sent into space by the Americans?
10 Which city did the Cowardly Lion want to get to?
11 In which century was Charles Darwin born?
12 Who was the director of the first Harry Potter movie?
13 What did the D stand for in Franklin D. Roosevelt's name?
14 Which actress did Cate Blanchett play in the movie "The Aviator"?
15 What is the surname of the advertising brothers Charles and Maurice?
16 What colour was the Trotter's Independent Trading van?
17 What is the capital of Costa Rica?
18 Which store group's slogan is "Never Knowingly Undersold"?
19 Scott Hamilton was a world champion in which sport?
20 Who wrote "Honeysuckle Rose" and "Ain't Misbehavin'"?
21 What do we call the place known by the Romans as Camulodunum?
22 In which place does Desperate Dan live?
23 What was the original meaning of the name Sarah in Hebrew?
24 Karl Landsteiner's work centred on discovering which groups?
25 Which rock star named his son Zowie?
26 Who wrote the novel "She"?
27 Where did the rumba originate?
28 Jason Allen Alexandar married which pop princess?
29 If it's 12 noon GMT what time is it in Cairo?
30 What was the first issued decimal coin in Britain?

Answers | **Pot Luck 74** *(see Quiz 166)*

1 Grace Kelly. 2 Victoria. 3 Peter Gabriel. 4 Moll Flanders. 5 A tidal wave. 6 109 seconds. 7 Salzburg. 8 Felix. 9 Cancer. 10 Liberia. 11 Ernest Hemingway. 12 S. 13 Spoonerism. 14 Coffee/Chocolate. 15 19th. 16 Berlin. 17 "A Ruby Murray". 18 Green. 19 Bach. 20 Duke of Wellington. 21 Robbie Williams. 22 Rembrandt. 23 "By the Way". 24 Niece. 25 Mad dogs and Englishmen. 26 Pete Sampras. 27 Yardley. 28 David Copperfield. 29 TV. 30 30s.

1 "The Magnificent Seven" was a remake of which 50s Japanese film?
2 In which film did John Wayne play his first leading role?
3 Which London-born actor played a boy adopted by Indians in "Last of the Mohicans"?
4 In which 1992 western with Gene Hackman did Clint Eastwood star and direct?
5 What was the sequel to "A Fistful of Dollars" called?
6 Who played the sheriff in "High Noon"?
7 Who was the female star of "Butch Cassidy and the Sundance Kid"?
8 Who played Bernardo in "The Magnificent Seven"?
9 Who co-starred with John Wayne in "The Man Who Shot Liberty Valance"?
10 Who played Wyatt Earp in the 1946 film "My Darling Clementine"?
11 Which musical western has the song "You Can't Get a Man with a Gun"?
12 Who was a singing "Calamity Jane"?
13 Which country singer starred in "True Grit"?
14 In which film did John Wayne play Davy Crockett?
15 Which then romantic partner of Clint Eastwood starred with him in "Bronco Billy" in 1980?
16 Who was the star of "Jeremiah Johnson" in 1972?
17 Which director was famous for his so-called "Cavalry Trilogy"?
18 Who was famous for playing the Man with No Name?
19 Which Indian tribe features in "Dances with Wolves"?
20 Who starred with Bob Hope in the comedy western "The Paleface"?
21 Which former child star starred in "Fort Apache" in 1948?
22 Which western star's theme song was "Back in the Saddle Again"?
23 Who starred in the musical western "Don't Fence Me" In in 1945?
24 Which 1994 western starred Mel Gibson and Jodie Foster?
25 In which 1969 musical western did Clint Eastwood sing?
26 Who was "Little Big Man"?
27 Who sang "Blaze of Glory" in "Young Guns II"?
28 Which director of westerns was born Sean Aloysius O'Fienne?
29 Who directed "Brokeback Mountain"?
30 Where was "A Fistful of Dollars" filmed?

| **Answers** | **The Media 1** *(see Quiz 167)* |

1 British Academy of Film and Television Arts. 2 Channel 4. 3 Director General. 4 Independent on Sunday. 5 Preston. 6 Autocue. 7 Parliament. 8 News. 9 The Discovery Channel. 10 A mounting for a camera. 11 Gaffer. 12 Sunday Times. 13 Sheepdog. 14 Expression!. 15 Lloyd's List. 16 Cardiff. 17 Japan. 18 Four. 19 Grip. 20 Daily Herald. 21 Sport Newspapers. 22 Financial Times. 23 Exchange and Mart. 24 Liverpool Echo. 25 Denmark. 26 Independent Local Radio. 27 Old Moore's Almanac. 28 Oracle. 29 Harlech Television. 30 Spectator.

1 Which actress had her wedding televised in April 1956?
2 What is Africa's largest lake and Australia's smallest mainland state?
3 Who was vocalist in Genesis before Phil Collins?
4 Which character was born in Newgate Prison in the Defoe novel?
5 What hit the ship in "The Poseidon Adventure" causing it to turn over?
6 To 20, how many seconds did Amir Khan's first professional fight last?
7 Which Austrian city was Mozart's birthplace?
8 Which famous cat was created by Otto Mesmer?
9 Who or what killed Eva Peron?
10 Which country boasts the world's largest registered shipping fleet?
11 Who wrote the novel "The Old Man and the Sea"?
12 In Morse code what letter is represented by three dots?
13 What describes inverting the initial letters of two words?
14 Which two flavours combined make mocha?
15 In which century was Charlotte Brontë born?
16 Who had an 80s No. 1 with "Take My Breath Away"?
17 How would Del Boy have ordered a curry?
18 What colour is the inside of a pistachio nut?
19 Which classical composer's "Air" has been used by Hamlet cigar ads?
20 Who was nicknamed the Iron Duke?
21 Which singing star dragged up in Little Britain's a Comic Relief special?
22 Who painted "The Night Watch"?
23 What was the third Red Hot Chili Peppers single to reach the top ten?
24 What relation was Queen Victoria to her predecessor on the throne?
25 According to Noël Coward, who go out in the midday sun?
26 Who was the first man to reach 13 Grand Slam titles in tennis?
27 Helena Bonham-Carter advertised which perfume house?
28 In which Dickens novel does Dora Spenlove appear?
29 What went from 405 lines to 625 lines?
30 In which decade of the 20th century was Melvyn Bragg born?

Answers | Pot Luck 73 *(see Quiz 164)*

1 "The Thick of It". 2 Acropolis. 3 Suez. 4 "If You Come Back". 5 Pole Vault. 6 Tunisia. 7 Fidel Castro. 8 Sebastian Loeb. 9 Chimpanzee. 10 Oz. 11 19th. 12 Chris Columbus. 13 Delano. 14 Katharine Hepburn. 15 Saatchi. 16 Yellow. 17 San Jose. 18 John Lewis. 19 Ice skating. 20 Fats Waller. 21 Colchester. 22 Cactusville. 23 Princess. 24 Blood. 25 David Bowie. 26 H. Rider Haggard. 27 Cuba. 28 Britney Spears. 29 2 p.m. 30 50-pence piece.

1 What does BAFTA stand for?
2 Jeremy Isaacs was the first chief executive of which channel?
3 Which title is given to the chief executive of the BBC?
4 Which London-based Sunday paper was founded in 1990?
5 In which town is Red Rose radio based?
6 What is the more common name for a teleprompt?
7 Who sets the rate for the television licence?
8 Izvestia was a Soviet newspaper. What does Izvestia mean?
9 Which channel has the slogan "Make the voyage"?
10 In a TV studio what is a dolly?
11 What is a studio's chief electrician called?
12 Which was the first British newspaper to issue a colour supplement?
13 In comics what was Black Bob?
14 What is the American Express magazine called?
15 Which daily publication is Britain's oldest?
16 Where is the Western Mail based?
17 In which country is Yomiuri Shimbun a daily newspaper?
18 How many Sky channels were there originally in 1989?
19 Which TV technician is responsible for hardware such as props, cranes etc.?
20 Which newspaper did the Sun replace in 1964?
21 Which newspaper group is David Sullivan associated with?
22 Which UK broadsheet has issues published in Frankfurt and New York?
23 Which publication, founded in 1868, consists wholly of adverts?
24 What is Liverpool's own regional daily paper called?
25 The idea of international copyright developed from measures in which country?
26 What does ILR stand for in the media?
27 What has been published anually since 1697?
28 Which telext system was replaced on ITV by Teletext UK?
29 What was HTV originally called?
30 Boris Johnson was a controversial editor of which publication?

| **Answers** | **Movies: Westerns** *(see Quiz 165)* |

1 The Seven Samurai. 2 Stagecoach. 3 Daniel Day-Lewis. 4 Unforgiven. 5 For a Few Dollars More. 6 Gary Cooper. 7 Katharine Ross. 8 Charles Bronson. 9 James Stewart. 10 Henry Fonda. 11 Annie Get Your Gun. 12 Doris Day. 13 Glen Campbell. 14 The Alamo. 15 Sondra Locke. 16 Robert Redford. 17 John Ford. 18 Clint Eastwood. 19 Sioux. 20 Jane Russell. 21 Shirley Temple. 22 Gene Autry. 23 Roy Rogers. 24 Maverick. 25 Paint Your Wagon. 26 Dustin Hoffman. 27 Jon Bon Jovi. 28 John Ford. 29 Ang Lee. 30 Italy.

1 Whom did the former model Victoria Lockwood marry?
2 How is the actress Estelle Skornik better known in the advertising world?
3 In which European country was Mariella Frostrup born?
4 What is Lord Lloyd-Webber's wife's first name?
5 Which Marquess is the brother of Victoria Hervey?
6 What are Steffi Graf's parents called?
7 Who is patron of the National Osteoporosis Society?
8 What is the name of the daughter of Michael Caine?
9 In which role is Marion Crawford best known?
10 Who was the first public-school-educated PM of the last third of the 20th century?
11 Who are the parents of Lady Gabriella Windsor?
12 Which TV personality is the wife of the editor Michael Wynn-Jones?
13 Whom was Brad Pitt engaged to before he married Jennifer Aniston?
14 How is the challenging former Mrs Nick Allott better known?
15 Who is sometimes known as TPT?
16 Whose file states she was Mrs Clyde Klotz?
17 Which two comedy actors have a daughter called Billie?
18 Whose name was Henriette Peace first linked with in 1997?
19 Who was Martin Bell's campaigning daughter in the 1997 General Election?
20 What is Earl Spencer's first name?
21 Who left "EastEnders" to have baby daughter Maia?
22 Which illness do cook Michael Barry and actress Mary Tyler Moore suffer from?
23 What is Carol Vorderman's university degree in?
24 Romantically, Dani Behr and Victoria Adams have been linked with which football club?
25 Charles Worthington is a famous name in which field?
26 Which actress was the first Mrs Mike Tyson?
27 Sue Barker and Penelope Keith's respective spouses have been members of which profession?
28 In whose garden was Alistair Coe found in 1997?
29 What would Claire Latimer provide for a society occasion?
30 Whom did Renate Blauel marry in 1984?

Answers	Sporting Records (see Quiz 170)

1 Bobby Robson. 2 Squash. 3 Bob Taylor. 4 Salford. 5 New England Patriots. 6 Ruud Gullit. 7 Sandwich. 8 First £1,000 soccer transfer. 9 David Campese. 10 Kapil Dev. 11 Pole vaulting. 12 Leyton Orient. 13 Smallwood. 14 Table tennis. 15 Notts County. 16 Tiger Woods. 17 60s. 18 Alan Shearer. 19 Angling. 20 Jim Clark. 21 Gipsy Moth IV. 22 Bonds. 23 Asaafa Powell. 24 Imran Khan. 25 Emerson Fittipaldi. 26 Liz McColgan. 27 Gliding. 28 Allan Border. 29 Most aces in a match (51). 30 Newbold.

1 Which Sinatra sang the Bond theme "You Only Live Twice"?
2 Which part of France would you come from if you were a Breton?
3 Mark Fish played soccer for which country?
4 Which South American country's name translates to "Rich Coast"?
5 How many inches wide should a wicket be?
6 "Dalziel and Pascoe" is set in which county?
7 Which London landmark was designed by David Marks and Julia Barfield?
8 In which county is the Duke of Norfolk's castle at Arundel?
9 A portrayal of Ray Charles landed which actor a 2005 Oscar?
10 Name Switzerland's largest city.
11 Who wrote the novel "Eyeless in Gaza"?
12 How many golfing majors did Jack Nicklaus win in total?
13 How is Lev Davidovich Bronstein better known?
14 Which link about a major cause of cancer was made by Sir Richard Doll?
15 What was the name of Darwin's survey ship?
16 Whose No. 1 debut album was called "Justified"?
17 How many finger holes are there in a tenpin bowling ball?
18 What was the name of Gene Autry's horse?
19 What is the capital of Liechtenstein?
20 The gemstone Sapphire is linked to which month?
21 Who has a friend called Pie-Face?
22 Who redesigned the Girl Guide and Brownie uniforms in 1990?
23 Who captained the MCC in the "Bodyline" series of the 30s?
24 At which American university was Condoleezza Rice the Provost?
25 What is produced by the lachrymal glands?
26 In which century was Beethoven born?
27 Which sea contains four ounces of salt to every pint of water?
28 Apiphobia is a fear of what?
29 Which piece of music was used as the Monty Python theme?
30 Which liner made her maiden voyage in 1946?

Answers	**Pot Luck 76** *(see Quiz 171)*

1 Ghana. 2 Opossum. 3 Cave paintings. 4 Lorna Doone. 5 Echo Beach. 6 Boy Scouts. 7 Brands Hatch. 8 Smoking. 9 Henley. 10 Bank Manager. 11 James Joyce. 12 Foxtrot. 13 Speed of sound. 14 "Second Thoughts". 15 Malachi. 16 Australia. 17 Phil Drabble. 18 19th. 19 Alaska. 20 Wendy Craig. 21 Rievaulx. 22 "Butter". 23 Field Marshal. 24 Port-au-Prince. 25 Andres Segovia. 26 Frankie Fraser. 27 Adam and the Ants. 28 20s. 29 Christopher Columbus. 30 Gladstone.

1 Who was Barcelona's boss for their record fourth European Cup Winner's Cup Final triumph in 1997?

2 In November '95 Jansher Khan won his seventh World Open title in which sport?

3 Which Derbyshire wicket-keeper set a career record number of dismissals from 1960 to 1988?

4 David Watkins scored 221 goals in a season for which rugby league club?

5 Which team were the first this century to win successive Super Bowl finals?

6 Who was the first overseas manager to win the FA Cup?

7 At which venue did Greg Norman set a lowest four-round Bittish Open total in 1993?

8 What record will Alf Common always hold?

9 Who was the first rugby union player to reach 50 international tries?

10 Who overtook Sunil Gavaskar's Test appearance record for India?

11 Sergei Bubka has broken a record over 30 times in which event?

12 Peter Shilton played his 1,000th league game with which club?

13 What was athlete Kathy Cook's maiden name?

14 Fred Perry was world champion in which sport before becoming a major tennis star?

15 Which soccer club is generally accepted to be the oldest in England?

16 Who is the youngest ever winner of the US Masters?

17 In which decade did Clive Lloyd first play Test cricket?

18 Who was the first player to hit 100 Premiership goals?

19 Bob Nudd had been a world champion in which sport?

20 Which British driver was first to have seven Grand Prix wins in a year?

21 Francis Chichester made his 60s solo round-the-world trip in which boat?

22 Which Billy set an appearance record for West Ham?

23 Who set a new record of 9.77 seconds for Men's 100m. in June 2005?

24 Who in the 80s and early 90s set a record for captaining Pakistan at cricket?

25 Who in 1972 became the youngest F1 Motor Racing world champ?

26 Which record beaker won the first major Marathon she entered?

27 George Lee has been three time world champ in which sport?

28 Which Australian holds the world record for most Test runs in cricket?

29 In Jan 2005 Joachim Johansson set which new world record in tennis?

30 What is Seb Coe's middle name?

Answers	**Famous Names** *(see Quiz 168)*

1 Earl Spencer. 2 Nicole. 3 Norway. 4 Madeleine. 5 Bristol. 6 Peter, Heidi. 7 Camilla Parker-Bowles. 8 Natasha. 9 Governess to Princesses Elizabeth and Margaret. 10 Tony Blair. 11 Prince and Princess Michael of Kent. 12 Delia Smith. 13 Gwyneth Paltrow. 14 Anneka Rice. 15 Tara Palmer-Tomkinson. 16 Gillian Anderson. 17 Lenny Henry and Dawn French. 18 Prince Andrew. 19 Melissa. 20 Charles. 21 Michelle Collins. 22 Diabetes. 23 Engineering. 24 Manchester United. 25 Hairdressing. 26 Robin Givens. 27 Policemen. 28 The Queen's (Buckingham Palace). 29 The food. 30 Elton John.

1 What is the former colony of the Gold Coast now called?
2 Which marsupial's native home is North America?
3 What was discovered at Lascaux in 1940?
4 Which work by Blackmore has a hero called John Ridd?
5 Which place was a hit for Martha and the Muffins?
6 Which organization had its first troop formed in 1908 in Glasgow?
7 Which racing circuit has a bend called Paddock?
8 What became illegal in 1984 on the London Underground?
9 Where is the world's oldest rowing club, Leander, based?
10 What was Captain Mainwaring's occupation?
11 Who wrote the novel "Finnegans Wake"?
12 If A is alpha and B is bravo what is F?
13 What is exceeded to produce a sonic boom?
14 In which sitcom did Bill Macgregor and Faith Grayshot appear?
15 Which is the last book of the Old Testament ?
16 Which country is partly surrounded by the Coral and Tasman Seas?
17 Who was the first presenter of "One Man and His Dog"?
18 In which century was J. M. Barrie born?
19 What did America buy from Russia for a mere two cents an acre?
20 Who played Ria Parkinson in "Butterflies"?
21 Harold Wilson became Baron of where when he became a peer?
22 What word can go before "cup", "scotch" and "fly"?
23 What is the army equivalent of the Royal Navy rank of Admiral of the Fleet?
24 What is the capital of Haiti?
25 Which guitarist was the Marquis of Salobrena?
26 Which Kray twin enforcer gave East End gangland tours in the 90s?
27 Who had a 80s No. 1 with "Stand and Deliver"?
28 In which decade of the 20th century was Marlon Brando born?
29 Which famous Italian explorer is buried in the Dominican Republic?
30 Who was the first British prime minister to take office four times?

| **Answers** | Pot Luck 75 *(see Quiz 169)* |

1 Nancy Sinatra. 2 Brittany. 3 South Africa. 4 Costa Rica. 5 Nine. 6 Yorkshire. 7 London Eye. 8 West Sussex. 9 Jamie Foxx. 10 Zurich. 11 Aldous Huxley. 12 18. 13 Leon Trotsky. 14 Smoking and cancer. 15 The Beagle. 16 Justin Timberlake. 17 Three. 18 Champion. 19 Vaduz. 20 September. 21 Dennis the Menace. 22 Jeff Banks. 23 Douglas Jardine. 24 Stanford. 25 Tears. 26 18th. 27 The Dead Sea. 28 Bees. 29 "Liberty Bell". 30 Queen Elizabeth.

Answers – page 416

1 Which veteran feline star of the Kattomeat adverts died in 1976?
2 Which outstanding female runner died of cancer at the age of 22?
3 What free item to schools did Education Secretary Thatcher cancel?
4 Who was Arsenal's double-winning captain?
5 Who led the Madison Square Garden concert for Bangladesh?
6 Which team bought Bob Latchford from Birmingham, making him Britain's costliest player?
7 Who was Randolph Hearst's kidnapped daughter?
8 Whom did Ruby Flipper replace?
9 What was Lord Louis Moutbatten doing when murdered by the IRA?
10 What was Gail's last name before her marriage to Brian Tilsley?
11 What did Brighton Council agree to on a section of the beach?
12 In which month did Princess Anne marry Captain Mark Phillips?
13 Singers Lyn Paul and Eve Graham went solo to break up which group?
14 What did Rolls-Royce declare in February 1971?
15 Which northern town was advertised for the vodka it produced?
16 Who was British prime minister during the Winter of Discontent?
17 Whom did Virginia Wade beat in the ladies singles final at Wimbledon?
18 Who wrote "Roots", adapted as a TV blockbuster?
19 In 1978 Pope John Paul I died after roughly how long in office?
20 Who were Jilly, Kelly and Sabrina?
21 What was Saigon renamed after the North Vietnamese takeover?
22 Percy Shaw passed away, but what had he passed on to road users?
23 Where was cricket's first World Cup Final held?
24 In which country was vanishing Labour MP John Stonehouse arrested?
25 What was the name of Edward Heath's Admiral's Cup yacht?
26 Where in Ireland did the Bloody Sunday shootings take place?
27 Who was leader of the Khmer Rouge in the Killing Fields?
28 In 1976, it was goodnight all for which copper after 20 years on TV?
29 Pele went on the dollar trail in 1975 with which team?
30 Who was Live at Treorchy?

Answers	Pop: Albums *(see Quiz 174)*

1 Ashton and Simpson. 2 "Wuthering Heights". 3 Every Picture Tells a Story. 4 Music from Big Pink. 5 Meat Loaf. 6 Slicker than Your Average. 7 Atomic Kitten. 8 Prince. 9 Virgin. 10 Spice. 11 Gilbert O'Sullivan. 12 The Seekers. 13 Queen. 14 Kelly Rowland. 15 Chet Atkins. 16 4,000. 17 Beautiful South. 18 Melanie B. 19 Blur. 20 Bowie. 21 Elton John. 22 Led Zeppelin. 23 No Parlez. 24 Madonna. 25 Abba. 26 Genesis. 27 Deep Purple. 28 Travis. 29 Brothers in Arms. 30 Abbey Road.

1 In which book would you find Magwitch?
2 Who opened the Manchester Ship Canal in 1894?
3 How old was Ronnie Barker when he died – 70, 76 or 79?
4 Which paper was formerly called the Daily Universal Register?
5 Which brothers in the film industry were Jack, Sam, Harry & Albert?
6 Which city was host for the 2006 World Cup third-place play-off?
7 Which horse ran the 1973 Grand National in record time?
8 What was the nickname of the landscape gardener Lancelot Brown?
9 Which American-owned store opened in 1909 in Oxford Street?
10 Which country was formerly known as Southern Rhodesia?
11 Who wrote the novel "The Honourable Schoolboy"?
12 Which cartoon strip began in L'il Folks in 1947?
13 Carlos Leon was the father of which world-famous singer's child?
14 Patricia Plangman is better known as which famous writer?
15 What was Sofia Coppola's follow-up movie to "The Virgin Suicides"?
16 In which century was Christopher Columbus born?
17 What runs every July in Pamplona?
18 What do the letters DPP stand for?
19 What is the only English anagram of GRAPHICALLY?
20 In Scrabble, how many points is the letter Z worth?
21 Who signs himself as Ebor?
22 Turnhouse Airport serves which city?
23 Which team first won rugby league's Challenge Cup at both Edinburgh and Cardiff?
24 Which American actress was the first to appear on a postage stamp?
25 Who was the mother of John the Baptist?
26 Which seemingly ageless singer is mother of Elijah Blue?
27 Brian Barwick has served as Chief Executive of which major sporting body?
28 Blackburn's ground Ewood Park stands by which river?
29 What is the height, in feet, of a football goal?
30 Whom did George W. Bush defeat to become US President in 2000?

Answers	Pot Luck 78 *(see Quiz 175)*

1 The Cotswolds. 2 Van Gogh. 3 Lionel Richie. 4 Bishop's Stortford. 5 1945. 6 Stella Artois. 7 The Severn Bridge. 8 Lorraine Braco. 9 Stop. 10 Cape Canaveral. 11 Pelham Grenville. 12 Sweden. 13 Million Dollar Baby. 14 Hyde. 15 "Ant". 16 Hanoi. 17 Clint Eastwood. 18 19th. 19 David Jason. 20 The Crucible. 21 Westminster Abbey. 22 Saint-Saens. 23 Charles Rolls. 24 Pickwick Papers. 25 Green. 26 Hannah. 27 D. H. Lawrence. 28 30s. 29 Tomato. 30 Colombo.

Quiz 174 | Pop: Albums

Answers – page 414

1 Which duo were Solid?
2 Which track on Kate Bush's "The Kick Inside" was a No. 1 single?
3 What was Rod Stewart's first No. 1 album?
4 "The Weight" by the Band was on which album?
5 "Dead Ringer" was the first No. 1 album for whom?
6 What was Craig David's second album called?
7 Which girl group released the album "Feel So Good" in 2002?
8 Who recorded "Graffiti Bridge"?
9 Mike Oldfield's "Tubular Bells" came out on which label?
10 What was the Spice Girls' first album called?
11 In the 70s which singer/songwriter recorded "Back to Front"?
12 Which 60s group came back in the 90s producing a "Carnival of Hits"?
13 Whose album was "Made in Heaven"?
14 "Simply Deep" was the debut album of which member of Destiny's Child?
15 Who was on "Neck and Neck" with Mark Knopfler?
16 On "Sgt Pepper", how many holes were in Blackburn, Lancashire?
17 Which group's best-of album was called "Carry On up the Charts"?
18 "Hot" was the first solo album by which former Spice Girl?
19 "Think Tank" was a No. 1 album in 2003 for which band?
20 Which David spent most weeks in the charts in 1973,1974 and 1983?
21 Who recorded "Captain Fantastic & the Brown Dirt Cowboy"?
22 Which group had eight No. 1 albums in a row from 1969 to 1979?
23 Which album did Paul Young record with an almost French title?
24 Who in 1987 became the first solo female to spend most weeks in the charts?
25 Which group produced their "Greatest Hits" before their Arrival?
26 Who had a mid-80s No. 1 with "Invisible Touch"?
27 Which heavy rock group recorded "Fireball" and "Machine Head"?
28 "12 Memories" was the fourth album by which Scottish group?
29 "Money for Nothing" first appeared on which Dire Straits album?
30 Which Beatles album featured a zebra crossing on the cover?

Answers	**The 70s** *(see Quiz 172)*

1 Arthur. 2 Lillian Board. 3 Milk. 4 Frank McLintock. 5 George Harrison. 6 Everton. 7 Patricia Hearst. 8 Pan's People (on "Top of the Pops"). 9 Fishing. 10 Potter. 11 Naturist bathing. 12 November. 13 New Seekers. 14 It was bankrupt. 15 Warrington. 16 Jim Callaghan. 17 Betty Stove. 18 Alex Haley. 19 One month (33 days). 20 Charlie's Angels. 21 Ho Chi Minh City. 22 Invented cat's-eyes. 23 Lord's. 24 Australia. 25 Morning Cloud. 26 Londonderry. 27 Pol Pot. 28 PC George Dixon. 29 New York Cosmos. 30 Max Boyce.

Quiz 175 | Pot Luck 78

LEVEL 2

1 Which range of hills has Cleeve Hill as its highest point?
2 Who painted a "Self Portrait with Bandaged Ear"?
3 Who co-wrote "We are the World" with Michael Jackson?
4 Where, on the River Stort, was the birthplace of Cecil Rhodes?
5 Which year was the Hiroshima bombing?
6 Which lager is the name of Britain's second-most important men's tennis tournament?
7 Which toll bridge crosses the River Severn?
8 In "The Sopranos" Dr Jennifer Melfi is played by which actress?
9 What is the first thing you should do if you have a motor accident?
10 What is Cape Kennedy now called?
11 What do P and G stand for in P. G. Wodehouse's name?
12 Which country has the internet code .se?
13 Morgan Freeman won 2005's best supporting actor Oscar for which film?
14 In which area of Greater Manchester did Dr Harold Shipman work?
15 What word can go after "gall" and before "hem"?
16 What is the capital of Vietnam?
17 Which actor portrayed Rowdy Yates in "Rawhide"?
18 In which century was Chopin born?
19 Whose was the voice of Dangermouse in the cartoon series?
20 Which Sheffield theatre opened in 1972?
21 Where are British monarchs crowned?
22 Whose Organ Symphony was used for the theme of "Babe"?
23 Who made the first non-stop double flight across the English Channel?
24 In which Dickens novel does Alfred Jingle appear?
25 What colour caps do the Australians cricket team wear?
26 Which girl's name means grace and favour in Hebrew?
27 Who wrote "The Rainbow"?
28 In which decade of the 20th century was Ray Charles born?
29 Alfresco, Golden Boy and Shirley are types of what?
30 What is the capital of Sri Lanka?

Answers | Pot Luck 77 *(see Quiz 173)*

1 Great Expectations. 2 Queen Victoria. 3 76 years. 4 The Times. 5 The Warner Brothers. 6 Stuttgart. 7 Red Rum. 8 Capability. 9 Selfridge's. 10 Zimbabwe. 11 John Le Carré. 12 Peanuts. 13 Madonna. 14 Patricia Highsmith. 15 Lost in Translation. 16 15th. 17 Bulls. 18 Director of Public Prosecutions. 19 Calligraphy. 20 Ten. 21 The Archbishop of York. 22 Edinburgh. 23 Bradford Bulls. 24 Grace Kelly. 25 Elizabeth. 26 Cher. 27 Football Association. 28 River Darwen. 29 Eight feet. 30 Al Gore.

1 Which Larry scripted "Seinfeld"?
2 Which ministry did Jim Hacker run before he became PM?
3 What are the names of Father Ted's equally eccentric colleagues?
4 What is the name of the Vicar of Dibley?
5 Who had an incompetent personal assistant called Bubble?
6 Which character does Chris Langham play in "The Thick of It"?
7 What are the surnames of Will and Grace?
8 Who was the slave played by Frankie Howerd in "Up Pompeii"?
9 What are the Porter children called in "2 Point 4 Children"?
10 Which 80s series took its name from a 50s Little Richard song title?
11 Whose son-in-law was to him a "randy Scouse git"?
12 In "Ab Fab", who was Edina's bizarre secretary?
13 In which show did Dr Sheila Sabatini appear?
14 What was Steptoe and Son's horse called?
15 Which character did Ronnie Corbett play in "Sorry!"?
16 Which US sitcom character was mother to Becky, Darlene and DJ?
17 Who is Ricky Gervais's co-writer?
18 What were Fletcher's two first names in "Porridge"?
19 In "Birds of a Feather" what is Dorien's husband called?
20 What is the TV news company called in "Drop the Dead Donkey"?
21 Who, collectively, had a landlord called Jerzy Balowski?
22 Which show had Diana and Tom at the Bayview Retirement Home?
23 Who was the caretaker, played by Deryck Guyler, in "Please Sir"?
24 What was Henry Crabbe's restaurant called?
25 Which actor was the "stupid boy" in "Dad's Army"?
26 Which spin-off about a couple followed "Man About the House"?
27 What was the occupation of Peter in "The Peter Principle"?
28 What was the profession of Victor Meldrew's neighbour Pippa?
29 In which sitcom did Charlie Burrows work for Caroline Wheatley?
30 Which sitcom had butler Brabinger and the Czech Mrs Polouvicka?

Answers	**On the Map** *(see Quiz 178)*

1 Bali. 2 San Andreas Fault. 3 Andes. 4 California. 5 Iceland. 6 Romania. 7 Archipelago. 8 Brown. 9 St Vincent. 10 Hobart. 11 Mountain. 12 Edinburgh. 13 Winchester. 14 Belize. 15 Zambesi. 16 Channel Islands. 17 Venezuela. 18 Columbus. 19 Bury St Edmunds. 20 Romney. 21 Canada. 22 St Paul's. 23 Cemetery. 24 Sudan. 25 North. 26 Parliament Square. 27 Yorkshire Dales. 28 Scotland (Highland Region). 29 Parishes. 30 Don.

Quiz 177 Pot Luck 79

Answers – page 421

LEVEL 2

1 What name is given to dried and germinated barley?
2 Which TV rat had a hit with "Love Me Tender"?
3 Where was the original Capodimonte factory in Italy?
4 On which ship did Sir Francis Drake receive his knighthood?
5 Which chemical formula represents ice?
6 Stephen Fleming captained which county to cricket's Championship?
7 Sutton Coldfield is a suburb of which city?
8 What fruit is grown by viticulturists?
9 On which day of the week are US elections always held?
10 What is the surname of Homer Simpson's workmate Carl?
11 Who wrote the novel "Coming Up for Air"?
12 What was Destiny's Child's debut single?
13 In which police series did Captain Dobey and Huggy Bear appear?
14 "Eyes Wide Shut" was the last movie made by which director?
15 Which of the Spice Girls was the first to marry?
16 With which sport do we associate the term "double axel"?
17 Who had a 50s No. 1 with "Dream Lover"?
18 To ten years, when was the storming of the Bastille?
19 Jonathan Edwards specialized in which athletics event?
20 Which birthstone is linked to April?
21 Bathophobia is a fear of what?
22 Corinthian, Doric and Ionian are all types of what?
23 In which century was Samuel Taylor Coleridge born?
24 How many points are there in a perfect hand of cribbage?
25 In which decade was the first Chelsea Flower Show?
26 What was Muhammad Ali's name when he was born?
27 In Morse code what letter is represented by two dots?
28 What is the name of Tony Blair's first-born daughter?
29 Who was the first presenter of "Points of View"?
30 Which is darker – muscovado or demerara sugar?

Answers	**Movies: The Oscars** *(see Quiz 179)*

1 Casablanca. 2 Clarice Starling. 3 On Golden Pond. 4 Forrest Gump. 5 The Philadelphia Story. 6 Muhammad Ali v. George Foreman in Zaire. 7 Chicago. 8 A roll of film. 9 The Color Purple. 10 Gone with the Wind. 11 Richard Burton. 12 Jessica Tandy. 13 Jeremy Irons. 14 Turned it down. 15 Kristin Scott Thomas. 16 Cabaret. 17 Fred Astaire and Ginger Rogers. 18 Best Director. 19 John Wayne. 20 Schindler's List. 21 Glenda Jackson. 22 Vanessa Redgrave. 23 Walt Disney. 24 Peter Finch. 25 Nun. 26 1920s. 27 Kathy Bates. 28 Three. 29 "Can You Feel the Love Tonight". 30 Anthony Minghella.

1 On which island is the holiday resort of Kuta?
2 What is the fault in San Francisco called?
3 What is the world's longest mountain range?
4 What is the third largest US state after Alaska and Texas?
5 Which country has IS as its international registration letters?
6 Where is Transylvania?
7 What is a sea containing many islands called?
8 What colour is the Bakerloo line on the London Underground map?
9 Which West Indian island has an active volcano named Soufrière?
10 What is the capital of Tasmania?
11 In Austria what is the Grossglockner?
12 Where are Waverley and Haymarket stations?
13 Where is the administrative HQ of Hampshire?
14 How was British Honduras subsequently known?
15 On which river is the Kariba Dam?
16 Herm is one of which group of islands?
17 Which South American country was named after Venice?
18 What is the capital of the US state of Ohio?
19 In which East Anglian town is the Greene King brewery based?
20 Which of the Cinque Ports has six letters in its name?
21 Which country has the longest coastline?
22 How is London Cathedral now known?
23 Which 77-acre site was founded at Kensal Green in London in 1832?
24 What is the largest country in Africa?
25 Which of the divisions of Yorkshire has the largest perimeter?
26 Which Square is in front of the Palace of Westminster?
27 After the Lake District which is England's largest National Park?
28 Which country of the British Isles has the largest county in terms of area?
29 What are the smallest units of local government in rural areas?
30 On which river does Sheffield stand?

Answers	TV Sitcoms *(see Quiz 176)*

1 Larry David. 2 Administrative Affairs. 3 Dougal, Jack. 4 Geraldine Granger. 5 Edina Monsoon. 6 Hugh Abbot. 7 Truman and Adler. 8 Lurcio. 9 Jenny, David. 10 "Tutti Frutti". 11 Alf Garnett. 12 Bubble. 13 "Surgical Spirit". 14 Hercules. 15 Timothy Lumsden. 16 "Roseanne". 17 Stephen Merchant. 18 Norman Stanley. 19 Marcus. 20 Globelink. 21 The Young Ones. 22 "Waiting for God". 23 Potter. 24 Pie in the Sky. 25 Ian Lavender. 26 "George and Mildred". 27 Bank manager. 28 Bus driver. 29 "The Upper Hand". 30 "To the Manor Born".

1 Which film ends, "Louis, I think this is the beginning of a beautiful friendship"?

2 Whom did Jodie Foster play in "The Silence of the Lambs"?

3 What was Henry Fonda's last film, for which he won an Oscar?

4 Who said, "Life is like a box of chocolates, you never know what you're going to get"?

5 James Stewart won his only Best Actor Oscar for which classic?

6 The film documentary "When We were Kings" told of which sports clash?

7 In which city is "The Sting" set?

8 What does the male figure stand on, on the Oscar statuette?

9 Which Whoopi Goldberg film had 14 nominations and no win at all?

10 Which film was the first all-colour winner of the Best Picture award?

11 From 1952 to 1977, which Brit had 10 nominations and never won?

12 Who was the oldest Best Actress award recipient when she won in 1989?

13 Which British star was the first Best Actor award winner of the 1990s?

14 What did Marlon Brando do with his 1972 Oscar?

15 Who played Katharine Clifton in "The English Patient"?

16 Best Director Bob Fosse was the only 70s winner whose film was not Best Picture that year. Which picture was it?

17 Who danced together for the last time at the 1966 Oscar ceremony?

18 Kevin Costner was nominated for Best Director and Best Actor for "Dances with Wolves" – which did he win?

19 Which cancer sufferer's last public appearance was at the 1979 Oscar ceremony?

20 Which was the first black-and-white film to win Best Picture after "The Apartment" in 1960?

21 Which British actress won two Oscars in the 70s?

22 Who criticized "militant Zionist hoodlums" in her '77 Oscar speech?

23 Who was given one large Oscar and seven small ones in 1938?

24 Who was the first posthumous recipient of the Best Actor award?

25 What is Susan Sarandon's occupation in "Dead Man Walking"?

26 In which decade were the first Academy Awards given?

27 Who won the Oscar for Best Actress for her role in "Misery"?

28 How many Oscars did Katharine Hepburn win after her 60th birthday?

29 Of the three "The Lion King" songs nominated, which won the Oscar?

30 Who directed "The English Patient"?

Answers | Pot Luck 79 *(see Quiz 177)*

1 Malt. 2 Roland. 3 Naples. 4 The Golden Hind. 5 H2O. 6 Nottinghamshire. 7 Birmingham. 8 Grapes. 9 Tuesday. 10 Carlson. 11 George Orwell. 12 "No, No, No". 13 "Starsky and Hutch". 14 Stanley Kubrick. 15 Mel B. 16 Figure skating. 17 Bobby Darin. 18 1789. 19 Triple jump. 20 Diamond. 21 Depth. 22 Orders (or styles) of architecture. 23 18th. 24 29. 25 1910s. 26 Cassius Clay. 27 I. 28 Kathryn. 29 Robert Robinson. 30 Muscovado.

1 How much did the wedding ring of the Owl and the Pussycat cost?
2 Which country was the first to retain the football World Cup?
3 Which "knight" played Catherine Zeta Jones's dad in "The Darling Buds of May"?
4 What do the Mexicans make from the Agave cactus?
5 Which horse was kidnapped in February 1983?
6 What trade was abolished in 1807 in England?
7 Whom did Maradona play for immediately before Napoli?
8 Who walked the length of the South Coast for charity in 1992?
9 Which doggy event was originally held in Newcastle?
10 In which country is Galle, scene of the tsunami of December 2004?
11 In which decade of the 20th century was Neil Armstrong born?
12 What was Al short for in Al Capone's name?
13 What is the only English anagram of GYRATED?
14 Which club has been managed by Ray Wilkins, Kevin Keegan and Paul Bracewell?
15 Who wrote "Brideshead Revisited"?
16 Who was the narrator of "Paddington" on TV?
17 In World War II, what were Chindits?
18 Where was "Home and Away" set?
19 Which monarch reigned for only 325 days?
20 If A is alpha and B is bravo what is R?
21 Who first won the Embassy World Snooker Championship twice?
22 In which century was Geoffrey Chaucer born?
23 Are there more days in the first six months or the last six months of the year?
24 "The Merryman and His Maid" is the subtitle of which light opera?
25 How long in years is a French presidential term?
26 How many edges does a cube have?
27 In which country did the US impose Operation Steel Curtain in 2005?
28 What is heraldic black called?
29 Clint Eastwood was born in which city?
30 Who had a 60s No. 1 with "I'm Alive"?

Answers	**Pot Luck 81** *(see Quiz 182)*

1 Dortmund and Munich. 2 Black-and-white. 3 Books of stamps. 4 Someone's life. 5 The Turkey. 6 Batons. 7 "Hit" or "Miss". 8 Four. 9 Arquette. 10 Green. 11 18th. 12 Jilly Cooper. 13 Pope Paul II. 14 Elijah Wood. 15 David Essex. 16 The Tempest. 17 37. 18 Chicago. 19 Principal Seymour Skinner. 20 "Her". 21 El Greco. 22 Zagreb. 23 Maria. 24 2 pm. 25 Joseph Stalin. 26 One. 27 Johannesburg. 28 Greenland. 29 Hydrogen. 30 Dorothy Wordsworth.

1 In which city is the National Railway Museum?
2 What is the maximum number of players in a game of poker?
3 Which game takes its name from the Chinese for sparrow?
4 How many pieces are on a chess board at the start of a game?
5 Which card game derives its name from the Spanish word for basket?
6 Which stately home is sometimes called the Palace of the Peak?
7 In which county would you visit Sissinghurst Gardens?
8 In which museum is the "Mona Lisa"?
9 How did Canterbury Cathedral announce it would emulate St Paul's in 1997?
10 In which city is Tropical World, Roundhay Park?
11 In which French château is there a Hall of Mirrors?
12 Which Suffolk Hall hosts days where Tudor life is re-created in great detail?
13 The Bluebell Railway straddles which two counties?
14 What does son et lumière mean?
15 What do you use to play craps?
16 How many dominoes are there in a double-six set?
17 How many different topics are there in a game of Trivial Pursuits?
18 In which month would you go to watch Trooping the Colour?
19 Where in Paris would you go to see Napoleon's tomb?
20 In which county is Whipsnade Park Zoo?
21 Chemin de fer is a type of which game?
22 Which is England's most visited zoo after London?
23 What is Margarete Steiff famous for making?
24 Which phenomenon might you be interested in if you went to Drumnadrochit?
25 UK Legoland is near which town?
26 What sort of leisure attraction is Twycross?
27 In which country is the De Efteling theme park?
28 The National Trust adminsters properties in which three countries?
29 Which tourist attraction is next door to Madamme Tussaud's in London?
30 Which two Cluedo weapons begin with the same letter?

Answers	**History: Who's Who?** *(see Quiz 183)*

1 Edward VII. **2** Bosworth Field. **3** Lord Louis Mountbatten. **4** Henry II. **5** Catherine Parr. **6** Spain. **7** George IV. **8** Robert Baden-Powell. **9** Henry. **10** Rasputin. **11** Farmer George. **12** Queen Anne. **13** Prussia. **14** Alexander the Great. **15** George V. **16** James I (James VI of Scotland). **17** Edward (later Edward II). **18** Anne Boleyn. **19** Philip II. **20** Edward II. **21** 1936. **22** Robert Walpole. **23** Clarence. **24** Stephen. **25** He drowned. **26** Mrs Wallis Simpson. **27** Three. **28** Napoleon Bonaparte. **29** James I. **30** Jane Seymour.

1 Which two cities were selected as hosts for World Cup semi-finals in 2006?
2 What two colours were five-pound notes before 1961?
3 Which necessity was first sold in Post Offices in 1904?
4 What do you save in order to win an Albert Medal?
5 Who conducted the Owl and the Pussycat's wedding ceremony?
6 What were first used by relay racers in 1893?
7 Which choice of verdict could the Juke Box Jury make?
8 How many sides does a tetrahedron have?
9 Which name did Courtney Cox add to her name after her marriage?
10 Which colour is the Libyan flag?
11 In which century was Robbie Burns born?
12 Who wrote the novel "Appassionata"?
13 In Feb. 2005, which world figure had tracheotomy at Rome's Gemelli hospital?
14 Which actor played Frodo Baggins in "The Lord of the Rings"?
15 Who had a 70s No. 1 with "Hold Me Close"?
16 Which Shakespeare play begins with a storm at sea?
17 What is the next highest prime number above 31?
18 Where did Frank Sinatra say was his "kind of town"?
19 Which character in "The Simpsons" used to be a Green Beret?
20 What word can go after "heat" and before "on"?
21 Which Greek artist painted the "View of Toledo"?
22 What is the capital of Croatia?
23 What is Jose Carreras's middle name?
24 If it's 12 noon GMT what time is it in Helsinki?
25 Which Russian succeeded Lenin?
26 In Scrabble, how many points is the letter E worth?
27 The rugby ground Ellis Park is in which city?
28 Which is the largest island in the world?
29 Which element has the atomic number 1?
30 Who wrote "Grasmere Journal"?

Answers | Pot Luck 80 (see Quiz 180)

1 A shilling. 2 Italy. 3 Sir David Jason. 4 Tequila. 5 Shergar. 6 The Slave Trade. 7 Barcelona. 8 Ian Botham. 9 Cruft's. 10 Sri Lanka. 11 30s. 12 Alphonse. 13 Tragedy. 14 Fulham. 15 Evelyn Waugh. 16 Michael Horden. 17 Jungle troops in Burma. 18 Summer Bay. 19 Edward VIII. 20 Romeo. 21 Steve Davis. 22 14th. 23 Last six. 24 The Yeomen of the Guard. 25 Seven. 26 12. 27 Iraq. 28 Sable. 29 San Francisco. 30 The Hollies.

1 Which British monarch succeeded Queen Victoria?
2 Richard III died at which battle?
3 Who was the last viceroy of India?
4 Which English monarch married Eleanor of Aquitaine?
5 Who was the last wife of Henry VIII?
6 Which country did Britain fight in the War of Jenkins' Ear?
7 Which King George did the Prince Regent become?
8 At the Siege of Mafeking who led the British forces?
9 The House of Lancaster kings were all called what?
10 Under what name is Gregor Efimovich better known?
11 Apart from Mad George which kinder nickname did George III have?
12 Which English queen married Prince George of Denmark?
13 Blucher commanded which country's troops at the Battle of Waterloo?
14 Who had a horse called Bucephalus?
15 Queen Elizabeth II's grandfather was which monarch?
16 Who was the Wisest Fool in Christendom?
17 Who was the first Prince of Wales?
18 Whose last words are reputed to be, "My neck is very slender"?
19 Which Spanish king sent his unsuccessful Armada?
20 Which monarch was murdered in Berkeley Castle?
21 In what year did Edward VIII abdicate?
22 In Britain, who first held the office that today is known as Prime Minister?
23 In the 15th century which Duke was drowned in Malmsey wine?
24 Who ruled England between Henry I and Henry II?
25 How did Lord Kitchener die?
26 Who with royal connections had the middle name Warfield?
27 In 1066 how many monarchs ruled England in the year?
28 Which ruler referred the English to a nation of shopkeepers?
29 Which monarch ordered the execution of Sir Walter Raleigh?
30 Which wife gave Henry VIII the male heir that he wanted?

| **Answers** | **Hobbies & Leisure** *(see Quiz 181)* |

1 York. 2 Eight. 3 Majong. 4 32. 5 Canasta. 6 Chatsworth. 7 Kent. 8 The Louvre.
9 Charge for admission. 10 Leeds. 11 Versailles. 12 Kentwell. 13 East and West
Sussex. 14 Sound and light. 15 Dice. 16 28. 17 Six. 18 June. 19 Les Invalides.
20 Bedfordshire. 21 Baccarat. 22 Chester. 23 Toy bears. 24 Loch Ness Monster.
25 Windsor. 26 Zoo. 27 Holland. 28 England, Wales and Northern Ireland. 29 The
Planetarium. 30 Rope, revolver.

1 What colour did the legendary keeper Lev Yashin play in?
2 Which host city was the most northerly in Germany 2006?
3 Bobby Robson left which club to join Barcelona?
4 Oscar Ruggeri became the highest-capped player for which country?
5 Who had the final kick of the 1994 World Cup Final?
6 In which decade did Bayern Munich first win the UEFA Cup?
7 Former Italian prime minister Silvio Berlusconi took over which club?
8 Thomas Ravelli became the most-capped player for which country?
9 The stadium the Monumental is in which country?
10 Which Dutchman came with Arnold Muhren to Ipswich in the 80s?
11 Alfredo di Stefano played for Argentina, Spain and which other country?
12 Which country does Andrei Shevchenko play for?
13 The club Feyenoord is based in which city?
14 Which club play at the Bernabeu Stadium?
15 Who was UK's first European Footballer of the Year this century?
16 What colour are Brazil's shorts?
17 How old was Maradona when he first played for Argentina?
18 Who captained Italy in the 1994 World Cup Final?
19 Gullit, Van Basten and Rijkaard lined up at which non-Dutch club?
20 The Fritz-Walter Stadium is in which German venue?
21 Who was first player from Ghana to play in the English league?
22 Which Arsenal manager signed Dennis Bergkamp?
23 How often is the African Nations Cup staged?
24 Who were the first African country to reach the World Cup quarter-finals?
25 Lars Lagerback took which country to Germany 2006?
26 Which club play at the Olympiastadion?
27 Which city hosted the final of Euro 2004?
28 What colour are Portugal's shorts?
29 Which country did Mario Kempes play for?
30 Since the 1950s, in which decade did Brazil not win the World Cup?

Answers | Animal World *(see Quiz 186)*

1 Ants and termites. 2 Yellow with black markings. 3 Okapi. 4 Omnivore. 5 Orang-utan. 6 Bones. 7 Mammals. 8 Caribou. 9 Grey. 10 Amphibian. 11 Cold-blooded. 12 Dog. 13 Fangs. 14 Camel. 15 Bat. 16 Deer. 17 Backbone. 18 Dodo. 19 Borzoi. 20 Blue. 21 Tasmania. 22 Underground. 23 Gorilla. 24 Barbary apes. 25 Milk. 26 Grizzly. 27 Otter. 28 Racoon. 29 America. 30 A monkey.

1 Las Ketchup who gave us "The Ketchup Song" came from which country?
2 Who was the longest-reigning British monarch before Victoria?
3 Which ponies were originally used in coal mines?
4 Who was the first post-war British winner of a British Grand Prix?
5 Was the Old Trafford Test the second, third or fourth in the 2005 Ashes?
6 What do Americans call the silencer on the car?
7 Which bird-shooting season runs from October 1 to February 1?
8 What is the name of Andy Capp's wife?
9 Who was the original owner of Today newspaper?
10 What name is given to America's most westerly time zone?
11 Who wrote the novel "Sharpe's Tiger"?
12 In which decade of the 20th century was George Harrison born?
13 What word can go before "beer", "bread" and "nut"?
14 Who lit the Eternal Flame on the grave of John F. Kennedy?
15 What is the capital of Colombia?
16 What do G and K stand for in G. K. Chesterton's name?
17 What specialist line of trade did Tom Keating follow?
18 What would a Mexican submerge into a beer to make a "Submarino"?
19 What night is Burns Night?
20 In which month was the 2005 Glastonbury Festival?
21 Who was the first TV newsreader to be knighted?
22 Which monarch was murdered at Pontefract Castle?
23 Which actress's real surname is Anistonopoulos?
24 Who was the first presenter of "A Question of Sport"?
25 Which club has members called Barkers?
26 Kenneth Starr was involved in impeachment against which US President?
27 Glen Cova and Joy are types of which fruit?
28 Was the first British "Who Wants to be a Millionaire?" millionaire male or female?
29 In which century was Lewis Carroll born?
30 Which Kid was John Cornelius better known as?

Answers | **Pot Luck 83** *(see Quiz 187)*

1 Fifteen (15). 2 Pepperland. 3 Blood cells. 4 Anne of Cleves. 5 Scarlet. 6 Emily Davison. 7 Austria. 8 Conservative Party. 9 Umbrellas. 10 Chest. 11 1901. 12 Scotland. 13 "Snap". 14 Othello. 15 Spike. 16 White. 17 Joseph Conrad. 18 Eight. 19 Red rose. 20 Manhattan. 21 Mercury Music Prize. 22 Opal. 23 1970s. 24 London. 25 Peter Mandelson. 26 Roses. 27 House of Commons. 28 Clouds. 29 Ladywood. 30 Melbourne.

1 What does the aardvark feed on?
2 What colour is an ocelot?
3 What is the only member of the giraffe family other than the giraffe itself?
4 What sort of animal feeds on plants and other animals?
5 Which ape's natural habitat is restricted to Sumatra and Borneo?
6 What are ossicles?
7 Which group has more teeth – mammals or reptiles?
8 What is the North American equivalent of the reindeer?
9 What colour is a coyote's coat?
10 What name is given to a creature equally at home on land and in water?
11 What term describes an animal which cannot control its body temperature and has to rely on its environment?
12 What was the first animal to be domesticated?
13 Which special mouth parts inject poison into prey?
14 The llama is a relative of which African animal?
15 Which is the only vertebrate capable of sustained flight?
16 The wapiti is a member of which family of animals?
17 What protects a vertebrate's nerve cord?
18 Which extinct animal's name is the Portuguese for "stupid"?
19 What is another name for the Russian wolfhound?
20 What colour tongue does a chow chow have?
21 Other than the Australian mainland the platypus is native to where?
22 Where does a gopher make its home?
23 What is the most intelligent of land animals after man?
24 What type of apes were imported into Gibraltar in the 18th century?
25 What do mammary glands produce?
26 The brown bear is also known by what name?
27 What is the only true amphibious member of the weasel family?
28 Which American native has a black masked face and a distinctive ringed tail?
29 The anteater is native to which continent?
30 What is a marmoset?

Answers	**World Soccer** *(see Quiz 184)*

1 Black. 2 Hamburg. 3 Porto. 4 Argentina. 5 Roberto Baggio. 6 1990s. 7 AC Milan. 8 Sweden. 9 Argentina. 10 Frans Thijssen. 11 Colombia. 12 Ukraine. 13 Rotterdam. 14 Real Madrid. 15 Michael Owen. 16 Blue. 17 16. 18 Franco Baresi. 19 AC Milan. 20 Kaiserslautern. 21 Tony Yeboah. 22 Bruce Rioch. 23 Every two years. 24 Cameroon. 25 Sweden. 26 Bayern Munich. 27 Lisbon. 28 Green. 29 Argentina. 30 1980s.

1 How many zeroes does a quadrillion have after its first digit?
2 Which kingdom was the setting for "Yellow Submarine"?
3 What do most humans lose 15 million of every second?
4 Who was the second wife that Henry VIII divorced?
5 What colour, traditionally, is an Indian wedding sari?
6 Who was the first suffragette martyr?
7 In which country is the Spanish Riding School?
8 In 2005, which party used the slogan "Are you thinking what we're thinking?"
9 What is the subject of Renoir's painting "Les Parapluies"?
10 Which part of the body is known as the thorax?
11 To five years, when was Louis Armstrong born?
12 What country is "Simpsons" character Groundskeeper Willie from?
13 What word can go after "brandy" and before "dragon"?
14 In Shakespeare, who kills Desdemona?
15 What is Snoopy's brother's name?
16 What colour were the wristbands for 2005's Make Poverty History campaign?
17 How is Teodor Josef Korzeniowsky better known?
18 How many records is a castaway allowed on "Desert Island Discs"?
19 What flower is on the shirts of the English Rugby Union team?
20 In which part of New York was "Kojak" set?
21 What prestigious award did Anthony Hegarty win in 2005?
22 Which birthstone is linked to October?
23 In which decade was "Blankety Blank" first screened in the UK?
24 In which city did Phileas Fogg begin his trip around the world?
25 Which grandson of 50s Labour home secretary Herbert Morrison played a leading part in the 1997 election?
26 Bourbon, Gallica and Rugosa are types of what?
27 Which House in England may not be entered by the Queen?
28 Nephophobia is a fear of what?
29 Clare Short has represented which Birmingham constituency?
30 What was the first Australian city to have hosted the Olympics?

Answers | **Pot Luck 82** (see Quiz 185)

1 Spain. 2 George III. 3 Shetland. 4 Stirling Moss. 5 Third. 6 A muffler. 7 Pheasant. 8 Flo or Florrie. 9 Eddy Shah. 10 Pacific. 11 Bernard Cornwell. 12 40s. 13 "Ginger". 14 Jacqueline Kennedy. 15 Bogota. 16 Gilbert Keith. 17 Art forger. 18 Tequila. 19 January 25th. 20 June. 21 Alastair Burnet. 22 Richard II. 23 Jennifer Aniston. 24 David Vine. 25 Variety Club. 26 Bill Clinton. 27 Raspberry. 28 Female. 29 19th. 30 The Milky Bar Kid.

1 All Cilla Black's 60s hits were on which record label?
2 What was the Beach Boys' first British No. 1?
3 Which same-surname artists both charted with "Memphis Tennessee"?
4 Which No. 1 starts "I'm in heaven when I see you smile"?
5 The Byrds' first two British hits were written by whom?
6 Who sang "Je T'Aime (Moi Non Plus)" with Serge Gainsburg in 1969?
7 Who was backed by the Stingers?
8 Who had No. 1s that had the colours red and black in the titles?
9 Which group featured drummer Anne Lantree?
10 Which US group sang "Rhythm of the Rain"?
11 What was the surname of Desmond and Molly in "Ob-La-Di-Ob-La-Da"?
12 Which Tom wrote and produced for the Seekers?
13 In the Ricky Valance song, who loves Laura?
14 "5-4-3-2-1" was the signature tune of which TV pop show?
15 Who sang "I'll Never Fall in Love Again"?
16 Which ex-Shadows hit No. 1 with "Diamonds"?
17 Who backed Tommy Bruce?
18 Jim Capaldi and Steve Winwood came together in which group?
19 Which animal did Cat Stevens first sing about in the charts?
20 Which husband-and-wife team wrote a string of Pet Clark hits?
21 Who were the first to have a No. 1 – the Beatles or the Stones?
22 In "A Whiter Shade of Pale" where were the vestal virgins leaving for?
23 On which label did Mary Hopkin record "Those were the Days"?
24 Gladys Knight and Marvin Gaye had separate hits with which song?
25 "Yeh Yeh" was a No. 1 for whom?
26 Which city did the Dave Clark Five come from?
27 Who became the first female singer to have three No. 1s?
28 Who wrote Chris Farlowe's "Out of Time"?
29 Which classic starts "Dirty old river"?
30 Whose last Top Ten hit of the 60s was "San Franciscan Nights"?

Answers | TV Times 2 (see Quiz 190)

1 Jonathan Edwards. 2 "St Elsewhere". 3 PE teacher. 4 Deal. 5 "Lewis". 6 Harmsworth Hospital. 7 Gerald Scarfe. 8 Dustmen. 9 Christopher Eccleston. 10 Bristol. 11 Mayday. 12 November. 13 Fraser. 14 Ma and Pa Larkin. 15 Alan Partridge. 16 Andrew Castle. 17 Arden House. 18 Jon Pertwee. 19 Goddard. 20 Terry Scott and June Whitfield. 21 Adrian Mole. 22 "Grace and Favour". 23 Advertising agency. 24 "Girls on Top". 25 Graham Norton. 26 Neil Morrissey. 27 Dr Kildare. 28 Wentworth Miller. 29 Timothy Spall. 30 12.

1 What would you measure on the cephalic index?
2 Which name links Gwent, Rhode Island, USA, and the Isle of Wight?
3 When was VAT introduced in Britain?
4 In the Tour de France, who wears the polka dot jersey?
5 Which breakfast dish was originally a hangover cure?
6 Who played Max in the 2005 movie remake of "The Producers"?
7 Where would you find the Doge's Palace?
8 What is the minimum number of points to win on a tennis tie-break?
9 What colour hair did Churchill have before he went bald?
10 What is the main range of hills in Gloucestershire?
11 Who wrote the novel "The Children of Men"?
12 What is the only English anagram of PIMENTOS?
13 What is studied by a heliologist?
14 In which century was Thomas à Becket born?
15 In Morse code what letter is represented by one dash?
16 Which golfer first won the US amateur title three years in a row?
17 Which London street is famous for men's tailoring?
18 Which was the frequency of Radio Luxembourg?
19 Which famous chair was kidnapped by students from the Cranfield Institute of Technology in 1978?
20 Which character did Bonnie Langford play in "Just William"?
21 What was Spain's General Franco's first name?
22 In the Chinese calendar which year follows the year of the dragon?
23 What is the RAF equivalent to the army rank of Major?
24 What was Jacques Cousteau's research ship called?
25 Which city does the Halle Orchestra come from?
26 How many different venues were selected for the 2006 World Cup in Germany?
27 What is the Archbishop of Canterbury's official residence?
28 Where in London did the statue Alison Lapper Pregnant appear in 2005?
29 In which decade of the 20th century was Jack Nicholson born?
30 What is the main flavour of aioli?

Answers	**Performing Arts** *(see Quiz 191)*

1 Theatre Royal Drury Lane. 2 Princess Diana. 3 The Magic Flute. 4 Puccini. 5 Six hours. 6 UK. 7 Paris. 8 Spamalot. 9 Tchaikovsky. 10 Bix Beiderbecke. 11 Ellington. 12 The Savoy. 13 Artie Shaw. 14 Olivier. 15 Beauty and the Beast. 16 Le Nozze di Figaro. 17 Hamlet. 18 Norma (Major). 19 Spanish. 20 Sam Wanamaker. 21 Kirov Ballet. 22 The Madness of George III. 23 Alan Ayckbourn. 24 Tom Stoppard. 25 The Queen Mother when Queen consort. 26 Evening Standard. 27 Olivier. 28 Cameron Mackintosh. 29 The Strand. 30 New York.

1 Which former triple jump champion presented "Songs of Praise"?
2 Which drama/comedy was set in St Elgius Hospital?
3 What was Zoë's job in "May to December"?
4 In "Lovejoy" what was Tinker's surname?
5 What was the name of the first "Morse" sequel?
6 Where were the first three series of "Animal Hospital" based?
7 Who drew the animated titles sequence for "Yes Minister"?
8 What was the job of the heroes of "Common as Muck"?
9 Who was the first Dr Who to play opposite Billie Piper?
10 Which city is "Casualty"'s Holby said to be?
11 What was the nickname of Sam Malone of "Cheers"?
12 In which month does the "Children in Need" appeal normally take place?
13 Who was the undertaker in "Dad's Army"?
14 Whose children included Primrose, Petunia, Zinnia and Montgomery?
15 Who was the sports commentator on "The Day Today"?
16 Which former tennis player has presented GMTV with Fiona Phillips?
17 Which House was the surgery for Drs Finlay and Cameron?
18 Who was the third Doctor Who?
19 What is the surname of Trisha of real-life drama daytime TV fame?
20 Which TV marriage began with "Happy Ever After" in 1969?
21 Which adolescent did Gian Sammarco play?
22 What was the sequel to "Are You being Served"?
23 Where did Tom Good work before he began the Good Life?
24 In which series did Dawn French as Amanda work for "Spare Cheeks" magazine?
25 Whose BBC chat show was called "The Bigger Picture"?
26 Who played Rocky in "Boon"?
27 Whose boss was Dr Gillespie?
28 Which star of "Prison Break" shares his first name with a UK golf course?
29 Who played Frank Stubbs in "Frank Stubbs Promotes"?
30 How many episodes of "Fawlty Towers" were made?

| **Answers** | **Pop: 60s** *(see Quiz 188)* |

1 Parlophone. **2** "Good Vibrations". **3** Chuck and Dave Berry. **4** "Diane" (The Bachelors). **5** Bob Dylan. **6** Jane Birkin. **7** B Bumble. **8** The Rolling Stones. **9** The Honeycombs. **10** The Cascades. **11** Jones. **12** Springfield. **13** Tommy. **14** "Ready Steady Go". **15** Bobbie Gentry. **16** Jet Harris and Tony Meehan. **17** The Bruisers. **18** Traffic. **19** Dog. **20** Hatch and Trent. **21** The Beatles. **22** The coast. **23** Apple. **24** "I Heard It Through the Grapevine". **25** Georgie Fame. **26** London. **27** Sandie Shaw. **28** Mick Jagger, Keith Richards. **29** "Waterloo Sunset". **30** The Animals.

1 Which is London's oldest theatre?
2 A ballet was staged in 2005 about which 20th-century princess?
3 How is Mozart's "Die Zauberflöte" known in English?
4 Who wrote "Tosca"?
5 Including intervals, approximately how long does Wagner's "Götterdämmerung" last?
6 Where is the Ballet Rambert based?
7 In which city is Europe's largest opera house?
8 "Monty Python and the Holy Grail" turned into which musical?
9 Who wrote the ballet "The Nutcracker"?
10 Which cornetist/pianist was considered to be the first great white jazz musician?
11 Which Duke's first names were Edward Kennedy?
12 Which London theatre was gutted by fire in 1990?
13 Which US clarinettist's real name was Arthur Jacob Arshawsky?
14 In 1984 the Society of West End Theatre Awards were renamed in honour of whom?
15 Which Disney-based musical features the song "Be Our Guest"?
16 How is "The Marriage of Figaro" known in Italian?
17 What is Shakespeare's longest play?
18 Which former prime minister's wife shares her name with a Bellini opera?
19 What nationality are two of the Three Tenors?
20 Which US director was the impetus behind the new Globe Theatre in London?
21 How is the Ballets Russes of Sergei Diaghilev now known?
22 What was "The Madness of King George" called as a play?
23 Which British playwright wrote the trilogy "The Norman Conquests"?
24 Which Czech-born playwright wrote "Jumpers" and "Arcadia"?
25 Who laid the foundation stone for the National Theatre on the South Bank?
26 Which newspaper presents awards for excellence in the London theatre?
27 Which of the three theatres within the National was named after the theatre's first Lord?
28 Who first produced "Les Misérables" in London?
29 In which street is London's Savoy Theatre?
30 In which city is the world's largest opera house?

Answers | Pot Luck 84 *(see Quiz 189)*

1 Human head. **2** Newport. **3** 1973. **4** The King of the Mountains. **5** Eggs Benedict. **6** Nathan Lane. **7** Venice. **8** Seven. **9** Red. **10** The Cotswolds. **11** P. D. James. **12** Nepotism. **13** The sun. **14** 12th. **15** T. **16** Tiger Woods. **17** Savile Row. **18** 208. **19** Mastermind chair. **20** Violet Elizabeth Bott. **21** Francisco. **22** Snake. **23** Squadron Leader. **24** The Calypso. **25** Manchester. **26** Twelve. **27** Lambeth Palace. **28** Trafalgar Square. **29** 30s. **30** Garlic.

1 Who made a scallop shell tribute to Benjamin Britten on a Suffolk beach?
2 Which Danish statue is a memorial to Hans Christian Andersen?
3 Where are rods and cones found in your body?
4 Which classic golf course is referred to as the Old Lady of golf?
5 What were the Boston Tea Party protesters unhappy about?
6 Which well-known trench was devised by Ferdinand De Lesseps?
7 What is the final round of "The Weakest Link" called, when there has been a tie thus far?
8 What was the name of Gwen Stefani's debut solo album?
9 Which state in America is the Gambling State?
10 Who finished the fastest solo non-stop sail around the world in February 2005?
11 On which island did Nelson Mandela serve most of his sentence?
12 What is the only English anagram of HEDONIST?
13 Who won the Australian Open as a Yugoslavian in 1993 and as American citizen in 1996?
14 Who was found guilty of the Oklahoma City bombing?
15 Who wrote the novel "Rob Roy"?
16 Which musical instrument does Tasmin Little play?
17 Who had a 60s No. 1 with "Mighty Quinn"?
18 How was Domenikos Theotocopolous better known?
19 Who shared the 1993 Nobel Peace prize with F. W. de Klerk?
20 Who is Chief of the Springfield Police Department?
21 If A is alpha and B is bravo what is V?
22 What was the sport of Emerson's brother Wilson Fittipaldi?
23 Which actor was the star in "Natural Born Killers"?
24 What name is given to the positive electrode of a battery?
25 Who was the first presenter of "Question Time"?
26 Which talk show host was turned into the subject of an opera?
27 What ship was Sir Francis Drake in when he circled the world?
28 In Norse mythology, who was god of thunder and war?
29 Which company's name was on the shirts of the 2005 Ashes-winning side?
30 In the Old Testament which book directly follows Numbers?

Answers	Pot Luck 86 *(see Quiz 194)*

1 The Rolling Stones. 2 Blackburn. 3 Wiltshire. 4 Labyrinth. 5 Miranda Hobbes. 6 Lenin. 7 Pasteurization. 8 Homer. 9 Malta. 10 19th century. 11 "Ton". 12 "Touch My Fire". 13 Helium. 14 Three. 15 Bat or bowl. 16 Oxford. 17 Mungo Jerry. 18 The Bounty. 19 Ravi Shankar. 20 Cumbria. 21 One. 22 Paul Sculthorpe. 23 Paris. 24 Australia. 25 Psychiatrist. 26 Great Expectations. 27 Ringo Starr. 28 True Grit. 29 Santiago. 30 Four.

1 T. Rex's "Children of the Revolution" featured in which movie?
2 In which musical do Tracy Lord and CK Dexter Haven appear?
3 In which musical is "The Duelling Cavalier" a film in the making?
4 Who sings "As Long as He Needs Me" in "Oliver!"?
5 Who directed "A Chorus Line"?
6 Which singer – famous for dubbing other actresses' voices – played Sister Sophia in "The Sound of Music"?
7 What was the follow-up to "Saturday Night Fever" called?
8 Who played Carlotta in the film of "Phantom of the Opera"?
9 What was the job of Joel Grey's character in "Cabaret"?
10 Which musical was based on a Harold Gray comic strip?
11 What instrument does Robert de Niro play in in "New York New York"?
12 Which musical does "The Ugly Duckling" come from?
13 Who sang "Moon River" in "Breakfast at Tiffany's"?
14 Which song in "Evita" was composed specially for the film?
15 How many Von Trapp children are there in "The Sound of Music"?
16 "Hopelessly Devoted to You" is sung in which movie?
17 Who are the two gangs in "West Side Story"?
18 Which character did Liza Minnelli play in "Cabaret"?
19 Which movie musical has the song "Feed the Birds"?
20 Who played Mama Rose in the 1993 movie "Gypsy"?
21 Which two musical legends starred in "Easter Parade"?
22 "Shall We Dance" features in which movie?
23 What was Stanley Holloway's role in "My Fair Lady"?
24 In which film does Fat Sam fight it out with Dandy Dan?
25 "The Bare Necessities" comes from which film?
26 In which film did Gordon Macrae play Billy Bigelow after Frank Sinatra dropped out?
27 Who played opposite Ewan McGregor in "Moulin Rouge"?
28 Which actress was I in "The King and I"?
29 In which musical would you see Lina Lamont?
30 Which musical movie features "The Cell Block Tango"?

Answers | Celebs *(see Quiz 195)*

1 Ireland. 2 Michael Jackson and Debbie Rowe. 3 Sulaiman. 4 Jackie Kennedy-Onassis. 5 Clothes design. 6 David Frost. 7 Paris Hilton. 8 Scarlet. 9 Larry Fortensky. 10 Underwear. 11 Linley. 12 Hairdressing. 13 Chanel. 14 Raine. 15 Queen Elizabeth II. 16 Costner. 17 Prunella Scales. 18 Sylvester Stallone. 19 Joan Collins. 20 Tony Blair. 21 Simpson's of Piccadilly. 22 Hawaii. 23 Barbara Hulanicki. 24 Marmaduke Hussey. 25 Dame Judi Dench. 26 Britt Ekland. 27 Lady Diana Spencer. 28 Mark McCormack. 29 Norman Hartnell. 30 Sharon Maughan.

1 Which rock band had songs censored for TV at Super Bowl XL?
2 What was the first Premiership side that Stephane Henchoz played for?
3 In which county is Silbury Hill, Europe's biggest man-made mound?
4 Which film featuring David Bowie is also an organ of balance?
5 Which character was a lawyer in "Sex and the City"?
6 Who founded the Communist newspaper Pravda in 1912?
7 What do we call the heating process which destroys enzymes in milk?
8 Who is the unproven author of the "Iliad"?
9 Which associate member of the EC is also a Commonwealth island?
10 In which century was Hans Christian Andersen born?
11 What word can follow "but", "car" and "bat"?
12 What was the name of the UK's 2005 Eurovision song?
13 Which element has the atomic number 2?
14 In music, how many sharps in the key of A?
15 What are substitutes in cricket not normally allowed to do?
16 The College of Brasenose is part of which university?
17 Who had a 70s No. 1 with "Baby Jump"?
18 What was Captain Bligh's most famous ship?
19 Which famous musician is the dad of Norah Jones?
20 In which county was HMP Slade from "Porridge"?
21 In Scrabble, how many points is the letter O worth?
22 Who was the first person named Man of Steel in successive years?
23 Which European city was the first home of the Statue of Liberty?
24 The composer Percy Grainger came from which country?
25 What is the profession of radio's Anthony Clare?
26 In which Dickens novel does Joe Gargery appear?
27 In the 60s whom did hairdresser Maureen Cox marry?
28 Which John Wayne movie won him his only Oscar?
29 What is the capital of Chile?
30 In measuring a horse, how many inches in a hand?

| **Answers** | Pot Luck 85 (see Quiz 192) |

1 Maggi Hambling. **2** Little Mermaid. **3** Eyes. **4** St Andrew's. **5** Tea taxes. **6** The Suez Canal. **7** Sudden Death. **8** Love, Angel, Music, Baby. **9** Nevada. **10** Ellen MacArthur. **11** Robben Island. **12** Dishonest. **13** Monica Seles. **14** Timothy McVeigh. **15** Sir Walter Scott. **16** Violin. **17** Manfred Mann. **18** El Greco. **19** Nelson Mandela. **20** Clancy Wiggum. **21** Victor. **22** Motor racing. **23** Woody Harrelson. **24** Anode. **25** Robin Day. **26** Jerry Springer. **27** The Golden Hind. **28** Thor. **29** Vodafone. **30** Deuteronomy.

1 Which country shares its name with Kim Basinger's daughter?
2 Who are the parents of Prince Michael Jr?
3 What is the son of Jemima and Imran Khan called?
4 Who was the famous sister of Lee Radziwill Ross?
5 In what field is Tommy Hilfiger a famous name?
6 Who is the son-in-law of the 17th Duke of Norfolk?
7 Often to be seen with her pet Chihuahua, which heiress was voted the worst dog owner ever in an online poll?
8 What colour dress did Paula Yates wear to marry Bob Geldof?
9 Who was Liz Taylor's eighth husband?
10 What type of clothes would you buy from Janet Reger?
11 Which Viscount attended Elton John's 50th birthday dressed as a lion?
12 In which field is Patrick Cameron famous?
13 Which fashion house does Stella Tennant model for?
14 What was Princess Diana's stepmother's first name?
15 When Sophie Rhys Jones married who became her mum in law?
16 Which Cindy's divorce settlement from her actor/director husband was reputedly in the region of £50 million?
17 Which actress is the mother of actor Sam West?
18 Who married Jennifer Flavin as his third wife?
19 Who is Tara Newley's famous mother?
20 Euan, Nicholas, Kathryn and Leo are children of which famous dad?
21 Mrs Anthony Andrews's family own which London store?
22 On which island was model Marie Helvin brought up?
23 Which Polish-born designer founded Biba?
24 Which ex-BBC Chairman's wife was Lady-in-Waiting to the Queen?
25 Which Oscar-winning Dame is the mum of Finty Williams?
26 Who has been married to Peter Sellers and Jim McDonnell?
27 Who used the pseudonym Deborah Smithson Wells when arranging fittings for her wedding dress?
28 Which agent married tennis star Betsy Nagelson?
29 Who made the wedding dresses of Princesses Elizabeth and Margaret?
30 Which actress was known as the lady in the Gold Blend commercials?

Answers	**Musical Movies** *(see Quiz 193)*

1 Moulin Rouge. 2 High Society. 3 Singing in the Rain. 4 Nancy. 5 Richard Attenborough. 6 Marni Nixon. 7 Staying Alive. 8 Minnie Driver. 9 Master of Ceremonies. 10 Annie. 11 Saxophone. 12 Hans Christian Andersen. 13 Audrey Hepburn. 14 "You Must Love Me". 15 Seven. 16 Grease. 17 Jets, Sharks. 18 Sally Bowles. 19 Mary Poppins. 20 Bette Midler. 21 Fred Astaire, Judy Garland. 22 The King and I. 23 Alfred P. Doolittle. 24 Bugsy Malone. 25 Jungle Book. 26 Carousel. 27 Nicole Kidman. 28 Deborah Kerr. 29 Singing in the Rain. 30 Chicago.

Quiz 196 Pot Luck 87

LEVEL 2

Answers – page 440

1 Which organ in the body produces bile?
2 Which county first won cricket's Benson & Hedges Cup twice?
3 Who are the main characters in Milton's "Paradise Lost"?
4 Which continent is wider in the south than in the north?
5 Which game is played to the Harvard rules?
6 Which Pennsylvanian power station had a nuclear accident in 1979?
7 Who was Lord Vestey's dessert-loving, opera-singing, grandmother?
8 How many cards does each player start with in gin rummy?
9 If you have herpes labialis, what are you suffering from?
10 Where would you find the Dogger Bank?
11 In which century was Lord Byron born?
12 Who wrote the novel "East of Eden"?
13 Which golfer declared that racially he was a "Cablinasian"?
14 What opened when Ali Baba said "Open sesame"?
15 Which band's singles include "Australia" and "A Design for Life"?
16 Which birthstone is linked to May?
17 What word can go after "machine" and before "dog"?
18 Who was called the Serpent of the Nile?
19 In the New Testament which book directly follows Romans?
20 Which journalist made the "Living with Michael Jackson" documentary?
21 Which sport includes sculls, strokes and slides?
22 Muslim cleric Abu Hamza was linked with which London mosque?
23 What year was set as the target for analaogue television to switch off?
24 Cynophobia is a fear of what?
25 "The Slave of Duty" is the subtitle of which light opera?
26 In which county do Bulls battle against Rhinos?
27 In Morse code what letter is represented by two dots?
28 Which TV personality said, "what a bobbydazzler!"?
29 What was the nickname of Julius Marx?
30 What special day was Friday 27th January, 2006?

Answers | **Pot Luck 88** *(see Quiz 198)*

1 Vonda Shepard. 2 Alphabetarian. 3 Malaria. 4 Henry VIII. 5 Mega. 6 Steve Carell. 7 Wedgwood. 8 Typewriting correction fluid. 9 The Canterbury Pilgrims. 10 White. 11 Bethnal Green & Bow. 12 Natasha Bedingfield. 13 J. R. R. Tolkien. 14 Vancouver Island. 15 19th. 16 Permissive. 17 Hungary. 18 One. 19 Ants. 20 Lotus. 21 "The Thorn Birds". 22 Tango. 23 Loch Ness Monster. 24 American GIs. 25 Beatrice. 26 36 years old. 27 Digitalis. 28 Blackcurrant. 29 Tin. 30 30s.

1 In 1990 Mr Frisk set a record time in which major race?

2 Which Earl of Derby gave his name to the race?

3 To a year each way, when was Red Rum's third Grand National win?

4 Which jockey rode Best Mate to a hat-trick of Cheltenham Gold Cup wins?

5 Which three races make up the English Triple Crown?

6 How did 19th-century jockey Fred Archer die?

7 Which Irish rider won the Prix de L'Arc de Triomphe four times?

8 To two years each way, when did Lester Piggott first win the Derby?

9 Which classic race was sponsored by Gold Seal from 1984–92?

10 Who rode Devon Loch in the sensational 1956 Grand National?

11 What colour was Arkle?

12 How long is the Derby?

13 Sceptre managed to win how many classics outright in a season?

14 Shergar won the 1981 Derby by a record of how many lengths?

15 Which National Hunt jockey retired in 1993 with most ever wins?

16 What was the nickname of Corbiere?

17 Who rode Nijinsky to victory in the Derby?

18 In which decade was the Prix de L'Arc de Triomphe first run?

19 Who triumphed in the Oaks on Ballanchine and Moonshell?

20 Which horse was National Hunt Champion of the Year four times in a row from 1987 on?

21 Which horse stopped Red Rum getting three in a row Grand National wins?

22 How many times did the great Sir Gordon Richards win the Epsom Derby?

23 The Preakness Stakes, Belmont Stakes plus which other race make up the American Triple Crown?

24 Which Frank established a record nine victories in the Oaks?

25 Which jockey was the first ever winner of the Derby?

26 What actually is Frankie Detorri's first name?

27 Who holds the world record of riding 9,531 winners?

28 Which horse was the first Derby winner ridden by Kieren Fallon?

29 What colour was Red Rum?

30 How old was Lester Piggott when he returned to racing in 1990?

Answers | The 80s *(see Quiz 199)*

1 Tumbledown. 2 July. 3 Iranian. 4 Moscow. 5 Gdansk. 6 Two million. 7 Jimmy Carter. 8 Scarman. 9 Ivan Lendl. 10 John Paul II. 11 "Do They Know It's Christmas?". 12 Nottingham Forest. 13 Norman Tebbit's father. 14 Commission in the Royal Marines. 15 In a car crash. 16 Best. 17 April. 18 Berkshire. 19 Yvonne Fletcher. 20 26. 21 Star Wars. 22 Black Monday (Stock Market crash). 23 Piper Alpha. 24 Peter Wright. 25 George Bush. 26 Noddy. 27 Michael Ryan. 28 October. 29 New York. 30 Roy Hattersley.

1 Which singer made regular appearances as herself in "Ally McBeal"?
2 What name is given to a student of the alphabet?
3 Which illness killed Oliver Cromwell?
4 Who commissioned Holbein's painting of Anne of Cleves?
5 What is the metric word for one million?
6 Which Steve plays the Gervais part in the US "Office" remake?
7 Which company developed the pottery called Jasper Ware?
8 What did Monkee Mike Nesmith's mother invent?
9 Which travellers met at the Tabard Inn, Southwark?
10 What colour blood cells do lymph glands produce?
11 Where is the constituency of Respect MP George Galloway?
12 "These Words" was the first No. 1 single for which female artist?
13 Who wrote the novel "The Silmarillion"?
14 On which Canadian island is the city of Victoria?
15 In which century was Isambard Kingdom Brunel born?
16 What is the only English anagram of IMPRESSIVE?
17 In which country was Joe Bugner born?
18 In Scrabble, how many points is the letter A worth?
19 Which creature lives in a formicary?
20 What make of car was Jim Clark driving when he died?
21 In which drama did Father Ralph de Bricassart and Meggie Cleary appear?
22 If A is alpha and B is bravo what is T?
23 Which monster hit the British headlines in 1933?
24 Who were "overpaid, oversexed and over here"?
25 Which name means bringer of joys in Latin?
26 How old was Dion Dublin when he moved to Celtic?
27 What drug is obtained from foxgloves?
28 Ben Lomond and Baldwin are types of which fruit?
29 Which element has the atomic number 50 and the symbol Sn?
30 In which decade of the 20th century was Alan Ayckbourn born?

Answers | Pot Luck 87 *(see Quiz 196)*

1 Liver. 2 Leicestershire. 3 Adam & Eve. 4 Antarctica. 5 American Football. 6 Three Mile Island. 7 Dame Nellie Melba. 8 10. 9 Cold sores. 10 The North Sea. 11 18th. 12 John Steinbeck. 13 Tiger Woods. 14 His cave. 15 Manic Street Preachers. 16 Emerald. 17 "Gun". 18 Cleopatra. 19 First Corinthians. 20 Martin Bashir. 21 Rowing. 22 Finsbury Park. 23 2012. 24 Dogs. 25 The Pirates of Penzance. 26 West Yorkshire. 27 M. 28 David Dickinson. 29 Groucho. 30 Holocaust Memorial Day.

1 Which controversial BBC Falklands film was broadcast in May 1988?
2 In which month was the marriage of Prince Charles and Lady Diana?
3 The SAS stormed which embassy in Knightsbridge?
4 Where did the 1980 Olympics take place?
5 Where did the Polish Solidarity movement start its strikes?
6 In August 1980 unemployment in Britain reached what figure?
7 Which US President ordered the aborted rescue of US hostages in Tehran?
8 Which Lord prepared a report following the Brixton riots?
9 Whom did Pat Cash beat in the final when he won Wimbledon?
10 Who became the first Pope to visit Britain in 400 years?
11 Which charity record was the last to reach No.1 in the 80s?
12 Who were Liverpool's opponents in the FA Cup semi-final Hillsborough disaster?
13 Who "got on his bike and looked for work"?
14 What did Prince Edward resign?
15 How did Princess Grace of Monaco die?
16 Which Tory MP Keith was involved in dodgy applications for shares?
17 In which month of 1982 did Argentine forces invade the Falkland Islands?
18 Nuclear protests were based at Greenham Common in which county?
19 Which police officer was shot outside the Libyan embassy?
20 To a year, how old was Bjorn Borg when he retired from tennis?
21 What did Reagan's Strategic Defence Initiative become known as?
22 What did Monday, October 19th, 1987 become known as?
23 Which North Sea oil rig exploded with the loss of over 150 lives?
24 Which former M15 man wrote "Spycatcher"?
25 Which American politician made the famous "watch my lips" speech?
26 In which books were golliwogs replaced by gnomes?
27 Which crazed gunman committed the Hungerford atrocities?
28 In which month was Michael Fish embarrassed by the gales of '87?
29 Where was the jumbo travelling to when it crashed at Lockerbie?
30 Who was Neil Kinnock's deputy when he became Labour leader?

Answers | **Horse Racing** *(see Quiz 197)*

1 Grand National. 2 12th. 3 1977. 4 Jim Culloty. 5 2,000 Guineas, Derby, St Leger. 6 Committed suicide. 7 Pat Eddery. 8 1954. 9 The Oaks. 10 Dick Francis. 11 Bay. 12 1 mile 4 furlongs. 13 Four. 14 Ten. 15 Peter Scudamore. 16 Corky. 17 Lester Piggott. 18 1920s. 19 Frankie Dettori. 20 Desert Orchid. 21 L'Escargot. 22 Once. 23 Kentucky Derby. 24 Buckle. 25 Sam Arnull. 26 Lanfranco. 27 Laffit Pincay Jr. 28 Oath. 29 Bay. 30 54.

Quiz 200 Easy Listening

Answers – page 444

1 Who wrote "For the Good Times"?
2 What was Will Young's second single to make No. 1?
3 Who made the Top Ten in 1952, had a 1968 No. 1 and was back in 1994?
4 Who had an album cryptically called "Last the Whole Night Long"?
5 Which instrument is associated with Mr Acker Bilk?
6 Which close harmony Sisters were Connee, Martha and Helvetia?
7 Who had a No. 1 with the title in brackets of "Voler A Empezar"?
8 Which Nat King Cole song was reissued and charted 30 years after the original?
9 In Sinatra's "High Hopes" what can't move a rubber-tree plant?
10 What was Lena Martell's only No. 1?
11 What was Perry Como's job before he became a singer?
12 Which 70s duo took the standard "Whispering Grass" to No. 1?
13 To two years, when did Johnny Mathis first have a Top Ten single?
14 Who did Gerry Dorsey become to sell thousands of 60s singles?
15 Who sang "I Just Want to Dance with You"?
16 Which Dickie had a 50s No. 1 with "Christmas Alphabet"?
17 Which singer/songwriter David fronted Bread?
18 What was Glenn Miller's main instrument?
19 Who wrote "Annie's Song"?
20 Where did Pat Boone write love letters?
21 Which city does James Galway come from?
22 How many were there in the Ink Spots?
23 Who had a British hit with "Guantanamera"?
24 Under what name did Brenda Gail Webb find fame?
25 Who wrote "This Guy's in Love with You"?
26 Whose singers invite radio listeners to "Sing Something Simple"?
27 Who had a 50s No. 1 with "Mary's Boy Child"?
28 What was Ken Dodd's huge 60s No. 1?
29 Which group used to accompany Herb Alpert?
30 Which song was No. 1 for Robson & Jerome and also for Gareth Gates?

Answers | TV Cops & Robbers *(see Quiz 202)*

1 "Crime Traveller". 2 Cadfael. 3 Jonathan Creek. 4 Mars. 5 Gardeners. 6 The Saint.
7 "Cagney and Lacey". 8 David. 9 "Bodyguards". 10 The Baron. 11 Peter Cushing.
12 Sun Hill. 13 Three. 14 "The Chief". 15 Bergerac. 16 Los Angeles. 17 Criminal
psychologist. 18 Afternoon. 19 Tony Curtis. 20 Danger Man. 21 Miss Marple. 22
Lynda LaPlante. 23 Jasper Carrott. 24 "Gideon's Way". 25 The Chinese Detective. 26
Poirot. 27 Lochdubh. 28 Pathologists. 29 New York. 30 Campion.

1 Which river is nearest to Balmoral Castle?
2 Which country and western singer appeared in "Gunfight"?
3 Which US probe was sent to land on Mars in 1997?
4 Which London park would you be in to ride along Rotten Row?
5 Which Swiss resort awards the Golden Rose TV awards?
6 How did Jane Austen's character Mr Woodhouse like his boiled egg?
7 Who was the first non-Englishman to play James Bond?
8 Which British airport was the first with its own railway station?
9 In 2005, which Russian vessel was trapped off the Kamchatka peninsula?
10 How many wives are allowed at one time under Islamic Law?
11 In which century was religious reformer John Calvin born?
12 Who had a 50s No. 1 with "Who's Sorry Now"?
13 If it's 12 noon GMT what time is it in Oslo?
14 A red variety of which fruit went on sale in Marks & Spencer, Feb. 2006?
15 Who wrote the novel "Anna Karenina"?
16 Which bridge joins a palace and a prison in Venice?
17 What word can follow "band", "mass" and "pass"?
18 Which battle came first – Agincourt or Bosworth Field?
19 What is the next highest prime number above 53?
20 In which American state are the Everglades?
21 Who took over Leeds soccer club in Jan. 2005?
22 Hollyoaks featured a map of which city in its opening credits?
23 Which banned insecticide was the first to be man-made?
24 What was Britney Spears's second No. 1 single?
25 What is the capital of Georgia of the former USSR?
26 Whose motto is Ich Dien?
27 Who was the first presenter of "Tomorrow's World"?
28 Where was the Bayview Retirement Home in "Waiting for God"?
29 In which decade was "Blue Peter" screened for the first time?
30 Which river was Jesus Christ baptized in?

Answers	**Pot Luck 90** *(see Quiz 203)*

1 Sean Connery. 2 "Mastermind". 3 Blue. 4 12. 5 19th. 6 Eat it. 7 O. 8 The Old Curiosity Shop. 9 Edward Heath. 10 Arsenal. 11 Lawyer. 12 Norman Foster. 13 Refraction. 14 Oxford. 15 Horses. 16 France. 17 Leeds Rhinos. 18 Women being members. 19 Bishop of Salisbury. 20 30s. 21 Keir Hardie. 22 "Turn". 23 White. 24 Sheena Easton. 25 Greece. 26 In the sea. 27 Queen Victoria. 28 H. G. Wells. 29 Cabbage. 30 A pancake.

1 Which 1997 series featured detectives Slade and Holly?
2 Which TV detective is based in Shrewsbury?
3 Maddy Magellan assisted which offbeat TV detective?
4 Which planet completes the crime fantasy TV series "Life on ...."?
5 What is the profession of sleuths Rosemary and Thyme?
6 Who had a business card which included a matchstick-man logo?
7 In which series did Detective Isbecki appear?
8 What was Callan's first name?
9 In which series did Louise Lombard star as Liz Shaw?
10 How was John Mannering better known?
11 Which horror actor played Sherlock Holmes in the 60s?
12 Chief Superintendent Charles Brownlow was in charge of which police station?
13 How many Angels did Charlie have?
14 Which drama featured Assistant Chief Constable Anne Stewart?
15 Who worked for the Bureau des Etrangers?
16 Where was "Columbo" set?
17 What is Cracker's job?
18 At what time of day was "Crown Court" first broadcast?
19 Who was the American half of "The Persuaders"?
20 How was 60s secret agent John Drake better known?
21 Which detective often embarrassed Inspector Slack?
22 Which writer created Superintendent Jane Tennison?
23 Who played the detective Bob Louis?
24 Which 60s series based on John Creasey's novels starred John Gregson?
25 How was Detective Sergeant Johnny Ho known?
26 Who had a secretary called Miss Lemon?
27 In which fictional town was "Hamish Macbeth" set?
28 In "Inspector Morse" what were the professions of Max and Dr Russell?
29 In "Dempsey and Makepeace" where was Dempsey from?
30 Whom did Magersfontein Lugg assist?

Answers	**Easy Listening** *(see Quiz 200)*

1 Don McLean. 2 "Light My Fire". 3 Louis Armstrong. 4 James Last. 5 Clarinet. 6 Boswell Sisters. 7 Julio Iglesias. 8 "When I Fall in Love". 9 An ant. 10 "One Day at a Time". 11 Barber. 12 Windsor Davies and Don Estelle. 13 1958. 14 Engelbert Humperdinck. 15 Daniel O'Donnell. 16 Valentine. 17 Gates. 18 Trombone. 19 John Denver. 20 In the sand. 21 Belfast. 22 Four. 23 The Sandpipers. 24 Crystal Gayle. 25 Bacharach and David. 26 Cliff Adams. 27 Harry Belafonte. 28 "Tears". 29 Tijuana Brass. 30 "Unchained Melody".

1 Which actor was James Bond in the "Thunderball" movie?
2 Which TV show's format was based on the producer's experience at the hands of the Gestapo?
3 What colour is Scooby Doo's collar in the cartoons?
4 How many pairs of ribs does a human adult have normally?
5 In which century was Paul Cézanne born?
6 What do you do with a wonton?
7 In Morse code what letter is represented by three dashes?
8 In which Dickens novel does Kit Nubbles appear?
9 Which politician sailed the yacht *Morning Cloud*?
10 Which side were Premiership runners up from 1999 to 2001?
11 In the musical "Chicago", what is the occupation of Billy Flynn?
12 Which architect Norman led the group that designed London's "gherkin"?
13 What describes the bending of light as it passes from one medium to another?
14 Which university athletics team had Jeffrey Archer as a member?
15 What was the favourite subject of the artist George Stubbs?
16 Which European country is split by the Canal Du Midi?
17 Who lost rugby league's Challenge Cup final in 2003 and 2005?
18 In April 1997, Leander Rowing Club overturned a 179-year ban on what?
19 Who signs with the name Sarum?
20 In which decade of the 20th century was Brigitte Bardot born?
21 Who was the first Labour leader?
22 What was Travis's second top ten hit?
23 What colour is Homer Simpson's T-shirt?
24 Who performed the title song in the Bond film "For Your Eyes Only"?
25 Which country includes the Peloponnese?
26 Where were Olympic swimming events held prior to 1908?
27 Who laid the foundation stone at the Victoria and Albert Museum?
28 Who wrote the novel "The History of Mr Polly"?
29 What variety of vegetable does kale belong to?
30 What is stuffed to make a blini or a blintz?

Answers | Pot Luck 89 *(see Quiz 201)*

1 The Dee. 2 Johnny Cash. 3 Pathfinder. 4 Hyde Park. 5 Montreux. 6 Very soft. 7 Sean Connery. 8 Gatwick. 9 Priz. 10 Four. 11 16th. 12 Connie Francis. 13 1 p.m. 14 Bananas. 15 Leo Tolstoy. 16 The Bridge of Sighs. 17 "Age". 18 Agincourt. 19 59. 20 Florida. 21 Ken Bates. 22 Chester. 23 DDT. 24 "Born to Make You Happy". 25 Tbilisi. 26 The Prince of Wales. 27 Raymond Baxter. 28 Bournemouth. 29 1950s. 30 The Jordan.

1 What is ciabatta?
2 What is the predominant flavour of fennel?
3 What type of pulses are used in hummus?
4 What flavour is the drink Kahlua?
5 What is added to butter in a *beurre manié* ?
6 What type of wine is traditionally used in zabaglione?
7 What is radicchio?
8 What do the Spanish call a medium dry sherry?
9 What is panettone?
10 What are the three main ingredients of an Hollandaise sauce?
11 In the kitchen, what would a mandolin be used for?
12 What is harissa?
13 Which liqueur is used in a White Lady?
14 What sweet substance is added to whisky to make Drambuie?
15 From which continent does couscous originate?
16 What is the dish of stuffed vine leaves called?
17 In wine bottle sizes what is another name for a double magnum?
18 In the food world what is rocket?
19 From which country does balsamic vinegar originate?
20 Which spirit is used in a Daiquiri?
21 In which century was chocolate introduced into the UK?
22 Everards beers were originally based near which town?
23 What type of meat is used in moussaka?
24 What is the main ingredient of rosti?
25 Which traditional pudding ingredient comes from the cassava plant?
26 What is ghee?
27 Slivovitz is made from which fruit?
28 From what is angostura obtained?
29 What type of milk is a basic ingredient of Thai cookery?
30 What is a bruschetta?

Answers	Pot Luck 91 *(see Quiz 206)*

1 Scotland. 2 Gleneagles, G8 Summit. 3 1990. 4 Thickens. 5 Thunder. 6 Mark Twain. 7 Glastonbury Tor. 8 Swansea. 9 17th. 10 Crevasse. 11 Geronimo. 12 Argon. 13 Michael Stipe. 14 Redcurrant. 15 Topaz. 16 1950s. 17 Blackburn Rovers. 18 The Crucible. 19 Andre Agassi & Steffi Graf. 20 A bittern. 21 Herrings. 22 Queen Elizabeth II. 23 Jackie Stewart. 24 Canada. 25 Oxfordshire, Berkshire. 26 "The News Huddlines". 27 720. 28 Nelly. 29 The Everglades. 30 A cock.

1 Who was the first Tory leader to have gone to a grammar school?
2 Who was acting leader of the Lib Dems after Charles Kennedy stood down?
3 In 1997 David Blunkett won which constituency?
4 What was the name of Harold Wilson's wife?
5 Who published the white paper "In Place of Strife"?
6 Mrs Thatcher became Baroness Thatcher of where?
7 In 2004, which former PM's son was linked in a plot involving a military coup?
8 Who was deputy prime minister when Harold Macmillan resigned?
9 Tony Blair had how many children when he became Prime Minister?
10 What was the Tory slogan on posters of a queue of the unemployed?
11 Who first became prime minister – Gladstone or Disraeli?
12 To two years, when did John Major first win Huntingdon?
13 Who was beaten to the Labour leadership by Michael Foot in 1980?
14 What was the name of the male model in the Jeremy Thorpe affair?
15 Prime Minister Arthur James Balfour belonged to which party?
16 Dennis Skinner is known as the Beast of where?
17 Who followed Anthony Crossland as Labour's Foreign Secretary?
18 Who said that Gorbachev was "a man we can do business with"?
19 Who was Labour leader when the party adopted the red rose symbol?
20 Which politician was responsible for the creation of the police force?
21 How may rounds were there in the Tory leadership election of 1997?
22 Who was acting Labour leader on the sudden death of John Smith?
23 Who is Kingston-upon-Hull's most famous MP?
24 John Redwood and William Hague have held which cabinet post?
25 Who was Britain's first Socialist MP?
26 Who courted disaster with a weekend at the Paris Ritz in September 1993?
27 Roy Jenkins, David Owen, Shirley Williams and who else were the Gang Of Four?
28 Prime Minister Andrew Bonar Law belonged to which party?
29 How many general elections did Mrs Thatcher win for the Tories?
30 What constituency did Sir Edward Heath represent for many years?

Answers	**Animation Movies** *(see Quiz 207)*

1 Bashful. 2 Nick Park. 3 Mortimer. 4 Snow White and the Seven Dwarfs. 5 Yellow Submarine. 6 Tim Rice. 7 Peter Kay. 8 Pinocchio. 9 Scar. 10 Arthur. 11 One Hundred and One Dalmatians. 12 Mickey Mouse. 13 "Whole New World". 14 Fantasia. 15 Orang-utan. 16 Jasmine. 17 Pongo and Perdita. 18 Rabbit. 19 Jungle Book. 20 Basil. 21 15. 22 Cinderella. 23 Donald Duck. 24 Pocahontas. 25 The Hunchback of Notre Dame. 26 The Return of Jafar. 27 Space Jam. 28 1930s. 29 Ostriches. 30 Spaniel.

1 Which country includes the Isle of Tiree ?
2 Where was Tony Blair when the London bombs exploded on 7th July 2005?
3 In which year did John Major become Prime Minister?
4 What is the only English anagram of KITCHENS?
5 Brontophobia is a fear of what?
6 Who wrote the novel "The Prince and the Pauper"?
7 Which Somerset hill is famed for its Arthurian associations?
8 Which Welsh town became a city in 1969?
9 In which century was Venetian painter Canaletto born?
10 What name describes a crack in a glacier?
11 Which leader of the Apache tribe died in 1909?
12 Which element has the atomic number 18 and the symbol Ar?
13 At Super Bowl XL whose song could be downloaded to raise cash for hurricane victims?
14 Which fruit provides the basis for Cumberland Sauce?
15 Which birthstone is linked to November?
16 In which decade is the movie "Vera Drake" set?
17 Rangers' Barry Ferguson played in the Premiership for which club?
18 Which Arthur Miller play is about witchcraft?
19 Which ex-Wimbledon and US champions of the 1990s married each other?
20 Which bird's cry is known as a boom?
21 Which fish are turned into rollmops?
22 Who opened the re-created Globe Theatre in 1997?
23 Which Briton has been F1 World Champion on the most occasions?
24 Which country was the nearest to where the Titanic was found?
25 Which counties does Thames Valley FM serve?
26 The 400th edition of which radio comedy went out in May 1997?
27 How many hours in April?
28 "Dilemma" was a 2002 No. 1 for Kelly Rowland and which rapper?
29 Which Florida national park is split by a road called Alligator Alley?
30 What bird was banned from fighting in Britain after 1848?

Answers | **Food & Drink 2** *(see Quiz 204)*

1 An Italian bread. 2 Aniseed. 3 Chick peas. 4 Coffee. 5 Flour. 6 Marsala. 7 Red-leaved lettuce. 8 Amontillado. 9 Fruit bread. 10 Butter, egg yolk, wine vinegar. 11 Slicing. 12 Hot spicy paste. 13 Cointreau. 14 Heather honey. 15 Africa. 16 Dolmas. 17 Jeroboam. 18 Salad leaf. 19 Italy. 20 Dark rum. 21 17th. 22 Leicester. 23 Lamb. 24 Potatoes. 25 Tapioca. 26 Clarified butter. 27 Plums. 28 Tree bark. 29 Coconut milk. 30 Fried or toasted bread.

1 Which of the Seven Dwarfs had the longest name?
2 Who created Wallace and Gromit?
3 What was Mickey Mouse originally called?
4 What was Disney's first full-length cartoon called?
5 Which film takes place in Pepperland?
6 Who wrote the song lyrics for "Aladdin"?
7 Who provided the voice of PC Mackintosh in "Curse of the Were-Rabbit"?
8 "When You Wish upon a Star" is from which Disney film?
9 What is Simba's uncle called in "The Lion King"?
10 "The Sword in the Stone" centres on the legend of which King?
11 Which film has the signal of the "twilight bark"?
12 Which character was the star of Disney's "Steamboat Willie"?
13 Which song from "Aladdin" in 1992 won an Oscar?
14 In which Disney film are Leopold Stokowski and the Philadelphia Orchestra seen?
15 What sort of animal is King Louie in "The Jungle Book"?
16 What is the Princess called in "Aladdin"?
17 Who were the original two Dalmatians in the 1961 classic?
18 What sort of creature was Thumper in "Bambi"?
19 Which was the first major Disney cartoon film released after Walt Disney's death in 1966?
20 What was the name of Disney's Great Mouse Detective?
21 How many puppies does Perdita produce in her first Dalmatian litter?
22 In which film is magic summoned by "Bibbidi-Bobbidi-Boo"?
23 Who had nephews called Dewey, Huey and Louie?
24 In which 90s film did "Colors of the Wind" appear?
25 Which 90s Disney film was based on a Victor Hugo story?
26 Which Disney film was the sequel to "Aladdin"?
27 Which 90s film starred Bugs Bunny and Michael Jordan?
28 In which decade was "Snow White and the Seven Dwarfs" released?
29 Which birds take part in the ballet in "Fantasia"?
30 What breed of dog is Lady in "Lady and the Tramp"?

Answers | Politics (see Quiz 205)

1 Ted Heath. 2 Sir Menzies Campbell. 3 Sheffield Brightside. 4 Mary. 5 Barbara Castle. 6 Kesteven. 7 Sir Mark Thatcher. 8 Rab Butler. 9 Three. 10 Labour isn't working. 11 Disraeli. 12 1983. 13 Denis Healey. 14 Norman Scott. 15 Conservative. 16 Bolsover. 17 David Owen. 18 Margaret Thatcher. 19 Neil Kinnock. 20 Robert Peel. 21 Three. 22 Margaret Beckett. 23 John Prescott. 24 Secretary for Wales. 25 James Keir Hardie. 26 Jonathan Aitken. 27 William Rogers. 28 Conservative. 29 Three. 30 Old Sidcup & Bexley.

1 Who is the Queen's only nephew?
2 Norman Kember was taken prisoner in 2005 in which country?
3 Which country do Hyundai cars originate from?
4 Who played Leo in the 2005 movie remake of "The Producers"?
5 Which director/writer guided the career of Katie Melua?
6 In which century was Catherine the Great born?
7 Which country does cricketer Ed Joyce come from?
8 What is the oldest mainline rail terminus in London?
9 Which area of London first installed parking meters?
10 Who wrote the novel "Busman's Honeymoon"?
11 Which cocktail was dedicated to Tom Harvey, the surfing star?
12 What is the naval equivalent of the army rank of General?
13 Which modern instrument was developed from the sackbut?
14 If A is alpha and B is bravo what is J?
15 What was Gandhi's profession before politics?
16 What is the capital of the Canadian province Alberta?
17 Which country has the internet code .al?
18 In which decade of the 20th century was Idi Amin born?
19 What is the largest bay in the world?
20 Who was elected Palestinian leader in 2005 after Yasser Arafat's death?
21 Which world-renowned writer lived at Bateman's in Sussex?
22 In which suburb was "2 Point 4 Children" set?
23 Which non-league club held Man. Utd to a 2005 FA Cup draw at Old Trafford?
24 In the story, who fell asleep on the Catskill Mountains?
25 What is the American equivalent of the British bilberry?
26 Vivian Stanshall was in which band?
27 In music, if a piece is in three flats which notes will be flat?
28 "Keep On Movin'" was the first No. 1 for which quintet?
29 What organization was set up by Agnes, Baden-Powell's sister?
30 In the Chinese calendar which year follows the year of the goat?

| **Answers** | **Pot Luck 93** *(see Quiz 210)* |

1 Martin Bell (at Tatton). **2** Bake them. **3** Ice hockey. **4** Band Aid. **5** "For". **6** Ten years. **7** Pierluigi Collina. **8** Leo Tolstoy. **9** Atomic Kitten. **10** Blue whale. **11** 15th. **12** Manhattan. **13** Cube. **14** Basil. **15** Ruth Rendell. **16** Portugal. **17** Lamentations. **18** Kate Winslet. **19** Anne Fine. **20** Ministry of Defence. **21** The Fast Show. **22** Zimbabwe. **23** Richard Nixon. **24** 30. **25** Two. **26** Latin. **27** Bad breath. **28** Leeds Tykes. **29** Goebbels. **30** Asparagus.

1 What can follow "milk" and "rag" in the plant world?
2 What sort of fruit is a mirabelle?
3 Which Princess had a rose named after her at the 1997 Chelsea Flower Show?
4 Which grain is used to make semolina?
5 Which term is used for plants which store moisture in their thick fleshy leaves or stems?
6 Which part of a plant protects it as a bud?
7 What shape is a campanulate flower?
8 What is a morel?
9 What does lamina mean when referring to a leaf?
10 Which part of the tree is cinnamon obtained from?
11 Which parts of the potato are poisonous?
12 If a leaf is dentate what does it mean?
13 What colour are the flowers of a St John's Wort?
14 What is a prickly pear?
15 What is the main vegetation of the South African veld?
16 Why is the grapefruit so called?
17 What colour are borage flowers?
18 What is kelp?
19 Which plant's name means lion's tooth?
20 What is another name for the lime tree?
21 What is to be found in a plant's anther?
22 How long is the life cycle of a biennial plant?
23 The sycamore is native to which continent?
24 How many leaves does the twayblade orchid have?
25 What colour are the fruits on the deadly nightshade?
26 What type of plants are traditionally seen in a herbarium?
27 Which tree did archers need to cultivate to make bows?
28 Which King reputedly sought refuge in an oak tree?
29 The loganberry is a cross between which fruits?
30 What colour is the blossom of the blackthorn?

Answers	**Wayne Rooney** *(see Quiz 211)*

1 Liverpool. 2 Macedonia. 3 David Moyes. 4 1985. 5 7th. 6 Australia. 7 Birmingham. 8 BBC Young Sportsperson of the Year. 9 Number 8. 10 Nicky Butt. 11 Arsenal. 12 Richard Wright. 13 Scorpio. 14 Portugal. 15 Newcastle. 16 Ferenbache. 17 Three. 18 Arsenal. 19 Switzerland. 20 Shrek. 21 Villarreal. 22 England won 4–2. 23 9. 24 6 goals. 25 Arsenal. 26 17 years 111 days old. 27 Tomasz Radzinkski. 28 Third. 29 Mark. 30 Wrexham.

1 Whom did David Soul campaign for in the 1997 General Election?
2 What do you do to mashed potatoes to make them Duchesse?
3 What sport do the Cardiff Devils play?
4 Which charity ceased in 1989 after 5 years and raising £90 million?
5 What word can go before "tress", "tune" and "ward"?
6 How often is a modern national census held in the UK?
7 Who was match referee for the 2002 FIFA World Cup Final?
8 Which famous Russian writer died on Astapova railway station?
9 The Bangles' "Eternal Flame" was covered by which other girl group?
10 Which creatures give birth to the world's biggest babies?
11 In which century was the astronomer Copernicus born?
12 Where in New York is "Sex and the City" set?
13 Height times breadth times 6 gives the surface area of which shape?
14 What is the main herb in pesto sauce?
15 Who wrote the novel "Simisola"?
16 In which country of mainland Europe did J. K. Rowling develop Hary Potter?
17 In the Old Testament which gloomy-sounding book directly follows Jeremiah?
18 Whose second marriage was to director Sam Mendes?
19 Who was Children's Laureate from 2001 to 2003?
20 Which Government department is the second biggest UK landowner?
21 Which show had the catchphrase, "suits you sir!"?
22 Bruce Grobbelaar kept goal for which country?
23 Who was the first US president to visit China?
24 How old did women have to be to vote in 1918?
25 In music, how many sharps in the key of D?
26 What language is the Magna Carta written in?
27 What is halitosis?
28 Which club did New Zealand scrum half Justin Marshall sign for in 2005?
29 Who was Hitler's propaganda minister 1933–45?
30 Which vegetable gives the flavour to a Bruxelloise sauce?

Answers | Pot Luck 92 (see Quiz 208)

1 Viscount Linley. 2 Iraq. 3 Korea. 4 Matthew Broderick. 5 Mike Batt. 6 18th. 7 Ireland. 8 London Bridge. 9 Mayfair. 10 Dorothy L. Sayers. 11 Harvey Wallbanger. 12 Admiral. 13 Trombone. 14 Juliet. 15 Lawyer. 16 Edmonton. 17 Albania. 18 20s. 19 Hudson Bay. 20 Mahmoud Abbas. 21 Rudyard Kipling. 22 Chiswick. 23 Exeter City. 24 Rip Van Winkle. 25 Blueberry. 26 The Bonzo Dog Doo Dah Band. 27 B, E, A. 28 Five. 29 Girl Guides. 30 Monkey.

1 In which city was Wayne born?
2 Rooney scored his first England goal against which country?
3 Which Everton manager gave Rooney his debut?
4 In which year was Rooney born?
5 Where did Everton finish in the Premiership in Rooney's first season?
6 Against which country did Rooney make his England debut?
7 Rooney was first sent off against which Premiership side?
8 Which BBC award did he win in 2002?
9 Which squad number did Rooney take at Man. Utd?
10 Which player left Man. Utd to make Rooney's number available?
11 Wayne first played in an FA Cup Final against which team?
12 Who was Everton's regular keeper in Rooney's first season?
13 What is Wayne's star sign – Taurus or Scorpio?
14 Who were the opponents in Euro 2004 when Rooney was injured?
15 Which other club bid for Rooney before the Man. Utd move?
16 Who were the opposition in Rooney's Man. Utd debut?
17 How many goals did he score in his Man. Utd debut game?
18 His first Premiership goal was against which club?
19 Rooney was booked against which country in Euro 2004?
20 Which animated character gives Rooney one of his nicknames?
21 Against which European club team was he red carded in Sept. 2005?
22 What was the score in the England v. Croatia Euro 2004 game?
23 What number does Rooney usually wear for England?
24 In his first season did Rooney score 6, 9, or 16 league goals?
25 A goal against which team made Wayne the youngest ever Premiership scorer?
26 He was 17 years and how many days old on his England debut – 111, 222 or 333?
27 Which Tomasz was Everton's top scorer in Wayne's first season?
28 Where did Man. Utd finish in the Premiership in Wayne's first season?
29 What is Wayne's middle name?
30 Wayne's first Everton goals were in the League Cup against which club?

Answers	**Plant World** *(see Quiz 209)*

1 "Wort". 2 Plum. 3 Princess of Wales. 4 Wheat. 5 Succulent. 6 Sepal. 7 Bell-shaped. 8 Mushroom. 9 Blade. 10 Bark. 11 Green parts including leaves. 12 Toothed or notched. 13 Yellow. 14 Cactus. 15 Grass. 16 Grows in grape-like clusters. 17 Blue. 18 Seaweed. 19 Dandelion (dent de lion). 20 Linden. 21 Pollen. 22 More than one year, but less than two. 23 Europe. 24 Two. 25 Black. 26 Dried plants. 27 Yew. 28 Charles II. 29 Raspberry and blackberry. 30 White.

Quiz 212 | Speed Stars

1 Which country did motor racing's Juan Manuel Fangio come from?

2 Who set a world record for the fastest ever maximum snooker break at the Crucible in April 1997?

3 Which England fast bowler received damages from "Wisden Cricket Monthly" over the article "Is It in the Blood?"?

4 What was the nost notable thing about Julio McCaw who raced against Jesse Owens?

5 In which event did Redgrave and Pinsent win Olympic gold?

6 Who was the first driver to register 50 Grand Prix victories?

7 In which British city did Kelly Holmes first race after Athens Gold?

8 In motor cycling, at what cc level was Barry Sheene world champ?

9 What was Mary Slaney's surname before her marriage?

10 Which Australian quick bowler is known as Pigeon?

11 To a year each way, when was James Hunt Formula 1 world champ?

12 Graeme Obree is connected with which sport?

13 Stephane Peterhansel won his second successive what in Jan. 2005?

14 To a year each way, how old was Nigel Mansell when he was F1 world champion?

15 What famous first will Diomed always hold?

16 Finishing third in which race made Fernando Alonso F1 world champ?

17 In April 1997 what did younger brother Florian give to Niki Lauda?

18 Colin Jackson's 60m. hurdle record was set in Sindelfingen – in which country?

19 Whom did Frank Williams recruit from IndyCar for the 1996 GP season?

20 Who succeeded Linford Christie as England's athletics team captain?

21 Which country does Donovan Bailey run for?

22 What nationality was Keke Rosberg?

23 Where in 1996 did Oliver Panis have his debut Grand Prix victory?

24 Who was the first man to swim 100m. in less than a minute?

25 Who was Man. Utd's left winger in the 60s European Cup triumph?

26 What are Daley Thompson's first two names?

27 Which Grand Prix did Damon Hill win first when he became 1996 world champion?

28 Which England fast bowler was nicknamed George?

29 Which horse was Lester Piggott's first Derby winner?

30 Bode Miller is associated with which sport?

Answers | **Soul & Motown** (see Quiz 214)

1 Supremes. 2 James Brown. 3 Whitney Houston. 4 1980s. 5 Georgia. 6 Billie Holiday. 7 Aretha Franklin. 8 Berry Gordy. 9 Organ. 10 Shot (by his father). 11 Aretha Franklin. 12 Gladys Knight. 13 "I Want You Back". 14 Michael Bolton. 15 Stevie Wonder. 16 Jimmy Ruffin. 17 The Wicked Pickett. 18 Four Tops. 19 1966. 20 The Commodores. 21 The Four Tops. 22 Michael Jackson. 23 James Brown. 24 Rose. 25 Smokey Robinson. 26 1960s. 27 "I Was Made to Love Her". 28 Stax. 29 Lionel Richie. 30 Floyd.

1 Which film featured the single "Vogue" by Madonna?
2 In medical terms, what does an ECG stand for?
3 Is Rolf Harris's birthday portrait of the Queen done in oils or watercolours?
4 With which two surnames did Aussie Evonne win Wimbledon?
5 Who played the con man in Spielberg's "Catch Me If You Can"?
6 Which canal linked Liverpool to London?
7 Which piece of attire took its name from a Pacific nuclear test site?
8 Who wrote the novel "Nostromo"?
9 Who was lost for six days in 1982's Paris–Dakar desert rally?
10 Which dessert is named after a ballerina?
11 Who invented the magnetic telegraph?
12 What word can go after "tea" and before "fast"?
13 Which word links a TV quiz show with space launches?
14 In which century was Botticelli born?
15 Who was Miss California in 1978?
16 What is the capital of Albania?
17 Which heroine was awarded Freedom of the City of London in 1908?
18 In Scrabble, how many points is the letter J worth?
19 In which country would you find the Great Sandy Desert?
20 In Morse code what letter is represented by four dots?
21 Alphabetically what is the last of the chemical elements?
22 What name is given to the larva of a fly?
23 Who became a Saint in 1909, nearly 500 years after she was killed?
24 In which Dickens novel does Jerry Cruncher appear?
25 What fruit can be made from the letters in TRANSCIENCE?
26 Which Asian capital city did George W. Bush visit in November 2005?
27 In which decade of the 20th century was Warren Beatty born?
28 Which pop star ran for Mayor of Detroit in 1989?
29 What name describes the loose rocks on the side of a mountain?
30 Which hat took its name from a novel by George Du Maurier?

Answers	Pot Luck 95 *(see Quiz 215)*

1 Nicholas. 2 Sunderland. 3 Monopoly. 4 The Samaritans. 5 Agate. 6 Patty and Selma Bouvier. 7 1970s. 8 Knesset. 9 Pennines. 10 Mrs Doubtfire. 11 A dotted line. 12 Iolanthe. 13 Ian Rush. 14 Thailand. 15 Boeing. 16 Rosamunde Pitcher. 17 3 p.m.. 18 Gardening. 19 Orange juice. 20 Shameless. 21 Clay. 22 16th. 23 Turkey. 24 Little Lord Fauntleroy. 25 Nottm Forest. 26 Marge & Homer. 27 Newcastle Upon Tyne. 28 India. 29 Amerie. 30 St Mark.

1 "Nathan Jones" was a 70s hit for which group?
2 The Famous Flames backed which classic soul performer?
3 Which pop star did Bobby Brown marry in 1992?
4 In which decade did Stevie Wonder have his first British No. 1?
5 In "Dock of the Bay" Otis Redding left his home in where when he headed for the Frisco Bay?
6 Whom did Diana Ross play in "Lady Sings the Blues"?
7 Who duetted with George Michael on "I Knew You were Waiting"?
8 Who founded Motown records?
9 What instrument did Booker T. play?
10 How did Marvin Gaye die?
11 Which female soul singer has recorded with the Eurythmics and George Benson?
12 In 1972, who recorded "Help Me Make It Through the Night"?
13 Which Jackson 5 hit of 1970 was remixed and back in 1988?
14 Who recorded the 90s album "Soul Provider"?
15 The song from the film "The Woman in Red" gave which star his first solo No. 1?
16 Who recorded the original "What Becomes of the Broken Hearted"?
17 What nickname was applied to Wilson Pickett?
18 "Reach Out I'll be There" was the first British No. 1 for which group?
19 To two years each way, when did Percy Sledge first chart with "When a Man Loves a Woman"?
20 Lionel Richie first charted with which group?
21 Levi Stubbs was lead singer with which group?
22 "One Day in Your Life" was a No. 1 for which superstar?
23 Who declared "Get Up I Feel Like Being a Sex Machine"?
24 What flower did Mary Johnson pick for his Rose?
25 Who wrote "Tracks of My Tears" and "My Guy"?
26 In which decade did Sam Cooke die?
27 What was Stevie Wonder's first British top ten hit?
28 Otis Redding recorded on the Atlantic and which other label?
29 Whom did Diana Ross duet with on "Endless Love"?
30 Which Eddie recorded the classic "Knock on Wood"?

Answers | **Speed Stars** *(see Quiz 212)*

1 Argentina. 2 Ronnie O'Sullivan. 3 Devon Malcolm. 4 Julio was a horse. 5 Coxless Pairs (Rowing). 6 Alain Prost. 7 Glasgow. 8 500 cc. 9 Decker. 10 Glenn McGrath. 11 1976. 12 Cycling. 13 Dakar Car Rally. 14 37. 15 First Derby winner. 16 Brazilian Grand Prix. 17 Kidney in a transplant. 18 Germany. 19 Jacques Villeneuve. 20 Roger Black. 21 Canada. 22 Finnish. 23 Monaco. 24 Johnny Weismuller. 25 John Aston. 26 Francis Morgan. 27 Australia. 28 Brian Statham. 29 Never Say Die. 30 Alpine skiing.

1 What is the name of Tony Blair's second-born son?
2 Which English town became a city in 1992?
3 Which game features a top hat, a boot and a racing car?
4 "Love Shine a Light" was written for the 30th anniversary of which organization?
5 What birthstone is linked to June?
6 Which two people work at Springfield DMV?
7 In which decade was "Emmerdale Farm" screened for the first time?
8 What is the Israeli parliament called?
9 Which range of Cumbrian hills has the highest point at Cross Fell?
10 How is the Robin Williams character Daniel Hillard better known?
11 How is a footpath indicated on a map?
12 "The Peer and the Peri" is the subtitle of which light opera?
13 Who returned to Liverpool in 1988 for £2.8 million from Juventus?
14 In which country is Khao Lak, scene of the tsunami of December 2004?
15 Who built the aircraft which dropped the bomb on Hiroshima?
16 Who wrote the novel "The Shell Seekers"?
17 If it's 12 noon GMT what time is it in Moscow?
18 Christopher Lloyd who died in Jan. 2006 was famous in which field?
19 What is added to champagne to make a Bucks Fizz cocktail?
20 Which Channel 4 series was about the Gallagher family?
21 What material is used to make a sumo wrestling ring?
22 In which century was Oliver Cromwell born?
23 What is the modern name for the country Asia Minor?
24 In literature, what title was inherited by Cedric Errol?
25 Spurs bought Andy Reid and Michael Dawson from which club?
26 Who are Bart Simpson's parents?
27 In which city was "Spender" set?
28 Which country has 845 languages with English and Hindi the main?
29 "Touch" and "All I Have" are albums by which artist?
30 Who is the patron saint of Venice?

Answers | Pot Luck 94 *(see Quiz 213)*

1 Dick Tracy. 2 Electrocardiogram. 3 Oils. 4 Goolagong/Cawley. 5 Leonardo DiCaprio. 6 Grand Union Canal. 7 Bikini. 8 Joseph Conrad. 9 Mark Thatcher. 10 Pavlova. 11 Morse. 12 "Break". 13 Countdown. 14 15th. 15 Michelle Pfeiffer. 16 Tirana. 17 Florence Nightingale. 18 Eight. 19 Australia. 20 H. 21 Zirconium. 22 Maggot. 23 Joan of Arc. 24 A Tale of Two Cities. 25 Nectarines. 26 Beijing. 27 30s. 28 Stevie Wonder. 29 Scree. 30 Trilby.

1 Who appeared with Fifi on Five's children animation show?
2 Which pre-school characters live in Home Hill?
3 Who presented the first series of "Live and Kicking"?
4 What were the Teenage Mutant Hero Turtles called?
5 In which show did Little Bo appear?
6 Who is the postmistress of Greendale?
7 What sort of creature is Children's BBC's Otis?
8 In which US state is "Sweet Valley High" set?
9 Which spacecraft was flown by Steve Zodiac?
10 Which character did Susan Tully play in "Grange Hill"?
11 Which comedian wrote the theme music for "Supergran"?
12 Where would you find Hugh, Pugh, Barney McGrew, Cuthbert, Dibble and Grubb?
13 Who numbered Bamabas, Willy and Master Bate in his crew?
14 Whom did Captains White, Blue, Grey and Magenta deal with?
15 Which "historical" series included Barrington, Rabies and Little Ron?
16 What sort of creature is Dilly?
17 How many legs did the Famous Five have on TV?
18 Where is the teenage drama series "Sweat" set?
19 What is the name of the Atomic intergalactic cartoon character?
20 In "Rag, Tag and Bobtail" what was Tag?
21 What is "Fablon" called on "Blue Peter"?
22 What did every contestant win on "Crackerjack"?
23 Who was the longest-lasting presenter of "Rainbow"?
24 The cartoon series about Willy Fogg was based on which book?
25 What sort of animal said, "I'm just a big silly old Hector"?
26 What day of the week was "The Woodentops" originally broadcast?
27 In "The Herbs" what were schoolteacher Mr Onion's pupils called?
28 Which characters live in Springfield?
29 Who has presented "How" and "How 2"?
30 What was Huckleberry Hound's favourite song?

| **Answers** | The 90s *(see Quiz 218)* |

1 43. 2 Tiger Woods. 3 Kuwait. 4 John Redwood. 5 "Unchained Melody" (Righteous Brothers). 6 Jefferson. 7 National Lottery. 8 President F. W. de Klerk. 9 Spurs. 10 John Bird and John Fortune. 11 Darren Gough. 12 The Guardian. 13 John Bryan. 14 Kenneth Clarke. 15 Barcelona. 16 George Carey. 17 Bowls. 18 Andrew Morton. 19 Robert Maxwell. 20 Tom Hanks. 21 Spongiform. 22 Baseball. 23 Whitney Houston. 24 Michael Heseltine. 25 Rod Stewart. 26 Annus horribilis. 27 22. 28 Road-rage attack. 29 George Bush. 30 Tony Adams.

1 Which harbour is the most famous on the island of Oahu?
2 What, in March 1988, ceased to be legal tender in England?
3 Who had the first-ever million-selling CD with "The Joshua Tree"?
4 What kind of vehicle was Charles Rolls of Rolls-Royce in when he died?
5 Which tree family is the basket-making osier a member of?
6 On which ground in England is the last cricket Test in a series held?
7 Which Italian ingredient helps to make a Harvey Wallbanger?
8 Who co-wrote with Bob Geldof the hit "Do They Know It's Christmas"?
9 Which sea did the Romans call *Mare Nostrum?*
10 Where is the largest gulf in the world?
11 The Stade is an area of shingle used by one of Britain's oldest fishing fleets. Where is it to be found?
12 What type of material was used by Rene Lalique for ornaments?
13 Who wrote the book "Aunts Aren't Gentlemen"?
14 Whose 100th single was called "The Best of Me"?
15 What do Australians call a budgerigar?
16 In Germany 2006, who made up Group D with Mexico, Portugal and Iran?
17 Which Liberal is known for the 1909 People's Budget?
18 Which "Friends" star appeared in "The Comeback" on TV?
19 Which country had Queen Wilhelmina as Queen until she died in 1962?
20 What is the official language of Haiti?
21 Which actor co-starred with Sandra Bullock in the film "Speed"?
22 Which country has Jakarta as its capital?
23 What are the Southern Lights also called?
24 If June 1 is a Sunday what day is July 1?
25 Which US state has the largest share of Yellowstone National Park?
26 What is craved by phagomanicas?
27 Which Spanish region is so named because of its many castles?
28 Which comic-strip photographer used the alias Peter Parker?
29 Which submarine was the focus of a rescue mission in 2000?
30 Which country hosted Expo '88 and celebrated its bicentenary?

Answers | **World Tour** *(see Quiz 219)*

1 Austria. 2 Sirocco. 3 Vancouver. 4 USA. 5 Indian. 6 Texas. 7 Ecuador. 8 Las Malvinas. 9 Harvard. 10 States with and without slavery. 11 China (16). 12 Florida. 13 Northern Territory. 14 The Zambesi. 15 Tanganyika, Zanzibar. 16 St Lawrence. 17 Fort Knox. 18 Vietnam. 19 Moscow. 20 Rio Grande. 21 New York. 22 Bechuanaland. 23 Venezuela. 24 Ellis Island. 25 K2. 26 Istanbul. 27 Texas. 28 Argentina. 29 Canaries. 30 McKinley.

1 How old was Tony Blair when he became Prime Minister?
2 Who first won the US Amateur Championship in 1994?
3 The invasion of which country sparked off the Gulf War?
4 Who was third in the 1997 Tory leadership election?
5 Which 25-year-old recording was 1990's best-selling single?
6 What is Bill Clinton's middle name?
7 Anthea Turner became the first female presenter of which live weekly event?
8 Who shared the 1993 Nobel Peace Prize with Nelson Mandela?
9 Paul Stewart scored an FA Cup Final goal for which team?
10 On TV, who were the Long Johns?
11 Which English fast bowler took the first wicket in the 1997 Ashes?
12 Jonathan Aitken withdrew from his court case against which paper?
13 Which royal financial adviser used toes for more than counting on?
14 In the 90s, who was Education Secretary, Home Secretary and Chancellor?
15 Which city hosted the 1992 Olympic Games?
16 Who succeeded Robert Runcie as Archbishop of Canterbury?
17 Andy Thomson became world indoor champion at what?
18 Which journalist helped write "Diana: Her True Story"?
19 Who made his last trip on the yacht Lady Ghislaine?
20 Who was the first man to win two Oscars in the 90s?
21 What does the S stand for in BSE?
22 Which sport's world series was cancelled due to the players' strike in 1994?
23 Who was No. 1 when Michael Jackson was No. 2 for five weeks with "Heal the World"?
24 Who stood against Margaret Thatcher for Tory leadership in 1990?
25 Whom did 22-year-old model Rachel Hunter marry in 1990?
26 According to Queen Elizabeth what was 1992?
27 How many teams were in the Premier League's first season?
28 What tragic British first was the death of Stephen Cameron in 1996?
29 Who was US President at the time of the Gulf War?
30 In 1990 which England soccer player was jailed for drink driving?

Answers | Children's TV *(see Quiz 216)*

1 The Flowertots. 2 The Teletubbies. 3 Andi Peters, Emma Forbes. 4 Leonardo, Michaelangelo, Raphael, Donatello. 5 The Roly Mo Show. 6 Mrs Goggins. 7 Aardvark. 8 California. 9 Fireball XL5. 10 Suzanne Ross. 11 Billy Connolly. 12 Trumpton. 13 Captain Pugwash. 14 The Mysterons. 15 Maid Marian and her Merry Men. 16 Dinosaur. 17 12. 18 Australia. 19 (Atomic) Betty. 20 Mouse. 21 Sticky back plastic. 22 Crackerjack pencil. 23 Geoffrey Hayes. 24 Around the World in Eighty Days. 25 Dog. 26 Friday. 27 The Chives. 28 The Simpsons. 29 Fred Dinenage. 30 Clementine.

1 Which country has the internet suffix .at?
2 Which wind blows from the Sahara to southern Italy?
3 Which Canadian island has Victoria as its capital?
4 Which country has the time zones Eastern, Central, Mountain and Pacific?
5 In which ocean are the Maldives?
6 Which US state is known as the Lone Star State?
7 In which country is Cotopaxi, the world's highest volcano?
8 How do the Argentinians refer to the Falkland Islands?
9 What is the USA's oldest educational institution called?
10 What did the Mason Dixon Line divide in the USA?
11 Which country has most neighbouring countries?
12 The Keys are islands off which US state?
13 Darwin is the capital of which Australian state?
14 Which river flows over the Victoria Falls?
15 Which two territories joined together to form Tanzania?
16 On which river are Quebec and Montreal?
17 Where are the US gold reserves?
18 In which country is the Mekong Delta?
19 Which capital is on the Moskva river?
20 Which river divides the USA and Mexico?
21 Where is Madison Square Garden?
22 How was Botswana known immediately prior to independence?
23 In which country is the world's highest waterfall?
24 Which US island was a registration point for immigrants until 1954?
25 Which of the world's highest mountains between India and China is not in the Himalayas?
26 How is Byzantium and Constantinople now known?
27 What is the second largest state of the US?
28 Tierra del Fuego is off which country?
29 Fuerteventura is in which island group?
30 Which is the highest mountain in North America?

Answers | **Pot Luck 96** *(see Quiz 217)*

1 Pearl Harbor. 2 £1 note. 3 U2. 4 An aeroplane. 5 Willow. 6 The Oval. 7 Galliano. 8 Midge Ure. 9 Mediterranean. 10 The Gulf of Mexico. 11 Hastings. 12 Glass. 13 P. G. Wodehouse. 14 Cliff Richard. 15 Parakeet. 16 Angola. 17 David Lloyd George. 18 Lisa Kudrow. 19 Holland. 20 French. 21 Keanu Reeves. 22 Indonesia. 23 Aurora Australis. 24 Tuesday. 25 Wyoming. 26 Food. 27 Castile. 28 Spiderman. 29 Kursk. 30 Australia.

1 Which leader of Bronski Beat also had solo hits?
2 Which British wild animal is quicker going uphill than downhill?
3 In which forest does the River Danube rise?
4 Who was the first person to score 100 runs and take 10 wickets in the same Test Match?
5 Who played Princess Margaret in "The Queen's Sister"?
6 How many legs has a crane fly?
7 Which part of your body could suffer from astigmatism?
8 Which City is the capital of the US state of Nevada?
9 What nationality is Leonard Cohen?
10 Which star has Marilyn Monroe's signature tattooed on her bottom?
11 What was the first thing to leave the Ark when the rain stopped?
12 "Funky Dory" was the debut album by which former S Clubber?
13 What is the opposite of aestivation?
14 Which tonic water flavour is taken from the cinchona tree?
15 What is the official language of Chile?
16 Who made the famous 70s album "Harvest"?
17 What is the longest river in France?
18 Who beat Kevin Curren in the '85 Wimbledon men's singles final?
19 Which train was known by the initials VSOE?
20 What comprises the diet of a pangolin?
21 Which country invented the duffel coat and bag?
22 Which British artist was greatly promoted by Delacroix in France?
23 Who beat President Marcos in the 1986 Philippines election?
24 What name are the Funchal Islands usually called?
25 Who wrote the book "Porterhouse Blue"?
26 What is the modern name for Hangman's Corner in London?
27 What are morels and chanterelles?
28 Was England's 2005 Test series win in South Africa the first for 20, 30 or 40 years?
29 Where was the first wartime meeting between Churchill, Roosevelt and Stalin held?
30 In a title of a Bizet opera what were the people fishing for?

Answers | Pot Luck 98 *(see Quiz 222)*

1 Colin Farrell. 2 Catalonia. 3 Townsend Thoresen. 4 Isle of Wight. 5 Holland. 6 Queen Nefertiti. 7 12. 8 Darts. 9 "Food Glorious Food". 10 M25. 11 Face transplant. 12 Madrid. 13 Clowder. 14 India. 15 Solicitor. 16 I. 17 Ralph. 18 Smell. 19 Rainbow Warrior. 20 Commit suicide. 21 Jeremy Beadle. 22 Paul McCartney. 23 Great Maple. 24 Venice. 25 Daniel and Natasha Bedingfield. 26 Black, green, red. 27 Nick Barmby. 28 Liza Goddard. 29 Feargal Sharkey. 30 Frederick Forsyth.

1 What was the first Lassie film called?

2 What was the most successful "creature" film of the 1970s ?

3 What was Clint Eastwood's co-star in "Every Which Way But Loose"?

4 What breed of dog was Beethoven?

5 Which country is the setting for "Born Free"?

6 Which animal adopts the piglet in "Babe"?

7 How many movie versions of "Black Beauty" had been made up to 1997?

8 In which decade was the first Lassie film made?

9 White Fang is a cross between which two animals?

10 What is Dorothy's dog called in "The Wizard of Oz"?

11 What was the sequel to "The Incredible Journey" called?

12 Which animals starred with Sigourney Weaver in a biopic of Dian Fossey?

13 Which film about rats had a theme song with lyrics by Don Black?

14 Which horse eventually had co-star billing with Gene Autry?

15 Which film was described as "Eight legs. Two fangs. And an attitude"?

16 What was the Lone Ranger's horse called?

17 What sort of creature is Flicka in "My Friend Flicka"?

18 Which two types of animal feature in "Oliver and Company"?

19 Which nation's army dog was Rin Tin Tin?

20 What is the principal lioness called in "Born Free"?

21 In which decade was one of the first successful animal films "Rescued by Rover" released?

22 Which studio made the seven official Lassie films?

23 Which fictional whale did Keiko play in a 1993 movie?

24 Who wrote the book on which "Babe" was based?

25 Which film was directed by Hitchcock from a Daphne Du Maurier novel, other than "Rebecca"?

26 What was the sequel to "Beethoven" called?

27 What breed of dog features in "K-9"?

28 Which 1971 film was the predecessor of "Ben" a year later?

29 Which creatures contributed to the most successful film of 1993?

30 What animal is the star of Disney's 1964 classic "The Three Lives of Thomasina"?

Answers	Hobbies & Leisure *(see Quiz 223)*

1 Go. 2 Pit. 3 Miss Scarlet. 4 Wax. 5 Bell ringing. 6 Blenheim. 7 January. 8 Bradford. 9 RSPB. 10 A rope. 11 Paraffin wax. 12 Dress with a tartan sash. 13 Cornwall. 14 Lace. 15 Hearts, clubs, diamonds, spades. 16 15. 17 Dagger, revolver. 18 Knotting, plaiting. 19 Sega. 20 Parc Asterix. 21 Gateshead. 22 Oxford. 23 Southport. 24 Victoria and Albert Museum. 25 York Minster. 26 Brent Cross. 27 Stonehenge. 28 Windsor. 29 Knowsley. 30 Princes Street.

1 Who played the title role in Oliver Stone's "Alexander"?
2 Barcelona is the capital of which region in Spain?
3 Who owned the capsized ferry *Herald of Free Enterprise*?
4 Which English county is completely surrounded by water?
5 The sport of speed skating originates from which country ?
6 Who was the wife of the Egyptian king, Ahkenaton?
7 How many yards is the penalty spot from a soccer goal line?
8 Which world-ranking sport takes place at the Circus Tavern, Purfleet?
9 Which musical song starts, "Is it worth the waiting for"?
10 Where did Chris Rea get held up, which led to the hit "Road to Hell"?
11 Isabelle Dinoire became the first to have what type of transplant?
12 What is the highest capital city in Europe?
13 Which term describes cats collecting together?
14 Which country invented snooker?
15 What was Bob Mortimer's job before joining up with Vic Reeves?
16 What is the chemical symbol for Iodine?
17 What is the name of Chief Wiggum's son in "The Simpsons"?
18 Which is the most sensitive of the human senses?
19 Which Greenpeace ship was sunk by the French in New Zealand?
20 What did Mary Alice Youngs do at the start of "Desperate Housewives"?
21 Who was the first presenter of "You've Been Framed"?
22 Who was the last of the Beatles to get married for a second time?
23 Which tree is the American version of the British Sycamore?
24 Which city is affectionately called the "Mistress of the Adriatic"?
25 Who were the first brother and sister to have solo No. 1 albums?
26 What three colours are on a roulette wheel?
27 Which English player Nick went from Everton to Liverpool in 2000?
28 Which actress has been married to Alvin Stardust and Colin Baker?
29 Who had a 80s No. 1 with "A Good Heart"?
30 Who wrote the novel "The Devil's Alternative"?

Answers	Pot Luck 97 *(see Quiz 220)*

1 Jimmy Somerville. 2 Hare. 3 Black Forest. 4 Ian Botham. 5 Lucy Cohu. 6 8. 7 Eyes. 8 Carson City. 9 Canadian. 10 Madonna. 11 A raven. 12 Rachel Stevens. 13 Hibernation. 14 Quinine. 15 Spanish. 16 Neil Young. 17 The Loire. 18 Boris Becker. 19 Venice Simplon Orient Express. 20 Ants or termites. 21 Belgium. 22 John Constable. 23 Corazon Aquino. 24 Madeira. 25 Tom Sharpe. 26 Marble Arch. 27 Mushrooms. 28 40 years. 29 Tehran. 30 Pearls.

1 What is the national game of Japan?
2 Which card game is based on dealing on the stock market?
3 Who is the only known unmarried person in Cluedo?
4 What is painted on to fabric in batik?
5 Carillon is a popular branch of what?
6 At which stately home would you see trees laid out in the form of troops at a famous battle?
7 In which month would you go to a Burns Night celebration?
8 Where is the National Museum of Geography?
9 The YOC is the junior branch of which society?
10 In bungee-jumping, what is a bungee?
11 Which type of wax is most commonly used in candle-making?
12 What is the traditional women's outfit in Scottish country dancing?
13 In which county would you visit St Michael's Mount?
14 What would you be making if you were following the bobbin or pillow method?
15 What order are trumps normally played at a whist drive?
16 How many counters does each player have at the start of a game of backgammon?
17 Which two Cluedo weapons are traditional weapons?
18 What are the two main activities in macrame?
19 Which manufacturer produces Sonic the Hedgehog computer games?
20 Which French theme park is named after a cartoon character?
21 Metroland is near which town?
22 In which city would you be if you went to the Ashmolean Museum?
23 In which resort is the golfing area of Birkdale?
24 How is the former Museum of Ornamental Art in London now known?
25 Which cathedral has ceiling decorations designed by "Blue Peter" viewers?
26 Which shopping centre in north-west London is near the foot of the MI?
27 Which world heritage site is near Amesbury in southern England?
28 Which is England's largest castle?
29 Which Safari Park is near Liverpool?
30 What is Edinburgh's main shopping street?

Answers	**Movies: Animal Stars** *(see Quiz 221)*

1 Lassie Come Home. 2 Jaws. 3 Orang-utan. 4 St Bernard. 5 Kenya. 6 Sheepdog. 7 Three. 8 1940s. 9 Dog and wolf. 10 Toto. 11 Homeward Bound. 12 Gorillas. 13 Ben. 14 Champion. 15 Arachnophobia. 16 Silver. 17 Horse. 18 Cats and dogs. 19 German. 20 Elsa. 21 1900s. 22 MGM. 23 Willy. 24 Dick King-Smith. 25 The Birds. 26 Beethoven's 2nd. 27 Alsatian. 28 Willard. 29 Dinosaurs (Jurassic Park). 30 A tabby cat.

1 Where was a concrete block Holocaust Memorial opened in 2005?
2 Which officer gives the results of a by-election?
3 Which gas was discovered in 1774 by Joseph Priestley?
4 What is the official language of Chad?
5 Which fruit has a variety called Ellison's Orange?
6 Which Disney film is based on a book by Dodie Smith?
7 Which country borders the Dead Sea together with Israel?
8 Bogota is the capital of which country?
9 Which sister group comprised Patty, Maxine and Laverne?
10 What event took place at Sears Crossing, Bedfordshire in August '63?
11 In which film did Michael Caine say, "Not a lot of people know that"?
12 Which former Fl champion has played golf in the Australian Open?
13 What was the UK's first all-colour newspaper?
14 Which England football manager was given the sack in 1974?
15 In which country was the Battle of Arnhem?
16 Whose best friend in the movies was a boy called Elliot?
17 Kimberley, South Africa is famous for producing which gem?
18 Which everyday steel was invented by Harry Brearley in 1913?
19 Which character did Bruce Willis play in "Moonlighting"?
20 What word can go before "pet", "ton" and "mine"?
21 At which major English tourist attraction are the Aubrey Holes?
22 Billy, Margaret and Brenda Chenowith are characters in which drama series?
23 Who invented 0 and 100 as freezing and boiling points of water?
24 Harvard University is in which US state?
25 In the food world what is Sudan 1?
26 Who wrote the novel "Wild Swans"?
27 Which swimmer hit gold for Britain in the 1980 Olympics?
28 Which European country owns the island of Elba?
29 Which artist painted his garden's water lilies and bridges?
30 What is an appaloosa?

Answers | **Pot Luck 100** *(see Quiz 226)*

1 Parking meter. 2 France. 3 Belize (formerly British Honduras). 4 Eagles. 5 Rudyard Kipling. 6 Bow Street. 7 Jokers. 8 Spice Girls. 9 The Menai. 10 Carbon monoxide. 11 Roman. 12 Saxophone. 13 River Lagan. 14 George Bush. 15 Czechoslovakia. 16 Spycatcher. 17 Commonwealth. 18 Portsmouth. 19 Translation (the Bible). 20 Max Bygraves. 21 Smallville. 22 Green. 23 A peacock. 24 Tungsten. 25 Starship Enterprise. 26 Dover Marine. 27 Marc Quinn. 28 People's car. 29 The nose. 30 Finnish.

1 How would you orally address an Archbishop?
2 Which seaside resort has Squires Gate airport?
3 How many rows of letter keys feature on a traditional keyboard?
4 Is type size measured in fonts or points?
5 What is the emergency phone number in the US?
6 In Braille which letter consists of a single dot?
7 What is the minimum number of computers that can be networked?
8 What is a TAM?
9 In telecommunications what is polling?
10 Which number can be used as an alternative to 999?
11 Which main product is sold on line by Jeff Bezos's company, founded 1994?
12 Which feared computer problem didn't happen at the end of 1999?
13 What do you dial if you do not want the person you are calling to know your phone number?
14 What would an Italian call a motorway?
15 What colour are telephone boxes in France?
16 What is the maximum weight you can send letters at the basic rate?
17 Which three cities are termini for the Eurostar service?
18 Which worldwide virus was detected in Hong Kong 1st May 2000?
19 What colour is a 1p postage stamp?
20 What colour is an airmail sticker?
21 Which two cities are the termini for the Anglia rail region?
22 Which underground line goes to Heathrow Terminals?
23 In which US city is O'Hare airport?
24 Where is bounced e-mail sent to?
25 What is the UK's oldest Sunday newspaper?
26 The Apple Mac logo has a piece missing from which side?
27 Which newspaper cartoon strip is translated into Latin with characters Snupius and Carolius Niger?
28 In New York easyEverything became the world's biggest what?
29 What colour is the logo for Virgin trains?
30 Which tennis star gave her name to a major 2001 computer virus?

Answers | TV Times 3 (see Quiz 227)

1 Christopher Eccleston. 2 Amy. 3 Gregory. 4 Eleanor, Robert. 5 "Have I Got News for You". 6 Kenny Everett. 7 "Red Dwarf". 8 Garraway. 9 Kate. 10 Holland Park. 11 Anthony Jay. 12 "ER". 13 John Torode. 14 Alaska. 15 MP. 16 Alan B'Stard. 17 Cissie and Ada. 18 Ork. 19 "Minder". 20 "Happy Days". 21 Haidresser's. 22 Pauline Quirke. 23 Compo and Clegg. 24 Elizabeth and Emmet. 25 Five. 26 "Solo". 27 Dogs. 28 1940s. 29 Vince and Penny ("Just Good Friends"). 30 Alf Garnett.

1 Which meter was invented in 1935 by C. C. Magee?
2 In which country is the port of St Malo?
3 Which territory was Britain's last in Latin America?
4 What is the USA's rugby union team called?
5 Who was the author of "Gunga Din"?
6 Which London police station, 230 years old, closed in 1992?
7 What was not included in a pack of cards until 1857?
8 Who had No. 1s with "Goodbye" and "Mama"?
9 Which bridge links the mainland to Anglesey?
10 Which fatal gas does burning coke emit?
11 Which civilization invented the arch?
12 Which musical instrument is played by Bart Simpson's sister?
13 Beside which river is Belfast's Waterfront Hall situated?
14 Who beat Michael Dukakis in the US Presidential election in 1988?
15 Where was tennis star Ivan Lendl born?
16 Which book had Peter Wright as a co-author?
17 In 1949, what did Eire leave?
18 In 2005, WBA's last-match win against which side kept them in the Premiership?
19 Miles Coverdale's greatest work was in which field?
20 Who released an autobiography titled "I Wanna Tell You a Story"?
21 Which town in Illinois was Superman's childhood home?
22 What colour are wild budgerigars?
23 Whose feathers according to superstition should not be in a house?
24 The letter W is the chemical symbol for what?
25 Which ship has the ID number NCC 1701?
26 Which Dover railway station closed after the Channel Tunnel rail link opened?
27 Who created the statue Alison Lapper Pregnant?
28 What does Volkswagen actually mean?
29 Where are the sweat glands of a cow?
30 What nationality was the composer Sibelius?

Answers | **Pot Luck 99** *(see Quiz 224)*

1 Berlin. 2 The Returning Officer. 3 Oxygen. 4 French. 5 Apple. 6 101 Dalmatians.
7 Jordan. 8 Colombia. 9 The Andrews Sisters. 10 Great Train Robbery. 11 Educating
Rita. 12 Nigel Mansell. 13 The Guardian. 14 Sir Alf Ramsey. 15 Netherlands. 16 E.T.
17 Diamonds. 18 Stainless. 19 David Addison. 20 "Car". 21 Stonehenge. 22 Six
Feet Under. 23 Celsius. 24 Massachusetts. 25 Toxic food dye. 26 Jung Chang. 27
Duncan Goodhew. 28 Italy. 29 Monet. 30 Horse.

1 Which future Dr Who starred in "Our Friends in the North"?
2 Who is Steve and Tracy's daughter in "Coronation Street"?
3 In "House", with Hugh Laurie, what is the doctor's first name?
4 What are the first names of the Doctors Bramwell in the TV series?
5 Which show featured Merton v. Hislop with Deayton as referee?
6 Whose characters included Marcel Wave and Sid Snot?
7 In which sci-fi series did the red-suited Kochanski appear?
8 Which Kate presented "GMTV"?
9 What was the name of Nick's first wife in "Heartbeat"?
10 In which area of London was the "Ab Fab" Monsoon household?
11 Who co-wrote "Yes Minister" with Jonathan Lynn?
12 Which series featured the Carol Hathaway/Doug Ross saga?
13 Who was on a desert island as a "Girl Friday" in the mid-90s?
14 In which American state is "Northern Exposure" set?
15 What was the Job in "No Job for a Lady"?
16 Who was Conservative MP for Haltemprice?
17 What were Les Dawson and Roy Barraclough's old gossips called?
18 Which planet was Mork from?
19 In which series was business conducted at the Winchester?
20 "Laverne and Shirley" was a spin-off from which 70s US series?
21 In what type of establishment was the series "Cutting It" set?
22 Which Bird starred as 22-stone Olive in "The Sculptress"?
23 Who were Blamire's two companions in 1973?
24 Who are Hyacinth Bucket's most frequently seen neighbours?
25 How many children were there in the Partridge family?
26 In which series did Felicity Kendal play Gemma Palmer?
27 Victoria Stilwell is an expert on which animals?
28 In which decade was "Shine On Harvey Moon" set?
29 Whose parents were Les and Rita, and Daphne and Norman?
30 Who was looked after by Mrs Hollingberry when his wife died?

Answers | **Communications** *(see Quiz 225)*

1 Your Grace. 2 Blackpool. 3 Three. 4 Points. 5 911. 6 A. 7 Two. 8 Telephone Answering Machine. 9 The ability to receive information from another fax machine. 10 112. 11 Books (Amazon). 12 Millennium bug. 13 141. 14 Autostrada. 15 Yellow. 16 60g. 17 London, Paris, Brussels. 18 I Love You. 19 Dark red. 20 Blue. 21 London, Norwich. 22 Piccadilly. 23 Chicago. 24 Sender. 25 The Observer. 26 Right. 27 Peanuts. 28 Internet cafe. 29 Red-and-grey. 30 Anna Kournikova.

Quiz 228 Pot Luck 101

Answers – page 473

LEVEL 2

1 What do Manolo Blahnik and Jimmy Choo make?
2 If you perform a rim shot, what instrument are you playing?
3 In the Chinese calendar which year follows the year of the rat?
4 What are you in if you are caught in a Haboob?
5 What was wrestler Big Daddy's real name?
6 What trade did a webster follow?
7 Who wrote the book "The Prodigal Daughter"?
8 Where does the River Seine empty?
9 What is the fourth letter of the Greek alphabet?
10 What day of the week did Solomon Grundy get married?
11 Which bone is the hardest in the human body?
12 Who was the last Chancellor of West Germany prior to reunification?
13 What was the pen name of Eric Blair?
14 In which decade was "Jim'll Fix It" screened for the first time?
15 Who solved the crime in "Death on the Nile"?
16 Who was the first presenter of "Wheel of Fortune" in the UK?
17 Who was John Major's last Party Chairman?
18 Which breed of dog does not have a pink tongue?
19 Who portrayed Jesus in the TV adaptation "Jesus of Nazareth"?
20 Which novel by Louisa May Alcott sold millions of copies?
21 Which city in India has an airport called Dum Dum?
22 What links a group of whales to a group of peas?
23 If a Vietnamese was depositing a dong, where would he be?
24 Which hat originates from Ecuador?
25 What medical procedure was Iceland the first country to legalize?
26 What was crossed on a tightrope by Charles Blondin in 1855?
27 Which country hosted the 2006 Winter Olympics?
28 What colour smoke announces the election of a new Pope?
29 Which birthstone is linked to December?
30 Which Canadian province has Halifax as its capital?

Answers	Halloween (see Quiz 230)

1 Samhain. 2 Cher. 3 Bobbing for apples. 4 Pope Boniface IV. 5 "Gros melons".
6 Hallowmas. 7 Fruits. 8 Jack O'Lantern. 9 Guy Fawkes Night. 10 Fruitloaf. 11
Transylvannia. 12 All Hallow's Eve. 13 Jamie Lee Curtis. 14 Edgar Allen Poe. 15 Sarah
Michelle Gellar. 16 Bram Stoker. 17 The Day of the Dead. 18 All Souls' Day. 19 The
Flying Broomstick. 20 Zombies. 21 Dr Frankenstein. 22 Macbeth. 23 Salem. 24
Pomona's Day. 25 Poltergeist. 26 Marilyn. 27 Gretel. 28 Trick or Treating. 29 Black
cats. 30 Pecan nuts.

1 Which country won League's World Cup from 1975 to 1995?
2 Which Scot was British Lions captain for the '93 New Zealand tour?
3 How old was Will Carling when he first captained England?
4 Who was top try scorer on the Lions 2005 tour of New Zealand?
5 How many countries had won the expanded Six Nations before Wales?
6 On his return to Union which Jonathan said, "It's a challenge I don't particularly need"?
7 Who did not play in 2005 after being named Great Britain league captain?
8 Where was Jeremy Guscott born?
9 Alphabetically, which team was last in the 2003 rugby union World Cup?
10 Which stadium hosted the League's 1995 World Cup Final?
11 The Ranfurly Shield is contested in which country?
12 Over half of the 1997 Lions squad came from which country?
13 In which decade was the John Player/Pilkington Cup begun?
14 Which English club did Franco Botica join when he left Wigan?
15 Which Michael has scored most points for Australia?
16 Which team ended Wigan's Challenge Cup record run in the 90s?
17 Which club were in the Heineken Cup finals of 2003, 2004 and 2005?
18 Which was the first team in the 90s other than Bath to win the Pilkington Cup?
19 Which two countries contest the Bledisloe Cup?
20 In the 1995 World Cup who were on the wrong end of an 89-0 score to Scotland?
21 What position did Sir Clive Woodward play at rugby?
22 In which decade was Fran Cotton born?
23 Which country did Grant Fox play for?
24 Gareth Thomas and which player captained Wales to 2005 Six Nations glory?
25 What was Martin Offiah's first League side?
26 Which player – a Frenchman – became the first to win 100 caps?
27 Which Belfast-born solicitor went on five British Lions tours?
28 Which Nick captained Australia from 1984 to 1992?
29 How many teams took part in the 2003 Rugby Union World Cup?
30 Where do St Helens play?

Answers	The Last Round *(see Quiz 231)*

1 David Foale. **2** Catherine Howard. **3** Three. **4** Cricket. **5** Tavistock Square. **6** Rachel Green. **7** Red. **8** 4929. **9** Thailand (2005). **10** Cornwall. **11** Modelling. **12** Annette Bening. **13** Michael Parkinson. **14** 60s (aged 68). **15** "Bad Girls". **16** The Home Service. **17** The Fugees. **18** Argentina. **19** Sigourney Weaver. **20** Omelette. **21** Garry Trudeau. **22** Chicken pox. **23** Sally Gunnell. **24** Nicole Kidman. **25** Arabic. **26** David Puttnam. **27** 672. **28** John Grisham. **29** Governor of California. **30** Grapefruit.

1 Which Celtic festival was the pre-Christian forerunner of Halloween?
2 Susan Sarandon, Michelle Pfeiffer and which other female star were "The Witches of Eastwick"?
3 Which traditional Halloween pastime is thought to derive from the symbol of the Pomona, the Roman goddess of fruit and gardens?
4 Which seventh century Pope designated November 1 All Saints' Day?
5 How did French explorer Jacques Cartier describe pumpkins in 1584?
6 How is All Saints' Eve, All Saints' Day and All Souls' Day collectively known?
7 Are pumpkins fruits or vegetables?
8 What Halloween prop comes from an Irish myth about "Stingy Jack"?
9 What autumn celebration in ancient England came in when worshipping saints ended in the Puritan Church?
10 What is the traditional Irish Halloween dish of barnbrack?
11 Where is Count Dracula's castle located?
12 The name Halloween is of Scottish origin, but what is it short for?
13 Who played Laurie Strode in John Carpenter's horror movie "Halloween"?
14 Who wrote the short story entitled "The Black Cat" in 1843?
15 Who played the eponymous role in "Buffy the Vampire Slayer"?
16 Who wrote the novel "Dracula"?
17 What 2 November Mexican festival has picnics held on dead relatives' graves
18 On which day do Catholics believe that the living may intercede on behalf of the dead through prayer?
19 According to folklore what is the preferred method of transport for witches?
20 According to voodoo belief, by what name are the living dead known?
21 Who secretly created an eight-foot monster out of separate body parts collected from a charnel house?
22 "Eye of newt, toe of frog" is a witch's charm in which Shakespeare play?
23 "The Crucible" by Arthur Miller is about which town's witchhunt?
24 The Romans merged which of their autumn festival with the Celtic Samhain?
25 In which horror movie are the Freeling family terrorised by ghosts?
26 Who was the only "normal-looking one" in the Munster Family?
27 Who, with Hansel, was lured into the wicked witch's gingerbread house?
28 Which modern Halloween custom comes from the poor begging for "Soul Cakes" on all All Souls' Day?
29 In the Middle Ages, what creatures were renowned as witches' familiars?
30 The pecan nut is a major food source for which indigenous population?

| **Answers** | **Rugby** *(see Quiz 229)* |

1 Australia. 2 Gavin Hastings. 3 22. 4 Shane Williams. 5 Two (England and France). 6 Davies. 7 Paul Sculthorpe (injured). 8 Bath. 9 Wales. 10 Wembley. 11 New Zealand. 12 England. 13 1970s. 14 Castleford. 15 Lynagh. 16 Salford Reds. 17 Toulouse. 18 Harlequins. 19 Australia, New Zealand. 20 Ivory Coast. 21 Centre. 22 1940s. 23 New Zealand. 24 Michael Owen. 25 Widnes. 26 Phillippe Sella. 27 Mike Gibson. 28 Fan-Jones. 29 Twenty. 30 Knowsley Road.

1 Who was the first British astronaut on the space station Mir?
2 Who was the second wife Henry VIII beheaded?
3 How many Popes were there in 1978?
4 What game is being played on the back of a £10 note?
5 In which London square was a bus destroyed on 7/7/05?
6 What is Jennifer Aniston's character's full name in "Friends"?
7 What colour are the seats in the House of Lords?
8 What numbers do Barclaycards begin with?
9 In which country did Andrew Murray reach his first ATP Tour final?
10 In which county did Britain's first lifeguard training centre open?
11 In which career is Jodie Kidd famous?
12 Who was the first Mrs Warren Beatty?
13 Who presented "Desert Island Discs" immediately before Sue Lawley?
14 Was comedian Dave Allen in his 50s, 60s or 70s when he died in 2005?
15 Which drama series was set in KMP Larkhill?
16 In the early 60s what was Radio 4 known as?
17 Who were Lauryn Hill, Wyclef Jean and Pras Michel?
18 Man. Utd defender Gabriel Heinze plays for which country?
19 Who played Ripley in the "Alien" movies?
20 A frittata is an Italian version of what?
21 Which cartoonist draws the "Doonesbury" strip?
22 Which childhood disease has the same virus as shingles?
23 Who was England ladies athletics team captain at the '96 Olympics?
24 Country singer Keith Urban was linked with which actress in 2005?
25 What is the official language of Morocco?
26 Who was the British producer of "The Killing Fields"?
27 How many hours were there in February 1997?
28 Who wrote "The Partner"?
29 What was Ronald Reagan's most senior political role before he became president?
30 If you buy pamplemousses in France what do you buy?

Answers	**Pot Luck 101** *(see Quiz 228)*

1 Shoes. 2 Drums. 3 Ox. 4 A sandstorm. 5 Shirley Crabtree. 6 Weaving. 7 Jeffrey Archer. 8 The English Channel. 9 Delta. 10 Wednesday. 11 The jawbone. 12 Helmut Kohl. 13 George Orwell. 14 1970s. 15 Hercule Poirot. 16 Nicky Campbell. 17 Brian Mawhinney. 18 Chow. 19 Robert Powell. 20 Little Women. 21 Calcutta. 22 They both collect in pods. 23 A Bank. 24 Panama. 25 Abortion. 26 Niagara Falls. 27 Italy. 28 White. 29 Turquoise. 30 Nova Scotia.

The Hard Questions

If you thought that this section of this book would prove to be little or no problem, or that the majority of the questions could be answered and a scant few would test you then you are sorely mistaken. These questions are the *hardest* questions *ever*! So difficult are they that any attempt to answer them all in one sitting will addle your mind and mess with your senses. You'll end up leaving the pub via the window while ordering a pint from the horse brasses on the wall. Don't do it! For a kick off there are 3,000 of them, so at 20 seconds a question it will take you over 16 hours and that's just the time it takes to read them. What you should do instead is set them for others – addle your friends' minds.

Note the dangerous nature of these questions though. These are you secret weapons use them accordingly unless, of course, someone or some team is getting your back up. In which case you should hit them hard and only let up when you have them cowering under the bench whimpering "Uncle".

These questions work best against league teams, they are genuinely tough and should be used against those people who take their pub quizzes seriously. NEVER use these questions against your inlaws.

1 Which school had a No 1 with "There's No One Quite Like Grandma"?

2 Which American answer to Band Aid sang "We are the World"?

3 Which musical did Lee Marvin's sole hit, "Wandrin' Star", come from?

4 According to 1950s star Kitty Kalen what do "Little Things Mean"?

5 Which pop duo recorded "In the Year 2525"?

6 Which member of the cast of "Dad's Army" sang "Grandad"?

7 Who recorded "Let It Be" in 1987 for a disaster fund?

8 Where had Charlene never been to in 1982?

9 Who said "Move Closer" in 1985?

10 What is Marie Osmond's only solo hit?

11 Which Beatles song did the Overlanders take to No 1?

12 With the theme song for which sporting event did Kiri Te Kanawa have her only chart hit in 1991?

13 Which music accompanied Des Lynam's top 50 hit?

14 Who had a No 1 hit in 1999 with "Everybody's Free (to Wear Sunscreen)"?

15 What colour were the spots on Mr Blobby?

16 Who were the first two one-hit wonders to reach the top with the same song?

17 Two members of which group sang on both of them?

18 Which Twins sang "When" in 1958?

19 Whom did Ricky Valance tell he loved her in 1960?

20 Which airways featured on Typically Tropical's only No 1?

21 What is John Denver's only solo UK single hit?

22 Who joined New Order on England New Order's "World in Motion"?

23 Which travel terminal provided a hit for Cats UK?

24 With which TV theme did Geoffrey Burgon have his only hit in 1981?

25 What was the Johnny Mann Singers' only hit?

26 Who got to No 3 in 1968 with "Judy in Disguise (With Glasses)"?

27 What did the Pipkins say "Gimme" in 1970?

28 Which qualification sang "I won't let you down" in 1982?

29 Which TV character gave Ken Barrie his only chart hit?

30 How many performers made up Las Ketchup who served up "The Ketchup Song"?

Answers	**Performance Arts** *(see Quiz 3)*

1 Vocal with no instrumental accompaniment. **2** The man. **3** Christopher Bruce. **4** Break dancing. **5** Piccolo. **6** Berlin. **7** Diaghilev. **8** Trombones and tubas. **9** Comedy. **10** Philip Pullman. **11** Mark Morris. **12** Saturday Night Fever. **13** Keyboard. **14** Cakes given as competition prizes. **15** Festival Ballet. **16** Boston, Charleston. **17** Three. **18** Paul Jones. **19** Samba. **20** Egypt. **21** Kazoo. **22** Lyre. **23** Festivities associated with the building of a new barn. **24** World War II. **25** Balanchine. **26** Ukulele. **27** Bullfighter's cloak. **28** Cannes. **29** Not touching partner. **30** Harriet Walter.

Quiz 2 | Pot-Luck 1 | Answers – page 478 | LEVEL 3

1 Who shot the Archduke Franz Ferdinand?
2 In fiction, what were Milly Molly Mandy's proper names?
3 Which monarchs sat on the Peacock Throne?
4 Of what is a lux a unit?
5 In the early 19th century what did George Shillibeer bring to London?
6 Who first claimed that the world was not flat but a sphere?
7 Who was the first woman to fly the Atlantic single-handed?
8 Which animals communicate by touch, smell and dance?
9 Around which French town is the champagne industry centred?
10 A track by which female artist was used as the theme to ITV's "Celebrity Love Island"?
11 At what speed in mph does a wind become a hurricane?
12 Who officially opened the 1936 Olympiad?
13 What was the name of the first talking cartoon?
14 Which competition was organized by Mecca Ltd to coincide with the 1951 Festival of Britain?
15 Who invented the coordinate system to compare relationships on a graph?
16 What colour is the ribbon of the Victoria Cross?
17 Who or what lived in Honalee?
18 Which profession would use the terms occlusion, isohyet and adiabatic?
19 What name is used to describe a baby salmon?
20 In which building did Charles and Camilla hold their civil wedding ceremony?
21 Who is the husband of Meera Syal?
22 Who anonymously entered a contest in Monaco to find his lookalike and came third?
23 Where in Spain was Pablo Picasso born?
24 Who was Edward VI's mother?
25 Which sea has no coast?
26 Who was the first Briton to organize a continental holiday tour?
27 What was the first US No 1 for Destiny's Child?
28 Who discovered oxygen in 1774?
29 Which bird can fly the fastest?
30 Which is the largest human organ?

Answers | Pot-Luck 2 (see Quiz 4)

1 Dublin. 2 Prostitute. 3 Pope John Paul II. 4 The Tories. 5 The Scottish red deer. 6 Frank Richards. 7 Number 13. 8 Yellow. 9 Scotland's largest cave. 10 The sixpence. 11 Chewing gum. 12 St Cecilia. 13 Nepal. 14 Sunny Afternoon. 15 Solomon. 16 Tom Cruise. 17 The White Tower. 18 Tetley. 19 The Huguenots. 20 The Anglican Church. 21 Greenland. 22 Burley. 23 Rosa Mota. 24 Jesus to a Child. 25 Baronet. 26 Aluminium. 27 Michael Caine. 28 A palindrome. 29 John Adams. 30 Lucy Davis.

1 How is a cappella music performed?
2 Which dancer performs a variation in a pas de deux?
3 Who stepped down as Artistic Director of the Rambert Dance Company in 2002?
4 Which dancing from the 1980s has dancers performing acrobatic feats?
5 Which instrument is also called the octave flute?
6 At which film festival is the Golden Bear awarded for best film?
7 Which impresario founded the Ballets Russes?
8 In a standard modern symphony orchestra which two brass instruments would be on the back row?
9 In 2005 Kim Cattrall made her West End debut at which theatre?
10 In 2003 the National Theatre premièred a stage version of a trilogy of books by which author?
11 Which US choreographer reworked "The Nutcracker" as "The Hard Nut"?
12 Which 1970s film is seen as greatly popularizing disco dancing?
13 What type of instrument is a celestea?
14 Why is a cakewalk so called?
15 What did the English National Ballet used to be called?
16 Which two dances take their names from US towns?
17 What is the minimum number of voices for performing a glee?
18 Which singer/radio DJ's name is also the name of a 19th-century dance?
19 Which dance is the bossa nova a type of?
20 Where are castanets thought to originate?
21 What is a mirliton another name for?
22 Which instrument are violins and violas descended from?
23 Why were barn-dances so called?
24 During which period did the jitterbug gain popularity?
25 Who founded the New York City Ballet?
26 Which instrument's name is the Hawaiian word for jumping flea?
27 In the paso doble what is the female dancer supposed to be?
28 At which film festival is the Palme d'Or awarded for best film?
29 What sort of dancing trend did the twist set?
30 Who won the 2005 Evening Standard Best Actress award for her performance in "Mary Stuart"?

Answers	Pop: One-Hit Wonders *(see Quiz 1)*

1 St Winifred's. 2 USA for Africa. 3 Paint Your Wagon. 4 A lot. 5 Zager and Evans. 6 Clive Dunn. 7 Ferry Aid. 8 Me. 9 Phyllis Nelson. 10 Paper Roses. 11 Michelle. 12 Rugby World Cup. 13 Fauré's Pavane. 14 Baz Luhrmanne. 15 Yellow. 16 Band Aid, Band Aid II, Do They Know It's Christmas. 17 Bananarama. 18 Kalin Twins. 19 Laura. 20 Coconut Airways. 21 Annie's Song. 22 England World Cup Squad. 23 Luton Airport. 24 Brideshead Revisited. 25 Up, Up and Away. 26 John Fred and the Playboy Band. 27 Dat Ding. 28 PhD. 29 Postman Pat. 30 Three.

1 Which city is known in its own language as Baile Atha Cliath?
2 Kitty Fisher was 18th-century London's most highly paid what?
3 Which pope was shot by Mehmet Ali Agca on May 13th, 1981?
4 Which political party takes its name from a band of Irish outlaws?
5 Which is the largest wild animal in the British Isles?
6 Who created Billy Bunter?
7 People who are terdekaphobic are afraid of what?
8 What colour is worn for funerals in Egypt?
9 What is the Great Smoo?
10 Which British coin ceased to be legal tender on June 30th, 1980?
11 What is manufactured from the sapodilla tree?
12 Who is the patron saint of music?
13 Which country is ruled by King Gyanendra?
14 Which song starts, "The taxman's taken all my dough..."?
15 Who was David's son in the Bible?
16 Whose first box office film was called "Risky Business"?
17 Which is the oldest part of the Tower of London?
18 Which company first introduced tea bags in Great Britain in 1952?
19 What were the French Protestants led by Henry of Navarre known as?
20 Which Church's doctrine is set out in the Thirty-Nine Articles?
21 Which country left the EC in 1985?
22 Which George led Ipswich Town into the Premiership in 2000?
23 Which marathon runner won Olympic gold in 1988, making her the first Portuguese woman to do so?
24 Which George Michael No 1 begins "Kindness in your eyes"?
25 What does the abbreviation Bt signify after a name?
26 In the Earth's crust which metal is the most abundant?
27 Which English actor played the disillusioned journalist in "The Quiet American"?
28 What type of word reads the same forwards and backwards?
29 Who was the second president of the United States?
30 Which actress played Dawn Tinsley in "The Office"?

Answers	**Pot-Luck 1** *(see Quiz 2)*

1 Gavrilo Princip. 2 Millicent Margaret Amanda. 3 The shahs of Persia. 4 Illumination. 5 A bus service (using horses). 6 Pythagoras. 7 Amelia Earhart. 8 Bees. 9 Epernay. 10 Jem. 11 73 mph. 12 Adolf Hitler. 13 Steamboat Willie. 14 Miss World. 15 René Descartes. 16 Purple. 17 Puff the Magic Dragon. 18 Meteorology. 19 Parr. 20 Guildhall, Windsor. 21 Sanjeev Bhaskar. 22 Charlie Chaplin. 23 Málaga. 24 Jane Seymour. 25 The Sargasso Sea. 26 Thomas Cook. 27 Bills, Bills, Bills. 28 Joseph Priestley. 29 The homing pigeon. 30 The liver.

1 Nanninga was the first sub to score in a World Cup Final ... for whom?
2 Which team are known as the Cherries?
3 What was strange about the tackle that ended the career of keeper Chic Brodie of Brentford back in 1970?
4 How many countries played in World Cup 2002 in Japan and South Korea?
5 Which club did Glenn Hoddle leave to become England manager?
6 Which country won the first World Cup held in 1930?
7 Which German club did Kevin Keegan play for?
8 Mike Walker and Martin O'Neill walked out on which chairman?
9 Who was the first uncapped player sold for over £1,000,000 in Britain?
10 What name is shared by Scunthorpe, Southend and Rotherham?
11 Fabien Barthez began his career with which French club?
12 Who was England's final substitute in the 2002 quarter-final defeat by Brazil?
13 Which country did Emlyn Hughes play for?
14 Emmanuel Petit joined Arsenal from which soccer club?
15 Which 4th Division team reached the first League Cup Final in 1962?
16 Who played in the first FA Cup Final ever to end 3–3?
17 Which team paid a record £1,000 for Alf Common in 1905?
18 Newcastle play at St James' Park but who plays at St James Park?
19 Who captained the Man Utd team that won the 1968 European Cup?
20 Who scored Scotland's only goal in the 1986 World Cup Finals in Mexico?
21 Where in England do you go to shout "Come on, you greens"?
22 An Italian boss replacing a Dutchman was a first at which English club?
23 Stokoe (Sunderland) and Revie (Leeds) were rival managers in the 1973 FA Cup Final. For which teams were they rivals as Cup Final players?
24 If you are at Turf Moor who is playing at home?
25 Which keeper played three games for Man Utd in the early 1990s and 23 games in 1999–2000?
26 Which club has been managed by Brian Clough and Jimmy Armfield?
27 Which player went from Juventus to Real Madrid for £46.5m in 2001?
28 Which team is known as "The Bairns"?
29 Which non-League team held Man Utd to a 0–0 draw in the third round of the 2005/6 FA Cup?
30 At which Lane did Wimbledon play when they entered the League?

Answers	**Great Buildings** *(see Quiz 7)*

1 Canterbury. 2 Winning an international competition. 3 Marble. 4 Etoile. 5 St Paul's.
6 Eiffel Tower. 7 Ivan the Terrible. 8 San Marco. 9 Cardinal Wolsey. 10 Devonshire.
11 Castle Howard. 12 It has sunk. 13 Castle Howard. 14 Mexico. 15 Versailles. 16 Chicago. 17 Cologne. 18 F. W. Woolworth. 19 Venus de Milo. 20 1894. 21 Extension to the National Gallery. 22 York Minster. 23 Montmartre. 24 Vatican, Rome. 25 Michelangelo. 26 Rangoon, Myanmar (Burma). 27 St Petersburg. 28 Coventry. 29 Amritsar. 30 To cover smoke stains. (It was set on fire by the British in 1814.)

1 Which organ in the body is affected by otitis?
2 Which was the first country, in 1824, to legalize trade unions?
3 Who replaced Christopher Eccleston as Dr Who?
4 Which is the smallest state of Australia?
5 In which castle was Edward II murdered?
6 In which year was North Sea oil discovered?
7 Californian and Stellar's are types of what?
8 What is a group of cats called?
9 Which former James Bond actor became a goodwill ambassador for UNICEF?
10 What is measured by an interferometer?
11 Which famous cliffs in Acapulco are used by daring divers?
12 Who broke Muhammad Ali's jaw in 1973?
13 Who was the voice of Shrek in "Shrek 2"?
14 Which airline's identification code is VS?
15 Which country decided by referendum against joining the European Union in 1994?
16 Who was the only English pope?
17 The kingdom of Navarre was divided between which two countries?
18 Which river does the water in real Irish Guinness come from?
19 In which Gilbert and Sullivan opera is eating a sausage roll a secret sign?
20 On which river is the Kariba Dam?
21 What is studied in the science of somatology?
22 Which football club was the first to use artificial turf?
23 Who succeeded Nelson Mandela as President of South Africa and leader of the ANC?
24 From which district in France do the majority of fine clarets come?
25 Who set up the first printing press in England in 1476?
26 In the film "Carry On Columbus" who played the title role?
27 If the image in the mirror shows the time as five past two, what time is it?
28 In heraldry what is meant by "couchant"?
29 Who was the leader of the first black band to play at Carnegie Hall?
30 Who was the Greek goddess of retribution?

Answers	Pot-Luck 4 (see Quiz 8)

1 252. 2 Strictly Come Dancing. 3 Mid Glamorgan. 4 Russ Abbot. 5. Gone with the Wind. 6 A monkey. 7 Corazón Aquino. 8 Borneo stick insect. 9 William Friese Green. 10 World War I. 11 Oldham, Lancs. 12 The issue of rum. 13 Richard II. 14 Edwin Land. 15 The weather forecast. 16 Bali. 17 Morgiana. 18 One vertebra fewer. 19 Telstar. 20 The monkfish. 21 From head to foot. 22 Nero. 23 West Point. 24 Egypt. 25 Organization of Petroleum Exporting Countries. 26 Mortimer. 27 The Princess Royal. 28 Millennium Bridge. 29 Bleak House. 30 A hoofed mammal.

1 Which is Britain's oldest cathedral?

2 Jørn Utzon designed the Sydney Opera House as a result of what?

3 What is the Taj Mahal made from?

4 In which Parisian square is the Arc de Triomphe?

5 What is the cathedral of the diocese of London?

6 What was the highest building in the world until 1930?

7 Who ordered the building of St Basil's Cathedral in Moscow?

8 Which library in Venice was described as "the richest and most ornate building since antiquity"?

9 Who had Hampton Court Palace built?

10 Which dukes does Chatsworth House in Derbyshire belong to?

11 Which stately home was used in the film "Brideshead Revisited"?

12 Why is the Washington Memorial smaller now than when it was built?

13 Which building did James Martin's cookery series "Castle in the Country" come from?

14 Other than in Egypt, where were pyramids built?

15 Which French château has a Hall of Mirrors?

16 In which US city is the Sears Tower?

17 Where was Europe's largest Gothic cathedral rebuilt after World War II?

18 Which chain store proprietor commissioned the then tallest inhabitable building in the world in 1913?

19 Which famous statue, brought back as war loot by Napoleon, is still housed in the Louvre?

20 When was Blackpool Tower built?

21 Which plan did Prince Charles describe as "a monstrous carbuncle"?

22 The memorial service for former "Countdown" presenter Richard Whiteley took place in which famous building?

23 In which area of Paris is the Basilica of Sacré Coeur?

24 Where is the largest church in the world?

25 Who designed it?

26 Where is the Shwa Dagon Pagoda?

27 In which city is Rastrelli's Winter Palace?

28 Which cathedral, opened in 1962, contains the ruins of the old cathedral?

29 Where in India is the Golden Temple, centre of the Sikh religion?

30 Why is the White House white?

Answers | Sport: Football *(see Quiz 5)*

1 Netherlands (in 1978). 2 Bournemouth. 3 It was against a dog that ran on to the field. 4 32. 5 Chelsea. 6 Uruguay. 7 Hamburg. 8 Robert Chase. 9 Steve Daley (in 1979). 10 United. 11 Toulouse. 12 Teddy Sheringham. 13 England. 14 Monaco. 15 Rochdale. 16 Crystal Palace v Man Utd (1990). 17 Middlesbrough. 18 Exeter. 19 Bobby Charlton. 20 Gordon Strachan. 21 Plymouth. 22 Chelsea (Vialli replacing Gullit). 23 Stokoe, Birmingham and Revie, Manchester City in 1956. 24 Burnley. 25 Mark Bosnich. 26 Leeds United. 27 Zinedine Zidane. 28 Falkirk. 29 Burton Albion. 30 Plough.

1 How many old pennies were there in a guinea?
2 "Dancing with the Stars" was the US spinoff of which UK TV series?
3 Which is the most densely populated Welsh county?
4 How is Russ Roberts better known?
5 What was Margaret Mitchell's only book?
6 What is a Mexican "black howler"?
7 Who was elected president of the Philippines in 1986?
8 Which is the world's longest insect?
9 Who invented the first motion picture camera?
10 The play "The Accrington Pals" deals with which conflict?
11 In which town was the first test tube baby born in 1978?
12 Which naval tradition ceased in 1970?
13 Which English king had to pawn his crown to raise money?
14 Who invented the Polaroid camera in 1947?
15 Which TV programme began broadcasting daily on July 29th, 1949?
16 Kuta Beach on which holiday island was the scene of a bomb in a nightclub in 2002?
17 What was Ali Baba's female slave called?
18 What does an Arab horse have fewer of than any other?
19 Which satellite sent the first live TV transmission between America and Europe?.
20 By what other name is the angel shark known?
21 What does "cap-a-pie" mean?
22 Which Roman emperor ordered St Peter to be crucified?
23 The British Military Academy is at Sandhurst; where is the American?
24 In which country did the study of geometry originate?
25 What is OPEC an acronym of?
26 What was Mickey Mouse's original name?
27 Which amateur jockey's first winner was Gulfland at Redcar in 1986?
28 Opened in 2000, what was the name of London's first new river crossing for 100 years?
29 In which novel does the character Quebec Bagnet appear?
30 What is an ungulate?

Answers	**Pot-Luck 3** *(see Quiz 6)*

1 The ear. 2 Britain. 3 David Tennant. 4 Tasmania. 5 Berkeley Castle. 6 1966. 7 Sea-lions. 8 A clowder. 9 Roger Moore. 10 The wavelength of light. 11 La Quebrada. 12 Ken Norton. 13 Mike Myers. 14 Virgin Atlantic. 15 Norway. 16 Nicolas Breakspear. 17 France and Spain. 18 The Liffey. 19 The Grand Duke. 20 Zambezi. 21 The body. 22 Queen's Park Rangers. 23 Thabo Mbeki. 24 Médoc. 25 William Caxton. 26 Jim Dale. 27 9.55 – five to ten. 28 Lying down. 29 Count Basie. 30 Nemesis.

1 Who was the first royal bride to include her family's motto on her marital coat of arms?
2 Who said "We live above the shop"?
3 Which club was Prince Charles not allowed to join at Cambridge?
4 Princess Anne was the only female competitor at the Montreal Olympics not to be given which test?
5 On which occasion did Elizabeth II make her last curtsey?
6 Where did Princess Diana's mother have a farm at the time of the royal engagement?
7 Who designed the feathered headdress the Duchess of Cornwall wore to her wedding to Prince Charles?
8 Whose autobiography was called "The Heart Has Its Reasons"?
9 Who said "She's more royal than the rest of us" about whom?
10 In which year this century were there three kings of Britain?
11 What are the first names of Princess Diana's sisters and brother?
12 What was tied in a Windsor knot and who introduced the fashion?
13 What did George V refer to as "a mixed grill"?
14 What was Princess Margaret's luxury on "Desert Island Discs"?
15 Which member of the Royal family became an Honorary Captain in the Royal Navy in July 2005?
16 How is the heir to the throne known in Scotland?
17 What name links Earl Spencer and the Duchess of Windsor's first husband?
18 What was Prince Charles' nickname for Mark Phillips?
19 Which army regiment did Prince Harry join after Sandhurst?
20 What are Prince Edward's first names?
21 What is the birthdate of Lady Louise Windsor?
22 Which close relative does Prince Charles share his birthday with?
23 Why is Prince Michael's middle name Franklin?
24 Who is the father of the Earl of St Andrews?
25 Who or what were Susan, Sugar, Honey, Whisky and Sherry?
26 Of the Queen's children who was the heaviest at birth?
27 Last century, how many second sons succeeded to the throne?
28 How many royals had held the title the "Princess Royal" before Princess Anne?
29 Who is the fifth grandchild of the Queen and Prince Philip?
30 Which monarch last century was left-handed?

Answers | Pot-Luck 5 *(see Quiz 11)*

1 Arsenal. 2 Bending the knee. 3 Harry S Truman. 4 Chromosomes. 5 Alistair Cooke. 6 Jupiter. 7 Kevin Spacey. 8 Salmon. 9 Hungary. 10 Longleat. 11 1947. 12 A lucifer. 13 Neptune. 14 Whooping cough. 15 IBM. 16 Neil Kinnock. 17 1965. 18 Fish. 19 The Royal College of Physicians. 20 Lord Protector. 21 Myanmar. 22 John Constable. 23 Italy. 24 1973. 25 Charles Lindbergh. 26 The leaves. 27 The Birdman of Alcatraz. 28 300. 29 Etymology. 30 Lake Titicaca.

1 Which minister resigned over findings in the Budd Report?
2 Which ex-Tory politician left prison in 2000, his possessions in a bin bag?
3 Jack Straw was appointed to which post after Labour's victory in 2001?
4 What was Mo Mowlam's real first name?
5 Over which Bill did Tony Blair's Labour government lose their first Commons vote?
6 Who resigned as Leader of the House of Commons in 2003 over Iraq?
7 Who was Tony Blair's youngest Secretary of State for Education?
8 Who replaced the MP for Sheffield Brightside as Secretary of State for Work and Pensions?
9 After the 2005 election Deputy PM John Prescott held which other post?
10 Which politician wrote a novel called "The Devil's Tune"?
11 Which leader of the SNP left the post in 2000 only to return later?
12 George Galloway was elected MP for which constituency in 2005?
13 Who was Shadow Home Secretary at the start of the new millennium?
14 Following the 2001 General Election who became Father of the House?
15 Who was the only woman in the final stages of the election for London Mayor in 2000?
16 In what year was London's congestion charge introduced.
17 Who replaced David Davis as Tory Party Chairman in 2002?
18 How old was John Major's successor when he became Tory Party leader?
19 Who became Home Secretary a few months before 9/11?
20 Who was Minister for the Civil Service at the time of David Cameron's election as Tory leader?
21 Who became Tory leader the day after the World Trade Center attack?
22 Which Tory MP has the first names Michael Andrew Foster Jude Kerr?
23 Which female was appointed Solicitor General in Tony Blair's government in 2001?
24 Helen Carey chaired which group that heckled Tony Blair?
25 Which Tory David was a former managing director of Tate & Lyle?
26 Which Transport Secretary resigned after Railtrack's collapse?
27 What did Ken Livingstone say was his top priority when he became Mayor of London?
28 Who replaced Blunkett as Secretary of State for Education?
29 Which post did Clare Short resign from over the Iraq war in 2003?
30 What was the title of Labour's 2001 election manifesto?

Answers	The Beatles (see Quiz 12)

1 Three. 2 Winston. 3 Pete Best. 4 Day Tripper. 5 Lucy in the Sky with Diamonds. 6 A record store. 7 Julian and Sean. 8 The White Album. 9 Thank Your Lucky Stars. 10 The Quarrymen. 11 Helen Shapiro. 12 Penny Lane/Strawberry Fields Forever. 13 Rattle their jewellery. 14 Stuart Sutcliffe. 15 Harmonica. 16 All four. 17 My Sweet Lord. 18 The Ed Sullivan Show. 19 Fred Lennon (John's long-absent father). 20 Parlophone. 21 Paul McCartney. 22 Evening Standard. 23 Yellow Submarine. 24 In His Own Write. 25 Four (John). 26 San Francisco (1966). 27 Silver Beetles. 28 Yesterday. 29 George Harrison. 30 MBE.

1 Which soccer team did England cricketer Denis Compton play for?
2 What are you doing if you are genuflecting?
3 Who was president of the United States at the end of World War II?
4 What are there 46 of in a normal human body cell?
5 Who died in 2004 just weeks after presenting his final "Letter from America"?
6 Which planet has at least 13 moons?
7 Which Hollywood movie star played Richard II at the Old Vic Theatre in London in 2005?
8 Parr, smolt and grilse are all stages in the growth of what?
9 Where does "Bull's Blood" originate?
10 What is the Marquis of Bath's Wiltshire home called?
11 In which year did India gain independence from Britain?
12 In the war song "Pack Up Your Troubles" what do you need to light a fag?
13 Which planet was discovered by Johann Galle in 1846?
14 What is pertussis more commonly known as?
15 Which company introduced its first commercial computer in 1953?
16 Which politician's books include "Making Our Way" and "Thorns and Roses"?
17 When was hanging abolished in Britain?
18 What do ichthyologists study?
19 Which body founded the anti-smoking organization, ASH, in 1971?
20 What title was Oliver Cromwell given in 1653?
21 To what did Burma change its name in 1989?
22 Which painter was born at East Bergholt?
23 In which country was King Juan Carlos of Spain born?
24 In which year did Ireland join the EC?
25 Who was the first solo aviator to fly the Atlantic non-stop?
26 Which part of a rhubarb plant is poisonous?
27 Convict Robert Stroud was better known as who?
28 What is the maximum score possible in a game of ten-pin bowling?
29 What name is given to the study of the origins of words?
30 What is the highest large lake in the world?

Answers	Royals *(see Quiz 9)*

1 Princess Diana. 2 Prince Philip. 3 Labour Club. 4 Sex test. 5 Her father's funeral. 6 Australia. 7 Philip Treacy. 8 Duchess of Windsor's. 9 The Queen about Princess Michael. 10 1936. 11 Jane, Sarah and Charles. 12 Tie, Edward VIII when Prince of Wales. 13 His ancestors. 14 Piano. 15 Prince Andrew. 16 Duke of Rothesay. 17 Earl Spencer. 18 Fog (thick and wet). 19 Blues and Royals (Household Cavalry). 20 Edward Antony Richard Louis. 21 8 November 2003. 22 Peter Phillips, his nephew. 23 Franklin Roosevelt was his godfather. 24 Duke of Kent. 25 Corgis. 26 Charles (7lb 6oz). 27 Two, George V and VI. 28 Six. 29 Princess Beatrice of York. 30 George VI.

1 How many Beatles were still alive when the album "1" first became No 1?
2 What was John Lennon's middle name?
3 Which original Beatle did Ringo Starr replace?
4 What was on the other side of the single "We Can Work It Out"?
5 Which Beatles song was banned by the BBC because its initials were said to be drug-related?
6 What did Brian Epstein manage before the Beatles?
7 What are John Lennon's two sons called?
8 How was the double album, "The Beatles", better known?
9 On which show did they make their first national TV appearance?
10 Which group did John Lennon form and name after his school in 1956?
11 Whom did the Beatles support on their first nationwide tour?
12 Which double-sided hit titles were Liverpool placenames?
13 On the Royal Variety Show John Lennon invited those in the cheaper seats to clap. What did he tell those in the more expensive seats to do?
14 Which Beatle died in Hamburg in 1962?
15 Which solo instrument did John Lennon play on "Love Me Do"?
16 How many Beatles appeared on one "Juke Box Jury" in 1963?
17 What was George Harrison's first solo hit?
18 On which show were the Beatles watched by 73 million in the US?
19 Who made a record called "That's My Life" in 1965?
20 What was the first label the Beatles recorded on with George Martin?
21 Who was the last Beatle to marry twice?
22 In which paper was John Lennon's remark that the Beatles were more popular than Jesus?
23 Which cartoon film did the Beatles make in 1969?
24 What was John Lennon's book published in 1964 called?
25 How many letters were in the title of Cynthia Lennon's biography of her first husband?
26 Where was the last live Beatles' performance?
27 What were the group known as immediately before being known as the Beatles?
28 Which Beatles song is the most recorded song of all time?
29 Who was the first Beatle to have a solo No 1 single this century?
30 What were the Beatles awarded by the Queen in 1965?

Answers	21st C British Politics *(see Quiz 10)*

1 David Blunkett. 2 Jonathan Aitken. 3 Foreign Secretary. 4 Marjorie. 5 Terrorism Bill. 6 Robin Cook. 7 Ruth Kelly. 8 John Hutton. 9 First Secretary of State. 10 Iain Duncan Smith. 11 Alex Salmond. 12 Bethnal Green. 13 Ann Widdecombe. 14 Tam Dalyell. 15 Susan Kramer. 16 2003. 17 Theresa May. 18 36. 19 David Blunkett. 20 Tony Blair. 21 Iain Duncan Smith. 22 Michael Ancram. 23 Harriet Harman. 24 WI. 25 David Davis. 26 Stephen Byers. 27 Transport. 28 Estelle Morris. 29 International Development Secretary. 30 Ambitions for Britain.

1 Australia's Barossa Valley is noted for which industry?
2 Who succeeded Ted Hughes as Poet Laureate?
3 Which French building did architects Nervi, Breuer and Zehrfuss create?
4 Which programme did the late John Peel present on Saturday mornings on Radio 4?
5 Who was the voice of Stuart Little in the 1999 movie?
6 After which mythological Greek character was the drug morphine named?
7 In which year did Britain go decimal?
8 What is the world's fastest-moving insect?
9 What was the capital of the Roman province of Britain before Londinium (London)?
10 How many minutes approximately does it take for one revolution of the London Eye?
11 At what height does a pony become a horse?
12 Which bird was selected in 1961 as the British national bird?
13 Who invented neon lights in 1911?
14 Which country was the first to insist upon car registration plates?
15 What was the original name of the flagship the "Golden Hind"?
16 Who was the first sovereign to be addressed as "Your Majesty"?
17 Which painting was stolen and kept for two years by V. Peruggio?
18 When did the first televised debate of the House of Lords take place?
19 What is the capital of Samoa?
20 In which country did the first Christmas stamp appear in 1898?
21 Which volcano erupted to give the greatest explosion in recorded history?
22 For what did the Swede Jenny Lind achieve fame?
23 How many legs has a lobster?
24 Who won the last FA Cup Final of the 20th century?
25 Which is the largest of the anthropoid apes?
26 Who is the magical spirit of the air in Shakespeare's "The Tempest"?
27 Who wrote the lyrics to "A Whiter Shade of Pale"?
28 How many Oscars for best director did Alfred Hitchcock win?
29 Which paper was first published as the "Daily Universal Register"?
30 Which grain is used to make malt whisky?

Answers | Pot-Luck 7 *(see Quiz 15)*

1 Two Little Boys. 2 The Iceni. 3 The Babylonians. 4 Michael Grandage. 5 Whoopi Goldberg. 6 Thierry Vigneron. 7 Edward II. 8 The Po. 9 Venus. 10 Leprosy. 11 Foot and mouth. 12 Tallahassee. 13 10,080. 14 Bangladesh. 15 Andrei Sakharov. 16 Eric Morecambe. 17 Goalkeeper. 18 2000. 19 Patricia. 20 Grapes. 21 Knock. 22 The Colour of Magic. 23 Manchester United. 24 Margaret Thatcher. 25 Stella Rimington. 26 Robbie Coltrane. 27 Dick Turpin. 28 The meaning of words. 29 Salisbury. 30 Lady Jane Grey.

1 What do you add to béchamel to make an aurore sauce?
2 What three main ingredients are added to mayonnaise to make a Waldorf salad?
3 What is a Kugelhupf?
4 In which country do red onions originate?
5 What is added to cheddar cheese to make Ilchester cheese?
6 What is laver?
7 What type of fish are Arbroath smokies?
8 What size eggs are between 60 and 65 grams?
9 What type of milk was mozzarella cheese originally made from?
10 What sort of meat is used in a guard of honour?
11 What is something cooked in if cooked "en papillote"?
12 What do you add to vegetables to make a salmagundi?
13 What are Pershore eggs and Marjorie's seedlings?
14 What are the two main ingredients of a Hollandaise sauce?
15 What colour top do bottles of unpasteurized milk have?
16 What is the chief ingredient of boxty bread?
17 In which English county is Brie made?
18 What is the main meat ingredient of faggots?
19 Which has most fat: double cream, crème fraîche or whipping cream?
20 What is Cornish yarg cheese coated with?
21 Which country does skordalia come from?
22 What shape is the pasta called farfalle?
23 What is the main ingredient of dal?
24 In Indian cuisine what is ghee?
25 Where does coulibiac originate and what is it?
26 Which term in Italian cooking means "soft but firm"?
27 What is a carbonade cooked in?
28 How is steak cooked if cooked blue?
29 How does paella get its name?
30 What is the main vegetable ingredient of moussaka?

Answers	**Marilyn Monroe** *(see Quiz 16)*

1 Mortensen. 2 Niagara. 3 Jane Russell. 4 Paris. 5 Joe DiMaggio. 6 Baseball player. 7 Nine months. 8 Bus Stop. 9 All About Eve. 10 Lauren Bacall and Betty Grable. 11 In the fridge. 12 Arthur Miller. 13 Billy Wilder. 14 Laurence Olivier. 15 Clark Gable. 16 Birthday cake. 17 Photographer's model. 18 Lee Strasberg's. 19 London. 20 16. 21 Four. 22 Jack Lemmon, Tony Curtis (they were in drag). 23 Sugar Cane. 24 Persistent absence. 25 On time. 26 Red satin sheet. 27 Frankie Vaughan. 28 Los Angeles. 29 Sleeping pill overdose. 30 Monkey Business.

1 Which song contains the line, "Each had a wooden horse"?
2 Which tribe rose in revolt against the Romans and was led by Boadicea?
3 Who were the first people to measure the year?
4 Who replaced Sam Mendes as Artistic Director of the Donmar Warehouse?
5 Who was the voice of the female hyena in "The Lion King"?
6 Who was the first pole-vaulter to clear 19 feet?
7 Who was the first Prince of Wales?
8 Which is the longest river in Italy?
9 Which is the brightest planet visible to the naked eye?
10 What is Hansen's Disease more commonly called?
11 In January 2002 it was announced that Britain was declared to be free of which disease?
12 What is the state capital of Florida?
13 How many minutes are there in a week?
14 What is the most densely populated country in the world?
15 Which scientist was known as the "father of the Soviet H-bomb"?
16 Which comedian died of a heart attack in May 1984 at the age of 58?
17 Which position did Pope John Paul II play in the Polish amateur soccer team?
18 In what year did the first British women reach the South Pole?
19 Alfred Hitchcock's daughter appeared in "Psycho". What is her name?
20 What does a viticulturist cultivate?
21 Which Irish village is famous for its shrine to the Virgin Mary?
22 Which book was the first in Terry Pratchett's series of Discworld novels?
23 Which football team was formerly known as Newton Heath?
24 Who signed the Single Act Treaty for Britain in 1986?
25 Who became the first director general of MI5 whose identity was not kept a secret?
26 How is Anthony McMillan better known?
27 Who, in 1948, was the first black boxer to win a British title?
28 Of what is semantics the study?
29 What was Harare called before 1982?
30 Who was the shortest-reigning British monarch?

| **Answers** | Pot-Luck 6 *(see Quiz 13)* |

1 Wine production. 2 Andrew Motion. 3 The Unesco headquarters. 4 Home Truths.
5 Michael J. Fox. 6 Morpheus. 7 1971. 8 Tropical cockroach. 9 Camulodunum
(Colchester). 10 30 minutes. 11 14.2 hands and over. 12 The robin. 13 Georges
Claude. 14 France. 15 The Pelican. 16 Henry VIII. 17 The Mona Lisa. 18 1985. 19
Apia. 20 Canada. 21 Krakatoa. 22 Soprano singer. 23 Eight. 24 Man Utd. 25 The
gorilla. 26 Ariel. 27 Keith Reid. 28 None. 29 The Times. 30 Barley.

1 Which surname other than Baker did Norma Jean use?
2 Which 1952 film gave Monroe her first big role?
3 Which actress co-starred with Monroe in "Gentlemen Prefer Blondes"?
4 To which city do the girls go to look for rich husbands?
5 Who was Monroe's second husband?
6 What type of sportsman was he?
7 How long had they been married before Monroe filed for divorce?
8 Which film had the title "The Wrong Kind of Girl" on TV?
9 Which 1950 film with Monroe in a minor role is famous for the line, "Fasten your seatbelts – it's going to be a bumpy night"?
10 Who were Monroe's two flatmates in "How to Marry a Millionaire"?
11 In "The Seven Year Itch" where does Monroe keep her underwear?
12 Whom did Monroe marry in June 1956?
13 Who directed Monroe in "The Seven Year Itch" and "Some Like It Hot"?
14 Who played the Prince to Monroe's Showgirl in the film?
15 Who died shortly after making "The Misfits" with Monroe?
16 Where did Monroe appear from when she sang "Happy Birthday" to President Kennedy?
17 What career did Marilyn Monroe embark on in 1946?
18 At which Actors' Studio did she study?
19 In which city was "The Prince and the Showgirl" made?
20 How old was Norma Jean when she first married?
21 How many times does Monroe sing "you" in one chorus of "I Wanna be Loved by You"?
22 Who played Monroe's friends Daphne and Geraldine in "Some Like It Hot"?
23 What was the name of the Monroe character?
24 Why was she fired from "Something's Got to Give" ?
25 Monroe said "I have been on a calendar but never ..." what?
26 What did Monroe pose on, on that notorious calendar?
27 Which English singer appeared with Monroe in "Let's Make Love"?
28 In which city did Monroe die?
29 What was the official cause of death?
30 In which film did she co-star with Cary Grant and Ginger Rogers?

Answers	**Food and Drink** *(see Quiz 14)*

1 Tomato purée. **2** Apple, celery and walnuts. **3** Cake. **4** Italy. **5** Beer and garlic. **6** Seaweed. **7** Haddock. **8** Three. **9** Buffalo. **10** Neck of lamb. **11** Paper. **12** Duck and chicken. **13** Plums. **14** Egg yolks and butter. **15** Green. **16** Potatoes. **17** Somerset. **18** Liver. **19** Double cream. **20** Nettle leaves. **21** Greece. **22** Bows or butterflies. **23** Lentils. **24** Clarified butter. **25** Russia, fish pie. **26** Al dente. **27** Beer. **28** Very rare. **29** From the pan it's cooked in. **30** Aubergines.

1 Condoleezza Rice became the first female provost at which American university?
2 Which was the first British daily paper to sell a million copies a day?
3 Which movie gave Jane Austen's story of Elizabeth Bennet and Mr Darcy a Bollywood twist?
4 In 1993 which film star bought himself a £12 million Gulfstream G-3 jet?
5 Swiss architect Charles-Edouard Jeanneret is better known as who?
6 What are also known as "The Decalogue"?
7 Who composed the tune to "Twinkle, Twinkle, Little Star"?
8 Which Arsenal manager completed the signing of Denis Bergkamp?
9 In Arthurian legend, what is the Holy Grail?
10 Why was income tax first levied in Britain?
11 Which herb is called milfoil?
12 How is the settlement the Town of Our Lady, the Queen of the Angels, by the Little-Portion River known today?
13 Which leading Nazi was born in Egypt?
14 What is psychometry?
15 In which novel does the land of Glubbdubdrib appear?
16 Which poet sold his home, Newstead Abbey, to pay his debts?
17 Who is the dictatorial father figure in Dickens' "Hard Times"?
18 What type of animal is a vmi-vmi?
19 Which animal was once called a foul marten?
20 In which year did women gain the vote in Switzerland?
21 The Strand Theatre in London was renamed after which writer and performer?
22 Where is Charles Darwin buried?
23 Where in the world can the largest cannon be seen?
24 Which bird is said to eat live sheep?
25 Who replaced Chris Woodhead as Chief Inspector of Schools?
26 Which British car was the first to sell over a million models?
27 In which city was the first underground railway?
28 What are the pointed pieces called on a ship's anchor?
29 Which detective lived in Cabot Cove, Maine?
30 What is a polyptych?

Answers | Charles Dickens *(see Quiz 19)*

1 Barrister. 2 Newman Noggs. 3 David Copperfield. 4 Gunshot wound. 5 Gordon riots. 6 Steerforth and Traddles. 7 Jarndyce v Jarndyce. 8 Mrs Sparsit. 9 Fanny and Tip. 10 Philip Pirrip. 11 Lizzy Hexam. 12 Jerry Cruncher. 13 Aunt. 14 Mr Dick. 15 Trent. 16 Miss Twinkleton's. 17 Ipswich and Bury St Edmunds. 18 Drowned attempting to rescue Steerforth. 19 Blacksmith. 20 Dogs. 21 Accidentally hangs himself. 22 Esther Summerson. 23 James Hawthorne. 24 They were debtors. 25 Transportation. 26 Barkis. 27 Mrs Bardell. 28 Mr Brownlow. 29 Sally. 30 Bentley Drummle.

1 What was Elvis Presley's middle name?
2 Which song did he sing to win a talent contest at the age of ten?
3 Which country guitarist produced Elvis's early RCA records?
4 What was his wife Priscilla's maiden name?
5 Which white gospel group provided vocal backings on Elvis's recordings in the 1950s and 1960s?
6 Which label signed Presley before selling his contract to RCA a year later?
7 What were Elvis's parents called?
8 What was Elvis's first film?
9 Where was he posted when he joined the army in 1958?
10 Which was his first ever recording, made at Sam Phillips' studio?
11 What was his first US No 1?
12 Who were vs Elvis in the 2002 remix that topped the singles charts?
13 Who took charge of Presley's career when he moved to RCA?
14 What was the fourth of four consecutive No 1s between November 1960 and May 1961?
15 What was Elvis Presley's music publishing company called?
16 Which Elvis hit owes a debt to the Italian song "O Sole Mio"?
17 In what year was Elvis's last No 1 single of the 20th century?
18 What was his first UK No 1?
19 Which city was the focus of Presley's work in the 1970s?
20 Which record went to No 1 after his death in 1977?
21 Which dancer co-starred with Presley in "GI Blues"?
22 Which is the only part of Britain Presley set foot on?
23 Which Elvis film was a western?
24 Because his movements were so controversial, only which part of Elvis was it suggested should be shown on TV?
25 Which operation did James Peterson carry out on Presley in March 1958?
26 In 2005 which Elvis single replaced an Elvis single as a UK No 1 single?
27 What was the name of Elvis's famous mansion and where was it?
28 Which double-sided single was the top seller of the 1950s in the US?
29 Which Elvis hit was a No 1 for Dusty Springfield?
30 What was Elvis's last No 1 record in the UK in his lifetime?

Answers	Pot-Luck 9 (see Quiz 20)

1 Oscar Wilde. 2 The Case of the Terrified Typist. 3 Hercules. 4 Aled Jones. 5 Hutton. 6 £3.60 per hour. 7 Ambulance driver. 8 Nano. 9 King Faisal. 10 Pinocchio. 11 Wembley Stadium, London. 12 The wettest place in Great Britain. 13 1922. 14 Scatterbrook. 15 Inchworm. 16 Teflon. 17 A flight. 18 Phobos. They are moons of Mars. 19 Ben Jonson. 20 Power station. 21 In autumn. Name for a colchinium. 22 Noel Coward. 23 Riche Havens. 24 A couple. 25 Anya Jenkins. 26 Smell. 27 Lou Reed. 28 The help the American Indians gave to the first white settlers. 29 Harry Allen. 30 An expert on China.

1 In "A Tale of Two Cities" what is the occupation of Sydney Carton?

2 In "Nicholas Nickleby" who is Ralph Nickleby's clerk?

3 Which of his novels did Dickens say he liked the best?

4 In Oliver Twist's burgling expedition with Bill Sikes what sort of injury does Oliver receive?

5 Which historical events are the background to "Barnaby Rudge"?

6 Who are David Copperfield's two vastly different schoolfriends?

7 Which court case is at the heart of "Bleak House"?

8 In "Hard Times" who is Mr Bounderby's housekeeper?

9 In "Little Dorrit" who are Amy's brother and sister?

10 In "Great Expectations" what is Pip's full name?

11 In "Our Mutual Friend" whom does Eugene Wrayburn marry?

12 In "A Tale of Two Cities" what is the name of the grave robber?

13 In "Oliver Twist" what is Rose's relation to Oliver discovered to be?

14 In "David Copperfield" whom does David's aunt Betsey Trotwood live with?

15 In "The Old Curiosity Shop" what is Little Nell's surname?

16 In "Edwin Drood" at whose school at Cloisterham was Rosa brought up?

17 Which two Suffolk towns are the background for scenes in "Pickwick Papers"?

18 In "David Copperfield" how did Ham die?

19 In "Great Expectations" what is the profession of Joe Gargery?

20 What are Nip and Bullseye?

21 In "Oliver Twist" how does Bill Sikes perish?

22 In "Bleak House" who is Lady Dedlock's daughter, at first assumed dead?

23 In "Hard Times" who tries to seduce Louisa Bounderby, née Gradgrind?

24 What offence had inhabitants of the Marshalsea prison committed?

25 In "Nicholas Nickleby" what is the final fate of Squeers?

26 In "David Copperfield" who was "willin'"?

27 In "Pickwick Papers" who is Mr Pickwick's landlady?

28 In "Oliver Twist" who adopts Oliver?

29 In "The Old Curiosity Shop" who is Samson Brass's sister?

30 In "Great Expectations" whom did Estella first marry?

Answers	Pot-Luck 8 (see Quiz 17)

1 Stanford University. 2 Daily Mail. 3 Bride & Prejudice. 4 Arnold Schwarzenegger. 5 Le Corbusier. 6 The Ten Commandments. 7 Mozart. 8 Bruce Rioch. 9 The cup used at the Last Supper. 10 To pay for the Napoleonic Wars. 11 Yarrow. 12 Los Angeles. 13 Rudolf Hess. 14 Measurement of mental qualities. 15 Gulliver's Travels. 16 Byron. 17 Thomas Gradgrind. 18 A pig. 19 Polecat. 20 1971. 21 (Ivor) Novello. 22 Westminster Abbey. 23 The Kremlin. 24 The kea parrot in New Zealand. 25 Mike Tomlinson. 26 Morris Minor. 27 London. 28 Flukes. 29 Jessica Fletcher. 30 Altarpiece with more than one panel.

1 Who said, "Philosophy teaches us to bear with equanimity the misfortunes of others"?
2 Which was the only case that Perry Mason ever lost in court?
3 Name the horse that pulled Steptoe and Son's rag-and-bone cart?
4 Which singer released the 2005 album "New Horizons"?
5 Who was the head of the inquiry investigating the death of Dr David Kelly?
6 In the UK, how much was the first minimum wage for those over 22?
7 What type of work did Ernest Hemingway do during World War I?
8 Which prefix denotes a one thousand millionth part?
9 Which Saudi Arabian king was assassinated in 1975?
10 In 1940 which classic Disney cartoon was made?
11 Where was the main arena for the 1948 Olympic Games?
12 Achnashellach is usually credited with what unfortunate title?
13 In which year did Mussolini seize power in Italy?
14 Where did Worzel Gummidge live?
15 What is a looper caterpillar called in the United States?
16 Polytetrafluoroethylene is usually known as what?
17 What name is given to swallows in the air?
18 What is the partner of Deimos?
19 Who was the first poet laureate?
20 What was the building that now houses the Tate Modern?
21 When would you see a naked lady in the garden?
22 Who wrote a song called the "The Stately Homes of England"?
23 Who opened the original Woodstock rock festival?
24 In "I Belong to Glasgow", how many drinks do I get on a Saturday?
25 "Buffy the Vampire Slayer" actress Emma Caulfield played which character?
26 If a person is anosmic, they have no sense of what?
27 How is Louis Firbank better known?
28 The Americans celebrate Thanksgiving in remembrance of what?
29 Who was Britain's last chief hangman?
30 What is a Sinologist?

Answers	**Elvis Presley** *(see Quiz 18)*

1 Aaron. 2 Old Shep. 3 Chet Atkins. 4 Beaulieu. 5 The Jordanaires. 6 Sun Records. 7 Vernon and Gladys. 8 Love Me Tender. 9 West Germany. 10 My Happiness. 11 Heartbreak Hotel. 12 JXL. 13 Colonel Tom Parker. 14 Surrender. 15 Elvis Presley Music. 16 It's Now or Never. 17 1977 (Way Down). 18 All Shook Up. 19 Las Vegas. 20 Way Down. 21 Juliet Prowse. 22 Scotland. 23 Charro. 24 Waist up. 25 Cut his hair for the army. 26 One Night/I Got Stung. 27 Graceland, Memphis. 28 Hound Dog/ Don't be Cruel. 29 You Don't Have to Say You Love Me. 30 The Wonder of You.

Quiz 21 | Sports Bag

Answers – page 497

LEVEL 3

1 In 2005 who became the biggest boxer to be WBA heavyweight champion?
2 Who after Ronnie O'Sullivan won two ranking snooker titles before his 19th birthday?
3 What two differences are there between the position and paddle of someone in a canoe and someone in a kayak?
4 In which two countries is curling most popular?
5 What is the longest-lasting, non-motorized sporting event in the world?
6 What is the biathlon a combination of?
7 What is Brian Gamlin of Bury credited with devising?
8 Which French rugby player (d. 2005) was called "The Little Corporal"?
9 What two types of bowling green are there?
10 In which part of London was the first equestrian jumping competition?
11 What are the three types of sword used in fencing?
12 Billiards probably gets its name from the French word "billiard". What is a billiard?
13 Who was first world champion at darts and which country did he represent?
14 What does karate mean, describing this kind of fighting?
15 What did the sport, baggataway, become?
16 Which country produced most winners of the World Rally Championship?
17 Which sport does the Fédération Internationale des Quilleurs control?
18 In which sport do you use a chistera?
19 Which sport is played on the largest pitch of any game?
20 Where is the world's oldest tobogganing club?
21 In Rugby League, who was the first person to be voted Man Of Steel in two consecutive seasons?
22 Which sport developed from a game called gossima?
23 Which sport has three lifts, squat, bench press and dead lift?
24 What is the object of sumo wrestling?
25 In judo which dan is the highest in the grading of black belts?
26 How does a hurl differ from a hockey stick?
27 How do you luge?
28 Aside from asymmetric bars, what are the three events for women gymnasts in the Olympics?
29 In which country was greyhound racing's first regular track?
30 How many players are there in a Gaelic football team?

Answers | **TV Gold** *(see Quiz 23)*

1 Boys from the Blackstuff. 2 Helen Flynn. 3 Simon Dee. 4 Fortunes of War. 5 A Premium Bond win. 6 Vanessa Redgrave. 7 Paul McCartney. 8 Wicksy. 9 Catering. 10 Trevor. 11 Eamonn Andrews. 12 The hairdressing salon. 13 As Time Goes By. 14 Richard Briers. 15 Man About the House. 16 Peter Duncan. 17 The Likely Lads. 18 The Last One: Part 2. 19 The Newcomers. 20 Our Man at St Mark's. 21 A Bit of a Do. 22 Frasier. 23 Shelley. 24 Terry Duckworth. 25 Fawlty Towers. 26 Strictly Come Dancing. 27 Denis Norden. 28 Neighbours. 29 Corky. 30 The Liver Birds.

Quiz 22 Pot-Luck 10

Answers – page 498

LEVEL 3

1 In which year did Concorde make its last commercial flight?
2 Which prince was the first to have a Royal baby born in an NHS hospital?
3 What gas propels the cork from a champagne bottle?
4 What is the smallest Test Match-winning margin by England over Australia?
5 When did Celtic first have numbers on the back of their shirts?
6 What colour cap is worn by an English cricketer capped for his country?
7 Which player went from Barcelona to Real Madrid for £35.7m in 2000?
8 By what name was the outlaw Harry Longbaugh better known?
9 What was Richard Burton's original name?
10 What is the name of the RAF free-fall parachute team?
11 In what year did Spain and Portugal join the EC?
12 Which Country and Western singer joined Bob Dylan on the latter's album, "Nashville Skyline"?
13 Who became Secretary of State for Health in 1999?
14 Which fruit contains the most calories?
15 What is the minimum age for a three-star cognac?
16 What publication was launched in 1920 by American bank clerk DeWitt Wallace?
17 In which Scottish castle did Madonna marry Guy Ritchie?
18 Which two French sides did Zinedine Zidane play for before moving to Italy in 1996?
19 Which king converted Leeds Castle, in Kent, into a royal palace?
20 Who in the Old Testament is eaten by dogs?
21 What tune is Liechtenstein's national anthem sung to?
22 Who wrote the words of the hymn "Jerusalem"?
23 Who was Priapus in Greek mythology?
24 Which charge card was launched in Britain in September 1963?
25 What is the name of the world's largest flower?
26 What opened in 1894 and closed in London's Strand in 1988?
27 Where did Indian ink originally come from?
28 Who said, "Make love in the afternoon ... It's the only time for it"?
29 Which romantic poet wrote "The Bride of Abydos"?
30 How is Thomas Derbyshire better known?

Answers | Pot-Luck 11 *(see Quiz 24)*

1 Mo Mowlam. 2 Eltham, London. 3 Pickles. 4 Fishing. 5 Wren. 6 Benjamin Franklin in September 1752. 7 Traffic islands. 8 1852 in London. 9 Case for a ship's compass. 10 William the Conqueror. 11 One. 12 Sicily and parts of mainland Italy. 13 Saccharine. It's an anagram. 14 James Purefoy. 15 Colin Baker. 16 Pam Shriver. 17 Halibut. 18 Texas. 19 Juno. 20 Admiral of the Fleet. 21 In India. 22 1945. 23 J. J. Thomson. 24 Long jump, high jump, triple jump and pole vault. 25 Sting. 26 Mega City 1. 27 168. 28 The Globe theatre. 29 A host. 30 President Mitterrand.

1 Which Alan Bleasdale offering won the BAFTA Drama award in 1982?
2 Which character was killed in episode two of spy drama "Spooks"?
3 Which 1960s TV personality ended his show in a white E-type Jaguar?
4 Which Alan Plater TV adaptation starred Kenneth Branagh as Guy Pringle?
5 Where did Ken Barlow's father get the money that enabled him to move out of Coronation Street?
6 Who played Josephine opposite Ernie Wise's Napoleon?
7 Who is the richest person to have accepted a bit-part on "Bread"?
8 Which Eastender thought his father was Pete Beale when it was Kenny?
9 What was Robin Tripp studying when he lived upstairs from the Ropers?
10 Who was Sid's next-door neighbour in "Bless This House"?
11 Which quiz and chat show host devised "Whose Baby"?
12 Which department at Crossroads Motel was run by Vera Downend?
13 Lionel Hardcastle and Jean Pargetter are characters in which long-running comedy?
14 Which "Good Life" star played the lodger in "Goodbye Mr Kent"?
15 Which series about two girls and a guy was "Three's Company" in the US?
16 Which "Blue Peter" presenter was in "Space 1999" and "Fallen Hero"?
17 Which comedy featured characters called Terry Collier and Bob Ferris?
18 What was the last episode of "Friends" called?
19 Which 1960s soap cast Haverhill in Suffolk as Angleton new town?
20 Which TV series starred Leslie Phillips and Donald Sinden as vicars?
21 Which comedy series married David Jason to Gwen Taylor?
22 "Freudian Sleep" and "The Placeholder" are episodes of which comedy?
23 Which Hywel Bennett series had the same title as a drama about a poet?
24 Who ran away to stay with Susan Barlow?
25 Where does Polly Sherman work?
26 David Dickinson, Esther Rantzen and Dennis Taylor have all featured on which popular entertainment show?
27 Who was Frank Muir's most regular writing partner?
28 Which television series, which celebrated its twentieth anniversary in 2005, was originally called "People Like Us"?
29 Who was always trying to borrow food in "Sykes"?
30 Which series linked Polly James and "District Nurse" Nerys Hughes?

Answers	**Sports Bag** *(see Quiz 21)*

1 Nicolay Valuev. 2 Ding Jun Hui. 3 Kayak, seated, double paddle; canoe, kneeling, single paddle. 4 Scotland, Canada. 5 Tour de France. 6 Cross-country skiing, shooting. 7 Dartboard numbering. 8 Jacques Fouroux. 9 Crown, level. 10 Islington. 11 Foil, épée, sabre. 12 Stick with a curved end. 13 Leighton Rees, Wales. 14 Empty hand. 15 Lacrosse. 16 Finland. 17 Ten pin bowling. 18 Pelota. 19 Polo. 20 St Moritz. 21 Paul Sculthorpe. 22 Table tennis. 23 Powerlifting. 24 Force opponent out of ring. 25 Tenth. 26 Flat on both sides. 27 Lie on your back;. 28 Floor, beam, vault. 29 US. 30 15.

1 Which Labour politician was appointed Chancellor of the Duchy of Lancaster in 1999 and died in 2005?
2 Where was Bob Hope born?
3 Which dog found the World Cup when it went missing in 1966?
4 Which British sport has the most participants?
5 What is the commonest bird in the British Isles?
6 Who designed the first lightning-conductor?
7 What road safety measure was introduced in the streets of Liverpool in 1860?
8 When and where was the first public lavatory opened in Britain?
9 What is a binnacle?
10 Which king built Windsor Castle?
11 How many lungs do snakes have?
12 Where can you find porcupines in Europe?
13 How can cane chairs be rearranged to produce something sweet?
14 Which actor played Mark Antony in the BBC drama production "Rome"?
15 Who played the sixth Dr Who?
16 Which ex-tennis player married actor George Lazenby, an ex-James Bond?
17 What is the common name for the fish Hippoglossus hippoglossus?
18 Destiny's Child formed in which US state?
19 Who was the Roman goddess of marriage?
20 What is the top rank in the Royal Navy?
21 Where was the decimal system developed?
22 When was the International Monetary Fund established?
23 Who discovered the electron?
24 In athletics, what are the four jumping events?
25 Who recorded the album "The Dream of the Blue Turtles"?
26 In which city does Judge Dredd work?
27 How many spots are there on a full set of 28 dominoes?
28 Which London landmark theatre was burnt down in 1613?
29 What is a group or flock of sparrows called?
30 Which President of France opened the Channel Tunnel along with Queen Elizabeth II?

Answers | **Pot-Luck 10** *(see Quiz 22)*

1 2003. 2 Prince Edward. 3 Carbon dioxide. 4 Two runs. 5 1994. 6 Blue. 7 Luis Figo. 8 The Sundance Kid. 9 Richard Jenkins. 10 The Falcons. 11 1986. 12 Johnny Cash. 13 Alan Milburn. 14 The avocado pear. 15 Five years. 16 Reader's Digest. 17 Skibo Castle. 18 Cannes & Bordeaux. 19 Henry VIII. 20 Jezebel. 21 God Save the Queen. 22 William Blake. 23 A fertility god. 24 American Express. 25 Rafflesia, which grows up to one metre across. 26 Lyons teashops. 27 China. 28 Arnold Wesker. 29 Lord Byron. 30 Tommy Cannon.

Quiz 25 | Geography: Capitals | Answers – page 501

1 What was the capital of Russia before Moscow?
2 What is the capital of Andorra?
3 What lies to the north of Algiers?
4 Which country has the last capital alphabetically?
5 What was Harare's former name?
6 Which Asian capital is at the head of the Mekong Delta?
7 Which capital is known as Leukosia or Lefkosa by its inhabitants?
8 Tashkent is the capital of which former Soviet republic?
9 Which capital is on the slopes of the volcano Pichincha?
10 Which is further north, Pakistan's new capital, Islamabad, or the former one, Karachi?
11 St John's is the capital of Antigua and Barbuda but on which island does it stand?
12 Which capital's former name was Christiania?
13 In Berlin which avenue runs east from the Brandenburg Gate?
14 Which capital is the largest city in Africa?
15 Where was Botswana's seat of government prior to 1965, after which it moved to Gaborone?
16 What was the capital of Italian East Africa between 1936 and 1941?
17 Which capital lies on the river Helmand?
18 In Paris what links the Arc de Triomphe and the Place de la Concorde?
19 Which new capital's main architect was Oscar Niemeyer?
20 Which capital's main industrial area is Piraeus?
21 In which capital is the Teatro Colón opera house?
22 What is the full name of the capital of Colombia?
23 Which capital's heating comes from natural hot springs?
24 What did New Delhi replace as the capital of British India in 1912?
25 On which sea is the Azerbaijani capital Baku?
26 Which capital is known as the Eternal City?
27 What is the capital of Bahrain?
28 Which capital began as the village of Edo?
29 Which capital in the West Indies is to be found on New Providence Island?
30 Which capital houses the Great Mosque and the Gate of God?

Answers	Pop: MOR *(see Quiz 27)*

1 Mike Batt. 2 Burt Bacharach and Hal David. 3 Barbra Streisand. 4 None. 5 Andy Williams. 6 Eva Casssidy. 7 Des O'Connor. 8 Jambalaya. 9 Roger Whittaker. 10 Herb Alpert. 11 James Last. 12 Mantovani. 13 Peter Skellern. 14 Mary Hopkin. 15 Jack Jones. 16 Charles Aznavour. 17 Barber. 18 Tony Christie. 19 Johnny Mathis. 20 Shirley Bassey. 21 Leo Sayer. 22 Bert Kaempfert. 23 Henry Mancini. 24 Syd Lawrence. 25 Stranger in Paradise. 26 Al Martino. 27 Nat King Cole. 28 Helen Reddy. 29 Shirley Bassey. 30 Gerry Goffin.

1 Whom did Paris select as the most beautiful goddess?
2 Who sails "The Black Pig"?
3 In which year did Hitler come to power in Germany?
4 Who formulated the periodic table of elements commonly used today?
5 Which Pope succeeded John Paul II?
6 Who discovered the three basic laws of planetary motion?
7 Who was the first secretary-general of the United Nations?
8 Which of Kelly Holmes' 2004 Olympic golds did she win first?
9 Which country's wine may be labelled DOCG?
10 Who designed Blenheim Palace?
11 Who is the only British prime minister to have been assassinated?
12 Who gave Henry II the right to invade and conquer Ireland?
13 What is the name of the nearest star, other than the Sun, to Earth?
14 When was the first appendix operation performed?
15 For what line of business was model manufacturer Airfix originally known?
16 Which gift did the Americans receive from the French in 1886?
17 Which other John challenged John Major for the Tory leadership in the 1990s?
18 What is a crapulous person full of?
19 What is sophistry?
20 Andrew Flintoff played which indoor game for Lancashire schools?
21 Which subatomic particle is named after the Greek word for "first"?
22 What was the name of the first feature-length animated film?
23 Which ex wife of a Rolling Stone starred in "High Society" in London's West End?
24 What is the colour of the bull on an archery target?
25 In which sport are Doggetts Coat and Badge awarded?
26 Who founded the first public library in the City of London?
27 By what name was Asa Yoelson better known?
28 The RAF motto is "Per Ardua Ad Astra". What does it mean?
29 The TV series "Jamie's Kitchen" featured which restaurant?
30 Which of the Seven Wonders of the Ancient World survives today?

Answers	**Sport: Cricket** *(see Quiz 28)*

1 Andy Caddick. **2** The Oval. **3** Shane Warne (in 1994). **4** Durham. **5** Kevin Pietersen. **6** Bob Woolmer. **7** Philip Eric. **8** Essex. **9** Kepler Wessels. **10** West Germany. **11** Shane Warne. **12** Darren Gough. **13** Matthew Hoggard. **14** Mark Burgess. **15** 355. **16** Yorkshire and Leicestershire. **17** Brian McMillan. **18** Wally Hammond. **19** New Zealand. **20** 1968. **21** Somerset. **22** Hubert. **23** Phil Neale. **24** Surrey. **25** Leicestershire. **26** "Jimmy" Binks. **27** Derbyshire. **28** Malcolm Nash (Sobers batting, in 1968). **29** Viv Richards. **30** Darren Gough.

1 Who wrote Katie Melua's hit "The Closest Thing to Crazy"?
2 Which partnership wrote "Walk On By" for Dionne Warwick?
3 Who has recorded with Neil Diamond, Barry Gibb and Don Johnson?
4 How many No 1 singles has Neil Diamond had?
5 Who recorded film themes "Moon River" and "Love Story"?
6 Who was the first artist to score three posthumous No 1 albums in the UK?
7 Who had a Top Twenty hit in 1969 with "Dick-A-Dum-Dum"?
8 Which Carpenters hit was the name of a food dish?
9 Whose hits mention Durham, Skye and the New World?
10 Which trumpeter was a co-founder of A & M Records?
11 Who in 1993 became second only to Elvis Presley with his number of album chart entries?
12 Which hugely successful orchestra leader was born Annunzio Paolo?
13 Who has recorded with northern brass bands and sung the songs of Fred Astaire and Hoagy Carmichael?
14 Who won "Opportunity Knocks" and was signed by the Apple label?
15 Which MOR singer's father was famous for his "Donkey Serenade"?
16 Which French singer's autobiography was called "Yesterday When I was Young"?
17 What was Perry Como's job before becoming a singer?
18 Who enquired about the whereabouts of Amarillo again in 2005?
19 Who has recorded with Deniece Williams and Gladys Knight?
20 Who was known as "The Tigress of Tiger Bay"?
21 Who had a transatlantic hit with "When I Need Love"?
22 Which German bandleader was the first to record the Beatles?
23 Who wrote film themes "Days of Wine and Roses" and the Pink Panther?
24 Which British orchestra emulated the sound of Glenn Miller?
25 What was Tony Bennett's first chart entry and only UK No 1?
26 Who was chosen for the role of Johnny Fontane (reputedly based on Frank Sinatra) in "The Godfather"?
27 Whose many hits included "When I Fall in Love" and "Too Young"?
28 Whose first US No 1 was the self-penned "I am a Woman"?
29 Who topped the bill in the first Royal Variety Show to be held in Wales?
30 Who was Carole King's songwriting partner in the 1960s?

Answers	Geography: Capitals *(see Quiz 25)*

1 St Petersburg. 2 Andorra la Vella. 3 Mediterranean. 4 Croatia (Zagreb). 5 Salisbury. 6 Phnom Penh. 7 Nicosia (Cyprus). 8 Uzbekistan. 9 Quito (Ecuador). 10 Islamabad. 11 Antigua. 12 Oslo. 13 Unter den Linden. 14 Cairo. 15 Mafeking. 16 Addis Ababa. 17 Kabul. 18 Champs Elysées. 19 Brasilia. 20 Athens. 21 Buenos Aires. 22 Santa Fé de Bogotà. 23 Reykjavik (Iceland). 24 Calcutta. 25 Caspian. 26 Rome. 27 Manama. 28 Tokyo. 29 Nassau. 30 Damascus (Syria).

1 Which bowler ended Brian Lara's record-breaking Test innings of 375?
2 At which ground did Malcolm take nine wickets in a 1994 Test innings?
3 After Hugh Trumble's Ashes hat-trick in 1904, who was the next Australian to repeat the feat?
4 With which county did Ian Botham end his playing career?
5 Which England player reached a century with a six in Faisalabad in 2005?
6 Who left Warwickshire in 1994 to become coach to South Africa?
7 What are Alan Knott's two middle names?
8 The Benson & Hedges Cup in 1979 was the first trophy for which county?
9 Who was skipper of South Africa in their 1994 return to England?
10 In which country was England batsman Paul Terry born ?
11 H. P. Tillakaratne was the 500th Test victim of which bowler?
12 In 1994 who gave his son the middle names David and Michael after the Australian batsman whom he dismissed the day after the baby's birth?
13 Which English player took a hat-trick against the West Indies in 2004?
14 Who led New Zealand to their first-ever victory against England in 1978?
15 To ten either way, how many Test wickets did Dennis Lillee take?
16 Which two counties did Dickie Bird play for?
17 Who topped the South African batting and bowling averages in the 1994 Test series against England?
18 Which England captain was the first Test outfielder to take 100 catches?
19 For which country did Peter Petherick take a Test hat-trick in 1976?
20 To three years, when was Yorkshire's last Championship win pre-2001?
21 Which English county did New Zealander Martin Crowe play for?
22 What is Clive Lloyd's middle name?
23 Who skippered both Lincoln at football and Worcester at cricket in 1993?
24 Which county did Jack Hobbs play for?
25 Which English county did the late Hanse Cronje play for?
26 Which Yorkshire wicket-keeper had the first names James Graham?
27 Which English county did Michael Holding play for?
28 Which bowler was the first to be hit for six sixes in an over?
29 Which West Indian player turned out for Antigua in the 1978 World Cup?
30 Who was the only Englishman to take a hat-trick against the Aussies last century?

| **Answers** | Pot-Luck 12 *(see Quiz 26)* |

1 Aphrodite. 2 Captain Pugwash. 3 1933. 4 Mendeleyev. 5 Benedict XVI. 6 Kepler.
7 Trygve Lie. 8 800 metres. 9 Italy (Denominazione di Origine Controllata e Garantita).
10 Sir John Vanbrugh. 11 Spencer Perceval. 12 The English pope, Adrian IV. 13 Proxima
Centauri. 14 1885. 15 Making combs. 16 Statue of Liberty. 17 John Redwood. 18
Alcohol. 19 False reasoning, meant to deceive. 20 Chess. 21 Proton. 22 Snow White
and the Seven Dwarfs. 23 Jerry Hall. 24 Gold or yellow. 25 Rowing. 26 Robert Ford.
27 Al Jolson. 28 Through difficulties to the the stars. 29 Fifteen. 30 Pyramids.

1 In which decade was flogging abolished in Britain?
2 What sort of word is made up from initial letters of other words?
3 What is a necropolis?
4 Where did the Vikings originally come from?
5 What is the coldest substance?
6 Who wrote the book "Chitty Chitty Bang Bang"?
7 In which sport is there a york round?
8 Who wrote the song "If"?
9 In cricket how many runs is a Nelson?
10 Which British prime minister once said, "Is a man an ape or an angel? Now I am on the side of the angels"?
11 By what name is Jim Moir better known?
12 When was the first free vertical flight of a twin-rotor helicopter?
13 What does an aphyllous plant not have?
14 For how long did Alexander the Great rule?
15 What is the central administrative body of the Catholic Church?
16 Which decade saw the introduction of instant coffee?
17 In which city was Ray Davies of the Kinks shot in the leg in 2004?
18 Who launched the "Daily Mail"?
19 Which co founder of "The Guinness Book Of Records" passed away in 2004?
20 Which film did newspaper magnate William Randolph Hearst inspire?
21 Which city is built on the site of the Aztec capital Tenochtitlan?
22 To which king in the Bible was Jezebel married?
23 Which famous American singer was described in "Life" magazine in 1974 as having a "half-melted vanilla face"?
24 What do you do in music when you play a piece "con brio"?
25 What punishment did the Vestal Virgins of Rome suffer if they betrayed their vows of chastity?
26 Which movie actress has twins Phinnaeus and Hazel?
27 Which is the largest seed in the world?
28 To 20 years each way, when was Hyde Park opened to the public?
29 Which country built the Mars probe known as Beagle 2?
30 Gilberto Silva joined Arsenal from which club side?

Answers	Pot-Luck 14 *(see Quiz 31)*

1 The Spectator. 2 His cousin, Celeste. 3 George II (Dettingen, 1743). 4 Hydrogen. 5 The Sea. 6 The Milky Way. 7 1963. 8 Chelonia. 9 72. 10 Blenheim. 11 The Third World. 12 Poppies. 13 About eight minutes. 14 Carl Koller. 15 Betty Boothroyd. 16 Richard Branson. 17 Jack the Ripper. 18 An instrument for enlarging or reducing drawings. 19 Jeffrey Archer. 20 Shanghai. 21 Electric current. 22 Long sight. 23 106. 24 Lord Palmerston. 25 Goodbye, Mr Chips. 26 Milk. 27 Paul Neal. 28 The 1920s. 29 Wanderly Luxemburgo. 30 The Picts.

1 What was the name of the first commercial atomic-powered ship?
2 Who devised the prototype for the "Beetle"?
3 What was the first car to be powered by a gas turbine?
4 Who first patented the seat belt in 1903?
5 Which rail line, opened in 1830, was the world's first inter-city service?
6 To three miles, how long is the M25?
7 In 1775 who invented the tram drawn by two horses?
8 What was the first hot-air balloon, called the Montgolfier, made of?
9 In air flight, what is the characteristic of aerodynes?
10 Where did the Wright brothers fly their first glider in 1900?
11 What was the first airliner, which was put into service in 1933?
12 Who invented the preselector gearbox for battle tanks in 1917?
13 Who founded the Great Western Railway using a seven-foot wide track?
14 Which famous ocean liner made its maiden voyage in May 1936?
15 Who invented the "air bag" anti-shock air cushion?
16 Who made the first airship flight in 1852 in a hydrogen-filled craft powered by a steam engine?
17 What does the "U" in U-Boat stand for?
18 What did French engineer Georges Messier invent in 1924?
19 Who in 1878 invented the electric staff which prevents trains on single-track lines colliding?
20 Who built the first submarine which was tested in the River Thames?
21 Who invented laminated windscreens in 1909?
22 What was the name of the first successful flying boat built in 1912?
23 Which brothers built the first American petrol-driven motor cars in 1892?
24 On which railway was the first buffet car created in 1899?
25 Which airline company first made a commercial flight in a Boeing 747 from New York to London?
26 Which German company created the electronically variable shock-absorber in 1987?
27 What first left Gare de l'Est in Paris on October 4th, 1883?
28 Who was Secretary of State for Transport when the first 12-lane section of the M25 was opened?
29 Which British doctor invented the disc brake in 1902?
30 Where was the first take-off by a manned helicopter in 1907?

| **Answers** | **European Community** *(see Quiz 32)* |

1 Six. 2 European Coal and Steel Community. 3 Euratom. 4 Ireland, Denmark. 5 Foreign secretaries. 6 Ten. 7 Italy. 8 Luxembourg. 9 Brussels. 10 European Council. 11 May. 12 Luxembourg. 13 Economic and Monetary Union. 14 Poland. 15 EU citizenship. 16 Pillars. 17 Subsidiarity. 18 Germany (99). 19 European Investment Bank. 20 Jacques Delors. 21 Butter. 22 De Gaulle. 23 Treaty of Brussels. 24 Roy Jenkins. 25 VAT payments. 26 Greenland. 27 Corporal punishment of children if parents disapproved. 28 EFTA. 29 Deputy foreign secretary. 30 Five years.

1 Which journal did Addison and Steele found?

2 Whom did Babar the Elephant marry?

3 Who was the last British king to lead an army into battle?

4 Of which element is tritium an isotope?

5 What was the title of the book that won the 2005 Man Booker Prize?

6 In which galaxy is the Earth?

7 In what year did Valentina Tereshkova become the first woman in space?

8 To which order of reptiles do turtles and tortoises belong?

9 At what age did Des O'Connor became dad of a new baby in 2004?

10 In which palace was Winston Churchill born?

11 Which expression was coined by Alfred Sauvy in the early 1950s to describe countries with underdeveloped economic structures?

12 In "Penny Lane" what is a nurse selling from a tray?

13 How long does the light of the Sun take to reach the Earth?

14 Who discovered the pain-killing properties of cocaine?

15 In 1994, which female politician became Chancellor of the Open University?

16 Whose first business enterprise on leaving school was a magazine called "Student"?

17 Who murdered Catherine Eddowes on September 30th, 1888?

18 What is an eidograph?

19 Which former MP became Baron of Weston Super Mare?

20 Which city has the largest population in the world?

21 What is controlled by a rheostat?

22 What would you have if you were hypermetropic?

23 How many times was Bobby Charlton capped for England?

24 Whose last words were, "Die, my dear doctor! That's the last thing I shall do!"?

25 Which James Hilton novel was turned into a film classic about school life?

26 What does a galactophagist like to drink?

27 What is the real name of Red Adair, the American fire-fighter?

28 In which decade did the "par avion" airmail stickers appear in Britain?

29 Who was dismissed as Real Madrid's coach following Beckham's red card against Getafe in Dec 2005?

30 Kenneth I ruled which people in the 9th century?

Answers	Pot-Luck 13 *(see Quiz 29)*

1 1940s. 2 Acronym. 3 Cemetery. 4 Gotland. 5 Solid helium. 6 Ian Fleming. 7 Archery. 8 David Gates. 9 111. 10 Benjamin Disraeli. 11 Vic Reeves. 12 1907, by Paul Cornu. 13 Leaves. 14 12 years. 15 The Curia. 16 1938, Nescafé. 17 New Orleans. 18 Alfred Harmsworth, Viscount Northcliffe, in 1896. 19 Norris McWhirter. 20 Citizen Kane. 21 Mexico City. 22 Ahab. 23 Elvis Presley. 24 Play vigorously. 25 Live burial. 26 Julia Roberts. 27 Double coconut. 28 1637. 29 Britain. 30 Athletico Madrid.

1 How many countries were in the EEC at its beginning in 1957?
2 What did the Treaty of Paris set up in 1951?
3 What was the European Atomic Energy Commission known as?
4 Who joined the EC in 1973 with Britain?
5 Who are the members of the Council of Ministers?
6 How many countries joined the EU in May 2004?
7 Former EU president Romano Prodi came from which country?
8 Which country held the EU presidency from January to June 2005?
9 Where is the Commission's headquarters?
10 What are the meetings of the heads of government called?
11 In which month is Europe Day?
12 Where is the secretariat of the European Parliament based?
13 What does EMU stand for?
14 Which of the states that joined the EU in May 2004 was the largest in terms of population?
15 What qualification do you need to stand for the European Parliament?
16 What did the Maastricht Treaty call each of the three areas of the EU?
17 Which principle in the Maastricht Treaty says the Community will act on policies which member states would find difficult to deal with alone?
18 Which country has the most MEPs?
19 What is the EU bank called?
20 Who preceded Jacques Santer as Commission president?
21 In 1987 what did the EC sell to the USSR for 6p per pound?
22 Which statesman vetoed Britain's entry into the EEC in the 1960s?
23 Which treaty allowed Britain's entry into the EC?
24 Who was the first British president of the EC Commission?
25 What did Margaret Thatcher threaten to withhold if the EC did not cut Britain's budget contribution in 1980?
26 Who voted to withdraw from the EC in February 1982?
27 What did the European Court outlaw in the same month?
28 Of which trading association was Britain a member prior to joining the EEC?
29 Which post did Ted Heath hold when Britain first tried to join the EEC?
30 How long is an MEP elected for?

Answers	**Transport** *(see Quiz 30)*

1 The Savannah. 2 Ferdinand Porsche. 3 Rover. 4 Gustave Desiré Liebau. 5 Liverpool to Manchester. 6 117 miles. 7 John Outram. 8 Pack-cloth covered with paper. 9 They are heavier than air. 10 Kitty Hawk. 11 Boeing 247. 12 Major Wilson. 13 I. K. Brunel. 14 The Queen Mary. 15 Daimler-Benz. 16 Henri Giffard. 17 Unterseeboot. 18 First hydraulic suspension system. 19 Edward Tyer. 20 Cornelius Drebbel. 21 E. Benedictus. 22 The Flying Fish. 23 Charles and Frank Duryea. 24 Great Central Railway. 25 Pan Am. 26 Boge. 27 The Orient Express. 28 Alistair Darling. 29 Dr Lanchester. 30 Lisieux, France.

1 When was Prohibition introduced in the United States?
2 Which metal melts at 30 degrees centigrade?
3 Which animals congregate in musters?
4 How many "sisters" make up the Pleiades?
5 Which group of ships was known as the "The First Fleet"?
6 What is the influence of gravity on plants called?
7 What colour is the wine Tokay?
8 Who wrote the novel "Birds without Wings"?
9 In which decade did the Falkland Islands first become a British colony?
10 In which war did the Battle of Isandhlwana take place?
11 In miles, how far from the Earth do meteors usually burn out?
12 Who was the third husband of Jennifer Lopez?
13 When did Green Shield stamps come into use in Britain?
14 In 1803 what did the United States double?
15 Which prison closed on March 21st, 1963?
16 What is an eponym?
17 How is Marie Gresholtz better known today?
18 What is special about the words rose, oven, send, ends?
19 What is the heaviest element in the world?
20 Who founded Eton?
21 How many players were on the field at the end of the 1990 World Cup Final?
22 Which sport was banned in England in 1849?
23 Who scripted, directed and appeared in "The Plank"?
24 In 1997, Bobbi McCaughey of Iowa gave birth to how many children?
25 What is nostology?
26 To five years either way, in which year did London's first airport open?
27 Who is the patron saint of Germany?
28 What type of meat did Prince Charles champion to "get back in its rightful place?
29 On which country did the United States declare war in 1898?
30 Which British university was the first to offer a degree in brewing?

Answers | Pop: Novelty Songs *(see Quiz 35)*

1 A Beatle. 2 Chuck Berry. 3 Bryan Hyland and Bombalurina. 4 Tie Me Kangaroo Down. 5 Julian Clary. 6 It ain't 'Alf Hot Mum. 7 DLT, Paul Burnett. 8 Mike Reid. 9 Liverpool FC. 10 Smear Campaign. 11 Mouldy Old Dough. 12 Napoleon XIV. 13 The Singing Nun. 14 Magic Roundabout. 15 Geordie Boys. 16 The Goons. 17 Lord Rockingham's XI. 18 Peter Sellers, Sophia Loren. 19 Aintree Iron. 20 Ivor Biggun. 21 Roland Rat. 22 7 days. 23 Hale, Pace. 24 Pinky, Perky. 25 Loadsamoney. 26 Splodgenessabounds. 27 Corporal Jones. 28 The Matchroom Mob. 29 1st Atheist Tabernacle Choir. 30 Brand New Key.

Quiz 34 | Speed Kings

Answers – page 510

1 Michael Schumacher won the 2004 F1 title with second place in which race?
2 Which British driver had five British Grand Prix wins during the 1960s?
3 Whom did Barry Sheene ride for when he won his world championships?
4 Who was the second Briton to be World Rally Champion?
5 Who was the only Australian motor racing world champion in the 1960s?
6 Which motor cyclist won 122 world championships?
7 Which driver was runner-up in the world championship in '63, '64 and '65?
8 Which Brazilian was world champion driver in 1972 and 1974?
9 What was the nationality of Mario Andretti?
10 Which driver won the world championship posthumously in 1970?
11 David Jefferies won Isle of Man's Senior TT three out of four years – what stopped him the other year?
12 What is the nationality of Nelson Piquet?
13 How many times did Graham Hill win the Monaco Grand Prix?
14 Which Belgian won Le Mans six times between 1969 and 1982?
15 Who was driving for Ferrari when they became the first manufacturer to have 100 Grand Prix wins?
16 Who was the British driver with most Grand Prix wins before Nigel Mansell?
17 How many times was Ayrton Senna world champion?
18 At which sport did Ivan Maugher win six world titles?
19 Which British motorcyclist won 14 Isle of Man Tourist Trophy titles?
20 Which Briton broke the world land speed record in the US in 1983?
21 What is the nationality of Keke Rosberg?
22 Who was world championship driver in 1964 and motorcycling champion seven times?
23 Who was the first Briton to win the world motor racing championship?
24 What did Brazilian Helio Castroneves win in both 2001 and 2002?
25 Which Briton was world champion in 1976 and retired three years later?
26 Who moved to the Stewart team from Jordan and then to Ferrari in 2000?
27 Who drove the McLaren to its first Grand Prix win in 1968?
28 What was Gilles Villeneuve's home country?
29 Which driver apart from Senna lost his life in the 1994 Formula 1 season?
30 Which Grand Prix did Damon Hill win for the first time in 1994?

Answers	**Pot-Luck 16** *(see Quiz 36)*

1 Lady Campanula Tottington. 2 Sir Christopher Meyer. 3 Noel Coward. 4 Six. 5 Gary Gilmore before his execution. 6 The sea horse. 7 The Phoenician. 8 Ten. 9 The Battle of Culloden in 1746. 10 Nine. 11 The International Red Cross. 12 Grumpy, Sleepy, Happy, Bashful, Sneezy, Dopey, Doc. 13 India. 14 Giant hailstones. 15 Baton Rouge. 16 A kiss. It is mistletoe 17 British Airways. 18 Charlie's Angels. 19 Roy Hattersley. 20 Orion. 21 Queen Victoria. 22 Beetles. 23 New Zealand. 24 Eaton Hall. 25 In 1812, during the Napoleonic Wars. 26 Silver. 27 Earth. 28 See in the dark. 29 Barbed wire. 30 Francis Scott Key.

1 What did Dora Bryan want for Christmas in 1963?

2 Who took his "Ding-a-ling" to No 1?

3 Which two versions of "Itsy Bitsy Teeny Weeny Yellow Polka Dot Bikini" have hit the charts 30 years apart?

4 On which of Rolf Harris's chart hits did we first hear a didgeridoo?

5 Which vocalist called himself the Joan Collins Fan Club?

6 Which TV series did the vocalists on "Whispering Grass" come from?

7 Which DJs were Laurie Lingo and the Dipsticks?

8 Which "EastEnders" star had a hit with "The Ugly Duckling"?

9 Who sang "Red Machine in Full Effect"?

10 Who was Mr Bean's backing group?

11 What are the only words on Lieutenant Pigeon's first No 1?

12 Who sang "They're Coming to Take Me Away Ha-Haaa" in 1966?

13 How was the Belgian Soeur Sourire known in Britain?

14 Which Jasper Carrott single was once banned by the BBC?

15 What was the title of Paul Gascoigne's Gazza Rap?

16 Who was "Walking Backwards for Christmas" in the 1950s?

17 Who got to No 1 in 1958 with "Hoots Mon"?

18 Who argued about "Bangers and Mash" in 1961?

19 What was the first thing Scaffold said "Thank U Very Much" for?

20 Who recorded with the Red Nosed Burglars and the D Cups?

21 Which Superstar recorded "Love Me Tender" nearly 30 years after Elvis Presley?

22 How long did it take Mr Blobby to reach No 1 in December 1993?

23 Who helped the Stonkers get a hit with "The Stonk"?

24 Which duo had a minor hit with "Reet Petite" in 1993?

25 What was the full title of Harry Enfield's 1988 hit?

26 "Two Pints of Lager and a Packet of Crisps Please" was a hit for which band?

27 Which "Dad's Army" character had a No 1 hit?

28 Who accompanied Chas and Dave on "Snooker Loopy"?

29 What was on the other side of Spitting Image's "Santa Claus is on the Dole"?

30 Which song did the Wurzels base their "Combine Harvester" on?

Answers	**Pot-Luck 15** *(see Quiz 33)*

1 1920. 2 Gallium. 3 Peacocks. 4 Seven. 5 Ships transporting the first convicts to Australia in 1788. 6 Geotropism. 7 White. 8 Louis De Bernieres. 9 1830s. 10 The Zulu War of 1879. 11 About 50 miles. 12 Marc Anthony. 13 1958. 14 Its size. 15 Alcatraz. 16 A word formed from a name. 17 Mme Tussaud. 18 They form a word square so the words read the same across and down. 19 Osmium. 20 Henry VI. 21 20. Argentina had two players sent off. 22 Cockfighting. 23 Eric Sykes. 24 Seven. 25 Study of senility. 26 1919. 27 St Boniface. 28 Mutton. 29 Spain. 30 Heriot-Watt.

1 Helena Bonham Carter was the voice of which character in "The Curse of the Were-Rabbit"?
2 Which former US ambassador's memoirs caused controversy in the autumn of 2005?
3 Which playwright told besuited actress Edna Furber that she looked like a man, and was given the reply "So do you"?
4 What was Patrick McGoohan's identity number in "The Prisoner"?
5 Whose last words were, "Let's do it"?
6 Which is the only fish able to hold objects in its tail?
7 From which alphabet did all the Western alphabets originate?
8 How many months were there in the old Roman year?
9 What is generally regarded as the last major battle on British soil?
10 How many sides has a nonagon?
11 Which medical body was set up at the Geneva Convention in 1864?
12 What are the names of all of Snow White's Seven Dwarfs?
13 In which country was "Release Me" singer Engelbert Humperdinck born?
14 In July 1923 what freak weather conditions killed 23 people in Rostov, USSR?
15 What is the state capital of Louisiana?
16 Viscum album provides an excuse for stealing what?
17 What did BOAC and BEA form on their merger?
18 What was the collective name of Sabrina, Jill and Kelly?
19 Who was Deputy Leader of the Labour Party under Neil Kinnock from 1983 to 1992?
20 In which constellation are the stars Bellatrix and Betelgeuse?
21 Who was the first British monarch to live in Buckingham Palace?
22 Which order in the classification of animals has most members?
23 Which country has a wine-producing area centred on Gisborne?
24 What is the Cheshire seat of the Duke of Westminster?
25 When did Britain last go to war against the United States?
26 With which metal is the Iron Cross edged?
27 Which planet lies between Venus and Mars?
28 What does scotopic vision allow you to do?
29 What did Lucien B. Smith first patent in 1867?
30 Who wrote the words of "The Star Spangled Banner"?

Answers	**Speed Kings** *(see Quiz 34)*

1 Belgian. 2 Jim Clark. 3 Suzuki. 4 Richard Burns 5 Jack Brabham. 6 Giacomo Agostini. 7 Graham Hill. 8 Emerson Fittipaldi. 9 American. 10 Jochen Rindt. 11 No race in 2001. 12 Brazilian. 13 Five. 14 Jacky Ickx. 15 Alain Prost. 16 Jackie Stewart. 17 Three. 18 Speedway. 19 Mike Hailwood. 20 Richard Noble. 21 Finnish. 22 John Surtees. 23 Mike Hawthorn. 24 Indianapolis. 25 James Hunt. 26 Rubens Barrichello. 27 Bruce McLaren himself. 28 Canada. 29 Roland Ratzenberger. 30 British.

1 In which part of London did Chaplin spend his early life?
2 What was his elder brother and fellow performer called?
3 What did the troupe, the Eight Lancashire Lads, do?
4 With which company did Chaplin travel to the United States in 1910?
5 For which company did Chaplin make his first films?
6 Who played the title role in "The Kid" in 1921?
7 Which film appeared in 1925 and had sound added in 1942?
8 Which wife of Chaplin co-starred in "Modern Times"?
9 How many times did Chaplin marry altogether?
10 Which was Chaplin's first sound film?
11 Whom did he choose to play the young ballerina in "Limelight"?
12 Which type of sound was heard in "City Lights" in 1931?
13 From which film, for which Chaplin wrote the music, did Petula Clark have a No 1 with "This is My Song"?
14 Which former silent movie star joined Chaplin in "Limelight"?
15 What is odd about Chaplin's comments on his ex-wife, Lita Grey, in his autobiography?
16 Who was Chaplin's last father-in-law?
17 What was his last wife called?
18 Which film distributing company did Chaplin found with D.W. Griffith, Douglas Fairbanks and Mary Pickford?
19 Who bought the company out in 1940?
20 Which of Chaplin's sons starred with him in "A King in New York"?
21 Which was the last film Chaplin made in the United States?
22 In which split-reel film did the Tramp first appear?
23 Which daughter of Chaplin starred in Doctor Zhivago?
24 How did Emil Jannings score over Chaplin in 1929?
25 Where did Chaplin live after being banned from the US in 1953?
26 Which award did Chaplin receive in 1975?
27 What did Chaplin win his Oscar for in "Limelight"?
28 On which day of the year did Chaplin die?
29 What happened on March 2nd the following year?
30 Who played the roles of Chaplin's parents in a 1989 TV series "The Young Chaplin"?

Answers	**Classic Women Writers** *(see Quiz 39)*

1 Clergyman. 2 Pride and Prejudice. 3 Harriet Smith. 4 Sense and Sensibility. 5 Jennifer Ehle. 6 Elizabeth, Anne, Mary. 7 Fanny Price. 8 Northanger Abbey. 9 Emma Thompson. 10 Charlotte. 11 Currer, Ellis and Acton Bell. 12 The Tenant of Wildfell Hall, Agnes Grey. 13 Brussels. 14 Their brother, Patrick Branwell. 15 Nicholls. 16 St John Rivers. 17 Lowood. 18 Villette. 19 Emily. 20 Mrs Gaskell. 21 Liverpool. 22 Isabella. 23 Edgar Linton. 24 George Eliot. 25 Eppie. 26 Middlemarch. 27 Dorlcote. 28 Carpenter. 29 Frankenstein. 30 Elizabeth Barrett Browning.

1 What is an encyclical?
2 Which famous TV cook died in 1994 at the age of 83?
3 What is the Latin name for the apple or fruit in general?
4 Which US city did Charles and Camilla first visit on their first overseas tour?
5 Which Hollywood film studio was founded in 1915 by Carl Laemmle?
6 Whom did the Walrus and the Carpenter invite to walk with them?
7 Where did the old London Bridge move to from the Thames?
8 In which language was the New Testament originally written?
9 Which famous dancer's legs were insured for $650,000?
10 Which Glenn Miller tune did Peter Sellers request for his own funeral?
11 In Roman mythology, who was the husband of Juno?
12 Where does the name Fray Bentos come from in connection with corned beef?
13 Who were the first group to have four consecutive double-sided hits?
14 In 2005 Tom Cruise announced his engagement to which actress?
15 Which Russian ruler imposed a beard tax?
16 What is blennophobia?
17 Which comic actor and writer co-wrote the book "Life and How to Survive It"?
18 Who wrote "The Napoleon of Notting Hill"?
19 Who played Hero in the 2005 BBC adaptation of "Much Ado About Nothing"?
20 What is the smallest breed of dog?
21 For how many months each year does a dormouse hibernate?
22 What were Franklin D. Roosevelt's four freedoms of democracy?
23 How was Alexander the Great's body preserved?
24 On the Chinese calendar which animal represents the year 2000?
25 How many "Monty Python" series were made?
26 The black swan is native to which country?
27 Who invented the game roulette?
28 Where was the wheel clamp first used in Europe?
29 To ten pence, what did the hourly minimum wage for over 21s rise to in 2005 in England?
30 What was the name of the captain of the "Titanic"?

Answers	Pot-Luck 18 *(see Quiz 40)*

1 Maria Friedman. 2 1950s. 3 Greece. 4 The giraffe. 5 A rodent. 6 "...and absolute power corrupts absolutely." 7 Mary Robinson. 8 Faraday. 9 The pigeon. 10 Ipswich players in 70s & 80s team. 11 Bakelite. 12 He designed the lions in Trafalgar Square. 13 The stethoscope. 14 L. S. Lowry. 15 Louis XIV of France (72 years, 110 days). 16 Speed of the film. 17 Shake hands. 18 First person on TV (at J. L. Baird's demonstration). 19 Seventy Two Virgins. 20 Archer fish of India. 21 Aramaic. 22 Richard Eyre. 23 1975. 24 Uncle Tom's Cabin. 25 Japan. 26 Dick Tracy. 27 Jesse Owens. 28 Bora. 29 Natal. 30 Viv Nicholson.

1 What was the occupation of Jane Austen's father?

2 Which Austen novel was originally called "First Impressions"?

3 Whom does Emma take under her wing in the novel of the same name?

4 Which Austen novel was first called "Elinor and Marianne"?

5 Who played Elizabeth Bennet in TV's "Pride and Prejudice" in 1995?

6 Who are Sir Walter Elliot's three daughters in "Persuasion"?

7 In "Mansfield Park" what is the name of the heroine?

8 In which Austen novel do we meet Catherine Morland?

9 Who wrote the screenplay for "Sense and Sensibility"?

10 Of the Brontë sisters that survived to adulthood who was the eldest?

11 Which pseudonyms did the Brontë sisters use when they published a collection of poems in 1846?

12 Which two novels did Anne Brontë write?

13 Where did Charlotte and Emily go to study languages in 1842?

14 Which member of the Brontë family died in the same year as Emily?

15 What was Charlotte's married name?

16 In "Jane Eyre" who cares for Jane after she flees Thornfield Hall?

17 In "Jane Eyre" what is the name of the asylum based on Cowan Bridge where Charlotte Brontë's sisters contracted the consumption from which they died?

18 Which novel by Charlotte reflects her life as a governess abroad?

19 Whom is the character of Shirley Keeldar based on in "Shirley"?

20 Which author of "Cranford" wrote the "Life of Charlotte Brontë" in 1857?

21 In which city does Mr Earnshaw first find Heathcliff?

22 Whom does Heathcliff marry?

23 Whom has Catherine Earnshaw married when Heathcliff returns from his three-year absence?

24 How is Mary Ann Cross better known?

25 Whom does Silas Marner adopt?

26 Which George Eliot novel is subtitled "A Study of Provincial Life"?

27 What is the name of the mill in "Mill on the Floss"?

28 What is the occupation of Adam Bede?

29 What is the title of Mary Wollstonecraft Shelley's "tale of terror"?

30 How is Elizabeth Moulton better known?

Answers | **The Movies: Charlie Chaplin** *(see Quiz 37)*

1 Lambeth. 2 Sydney. 3 Clog dancing. 4 Fred Karno. 5 Keystone. 6 Jackie Coogan. 7 The Gold Rush. 8 Paulette Goddard. 9 Four. 10 The Great Dictator. 11 Claire Bloom. 12 Music. 13 A Countess from Hong Kong. 14 Buster Keaton. 15 He never mentions her. 16 Eugene O'Neill. 17 Oona. 18 United Artists. 19 Sam Goldwyn. 20 Michael. 21 Limelight. 22 Kid Auto Races at Venice. 23 Geraldine. 24 Beat him to the first-ever Oscar. 25 Switzerland. 26 Knighthood. 27 Music score. 28 Christmas Day. 29 Coffin stolen. 30 Ian McShane and Twiggy.

1 Who originally took on the role of Marian Halcombe in "The Woman In White"?
2 In which decade did India go metric?
3 Which country held British plane-spotters on suspicion of spying in 2001?
4 The okapi is a relative of which animal?
5 What type of animal is the tucotucco?
6 Complete Lord Acton's phrase "Power tends to corrupt ... "?
7 Which former Irish President served as UN High Commissioner for Human Rights from 1997 to 2002?
8 Which famous scientist started out as a bookbinder's apprentice?
9 What is the fastest living creature regularly raced for sport?
10 In which trade did a Butcher, a Cooper and a Mariner work together?
11 What did Leo Baekeland invent in 1909?
12 Which animals in London are connected with Edwin Landseer?
13 What did 19th-century French physician René Laënnec develop?
14 Who said, "All the art in the world isn't worth a good potato pie"?
15 Who was the longest-reigning European monarch?
16 What does the DIN number denote in photographic film?
17 In polite society, what does a man do on two legs, a woman sitting down and a dog on three legs?
18 What famous first was achieved by William Tayton?
19 How many virgins feature in the title of a novel by Tory MP Boris Johnson?
20 Which fish "shoots" its food?
21 What language did Jesus speak?
22 Who was replaced as Director of the National Theatre by Trevor Nunn in 1997?
23 To ten years either way, until when were mules part of the British army?
24 In which American novel is there a character called Little Eva?
25 In which county is the Seikan tunnel?
26 Which comic-strip detective was created by Chester Gould?
27 Which athlete set six world records in less than an hour in 1935?
28 What is the name of the violent northwesterly wind that blows over the Adriatic?
29 Which land was first sighted by Vasco da Gama on a Christmas Day?
30 "Spend, spend, spend" was the cry of which winner of the football pools?

Answers | Pot-Luck 17 *(see Quiz 38)*

1 A letter sent by the pope to all Catholic archbishops. 2 Fanny Cradock. 3 Malum. 4 New York. 5 Universal. 6 The oysters. 7 Lake Havasu City, Arizona, United States. 8 Greek. 9 Fred Astaire's. 10 In the Mood. 11 Jupiter. 12 A port on the River Uruguay. 13 UB40. 14 Katie Holmes. 15 Peter the Great. 16 Fear of slime. 17 John Cleese. 18 G. K. Chesterton. 19 Billie Piper. 20 The chihuahua. 21 Six. 22 Of speech, of worship, from want, from fear. 23 It was kept in a large jar of honey. 24 The Dragon. 25 Four. 26 Australia. 27 Blaise Pascal. 28 Paris. 29 £5.05. 30 Edward J. Smith.

1 Which cocktail would you find in a toolbox?
2 What is the best-known type of Hollands called?
3 What is the Russian drink kvass made from?
4 What is Drambuie made from?
5 What spice is used in a whisky sling?
6 What turns gin into a pink gin?
7 What are the traditional ingredients in a daiquiri?
8 What is added to brandy to make a sidecar?
9 What is the principal spirit in a Harvey Wallbanger?
10 What is a cocktail of rye whisky, vermouth and angostura called?
11 What is the brandy Birngeist made from?
12 Which drink was Prince Charles caught ordering while at Gordonstoun?
13 If a cocktail is served "in a mist", how is it served?
14 What is a dry Manhattan called?
15 What is the fruit in an old-fashioned?
16 What makes a whisky a whisky sour?
17 What are the two main ingredients of a cuba libre?
18 Which former prime minister do you get if you mix cinzano, apricot brandy and angostura bitters?
19 What savoury ingredient do you include in a Sputnik?
20 What does an Alexandra taste of?
21 Which card game is a mix of cinzano bianco, gin and maraschino?
22 What do you add to champagne to make a champagne flip?
23 What type of plant is tequila made from?
24 Which distillery was the first to conform to the licensing laws which made other stills illegal in 1823?
25 With which US state is bourbon most associated?
26 What is the apple brandy of Normandy called?
27 Where is the original home of bacardi?
28 What is slivovitz made from?
29 What sort of drink is Barbancourt?
30 Where is the Talisker whisky distillery?

Answers	Sport: Rugby (see Quiz 43)

1 Seddon drowned in Australia. 2 J. P .R. Williams. 3 20 teams. 4 Zimbabwe. 5 Lawrence Dallaglio. 6 Toulouse. 7 Cardiff. 8 80 points. 9 New Zealand. 10 England. 11 Leicester. 12 Gavin Hastings. 13 M. J. K. Smith. 14 21times. 15 Bill Beaumont. 16 Currie Cup. 17 Peter Phillips (Princess Anne's son). 18 Australia. 19 Brisbane. 20 Auckland Warriors. 21 World Cup semi-final 2003. 22 Argentina. 23 Gareth Edwards. 24 Michael Dods. 25 Ranfurly Shield. 26 Devon. 27 England (1991). 28 Georgia. 29 1995 World Cup semi-final v England. 30 Small volcanic island.

1 What is the Duke of Argyll's stately home called?
2 In 2005 Max Egremont published a biography about which WWI poet?
3 Which spice comes from the crocus?
4 Who was the first person to sail single-handed non-stop around the world?
5 Which star is situated almost exactly above the North Pole?
6 What sort of creature is a tarantula hawk?
7 From which flower is digitalis obtained?
8 Whom did Harry Secombe play in the musical film "Oliver"?
9 Peter and Edmund were the boys, but which girls visited Narnia?
10 Which soccer club did Boris Becker have trials with?
11 Which single letter made the difference between two album titles of Robbie Williams?
12 Where was the world's first lighthouse, built of white marble?
13 Which politician shared the 1998 Nobel Peace Prize along with David Trimble?
14 In music what key is a piece written in if it has five flats?
15 Which tree has English, white and slippery varieties?
16 Which English county is known as the "county of sunsets"?
17 Which psychiatrist wrote "Bird of Paradise"?
18 Which artist includes "Away from the Flock" and "Mother and Child Divided" in his works?
19 Which politician had a dog called Pushinka?
20 Who in 1982 went topless at the England v Australia rugby game?
21 Which church leader had 27 wives?
22 Which opera star became Artistic Director of the Los Angeles Opera in 2000?
23 Who invented the first safety match?
24 What is the dog on "the Tweenies" called?
25 Which English queen banned mirrors as she grew old?
26 Which was the first stately home to open to the public?
27 When were driving tests first introduced in Britain?
28 Who was created by Mary Tourtel?
29 In Greek mythology which gift was given to Cassandra by Apollo?
30 Where would you find the vox humana and vox angelica together?

Answers	Modern History: Dictators *(see Quiz 44)*

1 Austria. 2 Art school. 3 Trying to overthrow the Bavarian government. 4 Night of the Long Knives. 5 Colonel Stauffenberg. 6 Axis. 7 Italian resistance. 8 Tonton Macoute. 9 First Consul. 10 Elba. 11 Generalissimo. 12 Man of steel. 13 National Movement. 14 1939. 15 Ferdinand Marcos. 16 Benigno Aquino. 17 Leopoldo Galtieri. 18 Very Mighty Ruler. 19 13. 20 Mao Tse Tung. 21 1979. 22 Born the same year. 23 General Zia. 24 Ceausescu. 25 Nicholas II. 26 Ho Chi Minh. 27 Pol Pot. 28 Tito. 29 Gaddafi. 30 Suharto.

Quiz 43 | Sport: Rugby

Answers – page 515

LEVEL 3

1 Why did A. E. Stoddart take over from R. L. Seddon as captain on the Lions' first tour of Australia and New Zealand?
2 Which rugby international won junior Wimbledon in 1966?
3 How many teams took part in the 2003 World Cup?
4 Which African side was invited to the Rugby Union World Cup in 1987?
5 Who was the only player involved in every minute of his side's games in the 2003 World Cup?
6 Who were the first French side to win the Heineken/European Cup twice?
7 For which club did fly half turned broadcaster Cliff Morgan play?
8 England scored a record how many points in February 2001?
9 Where was the first Rugby Union World Cup held?
10 Whom did Russian Prince Obolensky play for in 1936?
11 Which Union club first won the John Player Cup three years in a row?
12 Who kicked six penalty goals for Scotland on his debut in 1986?
13 Which England cricket captain was capped for England at rugby?
14 To two each way, how many times did Clive Woodward play for England?
15 Who preceded Steve Sale as England captain?
16 What is South Africa's inter-provincial tournament called?
17 Which member of the royal family played in a rugby international?
18 In which country do Randwick play?
19 In which city did England play Wales in the 2003 World Cup quarter-final?
20 Which team did Andy Platt and Dean Bell join after leaving Wigan?
21 In which big game did Jason Leonard establish himself as the world's most capped player?
22 Which country did Hugo Porta play for?
23 Who won 53 caps without missing a single game?
24 Who scored all Scotland's 19 points against France in 1996?
25 What is New Zealand's inter-provincial championship called?
26 Which County Champions this century had to go back to 1957 for their last championship?
27 Before 2003, who were the last hosts to be World Cup runners up?
28 In 2003's World Cup Richard Hill was injured against which team?
29 Which match was Jonathan Davies' last game of League for Wales?
30 What did New Zealanders suggest should be named after Jonah Lomu following the Rugby World Cup?

Answers	Spirits and Cocktails *(see Quiz 41)*

1 Screwdriver. 2 Schnapps. 3 Rye. 4 Scotch whisky and heather honey. 5 Nutmeg. 6 Angostura bitters. 7 Bacardi and lime juice. 8 Cointreau. 9 Vodka. 10 Manhattan. 11 Pears. 12 Cherry brandy. 13 On crushed ice. 14 Bronx. 15 Cherries. 16 Orange and lemon. 17 Rum and coca cola. 18 Mr Callaghan. 19 Cocktail onion. 20 Chocolate. 21 Canasta. 22 Egg yolk. 23 Cactus. 24 Glenlivet. 25 Kentucky. 26 Calvados. 27 Cuba. 28 Plums. 29 Rum. 30 Isle of Skye.

1 In which country was Hitler born?
2 What type of school did he attend in Munich?
3 Why was Hitler imprisoned in 1923?
4 What name was given to the occasion in 1934 when Hitler had members of his own party murdered by the SS?
5 Who tried to assassinate Hitler in 1944?
6 What name was given to the link between Hitler's Germany and Mussolini's Italy?
7 Which organization executed Mussolini?
8 Which civilian militia was established under Papa Doc Duvalier?
9 Which title did Napoleon take in 1799, instituting a military dictatorship?
10 What was Napoleon given sovereignty over after his abdication in 1814?
11 What title did Stalin assume when he became war leader?
12 What does the word "Stalin" mean?
13 What was Spain's only legal party after the Civil War?
14 When did Franco become absolute leader of Spain?
15 Who declared martial law in 1972 in the Philippines?
16 Which opposition leader in the Philippines was murdered in 1983?
17 Who was the leader of Argentina at the beginning of the Falklands War?
18 What does the name Genghis Khan mean?
19 How old was Ghenghis Khan when he succeeded his father?
20 Which leader launched his "Great Leap Forward" in 1958?
21 When did Saddam Hussein become president of Iraq?
22 Chaplin played a Hitler-like figure in "The Great Dictator" but what else did they have in common?
23 Which leader sanctioned the execution of President Bhutto in 1979?
24 Which Romanian leader was shot with his wife at Christmas 1989?
25 Who was the last tsar of Russia?
26 Which Vietnamese leader had a city named after him?
27 Who was the leader of the Khmer Rouge?
28 Which Communist leader's real name was Josip Broz?
29 Who overthrew King Idris to gain power in 1971?
30 Which Indonesian president was responsible for the invasion of East Timor in 1975?

Answers	Pot-Luck 19 (see Quiz 42)

1 Inveraray Castle. 2 Siegfried Sassoon. 3 Saffron. 4 Robin Knox-Johnston. 5 Polaris or the Pole Star. 6 A wasp. (It hunts spiders.) 7 Foxglove. 8 Mr Bumble. 9 Susan and Lucy. 10 Bayern Munich. 11 W (Sing/Swing When You're Winning). 12 Pharos. 13 John Hume. 14 D flat. 15 Elm. 16 Lincolnshire. 17 R. D. Laing. 18 Damien Hirst. 19 John F. Kennedy. 20 Erica Roe. 21 Brigham Young of the Mormons. 22 Placido Domingo. 23 Johan Edvard Lundstrom. 24 Doodles. 25 Queen Elizabeth I. 26 Wilton House, near Salisbury. 27 1935. 28 Rupert Bear. 29 The gift of prophecy. 30 On an organ. They are stops.

1 In which cathedral were the first Anglican women in Britain ordained?
2 What is the name of Jewish New Year?
3 Which Cardinal, who later became Pope, led the opening prayer at John Paul II's funeral?
4 Who was Canada's first prime minister?
5 What were the first words spoken on a film soundtrack?
6 Which film won more Oscars than any other movie?
7 Who provided the voice for Woody Woodpecker?
8 W. C. T. Dobson is credited in the 1840s with sending the first what?
9 Which female politician wrote a novel titled "The Clematis Tree"?
10 Which conductor said, "The English may not like music but they absolutely love the noise it makes"?
11 Which creature lost its tail in the doors of Noah's ark?
12 "In Utmost Good Faith" is the motto of which organization?
13 What is the devil's coach horse?
14 Who succeeded Laurence Olivier as director of the National Theatre?
15 How old was Bill Gates when he co founded Microsoft?
16 Who was the voice of Princess Fiona in "Shrek 2"?
17 Which Beautiful South song begins, "He was just a social drinker..."
18 What was the first book printed from movable type in 1456?
19 What is the Pentateuch?
20 How many teeth does a mature male horse have?
21 By what name is the marsupial Sarcophilus harrisi better known?
22 What was produced by Henry D. Perky of Denver, Colorado, in 1893?
23 What is the colour of lobsters' blood?
24 The Greek for a "circle of animals" gave its name to what?
25 What is the largest and heaviest satellite in the solar system?
26 Which No 1 single included the bracketed words "In Perfect Harmony"?
27 Who invented the first replaceable razor blade?
28 What kind of lights were first used in 1868 near Parliament Square?
29 Where was the world's first cast-iron bridge built?
30 Horatio Nelson lost his right eye in 1794 at Calvi during the French Revolutionary War. When and where did he lose his right arm?

Answers	Pot-Luck 21 *(see Quiz 47)*

1 Anne Boleyn. 2 Scout. 3 Albert Einstein. 4 £12. 5 Wales. 6 A ray. 7 1964. 8 Abdullah. 9 1856. 10 Winston Churchill (about Stafford Cripps). 11 24. 12 Elias. 13 All anagrams of animals. 14 The chinook. 15 Nick Hornby. 16 The Outlaws (in Richmal Crompton's books). 17 1965. 18 Tribophysics. 19 A labour. 20 Helium. 21 Francis II of France. 22 A reticulated python. 23 Gunner Parkin. 24 The Duke of Beaufort. 25 In 1842, after the First Opium War. 26 John Arbuthnot. 27 The Dog Star. 28 Tilda Swinton. 29 Richard Ingrams. 30 Tom Morris.

1 The Shadows' first record went to No 1 – what was it?
2 Who left the Shadows and recorded "Diamonds" on their own?
3 Whose first hit was "Lonely Bull" and then went on to be one of the most successful instrumentalists of all time?
4 What was Perez Prado's 1994/5 hit?
5 Which new record label was "Tubular Bells" recorded on?
6 Whose album was "Oxygène"?
7 Who won an Oscar for the music from "Chariots of Fire"?
8 Where and at what time was Kenny Ball chartwise in 1961?
9 Which film theme was a chart No 1 for the Hugo Montenegro Orchestra?
10 In 1994 which group had a No 1 with a record with the same name as themselves ?
11 Which military band had a hit with "Amazing Grace"?
12 Which clarinettist had an early 1960s hit with the theme for a TV serial?
13 Who recorded "Walk – Don't Run"?
14 Which instrument does Sandy Nelson play?
15 Which guitarist's real name is Brian Robson Rankin?
16 Which pianist's reply to criticism was "I cried all the way to the bank."?
17 Who recorded "Let's Have a Party" and "Let's Have Another Party"?
18 The theme from which TV serial gave Juan Martin a Top Ten hit?
19 Who was the leader of Manuel and his Music of the Mountains?
20 Who had a hit with "The Hustle"?
21 Which Vivaldi concertos were popularized by Nigel Kennedy?
22 Who had No 1s with "Side Saddle" and "Roulette"?
23 What was the title of the pieces on a theme by Paganini recorded by Julian Lloyd Webber?
24 Which instrument is Horst Jankowski playing in his "Walk in the Black Forest"?
25 Which group included Tristan Fry, Herbie Flowers and Kevin Peek?
26 Whose "March" took Joe Loss into the charts in 1964?
27 Which 1950s star was known as Mr Piano?
28 Who joined James Last on the recording "Together at Last"?
29 From which TV series did Jan Hammer's "Crockett's Theme" come?
30 Which guitarist had a hit with the theme from "The Deer Hunter"?

Answers | Geography: The Weather *(see Quiz 48)*

1 Egypt. 2 Boscastle. 3 Solstice. 4 Cumbria. 5 Cold front. 6 Fastnet. 7 Rockies. 8 Katrina. 9 Cirrus. 10 Mirage, Strait of Messina, Italy. 11 Doldrums. 12 Dry, warm, blowing down a mountain. 13 Alaska (wind). 14 Grey. 15 Russian wind. 16 Occluded front. 17 Typhoon. 18 Spain. 19 German Bight. 20 South Africa. 21 12. 22 Iran and Afghanistan. 23 Sirocco. 24 Rhône. 25 Australia. 26 Isobars. 27 Eye of the storm. 28 Sandstorm. 29 Excessive dust, e.g. after a volcanic eruption. 30 Andes.

1 Which queen of England had 11 fingers?

2 In "The Lone Ranger" what was the name of Tonto's horse?

3 Which world-famous scientist said that any man who likes marching had been given a brain for nothing: just the spinal column would have done?

4 To £5 either way, how much did a colour TV licence cost in 1974?

5 Former Tory Party leader Michael Howard was born in which country?

6 What type of fish is a torpedo fish?

7 In which year was Nelson Mandela sentenced to life imprisonment?

8 Who followed Hussein as King of Jordan?

9 To ten years either way, when was the Victoria Cross instituted?

10 Who said, "There but for the Grace of God, goes God"?

11 Into how many international time zones is the world divided?

12 What was Walt Disney's middle name?

13 What is the link between the words act, flow, loin and shore?

14 In the Rocky Mountains what is the dry wind that is warm in winter and cool in summer?

15 Published in 2001, which male novelist writes as a first-person female narrator in "How to be Good"?

16 Which group were made up of Douglas, Ginger, Henry and William?

17 When did Rhodesia declare UDI?

18 What is the physics of friction properly called?

19 What is the collective noun for several moles?

20 What does hydrogen fuse into in the Sun's core?

21 Who was Mary Queen of Scots' first husband?

22 What is the longest snake in the world?

23 Which character gave the name to the series "It ain't Half Hot Mum"?

24 Which duke owns Badminton, setting for the well-known horse trials?

25 To ten years, when did Hong Kong become a British crown colony?

26 Who invented the caricature John Bull?

27 How else is the star Sirius known?

28 Who played the White Witch in the 2005 movie version of "The Lion, The Witch and the Wardrobe"?

29 Who became editor of "The Oldie" magazine in 1992?

30 Who won the first British Open Golf Championship?

Answers	Pot-Luck 20 *(see Quiz 45)*

1 Bristol. 2 Yom Kippur. 3 Cardinal Ratzinger. 4 Sir John MacDonald. 5 You ain't seen nothing yet. 6 Ben Hur (11). 7 Mel Blanc. 8 Christmas Card. 9 Ann Widdecombe. 10 Sir Thomas Beecham. 11 Manx cat. 12 Lloyd's of London . 13 A beetle. 14 Peter Hall. 15 19. 16 Cameron Diaz. 17 The Woman in the Wall. 18 The Mazarin Bible. 19 First five books of the Bible. 20 40. 21 Tasmanian devil. 22 Shredded wheat. 23 Pale blue. 24 Zodiac. 25 Ganymede. 26 I'd Like to Teach the World to Sing. 27 King Camp Gillette. 28 Traffic lights. 29 Coalbrookdale in England, 1779. 30 1797 at the Battle of Cape St Vincent.

1 Which country has the driest inhabited area in the world?
2 Which Cornish village suffered a freak flood in the summer of 2004?
3 What name is given to an occasion when the equator is furthest from the Sun?
4 Which county is England's wettest?
5 Which usually travels faster, a cold front or a warm front?
6 Which sea area is immediately to the south of Ireland?
7 Over which mountains does the chinook blow?
8 Which 1990s Eurovision Song Contest winner shares her name with a devastating hurricane?
9 The name of which type of cloud is Latin for a lock of hair?
10 What is Fata Morgana and where would you see it?
11 What is the belt of light variable winds near the equator called?
12 What sort of wind is föhn wind?
13 Where would you experience a williwaw?
14 What colour are altostratus clouds?
15 What is the buran?
16 What is the name of a front where a cold front has overtaken a warm front?
17 What is a hurricane called in the Pacific?
18 Where is the tramontana?
19 Which sea area lies due east of Dogger and Humber?
20 Where does the berg wind blow?
21 What number does the Beaufort scale go up to in international use?
22 In which two countries does the Seistan sand wind blow?
23 What is the hot, dry North African wind which blows from the Sahara called?
24 Down which valley does the mistral blow?
25 Where would you experience a southerly buster?
26 What are lines joining places of equal atmospheric pressure called?
27 What is the centre of a hurricane called?
28 What does a haboob create?
29 What causes a blue moon?
30 Over which mountains does the pampero blow?

Answers	Pop: Instrumentals *(see Quiz 46)*

1 Apache. 2 Jet Harris and Tony Meehan. 3 Herb Alpert. 4 Guaglione. 5 Virgin. 6 Jean-Michel Jarre. 7 Vangelis. 8 Midnight in Moscow. 9 The Good, the Bad and the Ugly. 10 Doop. 11 Royal Scots Dragoon Guards. 12 Acker Bilk (Stranger on the Shore). 13 The Ventures. 14 Drums. 15 Hank B. Marvin. 16 Liberace. 17 Winnifred Atwell. 18 The Thorn Birds. 19 Geoff Love. 20 Van McCoy. 21 The Four Seasons. 22 Russ Conway. 23 Variations. 24 Piano. 25 Sky. 26 March of the Mods. 27 Joe Henderson. 28 Richard Clayderman. 29 Miami Vice. 30 John Williams.

1 In the autumn of 2005 which major US civil rights activist died?
2 Under what name did William White find fame on TV?
3 Difford and Tilbrook were songwriters for which group?
4 Who was Mussolini's mistress, who was executed with him?
5 What are the four groups that make up the ape family?
6 According to Lord Birkenhead, who devoted the best years of his life to preparing impromptu speeches?
7 Which creature is involved in the French equivalent of an April Fool?
8 Who was the first musician to be made a life peer?
9 What is the deepest lake in the world?
10 What is a male swan called?
11 Who said, "Genius is 1 per cent inspiration and 99 per cent perspiration"?
12 Which was the first country to make seat belts compulsory?
13 Who created and provided the voice of Basil Brush?
14 To ten years either way, when did Britain launch its first submarine?
15 In which country was Princess Margaret born?
16 In which decade did Pablo Picasso die?
17 Who said, "For years politicians have promised the moon. I am the first one to be able to deliver it"?
18 Who was FIFA world player of the year in both 1998 and 2000?
19 Which former politician published a biography of Winston Churchill in 2001?
20 What does the whale shark feed on?
21 Who left a fortune in his will to develop a new phonetic alphabet?
22 Who became the first female to win five track and field medals at the same Olympics?
23 Who was the first king to award medals to his troops for bravery?
24 Who wrote "Bambi"?
25 Where in China is the Forbidden City?
26 Who drew the cartoon comic-strip character Andy Capp?
27 Whose autobiography was called "Black, White and Gold"?
28 Who said of his troops, "I don't know what effect these men will have upon the enemy but, by God, they terrify me"?
29 What is nephology?
30 Henry III put three barleycorns in a line to make which measurement?

| **Answers** | Pot-Luck 23 *(see Quiz 51)* |

1 The trapdoor failed to open. 2 Trinity College, Dublin. 3 Hilary Spurling. 4 Peru. 5 Edinburgh Festival. 6 Paul Merton. 7 David Blunkett. 8 Frankie Laine. 9 Ross Perot. 10 Robert Ford. 11 Dawn French. 12 L.A. Law. 13 They both begin with the word "midnight". 14 18. 15 Miss Saigon. 16 Putrid pot. 17 Orange. 18 Lord Northcliffe. 19 Captain Blood. 20 Ruth Ellis. 21 1950s. 22 Attempting to swim the rapids at Niagara Falls. 23 Reginald Perrin. 24 25th January. 25 Peace. 26 The Humblebums. 27 July 29th, 1981. 28 Claire Rayner. 29 Paolo Wanchope. 30 Netherlands.

1 Which country won the first Eurovision song contest in 1956?
2 Which Austrian sang "Rock Me Amadeus" in 1986?
3 Who sang the song called "Volver a Empezar" in his own language?
4 Who was runner-up to Ireland's Linda Martin in the 1992 Eurovision?
5 From which countries were Enigma, who had a No 1 with "Sadness"?
6 "Raindrops Keep Falling on My Head" is Sacha Distel's only chart entry, but how many times did it do so?
7 Who was the first person to win Eurovision for Britain?
8 Whose first UK chart hit was "Joe Le Taxi"?
9 Which two songs has Cliff Richard sung in Eurovision?
10 What are the first names of Russian duo t.A.T.u.?
11 Which country came last in the 2005 Eurovision Song Contest?
12 "Young Parisians" was a hit for which UK band?
13 Which country won Eurovision with "A-Ba-Ni-Bi" and "Hallelujah"?
14 Who were the only UK Eurovision winners in the 1980s?
15 What was Nicole's "Ein bisschen Frieden" in English?
16 What is A-Ha's home country?
17 When Abba won Eurovision with "Waterloo" who represented Britain?
18 Who had a No 1 in 1981 with "Computer Love"?
19 In which year were there four Eurovision winners tying for first place?
20 What was Gigliola Cinquetti's 1974 hit whose second line was "Before you break my heart"?
21 Where do Clubhouse hail from, who had hits with "Do It Again – Billie Jean" and "Light My Fire"?
22 Which artist was the first to win Eurovision twice?
23 What was the New Seekers' 1972 Eurovision entry?
24 Which "Opportunity Knocks" winner represented Britain on Eurovision?
25 What nationality were Nina and Frederick who had a 1960 hit with "Little Donkey"?
26 Who was the first person to win Eurovision for Ireland?
27 What was the title of DJ Jurgen's one and only top ten hit?
28 For which event did Helmut Zacharias have a Melody hit in 1964?
29 Who won Eurovision for Britain in 1976?
30 The duo who had a hit "Take Your Shoes Off" came from which country?

Answers	**Sport: Tennis** *(see Quiz 52)*

1 Olga Morozova. **2** The Queen. **3** Pancho Gonzales and Charlie Pasarell. **4** Eight games all. **5** Jean Borotra. **6** Elena Dementieva. **7** Peter Fleming. **8** Roger Taylor. **9** Five. **10** Australian. **11** Arnaud Clement. **12** Kevin Curren. **13** Seventh. **14** Andrea Jaeger. **15** Daniela Hantuchova and Leos Friedl. **16** It was televised. **17** Donald Budge. **18** Rod Laver. **19** Jaroslav Drobny. **20** Steffi Graf. **21** 1968. **22** Margaret Court, Maureen Connolly. **23** Wear white flannels instead of shorts. **24** Boris Becker. **25** George VI (1926). **26** Twenty-five. **27** John and Tracy Austin. **28** MCC. **29** Manuel Santana. **30** Chuck McKinley.

1 In 1885, after being sentenced to death by hanging, how did John Lee survive three attempts by the hangman?
2 Where is the Book of Kells?
3 Who won the Whitbread Prize for her biography of Matisse.
4 Which country did Paddington bear come from?
5 Which festival was founded in 1947 and run by Rudolf Bing?
6 Which entertainer started life as Paul Martin?
7 In 2005 which high profile MP described the disability benefits system as "Crackers!"?
8 Who was the first performer to have British No 1 hits?
9 Which billionaire ran as an independent for the US Presidency in both 1992 and 1996?
10 Who shot Jesse James?
11 Which comedy actress founded the fashion label Sixteen47?
12 Which series featured the firm McKenzie, Brackman, Chaney and Kusak?
13 What is the lyrical link between "Memory" and "Green Door"?
14 How many French kings were named Louis?
15 Which musical on Broadway won Jonathan Pryce his first Tony award?
16 What is the exact translation of "potpourri"?
17 What flavour does the liqueur curaçao have?
18 Which legendary pressman said, "News is something that someone somewhere doesn't want to see printed"?
19 Which film first established Errol Flynn's fame as a swashbuckling actor?
20 Who was the last woman to be hanged in Britain?
21 In which decade did Disneyland open in California?
22 How did English Channel swimmer Matthew Webb die?
23 Joan Greengross was secretary to which fictional salesman?
24 When is Burns' Night?
25 In Greek mythology, what was Irene the goddess of?
26 Billy Connolly was a member of which group?
27 On what date was Prince Charles married to Lady Diana Spencer?
28 Which former nurse turned broadcaster writes in medical journals under the name of Ann Lynton?
29 Which all-time top scorer for Costa Rica has played club soccer in England?
30 In which country did the sport of speed skating originate?

Answers | Pot-Luck 22 (see Quiz 49)

1 Rosa Parks. 2 Larry Grayson. 3 Squeeze. 4 Claretta Petacci. 5 Chimpanzees, gorillas, gibbons and orang-utans. 6 Winston Churchill. 7 Fish. 8 Benjamin Britten. 9 Lake Baikal. 10 A cob. 11 Thomas Edison. 12 Czechoslovakia. 13 Ivan Owen. 14 1901. 15 Scotland. 16 1973. 17 Richard Nixon. 18 Zinedine Zidane. 19 Roy Jenkins. 20 Plankton. 21 George Bernard Shaw. 22 Marion Jones. 23 Charles I, in 1643. 24 Felix Salten. 25 Beijing. 26 Reg Smythe. 27 Kelly Holmes. 28 The Duke of Wellington. 29 Meteorological study of clouds. 30 Inch.

1 Whom did Chris Evert beat to win her first Wimbledon Singles title?
2 Who presented Virginia Wade with her Wimbledon trophy in 1977?
3 Who contested Wimbledon's longest-ever match?
4 At what score was the tie break used when it was first introduced at Wimbledon in 1971?
5 Which player was known as the "Bounding Basque"?
6 Who was runner-up in the 2004 Women's US Open Final?
7 With which doubles partner did John McEnroe have most success?
8 Which British man got to three Wimbledon semi-finals in the 60s and 70s?
9 Between 2000 and 2005 how many different players reached the women's final at Wimbledon?
10 What nationality did Hana Mandlikova take after leaving Czechoslovakia?
11 Whom did Andre Agassi beat to win the 2001 Australian Open final?
12 Whom did Becker beat to become the youngest Wimbledon champion?
13 What seed was 2005 Australian Open champion Serena Williams?
14 Who was the first player Martina Navratilova beat to win Wimbledon after her first three victories over Chris Evert ?
15 Which pair won the 2001 Mixed Doubles at Wimbledon?
16 What "first" happened at Wimbledon in 1937?
17 Who was the first player to win the Grand Slam?
18 Who was tennis's first millionaire?
19 Which exiled Czech beat Ken Rosewall at Wimbledon in 1954?
20 Who played her first professional match against Tracy Austin in 1982?
21 In which year did Wimbledon go open?
22 Who were the only two women to win Grand Slams before Steffi Graf?
23 What is Yvon Petra famous for being the last man to do?
24 Who said on losing his title in the second round at Wimbledon, "I lost a tennis match, not a war. Nobody got killed"?
25 Which future king played a doubles match at Wimbledon?
26 How many games did Rafael Nadal win in the 2005 French Open final?
27 Who were the first siblings to win the Wimbledon Mixed Doubles?
28 Whom did the LTA take over from in the management of tennis?
29 Which 1966 Wimbledon winner lost in 1967's first round?
30 Who was the only American to win the Men's Singles at Wimbledon in the 60s?

Answers | Pop: Euro Rockers *(see Quiz 50)*

1 Switzerland. 2 Falco. 3 Julio Iglesias (Begin the Beguine). 4 Michael Ball. 5 Germany and Romania. 6 Five. 7 Sandie Shaw. 8 Vanessa Paradis. 9 Congratulations, Power to All Our Friends. 10 Julia and Lena. 11 Germany. 12 Adam and the Ants. 13 Israel. 14 Bucks Fizz. 15 A Little Peace. 16 Norway. 17 Olivia Newton-John. 18 Kraftwerk. 19 1969. 20 Go. 21 Italy. 22 Johnny Logan. 23 Beg, Steal or Borrow. 24 Mary Hopkin. 25 Danish. 26 Dana. 27 Better Off Alone. 28 Tokyo Olympics. 29 Brotherhood of Man. 30 Romania.

1 Whom did Peeping Tom see naked?
2 Which author claimed the Man Booker Prize in 2005?
3 Who directed "The Seven Samurai"?
4 In which country was backpacker Peter Falconio murdered?
5 In Ancient Egypt what kind of bird is represented by Horus?
6 Which common water pollutant is believed to be harmful to babies?
7 What is the function of the Islets of Langerhans?
8 Which is the largest species of flatfish?
9 Where on the Pacific coast does the Trans-Siberian railway terminate?
10 Who designed the city of New Delhi?
11 Which new policy in 1958 was an attempt to achieve "true communism" in China?
12 Which element is the most toxic substance known?
13 Which philosopher invented "the Superman"?
14 Which singer is responsible for the Faenol Festival?
15 How did the suffragette Emily Davison meet her death in 1913?
16 What was the codename of the US development of the atom bomb?
17 Which planet has the Great Red Spot?
18 Lully was composer at the court of which king?
19 What do the French call the English Channel?
20 The classic text about which sport was written by Izaak Walton in 1653?
21 Brazilian Oscar Niemeyer followed which profession?
22 What is the link between saying "Madam, I'm Adam" and "Ma, I am"?
23 What did Thomas Blood try to steal in London in 1671?
24 What is the name of the southern lights?
25 What element gives amethyst its violet colour?
26 Which Bowie song includes the line: "The shrieking of nothing is killing me"?
27 Which former MP wrote "Charles and Camilla, Portrait of an Affair"?
28 Which technique developed by the painter Seurat uses small dabs of colour laid side by side?
29 At which fictional school is there a Ravenclaw House?
30 Which month is named after a two-faced god?

Answers	Pot-Luck 25 *(see Quiz 55)*

1 Marco Polo. 2 Once. 3 Ruth Kelly. 4 Robert Frost. 5 Ronnie Barker. 6 Auguste and Louis Lumière. 7 The Birth of a Nation. 8 Anther. 9 Four. 10 Jeremy Irons. 11 Telemetry. 12 Minoan. 13 1986. 14 IMF – The International Monetary Fund. 15 In a flying accident. 16 American Civil War. 17 Académie Française. 18 Jingles. 19 Jean Baptiste de Lamarck. 20 Madame Butterfly. 21 Lebanon. 22 The end of the watch. 23 Order of the Purple Heart. 24 Whitby. 25 None. 26 Unchained Melody. 27 Vienna. 28 Boulder Dam. 29 Karen Blixen. 30 Hendrik Verwoerd.

1 What was Sinatra's middle name?
2 What are his children called?
3 What was Sinatra's own record label, founded in 1961, called?
4 Who was Sinatra's most frequent arranger in the 1940s?
5 For which film did Sinatra win an Oscar in 1953?
6 Which character in "The Godfather" is said to be based on Sinatra?
7 Which famous Sinatra song was the first to become a hit after being featured in a TV show?
8 Where was Sinatra born on 12 December 1915?
9 Which Sinatra hit was also a hit in Britain for Matt Monro?
10 What was Sinatra's big 1966 hit – a No 1 in 13 countries?
11 Who was Sinatra's second wife?
12 What was Sinatra's first No 1 in Britain?
13 What was the English version of "Comme d'Habitude"?
14 Which album did he release three years after announcing his retirement?
15 Which song did Sinatra sing in "Robin and the Seven Hoods"?
16 In which musical did he co-star with Gene Kelly?
17 From which musical does "The Lady is a Tramp" come and whom did Sinatra sing it to in the film?
18 With which French singer did Sinatra duet in "Duets" in 1993?
19 Who was his male co-star in "Guys and Dolls"?
20 In which film did Sinatra co-star with Laurence Harvey, Janet Leigh and Angela Lansbury ?
21 Who sang with Sinatra on "Me and My Shadow"?
22 Which No 1 did Sinatra have with his elder daughter?
23 Which song won Sinatra a Grammy in 1965?
24 Who was Sinatra's third wife?
25 Which US cities feature in two of Sinatra's hit singles titles?
26 In which film did Sinatra sing the song with the lines "Have you heard, it's in the stars, next July we collide with Mars"?
27 Who was Sinatra's fourth wife, Barbara, previously married to?
28 In which year did Frank face his final curtain?
29 In which year did "My Way" first hit the UK charts?
30 With whom did he duet on his final top ten single during his own life time?

Answers	**American Literature** (see Quiz 56)

1 Spanish Civil War. 2 Henry James. 3 Edward Albee. 4 Death of a Salesman. 5 Billy Budd. 6 China. 7 Isaac Asimov. 8 F. Scott Fitzgerald. 9 James Fenimore Cooper. 10 Ambulance driver. 11 England. 12 Philip Marlowe. 13 Dashiel Hammett. 14 Catcher in the Rye. 15 The Armies of the Night. 16 John Steinbeck. 17 Eugene O'Neill. 18 Cuba. 19 The Wonderful Wizard of Oz. 20 Sylvia Plath. 21 The Crucible. 22 The Misfits. 23 Lillian Hellman. 24 Ezra Pound. 25 Mark Twain. 26 Gertrude Stein. 27 Cat on a Hot Tin Roof. 28 Washington Irving. 29 Travel. 30 Harold Robbins.

1 Which explorer's last words were, "I have not told half of what I saw"?
2 How many times was David Beckham sent off when playing for Man Utd?
3 Who was Education Minister at the time of the 2005 Labour Party Conference?
4 Who read "The Gift Outright" at President Kennedy's inauguration?
5 The British Comedy Awards have a Writer of the Year award named after which comic?
6 Which French brothers patented their cinematograph in 1895?
7 What is Griffith's film about the aftermath of the Civil War called?
8 What is the name of the body at the tip of a stamen?
9 How many pecks are there in a bushel?
10 Which actor links the films "Being Julia", "The Lion King" and "Kingdom of Heaven"?
11 What is the name given to the technique of measuring at a distance?
12 The existence of which civilization was confirmed by Arthur Evans' excavations on Crete?
13 In which year did the space shuttle Challenger explode?
14 What was set up after the Bretton Woods Conference in 1944?
15 How did the car manufacturer, Charles Stewart Rolls, die?
16 In which war was the Battle of Shiloh?
17 Which body ensures the purity of the French language?
18 What is the name of the metal discs set in the rim of a tambourine?
19 Which French zoologist is associated with the concept that acquired characteristics can be inherited?
20 How is the character Cio-Cio-San more usually known?
21 The late Rafik Hariri was a former PM of which country?
22 What does the ringing of eight bells mean on board a ship?
23 What is the earliest US military award for service beyond the call of duty?
24 At which place does the ship bringing Dracula to England land?
25 How many humps does a newborn camel have?
26 What is the most successful song written by Alex North and Hy Zaret?
27 Where were the first European coffee houses opened?
28 From 1933 to 1947 how was the Hoover Dam on the Colorado known?
29 Who wrote "Out of Africa"?
30 Which prime minister of South Africa was assassinated in 1966?

Answers | Pot-Luck 24 (see Quiz 53)

1 Lady Godiva. 2 John Banville. 3 Akira Kurosawa. 4 Australia. 5 Hawk. 6 Nitrate. 7 They secrete insulin. 8 Halibut. 9 Vladivostok. 10 Edwin Lutyens. 11 The Great Leap Forward. 12 Plutonium. 13 Friedrich Nietzsche. 14 Bryn Terfel. 15 She threw herself under the king's horse at the Derby. 16 Manhattan Project. 17 Jupiter. 18 Louis XIV. 19 La Manche. 20 Fishing. 21 Architect. 22 Both have the same letters reading forwards or backwards. 23 The crown jewels. 24 Aurora Australis. 25 Manganese. 26 Ashes to Ashes. 27 Gyles Brandreth. 28 Pointillism. 29 Hogwarts (Harry Potter). 30 January.

Quiz 56 | American Literature | Answers – page 528

1 Against what is Hemingway's "For Whom the Bell Tolls" set?
2 Which US-born novelist lived much of his life in France and England and became a British citizen in 1915?
3 Who wrote,"Who's Afraid of Virginia Woolf?"?
4 In which Arthur Miller play do you meet Willy Loman?
5 What is a novel by Herman Melville and an opera by Benjamin Britten?
6 Where are most of Pearl S. Buck's novels set?
7 Who wrote the short story "I Robot" in 1950?
8 Who died at the age of 44 with his novel "The Last Tycoon" unfinished?
9 Who wrote the "Leatherstocking" tales of frontier life with their hero Natty Bumpo?
10 "A Farewell to Arms" is based on Hemingway's own experience as what in World War I?
11 Where were Robert Frost's poems first published?
12 Which character appears in all nine of Raymond Chandler's novels?
13 Who wrote "The Maltese Falcon"?
14 Holden Caulfield appears in which, once controversial, novel?
15 Which Norman Mailer novel is based on a protest march?
16 Whose novels are about social conditions in his native California?
17 Which dramatist wrote "Long Day's Journey into Night"?
18 What is the setting for Hemingway's "The Old Man and the Sea"?
19 What is L. Frank Baum's most famous story?
20 Which US poet married Ted Hughes, later poet laureate?
21 Which Arthur Miller play is a comment on McCarthyism?
22 Which screenplay did Miller write for his wife Marilyn Monroe?
23 Who wrote plays with a political theme such as "The Little Foxes"?
24 Which poet spent time in a US mental hospital after supporting Mussolini and the Fascists in World War II?
25 Whose real name was Samuel Langhorne Clemens?
26 Who coined the phrase "the lost generations"?
27 In which Tennessee Williams play do you meet Big Daddy?
28 Who wrote the story of Rip van Winkle?
29 What type of writing is Paul Theroux associated with other than novels?
30 Whose most famous novel is "The Carpetbaggers"?

Answers	Pop: Frank Sinatra (see Quiz 54)

1 Albert. 2 Nancy, Frank, Tina. 3 Reprise. 4 Axel Stordahl. 5 From Here to Eternity. 6 Johnny Fontane. 7 Love & Marriage. 8 Hoboken. 9 Softly as I Leave You. 10 Strangers in the Night. 11 Ava Gardner. 12 Three Coins in the Fountain. 13 My Way. 14 Ol' Blue Eyes is Back. 15 My Kind of Town. 16 On the Town. 17 Pal Joey, Rita Hayworth. 18 Charles Aznavour. 19 Marlon Brando. 20 Manchurian Candidate. 21 Sammy Davis Jr. 22 Somethin' Stupid. 23 It was a Very Good Year. 24 Mia Farrow. 25 Chicago, New York. 26 High Society. 27 Zeppo Marx. 28 1998. 29 1969. 30 Bono.

1 Who was the first person to successfully climb the Matterhorn?
2 What was the name of the eldest of the Railway Children?
3 Whom did David Steel succeed as leader of the Liberal Party?
4 NaOH is the chemical formula for what?
5 What is the term for a group of monkeys?
6 Which movie-making operation bought Spielberg's Dreamworks in December 2005?
7 The scene of much brutality this millennium, Dafur is in which country?
8 What pigment comes from the cuttlefish?
9 In which country is the Napa Valley?
10 Who narrated the Paddington cartoon series?
11 Whose victory over the Danes is celebrated in Wiltshire's White Horse?
12 Which is the largest lake in the United Kingdom?
13 Which planet other than Venus does not have moons?
14 Which two people created "EastEnders"?
15 Which two words does the word modem come from?
16 In films how is Betty Joan Perske better known?
17 Who became Archbishop of York in 2005?
18 Which dancer plays the 25-year-old Billy at the end of "Billy Elliot"?
19 Which element has the symbol P?
20 Who said, "I want to be the white man's brother, not his brother-in-law"?
21 In what year was the first soccer World Cup broadcast on British TV in colour?
22 What's the link between Maria von Trapp of "The Sound of Music" and Patrick Troughton of "Dr Who" fame?
23 Who designed the Spitfire?
24 When did the EEC become the EC?
25 Which pope occupied the Holy See for only two days?
26 Which veteran comedian wrote "If I Don't Write It, Nobody Will"?
27 The names of British racehorses are limited to how many letters?
28 What was S Club 7's biggest hit?'
29 Which river forms part of the frontier between Spain and Portugal?
30 Of which country did Leonid Kravchuk become President in 1991?

Answers	**Pot-Luck 27** *(see Quiz 59)*

1 John Osborne. 2 Universal. 3 Sir Geoffrey Howe. 4 Dry ice. 5 A skulk. 6 Ellen MacArthur. 7 A seahorse. 8 Port. 9 Bedfordshire. 10 Adultery. 11 Stevie Wonder. 12 Horse. 13 1931. 14 Hazel. 15 Oxford Committee for Famine Relief. 16 Westminster Abbey. 17 Borstal, near Rochester, Kent. 18 Dame Kiri Te Kanawa. 19 Stalagmites. 20 Juventus. 21 The turkey. 22 Scarlett Johanssen. 23 Tony Hancock. 24 The Soviet Union. 25 1959. 26 Johnny Cash. 27 George II. 28 Silkworms. 29 Pope John Paul II. 30 Please Please Me.

1 Which comedian performed stunts in "Just Nuts" and "The Freshman"?
2 Who produced the "Keystone Kops" films?
3 Which actress starred in "Modern Times"?
4 About which actress did Kenneth Tynan say, "What one sees in other women drunk, one sees in her sober"?
5 Who was directed by D. W. Griffith in "Birth of a Nation" in 1916?
6 In which film does Rudolph Valentino play a father and his son?
7 Who directed the 1923 version of "The Ten Commandments"?
8 Which 1920 film with Douglas Fairbanks was based on the novel "The Curse of Capistrano"?
9 Who was the star of "The Paleface" in 1922?
10 In which year was the first version of "Ben Hur" made?
11 Which memorabilia were sold at Christie's in 1987 for £82,500?
12 Who was the "It" girl?
13 Who was the only woman in the quartet who founded United Artists?
14 What is Rudolph Valentino's job in "Blood and Sand"?
15 Which 1925 film starred John Gilbert as an American in the war in 1917?
16 Which 1926 film was remade in 1952 with James Cagney and Dan Dailey?
17 Although a silent movie, what did "Way Down East" contain?
18 Who played opposite Chaplin in "The Tramp"?
19 Which actress stars opposite Mack Sennett in "Mack and Mabel"?
20 Who asked D. W. Griffith to make the film "Hearts of the World"?
21 Who was Gaston de Tolignac, screenwriter of "Hearts of the World"?
22 Which English actor/playwright starred in "Hearts of the World"?
23 Who wrote and starred in the 1922 version of "Robin Hood"?
24 Which film about early aviation starred Clara Bow and Gary Cooper?
25 What nationality was the hero Valentino played in "The Four Horsemen of the Apocalypse"?
26 Which two roles did Mary Pickford play in "Little Lord Fauntleroy"?
27 What was Fatty Arbuckle's real first name?
28 Who played the title role in the 1928 version of "Sadie Thompson"?
29 Who won the first-ever Oscar for best actress for "Seventh Heaven"?
30 Where does the action of Buster Keaton's "The Navigator" take place?

Answers	**Sport: Golf** *(see Quiz 60)*

1 Tom Watson. 2 Augusta, Georgia. 3 Bobby Locke. 4 Retief Goosen. 5 Gary Player (South Africa). 6 Ben Hogan. 7 Ian Baker-Finch. 8 Tony Jacklin. 9 Supermex. 10 15 strokes. 11 Byron Nelson. 12 Southport. 13 Wentworth. 14 Jack Nicklaus. 15 Portugal. 16 Newport, Rhode Island. 17 Muirfield. 18 Great Britain and Ireland. 19 Nick Faldo. 20 Curtis Cup. 21 British Open. 22 Ian Woosnam beat Padraig Harrington (2001). 23 Bobby Jones. 24 Amateurs. 25 Lee Trevino. 26 Vijay Singh. 27 Christy O'Connor. 28 Bernard Gallacher. 29 Todd Hamilton. 30 Dwight D. Eisenhower.

1 Who wrote the play "Look Back in Anger"?
2 Which recording company did Prince sign with in 2005?
3 Who was Margaret Thatcher's first chancellor of the exchequer?
4 What is solid carbon dioxide commonly called?
5 What is the collective name for a group of foxes?
6 Which adventurer wrote "Race Against Time"?
7 What is the only male creature to carry and hatch eggs?
8 In polite circles, which drink should be passed to the left?
9 In which county is Woburn Abbey?
10 What shall you not commit according to the seventh commandment?
11 Who played every instrument on Cliff Richard's "She's So Beautiful"?
12 A centaur was a mythical creature halfway between a man and what?
13 When was the gold standard finally abandoned in Britain?
14 Which tree has the alternative name of "cob"?
15 What name was OXFAM originally registered as?
16 Where is the Jacobean playwright Ben Jonson buried?
17 Where was the first borstal in Britain?
18 Which female opera singer was appointed to the Order of Merit in 1995?
19 Which limestone formation found in caves grows upwards?
20 Which was the first Italian club side that Zinedine Zidane played for?
21 Which bird did Benjamin Franklin want to be the US emblem?
22 Which actress was the star of Woody Allen's Match Point?
23 Which comedian was known as "the lad himself"?
24 In 1920, which was the first country to legalize abortion?
25 In which year did the M1 motorway open?
26 Who started his career with the Tennessee Two?
27 Who was the last English monarch to be born abroad?
28 What do you breed if you are a sericulturist?
29 Who is the author of "Crossing the Threshold of Hope"?
30 What was the Beatles' first LP called in 1963?

Answers | Pot-Luck 26 (see Quiz 57)

1 Edward Whymper. 2 Roberta or Bobbie. 3 Jeremy Thorpe. 4 Caustic soda. 5 A troop. 6 Paramount Pictures. 7 Sudan. 8 Sepia. 9 United States. 10 Michael Hordern. 11 Alfred the Great. 12 Lough Neagh, Northern Ireland. 13 Mercury. 14 Julia Smith, Tony Holland. 15 Modulate, demodulate. 16 Lauren Bacall. 17 John Sentamu. 18 Adam Cooper. 19 Phosphorus. 20 Martin Luther King. 21 1970. 22 They died on the same day (March 30th, 1987). 23 Reginald Joseph Mitchell. 24 1965. 25 Stephen II. 26 Eric Sykes. 27 18 letters and spaces. 28 Don't Stop Movin. 29 The Guadiana. 30 Ukraine.

1 Which American won five British Opens between 1975 and 1983?
2 Where is the US Masters held?
3 Which South African won the British Open in 1949, 1950, 1952 and 1957?
4 Who won his second US Open at Shinnecock Hills, New York, in 2004?
5 Who was the first non-American post-war winner of the US Masters?
6 Which American played in the British Open only once and won it?
7 Faldo won the British Open in 1990 and 1992. Who won in 1991?
8 Who was the first Englishman to win the US Open after World War II?
9 What is Lee Trevino's nickname?
10 Tiger Woods won the 2000 US Open by a record of how many strokes?
11 Which US golfer had 11 successive tournament wins in 1945?
12 In which town is Royal Birkdale golf course?
13 Over which course is the World Matchplay Championship played?
14 Who won the US Masters in 1986 for a record sixth time?
15 In which country is Penina golf course?
16 Where was the first-ever US Open played in 1895?
17 What name did Jack Nicklaus give to his own golf course in honour of his favourite British course?
18 Who opposed the US in the Ryder Cup between 1973 and 1977?
19 Who won the English Amateur Championship in 1975 aged 18?
20 Which trophy is played for by women golfers from the United States in competition with Britain and Ireland?
21 Which is the oldest open championship in the world?
22 Who played in the World Matchplay Championship Final when a Welshman beat an Irishman?
23 Which golfer was responsible for the the US Masters?
24 What is the status of competitors in the Walker Cup?
25 Who won the US Masters to stop Tiger Woods claiming all majors in a year?
26 Which actor shared his name with the winner of the 1939 British Open?
27 Which Irish golfer played in ten successive Ryder Cup teams?
28 Who captained the European team to victory in the 1995 Ryder Cup?
29 Who got his PGA Tour card in 2003 at his eighth attempt and a year later landed a Major?
30 Which US president's home was alongside the course on which the US Masters is played?

Answers	The Movies: Silent Cinema (see Quiz 58)

1 Harold Lloyd. 2 Mack Sennett. 3 Paulette Goddard. 4 Garbo. 5 Lillian Gish. 6 Son of the Sheikh. 7 Cecil B. de Mille. 8 The Mark of Zorro. 9 Buster Keaton. 10 1926. 11 Chaplin's hat and cane. 12 Clara Bow. 13 Mary Pickford. 14 Matador. 15 The Big Parade. 16 What Price Glory? 17 A colour sequence. 18 Edna Purviance. 19 Mabel Normand. 20 British government. 21 D. W. Griffith. 22 Noel Coward. 23 Douglas Fairbanks. 24 Wings. 25 Argentinian. 26 Young Cedric and his mother. 27 Roscoe. 28 Gloria Swanson. 29 Janet Gaynor. 30 Transatlantic liners.

1 In 2005, who released the album "Affirmation"?
2 What colour was Rupert Bear's face in early books and annuals?
3 Where did the world's first controlled nuclear reaction take place in 1942?
4 What is the collective name for a group of bears?
5 In our solar system which planet is farthest from the Sun?
6 What colour was the Queen's outfit for the blessing of Charles and Camilla after their wedding?
7 Which big cat has the proper name Acinonyx jubatus?
8 Who ordered the building of the Pavilion at Brighton ?
9 What is the side away from the wind called on a ship?
10 What was Robin's real name in the Batman TV series?
11 Which fish walks on land?
12 What does the musical term Vivace mean?
13 What was the real title of the painting called "The Laughing Cavalier"?
14 Which king was known as "Silly Billy"?
15 Who designed the first mechanical adding machine in 1641?
16 In which country did a cultural revolution take place during 1966–69?
17 Who drew the Katzenjammer Kids for the "New York Journal" in 1910?
18 Who was the first Irish athlete to win gold in the European Championships?
19 Which scale measures the effects of an earthquake at a particular place?
20 What is the vitamin riboflavin?
21 Which is the second largest island in the world after Australia?
22 Which actress starred in "Bend It Like Beckham" and "ER"?
23 What was the surname of soul musician Booker T.?
24 What would the Chuckle Brothers be called if they used their real surnames?
25 In which Alpine range is the Swiss mountain, Jungfrau?
26 What nationality was the first non-US, non-Soviet spaceman?
27 To two years in what year was the final episode of "Dad's Army" originally screened?
28 Where in Italy was Mussolini executed?
29 Which means of transport features on Darkness's album cover "One Way Ticket to Hell ... and Back"?
30 What was the surname of the Windsors before they changed it?

Answers	Pot-Luck 29 *(see Quiz 63)*

1 Train à Grande Vitesse. 2 Giant Squid. 3 Edgar Degas. 4 Glasgow. 5 Mount of Olives. 6 Lincoln. 7 32. 8 A fox. 9 Bull & Finch. 10 John Hinckley. 11 Happiness. 12 A knight in armour. 13 Rowland Hill. 14 Stanley Baldwin. 15 Bree Van De Kamp. 16 Cherries. 17 The nine of diamonds. 18 Tent stitch. 19 Barbados. 20 Robbie Fowler. 21 A tax to buy off the Danish invaders. 22 The typewriter. 23 Education. 24 The Pearl Fishers. 25 2005. 26 Nose bleed. 27 Dow Jones Index. 28 Henry Hall. 29 Somnus. 30 Boxer & Laura.

1 How many number ones did Madonna have in the 1990s?
2 What was John Lennon's second No 1 hit, a month after his first?
3 Which was the first record to hit No 1 on two different occasions?
4 Who was the fourth artist to reach No 1 with the song "Unchained Melody"?
5 Which title was a No 1 for Kylie Minogue and Johnny Nash?
6 Elton John's first hit was in 1971. When was his first solo No 1?
7 How many singles were number one in 2003?
8 With which two groups did Gerry Marsden have the same No 1?
9 Which band had a No 1 with "Whatever People Say I am"?
10 What novelty record, by an Australian, was the first No 1 single of the 70s?
11 What were Art Garfunkel's first two hits at No 1?
12 Who took their first three hits to No 1 in 1984?
13 What was Christina Aguilera's fourth number one hit?
14 Who is the oldest person to have a No 1?
15 Who is runner-up to Madonna as female star with most weeks at No 1?
16 Who were the two different backing groups which accompanied Cliff Richard on two No 1 versions of "Livin' Doll"?
17 In 1954 "Oh Mein Papa" and "Oh! My Pa Pa" were recorded by different men with the same christian name, what is it?
18 Mother and son, Hilda and Rob Woodward, reached No 1 as what?
19 How many number ones did "Popstars" winners Hear'say have?
20 What were Rod Stewart's first two No 1 hits?
21 How many consecutive No 1s did the Beatles have between 1963 and 1966?
22 What were Abba's three consecutive No 1s in 1975–76?
23 Which song was Kylie Minogue's first hit to enter the chart at No 1?
24 "Ignition" was the second No 1 single for which male vocalist?
25 What were Adam Faith's two No 1s?
26 What was the Boomtown Rats' first No 1?
27 Who were the two acts who had No 1s with "Without You"?
28 Which No 1 links Elvis Presley and UB40?
29 Who sang with UB40 on their No 1 "I Got You Babe"?
30 Which song was a No 1 for Joe Cocker and Wet, Wet, Wet?

Answers	**Global Events** (see Quiz 64)

1 26th December. 2 Florida. 3 Madrid. 4 12. 5 Boscastle. 6 Paradise Square. 7 Saturn. 8 June. 9 Cuba. 10 Indian. 11 December. 12 Pacific. 13 Ukraine. 14 School. 15 202. 16 Paris. 17 Two. 18 Lebanon. 19 Columbia. 20 Saudi Arabia. 21 Afghanistan. 22 Slobodan Milosevic. 23 Libya. 24 Shoes. 25 Concorde. 26 March. 27 Space. 28 Vladimir Putin. 29 Sweden. 30 Isabel.

1 In France what do the initials TGV mean?

2 What is the largest living invertebrate?

3 Which French artist is known for his paintings of the ballet and dancers?

4 Which city comes from two Gaelic words and means "the place in the green hollow"?

5 Which hill marks the traditional site of the Ascension in the Bible?

6 Which is the third-largest cathedral in England?

7 How many pods or capsules does the London Eye have?

8 What type of animal was J. Worthington Foulfellow?

9 Exterior shots in "Cheers" featured a real bar. What was its name ?

10 Who shot Ronald Reagan in March 1981?

11 Of what is the bluebird a symbol?

12 Who would have worn a gorget, pauldron, beaver and greave?

13 Who instituted the penny post in England?

14 Who was the British prime minister when Edward VIII abdicated?

15 Steven Culp played the husband of which "Desperate Housewife"?

16 With what is the Belgian beer Kriek flavoured?

17 Which playing card is referred to as the "curse of Scotland"?

18 In needlework, which stitch may be described as "petit point"?

19 Which paradise holiday island is the most easterly of the West Indies?

20 Whose autobiography had the accurate, though not very original title "Robbie: My Autobiography"?

21 What, in English history, was the Danegeld?

22 With which invention of 1801 is the Italian, Pellegrine Tarri, credited?

23 Before he became party leader what was Neil Kinnock's shadow post?

24 In which work do Nadir and Zurga appear?

25 In what year did Placido Domingo make his proms debut?

26 What is epistaxis, a common complaint, the medical term for?

27 What is the US equivalent of the Financial Times Index?

28 Whose autobiography was entitled "Here's to the Next Time"?

29 What was the name of the Roman god of sleep?

30 In Rosemary & Thyme, what is Rosemary's surname and Thyme's first?

Answers | Pot-Luck 28 *(see Quiz 61)*

1 Beverley Knight. 2 Brown, although he was white-faced on inside colour pages. 3 Chicago. 4 A sleuth. 5 Pluto. 6 Cream. 7 Cheetah. 8 George IV, as Prince Regent. 9 The leeside. 10 Dick Grayson. 11 The climbing perch of India. 12 Lively. 13 Portrait of a Man. 14 William IV. 15 Blaise Pascal. 16 China. 17 Rudolph Dirks. 18 Sonia O'Sullivan. 19 Mercalli scale. 20 B2. 21 Greenland. 22 Parminder Nagra. 23 Jones. 24 The Elliot Brothers. 25 Bernese Alps. 26 Czech. 27 1977. 28 Como. 29 Train. 30 House of Saxe-Coburg.

1 On which date in 2004 was southeast Asia devastated by a tsunami?
2 In which US state was George W. Bush when the attacks began on 9/11?
3 Which European capital's railway station was attached in March 2004?
4 How many countries converted to the euro when it was first introduced?
5 Which Cornish town was a victim of freak flooding in August 2004?
6 What was the name of the Baghdad Square where Saddam Hussein's statue was toppled in 2003?
7 The space probe Cassini Hugens reached which planet in July 2004?
8 In which month in 2004 did the US hand power back to the Iraqis?
9 On which island was Camp X Ray?
10 An earthquake under which ocean caused Dec 2004's tsunami?
11 In which month of 2003 was Saddam Hussein captured after hiding in a cellar?
12 Islanders around which ocean were first to see the new millennium?
13 In 2004, which country had an election annulled and then rerun after accusations of fraud?
14 What type of building was besieged in Beslan in 2004 following the taking of hostages?
15 How many countries competed at the Athens Olympics in 2004?
16 In 2000, Concorde crashed near which European city?
17 How many hijacked civilian planes crashed into the World Trade Center on 9/11?
18 The militant movement Hezbollah was based in which country?
19 What was the name of the shuttle that broke up on returning to Earth in 2003 killing seven people on board?
20 Al Qaeda leader Osama Bin Laden was born in which country?
21 In which country was the Taleban based?
22 Which former Yugoslav president was charged with war crimes in 2001?
23 Which country vowed to give up its chemical weapons in a surprise move in December 2003?
24 Where did Richard Reid hide explosives on a 2001 Paris to Miami flight?
25 Which aircraft was taken out of service in October 2003?
26 In which month in 2003 did the US launch missiles against Iraq?
27 Yang Liwei was the first man from China to travel where?
28 Who was Russian President when the Iraq war began?
29 Which European country's Foreign Minister was stabbed to death in 2003?
30 Which hurricane hammered Washington DC in September 2003?

Answers | Pop: No 1s *(see Quiz 62)*

1 Two. 2 Woman 3 Bohemian Rhapsody. 4 Gareth Gates. 5 Tears on My Pillow. 6 1990. 7 Twenty-three. 8 The Pacemakers, the Crowd. 9 Arctic Monkeys. 10 Two Little Boys. 11 I Only Have Eyes for You, Bright Eyes. 12 Frankie Goes to Hollywood. 13 Beautiful. 14 Louis Armstrong. 15 Doris Day. 16 The Drifters, the Young Ones. 17 Eddie. 18 Lieutenant Pigeon. 19 Two. 20 Maggie May, You Wear It Well. 21 11. 22 Mamma Mia, Fernando, Dancing Queen. 23 Spinning Around. 24 R. Kelly. 25 What Do You Want, Poor Me. 26 Rat Trap. 27 Nilsson, Mariah Carey. 28 Can't Help Falling in Love. 29 Chrissie Hynde. 30 With a Little Help from My Friends.

1 On London's Shaftesbury Avenue which theatre is between the Lyric and the Gielgud?

2 What name is given to a young hawk taken from its nest for training?

3 Where in London would you find the sculpture of Prospero and Ariel?

4 Under which king was the Royal Observatory at Greenwich built?

5 Who, according to the Book of Samuel in the Bible, was born in Gath?

6 Which is the largest Gothic church in northern Europe?

7 What names are given to the old and new styles of calendar?

8 Musky Muskrat was the sidekick of which cartoon lawman?

9 What are Micmac, Cree and Ojibwa?

10 Which signal replaced the CQD signal in 1906?

11 What is the botanical emblem of Australia?

12 Who would wear an orphrey, morse and cope and carry a crozier?

13 What did the Polish oculist Dr L. Zamenhof invent?

14 Who was elected the first woman Lord Mayor of London in 1983?

15 In 1991 Jonathan Sacks took over which important post in Great Britain?

16 Which Scandinavian alcoholic spirit is made from potatoes?

17 In which country did the card game bridge originate?

18 Which Oscar-winning film features Colin Firth as Lord Wessex and Martin Clunes as Richard Burbage?

19 What are the Tonga Islands otherwise known as?

20 How many different albums reached number one in 2003?

21 Which English king invented a candle clock?

22 What Latin word is used to express the meaning "word for word"?

23 What did the American Hamilton Smith invent in 1858?

24 Where was the last battle between Britain and the United States?

25 In which London street is Hamley's toy shop?

26 What is the common name for the disease called trismus?

27 What is the French equivalent of the Stock Exchange?

28 Who composed the Symphony No 7, known as "the Leningrad"?

29 Who was the Greek goddess of victory?

30 Where are the birthplace and statue of King Alfred the Great?

Answers | Pot-Luck 31 *(see Quiz 67)*

1 Victoria Falls. 2 Chlorophyll. 3 Iolanthe. 4 The Vedas. 5 New Hampshire. 6 St Matthew. 7 Lactose. 8 Hong Kong harbour. 9 Lloyd George. 10 Morris Garages. 11 Lord Scarman. 12 A glider. 13 China. 14 Nil by Mouth. 15 1967. 16 Wedge. 17 Connecticut. 18 39 inquiries. 19 Countdown. 20 The Althing. 21 Jesuits. 22 Billy Elliot. 23 The kukri. 24 A dance. 25 Canada. 26 Touchstone. 27 Goering. 28 Caves. 29 The Atholl Highlanders. 30 Alpenstock.

1 Which hero is Beethoven's "Eroica" Symphony said to be named after?
2 Who were J. S. Bach's two sons?
3 What is the nationality of composer Isaac Albéniz?
4 On which instrument is Handel's "Harmonious Blacksmith" played?
5 What type of horns feature in Haydn's Symphony No 31 in D?
6 Whose ebony clarinet was Stravinsky's Clarinet Concerto written for, thus giving it the nickname "Ebony"?
7 In which country was Greek composer Iannis Xenakis actually born?
8 What was Vivaldi's profession aside from violinist and composer?
9 What type of works did John Wilbye compose?
10 To which composer is Bruckner's Symphony No 3 in D minor dedicated?
11 Who was Britten's Simple Symphony written for?
12 Which Gilbert and Sullivan opera has the subtitle "Flowers of Progress"?
13 Who wrote the tone poem "Tintagel"?
14 Which work provided Anthony Minghella with his operatic directorial debut?
15 Which American folk hero is the title of a ballet by Aaron Copland?
16 What is Debussy's dreamlike music often called?
17 What type of work is Elgar's "Dream of Gerontius"?
18 Which honorary degree was Haydn receiving when his Oxford Symphony was first performed?
19 Which modern English composer wrote the opera "Punch and Judy"?
20 Which two Russian revolutions does Shostakovich commemorate in his 11th and 12th symphonies?
21 What is the "joke" which gives Haydn's String Quartet in E flat its name?
22 Which Soviet republic did Khachaturian come from?
23 For which musical instrument were Liszt's "Liebesträume" written?
24 How many major symphonies did Mahler write?
25 What was Mussorgsky's first name?
26 Including interval time, how long does a performance of Richard Wagner's "Gotterdämmerung" last?
27 Which rival of Mozart has been accused, falsely, of poisoning him?
28 Who wrote "The Snow Maiden" and "The Golden Cockerel"?
29 What is the "Miracle" which gave Haydn's Symphony No 96 its name?
30 What were Johann Stamitz's "Mannheim rockets"?

Answers	Geography: Natural Phenomena *(see Quiz 68)*

1 Bam. 2 Cirrus. 3 Bogor, Java. 4 Snow. 5 Bracknell, north Wales. 6 Coriolis effect. 7 Krakatoa, near Java. 8 Sumatra. 9 St Elmo's fire. 10 Red, orange, yellow, green, blue, indigo, violet. 11 Tornado. 12 Aurora. 13 Tsunami (not tidal waves). 14 An annular eclipse. 15 Earthquake areas. 16 The International Ice Patrol. 17 Mauna Loa, Hawaii. 18 A waterspout. 19 Aurora Borealis. 20 Surtsey. 21 Empedocles. 22 Lebu, Chile. 23 Mount Erebus. 24 Geyser. 25 Pumice. 26 The Earth passes between the Sun and Moon. 27 Thermal. 28 Stalactites. 29 Fumarole. 30 The Mercalli scale.

1 What is the biggest tourist attraction in Zambia?
2 What name is given to the green colouring matter found in plants?
3 What was Reginald Perrin's middle name in the sit com with Leonard Rossiter?
4 What name is given to the four holy books of the Hindus?
5 Dan Brown was born in which American state?
6 Who is the patron saint of tax collectors?
7 What is the name of the sugar found in milk?
8 Where did the passenger liner "Queen Elizabeth" catch fire in 1972?
9 Who was the first prime minister to occupy Chequers?
10 What do the initials MG stand for on a sports car?
11 Who headed the inquiry into the Brixton Riots in 1981?
12 What kind of aircraft was the World War II Horsa?
13 Where did the Boxer Rising take place between 1898 and 1900?
14 Which movie was Gary Oldman's directorial debut?
15 In which year did the British breathalyzer law come into force?
16 In golf what is the traditional name for the number ten iron?
17 Which US state is called the Nutmeg state?
18 How many public inquiries were held before the go ahead was given for the M25?
19 On which TV programme does Susie Dent give her expert advice?
20 What is the Icelandic parliament called?
21 What were the names of the followers of Ignatius Loyola?
22 In which movie did the character in the title role say: "I don't want a childhood, I want to be a ballet dancer"?
23 What name is given to the knife which the Gurkha soldiers use?
24 What is a saraband?
25 In which country would you find the Laurentian Mountains?
26 What was the name of the jester in "As You Like It"?
27 Who created the German Luftwaffe?
28 What does a speleologist study?
29 What is the name of Britain's only private army?
30 What is the name of the long staff with an iron tip used in mountaineering?

Answers	**Pot-Luck 30** *(see Quiz 65)*

1 Apollo. 2 Eyas. 3 BBC Broadcasting House. 4 Charles II. 5 Goliath. 6 Cologne cathedral. 7 Julian, Gregorian. 8 Deputy Dawg. 9 American Indian Tribes. 10 SOS. 11 Wattle blossom. 12 A bishop. 13 Esperanto. 14 Lady Donaldson. 15 Chief Rabbi (of Great Britain). 16 Aquavit. 17 Turkey. 18 Shakespeare in Love. 19 Friendly Islands. 20 Twenty-five. 21 Alfred the Great. 22 Verbatim. 23 Washing machine. 24 New Orleans. 25 Regent Street. 26 Lockjaw. 27 The Bourse. 28 Shostakovich. 29 Nike. 30 Winchester.

1 Which Iranian city was partially destroyed by a Dec 2003 earthquake?
2 What is the highest standard cloud formation called?
3 Where is the most thundery place on earth?
4 What occurred in the Kalahari Desert on September 1st, 1981?
5 Where did the longest-lasting rainbow glow for three hours?
6 What name is given to the bending of the winds caused by the Earth spinning on its axis?
7 Which volcanic eruption gave the loudest sound ever recorded?
8 Which Indonesian island was nearest the epicentre of the earthquake in December 2004?
9 What is the name given to the lightning which clings to ships' masts?
10 What are the seven colours of the rainbow in their correct order?
11 What is the name for a column of swiftly spinning air?
12 What name is given to the phenomenon of bright lights in the atmosphere caused by the solar wind entering the ionosphere?
13 What are caused by changes in the level of the ocean floor?
14 What occurs when the central zone of the Sun is covered?
15 What are the "Ring of Fire" and "Alpine Belt"?
16 Which patrol group keeps track of all icebergs?
17 Which is the largest active volcano on Earth?
18 What forms when a tornado runs over water?
19 What is the scientific name for the Northern Lights?
20 Which island emerged from the sea off the coast of Iceland in 1963?
21 Which Greek philosopher made 5th-century BC studies of vulcanology?
22 Where did the strongest earthquake ever recorded take place in 1960?
23 Which is the only active volcano in Antarctica?
24 What is a vent in the Earth's crust that spouts a fountain of boiling water?
25 Which volcanic rock is so strongly charged with gas that it appears frothy and floats on water?
26 What occurs when a lunar eclipse take place?
27 What is a rising air current caused by heating from below called?
28 What are Tugela and the Buyoma?
29 What name is given to a volcanic opening that gives out gas and steam?
30 What scale, other than the Richter, measures earthquakes?

Answers	**Classical Music** *(see Quiz 66)*

1 Napoleon I. 2 Carl Philip Emanuel, Johann Christian. 3 Spanish. 4 Harpsichord. 5 Hunting horns. 6 Woody Herman. 7 Romania. 8 Priest. 9 Madrigals. 10 Wagner. 11 Young people. 12 Utopia Limited. 13 Sir Arnold Bax. 14 Madame Butterfly. 15 Billy the Kid. 16 Musical impressionism. 17 Oratorio. 18 Doctorate. 19 Harrison Birtwhistle. 20 1905, 1917. 21 Several false endings. 22 Armenia. 23 Piano. 24 Nine. 25 Modest. 26 Six hours. 27 Antonio Salieri. 28 Rimsky-Korsakov. 29 Chandelier said to have fallen, but injured no one. 30 Brilliant scale passages.

Quiz 69 | Pot-Luck 32

1 What, in computer terminology, do the initials COBOL stand for?
2 What are the two types of camel?
3 Which character announced "I'm not here" in times of crisis in "Drop the Dead Donkey"?
4 What name is given to the highest point of the heavens?
5 The September 11th USA attacks led to postponing news of the election of which new Tory leader?
6 In which city was the first boy scout troop registered?
7 On which date does International Labour Day fall?
8 Who created the popular 1920s cartoon character Felix the Cat?
9 Leap-Frog, the Gallant Hussar and Ampleforth are all types of what?
10 By what nickname was the criminal Albert De Salvo better known?
11 How many points has a Star of David?
12 What is the lace scarf worn over the head by Spanish women called?
13 Which Frenchman discovered the St Lawrence River?
14 Who was the BBC's principal TV commentator during the Queen's coronation?
15 What was Muse's first top ten hit?
16 Which drink do you associate with Holy Island in Northumberland?
17 Which English king reigned the longest?
18 In bridge, what jargon word describes "holding no trumps"?
19 What was the title of the first women's magazine ever published, in 1693?
20 What name is given to a whirling tornado-like cloud at sea?
21 Of which island republic is Antananarivo the capital?
22 Which movie, which began with the words "The hills are alive" celebrated its 40th anniversary in 2005?
23 With which invention is William Le Baron Jenny of the United States credited?
24 What was the title of John Wayne's final film?
25 Which stretch of water separates Sicily from Italy?
26 What is the Japanese word for goodbye?
27 Tom Naylor and Jacqueline King have both won what?
28 Which musical instrument do you associate with Dizzy Gillespie?
29 By what name is Portuguese West Africa now known?
30 Which photographer and cousin of the Queen died in November 2005?

| **Answers** | Pot-Luck 33 *(see Quiz 71)* |

1 Benjamin Britten's. 2 Helicon. 3 58. 4 Kestrel. 5 Dahlia. 6 Michael Buerk. 7 Sunday Times. 8 The Plymouth Brethren. 9 King Edward VII. 10 St Vincent. 11 Amalgam. 12 Clydebank. 13 Spoon. 14 Coco the Clown. 15 Sean O'Casey. 16 Susan Sarandon. 17 Ballistics. 18 Washington. 19 Hamilton. 20 All parts of a spinning wheel. 21 Belfast. 22 Fed Cup. 23 Kent. 24 Hindu. 25 Herbert Hoover. 26 Pistil. 27 The grouse family. 28 Two. 29 The Winchester. 30 Menelaus.

1 In which city was Yorkshire's Michael Vaughan born?
2 Which was the first English county that Anil Kumble played for?
3 Who was the last England captain to play South Africa before the ban?
4 Who won the county championships in every season from 1951 to 1958?
5 Where in the West Indies did Brian Lara score his record-breaking 375?
6 Who was the first player to make over 1,000 catches in first-class cricket?
7 What did ICC stand for before 1965?
8 Who were the first winners of the Women's World Cup in 1973?
9 What is Bob Willis's middle name?
10 Which England batsmen each scored double centuries against India in 1985 in the same innings?
11 Who was the first batsman to score 10,000 runs in Test cricket?
12 In which country are the first-class sides United Bank and National Bank?
13 Who were the first three members of the ICC?
14 What was the Nat West Trophy previously called?
15 Which New Zealander hit a double century in 153 balls vs England in 2002?
16 Who kept wicket for Yorkshire in 412 consecutive county championship games?
17 Who was England's most capped cricketer at the end of the 2002/03 Ashes series?
18 Who scored 322 runs against Warwickshire in less than a day in 1985?
19 In which country do first-class teams compete for the Plunkett Shield?
20 Who was Man of the Match in the 2003 World Cup Final?
21 What is the trophy played for by first-class inter-state sides in India?
22 Who captained England during the "bodyline" series?
23 Who was the first bowler to take 300 Test wickets?
24 Which bowler is nicknamed "The King of Spain"?
25 What was the title of Andrew Flintoff's autobiography?
26 Who said, "The bowler's Holding, the batsman's Willey"?
27 To three each way, how many Tests did it take Muttiah Muralitharan to reach the 400 wicket mark?
28 Michael Vaughan made his international debut against which country?
29 Which ex-England cricketer made his county debut in 1981 and retired on 22 June 2004?
30 Which cup succeeded the Shell Shield in the West Indies?

Answers	Animals (see Quiz 72)

1 Skomer vole. 2 Adder. 3 Sumatran tiger. 4 A small African antelope. 5 Ass. 6 Lizards. 7 Kangaroo hound. 8 Sea-cows. 9 Mongoose. 10 They act independently of each other. 11 South America. 12 Cockroaches. 13 Tiger. 14 Insects. 15 Fish, amphibians, reptiles, birds and mammals. 16 Animals which lay eggs. 17 Can precede "fly" to give the name of another creature. 18 Coypu. 19 Wombat. 20 Arthropods. 21 Types of beetle. 22 Desert fox. 23 Madagascar. 24 Leap. 25 China. 26 Viviparous. 27 Array. 28 Airedale terrier. 29 Worm. 30 Heavy horse.

1 Whose final opera was called "Death in Venice"?
2 Which Greek mountain is consecrated to the muses?
3 How old was John Paul II when he became Pope?
4 Which bird is sometimes called the windhover?
5 What is the national flower of Mexico?
6 Which newscaster's autobiography was called "The Road Taken"?
7 Which was the first British newspaper to issue a colour supplement?
8 Which religious sect was founded by J. N. Darby and E. Cronin?
9 Which British king was the first to own and drive a motor car?
10 Who is the patron saint of wine growers?
11 What name is given to an alloy of mercury?
12 In which shipyards were the "Queen Mary" and "QE2" built?
13 What is the traditional name for the number 3 wood in golf?
14 By what name is the Russian, Nicolai Poliakoff, better known?
15 Who wrote the classic Irish play "Cock-a-Doodle Dandy"?
16 Who won the '96 Oscar for Best Actress?
17 What name is given to the study of the paths taken by projectiles?
18 In which US city did Martin Luther King make his historic "I have a dream" speech?
19 Which city in Ontario is known as Steel City of Canada?
20 What do maiden, mother-of-all and footman have in common?
21 Which British city is served by Aldergrove airport?
22 In tennis, what name is given to the women's World Cup?
23 In which English county was Dame Kelly Holmes born?
24 Divali, or the Festival of Lights, is a celebration in which religion?
25 Who was president of the United States during the Wall Street crash of 1929?
26 What is the name given to the female reproductive organ of a flower?
27 To which group of birds does the capercaillie belong?
28 How many people (excluding the Queen's head) were on a 2005 Second Class Christmas stamp?
29 What was the name of the pub in "Minder"?
30 Who was the king of Sparta who was husband to Helen of Troy?

Answers	**Pot-Luck 32** *(see Quiz 69)*

1 Common Business Oriented Language. 2 Dromedary and Bactrian. 3 Gus Hedges.
4 Zenith. 5 Iain Duncan Smith. 6 Glasgow. 7 May 1st. 8 Pat Sullivan. 9 Morris
dances. 10 The Boston Strangler. 11 6. 12 Mantilla. 13 Jacques Cartier. 14 Richard
Dimbleby. 15 Time is Running Out. 16 Lindisfarne Mead. 17 George III. 18 Chicane.
19 The Ladies' Mercury. 20 Waterspout. 21 Madagascar. 22 The Sound of Music. 23
The skyscraper. 24 The Shootist. 25 The Straits of Messina. 26 Sayonara. 27 National
Lottery Jackpots. 28 Trumpet. 29 Angola. 30 Patrick Lichfield.

Quiz 72 | Animals

LEVEL 3

1 What creature is unique to Skomer Island, off the Pembrokeshire coast of Wales?
2 Which is the only snake to be found regularly north of the Arctic Circle?
3 What is the smallest tiger subspecies?
4 What is a dik-dik?
5 Which animal is the symbol of the US Republican Party?
6 What are goannas and anoles?
7 Which breed of dog is a cross between an Irish wolfhound and a greyhound?
8 What general name is given to manatees and dugongs?
9 Of which family is the linsang a member?
10 What is unusual about a chameleon's eyes?
11 What region is the arrow-poison frog a native of?
12 What group of insects include German, American and common?
13 Which animal might be Siberian or Caspian?
14 What do entomophagous animals eat?
15 What are the five groups of vertebrates?
16 What are oviparous animals?
17 What do horse, snake and scorpion have in common?
18 Which largest rodent became a serious pest in East Anglia?
19 What is the world's largest burrowing herbivorous mammal?
20 Which is the largest of all the animal phyla?
21 What are stag, rhinoceros and tiger other than animals in their own right?
22 What sort of animal is a fennec?
23 Where are the ayaye the remaining endangered animals?
24 What does an impala do when frightened?
25 What country are Père David's deer native to?
26 What name is given to a mammal which bears live young?
27 What is a group of hedgehogs called?
28 What is another name for an Old English terrier?
29 What is a sand mason?
30 What is a Clydesdale?

Answers | Sport: Cricket (see Quiz 70)

1 Manchester. 2 Northants. 3 M. J. K. Smith. 4 Surrey. 5 Antigua. 6 Frank Woolley. 7 Imperial Cricket Conference. 8 England. 9 Dylan. 10 Mike Gatting, Graeme Fowler. 11 Sunil Gavaskar. 12 Pakistan. 13 England, Australia, South Africa. 14 Gillette Cup. 15 Nathan Astle. 16 Jimmy Binks. 17 Alec Stewart. 18 Ian Botham. 19 New Zealand. 20 Ricky Ponting (Australia). 21 Ranji Trophy. 22 Douglas Jardine, Surrey. 23 Fred Trueman. 24 Ashley Giles. 25 Being Freddie. 26 Brian Johnston. 27 72 Tests. 28 South Africa. 29 Jack Russell. 30 Red Stripe Cup.

1 The Plains of Abraham overlook which city?
2 What were Vince's parents called in "Just Good Friends"?
3 Which French painter and sculptor created "The Pink Nude"?
4 By what other name is the constellation Pyxis known?
5 What is majolica?
6 The London Eye is located between Westminster Bridge and which mainline station?
7 To which family of flowers does the pimpernel belong?
8 In "Footballers' Wives" what was the name of Kyle Pascoe's stalker?
9 Whose final words were, "So little done, so much to do"?
10 Which is the smallest Canadian province?
11 What are the other three Christian names of Prince Charles?
12 The Three Stars is the national ice-hockey team of which country?
13 Which animated film features the voices of Timothy Spall, Julia Sawalha and Imelda Staunton?
14 Which is the only English city whose ancient walls are complete?
15 The Sam Maguire Trophy is the major competition in which sport?
16 What is the stage name of Carol Bongiovi's rock star son?
17 Mathurin Campbell is the real name of which female singer?
18 What is General Sherman in the Sequoia National Park?
19 Who along with Sitting Bull led the Native Americans at the Battle of Little Big Horn?
20 The Pindus are the principal mountain range of which country?
21 Who wrote the award-winning play "The History Boys"?
22 In yachting, what is a metal mike?
23 Who was the first Australian cricketer to be knighted?
24 What caused Prince Albert's death in 1861?
25 Who in 1989 said, "The Communist party has no God-given right to rule"?
26 What is a basenji?
27 Which planet did Mariner 9 photograph in 1971–72?
28 "Vision of a Knight" was the work of which Florentine painter?
29 What type of animal is a bariroussa?
30 By what other name do we know the Somers Islands?

Answers | **Pot-Luck 35** *(see Quiz 75)*

1 Missile Defence Alarm System. 2 A wild goat. 3 Lesley Garrett. 4 They are meteorites. 5 Exodus. 6 A minaret. 7 Pickpocket. 8 A distress signal. 9 Prince Henry of Portugal. 10 Glenn Miller, Chattanooga Choo Choo. 11 Nelson Mandela and F. W. de Klerk. 12 Joan Crawford. 13 NW8. 14 The Sorbonne, Paris. 15 Mexico. 16 Perth. 17 Launching missiles or stones. 18 Fidel Castro. 19 All are types of wine glass. 20 India. 21 Jenny Pitman. 22 Paraguay. 23 Ludicrus Sextus. 24 The Weir of Hermiston. 25 Bent Sorensen. 26 Shoulder blade. 27 Hungarian. 28 A single horse hair. 29 Steps. 30 Bamboo.

1 Which "Coronation Street" character was murdered by his daughter in 2005?

2 Whom did Malcolm Ryder try to poison so as to claim insurance?

3 Which EastEnder received a marriage proposal from Benny Bloom?

4 Which "Neighbours" character was killed in the fire at Lassiter's?

5 Who appeared on TV in 1974 as she held up a bank in San Francisco?

6 What feature was dropped from "The Great Egg Race" in 1981?

7 Whom did Connie Hall stab in 1988 in Dallas?

8 Who sat on a protesting lesbian during the 6 o'clock news in 1988 and who continued to read the news?

9 Which series ended when Tara King sent the main character into space?

10 Which soap saw Jason Gioberti die in its first episode?

11 Who rescued Bet when the Rovers Return caught fire?

12 Who presented the first British TV programme of birds in their natural habitat?

13 In addition to the "Blue Peter" team, who took part in the 1971 safari?

14 Who was ditched by Dame Edna for being boring?

15 How many people died in the Crossroads motel fire?

16 Who admitted that her face erupted when she first used Camay soap?

17 Who was the first British politician to have a televised state funeral?

18 Which sporting event was the first programme to be in colour?

19 What did Brian Connell have that no other newsreader had?

20 Which soap's first death was May Hardman on December 31st, 1960?

21 In which year were subtitles first included in the Queen's speech?

22 Which newsreader's drugs for epilepsy made him appear to be drunk?

23 What TV first did Gareth Jones achieve during a live transmission?

24 Whose was the first televised royal funeral?

25 Which "Blue Peter" team member was knocked out by a flying marrow?

26 What did Stephanie Rahn do in the "Sun" in 1970 to find herself on TV?

27 Which news programme was first to enter the Top 10 ratings in 1967?

28 Who made his first appearance in Albert Square in November 2002?

29 In "EastEnders", who accidentally ran over Tiffany Mitchell on New Year's Eve 1998?

30 Who was the first British newsreader to lose an earring on television?

Answers	**The Simpsons** *(see Quiz 76)*

1 Kent Brockman. 2 Yeardley Smith. 3 Kelsey Grammer. 4 Daddy. 5 Barney Gumble. 6 Herb Powell. 7 Jebediah Springfield. 8 Ned Flanders' grill. 9 Malibu Stacy dolls. 10 A Streetcar Named Desire. 11 Leonard Nimoy. 12 Milhouse van Houten. 13 Second. 14 Lute. 15 Leonard. 16 Scratchy. 17 He's a rabbi. 18 Ralph Wiggum. 19 Cough syrup. 20 Danny Elfman. 21 Vietnam War. 22 Charles Montgomery. 23 Agnes. 24 The Little Barber Shop of Horrors. 25 Ganesha. 26 Pink. 27 Happy Sumo. 28 Dark grey. 29 The Android's Dungeon. 30 Woodrow.

1 What is the meaning of the acronym MIDAS?

2 What type of animal is a markhor?

3 Which performer said, "Opera's an extreme sport, like jumping out of an aeroplane with a surfboard"?

4 What do Hoba, Baruberito and Williamette have in common?

5 In which Book of the Bible is found the story of the birth of Moses?

6 What is the high tower of a Muslim mosque called?

7 What type of person could have been referred to as a cutpurse?

8 What does it mean if the Union Jack is flown upside down from a ship?

9 Which European prince was known as "the Navigator"?

10 Who received the first gold disc and for which song?

11 Which two men were awarded the Nobel peace prize in 1993?

12 Which actress's story was portrayed in the 1983 film "Mommie Dearest"?

13 What is the postcode of the world famous studio at Abbey Road?

14 Which is the oldest of the European universities?

15 In which country is the volcanic mountain called Popocétapetl?

16 By what name is St Johnstown in Scotland now known?

17 In medieval times, what was a mangonel used for?

18 Who was the chief figure in the "26th of July" movement?

19 What do tulip, balloon and flute have in common?

20 Which country has the peacock as its national bird?

21 Which former trainer created the character Jan Hardy and her racing stable?

22 Of which country is Asunción the capital city?

23 Who was Frankie Howerd's master in "Up Pompeii"?

24 What was the name of Robert Louis Stevenson's last and unfinished novel?

25 Which composer created a new work based on Andersen's "The Little Mermaid" in 2005?

26 What is the other name for the scapula?

27 What nationality was the composer Bartók?

28 In Greek mythology what was the Sword of Damocles suspended by?

29 Which chart-topping quintet announced their split on Boxing Day 2001?

30 What is the world's tallest-growing grass?

Answers	**Pot-Luck 34** *(see Quiz 73)*

1 Quebec. 2 Rita, Les. 3 Henri Matisse. 4 Mariner's Compass. 5 Enamelled pottery. 6 Waterloo. 7 Primrose. 8 Sheena Hamilton. 9 Cecil Rhodes. 10 Prince Edward Island. 11 Philip Arthur George. 12 Sweden. 13 Chicken Run. 14 Chester. 15 Gaelic football. 16 Jon Bon Jovi. 17 Shola Ama. 18 Tree. 19 Crazy Horse. 20 Greece. 21 Alan Bennett. 22 Automatic helmsman. 23 Sir Donald Bradman. 24 Typhoid fever. 25 Mikhail Gorbachev. 26 A small hunting dog. 27 Mars. 28 Raphael. 29 A pig. 30 Bermuda.

1 What is the name of Springfield's newsreader?
2 Who is the voice of Lisa Simpson?
3 Which sitcom actor frequently guest starred as Sideshow Bob?
4 What was Maggie Simpson's first word?
5 Who was the Plow King?
6 What is the name of Homer's half brother?
7 Who founded the town of Springfield?
8 Who or what is Propane Elaine?
9 Waylon Smithers has the world's largest collection of what?
10 Marge Simpson once starred in a musical version of which play?
11 Which former "Star Trek" actor played himself in the episode "The Springfield Files"?
12 Kirk and Luann are the parents of which character?
13 In which season was the first Halloween special "Treehouse of Horror"?
14 Martin Prince plays which instrument?
15 What is the surname of Homer's colleague Lenny?
16 In the Itchy and Scratchy cartoons which character is the cat?
17 What does Krusty the Clown's father do?
18 Which character mistakenly thought Lisa was in love with him after she sent him a Valentine's card?
19 What was the secret ingredient in the cocktail the Flaming Homer?
20 Who composed the theme music to "The Simpsons"?
21 In which war did Principal Seymour Skinner fight?
22 What are Mr Burns' christian names?
23 What is the name of Groundskeeper Willie's shovel?
24 What was the title of the first Itchy and Scratchy episode Bart and Lisa wrote under Grampa's name?
25 There is a shrine to which Hindu god in the Kwik-E-Mart?
26 What colour is Otto's T-shirt?
27 What was the name of the sushi restaurant where Homer was poisoned by a piece of blowfish?
28 What colour is Snowball II?
29 What is the name of Springfield's comic book store?
30 What was the name of the man Bart made up to reply to Mrs Krabappel's personal ad?

Answers | TV: Memorable Memories *(see Quiz 74)*

1 Tommy Harris. 2 Meg Mortimer. 3 Ethel Skinner. 4 Gus Cleary. 5 Patty Hearst.
6 The actual egg race. 7 Ray Krebbs. 8 Nicholas Witchell and Sue Lawley. 9 The
Avengers. 10 Falcon Crest. 11 Kevin Webster. 12 Sir Peter Scott. 13 Princess
Anne. 14 Sir Cliff Richard. 15 One. 16 Katie Boyle. 17 Sir Winston Churchill. 18
Wimbledon. 19 A beard. 20 Coronation Street. 21 1981. 22 Reginald Bosanquet. 23
He died. 24 George VI's. 25 John Noakes. 26 Became the first topless page 3 girl. 27
News at Ten. 28 Alfie Moon. 29 Frank Butcher. 30 Angela Rippon.

1 What do the initials NASA stand for?
2 What is a palmiped?
3 In which city would you find the house of the painter Rubens?
4 What had Chloe and Jack become in Great Britain by the dawn of the new millennium?
5 Who was duped by a "Fake Sheikh" in January 2006?
6 Dodonpa, Goliath and Phantom's Revenge are all names of what?
7 What do Romney Marsh, Suffolk, Clun and Forest have in common?
8 Who was the singer on the radio classic "Take It from Here"?
9 Who succeeded Pope John Paul II?
10 In "Dad's Army" what was the occupation of Private Frazer?
11 What was Casanova's occupation at the time of his death?
12 Which Dutchman won the World Darts Championship in 2006?
13 Who wrote the forensic thriller "Predator"?
14 Which organization was founded in Ontario, Canada, by Mrs Hoodless in 1897?
15 What is the British equivalent to the US trademark Plexiglas?
16 Monte Marmolada is the highest peak of which mountain range?
17 Where in Britain would you find Roedean Girls' School?
18 Which Guy Ritchie film has the tagline "a disgrace to criminals everywhere"?
19 What was referred to as Black Forty-Seven?
20 2005 was which anniversary of the game of Monopoly?
21 What are Prince Andrew's three other first names?
22 Concord is the capital of which US state?
23 What is the opposite of oriental?
24 Which of Charles Dickens' novels was left unfinished in 1870?
25 Which Scottish mathematician invented logarithms?
26 What is the longest bone in the human body?
27 Who wrote "Anything Goes" and "Can Can"?
28 In Greek legend, which prophetess was the foreteller of doom?
29 Who was nicknamed "The Beard" by the US intelligence service?
30 The carnation is the national flower of which country?

Answers | Pot-Luck 37 (see Quiz 79)

1 Sidney Poitier. 2 The Reclining Figure. 3 1951. 4 The Royal Company of Archers. 5 Sweden. 6 A numismatist. 7 Friendship 7. 8 Harry Houdini. 9 Rifle shooting. 10 Beetles. 11 A mordant. 12 December 31st. 13 St James's Palace. 14 The Times. 15 Lawn Tennis. 16 C. T. Russell. 17 Rotary Club. 18 Paris and Brussels. 19 Goodbye, Farewell and Amen. 20 Christmas crackers. 21 Balalaika. 22 Wadi. 23 Whooping cough. 24 Northern Australia. 25 Trampolining. 26 Arundel Castle. 27 Antarctica. 28 Just Rewards. 29 Jo Grimond. 30 Britney Spears.

1 Which English county has the longest coastline?
2 Who is responsible for the blue plaques in London?
3 In which London borough are there the most blue plaques?
4 What was Marble Arch originally designed to be?
5 What is the stately home owned by the Spencer family in Northamptonshire called?
6 What are Grimes Graves and where are they?
7 Where is England's largest castle?
8 Which two English cathedrals have three spires each?
9 Which county used to be divided into Parts?
10 Which dukes are associated with Woburn Abbey?
11 Where would you go to watch a Furry dance?
12 Where are St Agnes, St Martin's and Bryher?
13 Which English county bordering the sea has the shortest coastline?
14 What is the eastern strait between the Isle of Wight and the English mainland called?
15 What is the main type of rock forming the North Downs?
16 Dunkery Beacon is the highest point where?
17 On which lake does Keswick stand?
18 Which part of England is associated with the novels of Arnold Bennett?
19 Under which London landmark are buried a razor, cigars and a portrait of Queen Victoria?
20 Where is there a Nelson's column other than the one in London ?
21 What is England's smallest mainland county?
22 Which stately home in Britain is the home of the Marquess of Bath?
23 In which city is Whip-ma-Whop-ma Gate?
24 How many parishes does Greater London have?
25 In which county is there a village called Middle Wallop?
26 Which Derbyshire village lost most of its population to plague in 1665 but prevented the spread of the disease?
27 Where would you find the Bell Harry tower?
28 Which English county has the smallest perimeter?
29 What are the chalk cliff headlands between Eastbourne and Seaford?
30 Where are trees laid out in the form of troops at a famous battle?

Answers	**Food and Drink: Gourmets** *(see Quiz 80)*

1 Egon Ronay. **2** Paul and Jeanne Rankin. **3** Heston Blumenthal. **4** Savoy, Carlton. **5** Michel Roux. **6** Alastair Little. **7** Italian. **8** Raymond Blanc. **9** Thailand. **10** Clement Freud. **11** Cork. **12** Simon Hopkinson. **13** Mireille Johnston. **14** Madhur Jaffrey. **15** Prue Leith. **16** The Greenhouse restaurant. **17** Darina Allen. **18** Michael Barry. **19** Terry Wogan. **20** John Tovey. **21** Evening Standard. **22** Vegetarian. **23** Caroline Conran. **24** Dorset. **25** Gareth Blackstock. **26** Jane. **27** Mr Beeton. **28** Ready Steady Cook. **29** Fanny and Johnny Cradock. **30** Philip Harben.

1 Who was the first black actor to win an Oscar?

2 Which sculpture by Henry Moore was stolen in December 2005?

3 In which year was the Festival of Britain?

4 What is the name of the Queen's bodyguard in Scotland?

5 Which country has had more monarchs – Norway or Sweden?

6 What is a person who collects coins called?

7 What was John Glenn's Mercury capsule called when he became the first American to orbit the Earth?

8 Under what name was Erich Weiss (1874–1926) better known?

9 With what sport is Bisley in Surrey associated?

10 If you were studying coleoptera what would you be examining?

11 In dyeing, what name is given to the substance used to fix the colour?

12 When is St Sylvester's night?

13 Where was the main residence of British sovereigns from 1698 to 1837?

14 What was the first newspaper to have a "Personal Column" on its front page?

15 Which game was patented under the name Sphairistike?

16 Which American founded the Jehovah's Witnesses?

17 Which club was founded by Paul Harris and others in Chicago in 1905?

18 Which two cities were the first two capitals to have a telephone link?

19 What was the final episode of M*A*S*H called?

20 Every year which invention by Tom Smith becomes a best seller?

21 What is the name of the Russian triangular guitar?

22 What name is given to a dry watercourse in a desert?

23 What is the common name for the illness pertussis?

24 Where is the Gulf of Carpentaria?

25 In which sport are the Triffus, Miller and Rudolf moves performed?

26 Which famous castle is the country seat of the Duke of Norfolk?

27 Adélie Land is a French territory on the coast of which continent?

28 What is the final novel in the series that began with "A Woman of Substance"?

29 Which British politician became leader of the Liberal Party in 1956?

30 Who was the first artist to release a single with Madonna?

| **Answers** | **Pot-Luck 36** *(see Quiz 77)* |

1 National Aeronautics and Space Administration. 2 A web-footed bird. 3 Antwerp. 4 Most popular first names for babies. 5 Sven-Goran Eriksson. 6 Roller coasters. 7 Breeds of sheep. 8 Alma Cogan. 9 Pope Benedict XVI. 10 Undertaker. 11 Librarian. 12 Jelle Klaasen. 13 Patricia Cornell. 14 Women's Institute. 15 Perspex. 16 Dolomites. 17 Brighton. 18 Lock, Stock and Two Smoking Barrels. 19 The potato famine in Ireland. 20 75th. 21 Albert Christian Edward. 22 New Hampshire. 23 Occidental. 24 The Mystery of Edwin Drood. 25 John Napier. 26 The femur (thigh bone). 27 Cole Porter. 28 Cassandra. 29 Fidel Castro. 30 Spain.

1 Who set up the Society of British Gastronomes?
2 Which couple had a TV show called "Gourmet Ireland"?
3 Whose restaurant was named Best Restaurant in The World by Restaurant magazine in 2005?
4 At which London hotels did Auguste Escoffier gain his reputation?
5 Which chef is associated with the world-class "Waterside Inn" at Bray?
6 Whose cookery book is called "Food of the Sun"?
7 What type of food does Valentina Harris specialize in?
8 Who is the chef/proprietor of "Le Manoir aux Quat' Saisons"?
9 Vatcharin Bhumichitr has written about the taste of which country?
10 Which writer, raconteur and food expert is a former Liberal MP for Ely?
11 In which city is Murphy's Irish stout brewed?
12 Which chef is the restaurant "Bibendum" associated with?
13 Which cook and writer produced a "Cook's Tour of France"?
14 Which expert on Indian cooking is also an accomplished actress?
15 Who founded a School of Food and Wine and was instrumental in improving British Rail sandwiches?
16 Where was Gary Rhodes chef when he shot to fame on TV?
17 Who founded the Ballymaloe Cook School in Ireland?
18 Which cook is a founder of Classic FM?
19 Who wrote the foreword to the collection of recipes in book form Delia Smith compiled as a response to Live Aid?
20 Who is chef/patron of the Miller Howe, Windermere?
21 Where did Delia Smith have a cookery column before achieving fame on TV?
22 What type of cuisine does Sarah Brown specialize in?
23 Which cook has been married to the founder of "Habitat"?
24 In which county is Hugh Fearnley-Whittingstall's River Cottage?
25 What was the name of the chef played by Lenny Henry?
26 What was the first name of Sophie Grigson's mother?
27 Who founded the magazine where Mrs Beeton's articles were printed?
28 Which TV programme consists of chefs producing a dish from a limited list of ingredients against the clock?
29 Which team wrote the Daily Telegraph's "Bon Viveur" column?
30 Who wrote "Man in the Kitchen" and was a TV cookery pioneer?

Answers	**Around England** *(see Quiz 78)*

1 Cornwall. 2 English Heritage. 3 Westminster. 4 Gateway to Buckingham Palace. 5 Althorp. 6 Flint mines, Norfolk. 7 Windsor. 8 Lichfield and Truro. 9 Lincolnshire. 10 Bedford. 11 Helston, Cornwall. 12 Scilly Isles. 13 Durham. 14 Spithead. 15 Chalk. 16 Exmoor. 17 Derwent Water. 18 The Potteries. 19 Cleopatra's Needle. 20 Great Yarmouth. 21 Tyne and Wear. 22 Longleat. 23 York. 24 None. 25 Hampshire. 26 Eyam. 27 Canterbury cathedral. 28 Isle of Wight. 29 Seven Sisters. 30 Blenheim.

1 Aluminium is extracted from which ore?
2 Which US statesman defined the "four freedoms"?
3 Which fairy story writer's bicentenary was celebrated in 2005?
4 Which word, meaning "I forbid" in Latin, means the right to prevent a law being enacted or an action being taken?
5 Who was the first golfer to win 15 career majors?
6 After Earth, which planet was orbited first by a man-made object?
7 Which instrument did Albert Schweitzer play?
8 Whom did Neil Kinnock describe as "the most courteous man in the western world"?
9 In cricket, who is the fielder who patrols the boundary behind the slips?
10 Who was the last emperor of the Incas?
11 Which gland in the body produces luteinizing hormone?
12 Who was the tightrope walker who repeatedly crossed Niagara Falls?
13 Which Australian cricketer needed to score only four in his final test innings to average 100, yet only got a duck?
14 Which theory compares the Earth to a living organism?
15 Which Italian opera composer said, "In the theatre the public will stand for anything except boredom"?
16 Which star of TV's "Lost" played the hobbit Merry in "The Lord of the Rings" trilogy?
17 Which painting medium uses egg yolk and water?
18 In the Sikh religion what is kesh?
19 Which twins are represented by the zodiacal sign Gemini?
20 Who said there are "lies, damned lies and statistics"?
21 Who is known as the founding father of eugenics?
22 What was the occupation of the "Wicked Lady" in the film?
23 Whose "guest" was six-year-old Stuart Lockwood in August 1990?
24 Which British actor played Magistrate Samuel Philips in "Sleepy Hollow"?
25 In how many films did James Dean appear?
26 What was the name of the landlord in "The Young Ones"?
27 What was Jim Hacker's wife called in "Yes Minister"?
28 What is the earliest known unit of length?
29 Who won "Strictly Come Dancing" the year after Jill Halfpenny won?
30 What is an astrolabe?

Answers | Pot-Luck 39 (see Quiz 83)

1 1922. 2 Tsunami. 3 Household management. 4 Chepstow. 5 1941. 6 Two. 7 Hammond organ. 8 Donna. 9 So that he could eat without leaving the gaming table. 10 Akihito. 11 T. S. Eliot. 12 White. 13 Insects. 14 Nitrogen oxides. 15 Medulla oblongata. 16 Turmeric. 17 DC Confidential. 18 Iron. 19 Chord. 20 Kemal Ataturk. 21 Crow. 22 Thornewill. 23 Sloane Square. 24 A violin bow. 25 Charlemagne. 26 He lost his sword arm. 27 Dakota Fanning. 28 Female. 29 P. T. Barnum's. 30 Lene Marlin.

1 Which horse gave Lester Piggott his first Royal Ascot winner?
2 Kieren Fallon's third Derby win was on which horse?
3 When were women first elected to membership of the Jockey Club?
4 As the Knavesmire is to York, so the Carholme was to which course?
5 Which was the first horse to win two Grand Nationals?
6 Who owned triple Grand National winner Red Rum?
7 Which Grand National winner of the 80s was named after a lighthouse?
8 Who was the first woman to ride in the Cheltenham Gold Cup in 1984?
9 Over which racecourse is the Greenham Stakes run?
10 Which horse was the first to win both the Derby and the St Leger?
11 In Britain who was the first National Hunt rider of over 1,000 winners?
12 In which year was the Derby first run?
13 Where in Doncaster did the St Leger take place before it was transferred to Town Moor?
14 Who won the flat racing jockeys' championship 26 times?
15 Who was the first trainer to turn out winners of more than £1 million in one flat racing season in Britain in 1985?
16 Which jockey won the 1970 St Leger on Nijinsky?
17 Over which racecourse is the Ebor Handicap run?
18 Which European flat race is run annually on the first Sunday in October?
19 In which years did Red Rum win the Grand National?
20 Who was the first woman to ride in the Grand National in 1977?
21 Which trainer, who died in 1983 aged 95, saddled 13 Classic winners?
22 Who was the first jockey to win both the Epsom and Kentucky Derbies?
23 Over which flat racing course is the Welsh Derby run?
24 When is a racehorse's official birthday south of the equator?
25 Which horse was the second Derby winner for the jockey who first won on Commander in Chief in 1993?
26 Who was Champion Jockey on the Flat sandwiched between Kieren Fallon's string of victories?
27 The Hambleton Cup, first run in 1612, is still run at which course?
28 Where did Jonjo O'Neill break his leg so badly that amputation was considered?
29 Which trainer's autobiography was called "The Glorious Uncertainty"?
30 Whom is the St Leger named after?

Answers	Modern History: US Politics (see Quiz 84)

1 Jefferson. 2 Henry Kissinger. 3 Kansas. 4 John F. Kennedy. 5 Gerald Ford. 6 Ronald Reagan. 7 Richard Nixon. 8 Rosalyn Carter. 9 Lyndon Johnson. 10 Bobby Kennedy. 11 Pamela Harriman. 12 William McKinley. 13 Alexander Haig. 14 Tipper. 15 Harry Truman. 16 Teddy Roosevelt. 17 Eisenhower. 18 George Bush. 19 Jesse Jackson. 20 Strategic Defence Initiative. 21 Polio. 22 Carl Bernstein, Bob Woodward, Washington Post. 23 Sadat, Begin. 24 Texas Rangers. 25 Ambassador to Britain. 26 Mary Jo Kopechne. 27 Nancy Reagan. 28 Spiro Agnew. 29 Washington. 30 Donald Rumsfeld.

1 When did Howard Carter and Lord Carnarvon find Tut's tomb?
2 What is the proper name for a tidal wave?
3 What does the word "economy" mean in the original Greek?
4 At which racecourse is the Welsh Grand National held?
5 In which year did the Japanese attack Pearl Harbor?
6 How many people feature on the front cover of John Peel's autobiography?
7 What was the electric tone-wheel organ invented in 1934?
8 What was the name of Kathy Beale's long-lost daughter in "EastEnders"?
9 Why did Lord Sandwich invent the sandwich?
10 Who succeeded Hirohito as emperor of Japan?
11 Who wrote "The Four Quartets"?
12 What colour is the cross of the Greek flag?
13 In which animals would you find compound eyes?
14 Which emissions from cars are acidic?
15 Which part of the brain controls the heart rate?
16 Which member of the ginger family is used to colour curries?
17 What were Christopher Meyer's controversial memoirs called?
18 What metallic element is found in fool's gold?
19 What name is given to the line which joins any two points on a circle?
20 Who in 1934 took the name meaning "Father of the Turks"?
21 What can be a bird or a North American Indian tribe?
22 What was the surname of the first married couple to walk to both South and North poles?
23 London's Cadogan Hall is near which famous square?
24 What did the baton replace for conducting an orchestra?
25 Who was crowned the first Holy Roman emperor in AD 800?
26 What injury did Lord Raglan, after whom the Raglan sleeve is named, sustain in battle?
27 Which child star has appeared in "Upton Girls" and "Sweet Home Alabama"?
28 Which gender of earwig has straight rather than curved pincers?
29 Whose circus did General Tom Thumb join at the age of five in 1843?
30 "Sitting Down Here" was a hit in 2000 for which artist?

Answers | Pot-Luck 38 *(see Quiz 81)*

1 Bauxite. 2 Franklin D. Roosevelt. 3 Hans Christian Andersen. 4 Veto. 5 Jack Nicklaus. 6 Mars. 7 Organ. 8 George Bush. 9 Third man. 10 Atahualpa. 11 Pituitary. 12 Charles Blondin. 13 Donald Bradman. 14 Gaia hypothesis. 15 Verdi. 16 Dominic Monaghan. 17 Tempera. 18 Uncut hair or beard. 19 Castor and Pollux. 20 Mark Twain. 21 Francis Galton. 22 Highwaywoman. 23 Saddam Hussein's in a TV broadcast. 24 Richard Griffiths. 25 Three. 26 Jerzy Balowski. 27 Annie. 28 Cubit. 29 Darren Gough and Lilia Kopylova. 30 Device used before the sextant for navigation.

1 The name of which US president is Bill Clinton's middle name?
2 Which US statesman won the Nobel Peace Prize in 1973, although the man he shared it with declined his award?
3 Which state did Robert Dole become senator for in 1968?
4 Under whose presidency was racial discrimination made illegal?
5 Which US president was born Leslie Lynch King?
6 Who is the only US president to have been divorced?
7 Who was the first US president to resign office?
8 Which First Lady was nicknamed the "Steel Magnolia"?
9 Which president initiated his "Great Society" programme?
10 Who was John F. Kennedy's attorney general?
11 Which American ambassador is the mother of Winston Churchill MP?
12 Which president other than John F. Kennedy was killed this century?
13 Which secretary of state announced to the world that he was in charge after the assassination attempt on Ronald Reagan?
14 What is Al Gore's wife called?
15 Which president ordered the dropping of the atomic bombs on Hiroshima and Nagasaki?
16 Which president's foreign policy was to "speak softly with a big stick"?
17 Whose memoirs were called "Mandate for Change" and "Waging Peace"?
18 Which president was a former director of the CIA?
19 Which Democrat founded what he called his "Rainbow Coalition"?
20 What was the official name of the so-called "Star Wars" programme?
21 What was the cause of Franklin D. Roosevelt's paralysis?
22 Which two journalists broke the story of the Watergate burglary and which paper did they work for?
23 Which leaders did Carter bring to Camp David to sign a peace treaty?
24 George W. Bush was part of a consortium that bought which baseball team?
25 Which post did Joseph Kennedy hold at the outbreak of World War II?
26 Whose death at Chappaquiddick stopped Ted Kennedy's ambitions?
27 Which First Lady was nicknamed the "Iron Butterfly"?
28 Who was Richard Nixon's first vice-president?
29 Where did Martin Luther King make his "I have a dream" speech?
30 Which Secretary of Defence held the post in two separate centuries?

Answers	Sport: Horse Racing *(see Quiz 82)*

1 Malka's Boy. **2** North Light. **3** 1977. **4** Lincoln. **5** Abd-el-Kader. **6** Noel Le Mare. **7** Corbière. **8** Linda Sheedy. **9** Newbury. **10** Champion. **11** Stan Mellor. **12** 1780. **13** Cantley Common. **14** Sir Gordon Richards. **15** Henry Cecil. **16** Lester Piggott. **17** York. **18** The Prix de l'Arc de Triomphe. **19** 1973, 1974 and 1977. **20** Charlotte Brew. **21** Cecil Boyd-Rochfort. **22** Steve Cauthen. **23** Chepstow. **24** August 1st. **25** Galileo (Michael Kinane). **26** Kevin Darley. **27** Thirsk. **28** Bangor. **29** Jenny Pitman. **30** Lt Col Anthony St Leger.

1 Marble is formed by the metamorphosis of which rock?
2 In which country was the playwright Tom Stoppard born?
3 Which constellation is named after the mother of Andromeda?
4 Where was Europe's first hard-paste porcelain made?
5 What kind of coolant is used in a fast reactor?
6 Who tells the tales of "The Thousand and One Nights"?
7 What was Queen Victoria first "not amused" by?
8 Who gave his name to the absolute scale of temperature?
9 At the end of 2005, what was Russia's only independent media corporation?
10 Who was Wyatt Earp's brother who, with Doc Holliday, fought the Clanton gang at the OK Corral?
11 What name is given to the technology of creating and reading codes?
12 Who replaced Geoffrey Howe as foreign secretary in 1989?
13 Who was the only US president whose terms of office were not consecutive?
14 Which children's author won the 2005 Blue Peter Book of the Year award?
15 Which radio presenter wrote "Melted into Air?"
16 Beriberi results from a lack of which vitamin?
17 Where does the Lhasa Apso dog originate?
18 What did Charles Dawson "discover" in the early 20th century that was proved a fake 40 years later?
19 In which year did the "Titanic" sink?
20 Who wrote "The Wealth of Nations"?
21 In which country did the first organized motor race take place?
22 How many time zones does mainland USA have?
23 Pidgin English originally evolved for trade between Britain and where?
24 How many reeds does an oboe have?
25 Which member of the "Gang of Four" was Mao Tse Tung's third wife?
26 Where was Celtic's first match after they signed Roy Keane?
27 In the international Code of Signals what does "Oscar" signify?
28 The biography "Three Act Life" was about which actor?
29 In which Wilkie Collins novel does the villain, Count Fosco, appear?
30 Where would you go to find a wild vampire bat?

Answers	Pot-Luck 41 *(see Quiz 87)*

1 Stratosphere. 2 Renal artery. 3 Sicily. 4 Dolly and Cissy. 5 Marcus Garvey. 6 Amritsar. 7 Lead. 8 Derek Roberts. 9 Iran. 10 Electoral college. 11 Sylvia and Christabel. 12 Neptune. 13 Sydney University. 14 Norway. 15 Wrestling. 16 A spore-producing body in a fern. 17 Jean Paul Gaultier. 18 Alice in Wonderland. 19 Cricket St Thomas. 20 Neil Simon. 21 Barbara Taylor Bradford. 22 Edward Hopper. 23 Ivana Trump. 24 78. 25 Mae West. 26 Christina Aguilera and Ricky Martin. 27 Belshazzar. 28 Red and yellow. 29 Hyperbole. 30 Gus Grissom.

1 What were the Supremes originally called?

2 What was the family relationship of the three Ronettes?

3 Which Ronettes hit was Phil Spector's only Grammy award?

4 What occupations did Martha Reeves, Rosalind Ashford and Annette Sterling have before they were Martha and the Vandellas?

5 Who sang "Stay" in 1993?

6 Which former Atomic Kitten took part in "Celebrity Love Island"?

7 The Girls Aloud hit "Jump" was taken from the soundtrack to which festive film?

8 Which quartet consisted of Susanna Hoffs, Annette Zilinskas and Debbi and Vicki Peterson?

9 Which group were "...in the Mood for Dancing" in 1979?

10 In 2001, which trio became the first US girl group to top the UK singles chart twice?

11 "Three" was the third album by which trio?

12 Which singer replaced Florence Ballard in the Supremes?

13 What was the Crystals first UK Top Ten hit?

14 BeBe Winans sang with which group on the No 1 hit "I Wanna be the Only One"?

15 Whose hit "We are Family" became an anthem for gay rights and the Pittsburgh Pirates baseball team?

16 Which of the Spice Girls' hits was the only one not to reach No 1?

17 Which band did Girls Aloud beat to win Popstar: The Rivals?

18 What was unusual about the Crystals' hit "He's a Rebel"?

19 Jessica, Melody, Kimberly, Nicole, Ashley and Carmit make up which group?

20 "Whole Again" was the first No 1 hit for which group?

21 Which girl group recorded the album "Saints and Sinners"?

22 Which duo were "Respectable" in 1987?

23 What was the real first name of Ronnie Spector, formerly Bennett?

24 The Sugababes' "Ugly" and "Push the Button" came from which album?

25 What was it raining according to the Weather Girls in 1984?

26 What was the first UK top ten hit for Destiny's Child?

27 Which actor is waiting in the title of the Bananarama hit?

28 Who married Dave Stewart and formed Shakespear's Sister?

29 Who backed Reparata on "Captain of Your Ship"?

30 Who had a 1960s hit with "Sweet Talkin' Guy"?

Answers	The Movies: Best of British (see Quiz 88)

1 Sir Ian McKellen. 2 Lion in Winter. 3 Rufus. 4 Brigitte Bardot. 5 Mike Newell. 6 Kind Hearts and Coronets. 7 Killing Fields. 8 Talbot Rothwell. 9 Prime of Miss Jean Brodie. 10 Don't Lose Your Head. 11 Lavender Hill Mob. 12 Room with a View. 13 I'm All Right Jack. 14 Oliver! 15 Lewis Gilbert. 16 Third Man. 17 Turin. 18 Harmonica. 19 Christy Brown. 20 Martita Hunt. 21 84 Charing Cross Road. 22 Gordon John Sinclair. 23 Italy, China. 24 Oh, Mr Porter! 25 Richard Briers. 26 Lauri Peters. 27 Peter Finch, Glenda Jackson, Murray Head. 28 How I Learned to Stop Worrying and Love the Bomb. 29 Albert Finney. 30 Gandhi.

1 In which part of the atmosphere is the ozone layer?
2 Which artery supplies the kidney with blood?
3 Which Italian region is the source of Marsala?
4 In "Dad's Army" what were Godfrey's two sisters called?
5 Who was the founder of the Back to Africa movement who largely inspired Rastafarianism?
6 In which Indian city did British troops open fire without warning on a crowd of 10,000 in 1919?
7 Which element gains its symbol from the Latin word "plumbum"?
8 Which Sun Hill Chief Inspector died in a car bomb in March 2002?
9 In which country did polo originate?
10 What is the name of the system by which the president of the US is elected?
11 What were Mrs Pankhurst's two suffragette daughters called?
12 Which planet has a Great Dark Spot?
13 Where was Enoch Powell a professor of Greek at the age of 25?
14 Which country's parliament is called the Storting?
15 Which sport has two main styles, called freestyle and Greco-Roman?
16 What is a "sorus"?
17 Which fashion designer created Madonna's famous conical bra?
18 Unsuk Chin's song cycle "Snag & Snarls" is based on which children's story?
19 In which village was Penelope Keith "To the Manor Born"?
20 Which playwright wrote "Barefoot in the Park" and "The Odd Couple"?
21 The biography "A Woman of Substance" was about which novelist?
22 Which painter caught the loneliness of city life in the 1930s and 1940s?
23 Who on the break-up of her marriage said "Gimme the Plaza, the jet and 150 million dollars"?
24 How many cards are there in a tarot pack?
25 Who said, "I used to be Snow White, but I drifted"?
26 Which vocalists released the single "Nobody Wants to be Lonely" in 2001?
27 In the Bible, which king of Babylon saw his own death prophesied?
28 What two colours are on a semaphore flag?
29 What is the deliberate use of exaggeration for emphasis called?
30 Who was the first man to go into space twice?

Answers	Pot-Luck 40 *(see Quiz 85)*

1 Limestone. 2 Czechoslovakia. 3 Cassiopeia. 4 Dresden. 5 Sodium. 6 Scheherazade. 7 An imitation of herself. 8 Kelvin. 9 Media Most. 10 Virgil. 11 Cryptography. 12 John Major. 13 Grover Cleveland. 14 Michael Morpurgo. 15 Sandi Toksvig. 16 Vitamin B1. 17 Tibet. 18 Piltdown Man. 19 1912. 20 Adam Smith. 21 France. 22 Four. 23 China. 24 Two. 25 Chiang Ch'ing. 26 Inverness (Caledonian Thistle). 27 Man overboard. 28 Anthony Hopkins. 29 The Woman in White. 30 South America.

1 Which actor from 2005's "The Magic Roundabout" was born in Burnley?

2 For which film did Katharine Hepburn win the first best actress BAFTA?

3 In "Love Actually" what is the name of Rowan Atkinson's jewellery salesman?

4 Who played opposite Dirk Bogarde in "Doctor at Sea"?

5 Who directed "Four Weddings and a Funeral"?

6 Which Ealing comedy was based on Roy Horniman's "Noblesse Oblige"?

7 Which 1984 film was based on "The Death and Life of Dith Pran"?

8 Who was the most prolific writer of "Carry On" scripts?

9 In which film did Maggie Smith call her girls "The crème de la crème"?

10 Which Carry On film was (very) loosely based on the Scarlet Pimpernel?

11 In which Alec Guinness film does a bank clerk carry out a bullion robbery?

12 Which 1986 film had "O Mio Babbino Caro" as its theme?

13 In which Boulting Brothers film did Ian Carmichael star as a graduate who starts work in a factory and causes a national strike?

14 Which musical was "the most non-U subject ever to be given a U certificate"?

15 Who directed "Educating Rita" and "Shirley Valentine"?

16 Which British film was the first non-French film to win the prestigious Palme d'Or at the Cannes Film Festival in 1949?

17 In which city does "The Italian Job" take place?

18 On what instrument is the music for the film "Genevieve" played?

19 Who was played by Daniel Day-Lewis in "My Left Foot"?

20 Who played Miss Haversham in David Lean's "Great Expectations"?

21 In which film was Anne Bancroft writing to a London bookseller?

22 What is John Gordon Sinclair called in the credits to "Gregory's Girl"?

23 "The Last Emperor" was a collaboration on film between Britain and which two other countries?

24 In which Will Hay movie does he play a haunted stationmaster?

25 Who plays Peter's father in Kenneth Branagh's "Peter's Friends"?

26 Who starred opposite Cliff Richard in "Summer Holiday"?

27 Which three actors made up the love triangle in "Sunday Bloody Sunday"?

28 What was the alternative title of "Dr Strangelove"?

29 Who turned down the role of T. E. Lawrence in "Lawrence of Arabia"?

30 Which film opens with the dedication "No man's life can be encompassed in one telling"?

Answers	**Pop: All-Girl Groups** *(see Quiz 86)*

1 The Primettes. 2 Two sisters, one cousin. 3 Walking in the Rain. 4 Motown secretaries. 5 Eternal. 6 Liz McClarnon. 7 Love Actually. 8 The Bangles. 9 The Nolans. 10 Destiny's Child. 11 Sugababes. 12 Cindy Birdsong. 13 Da Do Ron Ron. 14 Eternal. 15 Sister Sledge. 16 Stop. 17 One True Voice. 18 It wasn't the Crystals singing on the record. 19 The Pussycat Dolls. 20 Atomic Kitten. 21 All Saints. 22 Mel and Kim. 23 Veronica. 24 Taller in More Ways. 25 Men. 26 No, No, No. 27 Robert de Niro. 28 Siobhan Fahey. 29 The Delrons. 30 The Chiffons.

1 On the logo on an iPod which side of the apple is missing?
2 Which title did Bill Gates take on stepping down as Chief Executive Officer of Microsoft?
3 What do we call human-like robots?
4 What do the black bars and white spaces of bar codes represent?
5 What are optical fibres made from?
6 Who invented the mouse?
7 Which device converts chemical energy into electrical energy?
8 What was the name of the first communications satellite?
9 What does "laser" stand for?
10 Which separate companies invented and promoted the CD-ROM?
11 Which company developed the first electronic pocket calculator?
12 What device enables computers to send data down a telephone line?
13 Which software program was launched in 1982 by Lotus?
14 What name is given to a computer screen which responds to touch?
15 What does BASIC stand for?
16 What is the study of automated communication and control mechanisms in machines and humans called?
17 What do we call the wafer of silicon that carries miniaturized circuits?
18 What did the US company Diablo invent for use on typewriters?
19 How many bits or binary elements has a byte?
20 What is the largest bulletin board system (BBS) in the world?
21 What was the name of the first working electromechanical computer?
22 What is the name of the European Space Agency's satellite navigation system?
23 Who marketed the first dot matrix printers in 1957?
24 In digital communication terms what does MIME stand for?
25 What phrase applies to graphics programs which interact with people?
26 What was ARPANET a forerunner of?
27 What was launched in November 1985 by Microsoft?
28 Who invented the first calculating machine in 1642?
29 What term is given to part of a computer's memory that has its program permanently fixed?
30 Who developed the laser printer?

Answers | Foreign Literature *(see Quiz 91)*

1 Vaclav Havel. 2 Goethe. 3 Anton Chekhov. 4 Voltaire. 5 Dario Fo. 6 Pushkin. 7 Crimean War. 8 Actor. 9 Dostoyevski. 10 Czech. 11 Jakob, Wilhelm. 12 Rhinocéros. 13 The Blue Angel. 14 Honoré de Balzac. 15 Molière. 16 Omar Khayyam (Rubaiyat). 17 Aleksandr Solzhenitsyn. 18 Belgian. 19 Don Quixote. 20 Boris Pasternak (Doctor Zhivago). 21 Marcel Proust. 22 Aviator. 23 Les Fleurs du Mal. 24 Stendhal. 25 The Caucasian Chalk Circle. 26 Dreyfus. 27 Argentinian. 28 Simone de Beauvoir. 29 Jean-Paul Sartre. 30 George Sand.

1 Where was the Canadian goldrush which began in 1896?
2 Parsley belongs to which family?
3 Radioactivity is measured in which units?
4 What initials are used to describe chronic fatigue syndrome?
5 What device was originally used to explore the depths of an ocean?
6 What type of burial mounds date from the the early Bronze Age?
7 Which cricketer said about his autobiography, "I can honestly say that I've written one more book than I've read"?
8 In which year was the European Economic Community established?
9 Which "Casualty" character was played by an actor featured in "Strictly Come Dancing" 2005?
10 During which battle did the charge of the Light Brigade take place?
11 RP is the standard form of English accent – what do the letters stand for?
12 Which London bridge links St Paul's Cathedral to Tate Modern?
13 From which boat did Jacques Cousteau conduct his underwater research?
14 Which coin ceased to be legal tender from January 1st, 1991?
15 What is the feast of the Purification of the Virgin Mary?
16 From what colour rock is the Jordanian city of Petra carved?
17 In "Rising Damp" what is Rigsby's cat called?
18 What is the term for the energy obtained from hot underground rocks?
19 Where were the 2006 Winter Olympics held?
20 What does "lager" literally mean in German?
21 Who was appointed Chief Inspector of Schools in 1994?
22 What are crosses between bulldogs and terriers called?
23 Which element was used in the manufacture of the first florin?
24 To which Anglican movement did Newman, Pusey and Keble belong?
25 Which society was founded in London in 1884 to promote socialist ideas peacefully and to establish a socialist state in Britain?
26 Who was the French soldier whose constant drilling made his name a byword for strict discipline?
27 Which space probes failed to find life on Mars?
28 What was Beethoven's only opera?
29 What sort of creature was the best-selling robotic toy Teksta?
30 Where does the Australian Open Tennis Championship take place?

Answers | **Pot-Luck 43** *(see Quiz 92)*

1 Spike Milligan. 2 Samuel Goldwyn. 3 Rolf Harris. 4 Saitama in Japan. 5 Mass. 6 Man Ray. 7 Brookfield. 8 Baron Munchhausen. 9 The Rubicon. 10 Carbolic acid. 11 Pluto. 12 Pink. 13 Steve Waugh. 14 24. 15 Meriwether Lewis and William Clark. 16 Orchid. 17 Korea. 18 Trevor McDonald. 19 Fleur. 20 Etruscan. 21 Hindenburg. 22 John Stuart Mill. 23 Citroën. 24 Holly. 25 Farsi. 26 Cremona. 27 Descent of Man. 28 Fred Quimby. 29 The pressure of fluids. 30 Harrison.

1 Which Czech dramatist became president after the fall of communism?
2 Which German poet was prime minister to the Duke of Saxe-Weimar?
3 Which Russian dramatist married one of the actresses in his company?
4 Which French philosopher and writer was imprisoned in the Bastille and also wrote the fable "Candide"?
5 Which Italian dramatist wrote "Can't Pay, Won't Pay" in 1974?
6 Who wrote the novel Eugene Onegin?
7 In which war was "War and Peace" author Tolstoy on active service?
8 Before success as a writer what did Hans Christian Andersen do?
9 Which Russian novelist was sentenced to hard labour in Siberia in 1849 for printing socialist propaganda?
10 Franz Kafka wrote in German but what nationality was he?
11 What were the first names of the brothers Grimm?
12 In which Eugène Ionescu play do the characters turn into animals?
13 Which famous film is Heinrich Mann's "Professor Unrat" based on?
14 Who wrote a sequence of 94 novels under the title "La Comédie Humaine"?
15 Which French playwright's real name was Jean Baptiste Poquelin?
16 Which Iranian poet's most famous translator was Edward Fitzgerald?
17 Which Russian dissident's memoirs were called "The Oak and the Calf"?
18 What was the nationality of "Maigret" creator Georges Simenon?
19 What is Cervantes' parody of chivalric literature called?
20 Which Russian declined the 1958 Nobel prize after his novel about his mother country was published in Italy?
21 Who wrote "A la Recherche du Temps Perdu"?
22 What was the occupation of the author of "Le Petit Prince"?
23 What is the French title of Baudelaire's "The Flowers of Evil"?
24 Which French novelist's real name was Marie Henri Beyle?
25 Which Brecht play presents a dilemma about motherhood?
26 Whom was Zola defending in his open letter "J'accuse"?
27 What is the nationality of short-story writer Jorge Luis Borges?
28 Which French feminist writer wrote "The Second Sex"?
29 Which World War II member of the French resistance wrote "Nausea"?
30 How is Amandine Aurore Lucie Dupin better known?

| **Answers** | Hi-Tech *(see Quiz 89)* |

1 Right. 2 Chief Software Architect. 3 Androids. 4 Binary numbers. 5 Pure glass. 6 Douglas Engelbart. 7 Battery. 8 Telstar. 9 Light amplification by stimulated emission of radiation. 10 Philips invented, Sony promoted. 11 Texas Instruments. 12 Modem. 13 1-2-3. 14 Tactile screen. 15 Beginners All-purpose Symbolic Instruction Code. 16 Cybernetics. 17 Silicon chip. 18 Daisy wheel printer. 19 8. 20 CompuServe. 21 Coloccus. 22 Galileo. 23 IBM. 24 Multipurpose Internet Mail Extension. 25 Virtual reality. 26 Internet. 27 Windows. 28 Pascal. 29 Read Only Memory. 30 Canon.

1 Who played the part of Eccles in "The Goon Show"?

2 Which film mogul said, "include me out"?

3 Whose portrait of the Queen was unveiled in December 2005?

4 Where was the John Lennon Museum opened on October 9th 2000?

5 In the general theory of relativity what causes space-time to be modified?

6 How was the Parisian photographer Emmanuel Rudnitsky better known?

7 In "The Archers", at which farm do Phil and Jill Archer live?

8 Which 18th-century German soldier was famous for his exaggerated accounts of his adventures?

9 On crossing which river did Julius Caesar say, "The die is cast"?

10 What did Lister use to improve the hygiene of surgical operations?

11 What did the astronomer Clyde Tombaugh discover in 1930?

12 "Try This" was the third album by which female artist?

13 Which former sporting captain called his autobiography "Out of My Comfort Zone"?

14 In a standard cine film how many frames are shown each second?

15 Which two explorers did Jefferson send to find a land route to the Pacific?

16 Which type of flower has pods which are a source of vanilla?

17 Where does the martial art taekwondo originate?

18 Which newscaster said "Goodnight and goodbye" in December 2005?

19 In "May to December" what was Alec and Zoe's baby called?

20 Excavating the tombs of which civilization revealed lively paintings showing feasting, dancing and swimming?

21 Which airship exploded in New Jersey in 1937?

22 Which English economist sat as a Radical in Parliament during 1865–68 and urged votes for women?

23 Who made history with the first front-wheel drive vehicle in 1934?

24 In "Red Dwarf" what was the spaceship's computer called?

25 What is the official language of Iran?

26 In which Italian city did Antonio Stradivari and Niccolò Amati make their violins?

27 Which book by Darwin discussed human evolution?

28 Who was the producer of the Tom and Jerry cartoons until 1956?

29 What does a manometer measure?

30 What surname did the 9th and 23rd presidents of the US share?

| **Answers** | Pot-Luck 42 *(see Quiz 90)* |

1 Yukon. 2 Carrot family. 3 Becquerels. 4 ME. 5 A bathyscaph. 6 Round barrows. 7 Merv Hughes. 8 1957. 9 Woody. 10 Balaclava. 11 Received pronunciation. 12 Millennium Bridge. 13 Calypso. 14 5p pieces, which were the old shilling. 15 Candlemas. 16 Red. 17 Vienna. 18 Geothermal energy. 19 Turin. 20 Store. 21 Chris Woodhead. 22 Boston terriers. 23 Gold. 24 The Oxford Movement. 25 Fabian Society. 26 Jean Martinet. 27 Viking probes. 28 Fidelio. 29 Dog. 30 Flinders Park, Melbourne.

1 Which British dependent territory has a capital called the Valley?
2 The name of the capital of which country means "good air"?
3 Other than in Scotland, where is there a capital called Edinburgh?
4 What is the capital of Venezuela?
5 What is capital of Belarus?
6 What is the capital of the largest country in Europe after Russia?
7 Which US state's capital is the name of a lively 1920s' dance?
8 "One Night" in where is the name of a song from the musical "Chess"?
9 Oranjestad is the capital of Aruba but to whom does it belong?
10 Which fabric was originally made in Syria's capital?
11 In which US state's capital is the headquarters of the Mormon Church?
12 Which island's capital is Flying Fish Cove?
13 Which US state capital has the longest name?
14 In which capital was Gordon besieged for 10 months and then murdered?
15 Which African capital was sold to Italy in 1905?
16 What is the name of Greenland's capital, formerly Godthab?
17 Which country's capital is the end of a motor rally from Paris?
18 What shape is the Kremlin in Russia's capital, Moscow?
19 Which capital is linked to Almada by a bridge over the River Tagus?
20 Which US state capital is the name of the man credited with "discovering" America?
21 Which capital city has a state within it?
22 Which Arab capital's name is the name of a sweet dessert wine?
23 What did Abuja replace as Nigeria's capital?
24 Why is the Government Building in Wellington so notable?
25 Which Mexican state's name and state capital are also the name of a breed of small dog?
26 Which capital was founded in 1566 by the Knights of St John?
27 What is the capital of Malawi?
28 Which African capital's name was the name of a hit song by Tommy Steele in 1958?
29 "They Came to" which Middle Eastern capital in the title of a mystery by Agatha Christie?
30 Who sang about the capital of Catalonia in 1992?

Answers	**Sports Bag** *(see Quiz 95)*

1 Troon. 2 Geoff Howarth. 3 David Bryant. 4 Bradford. 5 Greyhound Racing Association. 6 Walter Swinburn. 7 1979. 8 Susan Brown. 9 Johnny Weissmuller. 10 Pat Smythe. 11 Curling. 12 Terry Griffiths. 13 Wimbledon. 14 Ayr. 15 Paavo Nurmi. 16 Four players. 17 100-metre breaststroke. 18 The Cresta Run. 19 Basketball. 20 Sonny Liston. 21 Parc des Princes. 22 Notts County. 23 Heather McKay. 24 Sandy Lyle. 25 Argentinian. 26 Doug Mountjoy. 27 Sampras and Agassi. 28 Hurst Park. 29 Multan. 30 Sydney, Australia.

1 What dye is named after a battle fought near Milan in 1859?
2 Which group of insects includes a hairstreak?
3 What component of CFCs causes destruction of ozone?
4 Which part of the gut absorbs water from the food?
5 Which pop star and pianist has a mother whose first name is Bong?
6 The mother and son of which king of England were both beheaded?
7 Which element is used in the preparation of light-sensitive film?
8 The Digambaras and the Swetambaras are sects of which religion?
9 What word for unthinking patriotism is derived from the name of one of Napoleon's admirers?
10 What metal is used for the filament in a light bulb?
11 Which planet has the lowest density?
12 Who was Millie, whose book was on the US bestsellers' list in 1990?
13 Margaret Thatcher and David Cameron share which star sign?
14 Which type of bond is most common in organic molecules?
15 How many wickets did Freddie Flintoff claim in the 2005 Ashes series?
16 Who was the first actress to turn up and accept a Razzie Award for Worst Actress?
17 Who converted the Louvre from a palace to an art gallery?
18 Which Marx brother was the piano player?
19 With which civilization did the legend of the phoenix begin?
20 Which veteran TV presenter called his autobiography "I Should Have been at Work"?
21 Whose theories of population growth helped Darwin form his theory?
22 What did social reformer George Williams found in 1844?
23 Whose plays include "Anna Christie" and "Mourning Becomes Elektra"?
24 In which battle were the British commander, Wolfe, and the French commander, Montcalm, both killed?
25 What is it called when the length of day controls the start of flowering?
26 Who wrote bad verse about the Tay Bridge disaster of 1879?
27 Who were the first to use tear gas in warfare and against whom?
28 Whose first film as a director was "Ordinary People"?
29 After a crash at Le Mans who stopped motor racing for over 30 years?
30 Which modern instrument was developed from the sackbut?

Answers | **Pop: The Rolling Stones** *(see Quiz 96)*

1 40 Licks. 2 Lennon and McCartney. 3 The Last Time. 4 Alexis Korner's. 5 Aftermath. 6 Sitar. 7 Drowned in pool. 8 Jean-Luc Godard. 9 Ned Kelly. 10 Jade. 11 Andy Warhol. 12 Jamaica. 13 Undercover. 14 Je suis un rock star. 15 David Bowie. 16 Willie and the Poor Boys. 17 Freejack. 18 Chuck Berry. 19 X-Pensive Winos. 20 Virgin. 21 Ian Stewart. 22 Muddy Waters. 23 Charlie Watts. 24 As Tears Go By. 25 Jeff Beck. 26 Have You Seen Your Mother Baby Standing in the Shadow? 27 Let's Spend the Night Together. 28 Brown Sugar. 29 Rolling Stones No 2. 30 2002.

1 On which British golf course is the hole called the "postage stamp"?
2 Which New Zealand cricket captain also captained Surrey?
3 Who was the first world champion at bowls in 1966?
4 Which is the home town of Joe Johnson, the snooker player?
5 Which sport's governing body carries the initials GRA?
6 Which jockey rode Shergar when it won the 1981 Derby?
7 When did Seve Ballesteros win the first of his Open championships?
8 Who was the first woman to compete in the Boat Race?
9 Which Olympic swimmer played the film role of Tarzan?
10 Who won the British Show Jumping Association Ladies' championship eight times?
11 The Air Canada Silver Broom is won in which sport?
12 Which Welshman won the world snooker championship in his first season as a professional?
13 At which course is the greyhound racing classic, the Laurels, run?
14 Over which course is the Scottish Grand National run?
15 Whose statue is outside the Olympic Stadium in Helsinki?
16 How many golfers before Tiger Woods had won all four majors?
17 At which event did Duncan Goodhew win an individual gold at the 1980 Moscow Olympics?
18 The St Moritz Tobogganing Club stages which famous race?
19 What is the modern name of "Pok-ta-Pok", which originated in Mexico?
20 Whom did Muhammad Ali beat to win the World Heavyweight boxing championship in 1964?
21 On which ground does France play its home rugby union matches?
22 Which is the oldest club in the Football League, founded in 1862?
23 Which woman squash player was unbeaten for 16 years from 1962?
24 Who became the first British golfer to win the European Open in 1979?
25 What nationality is lawn tennis player Gabriela Sabatini?
26 Whom did Steve Davis defeat in his first world snooker title final in 1981?
27 Which two tennis stars contested both the 1990 US Open and 2002 Open?
28 Which racecourse used to be alongside the Thames near Hampton Court?
29 Where did England lose the first Test to Pakistan in 2005?
30 Where is Randwick racecourse situated?

Answers | Geography: Capitals II *(see Quiz 93)*

1 Anguilla. 2 Argentina. 3 Tristan da Cunha. 4 Caracas. 5 Minsk. 6 Kiev, Ukraine. 7 West Virginia. 8 Bangkok. 9 Netherlands. 10 Damask. 11 Utah. 12 Christmas Island. 13 Jefferson City. 14 Khartoum. 15 Mogadishu. 16 Nuuk. 17 Senegal. 18 Triangular. 19 Lisbon. 20 Ohio. 21 Rome. 22 Muscat. 23 Lagos. 24 It's made of wood. 25 Chihuahua. 26 Valletta. 27 Lilongwe. 28 Nairobi. 29 Baghdad. 30 Montserrat Caballé, Freddie Mercury.

1 What was the name of the 2003 world tour?
2 Who wrote their first Top Twenty hit?
3 Which was their first No 1 to be written by Jagger and Richard?
4 In which blues band did both Mick Jagger and Charlie Watts perform?
5 From which album was the US chart entry "Mother's Little Helper"?
6 Which instrument did Brian Jones play, other than guitar, on "Their Satanic Majesties Request"?
7 How did Brian Jones die?
8 Which French director made The Stones film "One Plus One"?
9 Which Australian outlaw did Mick Jagger play on film?
10 What is the name of Mick Jagger's daughter by his first wife, Bianca?
11 Who designed the sleeve and logo on "Sticky Fingers"?
12 Where did they record the album "Goat's Head Soup"?
13 Which 1983 video for the title track was banned?
14 Which record was a hit for Bill Wyman in 1983?
15 Whom did Mick Jagger sing "Dancing in the Street" with at Live Aid?
16 What was the name of Bill Wyman's group that performed charity gigs?
17 Which sci-fi thriller did Mick Jagger appear in in 1992?
18 Who was the subject of the film "Hail Hail Rock 'n' Roll", for which Keith Richards directed the music?
19 Who were Keith Richards' band on "At the Hollywood Palladium"?
20 For which record label did the Stones sign a deal in 1991?
21 Who was dropped from the group in its early days because "he looked too normal"?
22 Whose song were the Rolling Stones named after?
23 Which Stone described his career as "five years of playing and 20 of hanging about"?
24 Which Jagger-Richard song was Marianne Faithfull's first hit?
25 Which famous guitarist played on Jagger's album "She's the Boss"?
26 Which 1960s Stones' hit had the longest title?
27 What was on the other side of "Ruby Tuesday"?
28 What was their first hit on their own Rolling Stones record label?
29 What was the Rolling Stones' second album called?
30 To a year either way, when did Mick Jagger become Sir Mick?

Answers | Pot-Luck 44 *(see Quiz 94)*

1 Magenta. 2 The Lycaenidae, a family of butterflies. 3 Chlorine. 4 Colon. 5 Myleene Klass. 6 James I (Mary Queen of Scots and Charles I). 7 Silver. 8 Jainism. 9 Chauvinism. 10 Tungsten. 11 Saturn. 12 George and Barbara Bush's dog. 13 Libra. 14 Covalent. 15 24 wickets. 16 Halle Berry. 17 Napoleon. 18 Chico. 19 Egyptian. 20 Des Lynam. 21 Thomas Malthus. 22 YMCA. 23 Eugene O'Neill. 24 Quebec. 25 Photoperiodism. 26 William McGonagall. 27 Germans against Russians in World War I. 28 Robert Redford. 29 Mercedes Benz. 30 Trombone.

1 Huntingdon is the birthplace of which ruler of England?
2 To whom is the Dunmow Flitch awarded each year?
3 About whom did Otto Preminger say, "Directing her was like directing Lassie. You need 14 takes to get each one of them right"?
4 In "The Archers", which character "died" in the run-up to Christmas 2005?
5 Which "Professionals" were played by Lewis Collins and Martin Shaw?
6 Which married couple were Time magazine's People of the Year in 2005?
7 Besides Hadrian, which Roman emperor had a wall built across Britain?
8 How are train robbers Parker and Longbaugh better known?
9 What are the Christian names of the two brothers who formed Bros?
10 Which soap star released an exercise DVD called "Busy Life Workout"?
11 In which year did the ten-shilling note cease to be legal tender?
12 In "The Odyssey", into what did the witch Circe change the sailors?
13 In heraldry, what colour is gules?
14 Rolf Harris was once Australian Junior Champion at what?
15 Which country won the soccer World Cup in 1982?
16 In Scotland what is or was a tawse?
17 King Jigme Singwe Wangchuck is king of which country?
18 Holi is a spring religious festival. In which religion?
19 Who wrote the poems "Ozymandias" and "Ode to the West Wind"?
20 What does a psephologist study?
21 Which large island is said to have been discovered by Eric the Red?
22 Which comedy drama had the theme song "That's Living Alright"?
23 In mythology which riddle was solved by Oedipus?
24 Which novelist wrote the book "Westward Ho!"?
25 Who wrote "A Wayne in a Manger"?
26 What was the first Red Hot Chili Peppers album to reach number one?
27 Who directed Mia Farrow in "Rosemary's Baby"?
28 If someone is lachrymose, what do they do a lot?
29 Who appoints the BBC's board of governors?
30 Between which towns was the railway for Stephenson's first locomotive?

Answers | Pot-Luck 46 *(see Quiz 99)*

1 Their shorthand could not be deciphered. 2 All Gas and Gaiters. 3 Arlene Phillips. 4 Red and green. 5 London bombings. 6 Vostok 1. 7 Battle of Actium. 8 12. 9 James Hanratty. 10 Her surname (credited as Emma). 11 Bill of Rights. 12 Albania. 13 Saturn. 14 Michael Jackson. 15 Yalta. 16 Sonja Henie. 17 Paraguay. 18 Six. 19 Amelia Earhart. 20 Francis Maude. 21 Methane. 22 Sibneft. 23 Barbara Hepworth. 24 Romania. 25 Gertrude Stein. 26 Edward Teller. 27 Noriega. 28 Printing. 29 The Empire Strikes Back. 30 Bovine spongiform encephalopathy.

1 Which studio had a lion as its symbol?
2 Why didn't some of the cast of "Gone with the Wind" see its première?
3 Whose roles included characters called McLain, McLintock and McQ?
4 Which future politician was beaten by Elizabeth Taylor for the role of Velvet Brown in "National Velvet"?
5 Who starred with Bergman and Grant in "Notorious"?
6 In which film did Bette Davis play Margo Channingt?
7 How was Ronald Reagan overlooked for a cinematic "White House"?
8 For which film were live leeches imported to Africa?
9 Which artist devised the dream sequence in "Spellbound"?
10 Who was voted king of Hollywood in 1937?
11 Which Astaire-Rogers film had the Oscar-winner "Cheek to Cheek"?
12 What was the first film co-starring Humphrey Bogart and Lauren Bacall?
13 In 1933 who choreographed "42nd Street" in which Ginger Rogers had a lesser role as Anytime Annie?
14 In which film did James Cagney play vaudevillian George M. Cohan?
15 Who was "The Hunchback of Notre Dame" in 1923?
16 Which classic was based on "The Tin Star" by John W. Cunningham?
17 In which movie did Gary Cooper play a farmer who became a war hero?
18 Who played "Mildred Pierce"?
19 Which 1948 classic was described as "Greed, gold and gunplay on a Mexican mountain of malice"?
20 What was Citizen Kane's real first name?
21 What was shown at the beginning of Paramount pictures?
22 Which John Wayne western was described as "'Grand Hotel' on wheels"?
23 What was Cary Grant's real name?
24 Which musical was the first to pair Mickey Rooney and Judy Garland?
25 What were the names of the four Warner Brothers?
26 What is the name of the drunk played by James Stewart in "Harvey"?
27 What did Cary Grant donate his salary from "The Philadelphia Story" to?
28 Which film star's real name was Reginald Truscott-Jones?
29 Which western hero is the subject of "My Darling Clementine"?
30 Which film opens with an office memo including the words "I killed Dietrichson. Me. Walter Neff, insurance salesman, 35 years old..."?

Answers	**Bestsellers** *(see Quiz 100)*

1 Blue. 2 Agatha Christie. 3 Webster's Dictionary. 4 Harper Lee. 5 Frederick Warne. 6 Thirteen and three-quarters. 7 Catch 22. 8 Guinness Book of Records. 9 Mickey Spillane. 10 The Remains of the Day. 11 Hold the Dream. 12 Catherine Cookson. 13 Cranberries. 14 Joan Collins'. 15 Nelson Mandela. 16 Dan Brown. 17 Peter Benchley. 18 Jung Chang. 19 Joanne Harris. 20 Delia Smith. 21 Wales. 22 Lady Chatterley's Lover. 23 Riders. 24 Kate Hannigan. 25 Alistair MacLean. 26 Ruth Rendell. 27 Danielle Steel. 28 Robert. 29 Mary Wesley. 30 Dr Benjamin Spock.

1 Why were Samuel Pepys' diaries not published until after 1825?
2 Which sit com was set in and around St Ogg's Cathedral?
3 Which person with "Strictly Come Dancing" links was involved in adapting "Saturday Night Fever" for stage?
4 Which two colours are mixed in a television to produce yellow?
5 Which event caused Tony Blair to leave the 2005 Gleneagles G8 summit?
6 What was Yuri Gagarin's spacecraft called?
7 In which battle did Rome defeat the forces of Antony and Cleopatra?
8 What is the atomic number for magnesium?
9 Who was hanged for the A6 murder?
10 What did Emma Bunton drop when she charted with "Free Me"?
11 What name is given to the first ten amendments to the US constitution?
12 Zog was king of which country from 1928 to 1939?
13 Which planet has the largest number of moons?
14 Whose first solo hit was "Got to be There"?
15 Where did Roosevelt, Churchill and Stalin meet in 1945?
16 Which Norwegian Olympic skating champion featured in many Hollywood films in the 1930s and 1940s?
17 Which country's currency is the guaraní?
18 How many carbon atoms are there in the phenol molecule?
19 In 1937 which woman flyer vanished without trace over the Pacific?
20 Who was the Conservative Party Chairman at the time of the 2005 leadership election?
21 What is the main constituent of natural gas?
22 What was the name of Roman Abramovich's oil company which he sold in 2005?
23 Which English sculptress exhibited her "Mother and Child" in 1930?
24 Which country had a secret police called Securitate, banned in 1990?
25 Who said, "Rose is a rose is a rose is a rose"?
26 Who worked on the Manhattan Project and later testified against its director, Robert Oppenheimer?
27 Which Central American dictator had the nickname "Pineapple Face"?
28 Which industry uses the gravure method?
29 Which was the second of the Star Wars films?
30 Often known as mad cow disease, what do the initials BSE stand for?

Answers | Pot-Luck 45 *(see Quiz 97)*

1 Oliver Cromwell. 2 The year's happiest newlywed couple. 3 Marilyn Monroe. 4 Betty Tucker. 5 Bodie and Doyle. 6 Bill and Melinda Gates. 7 Antoninus. 8 Butch Cassidy and the Sundance Kid. 9 Matt and Luke. 10 Debra Stephenson. 11 1970. 12 Pigs. 13 Red. 14 Swimming (backstroke). 15 Italy. 16 Strap, leather belt. 17 Bhutan. 18 Hinduism. 19 Shelley. 20 Elections, how people vote. 21 Greenland. 22 Auf Wiedersehen Pet. 23 The Riddle of the Sphinx. 24 Charles Kingsley. 25 Gervase Phinn. 26 By the Way. 27 Roman Polanski. 28 Cry. 29 The Queen. 30 Stockton and Darlington.

1 What colour was the flying Ford Anglia in "Harry Potter and the Chamber of Secrets"?

2 Which author said, "An archaeologist is the best husband a woman can have; the older she gets, the more interested he becomes in her"?

3 According to the Bob Hope/Bing Crosby song, which bestseller is Morocco bound as they were they were in the Road film?

4 Who wrote "To Kill a Mockingbird"?

5 Who has published Beatrix Potter's "Tale of Peter Rabbit" since 1902?

6 How old was Adrian Mole when he started writing his autobiography?

7 Which Joseph Heller book describes a "no win" situation?

8 Which book is the bestselling contemporary book of recent years?

9 Who created the detective Mike Hammer?

10 Which prize-winning novel by Kazuo Ishiguro became a successful film?

11 What was the second in Barbara Taylor Bradford's Emma Harte series?

12 Who holds the record as the novelist most borrowed from libraries?

13 Which fruit appears on the cover of Delia Smith's "Winter Collection"?

14 Whose sister wrote "Hollywood Wives"?

15 Whose autobiography was called "Long Walk to Freedom"?

16 Which author wrote with his wife, "187 Men to Avoid: A Guide for the Romatically Frustrated Woman"?

17 Who wrote the book on which the film "Jaws" was based?

18 Who wrote "Wild Swans"?

19 Which author, apparently with a sweet tooth, wrote "Blackberry Wine"?

20 Who cooked through the four seasons?

21 In the books about Inspector Morse where does Lewis come from?

22 About which book did a judge once ask if it was the sort of thing you would want your wife or servant to read?

23 Which book's hero is Rupert Campbell-Black and Jake his main rival?

24 What was Catherine Cookson's first novel?

25 Who wrote 30 books, with 28 of them selling a million in Britain?

26 Who sets her detective novels in Kingsmarkham?

27 Whose novels include "Lightning", "Accident" and "The Gift"?

28 What is the first name of Dr Atkins, author of a "New Diet Revolution"?

29 Whose first novel, "Jumping the Queue", came out when she was 70?

30 Who wrote a multi-million bestseller about child care in 1946?

Answers | **Hollywood Heyday** *(see Quiz 98)*

1 MGM. 2 All-white cinema. 3 John Wayne. 4 Shirley Williams. 5 Claude Rains. 6 All About Eve. 7 Rejected for Rick in Casablanca (White House). 8 The African Queen. 9 Salvador Dali. 10 Clark Gable. 11 Top Hat. 12 To Have and to Have Not. 13 42nd Street. 14 Yankee Doodle Dandy. 15 Lon Chaney. 16 High Noon. 17 Sergeant York. 18 Joan Crawford. 19 Treasure of the Sierra Madre. 20 Charles (Foster). 21 Mountain. 22 Stagecoach. 23 Archie Leach. 24 Babes in Arms. 25 Jack, Harry, Samuel, Albert. 26 Elwood. 27 War relief. 28 Ray Milland. 29 Wyatt Earp. 30 Double Indemnity.

1 In which country did Eddie Cochrane die?
2 What does the South African secretary bird kill and eat?
3 In Venice, what links the Ducal Palace with the state prison?
4 The African and French marigolds are both natives of which country?
5 In which speech did President Lincoln state that American government: was "of the people, by the people, for the people"?
6 Stephen Tompkinson, Eddie Izzard and Richard Wilson all guest starred on which comedy programme?
7 Who stood against Margaret Thatcher for the Tory leadership in 1989?
8 Which Israeli Prime Minister suffered a stroke in January 2006?
9 Which monarch had as one of his titles "The Lion of Judah"?
10 "The Happy Campers" was the first band formed by which Scottish solo singer?
11 Which forbidden river can no pure Hindu pass?
12 What was Madonna's first UK No 1 single when she was a 40 something?
13 Who is the patron saint of grave diggers?
14 In which part of the body is pepsin produced?
15 Bell metal is an alloy of which two metals?
16 Who wrote "Guy Mannering"?
17 What descriptive term is applied to Force 11 on the Beaufort scale?
18 Which Sunday paper was launched in January 1990?
19 What does the letter A stand for in Quango?
20 Who was the second Pope?
21 In which year was the first Wembley FA Cup Final to need a replay?
22 What did Del Boy in have written on the side of his car?
23 Who was the founder in 1945 of the Theatre Workshop, which moved to Stratford in east London in 1953?
24 The term "veteran" refers to cars made up to the end of which year?
25 What did the Germans codename "Operation Barbarossa"?
26 Which English king was nicknamed "The Hammer of the Scots"?
27 The marimba is an African form of which instrument?
28 Whose book "Flanimals" was published in 2004?
29 In "The Archers" what is the name of the church in Ambridge?
30 Whom did Stephen Hendry beat to become the youngest-ever world snooker champion in 1990?

Answers | **Eat and Drink: Pubs** *(see Quiz 104)*

1 Isle of Man TT course. 2 The Nutshell. 3 X. 4 Grand Stand Bar. 5 Grace Neill's Bar. 6 The Fighting Cocks. 7 North Yorkshire. 8 The George Inn. 9 The Horse Shoe. 10 Crown Liquor Saloon. 11 Medieval farmhouse. 12 The Dove. 13 Stalybridge. 14 Brazen Head Inn. 15 Earl Grey. 16 Woolpack, Malt Shovel. 17 Southport. 18 Coach & Horses. 19 Chichester. 20 Downham Tavern. 21 Lovejoy. 22 Olde Trip to Jerusalem 23 The Dove, Hammersmith 24 Recruitment centre for the Napoleonic Wars. 25 Blue Peter. 26 Munich. 27 Lou's Place. 28 The B.B.C. 29 The Snowdon Summit Bar. 30 Red Lion.

1 Who wrote "Wichita Lineman" and "By the Time I Get to Phoenix"?
2 Who co-wrote Eurovision "Puppet on a String" with Bill Martin?
3 Which songwriting pair penned hits in the rock 'n' roll era such as "Teenager in Love" and "Save the Last Dance for Me"?
4 Who won an Oscar for their writing of the title song of "Born Free"?
5 Along with Chris Martin and Guy Berryman who wrote the Coldplay album "A Rush of Blood to the Head"?
6 Who helped Shania Twain pen the hit "Man! I Feel Like a Woman!"?
7 Who wrote "Sailing", recorded by Rod Stewart?
8 Who replaced Bernie Taupin as Elton John's lyricist in 1979?
9 Who wrote the satirical "Dedicated Follower of Fashion"?
10 Which Neil Diamond song was the Monkees' first No 1?
11 What product was advertised in the Cook & Greenaway hit of 1971?
12 Who wrote Chris Farlowe's No 1 hit "Out of Time"?
13 Which singer sold more than 15 million records of the songs of Bacharach and David between 1962 and 1970?
14 Who wrote "It's Not Unusual" for Tom Jones?
15 Which songwriting trio established the Invictus and Hot Wax labels?
16 Which classical pianist became a pop writer with Howard Greenfield?
17 Which songwriting pair wrote "The Locomotion" for Little Eva?
18 Which 10cc member wrote "For Your Love" for The Yardbirds?
19 Which Lennon and McCartney song was Cilla Black's first single ?
20 Who was named "Officer of Arts and Letters" by France in 1993?
21 Which group was Stephen Stills with before Crosby, Stills, Nash and Young?
22 Which member of the Killers has a writing credit for all the tracks on their "Hot Fuss" album?
23 Who wrote Cliff Richard's first chart topper "Livin' Doll"?
24 Who wrote "Georgy Girl" and "I'll Never Find Another You"?
25 Who wrote the song which begins "I feel it in my fingers..."?
26 Who wrote the lyrics for Cliff Richard's "Heathcliff" musical?
27 Who wrote "If Not for You", a hit for Olivia Newton-John in 1971?
28 Who wrote the biggest-ever selling soundtrack album of its day in 1978?
29 How many tracks from David Gray's "White Ladder" album were written by him alone?
30 Which member of Fleetwood Mac wrote "Albatross"?

| **Answers** | Pot-Luck 49 *(see Quiz 105)* |

1 Glandular fever. 2 Time. 3 Richard Pryor. 4 Brighton Rock. 5 Opera. 6 King of Britain. 7 Kensal Green Cemetery. 8 The kidneys. 9 The checkered tablecloth once used for accounting. 10 Ignace Jan Paderewski. 11 "Clock" symphony. 12 Edith Mary Coates. 13 The River Rhine. 14 Burke. 15 Daily Universal Register. 16 Paul Rudd. 17 365. 18 Songthrush. 19 Jacques Brel. 20 Japan. 21 Henri Rousseau. 22 Noel Coward. 23 The Island of Sodor. 24 The Poor Clares. 25 Edward Kennedy. 26 Brazil. 27 Wind. 28 1577. 29 Heinrich Himmler. 30 Marcus.

1 What is Muckle Flugga?
2 Which Flemish painter produced "Adoration of the Kings"?
3 Who was described by the "Radio Times" as "The scummiest toerag in the great laundry basket of English history"?
4 Which French engineer conceived the idea of the Suez Canal?
5 On which day is Canada's Dominion Day or Canada Day celebrated?
6 What was the "Gluckauf" the first of its kind?
7 Who was the criminal who used a violin case for carrying his tools?
8 Which pop star had Slave written on his cheek, as a protest about his dealing with Warner?
9 In which needlecraft is honeycomb stitch worked?
10 Which two surveyors drew a line to set the boundary of Pennsylvania and Maryland?
11 What was the occupation of Mary Read and Anne Bonny?
12 Italian dictator Benito Mussolini previously had which two jobs?
13 Which US film director's work includes "Taxi Driver" and "Raging Bull"?
14 Peter Stringfellow, Lionel Blair and Peter Andre made guest appearances playing themselves on which programme?
15 On whose novel was the film "Lassie Come Home" based?
16 Which film was considered to be the first of the spaghetti westerns?
17 How is Shalimar described in the title of Salman Rushdie's novel?
18 Which film of 1934 gained an Oscar for the song "The Continental"?
19 Who was the voice of Donkey in Shrek 2?
20 What is the German term printed on labels of a high-quality wine?
21 What type of soup is Dubarry?
22 Which football team play at Tannadice Park?
23 When was the radio-only licence fee abolished?
24 Who joined French and Saunders in the quartet of "Girls on Top"?
25 In canasta, how many playing cards are needed?
26 Where would you find Amsterdam Island, Kerguelen and Crozet Island?
27 What is the Australian name for a kind of long, narrow lake?
28 Where would you find a canal in a national park in Britain?
29 For what is Peter the Hermit particularly known historically?
30 Why was Aberdeen's win over Celtic in the 1990 Scottish Cup Final a famous first?

Answers	**Sport: Football** *(see Quiz 106)*

1 Mark Walters. 2 Wigan. 3 Queen's Park. 4 Frank McLintock. 5 Steve McManaman. 6 Stoke City. 7 Cardiff. 8 Stelios Giannakopoulos. 9 Back Home. 10 A C Milan. 11 Aldershot. 12 Kevin Keegan. 13 Kenny Dalglish. 14 Solskjaer. 15 Blackpool. 16 Ron Saunders. 17 Queen Alexandra, Edward VII's consort. 18 Leeds United. 19 Ray Wilkins. 20 Real Madrid. 21 Northampton. 22 Millwall. 23 Parma. 24 David Batty. 25 Jasper Carrott. 26 Tommy Docherty. 27 Wembley. 28 Liverpool. 29 Gordon Strachan. 30 Ronaldinho.

1 On which famous course is the Sulby Glen Hotel?
2 What is the name of the tiny pub in Bury St Edmunds?
3 What was the previous name of the "Merry Harrier" in Devon which gave it the shortest pub name in the country?
4 What's the bar Galway Racecourse which is 210 feet long called?
5 What is said to be the oldest pub in Northern Ireland?
6 Which pub in St Albans is an 11th-century building?
7 In which county is the elevated Tan Hill Inn?
8 Which pub in Southwark is mentioned by Dickens in "Little Dorrit"?
9 Which pub in Drury Street, Glasgow, has one of the longest bars in Britain?
10 Which Belfast pub in Great Victoria Street is owned by the National Trust?
11 What was the Fleece Inn in Evesham before it became a licensed house?
12 What is the name of the pub, with the smallest bar room, in Upper Mall Chiswick?
13 Where is "The Old Thirteenth Century Cheshire Astley Volunteer Rifleman Corps Inn"?
14 What is the name of the 17th-century pub in Lower Bridge Street, Dublin?
15 Which Gloucestershire pub with a small bar room shares its name with a type of tea?
16 Which two pubs feature in the soap "Emmerdale"?
17 Where will you find "The Lakeside Inn" reputed to be Britain's smallest?
18 Which Soho pub was Jeffrey Barnard's regular haunt?
19 Where is the Gribble Inn which makes its own Black Adder II?
20 Which pub in Bromley, built in 1930, is said to be the country's largest?
21 Which antique dealer might you have met at the Butt & Oyster in Suffolk?
22 Which East Midlands pub served soldiers prior to going to fight the Crusades?
23 In which Hammersmith pub was "Rule Britannia" written?
24 Why is "The Napoleon" in Boscastle, Cornwall, so called?
25 Which pub in Polperro, Cornwall, shares its name with a TV programme?
26 In which city is the largest beer-selling establishment in the world?
27 What was the name of the pub destroyed by fire in "Neighbours" in 2005?
28 The George in Great Portland Street, London is which Auntie's local?
29 Where is the highest place you can buy beer in Wales?
30 What is the commonest name for a pub?

Answers	**Pot-Luck 50** *(see Quiz 107)*

1 As You Like It. 2 Stop Living the Lie. 3 Gold centre, then red, blue, black, white. 4 Tennis, anyone? 5 Margaret Beckett. 6 Victoria and Euston. 7 Admiral John Jellicoe. 8 Aeroflot. 9 Highest point of the city. 10 Silk screen painting. 11 Moldova. 12 3-tined fork. 13 A mollusc. 14 Apple. 15 Lizard. 16 American Indians in the United States. 17 Graham Sutherland. 18 The Coach. 19 Andromeda. 20 A mess of pottage. 21 Stained glass. 22 March 15th. 23 All are varieties of roses. 24 Clock face. 25 Dermot. 26 A large hat. 27 Wales. 28 Woodrow Wilson. 29 Grand National. 30 Tony Warren, creator of Coronation Street.

1 What illness is caused by the Epstein-Barr virus?
2 What is the first word of Madonna's hit "Hung Up"?
3 Which comedian and co-writer of "Blazing Saddles" died in December 2005?
4 In which of Graham Greene's novels does Pinkie appear?
5 Ellen Kent specializes in which type of touring entertainment?
6 What title is held by Shakespeare's "Cymbeline"?
7 Which cemetery is the resting place of Thackeray and Trollope?
8 Which organ of the body is affected by Bright's Disease?
9 How did the word "exchequer" come into being?
10 In 1919 which pianist was elected prime minister of Poland?
11 What is the nickname of Haydn's Symphony No 101 in D major?
12 Which mezzo-soprano created the role of Auntie in "Peter Grimes"?
13 On which river is the rocky cliff of the Lorelei located?
14 What was Calamity Jane's married name?
15 What was "The Times" first known as, in 1785?
16 "Friends" character Mike Hannigan was played by which actor?
17 How many islands make up the Calendar Islands in Casco Bay?
18 By what name is the mavis better known?
19 Who wrote the song known in English as "If You Go Away"?
20 Of which country is the Easter lily a native?
21 Whose jungle paintings inspired the 2005 film "Madagascar"?
22 Which British playwright said, "Never trust a man with short legs – brains too near their bottoms"?
23 What is the imaginary setting for the Rev. W. Awdry's "Railway Series"?
24 Which sisterhood established at Assisi around 1212 adopted the Franciscan rule and habit?
25 Which US politician shares his name with with Duke Ellington?
26 Nossa Senhora da Aparecida is the patron saint of which country?
27 What would be measured with an anemometer?
28 To five years either way, in what year did Francis Drake begin his voyage around the world?
29 Whom did Hitler choose to head the SS in 1929?
30 In "Birds of a Feather" what is Dorien's husband called?

Answers | Pot-Luck 47 *(see Quiz 101)*

1 England. 2 Snakes. 3 The Bridge of Sighs. 4 Mexico. 5 Gettysburg Address. 6 Father Ted. 7 Sir Anthony Meyer. 8 Ariel Sharon. 9 The emperor of Ethiopia. 10 KT Tunstall. 11 Attock. 12 Music. 13 St Anthony. 14 Stomach. 15 Copper and tin. 16 Sir Walter Scott. 17 Storm. 18 The Independent on Sunday. 19 Autonomous. 20 Saint Linus. 21 1970. 22 Trotter's Independent Trading Company. 23 Joan Littlewood. 24 1918. 25 The invasion of the Soviet Union. 26 Edward I. 27 Xylophone. 28 Ricky Gervais. 29 St Stephen's. 30 Jimmy White.

1 Which former Liverpool player's middle name was Everton?
2 After 19 games Peter Crouch managed his first Liverpool goal, but who were the opponents?
3 What is Scotland's oldest club?
4 Who captained Arsenal when they won the League and Cup in 1970–71?
5 Which English player featured in Real Madrid's 2002 Champions League Final triumph?
6 Which club, formed in 1863, won their first trophy 109 years later?
7 Which was the first Welsh side to win the FA Cup?
8 Which member of the Greek squad that won Euro 2004 played for Bolton?
9 What was the England World Cup Squad's No 1 hit in 1970?
10 Inzaghi, Rui Costa and Seedorf played together at which club?
11 Which football club folded in 1992 after 66 years in the League?
12 Which soccer player advertised "Brut" in the 1980s?
13 Who was the first Scot to make 100 appearances for his country?
14 Who hit Man Utd's late winner in the 1999 European Champions League Final?
15 With whom did Alan Ball begin his playing career?
16 Who was the first soccer manager to manage all three Birmingham clubs – Aston Villa, Birmingham and West Brom?
17 Who or what is Alexandra in Crewe Alexandra?
18 At which club were Robbie Fowler and Nigel Martyn team-mates?
19 Which England captain was sent off when captaining the side in 1986?
20 Who won the European Cup in the first five seasons from 1955 to 1960?
21 Which Football League club went from the fourth to the first division in five seasons in the 60s?
22 Which was the first 3rd division side to reach FA Cup semis?
23 Gianfranco Zola was a Chelsea player, but which club did he join them from?
24 Who missed the final penalty in England's 1998 World Cup campaign?
25 Who said on supporting Birmingham, "You lose some, you draw some"?
26 Which manager said he'd been in more courts than Bjorn Borg?
27 Which stadium hosted its first FA Cup semi-final in 1991?
28 Which team first won an FA Cup semi-final on a penalty shoot-out?
29 Who was the first Footballer of the Year in England and Scotland?
30 Who scored Brazil's winner in the 2002 World Cup game vs England?

Answers	Pop: Writers *(see Quiz 102)*

1 Jimmy Webb. 2 Phil Coulter. 3 Pomus and Shuman. 4 John Barry and Don Black. 5 Jonny Buckland and Will Champion. 6 Robert John "Mutt" Lange. 7 Gavin Sutherland. 8 Gary Osborne. 9 Ray Davies. 10 I'm a Believer. 11 Coca Cola (I'd Like to Teach the World to Sing). 12 Mick Jagger, Keith Richard. 13 Dionne Warwick. 14 Les Reed. 15 Holland Dozier Holland. 16 Neil Sedaka. 17 Gerry Goffin, Carole King. 18 Graham Gouldman. 19 Love of the Loved. 20 Elton John. 21 Buffalo Springfield. 22 Brandon Flowers. 23 Lionel Bart. 24 Tom Springfield. 25 Reg Presley. 26 Tim Rice. 27 Bob Dylan. 28 The Bee Gees. 29 Six. 30 Peter Green.

1 Sienna Miller was in which Shakespeare play, in the West End in 2005?

2 What was the first single by "Fame Academy" winner David Sneddon?

3 Starting at the centre, what are the five colours of an archery target?

4 What was the only line that Humphrey Bogart had in his first play?

5 In the 1990s, who was acting leader of the Labour Party after the sudden death of John Smith?

6 Name the first railway hotels opened in London in September 1839.

7 Who was the commander of the British fleet at the Battle of Jutland?

8 Which airline was originally called Dobrolet?

9 What is the literal meaning of acropolis ?

10 What is the common name for the craft known as serigraphy?

11 Who were the opponents when David Beckham made his first appearance for England?

12 What is a runcible spoon?

13 The shipworm is not a worm. What is it?

14 What is Gwyneth Paltrow's daughter called?

15 What is a chuckwalla?

16 Marlon Brando refused to accept his Oscar for "The Godfather" because of the oppression of which people?

17 Who painted the 80th-birthday portrait of Sir Winston Churchill?

18 In "Cheers" what was Ernie Pantouso's nickname?

19 Which constellation represents a princess in Greek mythology?

20 In the Book of Genesis, what did Esau get in return for his birthrigh?

21 Chartres cathedral in France is famed for what particular feature?

22 Julius Caesar was murdered on the Ides of March. What date was this?

23 What do Paddy McCready, Elizabeth of Glamis and Dorothy Perkins have in common?

24 In "Safety Last" where is stunt actor Harold Lloyd seen hanging from?

25 Whom did Harry Enfield play in "Men Behaving Badly"?

26 What kind of clothing is a dolly varden?

27 In which country was the explorer HM Stanley born?

28 Who was in office as president of the United States when the decision was taken to declare war on Germany during World War I?

29 Which major sporting event took place the same day as Charles and Camilla's wedding?

30 Whose autobiography was called "I was Ena Sharples' Father"?

Answers | Pot-Luck 48 *(see Quiz 103)*

1 The rock & lighthouse on Uist. 2 Brueghel. 3 Black Adder. 4 de Lesseps. 5 July 1st. 6 Custom-built oil tanker. 7 Charles Peace. 8 Prince. 9 Smocking. 10 Mason and Dixon. 11 Pirates. 12 Teaching, journalism. 13 Martin Scorsese. 14 Footballers' Wives. 15 Eric Knight's. 16 A Fistful of Dollars. 17 Shalimar the Clown. 18 The Gay Divorcée. 19 Eddie Murphy. 20 Kabinett. 21 Cream of cauliflower. 22 Dundee United. 23 1971. 24 Tracey Ullman, Ruby Wax. 25 108, two packs and four jokers. 26 Indian Ocean. 27 Billabong. 28 Brecon Beacons. 29 Led the First Crusade. 30 Decided on a penalty shoot-out.

1 What were the names of the three tunnels dug by POWs in "The Great Escape"?
2 Who had an 80s No. 1 with "Star Trekkin'"?
3 In which country is the city of Abu Dhabi?
4 Which shipping forecast area is due north of Shannon?
5 What is the only English anagram of LEOTARDS?
6 In which country are the Shakta Pantjukhina caves?
7 What was William Atheling's real name?
8 In Monopoly how much does it cost to buy the Angel Islington?
9 If it's noon at GMT, what time is it in Addis Ababa?
10 Who was the first player to be disqualified from Wimbledon?
11 Who wrote the novel "The Sea, the Sea"?
12 Which English county provided the setting for "The Farming Week"?
13 Who founded the Newman Haas Racing Indy Car Team?
14 In which decade were postal orders first issued in Britain?
15 Where on the M25 did Mrs Thatcher perform the official opening of the motorway?
16 Who wrote the non fiction title "Rebus's Scotland"?
17 In which fictitious town was "'Allo 'Allo" set?
18 Which ex-champ did Doug Flach beat in round 1 of Wimbledon '96?
19 Who defeated Tim Henman at Wimbledon 2005?
20 In which round did Tyson lose in his '96 clash with Evander Holyfield?
21 Who is the patron saint of wine merchants?
22 What was the first British Top Ten hit for Argent?
23 Lipari and Salina are in which island group?
24 On which river does St Petersburg stand?
25 Which magazine did Cherie Booth (Blair) guest-edit in 1996?
26 Prince Charles announced both his engagements in which month of the year?
27 From which language does the word "limousine" originate?
28 Whom did Norma Major write her first book about?
29 The airline Sansa is based in which country?
30 Which character was played by Prunella Scales in "After Henry"?

Answers | **Pot Luck 52** *(see Quiz 110)*

1 1940s. 2 Ghana. 3 Kingsley Amis. 4 Robert Terwilliger. 5 Chord. 6 Spanish. 7 The moon. 8 Algeria. 9 Free Parking. 10 Truffle. 11 T'Pau. 12 A meteorite. 13 J. C. Morton. 14 Walter Wolfgang. 15 Kriss Akabusi. 16 Simian Films. 17 Abdel Benazzi. 18 1500. 19 Rock Hudson. 20 Shot. 21 Over 300. 22 1440. 23 Patience. 24 Clement Ader. 25 Alan Mills. 26 Julia Roberts. 27 Sir John Houblon. 28 Moonee Ponds. 29 A lighthouse. 30 Dog Eat Dog.

1 Was Tony Blair's constituency majority in 2005: 8,449, 13,449 or 18,449?
2 Carole Caplin was a style guru for which famous female?
3 Who pulled out of the 2006 Lib Dem leadership race after newspaper "rent boy" stories?
4 Which Tory Shadow Arts Spokesman was sacked in November 2004?
5 Within five, in September 2005, how many Labour MPs were women?
6 When were pension arrangements for MPs first introduced?
7 Which disgraced former Minister of War died in March 2006?
8 In January 2005, which ex-MP said he had been HIV positive for 17 years?
9 When did Michael Howard first address the Tory conference as party leader?
10 In 2005 what was the full name of the Respect party?
11 Which city had six councillors found guilty of vote-rigging in 2005?
12 In September 2004 who became Chancellor of the Duchy of Lancaster?
13 Who played David Blunkett on television in "A Very Social Secretary"?
14 How old was Charles Kennedy when he became Lib Dem leader?
15 Whose web address is www.odpm.uk?
16 Who is the father of the MP made Secretary of State for International Development in 2003?
17 Where was Labour's Spring Conference held in 2006?
18 What was the Millennium Dome used for at Christmas in 2004?
19 Which UKIP MEP resigned in October 2004?
20 In 2005 what did BMG of the BMG Party stand for?
21 Who deputised for David Cameron at PMQs in February 2006?
22 With which MP did John Major have a four-year affair?
23 Who was the EU Trade Commissioner involved in the "bra" wars clothing subsidies?
24 In what year was the office of Leader of the Opposition first recognized with a salary?
25 What is the web address of the House of Lords?
26 What was the government majority at the start of Blair's third term as PM?
27 Which MP was featured in "Hello" magazine with one of the Cheeky Girls?
28 Which convicted conman was involved in the Cherie Blair Bristol flats saga?
29 The Lib Dem leader who resigned in 2005 was MP for which constituency?
30 The king of spin Alistair Campbell is a supporter of which soccer side?

Answers | Pop: Singers *(see Quiz 111)*

1 Boy George. 2 Dave Berry. 3 "South of the Border". 4 "Patches". 5 Coral. 6 Detroit. 7 HMS Ark Royal. 8 "Family Affair". 9 Marc Almond. 10 Moby. 11 11. 12 James Blunt. 13 The Chieftains. 14 Ricky Valance. 15 "Ring of Ice". 16 Louise Veronica. 17 The Belmonts. 18 D:Ream. 19 Archie Bell. 20 Tapestry. 21 Annie Lennox. 22 Ali Campbell. 23 Rosemary Clooney. 24 "I Won't Forget You". 25 Phil. 26 Barry Gibb. 27 Whitney Houston. 28 Gas fitter. 29 "Heartbreaker". 30 The Prince of Wails.

1 In which decade was Gérard Depardieu born?
2 In which country is the city of Accra?
3 Who wrote "Jake's Thing"?
4 In "The Simpsons" what is the real name of Sideshow Bob?
5 What name is given to a straight line that joins any two points on the circumference of a circle?
6 From which language does the word "bravado" originate?
7 Louis Daguerre took the first photograph of what?
8 The international car registration DZ applies to which country?
9 On a Monopoly board what is between Vine Street and the Strand?
10 What is the only English anagram of FRETFUL?
11 Who had an 80s No. 1 with "China in Your Hand"?
12 What is known to the Eskimos as Abnighito and is in Cape York Greenland?
13 What was Beachcomber's real name?
14 Which 82-year-old was thrown out of the 2005 Labour Party Conference?
15 Whose middle names are Kezie Uche Chukwu?
16 Which film company was founded by Liz Hurley and Hugh Grant?
17 Who captained France v. the Springboks in rugby in 1996?
18 What is the approximate distance of Athens airport from London in miles?
19 Which famous actor played Sammy Jo's father in "Dynasty"?
20 In which sport did Suzanne Allday achieve fame?
21 How many islands are in the Andaman group?
22 What is the sum total of the internal angles in a decagon in degrees?
23 How is Gilbert and Sullivan's "Bunthorne's Bride" better known?
24 Who invented the steam-powered aeroplane?
25 Who became Wimbledon referee in 1982?
26 Hazel Patricia and Phinnaeus Robert are children of which actress?
27 Who features on the most expensive banknote launched in April 1994?
28 In which Melbourne suburb was Dame Edna Everage brought up?
29 What type of building did Mary live in, in "The Life and Loves of a She-Devil"?
30 What was the first British Top Ten hit for Adam and the Ants?

Answers | Pot Luck 51 *(see Quiz 108)*

1 Tom, Dick & Harry. 2 Firm. 3 United Arab Emirates. 4 Rockall. 5 Lodestar. 6 Russia. 7 Ezra Pound. 8 £100. 9 3 p.m. 10 Tim Henman. 11 Iris Murdoch. 12 Northamptonshire. 13 Carl Haas. 14 1880s. 15 South Mimms. 16 Ian Rankin. 17 Nouvion. 18 Andre Agassi. 19 Dmitry Tursunov. 20 11th. 21 St Nicholas. 22 Hold Your Head Up. 23 Aeolian. 24 Neva. 25 Prima. 26 February. 27 French. 28 Dame Joan Sutherland. 29 Costa Rica. 30 Sarah France.

1 Whose first solo single had the catalogue reference Virgin BOY 100?
2 Which 60s singer was backed by the Cruisers on his first recordings?
3 What was the first Robbie Williams single not to make the UK top ten?
4 What was Clarence Carter's one and only hit?
5 On what label did Buddy Holly record?
6 Where in America was Diana Ross born?
7 Rod Stewart's "Sailing" was used for a BBC series about which ship?
8 What was the first US No. 1 single for Mary J. Blige?
9 Who was Marc of Marc and the Mambas?
10 How is Richard Hall better known?
11 "We Don't Talk Anymore" was Cliff's first No. 1 for how many years?
12 Which singer was on duty as a guard while the Queen Mother lay in state?
13 Whom did Van Morrison record the "Irish Heartbeat" album with?
14 Under what name did David Spencer record?
15 What was Jennifer Rush's follow-up to "The Power of Love"?
16 What are Madonna's two middle names?
17 In the 50s who was accompanying Dion on his first single?
18 Peter Cunnah sang his way to No. 1 with whom?
19 Which singer was backed by the Drells?
20 Both Carole King and Don McLean made an album called what?
21 Who was the most famous vocalist to sing with the Tourists?
22 Who is lead singer with UB40?
23 Who had a No. 1 with "Mambo Italiano"?
24 What was the first posthumous hit single for Jim Reeves?
25 Which Everly Brother sang the higher notes?
26 Who is the most successful singer to come from Douglas, Isle of Man?
27 Who played a character called Rachel Marron on film?
28 What was Joe Cocker's job before he became a singer?
29 What was Dionne Warwick's first Top Five hit in Britain?
30 What was Johnnie Ray's nickname?

Answers	**Westminster Village** *(see Quiz 109)*

1 18,500. 2 Cherie Blair. 3 Mark Oaten. 4 Boris Johnson. 5 97. 6 1964. 7 John Profumo. 8 Chris Smith. 9 2004. 10 Respect – the Unity Coalition. 11 Birmingham. 12 Alan Milburn. 13 Bernard Hill. 14 39. 15 Office of the Deputy Prime Minister. 16 Tony Benn. 17 Blackpool. 18 Shelter for the homeless. 19 Robert Kilroy Silk. 20 Blair Must Go. 21 William Hague. 22 Edwina Currie. 23 Peter Mandelson. 24 1937. 25 www.parliament.uk. 26 67. 27 Lembit Opik. 28 Peter Foster. 29 Ross, Skye & Lochaber. 30 Burnley.

1 Who wrote the novel "A Bend in the River"?
2 What was the first British Top Ten hit for Kenny Ball?
3 To 20, how many runs did Freddie Flintoff score in the 2005 Ashes series?
4 The airline Augusta Airways is based in which country?
5 Who led the British forces at the Battle of Princeton in 1777?
6 What number in Old Drum Lane was home to "Steptoe and Son"?
7 In which decade was Albert Finney born?
8 What was Acton Bell's real name?
9 What is the only English anagram of TRAGEDY?
10 On which river does Rangoon stand?
11 Who invented the swing-wing aeroplane?
12 If it's noon at GMT, what time is it in Casablanca?
13 From which language does the word "verandah" originate?
14 In Monopoly, what is the prize for winning a crossword competition?
15 Moluccas and Irian Jaya are in which island group?
16 Who played Christine in the film of "Phantom of the Opera"?
17 Where was Nelson Piquet's last Formula 1 Grand Prix race in 1991?
18 In which country was J. R. R. Tolkien born?
19 If something is "fluviatile" what is it?
20 Alaska became what number state of America?
21 Bonny Lad and White Windsor are types of what?
22 In which country is the city of Dakar?
23 Which novelist created the private investigator Hannah Wolfe?
24 In which Dickens novel does Susan Nipper appear?
25 Which Frenchman became Armenia's representative at UNESCO?
26 If A is Alpha and B is Bravo what is H?
27 Who wrote the novel "The English Patient"?
28 When is Lammas Day?
29 How many seats were in the Iraq parliament in 2006?
30 Which country does tennis player Marcos Baghdatis come from?

| **Answers** | Pot Luck 54 *(see Quiz 114)* |

1 Adverts. 2 Ken Boothe. 3 Svetlana Savitskaya. 4 Avenue Foch. 5 Italian. 6 Thames estuary. 7 John Stockton. 8 Erik Rotheim. 9 Liberal. 10 Alessandro Filipepi. 11 6,000. 12 Michael Moorcroft. 13 Stamford Brook. 14 Meryl Streep. 15 5-1. 16 1920s. 17 Aaliyah. 18 Golding. 19 Second cousin. 20 Between left thumb and forefinger. 21 "Manic Monday". 22 Marty McFly. 23 Edward Heath (1973). 24 Month of the grape harvest. 25 Nigel Mansell. 26. Dolly Parton economics. 27 Diana Rigg. 28 Lynette Scavo. 29 Cobbold. 30 USA.

1 In which two films did Paul Newman play "Fast Eddie" Felson?

2 Whom did Tom Cruise play in "Born on the Fourth of July"?

3 Whose first film, for Disney, was called "Napoleon and Samantha"?

4 Who played Sherman McCoy in "Bonfire of the Vanities"?

5 Which two superstars collaborated on the massive flop "Ishtar"?

6 Which film gave Michelle Pfeiffer her first Oscar nomination?

7 Who has been married to Judy Carne and Loni Anderson?

8 For which film did Meryl Streep win her second Oscar?

9 Which role did Kim Basinger play in "Batman" in 1989?

10 Who co-wrote the screenplay for "Yentl" with Barbra Streisand?

11 Which role did Elizabeth Taylor play in "The Flintstones"?

12 What was Disney's first PG movie, which starred Michael J. Fox?

13 Who was the star and executive director of the remake of "The Return of Martin Guerre"?

14 Who won the Best Supporting Actress award for "Cactus Flower"?

15 Who starred with Natalie Wood in "Splendor in the Grass" in 1961?

16 In which film did Jack Lemmon first direct Walter Matthau?

17 In which film did Russell Crowe play the 1994 Nobel Prize for Economics winner?

18 Aged 21, who wrote his autobiography "Absolutely Mahvelous"?

19 Who has played the Boston Strangler and Houdini on screen?

20 Who won an Oscar for playing an Irish cop in "The Untouchables"?

21 Who won an Oscar nomination for her first feature-film role as Robin Williams's mother?

22 Who played Sean Connery's son and Matthew Broderick's father in the same film?

23 Who posed nude covered in paint which looked like a man's suit?

24 Who was the attorney played by Kevin Costner in "JFK"?

25 Whom did Jack Nicholson play in "One Flew Over the Cuckoo's Nest"?

26 Which actor's directorial debut was "Confessions of a Dangerous Mind"?

27 Which actor won Australia's equivalent of an Oscar for "Tim"?

28 Who played Horace Vandergelder in "Hello Dolly!"?

29 Who was the Penguin in "Batman Returns"?

30 Whom did Cher play in Robert Altman's "The Player"?

Answers | Living World *(see Quiz 115)*

1 Use of feathers for the fashion trade. 2 Neotropical. 3 Demospongia. 4 Corals. 5 Red. 6 Harpy eagle. 7 Smell. 8 Three. 9 Starfish. 10 Bushman's clock. 11 Its diet. 12 On the sea bed. 13 Flightless bird. 14 Secretary bird. 15 Shellfish (not oysters!), worms, insects. 16 Cetacean or dolphin. 17 South America. 18 Andean condor. 19 Mongoose. 20 Sprat. 21 Mexico. 22 Dome of the shell. 23 Red mullet. 24 Cassowary. 25 Lizard. 26 Wishbone. 27 Plains wanderer. 28 Madagascar. 29 Dogfish. 30 Whole.

1 What is the only English anagram of STARVED?
2 Who had a 70s No. 1 with "Everything I Own"?
3 Who was the first woman to walk in space?
4 On a French Monopoly board, what is the equivalent to Oxford Street?
5 From which language does the word "piano" originate?
6 Where did the world-travelling aviator Amy Johnson vanish in flight?
7 In basketball, who smashed Magic Johnson's career assists record?
8 Who invented the aerosol?
9 Canadian Prime Minister Paul Martin was a member of which party?
10 What was Botticelli's real name?
11 What is the approximate distance of Bangkok airport from London in miles?
12 Who wrote the book "A Cure for Cancer"?
13 Which was the first London Underground station to have an automatic ticket barrier?
14 Which Oscar-winning actress guest starred on "The Simpsons" as Jessica Lovejoy?
15 What are the odds of rolling any combination totalling seven in dice-throwing?
16 In which decade was Dirk Bogarde born?
17 "I Care 4 U" was a posthumous hit album by which artist?
18 Which William won the Nobel Prize for Literature in 1983?
19 What relation is the actor Ralph Fiennes to the explorer Ranulph Fiennes?
20 Where does the actress Helen Mirren have a tattoo?
21 What was the first British Top Ten hit for the Bangles?
22 What was Michael J. Fox's character in the "Back to the Future" films?
23 Which prime minister introduced a 10.30 p.m. TV curfew?
24 In the French Republican calendar what did Vendemiare mean?
25 Who celebrated a Formula 1 win a lap too soon at Montreal in '91, losing to Nelson Piquet?
26 What did Kenneth Clarke call Gordon Brown's policy of "an unbelievable figure, blown out of all proportion with no visible means of support"?
27 Who played Vincent Price's daughter in "Theatre of Blood"?
28 Ryan O'Neal guest starred as the father-in-law of which Desperate Housewife?
29 Knebworth has been the home of which family for over 500 years?
30 In which country is the city of El Paso?

Answers	**Pot Luck 53** *(see Quiz 112)*

1 V. S. Naipaul. 2 "Midnight in Moscow". 3 402 runs. 4 Australia. 5 Lord Cornwallis. 6 24. 7 1930s. 8 Anne Brontë. 9 Gyrated. 10 Irrawaddy. 11 Grumman Co. 12 12 noon. 13 Portuguese. 14 £100. 15 Indonesia. 16 Emmy Rossum. 17 Montreal. 18 South Africa. 19 Belonging to or formed by rivers. 20 49th. 21 Broad Bean. 22 Senegal. 23 Sarah Dunant. 24 Dombey and Son. 25 Charles Aznavour. 26 Hotel. 27 Michael Ondaatje. 28 August 1st. 29 275 seats. 30 Cyprus.

1 RSPB founders campaigned specifically against the slaughter of birds for what purpose?
2 Which faunal region covers South/Central America and the Caribbean?
3 What is the largest class of sponges called?
4 Sea fans and sea whips are types of what?
5 What colour is the underside of the pipesnake's tail?
6 What is the world's largest eagle?
7 Which sense does the New World vulture have which the Old World vulture doesn't?
8 How many eyes does a tuatara have?
9 A sunstar is a type of what?
10 How is the early bird from Australasia, the butcherbird, also known?
11 How does the flamingo get its colour?
12 Where does a blenny live?
13 What is a ratite?
14 Which bird can walk up to 20 miles a day?
15 What do oystercatchers eat?
16 To which family does the grampus belong?
17 Which continent is the home of the electric eel?
18 What has the largest wingspan of any living bird?
19 The Puerto Rican boa is endangered due to which predator?
20 What does a white bait grow into?
21 Where does the axolotl come from?
22 Which part of a turtle is its carapace?
23 How is the goat fish also known?
24 Which flightless bird in addition to the emu is native to Australia?
25 What is a skink?
26 Which bone of birds is also called the furcula?
27 Which Australian male bird incubates the eggs and raises the young?
28 Where is the mesite native to?
29 Which fish is known as rock salmon when sold for food?
30 How does the monitor lizard consume its prey?

| **Answers** | **Movie Superstars** *(see Quiz 113)* |

1 The Hustler, The Color of Money. 2 Ron Kovic. 3 Jodie Foster. 4 Tom Hanks. 5 Warren Beatty, Dustin Hoffman. 6 Dangerous Liaisons. 7 Burt Reynolds. 8 Sophie's Choice. 9 Vicki Vale. 10 Jack Rosenthal. 11 Pearl Slaghoople. 12 Midnight Madness. 13 Richard Gere. 14 Goldie Hawn. 15 Warren Beatty. 16 Kotch. 17 A Beautiful Mind. 18 Billy Crystal. 19 Tony Curtis. 20 Sean Connery. 21 Glenn Close. 22 Dustin Hoffman. 23 Demi Moore. 24 Jim Garrison. 25 Randall Patrick McMurphy. 26 George Clooney. 27 Mel Gibson. 28 Walter Matthau. 29 Danny De Vito. 30 Herself.

Answers – page 592

1 Which shipping forecast area is south of Sole?

2 Which fictional village was the TV series "Dear Ladies" set in?

3 In which tennis major did the Williams sisters first play against each other in singles?

4 What was the lowest value on a Charles and Diana Royal Wedding stamp?

5 Who were the opponents when Alan Shearer became Newcastle's all-time top scorer?

6 What is the northern boundary of South America?

7 What was the first Spice Girls single to enter the chart at No. 1?

8 When did the US Supreme Court abolish the death penalty for minors?

9 Who wrote the novel "Nightmare Abbey"?

10 In which country is the city of Caracas?

11 What was Charlie Chaplin's first film?

12 How many islands are in the Azores group?

13 Who was President of the British Olympic Association from 1983?

14 Who won a Tony for his Broadway debut as Che in "Evita"?

15 Which soap had the characters Spanner and Craven and a drug dealer called Gibson?

16 Which character was played by Tim Healy in "Auf Wiedersehen Pet"?

17 If it's noon at GMT, what time is it in Mexico City?

18 What was the first British Top Ten hit for Shirley Bassey?

19 In which decade was Geoff Boycott born?

20 What is the only English anagram of GRIEVED?

21 What was Boz's real name?

22 Who was the first woman to be appointed captain of the Professional Golfers' Association?

23 Who invented the non-rigid airship?

24 In Monopoly, what dividend does the Bank pay you in Chance?

25 Who followed Arthur Balfour as prime minister of the UK?

26 Which ex-Miss Black Tennessee was Oscar-nominated for "The Color Purple"?

27 In which sport did Chris Baillieu achieve fame?

28 What is the capital of the Canadian province New Brunswick?

29 From which language does the word "steppe" originate?

30 Which performer undertook the Serious Moonlight Tour?

Answers | **Pot Luck 56** *(see Quiz 118)*

1 Hilary Swank. 2 Electric Company. 3 Elizabeth II. 4 Brussels Sprout. 5 Switzerland. 6 Bangladesh. 7 Paul Cattermole. 8 Diana Ross, Ryan O'Neal. 9 Monaco. 10 1,260. 11 Debbie Moore. 12 Jean Dominique Larrey. 13 Dutch. 14 New Edition. 15 Piers Morgan. 16 Prince Albert of Monaco. 17 CQD. 18 Philippa Vale. 19 Hawaiian. 20 Cricket. 21 1920s. 22 Ferns. 23 Friday. 24 Giovanni Antonio Canale. 25 Cambodia. 26 Sarah Ferguson, Duchess of York. 27 Kimbolton. 28 "Keep On Dancing". 29 7,000. 30 Gifted.

1 How many different French clubs did Eric Cantona play for before joining Leeds?

2 Who were Wigan's first ever opponents in the Premiership?

3 Who were the opponents when Michael Owen scored his first Newcastle goal?

4 What was the last English league club that George Best played for?

5 The world's first artificial pitch was built in which stadium in Texas?

6 Who got the last hat-trick against Man. Utd before Blackburn's Bentley in 2006?

7 Which city does the striker Chris Armstrong come from?

8 Who was the first manager to record six FA Cup Final wins?

9 Cec Podd created an appearance record for which club?

10 Which English club was first to be without a single British player in a squad for a game?

11 Which ground was featured in L. S. Lowry's painting "Going to the Match"?

12 Andy Cole scored his first League goal for which club?

13 Which team used to be called Shaddongate United?

14 Who scored for Manchester United in Cantona's "Kung-Fu" game v. Palace?

15 Which City play at home at Glebe Park?

16 To three, how many England clean sheets did Gordon Banks keep?

17 Colombia's Rene Higuita made an amazing scorpion kick save from which England player at Wembley in 1995?

18 Joel, Bryan and which other Glazer son joined Man. Utd's board in June 2005?

19 Which two teams were involved in Scotland's first ground share?

20 Steve D'Eath set an English clean sheet record while at which club?

21 At which club did Brian Horton follow Mark Lawrenson as manager?

22 Who scored the winning goal in the 1953 Matthews Final?

23 Which future international failed to impress Ipswich in trials in 1982?

24 Which teams played in the first international on an artificial pitch?

25 What were Barnet FC previously known as?

26 Lehmann saved which Man. Utd player's spot kick to win the 2005 FA Cup Final?

27 Whom did Hereford replace in the Football League in the 70s?

28 At which club did Steve Wigley take over from Paul Sturrock?

29 Which team was the first to retain the FA Cup in the 20th century?

30 Who was the boss for Alan Shearer's league debut?

Answers	**Around the UK** *(see Quiz 119)*

1 Ben Macdui. 2 Manchester. 3 Nith. 4 Edinburgh. 5 Bournemouth. 6 Aberdeen. 7 Neagh. 8 Aberystwyth. 9 Carlisle. 10 Leicester. 11 Kent. 12 Fenner's. 13 Jennie Lee. 14 Ten. 15 Perth. 16 Wakefield. 17 Towy. 18 Itchen. 19 Northern. 20 Leeds. 21 Douglas, Isle of Man. 22 Bangor. 23 Brighton. 24 The Octagon. 25 Dumfries. 26 Edinburgh, Heriot-Watt. 27 York. 28 The Parks. 29 St Andrews. 30 Colne.

1 Who won an Oscar for playing female boxer Maggie Fitzgerald?
2 In Monopoly, where would you land with a double six from Go ?
3 Who was the first reigning sovereign to visit a television studio?
4 Widgen and Welland are types of what?
5 In which country did the Scottish writer A. J. Cronin die?
6 In which country is the city of Dhaka?
7 Who left S Club 7 in 2002?
8 Who were originally suggested for the two main roles in "The Bodyguard" back in the 70s?
9 Which club did Thierry Henry play for when he first won the World Cup with France?
10 What is the sum total of the internal angles in a nonagon in degrees?
11 Who founded the Pineapple Dance Studios in London?
12 Who developed the ambulance?
13 From which language does the word "yacht" originate?
14 Who had an 80s No. 1 with "Candy Girl"?
15 Which former newspaper editor published his memoirs under the title "The Insider"?
16 Who became head of state in the month he acknowledged an illegitimate 22-month-old son?
17 What distress call did SOS replace?
18 Which character was played by Liza Goddard in "Bergerac"?
19 Niihau and Kahoolawe are in which island group?
20 In which sport did Enid Bakewell excel?
21 In which decade was Yasser Arafat born?
22 What does a pteridologist breed?
23 If Epiphany is on a Monday what day is Valentine's Day?
24 What was Canaletto's real name?
25 Which country has the internet code .kh, although neither letter is in its English name?
26 Which person with Royal Family links shares a birthday with singer Chris De Burgh?
27 At which palace did Catherine of Aragon die?
28 What was the first British Top Ten hit for the Bay City Rollers?
29 What is the approximate mileage of Buenos Aires airport from London?
30 What is the only English anagram of FIDGET?

Answers	Pot Luck 55 (see Quiz 116)

1 Finisterre. 2 Stackton Tressle. 3 Australian. 4 14p. 5 Portsmouth. 6 The Panama–Columbia boundary. 7 "Say You'll be There". 8 March 2005. 9 Thomas Love Peacock. 10 Venezuela. 11 Making a Living. 12 Nine. 13 Princess Anne. 14 Mandy Patinkin. 15 "The Archers". 16 Dennis Patterson. 17 6 a.m. 18 Banana Boat Song. 19 1940s. 20 Diverge. 21 Charles Dickens. 22 Beverley Lewis. 23 Henri Giffard. 24 £50. 25 Henry Campbell-Bannerman. 26 Oprah Winfrey. 27 Rowing. 28 Fredericton. 29 Russian. 30 Dave Bowie.

1 What is the highest peak in Scotland after Ben Nevis?

2 Where is the Whitworth Art Gallery?

3 On which river does Dumfries stand?

4 Where is the James Clerk Maxwell Telescope?

5 Which town has the car index mark AA?

6 Where is Dyce Airport?

7 Which Lough is in the centre of the Sperrin, Antrim and Mourne ranges?

8 Where is the National Library of Wales?

9 Which town's football ground is farthest away from any other?

10 Which English city has the first Jain temple in the western world?

11 In which county was there a £59 million robbery in February 2006?

12 What is Cambridge's county-class cricket ground called?

13 Which Milton Keynes theatre is named after a politician who was also a famous politician's wife?

14 How many bridges span the Tyne at Newcastle?

15 What was Scotland's capital in the 11th–15th centuries?

16 Where is Pontefract racecourse?

17 What is the longest river in Wales?

18 On which river does Winchester stand?

19 On which tube line is London's longest tunnel?

20 Which is farther north, Leeds or Halifax?

21 Where is Jurby Ronaldsway airport?

22 Where is the University College of North Wales?

23 Which town has a Theatre Royal and a Gardner Centre?

24 What is Bolton's theatre called?

25 Where is Queen of the South Football Club?

26 What are Edinburgh's two oldest universities called?

27 Which is farther east, Middlesbrough or York?

28 What is Oxford's county-class cricket ground called?

29 Where is the Royal and Ancient Golf Club?

30 On which river does Colchester stand?

Answers	**UK Football** *(see Quiz 117)*

1 Five. 2 Chelsea. 3 Blackburn. 4 Bournemouth. 5 Houston Astrodrome. 6 Dennis Bailey (for QPR, 1992). 7 Newcastle. 8 George Ramsay (all with Aston Villa). 9 Bradford City. 10 Arsenal (v. Palace Feb. 2005). 11 Burnden Park. 12 Fulham (on loan). 13 Carlisle. 14 David May. 15 Brechin. 16 35. 17 Jamie Redknapp. 18 Avram. 19 Clyde, Partick Thistle. 20 Reading. 21 Oxford. 22 Bill Perry. 23 Paul Gascoigne. 24 Canada v. USA. 25 Barnet Alston. 26 Paul Scholes. 27 Barrow. 28 Southampton. 29 Newcastle Utd. 30 Chris Nicholl (Southampton).

1 If it's noon at GMT, what time is it in Wellington?
2 Which soap was originally going to be called "One Way Street"?
3 Who wrote "The Pit and the Pendulum"?
4 What is the only English anagram of ORGANIST?
5 Since Christianity began when was the first visit by a Pope to the Holy Land?
6 The Bahamas is made up of approximately how many islands?
7 Prior to 2005 when did Wales last win rugby union's Nations Championship?
8 Who invented the balloon?
9 Who wrote "The Lady in the Van"?
10 What was the colour of the first decimal British 1/2p stamp?
11 Who had an 80s No. 1 with "Don't Leave Me This Way"?
12 In which decade was David Attenborough born?
13 Which Simpsons' character is a former boxer?
14 In which country are the Sistema del Trave caves?
15 Which secretary to Oliver North admitted shredding certain documents?
16 "Girlfriend," "Tearin' Up My Heart" and "Pop" were all hits for which boy band?
17 In March 2005 who was confirmed as the next President of the World Bank?
18 What was the first British Top Ten hit for the Beach Boys?
19 Where is the Circuit de Nevers, host of the French Formula 1 Grand Prix?
20 Whom did George Thomas succeed as Speaker in the Commons?
21 What was Lewis Carroll's real middle name?
22 Who was Jennifer Aniston's most famous godfather?
23 Which was the first film to be released simultaneously in cinemas and on video?
24 Which Olympic finalist won the Nobel Peace Prize in 1959?
25 On which river does Taunton stand?
26 Which cars won Le Mans consecutively from 1928 to 1930?
27 What was the name of the character killed in the shower in "Psycho"?
28 From which language does the word "plunder" originate?
29 The airline Gronlandsfly is based in which country?
30 In Monopoly, what do you receive when your Building Loan matures?

Answers	Pot Luck 58 *(see Quiz 122)*

1 Athole Still. 2 "Give Me the Night". 3 1930s. 4 £200. 5 Motor racing. 6 Maori.
7 Scissors Sisters. 8 Aland. 9 It threatened the practice of archery. 10 Somerset
Maugham. 11 Lamenting. 12 Brazil. 13 St George's. 14 Richard Mabey. 15
Thimphu. 16 B*Witched. 17 Yorkshire, Leicestershire. 18 Ned and Charles. 19 "The
Archers". 20 Lucien B. Smith. 21 May. 22 4,000. 23 Dijon. 24 Four. 25 Duke of
Grafton. 26 Abu Ghraib. 27 Robert Maxwell. 28 Ed McBain. 29 Argentina. 30 Jaime
Sommers.

1 Who was the housekeeper in "All Creatures Great and Small"?
2 Who narrated "Roobarb and Custard"?
3 Who replaced Anneka Rice on "Treasure Hunt"?
4 Which pseudonym did Ronnie Barker use when writing for "The Two Ronnies"?
5 Who sang the theme song for "Absolutely Fabulous"?
6 Who were the oarsmen in "Through Hell and High Water"?
7 Who was "concert chairman" at the "Wheeltappers and Shunters"?
8 Who devised the spoof news show "The Day Today"?
9 Who created the characters Mikki the Martian and Tich and Quackers?
10 Who was the first presenter of ITV's "World of Sport"?
11 Who played Shane O'Neill in TV's adaptation of "A Woman of Substance"?
12 Which job did Terry Wogan have before going into broadcasting?
13 Which TV presenter managed Dewsbury and Leeds rugby clubs?
14 Who played Mrs Bridges in "Upstairs Downstairs"?
15 Who had two chances to go for a charity million in "Who Wants to be a Millionaire?"?
16 Which character did Timothy Spall play in "Outside Edge"?
17 Who created "Soldier Soldier"?
18 Who was the first female presenter of "New Faces"?
19 Who are the "Hairy Bikers"?
20 What relation, if any, are the TV news journalists Jon and Peter Snow?
21 Who was known as the "godmother of soap"?
22 Who starred with Cilla Black in the first series of "Surprise Surprise"?
23 In which country was the actress Carmen Silvera born?
24 Who wrote the first series of "Black Adder"?
25 Who succeeded Robin Day as regular presenter of "Question Time"?
26 She played Katy in Corrie, but who played her dad in "Wild at Heart"?
27 Who wrote "The Phantom Raspberry Blower of Old London Town" for "The Two Ronnies"?
28 Which two MPs, unseated in 1997, were contestants on "University Challenge"?
29 Who achieved notoriety as the first person to use the F-word on British TV?
30 Which role did Robbie Coltrane play in "Tutti Frutti"?

Answers	**Books** *(see Quiz 123)*

1 Pocket books. 2 The Common Sense Book of Baby and Child Care. 3 Shelton's system. 4 49 (excluding covers). 5 Bentley Drummell. 6 1884. 7 Sophie Neveu. 8 Galsworthy. 9 René Goscinny. 10 Enid Blyton. 11 The Mysterious Affair at Styles. 12 Kazuo Ishiguro. 13 Ruth Rendell. 14 Lord Peter Wimsey, Harriet Vane. 15 John Mortimer. 16 1907. 17 Evelyn Waugh's Decline and Fall. 18 Queen's Bench Courtroom No. 7. 19 Alan Clark. 20 Isaac Bashevis Singer. 21 Philippa Carr, Jean Plaidy, Victoria Holt. 22 Ruth Prawer Jhabvala. 23 Endeavour. 24 Vera Brittain. 25 Elinor, Marianne. 26 A Kestrel for a Knave. 27 The Balkan Trilogy. 28 56. 29 Geraldine McCaughrean (Peter Pan). 30 Marilyn French.

1 Who was Sven-Goran Eriksson's agent during the "fake sheikh" fiasco?
2 What was the first British Top Ten hit for George Benson?
3 In which decade was David Bailey born?
4 In Monopoly how much does it cost to buy Vine Street?
5 In which sport did Tim Birkin excel early in the 20th century?
6 From which language does the word "kiwi" originate?
7 Jake Shears was frontman with which musical act?
8 Vardo and Lemland are in which island group?
9 Why did Edward III ban bowls?
10 Who wrote the novel "The Razor's Edge"?
11 What is the only English anagram of ALIGNMENT?
12 In which country is the city of Jaboatoa?
13 In which Windsor chapel did Charles and Camilla receive a blessing after their marriage?
14 Who wrote "Food for Free" about edible wild plants?
15 What is the capital of Bhutan?
16 Two members of which girl band were sisters of Boyzone's Shane Lynch?
17 Which two counties did Dickie Bird play for?
18 Who were the two Cherryble Brothers in "Nicholas Nickleby"?
19 What is Godfrey Baseley's most durable creation?
20 Who first patented barbed wire?
21 In what month did Mrs Thatcher first become prime minister?
22 What is the approximate distance of Chicago airport from London in miles?
23 Where did the Formula 1 racing driver Alain Prost obtain his maiden triumph?
24 How many successive years did Britain win the Davis Cup in the 30s?
25 What was Augustus Henry Fitzroy's title when he was UK prime minister?
26 American Lynndie England was charged with maltreating prisoners in which Iraqi jail?
27 Who was elected Labour MP for North Bucks in 1964?
28 How is Salvatore Lombino better known?
29 The international car registration RA applies to which country?
30 Which character was played by Lindsay Wagner in "The Bionic Woman"?

Answers	**Pot Luck 57** *(see Quiz 120)*

1 12 midnight. 2 "Neighbours". 3 Edgar Allan Poe. 4 Roasting. 5 1960s. 6 700. 7 1994. 8 Jacques and Joseph Montgolfier. 9 Alan Bennett. 10 Blue. 11 Communards. 12 1920s. 13 Moe Szyslak. 14 Spain. 15 Fawn Hall. 16 'N Sync. 17 Paul Wolfowitz. 18 "I Get Around". 19 Magny Cours. 20 Selwyn Lloyd. 21 Lutwidge. 22 Telly Savalas. 23 The Bitch, starring Joan Collins. 24 Philip Noel Baker. 25 Tone. 26 Bentleys. 27 Marion Crane. 28 German. 29 Greenland. 30 £150.

1 What were the first US equivalent of Penguin paperbacks?

2 What is the title of Dr Benjamin Spock's top best-seller?

3 In which shorthand system did Samuel Pepys write his diary?

4 How many pages did a book have to have to be termed a book according to UNESCO in 1950?

5 Who marries Estella in "Great Expectations"?

6 To ten years, when was the "Oxford English Dictionary" first published?

7 What is the name of the female French cryptologist in "The Da Vinci Code"?

8 Which John won the Nobel Prize for Literature in 1932?

9 Who wrote the Asterix books?

10 Which British author has written over 700 books and has sold over 60 million copies about one particular character?

11 What was the first Agatha Christie book in Penguin paperback?

12 Who won the Booker Prize for "Remains of the Day"?

13 In whose novels are Myfleet, Stowerton and Cheriton Forest found?

14 In "Busman's Honeymoon", who is on honeymoon?

15 Whose autobiography was called "Clinging to the Wreckage"?

16 To five years when did Rudyard Kipling win the Nobel Prize for Literature?

17 In which book would you find Captain Grimes, Mr Prendergast and Egdon Heath Prison?

18 In Leon Uris's "QBVII" what is QBVII?

19 Whose diaries tell of events at Saltwood and in government?

20 Who wrote the novel on which the Barbra Streisand film "Yentl" was based?

21 Which three pseudonyms did Eleanor Alice Burford Hibbert use?

22 Who wrote "Heat and Dust" later filmed by Merchant Ivory?

23 What did Colin Dexter eventually reveal to be Morse's first name?

24 Who followed up her first success with "Testament of Experience"?

25 Who are the two sisters in "Sense and Sensibility"?

26 Which novel was the film "Kes" based on?

27 How are the novels "The Great Fortune", "The Spoilt City" and "Friends and Heroes" known collectively?

28 To five, how many novels did Georgette Heyer write?

29 Who was asked to write a sequel to J. M. Barrie's story about a boy who never grew up?

30 Who wrote The Women's Room in 1977?

Answers	**TV Who's Who** *(see Quiz 121)*

1 Mrs Hall. 2 Richard Briers. 3 Annabel Croft. 4 Gerald Wiley. 5 Adrian Edmondson, Julie Driscoll. 6 Ben Fogle & James Cracknell. 7 Colin Crompton. 8 Armando Iannucci & Chris Morris. 9 Ray Alan. 10 Eamonn Andrews. 11 Liam Neeson. 12 Bank clerk. 13 Eddie Waring. 14 Angela Baddeley. 15 Jackie and Laurence Llewelyn-Bowen. 16 Kevin Costello. 17 Lucy Gannon. 18 Marti Caine. 19 Simon King & Dave Myers. 20 Cousins. 21 Julia Smith. 22 Christopher Biggins. 23 Canada. 24 Rowan Atkinson, Richard Curtis. 25 Peter Sissons. 26 Stephen Tompkinson. 27 Spike Milligan. 28 Malcolm Rifkind, David Mellor. 29 Kenneth Tynan. 30 Danny McGlone.

1 What were the names of Harold Wilson's two sons?
2 Which character was played by Julie Walters in "The Boys from the Black Stuff"?
3 The airline Air Littoral is based in which country?
4 Who had a 70s No. 1 with "Yes Sir, I Can Boogie"?
5 From which language does the word "paddy" originate?
6 Who invented artificial blood?
7 Utila in the Caribbean is part of which island group?
8 In 1968 who became the first Briton to win Olympic Gold at shooting for 44 years?
9 Whose wives include Dorothy Squires and Luisa Mattioli?
10 Who wrote "One-Upmanship"?
11 Which shipping forecast area is east of Finisterre?
12 Who played Bob Champion in "Champions"?
13 Hispy and Quickstep are types of what?
14 Which Formula 1 racing circuit has bends called Estoril, Lycée and Adelaide?
15 How old was Mae West when she died?
16 Who was the first host of "Crackerjack"?
17 What is the only English anagram of ALSATIANS?
18 What was Leslie Charteris's real name?
19 What are the odds of rolling any combination totalling nine in dice-throwing?
20 How many islands are in the Virgin group?
21 Which John won the Nobel Prize for Literature in 1962?
22 In Monopoly, what is the amount of the speeding fine?
23 Which racehorse trainer was the first to win over £1 million?
24 Which hospital ward was "The Singing Detective" in?
25 Who guided Oxford to ten successive boat race victories from 1976?
26 What was the first British Top Ten hit for the Beverley Sisters?
27 If it's noon at GMT, what time is it in Yokohama?
28 Helen Liddell entered Parliament after winning the by-election caused by which MP's death?
29 Which two jockeys' injuries brought about the setting up of the Injured Jockeys Fund in 1964?
30 Which Nazi was played by Ian Holm in "Holocaust"?

Answers | Pot Luck 60 *(see Quiz 126)*

1 L. S. Lowry. 2 Ancestral. 3 President Mogae. 4 Brooklands. 5 Laura and Tom (Parker Bowles). 6 VisiCalc. 7 Pentonville. 8 Alfred Hitchcock. 9 Ian Stark. 10 Saul Bellow. 11 Chinese. 12 Mohammed Al Fayed. 13 Chance. 14 Lord Sebastian Flyte. 15 Gilbert. 16 Windmill. 17 White sari with a blue border. 18 900. 19 Cullinan II. 20 Richard Gasquet. 21 Tower of London. 22 Evanglelista Torricelli. 23 The Tremeloes. 24 Michael and Margaret. 25 Prof. Sybil Trelawney. 26 Dining car on a train. 27 Badminton. 28 1,080. 29 Ohio. 30 Willie Carson.

1 What took the Les Baxter Orchestra, Al Hibbler and Liberace into the charts?
2 Frank Infante and Chris Stein first made No. 1 in which group?
3 Which record gave the 70s hearthrob David Cassidy a mid-80s hit?
4 Who wrote the Rolling Stones' first No. 1?
5 Which Beatle made it first to No. 1 with a solo single?
6 What was Peter Sarstedt's follow-up to "Where Do You Go to My Lovely?"?
7 What finally knocked Wet Wet Wet's "Love is All Around" off No. 1?
8 It was over 30 years ago, but what was Leo Sayers' first Top Ten hit?
9 What was A-Ha's first British Top Ten hit?
10 "Don't Cry for Me Argentina" was a big flop for whom after a previous No. 1 single?
11 What word links a door and a tambourine in No. 1 titles?
12 Who had a 70s hit with "Oh Babe What Would You Say"?
13 What was the first single since the 1960s to debut inside the US Top Ten?
14 Camp Grenada provided the setting for whose hit?
15 Kevin Parrot and Michael Coleman made No. 1 under what name?
16 What was Tracey Ullman's first UK Top Ten hit?
17 Which magazine produced the first record chart?
18 On which label did George Michael have his first solo No. 1s?
19 What was the fastest-selling single of 2004?
20 Eddie Reader had her first No. 1 with which group?
21 Which hit's title had the words "And That's the Truth" in brackets?
22 Who had his first UK hit in the 50s with "Young at Heart"?
23 First charting in 1971, when did Elton John have a solo No. 1?
24 How many Top Ten singles did New Kids on the Block have in 1990?
25 On what label did Oasis first make the charts?
26 Which artist has spent most weeks at No. 1 in a calendar year?
27 What was New Order's first UK Top Ten single?
28 What was Elvis's follow up to "It's Now or Never"?
29 Whom did Annie Lennox duet with on "Why"?
30 Who had their only UK hit with "Let Me Try Again"?

Answers	**Movie Tough Guys** *(see Quiz 127)*

1 Ray Liotta.. 2 Lee Van Cleef. 3 We were Soldiers. 4 Gert Frobe. 5 Medicine. 6 Steve Guttenberg. 7 Harvey Keitel. 8 Richard Gere. 9 The Blob. 10 Max Cady. 11 Gene Hackman. 12 Sands of Iwo Jima. 13 Charles Bronson. 14 James Cagney. 15 Clint Eastwood. 16 Patriot Games, Clear and Present Danger. 17 Ronald Reagan. 18 The Austrian Oak. 19 Duke Mantee. 20 Mean Streets. 21 James Cameron. 22 In the Heat of the Night. 23 Bananas. 24 Drum Beat. 25 Britt. 26 The Public Enemy. 27 A pregnant man. 28 Terry Molloy. 29 Kirk Douglas. 30 First Blood.

1 Which artist said, "I draw like a child … entirely out of my head"?
2 What is the only English anagram of LANCASTER?
3 In November 2004 who won a second term of office in Botswana?
4 Where was Britain's first motor-racing course, opening in 1909?
5 What are the first names of the Duchess of Cornwall's children?
6 What was the name of the first spreadsheet program developed by Apple in 1979?
7 In which prison was Dr Crippen executed?
8 Who featured on the 34p – the highest-priced – of the 1985 British Film Year stamps?
9 Who won double gold for three-day eventing at the European Championships in 1991?
10 Who wrote the novel "Herzog"?
11 From which language does the word "tea" originate?
12 Who bought Fulham FC in May 1997?
13 On a Monopoly board what is between Park Lane and Liverpool Street Station?
14 Whom did Anthony Andrews play in "Brideshead Revisited"?
15 Beru and Nonouti are in which island group?
16 What do the Americans mean by a pinwheel?
17 What is the dress of the order of the Missionaries of Charity founded by Mother Teresa?
18 What is the approximate distance of Rome airport from London in miles?
19 What is the diamond the Second Star of Africa also called?
20 Safin, Nadal and who else defeated Roger Federer in the 2005 season?
21 Josef Jakobs was the last man to be hanged where?
22 Who invented the barometer?
23 Who had an 60s No. 1 with "Silence is Golden"?
24 What were the names of James Callaghan's two children?
25 Which character did Emma Thompson play in Harry Potter movies?
26 In Germany what is a speisewagen?
27 In which sport did Ray Stevens excel?
28 What is the sum total of the internal angles in an octagon in degrees?
29 On which river does Cincinnati stand?
30 Who was the first Scot to be champion jockey?

Answers	Pot Luck 59 *(see Quiz 124)*

1 Robin and Giles. 2 Angie Todd. 3 France. 4 Baccara. 5 Malay. 6 Clark and Gollan. 7 Bay Islands. 8 Bob Braithwaite. 9 Roger Moore. 10 Stephen Potter. 11 Biscay. 12 John Hurt. 13 Cabbage. 14 Magny Cours. 15 88. 16 Eamonn Andrews. 17 Assailant. 18 Leslie Boyer Yin. 19 8-1. 20 Over 50. 21 Steinbeck. 22 £15. 23 Henry Cecil. 24 Sherpa Tensing Ward. 25 Daniel Topolski. 26 "I Saw Mommy Kissing Santa Claus". 27 9 p.m. 28 John Smith (Monklands East). 29 Tim Brookshaw, Paddy Farrell. 30 Himmler.

Quiz 127 | Movie Tough Guys

Answers – page 599

1 Who joined Robert De Niro and Joe Pesci on the poster for "Goodfellas"?
2 Who was lead villain to Clint Eastwood in "For a Few Dollars More"?
3 Which Mel Gibson movie tells of the first major battle of the Vietnam conflict?
4 Who played Goldfinger in 1964?
5 What did Humphrey Bogart study before entering the navy in the World War One?
6 Who was the star of the first four "Police Academy" films?
7 Which tough guy was Judas in Martin Scorsese's "The Last Temptation of Christ"?
8 Who was the violent hustler in "Looking for Mr Goodbar"?
9 Which film gave the real-life tough guy Steve McQueen his first lead role?
10 What was Robert De Niro's role in Scorsese's "Cape Fear" in 1991?
11 Who played Buck Barrow in "Bonnie and Clyde"?
12 Which film gave John Wayne his first Oscar nomination?
13 Who once said, "I look like a quarry that someone has dynamited"?
14 Which movie tough guy started out as a female impersonator?
15 Whose production company was called Malpaso?
16 What were Harrison Ford's first two films as the ex-CIA agent Jack Ryan?
17 Who played the crime boss to Lee Marvin's contract killer in "The Killers"?
18 What was Schwarzenegger's nickname after he won a record seven Mr Olympia titles?
19 Whom did Bogart play in one of his first movies "The Petrified Forest"?
20 What was the first Martin Scorsese film Robert De Niro appeared in?
21 Who directed Schwarzenegger in the "Terminator" films?
22 For which movie did Rod Steiger win his first Oscar?
23 In which film was Sylvester Stallone a thug threatening Woody Allen?
24 In which 1954 film was Charles Bronson first credited as Charles Bronson?
25 Who was the tough knife-thrower James Coburn played in "The Magnificent Seven"?
26 In which 30s movie did James Cagney push half a grapefruit into Mae West's face?
27 What unusual character did Schwarzenegger play in "Junior"?
28 What was the name of Brando's character in "On the Waterfront"?
29 Whose autobiography was called "The Ragman's Son"?
30 In which film did Stallone first play Rambo?

| **Answers** | Pop: Charts *(see Quiz 125)* |

1 "Unchained Melody". 2 Blondie. 3 "The Last Kiss". 4 Bobby & Shirley Womack. 5 George Harrison. 6 "Frozen Orange Juice". 7 "Saturday Night". 8 "The Show Must Go On". 9 "Take on Me". 10 Lena Martell. 11 Green. 12 Hurricane Smith. 13 "Speed of Sound" by Coldplay. 14 Allan Sherman. 15 Brian and Michael. 16 "Breakaway". 17 New Musical Express. 18 Epic. 19 "Do They Know It's Christmas". 20 Fairground Attraction. 21 "I'd Lie for You" (by Meat Loaf). 22 Frank Sinatra. 23 1990. 24 Seven. 25 Creation. 26 Frankie Laine. 27 "Blue Monday". 28 "Are You Lonesome Tonight". 29 Al Green. 30 Tammy Jones.

1 Which "Strictly Come Dancing" juror choreographed the dance group Hot Gossip?
2 What was Joseph Conrad's real name?
3 What did Dr Henry Durant first carry out in Britain in the 30s?
4 Which country has a top-selling newspaper called Esto?
5 What is another name for the scaly anteater?
6 To a hundred, how many names were in the first British telephone directory, published 1880?
7 Which shipping forecast area is north of Lundy?
8 Who was WBA's FA Cup Final keeper of the 60s?
9 What is the only English anagram of ANTIDOTES?
10 In March 2005, which team scored a goal to end Chelsea's clean-sheet record?
11 What was Colonel Thomas Blood disguised as when trying to steal the Crown Jewels?
12 The Caroline Islands belong to which country?
13 What did Bill Clinton call "the most powerful song I have ever heard"?
14 How many islands are in the Tristan da Cunha group?
15 Which TV series featured the Western Stagecoach Service?
16 If it's noon at GMT, what time is it in Vancouver?
17 In Monopoly, what is the fine for being drunk in charge?
18 Who invented the bicycle?
19 What is Michael Crawford's real name?
20 "The Killer in Me" and "Help" are episodes from the seventh series of which drama?
21 From which language does the word "tycoon" originate?
22 The Lugano Cup is awarded in which sport?
23 In which city was Cary Grant born?
24 What was the first British Top Ten hit for Big Country?
25 What was William Lamb's title when he was UK prime minister?
26 Which boxing champ shares his birth day and year with Glenda Jackson?
27 The airline Dragonair is based in which country?
28 Where was Britain's first road-race circuit, opening in 1933?
29 In what year did the Red Hot Chili Peppers have their first No. 1 album?
30 Which writer produced the work "Gargantua"?

Answers | Pot Luck 62 *(see Quiz 130)*

1 Authoress. 2 Voltaire. 3 Hugo Montenegro. 4 Blue. 5 Bristol. 6 Charles Edouard Jeanneret. 7 Sir Joseph Whitworth. 8 London. 9 The King's Singers (1997). 10 Leonardo da Vinci. 11 4,800. 12 La Cage Aux Folles. 13 Avenue Matignon. 14 Silverstone. 15 Poland. 16 Valencia. 17 Sixth. 18 D. H. Lawrence. 19 Sri Lanka. 20 Two points. 21 Benjamin Franklin. 22 Dateline. 23 Captain Marryat. 24 Fiddler's Dram. 25 Alexander. 26 Punch Tavern. 27 Carrot. 28 Magyar (Hungarian). 29 Nautilus. 30 Red (Vodafone).

1 In which city was Spain's King Juan Carlos born?
2 Who followed Lloyd George as prime minister of the UK?
3 Whom did Sanni Abacha overthrow in Nigeria in 1994?
4 How is Emperor Akihito known in Japan?
5 Whom became president of Georgia in 1992?
6 What was the name of Mrs Ceausescu who was executed with her husband?
7 Who became King of Sweden in 1973?
8 What was the nationality of the former UN Secretary General, Boutros Boutros Ghali?
9 Who won the 1990 elections in Burma while under house arrest?
10 Who went from vice-president to president of Ghana in 1967?
11 Archibald Philip Primrose was prime minister of where?
12 Who established Bloc Quebecois in 1990 in Canada ?
13 Other than politics, what is the profession of Jean-Bertrand Aristide of Haiti?
14 Who was the first science graduate to become British prime minister?
15 What post was Chief Buthelezi given in Mandela's cabinet in 1994?
16 Which faction did Robert Mugabe head before becoming prime minister of Zimbabwe?
17 Who was Bill Clinton's first Secretary of State?
18 In 1997 who was the only monarch who had been reigning longer than Elizabeth II?
19 Which Spanish prime minister took Spain into the EC?
20 Who became leader of Italy's Forza Italia Party in 1993?
21 Al Gore was senator of which state before becoming vice-president?
22 Who became the German president in 1994?
23 Who was the next non-Italian Pope after Adrian VI in 1522?
24 Whom did Lionel Jospin succeed as French prime minister in 1997?
25 Whom did T. N. I. Suharto overthrow to become president in 1967?
26 Who became Helmut Kohl's deputy in 1993?
27 Who is heir to the throne of Monaco?
28 In 2005, which former world leader announced his son had died of AIDS?
29 What is the nationality of Jacques Santer?
30 Who became Portugal's first civilian president for 60 years in 1986?

Answers | The Royals *(see Quiz 131)*

1 Lady Diana Spencer. 2 Princess Margaret. 3 Balmoral. 4 University Labour Club. 5 Hydro electric power plant. 6 Fabergé. 7 Countess of Wessex. 8 British Lung Foundation. 9 Four. 10 George Cross. 11 Rosemary. 12 Bryan Organ's. 13 Before her father's coffin at his funeral. 14 Berkshire (Windsor Castle). 15 Shand. 16 Converted to Roman Catholicism. 17 17 Bruton St, London W1. 18 George VI. 19 Architect. 20 Kanga. 21 The Duchess of Kent. 22 Prince Philip. 23 The Heart Has Its Reasons. 24 Wednesday. 25 Three. 26 Prince Philip. 27 Queen Victoria. 28 Dan Maskell. 29 War and Peace. 30 Duke of Kent.

1 What is the only English anagram (minus its hyphen) of SHARE-OUTS?
2 How is François Marie Arouet better known?
3 Who had a 60s No. 1 with "The Good, the Bad and the Ugly"?
4 What colour was "Monty Python's Big Red Book" cover?
5 At which city did Concorde make its first supersonic test flight?
6 What was Le Corbusier's real name?
7 Which mechanical engineer standardized screw threads?
8 Where were the first Olympics after the World War Two held?
9 Who first brought Lennon and McCartney music to the Proms?
10 Who painted "The Virgin of the Rocks"?
11 What is the approximate distance of Vancouver airport from London in miles?
12 Which musical contains "A Little More Mascara" and "Masculinity"?
13 On a French Monopoly board, what is the equivalent to the Strand?
14 Which Formula 1 circuit includes Maggotts Curve, Abbey Curve and Priory?
15 In which country is the city of Katowice?
16 Beckham and Gravesen both saw red playing for Real Madrid versus which side?
17 In the Bible which commandment says, "Thou shalt not kill"?
18 Which writer was born at 8a Victoria Street, Eastwood?
19 The international car registration CL applies to which country?
20 In Scrabble, how much is a letter D worth?
21 Who invented the bifocal lens?
22 Which agency was launched by John Patterson in 1966?
23 Who wrote "Mr Midshipman Easy"?
24 Which group went on a Day Trip to Bangor?
25 Baranof and Prince of Wales are in which island group?
26 What is the 20th-century name of Fleet Street's pub, the Crown and Sugarloaf?
27 Favourite and Figaro are types of what?
28 From which language does the word "goulash" originate?
29 What was the name of the first US nuclear submarine?
30 What colour was the company's name on England shirts in the 2005 Ashes?

Answers | Pot Luck 61 *(see Quiz 128)*

1 Arlene Phillips. 2 Jozef Korzeniowski. 3 Gallup opinion poll. 4 Mexico. 5 Pangolin. 6 255. 7 Irish Sea. 8 John Osborne. 9 Stationed. 10 Norwich. 11 Clergyman. 12 USA. 13 "Eleanor Rigby". 14 Five. 15 Wells Fargo. 16 4 a.m. 17 £20. 18 Kirkpatrick MacMillan. 19 Michael Dumble-Smith. 20 "Buffy the Vampire Slayer". 21 Japanese. 22 Walking. 23 Bristol. 24 "Fields of Fire". 25 Viscount Melbourne. 26 Terry Downes. 27 Hong Kong. 28 Donington Park. 29 2002. 30 François Rabelais.

1 Who was the first new royal to include her family's motto on her marital coat of arms?

2 Who said, "I have as much privacy as a goldfish in a bowl"?

3 Which royal residence did George V not visit during World War One?

4 Which club was Prince Charles not allowed to join by his college?

5 On 24 July 2005, the Queen won planning permission to build what at Windsor castle?

6 In 1907 who made models of Sandringham farm animals?

7 Which Royal's birthday is on 20 January?

8 Thirty per cent of the proceeds of Princess of Wales roses went to which charity at the Chelsea Flower Show?

9 How many British kings were emperors of India?

10 Which medal did Inspector Beaton receive after Princess Anne was attacked in the Mall in 1974?

11 What is the Duchess of Cornwall's middle name?

12 Whose portrait of Diana was damaged in the National Portrait Gallery in 1981?

13 When did Queen Elizabeth II last curtsey officially?

14 In which county near London does the Queen have an official residence?

15 What was Camilla's surname before marrying Andrew Parker Bowles?

16 Why did Lord Nicholas Windsor renounce his right to the throne in 2001?

17 Where was Queen Elizabeth II born?

18 Which 20th-century monarch is or was left-handed?

19 What was the Duke of Gloucester's profession before he became a duke?

20 What is the Prince of Wales's nickname for his friend Lady Tryon?

21 Sir William Worsley was the father of which royal?

22 Who said, "Constitutionally, I don't exist"?

23 What was the autobiography of the Duchess of Windsor called?

24 On what day of the week was Queen Elizabeth II born?

25 How many princes were given the title Prince of Wales in the 20th century?

26 Who is taller, Prince Philip or Prince Charles?

27 Which royal wrote "Our Life in the Highlands"?

28 Who taught Princess Anne to play tennis?

29 Which book did Princess Margaret choose for her desert island on "Desert Island Discs"?

30 Which Duke is the grandfather of Columbus, Cassius, Eloise and Estella?

Answers | World Leaders (see Quiz 129)

1 Rome. 2 Andrew Bonar Law. 3 General Babangida. 4 The Heisei Emperor. 5 Edvard Shevardnadze. 6 Elena. 7 Carl Gustaf XVI. 8 Egyptian. 9 Aung San Suu Kyi. 10 Omar Bongo. 11 UK. He was the Earl of Rosebery. 12 Lucien Bouchard. 13 Clergyman. 14 Margaret Thatcher. 15 Minister of the Interior. 16 ZANU – Zimbabwe African National Union. 17 Warren Christopher. 18 King Bhumipol of Thailand. 19 Felipe Gonzalez. 20 Silvio Berlusconi. 21 Tennessee. 22 Roman Herzog. 23 John Paul II. 24 Alain Juppé. 25 Achmed Sukarno. 26 Klaus Klinkel. 27 Prince Albert. 28 Nelson Mandela. 29 Luxembourgeois. 30 Mario Soares.

1 Where did Jacques Villeneuve take his first Formula 1 victory?
2 In Monopoly, how much is payed for school fees?
3 How many Top Ten singles did Busted have in 2003?
4 Which shipping forecast area is north of Rockall?
5 From which language does the word "bungalow" originate?
6 What was the title of the first Itchy and Scratchy cartoon?
7 What cabinet post did Michael Heseltine resign from over the Westland affair?
8 Transavia Airlines is based in which country?
9 In which Dickens novel does Thomas Traddles appear?
10 Who had an 60s No. 1 with "Do You Mind"?
11 How old was King George III when he died?
12 Who wrote "All Quiet on the Western Front"?
13 The first Boy Scouts to be registered were based in which city?
14 If A is Alpha and B is Bravo what is N?
15 What is the American equivalent to "University Challenge"?
16 How was novelist Henri Beyle better known?
17 If it's noon at GMT, what time is it in Tehran?
18 How many islands are in the Bismarck Archipelago group?
19 What was Robin Leigh-Pemberton's job between 1983 and 1993?
20 Who invented the burglar alarm?
21 What is the only English anagram of BARGAINED?
22 What was the first British Top Ten hit for Black Sabbath?
23 Whom was George Oldfield determined to catch?
24 Who created Dan Dare?
25 What does ALGOL stand for?
26 Whom did Martina Navratilova beat to win her ninth Wimbledon?
27 In which churchyard was Sir Winston Churchill buried?
28 Which World Cup venue was the most northerly in Germany 2006?
29 When did Britain first occupy Hong Kong?
30 What were the two main themes of the Proms season 2005?

| **Answers** | **Pot Luck 64** *(see Quiz 134)* |

1 W. Ritter. 2 "The Yeomen of the Guard". 3 Versatile. 4 Boris Yeltsin. 5 Have You Ever. 6 One. 7 Emma Geller Green. 8 Richmal Lambourn. 9 Sudan. 10 John McEnroe. 11 Sow. 12 Flight Lieutenant Simon Carter. 13 Arabic. 14 Hamburg. 15 Thunderclap Newman. 16 Newcastle. 17 Marengo. 18 Marlborough St. 19 900. 20 1910s. 21 Belfast City Hall. 22 August. 23 Gloriana. 24 Halifax Building Society turning into a bank. 25 Willie Whitelaw. 26 Arnold Ridley. 27 8-1. 28 4,000. 29 John Braine. 30 Galapagos.

1 Who scored 11 goals for QPR in their first season in Europe?
2 Who delighted in the nickname Ambling Alp?
3 Whom did Fernando Alonso collide with in the 2005 Hungarian Grand Prix?
4 Which brothers asked to wear England shirts while playing at Wimbledon during Euro '96?
5 Which great soccer manager was boss at Grimsby and Workington?
6 Who died during a bout with Drew Docherty in October 1995?
7 Who was Rob Andrew's first signing at Newcastle RFC?
8 Who were the only team not to score in soccer's Euro '96?
9 Who won cricket's Gillette Cup in 1970, '71 and '72?
10 Who took 5-67 on his first class debut, for Hants, in August 1996?
11 Which horse was Carson riding when he sustained serious injuries arguably hastening his retirement?
12 Who scored twice for Villa in the 50s FA Cup Final win over Man. Utd?
13 Whom did Steven Redgrave win Olympic Gold with in 1988?
14 Who was the first woman to be elected to the Wimbledon Championships Committee?
15 Whom did Monica Seles beat to win her first Grand Slam after her attack?
16 Which soccer keeper was known as the Flying Pig?
17 What did Robbie Paul win for scoring a hat trick in the 1996 Challenge Cup Final?
18 In the 1990s who first won the World Professional Snooker Championship after Stephen Hendry?
19 Mike Tyson announced retirement in June 2005 after defeat by whom?
20 Who followed Geoff Hurst as manager of Chelsea?
21 Who coached Torvill and Dean to Olympic success?
22 Who rode Red Rum for the third Grand National triumph?
23 Who was the first footballer to marry a managing director of football?
24 Who was the manager who brought Dwight Yorke to Aston Villa?
25 Who in 1995 was the first Grand National-winning favourite?
26 Who won the inaugural Turkish Grand Prix?
27 Who kept goal for Spurs in the 1981 FA Cup Final?
28 Who was the first woman to ride in the Derby?
29 What were the odds on Dettori's seven-race card win in 1996?
30 Who was Manchester United manager when they were last relegated?

Answers	**Mozart** (see Quiz 135)

1 Austria. 2 Six. 3 D minor. 4 Constanze. 5 Wolfgang. 6 Haydn. 7 The Marriage of Figaro. 8 30s. 9 Prague. 10 Violin & Viola. 11 Clarinet. 12 Lorenzo Da Ponte. 13 Cosi Fan Tutte. 14 Sister. 15 Vienna. 16 Maria Anna. 17 Salzburg. 18 Amadeus. 19 The Magic Flute. 20 50. 21 Cosi Fan Tutte. 22 Leopold. 23 George. 24 France. 25 Piano. 26 Salzburg. 27 Lange. 28 Amadeus Quartet. 29 Salieri. 30 Vienna.

1 Who invented the cable car?
2 The 18p stamp – the cheapest in the 1992 set – showed which Gilbert and Sullivan opera?
3 What is the only English anagram of RELATIVES?
4 Which Russian wrote "Against the Grain"?
5 What was S Club 7's fourth number one hit?
6 How many people (excluding the Queen) were on a 2005 First Class Christmas stamp?
7 Cali and Noelle Sheldon played which character in "Friends"?
8 What was Richmal Crompton's real name?
9 In which country is the city of Khartoum North?
10 Which Wimbledon winner was born the day Castro took over in Cuba?
11 On which river does Stafford stand?
12 Which character was played by David McCallum in "Colditz"?
13 From which language does the word "algebra" originate?
14 Thomas Gravesen joined Everton from which club?
15 Who had a 60s No. 1 with "Something in the Air"?
16 Chris Waddle first played for England while with which club?
17 What was the name of Napoleon Bonaparte's favourite horse?
18 In Monopoly, where would a throw of seven from Pall Mall land you?
19 What is the sum total of the internal angles in a heptagon in degrees?
20 In which decade were photographs first required on British passports?
21 In which building did the first civil partnership take place in the UK?
22 In which month does the oyster season open?
23 Which Benjamin Britten opera was commisioned for the Coronation of Queen Elizabeth II?
24 What made Mike Blackburn send out millions of letters in 1997?
25 Which Home Secretary talked about a "short, sharp shock"?
26 Who wrote the classic play "The Ghost Train"?
27 With two dice, what are the odds of rolling any combination totalling five?
28 What is the approximate distance of Karachi airport from London in miles?
29 Who wrote the novel "Room at the Top"?
30 Fernandina and Floreana are in which island group?

Answers	**Pot Luck 63** *(see Quiz 132)*

1 Nurburgring. 2 £150. 3 Four. 4 Bailey. 5 Hindustani. 6 Steamboat Itchy. 7 Defence Secretary. 8 Netherlands. 9 David Copperfield. 10 Anthony Newley. 11 81. 12 Erich Remarque. 13 Glasgow. 14 November. 15 "College Bowl". 16 Stendhal. 17 3.30 p.m. 18 About 200. 19 Governor of the Bank of England. 20 Edwin T. Holmes. 21 Gabardine. 22 Paranoid. 23 The Yorkshire Ripper. 24 Frank Hampson. 25 Algorithmic Orientated Language. 26 Zina Garrison. 27 Blaydon Churchyard. 28 Hamburg. 29 1841. 30 The Sea and Fairy Tales.

1 In which country was Mozart born?
2 Was Mozart, six, eight or ten when he went on his first music tour?
3 The unfinished Requiem was in which key?
4 Which Weber sister did Mozart marry at the age of 26?
5 What was Mozart's first name?
6 Mozart dedicated six string quartets to which composer Joseph?
7 How is "Le Nozze de Figaro" known in English?
8 Was Mozart in his 20s, 30s or 40 when he died?
9 Which symphony took its nickname from a Czech capital?
10 Mozart was an accomplished player on which string instruments?
11 Which instrument, invented in Mozart's lifetime, is the focus of a Concerto in A?
12 Who produced the libretto for "Don Giovanni"?
13 Which opera features the characters Fiordiligi and Ferrando?
14 Was Nannerl his sister or his wife?
15 In which Austrian city was "The Magic Flute" premiered?
16 What was the name of Mozart's older sister?
17 In which city was Mozart born?
18 What was Mozart's middle name and the name of a play and film about him?
19 How is "Die Zauberflöte" known in English?
20 Did he write approximately 10, 30 or 50 symphonies?
21 Which opera's title means "Thus Do All Women" in English?
22 What was the name of Mozart's famous father?
23 In London, Mozart played for the third English king to be called what?
24 The King of which country did Mozart play for at Versailles?
25 Mozart was one of the first great exponents of which relatively new keyboard instrument?
26 Mozart wrote all his violin concertos in which city?
27 According to Mozart's wife, a portrait by which artist was the best likeness of Mozart?
28 Which famous Quartet has one of Mozart's names in its name?
29 Which contemporary of Mozart is the narrator in the Peter Shaffer play about his life?
30 In which Austrian city did Mozart die?

Answers	**Sport: Who's Who** *(see Quiz 133)*

1 Stan Bowles. **2** Primo Carnera (boxer). **3** Ralf Schumacher. **4** Luke and Murphy Jensen. **5** Bill Shankly. **6** James Murray. **7** Dean Ryan. **8** Turkey. **9** Lancashire. **10** Liam Botham. **11** Meshhed. **12** Peter McParland. **13** Andrew Holmes. **14** Virginia Wade. **15** Anke Huber. **16** Tommy Lawrence. **17** Lance Todd Trophy + £10,000. **18** John Parrot. **19** Kevin McBride. **20** John Neale. **21** Betty Callaway. **22** Tommy Stack. **23** Paul Peschisolido. **24** Graham Taylor. **25** Rough Quest. **26** Kimi Raikkonen (2005). **27** Milija Aleksic. **28** Alex Greaves. **29** 25,095/1. **30** Tommy Docherty.

1 In which country are the San Agustin caves?
2 What was the title of the first episode of "The Simpsons"?
3 From which language does the word "divan" originate?
4 Who had a 60s No. 1 with "Michael"?
5 How was the Birmingham Royal Ballet previously known?
6 What is the capital of the Canadian province Saskatchewan?
7 How many islands are in the Shetland group?
8 When did Swansea become a city?
9 In which city was Felix Mendelssohn born?
10 If it's noon at GMT, what time is it in Sydney?
11 What is the only English anagram of DERANGING?
12 Alpha and Snow Cap are types of what?
13 In which city did Harold Macmillan deliver his "Wind of Change" speech?
14 Who became chairman of media regulator Ofcom in 2002?
15 How is Tiziano Vecelli better known?
16 Actor Bill Nighy released the 2003 single "Christmas is All Around" under which name?
17 Which Robert discovered the law of elasticity that is now known by his name?
18 To 10, what was the highest individual innings of the 2005 Ashes series?
19 In which country is the city of Kigali?
20 Who played the youngest child in the 2005 movie of the "Chronicles of Narnia"?
21 What was Daniel Defoe's real name?
22 Where was the first German Formula 1 Grand Prix staged in 1926?
23 Who scored the only goal of the Euro 2004 Final?
24 Who wrote "The Raj Quartet"?
25 How long after Jock Stein's death in 1985 was there another Wales v. Scotland game?
26 What was the first British Top Ten hit for Blondie?
27 In Monopoly, how much do you receive on 7% preference shares?
28 Whom did Ramsay MacDonald follow when he first became prime minister of the UK?
29 How old was Buddy Holly when he died?
30 The airline Kyrnair is based in which country?

Answers | Pot Luck 66 *(see Quiz 138)*

1 Tams. 2 Taoiseach (pronounced Tee-shock). 3 Jack London. 4 February. 5 San Francisco. 6 Greater Antilles. 7 21. 8 Vatican's Swiss Guards. 9 Turkish. 10 Mercedes Cars. 11 Beck. 12 John Ronald Reuel. 13 St Patrick. 14 Peace of Paris. 15 6,300. 16 "Like Clockwork". 17 Canada. 18 £260. 19 The Tracey Ullman Show. 20 Nicolas Appert. 21 Sir Edward Elgar. 22 Charlton Athletic. 23 Queen Anne. 24 Warwick. 25 Dr Andrei Sakharov. 26 William Hartnell. 27 Skylab. 28 Coastline. 29 Carpenter. 30 Mark Felt.

1 Who was the first young man to win the Junior Grand Slam?
2 Before Henman and Rusedski who were the last two Brits to be in the men's last eight together at Wimbledon?
3 In which country did Henman and Murray first play each other?
4 Where was Martina Hingis born?
5 How many times did Navratilova win the Wimbledon singles as a Czech?
6 Which unseeded player reached the final of the 2006 Australian Open?
7 What was Chris Evert's second married name?
8 Who is Vera Puzejova's daughter?
9 Who won the women's singles at the 1992 Olympics?
10 Tim Henman reached his first US Open quarter final when who withdrew in 2004?
11 Where was the US Open played before Flushing Meadow?
12 What is Boris Becker's eldest son called?
13 What did Major Wingfield call lawn tennis when he first showed off his new game?
14 Who were known as the Three Musketeers?
15 Who was the first European to win the women's singles at Roland Garros in the 70s?
16 Whom did Billie Jean Moffitt win her first women's doubles with?
17 With whom did Ann Jones win the Wimbledon mixed doubles in '69?
18 Who was the first male Brit to win a Wimbledon title after Fred Perry?
19 Where did Fred Perry die?
20 Whom did Chris Evert beat to win her first Wimbledon title?
21 Who was known as the Rockhampton Rocket?
22 Who was the first Swede to win the Australian men's singles?
23 Who contested Wimbledon's longest-ever match?
24 Which tennis trophy did Hazel Hotchkiss donate?
25 Who was the first man to hold all four Grand Slam titles at once?
26 Which two countries has Hana Mandlikova played for?
27 Where were the very first US Championships held?
28 Who was the last men's singles champion at Wimbledon before it became open?
29 Who was the first person to lose in the opening round in the defence of his championship?
30 Where were the Australian Championships held in 1906 and 1912?

Answers	Pop: No. 1s *(see Quiz 139)*

1 Pussycat. 2 Scott McKenzie. 3 Celine Dion. 4 Seal. 5 Destiny's Child. 6 "Two Little Boys" (Rolf Harris). 7 "The Fly" (U2). 8 Tony Visconti. 9 Rotherham. 10 October. 11 Joe Dolce Music Theatre. 12 Victoria Wood. 13 "His Latest Flame". 14 1957. 15 None. 16 "Sailor". 17 The Buggles. 18 Kris Kristofferson. 19 "Temptation". 20 David Gates. 21 Johnny Kidd. 22 St Winifred's School Choir. 23 "Goody Two Shoes". 24 San Pedro. 25 "Vincent". 26 Aneka. 27 "Angel". 28 "Oh Boy". 29 Shirley Bassey. 30 "You Spin Me Round (Like a Record)".

1 Who had a 70s No. 1 with "Hey Girl Don't Bother Me"?
2 Which title is the Irish prime minister also known by?
3 Who wrote "The Sea-Wolf"?
4 Waitangi Day, the national day of New Zealand, is in which month?
5 The movie "The Wild Parrots of Telegraph Hill" is set in which city?
6 Haiti and Puerto Rico are in which island group?
7 To three, how many caps did Sir Clive Woodward gain for England?
8 Which corps' 500th anniversary celebrations began in February 2006?
9 From which language does the word "kiosk" originate?
10 What was the Hockenheimring circuit originally built to test?
11 David Campbell is the real name of which singer?
12 What do the initials JRR stand for in J. R. R. Tolkien's name?
13 Which saint's flag has a saltire Gules in a field of Argent?
14 Canada was ceded to Britain by which treaty in 1763?
15 What is the approximate distance of Lima airport from London in miles?
16 What was the first British Top Ten hit for the Boomtown Rats?
17 In which country is the city of Kitchener?
18 In Monopoly how much does it cost to buy Coventry Street?
19 On which US television series were "The Simpsons" first seen?
20 Who invented canning?
21 Who features on the second most expensive banknote launched in June 1999?
22 Whom did Bolton Wanderers play in their last league game at Burnden Park?
23 Anne Hyde was the mother of which British monarch?
24 At which university did Steve Heighway get his BA degree?
25 Who was the first Russian to win the Nobel Peace Prize?
26 Who played Sergeant Major Bullimore in "The Army Game"?
27 Gerald Carr, Edward Gibson and William Pogue returned from what in 1974?
28 What is the only English anagram of SECTIONAL?
29 What was the trade of Abraham Lincoln's father?
30 In June 2005 who identified himself as informer Deep Throat in the Watergate Scandal?

Answers	**Pot Luck 65** *(see Quiz 136)*

1 Mexico. 2 Simpsons Roasting on an Open Fire. 3 Persian. 4 Highwaymen. 5 Sadlers Wells. 6 Regina. 7 100. 8 1969. 9 Hamburg. 10 10 p.m. 11 Gardening. 12 Cauliflower. 13 Cape Town. 14 Lord Currie. 15 Titian. 16 Billy Mack. 17 Hooke. 18 166 (Michael Vaughan). 19 Rwanda. 20 Georgie Henley. 21 Daniel Foe. 22 Avus Street Circuit, Berlin. 23 Angelos Charisteas. 24 Paul Scott. 25 12 years (May 1997). 26 "Denis". 27 £25. 28 Stanley Baldwin. 29 22. 30 Corsica.

Quiz 139 | Pop: No. 1s

Answers – page 611

1 Who were the first Dutch group to top the British charts?

2 Philip Blondheim had a 60s No. 1 under what name?

3 Which female spent 13 weeks on the chart before making No. 1 in February 1995?

4 Who was the uncredited vocalist of Adamski's "Killer"?

5 Who were the first American all-girl group to top the UK singles chart twice?

6 What was the final No. 1 of the hippy decade the 60s?

7 Which record ended Bryan Adams's 16-week record run at No. 1?

8 Who produced all the T. Rex No. 1s?

9 Where in England was the Music Factory Studios that mixed the Jive Bunny discs?

10 In which month did "Here Comes Summer" top the charts in 1959?

11 Who had a No. 1 with "Shaddap Your Face"?

12 Who was on the other side of Hale and Pace and the Stonkers' No. 1?

13 Which song was coupled with Elvis's "Little Sister"?

14 Jackie Wilson's "Reet Petite" made No. 1 in 1986, but in what year did it first chart?

15 How many instrumentals topped the charts in the 80s?

16 What was Petula Clark's first No. 1?

17 Under what name did Trevor Horn and Geoff Downes make No. 1?

18 Who wrote Lena Martell's chart-topper "One Day at a Time"?

19 What was the fourth and last No. 1 for the Everly Brothers?

20 Who wrote "Everything I Own"?

21 Who was the first artist at No. 1 to wear an eye patch?

22 Who were the last all-girl group to reach No. 1 before Eternal in 1989?

23 Which was the first No. 1 for Adam Ant as opposed to Adam and the Ants?

24 Which island is lamented in "La Isla Bonita"?

25 Which No. 1 begins, "Starry, starry night"?

26 Under what name did Mary Sandeman reach No. 1?

27 What was Shaggy's second No. 1 single to have one word in its title?

28 What was Mud's last No. 1?

29 Who had a 50s No. 1 with "As I Love You"?

30 What was the first Stock, Aitken and Waterman-produced No. 1?

Answers | Tennis (see Quiz 137)

1 Stefan Edberg. 2 Bobby Wilson, Mike Sangster. 3 Switzerland. 4 Kosice, Slovakia. 5 Twice. 6 Marcos Baghdatis. 7 Mill. 8 Helena Sukova. 9 Jennifer Capriati. 10 Nicolas Kiefer. 11 Forest Hills. 12 Noah. 13 Sphairistike. 14 Borotra, Cochet, Lacoste. 15 Sue Barker. 16 Karen Hantze. 17 Fred Stolle. 18 John Lloyd (Mixed 1983–4). 19 Australian Championships in 1995. 20 Olga Morozova. 21 Rod Laver. 22 Mats Wilander. 23 Pancho Gonzales, Charlie Pasarell. 24 Wightman Cup (she became Mrs Wightman). 25 Donald Budge. 26 Czechoslovakia, Australia. 27 Staten Island. 28 John Newcombe. 29 Manuel Santana. 30 New Zealand.

Quiz 140 Pot Luck 67

1 What was the first solo British Top Ten hit for Cher?
2 If it's noon at GMT, what time is it in Tangier?
3 Which Freeview news channel was wound up in December 2005?
4 What was George Eliot's real name?
5 Which shipping forecast area is west of forecast area Plymouth?
6 Which team in England's group lost all its games in the 2003 rugby union World Cup?
7 On which river does Calcutta stand?
8 How many islands are in the Bissagos group?
9 Who was widowed by the death of Stefano Casiraghi in 1990?
10 Who had a 70s No. 1 with "You to Me are Everything"?
11 The airline Flitestar is based in which country?
12 In the 1850s what did the discovery by Edward Hargreaves lead to?
13 Who won the Formula 1 German Grand Prix in three successive years, 1988/89/90?
14 In Monopoly, how much do you collect following a bank error?
15 What is the only English anagram of CONTINUED?
16 Matilda Alice Victoria Wood was known for what type of entertainment?
17 Which Road in Drumcree was the centre of unrest in July 1997?
18 At which airport did Concorde crash in 2000?
19 Who was the youngest MP after the 1997 general election?
20 In Bob Dylan's view what "don't work 'cos the vandals took the handles"?
21 The Consensus Front was an alliance of which people in Iraq?
22 What is the name of the albino in "The Da Vinci Code"?
23 Which singer featured on Eve's 2001 hit "Let Me Blow Ya Mind"?
24 In which month was John Lennon murdered?
25 Which beaten finalist said, "Pete [Sampras] doesn't let you breathe"?
26 Who invented the cannon?
27 The writer John Buchan became Governor General of where?
28 From which language does the word "floe" originate?
29 How was the actress Beatrice Stella Tanner better known?
30 Mary Shelley's novel was called "Frankenstein; or the…" what?

Answers | **Pot Luck 68** (see Quiz 142)

1 CMC. 2 Alfred, Lord Tennyson. 3 Bow Street. 4 Hungaroring. 5 Captain Cook. 6 The Mystery Of Edwin Drood. 7 Marwood. 8 Chicory Tip. 9 Sir Edward Heath. 10 Alvin Stardust. 11 Demanding. 12 North Frisian. 13 Duke of Portland. 14 720. 15 Braddock County. 16 J. B. Priestley. 17 Bolton. 18 Water Skiing. 19 Swedish. 20 John Buchan. 21 "I'm a Man". 22 Norman Hartnell. 23 Egypt. 24 Cucumber. 25 Alan McGee. 26 1960s. 27 Kuwait. 28 Ivor Wood. 29 Edward Heath. 30 6,700.

1 The Croatian currency kuna is divided into 100 what?
2 On which river does Berlin stand?
3 Which three major Spanish international airports begin with "V"?
4 Miskoic and Debrecen are major towns in which country?
5 Where was the World Council of Churches established in 1948?
6 Which country's official name is Republika e Shqipërisë?
7 What is Europe's lowest point below sea level?
8 On which river does the capital city of Croatia stand?
9 Who are the two heads of state of Andorra?
10 What is the capital of Saxony?
11 Which country has Letzeburgish as its most widely used language?
12 What is Europe's highest waterfall called?
13 Where is the European Investment Bank?
14 In which country has Alfred Moisiu been President?
15 What are the only armed forces in Monaco?
16 The Aland Islands belong to which country?
17 Which is the most northerly capital city in the world?
18 The Glomma is one of the principal rivers of which country?
19 Which three French regions begin with A?
20 Which country's highest point is Rysys?
21 Which has the greater area, Iceland or Ireland?
22 What is San Marino's second-largest town?
23 Where is Ulemiste Airport?
24 Which is farther north, Moscow or Copenhagen?
25 Where was the UN peacekeeping mission UNPROFOR in force?
26 What is Belgium's highest point?
27 On which river does Amsterdam stand?
28 Other than Denmark where is Danish currency used?
29 Where is Italy's principal stock exchange?
30 Gozo and Comino are to the north west of which island?

Answers	**Movies: Who's Who?** *(see Quiz 143)*

1 Louis Malle. 2 Hugh Bonneville & Jim Broadbent (Iris). 3 Anne Fine. 4 Kiefer Sutherland.
5 Tilda Swinton. 6 Patrick Swayze, Lisa Niemi. 7 Catherine Deneuve. 8 Gérard Depardieu.
9 Bo Derek's. 10 Divine. 11 Whoopi Goldberg. 12 Michael Gough. 13 Richard E. Grant.
14 Melanie Griffith. 15 Bernard Herrmann. 16 Charlton Heston. 17 Glenn Close. 18 John
Malkovitch. 19 Steve Martin. 20 Melina Mercouri. 21 Liza Minnelli. 22 Gwyneth Paltrow.
23 Val Kilmer. 24 Joanne Woodward. 25 Michael Douglas. 26 John Cleese & Julie Andrews.
27 Henry Mancini. 28 Joanne Whalley-Kilmer. 29 Natalie Wood. 30 Dr Kellogg.

1 How was Charlotte Church credited on the Jurgen Vries single "The Opera Song"?
2 Which literary figure was born at Somersby rectory in Lincolnshire?
3 On a Monopoly board what is between Marylebone Station and Community Chest?
4 At which circuit did Damon Hill achieve his first GP victory in 1993?
5 Who was massacred on Valentine's Day in 1779 at Kealakekua Bay?
6 Which Dickens novel was set in Cloisterham?
7 What is John Cleese's middle name?
8 Who had a 70s No. 1 with "Son of My Father"?
9 Who said William Hague had "no ideas, no experience and no hope"?
10 In the 1984 charts, who felt like Buddy Holly?
11 What is the only English anagram of MADDENING?
12 Amrum and Nordstrand are in which island group?
13 What was William Henry Cavendish's title when he was UK prime minister?
14 What is the sum total of the internal angles in a hexagon in degrees?
15 In which county was Southfork Ranch in "Dallas"?
16 Which writer used the assumed name Peter Goldsmith?
17 Chelsea claimed the 2005 title after playing which team?
18 Philippa Roberts was a world champion in which sport?
19 From which language does the word "gauntlet" originate?
20 Who wrote the book "Greenmantle"?
21 What was the first British Top Ten hit for Chicago?
22 Who designed Queen Elizabeth II's coronation gown?
23 The international car registration ET applies to which country?
24 Tokyo Slicer and Pepita are types of what?
25 Who founded the Creation record label?
26 In what decade did Malta become independent after British rule?
27 Massouma al-Mubarak was the first female minister in which country?
28 Which animator of "The Wombles" and "The Magic Roundabout" died in 2004?
29 Who was the second former British Prime Minister to die in 2005?
30 What is the approximate distance of Manila airport from London in miles?

Answers | Pot Luck 67 *(see Quiz 140)*

1 "All I Really Want to Do". 2 12 noon. 3 ITV News Channel. 4 Mary Ann Evans. 5 Sole. 6 Georgia. 7 Hooghy. 8 15. 9 Princess Caroline of Monaco. 10 The Real Thing. 11 South Africa. 12 Australian Gold Rush. 13 Ayrton Senna. 14 £200. 15 Unnoticed. 16 Music hall (Marie Lloyd). 17 Garvaghy. 18 Charles de Gaulle. 19 Christopher Leslie. 20 The pump. 21 Sunni Arabs. 22 Silas. 23 Gwen Stefani. 24 December. 25 Cedric Pioline. 26 Archimedes. 27 Canada. 28 Norse. 29 Mrs Patrick Campbell. 30 Modern Prometheus.

1 Who directed Brooke Shields in "Pretty Baby"?
2 Which two actors play John Bayley in the 2002 movie about his wife?
3 Who wrote the book that "Interview with the Vampire" was based on?
4 Whose first screen role was in "Max Dugan Returns" with his father?
5 Who played Queen Isabella in Derek Jarman's "Edward II"?
6 Which husband-and-wife team starred in "Steel Dawn" in 1987?
7 Who earned her first Oscar nomination in 1992 for "Indochine"?
8 Whose film US debut was opposite Andie MacDowell in "Green Card"?
9 David Letterman once introduced a plank of wood as whose acting coach?
10 How was Harris Glenn Milstead better known?
11 Who was the voice of Shenzi in "The Lion King"?
12 Who played Alfred in the 1989, 1992 and 1995 "Batman" films?
13 Who played the harassed executive in "How to Get Ahead in Advertising"?
14 Which 18-year-old divorcee made her screen debut in "Night Moves"?
15 Who died the night after conducting his score for "Taxi Driver" in '75?
16 Whose diary, "The Actor's Life", was published in 1978?
17 Andie MacDowell starred in the Tarzan film "Greystoke", but who was later asked to dub her voice?
18 Who played the Vicomte de Valmont in "Dangerous Liaisons"?
19 Whose first film role saw him enacting "Maxwell's Silver Hammer" in the "Sgt Pepper" movie?
20 Which actress and political activist was married to the director Jules Dassin?
21 Whose movie debut was in a film starring her mother, "In the Good Old Summertime", in 1949?
22 Who played the title role in the biopic about Ted Hughes' poet wife?
23 Who played Elvis's spirit in "True Romance"?
24 Who narrated Martin Scorsese's "The Age of Innocence"?
25 Who appeared in and co-produced "The China Syndrome"?
26 Who were the voices of King Harold and Queen Lilian in "Shrek 2"?
27 Who published his life story, "Did They Mention the Music"? in 1989?
28 Who has played Christine Keeler on film and Vivien Leigh on TV?
29 Who was the little girl who did not believe in Santa Claus in the 1947 film "Miracle on 34th Street"?
30 Who was the hero of "The Road to Welville", played by Anthony Hopkins?

Answers | Euro Tour *(see Quiz 141)*

1 Para. 2 Spree. 3 Valencia, Vigo, Vitoria. 4 Hungary. 5 Amsterdam. 6 Albania. 7 Caspian Sea. 8 Sava (capital: Zagreb). 9 President of France, Spanish Bishop of Urgel. 10 Dresden. 11 Luxembourg. 12 Ormeli. 13 Luxembourg City. 14 Albania. 15 Palace guard. 16 Finland. 17 Reykjavik, Iceland. 18 Norway. 19 Alsace, Aquitaine, Auvergne. 20 Poland. 21 Iceland. 22 Serraville. 23 Tallinn, Estonia. 24 Moscow. 25 Bosnia-Herzegovina and Macedonia. 26 Mount Botrange. 27 Amstel. 28 Greenland and the Faeroe Islands. 29 Milan. 30 Malta.

1 What was the first British Top Ten Hit for Clannad?
2 Curtis Jackson is the real name of which rapper?
3 What are the odds of rolling double six in dice-throwing?
4 How many islands are in the Seychelles group?
5 Who painted the "Girl with a Pearl Earring"?
6 Which Radio 2 presenter's first novel was called "Charlotte's Friends"?
7 What is the only English anagram of DIAMETRIC?
8 What was "Coronation Street" creator Tony Warren's autobiography called?
9 Which rock star had been a grave digger and a Brentford footballer?
10 In which country is the city of La Paz?
11 Who wrote the novel "Saturday Night and Sunday Morning"?
12 At which hotel did the G8 summit begin in July 2005?
13 Which Kirsty MacColl record did Gordon Brown choose on "Desert Island Discs"?
14 Which 19th-century trainer won the St Leger 16 times?
15 Who had the first British No. 1 with a song titled "Tears on My Pillow"?
16 Who was the first skipper to get a hat-trick of America's Cup wins?
17 What was Doug Fishbone's sculpture in Trafalgar Square in October 2004 made from?
18 From which language does the word "tattoo" originate?
19 Who won the 1989 Hungaroring Formula 1 Grand Prix, giving Ferrari their only success at the track?
20 If it's noon at GMT, what time is it in Cape Town?
21 How much is the doctor's fee in Monopoly?
22 Which British newspaper was founded in 1843?
23 The Rowe sisters were world champions in which sport?
24 Members of which sibling vocal group have starred in "Blood Brothers"?
25 What was Sir Allan Green, then Director of Public Prosecutions, cautioned for in 1992?
26 What do the initials AJ stand for in A. J. Cronin's name?
27 In which century was Nostradamus born?
28 What was the codename for Germany's 1941 Soviet Union invasion plan?
29 The airline NFD is based in which country?
30 Who was given a mess of pottage in return for his birthright in the Book of Genesis?

Answers	**Pot Luck 70** *(see Quiz 146)*

1 Byron. 2 Hedonists. 3 Spa-Francorchamps. 4 Blue. 5 Carrickfergus Castle. 6 December. 7 Psephologist. 8 Mexico. 9 Franz Kafka. 10 Stampy. 11 George Best. 12 The Times. 13 Andrew. 14 Shirley Chisholm. 15 Rumen. 16 25th October. 17 Frankie Laine. 18 St Ogg's. 19 Latin. 20 Lesser Antilles. 21 Rosie Barnes. 22 Norfolk (Sandringham). 23 Shrek. 24 Sir Adrian Boult. 25 6,000. 26 "The Little Shoemaker". 27 Freddie Starr. 28 Delaware. 29 Pineapple Face. 30 Boulevard de La Villette.

1 Where on TV would you have found Dr Fonseca and Dr Leroy?
2 In the Street what were Ken Barlow's parents called?
3 Who was the leader of the Daleks?
4 Other than "EastEnders" in which soap did Grant Mitchell appear?
5 Which adventurer battled against "The Face"?
6 Which future TV prime minister was one of Robin Hood's Merry Men?
7 Who first presented "Sunday Night at the London Palladium"?
8 Which programme replaced "Tonight"?
9 "Watchdog" was originally part of which programme?
10 Who succeeded Robert Wilson as host of "The White Heather Club"?
11 Who owned the corner shop in "Coronation Street" until 1974?
12 Which role did Gabrielle Drake play in "The Brothers"?
13 Who played Governor Faye Bowell in "Within These Walls"?
14 What was the name of the pub in "Albion Market"?
15 Who succeeded Keith Fordyce as presenter of "Thank Your Lucky Stars"?
16 Which star of "Jason King" was born Cyril Louis Goldbert?
17 Which role did Jane Wyman play in "Falcon Crest"?
18 Who were the first two teams on "University Challenge"?
19 Which three ports featured in "Triangle"?
20 Who was the host on "Stars and Garters"?
21 Who was the first Sports Personality of the Year in 1954?
22 In "Coronation Street" who was Linda Cheveski's mother?
23 Who were the first presenters of "Top Gear"?
24 Who played Dr Richard Moone in "Emergency Ward 10"?
25 Which arts programme did "The South Bank Show" replace?
26 Who played Emma Callon in "The Onedin Line"?
27 What was UKTV Gold's revival of Wogan called?
28 Which bandleader introduced "Television Dancing Club"?
29 Who created "Come Dancing"?
30 Who was the original choreographer of Pan's People?

| **Answers** | **Sporting Speed Stars** *(see Quiz 147)* |

1 New York Marathon. 2 Gay Lord. 3 Jesse Owens. 4 1926. 5 100 metre sprint. 6 Bruce McLaren. 7 Joyce Smith. 8 Nelson Piquet. 9 Ron Hutchinson (one win). 10 Lammtarra. 11 Roller skating. 12 Hungary. 13 Drum Taps. 14 Stephen Roche. 15 Heinz-Harald Frentzen. 16 Scobie Breasley. 17 Alan Morton. 18 Nelson Piquet. 19 Cecil Sandford. 20 Rallying. 21 Johnny Herbert. 22 Paul Seaton. 23 Sherry's Prince. 24 9 for 57 (v. SA, Oval 1994). 25 Mill Reef. 26 Carlos Pace. 27 John Surtees. 28 Leroy Burrell. 29 1,000 Guineas. 30 Thomas Kellar medal.

1 What was James Dean's middle name?

2 What is the only English anagram of DISHONEST?

3 Where is the Formula 1 motor racing circuit in Belgium?

4 Who won Best Pop Act at the 2003 Brit Awards?

5 The 80s British castle stamps showed Caernarfon, Edinburgh, Windsor and where?

6 In which month in 1960 was "Coronation Street" first screened?

7 What word is given to someone who studies elections and voting?

8 In which country is the city of Leon?

9 Who wrote the book "The Castle"?

10 What is the name of the elephant Bart Simpson won in a radio competition?

11 Who owned the nightclubs Blinkers and Slack Alice?

12 Which was the first paper to publish a daily weather chart?

13 Which name comes from the Greek and means manly?

14 Who was the first black woman elected to the US Congress, who died in 2005?

15 What is the first stomach of a cow called?

16 When is St Crispin's Day?

17 Under what name did Frank Paul Lo Vecchio become a singing star?

18 What was the name of the Cathedral in "All Gas and Gaiters"?

19 From which language does the word "premium" originate?

20 Leeward and Windward are in which island group?

21 Who was the only female Social Democrat MP when the party was wound up?

22 In which English county outside London does the Queen have a private residence?

23 Which movie won the first ever Best Animated Feature Oscar?

24 Who founded the BBC Symphony Orchestra in 1930?

25 What is the approximate distance of Hong Kong airport from London in miles?

26 What was the first British Top Ten hit for Petula Clark?

27 What is Freddie Starr's real name?

28 On which river does Philadelphia stand?

29 What nickname was given to the dictator President Noriega?

30 On a French Monopoly board, what is the equivalent to Pall Mall?

Answers | Pot Luck 69 (see Quiz 144)

1 "Theme from Harry's Game". 2 50 Cent. 3 35-1. 4 115. 5 Johannes Vermeer. 6 Sarah Kennedy. 7 Matricide. 8 I was Ena Sharples' Father. 9 Rod Stewart. 10 Bolivia. 11 Alan Sillitoe. 12 Gleneagles Hotel. 13 "Days". 14 John Scott. 15 Johnny Nash. 16 Russell Coutts. 17 Bananas. 18 Polynesian. 19 Nigel Mansell. 20 2 p.m. 21 £50. 22 News of the World. 23 Table tennis. 24 The Nolans. 25 Kerb crawling. 26 Archibald Joseph. 27 16th. 28 Operation Barbarossa. 29 Germany. 30 Esau.

1 What did Paula Radcliffe win in her first race after the Athens Olympics?

2 What was the name of Gordon Richards's first winning horse?

3 Which great athlete died at Tuscon, Arizona, in 1980?

4 In which year did Brooklands stage its first Formula 1 Grand Prix?

5 Armin Harry and Harry Jerome set world records in what?

6 Who was driving for McLaren when they won their first Fomula 1 race?

7 Which UK woman won the first two London Marathons?

8 Who won the first Formula 1 Grand Prix at Hungaroring in 1986, 38 seconds in front of Senna?

9 Who won the St Leger from 1967 to 1972 apart from Lester Piggott?

10 In 1995 on which horse did Walter Swinburn set a Derby record time?

11 Chloe Ronaldson was a speed star of the 60s, 70s and 80s at what?

12 At which 1992 race did Nigel Mansell secure enough points to win the Formula 1 World Championship?

13 Frankie Dettori won the Ascot Gold Cup in 1992 and 1993 on which horse?

14 Who was the first Irishmam to win the Tour de France?

15 Who partnered Jacques Villeneuve at the Williams team in 1997?

16 Who won the Derby on the unseasonably named Santa Claus?

17 Which Rangers speedy left winger made goals for Gallagher and James in the 1920s?

18 Who won the first Formula 1 world championship San Marino Grand Prix in 1981?

19 Who was the first British motorcycle rider to be world 125cc champ?

20 What was the sport of Stirling Moss's sister Pat?

21 Who, surprisingly, won the 1995 Formula 1 British Grand Prix at Silverstone?

22 Who was the first UK man to be European water skiing champ?

23 Which greyhound first won a hat trick of Grand National races?

24 What is Devon Malcolm's best return in a Test innings?

25 In the 70s, which horse gave Geoff Lewis his only Derby triumph?

26 Who gave his name to the Brazilian Formula 1 Grand Prix circuit?

27 Who was the first man to have been world champ on two wheels as well as four?

28 Who was the first person to officially run 100 metres in 9.9 seconds?

29 Which of the five Classics has Lester Piggott won least times?

30 Which medal is the highest honour in rowing?

Answers | TV Gold (see Quiz 145)

1 "EastEnders". 2 Frank & Ida. 3 Davros. 4 "Home & Away". 5 Adam Adamant. 6 Paul Eddington. 7 Tommy Trinder. 8 "24 Hours". 9 "Nationwide". 10 Andy Stewart. 11 Maggie Clegg. 12 Jill Hammond. 13 Googie Withers. 14 Waterman's Arms. 15 Brian Matthew. 16 Peter Wyngarde. 17 Angela Channing. 18 Reading and Leeds. 19 Felixstowe, Gothenburg, Rotterdam. 20 Ray Martine. 21 Christopher Chataway. 22 Elsie Tanner. 23 Angela Rippon, Barrie Gill. 24 John Alderton. 25 "Aquarius". 26 Jane Seymour. 27 "Wogan: Now and Then". 28 Victor Sylvester. 29 Eric Morley. 30 Flick.

1 Julia Roberts, Brad Pitt and George Clooney have guested in which TV series?

2 Remus and Sprite are types of what?

3 What is a paronomasia?

4 Who had a 70s No. 1 with "So You Win Again"?

5 If it's noon at GMT, what time is it in Ho Chi Minh City?

6 In whose fictitious fashion workshop was "The Rag Trade" set?

7 How much is received in Monopoly from the sale of stock?

8 Who invented the carpet sweeper?

9 Which UK paper size is 52 x 74 mm?

10 Which shipping forecast area is north of Malin?

11 Whom did Bryan Adams collaborate with on his first number one of the 21st century?

12 What did John Mason Neale write?

13 Which inventor of the microchip won the Nobel Prize for Physics in 2000?

14 What was founded in 1844 by George Williams?

15 Achluophobia is the fear of what?

16 Who was the first woman to win the tennis French Open two years running on more than one occasion?

17 What is the only English anagram of FOUNDLING?

18 What was the name of the first custom-built oil tanker?

19 Which three bishops always have seats in the House of Lords?

20 From which US state would a Nutmegger come from?

21 The airline Norontair is based in which country?

22 Who wrote "The Adventures of Peregrine Pickle"?

23 Which South African played in Ireland's first-ever victory over a county cricket side?

24 Whose final movie was "The Killers" in 1964?

25 What was Edward George Stanley's title when he was UK prime minister?

26 What is Joan Collins's middle name?

27 In which country is the city of Medellin?

28 Who became US Ambassador to the UN in 2005?

29 From which language does the word "robot" originate?

30 How many islands are in the Cape Verde group?

Answers | Pot Luck 72 *(see Quiz 150)*

1 Coventry Street. 2 540. 3 "Chain Gang". 4 Cannonball. 5 James Wight. 6 Eskimo. 7 Cycling. 8 Citroën. 9 Finland. 10 Anthony Burgess. 11 David Ginola. 12 The Delrons. 13 Alabama. 14 Cartoonist Vicky (Victor Weisz). 15 Metal strips were added. 16 Stockard Channing. 17 Wonder Woman. 18 Argentina. 19 John Paul II. 20 Fiji. 21 John W. Hyatt. 22 15th. 23 3,200. 24 The Aviator. 25 Nine. 26 Gradients. 27 Jim Clark. 28 Piltdown Man. 29 Perón. 30 Austria.

1 Which one-hit wonders sang "Gimme Gimme Good Lovin'"?
2 What was the first No. 1 single on the Apple label?
3 Which hit came from James Garner's film "A Man Could Get Killed"?
4 Which group backed Mike Berry?
5 Who had a hit with "Gin House Blues"?
6 Which label did the Bee Gees record on in the 60s?
7 What's the only 60s No. 1 to mention a soft fruit in the title?
8 Denny Doherty and Michelle Gillam were part of which group?
9 Who co-wrote "Sugar Sugar" with Jeff Barry?
10 Who sang about "Ramona", "Marie" and "Marta"?
11 Under what name did John Henry Deighton have his only No. 1?
12 Tony Hatch was an in-house producer for which company?
13 "A Whiter Shade of Pale" was released on which label?
14 Which No. 1 had the backing vocals "ook-a-chunka, ook-a-chunka"?
15 What was on the other side of Roy Orbison's "Blue Bayou"?
16 Freddie Heath and the Nutters became who for a 1960 No. 1?
17 What was the Stones' last No. 1 of the 60s (and 70s, 80s and 90s!)?
18 What was the Beatles' next album after "A Hard Day's Night"?
19 What was the number of the flight on which Ebony Eyes was killed?
20 What were the real surnames of the one-hit wonders Zager and Evans?
21 What was Billy J. Kramer's last chart success of the 60s?
22 What was Sinatra's follow-up to "Strangers in the Night"?
23 Clem Curtis was lead vocalist with which chart-topping group?
24 Who produced the Kinks' No. 1 hits?
25 Which group were first to get a cover of a Beatles album track to No. 1?
26 Who wrote the hippy anthem "San Francisco"?
27 Which No. 1 mentioned "a friend of Sacha Distel"?
28 What was Elvis's last hit of the 60s?
29 Who wrote "MacArthur Park"?
30 Who produced Cilla's No. 1 hits?

Answers | Food & Drink (see Quiz 151)

1 Lettuce. 2 Calves' stomachs. 3 Auvergne. 4 Buffalo milk. 5 Thiamin. 6 Ram's horn. 7 Chicken Marengo. 8 Pine nuts. 9 Parmigiano-Reggiano. 10 Wormwood. 11 Tomato purée. 12 In foil or paper. 13 USA. 14 A type of cider. 15 Angel hair. 16 Still water. 17 Japan. 18 President Thomas Jefferson. 19 Preservative. 20 Moulin Rouge. 21 Eggs. 22 Perrier water. 23 Wimpy. 24 Chopsticks. 25 Whey. 26 Haagen-Dazs ice cream. 27 Two legs and saddle. 28 Hass. 29 Bows – means butterflies. 30 Cake.

Quiz 150 | Pot Luck 72

Answers – page 622

1 In Monopoly, where would a double four from Vine Street land you?
2 What is the sum total of the internal angles in a pentagon in degrees?
3 What was the first British Top Ten hit for Sam Cooke?
4 What was the name of Damien Rice's debut single?
5 What was James Herriot's real name?
6 From which language does the word "kayak" originate?
7 Eileen Sheridan was a record-breaker at which sport?
8 Which car manufacturer made the first front-wheel-drive vehicle?
9 The international car registration SF applies to which country?
10 Who wrote the novel "Time for a Tiger"?
11 Which Frenchman has played for Aston Villa, Everton, Newcastle and Spurs?
12 Who sang with Reparata on "Captain of Your Ship"?
13 Which US state is known as the Camellia State?
14 Who first dubbed Harold Macmillan "Supermac"?
15 What happened to Bank of England £1 notes in 1940?
16 In "The West Wing" First Lady Abigail Bartlet is played by which award-winning actress?
17 What was the other name for Princess Diana of Paradise Island?
18 In which country is the city of Mendoza?
19 Which future pontiff became Archbishop of Krakow in 1964?
20 Viti Levu and Vanua Levu are in which island group?
21 Who invented celluloid?
22 In which century was Martin Luther born?
23 What is the approximate distance of Montreal airport from London in miles?
24 Which 2004 movie re-creates a scene from the 1930 movie "Hell's Angels"?
25 What was the Richter scale register of the earthquake causing December 2004's tsunami?
26 What is the only English anagram of ASTRINGED?
27 Who won the Belgian Formula 1 Grand Prix each year from 1962 to 1965?
28 Charles Dawson was involved in which discovery?
29 Which president gave backing to the Argentine Formula 1 Grand Prix circuit which opened in 1952?
30 In which country are the Schwersystem caves?

Answers | Pot Luck 71 (see Quiz 148)

1 Friends. 2 French Bean. 3 A play upon words. 4 Hot Chocolate. 5 7 p.m. 6 Fenner. 7 £50. 8 Melville Bissell. 9 A8. 10 Hebrides. 11 Chicane. 12 Hymns. 13 Jack Kilby. 14 Y.M.C.A. 15 Darkness or the night. 16 Chris Evert (Lloyd). 17 Unfolding. 18 Gluckauf. 19 London, Durham and Winchester. 20 Connecticut. 21 Canada. 22 Tobias Smollett. 23 Hansie Cronje. 24 Ronald Reagan. 25 Earl of Derby. 26 Henrietta. 27 Colombia. 28 John Bolton. 29 Czech. 30 10.

Answers – page 623

LEVEL 3

1 A batavia is a variety of what?
2 From where is rennet normally obtained?
3 Which part of France does Cantal cheese come from?
4 What was mozzarella cheese originally made from?
5 What is the chemical name of vitamin B1?
6 A rhyton was a drinking vessel in the shape of what?
7 Which chicken dish was named after a Napoleonic battle of June 1800?
8 What sort of nuts are used to make a pesto sauce?
9 What does authentic Parmesan cheese have stamped on its rind?
10 The leaves of which plant are the main ingredient of absinthe?
11 What do you add to a white sauce to make an aurore sauce?
12 How do you cook food en papillote?
13 Where is the home of the Anheuser-Busch Inc. brewery?
14 What is Ameleon?
15 What does the name of the pasta capelli d'angelo mean?
16 What sort of drink is Volvic?
17 Where is the Kirin Brewery based?
18 Who had signed the wine bottle sold for £105,000 at Christie's in 1985?
19 What are the ingredients with E numbers 200–29 used for in foods?
20 In which restaurant did Escoffier begin his career?
21 What is the main ingredient of a piperade?
22 Which drink is Les Bouillens famous for?
23 Which fast-food chain opened its first UK outlet in London in 1954?
24 What do the Chinese call "lively fellows"?
25 What is ricotta cheese made from?
26 What was Reuben Mattus's most famous creation of 1961?
27 What does a baron of lamb consist of?
28 Which type of avocado has a knobbly skin?
29 What shape is farfalle pasta?
30 What is a kugelhopf?

Answers	Pop: 60s *(see Quiz 149)*

1 Crazy Elephant. 2 "Hey Jude". 3 "Strangers in the Night". 4 The Outlaws. 5 Amen Corner. 6 Polydor. 7 "Blackberry Way". 8 Mamas and the Papas. 9 Andy Kim. 10 The Bachelors. 11 Chris Farlowe. 12 Pye. 13 Deram. 14 "Running Bear" (Johnny Preston). 15 "Mean Woman Blues". 16 Johnny Kidd and the Pirates. 17 "Honky Tonk Women". 18 Beatles for Sale. 19 1203. 20 Zager and Evans. 21 "Trains and Boats and Planes". 22 "Summer Wind". 23 The Foundations. 24 Shel Talmy. 25 The Overlanders ("Michelle"). 26 John Phillips. 27 "Where Do You Go to, My Lovely". 28 "Suspicious Minds". 29 Jim Webb. 30 George Martin.

1 Which Six Nations side didn't get to the quarter-finals in the 2003 World Cup?

2 In Monopoly, how much do you inherit in Community Chest?

3 What were immigrant workers picking at the Morecambe Bay tragedy, February 2004?

4 Who was Damon Hill's teammate with the 1997 Formula 1 Arrows Team?

5 Which Lord reported on the Brixton riots of 1981?

6 How many Top Ten singles did Catatonia have?

7 How did Ivan Owen's voice become widely heard on TV?

8 Who invented Portland cement?

9 Who had four Oscar nominations in four years in the 50s, winning at the fourth attempt?

10 Androphobia is the fear of what?

11 In which country is the city of Mogadishu?

12 What is the only English anagram of SIGNATORY?

13 Which character was played by David McCallum in "The Invisible Man"?

14 If A is Alpha and B is Bravo what is P?

15 How was Mikhail Khristodoulou Mouskos better known?

16 Who wrote "Corridors of Power"?

17 What was the character name of the second Alfie actor in "The Talented Mr Ripley"?

18 Who was Nigel Mansell's teammate in the year he won the Formula 1 World Championship?

19 How many islands are in the Scilly group?

20 On which river does Kilmarnock stand?

21 The adjective hircine refers to which creatures?

22 Where was the school besieged by Chechen rebels in September 2004?

23 What is the capital of the US State of Kansas?

24 Who was in goal for Brazil when they won the 2002 World Cup?

25 Who was painted by both Antony Williams and Susan Ryder?

26 If it's noon at GMT, what time is it in Panama City?

27 What was the first British Top Ten hit for Rita Coolidge?

28 In which Dickens novel does Dolly Varden appear?

29 What was Harry Lauder's real name?

30 From which language does the word "lemming" originate?

Answers	Pot Luck 74 (see Quiz 154)

1 4,200. 2 Inferiors. 3 Charles Blondin (Tightrope walker). 4 11-1. 5 Andy Williams. 6 Rolihlahla. 7 Gliding. 8 New Hampshire. 9 Fritz Walter Stadium. 10 Leek. 11 Wilfred Owen. 12 Queen Elizabeth II & Queen Victoria. 13 Azores. 14 Wore a leg iron. 15 Stirling Moss. 16 David Bailey. 17 Arabic. 18 Osnabruck (Hanover). 19 £320. 20 Connie Booth. 21 Original FA Cup entrants. 22 Barry Bucknell. 23 Insomnia. 24 Liberia. 25 "One Day I'll Fly Away". 26 Springfield Retirement Castle. 27 Willie Carson. 28 Storting. 29 St Swithin's. 30 Marble.

1 Which Italian king was assassinated in 1900?
2 In 1903 Panama was seceded from which country?
3 What was nationalized first in Britain, the railway or coal industry?
4 Where did the 1929 Hunger March to London begin?
5 The Chaco War broke out in 1928 between which two countries?
6 Which US Acts of the 1930s prevented involvement in non-American wars?
7 Who annexed Bosnia and Herzegovina in 1908?
8 Who first reached the North Pole in 1909?
9 Who was emperor of Japan during World War One?
10 What did the 1948 Marshall Plan provide?
11 In World War One who made up the Triple Entente?
12 What did the British Citizenship Act of 1948 guarantee?
13 Where in Europe did women gain the vote in 1971?
14 What did the Balfour Declaration of 1917 support?
15 How many independent republics was the USSR divided into in 1991?
16 Who clashed at the Battle of Midway Island in 1942?
17 Which dynasty was overthrown in China in 1912?
18 Who established a Nationalist Chinese Government in 1923?
19 Whose December 2005 stroke threw a naton into crisis?
20 Who was deposed from the Spanish throne in 1931?
21 In World War One how was the third battle of Ypres also known?
22 Where did a military coup bring about the first Marxist state in Africa?
23 Who seized power in Iran in 1921?
24 Where was there a war against Portuguese rulers 1962–74?
25 In which country was the Mau Mau uprising?
26 In which war was the Battle of Ebro River?
27 Who was head of the Turkish republic formed in 1923?
28 Immediately after which war was the PLO formed?
29 Whose murder took place at Birla House?
30 Contrary to tradition, whose presence was not required at the birth of Prince Charles?

| **Answers** | TV: Sitcoms *(see Quiz 155)* |

1 Aristotle. 2 Neville Hope. 3 1-2-1 Club. 4 George. 5 Peter Capaldi. 6 Lady Falkender.
7 Dick Van Dyke. 8 Miss Flood. 9 Erotica. 10 Bette. 11 Steptoe & Son. 12 Medford.
13 Phyllis and Sidney. 14 Mr Lewis. 15 Geraldine. 16 Footballer. 17 Yetta Feldman. 18 Valerie. 19 Mrs Edna Hawkins. 20 George and Pauline. 21 Restaurant in Fulham. 22 "Rising Damp". 23 "Gourmet Night". 24 Paddy. 25 Peter Cook. 26 Gash and Burney. 27 Chumley-on-the-Water. 28 Bygone Books. 29 Shirley Temple. 30 Greengrocer.

1 What is the approximate distance of Nairobi airport from London in miles?

2 What is the only English anagram of FIREIRONS?

3 Under what name did Jean Garvelet ply his high-risk trade?

4 What are the odds of rolling any combination totalling four in dice-throwing?

5 Who had a 50s No. 1 with "Butterfly"?

6 What is Nelson Mandela's middle name?

7 George Lee was three times world champion in which sport?

8 Concord is the capital of which US state?

9 Which stadium in Kaiserslautern hosted a 2006 World Cup game?

10 Musselburgh and Early Market are types of what?

11 Who wrote the poems "Mental Cases" and "Futility"?

12 Who appeared on stamps for the Penny Black's 150th anniversary?

13 Formigar and Terceira are in which island group?

14 What handicap did Sydney Smith overcome to win Wimbledon doubles?

15 Who was the first Englishman to win the British Grand Prix?

16 Who was the opponent in Amir Khan's first professional fight?

17 From which language does the word "assassin" originate?

18 George I was born at which castle?

19 In Monopoly how much does it cost to buy Bond Street?

20 Who co-wrote "Fawlty Towers" with John Cleese?

21 What links Hampstead Heathens, Reigate Priory and Maidenhead?

22 Whose first DIY programme was broadcast in 1957?

23 What plagued Mark Twain, Groucho Marx and Franz Kafka?

24 In which country is the city of Monrovia?

25 What was the first British Top Ten hit for Randy Crawford?

26 What is the old people's home called in "The Simpsons"?

27 Who rode Troy and Henbit to Derby triumphs?

28 What is the Norwegian parliament called?

29 In which teaching hospital was "Doctor in the House" set?

30 What is formed by the metamorphosis of limestone?

Answers	**Pot Luck 73** *(see Quiz 152)*

1 Italy. **2** £100. **3** Cockles. **4** Pedro Diniz. **5** Scarman. **6** Three. **7** Voice of Basil Brush. **8** Joseph Aspdin. **9** Marlon Brando. **10** Men. **11** Somalia. **12** Gyrations. **13** Dr Daniel Westin. **14** Papa. **15** Archbishop Makarios. **16** C. P. Snow. **17** Dickie Greenleaf. **18** Riccardo Patrese. **19** About 150. **20** Irvine. **21** Goats. **22** Beslan. **23** Topeka. **24** Marcos. **25** Queen Elizabeth II. **26** 7 a.m. **27** "We're All Alone". **28** Barnaby Rudge. **29** Hugh MacLennan. **30** Norwegian.

1 What was the name of Gomez Addams's pet octopus?
2 Which character did Kevin Whatley play in "Auf Wiedersehen Pet"?
3 What was the name of the club in the 80s sitcom "Dear John"?
4 What was Captain Mainwaring's first name in "Dad's Army"?
5 Who played enforcer Malcolm Tucker in "The Thick of It"?
6 Which former secretary was consultant on the first two series of "Yes Minister"?
7 Who starred in his own sitcom as Rob Petrie?
8 Who was the older secretary in "May to December"?
9 In "Up Pompeii" who was the daughter of Ludicrus and Ammonia?
10 In "2 Point 4 Children" what was Bill's mum called?
11 Which legendary sitcom transferred to London's Comedy Theatre in February 2006?
12 What was the surname of Terry and June in the sitcom?
13 Who were Timothy Lumsden's parents in "Sorry"?
14 Who was the Spencers' neighbour in the last series of "Some Mothers Do 'Ave 'Em"?
15 What was the goat called in "The Good Life"?
16 In "The Upper Hand" what did Charlie do before he was a housekeeper?
17 What was the name of the ghost in "So Haunt Me"?
18 Whom does the actress who played Phoebe in "Friends" play in "The Comeback"?
19 Who was Shelley's landlady in Pangloss Road?
20 What were the names of Adrian Mole's parents?
21 What and where was "Robin's Nest"?
22 Which sitcom resulted from a one-off play called "The Banana Box"?
23 In which "Fawlty Towers" episode did Cleese attack a car bonnet with a branch?
24 What was Miriam Karlin's militant character in "The Rag Trade"?
25 In "Blackadder" who played Richard III?
26 What were Rab C. Nesbitt's children called?
27 What was the fictitious setting for "The River" with David Essex?
28 Which company did Sarah first work for in "After Henry"?
29 By which film star's name did Alf Garnett refer to his son-in-law?
30 What is the "day job" of ARP Warden Hodges in "Dad's Army"?

Answers	**History: Turning Points** *(see Quiz 153)*

1 Umberto I. 2 Colombia. 3 Coal. 4 Glasgow. 5 Paraguay and Bolivia. 6 Neutrality Acts. 7 Austria. 8 Robert Peary. 9 Taisho. 10 US aid to Europe. 11 Germany, Austria-Hungary, Turkey. 12 British passports for Commonwealth citizens. 13 Switzerland. 14 Jewish state in Palestine. 15 15. 16 US and Japanese air forces. 17 Manchu. 18 Sun Yat-sen. 19 Ariel Sharon. 20 Alfonso XIII. 21 Passchendaele. 22 Congo. 23 Reza Khan. 24 Mozambique. 25 Kenya. 26 Spanish Civil War. 27 Mustapha Kemal. 28 Six-Day War of 1967. 29 Mahatma Gandhi. 30 Home Secretary.

1 "To You I Belong" was the third No. 1 for which girl group?

2 Charlottetown is the capital of which Canadian province?

3 Who invented the chronometer?

4 Gilles Villeneuve was killed during testing at which 1982 Formula 1 Grand Prix race?

5 What is the only English anagram of INTRODUCE?

6 Who wrote "The Gulag Archipelago"?

7 Who had an 80s No. 1 with "The Model"?

8 How was Ferdinand Joseph Lemott better known?

9 If it's noon at GMT, what time is it in Brasilia?

10 Who is the villain in the Wilkie Collins novel "The Woman In White"?

11 Who followed Lord North as prime minister of the UK?

12 In Monopoly, how much do you receive when your annuity matures?

13 In which country is the city of Monterrey?

14 Which shipping forecast area is east of Shannon?

15 The author Tom Wolfe was born on the same day as which Soviet leader?

16 Against which team did Alan Shearer hit his first Newcastle hat-trick?

17 How many islands are in the Caroline group?

18 What do the letters WG stand for in W. G. Grace's name?

19 What was the first British Top Ten hit for Bing Crosby?

20 Which TV play was based on the football-pools winner Viv Nicholson?

21 Anthophobia is the fear of what?

22 Who made the album "Bad Penny Blues"?

23 From which language does the word "census" originate?

24 Parson Lot was an assumed name of which writer?

25 Who was Foreign Secretary before John Major replaced him in 1989?

26 Which US state is known as the Badger State?

27 The picosecond is the smallest unit of what?

28 Whose three-volume autobiography was called "Diary of a Genius"?

29 The airline Malev is based in which country?

30 Who was Bradford City's manager when they were relegated from the Premiership?

Answers | Pot Luck 76 *(see Quiz 158)*

1 Simpson. 2 G. K. Chesterton. 3 200. 4 "The Love Cats". 5 150. 6 "When the Going Gets Tough". 7 Turkish. 8 Layer Cake. 9 Ellice. 10 Stan Laurel (born Arthur Jefferson). 11 Langley, Virginia. 12 Christie. 13 A portrait of Queen Victoria. 14 Steve Collins. 15 Trenton. 16 Della Street. 17 Piccadilly. 18 A7. 19 Sentamu – Archbishop of York. 20 The Post Office. 21 Cecil Day-Lewis. 22 Jerez. 23 Books (binding and selling). 24 Noiseless. 25 John F. Kennedy. 26 Five. 27 Frank Buckle. 28 Duke of Plaza Toro (Gondoliers). 29 Windsor Castle. 30 He's dead (American Beauty).

1 For what did "Four Weddings and a Funeral" win Oscar nominations?
2 What was the movie "Billy Elliot" called when it was shown at the Cannes Film Festival?
3 How many roles did Alec Guinness play in "Kind Hearts and Coronets"?
4 Who was Jane Seymour's first father-in-law?
5 What was Anthony Hopkins's role in "Bram Stoker's Dracula"?
6 Who played Stephen Ward in "Scandal"?
7 In which film did Emma Thompson play a 1940s European and a present-day Californian?
8 Which actor won a BAFTA for "Chariots of Fire"?
9 Which was Julie Andrews's first film with her husband Blake Edwards?
10 Who appeared with Robert Redford, when just six, in "The Great Gatsby"?
11 Who played Schindler's Jewish accountant in "Schindler's List"?
12 What was Roger Moore's second movie as James Bond?
13 Who starred in and composed the score for "Bedazzled"?
14 Which actor has been co-owner of London's Langan's Brasserie?
15 Who played General Allenby in "Lawrence of Arabia"?
16 The reciting of whose poem in "Four Weddings and a Funeral" resulted in a book of his poetry becoming a best-seller?
17 Who won an Oscar for Best Picture in 1968, which his nephew also starred in?
18 Who played Anne Boleyn in "A Man for All Seasons"?
19 What was Glenda Jackson's film debut?
20 What was Cilla Black's first feature film?
21 Who wrote an autobiography "Beginning" in 1989, aged 28?
22 Who is the actress wife of the Oscar-winning director of "Ray"?
23 Who said she was "the only sex symbol England produced since Lady Godiva"?
24 Who played opposite Hayley Mills in "The Family Way"?
25 Who played Poirot in "Murder on the Orient Express"?
26 Which character did Alec Guinness play in "Dr Zhivago"?
27 Which "Carry On" film was called "Carry On Venus in the US"?
28 Who directed "Whistle Down the Wind" in 1961?
29 Who wrote of his relationship with his actress wife in "Meeting Mrs Jenkins"?
30 Who played Noël Coward in "Star!"?

Answers	**Plant World** *(see Quiz 159)*

1 Meilland. 2 Wild cherry. 3 Borlotti beans. 4 Egypt. 5 Sap. 6 Poisonous mushroom. 7 Hydroponics. 8 Red. 9 Starch. 10 Latex. 11 Gold/orange. 12 Calcifuge. 13 Insects. 14 Weigelas. 15 Brambles. 16 Lichens. 17 Salt. 18 Pappus. 19 Tomatoes. 20 Figs. 21 Carrot. 22 Its cap. 23 The stems of plants. 24 Old tree or log. 25 Study of plant diseases. 26 Tea. 27 Coconut palm. 28 Pertaining to the soil. 29 Giant cactus. 30 Unopened flower buds.

1 What does S stand for in Ulysses S. Grant's name?
2 Who wrote the book "The Napoleon of Notting Hill"?
3 What is the approximate distance of Paris airport from London in miles?
4 What was the first British Top Ten hit for the Cure?
5 How many degrees are there in each internal angle of a dodecagon?
6 What was Boyzone's fifth No. 1 single?
7 From which language does the word "horde" originate?
8 In which movie did Pierce Brosnan's successor as 007 play X?
9 Nanumea and Nukulailai are in which island group?
10 Who was the most famous comedian to be born in Ulverston, north-west England?
11 Where is the HQ of the CIA?
12 Who had a 70s No. 1 with "Yellow River"?
13 What is buried under Cleopatra's Needle with a razor and cigars?
14 Who inflicted Chris Eubank's first defeat as a professional fighter?
15 What is the capital of the US State of New Jersey?
16 What was the name of Perry Mason's secretary?
17 On a Monopoly board what is between Water Works and Go To Jail?
18 Which UK paper size is 74 x 105 mm?
19 Which Archbishop has the middle names Mugabi Tucker?
20 Whom did Keith Richards work for before becoming a Rolling Stone?
21 Which Irish poet wrote detective novels under the pseudonym Nicholas Blake?
22 Where was the Spanish Formula 1 Grand Prix held prior to 1991?
23 What did the physicist and chemist Michael Faraday train to work with?
24 What is the only English anagram of LIONESSES?
25 Who was US president when racial discrimination was made illegal?
26 Before the 20th century how many moons of Jupiter had been discovered?
27 Lestor Piggott overtook whose record for English classic wins?
28 In light opera, who "led his regiment from behind"?
29 Which place was first intended to be the venue for Prince Charles and Camilla's wedding?
30 What is unusual about the narrator of Sam Mendes's first feature film?

Answers | Pot Luck 75 *(see Quiz 156)*

1 B*Witched. 2 Prince Edward Islands. 3 John Harrison. 4 Belgium. 5 Reduction. 6 Alexander Solzhenitsyn. 7 Kraftwerk. 8 Jelly Roll Morton. 9 9 a.m. 10 Count Fosco. 11 Lord Rockingham. 12 £100. 13 Mexico. 14 Fastnet. 15 Mikhail Gorbachev. 16 Leicester. 17 About 680. 18 William Gilbert. 19 "Isle of Innisfree". 20 "Spend, Spend, Spend". 21 Flowers. 22 Humphrey Lyttelton. 23 Latin. 24 Charles Kingsley. 25 Geoffrey Howe. 26 Wisconsin. 27 Time. 28 Salvador Dali. 29 Hungary. 30 Jim Jefferies.

1 Who bred the first Peace rose?
2 What sort of tree is a gean?
3 How are Boston or pinto beans also known?
4 Where did liquorice originate?
5 Which part of asafoetida is used as a spice?
6 What is a clouded agaric?
7 What is the practice of growing plants in liquid nutrients instead of soil called?
8 What colour is the pigment leghaemoglobin found in legumes?
9 The breakdown of what produces malic acid?
10 What is the milky juice of the dandelion called?
11 What colour is a cloudberry?
12 What term applies to a plant which is lime-hating?
13 What does the bladderwort live on?
14 Which shrubs are also known as bush honeysuckles?
15 What does a batologist study?
16 What is litmus obtained from?
17 A halophyte tolerates soil or water containing what?
18 What is the ring of fine down on a dandelion called?
19 What would you grow if you grew Peruvian apples?
20 What fruit is produced on a banyan tree?
21 Which common vegetable family does chervil belong to?
22 What is a toadstool's pileus?
23 Cauliflowers are vegetables but technically what are caulis?
24 Where would you normally find a bracket fungus?
25 What is phytopathology?
26 What is Camellia sinensis more commonly called?
27 From what is the oil copra obtained?
28 What does edaphic mean?
29 What is a saguaro?
30 Which part of the plants are the cloves you buy as a spice?

Answers	**Movies: The Brits** *(see Quiz 157)*

1 Best Film, Writer (Richard Curtis). 2 Dancer. 3 Eight. 4 Richard Attenborough. 5 Dr Van Helsing. 6 John Hurt. 7 Dead Again. 8 Ian Holm. 9 Darling Lilli. 10 Patsy Kensit. 11 Ben Kingsley. 12 The Man with the Golden Gun. 13 Dudley Moore. 14 Michael Caine. 15 Jack Hawkins. 16 W. H. Auden. 17 Carol Reed (Oliver! – Oliver Reed). 18 Vanessa Redgrave. 19 This Sporting Life. 20 Work is a Four Letter Word. 21 Kenneth Branagh. 22 Helen Mirren. 23 Diana Dors. 24 Hywel Bennett. 25 Albert Finney. 26 Zhivago's half-brother Yeugraf. 27 Carry On Jack. 28 Bryan Forbes. 29 Richard Burton. 30 Daniel Massey.

1 What was Alicia Markova's real name?
2 Who wrote the opera "The Tempest", premiered at the Royal Opera in 2004?
3 The 2003 rugby union World Cup was played in how many cities?
4 Who invented the mechanical clock?
5 Astraphobia is the fear of what?
6 What is the only English anagram of MEANS TEST?
7 Why was the release of "Gangs of New York" postponed for a year?
8 Springfield is the capital of which US state?
9 In which movie did the star of "The Cider House Rules" play murderess Aileen Wuornos?
10 Who had an 80s No. 1 with "Give It Up"?
11 If it's noon at GMT, what time is it in Halifax, Nova Scotia?
12 When was the first race meeting at Royal Ascot?
13 Whose recording of which piece was the first classical record to sell over a million copies?
14 How many islands are in the Queen Charlotte group?
15 In which century was John Bunyan born?
16 What was Patrick Vieira's first football club?
17 From which language does the word "ombudsman" originate?
18 In Scrabble what is the letter T worth?
19 What was the number of the Trotter's flat in Nelson Mandela House?
20 A set of British stamps was issued in 1990 for which charity's 150th anniversary?
21 On which river does Milan stand?
22 What word is given to the fear of bees?
23 Whose autobiography was called "Child of Change"?
24 In how many Test matches did Ian Botham captain England?
25 What was the first British solo Top Ten hit for Roger Daltrey?
26 In which country is the city of Murcia?
27 In Monopoly, how much do you receive for your birthday if there are four players?
28 Longleat is the stately home of whom?
29 The airline Crossair is based in which country?
30 Sabine and Saladin are types of what?

Answers | **Pot Luck 78** *(see Quiz 162)*

1 Justin. 2 Boulevard de Belleville. 3 The Simon Park Orchestra. 4 Henry James. 5 Italian. 6 Bahamas. 7 Fred Noonan. 8 Dido. 9 Newcastle Utd and Everton. 10 Leslie Poles. 11 Samuel de Champlain. 12 The Pickwick Papers. 13 Leicester. 14 The name Winston. 15 "Eloise". 16 24. 17 1954. 18 Christiaan Huygens. 19 Olivier Panis. 20 No place (Greek). 21 5,800. 22 Kiefer Sutherland. 23 Carnation. 24 On the moon. 25 Lord Grenville. 26 Monte Marmolada. 27 Derby-winning horses. 28 Delaware. 29 Mobilises. 30 Viktor Yanukovych, Viktor Yushchenko.

1 Who was Tiger Woods's caddie for his first Masters win?
2 When did Great Britain first win the Walker Cup?
3 Where did Nick Faldo win his first British Open?
4 What was Jack Nicklaus's nickname in his first Walker Cup in the 50s?
5 What is the name of Hole 8 at Troon?
6 In the 1996 US Masters, by how many strokes did Norman lead Faldo before the final round?
7 Who won the British Open the year after Lee Trevino's first triumph?
8 Henry Cotton won the British Open at Sandwich, Muirfield and where?
9 Who was the first South African to win the British Open?
10 Which champion's father was a pro at Hawkstone Park golf course?
11 On which course did Tiger Woods win his first British Open?
12 Where in America did Great Britain and Ireland first win the Walker Cup?
13 Who got the nickname the Walrus?
14 What did Jack Nicklaus score on his last Major round at the British Open in 2005?
15 After World War Two, who got the first three-in-a-row hat-trick of British Opens?
16 Who set the course record of 64 at Troon in the Open of 1989?
17 Horton Smith was the first winner of which major event?
18 Which management group did Tiger Woods sign up to on turning pro?
19 What was the original prize for winning the British Open?
20 Michael Campbell won the 2005 US Open by how many shots from Tiger Woods?
21 Who was the first New Zealander to win the British Open?
22 In which decade was the Walker Cup staged at an English course?
23 Who got the nickname Dough Boy?
24 In what capacity did Devereux Emmet leave his mark on golf?
25 Who was the last golfer before Faldo to be BBC Sports Personality of the Year?
26 What first did Peter Butler manage in the 1973 Ryder Cup?
27 Which golfer's first tour victory was the 1982 Swiss Open?
28 Which course contains the Rabbit and the Seal?
29 Tom Lehman became the first American since whom to win an Open at Royal Lytham?
30 Where was the great Harry Vardon born?

Answers | Pop: Who's Who (see Quiz 163)

1 Coldplay (A Rush of Blood to the Head). 2 Paul Anka. 3 Mickie Most. 4 Beats International. 5 Red Hot Chili Peppers. 6 Marco Pirroni. 7 John Barry Orchestra. 8 Boomtown Rats. 9 Renée of Renée and Renato. 10 Dave Ball. 11 Craig Logan. 12 Kenny Ball and his Jazzmen. 13 Belinda Carlisle. 14 Procul Harum. 15 Lose Yourself. 16 Geno Washington. 17 New Edition. 18 Boy George. 19 John Gorman. 20 Helen Shapiro. 21 Jeff Lynne. 22 The Jordanaires. 23 Mr Blobby. 24 Dusty Springfield's ("You Don't Have to Say You Love Me"). 25 Earth Wind and Fire. 26 Eddie Cochran. 27 2 Unlimited. 28 Shaggy. 29 Brook Benton and Dinah Washington. 30 Radiohead.

1 Who attempted to blackmail Desperate Housewife Gabrielle Solis?

2 On a French Monopoly board, what is the equivalent to Old Kent Road?

3 Who had an 80s No. 1 with "Eye Level"?

4 Who wrote "The Turn of the Screw"?

5 From which language does the word "parasol" originate?

6 Cat Crooked and Acklins are in which island group?

7 Who died with Amelia Earhart on her round-the-world attempt?

8 Who is Florian Cloud de Bounevialle Armstrong?

9 Steve Watson and Alessandro Pistone were colleagues at which two Premiership clubs?

10 What do the letters LP stand for in L. P. Hartley's name?

11 Which explorer founded Quebec?

12 In which Dickens novel does Job Trotter appear?

13 Where in Britain did the first women traffic wardens go on duty?

14 What did John Lennon share with Gary Lineker?

15 What was the first British Top Ten hit for the Damned?

16 What is the maximum number of Knights and Lady Companions of the Order of the Garter?

17 In which year did food rationing end in Britain?

18 Who invented the pendulum clock?

19 Who broke both legs in a Montreal 1997 Formula 1 Grand Prix crash ?

20 What does the word "Utopia" mean?

21 What is the approximate distance of Rio de Janeiro airport from London in miles?

22 Who plays the sniper who keeps ringing the booth in the "Phone Booth"?

23 What is the national flower of Spain?

24 Where is the Marsh of Sleep located?

25 What was William Wyndham's title when he was UK prime minister?

26 What is the highest peak of the Dolomites called?

27 What's the link between Blue Peter, Pearl Diver and Sir Peter Teazle?

28 Which US state is known as the Diamond State?

29 What is the only English anagram of OMNISSIBLE?

30 Who were the two main contenders in the controversial 2004 Ukraine elections?

| **Answers** | **Pot Luck 77** *(see Quiz 160)* |

1 Lillian Marks. 2 Thomas Ades. 3 Ten. 4 I-Hsing. 5 Lightning. 6 Statesman. 7 9/11 attacks. 8 Illinois. 9 Monster (Charlize Theron). 10 K.C. and the Sunshine Band. 11 8 a.m. 12 1711. 13 Dame Joan Hammond – Puccini's Turandot. 14 150. 15 17th. 16 Cannes. 17 Swedish. 18 One. 19 368. 20 RSPCA. 21 Olono. 22 Apiphobia. 23 Chess player Gary Kasparov. 24 12. 25 "Giving It All Away". 26 Spain. 27 £30 (£10 each from the three other players). 28 Marquess of Bath. 29 Switzerland. 30 Lettuce.

1 Who released an album giving the website details of the campaign for fairer trade?

2 Who was the first person to write a British No. 1 both for himself and for someone else?

3 Who produced "House of the Rising Sun" for the Animals?

4 With what did the ex-Housemartin Norman Cook next hit No. 1?

5 Who were formed by Anthony Kiedis and Michael Balzary?

6 Which ex-Siouxsie and the Banshees guitarist penned the Adam Ant No. 1s?

7 Whose first Top Ten hit was "Hit and Miss"?

8 Who were the next Irish group to top the British charts after the Bachelors?

9 Who was Hilary Lefter when she hit the top of the charts in 1982?

10 Who was the synthesizer player in Soft Cell?

11 Who wasn't one of the brothers in Bros?

12 Acapulco, Casablanca and Moscow feature in whose record titles?

13 Who left the Go Gos in '85 and had her first UK No. 1 in 1988?

14 Whose last single, in 1975, was called "Pandora's Box"?

15 What was the first Eminem single to be No. 1 in the UK and US?

16 Who led the Ram Jam Band in the 60s?

17 In which band did Bobby Brown make No. 1 in 1983?

18 In Praise of Lemmings wisely changed their name but kept which name-change singer?

19 Who made up Scaffold with Roger McGough and Mike McGear?

20 Who was the first British female to have two consecutive No. 1s?

21 Who wrote the hits for ELO?

22 Who provided backing vocals on Elvis's "It's Now or Never"?

23 Whose first hit song started out with the title "Mr Jellybun"?

24 Whose first No. 1 was originally called "Io Che No Vivo Senza Te"?

25 The percussionist of which band duetted with Phil Collins on "Easy Lover" in 1985?

26 Who had the second posthumous No. 1 in the British charts?

27 Who were Anita Dels and Ray Slijngaard?

28 Who was born Orville Richard Burrell in Jamaica in 1968?

29 Who had the original hit with "A Rockin' Good Way" in 1960?

30 Who first made the album charts with "Pablo Honey"?

Quiz 164 | Pot Luck 79

1 What did George Shillibeer introduce in London in 1829?
2 Who made his first start for Man. Utd for 20 months in January 2006 against Burton Albion?
3 Who is credited with having conceived the first automatic digital computer?
4 Who had a 70s No. 1 with "Up Town Top Ranking"?
5 What is the only English anagram of SCHEMATIC?
6 What did Lovejoy affectionately call his Morris Minor?
7 Which Samuel won the Nobel Prize for Literature in 1969?
8 The comic actor Eric Idle was born on the same day as which British prime minister?
9 What is Denis Healey's middle name?
10 How many islands are in the Cyclades group?
11 Which shipping forecast area is east of Fastnet?
12 Which poet referred to himself as Merlin in a summing-up of his poetical career?
13 What is the capital of the US State of Florida?
14 Which Prince died three days after the death of John Paul II?
15 In 1973 Mrs Susan Shaw became the first woman to set foot where?
16 Batrachophobia is the fear of what?
17 In which country are the Abisso Olivifer caves?
18 What was U2's first No. 1 single of the 21st century?
19 Who wrote "Keep the Home Fires Burning"?
20 What was the first British solo Top Ten hit for Doris Day?
21 In the Monopoly Community Chest, how much is the insurance premium?
22 The airline Linjeflyg is based in which country?
23 In 2002, what was the highest-ever grossing French film in the US?
24 Which Royal has Albert Christian Edward as his three other names?
25 What are the odds of rolling any combination totalling eleven in dice-throwing?
26 What is the opposite of occidental?
27 From which language does the word "bazaar" originate?
28 Harry Dobson had a 6 per cent stake in which high-profile business?
29 Which country's secret police is called Savak?
30 If it's noon at GMT, what time is it in Managua?

Answers	Pot Luck 80 (see Quiz 166)

1 Blair General Hospital. 2 Enigma. 3 David Coleman. 4 Morocco. 5 144. 6 Italian. 7 Onion. 8 Peritonitis. 9 Arthur C. Clarke. 10 Surfers Paradise, Australia. 11 Peter Sellers. 12 Laura Solon. 13 Maine. 14 Spottable. 15 "Footballers' Wives". 16 Dodecanese. 17 14th February. 18 Phyllis Dorothy. 19 Damon Hill. 20 "Candida". 21 François Hennebique. 22 Go to Jail. 23 Leeches. 24 6,800. 25 Eliza Dushku. 26 Gosford Park. 27 Sunday Post. 28 Martine McCutcheon. 29 Neckar. 30 Fort Sill (Oklahoma).

1 Which company marketed the first diesel-engined private car?
2 Which north-west town has Central and Bank Quay stations?
3 What was the first vehicle-registration plate in Britain?
4 How many London Underground lines begin with letters in the second half of the alphabet?
5 In July 2005 which airline catering suppliers' strike caused long delays?
6 Who was with Jean Pierre Blanchard in the first balloon crossing of the English Channel?
7 Which two Great Lakes does the Welland Canal link?
8 Who was the first person to walk in space without a safety line?
9 What did TML stand for in Channel Tunnel construction?
10 In which American state was the first railway station opened?
11 Which airline did British Airways acquire in 1988?
12 Where is Baltasound Airport?
13 What did Enrico Forlanini develop in 1898?
14 The first part of London Underground's ran from Paddington to where?
15 Which was Thor Heyerdahl's third raft after Kontiki and Ra?
16 Which nuclear submarine made the first underwater circumnavigation of the globe?
17 Where was the flight from London going to when Concorde entered supersonic service in 1976?
18 Which spacecraft took the first close ups of Mars?
19 What was the first turbine-driven steamship called?
20 Where were the Apollo 1 astronauts when they perished in the 60s?
21 Who were the first two countries to offer flags of convenience?
22 Which two rivers does the Albert Canal link?
23 How many major private rail companies were nationalized in 1947?
24 What does the Seikan Tunnel link?
25 Which airport company was the first to float on the Stock Exchange?
26 What was the Queen Elizabeth called when it was destroyed by fire in Hong Kong?
27 Who was the first person to fly over both Poles and the Atlantic?
28 Which report recommended changes after the 1987 King's Cross fire?
29 Where is the deepwater port of Tuticorin?
30 What did the Soviets call their first nuclear-powered ship?

Answers | TV Detectives (see Quiz 167)

1 Charley Farley and Piggy Malone. 2 "Johnny Todd". 3 Auguste Dupin. 4 Piet. 5 George Cross. 6 "Target". 7 Inspector Tsientsin. 8 Trout Inn. 9 Starsky and Hutch. 10 Taggart. 11 Denise Welch. 12 Special Branch. 13 Wyvern. 14 Kelly Garrett. 15 Radio West. 16 Exeter. 17 Sexton Blake. 18 College porter. 19 LA Coroner's Office. 20 Suzanne "Pepper" Anderson. 21 Whitehaven Mansions. 22 Barstock CID. 23 1960 Mark 2. 24 Through the Del Floria tailor's shop. 25 Inspector Claude Eustace Teal. 26 Inspector Wexford. 27 Seven. 28 Answerphone message. 29 Laura Holt. 30 Granada.

Quiz 166 Pot Luck 80

Answers – page 638

LEVEL 3

1 In which hospital was "Dr Kildare" set?
2 Who had a 90s No. 1 with "Sadness Part 1"?
3 Which sports commentator was a champion mile runner for Cheshire?
4 In which country is the city of Oujda?
5 How many degrees are there in each internal angle of a decagon?
6 From which language does the word "scenario" originate?
7 Turbo and Stuttgarter Giant are types of what?
8 What was Rudolph Valentino's cause of death?
9 Who wrote "The City and the Stars"?
10 Where did Nigel Mansell achieve his first pole position and win in an Indy car race?
11 Who featured on the 17p – the cheapest – of the 1985 British Film Year stamps?
12 Who in 2005 was only the second woman to win the Perrier Comedy Award?
13 Augusta is the capital of which US state?
14 What is the only English anagram of TABLETOPS?
15 "Extra Time" is a spin off from which glossy drama?
16 Tilos and Astipalaia are in which island group?
17 What special birthday links Kevin Keegan and P. G. Wodehouse?
18 What do the letters PD stand for in P. D. James's name?
19 Who won the inaugural Melbourne Formula 1 Grand Prix in 1996?
20 What was the first British Top Ten hit for Dawn?
21 Who invented reinforced concrete?
22 In Monopoly, where would double one from Water Works land you?
23 The adjective hirudinal refers to which creatures?
24 What is the approximate distance of Singapore airport from London in miles?
25 Which "Buffy the Vampire Slayer" cast member was born on 30 December 1980?
26 The plot of which 2002 movie centres on the murder of Sir William McCordle?
27 Which Dundee-based paper first appeared in 1920?
28 "Perfect Moment" was a No. 1 in 1999 for which former EastEnder?
29 On which river does Stuttgart stand?
30 Geronimo died at which US Fort?

Answers	Pot Luck 79 *(see Quiz 164)*

1 First regular bus service. 2 Ole Gunnar Solskjaer. 3 Charles Babbage. 4 Althia and Donna. 5 Catechism. 6 Miriam. 7 Beckett. 8 John Major. 9 Winston. 10 About 220. 11 Lundy. 12 Alfred, Lord Tennyson. 13 Tallahassee. 14 Prince Rainier. 15 Floor of the London Stock Exchange. 16 Reptiles. 17 Italy. 18 "Beautiful Day". 19 Ivor Novello. 20 "My Love and Devotion". 21 £50. 22 Sweden. 23 Amelie. 24 Prince Andrew. 25 17.5-1. 26 Oriental. 27 Persian. 28 Manchester United. 29 Iran. 30 6 a.m.

1 Who were the private investigators played by the Two Ronnies?

2 Which folk song was the "Z Cars" theme based on?

3 Which Edgar Allan Poe detective did Edward Woodward play in the "Detective" series?

4 What was Van de Valk's first name?

5 Which medal had Detective Inspector Frost won?

6 Which TV drama featured Detective Steve Hackett?

7 Which character did David Suchet play in "Reilly – Ace of Spies"?

8 Which Oxford pub was the setting for the Morse episode "The Wolvercote Tongue"?

9 Who had a street contact called Huggy Bear?

10 Who was assisted by Detective Sergeant Peter Livingstone?

11 Which future "Coronation Street" actress played Jimmy Nail's wife in "Spender"?

12 Craven and Haggerty starred in which series?

13 Where did the action of "Softly Softly" take place?

14 Which agent was played by Jaclyn Smith in "Charlie's Angels"?

15 Whom did Eddie Shoestring work for?

16 In which college did Morse collapse at the end of "The Remorseful Day"?

17 Which detective had a bloodhound called Pedro and a Rolls-Royce called the Grey Panther?

18 Which walk-on part did Colin Dexter have in the Morse sequel "Lewis"?

19 Where did Quincy work?

20 Which role did Angie Dickinson play in "Police Woman"?

21 In the TV series what was Hercule Poirot's London address?

22 Which police force was Henry Crabbe retired from?

23 What year and model were Morse's most famous red Jaguar?

24 What was the secret entrance to the headquarters of U.N.C.L.E.?

25 Which police officer was a regular adversary of Simon Templar?

26 Whom did Inspector Mike Burden assist?

27 How many Babies did Rockliffe have in the 80s series?

28 What did each episode of "The Rockford Files" begin with?

29 Who owned Remington Steele Investigations?

30 Which TV company made the "Prime Suspect" series in the UK?

Answers | **Travel & Transport** *(see Quiz 165)*

1 Mercedes Benz. 2 Warrington. 3 A1. 4 Three (Northern, Piccadilly, Victoria). 5 Gate Gourmet. 6 John Jeffries. 7 Ontario to Erie. 8 Bruce McCandless. 9 TransManche Link. 10 Baltimore. 11 British Caledonian. 12 Unst, Shetland. 13 Hydrofoil. 14 Farringdon Street. 15 Tigris. 16 USS Triton. 17 Bahrain. 18 Mariner 4. 19 Turbinia. 20 Cape Kennedy (fire at a ground test). 21 Liberia and Panama. 22 Meuse, Scheld. 23 Four. 24 Islands of Honshu and Hokkaido. 25 BAA. 26 Seawise University. 27 Richard Evelyn Byrd. 28 Fennel Report. 29 India. 30 Lenin.

Answers – page 644

1 In which month is Venezuela's national day?

2 How was Angelo Giuseppe Roncalli better known?

3 What was the nickname of the Locomotives and Highway Act of 1865?

4 Who wrote "Tortilla Flat"?

5 To one season, when did Tony Adams make his Arsenal debut?

6 Where was the first Formula 1 World Championship race held outside Europe in 1953?

7 Which newspaper first introduced box numbers in the UK?

8 What was Molière's real name?

9 If it's noon at GMT, what time is it in Montevideo?

10 In which city was "Ally McBeal" set?

11 In Scrabble what is the letter L worth?

12 Which film was based on Sir Laurence Van Der Post's novel "The Seed and the Sower"?

13 In Monopoly, how much is paid to the Hospital in Community Chest?

14 How many islands are in the Philippines group?

15 What was the Oscar winner for "Monster's Ball" called when she became a Bond girl?

16 What is the name of Scotland's largest cave?

17 What was the fourth Radiohead album to top the charts?

18 What are the Sudanese Dunka tribe recognized to be?

19 Who led the French Protestants known as the Huguenots?

20 Which UK paper size is 105 x 148 mm?

21 What is the only English anagram of SUBLINEAR?

22 Which bridge was opened by Lady Thatcher in Hong Kong giving access to the airport of Lantau Island?

23 Who was the barman in "Shameless", as played by Dean Lennox Kelly?

24 In which US state would a Hoosier be a native inhabitant?

25 From which language does the word "parallax" originate?

26 What was George Hamilton-Gordon's title when he was UK prime minister?

27 Who invented contact lenses?

28 Belonophobia is the fear of what?

29 What was the first British Top Ten hit for Depeche Mode?

30 The airline Bell-Air is based in which country?

Answers | Pot Luck 82 *(see Quiz 170)*

1 "Time is Tight". 2 Marginal. 3 Mayfair. 4 £140. 5 Gregor Pincus. 6 Arizona. 7 Capricorn. 8 David Broome. 9 French. 10 Melanie Chisholm. 11 Balearic. 12 Robert Frost. 13 The Bank of England. 14 Muhammad Ali. 15 The Metro. 16 6,000. 17 Jorn Utzon. 18 Fred Baldasare. 19 Jakob Eberst. 20 4th. 21 46. 22 Starship. 23 The Cornfield. 24 Canada. 25 Nigeria. 26 US President Wilson. 27 Edward Whymper. 28 Taxation. 29 Ayrton Senna and Roland Ratzenberger. 30 Bradford City.

1 Other than wife what relation was Eleanor Roosevelt to Franklin D.?
2 What was the profession of Roger Moore's father?
3 What is the real name of the author Nigel West?
4 Which celebrity photographer wrote "My Royal Past"?
5 Who captained the first all-female crew to sail round the world?
6 Who was Mia Farrow's second husband?
7 Who was the oldest member of the Royal Family at her death, in 2004?
8 What is David Bailey's middle name?
9 Which contest was Kiki Haakonson the first winner of?
10 Which MP competed at the Tokyo Olympics and was UK 100m. record holder 1967–74?
11 Which son of the late US Ambassador to Paris, Pamela Harriman, has been a British MP?
12 Which forename is shared by Princess Beatrice, Zara Phillips and Lady Louise Windsor?
13 Who won Best Actor Oscar the night the first black Best Actress won?
14 How many Princesses Royal were there before Princess Anne?
15 Which Guinness heiress overdosed at Oxford University in the 80s?
16 Who is Wath-on-Dearne Comprehensive School's most famous old boy?
17 What was US President Nixon's wife called?
18 How was the designer Miss Mountney of Merthyr Tydfil better known?
19 Who said she was famous first as someone's daughter, then someone's wife, and probably finally as someone's mother?
20 In which musical did Darius Danesh star in January/February 2006?
21 What relation, if any, is Vanessa Redgrave to Jemma Redgrave?
22 Who became Earl of Chester in 1958?
23 Who was Britain's youngest-ever city councillor at 21, and youngest – then – MP aged 28?
24 What are Prince Edward's four given names?
25 Where was Pierre Cardin born?
26 How was Vera Jane Palmer better known?
27 Who tried to assassinate Pope John Paul II in 1981?
28 Who was the first woman general of the Salvation Army?
29 Which prime minister was a former football referee and coach?
30 Whose second shop was called Nostalgia of Mud?

Answers | **Screen Greats** *(see Quiz 171)*

1 Grand Hotel. 2 Clark Gable, Jean Harlow. 3 James Stewart. 4 Claudette Colbert. 5 Robert Mitchum. 6 Thoroughbreds Don't Cry. 7 Blue Skies. 8 Rita Hayworth. 9 Orson Welles. 10 Olivia de Havilland. 11 Stromboli. 12 Spencer Tracy & Katharine Hepburn. 13 Bette Davis. 14 Claude Rains. 15 Susan Hayward. 16 Paramount. 17 Deborah Kerr. 18 Lola-Lola. 19 Donald O'Connor. 20 Debbie Reynolds. 21 Joan Crawford. 22 Humphrey Bogart. 23 Gene Kelly. 24 Neath, Wales. 25 W. C. Fields. 26 Safety Last. 27 Lita Grey. 28 Mack Sennett. 29 Ginger Rogers. 30 Rita Hayworth.

1 What was the first British Top Ten hit for Booker T. and the MGs?

2 What is the only English anagram of ALARMING?

3 In which part of London were parking meters first introduced?

4 In Monopoly how much does it cost to buy Whitehall?

5 Who invented the contraceptive pill?

6 Which US state is known as the Apache State?

7 Which star sign links the TV presenter Michael Aspel and the botanist David Bellamy?

8 Who was the first Briton to win the World Show Jumping Championships?

9 From which language does the word "fuselage" originate?

10 Which female was first to have a UK No. 1 single solo, part of a duo, a quartet and a quintet?

11 Cabrera and Formentera are in which island group?

12 Who wrote the poem "After Apple Picking"?

13 Sir John Houblon was the first governor of what?

14 Who had his jaw broken in 1973 by Ken Norton?

15 What was the work of Fulgence Bienvenue in Paris?

16 What is the approximate distance of Tokyo airport from London in miles?

17 Who designed the Sydney Opera House?

18 Who was the first person to swim the Channel underwater?

19 What was Jacques Offenbach's real name?

20 In which century was Alexander the Great born?

21 How many chromosomes are there in a normal human body cell?

22 Who had an 80s No. 1 with "Nothing's Going to Stop Us Now"?

23 At the scene of which of his pictures did Van Gogh shoot himself?

24 In which country was the actress Lynda Bellingham born?

25 The international car registration WAN applies to which country?

26 Who officially opened the Panama Canal?

27 Who was the first Englishman to climb the Matterhorn?

28 What law did Margaret Thatcher specialize in when she studied for the Bar?

29 Which two Formula 1 Drivers lost their lives at Imola in 1994?

30 Chris Hutchings had a short spell as manager of which club in the Premiership?

Answers | Pot Luck 81 *(see Quiz 168)*

1 July. 2 Pope John XXIII. 3 The Red Flag Act. 4 John Steinbeck. 5 1983–84. 6 Buenos Aires, Argentina. 7 Daily Telegraph. 8 Jean-Baptiste Poquelin. 9 9 a.m. 10 Boston. 11 One. 12 Merry Christmas Mr Lawrence. 13 £100. 14 Over 7,100. 15 Jinx (Halle Berry). 16 The Great Smoo. 17 Hail to the Thief. 18 Tallest people in the world. 19 Henry of Navarre. 20 A6. 21 Insurable. 22 The Tsing Ma Bridge. 23 Kev. 24 Indiana. 25 Greek. 26 Lord Aberdeen. 27 Adolph E. Fick. 28 Needles. 29 "You Just Can't Get Enough". 30 New Zealand.

1 In which movie did Greta Garbo say, "I want to be alone"?
2 Which two Hollywood greats were the stars of "Red Dust" in 1932?
3 Which Oscar-winner in 1940 received the DFC and the Croix de Guerre?
4 How was Lily Cauchoin better known?
5 Ernest Borgnine said who was "the best two-fisted drinker I've ever known"?
6 In which film did Judy Garland first team with Mickey Rooney?
7 What was the second film in which Bing Crosby co-starred with Fred Astaire?
8 Who starred opposite Fred Astaire in "You'll Never Get Rich"?
9 About whom did Marlene Dietrich say, "People should cross themselves when they say his name"?
10 Who played Maid Marian to Errol Flynn's Robin Hood in 1938?
11 What was the first Ingrid Bergman film directed by Roberto Rossellini?
12 Who were first teamed in "Woman of the Year" in 1942?
13 Kim Carnes sang about whose "Eyes"?
14 Who played Ingrid Bergman's husband in "Notorious"?
15 Who was born Edythe Marrener?
16 Which studio signed Gary Cooper in the late 20s?
17 Whose promotion for her first Hollywood film advised Americans that her name rhymed with "star"?
18 Who was Marlene Dietrich in "The Blue Angel"?
19 Who played the title role in "The Buster Keaton Story"?
20 Who had a career in films after being crowned Miss Burbank 1948?
21 Who married the chairman of Pepsi-Cola in 1955 and remained on the board of directors after his death?
22 Who played Captain Queeg in "The Caine Mutiny" in 1954?
23 Who found fame playing the lead in "Pal Joey" on Broadway in 1940?
24 Where was Ray Milland born?
25 Who replaced Charles Laughton as Mr Micawber in the 1935 film "David Copperfield"?
26 In which 1923 film did Harold Lloyd hang from the hands of a skyscraper clock?
27 Which wife was not mentioned by name in Chaplin's autobiography?
28 Whose life story was told in the 1939 movie "Hollywood Cavalcade"?
29 Who played "Anytime Annie" in 42nd Street?
30 Whose pin-up photo was on the atomic bomb that was dropped on Bikini?

Answers | **Famous Names** *(see Quiz 169)*

1 Cousin. 2 Policeman. 3 Rupert Allason. 4 Cecil Beaton. 5 Tracy Edwards. 6 Andre Previn. 7 Princess Alice, Duchess of Gloucester. 8 Royston. 9 Miss World. 10 Menzies Campbell. 11 Winston Churchill. 12 Elizabeth. 13 Denzel Washington. 14 Six. 15 Olivia Channon. 16 William Hague. 17 Thelma. 18 Laura Ashley. 19 Cherie Booth. 20 Chicago. 21 Aunt. 22 Prince Charles. 23 David Alton. 24 Edward Antony Richard Louis. 25 Venice. 26 Jayne Mansfield. 27 Mehmet Ali Aga. 28 Evangeline Booth. 29 James Callaghan. 30 Vivienne Westwood.

Quiz 172 | Pot Luck 83

Answers – page 648

LEVEL 3

1 At which Formula 1 Grand Prix circuit are the Tamburello and Acque Minerale?
2 Who left the FA after a scandal involving Mark Palios and Sven-Goran Eriksson?
3 What was Willie Carson's last ride to win the Derby?
4 In Monopoly, how much is won for second prize in a beauty contest?
5 Which shipping forecast area is east of Fair Isle?
6 If A is Alpha and B is Bravo what is U?
7 Dromophobia is the fear of what?
8 Who had a 50s No. 1 with "Hernando's Hideaway"?
9 Where did Shirley Williams become a professor when she left politics?
10 How many countries competed in the first soccer World Cup?
11 What is the capital of the US State of Kentucky?
12 In Scrabble what is the letter M worth?
13 Which club did Arsenal buy Pascal Cygan from?
14 John Solomon represented England at which sport?
15 From which language does the word "cherub" originate?
16 In fiction, who was David Copperfield's first wife?
17 When did the Bank of England move to Threadneedle Street?
18 What was the first British Top Ten hit for Bow Wow Wow?
19 Which "West Wing" actor died from a heart attack in December 2005?
20 Who invented corrugated iron?
21 Ailsa Craig and Dobies Allrounder are types of what?
22 On which river does Lisbon stand?
23 Marlon Brando was born on the same day as which US actress/singer?
24 If it's noon at GMT, what time is it in Karachi?
25 How many islands are in the Dodecanese group?
26 Which movie had the tag line, If You Can't be Famous, be Infamous?
27 What is the only English anagram of ANIMATED?
28 Which city on the signpost in "M*A*S*H*" is 6,133 miles away?
29 In which country is Dalaman Airport?
30 "Fools" by Rachel Stevens features on the soundtrack to which film?

Answers | Pot Luck 84 *(see Quiz 174)*

1 Tarragon. 2 Kaiser Chiefs. 3 Joseph Conrad. 4 Winifred Atwell. 5 Taurus. 6 Cyclades. 7 Ralph Scheider. 8 Appeared on a set of stamps (1991). 9 Seb Coe (after Olympic bid success). 10 5,000. 11 Eric Oliver. 12 1980. 13 Katharine Hepburn. 14 Internazionale. 15 Rubens Barrichello. 16 Benjamin Franklin & George Washington. 17 Spanish. 18 Park House, Sandringham. 19 "Mary Had a Little Lamb". 20 Feyenoord. 21 Whitechapel. 22 "Make It with You". 23 11-1. 24 North Dakota. 25 Jack Giles. 26 Three. 27 Frank Zappa. 28 "Abu Hanza". 29 Chance. 30 Six Feet Under.

1 Which TV company was formed when ABC merged with Associated Rediffusion in the late 60s?

2 What was the BBC's first broadcast on June 7 1946 after the station had been closed down for seven years?

3 What is Rupert Murdoch's first name?

4 Which country has a national newspaper B.T., founded in 1916?

5 What did Sergey Brin and Larry Page found?

6 Peter Benenson, who died in 2005, founded which global organization?

7 Which BBC channel was launched in 1991?

8 Which newspaper is older – the Daily Express or the Daily Mirror?

9 What is ENG?

10 Who set up Britain's oldest daily trade newspaper?

11 In the US what does Nielsens show?

12 The world's largest business merger joined AOL with which media corporation?

13 Where was the SECAM TV transmission system developed?

14 What is Britain's oldest national newspaper?

15 Which SES broadcast satellite was launched in December 1978?

16 In the 60s, what was an oater?

17 Which actress posed nude with Keira Knightley on a "Vanity Fair" cover?

18 Who commissioned the infamous Danish cartoons depicting Muhammad?

19 What is the oldest weekly publication in the UK?

20 What is the total of the numbers in a standard sudoku puzzle?

21 Which town did Sky use as its UK satellite/cable testing ground?

22 Who was the first chairman of the Broadcasting Standards Authority?

23 What is the major daily paper of Denver Colorado called?

24 Which Sunday paper was founded in 1989?

25 In which three cities are Scotland's three major evening newspapers?

26 Which colour is at the top of an Apple colour logo?

27 Where was the Agenzia Internazionale Fides agency set up in 1926?

28 Which version of the Daily Mail was launched in February 2006?

29 Ricky Gervais started his podcasts linked with which newspaper?

30 What does JPEG stand for?

Answers	History: Who's Who? *(see Quiz 175)*

1 Richard III. 2 1735. 3 Wettin. 4 Rome. 5 George I. 6 It was the shortest. 7 Joseph Bonaparte. 8 Duke of Clarence. 9 Lloyd George. 10 Sophia Dorothea of Celle. 11 George III and George V. 12 Earl of Wilmington. 13 George IV. 14 Henry II. 15 Alexander III. 16 William Hamilton. 17 Henri Rousseau. 18 John D. Rockefeller. 19 Michael Barrett. 20 Mrs Oliva Dionne. 21 John Paul II. 22 James Buchanan. 23 Robert and Edward Kennedy. 24 Casanova. 25 Edward II. 26 George I. 27 Christian IX of Denmark. 28 Elias Ashmole. 29 Lloyd George. 30 White Lodge, Richmond.

1 What is the only English anagram of ARROGANT?
2 Nick Hodgson and Nick "Peanut" Baines are members of which band?
3 Who wrote "An Outcast of the Islands"?
4 Who had a 50s No. 1 with "Poor People of Paris"?
5 Which star sign links Eric Bristow and Joe Brown?
6 Tinos and Siros are in which island group?
7 Who invented the credit card?
8 What links the roses Silver Jubilee, *Rosa moyesii* and Harvest Fayre?
9 Who said in 2005, "It's massive, it's huge, it's the biggest prize in sport"?
10 What is the approximate distance of Bejing Airport from London in miles?
11 Who was the first-ever world sidecar champion?
12 In what year did the sixpence cease to be legal tender?
13 Whose last major film appearance was with Warren Beatty in "Love Affair"?
14 Which Italian club cancelled their tour of the UK after the 2005 London bombings?
15 Which lucky Formula 1 driver, who crashed heavily at Imola in 1994, escaped without injury?
16 Who appeared on the first two US adhesive stamps?
17 From which language does the word "cafeteria" originate?
18 At which house was Diana, Princess of Wales, born?
19 Which famous nursery rhyme was written by Sarah Josepha Hall?
20 Jerzy Dudek joined Liverpool from which club?
21 Where in London was the first Salvation Army Revival Meeting?
22 What was the first British Top Ten hit for Bread?
23 What are the odds of rolling any combination totalling four in dice-throwing?
24 Bismarck is the capital of which US state?
25 Who won the first ten UK Closed Pro Squash Championships?
26 In Scrabble what is the letter B worth?
27 Who said, "Rock journalism is people who can't write interviewing people who can't talk for people who can't read"?
28 Adam Eaman was a false name used by which Muslim cleric?
29 On a Monopoly board what is between Angel Islington and Euston Rd?
30 "The Will" and "Life's Too Short" are episodes from the first series of which TV drama?

Answers	**Pot Luck 83** *(see Quiz 172)*

1 Imola, San Marino. 2 Faria Alam. 3 Erhaab. 4 £10. 5 Viking. 6 Uniform. 7 Crossing streets. 8 The Johnston Brothers. 9 Harvard University. 10 13. 11 Frankfort. 12 3. 13 Lille. 14 Croquet. 15 Hebrew. 16 Dora Spenlove. 17 1734. 18 "Go Wild in the Country". 19 John Spencer. 20 Pierre Carpentier. 21 Onion. 22 Tagus. 23 Doris Day. 24 5 p.m. 25 12. 26 Chicago. 27 Diamante. 28 Toledo. 29 Turkey. 30 The Princess Diaries 2.

1 Which English monarch had a horse called White Surrey?

2 When was Paul Revere's ride to warn of the British advance?

3 What was the family name of Prince Albert of Saxe-Coburg-Gotha?

4 In which city did the Old Pretender die?

5 Which monarch communicated with his ministers in French?

6 Why did George V say "La Bohème" was his favourite opera?

7 Who was Napoleon Bonaparte's eldest brother?

8 Who was George V's elder brother?

9 Who was the first prime minister to occupy Chequers?

10 Who was George II's mother?

11 Who were the last two British monarchs to have two children who became British monarchs?

12 Who followed Sir Robert Walpole as prime minister of the UK?

13 Who was the first Hanoverian monarch to visit Ireland and Scotland ?

14 Which English king had the nickname Curtmantle?

15 Who was the father of the last Tsar of Russia?

16 Who attempted to assassinate Queen Victoria in 1849?

17 Which French painter was known as "Le Douanier"?

18 Who was the founder of the Standard Oil Company?

19 Who died in Britain's last public execution?

20 Who gave birth to Emile, Yvonne, Cecile, Marie and Annette in 1934?

21 Who was the first reigning pope to visit Britain?

22 Who was the first unmarried president of the USA?

23 Who opened Regent's Park Children's Zoo in 1938?

24 Who died at his Castle of Dux in Bohemia in 1798?

25 Which king was buried in Gloucester Cathedral in the 14th century?

26 Which British monarch had mistresses nicknamed the Elephant and the Maypole?

27 Who was the father of Edward VII's consort Alexandra?

28 Who founded Britain's first museum in 1683?

29 Who followed Herbert Henry Asquith as prime minister of the UK?

30 Where was Edward VIII born?

Answers	The Media (see Quiz 173)

1 Thames Television. 2 "Mickey Mouse". 3 Keith. 4 Denmark. 5 General Electric. 6 Amnesty International. 7 World Service Television. 8 Daily Express. 9 Electronic News Gathering. 10 Licensed Victuallers' Association. 11 TV audience ratings. 12 Time Warner. 13 France. 14 Glasgow's Herald. 15 Astra. 16 TV western. 17 Scarlett Johansson. 18 Fleming Rose. 19 The Lancet. 20 405. 21 Swindon. 22 Lord Rees Mogg. 23 Denver Rocky Mountain News. 24 Sunday Correspondent. 25 Edinburgh, Glasgow, Dundee. 26 Green. 27 Vatican City. 28 Irish Daily Mail. 29 The Guardian. 30 Joint Photographic Experts Group.

1 From which language does the word "bantam" originate?
2 In which country are the Anou Ifflis caves?
3 Who won the first "Pot Black" Trophy?
4 Who wrote "A Connecticut Yankee in King Arthur's Court"?
5 Which US state is known as the Panhandle State?
6 Who was prime minister of the UK in between William Pitt's two terms in office?
7 In Monopoly, how much is the income tax refund?
8 Which Scottish writer and statesman was the first Baron Tweedsmuir?
9 Who had a 50s No. 1 with "Whole Lotta Woman"?
10 What do the letters CS stand for in C. S. Lewis's name?
11 What is the capital of the Canadian province Yukon Territory?
12 Javine Hylton, the UK's 2005 Eurovision entrant, once starred in which West End musical?
13 What did Hippolyte Mega Mouries patent in Paris in 1869?
14 Where in California is Disneyland?
15 Who scored the last league goal at Maine Road?
16 Eisoptrophobia is the fear of what?
17 The son of which actress played Tony Armstrong-Jones in "The Queen's Sister"?
18 Who invented the automatic dishwasher?
19 At which ground did Shane Warne take his 600th Test match wicket?
20 If it's noon at GMT, what time is it in Quebec?
21 Which hurricanes hit Florida in September 2004?
22 Who founded the Sûreté?
23 Who played Jimmy "Rabbit" Smith Jnr in his debut movie with Kim Basinger?
24 What is the only English anagram of PARTISAN?
25 Who features on the least expensive banknote launched in May 2002?
26 In which country is Findel Airport?
27 How did the Channel swimmer Matthew Webb perish?
28 How many islands are in the Pelagian group?
29 In Scrabble what is the letter G worth?
30 Which team were the first European side to get to Germany 2006, apart from the hosts?

Answers | Pot Luck 86 *(see Quiz 178)*

1 Five. 2 "Pearl's a Singer". 3 Peter Lorre. 4 Parsnip. 5 Uzbekistan. 6 Emmanuel Petit. 7 A5. 8 Helena. 9 Robert Burns. 10 Herman Hesse. 11 Crimpton on Sea. 12 Rue La Fayette. 13 Wasps. 14 "Nine Million Bicycles". 15 Dave Lee Travis. 16 Frederic Dannay and Manfred Lee. 17 Dreamweavers. 18 George Bush. 19 Earliest. 20 Tobogganing. 21 Nero. 22 Bay. 23 Adrien Brody. 24 Deimos. 25 2,800. 26 Germain Sommelier. 27 German. 28 McConnell. 29 J. R. R. Tolkien. 30 Alan Bennett.

1 What were Roobarb and Custard?
2 Who narrated "Tales of the Riverbank"?
3 Who narrates the series which includes Elly and Pato?
4 In which decade did "Watch with Mother" finish?
5 Which part did Letitia Dean play in "Grange Hill"?
6 Which female presented "Lift Off" in the 70s?
7 On which Farm did Worzel Gummidge live?
8 Who were the twins in "The Woodentops"?
9 Where did Torchy the Battery Boy live?
10 Who narrated "The Wombles"?
11 In "TISWAS" what was Bob Carolgees's punk dog called?
12 Who designed the Italian sunken garden on "Blue Peter"?
13 Who took over from Ringo Starr narrating "Thomas the Tank Engine"?
14 Where did Supergran's adventures take place?
15 Which two inventors invented Supercar?
16 Who are Dib-dab, Scribble and Stick?
17 In "Stingray" what did WASP stand for?
18 Who ran the sweetshop in the early days of "Sesame Street"?
19 What was the first weekend programme which Phillip Schofield presented regularly?
20 In "Rainbow" what colour were Moony and Sunshine?
21 Which humans appeared with Pussy Cat Willum?
22 What is the parish of the Reverend Timms?
23 Who were the first presenters of "Television Top of the Form"?
24 Who was the voice of Penfold in the "Dangermouse" series?
25 Which Tracy piloted Thunderbird 2?
26 Which clay model accompanied Tony Hart's programmes and who created him?
27 Who has presented "Screen Test" and "Blue Peter"?
28 What was the name of the Pogles' pet squirrel?
29 What were Bit and Bot on "Playschool"?
30 In "Vision On" what were Phil O'Pat and Pat O'Phil made from?

Answers | Pop: Albums *(see Quiz 179)*

1 White Flag. 2 Cecilia. 3 Nursery Cryme. 4 A Hard Day's Night. 5 Harvest. 6 Let's Dance. 7 Michael Nyman. 8 Brain Salad Surgery. 9 Ringo Starr. 10 Roller skating. 11 Fulfillingness' First Finale. 12 Life Thru a Lens. 13 Paul Simon. 14 Timeless, Romanza. 15 Tuesday Night Music Club. 16 Yellow. 17 Phantom of the Opera. 18 Super Trouper. 19 Carly Simon. 20 Band on the Run. 21 Bonnie Tyler. 22 Richard Burton. 23 Red Hot Chili Peppers (Californication). 24 Marianne Faithfull. 25 "Rock This Country". 26 Kylie Minogue. 27 Ten. 28 Janis Joplin. 29 Loudmouth. 30 Ear.

1 How many times did Graham Hill win the Formula 1 Monaco Grand Prix?
2 What was the first British Top Ten hit for Elkie Brooks?
3 How is Laszlo Lowenstein better known?
4 Tender and True and White Gem are types of what?
5 In which country is the city of Tashkent?
6 Which Chelsea player was against his old club Arsenal in the 2002 FA Cup Final?
7 Which UK paper size is 148 x 210 mm?
8 What is the capital of the US State of Montana?
9 Who was said to have "loved mankind in general and women in particular"?
10 Who wrote "Der Steppenwolf"?
11 In which fictitious resort was "Hi-De-Hi" set?
12 On a French Monopoly board, what is the equivalent to Piccadilly?
13 The adjective vespine refers to which creatures?
14 What was the first single released from Katie Melua's "Piece by Piece" album?
15 Who joined the DJ Paul Burnett to become Laurie Lingo & the Dipsticks?
16 What was Ellery Queen's real name?
17 Who had an 50s No. 1 with "It's Almost Tomorrow"?
18 Who was the US Navy's youngest pilot in World War Two?
19 What is the only English anagram of ATELIER?
20 St Moritz is home to the world's oldest sporting club in what?
21 Whose second wife was Poppaea?
22 Roatan and Guanja are in which island group?
23 Who became the then youngest Best Actor Oscar winner in 2003?
24 What is the partner of Phobos, the moon of Mars?
25 What is the approximate distance of Teheran airport from London in miles?
26 Who invented the pneumatic drill?
27 From which language does the word "poltergeist" originate?
28 What was Mindy's surname in the TV series "Mork and Mindy"?
29 Who created the fictional place Rivendell?
30 Who produced a collection of prose called "Writing Home"?

Answers | Pot Luck 85 (see Quiz 176)

1 Malay. 2 Algeria. 3 Ray Reardon. 4 Mark Twain. 5 West Virginia. 6 Henry Addington. 7 £20. 8 John Buchan. 9 Marvin Rainwater. 10 Clive Staples. 11 Whitehorse. 12 The Lion King. 13 Margarine. 14 Anaheim. 15 Michael Svensson. 16 Mirrors. 17 Maggie Smith. 18 Mrs W. A. Cockran. 19 Old Trafford. 20 7 a.m. 21 Frances and Ivan. 22 Eugene Vidocq. 23 Eminem. 24 Aspirant. 25 Elizabeth Fry. 26 Luxembourg. 27 Drowned (Niagara Falls). 28 3. 29 2. 30 Ukraine.

1 What was the first track on Dido's "Life for Rent"?
2 Which girl's name provides a track on "Bridge Over Troubled Water"?
3 On which album did Phil Collins make his vocal debut for Genesis?
4 "Can't Buy Me Love" first appeared on which Beatles album?
5 "Dark Side of the Moon" was first released on which label?
6 Which album's sleeve featured David Bowie wearing boxing gloves?
7 Who recorded the soundtrack for the Oscar-winning film "The Piano"?
8 What type of surgery did Emerson, Lake and Palmer come up with?
9 Which Beatle holds a trumpet on the "Sgt Pepper" album sleeve?
10 What are Gallagher and Lyle doing on the back cover of "Breakaway"?
11 What was Stevie Wonder's follow-up album to "Innervisions"?
12 What was the first Robbie Williams album to spend more than 100 weeks on the chart?
13 Who recorded the album "Graceland"?
14 Which albums did Sarah Brightman and Andrea Bocelli release separately, each containing "Time to Say Goodbye"?
15 What was Sheryl Crow's debut album?
16 What colour stripe along with red and blue is on Police's "Synchronicity" sleeve?
17 What was the first original-cast recording of a show to top the charts?
18 "The Winner Takes It All" comes from which Abba album?
19 Whose first album was "No Secrets"?
20 Which album sleeve has the boxer John Conteh among the faces?
21 Who was the second British female artist to top the album charts?
22 Who was the narrator on Jeff Wayne's "War of the Worlds"?
23 Which group made an album including the tracks "Scar Tissue" and "Porcelain"?
24 Which 60s character made a comeback in 1979 with "Broken English"?
25 What is the closing track on Shania Twain's "Come On Over"?
26 Who was the first solo artist to be a year's top-seller with a debut disc?
27 How many albums were in the first Melody Maker chart in 1958?
28 "Pearl" was a posthumously released album from which singer?
29 What was subtitled "The Best of the Boomtown Rats and Bob Geldof"?
30 What part of the body was on the sleeve of Pink Floyd's "Meddle"?

Answers | Children's TV *(see Quiz 177)*

1 Green dog, pink cat. 2 Johnny Morris. 3 Stephen Fry. 4 1980s. 5 Lucinda. 6 Ayshea Brough. 7 Scatterbrook Farm. 8 Jenny and Willy. 9 Topsy Turvy Land. 10 Bernard Cribbins. 11 Spit. 12 Percy Thrower. 13 Michael Angelis. 14 Chisleton. 15 Professor Popkiss and Dr Beaker. 16 Doodle Doers. 17 World Aquanaut Security Patrol. 18 Mr Hooper. 19 "Saturday Superstore". 20 Mauve, Yellow respectively. 21 Wally Whyton, Muriel Young. 22 Greendale. 23 Geoffrey Wheeler and David Dimbleby. 24 Terry Scott. 25 Virgil. 26 Morph, Nick Park. 27 Mark Curry. 28 Tog. 29 Goldfish. 30 Pipe cleaners.

1 What was Raphael's real name?
2 Which post was held by Elizabeth Manningham-Buller in January 2005?
3 What is the only English anagram of ALLEGORIST?
4 Who had a 60s No. 1 with "You're Driving Me Crazy"?
5 In which country is General Manuel Marquez de Leon Airport?
6 In which century was Sir Humphrey Davy born?
7 In Scrabble what is the letter F worth?
8 Which shipping forecast area is south of Humber?
9 Who won the second series of "I'm a Celebrity..."?
10 Which TV teddy was 40 in 1992?
11 In 1980 who described Ronald Reagan's monetarist policy as "voodoo economics"?
12 Actress Debra Winger was born on the same day as which Soviet gymnast?
13 Who won the Best Actor Oscar the year Tony Blair began his third term in office?
14 Who invented the electric oven?
15 From which language does the word "ketchup" originate?
16 How many islands are in the Falklands group?
17 Which team was Alain Prost with for his 80s hat-trick of Monaco wins?
18 Who wrote the novel "A Handful of Dust"?
19 In which country is the city of Tbilisi?
20 Who was the first Italian to have a No. 1 album in the UK?
21 What was the first British Top Ten hit for Bronski Beat?
22 In which sport were Wilfred and Herbert Baddeley famous?
23 What was Quentin Tarantino's next movie after "Jackie Brown"?
24 Who was the first US Homeland Security Secretary, a post created in October 2001?
25 If it's noon at GMT, what time is it in Delhi?
26 Des Moines is the capital of which US state?
27 Ergasiophobia is the fear of what?
28 Which star of TV's "Coupling" was Commodore Norrington in "Pirates of the Caribbean"?
29 Whose statue of Baroness Thatcher was vandalized in 2002?
30 On which river does Munich stand?

Answers	Pot Luck 88 *(see Quiz 182)*

1 William Sturgeon. 2 A giant hedgehog. 3 Gaetano Donizetti. 4 Sir Freddie Laker. 5 Dutch. 6 Foo Fighters.. 7 140. 8 1st edition Dennis the Menace comic. 9 Albania. 10 Athletics. 11 Georgia. 12 Richard Austen. 13 The Old Curiosity Shop. 14 Hayley Mills. 15 Cook. 16 Stagnation. 17 Bill Bryson. 18 Flower. 19 3,200. 20 "United We Stand". 21 Danielle Steele. 22 Colorado. 23 Pinza. 24 Joel Chandler Harris. 25 Marriage. 26 Denis Lawson. 27 Benjamin Disraeli. 28 Lord Byron. 29 Olivier Panis. 30 Northumberland Avenue.

1 Which 90s England player had the middle names Edward Riche?
2 Who was the first player to score over 200 in an English Sunday league game?
3 How many runs did Kevin Pietersen make in his final 2005 Ashes innings?
4 Who was the first England cricketer to be fined for conduct during a Test?
5 What sport – other than cricket – did Graeme Hick play for Zimbabwe?
6 Who scored the first fifty in a one-day international?
7 Who is the only player to represent both Australia and South Africa?
8 What is Ben Hollioake's middle name?
9 Shane Warne hit his maiden first-class century against which county?
10 Which England spinner shared his debut with Shane Warne's Test arrival in England?
11 When did Essex first win the county championship?
12 Which one-cap Neil took 2 for 148 and hit 38 runs in his one innings?
13 Where was the England bowler Andy Caddick born?
14 Which was England's third test ground after The Oval and Lord's?
15 Who was the first keeper to make 10 test dismissals?
16 Which England cricketer was named after the Australian Neil Harvey?
17 Who in 1966, aged 16 years, 180 days, was Northants' youngest player?
18 Bob Willis's eight for 43 ended the Ashes third Test of 1981, but how many wickets did he take in the first innings?
19 Which team were the first after Lancashire to win the John Player League?
20 Which England player had the middle name Cleophas?
21 Who scored the first century in a one-day international?
22 In which decade did Derby first win the county championship?
23 Which wicketkeeper was sacked in June, 2005, after positive drug tests?
24 Who were the last two Aussie batsmen as England won the 2005 Edgbaston Test?
25 At which ground did Jim Laker take 19 test wickets in 1956?
26 And how many runs did Laker score in that fourth Test against Australia?
27 How many members of England's 2005 Ashes team did not play a Test in India in 2006?
28 What is David Gower's middle name?
29 Who were the opposition when Mike Atherton played his first Test?
30 Which substitute English fielder ran out Ricky Ponting at Trent Bridge, 2005?

Answers | **Performing Arts** (see Quiz 183)

1 Juditha Triumphans. 2 Oldham. 3 Titus Andronicus. 4 50. 5 W. H. Auden. 6 Joan of Arc. 7 Milan La Scala Orchestra. 8 Oliver Knussen. 9 Saint-Saëns (3rd). 10 Scarlatti. 11 "Titan". 12 Peggy van Praagh. 13 Alban Berg. 14 Wenzel Muller. 15 Vivaldi. 16 Dance Theatre of Harlem. 17 League of New York Theatres. 18 Pam Gems. 19 Two Gentlemen of Verona. 20 Nine. 21 Nigel Hawthorne. 22 Anton Dolin. 23 Rome. 24 Mouth organ. 25 "Leningrad". 26 English National Ballet. 27 John Webster. 28 The Producers. 29 Harrison Birtwistle. 30 Balanchine.

1 Who invented the electromagnet?

2 What was Dinsdale in "Monty Python's Flying Circus"?

3 Who wrote the opera "Don Pasquale"?

4 Which transport entrepreneur passed away in Miami, February 2006?

5 From which language does the word "schooner" originate?

6 Who made the albums "One by One" and "The Colour and the Shape"?

7 How many degrees are there in each internal angle of a nonagon?

8 What was the most expensive item stolen in the British Library's 1997 move?

9 In which country is the city of Tirana?

10 In which sport was Emmanuel McDonald Bailey famous?

11 Which US state is known as the Empire State of the South?

12 What were R. A. (RAB) Butler's first two names?

13 In which Dickens novel does Sampson Brass appear?

14 Which actress's first film was "Tiger Bay"?

15 Mangaia and Palmerstone are in which island group?

16 What is the only English anagram of ANTAGONIST?

17 Who replaced Peter Ustinov as Chancellor of Durham University?

18 What is a Rafflesia the largest of in the world?

19 What is the approximate distance of Bahrain airport from London in miles?

20 What was the first British Top Ten hit for the Brotherhood of Man?

21 Who wrote "Thurston House", "Palamino" and "Fine Things"?

22 Which US state is directly north of New Mexico?

23 On which horse did Gordon Richards have his only Derby success?

24 What was Uncle Remus's real name?

25 Juno was the Roman goddess of what?

26 Which uncle of Ewan McGregor played John Jarndyce in the 2005 "Bleak House"?

27 Who wrote "Vivian Grey"?

28 Who in 1812 said, "I awoke one morning and found myself famous"?

29 Who gave Ligier their first Formula 1 Grand Prix win since 1981 when he won at Monaco in 1996?

30 In Monopoly, if you were on Income Tax and got double five, where would you land?

Answers | Pot Luck 87 *(see Quiz 180)*

1 Raffaello Santi. 2 Head of MI5. 3 Legislator. 4 The Temperance Seven. 5 Mexico. 6 18th. 7 Four. 8 Thames. 9 Phil Tufnell. 10 Sooty. 11 George Bush. 12 Olga Korbut. 13 Jamie Foxx (for Ray). 14 Bernina Hotel, Switzerland. 15 Chinese. 16 Over 200. 17 McLaren. 18 Evelyn Waugh. 19 Georgia. 20 Pavarotti. 21 "Smalltown Boy". 22 Tennis. 23 Kill Bill. 24 Tom Ridge. 25 5.30 p.m. 26 Iowa. 27 Surgery. 28 Jack Davenport. 29 Neil Simmons. 30 Isar.

1 What was Vivaldi's only oratorio called?
2 Where was the composer William Walton born?
3 What was Shakespeare's first tragedy?
4 For how many instruments is Xenakis's "Pithoprakta" for?
5 Who wrote the text for Benjamin Britten's "On This Island"?
6 Who is the subject of Jean Anouilh's play "L'Alouette"?
7 Which major European orchestra is the oldest?
8 Who wrote "Where the Wild Things are" in 1980?
9 Who first used the organ in a symphony?
10 Who wrote the earliest concerto for flute?
11 What is the nickname of Mahler's Symphony No. 1 in D?
12 Who founded the Australian Ballet?
13 Who wrote the controversial opera "Lulu"?
14 Which Austrian wrote around 250 operas before his death in 1835?
15 Who wrote the earliest concerto for piccolo?
16 Which company for black dancers did Arthur Mitchell form in 1969?
17 Who gives Tony Awards?
18 Who wrote "Marlene" about Dietrich?
19 What was Shakespeare's first comedy?
20 How many symphonies did Bruckner write?
21 Who won the Leading Actor Tony in 1991 for "Shadowlands"?
22 How was the classical dancer Sydney Healey-Kay better known?
23 Where is the Santa Cecelia Academy Orchestra based?
24 Which instrument was invented in 1821 and had the first concerto written for it in 1951?
25 What is the nickname of Shostakovich's Symphony No. 7 in C written during World War Two?
26 What did the Festival Ballet change its name to?
27 Who wrote "The Duchess of Malfi"?
28 In Feb. 2005 which show won the Critics' Circle Theatre Award for Best Musical?
29 Who wrote the opera "Punch and Judy"?
30 Who was the founding choreographer of the New York City Ballet?

Answers | Cricket *(see Quiz 181)*

1 Jason Gallian. 2 Alistair Brown. 3 158. 4 Michael Atherton (Lord's 1994). 5 Hockey. 6 John Edrich. 7 Kepler Wessels. 8 Caine. 9 Kent (May 2005). 10 Peter Such. 11 1979. 12 Williams. 13 Christchurch, New Zealand. 14 Old Trafford. 15 Bob Taylor. 16 Neil Harvey Fairbrother. 17 Peter Willey. 18 None. 19 Worcestershire. 20 Gladstone Small. 21 Dennis Amiss. 22 1930s. 23 Kevin Piper. 24 Brett Lee & Michael Kasprowicz. 25 Old Trafford. 26 Three. 27 Four (Trescothick, Vaughan, Giles, S. Jones). 28 Ivon. 29 Australia. 30 Gary Pratt.

Quiz 184 | Pot Luck 89

Answers – page 660

LEVEL 3

1 Who became the first team to lose four consecutive Charity Shields?
2 Where in new South Wales is "I'm a Celebrity..." set?
3 Who had a 70s No. 1 with "Double Barrel"?
4 The Spanish Formula 1 Grand Prix is held on the outskirts of which city?
5 How many main islands are in the Novaya Zemlya group?
6 Gatophobia is the fear of what?
7 In which town in Texas was Roy Orbison born?
8 On which Isle was the entertainer Rod Hull born?
9 Which parliamentary constituency did William Hague first contest?
10 If it's noon at GMT, what time is it in Honolulu?
11 From which language does the word "khaki" originate?
12 Who wrote "Love and Mr Lewisham"?
13 Which band won the £20,000 Mercury Music Prize in 2004?
14 Which US state is north of Wyoming?
15 Shaft, Meteor and Onward are types of what?
16 In which country is Varna International Airport?
17 Who invented the endoscope?
18 What are the odds of rolling any combination totalling ten in dice-throwing?
19 Who in 1952 wrote "Water Music", in which the pianist blows whistles under water?
20 Who directed the British winner of the 2004 Venice Film Festival Golden Lion Prize?
21 In which sport was William James Bailey famous?
22 In 2004 who replaced Helen Boaden as Controller of BBC Radio 4?
23 What is the only English anagram of CANE CHAIRS?
24 Niels Henrik Abek pioneered several branches of modern what?
25 Who won Emmy awards as an actor, writer and director of "M*A*S*H"?
26 The adjective aquiline refers to which creatures?
27 What is the capital of the US state of Idaho?
28 What was the name of the first Steps album to reach number one?
29 Who was Mohammed Reza Pahlavi?
30 What was the first British solo Top Ten hit for Bobby Brown?

Answers | Pot Luck 90 *(see Quiz 186)*

1 £180. 2 Munich. 3 Libya. 4 Greek. 5 1986. 6 Bowls. 7 Pope Paul VI. 8 J. J. Barrie. 9 Peter Chamberlen. 10 Gilles Villeneuve. 11 Harmonicas. 12 White. 13 Sudan 1. 14 Nelson. 15 New Mexico. 16 Shaggy. 17 "Bones". 18 Ernest Hemingway. 19 5,300. 20 John Boynton. 21 Alcohol. 22 The Black Pig. 23 Football shirt (Tear stained from 1990). 24 Maryland. 25 Meryl Streep & Al Pacino. 26 Greenland. 27 "Living in America". 28 Lefkosa or Leukosia. 29 Pichincha. 30 Bismarck Archipelago.

1 What was the second "Road" film?
2 Which comedy included the song "Somewhere in My Memory"?
3 In which city does "Sister Act 2" take place?
4 In which industry did Helen Fielding's Chardonnay-loving heroine work?
5 Which two performers won BAFTAs for "A Fish Called Wanda"?
6 What is the name of the jewel thief in "The Pink Panther"?
7 Who starred opposite Michell Pfeiffer in "One Fine Day"?
8 What was the Doris Day remake of "My Favorite Wife" called?
9 In which film was Chaplin's Little Tramp seen for the last time?
10 Who wrote the books on which the "St Trinians" films were based?
11 What was Morecambe and Wise's first film called?
12 What is Nicole Kidman's job in "To Die For"?
13 Which classic comedy won BAFTA best film in 1951?
14 What was the first film the Marx Brothers made in Hollywood?
15 After which 1923 film did Harold Lloyd marry his leading lady Mildred Davis?
16 What was the follow-up to "A Fish Called Wanda" called?
17 In which 1936 film did Laurel and Hardy each play their own twins?
18 In which 1983 movie did Dan Aykroyd team with Eddie Murphy?
19 What was Woody Allen's first film as screenwriter and actor?
20 Who was the bungling Sherlock Holmes in "Without a Clue" in 1988?
21 Who wrote and starred in "L.A. Story"?
22 Which village is the setting of the movie where the WI strips for charity?
23 What was the second "Carry On" film?
24 Which "Pink Panther" sequel mentions neither the Pink Panther nor Inspector Clouseau in the title?
25 Which comedy team first appeared in "One Night in the Tropics"?
26 Who played opposite Debbie Reynolds in "Tammy and the Bachelor"?
27 Who was the witch in "Spellbinder"?
28 Which 1982 film told of a concert party in Singapore in 1948?
29 Who wrote "Ghostbusters" with Harold Ramis?
30 Which was the first of the Rock Hudson/Doris Day comedies?

Answers	Celebs *(see Quiz 187)*

1 Jamie Lee Curtis (Jake Gyllenhaal). 2 Graca Machel. 3 Mia Farrow. 4 Kennedy. 5 Hear'Say (Myleene Klass). 6 Menzies Campbell. 7 Julio Iglesias. 8 Christian Dior. 9 Mrs Steven Spielberg. 10 Tim Campbell. 11 Tara Newley. 12 John Paul Getty. 13 Joaquin Cortes. 14 Hello, She Lied. 15 "Tantrums and Tiaras". 16 Jeremy Vine (Tim is the comic). 17 George Clooney. 18 Jane Seymour. 19 Princess Di's mum. 20 Marisa Berenson. 21 Fergie's sister. 22 Duke of Gloucester. 23 Lisa Potts. 24 David Hicks. 25 Darius Guppy. 26 The Bushes' cat Millie. 27 Ivana Trump. 28 Grimaldi. 29 Mick Jagger. 30 Lord Snowdon.

1 In Monopoly how much does it cost to buy Bow Street?
2 Which venue was the most southerly in Germany 2006?
3 Which country's capital city is Tripoli?
4 From which language does the word "elastic" originate?
5 In what year were the British Halley's Comet stamps issued?
6 In which sport was Edwin Percy Baker famous?
7 How was Giovanni Battista Montini better known?
8 Who had an 70s No. 1 with "No Charge"?
9 Who invented obstetric forceps?
10 Which Formula 1 racing driver gave his name to the Grand Prix circuit in Montreal?
11 What is the only English anagram of MARASCHINO?
12 On which river does Indianapolis stand?
13 In February 2005 traces of which dye led to some food products being withdrawn from sale?
14 In cricket, what name is given to 111 runs?
15 Which US State is directly east of Arizona?
16 How is Orville Burrell better known?
17 In which US series did David Boreanaz play Seeley Booth?
18 Who wrote the novel "Death in the Afternoon"?
19 What is the approximate distance of San Francisco airport from London in miles?
20 What do the letters JB stand for in J. B. Priestley's name?
21 If you are crapulous, what are you full of?
22 What is the name of the ship sailed by Captain Pugwash?
23 Which piece of Paul Gascoigne memorabilia fetched £28,680 at auction in September 2004?
24 Annapolis is the capital of which US state?
25 Who won best actor and actress Emmys for "Angels in America" in 2004?
26 In which country is the mineral cryolite found?
27 What was the first British Top Ten hit for James Brown?
28 What would a Cypriot call his capital of Nicosia?
29 Which volcano has the capital Quito, Ecuador, on its edge?
30 New Britain and Admiralty are in which island group?

Answers	**Pot Luck 89** *(see Quiz 184)*

1 Man Utd. 2 Murwillumbah. 3 Dave and Ansil Collins. 4 Barcelona. 5 Two. 6 Cats.
7 Wink. 8 Isle of Sheppey. 9 Wentworth (Yorks). 10 2 a.m. 11 Hindustani. 12 H. G.
Wells. 13 Franz Ferdinand. 14 Montana. 15 Pea. 16 Bulgaria. 17 Pierre Segalas. 18
11-1. 19 John Cage. 20 Mike Leigh (for Vera Drake). 21 Cycling. 22 Mark Damazer.
23 Saccharine. 24 Mathematics. 25 Alan Alda. 26 Eagles. 27 Boise. 28 Steptacular.
29 The last Shah of Iran. 30 My Prerogative.

1 Which actress is the godmother of the star of "Brokeback Mountain", "Jarhead" and "Proof"?

2 Who was Nelson Mandela's companion on his July 1997 trip to London?

3 Who wrote her memoirs in "What Falls Away"?

4 Whose family estate is at Hyannis Port?

5 Aled Jones's Sunday slot on Classic FM was replaced by a member of which former band?

6 Who said, "I believe in open minds not open-neck shirts"?

7 Which singer was the celeb Isabel Preysler married to?

8 Which fashion house did John Galliano first design for in 1997?

9 What is Kate Capshaw's married name?

10 Who was the 2005 winner of the entrepreneurial show hosted by the founder of Amstrad?

11 Which daughter of Joan Collins married in 1997?

12 Who owns a motor yacht called Talitha G?

13 Who was Naomi Campbell staying with in the Canaries when she was rushed to hospital in 1997?

14 Pamela Anderson won a court case over her withdrawal from which film?

15 What was the name of the Elton John documentary made by David Furnish?

16 Which radio presenter's brother held the 2004 world record for telling jokes in an hour?

17 Which 2005 Oscar nominee starred in "Return of the Killer Tomatoes"?

18 Who is Mrs James Keach?

19 How did Frances Roche become widely known?

20 Which actress is the granddaughter of the designer Elsa Schiaparelli?

21 In which capacity did Jane Makim attend Prince Andrew's wedding?

22 Whose family home is at Barnwell Manor?

23 Who was awarded the second-highest civilian medal for bravery in 1997?

24 Which interior designer was the son-in-law of Lord Mountbatten?

25 Who was Earl Spencer's best man who was jailed for fraud?

26 Who produced six offspring in the Lincoln Bedroom at the White House?

27 Which rich divorcee did Riccardo Mazzucchelli marry?

28 Which royal family name was Princess Stephanie born with?

29 Which rock star has granddaughters called Assisi and Amba?

30 Which ex-royal's family home was at Nymans in Sussex?

Answers | Movie Comedies (see Quiz 185)

1 Road to Zanzibar. 2 Home Alone. 3 Las Vegas. 4 Book publishing (Bridget Jones's Diary). 5 John Cleese, Michael Palin. 6 The Phantom. 7 George Clooney. 8 Move Over Darling. 9 The Great Dictator. 10 Ronald Searle. 11 The Intelligence Men. 12 Weather girl. 13 The Lavender Hill Mob. 14 Monkey Business. 15 Why Worry? 16 Fierce Creatures. 17 Our Relations. 18 Trading Places. 19 What's New Pussycat? 20 Michael Caine. 21 Steve Martin. 22 Rylstone. 23 Carry On Nurse. 24 A Shot in the Dark. 25 Abbott and Costello. 26 Leslie Nielsen. 27 Kelly Preston. 28 Privates on Parade. 29 Dan Aykroyd. 30 Pillow Talk.

1 Which shipping forecast area is south of Forties?
2 Who, in March 2005, was the first recipient of the Victoria Cross for 23 years?
3 How many islands are in the Faroe group?
4 In motor racing, what is the ECU?
5 For which album did Ray Charles win a posthumous Best Album Grammy?
6 If it's noon at GMT, what time is it in Bombay?
7 From which language does the word "cigar" originate?
8 In which US state would a Downeaster be a native inhabitant?
9 In which country is Trivandrum Airport?
10 Who had an 80s No. 1 with "99 Red Balloons"?
11 What is a dasyure?
12 The botanist Gregor Mendel belonged to which order of monks?
13 Which ex-Corrie character starred in "Dancing on Ice"?
14 In which country, as well as Spain, is the city of Valencia ?
15 What name is given to a plant that doesn't have leaves?
16 In Scrabble what is the letter K worth?
17 What did Wonder Woman's lasso always make people do?
18 Helminthophobia is the fear of what?
19 How many main islands are in the Hawaiian group?
20 Who had "The Battle of the Books" published in 1704?
21 What did Shevardnadze call the idea that "each country should construct its foreign policy on a 'My Way' basis"?
22 What was the first British Top Ten hit for Joe Brown and the Bruvvers?
23 Whose debut film "Top Spot" was withdrawn as its creator objected to its 18 certificate?
24 What was Henry John Temple's title when he was UK prime minister?
25 Which US state is directly south of Georgia?
26 In February 2005 the last competition for the Waterloo Cup took place, in which activity?
27 Gene Wilder was born on the same day as which racing driver?
28 Which UK paper size is 420 x 594 mm?
29 Whose first book was called "Jigsaw"?
30 What is the only English anagram of INTERLACED?

| **Answers** | **Pot Luck 92** *(see Quiz 190)* |

1 135. 2 The Four Pennies. 3 Reinvented. 4 Electric Company. 5 Nero. 6 Casablanca. 7 Wimbledon. 8 Philippines. 9 The Daily Mail. 10 Nelson Mandela. 11 Venezuela. 12 Owens Illinois. 13 The Creeper (In 2006). 14 Jezebel. 15 Romanian (Anamaria Marinca). 16 Colin Moynihan. 17 Minnesota. 18 Arthur Conan Doyle. 19 200. 20 Con Brio. 21 Tuscany Valley. 22 Babar the Elephant. 23 Mintonette. 24 1,600. 25 17th. 26 Malay. 27 Arkansas. 28 Comoros. 29 Potato. 30 1989.

1 Allegheny and Blue Ridge are in which mountain range?
2 Where is the N'Gorongoro Crater?
3 The Commonwealth of Australia set up in 1901 comprised two territories and how many states?
4 Flores, Corvo and Pico belong to which group of islands?
5 Which city had a street called the Bowery?
6 Who links the Cenotaph in London and New Delhi?
7 What do the straits of Magellan separate?
8 On which river does Adelaide stand?
9 What is the capital of the Canadian province Manitoba?
10 Fagatogo is the capital of what?
11 What are the three volcanic islands of the British Virgin Islands?
12 Avarua is on which of the Cook Islands?
13 What are the Monte Titano peaks made from?
14 Who owns Bouvet Island?
15 How many official languages does South Africa have?
16 In which country is the largest expanse of sand in the world?
17 The Fouta Djallon mountains are to the south of which country?
18 On which river does Nashville stand?
19 Lake Kivu forms much of the western boundary of which country?
20 What is the former name of Nizhny Novgorod?
21 Where is the Kara-Kum Desert?
22 Doi Inthanon is the highest point of which country?
23 What is the capital of Anguilla?
24 Where is the largest phosphate deposit in the world?
25 Flying Fish Cove is on which island?
26 Which country lies between Guyana and French Guiana?
27 What does the Nile split into at Khartoum?
28 Aruba is off which country's coast?
29 Which islands were annexed to the Clunies-Ross family until 1978?
30 In the US which state is immediately west of Colorado?

| **Answers** | Musicals *(see Quiz 191)* |

1 Hair. 2 South Pacific. 3 Sweet Charity. 4 Frank Loesser. 5 Smokey Joe's Cafe. 6 Always. 7 "Oh What a Beautiful Morning". 8 Blood Brothers. 9 The Shadows. 10 Cats. 11 "With One Look". 12 Steve Harley. 13 Buddy. 14 Memories. 15 Martin Guerre. 16 Chess. 17 Grease. 18 Judi Dench. 19 Phantom of the Opera. 20 Funny Girl. 21 Marti Webb, Wayne Sleep. 22 Charles Hart & Richard Stilgoe. 23 Stephen Fry 24 Patti LuPone. 25 Cameron Mackintosh. 26 Dr Barnardo. 27 Anita Dobson. 28 Marvin Hamlisch. 29 Tim Currie. 30 Fagin.

1 How many degrees are there in each internal angle of an octagon?

2 Who had an 60s No. 1 with "Juliet"?

3 What is the only English anagram of INTERVENED?

4 On a Monopoly board what is between Pall Mall and Whitehall?

5 What was the name of the caterpillar in "Dangermouse"?

6 Which port is known in Arabic as Dar el-Beida?

7 Egil Olsen and Terry Burton have managed which soccer club?

8 In which country was the actress Susan Penhaligon born?

9 What was launched by Alfred Harmsworth and Viscount Northcliffe in 1896?

10 Which world figure received an honorary Order of Merit in 1995?

11 The international car registration YV applies to which country?

12 Who invented industrial glass fibre?

13 Ian Richardson's first West End stage appearance this century was in which play?

14 In the Bible, who was King Ahab married to?

15 What is the nationality of the BAFTA Best Actress of 2004?

16 Which ex-Sports Minister became Chairman of the British Olympic Association in 2005?

17 Which US state is north of Iowa?

18 Who wrote "The White Company"?

19 How many 2.5-mile laps are completed in the car race, the Indy 500?

20 What term is given to a piece of music played vigorously?

21 In which valley was "Falcon Crest" set?

22 Which animated animal was married to his cousin, Celeste?

23 What was the original name of volleyball?

24 What is the approximate distance of Moscow airport from London in miles?

25 In which century was Daniel Defoe born?

26 From which language does the word "caddy" originate?

27 Which US state is known as the Bear State?

28 Moheli and Mayotte are in which island group?

29 Vanessa and Wilja are types of what?

30 Which year first saw red noses on cars in support of Comic Relief?

Answers | **Pot Luck 91** *(see Quiz 188)*

1 Dogger. 2 Private Johnson Beharry. 3 22. 4 Electronic Control Unit. 5 Genius Loves Company. 6 5.30 p.m. 7 Spanish. 8 Maine. 9 India. 10 Nena. 11 A marsupial. 12 Augustinian. 13 Martin Platt (actor Sean Wilson). 14 Venezuela. 15 Aphyllous. 16 Five. 17 Tell the truth. 18 Worms. 19 Eight. 20 Jonathan Swift. 21 Sinatra Doctrine. 22 "A Picture of You". 23 Tracey Emin. 24 Viscount Palmerston. 25 Florida. 26 Hare coursing. 27 Jackie Stewart. 28 A2. 29 Barbara Cartland. 30 Credential.

1 Which Broadway musical was the first to include nudes on stage?
2 Which musical opens on Emile de Becque's plantation?
3 "Big Spender" comes from which show?
4 Who wrote the lyrics for "Guys and Dolls"?
5 Which musical is based on the songs of Leiber and Stoller?
6 Which new 90s musical starred Sheila Ferguson, formerly of the Three Degrees?
7 Which song opens the music for "Oklahoma"?
8 Which musical has the songs "Light Romance" and "My Child"?
9 Who next charted with "Don't Cry for Me, Argentina" after Julie Covington?
10 Elaine Paige's first Top Ten hit was from which musical?
11 What was Barbra Streisand's first hit from "Sunset Boulevard"?
12 Who duetted with Sarah Brightman on the chart single, "Phantom of the Opera"?
13 Paul Hipp first played the title role in which musical?
14 Which album was subtitled "The Best of Elaine Paige"?
15 Which musical has the same theme as the Richard Gere film "Sommersby"?
16 Frederick Trumper was one of the heroes in which show?
17 Ian Kelsey of "Emmerdale" went on to star in which musical?
18 Whose withdrawal from "Cats" meant Elaine Paige starred in it?
19 Which Lloyd Webber show gave Cliff Richard a hit single?
20 Which musical does the song "People" come from?
21 Who were the first "Song" and "Dance" of "Song and Dance"?
22 Who wrote the lyrics of "Love Changes Everything"?
23 Which English comedian and novelist was said to have been made a millionaire in his 20s with his work on the West End hit "Me and My Girl"?
24 Who was the first Norma Desmond in "Sunset Boulevard" in London?
25 Who sponsored Oxford University's first professorship in drama and musical theatre?
26 Who was the subject of Rice and Lloyd Webber in "The Likes of Us"?
27 Who played opposite Adam Faith in the doomed "Budgie"?
28 Which musical writer wrote "Sunshine Lollipops and Rainbows" for Lesley Gore?
29 Who was the original King Arthur in the musical "Spamalot"?
30 Which role has been played by Barry Humphries, Jonathan Pryce and Russ Abbot?

Answers | World Tour (see Quiz 189)

1 Appalachian Mountains. 2 Serengeti National Park, Tanzania. 3 Six. 4 Azores. 5 New York. 6 Sir Edward Lutyens (designed the first, planned the second). 7 Tierra de Fuego and South American mainland. 8 Torrens. 9 Winnipeg. 10 American Samoa. 11 Tortola, Virgin Gorda, Jost van Dyke. 12 Rarotonga. 13 Limestone. 14 Norway. 15 11. 16 Saudi Arabia. 17 Senegal. 18 Cumberland. 19 Rwanda. 20 Gorky. 21 Turkmenistan. 22 Thailand. 23 The Valley. 24 Bu Craa, Western Sahara. 25 Christmas Island. 26 Suriname. 27 Blue Nile, White Nile. 28 Venezuela. 29 Cocos Islands. 30 Utah.

1 On which river does Melbourne stand?
2 How did Barbara Betts become known in public life?
3 Who had an 80s No. 1 with "Save Your Love"?
4 Who was the first qualifier to win the Embassy World Championship this century?
5 Which band is named after a soccer team that Lucas Radabe once played for?
6 Lyon, Nord and Saint-Lazare are three stations on a French Monopoly board – what's the fourth?
7 What is the capital of the US state of Mississippi?
8 What were Bart Simpson's first words?
9 Who was the first indy car rookie to start from pole and win in 84 years?
10 In which country is the city of Windhoek?
11 What is the only English anagram of INTOXICATE?
12 The drunken midwife Sarah Gamp appeared in which Dickens novel?
13 What was the first British Top Ten hit for Canned Heat?
14 How many islands are in the Marquesas group?
15 If A is Alpha and B is Bravo what is K?
16 St Boniface is the patron saint of which country?
17 Who wrote Jamelia's hit single "See It in a Boy's Eyes"?
18 In which country is Turku Airport?
19 Who wrote "The Once and Future King"?
20 Which US state is south of Kansas?
21 Which Stephen Poliakoff play was about one of George V and Queen Mary's children?
22 In Scrabble what is the letter W worth?
23 Linonophobia is the fear of what?
24 In which country are the Siebenhengste System caves?
25 Which Swede did Frank Bruno beat in 1985 to become European heavyweight champ?
26 Which star sign links Steve Davis and Jim Bowen?
27 Who invented heat-resistant glass?
28 If it's noon at GMT, what time is it in La Paz?
29 Who became Earl of Merioneth and Baron Greenwich in 1947?
30 The adjective murine refers to which creatures?

Answers | **Pot Luck 94** (see Quiz 194)

1 Murrayfield, Edinburgh. **2** Claude-Joseph Rouget de Lisle. **3** Eiffel Tower. **4** 17.5-1.
5 Holography. **6** Triceratops. **7** Wyoming. **8** Kiss. **9** Amandine-Aurore-Lucile (Lucie)
Dudevant. **10** Pilot. **11** Black Magic. **12** Hindi. **13** Oregon. **14** A Muster. **15** Floors
Castle. **16** Bissagos. **17** Ayrton Senna. **18** 3,200. **19** Dashiell Hammett. **20** "It Must
be Him". **21** Canadian Arctic Archipelago. **22** Four. **23** Maryland, Pennsylvania. **24** US
Women's Open Golf. **25** Acton Town. **26** Rue de Courcelles. **27** Japan. **28** Terminates.
29 Hemingway. **30** Wrestling.

1 Who scored Chelsea's first goal in the 2004–05 season?
2 Who was the first player to win the Premier League eight times?
3 Which winners included the players Warhurst and Wilkins?
4 Which winner had played for Marseille, Bordeaux and Nimes?
5 Brazilian World Cup winner Gilberto Silva joined Arsenal from which club?
6 Which title-winning striking force were reunited at Blackburn Rovers?
7 Wright, Seaman and who else kept goal in Arsenal's 2001–02 triumph?
8 In which month did Chelsea win the title in 2005?
9 To two goals, how many did Alan Shearer score when Blackburn won the title?
10 How many times did David Beckham win the title with Man. Utd?
11 Which title winner had played for Crewe and Juventus?
12 Who scored the goal inflicting Chelsea's only 2004–05 Premiership defeat?
13 Which keeper played 45 minutes as Man. Utd won the 2002–03 title?
14 Which 1990s winner delighted in the nickname "Choccy"?
15 How many players played in every Premiership game for Chelsea 2004–05?
16 Arsenal finished the 2002 season by winning how many consecutive games?
17 Which Czech Republic star played in Man. Utd's 1996–97 side?
18 Who lost their last game and would have lost the title had their rivals won?
19 What is Roy Keane's middle name?
20 Who left Oldham, won several titles then moved to Wolves?
21 Which title winner had played for BK Halmstad?
22 Which of Arsenal's 2001–02 winning squad signed from Glasgow Rangers?
23 Who was second highest Premiership scorer for Chelsea 2004–05?
24 Who was Man. Utd's most regular keeper for the 1999–2000 season?
25 Who was Blackburn's only ever present player in the 1994–95 triumph?
26 Which full-back won the old League Championship twice and two Premier titles?
27 To three, what was Chelsea's amazing goal difference in 2004–05?
28 How many French players in the final of the 1998 World Cup have won the title?
29 Who was the first player to win the Premier League with different clubs?
30 How many points did Chelsea drop at home in the Premiership 2004–05?

Answers | Olympics (see Quiz 195)

1 200m. Individual Medley. 2 Marie-Jose Perec. 3 Cuba, Japan. 4 Lanier. 5 Belarus. 6 Marlo Kindelan. 7 Garmisch-Partenkirchen. 8 Tim Henman & Neil Broad. 9 Christa Luding, née Rothenburger. 10 Cortina (1956). 11 St Moritz. 12 Twice (1908, 1948). 13 Head garland of wild olive leaves. 14 Three. 15 Equestrian dressage. 16 Armenia, Azerbaijan. 17 Kenny Harrison. 18 Penny Heyns. 19 1994. 20 Carl Lewis. 21 Ian Walker, John Merricks. 22 Seppo Raty. 23 Mark Phillips. 24 Paul Palmer. 25 Steve Redgrave. 26 Mountain biking. 27 Over transport problems. 28 One. 29 Krisztina Egerzegi. 30 Eric Heiden (speed skating).

1 Where was the final Live8 concert held?
2 Who wrote "La Marseillaise"?
3 The world's second TV service was beamed from which landmark?
4 What are the odds of rolling any combination totalling three in dice-throwing?
5 What was pioneered by the physicist Dennis Gabor?
6 What creature appeared on the most expensive of the British 1991 dinosaur stamps?
7 Cheyenne is the capital of which US state?
8 The "teacher" in TV's "Rock School" fronted which band?
9 What was George Sand's real name?
10 Who had an 70s No. 1 with "January"?
11 Which craft won the America's Cup in 1995 and 2000?
12 From which language does the word "jungle" originate?
13 Which US state is south of the State of Washington?
14 What term describes peacocks congregating together?
15 Which castle is the Scottish home of the Duke of Roxburgh?
16 Roxa and Caravela are in which island group?
17 Which Formula 1 driver won the Monaco Grand Prix each year 1989–93?
18 What is the approximate distance of Lagos airport from London in miles?
19 Who wrote "The Thin Man"?
20 What was the first British Top Ten hit for Vikki Carr?
21 Banks and Baffin are in which island group?
22 In Scrabble what is the letter H worth?
23 The Mason-Dixon line is the boundary between which two states?
24 Patty Berg was the first winner of which major sporting event?
25 Alphabetically, what is the first station on the London Underground?
26 On a French Monopoly board, what is the equivalent to Euston Road?
27 In which country was the actress Victoria Principal born?
28 What is the only English anagram of MAIN STREET?
29 Which Ernest won the Nobel Prize for Literature in 1954?
30 In which sport was Edward Barrett famous?

Answers | **Pot Luck 93** *(see Quiz 192)*

1 Yarra. 2 Barbara Castle. 3 Renée and Renato. 4 Shaun Murphy. 5 Kaiser Chiefs.
6 Montparnasse. 7 Jackson. 8 "Aye Carumba!". 9 Nigel Mansell. 10 Namibia. 11 Excitation. 12 Martin Chuzzlewit. 13 "On the Road Again". 14 10. 15 Kilo. 16 Germany. 17 Chris Martin. 18 Finland. 19 T. H. White. 20 Oklahoma. 21 The Lost Prince. 22 Four. 23 String. 24 Switzerland. 25 Anders Eklund. 26 Leo. 27 Carl Zeiss. 28 8 a.m. 29 Prince Philip. 30 Mice.

1 Which race gave Michelle Smith her third gold medal in Atlanta?
2 Who was the first Olympic athlete to win the 200m./400m. double gold?
3 Who were the finalists in basketball in the 1996 Games?
4 On which Olympic lake did Steve Redgrave win a fourth gold?
5 With whom did Britain tie for 35th place in the medals table in Atlanta?
6 Who defeated Amir Khan in the 2004 Olympic final?
7 Where were the 1936 Winter Olympics held?
8 Who were beaten by the Woodies in the 1996 men's doubles final?
9 Who was the first woman to win gold at winter and summer Games?
10 Before Turin where was the last Winter Olympics to be held in Italy?
11 Between 1928 and 1948 where were the Winter Olympics held twice?
12 How many times have the Olympics been held in Britain?
13 What were victors given in the ancient Olympics?
14 How many of Mark Spitz's seven golds in 1972 were for team events?
15 In which event did Hilda Johnstone compete in the 1972 Games aged 70?
16 Which two countries beginning with A won first-time medals in 1996?
17 Who beat Jonathan Edwards in the Triple Jump final in Atlanta?
18 In Atlanta who became South Africa's first gold medallist since 1952?
19 In which year were the Winter Olympics first held in the middle of the four-year cycle of the summer games?
20 Who was the second track and field athlete in Olympic history to win four successive titles in the same event?
21 Who won silver medals for Britain for yachting in Atlanta?
22 Whom did Steve Backley beat into third place in 1996?
23 Whose horse Cartier forced him to withdraw from the Three-Day Event competition in 1988?
24 Who won Britain's first medal of the Atlanta Games?
25 Who carried the Olympic flag for the UK in Barcelona?
26 In which event, new in Atlanta, did Paolo Pezzo win gold?
27 Why did the Modern Pentathletes stage a sit-down protest at Atlanta?
28 How many people died because of the Centennial Park bomb?
29 Which woman won a record fifth individual swimming gold in 1996?
30 Who held the record from 1980 for most individual golds in one Games?

Answers	Premiership Winners *(see Quiz 193)*

1 Eidur Gudjohnsen. 2 Ryan Giggs. 3 Blackburn. 4 Eric Cantona. 5 Atletico Mineiro. 6 Cole and Dwight Yorke. 7 Stuart Taylor. 8 April. 9 34 goals. 10 Six times. 11 David Platt. 12 Anelka (Man City). 13 Ricardo Felipe. 14 Brian McClair. 15 One (Lampard). 16 13 games. 17 Karel Poborsky. 18 Blackburn. 19 Maurice. 20 Denis Irwin. 21 Freddie Ljungberg. 22 Giovanni van Bronckhorst. 23 Eidur Gudjohnsen. 24 Mark Bosnich. 25 Alan Shearer. 26 Lee Dixon. 27 57. 28 Three (Barthez, Petit, Vieira). 29 Henning Berg (Blackburn, Man. Utd). 30 Ten.

1 Who was chairman of the Football League when London was awarded the 2012 Olympics?

2 Which Turner Prize winner collected his award dressed as a woman?

3 Which country did Surya Bonaly represent at skating?

4 Who had an 80s No. 1 with "A Little Peace"?

5 Who invented the glider?

6 Mysophobia is the fear of what?

7 Which shipping forecast area is west of Dogger?

8 Who wrote "To the Lighthouse"?

9 In which country is the city of Aleppo?

10 The drama "See No Evil" was about which crime?

11 Mergoles and Kelvedon Marvel are types of what?

12 To 50, Chelsea's 2004–05 record of playing without letting in a goal was how many minutes?

13 Which US state is directly south of New Mexico?

14 Ernest Barry was a world champion which sport?

15 In Scrabble what is the letter P worth?

16 If it's noon at GMT, what time is it in Guatemala City?

17 Which author has used the pseudonym Richard Bachman?

18 In which US state was anaesthesia used for the first time in an operation?

19 What is the capital of the Canadian province Northwest Territories?

20 What was unusual about the first edition of "Newsnight"?

21 What was the Hoover Dam originally known as?

22 On which Indonesian island is the Rinjani volcano to be found?

23 Which star sign links actors Christopher Biggins and Lionel Blair?

24 Which US state is known as the Sooner State?

25 What is the only English anagram of MODERATORS?

26 In which country is Townsville Airport?

27 In which century was Franz Schubert born?

28 Whom did Neville Chamberlain follow as prime minister of the UK?

29 On a French Monopoly board, how much is the fine on Impôts sur le Revenu?

30 Who presented the Brit Awards in '95, '96 and 2005?

| **Answers** | **Pot Luck 96** *(see Quiz 198)* |

1 "My Best Friend's Girl". 2 4,500. 3 Old Kent Road. 4 C. S. Forester. 5 Interlagos. 6 Southampton. 7 Deer. 8 Nebraska. 9 Jukebox. 10 Sweet Sensation. 11 120. 12 Harold Wilson. 13 Badger-digging. 14 Transience. 15 Scotland. 16 A1. 17 Minnesota. 18 The Most Honourable Order of the Bath. 19 Rex. 20 32. 21 Chonos Archipelago. 22 Germany. 23 Yashin. 24 1970s. 25 Arabic. 26 Prince of Wales. 27 Stamped with a lion symbol. 28 Irving Berlin. 29 Golf. 30 St Paul.

1 How is Caryn Johnson better known?
2 Cate Blanchett played which actress to win her 2005 Oscar?
3 Which actress's novels include "Delusions of Grandma"?
4 Which actress sang under the pseudonym Rainbo?
5 Who was the chain-smoking scientist in "Brainstorm"?
6 Who played the actress born Lucille Le Sueur in 1981?
7 Whose first Oscar nomination was in "The Sterile Cuckoo" in 1969?
8 Who won an Oscar without speaking in 1993?
9 Who was known as Anna Marno when she first went to Hollywood?
10 Who replaced Jean Harlow in the 1953 remake of "Red Dust"?
11 A film of whose wedding was released by MGM in Technicolor?
12 Who made her film debut in Hitchcock's "The Trouble with Harry"?
13 Who at 19 was Charlie Chaplin's oldest bride when he was 44?
14 Who married a French editor and wrote a book "Every Frenchman Has One"?
15 Who was created Miss New Orleans 1931?
16 Which two films did Marilyn Monroe make after playing Sugar Kane?
17 In which TV soap did Demi Moore find fame?
18 Who was the daughter of Lana Turner who stabbed Lana's boyfriend to death?
19 Who played the investigator V. I. Warshawski on film and on Radio 4?
20 Who was the only female founder of United Artists?
21 Which film gave Elizabeth Taylor her third successive Oscar nomination in the 50s?
22 Which actress was called the Look on arriving in Hollywood?
23 Who was Honey Hornee in "Wayne's World II"?
24 Who was Warren Beatty's first wife?
25 Which actress had a son called Satchel?
26 Who was directed by her husband in "Rachel Rachel"?
27 Who played her sister as a child in "The Searchers" in 1956?
28 Whose autobiography was called "Goodness Had Nothing to Do with It"?
29 Who was born in 1932 as Edna Rae Gillooly?
30 Who played Jerry Lewis's child bride cousin in "Great Balls of Fire!"?

Answers | **Animal World** *(see Quiz 199)*

1 Vegetation above ground. 2 Capybara. 3 Barn Owl. 4 In its ear. 5 Insects. 6 Three. 7 Oxen. 8 Guanaco. 9 Live young. 10 Antelope. 11 30. 12 Red blood cell. 13 Highland collie. 14 London Zoo. 15 Bandicoot. 16 Colugo. 17 The Cat Fanciers Association of the US. 18 Strictly monogamous. 19 Madagascar. 20 Fisher. 21 Spiral. 22 When they stand up on hind legs and tail. 23 Squid. 24 Squamata. 25 Cold-blooded animal. 26 Snake. 27 Fox, badger or otter hunting. 28 Scaled waterproof skins, shelled yolk-bearing eggs. 29 Venomous snake. 30 Great Dane.

1 What was the first British Top Ten hit for the Cars?
2 What is the approximate distance of Bombay airport from London in miles?
3 In Monopoly, where would a double six from Piccadilly land you?
4 Who wrote "The African Queen"?
5 Which São Paolo suburb hosts the Brazilian Formula 1 Grand Prix circuit?
6 Which city is Craig David from?
7 The adjective cerine refers to which creatures?
8 Which US state is directly south of South Dakota?
9 The Palais Royal Saloon, San Francisco, had the first what installed?
10 Who had a 70s No. 1 with "Sad Sweet Dreamer"?
11 How many degrees are there in each internal angle of a hexagon?
12 Who was the first Labour prime minister to meet a pope?
13 The dachshund was originally bred for what purpose?
14 What is the only English anagram of NECTARINES?
15 Which country's flag has a saltire Argent in a field of Azure?
16 Which UK paper size is 594 x 841 mm?
17 Which US state is the setting for "The Little House on the Prairie"?
18 Which order of chivalry has the motto Tria juncta in uno – Three joined in one?
19 In "Desperate Housewives", who was Bree's late husband?
20 What number did Theo Walcott have on his first Arsenal shirt?
21 Melchior and James are in which island group?
22 In which country was the actor Andrew Sachs born?
23 Puskas and who chaired Stanley Matthews off after his last game?
24 In what decade was Pluto's moon Charon discovered?
25 From which language does the word "minaret" originate?
26 Who has a residence at Birkhall, Ballater, Aberdeenshire?
27 What happened to British eggs for the first time in June 1957?
28 Who wrote the scores for the films "Easter Parade" and "Blue Skies"?
29 In which sport was Pamela Barton famous?
30 What is the capital of the US state of Minnesota?

Answers	Pot Luck 95 *(see Quiz 196)*

1 Lord Mawhinney. 2 Grayson Perry. 3 France. 4 Nicole. 5 George Cayley. 6 Dirt. 7 Tyne. 8 Virginia Woolf. 9 Syria. 10 Moors Murders. 11 Runner bean. 12 1,025 minutes. 13 Texas. 14 Rowing. 15 Three. 16 6 a.m. 17 Stephen King. 18 Georgia. 19 Yellowknife. 20 No one saw it due to a strike. 21 Boulder Dam. 22 Lombok. 23 Sagittarius. 24 Oklahoma. 25 Astrodome. 26 Australia. 27 18th. 28 Stanley Baldwin. 29 F20,000. 30 Chris Evans.

1 What does a browser forage for?
2 What is the largest living rodent?
3 What type of owl featured on the British Nature Conservation stamps of the 80s?
4 Where would a mammal have a malleus?
5 Echidna feed chiefly on what?
6 How many chambers does a camel have in its stomach?
7 What sort of creatures were the now extinct aurochs?
8 Which camelid is the ancestor of the llama and the alpaca?
9 What does a therian mammal produce?
10 In the animal world what is a bongo?
11 How many bones are there in the human arm?
12 What is an erythrocyte?
13 What is another name for the bearded collie?
14 Where is the world's largest zoological library?
15 Which marsupial has the highest reproductive rate?
16 What is another name for the flying lemur?
17 What is the world's largest pedigree cat registry?
18 Which unusual sexual characteristic does the Patagonian hare have?
19 The lemur is native to where?
20 Which species of marten can penetrate a porcupine's defences?
21 What shape are a bushbuck's horns?
22 In mongooses what is the tripod position?
23 What is the principal food of the sperm whale?
24 Which order of reptiles do snakes and lizards belong to?
25 What is a poikilotherm?
26 What is a taipan?
27 What were Dandie Dinmonts originally bred for?
28 Which two main features do reptiles have which amphibians don't?
29 What is a krait?
30 How is the German mastiff also known?

1 Tam Dalyell became Father of the House in 2001 – when did he enter parliament?

2 On which river does Perth, Australia, stand?

3 What was the lowest value of a British Andrew-and-Fergie wedding stamp?

4 Which pair won the Mixed Doubles at the 2005 Australian Open?

5 Who had an 80s No. 1 with "Feels Like I'm in Love"?

6 In Scrabble what is the letter C worth?

7 What is the first name of the medic in the title role of the US series starring Hugh Laurie?

8 St Jude's Institute formed the soccer club now known as what?

9 In which country is the city of Constantine?

10 From which language does the word "hammock" originate?

11 In which century was Cyrano de Bergerac born?

12 Who were the opponents in Bolton's first-ever European soccer game?

13 Nosophobia is the fear of what?

14 Which US state is directly east of Minnesota?

15 Fresh breeze equals which number on the Beaufort Scale?

16 What was the first British Top Ten hit for CCS?

17 On a French Monopoly board, how much does it cost to buy a utility?

18 Pele was born on the same day as which English Test cricketer?

19 In which country is Yundam Airport?

20 Selene is the Greek goddess of what?

21 Sammy Duvall was an 80s world champion in which sport?

22 What is the only English anagram of PERCUSSION?

23 If it's noon at GMT, what time is it in Rio de Janeiro?

24 What was Stendahl's real name?

25 How many islands are in the Mariana group?

26 Whom did Steve Davis beat in the final when he first became world champion?

27 In what year was the George Cross created?

28 Dave Bickers was a British 60s champion in which sport?

29 What is the approximate distance of Johannesburg airport from London in miles?

30 Juneau is the capital of which US state?

---

1 In which show did Yogi Bear first appear?
2 Whose partners included Crazylegs Crane and the Aardvark?
3 Who was the most famous voice of Bugs Bunny?
4 Which Simpsons character has the catchphrase "Hi everybody"?
5 In "The Flintstones" what was Baby Rubble called?
6 Where did the Jetsons live?
7 What was Scooby-Doo's nephew called?
8 What was Bedrock's newspaper called?
9 In which series did Rock and Gravel Slag first appear?
10 What was the first name of Mr Magoo?
11 Who narrated Mr Benn?
12 What was the name of the four Banana Splits?
13 Whose gang included Brain, Spook and Benny the Ball?
14 Which vegetarian vampire was voiced by David Jason?
15 What was the racoon called in "Deputy Dawg"?
16 Who first produced the "Tom and Jerry" cartoons?
17 Whose catchphrase was "Drat and triple drat"?
18 Where did George Jetson work?
19 What were the first names of Hanna and Barbera?
20 What was Nero in "Dangermouse"?
21 What colour is Marge Simpson's necklace?
22 Which cartoon character was first seen in "Le Petit Vingtieme"?
23 What grade is Lisa Simpson in at Springfield Elementary?
24 For which railway company did Ivor the Engine work?
25 Where was the series "Marine Boy" made?
26 In "The Flintstones" what was Wilma's vacuum cleaner?
27 What did Paddington's friend Mr Gruber do for a living?
28 What was the old name of the Djebel Amilah in Tintin's adventure "The Crab with the Golden Claws"?
29 Who had adventures with her dog Alistair?
30 What does Top Cat steal in the closing credits of the cartoon?

Answers	**Communication** *(see Quiz 203)*

1 Sound navigation and ranging. 2 Transistor. 3 Electronic funds transfer. 4 1,000. 5 Coordinate geometry. 6 Router. 7 Algeria. 8 Anthony Trollope. 9 Electrically erasable read-only memory. 10 NW Alaska, Brasilia. 11 ANIK-B. 12 American Standard Code for Information Interchange. 13 Andorra – it was free. 14 25 billion. 15 Telegraphones. 16 .hr. 17 Gramophone. 18 Troll. 19 Baltimore. 20 Seafloor/Bahamas. 21 KDKA. 22 Bellsouth network. 23 Sea crossing. 24 Cornwall to Newfoundland. 25 Monaco. 26 02. 27 EMI. 28 Sky Pod. 29 Merlin network. 30 Austria.

1 When did Italy adopt a double race format for Formula 1 at Imola and Monza?
2 Who wrote "The Third Man"?
3 Sioux and Sleaford Abundance are types of what?
4 What did both East Timor and Switzerland join in 2002?
5 What is the only English anagram of PERSISTENT?
6 Hierro and Gomera are in which island group?
7 What was Robert Banks Jenkinson's title when he was UK prime minister?
8 In which sport was Blanche Bingley famous?
9 "New Beginnings" was the debut album from which ex-Boyzone singer?
10 Who had a 70s No. 1 with "Barbados"?
11 Who invented linoleum?
12 In which country is the city of Da Nang?
13 Which series' backdrop is Chicago's Joliet Correctional Center?
14 Who were the opponents for Bobby Charlton's first international?
15 Who are the patron saints of Sweden?
16 In the 40s who were England's regular Test openers?
17 In Monopoly how much does it cost to buy Pentonville Road?
18 What was the first British Top Ten hit for Ray Charles?
19 From which language does the word "chassis" originate?
20 Which US state is known as the Gem State?
21 Which star sign links Richard Briers and Keith Chegwin?
22 In which General Hospital was "Emergency Ward 10" set?
23 The Corbillon Cup is awarded in which sport?
24 What is the approximate distance of Sydney airport from London in miles?
25 On a six-string guitar, what note is played fifth fret, top string?
26 In which Dickens novel does Bradley Headstone appear?
27 Which US state is directly north of Indiana?
28 What was filmed in Kewferry Road, Northwood, Middlesex in the 70s?
29 In which country was the comedienne Pamela Stephenson born?
30 What was Tom Stoppard's original name?

Answers	**Pot Luck 97** *(see Quiz 200)*

1 1962. **2** Swan. **3** 12p. **4** Scott Draper and Samantha Stosur. **5** Kelly Marie. **6** Three. **7** Greg. **8** QPR. **9** Algeria. **10** Spanish. **11** 17th. **12** Lokomotiv Plovdiv. **13** Disease. **14** Wisconsin. **15** Five. **16** "Walkin'". **17** F15,000. **18** Geoffrey Boycott. **19** Gambia. **20** The moon. **21** Water skiing. **22** Supersonic. **23** 9 a.m. **24** Marie-Henri Beyle. **25** 14. **26** Doug Mountjoy. **27** 1940. **28** Moto Cross. **29** 5,700. **30** Alaska.

1 In communications what does SONAR stand for?

2 What did Bardeen, Shockley and Brattain invent in 1948?

3 What is EFT?

4 How many megabits are there in a gigabit?

5 What is the full name of the computer language COGO?

6 What is a computer that links one network to another called?

7 Which country has the internet code .dz?

8 Which Post Office clerk suggested roadside postboxes be erected in Guernsey?

9 What does EEROM mean?

10 What are the two extremities of the Pan-American Highway?

11 What was the first regular direct broadcasting system called?

12 What does ASCII stand for?

13 In 1997 which country had the cheapest postal service?

14 According to Ferris research how many billion emails are sent every day?

15 What were early tape recorders, pioneered by Poulsen, called?

16 What is the internet code of Croatia?

17 What did Emile Berliner first demonstrate in 1888?

18 Which word from folklore describes a troublemaker in internet slang?

19 Samuel Morse sent the first electric telegram from Washington to where?

20 What postmark did the first undersea post office have?

21 What was the name of the first radio station in the USA?

22 What was the name of the huge telecommunications exchange at the Atlanta Olympics?

23 On the international E-road network what do three dots mean?

24 The first transatlantic radio message was sent from where to where?

25 Which country in 1997 had the greatest number of telephone subscribers per head of population?

26 BT Cellnet became which mobile network operator?

27 Which British company pioneered stereophonic sound?

28 What is the name of the restaurant on Canada's CN Tower?

29 On which network is the Lovell telescope at Jodrell Bank?

30 Is .at the internet code for Argentina, Austria or Australia?

Answers | TV: Cartoons (see Quiz 201)

1 "Huckleberry Hound Show". 2 Pink Panther. 3 Mel Blanc. 4 Dr Nick Riviera. 5 Bamm Bamm. 6 Orbit City. 7 Scrappy-Doo. 8 The Daily Slate. 9 "Wacky Races". 10 Quincy. 11 Ray Brooks. 12 Fleegle, Bingo, Drooper and Snorky. 13 Top Cat (in "The Boss Cat"). 14 Count Duckula. 15 Ty Coon. 16 Fred Quimby. 17 Dastardly. 18 Spacely Space Sprockets. 19 William, Joseph. 20 Caterpillar. 21 Red. 22 Tin Tin. 23 Second. 24 Llantissily Rail Traction Co. Ltd. 25 Japan. 26 Baby elephant on roller skates. 27 Antiques dealer. 28 Karaboudjan. 29 Crystal Tipps. 30 A bottle of milk.

1 Ochlophobia is the fear of what?
2 If it's noon at GMT, what time is it in Lima?
3 Who had a 50s No. 1 with "Hoots Mon"?
4 What is America's third largest city in terms of population?
5 Who are Iver, Tula, Groove, Roma?
6 In which country is the city of Chittagong?
7 From which language does the word "iceberg" originate?
8 What is the capital of the US state of Louisiana?
9 Which country lost their Formula 1 Grand Prix after 1981 but re-entered the staging in 1995?
10 What was Tintoretto's real name?
11 On a French Monopoly board, what street is the equivalent of Mayfair?
12 Which shipping forecast area is east of Dogger and Humber?
13 Which batsman became Shane Warne's 600th Test victim?
14 Who won the Best Actress Oscar the year Prince Charles married Camilla?
15 In which country was the actress Angela Thorne born?
16 The adjective "leporine" refers to which creatures?
17 Teddy Bourne competed in three Olympics at which event?
18 How many islands are in the Kuril group?
19 What was the first British Top Ten hit for Glen Campbell?
20 Who wrote the novel "The Curious Incident Of The Dog In The Night-Time"?
21 Alice Perrers was the mistress of which monarch?
22 Which US state is North of Arkansas?
23 What is the only English anagram of SHATTERING?
24 Where was the first by-election held after the 1997 general election?
25 Who invented margarine?
26 In Scrabble what is the letter Y worth?
27 Who was Benfica's boss when they dumped Man. Utd out of Europe in 2005–06?
28 Which US state is known as the Wolverine State?
29 By what name was the first female winner of "I'm a Celebrity..." known when she won?
30 In which country is Yoff Airport?

Answers | **Pot Luck 100** *(see Quiz 206)*

1 "I Hear You Now". 2 108. 3 Willie Rennie. 4 Tiziano Vecellio. 5 Chagos. 6 Misconstrue. 7 Germany. 8 Juan Carlos Ferrero. 9 Ealing, Enfield and Islington. 10 M/A/R/R/S. 11 John Fowles. 12 Monaco. 13 Leon Brittan. 14 800. 15 Detective Inspector. 16 Super Tax. 17 Equestrianism. 18 November. 19 Percy Le Baron Spencer. 20 Michigan. 21 Michael Howard. 22 John Le Carré. 23 Friday. 24 Charles Darwin. 25 Mazanares. 26 "Coupling". 27 Ohio. 28 Italian. 29 Duchess of Gloucester. 30 Four.

1 What was the last battle between Britain and America?
2 Who fought whom in the late 19th-century War of the Pacific?
3 In which war were Britain the victors in 1842?
4 What was the first battle in the American War of Independence?
5 Which British Army general was born at Westerham vicarage in 1788?
6 What was the largest carrier battle of World War Two?
7 Who was defeated at the battle of Pharsalus in 48 BC?
8 During which war was the battle of the Alamo?
9 In which battle were tanks first used?
10 Who was the German commander at Verdun in 1916?
11 What was the last major naval battle of World War Two?
12 Where did the Russians have their final conflict in Germany in World War One?
13 In which war did the Battle of Solferino take place in 1859?
14 In World War Two, the battle of Coral Sea stopped a Japanese attack on where?
15 The site of the battle of Koniggratz in 1866 is now in which country?
16 Canada fell under British control after which battle of the Seven Years War?
17 Which treaty led to the withdrawal of US troops from Vietnam?
18 In which war was the battle of Tsushima?
19 Conflict between which two tribes brought about the Biafran war?
20 After which major battle did the French leave Vietnam?
21 At which World War One battle did the Germans use poison gas for the first time?
22 Which ships were involved in the first battle of the Atlantic in 1939?
23 Which British territory was captured on Christmas Day 1941?
24 Who was defeated at the battle of Lepanto in 1571?
25 Who fought the Romans in the Battle of Mons Grapius in AD 84?
26 Who was in charge of the Russian army when the Germans were defeated at Stalingrad?
27 Which war was precipitated by the rejection of the Nineteen Propositions?
28 Which treaty ensured the Boers lost their independence in 1902?
29 Which three countries along with Germany invaded Russia in 1941?
30 Which World War One campaign began with the arrival of Indian troops at Abadan?

Answers	Folk & Blues (see Quiz 207)

1 Judy Dyble. 2 Phil Ochs. 3 Paris. 4 Rolling Thunder Review. 5 "The Times They are A-Changin'". 6 Blind Willie McTell (Ralph McTell). 7 The Humblebums. 8 Conor. 9 Travers (Peter, Paul and Mary). 10 Blind Lemon Jefferson. 11 Rhymes and Reasons. 12 Riley. 13 Troubador. 14 Elektra. 15 Martin Carthy. 16 John Lee Hooker. 17 Sandy Denny. 18 Alexis Korner. 19 Al Stewart. 20 Basket of Light. 21 Wilson. 22 Chicago. 23 Cecil Sharp. 24 Macclesfield. 25 Al Kooper. 26 T-Bone Walker. 27 West Virginia. 28 Brain haemorrhage. 29 Bob Dylan. 30 Sam Hopkins.

1 What was the first British Top Ten hit for Jon and Vangelis?
2 How many degrees are there in each internal angle of a pentagon?
3 In 2006 who won the Dunfermline and West Lothian by-election for the Lib Dems?
4 What was Titian's real name?
5 Banhos and Salomon are in which island group?
6 What is the only English anagram of CONSUMERIST?
7 In which country is the city of Duisburg?
8 Whom did Andy Roddick beat in the final to win his first tennis major?
9 Which are the only London boroughs to begin with a vowel?
10 Who had an 80s No. 1 with "Pump Up the Volume"?
11 Who wrote the book "The Collector"?
12 Where is the Autodromo Enzo e Dino Ferrari circuit?
13 Who was MP for Richmond, North Yorks, before William Hague?
14 What is the approximate distance of Madrid airport from London in miles?
15 What was Regan's rank in the last episode of "The Sweeney"?
16 On a Monopoly board what is between Park Lane and Mayfair?
17 In which sport was George Bowman famous?
18 What month did Channel 4 go on the air in 1982?
19 Who invented the microwave oven?
20 Lansing is the capital of which US state?
21 Which former party leader received the Order of Merit in 2005?
22 Who said, "Spies, like prostitutes, are always going to be with us"?
23 If March 1 is on a Monday in a leap year, what day was January 1?
24 Who features on the second least expensive banknote launched in November 2000?
25 On which river does Madrid stand?
26 Sally, Geoff, Susan and Patrick were characters in which sitcom?
27 Which US state is west of Pennsylvania?
28 From which language does the word "manifesto" originate?
29 Which Duchess is the daughter of Asger Henriksen and Vivian van Deurs?
30 In Scrabble what is the letter V worth?

Answers	Pot Luck 99 (see Quiz 204)

1 Crowds. 2 7 a.m. 3 Lord Rockingham's XI. 4 Chicago. 5 The Hoobs. 6 Bangladesh. 7 German. 8 Baton Rouge. 9 Argentina. 10 Jacopo Robusti. 11 Rue De La Paix. 12 German Bight. 13 Marcus Trescothick. 14 Hilary Swank (Million Dollar Baby). 15 Pakistan. 16 Hares. 17 Fencing. 18 56. 19 "Wichita Lineman". 20 Mark Haddon. 21 Edward III. 22 Missouri. 23 Straighten. 24 Uxbridge. 25 Hippolyte Merge-Mouries. 26 Four. 27 Ronald Koeman. 28 Michigan. 29 Kerry McFadden. 30 Senegal.

1 Who was the original female vocalist in Fairport Convention?

2 Who wrote "There but for Fortune"?

3 In which city was Alexis Korner born?

4 What was Bob Dylan's 1976 tour called?

5 Which cover version sneaked in the charts for Ian Campbell in 1965?

6 Whom did Ralph May take his stage name from?

7 What name did Billy Connolly and Gerry Rafferty sing under?

8 What was the name of Eric Clapton's son whose death inspired "Tears in Heaven"?

9 Who made up the trio with Yarrow and Stookey?

10 In the 1920s, who recorded "Match Box Blues" and "That Black Snake Moan"?

11 What was John Denver's first album called?

12 What is B. B. King's actual first name?

13 What was the name of London's leading folk club in the 60s?

14 Tom Paxton's "Ramblin' Boy" album came out on which label?

15 Simon and Garfunkel took the song "Scarborough Fair" from whom?

16 Who used the pseudonyms Birmingham Sam and Delta John?

17 Who wrote "Who Knows Where the Time Goes"?

18 Which blues man had a speaking part on Hot Chocolate's hit "Brother Louis"?

19 Who recorded the album "Bedsitter Images"?

20 Pentangle's "Night Flight" came from which album?

21 What was Woody Guthrie's middle name?

22 Smitty's Corner and Pepper's Lounge were blues clubs in which city?

23 Who published in 1907 "English Folk Songs: Some Conclusions"?

24 John Mayall comes from which untraditional birthplace of bluesmen?

25 Who played organ on Dylan's "Like a Rolling Stone"?

26 Who made the album "Stormy Monday Blues"?

27 According to John Denver which state is "almost heaven"?

28 How did Sandy Denny die?

29 Which folk hero played piano in Bobby Vee's band the Shadows?

30 What was Lightnin' Hopkins's real name?

Answers	**War Zones** *(see Quiz 205)*

1 Battle of New Orleans. **2** Chile v. Peru & Bolivia. **3** First Opium War in China. **4** Battle of Bunker Hill. **5** James Wolfe. **6** Philippine Sea. **7** Julius Caesar. **8** Texan War of Independence. **9** Cambrai. **10** Falkenhayn. **11** Leyte Gulf. **12** Tannenburg. **13** Italian War of Unification. **14** New Guinea. **15** Czech Republic. **16** Heights of Abraham. **17** Peace of Paris. **18** Russo-Japanese War. **19** Ibo, Hausa. **20** Dien Bien Phu. **21** Ypres (1915). **22** Graf Spee & HMS Exeter. **23** Hong Kong. **24** Turkish navy. **25** Scottish tribes. **26** Zhukov. **27** English Civil War. **28** Treaty of Vereeniging. **29** Finland, Hungary & Rumania. **30** Mesopotamian Campaign.

1 What was the first British Top Ten hit for Eartha Kitt?
2 On a French Monopoly board, how much does it cost to buy a station?
3 Who was the first British conductor to have his life dramatized on TV?
4 From which language does the word "typhoon" originate?
5 In which country is the city of La Plata?
6 Whose last Formula 1 Grand Prix race of his career was at Adelaide in 1985?
7 What was Robert Gascoyne-Cecil's title when he was UK prime minister?
8 Bert Turner got an FA Cup Final goal and an own goal playing for whom?
9 Which UK paper size is 841 x 1189 mm?
10 Who invented the parking meter?
11 In which country are the world's deepest caves?
12 Which playwright received the Order of Merit in 2000?
13 In which country was Alan Whicker born?
14 Mike Avory and Pete Quaife were members of which pop group?
15 What is the approximate distance of Frankfurt airport from London in miles?
16 What was Michael Angelo Titmarsh's real name?
17 How many clusters of islands are in the Maldives group?
18 In which US state would a Bay Stater be a native inhabitant?
19 Odynophobia is the fear of what?
20 Who had a hit in 1975 with "Loving You"?
21 If it's noon at GMT, what time is it in Riyadh?
22 Model White and Green Globe are types of what?
23 Which soccer club left the Scottish League in the 1960s?
24 Which US state is directly east of New Hampshire?
25 Lauren Ambrose played which character in "Six Feet Under"?
26 What are Phoebe, Mimas and Rhea?
27 In which country is Spokane Airport?
28 What is the only English anagram of INTERSPERSE?
29 Who wrote books about the Wombles?
30 In which sport was Beryl Burton famous?

Answers	**Pot Luck 102** *(see Quiz 210)*

1 Italian. 2 18th. 3 India. 4 "Everybody's Got to Learn Sometime". 5 "We Belong Together". 6 Caisse de Communauté. 7 28.9%. 8 20th C. 9 Colorado. 10 H. Rider Haggard. 11 The Battle of Wounded Knee. 12 Squash. 13 Berg's Wozzeck. 14 10. 15 Thomas à Becket. 16 Germany. 17 Cape Verde. 18 "Home & Away". 19 3,400. 20 Tom Robinson Band. 21 Parliaments. 22 Apollo 17. 23 Nereid. 24 Berlin. 25 1973. 26 Vatican City. 27 New York. 28 Graham Hill. 29 Vengeance. 30 Countess of Wessex.

1 Which country were the first to play in two union World Cup Finals?
2 As a player Willie John McBride went on how many Lions tours?
3 To five years, when did France first win the Five Nations outright?
4 Who won league's first Man of Steel award?
5 Lawrence Dallaglio's Lions tour ended in June 2005 in a game against which side?
6 Who is Argentina's leading all-time point-scorer?
7 Who didn't collect his loser's medal after the 1996 Pilkington Cup Final?
8 Keith Elwell played in 239 consecutive games for which league side?
9 Who scored 45 individual points for New Zealand against Japan in 1995?
10 Which university did Will Carling go to?
11 Who is the only person to captain the Lions and the English cricket team?
12 Who said at the wedding of the All-Black Glen Osborne, "I'm not the best man: I'm one of the security guards"?
13 Who scored most tries in the first Super League season?
14 Which country first completed the Grand Slam in 1968?
15 How old was Barry John when he retired from playing rugby?
16 Which coach was sacked by St Helens for gross misconduct in May 2005?
17 Rory Underwood began his senior career with which club?
18 What is Martin Offiah's middle name?
19 Gavin Hastings scored how many points in the 1995 World Cup game against Ivory Coast?
20 Ellery Hanley first won the Man of Steel award while with which club?
21 In which decade were Orrell founded?
22 Which club did Gareth Edwards play for?
23 Who was Warrington's first player to win the Man of Steel award?
24 In the 1995 World Cup which two players scored seven tries?
25 Who set a new Super League record with six tries in a Sept. 2005 game?
26 Which team won league's Challenge Cup before Wigan's eight-in-a-row run?
27 The full-back J. P. R. Williams played once in a 1978 international in which position?
28 Who was the first man to play for, then coach an England Grand Slam team?
29 Where was Tony Underwood born?
30 Andrew Johns's much-heralded move to Warrington Wolves lasted how many games?

Answers | Movies: Oscars *(see Quiz 211)*

1 Diane Ladd, Laura Dern. 2 Frank Borzage. 3 Sessue Hayakawa. 4 Costume design. 5 Kitty Foyle. 6 Sophia Loren. 7 Sally Field. 8 Broadway Melody. 9 Marlee Matlin (Children of a Lesser God). 10 Geraldine Page. 11 Spencer Tracy. 12 Ingrid Bergman. 13 It Happened One Night. 14 Cimarron, Cavalcade. 15 Clint Eastwood (Million Dollar Baby). 16 Glenda Jackson. 17 11 nominations, no winners. 18 Mr Skeffington. 19 "Somewhere in My Memory". 20 Deborah Kerr. 21 Keisha Castle-Hughes. 22 Charlie Allnut (The African Queen). 23 Giant. 24 The Man Who Knew Too Much. 25 Hollywood Roosevelt Hotel. 26 Margaret Rutherford. 27 Louise Fletcher (One Flew Over the Cuckoo's Nest). 28 Going My Way. 29 Hayley Mills. 30 All About Eve (14).

1 From which language does the word "balcony" originate?
2 In which century was the US novelist James Fenimore Cooper born?
3 In which country is the city of Nagpur?
4 What was the first British Top Ten hit for the Korgis?
5 "I didn't mean it when I said I didn't love you so" opens which Mariah Carey song?
6 On a French Monopoly board, what is the equivalent to Community Chest?
7 To 1%, Magnier and McManus sold what percentage stake in Man. Utd to Malcolm Glazer?
8 In which century were the greatest number of Princesses Royal created?
9 Which US state is known as the Centennial State?
10 Who wrote the novel "King Solomon's Mines"?
11 What was the last major conflict between native North Americans and US troops?
12 Don Butcher was a champion in which sport?
13 What did Welsh National Opera first perform after 2005's move to Cardiff's Millennium Centre?
14 Whole gale equals which number on the Beaufort Scale?
15 Whom did Fitzurse, de Tracy, de Merville and le Breton murder?
16 In which country was Bruce Willis born?
17 Boa Vista and Sao Nicolau are in which island group?
18 "Headland" was a spin-off of which TV series?
19 What is the approximate distance of New York airport from London in miles?
20 Who had a hit in 1977 with "2-4-6-8 Motorway"?
21 What is the only English anagram of PATERNALISM?
22 Which was the sixth and last US mission to the Moon in the 20th century?
23 What name was given to the second of Neptune's moons to be discovered?
24 In which city was André Previn born?
25 When did Denmark join the European Union?
26 The international car registration V applies to vehicles from where?
27 Which US state is directly west of Vermont?
28 Who was the first Formula 1 driver to win at Monaco in three successive years 1963–5?
29 In Greek mythology, Attis is the god of what?
30 Who is Colonel in Chief, Queen Alexandra's Royal Army Nursing Corps?

Answers | **Pot Luck 101** *(see Quiz 208)*

1 "Under the Bridges of Paris". 2 F20,000. 3 Sir Thomas Beecham. 4 Chinese. 5 Argentina. 6 Niki Lauder. 7 Marquess of Salisbury. 8 Charlton (1946). 9 A0. 10 Carlton C. Magee. 11 France. 12 Tom Stoppard. 13 Egypt. 14 The Kinks. 15 400. 16 William Makepeace Thackeray. 17 19. 18 Massachusetts. 19 Pain. 20 Minnie Riperton. 21 3 p.m. 22 Turnip. 23 Third Lanark. 24 Maine. 25 Claire Fisher. 26 Satellites of Saturn. 27 USA. 28 Enterprises. 29 Elizabeth Beresford. 30 Cycling.

1 Who were the first mother and daughter to receive simultaneous Oscar nominations?
2 Who won the first Best Director Oscar?
3 Who was nominated for his role as the prison camp commander in "The Bridge on the River Kwai"?
4 Milera Canonero won an Oscar for "Chariots of Fire" for what?
5 For which film did Ginger Rogers win her only Oscar?
6 Who was the first person to receive an Oscar for a role played entirely in a foreign language?
7 Whose second Oscar prompted her "You like me" speech?
8 What was the first talkie to win an Oscar?
9 Who won an award in her first film, based on a Mark Medoff play?
10 Which actress won her first Oscar after her eighth nomination?
11 Who was the first Best Actor in successive years?
12 Of all the star cameos, who won the only Oscar for "Murder on the Orient Express"?
13 What was the first movie to win Best Actor, Actress, Director and Film?
14 Which two 30s Best Films had one-word titles?
15 Who directed Morgan Freeman to win his first Oscar?
16 Who was the first Best Actress to win the award twice in the 70s?
17 In Oscar terms what links "The Color Purple" and "The Turning Point"?
18 For which 1944 film did Bette Davis win her fifth successive nomination?
19 Which song from "Home Alone" as Oscar nominated?
20 Who received an honorary Oscar in 1994 after six unsuccessful nominations in 12 years?
21 In 2004 who was the then youngest ever Oscar nominee?
22 Which character won Humphrey Bogart an Oscar in 1951?
23 For which film did Rock Hudson receive his only nomination?
24 In which film was "Que Sera Sera" an Oscar-winner?
25 Where were the first Oscars presented?
26 Who was Best Supporting Actress winner in 1963 for "The VIPs"?
27 Who won an Oscar playing Nurse Ratched?
28 In which film did "Swinging on a Star" win an Oscar?
29 In 1960 who received a miniature statuette for her "outstanding juvenile performance"?
30 Which 50s film had most Oscar nominations?

Answers | Rugby (see Quiz 209)

1 New Zealand. 2 Five. 3 1959. 4 David Ward. 5 Bay of Plenty. 6 Hugo Porta. 7 Neil Back. 8 Widnes. 9 Simon Culhane. 10 Durham. 11 Andrew Stoddart. 12 Jonah Lomu. 13 Paul Newlove. 14 France. 15 27. 16 Ian Millward. 17 Middlesbrough. 18 Nwokocha. 19 44. 20 Bradford Northern. 21 1920s. 22 Cardiff. 23 Jonathan Davies. 24 Marc Ellis, Jonah Lomu. 25 Lesley Vainikolo. 26 Halifax. 27 Flanker. 28 Roger Uttley. 29 Malaysia. 30 3 games.

1 Who had a hit in 1985 with "My Toot Toot"?

2 Which Malian guitarist recorded the albums "Talking Timbuktu" and "In the Heart of the Moon"?

3 Which shipping forecast area is south of Shannon and Fastnet?

4 What is the only English anagram of PROCREATION?

5 Which city introduced Britain's first trolley-bus service?

6 To whom was the George Cross awarded collectively in 1999?

7 Who invented the slide rule?

8 In which country is the city of Nanning?

9 Who is the voice of Mr Burns, Otto and Ned Flanders in "The Simpsons"?

10 Joan Rivers was born on the same day as which opera singer?

11 If it's noon at GMT, what time is it in Rangoon?

12 In Scrabble what is the letter N worth?

13 In which Dickens novel does Jeremiah Flintwinch appear?

14 How many islands are in the Laccadive group?

15 What blood group did the Vulcan Mr Spock have?

16 What was the first British Top Ten hit for the Trammps?

17 From which language does the word "skippe" originate?

18 On which river does Pittsburgh stand?

19 "The Talented Mr Ripley" was a remake of which René Clair film of 1960?

20 Which flag has cross Gules in a field of Argent?

21 What is the approximate distance of Mexico City airport from London in miles?

22 Who is the "Crocodile Hunter" on TV?

23 In which sport was Philip Mario Caira famous?

24 What is the capital of the US state of Pennsylvania?

25 Phagophobia is the fear of what?

26 If A is Alpha and B is Bravo what is U?

27 Who invented the car speedometer?

28 What was Toploader's debut album called?

29 How much was the weekly family allowance when first introduced?

30 In which country is Pago Pago Airport?

---

1 India. 2 William Golding. 3 "Hold Me Tight". 4 11. 5 Nevada. 6 Ely.
7 Rationale. 8 Joseph Glidden. 9 Caroline. 10 92. 11 New Lyne. 12 35-1. 13
Shannon Sickles. 14 Whitechapel. 15 Harry Longbaugh. 16 Cabbage. 17 Speed
skating. 18 Countdown. 19 Utah. 20 Arabic. 21 Chile. 22 Too2Much. 23 Justin
Timberlake. 24 Lyn St James. 25 Sir Winston Churchill. 26 Toaster. 27 South Africa.
28 Customs and Excise. 29 Musical Youth. 30 2,200.

1 Who said, "Take it easy driving – the life you save might be mine"?
2 What was suggested that you "Buy some for Lulu"?
3 How much did "1001" clean your carpet for?
4 What did Patsy Kensit advertise in her first TV ad?
5 Pook's "Blow the Wind" was used to advertise what?
6 Which programme was interrupted with the first commercial on UK TV?
7 Who wrote "O Sole Mio", which advertised Wall's Cornetto?
8 Which brand of what featured in the first UK TV ad?
9 Who wrote "The Flight of the Bumble Bee", which urged us to buy Black & Decker paint-stripper?
10 Whose watches were advertised to the music of Ramirez?
11 Which Bobby Hodgens and Siobhan Fahey song hit No. 1 after being used in a VW ad?
12 Which Muddy Waters hit was reissued after it was used to advertise Levi's?
13 Which Mozart opera helped to sell the Citroën ZX?
14 Verdi's "Dies Irae" was used to advertise which newspaper?
15 Who were the original jingle artists for the song that became "I'd Like to Teach the World to Sing"?
16 Georgie Fame's "Get Away" started out as a jingle for what?
17 Jack Nicklaus advertised Spanish houses for which company?
18 In the BT "EastEnders" ad what was the late Arthur Fowler doing?
19 Whose music – the theme from "Raging Bull" – advertised Heineken Export?
20 Whose wines were trumpeted to Pachelbel's "Canon in D Major"?
21 Which upmarket scent was advertised to Vivaldi's "Four Seasons"?
22 Which music by whom advertised Hamlet cigars?
23 Who wrote "The Force of Destiny" (La forza del destino), in Stella Artois ads?
24 The Clash's only No. 1 was used to advertise what?
25 What was being advertised in the jingle which began "You'll wonder where the yellow went"?
26 Elgar's Cello Concerto advertised which brand of spring water?
27 Which model ditched everything but her ex's VW keys?
28 What was Lorraine Chase advertising when she said "Nah, from Luton Airport"?
29 According to the ad, what did PAL stand for?
30 Which drink was advertised to the music of Offenbach's "Barcarolle"?

Answers | Famous Queens (see Quiz 214)

1 Egypt. 2 Queen's Park. 3 Billy Ocean. 4 Queen Elizabeth I. 5 Anne Boleyn. 6 Princess Diana. 7 Marie Antoinette. 8 Aleksandr Pushkin. 9 Mary Queen of Scots. 10 Mary II. 11 Humphrey Bogart. 12 Mary I (Mary Tudor). 13 Queen Guinevere. 14 Catherine of Aragon. 15 Brisbane. 16 Carrot. 17 Cricket. 18 Boadicea. 19 Queen Gertrude. 20 The Sex Pistols. 21 Catherine de Medici. 22 Steve McQueen. 23 Boxing. 24 The Queen of Sheba. 25 Queen of Puddings. 26 Cleopatra. 27 The Queen of Hearts. 28 Queen Isabella. 29 KC and the Sunshine Band. 30 Bohemia.

1 Queen Nefertiti ruled over which ancient land?
2 Which football club won the Scottish FA Cup 10 times between 1874 and 1893?
3 Who had chart hit with "Caribbean Queen"?
4 Which queen said: "I know I have the body of a weak and feeble woman, but I have the heart and stomach of a king, and of a king of England too."
5 Which one of Henry VIII's wives was accused of adultery and incest and beheaded in the Tower of London?
6 Who was dubbed "The Queen of Hearts" on her death?
7 Which queen recommended her starving subjects to eat cake?
8 Who wrote "The Queen of Spades and Other Stories"?
9 Which queen's involvement in the Babington Plot resulted in her trial and execution?
10 Which queen of England ruled jointly with William of Orange?
11 Who played the male lead in "The African Queen"?
12 Who succeeded Edward VI?
13 Which queen was adulterously involved with Sir Lancelot?
14 Which queen was the first of Henry VIII six wives?
15 What is the State capital of Queensland, Australia?
16 What sort of wild vegetable is Queen Anne's lace?
17 What sport is played at Queen's Park Oval?
18 Which queen of the Ancient Britons led an uprising against the Romans?
19 Who was Hamlet's mother?
20 Which punk rockers had a hit with "God Save the Queen"?
21 Which French queen presided over the St Bartholomew's Day Massacre?
22 Who played the Cincinnatti Kid in the movie of the same name?
23 Which sport is governed by the Queensberry rules?
24 Which Biblical queen tested the wisdom of Solomon?
25 Which traditional British dessert consists of a baked, breadcrumb-thickened egg custard, spread with jam and topped with meringue?
26 Which queen committed suicide by clasping an asp to her bosum?
27 Which bad-tempered monarch does Alice encounter in her adventures in Wonderland?
28 Which queen's marriage to Ferdinand of Aragon united the Spanish peninsula?
29 Who had a transatlantic chart hit in 1974 with "Queen of Clubs"?
30 Which seventeeth-century European state was briefly ruled by the Winter Queen?

Answers	**Pot Luck 103** *(see Quiz 212)*

1 Denise La Salle. 2 Ali Farka Toure. 3 Sole. 4 Incorporate. 5 Leeds. 6 Royal Ulster Constabulary. 7 William Oughtred. 8 China. 9 Harry Shearer. 10 Luciano Pavarotti. 11 6.30 p.m. 12 One. 13 Little Dorrit. 14 27. 15 T-negative. 16 "Hold Back the Night". 17 Dutch. 18 Ohio. 19 Purple Noon. 20 Flag of St George. 21 5,500. 22 Steve Irwin. 23 Weightlifting. 24 Harrisburg. 25 Eating. 26 Uniform. 27 Thorpe & Salter. 28 Onka's Big Moka. 29 Five shillings (25p). 30 Samoa.

1 In which country is the city of Srinagar?
2 Who wrote the novel "Rites of Passage"?
3 What was the first British Top Ten hit for Johnny Nash?
4 How many sides has an undecagon?
5 Carson City is the capital of which US state?
6 Which cathedral's 800th anniversary was marked by a 1989 set of stamps?
7 What is the only English anagram of ALIENATOR?
8 Who first manufactured barbed wire?
9 Belau and Kusac are in which island group?
10 To five, how many league games did Gazza play for Newcastle?
11 Which electronics firm featured in the TV series "Making Out"?
12 What are the odds of rolling double one in dice-throwing?
13 Who was Grainne Close's partner in the UK's first civil partnership ceremony?
14 In Monopoly, if you were on Liverpool Street Station and got double four, where would you land?
15 What was the name of the outlaw nicknamed the Sundance Kid?
16 Hargenger and Spivoy are types of what?
17 In which sport was John Dennis Cronshey famous?
18 Which long-running TV show was screened on Saturday for the first time in January 2006?
19 Which US state is directly west of Colorado?
20 From which language does the word "sherbet" originate?
21 The airline Ladeco was formed in which country?
22 Which Soho club staged Elton John's 2005 stag night cabaret?
23 Which male was on stage when Janet Jackson's breast appeared at the Super Bowl?
24 Which female driver was the 1992 Indy 500 Rookie of the Year?
25 Which statesman won the Nobel Prize for Literature in 1953?
26 What kitchen aid did Charles Strite invent?
27 In which country was the TV Presenter Bob Holness born?
28 What did the people who appeared in "The Duty Men" work for?
29 Who had a hit in 1982 with "Pass the Dutchie"?
30 What is the approximate distance of Cairo airport from London in miles?

| **Answers** | TV: Ads *(see Quiz 213)* |

1 James Dean. 2 Smarties. 3 Less than half a crown (25p). 4 Bird's Eye frozen peas. 5 Orange phone. 6 "Channel Nine". 7 Di Capua. 8 Gibbs SR toothpaste. 9 Rimsky Korsakov. 10 Citizen. 11 "Young at Heart". 12 "Mannish Boy". 13 The Marriage of Figaro. 14 Today. 15 Hillside Singers. 16 Petrol. 17 Polaris World. 18 Working on his allotment. 19 Mascagni. 20 Thresher. 21 Chanel No. 19. 22 Bach's "Air on a G String". 23 Verdi. 24 Levi's. 25 Pepsodent toothpaste. 26 Buxton. 27 Paula Hamilton. 28 Campari. 29 Prolongs Active Life. 30 Bailey's Irish Cream.

How to Set Up Your Own
Pub Quiz

It isn't easy, get that right from the start. This isn't going to be easy. Think instead of words like "difficult", "taxing", "infuriating". Consider yourself with damp palms and a dry throat and then, when you have concentrated on that, put it out of your mind and think of the recognition you will receive down the local, imagine all the regulars lifting you high upon their shoulders dancing and weaving their way around the pub. It won't help but it's good to dream every once in a while.

What you will need:

- A good selection of Biros (never be tempted to give your own pen up, not even to family members)
- A copy of *The Official Biggest Pub Quiz Book Ever!*
- A set of answer sheets photocopied from the back of the book
- A good speaking voice and possibly a microphone and an amp
- A pub
- At least one pint inside you
- At least one more on your table
- A table

What to do:

Choose your local to start with; there is no need to get halfway through your first quiz and decide you weren't cut out for all this and then find yourself in the roughest pub in Christendom 30 miles and a long run from home.

Chat it through with the landlord and agree on whether you will be charging or not; if you don't then there is little chance of a prize for the winners other than a free pint each and this is obviously at the landlord's discretion – if you pack his pub to bursting then five free

pints won't worry him, but if it's only you and a couple of others then he may be less than unwilling, as publicans tend to be.
If you decide on an entry payment keep it reasonable; you don't want to take the fun out of the quiz; some people will be well aware that they have very little hope of winning and will be reluctant to celebrate the fact by mortgaging their house.

Once location and prize are all sorted then advertising the event is paramount. Get people's attention, sell, sell, sell or, alternatively, stick up a gaudy-looking poster on the door of the bogs. Be sure to specify all the details, time, prize and so on – remember you are selling to people whose tiny attention span is being whittled down to nothing by alcohol.

After this it is time for the big night. If you are holding the event in the "snug" which seats ten or so you can rely on your voice, if not you should get hold of a good microphone and an amplifier so that you can boom out your questions and enunciate the length and breadth of the pub (once again, clear this with the landlord and don't let liquid anywhere near the electrical equipment). Make sure to practise, and get comfortable with the sound of your own voice and relax as much as possible, try not to rely on alcohol too much or "round one" will be followed by "rown' too" which will eventually give way to "runfree". Relax your voice so that you can handle any queries from the teams, and any venomous abuse from the "lively" bar area.

When you enter the pub make sure you take everything listed above. Also, make sure you have a set of tie-break questions and that you instruct everybody who is taking part as to the rules – and be firm. It will only upset people if you start handing out impromptu solutions, and let's face it the wisdom of Solomon is not needed when you are talking pub quiz rules; "no cheating" is a perfectly healthy stance to start with.

Finally, keep the teams to a maximum of five members, hand out your answer papers and pens and, when everybody is good and settled, start the quiz. It might not be easy and it might not propel you to international stardom or pay for a life of luxury but you will enjoy yourself. No, really.

1 _____   16 _____

2 _____   17 _____

3 _____   18 _____

4 _____   19 _____

5 _____   20 _____

6 _____   21 _____

7 _____   22 _____

8 _____   23 _____

9 _____   24 _____

10 _____   25 _____

11 _____   26 _____

12 _____   27 _____

13 _____   28 _____

14 _____   29 _____

15 _____   30 _____

ANSWERS

1 _____

2 _____

3 _____

4 _____

5 _____

6 _____

7 _____

8 _____

9 _____

10 _____

11 _____

12 _____

13 _____

14 _____

15 _____

16 _____

17 _____

18 _____

19 _____

20 _____

21 _____

22 _____

23 _____

24 _____

25 _____

26 _____

27 _____

28 _____

29 _____

30 _____

ANSWERS

1 _____

2 _____

3 _____

4 _____

5 _____

6 _____

7 _____

8 _____

9 _____

10 _____

11 _____

12 _____

13 _____

14 _____

15 _____

16 _____

17 _____

18 _____

19 _____

20 _____

21 _____

22 _____

23 _____

24 _____

25 _____

26 _____

27 _____

28 _____

29 _____

30 _____

ANSWERS

1 _____

2 _____

3 _____

4 _____

5 _____

6 _____

7 _____

8 _____

9 _____

10 _____

11 _____

12 _____

13 _____

14 _____

15 _____

16 _____

17 _____

18 _____

19 _____

20 _____

21 _____

22 _____

23 _____

24 _____

25 _____

26 _____

27 _____

28 _____

29 _____

30 _____

ANSWERS

1 _____	16 _____
2 _____	17 _____
3 _____	18 _____
4 _____	19 _____
5 _____	20 _____
6 _____	21 _____
7 _____	22 _____
8 _____	23 _____
9 _____	24 _____
10 _____	25 _____
11 _____	26 _____
12 _____	27 _____
13 _____	28 _____
14 _____	29 _____
15 _____	30 _____

ANSWERS

1 _____

2 _____

3 _____

4 _____

5 _____

6 _____

7 _____

8 _____

9 _____

10 _____

11 _____

12 _____

13 _____

14 _____

15 _____

16 _____

17 _____

18 _____

19 _____

20 _____

21 _____

22 _____

23 _____

24 _____

25 _____

26 _____

27 _____

28 _____

29 _____

30 _____

ANSWERS

1 _____

2 _____

3 _____

4 _____

5 _____

6 _____

7 _____

8 _____

9 _____

10 _____

11 _____

12 _____

13 _____

14 _____

15 _____

16 _____

17 _____

18 _____

19 _____

20 _____

21 _____

22 _____

23 _____

24 _____

25 _____

26 _____

27 _____

28 _____

29 _____

30 _____

ANSWERS

1 _____

2 _____

3 _____

4 _____

5 _____

6 _____

7 _____

8 _____

9 _____

10 _____

11 _____

12 _____

13 _____

14 _____

15 _____

16 _____

17 _____

18 _____

19 _____

20 _____

21 _____

22 _____

23 _____

24 _____

25 _____

26 _____

27 _____

28 _____

29 _____

30 _____

ANSWERS

1 _____

2 _____

3 _____

4 _____

5 _____

6 _____

7 _____

8 _____

9 _____

10 _____

11 _____

12 _____

13 _____

14 _____

15 _____

16 _____

17 _____

18 _____

19 _____

20 _____

21 _____

22 _____

23 _____

24 _____

25 _____

26 _____

27 _____

28 _____

29 _____

30 _____

ANSWERS

1 _____

2 _____

3 _____

4 _____

5 _____

6 _____

7 _____

8 _____

9 _____

10 _____

11 _____

12 _____

13 _____

14 _____

15 _____

16 _____

17 _____

18 _____

19 _____

20 _____

21 _____

22 _____

23 _____

24 _____

25 _____

26 _____

27 _____

28 _____

29 _____

30 _____

ANSWERS

1 _____

2 _____

3 _____

4 _____

5 _____

6 _____

7 _____

8 _____

9 _____

10 _____

11 _____

12 _____

13 _____

14 _____

15 _____

16 _____

17 _____

18 _____

19 _____

20 _____

21 _____

22 _____

23 _____

24 _____

25 _____

26 _____

27 _____

28 _____

29 _____

30 _____